P9-DYE-410

THE ENCYCLOPEDIA OF CREATIVE COOKING

Compiled by Jane Solmson
Edited by Charlotte Turgeon

WEATHERVANE BOOKS

New York

We would like to thank the National Marine Fishery Service, Department of Commerce, for their help in supplying us with some of the seafood pictures in this book.

Photographic compilation
Copyright © MCMLXXX by Ottenheimer Publishers, Inc.
All rights reserved.

This 1985 edition is published by Weathervane Books, distributed by Crown Publishers, Inc., by arrangement with Ottenheimer Publishers, Inc.

Manufactured in Italy.

Library of Congress Cataloging in Publication Data
Main entry under title:

The Encyclopedia of creative cooking.

   Includes index.
   1. Cookery.   I. Solmson, Jane.   II. Turgeon,
Charlotte Snyder, 1912-
TX651.E55   1982   641.5   80-52823
                                     AACR2

ISBN: 0-517-309726
hg

CONTENTS

CANAPÉS

brie-cheese canapés

¼ pound brie cheese
½ stick sweet butter
12 almonds
1 teaspoon peanut oil
¼ teaspoon curry powder
¼ teaspoon salt
¼ teaspoon pepper
Toasted white-bread squares

Allow cheese and butter to come to room temperature; mix together well.

Heat almonds in oil over low heat until toasted lightly; be careful, they burn easily. Drain on paper towels. Sprinkle with curry powder, salt, and pepper. Chop in nut grinder or pulverize in blender or food processor.

Add two-thirds of nuts to cheese. Spread mixture on toasted bread squares. Sprinkle tops with remaining chopped nuts. Yield 16 to 20.

crab-meat spread

1 can (7½ ounces) king crab meat, drained, flaked
1 teaspoon prepared horseradish
½ teaspoon seasoned salt
¼ teaspoon lemon juice
Dash of white pepper
½ cup plain yogurt

Combine crab meat, horseradish, salt, lemon juice, and pepper. Fold in yogurt. Cover; chill.

Use to spread on crackers as canapés, or use as a dip. Yield about 1¼ cups.

seafood pretties

Cut fancy shapes (stars, diamonds, circles, etc.) from thinly sliced white, whole wheat, or rye bread. Spread with cream cheese or a favorite cheese spread; top with rolled smoked salmon, whitefish or salmon caviar, sardines, pickled herring, cooked lobster tail, or king crab. Garnish with additional cream cheese put through a pastry tube and bits of pimiento, green pepper, or ripe or stuffed olives. Arrange on a platter; garnish with watercress. Yield as desired.

stuffed-olive canapés

1 loaf sliced bread
Butter
5 ounces cream cheese, softened
⅛ teaspoon freshly ground pepper

seafood pretties

¼ teaspoon celery salt
¼ teaspoon lemon juice
½ teaspoon cream
1 bunch parsley
1 can pitted black olives, drained
1 small bottle pitted green olives

Preheat broiler.

Dip 1½-inch fluted cookie cutter in water; cut 24 rounds from bread slices. Wet cutter several times while cutting bread. Spread both sides of each bread round with butter. Place rounds on large baking sheet. Broil on each side until lightly browned. Reduce oven temperature to 225°F. Bake rounds until they are crisp and dry croutons.

Blend cream cheese with fork until fluffy. Stir in pepper, celery salt, and lemon juice, and cream until smooth. Stir in additional cream, if cream cheese mixture is too stiff for easy spreading.

Remove stems from parsley; chop leaves fine.

Spread 1 side of each crouton with cream-cheese mixture.

Spoon remaining cream-cheese mixture into pastry bag fitted with medium-size star tube. Pipe small dot of cream-cheese mixture in center of each crouton. Place olives securely in cream-cheese mixture. Pipe a rosette into and on top of each olive.

Cut remaining olives into petal shapes; insert into stuffed olives. Sprinkle parsley thickly onto each crouton base, as shown in illustration. These can be chilled a short time until ready to serve. Too long a period of refrigeration will cause croutons to become soggy. Yield 24.

stuffed-olive canapés

CAVIAR

caviar crown

1 jar (4 ounces) salmon caviar
1 jar (3½ ounces) whitefish caviar
2 packages (8 ounces each) cream cheese, softened
2 tablespoons lemon juice
2 tablespoons chopped green onion
1 teaspoon Worcestershire sauce
Parsley
Assorted party breads or melba toast

Drain caviars.

Cream the cheese and seasonings. Place cheese mixture in center of serving plate. Shape into circle about 7 inches in diameter and 1 inch thick, similar to a layer cake. Cover a 4-inch circle in the center with salmon caviar. Cover the remaining 1½ inches on top and sides with whitefish caviar. Place small sprigs of parsley around edge of salmon caviar. (A ring of overlapping slices of tiny stuffed olives or a ribbon of cream cheese put through pastry tube can be substituted for parsley.) Garnish base of cheese mixture with parsley.

Serve with party breads or melba toast.

Note: For large parties, fix several small crowns, using ½ recipe for each one.

Divide cheese mixture in half. Make 2 cheese circles about 3½ inches in diameter and 1 inch thick. Cover 2-inch circle in center of each with salmon caviar and remaining outside edges with whitefish caviar. Proceed as directed above. Yield approximately 2 cups.

caviar pie

3 hard-cooked eggs, finely chopped
5 tablespoons unsalted butter
1 tablespoon finely chopped Bermuda onion
1 jar (4½ ounces) red or black caviar, drained
1 cup dairy sour cream
Assorted crackers
Lemon wedges

Stir together eggs, butter, and onion.

Line small shallow dish or soup plate with plastic wrap. Press mixture into it. Refrigerate until mixture hardens.

Turn out mold; cover with caviar. Frost with sour cream.

Serve with crackers and lemon wedges. Yield: 8 to 10 servings as cocktail spread; 4 as first course.

caviar rounds

2 cups sifted flour
¾ teaspoon salt
2½ teaspoons baking powder
⅓ cup shortening
½ cup Sourdough Starter (see Index)
½ cup milk (approximately)
1 cup caviar

Sift dry ingredients together. Cut in shortening until mixture is like coarse cornmeal. Add sourdough starter and enough milk to form a soft dough.

Roll or pat dough on floured board to ½ inch thick. Cut it with 1¼-inch-round biscuit cutter. Place half of biscuits on ungreased cookie sheet. With ¾-inch biscuit cutter cut centers from remaining circles. Place rings on tops of biscuits.

Bake rounds in 450°F oven 10 to 12 minutes or until golden brown. Remove from oven; fill center wells with caviar. Yield 20 rounds.

caviar rounds

caviar and salmon checkerboard

CHEESE

cheddar-cheese puffs

2 cups grated cheddar cheese
½ cup butter or margarine, softened
1 cup flour, sifted
½ teaspoon salt
½ teaspoon paprika
48 small green olives, stuffed with pimientos

Blend cheese with butter. Add flour, salt, and paprika; mix well. Mold 1 teaspoon dough around each olive to cover. At this point you can refrigerate or freeze puffs for up to 10 days.

Bake puffs at 400°F for 15 minutes. Serve hot. Yield 48.

deluxe cheeseball

½ to 1 pound soft cheddar cheese (found in dairy stores) or cheddar cold pack, room temperature
½ pound cream cheese, room temperature
3 ounces pimiento cream cheese, room temperature
6 to 8 ounces crumbled blue cheese for salads, room temperature
2 tablespoons freshly grated or dry minced onion
1 teaspoon Worcestershire sauce
Chopped nuts or paprika for garnish

Combine all ingredients except nuts or paprika in large bowl; mix thoroughly with heavy-duty mixer. Mixture is very thick, so lighter mixers may not be powerful enough unless all cheeses have been at room temperature for quite a few hours.

Refrigerate until firm enough to form into ball, apple, or even banana shape!

Garnish with paprika or nuts; decorate accordingly.

Rewrap in plastic wrap; refrigerate until serving. Yield 12 servings as an hors d'oeuvre.

cheese crisps

½ pound cheddar cheese, grated (2 cups)
⅓ cup grated Parmesan cheese
½ cup butter or margarine, room temperature
¼ cup water
¾ cup whole-wheat pastry flour
⅓ cup all-purpose flour
1 tablespoon toasted wheat germ
¼ teaspoon salt
Dash of cayenne (optional)
1 cup rolled oats
⅛ teaspoon paprika

Thoroughly blend cheeses, butter, and water. Add flours, wheat germ, salt, and cayenne; mix well. Stir in rolled oats.

Divide dough in half. Form into 2 rolls, each

caviar and salmon checkerboard

Brown-bread slices, ¼ inch thick
White-bread slices, ¼ inch thick
Softened unsalted butter
8 ounces black caviar (sturgeon or cod)
¼ ounces very thinly sliced smoked salmon
1 lemon, cut in half

Trim crusts evenly from brown and white bread. Butter slices. Cut forty 1¼-inch squares from brown bread and forty-one 1¼-inch squares from white bread. Spread caviar on each brown bread square.

Cut forty-one 1¼-inch squares from smoked salmon. Place 1 salmon square on each white bread square.

Arrange squares on large serving platter as shown in illustration. Garnish edges of checkerboard with parsley. Squeeze lemon juice over all squares just before serving.

Small checkerboards can be formed on small salad plates and served as a first course.

When serving the caviar and smoked salmon, do not forget to squeeze lemon juice over the checkerboard just before serving. Yield 81 appetizers.

about 1½ inches in diameter (about 6 inches long). Wrap tightly; refrigerate until well chilled, about 4 hours, or up to 1 week.

Slice ⅛ to ¼ inch thick; sprinkle with paprika.

Bake on greased baking sheet at 400°F 8 to 10 minutes. Cool on rack.

If less uniform shape is desired, dough can be shaped into small (1¼-inch) balls immediately after mixing; flatten with hands onto baking sheet. Sprinkle with paprika. Bake in 400°F oven 8 to 10 minutes, until golden brown. Yield 4 dozen.

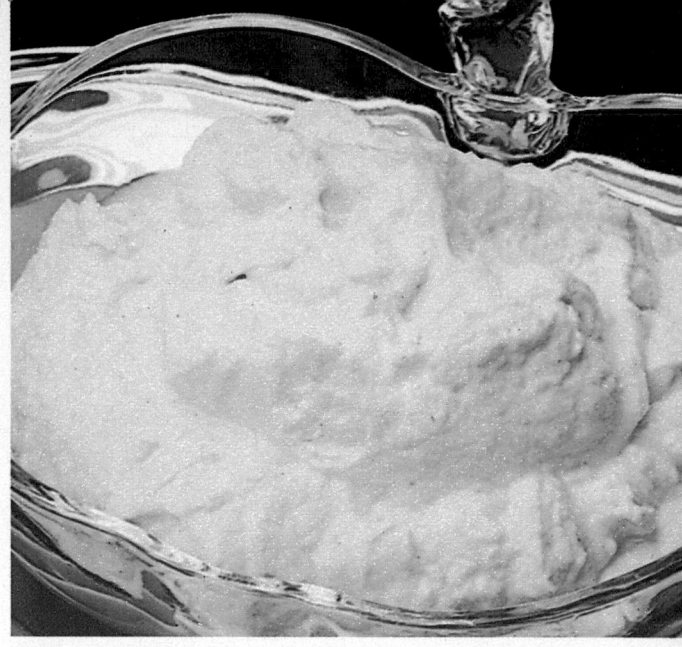

cottage-cheese tartare

cottage-cheese tartare

This dish can be served as beef tartar is, as a cocktail appetizer, or as a first course.

1 12-ounce container cottage cheese
⅓ cup yogurt
1 tablespoon prepared Dijon mustard
Salt and white pepper to taste
2 tablespoons capers
2 or 3 tomatoes, cut into thin wedges
3 or 4 tablespoons chopped chives or thinly sliced
**   scallions**
1 large onion, chopped
4 to 6 ounces small cooked shrimp

Paprika
Caraway seeds
Assorted crackers and snack breads

In blender or food processor cream together cottage cheese, yogurt, and mustard until smooth. Season to taste with salt and pepper.

Arrange capers, tomatoes, chives, onion, and shrimp on platter with tartare. Also have on hand paprika and caraway seeds to be used as garnish.

Serve tartare on crackers or snack breads. Top with any other ingredients, singly or in combination. Sprinkle with paprika or caraway seeds, if desired. Yield 4 to 6 servings.

creamed blue cheese

creamed blue cheese

6 ounces blue cheese, crumbled
¾ cup butter
⅛ teaspoon white pepper
Ground pistachio nuts

Cream blue cheese until light and smooth.

Cream butter in a separate bowl until fluffy.

Combine cheese and butter; blend well. Add pepper; mix thoroughly.

Line small, decorative mold with about 3 thicknesses of cheesecloth, leaving enough over rim to bring over top.

Press cheese mixture firmly into mold; bring corners of cheesecloth up over top.

Store in refrigerator overnight.

Grasp corners of cheesecloth; lift cheese mixture out of mold. Remove cheesecloth. Turn into serving dish. Sprinkle pistachio nuts thickly over top. Let set at room temperature to soften.

Serve with fresh celery sticks, cauliflower florets, or assorted crackers. Yield 8 to 10 servings.

fried-cheese profiteroles

⅓ cup all-purpose flour
⅓ freshly grated Parmesan cheese
¼ cup butter, softened
2 eggs
Paprika

Blend flour with cheese.

Combine butter with ½ cup water in small saucepan. Bring to boil, stirring until butter melts. Add flour mixture all at once; stir vigorously with wooden spoon until mixture is smooth and leaves sides of pan, forming a ball. Remove from heat. Add 1 egg; beat 1 minute, until well mixed. Repeat procedure with remaining egg; beat until smooth and thickened.

Let stand, covered, at room temperature until completely cool. Do not refrigerate.

Spoon mixture into pastry bag with ½-inch tip affixed. Pipe ½-inch pieces or drop by teaspoonfuls into 350°F oil in deep-fat fryer. Fry until golden; drain well on absorbent toweling. Sprinkle with paprika. Yield 40 to 50 small puffs.

liptauer cheese

½ cup salted butter, softened
4 ounces cream cheese, softened
1 teaspoon (heaping) caraway seeds
1 teaspoon drained pickled capers
1 teaspoon (heaping) Dijon mustard
1¼ teaspoon Hungarian paprika
1 boned anchovy fillet
Pretzels

Cream butter in small mixing bowl with electric

liptauer cheese

mixer until light and fluffy.. Add cream cheese; beat until smoothly blended.

Chop caraway seeds in blender or food processor; add to butter mixture.

Chop capers finely; add to mixture. Add mustard and paprika.

Rinse, dry, and chop anchovy. Stir into cheese mixture; blend well.

Shape into neat rectangle on serving plate; border with pretzels. Serve with additional pretzels or crackers. Yield 4 to 6 servings.

paprika cookies

½ cup (1 stick) butter or margarine
¾ cup grated cheese
1 cup flour
1 teaspoon Hungarian paprika
½ teaspoon salt
½ teaspoon dry mustard
½ tablespoon poppy seeds

Preheat oven to 375°F.

Mix butter and cheese together until soft and creamy.

Sift flour, paprika, salt, and mustard together; add to butter and cheese. Beat until well blended.

Flour your hands lightly; roll heaping teaspoons of mixture into small balls. Place on greased baking sheets; flatten a little. Sprinkle with poppy seeds.

Bake 15 to 20 minutes or until golden brown. Loosen cookies, but leave on baking sheets to cool. Yield about 18 cookies.

paprika cookies

Bring water and butter to boil, stirring until butter melts. Add flour and salt all at once. (Remember to spoon flour into dry measuring cup; level. Do not scoop). Reduce heat. Cook, stirring vigorously, over low heat until mixture is smooth and forms soft ball, 1 to 2 minutes. Remove from heat; cool slightly. Add eggs one at a time; beat well after each addition.

Turn half of batter into mixing bowl; stir in chopped dried beef.

Add cheese to remaining half of batter. Drop by level teaspoonfuls or pipe with pastry tube in ½-inch piles onto greased baking sheet. Bake in preheated 400°F oven 20 to 25 minutes or until golden brown and firm to touch. Serve warm or cold. Yield about 9 dozen.

petite appetizer puffs

1 cup water
½ cup butter
1 cup enriched flour
⅛ teaspoon salt
4 eggs
½ cup finely chopped dried beef
¼ cup grated Parmesan or Romano cheese

swiss-cheese squares

2 cups all-purpose white flour
2½ teaspoons baking powder
½ teaspoon baking soda
1 teaspoon salt
⅓ cup shortening
½ cup sourdough starter (see Index)
½ cup buttermilk
1 cup grated Swiss cheese
1 egg, beaten
3 tablespoons poppy seeds

Combine flour, baking powder, baking soda, and salt. Cut in shortening until mixture resembles dry cornmeal. Add sourdough starter and enough

petite appetizer puffs

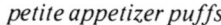

swiss-cheese squares

milk to form soft dough that cleans side of bowl. Add Swiss cheese; knead lightly into dough. Pat or roll dough to ½ inch thick. Cut into squares, using serrated knife or cookie cutter. Brush tops with beaten egg. Sprinkle with poppy seeds.

Place squares on ungreased cookie sheet. Bake in preheated 450°F oven 10 minutes or until golden brown. Serve warm or cold. Yield 1½ dozen.

vareneky

This is a nice way to start a meal in the evening, or serve it for lunch.

2 cups flour
1 egg
Pinch of salt
1 cup potato water or milk
1 teaspoon oil

Blend all ingredients. Knead into stiff dough. Roll out very thin; cut into circles, using glass or pastry cutter. Fill with your choice of fillings. Simmer 10 minutes in 4 quarts salted water.

Serve with sour cream or melted butter.

Potato and cheese and cabbage or mushroom-filled vareneky (any filling except fruit) are better if they are fried slightly in butter before serving. Yield 6 to 8 servings.

cottage cheese filling

1 cup cottage cheese
1 teaspoon butter
1 egg
1 tablespoon sugar

Mix well and fill.

mashed potato filling

2 pounds cooked potatoes, mashed with butter and salt
6 slices American cheese or, for a tangier flavor, ½ pound sharp cheese

other suggested fillings

Rice and mushrooms
Fried sauerkraut
Cooked meat

DIPS

apple-nut horseradish dip

2 apples, peeled, cored
1 tablespoon lemon juice
¼ cup yogurt
1 tablespoon prepared horseradish
2 tablespoons minced or ground walnuts

Grate apples; immediately combine with lemon juice to prevent discoloration. Blend in remaining ingredients.

Serve dip at once with chips, crackers, or vegetable dippers. Yield about 1 cup.

avocado dip

For raw vegetables or corn chips.

3 ripe avocados
1 tomato, peeled, seeded
1 small red onion, finely diced
1 tablespoon chopped hot jalapeno pepper
Dash of ground coriander
1 tablespoon lemon juice
1 tablespoon vinegar
2 tablespoons salad oil
1 teaspoon salt

apple-nut horseradish dip

Mince avocados and tomato. Stir in all other ingredients.

You can use scooped-out avocado shells for serving dishes if this is to be served at table. For cocktail parties use a pretty bowl.

If made ahead of time, put avocado seeds in mixture to keep it green. Yield 2 cups.

clamdigger dip

1 can (7½ or 8 ounces) minced clams
1 package (8 ounces) cream cheese, softened
1 tablespoon lemon juice
1 tablespoon grated onion
1 teaspoon chopped parsley
1 teaspoon Worcestershire sauce
¼ teaspoon salt
⅛ teaspoon liquid hot pepper sauce
Assorted chips, crackers, or raw vegetables

Drain clams; reserve liquid.

Cream the cheese. Add seasonings and clams; mix thoroughly. Chill at least 1 hour to blend flavors.

If necessary to thin dip, add clam liquid gradually.

Serve with chips, crackers, or vegetables. Yield 1⅓ cups.

garden dip

⅔ cup low-fat cottage cheese
1 tablespoon finely grated onion
1 tablespoon finely grated carrot
1 teaspoon finely chopped green pepper
½ teaspoon salt
Dash of garlic salt
1 cup plain yogurt

In small bowl mash cottage cheese with fork. Add onion, carrot, pepper, salt, and garlic salt; beat until fairly smooth. Stir in yogurt. Cover; chill several hours.

Serve as dip with chips or raw vegetables. Yield 1¾ cups.

greek caviar dip (taramosalata)

½ of 8-ounce jar of tarama
1 small onion, finely grated
1 egg yolk
4 slices white bread (stale)
¼ cup lemon juice
½ cup olive oil

Place tarama in blender jar; whirl at low speed to smooth paste. Add onion and egg yolk; whirl to mix.

Remove crusts from bread; soak bread in water. Squeeze to dry. Tear it into pieces. Add to fish-roe

mixture; whirl until well blended. Add lemon juice and olive oil alternately while whirling at medium speed. Blend at high speed until well combined.

Chill; serve with melba toast, pita bread, or lavash (Arabic crisp flatbread) and crisp raw vegetables. Yield 1½ cups.

green mayonnaise with fresh vegetables

¼ teaspoon sugar
½ teaspoon dry mustard
¾ teaspoon salt
1 large (or 2 small) egg yolk
2 tablespoons fresh lemon juice
¾ cup vegetable oil plus ¼ cup French olive oil or
** 1 cup vegetable oil**
2 tablespoons chopped parsley
1 teaspoon fresh or frozen chives
1 teaspoon fresh or dried tarragon (optional)

Fresh vegetables for dipping, such as mushrooms, cherry tomatoes, cauliflower florets, zucchini sticks, green-pepper slices, cucumber slices, carrot sticks.

Mix sugar, mustard, salt, egg yolk, and 1 tablespoon lemon juice in 1-quart bowl. Using wire whisk, very slowly add oil, a drop at a time, until about ¼ cup is added. Once a thick emulsion has formed, oil can be added 1 teaspoon at a time. When mixture is very thick, add remaining lemon juice. Slowly beat in remaining oil. Add herbs; mix well. Chill.

Arrange chilled vegetables attractively on large platter, with mayonnaise in center as a dip. Yield 8 servings.

Note: If mayonnaise separates, place 1 teaspoon cold water or an egg yolk in a separate bowl. Slowly beat in mayonnaise. When emulsion is re-formed, continue adding oil as above.

guacamole

guacamole

2 avocados, peeled, mashed
1 cup fresh tomatoes, peeled, cut up
⅓ cup salad dressing
¼ cup chopped onion
1 teaspoon salt
Lettuce
4 slices crisply cooked bacon, crumbled

Combine avocados, tomato, salad dressing, onion, and salt. Mix well; chill. Place in individual bowls. Serve on plates.

Sprinkle with bacon garnished with tomato wedges and tortilla chips.

Serve as a first course or luncheon, or serve ungarnished as a dip. Yield 4 to 6 servings.

hot clam dip

3 tablespoons butter
1 onion, chopped very fine
½ green pepper, chopped very fine
1 clove garlic, minced (optional)
2 cans (7½-ounce) minced clams
1 cup grated mild cheddar cheese (¼ pound)
¼ teaspoon cayenne
4 tablespoons catsup
1 tablespoon Worcestershire sauce
3 tablespoons sherry

Melt butter in double boiler. Sauté onion and green pepper 5 minutes over direct heat.

Drain clams.

Cut cheese into small pieces.

Put all ingredients in double boiler. Cook over water until cheese melts; stir often.

Serve hot in chafing dish with Melba toast or party rye. More cayenne or some Tabasco can be added if desired. Yield 6 servings.

shrimp dip

½ pound fresh or frozen shrimp, cooked and
**   cleaned, or 1 5-ounce can (1 cup)**
1 cup cream-style cottage cheese
3 tablespoons chili sauce
2 teaspoons lemon juice
½ teaspoon onion juice
¼ teaspoon Worcestershire sauce
About ⅓ cup milk

Finely chop shrimp. Combine shrimp, cheese, chili sauce, lemon juice, onion juice, and Worcestershire sauce; blend in blender. Gradually beat in enough milk to give good dipping consistency.

Serve with potato chips, crackers, or celery. Yield about 2 cups.

EGGS
egg and anchovy mousse

6 hard-boiled eggs
2 2-ounce cans anchovy fillets
3¼ teaspoons lemon juice
½ cup butter, softened
¼ teaspoon white pepper
¼ cup mayonnaise

Slice eggs; process in food processor.

Drain anchovy fillets well on absorbent paper; place on chopping block. Sprinkle with ¼ teaspoon lemon juice. Mash into smooth paste.

Place butter in mixer bowl; beat with electric mixer until light and fluffy. Add anchovy mixture gradually; beat well after each addition. Add eggs, 2 tablespoons at a time, mixing well. Stir in pepper and mayonnaise; beat until well blended.

Spoon egg mixture onto serving plate; shape into a mound with knife. Chill overnight for flavors to blend. Make a pattern with fork tines around side.

For an effective garnish save ½ cup mousse; divide into 2 portions. Add a drop of red vegetable coloring to 1 portion and a drop of green coloring to other portion. Using appropriate pastry tips, fashion leaves and stems with green and a rose on top. Yield 25 to 30 servings.

egg and anchovy mousse

egg rolls

You can purchase ready-made egg roll skins in supermarkets or Oriental specialty stores.

dipping batter

**1 egg
1 tablespoon cornstarch
1½ teaspoons baking powder
1 cup flour
1 tablespoon sugar
2 teaspoons salt
½ teaspoon MSG
1¼ cups milk
1¾ cups water**

filling

**1 cup shredded bamboo shoots
½ pound bean sprouts, rinsed, well-drained
1½ cups shredded water chestnuts
3½ cups slivered cooked chicken
¾ cup slivered barbecued pork
¾ cup finely chopped fresh parsley
1 cup chopped fresh mushrooms
½ cup finely chopped scallion
Salt and freshly ground black pepper to taste
Oil**

Beat egg slightly. Sift together dry ingredients; mix with egg. Slowly stir in milk and water; stir until smooth.

All filling ingredients should be cut finely. Mix filling ingredients (except oil) together. Sauté in a little oil about 10 minutes; stir occasionally. Let mixture cool.

Spoon about ½ cup onto egg-roll skin. Fold like an envelope. Dip in batter. Fry in hot oil (375°F) about 5 minutes; turn carefully to brown both sides.

Serve whole when served at table. Cut into pieces and use mustard or sauce as a dip for a cocktail party. Yield 2 dozen.

egg rolls

pickled eggs

Place as many eggs as you wish to pickle in heavy saucepan; cover with water. Salt water heavily. This will make shells easy to remove. Bring to boil over medium heat. Reduce heat to maintain slow boil; cook eggs 15 minutes. Remove from heat; cool under cold running water.

Remove shells; place eggs in pickling jar. Add water to cover 1 to 2 inches above eggs. Remove eggs carefully; let dry on paper toweling.

Measure water from jar in order to replace same amount with mixture of ¾ red wine vinegar and ¼ water. Place vinegar mixture in saucepan. For each quart of vinegar mixture add 1 small dried red pepper, 1 clove of garlic, 4 peppercorns, 2 whole cloves, and 1-inch piece of gingerroot, quartered. Bring to boil. Reduce heat; simmer 5 minutes. Let cool to room temperature.

Place eggs in pickling jar. Pour vinegar mixture over eggs; cover tightly. Let stand at least 1 week.

Eggs, as they pickle, will produce a strong odor. Open every day during first week to let fumes escape. After a week or so this odor will disappear and they will have a most delectable pickled aroma. Yield as desired.

MEAT

antipasto tray

**Carrot or celery sticks
Cheese cubes: mozzarella, provolone, cheddar, feta, or Edam
Cocktail tomatoes
Hard-cooked eggs, sliced
Fish: tuna (best quality), shrimp, or sardines
Thin meat slices: salami, pepperoni, roast beef, or ham
Pimientos or roasted peppers topped with anchovy fillets
Melon slices wrapped with proscuitto ham
Olives: black or green**

Choose an assortment from the above; arrange on a pretty tray or lazy susan. Selection should be made for flavor contrast and eye appeal. Yield as desired.

cocktail meatballs

**1 pound lean hamburger
1 teaspoon garlic powder
1 12-ounce bottle chili sauce
1 10-ounce jar grape jelly**

Mix hamburger with garlic powder; shape into small balls. Pan-fry until well cooked; drain.

Mix chili sauce and jelly. Add meatballs; heat mixture.

Serve warm in chafing dish with toothpicks neatly. Yield 12 servings as cocktail appetizer

ham appetizer

2 tablespoons finely chopped green pepper
2 tablespoons finely chopped celery
2 tablespoons finely chopped pimiento
¼ teaspoon Dijon mustard
2 teaspoons lemon juice
2 teaspoons olive oil
Salt and pepper
4 slices cooked ham
Stuffed olives or gherkins for garnish

Mix green pepper, celery, and pimiento together.

Mix mustard with lemon juice and oil. Add salt and pepper to taste. Pour over vegetables; mix well. Divide equally between ham slices. Fold over; secure with toothpicks.

Arrange on serving dish; garnish with stuffed olives or gherkins cut into fan shapes.

This can be served as a first course for a dinner party; as a luncheon dish; or each roll can be cut into 4 portions, speared with toothpicks, and served on a canapé tray. Yield 4 servings.

ham appetizer

meat-stuffed grape leaves

Olive oil
2 pounds ground lamb
1½ cups chopped onions
1 15-ounce can tomato sauce
¼ cup lemon juice
¼ cup chopped fresh parsley
¼ cup currants
½ cup pine nuts
½ teaspoon cinnamon
1 teaspoon paprika
½ teaspoon allspice
1 recipe Risotto (see Index)
2 1-quart jars grape leaves

Heat ⅓ cup oil in large frying pan. Add lamb; cook over medium heat, stirring constantly, until lamb loses red color. Add onions; cook, stirring, until lamb is lightly browned. Add tomato sauce, lemon juice, parsley, currants, pine nuts, cinnamon, paprika and allspice; mix well. Reduce heat; simmer until most of liquid has evaporated. Stir in Risotto until well mixed; cool.

Wash grape leaves in hot water. Cut off stems; open leaves.

Shape 1 to 2 teaspoons lamb mixture, according to the size of leaves, into rolls; place near stem ends of leaves. Fold over sides of leaves; roll up from stem end.

Grease large casserole heavily with olive oil. Place layer of grape leaves over bottom of casserole in layers; cover casserole.

Bake in preheated 350°F oven 45 minutes.

Serve hot or cold. If served cold, do not uncover until *dolmas* have cooled, to prevent discoloration of leaves. Yield 70 to 80 *dolmas*.

melon with prosciutto

½ of large ripe honeydew or cantaloupe
¼ pound prosciutto ham
Pepper mill

Remove seeds and rind from melon; slice into crescents.

Cut ham slices; wrap piece of ham around each piece of melon.

Arrange on platter; grind fresh pepper over ham and melon just before serving. Lemon or lime wedges are a suitable garnish. Yield 4 to 6 servings.

mustard veal tongues

1 dozen veal tongues
Bay leaves
Whole peppers
1 tablespoon salt
4 tablespoons vinegar

Use enough water to cover tongues; bring to

rapid boil. Drop thoroughly cleaned tongues into water to which the other ingredients have been added. Cook until quite tender. Skin; cut in lengthwise halves. Put tongues in large jar or jars; pour following sauce over them:

sauce

1½ cups Dijon or French's prepared mustard
2¼ cups tongue broth
4 to 5 onions, sliced thin
Bay leaves
Whole peppers
Sugar to taste

Bring ingredients to slow boil, watching very carefully and stirring while cooking. Let tongues marinate several hours before serving hot or cold. Yield 12 servings.

oriental cocktail kebabs

1 15¼-ounce can pineapple chunks, drained
1-pound package brown-and-serve sausages, cooked according to package directions, cut into thirds
1 8-ounce can water chestnuts, halved
2 green peppers, cut into ¾-inch squares
¼ pound small mushrooms, stemmed
Reserved syrup from drained pineapple
4 tablespoons soy sauce
3 slices fresh gingerroot
3 tablespoons brown sugar
2 tablespoons dry sherry

Alternate pieces of pineapple, sausage, water chestnuts, green pepper, and mushrooms on toothpicks.

Combine remaining ingredients; heat in skillet. Add kebabs. Cover; simmer 10 minutes. Remove from skillet; serve warm as a dinner or cocktail appetizer. On the latter case stand the kebabs up in a wire-mesh trivet, leaving the exposed toothpicks dry. Yield 40 to 50.

pepperoni pizza hors d'oeuvres

1 can (10¼ ounces) marinara sauce
4 English muffins, split, toasted
1 cup shredded mozzarella cheese
1 package (4 ounces) sliced pepperoni

Spread marinara sauce evenly over English muffin halves. Sprinkle with cheese. Arrange 4 pepperoni slices on each muffin half.

Broil 4 to 5 inches from source of heat 2 to 3 minutes or until cheese bubbles and browns. Cut each muffin half into 4 wedges. Yield 32.

pigs in blankets

6 frankfurters
Prepared mustard
6 thin fingers cheese
Flaky pastry
Egg or milk to glaze

Preheat oven to 450°F.

Split frankfurters. Spread very lightly with mustard; insert a finger of cheese in each.

Roll pastry thin; cut into 6-inch squares. Place 1 frankfurter diagonally on each square; bring together other two diagonal corners of pastry so that ends of frankfurters are exposed.

Put onto baking sheet; glaze with egg or milk. Bake 20 minutes.

meat-stuffed grape leaves

pigs in blankets

Serve hot with broiled tomatoes, cold with salad as a table appetizer, or cut into small pieces and spear with toothpicks for the cocktail variety. Serve hot, with or without a mustard sauce. Yield 6 servings.

sausage pies

1 recipe double pie crust
¾ pound sausage
20 to 24 cherry tomatoes, halved

Prepare pie crust; set aside.

Break up sausage in heavy skillet; cook until all pink has disappeared, about 10 minutes. Drain off fat on paper towels.

Roll out pie-crust dough; cut into 4-inch squares. Moisten corner of each square with a little cold water. Place squares on lightly greased baking sheet. Spoon drained sausage, about 1 spoonful per square, into center of each square. Pinch corners to seal, but don't close completely.

Bake at 450°F 12 to 15 minutes. Place half of cherry tomato, cut-side-down, on top of sausage—this is why you didn't seal the pie crust. Bake 10 minutes more or until pie crust is golden brown. Serve at once. Yield 20 to 24.

swedish meatballs

This recipe improves if made one day ahead of time.

1 pound ground beef
¼ pound ground veal
¼ pound ground pork
2 cups bread crumbs
½ cup milk
1 onion, diced fine
2 tablespoons butter
2½ teaspoons salt
¼ teaspoon pepper
2 teaspoons nutmeg
2 teaspoons paprika
1 teaspoon dry mustard
3 beaten eggs
4 tablespoons butter or margarine

Have meat ground together twice.

Soak bread crumbs in milk. Add meat; mix.

Sauté onion in large skillet in 2 tablespoons butter.

Mix together seasonings, eggs, onion, and meat in bowl. Mix well; form into 48 small balls.

Melt butter in skillet; brown meatballs on all sides. Remove; set aside to make sauce.

sauce

¼ teaspoon minced garlic
5 tablespoons butter
2 teaspoons tomato paste
1 teaspoon beef concentrate
2 cups bouillon or soup stock
1 teaspoon aromatic bitters (optional)
1 cup sour cream

Add garlic and 1 tablespoon butter to fat left in skillet. Sauté 1 minute. Blend in 4 more tablespoons butter, tomato paste, beef concentrate, and stock. Add bitters; stir mixture over low heat until it thickens. Pour sauce into lighted chafing dish. Stir in sour cream. Add meatballs to sauce, stirring once or twice to be sure all heats through.

Sauce can be poured into casserole dish and heated in oven, if preferred. Yield 48 balls.

water chestnuts with bacon

⅓ to ½ pound bacon
1 6-ounce can water chestnuts
Toothpicks
1 tablespoon soy sauce
1 tablespoon dry sherry

Wrap ½ slice bacon around each water chestnut; fasten with toothpick. Place water chestnuts in ovenproof dish; brush with mixture of soy sauce and sherry. Bake at 350°F 15 to 20 minutes. Yield about 20.

19

swedish meatballs

NUTS

curried nuts

¼ cup olive oil
1 tablespoon curry powder
1 tablespoon Worcestershire sauce
⅛ teaspoon cayenne
2 cups nuts (assorted are best)

Combine oil and seasonings in medium-size skillet. When mixture is hot, add nuts; stir constantly until nuts are completely coated.

Line baking pan with brown paper. Spread out nuts. Bake at 300°F 10 minutes. Nuts should be crisp and tasty. Yield 2 cups.

glacé nuts

1½ cups nuts, salted or unsalted
2 cups sugar
¼ teaspoon cream of tartar
1 cup hot water
⅛ teaspoon salt

Mix sugar, cream of tartar, hot water, and salt in small saucepan; place over hot fire. Stir until sugar has dissolved. Let syrup boil until it reaches 293°F, or hard-crack stage. Remove from fire at once; place in pan of hot water while dipping nuts.

Hold nuts separately with tweezers or on long pin; dip in syrup to cover. Place dipped nuts on waxed paper to dry. Reheat syrup carefully if it becomes too thick. Yield 1½ cups.

salted almonds

2 cups shelled almonds
¼ cup salad oil
Salt to taste

Pour almonds into boiling water in large saucepan. Remove from heat; let stand about 5 minutes or until skins are soft. Drain; remove skins. Spread almonds on cookie pan; let stand until dry. Sprinkle with oil; stir until almonds are coated evenly. Sprinkle with salt; stir again.

Bake in preheated 350°F oven until lightly browned, stirring frequently. Cool; store in airtight container. Yield 2 cups.

spiced cocktail nuts

4 tablespoons butter
1 tablespoon Worcestershire sauce
½ teaspoon hot pepper sauce
1 tablespoon seasoned salad salt
1 teaspoon salt
1 teaspoon garlic salt
¼ teaspoon pepper
1 pound walnuts, almonds, or filberts (a mixture of nuts is also good)

Melt butter; add remaining ingredients, except nuts. Stir until well blended. Add nuts; toss. Cook over low heat 15 minutes; stir occasionally. Cook 5 minutes in 350°F oven, until crispy. Drain on paper towels. Store in airtight container. Yield 4½ cups.

toasted pecans

12 cups pecans
¼ pound butter
Salt

Place pecans in rectangular oven dish. Toast in 250°F oven 30 minutes. Add butter over all by

slicing or dotting it over nuts. Stir once or twice, until pecans and butter have mixed well. Nuts will be greasy at this point. Sprinkle generously with salt. Toast pecans 1 hour; salt again several times. Stir as you go. When done, butter will be completely absorbed and nuts crisp. Yield 12 cups.

OLIVES

olive–ham turnovers

turnover pastry

2 cups flour
½ teaspoon salt
⅔ cup Garlic Mayonnaise
Dash of cayenne
2 tablespoons cold water

turnover filling

⅔ cup ground Serrano or other smoked ham
⅔ cup chopped ripe olives
3 to 4 tablespoons mayonnaise

Heat oven to 425°F.

Sift flour with salt. Add garlic mayonnaise, cayenne, and water; mix. Turn onto lightly floured board; roll thin. Cut into 2½-inch squares.

Mix together filling ingredients. Put generous ½ teaspoon filling on each pastry square. Moisten edges with water; fold over into triangles; pinch edges to seal. Bake 15 minutes or until pastry browns. Yield 2½ dozen.

garlic mayonnaise

1 egg
½ teaspoon salt
½ teaspoon garlic powder
Dash of cayenne pepper
1 cup olive oil
3 tablespoons fresh-squeezed lemon juice

Combine egg, salt, garlic powder, cayenne, and ¼ cup oil in blender container; blend thoroughly. With blender running, very slowly add ½ cup oil. Gradually add lemon juice and remaining ¼ cup oil; blend until thick. Occasionally scrape sides of bowl. Yield 1 cup.

olives in blankets

Wrap slice of bacon around each olive. Fasten with toothpicks. Broil at moderate temperature until bacon is crisp. Serve hot. Yield as desired.

stuffed olives

1 6-ounce can jumbo pitted black olives
1 2-ounce can anchovy fillets
2 tablespoons olive oil
1 clove garlic, minced
2 tablespoons finely chopped parsley
12 stemmed cherry tomatoes
½ of medium green pepper, thinly sliced

Drain olives.

Drain anchovy fillets; cut each in half.

Stuff each olive with half an anchovy fillet. Place in serving bowl.

Combine olive oil, garlic, and parsley; pour over olives. Mix well. Chill several hours. Bring to room temperature before serving.

Garnish with cherry tomatoes and green peppers. Provide cocktail picks for guests to spear these. Yield 6 servings.

PÂTÉ

chicken-liver pâté

2 tablespoons butter
½ pound chicken livers
2 eggs, hard-cooked
1 package (3-ounce) cream cheese, softened
1 tablespoon finely chopped parsley
¾ teaspoon salt
⅛ teaspoon pepper
1 tablespoon cognac

Heat butter in medium frypan. Cook chicken livers, stirring occasionally, over medium heat 10 minutes or until tender; drain.

Chop livers and eggs in food grinder, blender, or food processor, a little at a time.

With wooden spoon, work cheese until light and fluffy. Mix into liver mixture along with remaining ingredients. Refrigerate several hours.

Serve pâté with hot toast or crackers. Yield ¼ cups.

chicken pâté cream

Bacon fat
2 tablespoons butter
1½ pounds chicken livers
½ pound unsalted pork fat, ground
2 tablespoons dry sherry
2 tablespoons brandy
½ teaspoon freshly ground pepper
3 green onions or shallots, chopped
1 clove garlic, minced
1½ teaspoons salt

Coat 7-inch soufflé mold well with cold bacon fat.

Melt butter in skillet. Sauté livers until all pink has disappeared.

Combine livers, port fat, sherry, brandy, pepper, onions, garlic, and salt; mix well. Place mixture in blender or food-processor container, a small amount at a time; blend until thoroughly pureed. Blending may take longer than usual; pork fat is not easily pureed. Spoon mixture into prepared mold; cover with aluminum foil. Place mold in baking dish. Pour hot water half the depth of mold.

Bake in preheated 350°F oven 1 hour. Remove from oven; let cool. Invert onto serving platter; chill in refrigerator overnight.

Serve with French bread or crackers. Yield about 2 cups.

hot pâté with garlic bread

½ pound finely ground lean beef
½ pound finely ground lean pork
½ pound mild pork sausage
2 cloves garlic, pressed
2 tablespoons grated onion
¼ teaspoon basil
¼ teaspoon marjoram
¼ teaspoon thyme
¼ teaspoon oregano
1 teaspoon salt
½ teaspoon freshly ground pepper
½ cup Basic Beef Stock (see Index)
3 tablespoons sherry
1 tablespoon brandy

Combine beef, pork, and sausage and grind through a food chopper 3 times or spin in a food processor until smooth, using the on-off method.

hot pâté with garlic bread

Add garlic, onion, basil, marjoram, thyme, oregano, salt, and pepper. Mix with wooden spoon until thoroughly blended. Add stock, sherry, and brandy; blend until smooth. Turn into buttered 1-quart earthenware mold; cover. Set in baking pan; pour in boiling water to half the depth of mold.

Bake in preheated 325°F oven 1 hour and 15 minutes. Increase oven temperature to 350°F. Remove cover; bake 30 minutes or until brown.

Slice; serve with hot garlic bread. Serve on small slices of bread as a cocktail appetizer or as a first course. Yield about 3 cups.

party liver pâté

¼ pound butter or chicken fat
1 large onion, chopped fine
1 pound chicken livers
1 tablespoon Worcestershire sauce
Salt and pepper to taste

Melt butter in medium skillet; lightly tan chopped onion. Add chicken livers; cook until slightly pink at center, about 5 minutes. Remove from heat.

Put entire mixture through food mill until

ground very smooth. If you use a colander instead of a food mill, you may want to put the liver mixture through twice to ensure a smooth texture. Add Worcestershire sauce and salt and pepper; mix together well with spoon.

Shape pâté into greased mold for a party. Turn out on serving plate; surround with party crackers so that guests can help themselves. Yield 10 to 16 servings.

simple pâté maison

6 slices salt pork
6 slices bacon, diced
1½ cups chopped onions
1 pound calves liver
1 pound chicken livers
1¾ teaspoons salt
1 teaspoon pepper
3 egg yolks
2 eggs
¼ cup Maderia
½ teaspoon chervil
½ teaspoon tarragon leaves
½ teaspoon nutmeg
¼ teaspoon allspice

Rinse salt pork in cold water to remove some of salt. Drain thoroughly. Line 7-inch soufflé mold with salt pork slices.

Cook bacon in skillet until fat is rendered.

Sauté onions in bacon fat until tender and lightly browned.

Cut the liver into 1-inch pieces; halve chicken livers. Add livers, 1 teaspoon salt and ½ teaspoon pepper to onion mixture. Sauté until all pink has disappeared from livers. Place liver mixture in

party liver pâté

blender container or in food processor a small amount at a time. Blend until thoroughly pureed, adding egg yolks, eggs, and Madeira. Spoon liver mixture into large bowl. Stir in remaining salt, pepper, and spices. Pour liver mixture into prepared mold; cover with aluminum foil. Place mold in larger baking dish; add water halfway to top of mold.

Bake in preheated 375°F oven 2 hours. Cool pâté well; invert onto serving platter. Refrigerate at least 8 hours to chill thoroughly.

Pâté can be sliced thin and served with French bread or crackers or as a separate course with a green salad. Yield about 30 servings as a spread.

simple pâté maison

QUICHE

broccoli quiche

Pastry for single-crust 9-inch pie (see Index)
¼ cup grated Parmesan cheese
2 cups chopped fresh broccoli
1 cup shredded Swiss cheese
¼ cup sliced scallions
3 eggs
⅔ cup chicken broth
½ cup heavy cream
½ teaspoon salt
¼ teaspoon Tabasco pepper sauce

Line 10-inch quiche dish or 9-inch pie plate with pastry. Prick bottom and corners of pastry with fork. Bake in 450°F oven 5 minutes. Remove from oven; sprinkle with 2 tablespoons Parmesan cheese. Layer half the broccoli over Parmesan cheese. Continue with layers of half Swiss cheese and scallions; repeat with remaining broccoli, Swiss cheese, and scallions.

Beat eggs. Add chicken broth, cream, salt, and Tabasco; mix well. Pour over broccoli mixture in pastry shell. Sprinkle with remaining 2 tablespoons Parmesan cheese.

Bake 10 minutes at 450°F. Reduce heat to 325°F; bake 20 to 25 minutes longer or until knife inserted in center of pie comes out clean. Let stand 5 to 10 minutes before cutting. Yield 10 to 12 servings.

cheese, bacon, and onion quiche

1 single-crust Basic Pastry (see Index; do not bake)
6 slices bacon, cut into 2-inch pieces
1 small onion, chopped
3 eggs
½ cup milk
½ cup heavy cream
1 cup shredded Swiss cheese
½ teaspoon salt
⅛ teaspoon pepper

Line quiche or pie pan with pastry.

Cook bacon until crisp. Drain; place in pie shell.

Sauté onion in bacon fat until lightly browned. Drain off fat. Off heat, stir in eggs, milk, cream, cheese, and seasonings. Pour into pastry-lined pan.

Bake in preheated 375°F oven 25 minutes or until knife plunged into custard comes out clean.

Serve hot, warm, or cold. Yield 4 servings.

corn–cheese quiche

1 Single-Pie Crust pastry, unbaked (see Index)
3 ears corn (or about 1 cup kernels)
4 eggs
1 cup milk
½ cup light (table) cream
½ cup freshly grated Parmesan cheese
2 tablespoons finely chopped onion

corn-cheese quiche

1 teaspoon salt
¼ teaspoon pepper
6 slices bacon
Parsley for garnish

Roll out pastry on floured board to ⅛ inch thick; fit into 9-inch quiche or pie pan.

Cut kernels off corncobs; reserve.

Beat eggs in large mixing bowl. Stir in milk, cream, cheese, onion, salt, and pepper; mix well. Add corn. Pour into pie shell. Bake in preheated 375°F oven 20 minutes.

Meanwhile fry bacon until almost done; drain on paper towels. Arrange bacon on top of pie. Bake 10 minutes or until knife inserted in custard comes out clean.

Garnish quiche with parsley; serve hot. Yield 6 servings.

greek spinach and cheese turnovers

1 egg
½ medium onion, finely chopped
¼ pound crumbled feta cheese
4 ounces cream cheese
5 ounces (½ of 10-ounce package) frozen chopped spinach, thawed, drained
1 tablespoon chopped parsley
½ teaspoon dillweed
½ teaspoon garlic powder
6 sheets phyllo or 4 frozen patty shells (omit butter when using patty shells)
1 stick butter, melted

In blender or mixer bowl combine egg, onion, and feta cheese; beat to combine. Add cream cheese; combine well. Add spinach and seasonings; mix just until blended. Chill 1 hour.

phyllo dough

Phyllo must be handled with great care, since it is very delicate and dry to the touch. Carefully unroll as many sheets needed; store remainder immediately.

Place the sheets not immediately in use between linen tea towels to prevent drying. If weather is very hot and dry, sprinkle a little water on towels.

Phyllo sheets are generally 16 × 22 inches. Stack 2 leaves together, cutting through both sheets. Cut strips 2 inches wide by 16 inches long. Brush with melted butter. Place a teaspoon of filling on one end of strip. Fold one corner of strip to opposite side, forming a triangle and enclosing filling. Continue folding as you would an American flag, to end of strip, maintaining triangular shape. Brush with melted butter.

Place on ungreased cookie sheet. Bake at 375°F 20 minutes. Serve hot.

greek spinach and cheese turnovers

puff pastry dough

Defrost patty shells at room temperature 15 to 20 minutes. Form each shell into a ball; roll on floured pastry cloth to 11 × 11-inch square. Cut into 16 individual squares. Place ½ teaspoon filling on each square. Fold to form a triangle; seal with milk.

Bake at 450°F 12 minutes. Yield: About 33 if made with phyllo; about 64 if made with puff pastry.

Note: These can be baked, then frozen. Reheat on cookie sheet at 350°F 15 minutes.

mushroom and onion quiche

If you have a pre-made shell in the freezer you are always prepared for the unexpected with this recipe.

Pastry for single-crust 9-inch pie (see Index)
3 tablespoons butter or margarine
2 onions, peeled, chopped
1 can button mushrooms (about 1 cup)
2 eggs
½ can evaporated milk (about 1 cup)
½ cup grated cheese
Pinch of dry mustard

Preheat oven to 400°F.

Line deep 8-inch pie plate with pastry.

Heat 2 tablespoons butter in sauté pan; cook onion until transparent. Drain well; put into pastry shell with most of mushrooms, cut in halves. Leave a few uncut for decoration.

Beat eggs, stir in evaporated milk, grated

cheese, and seasoning. Pour over mushrooms. Bake about 35 minutes.

Sauté remaining mushrooms a few minutes in 1 tablespoon butter. Drain; cut into thin slices.

When pie is cooked, decorate with sliced mushrooms. Yield 4 to 5 servings.

spinach quiche

1½ to 2 pounds fresh spinach, cooked, drained
⅛ teaspoon freshly grated nutmeg (or same amount bottled)
1 tablespoon fresh tarragon or 1 teaspoon dried
1 tablespoon freshly squeezed lemon juice
Salt
Freshly ground black pepper
2 tablespoons chopped fresh parsley
9-inch pastry shell (see Index) that has been baked five minutes
½ cup feta cheese
4 eggs
½ cup plain yogurt
¾ cup cream

Cook spinach until tender. Drain liquid thoroughly by squeezing small handfuls between palms of your hands. Chop very fine. Combine spinach with nutmeg, tarragon, lemon juice, salt and pepper to taste, and parsley; spread on bottom of pastry. Sprinkle cheese on top.

Beat eggs lightly with yogurt. Cream; blend well. Pour over spinach mixture.

Bake in 350°F oven about 30 minutes, or until custard is set.

This is an excellent accompaniment to roast lamb or chicken. It also makes a fine brunch entree. Yield 6 to 8 servings.

SANDWICHES

appetizer egg and asparagus sandwiches

½ recipe Basic Emergency Aspic (see Index)
10 slices thin-sliced pumpernickel or whole-wheat bread
10 slices Monterey Jack cheese
6 hard-boiled eggs
20 small gherkins
1 1-pound can white asparagus tips

Prepare aspic: Substitute chicken consommé for beef consommé; let chill until syrupy.

Remove crusts from bread; cut into 2 rectangles. Spread generously with mayonnaise; top with rectangle of cheese.

Cut eggs crosswise into ¼-inch slices. Place 3 slices on each rectangle.

Cut gherkins.

Place 1 gherkin and 1 asparagus spear on each sandwich. Place sandwiches on rack over jelly-roll pan. Spoon aspic carefully over each sandwich; coat evenly. Place rack on cookie sheet. Refrigerate until firm.

Return excess aspic in jelly-roll pan to remaining aspic; do not stir. Chill aspic as needed to keep at syrupy stage. Repeat coating and chilling several times, until sandwiches are thickly glazed. Refrigerate until ready to serve.

Garnish serving tray with any remaining asparagus. Yield 20.

appetizer egg and asparagus sandwiches

danish cheese appetizer sandwiches

appetizer peanut-butter sandwiches

16 pieces bread, crusts removed, quartered or cut into triangles
1½ cups peanut butter
¼ pound butter
1 cup shredded carrots
1½ cups finely chopped celery
2 teaspoons salt
Stuffed green olives for garnish

Set bread aside; save crusts for future bread stuffing.

Mix rest of ingredients, except olives, to form smooth spread; spread onto each piece of bread. Top with stuffed green olive for color; arrange on serving plate. Yield about 60.

danish cheese appetizer sandwiches

Dark rye bread
Butter
White cheddar-process cheese slices
Unskinned tomato
Pimiento-stuffed olive slices
Danish black bread
Roquefort cheese wedges
Pitted black olives
Whole-wheat bread
Caraway Swiss-cheese slices
Heart of lettuce leaves

Spread rye bread slices with butter; cover with slices of Cheddar cheese. Decorate cheese with tomato slivers and half slices and with green-olive slices.

Butter black-bread slices with 4 Roquefort-cheese wedges; top with 2 black olives on each slice.

Butter whole-wheat bread; cover with slices of caraway Swiss cheese. Overlap a row of green olives down 2 sides of each sandwich. Place a roll slice of Swiss cheese diagonally across each sandwich. Garnish sandwiches with lettuce leaves and tomato slivers. Yield as desired.

SEAFOOD

anchovy puffs

½ cup margarine or butter
3 ounces cream cheese
1 cup flour
Anchovy paste

Blend margarine and cream cheese. Mix with flour; chill.

Roll out very thin; cut with small biscuit cutter. Spread each piece with small amount of anchovy paste. Fold; pinch sides together. Bake in 400°F oven 10 minutes. Yield 6 servings.

anchovy sticks

10 slices bread, toasted and buttered
½ cup chopped green onions
½ cup chopped parsley
¼ pound butter
40 anchovy fillets

Cut each piece of buttered toast into 4 1-inch strips.

Mix together onions and parsley. Sprinkle mixture over toast strips. Top with 1 anchovy fillet on each toast stick; dot with butter. Bake sticks at 375°F just long enough to heat through.

Serve sticks hot; allow 2 or 3 per person. Yield 40.

angels on horseback

avocado pear cream

flesh; be careful not to break skin. Reserve empty shells. Put flesh into bowl; mash well. Add vinegar, anchovies, onion; season with salt, cayenne, and sugar. Chill. Fold in whipped cream just before serving. Fill pear shells; sprinkle with paprika. Garnish with black olives; serve with melba toast. Yield 4 servings.

clam macadamia puffs

Clam dip must be the most overused canapé spread in the world. A little ingenuity and a few macadamia nuts can revitalize this old favorite. Your guests won't recognize it! Best of all, you can make it on the morning of a party.

1 8-ounce package cream cheese, softened
1 can minced clams, drained
1 teaspoon minced green onion
½ cup chopped macadamia nuts (bits)
Salt to taste
Dash of red pepper
¾ teaspoon Worcestershire sauce
1 tablespoon macadamia nuts (fine)
1 teaspoon paprika

Whip cheese thoroughly. Add clams; mix well. Add onion, chopped macadamias, salt, red pepper, and Worcestershire; whip again. Test for salt. Refrigerate in covered dish.

When ready to serve, heap mixture generously on salty crackers; bake 20 minutes in 300°F oven. Decorate with a sprinkle of ground macadamias and paprika. Yield about 20.

crab balls

1 pound crab meat
4 tablespoons butter or margarine
1 teaspoon salt
⅛ teaspoon cayenne pepper
1 teaspoon dry mustard
1 teaspoon dehydrated parsley flakes
2 teaspoons Worcestershire sauce
½ cup soft bread crumbs
2 egg yolks, lightly beaten
½ cup flour
Oil for frying

Pick over crab meat; remove any bits of shell and cartilage. Flake crab meat; place in mixing bowl.

Melt butter in small saucepan. Add seasonings, bread-crumbs, and egg yolks to crab; mix well. Refrigerate 2 to 3 hours or until stiff enough to be handled easily.

Form into 35 small balls the size of a walnut; dredge in flour.

Heat several inches of oil in heavy saucepan or

angels on horseback

1 can (12 ounces) oysters, fresh or frozen (preferably small)
2 tablespoons chopped parsley
½ teaspoon salt
Paprika
Pepper
10 slices bacon, cut into thirds

Thaw frozen oysters; drain. If oysters are large, cut in half. There should be 30 pieces. Sprinkle with parsley and seasonings. Place an oyster on each piece of bacon. Wrap bacon around oyster; secure with toothpick. Place on broiler pan. Broil about 4 inches from source of heat 8 to 10 minutes or until bacon is crisp. Turn carefully. Broil 4 to 5 minutes longer or until bacon is crisp. Yield approximately 30 hors d'oeuvres.

avocado pear cream

2 ripe avocado pears
1 tablespoon white-wine vinegar
4 anchovy fillets, finely chopped
2 teaspoons finely chopped onion
Cayenne pepper
1 teaspoon sugar
½ cup whipping cream
Paprika
Ripe olives

Cut pears in half; remove seeds. Scrape out all

deep-fat fryer to 360°F. Fry crab balls until golden brown; serve hot.

Garnish with parsley and lemon wedges. Yield 35.

crab–cheese pie

1 can (6 to 8 ounces) Alaska Snow crab meat
1½ cups grated Cheddar or Jack cheese
2 eggs, beaten
½ cup milk
2 tablespoons minced green onions (scallions)
1 can (8 ounces) refrigerated crescent rolls

Drain and slice crab meat. Combine with cheese, eggs, milk, and onions.

Line 9-inch pie plate with 5 triangles of dough. Press together to form crust. Spoon in crab mixture. Top with remaining triangles. Bake at 325°F 50 to 60 minutes. Yield 5 to 6 servings.

crab dabs

crab dabs

1 can (12 ounces) dungeness or other crab meat, fresh or frozen or 2 cans (6½ or 7½ ounces each) crab meat
⅓ cup fine soft bread crumbs
2 tablespoons dry sherry
1 teaspoon chopped chives
1 teaspoon dry mustard
¼ teaspoon salt
10 slices bacon, cut into thirds

Thaw frozen crab meat. Drain crab meat; remove any shell or cartilage. Chop crab meat.

Combine all ingredeints except bacon; mix thoroughly. Chill 30 minutes. Portion crab mixture with a tablespoon; shape into small rolls. Wrap bacon around crab rolls; secure with toothpicks. Place crab rolls on broiler pan. Broil about

4 inches from source of heat 8 to 10 minutes or until bacon is crisp. Turn carefully. Broil 4 to 5 minutes longer or until bacon is crisp. Yield about 30 hors d'oeuvres.

festive seafood cocktail

3 pounds Boiled Shrimp (see Index)
1½ cups catsup
2 tablespoons fresh lemon juice
1 tablespoon Worcestershire sauce
1½ teaspoons sugar
Dash of hot sauce
Salt and freshly ground pepper to taste

Place shrimp in refrigerator; chill thoroughly.

Combine remaining ingredients for sauce; mix thoroughly. Chill well.

Arrange shrimp in cocktail icers or stemmed dessert glasses; spoon sauce over shrimp. Yield about 6 servings.

gefilte fish

8 to 10 pounds fish (rock, shad, white and/or pike)
1 onion, whole
Carrots, sliced
Salt and pepper
1 large onion, grated
½ stick margarine
2 eggs
½ cup matzo meal
½ cup fish stock

Fish should be filleted and ground. This yields about 4 to 5 pounds ground fish. Reserve heads and bones. Place heads, bones, several sliced carrots, whole onion, salt, and a lot of pepper in large pot of water; bring to boil.

Sauté grated onion in margarine.

In wooden bowl, using hand chopper, mix all remaining ingredients with fish. Adjust fish seasoning, adding freshly ground pepper to reduce fishy taste.

Form medium-size balls; place in boiling water. Simmer, uncovered, 3 hours. Yield 20 pieces.

greek fish appetizers

All-purpose flour
1 teaspoon salt
⅛ teaspoon paprika
3 tablespoons vegetable oil
1 cup milk
½ teaspoon Worcestershire sauce
2 teaspoons grated onion
2 cups cooked flaked whitefish
1 egg
Fine dry bread crumbs

Mix 6 tablespoons flour, salt, and paprika in small saucepan. Stir in oil; mix until smooth. Add milk; mix well. Cook over low heat, stirring constantly, until thick and smooth. Remove from heat; stir in Worcestershire sauce, onion, and whitefish. Refrigerate until chilled.

Beat egg with 2 tablespoons water.

Shape whitefish mixture into small balls, using 1 teaspoon for each; roll in flour. Dip in egg; roll in bread crumbs.

Cook in deep fat at 350°F until well browned; drain on paper toweling.

Place on serving plate; insert end of small skewer or pick in each ball. Yield about 48.

greek fish appetizers

festive seafood cocktail

hen-house homards

1 pound cooked lobster meat, fresh or frozen
⅔ cup mayonnaise or salad dressing
1 tablespoon chili sauce
1 teaspoon chopped green pepper
1 teaspoon grated onion
1 teaspoon chopped pimiento
16 hard-cooked eggs
Parsley

Thaw frozen lobster meat. Drain lobster meat. Remove any shell or cartilage. Chop lobster meat.

Combine mayonnaise, seasonings, and lobster.

Cut eggs in half lengthwise; remove yolks.* Fill each egg white with 1 tablespoon lobster mixture. Sprinkle with parsley; chill. Yield 32 hors d'oeuvres.

*Egg yolks may be used in other recipes.

lobster boats

hen-house homards

lobster boats

½ pound cooked lobster meat, fresh or frozen
24 fresh mushrooms, approximately 1½ inches in
    diameter
¼ cup condensed cream of mushroom soup
2 tablespoons fine soft bread crumbs
2 tablespoons mayonnaise or salad dressing
¼ teaspoon Worcestershire sauce
⅛ teaspoon liquid hot pepper sauce
Dash of pepper
Grated Parmesan cheese

Thaw frozen lobster meat. Drain lobster meat. Remove any shell or cartilage. Chop lobster meat.

Rinse mushrooms in cold water. Dry mushrooms; remove stems.

Combine soup, crumbs, mayonnaise, seasonings, and lobster. Stuff each mushroom cap with a tablespoonful of lobster mixture. Sprinkle with cheese.

Place mushrooms on well-buttered baking pan,

15 × 10 × 1 inch. Bake in 400°F oven 10 to 15 minutes or until lightly browned. Yield 24 hors d' oeuvres

oysters on the half shell

24 oysters
Beds of lettuce or crushed ice
Lemon wedges
Tabasco sauce

Wash oysters well to remove sand and grit.

Prepare beds of lettuce or ice.

Open oysters with oyster knife just before serving. Discard top shell; loosen oyster from bottom of shell by cutting ligaments.

Serve oysters immediately. Garnish with lemon wedges; accompany with Tabasco. Pass lots of whole-wheat soda bread. Yield 4 servings.

oysters on the half shell

party salmon ball

1 pound can salmon
8 ounces cream cheese, room temperature
1 tablespoon lemon juice
2 teaspoons grated onion
1 teaspoon prepared horseradish
¼ teaspoon salt
3 drops liquid smoke

½ **cup chopped pecans**

Drain salmon thoroughly; flake carefully with fork or your fingers. Combine salmon with softened cream cheese. Add next 5 ingredients; mix thoroughly. Cover bowl. Refrigerate a few hours, until firm.

Shape salmon into ball; roll in nuts. Wrap tightly in plastic wrap; return to refrigerator until serving.

Serve with firm, unflavored crackers. Yield 10 to 12 cocktail appetizers.

rock lobster appetizers

12 2-ounce frozen rock lobster tails
6 tablespoons butter
6 tablespoons all-purpose flour
1½ cups half-and-half cream
1 teaspoon grated lemon rind
1 teaspoon paprika
2 eggs, separated
Salt and freshly ground pepper to taste
½ **cup freshly grated cheddar or Parmesan cheese**

Drop frozen lobster tails into kettle of boiling salted water; bring to boil again. Drain lobster tails immediately; drench with cold water. Remove underside membrane with scissors; pull out lobster meat, reserving shells. Dice lobster meat.

Melt butter in top of double boiler over boiling water. Stir in flour until smooth. Add cream gradually, stirring constantly; cook until thickened. Add lemon rind and paprika.

Stir small amount of sauce into beaten egg yolks; stir mixture back into sauce. Cook 2 minutes, stirring constantly. Season with salt and pepper.

Combine lobster meat and half the sauce, mixing well. Spoon lobster mixture into reserved shells; place shells on baking sheet.

Heat remaining sauce. Add cheese; stir until melted. Cool slightly; fold in stiffly beaten egg whites. Spoon egg-white mixture over lobster mixture in shells.

Bake in preheated 350°F oven 25 to 30 minutes or until puffed and lightly browned.

Serve in chafing dish over hot water. Yield 6 servings as first course-appetizers.

seafood avocado appetizers

4 large avocados
Lemon juice
4 tablespoons Vinaigrette Aux Fines Herbes (see Index)
4 tablespoons Madeira
1 cup mayonnaise
⅛ **teaspoon hot sauce**
1 teaspoon paprika
Salt to taste
2 teaspoons lemon juice
1 cup fresh crab meat, flaked
1 cup cooked small shrimp

Cut avocados; remove the seeds. Brush cut sides of avocados with lemon juice. Spoon 2 tablespoons vinaigrette into each cavity of 2 avocado halves. Spoon 2 tablespoons of Madeira into each cavity of 2 more avocado halves.

Place mayonnaise in mixing bowl. Add hot sauce, paprika, salt, and lemon juice; mix well. Divide in half.

Add crab meat to half of mayonnaise mixture; stir until combined. Mound crab-meat mixture on

rock lobster appetizers

![seafood avocado appetizers]

seafood avocado appetizers

2 more avocado halves; garnish each mound with 1 shrimp.

Add remaining shrimp to remaining mayonnaise mixture; mix well.

Place half of shrimp mixture on each of remaining avocado halves.

Place halves on serving platter as shown in illustration; garnish as desired. Each guest can make his own choice. Yield 8 servings as a first course or luncheon dish.

seafood cocktail

1 orange
2 tablespoons kirsch
12 blue grapes, halved, seeds discarded
Lettuce leaves
1 small can white asparagus tips (optional; available in specialty food stores)
12 ounces canned or cooked seafood (shrimp, lobster, scallops, or crab meat)

cocktail dressing

¼ cup mayonnaise
¼ cup plain yogurt
1 teaspoon catsup
1 teaspoon prepared horseradish
Freshly ground black pepper to taste
Few drops Worcestershire sauce, to taste
1 tablespoon lemon juice
Salt and pepper to taste

garnishes

Whole blue grapes
Unpeeled orange slices, halved
Cooked crab claws

Peel orange; remove as much white membrane as possible. Cut into slices and each slice into quarters. Sprinkle with kirsch.

Prepare dressing by blending together all dressing ingredients.

Arrange orange pieces in 4 champagne glasses lined with lettuce leaves. Add grape halves and asparagus tips. Arrange selected seafood on top. Pour dressing over all.

Serve seafood cocktail at once, garnished with whole grapes, half slice of unpeeled orange, and a crab claw. Yield 4 servings.

seafood cocktail

shrimp balls

1 medium onion, grated
1½ pounds raw shrimp, shelled, deveined, grated
1 medium raw potato, grated
1 egg, slightly beaten
Salt and pepper to taste
Fat for deep frying

Grind or grate onion and shrimp into large bowl.

Grind potato; pat dry with paper toweling. Stir in egg, salt, and pepper. Potato is the thickening; batter will be thick.

Heat deep fat; drop batter in by spoonfuls. Fry until golden brown; remove with slotted spoon. Drain on paper towels. Serve hot. Yield 36 to 48.

shrimp muffin hors d' oeuvres

3 English muffins, split
1 egg
1 tablespoon cornstarch
1 teaspoon soy sauce
½ teaspoon sugar
½ pound raw shrimp, shelled, deveined, finely chopped
1 quart (about) corn oil
Salt

Toast muffin halves just enough to give light crispness; do not brown. Tear each muffin half in two.

Mix together egg, cornstarch, soy sauce, and sugar until smooth. Stir in shrimp. Spread shrimp mixture evenly over 12 muffin quarters.

Pour corn oil into heavy 3-quart saucepan or deep fryer, filling no more than ⅓ full. Heat over medium heat to 375°F. Carefully add muffins, a few at a time, shrimp-side-down. Fry about 2 minutes or until light golden. Turn; fry about 1 minute to brown other side. Remove from oil with slotted spoon; drain on paper towels. Sprinkle with salt. Serve hot. Yield 12.

shrimp tree

3 pounds shrimp, fresh or frozen
2 quarts water
½ cup salt
4 large bunches curly endive
1 styrofoam cone, 2½ feet high
1 small box round toothpicks

If shrimp is frozen, thaw. Place shrimp in boiling salted water; cover. Simmer about 5 minutes or until shrimp are pink and tender; drain. Peel shrimp. Remove sand veins; wash. Chill.

Separate and wash endive; chill.

Fasten endive to styrofoam cone with toothpick halves. Start at outside edge of base; work up. Cover fully with greens to resemble tree. Attach shrimp artistically to tree with toothpicks.

Place tree on large plate or tray; add leftover shrimp around base. Top tree with ribbon, tinsel, or your favorite ornament. Provide cocktail sauce for dunking.

You can keep a bowl of prepared shrimp in the refrigerator and replenish tree as needed. Yield as desired.

stuffed clams

2 dozen clams (little-neck or rock)
¾ cup dry white wine
¼ cup water
½ teaspoon salt
3 tablespoons olive oil
½ cup chopped onion
½ cup raw long-grain rice
¼ teaspoon pepper
½ teaspoon allspice
¼ teaspoon cinnamon
3 tablespoons currants
3 tablespoons pine nuts
2 tablespoons chopped parsley

Scrub clams; soak in several changes of cold water to remove sand. Place in skillet with wine, water, and salt. Cover; steam until the shells open. Discard any clams that do not open. Cool; remove clams from shells. Save shells; strain pan juices.

Heat oil in medium saucepan. Sauté onion until golden. Add rice and 1 cup juices; bring to boil. Cover; reduce heat to low. Cook 15 minutes. Add pepper, spices, currants, pine nuts, and parsley. Cook 5 minutes; cool.

Dice clams; and add to pilaf.

Stuff shells with rice mixture; chill. Serve as a meal appetizer. Yield 24 appetizers.

tuna puffs

2 cans (6½ or 7 ounces each) tuna
1 cup finely chopped celery
½ cup mayonnaise or salad dressing
2 tablespoons chopped onion
2 tablespoons chopped sweet pickle
Salt to taste
Puff Shells

Drain and flake tuna.

Combine all ingredients except puff shells; mix thoroughly.

Cut tops from puff shells. Fill each shell with approximately 2 teaspoonfuls salad. Yield about 55 hors d' oeuvres.

tuna puffs

puff shells

½ cup boiling water
¼ cup butter or margarine
Dash of salt
½ cup flour
2 eggs

Combine water, butter, and salt in saucepan; bring to boil. Add flour all at once; stir vigorously until mixture forms a ball and leaves sides of pan. Remove from heat. Add eggs, one at a time; beat thoroughly after each addition. Continue beating until stiff dough is formed. Drop by level teaspoonfuls onto well-greased cookie sheet, 15 × 12 inches.

Bake in 450°F oven 10 minutes. Reduce heat to 350°F; bake about 10 minutes. Yield about 55.

SNACKS

garlic-butter chips

¾ cup butter or margarine
2 to 3 cloves garlic, cut into slivers
Potato chips

Preheat oven to 350°F.

Heat butter with garlic a few minutes; remove garlic.

Brush potato chips with garlic butter; place on baking sheets lined with paper towels. Heat 5 minutes; drain on clean paper towels. Yield as desired.

garlic-butter chips

quark snacks

quark snacks

2 cups all-purpose white flour
3 teaspoons baking powder
1 teaspoon salt
¼ cup all-vegetable shortening
¾ cup milk (about)
2 egg yolks, beaten
3 tablespoons caraway seeds

cottage-cheese filling

1 cup dry-curd cottage cheese
2 tablespoons dried parsley flakes
1 teaspoon salt
2 tablespoons chopped pimiento

Combine dry ingredients; cut in shortening to resemble coarse meal. Add milk to form soft dough. Knead dough 6 times. Roll on floured surface to ¼ inch thick. Brush half the biscuits with egg yolks; sprinkle with caraway seeds.

Bake biscuits at 450°F 10 minutes or until golden brown.

Make Cottage-Cheese Filling by combining cottage cheese, parsley flakes, salt, and pimiento.

To serve, spread Cottage-Cheese Filling on plain biscuits; top with caraway-seed biscuits. Yield 20.

snack mix

2 cups Grapenuts cereal
½ cup shredded coconut
2 cups raisins
½ cup crushed walnuts

Mix together and enjoy. Yield 5 cups.

sweet or salty pretzels

1 package dry yeast
½ cup lukewarm milk
4 or more cups flour
1 teaspoon sugar
½ teaspoon salt
2 egg yolks
½ pound butter
2 tablespoons kosher salt or 4 tablespoons
  fine sugar

Dissolve yeast in milk.

Put flour in large bowl; make depression in center. Add dissolved yeast and milk, sugar, and salt. Add 1 egg yolk; mix well. Liberally dot mixture with ¼ pound butter. Knead it quickly and lightly. Roll out dough on floured board to a large square. Dot with ¼ pound butter. Fold in thirds. Cover dough; set in refrigerator on a lightly floured plate.

Put dough on flour-covered work surface; roll it out again to a square. Work butter into batter. Knead dough 4 times; let rest in refrigerator.

Repeat process again; let dough rest 30 minutes at room temperature.

Roll out dough final time to about 1 inch thick and 10 inches long, so that you can cut sticks about 1 inch wide. Cut and form these sticks into pretzel shapes. Put onto greased cookie sheet. Brush with egg yolk. Sprinkle with coarse salt or sugar.

Bake pretzels at 425°F 20 minutes. Allow to cool before serving. Yield 18 or 19.

tortilla chips

1 dozen corn tortillas
Oil for frying
Salt

Defrost tortillas if frozen. Cut each tortilla into 8 wedges.

Use small heavy skillet, electric skillet, or deep fryer to heat at least 1 inch cooking oil to 360°F. Fry tortilla pieces, a few at a time, until crisp and lightly browned. Remove from oil with slotted spoon. Drain chips on paper towels; salt lightly.

Serve with dips or refried beans. Yield 8 dozen.

tv snacks

1 small box Cheerios
1 box Wheat Chex
1 box Rice Chex
1 box pretzel sticks
½ pound nuts
¼ pound butter
⅔ cup peanut oil

sweet or salty pretzels

4 tablespoons Worcestershire sauce
2½ tablespoons garlic salt

Preheat oven to 250°F.

Put cereals, pretzel sticks, and nuts into roasting pan.

Melt butter in pan. Blend in oil, Worcestershire sauce, and garlic salt. Sprinkle over dry ingredients; mix through. Bake 1½ hours; stir several times while baking.

When done, remove from oven; spread on absorbent paper 20 minutes. When cool, put into jars; seal. Yield as desired.

VEGETABLES

rice-stuffed grape-vine leaves

These can be frozen in a covered container. Thaw them in the refrigerator 24 hours before serving.

1 1-pound jar vine leaves
1½ tablespoons olive oil
1 medium onion, finely chopped
½ cup pine nuts
¾ cup raw long-grain rice
½ cup golden raisins
2½ cups water
2 tablespoons finely chopped parsley
½ teaspoon salt
Freshly ground pepper
½ teaspoon cinnamon
2 medium tomatoes, peeled, seeded, chopped

Juice of 1 lemon
¼ cup olive oil
Lemon wedges for garnish

Unfold vine leaves. Rinse carefully under cold running water; drain.

Heat 1½ tablespoons oil in saucepan. Add onion; sauté until limp. Add pine nuts; cook over medium heat 5 minutes. Add rice, raisins, and 1½ cups water. Cover; cook 20 minutes or until all liquid is absorbed. Stir in parsley, salt, pepper, cinnamon, and tomatoes.

With stem end of leaf toward you, place approximately 1 tablespoon filling on each vine leaf. Fold up stem end to enclose filling. Fold sides to center; roll to form a neat package. Do not try to secure rolls with toothpicks; they are fragile and will tear easily.

Place thin layer of unfilled vine leaves in bottom of large, heavy saucepan. Tightly pack rolls in pan, seam-side-down, in layers. Sprinkle each layer with some of lemon juice and part of the ¼ cup oil. Add 1 cup water; place heavy kitchen plate on top of rolls in pan to weight them down. Cover pan; bring rolls to boil. Reduce heat to simmer; cook 30 minutes. Remove from heat; cool.

Carefully remove stuffed leaves from pan; serve them cold, garnished with lemon wedges. Yield 30 to 40 appetizers; 6 servings as a first course.

stuffed mushrooms

8 ounces cooked crab, shrimp, or lobster, minced
4 water chestnuts, minced

1 scallion, minced
2 teaspoons soy sauce
1 teaspoon dry sherry
1 teaspoon sugar
1 teaspoon cornstarch
1 egg
12 mushroom stems, minced, browned in a little oil
12 large mushrooms, stems removed
Parsley (optional)

Combine all ingredients except mushroom caps and parsley. Fill mushroom caps with mixture. Bake at 350°F 20 minutes. Serve hot, garnished with parsley. Allow 2 or 3 to a person for a first course, or use smaller mushrooms, and serve on melba rounds as finger food. Yield 12 appetizers.

stuffed zucchini hors d'oeuvres

3 small zucchini, unpeeled
4 ounces cream cheese, softened
3 slices bacon, crisped, crumbled
1 clove garlic, minced
1 teaspoon chopped parsley
¼ teaspoon black pepper.

Cut off zucchini ends; scoop out centers with long-handled spoon.

Mix together remaining ingredients. Stuff mixture firmly into center of zucchini, using a pastry bag with a wide-mouthed tip or a small spoon; chill. To serve, cut into ½-inch slices. Yield 4 to 6 servings.

rice-stuffed grape-vine leaves

BATTERS

basic tempura batter

2 cups sifted all-purpose flour
3 egg yolks
2 cups ice water

Sift flour 3 times.

Combine egg yolks and water in large bowl over ice; beat with whisk until well blended. Add flour gradually, stirring and turning mixture from bottom with a spoon. Do not overmix. Flour should be visible on top or batter will become gummy. Keep batter over ice while dipping and frying. Cold beer can be substituted for water, if desired. Yield about 4½ cups.

beer tempura batter

2 eggs
1⅓ cups sifted all-purpose flour
1 teaspoon salt
1 cup flat beer

Place eggs, flour, and salt in bowl; mix well. Gradually stir in beer; beat just until smooth. Let stand 1 hour, or refrigerate overnight. Yield approximately 2 cups.

golden tempura batter

1 large egg
1 cup water
1¼ cups sifted all-purpose flour

Beat egg and water together. Add flour all at once; beat just until smooth. Let stand 1 hour, or refrigerate overnight. Yield approximately 2 cups.

CURED BEEF

CORNED BEEF

boiled corned beef

1 (3- to 5-pound) corned-beef round

Place corned beef in Dutch oven or heavy pan; cover with cold water. Bring slowly to boil. Simmer, covered, 3½ to 5 hours or until tender. Remove from broth; let stand 15 minutes before slicing.

Cabbage wedges and potatoes can be cooked in broth for old-fashioned corned beef and cabbage. Yield 4 to 6 servings.

caribbean corned-beef kabobs

Preheat oven to 350°F.
Preheat broiler.

2 medium onions
2 tablespoons oil
1 cup rice
3 cups beef stock (or water with cube)
1 orange
2 to 3 tablespoons butter
¼ cup pineapple juice
1 teaspoon Worcestershire sauce
1 teaspoon cornstarch
4 thick slices corned beef (canned or home-cooked)
8 strips bacon
2 bananas
12 pineapple chunks (fresh or canned)
8 button mushrooms
4 bay leaves

Make risotto first: Cook 1 finely chopped onion in oil 5 minutes without browning. Add rice; cook 2 to 3 minutes. Add 2 cups stock and seasoning; stir well. Cook in oven about 30 minutes, until all stock is absorbed. Grate about half the orange rind over rice; mix in juice of orange with 1 teaspoon melted butter. Turn into buttered cake tin; keep warm in oven.

For gravy: Cook 1 finely chopped onion in 1 cup stock for about 15 minutes. Add pineapple juice, Worcestershire sauce, and remaining grated orange rind, without pith.

Mix cornstarch with 1 tablespoon cold water until smooth. Add to gravy; boil 1 minute to thicken.

Cut each slice of corned beef into 4 chunks; wrap each in half slice of bacon. Arrange on 4 skewers alternately with banana and pineapple chunks, mushrooms, and half bay leaves. Brush well with melted butter. Broil (or barbecue) 10 minutes, turning all the time.

Turn rice mold onto warmed serving dish. Lay kabobs on top or alongside. Serve gravy separately. Yield 4 servings.

caribbean corned-beef kabobs

corned beef and cabbage hash

¼ cup butter
¼ cup vegetable oil
3 cups thinly sliced onions
4 cups shredded cabbage
Salt
2 medium potatoes, diced
1½ cups chopped cooked corned beef or
   1 12-ounce can corned beef, flaked
2 tablespoons tomato puree
¼ teaspoon freshly ground pepper

Heat butter and oil in large frypan. Add onions; cook until transparent. Place cabbage in saucepan. Add ½ cup water and ½ teaspoon salt. Cook over low heat until crisp-tender, about 12 minutes.

Cook potatoes in small amount salted water until tender.

Drain cabbage and potatoes well. Combine onions, cabbage, potatoes, and corned beef. Stir

corned beef and cabbage hash

in puree. Season with salt and pepper. Pack into loaf pan.

Bake in preheated 375°F oven 30 minutes.

Invert onto serving platter. Serve with poached eggs, if desired. Yield 5 to 6 servings.

corned beef, cabbage, and red pepper stew

1 medium-sized head cabbage
1 large onion
2 red bell peppers
1½ pound boiled corned beef or 2 cans (12 ounces each) corned beef
1 cup water
4 drops Tabasco Sauce
2 teaspoons soy sauce
2 tablespoons vinegar
1 teaspoon sugar

Cut cabbage into 1-inch-wide wedges.

Slice onion into rings.

Remove stems and seeds from peppers; slice into ¼-inch-wide strips.

corned-beef—stuffed potatoes

Cut corned beef into thin slices.

Using Dutch oven or other heavy pan, arrange half the cabbage on bottom; top with half the onion, peppers, and beef slices. Repeat layers, using remaining cabbage, onion, peppers, and beef.

Combine water, Tabasco, soy sauce, vinegar, and sugar; pour over foods in pan. Cover; bring to boil. Reduce heat; simmer gently until tender (about 30 minutes).

Serve in wide soup bowls or deep plates. Yield 6 to 8 servings.

corned-beef patties

3 cups riced potatoes
2 cups minced corned beef
¼ cup tomato puree
1 teaspoon salt
½ teaspoon white pepper
4 eggs, beaten
Flour
Dry bread crumbs
¼ cup bacon drippings
¼ cup butter

Boil 4 or 5 potatoes until tender. Drain, dry. Force through ricer or spin briefly in food processor.

Combine potatoes, corned beef, tomato puree,

salt, pepper, and 2 eggs; mix well. Shape into patties. Chill thoroughly.

Dredge patties in flour; dip in remaining eggs. Coat well with bread crumbs.

Melt bacon drippings and butter in griddle over medium heat until hot. Fry patties slowly until browned on both sides. Serve immediately. Yield 8 to 10 servings.

corned-beef— stuffed potatoes

4 large baking potatoes
1½ cups minced cooked corned beef
¼ cup butter or margarine
Salt and pepper to taste
⅛ cup minced fresh parsley
4 eggs

Bake potatoes at 400°F 1 hour or until done. Cut slice off top of each potato; scoop out centers. Leave ¼ to ½ inch potato around walls. Mash potatoes. Stir in corned beef and butter. Add salt and pepper. Divide mixture among potatoes; reheat.

Meanwhile poach eggs.

Sprinkle potato tops with parsley; top with cooked eggs. Serve as main dish. Yield 4 servings.

delta short ribs

3 pounds beef short ribs, cut into serving pieces
Salt
Pepper
Flour
1 tablespoon butter

corned-beef patties

2 (1-pound) cans stewed tomatoes
⅓ cup snipped celery leaves
¼ cup green pepper, chopped
1 teaspoon salt
¼ teaspoon chili powder
⅓ cup seedless raisins
1 tablespoon lemon juice
Cooked rice
4 to 6 thin slices lemon, twisted

Salt and pepper ribs; coat with flour. Brown on all sides in hot butter in Dutch oven over medium heat. Add tomatoes, celery, green pepper, salt, and chili powder. Simmer 2½ hours. Stir in raisins and lemon juice; simmer 10 minutes.

Serve over rice; garnish with lemon slices.

Skim fat from gravy; serve separately. Yield 6 servings.

new england boiled dinner

1 (3 to 4 pounds) corned-beef brisket
1 garlic clove, minced
1 bay leaf
6 medium-size potatoes
3 carrots, cut in halves
2 small onions, cut in quarters
1 small head cabbage, cut in sixths

Place corned beef in Dutch oven; barely cover beef with water. Add garlic and bay leaf; bring to boil. Reduce heat; simmer, covered, until meat is tender when pricked with fork. 3 to 4 hours.

Remove meat from broth; keep warm. Add potatoes, carrots, and onions to broth. Cover; cook 10 minutes. Add cabbage; cook, covered, 20 minutes. Remove bay leaf. Yield 6 servings.

DRIED BEEF

chipped beef deluxe

2 tablespoons fat or oil
½ cup chopped celery
2 tablespoons chopped green pepper
2 tablespoons chopped onion
1 (10½-ounce) can condensed cream of
   mushroom soup
½ cup water
1 (4-ounce) package dried beef
2 tablespoons chopped pimiento
2 hard-cooked eggs, diced
3 cups cooked noodles (about 6 ounces uncooked)

Heat fat. Add raw vegetables; cook until they begin to brown. Stir soup, water, and beef into vegetables. Cook, stirring as needed, until thickened. Add pimiento and eggs. Serve on noodles. Yield 6 servings.

Note: In place of mushroom soup and water, you can use 2 cups milk and ¼ cup flour. Gradually blend milk into flour.

creamed dried beef

1 (4-ounce) package dried beef
2 tablespoons butter
¼ cup chopped onion
1 can condensed cream of celery soup
⅓ cup water
1 cup evaporated milk
⅛ teaspoon Worcestershire sauce

Pull dried beef into small pieces. If beef is very salty, rinse first in warm water; drain well.

frankfurter casserole

frankfurters with sauerkraut

Melt butter over low heat in 2-quart saucepan. Add onion; cook until onion is yellow and transparent. Add beef; cook gently until edges curl. Blend in soup. Stir in water, evaporated milk, and Worcestershire sauce. Bring to serving temperature. Serve over baked potato or toast. Yield 4 servings.

Note: A 5-ounce jar of dried beef can be substituted for the package if desired.

FRANKFURTERS

batter-dipped all-beef hot dogs

For most people hot dogs mean a steamed, boiled, or grilled frankfurter stuck into a roll and covered with condiments. There are other ways to serve them. Buy the best. The cheaper varieties contain all kinds of unknown ingredients.

½ cup cornmeal
½ cup sifted flour
1 teaspoon salt
½ teaspoon pepper
½ cup fluid milk
1 egg, beaten
2 tablespoons melted fat or oil
12 all-beef hot dogs
Fat or oil for deep frying

Mix cornmeal, flour, salt, and pepper in bowl. Add milk, egg, and fat; stir until smooth.

Dip hot dogs into batter; drain over bowl.

Fry in heated fat 2 to 3 minutes, until golden brown, turning once. Remove from fat; drain. Yield 6 servings.

frankfurter casserole

2 tablespoons cooking fat
1½ cups diced potatoes
1 cup finely chopped onion
2 green peppers, seeded, thinly sliced
8 all-beef frankfurters, cut into 1-inch slices
4 tablespoons water
Salt and pepper

Heat fat in skillet with tightly fitting lid. Add potatoes and onion; cook over low heat about 10 minutes. Add green peppers and frankfurters; mix well. Cook 5 minutes. Add water, salt and pepper to taste. Cover; cook 10 minutes. Yield 4 servings.

frankfurters with sauerkraut

1 1-pound can or bulk sauerkraut
1 small onion, minced
2 tablespoons bacon drippings
1½ teaspoons caraway seed (optional)
Freshly ground pepper to taste
1 medium potato, grated
1 cup dry white wine (optional)
1 pound frankfurters

Place sauerkraut in colander. Rinse thoroughly with cold water; drain well.

Saute onion in bacon drippings in large frypan until transparent but not browned. Add sauerkraut, caraway seed, pepper, potato, and 1 cup water or dry white wine. Simmer, covered, 30 minutes or until liquid is absorbed.

Place frankfurters in steamer pan over hot water; steam 20 minutes.

Turn sauerkraut into serving dish; arrange frankfurters on top. Yield 4 to 6 servings.

hot dogs san francisco style

½ recipe Basic White Bread (see Index)
8 all-beef hot dogs
½ cup catsup
8 ounces mozzarella cheese, shredded
½ cup fried bacon crumbs

Prepare bread dough; let rise. Divide in half; use one half for small loaf of bread. Roll remaining half of dough into ½-inch-thick rectangle. Cut into 8 equal pieces. Wrap each hot dog in dough. Place on greased cookie sheet. Let rise 30 minutes.

Bake in preheated 375°F oven 20 minutes or until rolls are golden brown. Remove from oven.

Split rolls; pull hot dogs from buns so that one end is exposed, as illustrated. Pour 1 tablespoon catsup in each split bun. Top catsup with 1 ounce cheese. Return hot dogs to oven. Bake until cheese has melted. Remove from oven. Garnish with bacon crumbs. Serve at once. Yield 8 servings.

GROUND BEEF

american enchiladas

Ground or shredded beef is the housewife's best friend because it is so versatile, comparatively inexpensive, and easy to prepare.

cornmeal crepes
¾ cup flour
½ cup cornmeal

hot dogs san francisco style

american enchiladas

1¼ cups buttermilk
¼ teaspoon baking soda
3 eggs
1 tablespoon butter, melted

sauce
2 tablespoons olive oil
1 pound ground beef
¼ cup chopped onion
1 teaspoon chili powder
½ teaspoon ground cumin
½ teaspoon salt
¼ teaspoon pepper
1 (8-ounce) can tomato sauce
Tomato wedges and pasley for garnish

Measure all crepe ingredients into jar of electric blender or food processor; blend 30 seconds. Scrape down sides of blender; blend 1 minute. Refrigerate 1 hour.

Meanwhile, make sauce. Heat oil in large skillet. Brown meat and onion; stir frequently. Drain off excess fat. Add chili powder, cumin, salt, pepper, and tomato sauce; simmer 20 minutes. Keep sauce warm while making crepes.

Heat lightly oiled skillet or small crepe pan over moderate heat until drop of water sizzles and dances on hot pan. Stir batter. Pour scant ¼ cup batter into pan; tilt pan in all directions to coat bottom. Cook until bottom is lightly browned and edges appear dry. Turn; cook a few seconds, until lightly browned. Stack on a towel, with paper towels between each. Keep crepes warm in oven as others are cooked. When all crepes are made, fill each with some meat mixture. Roll crepes; place on warm platter.

Garnish enchiladas with fresh tomato wedges and parsley. Yield 6 servings.

barbecued beef steak on a bun

1½ to 2 pounds beef top round steak, ¾ to 1-inch thick
2 tablespoons flour
2½ teaspoons salt
⅛ teaspoon pepper
2 tablespoons cooking fat
1 small onion, finely chopped
½ cup water
¼ cup firmly back brown sugar
2 tablespoons prepared mustard
¼ teaspoon celery salt
Dash of ground cloves
1 can (6 ounces) tomato paste
¼ cup cider vinegar
1½ teaspoons Worcestershire sauce
Few drops of hot pepper sauce
1 small green pepper, cut into strips
6 Kaiser rolls or 8 hamburger buns, split

Partially freeze steak; cut into strips ⅛ inch thick and 2 to 3 inches long.

Combine flour, 1 teaspoon salt, and pepper. Dredge strips; brown in fat in large frying pan. Pour off drippings. Add onion and water to strips; cover tightly. Cook slowly 30 minutes.

Combine brown sugar, mustard, 1½ teaspoons salt, celery salt, and cloves; sprinkle over strips. Stir in tomato paste, vinegar, Worcestershire sauce, and hot pepper sauce. Cook, covered, 20 minutes; stir occasionally. Add green pepper; cook 10 minutes. Serve on rolls. Yield 6 to 8 servings.

barbecued meatballs

1 pound ground beef
¾ cup bread crumbs
½ cup milk
½ cup chopped onions
1 teaspoon salt
½ teaspoon pepper
½ teaspoon oregano

beef shreds with carrots and green peppers

1 egg
Barbecue Sauce

Combine ingredients; form into 1-inch meatballs. Brown in skillet; drain.

barbecue sauce
1 can (10½-ounce) tomato puree
¼ cup molasses
¼ cup brown sugar
¼ cup vinegar
1 teaspoon sweet basil

Simmer, covered, in skillet used for meatballs, about 15 minutes to allow flavors to blend. Delicious over rice or noodles. Yield 3 to 4 servings.

beef and blue patties

2 pounds ground beef
1 teaspoon salt
⅓ teaspoon pepper
½ cup dairy sour cream
¼ cup crumbled blue cheese

Lightly mix ground beef, salt, and pepper; shape into 6 patties, ½ inch thick. Place patties on rack in broiler pan so surface of meat is 3 to 4 inches from heat. Broil 6 to 8 minutes on each side, depending on degree of doneness desired.

Meanwhile combine sour cream and blue cheese. About 2 minutes before end of broiling time, top each patty with about 1½ tablespoons cheese mixture; continue broiling. Yield 6 servings.

beef and pork with bean sprouts

½ pound finely chopped beef (chuck or round)
½ pound finely chopped pork (butt or shoulder)
2 tablespoons soy sauce
1 tablespoon vinegar
1 clove garlic, grated
1 teaspoon grated gingerroot
2 tablespoons vegetable oil
¼ to ½ cup green beans, cut into 1-inch pieces
¼ pound mushrooms, sliced in "T" shapes
1 cup bean sprouts
½ tablespoon cornstarch in ½ cup chicken or beef broth

Marinate beef and pork in combined soy sauce, vinegar, garlic, and gingerroot 20 to 30 minutes.

Heat oil in wok or skillet. Stir-fry beans 2 to 3 minutes; push up to sides. Stir-fry mushrooms 2 to 3 minutes; push up to sides. Additional vegetable oil may be needed. Stir-fry sprouts 1 to 2 minutes; push up to sides. Stir-fry beef and pork 3 to 4 minutes, until well done. Return vegetables to meat in center of pan. Add cornstarch mixture; heat until sauce is thickened and clear. Serve at once with rice. Yield 4 servings.

beef tartare

bobotee

beef shreds with carrots and green peppers

1 tablespoon vegetable oil
2 thin slices gingerroot
1 clove garlic, cut in half
1 large green pepper, cut into thin strips
2 carrots, shredded
1 onion, sliced
1 cup bean sprouts
1 pound cooked beef, thinly sliced
4 water chesnuts, sliced
2 tablespoons soy sauce
1 tablespoon cornstarch in 2 tablespoons water
½ cup chicken broth

Heat oil in frypan or wok; quickly brown ginger and garlic. Remove and discard ginger and garlic.

Stir-fry pepper and carrots 3 to 4 minutes; remove and reserve.

Add onion to frypan; stir-fry 2 minutes. Reserve with pepper and carrot mixture.

Stir-fry sprouts 1 minute; reserve with other vegetables.

Stir-fry beef strips and water chestnuts until heated.

Return vegetables to beef in frypan.

Combine soy sauce, cornstarch mixture, and broth; add to beef—vegetable mixture. Heat until sauce boils and thickens and ingredients are heated through. Serve on plate of hot rice. Yield 4 servings.

beef tartare

1 pound chuck, round sirloin, or tenderloin steak
Freshly ground black pepper
4 large raw onion rings
4 raw egg yolks
2 teaspoons capers
4 anchovy fillets
Few chives (optional)
Fresh horseradish (optional)
4 lemon quarters

Buy and grind steak as near to serving time as possible; meat becomes dark in color if left standing. Add only pepper to meat. Shape meat into 4 equal-size cakes; make depression in center of each with spoon. Place onion ring around depression; put egg yolk into center of each. Sprinkle few capers on top of egg yolk. Lay 1 curled anchovy fillet on top of each yolk or present garnishes on side. Decorate with few chives or fresh horseradish. Serve with rye bread and butter, or French bread and lemon quarters. Yield 4 servings.

bobotee

2 pounds ground beef
2 thick slices white bread
1 cup milk
3 onions, chopped
Butter
3 tablespoons curry powder (or paste)
½ tablespoon sugar
Salt
Juice of 1 lemon
10 almonds, slivered
3 eggs
¼ cup strong beef stock
2 bay leaves
½ cup chopped parsley

Preheat oven to 350°F.

Grind meat fairly coarsely.

Soak bread in some of milk. Squeeze until dry; retain milk.

Fry onions in butter. Add curry powder; fry 1

minute. Add meat, sugar, salt, lemon juice, and almonds.

Beat eggs; add half to meat mixture. Whisk other half into milk. Thoroughly mix bread into meat mixture; add stock. Put meat mixture into buttered ovenproof dish; smooth top. Pour egg-and-milk mixture over; add bay leaves. Cook in oven 30 minutes or until set. Remove from oven.

Decorate top with chopped parsley. Serve with plain boiled rice and chutney. Yield 8 servings.

chili bulgur

1 medium-size onion
½ green pepper (optional)
1 pound ground beef
2 teaspoons salt
¾ cup uncooked bulgur
3½ cups cooked or canned tomatoes
1 tablespoon chili powder

Chop onion.

Chop pepper.

Crumble ground beef in heated frypan. Add onion, pepper, salt, and bulgur. Cook and stir over medium heat until meat is browned. Drain off fat. Add tomatoes and chili powder. Cover; boil gently 20 to 25 minutes, until bulgur is tender. Yield 6 servings.

chili con carne

2 tablespoons vegetable oil
½ cup thinly sliced onion
½ cup diced green pepper
1 clove garlic, crushed
¾ pound ground beef
¾ cup boiling water
1 can (about 20 ounces) peeled tomatoes
1 to 2 tablespoons chili powder (according to taste)
⅛ teaspoon paprika
Salt
2 cups canned kidney beans

Heat oil in kettle. Cook onion, pepper, and garlic about 10 minutes. Add meat. Increase heat; stir until meat has browned. Add water, tomatoes, chili powder, paprika, and a little salt. Cover; cook over low heat about 45 minutes. Add beans; cook 30 minutes. Adjust seasoning to taste before serving.

Eat with dry salted crackers or with rice. Yield 4 to 5 servings.

chili elegante

1½ cups red chili beans or
   1 No. 2 can (2½ cups) kidney beans
1 large onion, sliced

1 green pepper, chopped
1 pound ground beef
3 tablespoons fat
2 (1-pound) cans (4 cups) tomatoes
1 to 2 tablespoons chili powder
1½ teaspoons salt
3 whole cloves
1 bay leaf
Dash of paprika
Dash of cayenne pepper
¼ cup dry sherry

Soak dry chili beans overnight. Cook in boiling, salted water until tender; drain.

Brown onion, green pepper, and meat in hot fat. Add tomatoes, seasonings, and dry sherry. Simmer 2 hours; add water if necessary. Add beans; heat thoroughly. Yield 6 servings.

chili con carne

cranberry meatballs

1 pound lean ground meat
1 (16-ounce) can whole cranberries
1 bottle tangy catsup
1 tablespoon brown sugar
Few drops lemon juice

Prepare meatballs as in recipe for Barbecued Meatballs, (see Index).

Mix together cranberries, catsup, sugar, and lemon juice. Combine with meatballs; place in lightly greased casserole. Bake uncovered at 350°F about 1 hour.

Serve with boiled sweet potatoes or cooked brown rice. Yield 4 servings.

croquettes

1 pound cooked potatoes
1 small onion
2 to 3 cups cooked ground beef
1 tablespoon chutney
1 tablespoon chopped herbs
½ teaspoon salt
⅛ teaspoon white pepper
Tomato puree (optional)
2 to 3 tablespoons flour
2 eggs, beaten
Dry white crumbs
Fat for deep frying
A bunch of parsley

Boil and mash potatoes.

Finely chop onion.

Mix potatoes and onion with meat, chutney, herbs, and seasoning. Add a little tomato puree if mixture is too dry. Put mixture on floured board. Make into long roll; cut into sections about 1 inch thick and 3 inches long. Roll in seasoned flour. Brush all over with eggs; roll in bread crumbs. Deep-fry in smoking-hot fat until well browned; drain. Serve with parsley fried in deep fat a few seconds and pass a well-flavored sauce. Yield 4 servings.

danish meat patties

1 pound lean ground beef
1 medium onion, coarsely chopped
2 tablespoons all-purpose flour
¼ cup club soda
1 egg, beaten
1 teaspoon salt
½ teaspoon freshly ground pepper
2 tablespoons vegetable oil
2 pounds small new potatoes
2 tablespoons melted butter
3 tablespoons chopped chives

Combine ground been and onion in large bowl;

danish meat patties

blend well. Stir in flour, soda, egg, and seasonings. Chill 1 hour.

Shape into six 4 × 2 × 1-inch-thick oval patties; dredge with additional flour.

Heat oil in a large skillet. Add patties. Cook over moderate heat until browned and cooked through; turn once. Drain well on paper toweling; keep warm. At the same time cook well-washed potatoes in boiling, salted water until tender, 15 to 20 minutes. Drain potatoes; remove skins or not, as you prefer.

Arrange patties and potatoes on heated serving platter. Pour melted butter over potatoes; sprinkle with chives. Serve with sour cream, if desired. Yield 6 servings.

dumpling steak

2 pounds ground beefsteak
3 large onions, chopped fine
5 tomatoes, skinned, seeded, and chopped
1 teaspoon salt
¼ teaspoon black pepper
Paprika to taste
1 tablespoon butter
Tomato quarters for garnish
Parsley for garnish
Onion rings for garnish

Mix meat with onions and tomatoes. Add salt, pepper, and paprika. Form into large, round dumpling; set in well-greased casserole. Dot top with specks of butter. Bake it at 400°F 1 hour.

Decorate finished dumpling with tomato, parsley, and onion. Yield 6 to 8 servings.

dumpling steak

german meat loaf

1 pound ground beef
1 egg
¼ cup milk
⅓ cup dry bread crumbs
½ cup chopped onion
½ teaspoon salt
1 teaspoon Worcestershire sauce
¼ teaspoon pepper
1 small head cauliflower
1 cup grated sharp cheddar cheese
1 cup evaporated milk
3 tomatoes, halved

Mix beef, egg, milk, crumbs, onion, and seasonings to make meat loaf. Mold into ring in 2-quart-round baking dish.

Parboil cauliflower 5 minutes. Place in center of meat loaf.

Mix cheese and milk, pour over cauliflower.

Bake at 350°F 45 minutes to 1 hour. Last 5 minutes of baking, place tomatoes on top of meat loaf. Yield 4 servings.

gingersnap meatballs

Goes well with noodles.

1 pound lean ground beef
¾ cup bread crumbs
1 medium onion, minced fine
2 teaspoons salt
¼ teaspoon black pepper
6 teaspoons lemon juice
2 tablespoons water
4 tablespoons margarine or shortening
2½ cups beef broth
½ cup brown sugar
¾ cup gingersnap crumbs

Mix meat, bread crumbs, onion, salt, pepper, 3 teaspoons lemon juice, and water in bowl. Mix well; form into 1-inch balls.

Heat shortening in medium skillet; brown meatballs. Remove balls from pan.

Add beef broth and 3 teaspoons lemon juice to pan drippings. Bring to boil; add brown sugar and gingersnap crumbs. Add meatballs to sauce; cook, covered, 10 minutes. Stir once; allow to simmer uncovered 5 minutes. Taste sauce for seasoning. Yield 4 to 6 servings.

hamburger parmesan

1½ pounds ground round beef
½ teaspoon salt
⅛ teaspoon pepper
¼ cup unsifted flour
2 eggs, beaten
1 cup fine, dry, bread crumbs
3 tablespoons fat or oil

gingersnap meatballs

6 slices mozzarella cheese
1 (4-ounce) can mushroom pieces, drained
1 (15-ounce) can spaghetti sauce
3 tablespoons grated Parmesan cheese

Preheat over to 400°F.

Gently mix beef with salt and pepper. Shape into 6 patties about ½ inch thick. Coat each patty with flour; dip into eggs. Coat with bread crumbs. Brown in fat. Arrange in single layer in baking pan, about 13 × 9 × 2 inches. Top each patty with slice of mozzarella cheese. Place mushroom pieces on top of cheese-covered patties. Top with spaghetti sauce. Sprinkle with Parmesan cheese.

Bake 25 minutes or until sauce is bubbly and cheese is melted. Yield 6 servings.

hawaiian sweet-and-sour meatballs

1½ pounds ground beef
2 eggs
4 tablespoons cornstarch
1 onion, minced
¼ teaspoon pepper
¼ teaspoon nutmeg
1 teaspoon salt
¼ teaspoon garlic powder or minced garlic
2 tablespoons salad oil
1¼ cups pineapple juice
1 tablespoon soy sauce
3 tablespoons vinegar
⅓ cup water
½ cup brown sugar
2 cups fresh pineapple and papaya chunks
2 green peppers, cut bite-size

Blend together beef, eggs, 1 teaspoon cornstarch, onion, pepper, nutmeg, salt, and garlic. Form into 1-inch balls.

Heat oil in skillet; brown meatballs on all sides.

In large saucepan add remaining cornstarch, soy sauce, vinegar, water, and brown sugar to pineapple juice. Cook until thickened; stir constantly. Add meatballs, fruit, and peppers. Cook 5 minutes or until fruit is well heated. Yield 4 to 6 servings.

jambolaya

¾ cup uncooked long-grained rice
3 tablespoons oil
1 clove garlic, diced
2 green peppers, chopped
1 cup chopped onion
1 pound ground beef
¼ teaspoon paprika
½ teaspoon Worcestershire sauce
1 tablespoon chopped parsley

1 small bay leaf
1 (No. 2) can tomatoes (2½ cups)
¼ teaspoon chili powder
1½ teaspoon salt
¼ teaspoon black pepper

Cook rice.

Place oil in heavy skillet; sauté garlic. Sauté pepper and onion until soft. Push to one side of pan; brown meat. Add rest of ingredients. Cover, simmer gently 30 minutes.

Add rice; stir. Simmer 20 minutes. Yield 4 to 6 servings.

meatballs königsberg-style

meatballs
1 hard roll
¾ cup water
1 pound lean ground beef
1 strip bacon, diced
4 anchovy fillets, diced
1 small onion, chopped
1 egg
½ teaspoon salt
¼ teaspoon white pepper

broth
6 cups water
½ teaspoon salt
1 bay leaf
1 small onion, peeled, halved
6 peppercorns

gravy
1½ tablespoons butter or margarine
1½ tablespoons flour
1 tablespoon capers, drained
Juice of ½ lemon
½ teaspoon prepared mustard
1 egg yolk
¼ teaspoon salt
¼ teaspoon white pepper

Soak roll in water about 10 minutes. Squeeze dry; place in mixing bowl with ground beef. Add bacon, anchovy fillets, onion, egg, salt and pepper; mix thoroughly.

Prepare broth by boiling water seasoned with salt, bay leaf, onion, and peppercorns.

Shape meat mixture into balls about 2 inches in diameter. Add to boiling broth; simmer over low heat 20 minutes. Remove meatballs with slotted spoon. Set aside; keep warm. Strain broth through sieve. Reserve broth; keep warm.

To prepare gravy, heat butter in frypan; stir in flour. Cook 3 minutes, stirring constantly. Slowly blend in 2 cups reserved broth. Add capers, lemon juice, and mustard; simmer 5 minutes.

Remove a small amount of sauce to blend with egg yolk. Stir egg yolk back into sauce. Season

meatballs königsberg-style

with salt and pepper.

Place reserved meatballs into gravy; reheat if necessary. Serve on a preheated platter. Yield 4 servings.

meat loaf

1½ pounds ground beef
3 slices soft white bread, torn into very small
 pieces
1 cup tomato juice or milk
½ cup finely chopped onion
2 tablespoons chopped parsley
1 egg, beaten
1 teaspoon salt
¼ teaspoon pepper

Mix ingredients thoroughly. Press into 9 × 5 × 3-inch loaf pan or shape into loaf.

Bake uncovered at 350°F about 1½ hours. Remove from oven; drain off excess fat. Yield 6 servings.

meat—potato cakes

1 small onion, chopped
2½ cups cut-up, canned chopped meat or canned
 luncheon meat
2 cups cold mashed potatoes
1 egg

Mix all ingredients. Shape into 12 patties. Brown on both sides in greased frypan over medium heat. Yield 6 servings, 2 patties each.

mock stroganoff

1 pound ground beef
¼ cup chopped onion
1 crushed garlic clove
1 can condensed cream of mushroom soup
⅓ cup milk
2 tablespoons sherry
½ cup sour cream
Salt
Cooked noodles or rice
Chopped parsley

Lightly brown meat in skillet with onion and garlic, stirring. Add soup and milk; heat well, stirring. Reduce heat; stir in sherry, then sour cream. Season to taste.

Serve over noodles; garnish with parsley. Yield 4 to 6 servings.

pizza hamburgers

1½ pounds ground beef
¼ cup grated Parmesan cheese
¼ cup finely chopped onion
¼ cup chopped stuffed olives

pizza hamburgers

1 teaspoon oregano
1 small can tomato purée
Salt
Black pepper
8 thin slices Bel Paese cheese (or mozzarella)
4 tomatoes
4 hamburger buns, split, toasted

Mix meat, grated cheese, onion, olives, oregano, and tomato purée together. Season with salt and black pepper. Shape into 8 patties. Broil on grid or under broiler (medium heat) about 10 minutes. Turn; place slice of cheese and half tomato on each. Cook a few minutes, until cheese melts and hamburgers are cooked.

Serve on hamburger buns. Yield 8 servings.

stuffed chilies

2 medium onions, chopped
1 clove garlic, crushed
2 tablespoons oil
½ pound ground beef
½ pound ground pork
1 cup chopped fresh tomatoes
1 teaspoon salt
½ teaspoon pepper

4 tablespoons sliced almonds
4 tablespoons raisins
8 whole canned chilies
½ cup flour
4 eggs
Oil for frying

Sauté onions and garlic in 2 tablespoons oil until onion is transparent. Add ground meats; stir until meat is crumbly. Add chopped tomatoes, seasonings, almonds, and raisins; simmer.

Remove chili seeds; leave skins whole. Stuff with meat filling; roll well in flour. Dip in following egg batter: Beat egg whites until stiff; beat egg yolks. Combine egg yolks with egg whites.

Fry chilies in deep fat at 375°F until golden brown. Remove; drain on paper toweling. Yield 8 servings.

stuffed peppers

6 medium green peppers
Salt
1 pound ground beef
⅓ cup chopped onion
1 tablespoon fat
2 cups stewed tomatoes or 1 (1-pound) can
¾ cup cooked rice
2 tablespoons Worcestershire sauce
Pepper
1 cup shredded sharp American cheese

Cut off tops of peppers; remove seeds and membranes. Precook in boiling salted water 5 minutes; drain. Sprinkle insides with salt.

Brown meat and onion in hot fat. Add tomatoes, rice, Worcestershire sauce, salt, and pepper. Cover; simmer until rice is tender, about 5 minutes. Add cheese.

sweet-and-sour chinese meatballs

Stuff peppers. Stand up in baking pan. Bake, uncovered, in 350°F oven 25 minutes or until hot. Sprinkle with more cheese. Yield 6 servings.

sweet-and-sour beef

1 tablespoon shortening
2 pounds cubed lean stewing beef
½ teaspoon salt
2 cups canned tomatoes
⅓ cup brown sugar
⅓ cup vinegar
½ cup finely chopped onion
½ bay leaf
1 green pepper, cut into thin strips

Melt shortening in large skillet; brown beef on all sides. Add salt, tomatoes, brown sugar, vinegar, onion, and bay leaf. Cover skillet; lower heat. Let simmer about 2 hours, until beef is tender. Add pepper strips to beef; cook 10 minutes to blend all flavors. Serve with hot rice or noodles. Yield 6 to 8 servings.

sweet-and-sour chinese meatballs

1 pound extra-lean ground beef
¾ teaspoon salt
½ teaspoon pepper
½ teaspoon grated fresh gingerroot
2 tablespoons vegetable oil
1 green pepper, cut into ¼-inch cubes
1 onion, chopped
1 carrot, grated
2 tablespoons vinegar
2 tablespoons brown sugar
1 teaspoon soy sauce
1 teaspoon dry sherry
1 tablespoon cornstarch stirred into ½ cup cold chicken or beef broth

Blend together ground beef, salt, pepper, and ginger. Shape into 1-inch meatballs.

Heat oil in wok or skillet; brown meatballs on all sides about 2 minutes. Add remaining ingredients. Cook over moderate heat, stirring constantly, until mixture thickens. Cook 5 minutes. Serve at once with rice. Yield 4 servings.

tagliatelle bolognese

1 onion, chopped
1 carrot, diced
1 stalk celery, diced
½ green pepper
2 tablespoons water
1 tablespoon dry vermouth
1 pound lean ground beef

sweet-and-sour beef

tagliatelle bolognese

2 (8-ounce) cans tomato sauce
1 clove garlic, minced
1 bay leaf
1 cup beef bouillon
½ teaspoon salt
¼ teaspoon pepper
¾ pound tagliatelle or other pasta
¼ cup grated Parmesan cheese

In large frypan sauté onion, carrot, celery, and green pepper in water and vermouth until onion turns translucent. Remove vegetables with slotted spoon; set aside.

Brown ground beef in same pan; add more vermouth if necessary to prevent sticking. Drain beef. Add vegetables, tomato sauce, garlic, bay leaf, bouillon, salt, and pepper. Gently simmer, uncovered, 30 minutes.

Meanwhile cook pasta according to package directions. Do not overcook. When pasta is done to taste, adjust seasonings in sauce. Discard bay leaf.

Turn pasta into hot serving dish; pour cooked meat sauce into center. Sprinkle with Parmesan cheese. Yield 4 servings.

tamale pie

½ pound ground beef
½ pound bulk pork sausage
1 large onion, sliced
⅛ teaspoon minced garlic
1 (16-ounce) can tomatoes with juice
1 (12-ounce) can whole-kernel corn, drained
1 tablespoon chili powder
1 teaspoon salt
¼ teaspoon pepper

cornmeal pastry
1 cup cornmeal
2 medium eggs
1 cup milk
18 green olives, chopped
Olive slices for garnish

Cook meats with onion and garlic until browned. Stir in tomatoes with juice, corn, and seasonings. Simmer 10 minutes. Pour into greased oblong baking dish.

Prepare cornmeal crust by mixing cornmeal, eggs, milk, and chopped olives. Spread over hot mixture. Decorate top with few olive slices. Bake at 350°F 30 to 35 minutes. Serve tamale pie warm. Yield 4 to 6 servings.

tomato ground beef

1 tablespoon shortening
1 large onion, diced
1 green pepper, diced
1½ pounds ground beef
1 carrot, diced
1 can tomato soup, undiluted
1 teaspoon salt
1 teaspoon garlic salt
¼ teaspoon freshly ground black pepper

Heat shortening in medium skillet; sauté onion and green pepper until lightly browned. Add beef and carrot. Sauté 1 minute. Add soup. Add seasonings; simmer about 5 minutes to blend flavors.

To make this a complete meal, add 1 cup cooked rice, or serve over cooked noodles or spaghetti. Yield 4 to 6 servings.

ROASTS

beef in red wine

3 to 4 pounds boneless beef (rump, sirloin tip, or round)
½ teaspoon salt
¼ teaspoon freshly ground black pepper

tomato ground beef

beef in red wine

marinade
3 cups red wine
1 cup water
½ cup sliced onions
¼ cup sliced carrots
1 clove garlic, minced
1 bay leaf, crumbled
2 teaspoons chopped fresh parsley
1 teaspoon thyme

braising ingredients
2 tablespoons vegetable oil
2 strips lean bacon, cubed
1 ounce brandy, warmed
1 veal or beef knuckle
1 tomato, peeled, quartered
1 tablespoon chopped fresh parsley
1 bay leaf
3 green onions, chopped
1 cup beef bouillon
½ teaspoon salt

vegetables
10 small white onions, peeled
8 carrots, peeled, shaped like small balls
Parsley for garnish
2 tablespoons flour
2 tablespoons butter
3 tablespoons Madeira
2 tablespoons cognac

Rub beef with salt; sprinkle with pepper.

Blend all marinade ingredients. Pour marinade into glass or ceramic bowl. Add beef; turn it several times, so that all sides are coated with marinade. Cover; marinate in refrigerator 12 to 24 hours. Turn beef occasionally.

Remove beef from marinade, drain. Pat dry with paper towels. Strain; reserve marinade.

Heat oil in large Dutch oven. Add bacon; cook until transparent. Add beef; brown well on all sides. Drain off fat. Pour warm brandy over meat. Ignite; wait until flames die down. Add remaining braising ingredients; cover pan. Place in preheated 350°F oven. During cooking, occasionally pour some reserved marinade over beef. Cook meat 3 hours.

Meanwhile, prepare vegetables. Add onions and carrots to Dutch oven; braise 1 hour.

When meat and vegetables are tender, remove from oven; place on preheated platter. Surround with onions and carrots. Garnish with parsley. Keep food warm.

Strain sauce through fine sieve. Skim off fat, if necessary.

Cream together flour and butter. Thicken pan sauce with all or part of this. Stir and heat to boiling 1 to 2 minutes. Add Madeira and cognac. Adjust seasonings

Spoon some sauce over meat; serve rest separately. Yield 6 servings.

beef with sauerkraut

2½ to 3 pounds brisket of beef
3 tablespoons bacon fat
1 large onion, peeled, sliced
2 pounds sauerkraut
2 cups boiling water
Salt and pepper
Few caraway seeds

Heat fat in pan. Add onion; sauté until lightly browned. Put in meat; arrange sauerkraut on top. Add boiling water; cover. Simmer over low heat 2 to 2½ hours or until meat is tender. Add salt and pepper to taste and a few caraway seeds. Serve with boiled potatoes. Yield 6 servings.

boiled beef and carrots

3 to 4 pounds bottom round of beef
1 large onion stuck with 2 cloves
6 peppercorns
1 bay leaf
Parsley stems
Sprig of thyme
Salt
8 to 10 medium carrots
2 small turnips
3 celery stalks
4 to 6 small onions, whole
2 cups flour (all-purpose)
8 tablespoons suet (or butter)
3 tablespoons chopped parsley
½ tablespoon thyme
½ tablespoon marjoram
Pepper

Into large pot put beef, large onion, peppercorns, bay leaf, parsley stems, sprig of thyme, enough water to cover meat, and a little salt. Slowly bring to boil, remove any scum that rises to surface. Put lid on pot; simmer 1 hour.

Peel and quarter carrots and turnips lengthwise.

Remove herbs and large onion from pot.

Add carrots, turnips, celery, and small onions to pot, simmer 1 hour.

Make dumplings: Sift flour with pinch of salt. Mix in finely shredded suet, herbs, and pepper. Mix in water to make light dough. Divide into pieces about size of small walnut, rolling between hands. Drop dumplings into boiling liquid around meat; cover pot. Cook about 15 to 20 minutes.

Serve on large dish with vegetables and dumplings. Serve gravy separately in sauceboat. Yield 6 servings.

burgundian roast sirloin

1 (5-pound) sirloin tip roast
1 recipe Marinade for Beef (see Index)

Place roast in shallow dish; cover with marinade. Marinate in refrigerator overnight or at room temperature several hours. Turn roast several times while marinating to soak completely.

Place roast on rack in shallow roasting pan. Pour 1 cup water in pan.

Set meat thermometer to temperature for desired doneness; insert thermometer in roast.

beef with sauerkraut

boiled beef and carrots

Bake in preheated 325°F oven until thermometer dial reaches desired temperature. Add small amount water as needed to prevent roasting pan from becoming too dry. Yield 10 to 12 servings.

cranberry pot roast

**3 to 4 pounds beef arm pot roast,
  cut 2 inches thick**
2 tablespoons cooking fat, if needed
2 teaspoons salt
¼ teaspoon pepper
4 whole cloves
1 stick cinnamon
½ cup water
3 tablespoons prepared horseradish
6 medium carrots
6 small onions
½ cup cranberry sauce (whole-berry)
2 tablespoons flour

Brown meat in own fat (trimmed from meat) or in cooking fat, if needed, in large frying pan. Pour off drippings. Sprinkle salt and pepper over meat. Add cloves and cinnamon.

Combine water and horseradish; add to meat. Cover tightly; cook slowly 2½ hours. Turn meat.

Cut carrots into 2-inch pieces.

Cut onions in half lengthwise.

Add vegetables to meat. Cook, covered, 40 minutes or until meat and vegetables are tender. Remove meat and vegetables to warm platter.

Blend cranberry sauce with flour; combine with cooking liquid. Cook, stirring constantly, until thickened. Reduce heat; cook 3 minutes. Yield 6 to 8 servings.

Note: For beef blade roast, reduce initial cooking time 30 to 45 minutes.

football brisket

1 envelope powdered onion soup mix
2 cups water
3 to 4 pounds brisket of beef
Pepper

¾ cup catsup
½ cup beer
¼ cup flour

Mix onion soup mix with water in roasting pan.

Season meat with a little pepper, if desired. Place meat in pan; cover tightly. Cook at 325°F 2 to 2½ hours or until meat is just about tender. Remove meat.

Place gravy in bowl; put bowl in freezer. When fat hardens remove from gravy. Combine gravy with catsup, beer, and flour.

Slice meat. Place in roasting pan; cover with gravy mixture. Bake at 325°F 40 minutes, until the meat is tender. Taste for seasoning. Yield 6 to 8 servings.

marinated beef roast

1 clove garlic, minced
1 teaspoon ground black pepper
1 bay leaf
1½ cups dry red wine
2 tablespoons lemon juice
1 (4-pound) rolled rump roast
3 tablespoons olive oil
2 tablespoons flour
2 tablespoons water

Combine garlic, pepper, bay leaf, wine, and lemon juice in enamelware pan or deep glass casserole. Add roast; turn several times to coat with mixture. Cover; let marinate in refrigerator at least 24 hours; turn occasionally.

Heat oil over moderate heat.

Remove roast from marinade; pat dry. Brown on all sides in hot oil.

Meanwhile, preheat oven to 375°F.

Pour marinade over roast in Dutch oven; cover tightly. Place in oven; cook 2 hours. Uncover; bake 30 minutes. Transfer pan to stove; remove meat to warm platter.

Make a paste with flour and water; thicken pan gravy.

Slice roast. Serve with gravy and oven-fried potato wedges or boiled or mashed potatoes. Yield 8 to 10 servings.

pot roast

1 clove garlic
3 to 4 pounds shoulder, blade of beef, or chuck
   steak
Flour
Salt and pepper
2 tablespoons oil
1 or 2 carrots, peeled, chopped
1 or 2 stalks celery, chopped
2 to 3 tablespoons chopped green pepper
1 small turnip, peeled, diced

1 onion, peeled, stuck with 3 cloves
2 cups boiling stock or water
Cooked rice or noodles

Cut garlic clove; rub over meat.

Sprinkle meat liberally with flour to which some salt and pepper have been added.

Heat oil in large, heavy kettle. Put in meat; brown well on one side. Turn meat. Add carrots, celery, green pepper, and turnips. Cook until meat is browned on underside. Pour off excess fat. Add onion and stock. Cover tightly; cook over low heat 2 to 2½ hours. Turn meat occasionally; add stock or water as required. Adjust seasoning.

Serve with rice or noodles and pot liquid, thickened with 1 tablespoon flour mixed to smooth paste with 2 tablespoons cold water. Add to hot liquid; stir until thickened. (Any meat left over is very good served cold.) Yield 6 servings.

pot roast and stuffed cabbage

¼ cup flour
2 teaspoons salt
⅛ teaspoon pepper
3 to 3½-pound beef arm pot roast
3 tablespoons lard or drippings
¼ cup water
½ bay leaf
1 small head cabbage
3 cups cooked rice
2 ounces shredded Cheddar cheese
¼ teaspoon marjoram
⅛ teaspoon sage
1 can (16 ounces) tomatoes
1 large onion, chopped

Combine flour, salt, and pepper. Dredge meat; reserve excess flour. Brown meat in lard. Pour off drippings. Sprinkle reserved excess flour over meat. Add water and bay leaf; cover tightly. Cook slowly 2 hours or until meat is almost tender.

Remove center core of cabbage; cook in boiling, salted water 12 to 15 minutes. Remove 8 leaves. Thinly slice remaining cabbage. Drain thoroughly; reserve.

Combine rice, cheese, marjoram, and sage.

Drain tomatoes; reserve liquid. Cut pulp into small pieces. Add half of pulp to rice mixture. Divide into 8 equal portions; roll each portion in cabbage leaf. Secure with small wooden picks.

Combine remaining tomato pulp and liquid with sliced cabbage and onion; add to meat. Place cabbage rolls on top of meat. Cook slowly, covered, 30 minutes or until meat is tender.

Remove picks from cabbage rolls. Remove meat and cabbage rolls to warm platter.

Stir cabbage and cooking liquid to combine. Serve sauce with meat and cabbage rolls. Yield 8 servings.

Note: Arm pot roast is an economic beef cut from chuck section that can be easily identified by its round bone. A blade pot roast can be substituted. In this case, reduce initial cooking time by 30 to 45 minutes, as blade pot roast cooks more quickly.

roast beef au jus and yorkshire pudding

yorkshire pudding
1 cup all-purpose flour
¾ teaspoon salt
2 large eggs
1 cup milk

1 cup shortening for roasting
4 pounds rolled rib roast
2 pounds potatoes
1 cup stock
½ cup grated fresh horseradish
   (or horseradish sauce)
   Preheat oven to 450°F.
   Prepare batter: Sift flour into mixing bowl. Add salt; make hollow in center. Add eggs and a little milk. Stir and draw flour into center gradually until smooth. Add remaining milk; beat well. Let stand 30 minutes.
   Melt shortening in roasting pan. Place roast (thawed, if frozen) in pan; baste well. Roast 15 minutes per pound; baste every 15 minutes.
   Peel potatoes; boil 5 minutes. Drain; scratch with fork to make crisp. After 15 minutes put in pan with meat; cook about 45 minutes.
   After 30 minutes, pour off about 1 tablespoon fat drippings from meat into small, open pan; reheat. Add batter; place at top of oven until well-risen and brown, about 30 minutes.
   When roast is cooked, place on heated platter with potatoes and Yorkshire pudding; keep warm. Pour off all clear fat; make gravy with juices in roasting pan, adding stock. Stir and scrape well to loosen all meaty brown bits. Season to taste; strain.
   Serve with grated horseradish or horseradish sauce. Yield 8 servings.

sauerbraten with gingersnap gravy

4-pound beef rump roast
2 onions, thinly sliced
8 peppercorns
4 cloves
1 bay leaf
1 cup mild white vinegar
1 cup water
½ cup cider vinegar
¼ cup vegetable oil
½ teaspoon salt
2 cups boiling water
10 gingersnaps, crushed
½ cup sour cream
1 tablespoon flour

   Place beef in deep ceramic or glass bowl. Add onions, peppercorns, cloves, and bay leaf. Pour white vinegar, water, and cider vinegar over meat. Chill, covered, 4 days. Turn meat twice each day.

   Remove meat from marinade; dry well with paper towels. Strain marinade into bowl. Reserve onions and 1 cup marinade.

   In Dutch oven brown meat on all sides in hot oil. Sprinkle with salt. Pour boiling water around meat. Sprinkle in gingersnaps; simmer, covered, 1½ hours. Turn often. Add 1 cup reserved marinade; cook 2 hours or more, until tender. Remove meat; keep warm. Strain cooking juices into large saucepan.

   Mix sour cream with flour in small bowl. Stir into cooking juices. Cook, stirring, until sauce is thickened and smooth.

   Slice meat into ¼-inch slices; add to hot gravy.

   Arrange meat on heated platter; pour extra sauce over. Yield 8 to 10 servings.

savory pot roast

1 4-pound pot roast
½ teaspoon salt
¼ teaspoon pepper
2 tablespoons flour
4 tablespoons butter
3 onions, sliced
3 carrots, peeled, sliced
2 stalks celery, sliced
½ cup tomato sauce
2 cups water
1 bay leaf
½ cup red wine
   Wipe meat with damp cloth.
   Combine salt, pepper, and flour. Rub into surface of roast.
   Melt butter in Dutch oven. Brown roast on all sides. Add onions; brown. Add carrots, celery, tomato sauce, water, bay leaf, and red wine. Cover; simmer 3 hours.
   Slice meat. Serve with pan juices, accompanied by rice or potatoes. Yield 8 servings.

scandinavian beef pot roast

scandinavian beef pot roast

1 (3½-pound) pot roast
Salt and pepper
Ginger
¼ cup olive oil
3 large onions
1 garlic clove
½ cup Burgundy
12 diced pitted prunes
2 cups weak tea
1 (4½-ounce) can olives, drained
1 (2-ounce) can mushrooms, drained
Beurre Manié

Sprinkle roast generously with salt, pepper, and ginger.

Pour oil into shallow frying pan over medium heat.

Peel and thinly slice onions.

Peel and crush garlic.

Sauté onions and garlic in hot oil until onions are soft and golden.

Place prepared roast in Dutch oven or deep casserole. Pour onion mixture on top. Add Burgundy. Bake, covered, in preheated 300°F oven 2 hours.

Cover prunes with hot strained tea. Let prunes stand until cold, then drain away all but ¾ cup liquid.

Add ¾ cup liquid, prunes, and olives to roast; cover. Bake about 2 hours or until roast is tender.

Lift roast onto serving platter. Surround with mushrooms, prunes, and olives.

Stir pan liquid into saucepan; bring to boil. Thicken with Beurre Manié. Sauce can be poured over roast or served separately as an accompaniment. Yield 6 servings.

beurre manié

A classic recipe used to thicken sauces and gravies.

2 tablespoons soft butter
¼ cup all-purpose flour

Combine butter and flour in small bowl; mix until well blended. Roll mixture into small balls. Add balls to boiling liquid, one by one; stir constantly with whisk. Add as many balls as needed for desired thickness.

spicy pot roast

1 (3- to 4-pound) rolled rump roast
½ cup flour
2 tablespoons cooking oil
1 cup chopped onion
2 garlic cloves, minced
1 teaspoon beef bouillon granules
1 teaspoon celery seed
1 teaspoon ground cumin
1 teaspoon salt
½ teaspoon pepper
1 (8-ounce) can tomato sauce
½ cup water
½ cup cold water
Hot cooked rice

Coat roast on all sides with ¼ cup flour. Brown on all sides in Dutch oven or heavy casserole in hot oil. Add onion, garlic, beef bouillon granules, celery seed, cumin, salt, pepper, tomato sauce, and ½ cup water. Cover with tight-fitting lid.

Cook over low heat until tender, 3 to 3½ hours. Remove meat; keep warm.

Measure pan juices; add water, if necessary, to make 2½ cups.

Blend together ¼ cup flour and ½ cup cold water; stir into pan juices. Cook and stir until bubbly and smooth. Strain over sliced meat and rice. Yield 8 servings.

stuffed boneless beef roast

1 (3½-pound) fresh beef brisket
4 slices bacon, diced
1 cup chopped onions
8 cups stale bread cubes
1 teaspoon oregano
¼ teaspoon finely chopped parsley
2 eggs, lightly beaten
Salt and freshly ground pepper to taste

Have butcher cut large pocket in brisket.

Sauté bacon about 3 minutes. Add onions;

stuffed boneless beef roast

cook, stirring frequently, until lightly browned.

Combine bread cubes with bacon mixture in large mixing bowl; toss lightly. Add oregano, parsley, and eggs; toss with fork until well combined. Season with salt and pepper. Sprinkle about 3 tablespoons water over stuffing if mixture seems too dry. Pack stuffing evenly into pocket of brisket. Secure opening with skewers. Score top of roast lightly. Sprinkle with pepper; rub into roast. Place in lightly greased shallow baking pan. Cover loosely with aluminum foil. Bake in preheated 350°F oven 1 hour and 45 minutes.

Remove foil; bake 30 minutes.

Remove from oven; place on serving platter. Pour pan juices over top of roast, if desired. You can double stuffing recipe and bake additional amount separately if desired.

Serve with Broiled Tomatoes (see Index). Yield 8 to 10 servings.

sweet-and-sour brisket

5- to 6-pound brisket
2 onions, sliced
1 clove garlic, minced
¾ cup brown sugar
½ cup vinegar
1 cup catsup
1 cup water
1 tablespoon salt
Ground pepper to taste

Place brisket on onions and garlic.

Mix other ingredients; pour over brisket. Cover; roast in 350°F oven until tender, approximately 4 hours. Yield 10 to 12 servings.

tenderloin beef wellington

4 to 5 tablespoons oil or shortening
1 fillet tenderloin beef, 2 to 2½ pounds
1 clove garlic
Pepper
3 tablespoons butter
1 onion, finely chopped
1 cup finely chopped mushrooms
2 tablespoons brandy
1 tablespoon mixed herbs
1 package puff pastry
1 egg

Preheat oven to 400°F.

Heat oil or shortening in oven. Rub over fillet with cut piece of garlic. Season with pepper. Roast about 20 to 25 minutes. Allow to cool. (Reset oven to 450°F for pastry.)

Melt butter. Cook onion and mushrooms 5 minutes, until onion is soft. Add brandy, seasoning, and herbs; let cool.

Roll pastry thinly on floured board to size that

will completely cover tenderloin. Lay cooled meat in center; spoon mushroom-and-onion mixture over top. Brush pastry edges with water. Fold over top; pinch together to make pattern. Fold pastry carefully over ends to seal. Decorate with leaves made from leftover pastry. Brush whole surface with beaten egg, to glaze. Bake 20 to 30 minutes, until pastry is browned. Cut in slices to serve. Yield 4 servings.

STEAK

anchovy steaks

4 large, tender steaks (sirloin or club steaks)
Oil
1 clove garlic
3 tablespoons butter
1 to 2 tablespoons anchovy paste
Squeeze of lemon juice
Freshly ground black pepper

Preheat broiler.

Brush steaks with oil and crushed garlic. Let marinate at least an hour, longer if possible.

Cream butter until soft. Add anchovy paste gradually, using amount to taste. Add lemon juice and pepper. Make into 4 balls or pats. Put in refrigerator to chill.

When broiler is very hot, put steaks under. Cook 3 to 6 minutes on each side, depending on thickness of steaks and personal taste.

When ready, put pat of anchovy butter on each steak. Serve at once with Broiled Tomatoes (see Index), French-fried potatoes, and green salad. Yield 4 servings.

barbecued sirloin steak

Sirloin, Porterhouse or T-bone steaks, 1½ to 2 inches thick

Do not attempt to start cooking until coals are hot. There should be no flames—just glowing coals; rack should be about 6 inches above top of coals.

Trim some fat from meat; use to rub over hot rack so steaks will not stick. (If you spear piece of fat with fork, there is no danger of burned fingers.)

Put steaks on rack. Broil on one side until well browned about 20 minutes. Turn over with tongs. Sprinkle browned side with salt and pepper. (If fire blazes up from meat drippings, extinguish flames with few drops of water.) Broil until steaks are cooked as desired. Serve with pat of plain or herb butter (see Index) on each steak. Yield as desired.

beef fillet mexicana

1 tablespoon butter or margarine
1 large onion, chopped
1 green pepper, chopped
1 red pepper, chopped
2 tablespoons tomato paste
½ cup hot beef bouillon
¾ teaspoon salt
⅛ teaspoon white pepper
Few drops Tabasco sauce
4 servings beef fillet, 4 ounces each (or use rib-eye
    steaks)
¼ to ½ teaspoon freshly ground black pepper
2 tablespoons vegetable oil
2 tablespoons tequila (or vodka)
⅛ teaspoon cayenne pepper

Heat butter in frypan; sauté onion until golden. Add green and red peppers; cook 2 minutes.

Blend tomato paste with hot bouillon; pour over vegetables. Season with ½ teaspoon salt, white pepper, and Tabasco. Cover; simmer 10 minutes.

Meanwhile, pat meat dry with paper towels. Rub generously with coarsely ground black pepper.

Heat oil in skillet until very hot; cook meat 3 minutes on each side.

Arrange vegetables on preheated platter; place steaks on top.

Add tequila or other clear liquor to pan drippings; scrape any particles from bottom of pan. Season with cayenne and ¼ teaspoon salt. Pour over meat; serve immediately. Yield 4 servings.

beef flank steak
with mushroom stuffing

½ teaspoon salt
¼ teaspoon white pepper
2 pounds flank steak
1 teaspoon Dijon-style mustard

mushroom stuffing
2 tablespoons vegetable oil
1 small onion, chopped
4-ounce can mushroom pieces, drained, chopped
¼ cup chopped parsley
2 tablespoons chopped chives
1 tablespoon tomato paste
¼ cup dried bread crumbs
¼ teaspoon salt
¼ teaspoon pepper
1 teaspoon paprika

gravy
3 strips bacon, cubed
2 small onions, finely chopped

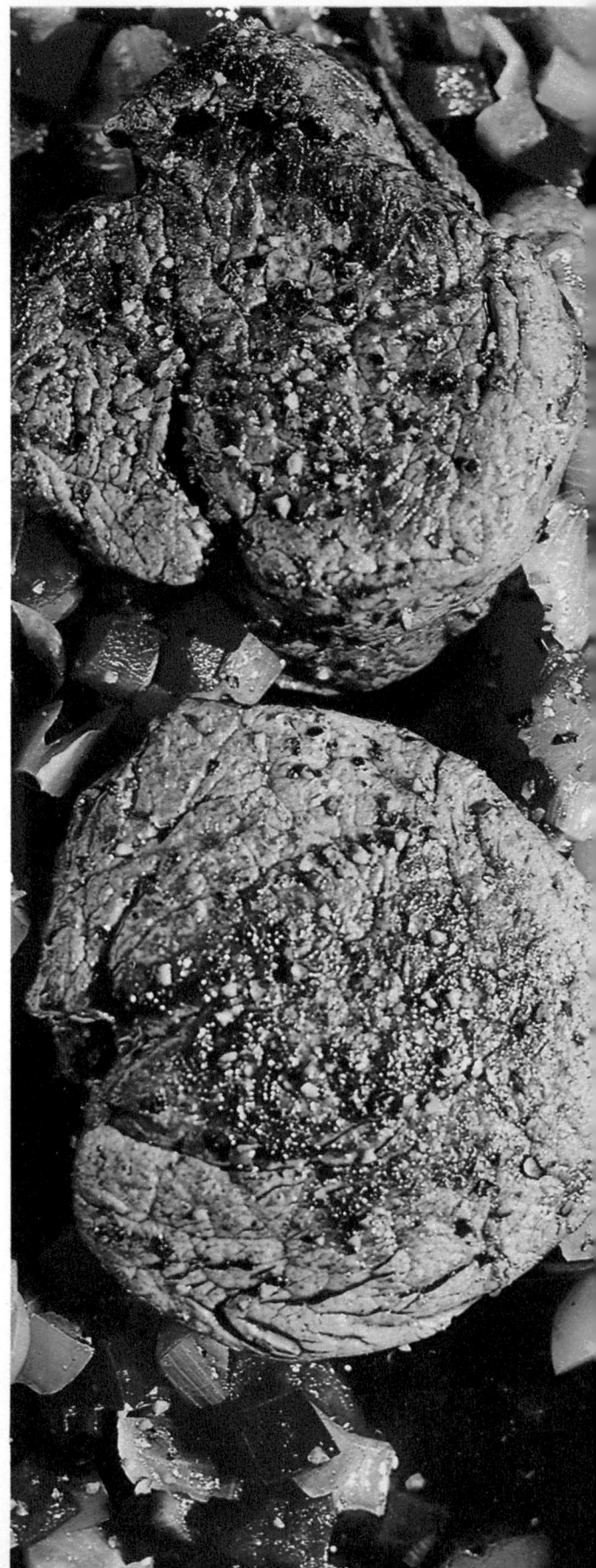

beef fillet mexicana

beef flank steak with mushroom stuffing

1 cup hot beef broth
1 teaspoon Dijon-style mustard
2 tablespoons tomato catsup

Lightly salt and pepper steak on both sides. Spread one side with mustard.

Prepare stuffing. Heat oil in frypan. Add onion; cook 3 minutes, until lightly browned. Add mushrooms; cook 5 minutes. Stir in parsley, chives, tomato paste, and bread crumbs. Season with salt, pepper, and paprika.

Spread stuffing on mustard side of steak. Roll up jelly-roll fashion; tie with thread or string.

Prepare gravy. Cook bacon in Dutch oven or heavy casserole until partially done. Add meat roll; brown on all sides, approximately 10 minutes. Add onions; saute 5 minutes. Pour in beef broth; cover Dutch oven. Simmer 1 hour. Remove meat to preheated platter.

Season pan juices with mustard. Salt and pepper to taste; stir in catsup. Serve gravy separately. Yield 6 servings.

beef round over noodles

2 tablespoons peanut or corn oil
1 teaspoon soy sauce
½ teaspoon sugar
2 teaspoons sherry
3 cups thinly sliced onions
2 teaspoons cornstarch
1 tablespoon soy sauce
1½ pounds beef round, cut into 1-inch pieces
1 tablespoon Worcestershire sauce
1 teaspoon garlic salt or 1 clove garlic, minced
1 can mushrooms (optional)

Heat oil in large skillet with 1 teaspoon soy sauce, sugar, and 1 teaspoon sherry. Sauté onions.

Mix cornstarch, 1 tablespoon soy sauce, and 1 teaspoon sherry in bowl. Dredge meat in mixture; coat every piece. Put meat in onion mixture; brown. Stir in Worcestershire sauce and garlic salt. Cover skillet; let simmer 1 hour adding mushrooms, if desired, for last 10 minutes; stir occasionally.

Serve on bed of noodles. Yield 4 to 6 servings.

beef slices peking

beef round over noodles

beef slices peking

marinade
3 tablespoons soy sauce
1 tablespoon sherry
1 pound lean beef
1 cup oil
2 tablespoons flour
2 leeks, thinly sliced
2 garlic cloves, minced
½ teaspoon powdered ginger
2 tablespoons soy sauce
⅛ teaspoon ground anise
½ cup beef broth
1 teaspoon cornstarch

Blend 3 tablespoons soy sauce and sherry in deep bowl.

Freeze meat slightly; slice paper-thin. Add beef slices to soy sauce and sherry; coat well. Cover; let stand 1 hour.

Heat oil in large skillet.

Thoroughly drain beef on paper toweling. Sprinkle with flour; add to hot oil. Deep-fry 3 minutes. Remove meat with slotted spoon; drain. Set aside; keep warm.

Pour 4 tablespoons hot oil into another skillet. Throw away rest of frying oil. Reheat oil, add leeks and garlic. Cook 5 minutes, stirring. Add meat. Season with ginger, 2 tablespoons soy sauce, and anise. Pour in beef broth; cover. Simmer over very low heat 1 hour. At end of cooking time, bring to quick boil.

Blend cornstarch with small amount of cold water. Add to skillet; stir constantly until sauce is slightly thickened and bubbly. Correct seasoning, if necessary. Serve immediately with Boiled Rice (see Index). Yield 2 servings.

beef with snow pea pods and water chestnuts

1 pound beef (top round), sliced very thin
2 tablespoons soy sauce
2 tablespoons dry sherry
2 tablespoons vegetable oil
12 to 16 snow-pea pods, strings removed
6 to 8 water chestnuts, sliced
½ cup chicken broth or stock
1 tablespoon cornstarch in 2 tablespoons cold
   water

Walnuts (optional)

Freeze meat partially; slice thin.

Combine 1 tablespoon soy sauce and 1 tablespoon dry sherry in small bowl. Add beef; let stand 20 to 30 minutes.

Heat oil in wok or skillet. Stir-fry pea pods 1 to 2 minutes or just until green color brightens; push aside.

Stir-fry water chestnuts 1 minute; push aside.

Stir-fry beef 3 to 4 minutes. Return pea pods and water chesnuts to beef in wok. Add broth, 1 tablespoon soy sauce, 1 tablespoon dry sherry, and cornstarch mixture. Heat until sauce boils and is thickened and clear.

Garnish with walnuts. Serve at once with rice. Yield 4 servings.

beef strips and carrots

1 pound carrots
⅔ cup carbonated soda water
1 cup white wine
1 teaspoon salt
¼ teaspoon sugar
1 pound sirloin steak
2 tablespoons vegetable oil
2 small onions, diced
¼ teaspoon white pepper
½ cup heavy cream
1 tablespoon chopped parsley

Peel carrots; cut into thin slices (crosswise at slant). Place in saucepan with soda water, wine, ½ teaspoon salt, and sugar. Cover; simmer 25 minutes or until tender.

Meanwhile cut meat into very thin slices.

Heat oil; sauté onions about 5 minutes. Add beef slices; cook 5 minutes, stirring often. Season with ½ teaspoon salt and pepper. Add to carrots; mix carefully. Stir in cream; heat through but do not boil. Correct seasonings if necessary. Sprinkle with chopped parsley. Yield 4 servings.

beef stroganoff

1 to 1½ pounds beef tenderloin
1 or 2 onions
8 to 10 medium size mushrooms
4 to 5 tablespoons butter
Salt and pepper
1 cup sour cream
Grating nutmeg

Cut beef into strips about 2½ inches long and ½ inch thick.

Slice onions and mushrooms finely.

Melt 2 tablespoons butter in frying pan; cook onions slowly until golden brown. Remove from pan; keep warm. Add a little more butter. Cook mushrooms about 5 minutes; add to onions.

Melt remaining butter. When foaming, put in

about half the strips of steak. Fry quickly about 5 minutes, until brown on all sides. Remove; repeat with remaining steak.

Replace all meat and vegetables in pan. Shake over heat, adding salt, pepper, and nutmeg. Add sour cream; heat until it nearly boils. Serve immediately with plain Boiled Rice (see Index). Yield 4 servings.

beef sukiyaki

2 pounds beef sirloin, cut into strips
1 large Bermuda onion
3 stalks celery
¼ pound fresh mushrooms
12 scallions
8 ounces canned water chestnuts
¼ pound fresh spinach

beef stroganoff

1 tablespoon oil
¾ cup beef bouillon
½ cup soy sauce
¼ cup vermouth
1 tablespoon sugar

Have butcher cut sirloin into thin strips. If you are cutting it, partially freeze it to make it easier to slice.

Slice onion; put aside.

Slice celery at an angle into thin slices; set aside.

Thinly slice mushrooms; set aside.

Slice scallions into approximately 1½-inch pieces.

Drain water chestnuts; slice in half.

Wash spinach; tear into pieces.

Arrange meat and vegetables on large platter.

Put oil into extra-large skillet or wok. Brown meat; push to side of pan. Add all vegetables except spinach. Stir in bouillon, soy sauce, vermouth, and sugar; let sizzle 5 minutes. Add spinach; cover. Cook 2 minutes. Serve with rice. Yield 3 to 4 servings.

braised beef with vegetables

1 red pepper
1 green pepper
1 small Spanish onion
2 medium tomatoes
2 medium zucchini
2 tablespoons vegetable oil
4 slices round steak, each approximately 4 ounces
½ teaspoon salt
⅛ teaspoon pepper
⅛ teaspoon dried basil
½ cup white wine

Cut peppers in half. Remove seeds; slice into thin strips.

Slice onion. Peel tomatoes; cut into eighths.

Clean zucchini; cut into ½-inch-thick slices.

Heat oil in large frypan or Dutch over. Add all vegetables; cook about 10 minutes, stirring occasionally.

Trim fat from steak.

Lightly grease ovenproof casserole; place ⅓ of vegetable mixture in dish. Arrange steak on top. Sprinkle with salt, pepper, and basil. Cover with rest of vegetables. Pour wine over vegetables; cover casserole. Cook in preheated 350°F oven 50 minutes. Ten minutes before end of cooking time, remove cover to reduce liquid. Yield 4 servings.

braised beef with vegetables

broiled sirloin with mushrooms

broiled sirloin
with mushrooms

4 1-inch thick sirloin steaks
½ clove garlic
1 teaspoon salt
½ teaspoon freshly ground black pepper
½ cup butter
2 cups sliced mushrooms

Rub steaks with garlic. Sprinkle with half the salt and pepper. Score fatty edges of steak. Place on broiling pan 3 inches from heat. Broil on one side to desired degree of doneness. Turn; season uncooked side with remaining salt and pepper. Return meat to broiler; cook to desired doneness.

While steak is broiling, melt butter. Add mushrooms; sauté until golden brown and tender.

Arrange steaks on serving platter; cover with sautéed mushrooms. Yield 4 servings.

filet mignon in wine

chinese stir-fried beef and mushrooms

½ **pound dried Chinese mushrooms**
3 **pounds lean steak, cut into thin strips**
¼ **cup flour**
1 **tablespoon sugar**
½ **cup sherry**
½ **cup soy sauce**
¾ **cup oil**
1 **(2-inch) slice fresh gingerroot, minced**
1 **cup chopped onions**
2 **cups beef bouillon**
Salt to taste

Soak mushrooms in water 30 minutes. Drain well; set aside.

Cut steak into strips.

Combine flour, sugar, sherry, and soy sauce in bowl. Add beef; marinate 30 minutes. Stirring frequently.

Heat ½ cup oil in wok or skillet; stir-fry gingerroot 1 minute. Add beef with marinade; stir-fry until beef changes color. Remove beef from wok.

Add remaining oil to wok. Add onions; stir-fry until almost tender. Add mushrooms; stir-fry until soft. Place beef in wok; stir-fry about 2 minutes. Add bouillon. Bring to boil; reduce heat. Add salt; cover. Cook 2 minutes. Yield 8 to 10 servings.

chinese stir-fried beef and mushrooms

filet mignon in wine

4 **2-inch-stick filets**
1 **teaspoon salt**
½ **teaspoon peppermill-ground black pepper**
¼ **cup butter**
4 **small onions, peeled, halved**
1 **cup red wine**

Rub filets with salt and pepper.

Melt butter in heavy frying pan. Add steaks; brown on both sides. Reduce heat to simmer. Add onions and wine. Cover skillet tightly; simmer steaks 30 minutes. Yield 4 servings.

filet mignon, broiled

Place 1¼-inch-thick filets on rack in broiling pan. Set oven at broil; preheat several minutes. Place broiling pan in highest position in broiler; allow 2 to 3 minutes on each side to sear fillets. Lower pan to middle position; broil 2 minutes on each side for rare, 3 minutes and 30 seconds for medium, and 4 minutes for well-done.

Serve on heated platter with pat of Maître d'Hôtel butter on each steak.

filets mignons

filets mignons rossini

filet mignon, grilled

Place grill rack about 4 inches above red-hot coals. Place 1½-inch-thick filets on grill; sear about 2 to 3 minutes on each side. Cook 2 minutes and 30 seconds on each side for medium-rare.

filets mignons rossini

2½ pounds filet beef (cut into 1- to 1½-inch-thick slices)
1 tablespoon butter or margarine
2 tablespoons chopped onions
1 slice bacon, diced
½ tablespoon flour
1 teaspoon tomato puree
8 large mushrooms, stems chopped
2 cups beef stock (or water and beef cube)
¼ cup red wine (optional)
Salt and pepper
1 teaspoon chopped parsley and thyme
1 cup butter
8 slices white bread
1 cup cooking oil
1 can paté de foie gras
Watercress

Preheat oven to 350°F.

First make sauce: Melt butter. Add onions and bacon. Slowly cook to golden color; stir well. Add flour; cook until just turning light brown. Add tomato puree, chopped mushrooms, stock, wine, salt, and pepper. Bring to boil; simmer 15 minutes. Add parsley and thyme; cook a few minutes. Strain through fine sieve into serving dish; keep warm.

Put mushroom tops into buttered dish; put small pat of butter, salt, and pepper on each. Cook in oven 10 minutes.

Cut bread into slices same size as filets.

Heat oil; add 1 tablespoon butter. When foaming, fry bread until golden brown on both sides. Drain; keep warm.

Melt ½ cup butter in large frying pan. When foaming, cook filets 4 to 6 minutes each side, according to taste. (Or brush with melted butter and broil 5 to 8 minutes each side.)

Place filets on fried bread. Top each with slice of paté and a mushroom. Spoon a little sauce over each steak; serve the rest separately. Garnish with watercress. Yield 8 servings.

german beef rolls

4 pieces steak roll or sandwich steaks, each about 6 ounces
2 teaspoons Dijon-style mustard
½ teaspoon salt
¼ teaspoon pepper
2 large pickles, cut into long, thin strips
2 ounces salt pork (or 2 strips bacon), cut into thin strips
1 large onion, chopped
¼ cup vegetable oil
1½ cups hot beef broth
4 peppercorns
½ bay leaf

1 tablespoon cornstarch

Lay steaks on flat surface. Spread each with mustard; sprinkle with salt and pepper.

Divide pickles, salt pork, and onion among steaks as shown. Roll up steaks jelly-roll fashion; secure with beef-roll clamps, toothpicks, or thread.

Heat oil in heavy saucepan. Add steak rolls; brown well on all sides, about 15 minutes. Pour in broth, peppercorns, and bay leaf. Cover; simmer 1 hour and 20 minutes.

Remove beef rolls; discard clamps. Arrange on preheated platter.

Blend cornstarch with small amount cold water; stir into gravy. Bring to boil; cook until thick and bubbly. Correct seasonings; serve gravy separately. Yield 4 servings.

grilled sirloin steak

Place grill rack about 4 inches above red-hot coals. Sear steak about 5 minutes each side, then grill 3 minutes each side for medium-rare. Allow 6 to 10 ounces per serving. Serve with butter seasoned with salt and freshly ground black pepper or with Béarnaise Sauce (see Index). Yield as desired.

grilled steaks

marinade

½ cup soy sauce
4 tablespoons minced onions
2 cloves garlic, minced
1 tablespoon minced fresh gingerroot
¼ cup rice wine, or dry white wine
4 small steaks of your choice, boneless
Cherry tomatoes for garnish

Mix together marinade ingredients. Pour over steaks. Refrigerate overnight or let sit at room temperature 3 to 4 hours.

Broil in oven or on grill or hibachi. Baste with marinade while steaks are grilling. When almost done, grill tomatoes; use for garnish. Yield 4 servings.

london broil

2 (2-pound) flank steaks
1 cup salad oil
1 cup dry red wine
4 tablespoons soy sauce
2 tablespoons chopped green onions
1 clove garlic, chopped

german beef rolls

grilled steaks

1 teaspoon salt
¼ teaspoon pepper

Place steaks in shallow pan.

Combine remaining ingredients; pour over meat. Marinate at least 4 hours (or overnight).

Broil 5 to 7 minutes on each side 3 inches from heat. Baste frequently. Slice thinly on diagonal. Yield 8 servings.

pepper steaks

2 tablespoons peppercorns
4 large sirloin steaks (1 inch thick)
3 to 4 tablespoons oil
¼ cup butter
½ cup white wine
2 tablespoons brandy (optional)
Little lemon juice
Salt and pepper

Preheat broiler.

Press the crushed pepper well into steaks, using wooden spoon.

Heat oil in pan; add half of butter. When foaming, fry steaks 4 to 6 minutes on each side, longer if preferred. Add remaining butter, if needed. Remove to heated dish to keep warm.

Add wine, brandy, and lemon juice to juices in pan; bring to boil. Season with salt and pepper; pour over steaks. Serve at once.

Pepper can be scraped off before adding sauce, if preferred. Yield 4 servings.

polish steak with mushroom caps

1 teaspoon salt
½ teaspoon peppermill-ground black pepper
4 (2-ounce) filets mignons
¼ cup butter
1 cup fresh mushroom caps
¼ cup mayonnaise
2 teaspoons horseradish
4 slices toast
4 lemon slices
Dillweed

Salt and pepper both sides of filets.

Melt butter in heavy skillet; sauté steaks to desired doneness. Remove from skillet. Add mushrooms; sauté until done.

Combine mayonnaise and horseradish. Spread each toast slice with mixture.

To serve, place steaks on toast slices; top each with ¼ cup mushrooms. Garnish with lemon slice and dillweed. Yield 4 servings.

ragout á la berghoff

¾ cup butter
3½-pound boneless round steak, cut into thin
   strips
1 cup chopped onion
1½ cups chopped green pepper
1 pound mushrooms, sliced
½ cup flour
2 cups beef broth, canned or homemade
1 cup dry white wine
1 teaspoon salt
1 teaspoon Worcestershire sauce
Few drops Tabasco sauce (to taste)

Melt ½ cup butter in large frypan. Brown meat over medium-high heat. Remove browned meat.

Sauté onion in remaining butter 2 minutes. Add pepper and mushrooms. Cook 3 minutes.

Melt ¼ cup butter; add flour. Slowly add broth; cook until thickened. Stir in wine and seasonings. Add meat-and-mushroom mixture;

polish steak with mushroom caps

cover. Simmer 45 minutes to 1 hour, until meat is tender.

Serve with buttered noodles or dumplings. Yield 8 servings.

shallow-fried round steaks

1 (1½-pound boneless round steak),
   cut about ½ inch thick
1 recipe Marinade For Beef (see Index)
2 tomatoes
Olive oil
Salt and freshly ground pepper to taste
¼ cup butter
2 tablespoons beef extract
4 teaspoons finely chopped chives
Chives Butter (see Index)

beef extract over steaks; cook 1 minute. Steaks will be medium-rare.

Place on meat platter; place tomatoes around steaks.

Sprinkle 1 teaspoon chives on 4 pats Chives Butter; place 2 pats on each steak. Garnish with watercress, if desired. Yield 2 to 4 servings.

silver baked steak

4 large sirloin, club, or T-bone steaks
Oil
1 clove garlic, crushed (optional)
Black pepper
1 medium onion
1 cup chopped mushrooms

shallow-fried round steaks

Cut steak in half; place in shallow dish. Pour marinade over steaks. Refrigerate at least 24 hours; turn occasionally. Drain steaks; set aside.

Remove stem ends from tomatoes; cut in half. Place in shallow baking pan, cut-side-up; brush lightly with oil. Broil 6 inches from source of heat until tender and lightly browned. Sprinkle with salt and pepper; keep warm.

Place butter in large frypan over high heat until bubbly and light brown. Place steaks in butter; cook 30 seconds. Turn; cook 30 seconds. Reduce heat to low; cook 2 minutes on each side. Spoon

1 small green pepper
4 or 5 small tomatoes (or 1 tablespoon tomato
   puree)
Salt
1 tablespoon mixed herbs
2 tablespoons butter
Chopped parsley

Preheat oven to 350°F.

Beat steaks to tenderize; brush over with oil, garlic, and black pepper. Leave at least 1 hour.

Meanwhile, cut 4 squares of foil large enough to wrap 1 steak in each.

steak diane

Chop onion, mushrooms, green pepper, and tomatoes; cook few minutes in a little oil. Add salt and pepper to season.

Heat broiler; broil steaks about 1 to 2 minutes each side, or fry same length of time. Put each steak on center of foil square. Pile tomato-and-onion mixture on each steak; sprinkle with herbs. Fold foil over to seal.

Bake in oven 15 minutes for rare, 20 minutes for medium, and 25 to 30 minutes for well-done steak.

Open; serve on foil with pat of butter rolled in chopped parsley on top of each. Yield 4 servings.

steak diane

If you use a less expensive cut of been than strip sirloin, marinate steak overnight before cooking. Cook Steak Diane quickly to retain tenderness. Always serve it on a heavy, preheated platter to keep the juices hot and to heighten the full flavor.

3 well-marbled strip sirloin steaks, cut ½ inch thick
2 tablespoons butter
2 tablespoons cooking oil
2 tablespoons brandy
2 tablespoons minced shallots or green onions
1 tablespoon freshly chopped parsley
1 (10½-ounce) can beef consommé, chilled
Salt and pepper to taste
1 teaspoon Worcestershire sauce

Pound steaks with mallet or wine bottle to ¼ inch thick. Pierce steaks with tines of fork on one end; roll up steaks. Unroll 1 steak into sizzling butter and oil in heavy skillet. Cook 1 minute on each side. Remove to heated platter.

Place remaining steaks, one at a time, in hot-oil mixture; cook 1 minute on each side. Return steaks on platter to skillet. Turn heat to high; pour brandy over steaks. Ignite brandy; shake pan until flame is extinguished. Reduce heat; cook 1 minute. Add shallots; cook 2 minutes. Sprinkle with parsley, stirring well. Add consommé, 1 spoonful at a time, to steak mixture in skillet; bring to boil. Spoon about 2 tablespoons pan liquid onto warm platter. Remove steaks to platter; keep warm.

Cook pan liquid vigorously until reduced by half. Season with salt and pepper; stir in Worcestershire sauce. Spoon sauce over steaks; serve immediately. Serve with French-fried potatoes if desired. Yield 6 servings.

steak in savory marsala sauce

steak and mushroom kabobs

1 pound tenderloin steak
12 small mushroom caps
½ cup red wine
½ cup corn oil
1 teaspoon Worcestershire sauce
1 clove garlic, crushed
2 tablespoons catsup
1 teaspoon sugar
½ teaspoon salt
1 tablespoon vinegar
Pinch of dried marjoram
Pinch of dried rosemary

Cut steak into small cubes.

Mix all other ingredients together in bowl. Add steak; marinate at least 2 hours.

Alternate steak and mushrooms on skewers. Cook until meat is tender, about 15 minutes. Baste frequently with marinade. Yield about 8 skewers.

steak in savory marsala sauce

1 (1½-inch) sirloin steak
1 medium onion, grated

3 tablespoons all-purpose flour
1½ cups Basic Beef Stock (see Index)
½ cup Marsala wine
½ pound fresh mushrooms, sliced
Salt and pepper to taste
4 lemon slices

Trim steak; slash fat at 1-inch intervals. Broil steak about 6 inches from source of heat 8 minutes. Turn; broil 7 minutes for medium-rare. Place steak on serving platter; keep warm.

Pour ¼ cup pan juices into heavy saucepan. Add onion to hot juices; sauté about 4 minutes, stirring frequently. Stir in flour to make thick paste. Stir in stock and Marsala; cook until thickened and flavors are blended. Add mushrooms and seasonings; cook 3 minutes.

Cut steak diagonally into ½-inch slices. Pour sauce over steak; garnish with lemon slices. Yield about 4 servings.

steaks bercy

herb butter
4 ounces softened butter
1 tablespoon finely chopped parsley
1 tablespoon finely chopped chives
1 teaspoon dried chervil

1 teaspoon dried tarragon
1 tablespoon grated shallots or onion
Dash of pepper
4 filets mignons steaks
2 tablespoons vegetable oil
½ teaspoon salt
⅛ teaspoon pepper
4 lemon slices
Watercress
French-fried potatoes (cut very thin, dried on
　towels, deep-fried)

Make Herb Butter first by blending all ingredients. Spoon onto sheet of waxed paper; shape into roll about 1½ inches in diameter. Chill in freezer while steak is prepared. Cut into 4 thick slices just before serving.

Brush steaks with oil. Depending on thickness, broil about 5 minutes on each side or to desired doneness. Season with salt and pepper.

Arrange steaks on preheated platter. Place 1 lemon slice on each steak; top with slice of Herb Butter. Garnish with watercress and potatoes. Yield 4 servings.

steaks esterhazy

¼ pound mushrooms, diced
1 small carrot, diced
1 shallot or green onion, minced
2 tablespoons butter
1 teaspoon paprika
½ teaspoon salt
1 cup sour cream
1 teaspoon Worcestershire sauce
4 servings beef sirloin, T-bone, or fillet steaks

Sauté mushrooms, carrot, and shallot in butter. Add paprika, salt, sour cream, and Worcestershire sauce. Simmer 2 minutes; do not boil.

Broil steaks; top with sauce. Yield 4 servings.

steaks bercy

swiss steak

2 pounds eye of round
½ cup flour
2 teaspoons salt
2 teaspoons paprika
2 onions, sliced
1 large can tomatoes
1 can tomato sauce
2 to 3 cups water
½ teaspoon pepper
½ cup shortening

Cut meat in slices about ³/₈-inch thick. Dip into flour seasoned with salt and paprika.

Sauté onions until yellow. Remove onions with slotted spoon; leave fat in pan.

Brown meat slices; remove from pan.

Put remaining seasoned flour into pan; stir. When flour and fat are mixed thoroughly, add boiling water. Stir until gravy is made. Add tomatoes and tomato sauce; if too thick, add more water. Bring to boil. Strain; pour over meat and onions that have been put into casserole.

Bake, tightly covered, in 325°F oven until meat is tender, approximately 2 hours. Serve over fluffy rice. Yield 8 servings.

teriyaki

2½ to 3 pounds sirloin steak, cut about
 ½ inch thick
1 cup soy sauce
⅓ cup dry sherry
4 tablespoons brown sugar
1½ teaspoons ground ginger
2 teaspoons grated onion
1 clove garlic, crushed
18 chunks canned pineapple
18 small mushroom caps
2 tablespoons pineapple juice
1 tablespoon cornstarch

Cut steak into 1-inch squares.

Mix together soy sauce, sherry, sugar, ginger, onion, and garlic. Add meat; marinate 3 hours.

Place steak, pineapple, and mushrooms on skewers, starting and finishing with meat. Broil or grill about 4 to 5 minutes, until cooked to taste; turn once or twice to brown evenly.

Mix pineapple juice slowly into cornstarch. Add marinade; cook, stirring constantly, until sauce thickens. Serve with kabobs. Yield enough for 6 to 8 skewers.

teriyaki steak

4 boneless steaks, about ½ pound each

marinade
1 clove garlic, finely minced
1 sugared or candied ginger, finely minced
1 tablespoon brown sugar
Salt
Pepper, freshly ground
Pinch of monosodium glutamate (MSG)
½ cup red wine or sherry

teriyaki

teriyaki steak

6 tablespoons soy sauce
½ cup white wine
Juice of half a lemon

stuffed-tomato garnish
4 medium tomatoes
Salt
White pepper
4 tablespoons bean sprouts, canned or fresh
1 tablespoon tomato catsup

Combine marinade ingredients in shallow dish large enough to hold steaks. Stir until well blended. Add steaks; coat well. Marinate 12 hours; turn steaks frequently. Drain steaks; arrange on broiler pan. Place under preheated broiler; broil 4 minutes on each side.

Meanwhile, remove stems from tomatoes; cut off approximately ½-inch slices from bottoms. Scoop out seeds; discard. Sprinkle insides with salt and pepper.

Place bean sprouts and catsup into small skillet; heat 5 minutes. Spoon into tomatoes.

Arrange steaks on preheated serving platter. Garnish with stuffed tomatoes. Serve with rice. Yield 4 servings.

Note: If using fresh bean sprouts, boil 2 minutes, then rinse with cold water before using.

teriyaki steak bits

½ cup soy sauce
1 clove garlic, chopped fine
1 teaspoon ground ginger
2 tablespoons sugar
2 tablespoons sherry wine
1½ pounds steak, cut into 1-inch cubes
2 or more tablespoons margarine

Combine soy sauce, spices, sugar, and wine to make marinade. Marinate meat at least 1 hour. Drain meat; reserve liquid.

Melt 2 tablespoons margarine in medium skillet. Brown meat cubes quickly on all sides.

Place meat in chafing dish; pour sauce over. Stir occasionally. (You won't have to stir much, as guests will eat steak on handy toothpicks very quickly.) If you like, add pineapple chunks to chafing dish. Yield 6 to 8 servings.

tokyo steak

Salt
Ground ginger to taste
Pepper to taste, freshly ground
2 tablespoons rice wine or sherry
4 filet mignon steaks, about 6 ounces each
1½ tablespoons butter
1 (11-ounce) can mandarin oranges
1 tablespoon capers
1 tablespoon butter, cut into small pieces

Combine salt, ginger, pepper, and wine; blend well. Rub onto steaks.

Heat 1½ tablespoons butter in heavy skillet. Add steaks; sauté 2 minutes on each side. Arrange oranges and capers on top of steaks; dot with remaining butter. Place skillet under preheated broiler; broil 3 minutes. Serve steaks immediately on preheated plates. Yield 4 servings.

teriyaki steak bits

VARIETY MEATS

LIVER

braised liver and onions

1½ pounds sliced beef liver
½ cup flour
2 tablespoons fat or oil
1½ teaspoons salt
¼ teaspoon pepper
1 large onion, sliced
¼ cup water

Remove skin and large veins from liver; coat with flour.

Heat fat in large frypan over moderate heat; brown liver on one side. Turn liver; sprinkle with seasonings. Cover with onion. Add water; cover pan tightly. Cook over low heat 20 to 30 minutes or until liver is tender. Yield 6 servings.

creole liver

1 (8-ounce) can tomato sauce
1 (16-ounce) can tomatoes
½ cup chopped green pepper
½ cup chopped celery
½ cup chopped onion
½ teaspoon salt
⅛ teaspoon pepper
1¾ pounds beef liver, cut into strips
2 tablespoons fat or oil
3 cups cooked rice (about 1 cup uncooked)

Mix tomato sauce and tomatoes with green pepper, celery, onion, salt, and pepper. Simmer 15 minutes.

Cook liver in fat until lightly browned. Add to tomato mixture; simmer 30 minutes or until liver is tender. Serve over rice. Yield 6 servings.

risotto alla bolognese

½ to ¾ pound calf liver
1 onion
1 clove garlic
1 cup quartered mushrooms
2 to 3 tablespoons butter
1 cup long-grain rice
1 dessert spoon tomato puree
2½ to 3 cups stock
Salt and pepper

tokyo steak

risotto alla bolognese

1 tablespoon mixed herbs
1 cup grated Parmesan cheese

Cut liver into chunks.
Chop onion fine.
Crush garlic.
Quarter mushrooms.

Melt butter; cook onion and garlic a few minutes with lid on pan. Add liver; cook quickly until it changes color. Remove from heat. Add mushrooms, rice, tomato puree, 2½ cups stock, salt, and pepper. Bring to boil; stir all the time. Reduce heat; simmer gently 25 to 30 minutes. Stir occasionally; add extra stock if rice becomes dry. When cooked, rice should have absorbed all moisture. Sprinkle top with chopped herbs. Serve with grated cheese. Yield 4 servings.

OXTAIL

braised oxtails

3 tablespoons butter or fat
1 onion, chopped
2 carrots, sliced
1 small turnip, diced
1 stalk celery, chopped
2 tablespoons flour
2 oxtails
1 teaspoon salt
⅛ teaspoon pepper
2 cloves

Melt butter in saucepan. Add onion, carrots, turnip, and celery. When very lightly browned, stir in flour; blend well.

Cut oxtails into 2- to 3-inch pieces; add to pan. Add salt, pepper, cloves, and 2 cups water. Bring to boil, stirring constantly. Reduce heat; let simmer 2 to 3 hours.

Serve oxtails hot with liquid for gravy. Yield 6 to 8 servings.

french grilled oxtail

1 large lean oxtail cut into even-sized pieces
Several parsley stalks
1 bay leaf
1 sprig thyme
6 or 7 peppercorns
2 onions
2 carrots
6 to 7 tablespoons butter
4 to 5 tablespoons dried white bread crumbs

Preheat broiler.

Soak oxtail pieces at least 3 hours in cold salted water (overnight if possible). Drain; put into pan of boiling water containing herbs, peppercorns, 2 onions, and carrots. Cook slowly 2 to 3 hours or until meat is tender. Drain; reserve liquid to use as gravy with vegetables if desired. Dry oxtail.

Melt 3 to 4 tablespoons butter; roll each oxtail in this, then in bread crumbs.

Heat broiler until red-hot. Broil oxtail pieces until brown and crisp; turn frequently. Serve with Sauce Robert. Yield 4 servings.

sauce robert

3 tablespoons butter
1 onion, chopped
3 tablespoons wine vinegar
1 tablespoon flour
1 cup brown stock
1 tablespoon chopped gherkins
2 teaspoons French mustard
Salt and pepper

Melt butter; cook onion slowly 6 to 8 minutes. Add vinegar; boil few minutes. Add flour, then stock; bring to boil. Cook 10 minutes. Add gherkins, mustard, salt, and pepper. Reheat; serve.

french grilled oxtail

TONGUE
apricot tongue

1 small beef tongue
Water
¼ cup soy sauce
2 cloves garlic, cut

sauce
⅔ cup brown sugar
¾ cup catsup
¼ teaspoon grated fresh gingerroot, or
  ½ teaspoon powdered ginger
1 tablespoon soy sauce
1 package dried apricots

Place tongue in large pot; add water to cover. Mix in ¼ cup soy sauce and garlic. Bring to boil; simmer 2 to 3 hours until tongue is tender. Cool; remove skin. Trim base. Put back in pot to reheat. Slice before serving.

Make sauce: Combine all ingredients in saucepan; simmer slowly until apricots are soft.

Pour sauce over sliced tongue. Yield 4 servings.

cooked pickled tongue

1 (2- to 3-pound) pickled tongue

Wash tongue; cover with boiling water. Cook ½ hour; pour off water. Add fresh boiling water to cover; cook over low heat 2 to 2½ hours, until tender. Test with fork. If water cooks out, add more boiling water during cooking period. Cool, peel. Trim base; slice.

Serve on bed of rice or serve cold with Dijon mustard. Yield 6 servings.

cooked pickled tongue

red-stewed beef tongue

1 small fresh beef tongue (2 pounds)
Boiling water to cover meat
½ clove garlic
1 tablespoon oil
2 tablespoons cooking wine
2 tablespoons dark soy sauce per pound of meat
1 teaspoon sugar per pound of meat

Immerse tongue completely in boiling water. Turn off heat; let soak 1 minute. Remove tongue from water. Use blunt knife to peel off skin and trim base.

Brown garlic in oil in wok or skillet. Brown tongue on both sides. Lower heat; add cooking wine. For each pound of tongue, add 2 tablespoons dark soy sauce. Cook over low heat 1½ to 2 hours. Turn tongue at 20-minute intervals. Add water to maintain quantity of cooking liquid at 6 to 8 tablespoons. During last 20 minutes, add 1 teaspoon sugar per pound. Yield 4 servings.

smoked tongue with creole sauce

1 (2-pound) smoked beef tongue
1 large onion, chopped
1 carrot, chopped
2 stalks celery, chopped
2 cloves
1 recipe Creole Sauce

Place tongue in large kettle; cover with water. Add onion, carrot, celery, and cloves. Cover; bring to boil. Reduce heat; simmer about 2 hours or until fork-tender. Remove tongue from liquid; let cool. Peel off outer skin; trim base.

Add enough tongue broth to Creole Sauce to thin to desired serving consistency. Pour Creole Sauce into serving platter to depth of ¼ inch.

Cut tongue into thin slices, starting at base. Arrange slices in sauce. Cut slices toward tip at an angle, so pieces will not be too small. Serve with remaining sauce. Tongue can be reheated in liquid if desired. Yield 6 to 8 servings.

creole sauce

4 medium onions
4 green sweet peppers
1 pound fresh mushrooms
¼ cup olive oil
3 tablespoons sugar
1 bay leaf
1 teaspoon allspice
¼ cup wine vinegar
2 (1-pound) cans Italian tomatoes
Salt and cayenne pepper to taste

Slice onions lengthwise into thin strips.

Cut peppers in half lengthwise; remove seeds and membrane. Cut halves into strips same width as onions.

Cut mushrooms with stems attached into lengthwise slices about ⅛ inch thick.

Sauté vegetables lightly in oil in large saucepan over medium heat until wilted but not brown. Add remaining ingredients. Simmer, covered, over very low heat 2 hours. Stir frequently, mashing tomatoes. Sauce will be thick. Yield 3 to 4 cups.

sweet-sour tongue

1 fresh tongue, 2 to 3 pounds
Salt to taste
1 onion
1 lemon, sliced thin
1 cup raisins
¼ teaspoon cinnamon
¼ teaspoon allspice
Pepper to taste
¾ cup vinegar
1 cup brown sugar
10 gingersnaps

Cover tongue with water; cook with salt and onion until tender. Skin tongue, trim base, and slice.

Strain gravy. Add lemon, raisins, cinnamon, allspice, pepper, vinegar, brown sugar, and gingersnaps (softened in water); boil. Add sliced tongue; and boil a few minutes. Yield 6 to 8 servings.

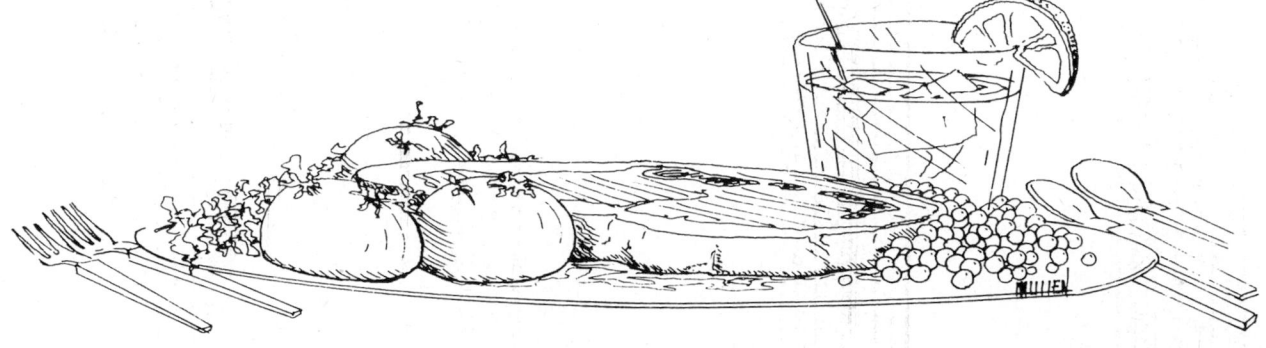

banana shake

BEVERAGES

café brûlot

3 tablespoons sugar
Thinly peeled rind of 1 small orange
1 vanilla pod or 1 teaspoon vanilla extract
1½ cups brandy
6 cups piping-hot black coffee

Place sugar, orange rind, and vanilla pod in heatproof bowl; bruise rind with wooden spoon.

Pour brandy into small saucepan; place over low heat until heated through. Pour over sugar mixture. Ignite; stir constantly 30 seconds. Extinguish flames with hot coffee. Remove orange rind and vanilla pod.

Serve in coffee cups. Do not serve with cream or additional sugar. Yield about 20 demitasse cups.

apple–pineapple cooler

3 cups unsweetened apple juice
2 cups unsweetened pineapple juice
1 cup orange juice
2 tablespoons freshly squeezed lime or lemon juice
Orange slices to garnish

Combine ingredients; chill. Garnish glasses with orange slices. Yield 1½ quarts.

banana shake

1 banana
1 tablespoon lemon juice
4 tablespoons sugar
1 cup milk
1 cup plain yogurt
Whipped cream (garnish)

Puree banana, lemon juice, and sugar in blender or food processor until smooth. Add milk and yogurt; blend until thoroughly mixed.

Pour at once into glasses. Top with dab of whipped cream. Yield 3 cups.

café brûlot

caribbean punch

caribbean punch

Juice of 12 oranges
Juice of 12 lemons
3 cups white rum
½ cup (packed) brown sugar
1 teaspoon cinnamon
1 teaspoon cloves
1 teaspoon nutmeg
1 teaspoon ginger
12 cups crushed ice

Mix juices, rum, brown sugar, and spices.

Place crushed ice in punch bowl; pour rum mixture over ice. Cover with cloth; let stand 10 minutes. Remove cloth; stir mixture well. Add 2 trays ice cubes; garnish with orange slices.

Dip rims of glasses in ice water, then in sugar for frosted effect, if desired. Ladle punch into glasses; garnish each glass with orange slice and long orange-peel strip. Yield about 20 (¾-cup) servings.

champagne punch

1 cup orange juice, chilled
2 cups lemon juice, chilled
2½ cups Basic Sugar Syrup (see Index)
1 quart sauterne, chilled
2 quarts soda water, chilled
1 quart champagne, chilled

Combine juices, syrup, and sauterne; pour into punch bowl. Just before serving, pour soda water into punch mixture. Add champagne; stir once or twice, just to mix. Add ice cubes to punch. Serve in champagne glasses. Yield about 20 cups.

chocolate yogurt brandy

2 scoops chocolate ice cream
1 cup plain yogurt
2 tablespoons brandy
Whipped cream
Cocoa

Place ice cream, yogurt, and brandy in blender or food processor; blend until smooth. Pour into tall glass. Garnish with whipped cream and pinch of cocoa. Yield about 1½ cups.

chocolate yogurt brandy

christmas wassail

2 quarts apple cider
2 cups orange juice
1 cup lemon juice
1½ cups pineapple juice
4 to 6 whole cloves
Sugar or honey to taste
½ fifth of vodka (optional)
3 small oranges
Cloves

Combine cider, juices, cloves, and sugar; bring to simmer. Strain; add vodka.

Stud each orange with cloves; float in punch. Ladle into punch glasses. Serve hot. Yield 12 servings.

coffee copenhagen

8 cups hot coffee
1 cup rum
¾ cup sugar
2 sticks cinnamon or 1 teaspoon ground cinnamon
12 whole cloves

Combine all ingredients in slow cooker. Cover; keep warm on low up to 2 hours. Ladle into mugs or tall, heavy glasses. Yield 8 servings.

créme de menthe pickup

1 tablespoon grenadine
Sugar
½ cup cold milk
½ cup plain yogurt
¼ cup créme de menthe
2 tablespoons cointreau

Pour grenadine into small, shallow bowl.
Place sugar in second dish.
Dip rims of glasses in grenadine, then in sugar.
Blend milk, yogurt, créme de menthe, and cointreau in blender until smooth.
Pour into prepared glasses; serve immediately. Yield 2 servings.

cucumber cooler

1 cup chilled unsweetened pineapple juice
1 cup peeled, seeded cucumber chunks
½ cup watercress
2 sprigs parsley
½ cup finely crushed ice

Place all ingredients in blender; blend until smooth. Yield 2 servings.

créme de menthe pickup

frozen black coffee

2½ cups strong coffee
1¼ cups Basic Sugar Syrup (see Index)
Sugar
1 recipe Basic Chantilly Cream (see Index)

Combine coffee and syrup; mix well. Pour into refrigerator trays; freeze until icy crystals form.

Dip edges of tall glasses in cold water, then into sugar to frost. Spoon coffee mixture into glasses; top with Chantilly cream. Serve immediately. Yield 4 servings.

fruit-juice appetizer

1 (10-ounce) package frozen raspberries, thawed
1 can pineapple-grapefruit juice
4 lemon wedges

frozen black coffee

Place raspberries and juice in blender. Blend 30 seconds on low speed, until thoroughly blended. Strain to remove seeds. Chill; serve with lemon garnish. Yield 4 servings.

fruit–tea punch

2 cups boiling water
4 tea bags black tea
¼ cup lemon juice
2 cups orange juice
1 tablespoon honey
1 lemon
2 oranges
2 cups fresh strawberries
1 bottle soda water

Pour boiling water over tea bags; steep 3 minutes. Remove tea bags. Blend in juices; sweeten with honey.

Cut peel from lemon and oranges; section fruit. Remove all membranes; add to tea.

Wash and hull strawberries; cut in half. Add to tea; cover. Refrigerate punch at least 6 hours to blend flavors. Just before serving, add bottle of soda water. Yield about 10 cups.

fruit–tea punch

hot buttered rum

fruited wine bowle

4 cups fresh fruit, such as nectarines, peaches, apricots, strawberries, plums
2 tablespoons sugar
1 cup brandy
2 bottles dry white wine, chilled
1 bottle champagne, chilled

Mix fruit and sugar. Pour brandy over. Let marinate 24 hours or more.

Place fruit and brandy into large punch bowl. Add wine and champagne; mix. Remove fruit from punch.

Serve punch in separate dish with toothpicks. Ladle into punch cups. Keep chilled. Yield about 14 (6-ounce) punch-cup servings.

93

grape frost

Frothy and refreshing.
1 cup grape juice
1 cup plain yogurt
4 or 5 ice cubes

Place all ingredients in blender; blend until smooth. Serve at once. Yield 2 servings.

hot buttered rum

2 ounces light rum
Juice of 1 small lemon
1 small strip lemon peel
1½ teaspoons brown sugar
1½ tablespoons butter

Place long spoon in tall glass. Pour rum into glass. Add lemon juice and peel. Pour enough boiling water into glass over handle of spoon to fill glass. Stir in brown sugar. Add butter; stir until melted.

Garnish with slice of lemon and additional lemon peel. Yield 1 serving.

hot chocolate

1½ squares (1½ ounces) unsweetened chocolate
¼ cup sugar
¼ teaspoon salt
1 cup boiling water
3 cups hot milk
½ teaspoon vanilla extract
Marshamllows

Melt chocolate in top of double boiler over hot water. Stir in sugar and salt. Add water gradually; stir until smooth. Add milk; cook 2 minutes. Add vanilla.

To serve, put marshmallow into each cup; add hot chocolate. Yield about 2 pints.

hot chocolate

hot chocolate mexican-style

hot chocolate mexican-style

2 (1-ounce) squares unsweetened chocolate
½ teaspoon vanilla
1 teaspoon ground cinnamon
4 tablespoons heavy cream
2 cups milk
2 egg yolks
2 tablespoons sugar
3 ounces brandy
4 cinnamon sticks

Combine chocolate, vanilla, cinnamon, and cream in saucepan. Place over very low heat; stir until chocolate is melted. Add milk slowly to chocolate mixture; mix well. Warm over very low heat. Do not allow mixture to boil.

Beat egg yolks and sugar until foamy. Slowly pour part of chocolate mixture into egg yolks, beating well. Pour egg-yolk mixture into saucepan; beat. Add brandy to chocolate mixture; beat until mixture is frothy.

Serve hot chocolate immediately in small cups with cinnamon sticks as stirrers. Yield 4 servings.

Note: A simpler method for making delicious chocolate is: For each cup chocolate, heat 1 cup milk until quite hot (do not boil). Pour over 1 ounce (per cup of milk) grated Mexican chocolate; stir until melted. Whip with rotary beater until frothy; serve. If Mexican chocolate unavailable, substitute 1 ounce unsweetened chocolate, grated, and ¼ teaspoon ground cinnamon for each ounce Mexican chocolate.

ice-cream brandy punch

2½ cups milk
½ cup brandy
1 egg
1 pint vanilla ice cream

Place milk, brandy, and egg into bowl; beat well. Add ice cream cut into small pieces; beat until frothy.

Pour into punch bowl; serve immediately. Yield 6 to 8 glasses.

iced coffee with whipped cream

1 cup sugar
1½ cups milk
1 vanilla pod
1½ cups cold coffee
¾ cup whipping cream
Unsweetened whipped cream

Combine sugar, milk, and vanilla pod in heavy saucepan; bring to boil, stirring until sugar is dissolved. Remove from heat; let stand until cold. Remove vanilla pod; rinse and dry for future use.

Combine milk mixture, coffee, and whipping cream, mixing well; pour into refrigerator trays. Place in freezing compartment; let stand until partially frozen.

Stir; pour into tall glasses, filling ⅔ full. Top with spirals of whipped cream; serve immediately.

Coffee mixture can be made ahead and frozen. Let thaw until mushy. Yield 6 servings.

irish coffee

4 heaping teaspoons instant coffee powder
4 full teaspoons sugar
4 jiggers Irish whiskey

4 cups boiling water
Whipped cream

Divide coffee, sugar, and whiskey among 4 cups; mix well. Add boiling water until almost full. Spoon whipped cream on top in mounds. Serve immediately. Yield 4 servings.

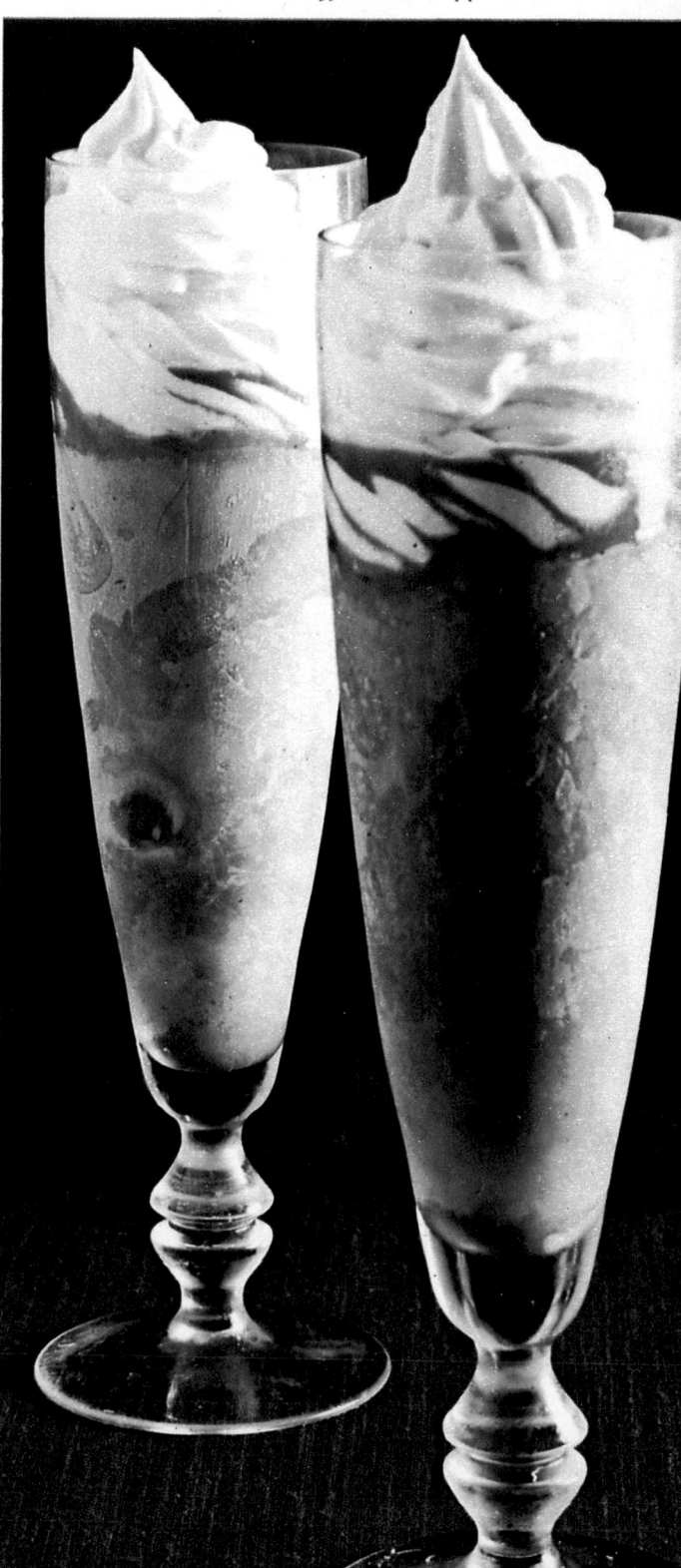

iced coffee with whipped cream

lamb's wool

8 apples, peeled, cored, coarsely chopped
¼ cup butter
2 quarts beer or ale
1 cup sugar
½ teaspoon nutmeg
½ teaspoon ginger

Combine all ingredients in slow cooker. Cover; cook on low 2 to 3 hours.

Remove apples; mash or sieve. Return to beer mixture. Serve very hot. Yield 8 servings.

lamb's wool

lemon sherry cocktail

Juice of 1 lemon
Juice of ½ orange
1 teaspoon honey
2 jiggers sherry
3 ice cubes
1 lemon slice
1 orange slice
2 maraschino cherries

Shake juices, honey, and sherry in cocktail shaker.

Crush ice cubes; place in tall glass. Pour lemon cocktail over ice.

lemon sherry cocktail

Peel lemon and orange slices; cut into small pieces. Add to drink. Garnish with cherries; serve. Yield 1 serving.

mulled wine

½ cup sugar
¼ cup water
2 orange slices
6 cloves
2 cinnamon sticks
½ cup orange juice
1 bottle red Bordeaux wine

Boil sugar, water, orange slices, cloves, and cinnamon 5 minutes. Remove from heat. Add juice and wine. Keep hot but do not boil. Serve with cinnamon sticks or orange slices.

Cider can be substituted for wine. Sweeten to taste. Yield 6 servings.

orange delight

½ cup orange juice
1 tablespoon lemon juice
2 tablespoons honey
1 cup plain yogurt
Orange peel (garnish)

Combine and shake all ingredients except peel.

Pour into tall glass. Garnish rim with curled strip of orange peel (or slice of orange). Yield about 1½ cups.

orange delight

pina colada

1 cup coconut juice (available canned)
1 cup pineapple juice
4 to 6 tablespoons honey or sugar
8 to 10 ice cubes
½ cup rum

Combine all ingredients in blender jar; blend until smooth. Serve at once. Yield about 2 cups.

pink lady

¾ cup sugar
2 cups chilled cranberry juice

2 cups chilled pineapple juice
4 cups chilled ginger ale
Vanilla ice milk

Place sugar in pitcher. Add cranberry juice slowly; stir until sugar is dissolved. Add pineapple juice; chill thoroughly. Add ginger ale; pour into serving glasses. Add 1 serving spoon of ice milk to each glass; stir until foamy. Serve immediately. Yield about 8 servings.

planter's punch

4 tablespoons fresh lime juice
4 ounces dark Jamaican rum
2 teaspoons grenadine
2 teaspoons Triple Sec
Soda water
4 orange slices

Combine lime juice, rum, grenadine, and Triple Sec in mixer glass; mix well. Pour over ice in highball glasses; fill with soda water. Place orange slices in glass. Yield 2 servings.

sangria

1 large orange
1 large lemon
⅛ teaspoon cinnamon
⅛ teaspoon nutmeg
Sugar to taste
1½ ounces brandy
1 fifth of claret
1 cup chilled club soda

Cut 2 thick slices from center of orange, then from center of lemon. Remove seeds from slices; set aside.

Squeeze juice from remaining parts of orange and lemon; strain into 2-quart container. Add spices, sugar, brandy, claret, and orange and lemon slices; mix well. Cover; let stand 1 hour.

Pour claret mixture and soda into large decanter or serving pitcher. Pour over ice in tall, chilled glasses; garnish each glass with an orange slice.

White Bordeaux wine can be used instead of claret. Yield about 6 servings.

strawberry shake

½ cup (or more) strawberries
2 tablespoons honey
1 cup cold milk
1 cup plain yogurt
Large whole strawberries

Puree ½ cup strawberries and honey in blender or food processor. Add milk and yogurt; blend until smooth. Pour into glasses; garnish each with whole strawberry. Yield about 2 cups.

sangría

Combine all ingredients in slow cooker. Cover; cook on low 1 to 2 hours. Serve hot. Yield about 2 quarts.

tropical punch

1 (46-ounce) can red fruit punch
1 (6-ounce) can frozen lemonade concentrate
6 cups cold water
1 (6-ounce) can frozen orange-juice concentrate
1 (6-ounce) can frozen grape-juice concentrate
3½ cups ginger ale, chilled

Combine punch and frozen concentrates with water. Pour over ice in large punch bowl. Carefully pour in ginger ale. Yield 30 to 35 servings.

Note: Use an ice ring with orange slices and fresh mint leaves frozen in it.

tropical twist

3 cups chilled unsweetened pineapple juice
2 ripe bananas
4 teaspoons honey
Juice of 1 lime
1 cup finely crushed ice

Place all ingredients in blender; blend until smooth. Yield 4 servings.

swedish glogg

1 bottle port (⁴/₅ quart)
1 bottle claret (⁴/₅ quart)
½ cup apricot brandy
½ cup raisins or currants
6 dried apricot halves, chopped
12 blanched almonds
4 whole cloves
2 sticks cinnamon
4 whole cardamom

strawberry shake

vanilla shake with chartreuse

vanilla shake with chartreuse

1 cup plain yogurt
2 scoops vanilla ice cream
2 tablespoons French chartreuse
Maraschino cherry

Blend first 3 ingredients in blender or food processor until smooth. Pour into glass; garnish with cherry on toothpick. Yield about 1½ cups.

BREADS

almond raisin bread

2 cups all-purpose flour
¾ cup granulated sugar
½ cup brown sugar
1½ teaspoons baking soda
1½ teaspoons salt
1 teaspoon cinnamon
½ teaspoon nutmeg
½ cup butter or margarine
1½ cups applesauce
2 eggs
½ cup chopped figs
¾ cup raisins
¼ cup citron
¾ cup blanched whole almonds
½ cup powdered sugar, sifted

Combine flour, granulated and brown sugars, soda, salt, cinnamon, and nutmeg in mixing bowl. Add butter and applesauce; beat on low speed of electric mixer 2 minutes, being sure to scrape sides of bowl. Add eggs; beat 2 minutes. Stir in fruits and nuts. Pour batter into greased and floured 9-inch loaf pan.

Bake bread at 350°F 1½ hours or until done. Cool slightly before removing from pan.

Dust warm bread with powdered sugar; serve warm. Yield 12 servings.

austrian kugelhopf

¾ cup chopped almonds
½ cup raisins
1½ teaspoons grated lemon rind

almond raisin bread

austrian kugelhopf

6 cups all-purpose flour, sifted
1 cup sugar
1 teaspoon salt
2 envelopes yeast
¼ cup lukewarm water
2 cups lukewarm milk
2 eggs, well beaten
⅓ cup melted butter
1 teaspoon vanilla extract
Confectioners' sugar

Combine almonds, raisins, and lemon rind with ½ cup flour; toss until well coated.

Combine sugar, salt, and 2½ cups flour in large mixing bowl.

Sprinkle yeast over water; stir until dissolved.

Add milk to sugar mixture; stir until well mixed. Add yeast mixture; beat with wooden spoon until smooth. Beat in eggs thoroughly. Add butter gradually; beat constantly. Stir in vanilla extract. Add remaining flour; beat until smooth and satiny. Add raisin mixture; mix thoroughly. Cover with towel. Let rise in warm place 1½ hours or until double in bulk.

Stir down dough; turn into large, buttered bundt pan. Cover with towel; let rise 1 hour.

Bake in preheated 350°F oven about 50 minutes, until cake tester comes out clean. Remove from pan; cool on wire rack. Cover; let stand 1 day.

Sprinkle with confectioners' sugar before slicing. Yield about 20 servings.

banana bread

1¾ cups unsifted flour
1 tablespoon baking powder
½ teaspoon salt
¾ cup sugar
½ cup shortening
2 eggs
1 cup mashed bananas

Preheat oven to 350°F.

Grease 9 × 5-inch pan.

Mix flour, baking powder, and salt thoroughly.

Mix sugar, shortening, and eggs together until light and fluffy. Mix in bananas. Add dry ingredients; stir just until smooth. Pour into prepared pan. Bake until firmly set when lightly touched in center top, 50 to 60 minutes. (Bread may crack across top.) Cool on rack. Remove from pan after 10 minutes.

date-nut banana bread

Add ½ cup chopped dates and ½ cup chopped nuts with mashed bananas.

orange banana bread

Mix 1 tablespoon grated orange rind with creamed shortening, sugar, and eggs. Yield: 5 × 9-inch loaf; 18 (1½-inch) slices.

basic large sweet brioche

½ cup butter
⅓ cup extra-fine sugar
1½ teaspoons salt
1 package yeast
¼ cup warm water
¼ cup warm milk
4 eggs
3½ cups all-purpose flour
1 recipe Egg Wash (see Index)

Beat butter in large mixing bowl with wooden spoon or electric mixer until creamy. Add combined sugar and salt gradually; cream until well blended.

Sprinkle yeast over warm water in small bowl; stir until dissolved.

Add milk, yeast, eggs, and flour to creamed

mixture. Beat vigorously with wooden spoon 2 minutes or until smooth; scrape sides of bowl frequently. Cover; let rise in warm place about 2 hours or until double in bulk.

Stir down; beat vigorously with wooden spoon 2 minutes. Cover with aluminum foil; refrigerate overnight.

Stir down; turn onto lightly floured surface. With floured hands shape ¾ of dough into ball. Place in well-buttered, fluted brioche mold. Snip a cross in center with scissors; push dough to sides to form a well. Moisten inside of well with water.

Shape remaining dough into pear shape to form head. Push pointed end into well in the center of large ball. Cover; let rise in warm place 1 hour and 20 minutes or until double in bulk.

Bake in preheated 400°F oven 1 hour or until cake tester comes out clean. Brush with Egg Wash 5 minutes before removing from oven. An aluminum-foil tent can be placed over brioche if it browns too quickly. Remove from oven; turn onto wire rack to cool.

Fill brioche with sweet or savory filling. Remove head; trim. Pull out dough in center of brioche to leave shell ½ to ¾ inch thick. Fill as desired. Yield 1 large brioche.

basic large sweet brioche

sweet filling for brioche
Apricot Jam
1 recipe Basic Confectioners' Custard (see Index)
1 recipe Basic Chantilly Cream (see Index)
Slivered almonds
Brush inside of brioche shell with thick coating of jam. Spoon custard into shell. Fill remainder of shell with Chantilly Cream. Sprinkle with almonds.

basic white bread

1½ cups lukewarm water
2 packages yeast
7½ cups all-purpose flour
3 tablespoons sugar
1 cup milk
1 tablespoon salt
¼ cup butter
1 recipe Anglais Glaze (see Index)
Place water in large warm bowl or crock. Sprinkle yeast over water; stir until dissolved. Cover; let stand 15 minutes.

Combine 1½ cups flour and 2 tablespoons sugar. Beat mixture carefully into yeast mixture with wooden spoon until free from lumps. Cover with towel; let rise in warm place 30 minutes.

Scald milk; stir in salt and remaining sugar. Add butter; stir until dissolved. Cool to lukewarm. Add to yeast mixture. Add enough remaining flour to make soft dough.

Turn onto lightly floured board. Knead 10 minutes or until smooth and elastic; add flour if needed. Place in greased bowl; turn dough to grease top. Cover with towel; let rise in warm place 1 hour or until double in bulk.

Turn dough onto lightly floured board; divide in half. Shape into loaves. Place in 2 well-greased 9 × 5-inch loaf pans or 3 smaller shaped molds. Cover; let rise 1 hour or until double in bulk.

Bake at 400°F 10 minutes. Brush tops with Anglais Glaze, using pastry brush. Bake 15 minutes. Turn loaves onto wire racks to cool. Yield 2 (9 × 5-inch) loaves.

basic whole–wheat bread

¾ cup milk
¼ cup firmly packed brown sugar
1 tablespoon salt
⅓ cup butter
⅓ cup molasses
1½ cups lukewarm water
2 packages yeast
6 cups stone-ground whole-wheat flour
1½ cups flour
1 recipe Egg Wash (see Index)
Scald milk in small saucepan. Add brown sugar, salt, butter, and molasses. Stir until dissolved; let stand until lukewarm.

Pour water into warm, large mixing bowl. Sprinkle yeast over water; stir until dissolved. Pour in milk mixture, stirring constantly. Stir in 4 cups whole-wheat flour, 1 cup at a time, mixing until smooth. Stir in remaining whole-wheat flour. Sprinkle with part of regular flour.

Turn dough onto floured surface. Knead in remaining flour about 10 minutes or until dough is smooth and elastic. Place dough into well- buttered bowl; turn to grease top. Cover with towel; let rise in warm place 1 hour or until double in bulk.

Turn dough onto lightly floured surface; divide in half. Shape into loaves. Place in 2 well-greased 9 × 5-inch loaf pans. Cover; let rise in warm place about 1 hour or until double in bulk.

Bake at 400°F 10 minutes.

Brush with Egg Wash; bake 15 minutes. Yield 2 (9 × 5-inch) loaves.

basic whole-wheat bread

biscuits

2 cups flour
1 tablespoon baking powder
1 teaspoon salt
⅓ cup shortening
About ¾ cup milk

Mix dry ingredients thoroughly. Mix in shortening only until mixture is crumbly. Add most of milk; stir to mix. Add more milk as needed to make dough that is soft but not too sticky to knead.

Knead dough gently on lightly floured surface 10 to 12 times. Form into ball. Pat or roll dough to ½ to ¾ inch thick. Cut with floured biscuit cutter or cut into squares with knife. Place on ungreased baking sheet: 1 inch apart for crusty biscuits; together for softer biscuits.

Bake at 450°F 12 to 15 minutes, until golden brown.

cheese biscuits

Combine ¾ cup shredded sharp or extra-sharp cheese with dry ingredients before adding fat.

sweet biscuits or shortcake

Combine 1 tablespoon sugar with dry ingredients. Use ¼ cup butter or margarine for fat. Reduce milk to ⅔ cup. Bake at 425°F 10 to 15 minutes. Yield 12 biscuits.

bran date bread

2 teaspoons baking soda
1 8-ounce package dates, cut up
1⅔ cups boiling water
1 cup margarine
2 cups granulated sugar
2 eggs, beaten
½ cup Sourdough Starter (see Index)
1½ cups all-purpose unbleached white flour
1 cup whole-wheat flour
½ cup unprocessed wheat bran
⅓ cup wheat germ
2 cups sliced almonds

Mix baking soda and dates. Pour boiling water over; let stand until cool.

Cream margarine and sugar. Add eggs; beat until smooth.

Combine Sourdough Starter and date mixture.

Combine flours, wheat bran, and wheat germ. Add dates and flour mixture alternately to creamed mixture; mix well after each addition. Fold in nuts.

Pour batter into well-greased and floured small loaf pans. Bake at 375°F 10 minutes. Lower temperature to 350°F; bake 50 minutes or until done.

Remove bread from oven. Let stand 10 minutes before removing from pans. Yield 3 small loaves.

bran date bread

brioches

1 package active dry yeast
1 cup warm water
1 cup Sourdough Starter (see Index)
1 cup all-purpose unbleached white flour
½ cup sugar
1 cup butter, melted
1 teaspoon salt
5 eggs, beaten
5 to 5½ cups all-purpose unbleached white flour
1 egg, beaten
1 tablespoon water

bread sticks

bread sticks

1 package active dry yeast
2 cups warm water
½ cup Sourdough Starter (see Index)
2 cups unbleached white flour
2 tablespoons granulated sugar
1¼ cups butter, melted
2 teaspoons salt
3½ to 4 cups unbleached white flour
2 tablespoons caraway seeds
2 tablespoons poppy seeds
2 tablespoons coarse salt or sea salt

Dissolve yeast in water. Stir in Sourdough Starter; blend well. Add 2 cups flour; mix well. Let rise overnight or about 12 hours.

Stir down sponge. Add sugar, ½ cup butter, and salt. Add about 3 cups flour to form stiff dough.

Pour remaining flour onto kneading surface. Pour bread sponge on flour. Knead until all flour has been worked into dough. Continue kneading until dough is smooth and elastic. Place in greased bowl; remember to grease top of dough. Cover; let rise until double in bulk.

Punch down dough. Cover with bowl; let rest 10 minutes. Divide into 24 equal balls. Divide each ball into 2 equal parts; form each part into thin stick about 6 to 8 inches long. Place sticks side by side; twist. Repeat process with remaining dough balls.

Place on ungreased cookie sheet. Brush with remaining melted butter. Top with one of seeds or salt. Cover; let rise 30 minutes.

Place sticks in preheated 400°F oven in which pan of hot water has been placed on oven floor. Bake 10 to 15 minutes or until golden brown. Cool sticks. Yield 2 dozen.

Dissolve yeast in water. Add Sourdough Starter; blend thoroughly. Mix in 1 cup flour; cover. Let stand overnight.

Stir sponge to dissolve crust. Add sugar, butter, salt, and 5 eggs; mix well. Add enough remaining flour to make soft dough. Turn onto floured pastry cloth; knead until dough is smooth. Place in greased bowl; cover. Let rise until double in bulk.

Punch down dough; divide into 24 equal parts. Cut small piece of dough from each of 24 pieces. Shape large pieces of dough into round balls; place in greased brioche pans or greased muffin tins. Make indentation in center of each large ball. Form small pieces of dough into balls; place in indentations in large balls. Cover pans; let rise until double in bulk.

Mix egg and water. Brush brioches with mixture. Bake in preheated 375°F oven 15 minutes or until golden brown. Cool on racks. Yield 2 dozen.

caraway rye loaf

Dough can be formed into 2 smaller loaves.

1 cake compressed yeast or 1 package active dry yeast
2 cups warm water
½ cup Sourdough Starter (see Index)
2 cups all-purpose unbleached white flour
¼ cup molasses
1 teaspoon salt
3 tablespoons shortening, melted
2 tablespoons caraway seeds
4 to 4½ cups rye flour
¼ cup cornmeal
1 egg, beaten

Dissolve yeast in water. Add Sourdough Starter; blend thoroughly. Mix in white flour; cover. Set in warm place 12 hours or overnight.

Stir mixture to dissolve crust on top. Add molasses, salt, shortening, and caraway seeds; mix well. Add rye flour until soft dough has formed.

Pour 1 cup rye flour on kneading surface. Pour dough on flour. Knead flour into dough. Add enough remaining flour to form medium-stiff dough. Knead 10 minutes or until folds form in dough.

Place dough ball in greased bowl. Grease top; cover. Let rise until double in bulk.

Punch down dough. Knead 2 minutes. Form into oblong loaf. Place loaf on greased cookie sheet that has been dusted with cornmeal; cover. Let rise until double in bulk.

Place loaf in 400°F oven 10 minutes. Remove from oven. Brush with beaten egg. Return to oven. Bake 35 to 40 minutes or until done. Cool on rack. Yield 1 oblong loaf.

caraway rye loaf

brioches

cheese bread

1 recipe Basic White Bread (see Index)
1¾ cups freshly grated Parmesan cheese
2 tablespoons freshly grated Emmenthal or Swiss
  cheese
1 recipe Anglais Glaze (see Index)

Prepare Basic White Bread according to recipe directions; add 1½ cups Parmesan to yeast mixture with second addition of flour. Place in 2 prepared loaf pans.

Bake at 400°F 10 minutes. Brush with Anglais Glaze; bake 10 minutes. Brush with Anglais Glaze. Sprinkle mixture of remaining Parmesan and the Emmenthal cheese over top of loaves. Bake 5 minutes. Remove from pan; cool on wire rack. Yield 2 loaves.

cheese bread

cornbread

1 cup cornmeal
1 cup flour
1 tablespoon baking powder
½ teaspoon salt
2 to 4 tablespoons sugar (optional)
1 egg
1 cup milk
¼ cup melted fat or oil

Mix cornmeal, flour, baking powder, salt, and sugar. Set aside.

Beat egg. Add milk. Add fat. Add to cornmeal mixture, stir just enough to mix. Fill greased pan half full.

Bake at 425°F 20 to 25 minutes, until lightly browned. Yield 6 servings.

cornmeal muffins

Use recipe for Cornbread. Fill greased muffin pans half full of cornmeal mixture. Baking time will be 15 to 20 minutes. Yield 12 servings.

cheese cornbread

Use 2 eggs in recipe for Cornbread, Stir 1½ cups cut-up cheese into batter before putting into baking pan.

105

crescent rolls

**1 cake compressed yeast or 1 package active dry
  yeast**
1 cup warm water
½ cup Sourdough Starter (see Index)
⅓ cup nonfat dry milk
1 cup all-purpose white flour
½ cup shortening, melted
½ cup granulated sugar
2 eggs, beaten
1 teaspoon salt
3½ to 4½ cups all-purpose white flour
½ cup margarine, melted

Dissolve yeast in water. Add Sourdough Starter; mix well. Add dry milk and 1 cup flour; cover. Let stand overnight to develop sponge.

Stir down sponge to dissolve crust. Add shortening, sugar, eggs, and salt; mix well. Add enough remaining flour to make soft dough.

Turn dough onto floured surface; knead until dough is smooth. Place in greased bowl; cover. Let rise until double in bulk.

Punch down dough; divide into thirds. On floured surface roll each third to 9-inch circle. Brush circles with margarine. Cut each circle into

crescent rolls

9 equal wedges. Roll each wedge, starting with wide end. Place on greased cookie sheet. Put ends of wedges on bottom to prevent rolls from unrolling. Curve ends of rolls to form crescent shapes; cover. Let rise until double in bulk.

Bake in preheated 400°F oven 10 to 12 minutes or until golden brown. Yield 27 rolls.

danish christmas bread

2 packages dry yeast
¼ cup lukewarm water
½ cup milk, scalded
⅓ cup sugar
1 teaspoon salt
⅔ cup butter
5 cups sifted all-purpose flour
1½ teaspoons vanilla extract
4 eggs, beaten
¼ cup warm water
2 tablespoons dark corn syrup
Confectioners' sugar
¼ cup chopped mixed candied fruits

Dissolve yeast in lukewarm water.

Mix milk, sugar, salt, and butter in large bowl; cool to lukewarm. Add 2 cups flour; mix well. Add yeast, vanilla, and eggs; mix until blended. Add enough remaining flour to make soft dough; mix well.

Knead on lightly floured surface, adding more flour as needed, 10 minutes or until smooth and elastic. Place in greased bowl; turn to grease surface. Cover; let rise in warm place until double in bulk.

Punch down dough; shape into round loaf. Place on greased baking sheet. Cover; let rise until double in bulk.

Bake in preheated 350°F oven 20 minutes. Mix warm water and syrup; brush on bread. Bake about 30 minutes, until well browned. Brush with syrup mixture again; place bread on rack to cool.

Sprinkle with confectioners' sugar, then with candied fruits. Yield about 15 servings.

dilled croutons

A delicious and economical addition to a tossed salad.

1-pound loaf day-old bread
1 cup butter
2 teaspoons onion salt
2 tablespoons dried parsley flakes
1 teaspoon dried dillweed

Cube bread into ½-inch cubes. Spread cubes evenly over baking sheet. Let dry 2 days or until cubes lose moisture and become hard.

Melt butter in large skillet. Pour butter from

stollen

skillet into a bowl. Add onion salt, parsley, and dillweed; mix well.

Reheat skillet in which butter was melted. Add croutons; distribute evenly over skillet surface. Pour melted-butter mixture over croutons. Stir to distribute evenly. Fry croutons until golden brown and thoroughly heated; cool. Store up to 1 month in airtight container. Yield 2 quarts.

easter anise loaf

2 envelopes active dry yeast
¼ cup lukewarm milk
1 teaspoon sugar
½ cup (1 stick) butter
⅔ cup sugar

danish christmas bread

1 tablespoon grated lemon rind
¾ teaspoon aniseed
1 teaspoon salt
¾ cup scalded milk
4 eggs, beaten
6 cups all-purpose flour
¾ cup currants
5 hard-boiled eggs, dyed red with food coloring

In small bowl proof yeast with ¼ cup milk and 1 teaspoon sugar.

In large bowl combine butter (softened, cut into bits), sugar, lemon rind, aniseed, and salt. Add scalded milk (while still hot); stir well. Cool mixture to lukewarm. Add yeast mixture. Add 4 eggs and 2 cups flour; beat with electric mixer on medium speed 2 minutes. By hand mix in 2½ cups

easter anise loaf

flour and currants. Dough should be soft and slightly sticky.

Turn dough onto well-floured board; knead in 1½ cups flour. Knead 10 minutes or until dough is smooth and satiny. Form dough into ball; place in greased bowl. Turn dough in bowl to grease top. Cover; let rise in warm place 1½ hours or until double in bulk.

Punch down dough. Divide into 3 equal pieces; shape each piece into 20-inch rope. Braid 3 dough ropes; form into circle. Press ends together. Place on greased baking sheet. Press dyed eggs into braid at intervals. Brush with melted butter. Cover; let rise in warm place until double in bulk.

Bake in preheated 325°F oven 45 to 50 minutes or until golden brown. Cool on cake rack. Yield 1 loaf.

egg braid

1 package active dry yeast
1 cup warm water
1 cup Sourdough Starter (see Index)
1 cup all-purpose white flour
⅓ cup granulated sugar
2 eggs, beaten
½ cup butter, melted
1 teaspoon salt
4 to 4½ cups all-purpose white flour
2 eggs, beaten

Dissolve yeast in water. Add Sourdough Starter. Mix in 1 cup flour. Let mixture set 12 hours or overnight to develop sponge.

Stir sponge to dissolve crust. Add sugar, 2 eggs, butter, and salt; mix well. Add 2½ cups flour to sponge; mix well.

Pour 1 cup flour on kneading surface. Pour sponge mixture on flour. Cover with 1 cup flour. Knead until flour is worked into dough. Continue adding flour until stiff dough has formed. Knead dough 10 minutes or until folds form. Place in greased bowl. Grease top. Cover; let rise until double in bulk.

Punch down dough. Knead 2 minutes. Divide dough into 2 equal balls; divide 1 ball into 8 equal parts. Roll 8 parts until approximately 12 inches long. Place these 8 strips side by side; braid by folding 1 strip over other in numerical order. Tuck in edges. Prepare second dough ball in same manner. Place braids on greased cookie sheets. Cover; let rise until double in bulk.

Brush braids with 2 eggs. Bake in preheated 350°F oven 30 minutes or until golden brown. Remove from oven; brush with oil. Cool on rack. Yield 2 braids.

french bread

1 package active dry yeast
1½ cups warm water
1 cup Sourdough Starter (see Index)
1½ cups all-purpose white flour
3 tablespoons granulated sugar
2 teaspoons salt
4½ to 5 cups all-purpose white flour
¼ cup yellow cornmeal

Dissolve yeast in water. Stir in Sourdough Starter; blend well. Add 1½ cups flour; mix well. Let mixture rise overnight or about 12 hours to develop sponge.

Stir down sponge. Add sugar and salt; mix well. Add 3 to 3½ cups flour; work in.

Pour remaining flour onto kneading surface. Pour sponge mixture on flour. Knead until all flour has been worked into dough. Continue kneading until folds form (about 10 minutes). Place dough in greased bowl. Grease top of dough. Cover; let rise in warm place until double in bulk. Punch down.

Turn dough onto lightly floured board. Divide into 2 equal portions; roll each portion into 15 × 10-inch oblong. Beginning at widest side, roll up tightly; pinch edges together. Taper ends by gently rolling dough back and forth. Place loaves on

french bread

greased baking sheets sprinkled with cornmeal. Cover; let rise in warm place about 1 hour or until double in bulk.

With sharp razor make diagonal cuts on top of each loaf. Place loaves in cold oven in which pan of boiling water has been placed. Set oven at 450°F; bake loaves about 35 minutes or until golden crust has formed. Remove from oven. Cool on wire rack. Yield 2 loaves.

fried croutons

For small croutons cut crust from dried slices of day-old bread. Cut slices into about ½-inch squares.

Melt ¼ cup butter for each 2 cups bread squares in heavy saucepan or skillet. Toss bread squares in butter to coat evenly, using pancake turner. Fry over medium heat until croutons are golden; toss continuously. Turn out on paper toweling to drain and cool.

Use in salads or soups. Can be stored in airtight container several days. Yield as desired.

garlic bread

1 loaf Italian bread
½ cup soft butter or margarine
1 teaspoon parsley flakes
¼ teaspoon crumbled oregano
¼ teaspoon dried dillweed
1 clove garlic, minced
Grated Parmesan cheese

Cut bread diagonally into 1-inch slices; do not cut all the way through.

Blend butter, parsley, oregano, dillweed, and garlic. Spread mixture on both sides of bread slices. Shape aluminum foil around loaf of bread. Twist ends; leave top open. Sprinkle top liberally with cheese and parsley flakes. Heat in 400°F oven 10 minutes. Yield 1 loaf.

german beer coffee cake

2 cups (packed) dark brown sugar
1 cup butter, softened
2 eggs
1 teaspoon cinnamon
½ teaspoon allspice
½ teaspoon ground cloves
3 cups sifted all-purpose flour
2 teaspoons baking soda
½ teaspoon salt
1 cup chopped walnuts
2 cups chopped dates
2 cups beer
Confectioners' sugar

Combine brown sugar and butter in mixing bowl; cream until smooth and well blended. Add

garlic bread

the eggs one at a time; beat well after each addition.

Sift cinnamon, allspice, cloves, flour, soda, and salt together.

Dust walnuts and dates with small amount of mixture. Add remaining flour mixture alternately with beer to creamed mixture; blend well after each addition. Stir in walnuts and dates. Spoon batter into large well-buttered and floured tube or bundt pan.

Bake in preheated 350°F oven 1¼ hours or until cake tester comes out clean. Let stand 5 minutes; invert on a wire rack.

Sprinkle confectioners' sugar; place on serving plate. Yield 18 to 20 servings.

german beer coffee cake

hamburger buns

hamburger buns

1 package active dry yeast
2 cups warm water
½ cup Sourdough Starter (see Index)
6 cups all-purpose white flour
2 tablespoons honey
⅔ cup nonfat dry milk
2 teaspoons salt
¼ cup oil
2 eggs, beaten
1 cup unprocessed wheat bran
¼ cup margarine, melted

Dissolve yeast in water. Add Sourdough Starter. Mix in 2 cups flour. Let stand 12 hours or overnight to develop starter.

Stir to dissolve crust. Add honey, milk, salt, oil, and eggs; mix well. Stir in bran. Add 2 cups flour; work in.

Pour 1 cup flour on kneading surface. Pour sponge on flour. Dust top of dough with flour. Work flour into dough. Add remaining flour until soft dough has formed. Knead 10 minutes. Place dough ball in greased bowl. Grease top of ball. Cover; let rise until double in bulk.

Punch down dough. Knead 2 minutes. Shape dough into 12 round balls. Place on greased cookie sheet; flatten balls slightly. Brush with melted margarine; cover. Refrigerate 2 hours.

Uncover dough balls. Let stand at room temperature 10 minutes.

Bake buns in preheated 400°F oven 20 to 25 minutes or until golden brown. Slice before serving. Yield 12 large buns.

hazelnut coffee cake

¾ cup brown sugar
1 cup all-purpose white flour
1 cup whole-wheat flour
1 teaspoon baking soda
1 teaspoon baking powder
1 teaspoon cinnamon
1 teaspoon nutmeg
½ teaspoon salt
⅔ cup milk
1½ ounces liquid egg substitute
¼ cup honey
½ cup ground hazelnuts
1 cup powdered sugar, sifted
1 to 2 tablespoons hot milk
½ cup whole hazelnuts

Mix brown sugar, flours, soda, baking powder, cinnamon, nutmeg, and salt.

Combine milk, egg substitute, and honey. Add liquid mixture to dry ingredients; blend well. Fold in ground hazelnuts. Pour mixture into greased 9-inch loaf pan. Bake at 350°F 60 minutes or until done. Cool slightly; remove from pan.

Combine powdered sugar and hot milk; beat until smooth. Drizzle over top of cake in lattice design, as illustrated. Place whole hazelnuts between lattice design. Yield 12 servings.

health bread

2 cups unbleached all-purpose flour
1 cup whole-wheat flour
1 tablespoon toasted wheat germ
2 packages active dry yeast
1 cup rolled oats (regular or quick-cooking)
1 cup whole-bran cereal
1 cup seedless raisins
1½ cups low-fat cottage cheese
2 tablespoons vegetable oil
1 tablespoon salt
½ cup honey
2½ cups boiling water
About 4½ cups additional unbleached all-purpose flour

hazelnut coffee cake

Stir together 2 cups flour, whole-wheat flour, wheat germ, and yeast in large mixing bowl. Set aside.

In separate bowl combine rolled oats, bran cereal, raisins, cottage cheese, oil, salt, and honey. Cover with boiling water; stir until thoroughly mixed. Cool to lukewarm. Add to dry ingredients in mixer bowl. Beat ½ minute at lowest speed of electric mixer; scrape bowl constantly. Beat 3 minutes at highest speed. Stir in about 4½ cups flour by hand, until mixture forms moderately stiff dough.

Turn onto floured board. Knead until smooth and elastic, about 10 minutes. Place in greased bowl; turn once to grease surface. Cover with dampened towel; let rise until double in bulk, about 1 hour.

Punch down dough; divide into thirds. Cover; let rest 10 minutes. Shape into 3 loaves. Place in 3 greased 8½ × 4½ × 2½-inch loaf pans. Brush tops lightly with vegetable oil. Cover; let rise until double, about 35 to 45 minutes.

Bake in 375°F oven 35 to 40 minutes, until golden brown. Remove bread from pans; let cool on rack. Yield 3 loaves.

italian croutons

A pick-up for your dinner salad.
1 loaf sourdough French Bread (see Index), cubed
½ cup butter, melted
½ cup grated Romano cheese
2 tablespoons oregano
2 tablespoons garlic powder
1 tablespoon basil leaves
1 teaspoon salt
1 teaspoon freshly ground pepper

Toss bread cubes and butter, then toss with cheeses and herbs until well mixed. Spread on ungreased jelly-roll pan.

Bake at 250°F until crisp and golden brown. Stir every 15 minutes. Cool; store in airtight container. Keeps well 1 month. Yield 1 quart.

kielbasa and cheese loaf

¾ cup warm water
1 package hot-roll mix
1 egg, beaten
½ cup grated Swiss cheese
½ cup cooked, finely chopped Kielbasa
¼ cup butter, melted

Pour water into medium-size bowl. Sprinkle yeast from roll mix over water; stir until dissolved. Add egg; mix well. Blend in flour from roll mix, Swiss cheese, and Kielbasa. Blend until all ingredients are combined and form sticky dough ball. Cover; let rise in warm place until double in bulk, about 45 minutes.

Punch down dough. Work dough on floured surface to form oblong roll. Place on greased baking sheet. Cover loosely; let rise in warm place until light and double in size, about 30 minutes.

Brush top of loaf with melted butter. Bake in preheated 400°F oven 30 minutes or until golden brown. Remove from oven; cool on rack. Yield 1 loaf.

italian croutons

kielbasa and cheese loaf

lucia bread

1 package dry yeast
½ cup lukewarm milk
¼ cup sugar
3 to 4 cups flour
1 egg
½ teaspoon saffron
½ teaspoon salt
4 tablespoons butter
Extra flour for kneading
1 egg yolk for glazing
Dried currants for garnish

Dissolve yeast in 2 tablespoons lukewarm milk. Mix with sugar, flour, egg, and 2 tablespoons milk to make dough. Cover; place in warm spot to rise 15 minutes.

Put saffron into bowl with 4 tablespoons milk. Add salt.

Melt but do not heat butter. Pour over saffron mixture. Add mixture to risen dough. Knead thoroughly until dough does not stick to bowl.

Cover; place in warm spot to rest 30 minutes. If necessary or desired, knead and let rise again.

On floured board roll out dough to ½ inch thick. Shape into rolls about 8 inches long. These can be worked into shapes of spirals, pretzels, or crosses. Place on greased baking sheet.

Glaze with beaten egg yolk; dot with currants. Bake at 425°F about 15 minutes.

Serve warm with plenty of butter and hot coffee. Yield about 24 pieces.

plum kuchen

½ cup soft butter or margarine
½ cup sugar
2 eggs
¾ teaspoon almond extract
½ teaspoon vanilla
1 cup flour
1 teaspoon baking powder
½ teaspoon coarse salt
20 plum halves

topping
½ cup sugar
1 teaspoon cinnamon
¼ teaspoon nutmeg

Preheat oven to 400°F.

Grease 9-inch-round pan.

Cream butter and ½ cup sugar until light and fluffy. Beat in eggs one at a time; add flavorings, beat well.

Sift flour, baking powder, and salt together; blend in. Pour batter into pan. Arrange plum halves in batter, cut-side-down.

Mix together topping ingredients; sprinkle over plums and batter. Bake 30 minutes.

Serve warm or cold with whipped cream, if desired. Yield 6 servings.

popovers

1 cup flour
¼ teaspoon salt
2 eggs, beaten
1 cup milk (scant measure)
1 tablespoon shortening, melted

Preheat oven to 450°F.

Sift flour and salt together.

Mix eggs, milk, and shortening; add gradually to flour. Beat until smooth, with egg whisk or electric mixer. Should take about 1 minute. Pour into greased popover tins, Pyrex cups, or muffin pans to ⅓ full.

Bake 20 minutes at temperature given. Reduce heat to 350°F; bake 15 minutes, until popovers are firm. Yield about 8 large popovers.

lucia bread

poppy-seed kuchen

½ cup milk
½ cup half-and-half or light cream
¾ cup butter
1 cup granulated sugar
1 teaspoon salt
1 package active dry yeast
2 eggs, beaten

poppy-seed kuchen

BREADS

4 to 5 cups all-purpose white flour
1 cup raisins
½ cup water
¼ cup vodka
1 can poppy-seed filling
1 cup chopped English walnuts
⅔ cup all-purpose flour

Combine milk and half-and-half; scald. Add ½ cup butter, ½ cup sugar, and salt to milk mixture; stir until butter dissolves. Cool to lukewarm. Add yeast; mix well. Add eggs and 4 cups flour. Stir until flour is worked in and dough forms.

Turn dough onto floured surface; work in enough remaining flour to form medium-stiff dough. Knead 10 minutes or until smooth dough forms. Place in greased bowl; cover. Let rise until double in bulk, about 1 hour.

While dough is rising, combine raisins, water, and vodka in small saucepan. Simmer until raisins absorb all liquid.

Combine poppy-seed filling, nuts, and raisins; mix well.

Punch down dough; divide into 2 equal parts. Roll each dough ball into a 12 × 10-inch rectangle. Spread filling evenly over rectangles.

Combine ¼ cup butter, ¼ cup sugar, and flour; mix well. Spread over poppy-seed filling. Cover; let rise until double in bulk.

Bake in 350°F oven 30 minutes or until dough is golden brown. Yield 2 kuchen.

soda scones

soda scones

3 cups sifted all-purpose flour
½ teaspoon soda
2 teaspoons cream of tartar
½ cup butter, softened
1 tablespoon sugar
¼ cup milk

¼ cup water
1 egg, beaten

Sift flour, soda, and cream of tartar into large bowl. Work in butter with fingers until of fine-meal consistency. Add sugar; blend thoroughly.

Combine milk and water; stir into flour mixture to form medium-soft dough. Press dough lightly into 10 × 8-inch rectangle on lightly floured surface. Cut into 1 × 3-inch triangles.

Brush tops with egg; place on baking sheet. Bake in preheated 400°F oven 20 minutes or until lightly browned.

Serve hot with butter and jam. Yield 16.

sourdough starter I

The original recipe for sourdough starter.

2 cups warm water
2 cups all-purpose white flour

Using stone jar or crock, combine water and flour. Place mixture in warm place 3 to 4 days, until bubbly and sour smelling. Refrigerate starter.

Each time it is used, replenish with equal parts water and flour; mix well. Cover; refrigerate. Starter will be ready when you next bake. Never use all your sourdough starter in a recipe. Reserve enough to keep it going.

sourdough starter II

1 package active dry yeast
2 cups warm water
2 cups all-purpose white flour

Using stone jar or crock, dissolve yeast in warm water. Stir in flour. Place mixture in warm place 3 to 4 days or until bubbly and smells sour. Refrigerate it.

Replenish as in preceding recipe. If sourdough starter gets too sour, add a little baking soda to recipe—½ teaspoon to 3 cups flour.

stollen

2 packages dry yeast
¼ cup warm water
1 cup scalded milk
½ cup butter
¼ cup sugar
1 teaspoon salt
¼ teaspoon ground cardamom
4½ cups sifted all-purpose flour
1 egg, slightly beaten
1 cup seedless raisins
¼ cup currants

¼ cup chopped mixed candied fruits
2 tablespoons grated orange rind
1 tablespoon grated lemon rind
¼ cup chopped blanched almonds
2 tablespoons melted butter
Confectioners' sugar

Dissolve yeast in warm water.

Combine milk, ½ cup butter, sugar, salt, and cardamom in large bowl; cool to lukewarm. Stir in 2 cups flour; mix well. Add yeast and egg; mix until blended. Stir in fruits, grated rinds, and almonds. Stir in enough remaining flour to make soft dough.

Turn out onto lightly floured surface. Knead 10 minutes or until smooth and elastic; add more flour as needed. Place in greased bowl; turn to grease surface. Cover; let rise in warm place 1 hour and 45 minutes or until double in bulk.

Punch down dough; turn out onto lightly floured surface. Cover; let rest 10 minutes. Shape into long, oval loaf; place on greased baking sheet. Cover; let rise in warm place 1 hour, until double in bulk.

Bake in preheated 375°F oven 20 minutes. Reduce oven temperature to 350°F; bake about 40 minutes, until lightly browned. Brush with melted butter; place on rack to cool.

Sprinkle with confectioners' sugar, then with additional candied fruits. Yield about 15 servings.

torrijas

8 to 10 (½- or 1-inch thick) bread slices
1 cup sifted confectioners' sugar
1½ teaspoons cinnamon
2 eggs
2 tablespoons sherry

Cut 2 circles from each bread slice with 2¼-inch-round cookie cutter.

Sift sugar and cinnamon together; set aside.

Place eggs in small mixer bowl; beat with electric mixer until fluffy. Strain eggs. Stir in sherry.

Dip each bread round into egg mixture. Fry in 380°F oil in deep-fat fryer until lightly browned on each side. Watch carefully; Torrijas brown quickly. Remove from oil with slotted spoon; drain on absorbent paper.

Coat well with sugar mixture; serve immediately. Yield 16 to 20.

viennese coffee braid

2 packages dry yeast
4 tablespoons sugar
2⅓ cups milk, warmed

BREADS

7 cups sifted all-purpose flour
2 cups seedless raisins
1½ teaspoons salt
1 cup crushed sliced almonds
6 tablespoons butter, softened
3 eggs
1 egg yolk

Combine yeast with 1 tablespoon sugar in 1-pint bowl. Add ⅔ cup milk gradually, stirring until smooth. Add ⅓ cup flour, small amount at a time; stir until smooth. Cover with a cloth. Set in warm place; let rise 30 minutes.

Place remaining flour, sugar, raisins, salt, and almonds in extra-large mixing bowl. Blend with wooden spoon until raisins are well coated. Add 4 tablespoons butter and yeast mixture; mix well. Stir in eggs. Add remaining milk gradually, work-ing into a dough. When thoroughly mixed, turn out onto floured surface, preferably wooden or marble. Knead with heel of your hand. Alternate kneading with slapping dough hard with palm of hand. Continue kneading and slapping about 10 minutes, until dough is smooth and soft. Return dough to large bowl. Cover; let rise in warm place 1 hour.

Turn out onto floured surface; punch down dough hard with your fist. Return to bowl. Cover and let rest for 30 minutes. Divide dough into 3 parts, graduated in size. The 3 pieces, from small to large, will weigh about 15, 20, and 28 ounces.

Roll out largest piece about 19 inches long. Cut into 3 (2-inch wide) strips.

Melt remaining butter. Dab a little on one end of each strip of dough; pinch together. Make 3-strand braid. Lift braid onto floured, 16-inch long

viennese coffee braid

baking sheet. Brush top with melted butter. Roll second-largest piece of dough into 17-inch-long strip. Cut into 3 (2-inch-wide) strips. Pinch together at one end as with first braid. Repeat braiding; place this braid on top of first. Brush with butter. Repeat procedure with smallest piece of dough, cutting 14-inch-long strips. Braid; place on top. Brush with additional melted butter.

Mix egg yolk with 1 tablespoon water; brush over braid. Cover lightly with tea towel; set in warm place. Let rise 1 hour.

Place in preheated 350°F oven, one shelf above center. Bake 1 hour. Remove from oven; place on cooling rack. Dust liberally with confectioners' sugar. Yield 1 braid.

torrijas

yankee spoon bread

1 package frozen kernel corn
3 cups milk
1 cup cornmeal
2 tablespoons plus 2 teaspoons butter
Salt
1 teaspoon baking powder
3 eggs, separated

Preheat oven to 325°F.

Cook corn according to directions. Drain; cool. Heat 2 cups milk.

Mix cornmeal with remaining cup of milk; add to hot milk. Cook until thick; stir constantly. Add butter and salt; let cool. Add corn, baking powder, and slightly beaten egg yolks, mixing well.

Beat egg whites until stiff; fold into cornmeal mixture. Pour all into casserole. Bake about 45 minutes. Yield 6 to 8 servings.

CAKES

almond jelly layers

almond jelly layers

2¼ cups cake flour
1½ cups granulated sugar
4 teaspoons baking powder
1 teaspoon salt
½ cup shortening
1 cup milk
1 teaspoon vanilla
2 eggs
2 cups currant jelly, room temperature
2 cups chopped almonds

Combine flour, sugar, baking powder, and salt. Add shortening, ¾ cup milk, and vanilla. Beat on low speed 2 minutes. Add eggs and remaining milk. Beat 2 minutes.

Grease and flour 3 (8-inch) cake pans. Divide batter evenly among pans. Bake in 350°F oven 20 minutes or until done. Remove from pans; cool.

Whip jelly until spreadable. Spread between layers; stack layers. Cover sides of cake with thin coat of jelly; cover sides with 1 cup almonds before jelly sets. Pour remaining jelly on top of cake; cover top evenly. Spread remaining almonds around edge of cake and in circular design in center of cake, as illustrated. Let jelly set before serving. Yield 12 servings.

angel almond layer

1 Angel-Food Cake (see Index)
1 cup strawberry jam
8 egg whites
¼ teaspoon cream of tartar
½ cup granulated sugar
¼ cup thinly sliced almonds

Prepare angel-food cake as directed. Pour into loaf angel-food pan. Bake as directed. Invert pan;

cool. Remove cake from pan. Cut cake in half horizontally; spread jam between layers.

Whip egg whites until foamy. Gradually beat in cream of tartar and sugar until egg whites stand in peaks. Spread on sides and top of cake. Sprinkle almonds over meringue.

Bake in 450°F oven 3 minutes or until meringue starts to turn light brown. Yield 12 servings.

angel almond layer

apple cake

angel-food cake

1 cup sifted cake flour
1½ cups sugar
¼ teaspoon salt
12 egg whites
1¼ teaspoons cream of tartar
1¼ teaspoons almond extract

Sift flour with ¾ cup sugar and salt 4 times.

Beat egg whites with cream of tartar until soft peaks form. Add remaining sugar, 2 tablespoons at a time; beat well after each addition. Sift ¼ cup flour mixture over egg whites; fold in carefully. Fold in remaining flour mixture by fourths. Turn into 10-inch tube pan.

Bake in preheated 375°F oven 35 to 40 minutes or until cake tests done. Invert pan on funnel; cool completely. Remove from pan. Yield 10 to 12 servings.

apple cake

4 to 6 tart apples (medium size)
2 lemons, juiced
3 tablespoons sugar
3 tablespoons butter
¾ cup sugar
2 egg yolks (do not put 2 yolks together; they will be used individually)
½ lemon, juiced, peel grated
1 teaspoon baking powder
1½ cups flour
¾ cup milk
1 tablespoon rum
2 egg whites
1 teaspoon butter (to grease pan)
1 teaspoon vegetable oil
3 tablespoons powdered sugar

Peel apples. Cut in half; core. Cut decorative lengthwise slits in apples, about ½ inch deep (see picture). Sprinkle with lemon juice and 3 table-spoons sugar; set aside.

Cream butter and ¾ cup sugar together. Beat in egg yolks one at a time. Gradually beat in lemon juice and grated peel.

Sift baking powder and flour together; gradually add to batter. Blend in milk and rum.

In a small bowl beat egg whites until stiff; fold into batter.

Generously grease springform pan. Pour in batter; top with apple halves. Brush apples with oil.

Bake in preheated 350°F oven 35 to 40 minutes. Remove from pan; sprinkle with powdered sugar. Yield 6 servings.

baba au rum

½ cup milk
⅓ cup butter

1 teaspoon salt
1¼ cups granulated sugar
1 package active dry yeast
¼ cup warm water
2 eggs, beaten
½ teaspoon grated lemon peel
2¼ cups all-purpose white flour
½ cup water
½ cup molasses
½ cup rum
½ cup powdered sugar

Scald milk. Add butter, salt, and ¼ cup granulated sugar until melted. Cool to lukewarm.

Dissolve yeast in warm water. Add to lukewarm milk; mix well. Stir in eggs and lemon peel. Add flour; beat until smooth. Cover; let rise 5 hours.

Beat down until smooth and elastic. Fill greased tube pan or Baba mold. Let rise uncovered 30 minutes.

Bake in 425°F 20 minutes or until done. Remove from pan at once.

Combine ½ cup water, 1 cup sugar, and molasses in heavy saucepan. Bring to boil; boil rapidly 10 minutes. Cool slightly; add rum. Place Baba in serving dish; soak with rum sauce 24 hours prior to serving.

To serve, dust with powdered sugar. Yield 12 servings.

babka

½ cup milk
⅓ cup shortening
1 teaspoon salt

babka

baba au rum

¼ **cup granulated sugar**
1 package active dry yeast
¼ **cup warm water**
2 eggs
½ **teaspoon dried lemon peel**
2¼ **cups all-purpose flour**
1 cup raisins
¼ **cup chopped almonds**

Scald milk. Add shortening, salt, and sugar; stir until melted. Cool to lukewarm.

Add yeast to water; stir until dissolved. Add to lukewarm milk mixture; mix well.

Beat eggs; add with lemon peel to milk mixture. Add flour; beat until smooth. Cover; let rise about 6 hours.

Punch down. Add raisins; beat until smooth and elastic.

Generously grease brioche pan; sprinkle bottom with almonds. Pour dough into pan. Let rise, uncovered, about 20 minutes.

Bake in 425°F oven 20 minutes. Unmold immediately. Yield 12 servings.

basic chocolate cake

½ **cup butter or margarine**
2 cups sugar
3 eggs
1½ **teaspoons vanilla**
3 squares unsweetened chocolate, melted, cooled
2 cups sifted cake flour
2 teaspoons baking soda
½ **teaspoon salt**
1 cup sour cream
1 cup boiling water

Beat butter and sugar together in large bowl. Add eggs; beat until light and fluffy. Beat in vanilla and chocolate.

Sift together dry ingredients. Add alternately with sour cream to butter mixture; beat well after each addition. Stir in boiling water. (Batter will be thin.) Pour into 2 greased and floured 9-inch layer-cake pans.

Bake in preheated 350°F oven 35 minutes or until cake tests done. Cool in pan on wire racks 10 minutes. Turn out onto racks; cool completely. Fill and frost as desired. Yield 12 servings.

basic close-textured sponge cake

1 cup sifted cake flour
1 cup sifted self-rising flour
¾ **cup cornstarch**
1 cup butter
1 cup extra-fine sugar
4 large eggs
½ **cup milk**

Use 2 (9-inch) or 1 (12-inch) springform cake pans. Butter and lightly flour bases; do not prepare sides.

Sift flours and cornstarch together twice.

Cream butter in large mixing bowl with electric mixer at medium speed about 2 minutes or until creamy and smooth. Add sugar; cream 2 minutes or until light and fluffy. Beat in 2 heaping tablespoons flour mixture. Add 1 egg; beat until smooth. Continue adding part of flour mixture, then 1 egg until all ingredients are used. Add milk; beat until well mixed. Spoon batter equally and evenly into prepared pans.

Bake in preheated 350°F oven 25 minutes. Cool on racks about 5 minutes; remove layers from pans. Let cool completely on cake racks. Frost as desired. Yield 10 to 12 servings.

basic sponge cake

basic sponge cake

1 cup cake flour
¼ **teaspoon salt**
6 eggs, separated
1 cup extra-fine sugar
1 tablespoon lemon juice
Grated rind of 1 lemon
Confectioners' sugar

Grease and lightly flour bottom of 9¼ × 5¼ × 2¾-inch loaf pan.

Sift flour and salt together.

Beat egg yolks until thick and lemon-colored.

Beat egg whites in large mixing bowl with electric mixer at high speed until stiff but not dry. Add extra-fine sugar, about 2 tablespoons at a time; beat thoroughly after each addition. Beat in lemon juice and rind. Fold in egg yolks with rubber spatula or wire whisk. Cut and fold in flour mixture, small amount at a time. Continue folding 2 minutes after last addition. Fill prepared pan ¾ full; smooth batter evenly into corners and over top. (There will be batter left over.)

Bake in preheated 350°F oven 30 to 35 minutes or until cake tests done. Let cake cool in pan about 5 minutes. Turn onto rack to cool completely. Sprinkle with confectioners' sugar.

Pour remaining batter into 12 cupcake liners in muffin pan; fill about ½ full. Bake at 350°F about 18 minutes or until lightly browned. Yield 9¼ × 5¼ loaf and 12 cupcakes.

basic white cake

2⅔ cups sifted cake flour
1½ cups sugar
4 teaspoons baking powder
1 teaspoon salt
⅔ cup vegetable shortening
1¼ cups milk
1 teaspoon vanilla
4 egg whites, beaten

Grease bottoms of 2 (9-inch) round layer-cake pans. Line pans with waxed paper; grease and flour paper.

Combine flour, sugar, baking powder, salt, shortening, ¾ cup milk, and vanilla in large bowl; beat until well blended. Add remaining milk and egg whites; beat well. Pour into pans.

Bake in preheated 350°F oven 30 minutes or until cake tests done. Cool in pans on wire racks 10 minutes. Turn out onto racks. Remove paper; cool completely. Fill and frost as desired. Yield 12 servings.

basic yellow cake

¾ cup butter or margarine, softened
1⅔ cups sugar
2 eggs
2 teaspoons vanilla
3 cups sifted cake flour
2½ teaspoons baking powder
½ teaspoon salt
1⅓ cups milk

Beat butter, sugar, eggs, and vanilla in large bowl.

Sift dry ingredients together. Add alternately with milk to butter mixture; beat until smooth after addition. Pour into 2 greased and floured 9- inch layer-cake pans.

Bake in preheated 350°F oven 30 minutes or until cake tests done. Cool in pans on wire racks 10 minutes. Turn out onto racks; cool completely. Fill and frost as desired. Yield 12 servings.

birthday layers

2 (9-inch) Basic White-Cake layers (see Index)
4 cups powdered sugar, sifted
¼ cup hot milk
1 tube pink decorator's icing

Slice cake layers in half, using sharp knife or string.

Combine sugar and milk; mix until smooth. Spread thin layer of icing between cake layers. Spread remaining icing over edges and top of

birthday layers

cake. Let icing set before decorating.

Using small heart cookie cutter, evenly space heart designs around edge of cake. Using decorator's icing, fill in heart outlines with icing. Write desired age in center of cake. Place on serving platter. Arrange candles around outside of cake. Yield 12 servings.

black forest cherry cake

6 eggs
1 cup sugar
1 teaspoon vanilla
4 squares unsweetened baking chocolate, melted and cooled
1 cup sifted flour
syrup
¼ cup sugar
⅓ cup water
2 tablespoons kirsch
butter-cream filling
1½ cups confectioners' sugar
⅓ cup unsalted butter
1 egg yolk
2 tablespoons kirsch liquer
topping
2 cups drained canned sour cherries, patted dry
2 tablespoons confectioners' sugar
1 cup heavy cream, whipped
8-ounce semisweet chocolate bar

Beat eggs, sugar, and vanilla together until thick and fluffy, about 10 minutes. Alternately fold chocolate and flour into egg mixture, ending with flour. Pour batter into 3 well-greased and floured 8-inch-round cake pans. Bake in preheated 350°F oven 10 to 15 minutes, until cake tester inserted in center comes out clean. Cool cakes in pans 5 minutes; turn onto racks to cool completely.

Make syrup. Mix together sugar and water; boil 5 minutes. When syrup has cooled, stir in kirsch.

Prick cake layers; brush syrup over all 3 layers.

Make butter-cream filling. Beat together sugar and butter until well-blended. Add egg yolk; beat until light and fluffy, about 3 to 5 minutes. Fold in kirsch.

Assemble cake. Place 1 layer on cake plate. Spread with filling. Drop ¾ cup cherries evenly over filling. Place second layer on cake. Repeat. Place third layer on top.

Fold confectioners' sugar into whipped cream. Cover sides and top of cake with whipped cream. Decorate top of cake with remaining ½ cup cherries.

To make chocolate curls from chocolate bar, shave bar (at room temperature) with vegetable peeler. Refrigerate curls until ready to use.

Press chocolate curls on sides of cake; sprinkle a few on top. Chill until serving time. Yield 8 to 10 servings.

butterscotch cake

½ cup (1 stick) butter
1 cup lightly packed brown sugar
1 egg
2 cups flour, sifted
3 teaspoons baking powder
½ cup milk

butterscotch frosting
¾ cup lightly packed brown sugar
2 tablespoons milk
Pinch of salt
2 tablespoons butter
½ cup confectioners' sugar, sifted
Chopped browned almonds

butterscotch cake

candy cake

candy cake

1 recipe Milk-Chocolate Icing
2 (9-inch) Basic Chocolate-Cake layers (see Index)
12 assorted chocolates

Prepare Milk-Chocolate Icing as directed. Spread between cake layers; stack layers. Frost top and sides of cake; smooth surface with frosting knife. Arrange chocolates on top of cake to indicate serving pieces.

Do not refrigerate, as temperature change will discolor chocolates. Yield 12 servings.

milk-chocolate icing
½ cup butter
1 pound powdered sugar, sifted
¼ cup milk
1 small plain milk-chocolate bar, melted

Cream butter until smooth. Beat in sugar, small amount at a time; beat well after each addition. Add milk and chocolate; beat until icing becomes light and fluffy. Yield approximately 2 cups.

Preheat oven to 375°F.

Grease 8-inch layer pan.

Cream butter and sugar until light and fluffy. Beat in egg. Fold in sifted flour and baking powder alternately with milk. Turn into prepared pan.

Bake 40 to 45 minutes. Turn onto cooling rack. When cold, top with Butterscotch frosting.

Make frosting. Put brown sugar, milk, salt, and butter into pan; stir over low heat until mixture boils. Cook steadily, without stirring, 5 minutes. Remove from stove. While still just warm, beat in confectioners' sugar. Add extra, if necessary, to give spreading consistency.

Spread almonds on baking sheet; brown lightly under broiler. Watch carefully; they burn easily.

Arrange almonds around edge of frosted cake. Yield 6 to 8 servings.

cherry and orange dessert

Bake ¾ to 1 hour, until cake is firm when lightly pressed on top. Leave in pan for few minutes before turning out. When cold, split into 3 sections.

Whip cream (reserve some for decorating). Add half the cherries and orange sections to rest. Add cognac. Sandwich each layer with fruit-and-cream mixture.

Spread some of remaining cream lightly around sides of cake. Cover with almonds. Decorate top of cake with rings of cherries and orange sections.

Boil ½ cup juice from cherries with ¼ cup sugar until reduced to a glaze; spoon over fruit. Decorate with rosettes of cream. Yield 6 to 8 servings.

chilled cheesecake

3 tablespoons melted butter
¾ cup graham-cracker crumbs
Sugar
¼ teaspoon cinnamon
¼ teaspoon nutmeg
2 envelopes unflavored gelatin
2 eggs, separated
1 cup milk
1 teaspoon grated lemon rind
1 tablespoon lemon juice
1 teaspoon vanilla extract
3 cups creamed cottage cheese
1 cup whipping cream, whipped

cherry and orange dessert cake

3 eggs
³⁄₈ cup sugar
³⁄₈ cup flour, sifted
¼ cup sweet (unsalted) butter, melted
1½ cups whipping cream
1 can pitted red cherries, chopped, juice reserved
1 can orange sections
2 tablespoons cognac or rum
¼ cup browned flaked almonds
¼ cup sugar

Preheat oven to 350°F.

Grease and line 6-inch-round baking pan with greased paper.

Whisk eggs and sugar in top of double boiler until thick enough to form a ribbon. Remove from stove; whisk until cool. Fold in flour, using metal spoon. Fold in butter. Pour into pan.

128

chilled cheesecake

chocolate-covered pear layer

Combine butter, graham-cracker crumbs, 2 tablespoons sugar, cinnamon, and nutmeg in bowl. Press ½ cup crumb mixture into 8- or 9-inch springform pan.

Combine gelatin and ¾ cup sugar in medium saucepan.

Beat egg yolks. Stir in milk gradually. Stir into gelatin mixture; place over low heat. Cook, stirring constantly, 3 to 5 minutes or until gelatin dissolves and mixture is slightly thickened. Remove from heat. Stir in lemon rind, lemon juice, and vanilla.

Beat cottage cheese with electric mixer at high speed 3 to 4 minutes or until smooth. Stir into gelatin mixture. Chill, stirring occasionally, until mixture mounds slightly when dropped from spoon.

Beat egg whites until stiff but not dry. Gradually add ¼ cup sugar; beat until very stiff. Fold into gelatin mixture; fold in whipped cream.

Turn into prepared pan; sprinkle with remaining crumb mixture. Chill 3 to 4 hours or until firm. Loosen sides of pan with sharp knife; release springform.

An 8-cup loaf pan can be used instead of springform pan. Grease loaf pan lightly. Cut waxed paper to fit pan; line pan. Invert onto serving plate to unmold; remove waxed paper. Yield 12 servings.

chinese almond torte

2 eggs
1½ cups sugar
¼ cup sifted all-purpose flour
2½ teaspoons baking powder
¼ teaspoon salt
2 teaspoons almond extract
½ cup slivered almonds
1 medium apple, finely chopped

Preheat oven to 350°F.

Beat eggs until light. Gradually add sugar; beat until thick and lemon-colored.

Sift together flour, baking powder, and salt. Fold into egg mixture. Add almond extract, nuts, and apple; fold in gently. Pour into 8-inch-square baking pan. Bake 25 minutes. Yield 6 servings.

chocolate-covered pear layer

10 canned pear halves, drained
1 (9-inch) Basic Yellow-Cake layer (see Index)
½ cup corn syrup
¼ cup hot water
¼ cup butter
1 12-ounce package chocolate chips
1 can pressurized whipped topping

Slice each pear half into 3 equal slices. Arrange in circle around outer edge of cake layer.

Combine corn syrup, hot water, and butter in saucepan; heat to boiling. Remove from heat. Stir in chocolate chips until well blended. Cool to warm.

Cover cake with warm glaze. Let glaze set before decorating with whipped topping, as illustrated. Yield 12 servings.

chocolate dessert cake

2 squares (2 ounces) unsweetened chocolate
2 cups flour
¼ teaspoon salt
1 teaspoon baking soda
¼ teaspoon bicarbonate of soda
½ cup butter or margarine
¾ cup sugar
2 eggs
1 cup beer or ale
½ cup coarsely chopped pecans

filling
¼ cup softened butter
¾ cup confectioners' sugar
1 tablespoon beer or ale
2 squares (2 ounces) unsweetened chocolate

Grease and line 2 (8-inch) cake pans.
Melt chocolate; let cool.
Sift flour, salt, baking soda, and bicarbonate together.

Beat butter and sugar together until light and creamy. Beat in eggs one at a time. Add chocolate-and-flour mixture alternately with beer; beat well. Fold in pecans. Put into prepared pans. Bake 25 to 30 minutes at 350°F. Leave in pans to cool 5 minutes before turning out.

Make filling. Beat butter and sugar until creamy. Add beer and chocolate; beat well. Chill until required.

To finish, sandwich cakes with half the filling; spread rest on top. Decorate with extra pecans or whipped cream if desired. Yield 8 to 10 servings.

coffee cream-roll cake

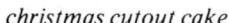
christmas cutout cake

christmas cutout cake

Cutouts from Christmas cards or coloring book
1 (9-inch) Basic Chocolate-Cake layer (see Index)
1 cup powdered sugar, sifted

Cut out holiday figures to fit dimensions of cake. Arrange on cake layer in attractive design. Dust top of cake with powdered sugar. Remove designs. Cover cake until serving time, to prevent dryness. Yield 10 servings.

coffee cream-roll cake

2½ cups sweet cracker crumbs
¾ cup confectioners' sugar, sifted
⅓ cup ground almonds
½ cup hot black coffee
½ teaspoon vanilla extract

Put cracker crumbs into bowl with sugar and almonds. Make well in center. Add coffee and vanilla; mix to soft dough.

Sift a little extra sugar onto large sheet of grease-proof paper. Roll out mixture onto paper to rectangular shape about 9 × 12 inches. Spread evenly with desired filling. Holding paper with both hands, gently roll into Swiss-roll shape. Keep in paper; refrigerate until firm. Yield 6 servings.

butter-cream filling

¾ cup sugar
⅓ cup water
½ cup (1 stick) butter
1 to 2 teaspoons rum

Put sugar and water into pan; stir over low heat until sugar has dissolved. Boil 5 minutes. Remove from heat; cool.

Beat butter until creamy. Gradually add cold syrup; beat well between each addition. Add rum to taste.

cream filling

1 cup whipping cream
¼ cup confectioners' sugar
1 to 2 teaspoons rum

Beat cream until stiff. Gradually add sugar and rum.

cream-cheese mocha cake

½ cup strong coffee, hot
⅓ cup cocoa
½ cup butter or margarine
1 cup brown sugar
1 cup granulated sugar
3 egg yolks
1 teaspoon baking soda
½ cup sour cream
2 cups all-purpose flour
3 egg whites, beaten stiffly
2 batches Cream-Cheese Frosting (see Index)

Gradually add coffee to cocoa, stirring constantly; let stand until cool.

Cream butter and sugars until light and fluffy. Add egg yolks; beat until batter is thick. Add coffee-and-cocoa mixture.

Dissolve soda in cream. Add alternately to sugar mixture with flour; beat well after each addition. Fold in egg whites. Pour batter into 2 well-greased and floured 9-inch cake pans.

Bake in 350°F oven 35 to 40 minutes or until

cream-cheese mocha cake

done. Remove from pans; cool.

Prepare frosting as directed. Spread between cake layers; stack layers. Spread over sides and top of cake. Score top of cake to indicate serving pieces. Using ribbon-edge piping tip and frosting-filled pastry bag, form a flower on each serving piece, as illustrated. Yield 12 servings.

crown-jewel cake

1 cup all-purpose white flour
1 cup whole-wheat flour
2 teaspoons baking powder
1½ teaspoons baking soda
½ teaspoon salt
2 teaspoons apple-pie spice
1 cup granulated sugar
1 cup brown sugar
1½ cups oil
4 eggs, beaten
2 cups grated carrots
1 (8½-ounce) can crushed pineapple, drained
½ cup chopped almonds
2 cups powdered sugar, sifted
2 to 3 tablespoons hot milk
½ cup candied druit
½ cup slivered almonds

Combine flours, baking powder, soda, salt, and apple-pie spice. Add granulated and brown sugars, oil, and eggs; mix with electric beater 2 minutes. Add carrots, pineapple, and nuts; stir in. Pour into 2 greased and floured 9-inch cake pans.

Bake at 350°F 35 to 40 minutes or until done.

Cool; remove from pans.

Combine powdered sugar and enough hot milk to form pourable icing; mix until smooth. Spread small amount of icing between layers; stack layers. Drizzle remaining icing over top and sides of cake.

Combine fruit and almonds. Sprinkle over top of cake. Yield 12 servings.

cupcakes

2 cups sifted flour
½ teaspoon salt
2 teaspoons baking powder
½ cup (1 stick) butter
1¼ cups sugar
2 eggs
1 cup milk
1 teaspoon vanilla extract

Preheat oven to 375°F.

Line 24 muffin pans with paper liners, or grease pans and sprinkle lightly with flour.

Sift flour, salt, and baking powder together.

Cream butter. Add sugar; beat until light and fluffy. Beat in eggs one at a time. Add flour mixture alternately with milk; beat well after each addition. Stir in vanilla. Put into prepared pans; bake about 20 minutes.

When cool, sprinkle with confectioners' sugar or cover with frosting. Yield 24.

easter bunny cookie-cutter cake

2 cups powdered sugar, sifted
2 tablespoons hot milk
1 teaspoon vanilla
2 (9-inch) Basic Chocolate-Cake layers (see Index)

crown-jewel cake

Combine sugar, milk, and vanilla; mix until smooth and free from lumps. Spread ¼ cup icing between cake layers.

Place rabbit cookie cutter in center of top of cake. Spoon icing over top of cake; let drizzle down sides. Remove cookie cutter; form rabbit's eye with dot of frosting. Let frosting set before serving. Yield 12 servings.

easy jam sponge cake

2 eggs
1 egg yolk
⅔ cup confectioners' sugar
½ cup cake flour
¼ teaspoon salt
¼ teaspoon vanilla extract
1 12-ounce jar black-currant jam

Line bottom of 9-inch layer-cake pan with buttered waxed paper; sprinkle with flour.

Combine eggs, egg yolk, and sugar in mixing bowl. Beat with electric mixer until very thick and creamy.

Sift flour and salt together. Carefully fold into egg mixture. Add vanilla. Turn batter into prepared pan.

Bake in preheated 350°F oven 30 minutes. Cool on rack 5 minutes. Turn out; cool completely.

Split cake in half crosswise; spread jam between layers. Sprinkle top of cake generously with additional confectioners' sugar. Yield about 8 servings.

french meringue cake

1 recipe Basic Meringues mixture (see Index)
1 recipe Basic Coffee Butter Cream
Toasted almonds, sliced
Confectioners' sugar sifted

Drop meringue mixture by heaping tablespoonfulls onto cookie sheets lined with oiled brown paper.

Bake in preheated 250°F oven 55 minutes. Remove from paper onto racks. Cool; crumble

easter bunny cookie-cutter cake

into large bowl. Add 2 cups butter cream to meringue crumbs; mix until crumbs hold together. Divide into 2 equal parts. Place each part between 2 sheets waxed paper; pat into 7 × 8-inch rectangles. Chill about 20 minutes or until layers are firm.

Remove both sheets waxed paper from 1 rectangles; place rectangle on serving platter. Spread with thin layer of butter cream.

Remove 1 sheet waxed paper from remaining rectangle. Place rectangle, waxed-paper-side-up, over butter-cream-covered rectangle; remove waxed paper.

Spread remaining butter cream over top and sides of cake. Arrange almonds over top. Sprinkle with confectioners' sugar just before serving.

easy jam sponge cake

Cake sides can be piped with remaining butter cream, if desired. Yield 20 servings.

basic coffee butter cream
1 cup unsalted butter, softened
5 cups sifted confectioners' sugar
2 egg yolks
¼ cup Basic Coffee Syrup (see Index)

Cream butter in large mixing bowl with electric mixer until light and fluffy. Add half the sugar; beat until smooth. Add egg yolks; blend well. Mix in remaining confectioners' sugar. Pour in coffee syrup; beat until well combined and fluffy. Yield Enough to fill, frost, and decorate a 9-inch 2-layer cake

german cheesecake

1½ pints sour cream
32 ounces cream cheese, room temperature
7 eggs
5 teaspoons vanilla
1 cup sugar
1 box graham cracker crumbs or 1 package (22 crackers) graham crackers, crumbled
2 tablespoons sugar
6 tablespoons butter or margarine, melted

Use 10-inch spring pan.

Mix sour cream, cream cheese, eggs, vanilla, and sugar in large mixing bowl; beat 25 minutes on medium speed.

Meanwhile, combine crumbs, sugar, and melted butter; mix well. Press onto bottom and sides of pan. Chill in freezer 15 minutes. Pour batter into pan.

Bake at 375°F 1¼ hours or until top is very brown. Turn off oven; let stay 2 hours with oven door ajar. Can top with cherry-pie filling. Yield 10 to 12 servings.

gingerbread

½ cup butter or margarine
½ cup packed brown sugar
1 egg
½ cup molasses
1½ cups flour
½ teaspoon salt
¾ teaspoon baking soda
½ teaspoon ginger
½ teaspoon cinnamon
½ cup boiling water

Beat butter and sugar until creamy. Add egg and molasses; beat well.

Mix dry ingredients thoroughly. Add to molasses mixture alternately with boiling water. Beat after each addition. Pour into greased 8 × 8 × 2-inch baking pan.

Bake at 350°F 35 to 40 minutes. Serve warm. Yield 6 to 9 servings.

ginger walnut loaf

ginger walnut loaf

1 Gingerbread cake (see Index)
½ cup honey
2 cups coarsely chopped walnuts

Bake Gingerbread in loaf pan. Remove from oven; wait 5 minutes before removing from pan. Remove from pan. Coat top with honey. Spread walnuts over top; press gently into honey coating. Yield 10 servings.

golden bundt cake

3 cups sugar
1½ cups butter or margarine
5 eggs
3 cups unsifted flour
¼ teaspoon salt
5-ounce can evaporated milk plus water to make 1 cup
2 teaspoons vanilla

Beat sugar and butter until light and fluffy, about 5 minutes. Beat in eggs one at a time; beat well after each addition.

Mix flour and salt. Alternately add flour and milk, ending with flour. Fold in flavoring.

Start in cold oven. Bake in greased tube pan at 325°F 1 hour and 45 minutes, until done. Do not open door. Remove from pan and cool on wire rack. Yield 10 to 12 servings.

gypsy john

chocolate cake
1 cup cake flour
¼ cup unsweetened cocoa
1 teaspoon baking powder·
¼ teaspoon salt
3 large eggs
1 cup sugar
⅓ cup water
1 teaspoon vanilla

Sift together flour, cocoa, baking powder, and salt twice; set aside.

Line jelly-roll pan with waxed paper; grease.

Place eggs in small mixing bowl. Beat with electric mixer 5 minutes or until thick and lemon-colored. Slowly beat in sugar, tablespoon at a time. Mixture will become very thick. Transfer to large mixing bowl. Beat in water and vanilla. Slowly add flour mixture; beat until smooth. Pour into prepared pan; spread evenly to corners.

Bake in preheated 375°F oven 12 to 15 minutes or until cake tests done. Loosen from pan. Turn out on rack; remove waxed paper. Invert; cool completely.

Cut cake in half crosswise. Place 1 piece of cake on small cookie sheet. Top with Chocolate Filling; spread to form even layer 1½ inches thick. Top with remaining cake layer. Chill at least 1 hour.

Spread icing over top of cake. Chill until icing sets.

Cut cake into 12 squares; arrange on decorative plate. Yield 12 servings.

chocolate filling
10 squares semisweet chocolate, broken into pieces
2 cups heavy cream
2 tablespoons rum

Combine chocolate and cream in heavy saucepan. Heat slowly, stirring constantly, until chocolate melts. Transfer to medium-size mixing bowl. Stir in rum. Chill 1 to 2 hours. Beat with electric mixer until stiff and thick.

chocolate icing
¼ cup light corn syrup
2 tablespoons hot water
2 tablespoons butter
1 (6-ounce) package semisweet chocolate bits

Combine corn syrup, water, and butter in small saucepan. Bring to boil; cook until butter melts. Remove from heat. Add chocolate bits; stir until chocolate melts. Cool to room temperature.

hazelnut layer cake

½ pint whipping cream
¼ cup granulated sugar
1 teaspoon vanilla
½ cup ground hazelnuts
1 (9-inch) Basic White-Cake layer (see Index)
12 whole hazelnuts

Whip cream until it starts to hold its shape. Continue to beat, gradually adding sugar and vanilla. Fold in ground hazelnuts. Spread whipped cream smoothly over cake. Mark serving pieces in topping. Garnish each serving piece with whipped-cream rosette and whole hazelnut. Refrigerate. Yield 12 servings.

honey treats

1 (8-inch) loaf Pound Cake (see Index)
½ cup honey

hazelnut layer cake

Slice cake into 2-inch squares. Place on cooling rack.

Warm honey; drizzle over cake squares.

To serve, place sweetened cakes on serving platter or into individual paper cups. Yield 12 servings.

honey treats

layered chocolate dessert cake

1½ cups milk
4 squares unsweetened chocolate
1½ cups sugar
½ cup butter
1 teaspoon vanilla extract
2 eggs
2 cups sifted all-purpose flour
¾ teaspoon salt
1 teaspoon baking soda
1 recipe Mocha Butter Cream (see Index)
½ recipe Special Chocolate Icing (see Index)

Line bottom of 13 × 8 × 2-inch baking pan with waxed paper; grease and flour the waxed paper.

Place 1 cup milk, chocolate, and ½ cup sugar in top of double boiler. Place over boiling water; cook, stirring constantly, until chocolate is melted. Remove from boiling water; cool.

Cream the butter and remaining sugar in large mixing bowl with electric mixer. Add vanilla and eggs; beat well. Beat in chocolate mixture.

Sift flour with salt; add to chocolate mixture alternately with remaining milk. Beat 2 minutes at medium speed.

Dissolve soda in 3 tablespoons boiling water. Add to batter; beat 1 minute. Pour into prepared pan.

Bake at 350°F 30 to 35 minutes or until cake tests done. Cool in pan 10 minutes. Remove from pan; cool on rack.

Trim edges from cake; cut cake crosswise into 3 equal portions. Cover 2 portions with Mocha But-

layered chocolate dessert cake

ter Cream; stack one on top of other. Place on cake plate. Top with remaining portion. Spread top and sides with thin layer of Mocha Butter Cream. Pour most of icing over top and sides of cake. Chill until firm.

Drizzle remaining icing over top of cake, if desired; chill until firm. Yield about 12 servings.

lemon spice dessert cake

cake
⅓ cup butter or margarine
¾ cup sugar
1 egg
1½ cups cake flour
½ teaspoon salt
¼ teaspoon grated nutmeg
¼ teaspoon ground cinnamon
¼ teaspoon ground ginger
2 teaspoons baking powder
4 tablespoons water
4 tablespoons lemon juice
½ cup seeded or seedless raisins
1 teaspoon grated lemon rind

topping
2 tablespoons soft butter or margarine
½ cup light brown sugar
¼ teaspoon grated nutmeg
¼ teaspoon ground cinnamon
¼ teaspoon ground ginger
⅛ teaspoon salt
2 tablespoons flour

Preheat oven to 350°F.

Grease and flour cake pan about 8 × 8 × 2 inches.

Cream the butter and sugar until light and fluffy. Add egg; beat well.

Set aside 2 tablespoons flour. Sift rest with salt, spices, and baking powder; add to creamed mixture alternately with water and lemon juice mixed together.

Dredge raisins with reserved flour; stir with lemon rind into cake mixture. Pour into prepared pan.

Toss all topping ingredients together with fork; sprinkle over cake batter.

Bake 45 to 50 minutes. Leave in the pan until cold. Cut into squares. Yield 6 servings.

miniature cheesecakes

¾ stick butter or margarine
1½ cups graham-cracker crumbs
½ pound dry cottage cheese
½ pound cream cheese
½ pint sour cream
¾ cup sugar
3 eggs

neopolitan torte

1 teaspoon vanilla
1 can cherry and/or blueberry pie filling

Melt butter. Combine with crumbs; set aside. With mixer combine cottage cheese, cream cheese, and sour cream until blended. Add sugar, then eggs and vanilla. Spin in blender or food processor 1 minute or until smooth.

Line miniature muffin tins with paper cupcake liners. Put 1 teaspoon crumb mixture in each liner; press down. Fill ¾ full with cheese mixture.

Bake at 350°F exactly 12 minutes. When cool, top each with 1 teaspoon pie filling. Chill until topping sets. Can be frozen. Yield 4 dozen.

neopolitan torte

dough
¾ cup butter
1 cup sugar
2 eggs
½ cup ground almonds
1½ teaspoons grated lemon rind
3½ cups flour
filling
1⅓ cups raspberry jam (very thick, with lots of fruit)
glaze and garnish
2 cups sifted confectioners' sugar
2 tablespoons hot water
2 tablespoons maraschino cherry liqueur
Few drops red food coloring
½ cup whipping cream
6 candied cherries, halved

Cream butter and sugar well. Beat in eggs one at a time. Add almonds and lemon rind; mix. Slowly add flour, mixing in well by hand. Form into large ball; cover. Refrigerate 1 hour.

Divide dough into 5 equal parts.

Grease detached bottom of 10-inch springform pan.

Roll dough 1 part at a time; cut to fit springform pan. Place 1 layer of dough on bottom section of pan. Spread with ⅓ cup jam. Top with another layer of dough; spread with jam. Repeat until all dough is used.

Place ring around pan. Bake at 400°F in bottom oven rack 45 minutes. Cool; place on platter.

Mix confectioners' sugar, water, liqueur, and coloring to form smooth glaze. Smooth over top of cake.

Whip cream until stiff. Place in pastry bag fitted with rose tip; pipe 12 rosettes around edge of cake. Top each rosette with ½ of a candied cherry. Yield 12 servings.

normandy sand cake

1½ cups cake flour, sifted
1 teaspoon baking powder
⅛ teaspoon nutmeg
½ cup unsalted butter, softened
1 cup sugar
3 eggs
6 tablespoons Madeira
½ teaspoon grated lemon rind
Confectioners' sugar

normandy sand cake

orange cheesecake

Sift flour, baking powder, and nutmeg together.

Cream butter and sugar together, using electric mixer at medium speed, 5 minutes or until thick and creamy. Add eggs one at a time; beat well after each addition. Add flour mixture alternately with Madeira, beginning and ending with flour mixture; beat well after each addition. Stir in lemon rind. Pour batter into well-greased and floured loaf pan.

Bake in preheated 350°F oven 25 to 30 minutes or until cake tests done. Let cake cool in pan 5 minutes; turn out on rack to cool completely. Dust with sifted confectioners' sugar before serving. Yield 6 to 8 servings.

orange cheesecake

1 cup sifted all-purpose flour
¼ cup sugar
1 tablespoon grated orange rind
½ cup butter
1 egg yolk
½ teaspoon vanilla extract

Combine flour, sugar, and orange rind. Add butter; cut in with pastry blender until of a coarse meal consistency. Add egg yolk and vanilla; blend well. Place ⅓ of dough on bottom of 9-inch springform pan; pat out evenly to cover bottom.

Bake in preheated 400°F oven 5 minutes or until golden brown. Remove from oven; cool.

Pat remaining dough evenly around sides to ½ inch from top. Set aside; prepare filling.

Pour filling into prepared pan; place on cookie sheet.

Bake in preheated 400°F oven 8 to 10 minutes

138

or until crust is lightly browned. Reduce oven temperature to 225°F; bake 1 hour and 20 minutes. Cool to room temperature; refrigerate until well chilled. Garnish with fresh orange sections. Yield 12 to 18 servings.

orange cheese filling

5 (8-ounce) packages cream cheese, softened
1¾ cups sugar
3 tablespoons all-purpose flour
1 tablespoon grated orange rind
¼ teaspoon salt
¼ teaspoon vanilla extract
5 eggs
2 egg yolks
¼ cup frozen Florida orange-juice concentrate, thawed

Combine cream cheese, sugar, flour, orange rind, salt, and vanilla in large mixer bowl. Beat with electric mixer at low speed until smooth. Add eggs and egg yolks one at a time; beat well after each addition. Stir in orange-juice concentrate.

peach marshmallow dessert cake

peach marshmallow dessert cake

3 tablespoons butter
¼ cup sugar
½ cup corn syrup
1 egg
2 cups cake flour
2 teaspoons baking powder
¼ teaspoon salt
½ cup milk
8 peach halves
1⅓ cups brown sugar
1 teaspoon ground cinnamon
8 marshmallows

Preheat oven to 350°F.

Grease 8 × 12-inch baking pan.

Cream 2 tablespoons butter, sugar, and corn syrup together. Add egg; beat well.

Sift flour, baking powder, and salt; add to creamed mixture alternately with milk. Pour into prepared pan; arrange peach halves on top.

Cream 1 tablespoon butter with brown sugar and cinnamon; sprinkle over peaches.

Bake 40 minutes. Place marshmallows on top of each peach half; return to oven to brown. Yield 8 servings.

peanut-butter layer cake

peanut-butter layer cake

2 eggs
½ cup granulated sugar
2¼ cups cake flour
3 teaspoons baking powder
1 teaspoon salt
¼ teaspoon baking soda
1 cup well-packed brown sugar
⅓ cup peanut butter
⅓ cup vegetable oil
1¼ cups milk

peanut-butter frosting
¼ cup peanut butter
3 cups sifted confectioners' sugar
4 to 5 tablespoons milk
¼ cup peanuts

Preheat oven to 350°F.

Grease and flour 2 (8- or 9-inch) layer-cake pans.

Bake cake. Separate eggs. Beat whites until fluffy. Add granulated sugar; beat until stiff and glossy.

Sift flour, baking powder, salt, and baking soda together into bowl. Add brown sugar, peanut butter, oil, and ½ the milk; beat well. Add remaining milk and egg yolks; beat again. (If using mixer, beat 1 minute each time at medium speed.) Fold in egg-white mixture lightly. Put into prepared pans.

Bake 30 to 35 minutes. Leave in pans to cool a little; turn onto rack.

Prepare frosting. Blend peanut butter with sugar. Add enough milk to make creamy consistency. Use to sandwich layers together; spread rest over top. Sprinkle top edge with peanuts. Yield 8- or 9-inch layer cake.

pineapple carrot cake

2 cups flour
2 teaspoons baking soda
1¼ teaspoons salt
2 teaspoons cinnamon
4 eggs
2 cups sugar
1 cup oil or melted butter
2 cups grated carrots
2 cups crushed pineapple (drained)
1 cup walnuts or fresh coconut

Sift together dry ingredients; set aside.

Mix eggs, sugar, and oil, stirring well. Add carrots, pineapple, and nuts; beat after each addition. Add sifted ingredients; stir well. Pour into greased and floured 9 × 13-inch pan.

Bake at 350°F 40 minutes.

Frost with whipped-cream icing or cream-cheese icing. Yield 6 servings.

pineapple meringue dessert cake

½ cup cake flour
¾ teaspoon baking powder
Pinch of salt
2 eggs
¾ cup sugar
¼ cup butter or margarine
½ teaspoon vanilla extract
3½ tablespoons milk
Blanched almonds, chopped
1 cup (No. 1 can) drained crushed pineapple
½ cup whipping cream

Preheat oven to 300°F.

Grease 2 (8-inch) layer pans.

Sift flour, baking powder, and salt together.

Beat egg yolks until thick and honey-colored.

Gradually beat in ¼ cup sugar. Add well-creamed butter and vanilla; mix well. Beat in flour and milk. Spread mixture evenly between 2 layer pans; chill.

Beat egg whites stiffly. Fold in ½ cup sugar; spread on top of each cake. Sprinkle thickly with almonds, pressing them into surface of cakes.

Bake for about 50 minutes.

When cold, sandwich layers with a little pineapple and whipped cream mixed together. Cover top with remaining pineapple and whipped cream. Yield 8 servings.

polish easter cake

½ **cup milk**
½ **cup granulated sugar**
½ **teaspoon salt**
¼ **cup butter**
¼ **cup warm water**
1 package active dry yeast
2 eggs, beaten
2½ **cups all-purpose white flour**
½ **cup chopped almonds**
½ **cup raisins**
½ **teaspoon grated lemon peel**
1 cup confectioners' sugar
1 tablespoon milk
Whole candied cherries

Scald ½ cup milk. Stir in sugar, salt, and butter. Cool to lukewarm.

Pour lukewarm water into large bowl. Sprinkle yeast over water; stir until dissolved. Add milk mixture, eggs, and flour; beat vigorously 5 min-utes. Cover; let rise in warm place, free from draft, for 1½ hours or until double in bulk.

Stir down batter; beat in almonds, raisins, and lemon peel. Pour batter into greased and floured 1½-quart Charlotte mold or deep cake pan. Let rise 1 hour.

Bake in 350°F oven 50 minutes. Let cool in pan 20 minutes; remove.

Beat together confectioners' sugar and 1 tablespoon milk to form glaze.

To serve, place cake on serving platter; drizzle glaze on top. Garnish with cherries. Yield 8 servings.

polish easter cake

pineapple meringue dessert cake

queen-of-hearts crown cake

pound cake

1 cup butter or margarine
1½ cups sugar
5 eggs
2 cups sifted cake flour
1½ teaspoons salt
1 teaspoon vanilla

Cream butter and sugar together. Add eggs one at a time; beat well after each addition. Add sifted dry ingredients. Add vanilla; beat thoroughly.

Bake in greased loaf pan in 350°F oven 1 to 1¼ hours or until cake tests done. Cool in pan on wire rack 10 minutes. Turn out onto rack; cool completely before serving. Yield 8 servings.

queen-of-hearts crown cake

4 egg whites
¼ teaspoon cream of tartar
Dash of salt
¼ cup granulated sugar
1 (9-inch) Basic White-Cake layer (see Index)
½ cup toasted almonds
1 cup cherry pie filling

Whip egg whites until stiff. Gradually beat in cream of tartar, salt, and sugar until egg whites stand in peaks. Spread sides of cake with meringue. Cover with almonds. Spread cherry pie filling on top of cake to within 1 inch from edge of cake.

Fill pastry bag with meringue. Using large rosette tip, form double row of meringue rosettes around edge of cake.

Bake in preheated 425°F oven 4 minutes or until tips of meringue turn brown. Yield 12 servings.

quick apple cake

1¾ cups sifted cake flour
1 teaspoon baking powder
½ teaspoon soda
½ teaspoon salt
Sugar
½ cup melted butter
1 egg
Buttermilk
1 teaspoon vanilla extract
2 tart apples, peeled, sliced thin
1 teaspoon cinnamon

Sift flour, baking powder, soda, salt, and 1 cup sugar into mixing bowl.

Pour ¼ cup butter into 1-cup measuring cup. Add egg. Fill cup with buttermilk. Pour into flour mixture; beat vigorously 1 minute or until batter is smooth. Stir in vanilla.

Pour remaining butter into ovenproof skillet or baking dish. Pour batter into skillet. Arrange apples over top.

Combine cinnamon with 2 tablespoons sugar; sprinkle over apples.

Bake in a preheated 350°F oven 35 to 40 minutes.

Serve hot from skillet, or cool 5 minutes, then invert onto rack. Slide onto serving dish. Yield 8 to 10 servings.

royal orange-crown cake

2 (8-inch) Basic White-Cake layers (see Index)
1 pint whipping cream
½ cup granulated sugar
1 teaspoon vanilla
1 cup mandarin orange sections, drained

Split cake layers in half with sharp knife or string.

Whip cream until fluffy. Gradually beat in sugar and vanilla until cream stands in soft peaks. Spread 1 cup whipped cream between 4 cake layers; stack one on top of other. Frost outside of cake with remaining whipped cream. Decorate cake with mandarin orange sections, as illustrated. Yield 8 servings.

ruby ring-around cake

1 9-inch Basic White-Cake layer (see Index)
4 egg whites
1 teaspoon cream of tartar
¼ cup granulated sugar
1 cup fresh cranberries

Hollow 1-inch center from cake layer.

Beat egg whites until foamy. Gradually add cream of tartar and sugar; beat until meringue

royal orange-crown cake

stands in stiff peaks. Reserve ¾ cup meringue for rippled topping. Fill center of cake with meringue; sprinkle top with cranberries.

Fill pastry bag with remaining meringue. Using ripple-edge tip, form circular meringue ribbon, as illustrated.

Bake in 400°F oven 4 minutes or until meringue begins to turn light brown. Yield 12 servings.

ruby ring-around cake

sour–cream cheesecake

1½ cups shortbread cookie crumbs
½ cup unsalted butter, melted
1 (12-ounce) carton cottage cheese
1 tablespoon lemon juice
¼ teaspoon grated lemon rind
1 egg, beaten
¼ cup sifted confectioners' sugar

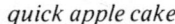

quick apple cake

sour-cream cheesecake

⅛ teaspoon vanilla extract
1 cup sour cream

Line bottom of 10 × 4-inch loaf pan with removable sides with greased and floured aluminum foil.

Combine crumbs and butter; mix well. Press mixture firmly over bottom of prepared pan.

Drain cottage cheese well; place in blender or food-processor container. Blend until free of large lumps.

Combine cottage cheese, lemon juice, lemon rind, egg, sugar, and vanilla in mixing bowl; mix well. Fold in sour cream. Spoon mixture evenly over crumb mixture; smooth the top.

Can pipe with ¼ recipe Basic Cream-Puff Pastry, (see Index) if desired.

Bake at 350°F about 50 minutes or until cheesecake tests done. Cool well. Refrigerate overnight.

You can add ¼ cup chocolate chips or raisins to cheese mixture before baking, if desired. Yield about 8 servings.

spaceship cake

½ recipe Basic Chocolate Cake (see Index)
2 cups slivered almonds
5 tablespoons hot water
½ cup light corn syrup
¼ cup butter or margarine, melted
2 cups chocolate chips
2½ cups commercial hot-fudge sauce (can be used in place of last 4 ingredients above)

Prepare cake batter as directed. Pour batter into long, shallow loaf pan. Bake at 350°F 20 minutes or until done. Cool slightly before removing from pan.

Place cake on cake rack, top-side-down. With sharp knife, cut off sharp corners of cake. Stick almonds into cake in staggered-row design, as illustrated. Cover to prevent drying.

Combine hot water, corn syrup, and butter in top of double boiler. Bring mixture to boil; boil until butter melts. Remove from heat; stir in chocolate chips. Beat until sauce is combined. (Or,

heat hot-fudge sauce over double boiler until it drips from spoon.) Cool sauce to warm; spoon slowly over cake with almonds. (This process must be done slowly to allow sauce time to adhere to nuts and cake.) Let sauce set before serving. Yield 10 servings.

spanish sponge cake

1¼ cups butter, softened
1 tablespoon grated lemon rind
1 cup sugar
3 eggs
1½ cups sifted all-purpose flour
¼ teaspoon salt
½ cup blanched sliced almonds
½ cup chopped candied cherries

Combine butter and lemon rind in large bowl; beat with electric beater until light and fluffy. Gradually add ¾ cup sugar; beat after each addi-

spaceship cake

tion until smooth. Add 1 egg, 1 tablespoon flour and salt; beat until smooth. Add remaining eggs alternately with flour; beat thoroughly after each addition. Spoon into well-greased and floured 9-inch-square cake pan; spread evenly.

Combine almonds and cherries; sprinkle over cake mixture. Sprinkle with the remaining sugar.

Bake in preheated 350°F oven 35 minutes or until golden brown. Yield about 9 servings.

sponge cupcakes

1 cup cake flour
1 cup self-rising flour
½ cup butter, softened
1 cup extra-fine sugar
2 eggs
½ cup raisins
1 tablespoon milk
1 teaspoon vanilla

Combine flours.

Cream butter with sugar in large mixing bowl with electric mixer at medium speed. Add ½ cup flour mixture and 1 egg; beat well. Add ½ cup flour mixture and remaining egg; beat until well blended.

Dust raisins lightly with small amount of remaining flour.

Add remaining flour to mixing bowl gradually; beat after each addition until well blended. Add milk and vanilla; mix well. Stir in raisins. Spoon

sponge cupcakes

into paper-lined muffin cups; fill ½ full.

Bake in 375°F oven on middle shelf 18 to 20 minutes. To test for doneness insert toothpick in center of cupcake; when the toothpick comes out clean, cupcake is done.

Chopped candied cherries, grated coconut, currants, or chocolate chips can be substituted for raisins. Yield 18.

spanish dessert sponge cake

steamed coconut cakes

½ cup sugar
3 eggs
¾ cup sifted all-purpose flour
2 pinches of salt
¼ teaspoon vanilla extract
2 tablespoons butter, softened
1 cup red currant jelly
1 cup freshly grated coconut

Combine sugar and eggs in medium-size mixing bowl. Place bowl in larger mixing bowl, filled ⅓ full with boiling water. Beat eggs and sugar with electric mixer at medium speed about 5 minutes or until thick and foamy. Remove bowl from water.

Combine flour and salt; fold into egg mixture, a very small amount at a time. (This must be done very slowly and carefully.) Fold in vanilla. Drop butter over top in small pieces; fold in carefully. (Butter should be very soft but not melted.) Spoon into 6 very heavily buttered individual molds or custard cups. Cover with buttered waxed paper and aluminum foil. Place on rack in steamer; add boiling water to just below rack. Cover; steam 30 minutes. Remove covers; unmold.

Melt the jelly in small saucepan. Place coconut in shallow bowl. Using small fork dip cakes in jelly to coat bottoms and sides. Roll in coconut. Place on rack to dry. Garnish as desired. Yield 6 servings.

steamed coconut cakes

strawberry cream-puff dessert cake

1 recipe Basic Sweet Cream-Puff (see Index)
1 recipe Basic Chantilly Cream (see Index)
1 cup crushed strawberries
3 cups whole strawberries
Confectioners' sugar

strawberry cream-puff dessert cake

Trace a ring on lightly greased and floured baking sheet. Spoon Cream-Puff Pastry in large dollops on tracing mark. Smooth top with small spatula; fill in between dollops.

Bake in preheated 450°F oven 8 minutes. Reduce oven temperature to 350°F; bake 30 to 40 minutes or until dry. Cool on wire rack; split in half crosswise.

Place bottom half of ring on serving dish; spread with about ½ of Chantilly cream. Cover with crushed strawberries. Place top half of ring over strawberries.

Spoon the remaining Chantilly Cream into pastry bag with large star tube affixed. Pipe around base; pipe dollops of cream over top. Arrange whole strawberries around base and inside edge. Dust with confectioners' sugar. Place remaining whole strawberries in center. Serve immediately. Yield 8 to 10 servings.

strawberry layer cake

½ pint whipping cream
¼ cup sugar
1 tablespoon rum or Triple See
1 (9-inch) Basic White-Cake layer (see Index)
2 cups strawberry halves

Whip cream until stiff. Fold in sugar and rum. Spread generously over top and sides of cake layer; refrigerate.

Just prior to serving; arrange strawberries in circles over top of cake. Yield 8 servings.

sugar-plum cake

2 (9-inch) Basic Yellow-Cake layers (see Index)
2 cups whipped cream
1 cup toasted almonds
Gum drops
Candied fruit

Frost cake layers with whipped cream; be sure sides and top are covered. Cover sides and top edge with toasted almonds.

Place small amount whipped cream in icing bag. Using rosette tip, pipe rosettes in circle on top of cake, as illustrated. Decorate each whipped-cream rosette with gum drop or with candied fruit. Refrigerate until ready to serve. Yield 12 servings.

sweet cream-cheese dessert cake

1 recipe Easy Jam Sponge Cake (see Index)
2 egg yolks
½ cup confectioners' sugar
1½ teaspoons kirsch
4 (3-ounce) packages cream cheese, softened
Juice of 1 orange, strained
1 recipe Basic Chantilly Cream (see Index)
1 pint whole strawberries

Prepare cake as instructed. Let cool, but do not slice and fill.

Combine egg yolks and sugar in mixer bowl; beat with electric mixer until thick and creamy.

sugar-plum cake

egg braid

Gradually pour in kirsch; beat well.

Cut cream cheese into small cubes. Add to egg-yolk mixture gradually; beat well after each addition. Beat 10 minutes or until smooth.

Line small mold with plastic wrap; let wrap extend over edge of mold. Spoon cream-cheese mixture into mold; place in freezer 2 hours.

Trim edge from cake to fit mold; place on edge from cake to fit mold; place on serving dish. Sprinkle cake with orange juice.

Lift cheese mixture in plastic wrap from bowl; invert onto cake. Remove plastic wrap carefully. Spread rim of the cake with Chantilly Cream, using pastry bag filled with star tube. Pipe little mounds of cream around base; top with strawberries.

Serve with strawberries and remaining Chantilly Cream. Yield 8 servings.

sweetheart spice cake

Butter
1 cup sugar
3 eggs
½ cup light molasses
2¾ cups sifted cake flour
1 teaspoon baking soda
1 teaspoon cinnamon
¾ teaspoon salt
Milk
1½ tablespoons grated orange rind
¾ cup cherry preserves
1 recipe Sweetheart Frosting
1 cup shredded coconut
Red food coloring

Cut 2 pieces waxed paper to fit bottoms of 2 heart-shaped cake pans that measure 9 inches at widest part and 1½ inches in depth. Grease bottoms of pans with butter; place waxed paper over butter. Grease waxed paper with butter; coat lightly with flour.

Place ¾ cup butter in large mixer bowl; beat with electric mixer until light. Add sugar gradually; beat until smooth after each addition. Add eggs one at a time; beat well after each addition. Stir in molasses until well blended.

Sift flour with soda, cinnamon, and salt. Add to egg mixture alternately with 1 cup milk; beat well after each addition. Stir in orange rind. Pour batter into prepared pans.

Bake in preheated 350°F oven 30 to 35 minutes or until cake tester inserted in center comes out clean. Cool in pans 5 minutes. Invert onto wire racks; remove waxed paper carefully. Cool completely.

Spread cherry preserves between layers; frost sides and top of cake with Sweetheart Frosting.

Place coconut in pint jar. Add ½ teaspoon of

sweet cream-cheese dessert cake

milk and enough food coloring for desired tint. Cover jar; shake vigorously until coconut is tinted. Decorate top edge and base of cake with coconut. Yield 12 to 15 servings.

sweetheart frosting
1½ cups sugar
½ cup water
3 egg whites
⅛ cream of tartar
1 teaspoon vanilla extract

sweetheart spice cake

Combine sugar and water in heavy saucepan; stir well. Bring to boil; cook, without stirring, to hard-ball stage (250°F on candy thermometer).

Place egg whites and cream of tartar in large mixer bowl; beat until stiff peaks form. Pour hot syrup into egg whites very gradually, beating constantly, then beat 7 minutes or until stiff peaks form. Beat in the vanilla.

swiss carrot cake

2 cups sifted all-purpose flour
2 teaspoons baking powder
1½ teaspoons baking soda
1 teaspoon salt
2 teaspoons cinnamon
1½ cups salad oil
2 cups sugar
4 eggs
2 cups grated carrots
1 small can crushed pineapple
1½ cups chopped walnuts or pecans
1 teaspoon vanilla extract

Sift flour, baking powder, soda, salt, and cinnamon together.

Combine oil and sugar in large mixing bowl; beat thoroughly with electric mixer. Add eggs one at a time; beat well after each addition. Sift flour mixture into egg mixture; beat thoroughly. Stir in

remaining ingredients. Spread batter evenly into well-greased and floured 9 × 13-inch pan or 2 loaf pans.

Bake in preheated 350°F oven 1 hour or until cake tests done. Let cool in pan 5 minutes; turn onto cake rack to finish cooling.

Dust with sifted confectioners' sugar to serve. Yield 12 to 15 servings.

upside-down apple cake

4 or 5 tart cooking apples
Lemon juice
2 tablespoons butter
1 cup packed light brown sugar, sifted
1 egg
1 cup sugar
1 cup whipping cream
1 teaspoon vanilla extract
2 cups all-purpose flour
2 teaspoons baking powder
Confectioners' sugar

Peel apples; remove cores. Slice apples paper-thin; sprinkle lightly with lemon juice to keep from discoloring.

Place butter in 9-inch-round shallow baking dish. Place in preheated 325°F oven until melted; remove from oven. (Do not turn off heat.) Sprinkle brown sugar over butter. Overlap apple

swiss carrot cake

slices in dish; work from center to outside, with only ¼ inch between each overlap, until bottom is covered.

Place egg in medium-size mixing bowl; beat well with electric mixer. Add sugar gradually; beat until mixed.

Mix cream and vanilla.

Sift flour with baking powder. Add to egg mixture alternately with cream mixture; beat well after each addition. Pour over the apples.

Bake about 35 minutes or until cake tester inserted in center comes out clean. Let cool 10 minutes. Turn onto rack; cool.

Place on cake plate; cut into servings. Sprinkle each serving with confectioners' sugar. Yield 6 to 8 servings.

vegetable-garden cake

3 eggs, beaten until fluffy
1 cup oil
2 cups granulated sugar
1½ cups tightly packed shredded zucchini
½ cup tightly packed shredded carrots
2 cups all-purpose flour
1 teaspoon salt
2 teaspoons baking soda
½ teaspoon baking powder
1 teaspoon vanilla
½ cup ground almonds
½ teaspoon cinnamon

milk glaze
½ cup sifted confectioners' sugar
2 teaspoons hot milk
¼ teaspoon vanilla
½ cup powdered sugar, sifted
10 marzipan carrots

upside-down apple cake

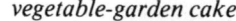

vegetable-garden cake

viennese sachertorte

Combine eggs, oil, and sugar; mix well. Stir in zucchini and carrots. Add remaining ingredients; stir until well moistened. Pour into 2 greased and floured 9-inch cake pans.

Bake at 350°F 25 to 30 minutes or until done. Cool slightly before removing from pans. Freeze 1 cake layer for use at another time.

Prepare milk glaze by mixing sugar, milk, and vanilla until smooth.

Cover top of cake generously with glaze. Place small amount of glaze on teaspoon; drizzle glaze in scalloped design around edges as illustrated. Dust top of cake with powdered sugar. Arrange marzipan carrots around outer edge of cake. Yield 10 servings.

viennese sachertorte

1 cup chocolate chips
8 egg yolks, slightly beaten
½ cup unsalted butter, melted
1 tablespoon vanilla extract
10 egg whites
¼ teaspoon salt
¾ cup sugar
1 cup sifted cake flour
1 recipe Apricot Glaze (see Index)
½ recipe Special Chocolate Icing (see Index)

Butter and lightly flour bottoms of 2 (9-inch) sliding-based cake pans.

Melt the chocolate chips; cool slightly.

Combine egg yolks with chocolate chips in small mixer bowl; blend well. Add butter and vanilla; stir until smooth and thoroughly blended.

Beat egg whites and salt until frothy. Add sugar

1 tablespoon at a time; beat well after each addition. Beat until stiff peaks form. Fold ⅓ of egg whites into chocolate mixture thoroughly; fold chocolate mixture gently into egg whties. Fold flour gradually into chocolate mixture until smooth and just blended, using rubber spatula. Pour batter into prepared cake pans.

Bake in preheated 350°F oven 25 to 30 minutes or until layers test done. Remove from oven; cool on wire racks 1 minute. Remove layers from pans; let cool completely.

Spread Apricot Glaze between layers and over top of cake. Pour chocolate icing over all, smoothing with wet spatula. Chill cake 3 hours or until glaze is set.

Remove from refrigerator 30 minutes before serving.

Sachertorte can be piped with Basic Chantilly Cream (see Index). Each layer can be glazed, frosted, and served as shown in illustration, or individually, if desired. Yield 20 to 24 servings.

violet garden cake

1 recipe Sweetheart Spice Cake (see Index)
5 to 6 drops green food coloring
1 (9-ounce) container whipped topping
2 dozen crystallized violets

Follow cake recipe. Bake half in greased and floured 8-inch layer cake tin and half in 1½-quart greased and floured ovenproof mixing bowl at 350°F 30 minutes or until done. Remove, unmold and cool. (Wrap layer cake in thick plastic wrap; freeze for future use.)

Fold food coloring into whipped topping until

151

violet garden cake

topping is evenly tinted. Fill pastry bag with whipped topping. Using rosette tip, cover cooled cake with whipped-topping rosettes, as illustrated. Arrange crystal violets randomly over frosted cake. Refrigerate at least 2 hours to set before serving. Yield 8 servings.

walnut torte

½ pound shelled walnut meats
9 eggs, separated
1 cup sugar
½ cup zwieback crumbs
1 tablespoon grated orange peel

½ teaspoon salt
1 teaspoon ground cinnamon
½ teaspoon ground cloves
2 teaspoons baking powder
¼ cup brandy
3 tablespoons water
1 teaspoon vanilla extract
Whipped cream
Whole hazelnuts or almonds, or walnut halves,
    for garnish

Grind walnuts through medium blade of food chopper. (You should have 3 cups.)

Beat egg yolks and sugar until thick and lemon-colored.

Mix ground nuts, zwieback crumbs, orange peel, salt, cinnamon, cloves, and baking powder. Stir into egg-yolk mixture. Add brandy and water.

Beat egg whites until stiff but not dry. Fold into nut mixture. Pour into greased 9-inch springform pan or 2 (9-inch) layer-cake pans.

Bake at 350°F 30 to 35 minutes or until cake tests done in center. (Bake 9-inch layers 20 to 25 minutes.) Cool in pan. When cold, remove from pan.

Garnish with vanilla-flavored whipped cream and whole hazelnuts. Yield 12 servings.

walnut torte

yolk mixture.

Line bottom of 10-inch tube pan with waxed paper. Pour batter into pan.

Bake in 375°F oven 1 hour or until done. Invert cake; cool thoroughly. Remove from pan.

Whip cream; add ½ cup granulated sugar and 2 teaspoons vanilla at end of whipping period.

Place cake, top-side-down, on serving platter; cover center hole with small plastic or cardboard disk. Frost cake with whipped cream. Using pastry tube, decorate edge with whipped-cream flowers. Press toasted almonds around sides of frosted cake. Garnish each whipped-cream flower with fresh raspberry. Refrigerate torte prior to serving. Yield 12 servings.

wheat-germ carrot cake

1½ cups cooking oil
2 cups packed brown sugar
4 eggs
1 tablespoon grated orange peel
1½ teaspoons pure vanilla extract
3 cups grated carrot
1½ cups vacuum-packed wheat germ, regular or sugar and honey
2 cups flour
3 teaspoons baking powder
1½ teaspoons salt
1½ teaspoons cinnamon
¾ teaspoon nutmeg
1 cup raisins
¾ cup chopped pecans

Beat together oil, sugar, and eggs. Mix in orange peel, vanilla, and carrot.

Combine wheat germ, flour, baking powder, salt, cinnamon, and nutmeg. Stir into carrot mixture. Mix in raisins and pecans. Turn into greased and floured 10-inch bundt pan.

Bake in 350°F oven 60 to 70 minutes or until pick inserted into center comes out clean. Cool in pan 10 minutes. Remove from pan to rack to finish cooling. Serve with cream cheese sauce. Yield 12 or more servings.

cream-cheese sauce
2 (3-ounce) packages cream cheese
2 tablespoons soft butter
1 cup powdered sugar
1 teaspoon vanilla

Beat cream cheese with butter until creamy. Beat in sugar and vanilla. If necessary, stir in about 4 teaspoons milk to get a fluffy consistency.

warsaw party torte

warsaw party torte

½ pound almonds, ground
6 tablespoons all-purpose white flour
1 teaspoon cream of tartar
10 egg yolks
1¾ cups granulated sugar
3 teaspoon vanilla
10 egg whites
3 cups whipping cream
1 cup slivered almonds, toasted
12 fresh red raspberries

Combine ground almonds, flour, and cream of tartar.

Beat egg yolks until light and fluffy. Gradually beat 1¼ cups sugar into yolks; beat until mixture is thick and smooth. Stir in 1 teaspoon vanilla. Fold in flour mixture.

Beat egg whites until very stiff. Fold into egg-

CAKE DECORATING

chocolate curls

Pour softened chocolate chips as thinly as possible, ⅛ to ¼ inch, onto very cold surface. Marble is best; if not available, ice down kitchen counter or table. Let chocolate harden about 2 hours or until it has lost its gloss. Hold knife at slight angle as shown in picture; pull it across chocolate surface, using pivot-like motion. Result will be beautiful chocolate curls that can be used to decorate cakes or other desserts.

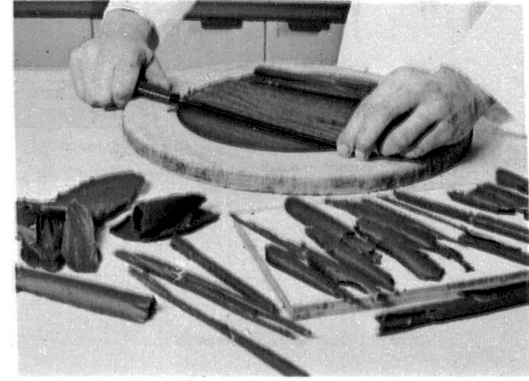

chocolate leaves

Wash rose leaves. Melt chocolate chips. Pull single leaf, upside down, over surface of melted chocolate.

Remove extra chocolate by tapping leaf against side of bowl. Place leaf, chocolate-side-up, on cookie sheet; place in refrigerator to harden.

When chocolate has chilled and hardened, peel off leaves. Chocolate leaves will be perfect, with veins from real leaf imprinted in chocolate.

crystallized violets

In France candied violets are used for cake decorations or to enhance a frozen soufflé or a dish of candy. Although they lend a cosmopolitan touch to gourmet desserts, they are very costly to buy in this country; but, with a little patience, you can make your own. Make them in spring when violets grow wild; store enough to use through the entire year.

36 violets
1 egg white
½ cup sugar
8 to 10 drops violet extract (optional)
Purple food coloring (optional)

Buy or pick 3 dozen violets. If picking them, be sure they have not been sprayed with pesticide. Remove stems; leave just flower. Dry flowers very carefully with soft paper towel or tissue.

Beat egg white until foamy but not stiff. Dip each flower in egg white, then in sugar; coat thoroughly. Use toothpick to manipulate flowers; keep petals open. Place flowers on cookie tin. Turn on oven to lowest heat for 5 minutes. Turn heat off; place pan of violets in oven. Let dry overnight. Will keep forever stored in airtight container in cool place.

To color violets a deeper purple than they are naturally, add few drops of vegetable coloring to egg white before beating. For a violet flavor, add extract to egg white before beating. Violet extract is available in some drugstores and some gourmet food stores. It is not necessary. Yield 36.

variations
Mint leaves or rose petals can be crystallized same as violets. It is not necessary to use added coloring or flavor for these leaves.

basic divinity

½ cup water
½ cup light corn syrup
2 cups sugar
¼ teaspoon salt
2 egg whites
1 teaspoon vanilla
½ cup chopped nuts

Lightly oil inside of heavy 2-quart saucepan. Combine water and corn syrup in pan. Cook over moderate heat until mixture boils. Remove from heat. Add sugar and salt. Cook over moderate heat, stirring constantly, until sugar is completely dissolved. Cover; cook until mixture comes to boil. Uncover immediately. Clip on candy thermometer. Cook over medium heat, *without stirring,* until thermometer registers 260°F (hard-ball stage).

Begin beating egg whites while syrup is cooking—have syrup reach 260°F about same time egg whites are beaten very stiff. Start beating egg whites at about time syrup reaches soft-ball stage; it usually goes fairly rapidly after that point. Beat egg whites very stiff.

As soon as syrup has reached 260°F begin pouring it over egg whites *with mixer running.* This is why stationary electric mixer is so important in divinity-making. Recruit a helper at this point if there is no electric mixer. Pour syrup in slow but steady stream. Add vanilla at some point during mixing; beat until divinity is quite thick and loses glossy look. It will hold shape when dropped from tip of spoon when it is ready. Add nuts very quickly. Drop by spoonful onto well-oiled cookie tin. Work as rapidly as possible, so divinity does not cool down in bowl. Store in absolutely airtight container in cool place. The flavor of divinity, like most candy, improves after a day or two of ripening. Yield 36 to 50 pieces.

fruit divinity

Follow directions for Basic Divinity. Add ½ cup raisins or ½ cup chopped candied fruit. For very festive look, use ½ cup chopped candied cherries.

honey divinity

Omit corn syrup in Basic Divinity recipe; substitute ½ cup honey.

maple divinity

Add ½ cup pure maple syrup to water and corn syrup in Basic Divinity recipe.

orange divinity

Add 2 or 3 teaspoons grated orange rind to basic recipe. For very special orange divinity also add ¼ cup chopped candied orange rind while beating.

peppermint divinity

Omit nuts and vanilla from Basic Divinity; substitute 1 teaspoon peppermint flavoring. One-half cup crushed peppermint candy can be added to mixture while beating.

basic marshmallows

2 envelopes unflavored gelatin (2 tablespoons)
½ cup cold water
2 cups sugar
¾ cup light corn syrup
¾ cup water
2 teaspoons vanilla
¼ cup confectioners' sugar mixed with ¼ cup cornstarch

Combine gelatin and ½ cup cold water in large electric-mixer bowl. Let mixture stand while preparing sugar syrup.

Lightly oil 2-quart saucepan. Combine sugar, corn syrup, and ¾ cup water in saucepan. Cook over medium heat, stirring constantly, until sugar dissolves. Cover; bring to boil. Remove cover as soon as mixture boils; cook, without stirring, to 245°F (firm-ball stage). Remove from heat. Attach electric beater; with mixer beating, pour hot syrup slowly into softened gelatin. Entire process should take about 15 minutes. Add vanilla at very end of beating process. At this point marshmallow mixture should be very light and fluffy.

Lightly oil 8 × 8 × 2-inch pan. Sprinkle half the confectioners' sugar-cornstarch mixture over bottom; pour marshmallow mixture over this. Chill overnight in refrigerator.

When ready to cut marshmallows, sprinkle rest of confectioners' sugar-cornstarch mixture over top of marshmallow. Lift entire piece out of pan onto cutting board. Use very sharp scissors, dipped into cold water periodically, to cut marshmallow into 1-inch pieces. Roll pieces in confectioners' sugar-cornstarch mixture; there will be enough left in bottom of pan for this step. Let marshmallows dry on cooling rack an hour or two. Store in airtight container. Will stay moist at least 3 weeks. Yield 64 (1-inch) or 128 (½-inch) marshmallows.

chocolate marshmallows

Follow Basic Marshmallows recipe; add 2 squares unsweetened chocolate, melted and cooled, to marshmallow during beating step.

fruit-and-nut marshmallows

Add 1 cup candied fruit, chopped nuts, dates,

figs, or raisins after marshmallow is beaten and before it is spread to cool.

fruity marshmallows

Substitute fruit juice for water when softening gelatin.

Important note: Do not use fresh pineapple juice; it will prevent marshmallows from jelling. Canned pineapple juice can be used, or cook fresh juice before using.

minty marshmallows

Omit vanilla; substitute few drops oil of peppermint or 1 teaspoon peppermint extract.

toasted-coconut marshmallows

Instead of using confectioners' sugar and cornstarch to coat marshmallows, sprinkle pan with 1 cup lightly toasted coconut. After marshmallow mixture has cooled, sprinkle top with 1 cup lightly toasted coconut. After marshmallows are cut to desired size, roll each piece in coconut that has fallen off.

basic vanilla caramels

Caramels are rich, chewy, and delicious. Many candy-makers have been discouraged from making them by the long and tedious process described in old cookbooks. Modern candy-makers use a simple shortcut. They add the butter and cream after the syrup has reached the firm-ball stage. Making caramels in stages in this manner cuts the cooking down to a reasonable time and also makes a better-tasting candy.

2 cups sugar
1 cup corn syrup
2 cups heavy cream, lukewarm
½ cup butter
1 teaspoon vanilla

Lightly oil inside of 3-quart saucepan. Combine sugar and corn syrup in pan; cook over low heat, stirring constantly, until sugar is completely dissolved and mixture comes to boil. Clip on candy thermometer; cook, stirring occasionally, until thermometer registers 250°F (firm-ball stage). Add warm cream very slowly so mixture never stops boiling. Cook until temperature again reaches 250°F. Add butter, bit by bit, so mixture never stops boiling. Stir a little to blend; let mixture cook to 250°F again. Remove from heat; add vanilla. Pour in steady stream into lightly oiled 9 × 9 × 2-inch pan. Do not scrape pan. Mark in 1-inch squares, but do not cut all the way through. After caramel has cooled completely, it can be turned out onto cutting board and cut into marked squares. Wrap individual pieces immediately in plastic wrap or waxed paper; store in airtight container. Yield 81 (1-inch) pieces.

wrapped caramels

butterscotch caramels

Substitute 1 cup light brown sugar and 1 cup granulated sugar for 2 cups sugar in basic recipe.

caramel-nut-fudge roll

Prepare 1 recipe Traditional Chocolate Fudge (see Index); shape into long roll about 1 to 1½ inches in diameter. Pour caramel into shallow pan. When cool enough to handle, turn out of pan onto cutting board. Cut strip large enough to wrap around fudge. Roll caramel in coarsely chopped nuts or chocolate sprinkles. Cut into slices when completely cool.

caramel-nut roll

Use either vanilla or chocolate caramel. Allow to cool slightly. Shape into long roll about 1½ to 2 inches in diameter; roll in coarsely chopped nuts. When completely cool, cut into slices.

chocolate caramels

Add 2 (2-ounce) squares bitter chocolate to sugar and corn syrup.

coffee caramels

Add 1 teaspoon instant coffee crystals to sugar and corn syrup.

nut caramels

Add 1 cup chopped nuts to syrup with the butter.

brandy balls

1 cup semisweet chocolate chips, 1 (6-ounce) package
1 5-ounce can evaporated milk
2½ cups cookie crumbs
½ cup confectioners' sugar, sifted

brandy balls

1 cup coarsely chopped pecans
⅓ cup brandy

Combine chocolate chips and milk in 2-quart saucepan. Cook over low heat, stirring constantly, just until chocolate is melted and mixture well blended. Remove from heat.

Combine remaining ingredients; add to melted-chocolate mixture, mixing well. Cool about ½ hour. Shape mixture into small balls about 1 inch in diameter. Finished balls can be rolled in confectioners' sugar, cocoa, candy sprinkles, ground nuts, or flaked coconut. For very pretty tray of brandy balls, use variety of coatings. Let finished brandy balls air-dry an hour or two; store in airtight container in refrigerator. Bring to room temperature before serving. Yield 48 1-inch balls.

raisin-rum balls

Soak ½ cup seedless raisins in ⅓ cup rum; drain well. Use rum in place of brandy in recipe as directed. Form balls with several raisins in center. For shortcut, mix raisins into other ingredients.

candied grapefruit or orange rind

Rind from 3 grapefruits or 6 oranges
Water
Salt
½ cup water
2½ cups sugar
Granulated sugar

Using fingers, pull out all membrane and some of soft white inner rind from fruit; leave some, however. This is a matter of experience and judgement, and it is impossible to tell exactly how much white inner rind to leave. Cut rind into even strips about ⅛ inch wide. About 6 or 7 cups of rind strips are needed. Place in large saucepan; add enough cold water to cover well. Measure water as it is added. Add 2 tablespoons salt per quart of water. Bring to boil; boil gently 20 minutes. Drain

rind well. Cover again with cold water—do not add salt—and bring to boil. Cook gently 15 minutes. Drain; repeat step again. Drain well. Add ½ cup water and 2½ cups sugar; heat slowly, stirring to dissolve sugar. Bring to boil; cook slowly until all syrup is absorbed and rind looks clear. This may take as long as an hour, but it really needs no attention while slowly cooking.

Spread large baking tin with sugar When rind is done, roll few strips at a time in sugar.

Heat oven to 250°F; turn off heat. Place pan of sugared rind in oven; leave overnight to dry. Will keep indefinitely stored in airtight container in cool place. Yield about 1 pound.

Note: This recipe can be doubled.

chocolate candied rind

To dip candied rind in chocolate, roll finished candied rind in confectioners' instead of granulated sugar; omit oven drying. Cool strips to lukewarm; dip in 88°F melted chocolate coating.

chocolate cherry cordials

1 (12-ounce) package chocolate chips, melted
3 tablespoons kirsch
1½ tablespoons grenadine syrup
24 candied cherries

Spoon small amount chocolate into each of 24 paper or foil candy cases; coat sides and bottoms well. Chill not more than 5 minutes to set chocolate.

Combine kirsch and grenadine syrup; chill well.

Place cherry in each case. Drizzle enough kirsch mixture over each cherry to cover halfway. Spoon melted chocolate over each cherry to fill case. Chill 5 minutes or until chocolate is set. Place in airtight container; let stand at least 24 hours before using.

Peel casings from candy. Eat carefully; syrup will drip. Yield 24.

chocolate divinity

½ cup water
½ cup light corn syrup
1 cup firmly packed light brown sugar
1 cup granulated sugar
2 (1-ounce) squares unsweetened chocolate
⅛ teaspoon nutmeg
2 egg whites
1 teaspoon vanilla
½ cup semisweet-chocolate bits

Lightly oil inside of heavy 2-quart saucepan. Combine water and corn syrup in pan. Cook over moderate heat until mixture boils. Remove from heat. Add sugars, chocolate, and nutmeg. Cook over moderate heat, stirring constantly, until sugars are completely dissolved and chocolate is melted. Wipe down sugar crystals above liquid line, using clean pastry brush dipped in cold water. Cook without stirring until mixture boils. Wipe down sugar crystals. Clip on candy thermometer. Cook over moderate heat to 260°F (hard-ball stage).

Begin beating egg whites before syrup is finished cooking, so egg whites will be beaten stiff and syrup will have reached 260°F about same time. Start when soft-ball stage is reached. Beat egg whites very stiff. Keep mixer going or enlist aid of another person. Pour chocolate syrup in steady stream over egg whites. Add vanilla while beating. When mixture is quite thick and has lost glossy look, stir in chocolate bits. Working rapidly, drop by spoonfuls onto well-greased cookie sheet. Store in absolutely airtight container in cool place. Leave for day or two so flavor can ripen. Yield 50 pieces.

chocolate fondant

3 cups sugar
1½ cups water
1 tablespoon light corn syrup
2 (1-ounce) squares unsweetened chocolate
1 teaspoon vanilla

Lightly oil inside of 3-quart saucepan. Combine sugar, water, corn syrup, and chocolate in pan. Stirring constantly, cook over low heat until sugar and chocolate are completely melted. After mixture is thoroughly blended, wipe down sugar crystals above liquid line; use clean pastry brush dipped in cold water. Let mixture come to boil; do not cover. When mixture boils, wipe down sugar crystals again. Clip on candy thermometer. Boil without stirring to 238°F (soft-ball stage). Remove from heat. Pour in slow but steady stream onto either marble slab or wet large cookie sheet that has been placed on cooling rack. Placing baking sheet on rack will allow mixture to cool evenly, since air can circulate around it; will also protect surface under it from burning. Cool to 110°F (lukewarm). Add vanilla. Begin working fondant with heavy spatula. When fondant thickens; oil hands; knead gently until it forms a ball. Place fondant ball in airtight container; let mellow overnight before using. Yield 1¼ pounds.

chocolate-brandy fondant
Omit vanilla; add 1 teaspoon brandy extract.

chocolate-cream fondant
Follow above recipe; add 2 tablespoons margarine as fondant is worked.

chocolate-rum fondant
Omit vanilla; add 1 teaspoon rum extract.

chocolate rum-raisin fondant
Omit vanilla; add 1 teaspoon rum flavoring and ½ cup chopped raisins.

mocha fondant
Omit vanilla; add 1 teaspoon instant coffee concentrate to water.

foolproof chocolate fudge

This recipe will work no matter what the weather.
1⅔ cups sugar
⅔ cup evaporated milk
1 6-ounce package semisweet chocolate bits
1½ cups miniature marshmallows
Dash of salt
Dash of nutmeg
4 tablespoons butter or margarine

Lightly oil inside of 1½- to 2-quart saucepan. Combine sugar and milk in saucepan; cook over medium heat, stirring constantly, until sugar is completely dissolved and mixture comes to boil. Boil, sitrring constantly, 5 minutes. Remove from heat; add chocolate bits, marshmallows, salt, nutmeg, and butter. Stir until chocolate and marshmallows are melted. Beat until thick and not glossy. Spread in oiled 8 × 8 × 2-inch pan. When cool, cut into squares.

Can be cooled in refrigerator and should be stored in refrigerator in very hot weather. Bring to room temperature before serving. Yield 1¼ pounds.

foolproof chocolate-coconut fudge
After fudge has been cut into squares, roll each square in shredded coconut.

foolproof chocolate-fruit fudge
Mix 1 cup raisins, chopped candied fruit, dates, figs, or any kind of dried fruit into fudge before spreading mixture into pan.

foolproof chocolate-marshmallow fudge
Spread 1 cup miniature marshmallows on bottom of well-oiled pan before spreading fudge mixture in pan.

foolproof chocolate-nut fudge
Mix 1 cup nuts into fudge mixture before spreading.

marshmallow crispies

¼ cup butter or margarine
4 cups tightly packed marshmallows
6 cups crisp rice cereal

Melt butter in 3-quart saucepan. Add marshmallows; cook over low heat, stirring constantly. When marshmallows are completely melted, add rice cereal; stir just until all blended. Immediately press mixture into well-oiled, shallow pan about 12 × 9 inches. When cool, cut into 1-inch squares. Yield 96 (1-inch) squares.

chocolate-chip marshmallow crispies

Add 1 cup semisweet chocolate chips to rice cereal.

nutty marshmallow crispies

Add 1 cup chopped walnuts to rice cereal.

mocha divinity

½ cup strong black coffee or ½ cup water and 2
  teaspoons instant coffee
½ cup light corn syrup
1 cup firmly packed light brown sugar
1 cup granulated sugar
¼ teaspoon salt
2 (1-ounce) squares unsweetened chocolate
2 egg whites
1 teaspoon vanilla
½ cup chopped nuts

Lightly oil inside of heavy 2-quart saucepan. Combine coffee and corn syrup in pan. Cook over moderate heat until mixture boils. Remove from heat. Add sugars, salt, and chocolate. Cook over moderate heat, stirring constantly, until sugars are completely dissolved and chocolate is melted. Wipe down sugar crystals above liquid line; use clean pastry brush dipped in cold water. Cook without stirring until mixture boils. Wipe down sugar crystals again. Clip on candy thermometer. Cook over moderate heat, *without stirring,* until mixture reaches 260°F (hard-ball stage).

Begin beating egg whites before syrup is quite finished so egg whites will be beaten stiff and syrup will reach 260°F about same time.

When syrup reaches 260°F, pour over egg whites in steady stream with beater still running. If attempting this without electric mixer, try to have someone help at this stage; it is almost impossible to beat and pour at same time. Add vanilla while mixing; beat until mixture is quite thick and no longer glossy. Stir in nuts. Drop by spoonfuls onto well-oiled cookie sheet. Store in absolutely airtight container in cool place. Let stand day or two so flavor can ripen fully. Yield 50 pieces.

nut balls

¼ cup corn syrup
1 tablespoon vanilla
⅛ tablespoon salt
½ cup powdered milk
¼ cup chopped nuts

Put syrup, vanilla, and salt into bowl; mix together. Add powdered milk and chopped nuts. Stir with knife until well blended. Pat into ball;

place on board sprinkled lightly with sugar. Knead until creamy. Let stand until firm enough to shape into 1-inch balls. Roll in sugar. Yield ½ pound.

nut and raisin squares

1 cup flour
¼ teaspoon baking soda
¼ teaspoon salt
½ teaspoon ground ginger
1 cup seeded raisins
1 cup chopped nuts
¼ cup shortening
¼ cup firmly packed brown sugar
2 eggs
¼ teaspoon vanilla extract
½ cup molasses

Preheat oven to 350°F.
Grease shallow 9-inch-square pan.
Sift flour, soda, salt, and ginger together. Stir in raisins and nuts.

Cream shortening and sugar. Beat in eggs one at a time. Add vanilla and molasses. Add flour-and-nut mixture; blend well. Pour into prepared pan; bake about 30 minutes.

Mark into squares; let cool in pan before removing. Yield 25.

peanut-butter chews

1 cup peanut butter
1 cup light corn syrup
1 cup nonfat dry milk (not instant) or 2 cups
  instant nonfat dry milk
1 cup confectioners' sugar

Mix all ingredients together. Press ½-inch thick in pan. Cut into pieces. Chill before serving. Yield 24 pieces.

penuche

2 cups firmly packed light brown sugar
¾ cup milk
1 tablespoon light corn syrup
Dash of salt
2 tablespoons butter
1 teaspoon vanilla
1 cup broken nut meats

Lightly oil inside of 2-quart saucepan. Combine sugar, milk, corn syrup, and salt in pan. Cook over medium heat, stirring constantly, until sugar is completely dissolved and mixture comes to boil. Wash down sugar crystals above liquid line, using clean pastry brush dipped in cold water. Clip on candy thermometer; cook mixture to soft-ball stage (238°F). If syrup looks curdled, *do not worry;* it will become creamy as it is beaten. Remove from heat immediately. Add butter; *do not stir.* Cool to 110°F or until pan feels warm to touch. Add vanilla; beat vigorously until mixture becomes thick and loses glossy look. Add nuts; spread in well-oiled 8 × 8 × 2-inch pan to cool. Cut into squares when cool. Yield 1 pound.

peppermint cushions

2 cups sugar
¾ cup water
2 tablespoons light corn syrup
2 tablespoons butter or margarine
Few drops oil of peppermint or 2 teaspoons
  peppermint extract

Lightly oil inside of 2-quart saucepan. Combine sugar, water, and corn syrup in pan. Cook over medium heat, stirring constantly, until sugar dissolves completely and mixture comes to boil. Wipe down sugar crystals above liquid line, using clean pastry brush dipped in cold water. Clip on candy thermometer. Boil without stirring until thermometer registers 245°F (firm-ball stage). Add butter little at a time so mixture does not stop boiling. It may be necessary to stir to blend butter into syrup. Cook until thermometer registers 290°F (hard-crack stage). Remove from heat immediately. Pour at once onto well-oiled jelly-roll pan. Add flavoring; blend with heavy spatula. As soon as mixture is cool enough to handle, oil fingers. Pull mixture into long rope; keep pulling and re-forming until mixture is opaque. Pull into long

rum balls

sausage shape about ¾ inches in diameter. Cut with oiled scissors into pieces about 1 inch long, giving mixture half turn after each cut to form into cushion shape. Wrap each piece separately. Store in cool, not refrigerated, place. Yield 1 pound.

rum balls

1 cup cookie crumbs, chocolate or vanilla
1 cup confectioners' sugar
1½ cups finely chopped walnuts
2 tablespoons light corn syrup
4 tablespoons rum
2 tablespoon cocoa

Combine cookie crumbs, sugar, 1 cup walnuts, corn syrup, rum, and cocoa; mix well. Form into 1-inch balls. Roll each ball in reserved walnuts. Air-dry about 1 hour. Store in airtight container in cool place. Will keep several weeks. Yield 36 1-inch balls.

variations

Garnish each finished ball with ½ candied cherry or ½ walnut pressed into top.

Reduce nuts to 1 cup. Roll finished balls in sugar or shredded coconut.

saltwater taffy

2 cups sugar
1 cup light corn syrup
1 cup water
1½ teaspoons salt
2 teaspoons glycerine (can be purchased at
  drugstore)
2 tablespoons butter or margarine
2 teaspoons vanilla or flavoring of your choice

Lightly oil inside of 2-quart saucepan. Combine sugar, corn syrup, water, salt, and glycerine in pan. Cook over low heat, stirring constantly, until sugar is completely dissolved and mixture comes to boil. Wipe down sugar crystals above liquid line, using clean pastry brush dipped in cold water. Clip on candy thermometer. Cook without stirring until thermometer registers 260°F (hard-ball stage). Remove from heat. Add butter. Pour hot syrup onto oiled jelly-roll tin. Put tin on cooling rack before pouring hot syrup from pan. This protects surface underneath from being damaged by extreme heat and also allows syrup to cool faster. Let taffy cool. Add vanilla. Begin working taffy with heavy spatula by pushing outer edges into center of taffy. When taffy is cool enough to handle, oil fingers well; start working by hand. Gather taffy into ball; stretch into rope. Pull taffy until light in color and texture. Work by first pulling it into long rope, then doubling and re-doubling taffy, then pulling it into long rope again. Two people can do this together. When pulled enough, form into long rope about ¾ inch thick. Cut into 1-inch pieces, using well-oiled scissors. Wrap each piece separately. Store in cool place. Yield about 1¼ pounds.

traditional chocolate fudge

2 (1-ounce) squares unsweetend chocolate
2 cups sugar
1 cup milk
1 tablespoon light corn syrup
Dash of salt
2 tablespoons butter or margarine
1 teaspoon vanilla
Dash of nutmeg (optional)

Lightly oil inside of 1½- to 2-quart saucepan. Combine chocolate, sugar, milk, corn syrup, and salt in saucepan. Cook over medium heat, stirring constantly, until sugar dissolves and mixture comes to boil. Wash down crystals on inside of pan above liquid line, using clean pastry brush dipped in water. If using candy thermometer, clip it onto pan; allow mixture to cook until thermometer registers 238°F (soft-ball stage). If not using candy thermometer, test for soft-ball stage (syrup forms soft ball in cold water). Do not stir while mixture is cooking; when it reaches proper temperature, remove from heat immediately. Add butter, *but do not stir.* Cool to 110°F. If not using thermometer, cool until bottom of pan feels lukewarm. Add vanilla and nutmeg. Start beating vigorously; beat until mixture loses its glossy look. Pour into well-oiled 8 × 8 × 2-inch pan. Cut into squares when cool.

Store in airtight container in cool place. Let stand day or two to allow flavor to develop. Yield 1¾ pounds.

kneaded fudge

This fudge can be kneaded in an electric mixer. As it becomes very thick, change beater to a bread hook and knead fudge just like bread dough until it is very creamy and can be shaped by hand. Imagination can take over then. Make small fudge balls; roll in cocoa or chopped nuts. A nice change from traditional fudge squares is fudge roll: form long sausage-shaped roll; slice into rounds. Roll can be coated with chopped nuts or shredded coconut, then sliced.

mocha fudge

Add 1 teaspoon instant coffee to mixture as it cooks.

nut fudge

Mix 1 cup unsalted roasted nuts into fudge after it is beaten and before it is spread in pan to cool. If kneaded method is used, nuts can be kneaded into fudge.

truffles

3 (1-ounce) squares unsweetened chocolate
1¼ cups sifted confectioners' sugar
⅓ cup butter
3 egg yolks
1 teaspoon vanilla or 2 tablespoons cognac
Melted chocolate, cocoa, ground nuts, chocolate jimmies, or coconut

Melt 3 chocolate squares over hot, not boiling, water.

Meanwhile combine sugar and butter in mixing bowl; cream together. Add egg yolks one at a time; blend well after each addition. Stir in 3 melted chocolate squares and flavoring. Chill mixture until firm enough to handle easily. Break off small pieces; form into ½-inch balls. Roll in a favorite coating. (It is very nice to use several different coatings and arrange finished truffles in very pretty pattern on serving dish.) Allow finished balls to dry and firm on baking sheet about an hour before storing in airtight container in very cool place. These keep about a week. Yield 50 ½-inch balls.

turtles

1 pound cashew nuts
1 recipe Vanilla Caramels (see Index)
8 ounces semisweet chocolate, melted, or 1⅓ cups semisweet chocolate bits, melted

Lightly oil large baking sheet or cookie tin.

Arrange 60 groups of cashew nuts, 4 to each group.

Allow caramel syrup to cool slightly in pan, but be sure it is still liquid. Spoon tablespoon of liquid caramel over cashew nuts. Let cool 10 to 15 minutes. Spoon melted chocolate over top of each caramel turtle. Allow to cool completely until quite firm. Yield 60 turtles.

Hint: Lacking time to make vanilla caramels from scratch, buy 1-pound package of commerical caramels. Melt in top of double boiler with 2 tablespoons water; use in above recipe.

yogurt fudge

2 cups firmly packed light brown sugar
1 cup unflavored yogurt
Dash of salt
2 tablespoons butter
1 cup firmly packed marshmallows, miniature or standard
1 teaspoon vanilla

Lightly oil inside of 1½- to 2-quart saucepan. Combine sugar, yogurt, and salt in pan. Cook over low heat, stirring constantly, until sugar is completely dissolved and mixture comes to boil.

Wipe down sugar crystals above liquid line, using clean pastry brush dipped in cold water. Cook until mixture reaches soft-ball stage (238°F). If syrup looks curdled, *do not worry;* it will become creamy as it is beaten. Remove from heat immediately. Add butter and marshmallows; *do not stir.* Allow mixture to cool to 110°F or until pan feels warm to touch. Add vanilla; beat vigorously until fudge is thick and has lost glossy look. Pour into 8 × 8 × 2-inch pan to cool. Cut into squares when cool. Yield 1 pound.

yogurt-nut fudge

Add ½ cup chopped or broken nut meats to mixture before spreading in pan to cool.

yogurt pralines

3 cups sugar
½ teaspoon baking soda
1 cup unflavored yogurt
2 tablespoons light corn syrup
2 tablespoons butter
1 teaspoon vanilla
2 cups pecans

Lightly oil inside of 4-quart saucepan. (This is going to foam!) Combine sugar, soda, yogurt, and corn syrup in pan. Cook over low heat, stirring constantly, until sugar is dissolved. Wipe off sugar crystals above liquid line, using clean pastry brush dipped in cold water. Allow mixture to come to boil. Clip on candy thermometer; cook until thermometer registers 234°F (soft-ball stage). Remove from heat. Stir in butter, vanilla, and pecans. Beat with wooden spoon just until mixture thickens and begins to look cloudy. Drop by spoonful onto well-oiled cookie tin. Let cool completely. Store in airtight container in cool place. Yield 12 to 15 pralines.

brown-sugar yogurt pralines

Substitute 1½ cups light brown sugar and 1½ cups granulated sugar for 3 cups sugar.

rich yogurt pralines

Substitute 1 cup commerical sour cream for yogurt.

MEAT

beef burgundy

2 pounds beef chuck or round
2 tablespoons flour
Salt and pepper
2 tablespoons oil
1 cup chopped lean bacon
15 to 18 small white onions
5 or 6 small carrots
1 clove garlic, crushed
1 tablespoon tomato paste
¾ cup red wine

beef burgundy

1 cup beef broth or bouillon
1 cup sliced mushrooms

Preheat oven to 250°F.

Cut meat into 2-inch cubes; dredge with flour mixed with salt and pepper.

Heat oil in skillet. Sauté meat until well browned; remove to casserole.

Sauté bacon in skillet a few minutes. Add onions, carrots, and garlic; cook until onions begin to brown. Put bacon and vegetables into casserole with meat.

Stir remaining flour into fat left in skillet; cook until it begins to brown. Add tomato paste, wine, and broth; stir until boiling. Taste for seasoning; pour over meat and vegetables. Cover tightly; cook about 3 hours. Add mushrooms; cook 15 to 20 minutes.

Serve with lima beans, green peas, or other green vegetables; a tossed salad; and garlic bread. Yield 5 or 6 servings.

beef casserole with beer (carbonnade de boeuf flamande)

4 cups Basic Beef Stock (see index) or 1 can beef
  bouillon
5 pounds lean stew beef
1½ cups Basic Seasoned Flour (see Index)
2 tablespoons butter or margarine
2 tablespoons peanut or corn oil
1½ cups minced onions
24 small whole onions or shallots, peeled
Salt and freshly ground pepper to taste
4 cups strong beer or ale

Pour stock into saucepan; boil until reduced to ¾ cup liquid (or heat canned bouillon.) Cut beef into large chunks.

Place flour in plastic bag. Add beef; shake until coated. Remove beef; reserve remaining flour.

Heat butter and oil in heavy skillet. Add beef; cook until brown, stirring with wooden spoon. Remove beef from skillet; set aside.

Coat minced onions with reserved flour. Brown in skillet; add shortening, if needed. Arrange half of minced onions in casserole; cover with half of beef. Cover beef layer with remaining minced onions; top with remaining beef. Add whole onions. Season with salt and pepper. Pour stock and beer over beef mixture.

Bake, covered, in preheated 350°F oven, 1 rack below center, 2 hours or until beef is tender.

Place in serving dish; garnish with fresh parsley, if desired. Yield about 12 servings.

beef casserole with beer

beef with dumplings

2 tablespoons flour
1½ teaspoons salt
¼ teaspoon pepper
2 pounds lean beef chuck
3 tablespoons oil
3 medium onions, peeled
3 cloves
4 carrots, peeled, cut into lengthwise strips
1½ cups beef consommé
1 tablespoon red or white wine vinegar
1 package biscuit mix
3 tablespoons chopped chives

Preheat oven to 350°F.

Sift flour with salt and pepper.

Cut meat into 1-inch cubes; dredge well with flour.

Heat oil in casserole. Add meat and onions (each stuck with a clove); stir until meat is well browned. Add carrots, consommé, and vinegar; bring to boil. Cover; remove to oven. Cook about 1 hour.

Make dumplings according to instructions on package. Drop into casserole in spoonfuls; replace

lid. Cook 30 minutes. Sprinkle with chives before serving. Yield 4 or 5 servings.

beef-and-rice casserole

½ pound bacon slices
2 pounds boneless beef chuck
2 onions, peeled, sliced
¾ cup uncooked rice
1 cup dry red wine
1½ cups beef consommé
1 clove garlic, crushed
1 sprig fresh or ½ teaspoon dried thyme
1 teaspoon chopped parsley
¼ teaspoon saffron
1 cup chopped fresh tomatoes
½ cup grated Parmesan cheese

Preheat oven to 325°F.

Cut bacon into strips; fry in skillet until crisp. Remove to large casserole.

Cut meat into cubes; brown in bacon fat. Transfer to casserole, using slotted spoon.

Add onions and rice to remaining fat. Stir until rice begins to color; set aside.

164

Put wine, consommé, garlic, thyme, parsley, and saffron into casserole. Cover; cook 1 hour.

Remove casserole from oven. Skim off excess fat; stir in rice-and-onion mixture and tomatoes; cover. Return to oven another hour; check occasionally to see if extra liquid is required. Before serving, adjust seasoning and stir in cheese. Yield 4 or 5 servings.

bittersweet lamb casserole

2 to 2½ pounds loin or shoulder lamb chops
2 tablespoons oil
3 tablespoons vinegar
1 can (6 to 8 ounces) orange juice

casserole of beef with walnuts

2 teaspoons Worcestershire sauce
½ teaspoon salt
⅛ teaspoon freshly ground pepper
Pinch of dry mustard
Pinch of paprika
½ teaspoon each celery seed, basil, oregano
3 or 4 cloves
2 teaspoons sugar
Cooked rice or noodles

Preheat oven to 350°F.

Brown chops in hot oil. Put into casserole with 1 cup water and vinegar. Cover; cook 1 hour.

Put orange juice, Worcestershire sauce, seasonings and flavorings into small pan; simmer, uncovered, 10 minutes.

When meat has cooked 1 hour, stir in orange-juice mixture; cook another hour. Serve with rice or noodles. Yield 4 to 6 servings.

calico casserole

1 pound ground beef
1 cup chopped onions
1 cup chopped celery
1 (10-ounce) package frozen mixed vegetables
2 (8-ounce) cans tomato sauce
½ cup water
1 teaspoon Worcestershire sauce
½ teaspoon salt
⅛ teaspoon pepper
2 cups cooked macaroni

Brown beef. Add onions, celery, and mixed vegetables; cook until onion is well done. Drain accumulated fat. Add tomato sauce, water, and seasonings; cook until vegetables are tender but crisp.

Place hot cooked macaroni in casserole; pour beef-vegetable mixture over it.

Beef-vegetable mixture can be served separately with cooked macaroni. Yield 6 to 8 servings.

casserole of beef with walnuts

2 tablespoons drippings
1½ to 2 pounds beef chuck
12 small white onions, peeled
1 tablespoon flour
¼ cup red wine
Bouquet Garni (see Index)
1 clove garlic
1½ to 2 cups beef bouillon
1 small bunch celery
1 tablespoon butter or margarine
¼ cup walnut meats
Rind of ½ orange, shredded, blanched

Preheat oven to 325°F.

Heat drippings in sauté pan; brown meat. Remove to casserole.

Sauté onions in remaining fat until they just begin to color; put with meat.

Pour off excess fat, leaving about 1 tablespoon. Stir in flour. Add wine, bouquet garni, garlic (crushed with a little salt) and 1½ cups bouillon. Stir until boiling; pour over contents of casserole. Add extra bouillon, if necessary, just to cover meat. Add a little seasoning. Cover tightly; cook about 2 hours.

Trim celery; cut into crosswise strips.

Heat butter. Add celery, walnut meats, and pinch of salt. Toss over heat a few minutes.

When ready to serve, scatter celery, walnut meats, and orange rind over meat. Yield 4 to 5 servings.

curried-lamb casserole

½ cup prunes
½ cup dried apricots
4 thick lamb chops
1 tablespoon oil
¼ cup sultana raisins
1 lemon, thinly sliced
1 cup rice
2 teaspoons curry powder
Salt and pepper

Preheat oven to 350°F.

Soak prunes and apricots in cold water at least 3 hours; drain.

Trim chops; sauté in hot oil a few minutes.

Put layer of fruit in deep, buttered casserole with tight-fitting lid. Sprinkle with raisins. Add 1 or 2 slices lemon and some of rice. Sprinkle with curry powder, salt, and pepper. Continue in alternate layers until all ingredients are used. Place chops on top; pour in 3 cups water. Cover tightly; cook 1 to 1¼ hours, until most liquid has been absorbed. Adjust seasoning. Serve with tossed green salad. Yield 4 servings.

dublin coddle

1 pound large pork-sausage links
4 to 6 thick slices bacon (approximately ½ pound), cut into 2-inch pieces
¾ pound onions (3 medium)
1½ pounds potatoes (4 medium)
Black pepper
Finely chopped parsley

Prick sausages in several places. Place sausage and bacon in skillet. Barely cover with water (about 3 cups); bring to boil. Cover; simmer 10 minutes. Drain; reserve liquid.

Peel and slice onions.

Peel and thinly slice potatoes.

Layer sausage, bacon, onions, and potatoes in 2½-quart casserole. Lightly pepper layers. Pour broth from sausages into casserole barely to cover meat and vegetables (about 2½ cups). Cover casserole with waxed paper.

Bake at 350°F 1 hour or until potatoes are tender. Sprinkle with parsley. Yield 4 to 5 servings.

enchilada casserole

3 tablespoons cooking oil
8 corn tortillas
1 pound ground beef
1 small onion, chopped (¼ cup)
1 (16-ounce) can refried beans
¼ cup hot taco sauce
½ teaspoon salt
Dash of garlic powder
⅓ cup sliced pitted ripe olives
1 (10-ounce) can enchilada sauce
1½ cups shredded cheddar cheese (6 ounces)

Heat oil in medium skillet. Dip tortillas in hot oil on both sides to soften; set aside.

Cook ground beef and onion in same skillet until meat is browned. Remove from heat; drain off fat. Stir beans, taco sauce, salt, garlic powder, and olives into beef mixture. Fill tortillas with mixture; roll up.

Place enchilada sauce into 2-quart glass baking dish (12 × 8 × 2 inches). Roll filled tortillas in sauce to moisten all surfaces. Place seam-side-down in sauce. Cover with aluminum foil.

Bake in 350°F oven 30 minutes or until hot. Sprinkle with cheese; bake, uncovered, 2 or 3 minutes or until cheese is melted. Yield 4 servings.

fiesta casserole

¾ cup hominy grits
1 cup milk
½ pound ground beef
½ pound bulk pork sausage
1 onion, chopped
1 green pepper, chopped
1 (4½-ounce) can chopped ripe olives
1 (17-ounce) can cream-style corn
1 (8-ounce) can tomato sauce
1 (2-ounce) can mushroom stems and pieces
1 teaspoon salt
1 tablespoon chili powder
Pepper

Combine grits and milk in large bowl; let stand 1 hour or longer.

Cook beef, sausage, onion, and green pepper in skillet until meat is browned and onion and green pepper are tender. Add to grits mixture. Add olives, corn, tomato sauce, mushrooms, salt, chili powder, and pepper to taste; mix well. Turn into greased 12 × 7-inch baking dish.

Bake, uncovered, at 325°F 45 minutes to 1 hour. Yield 6 servings.

french white-bean casserole

1 (1-pound) package dried white beans
2 teaspoons salt
½ cup diced salt pork
1½ cups diced cooked ham
2 cups chopped onions
1½ cups diced carrots
2 cups diced skinned tomatoes
3 small cloves garlic, pressed
2 bay leaves
2 tablespoons chopped parsley

french white-bean casserole

½ teaspoon oregano
1 freshly ground pepper
4 cups Basic Chicken Stock (see Index) or 3 (10½ ounce) cans chicken broth
½ pound hard salami, slivered
2 cups diced cooked dark chicken meat
2 cups fine soft bread crumbs

Rinse beans thoroughly in cold, running water. Place beans in large saucepan; add enough water to cover. Bring to boil; boil 2 minutes. Remove from heat; let stand 1 hour. Bring to boil again; stir in salt. Reduce heat; simmer 1½ hours or until almost tender.

Fry pork over low heat until golden. Stir in ham, onions, carrots, and tomatoes. Add garlic, bay leaves, parsley, oregano, and pepper; blend thoroughly. Stir in stock; bring to boil. Reduce heat to low; simmer 30 minutes.

Drain beans; place in 4-quart casserole. Add salami and chicken. Pour sauce over all; stir to blend thoroughly.

Bake, covered, in preheated 350°F oven 30 minutes; stir at 10-minute intervals. Sprinkle bread crumbs evenly over top; pat gently. Reduce oven temperature to 300°F. Bake 30 minutes or until crumbs are browned. Yield 8 to 10 servings.

ginger beef

1 cup onions, minced
2 cloves garlic, pressed
2 teaspoons turmeric
2 teaspoons ginger
1 teaspoon chili powder
1 teaspoon salt
3 pounds lean beef, cut into cubes
½ cup peanut oil
8 fresh tomatoes, peeled, cut into large pieces
4 cups beef bouillon
Boiled rice
Strips of red sweet pepper for garnish

Combine onions, garlic, turmeric, ginger, chili powder, and salt in bowl; mix well.

Place beef in shallow dish. Sprinkle with onion-garlic mixture; refrigerate 3 hours, stirring occasionally. Heat oil in large skillet; stir-fry beef until browned on all sides. Place beef in casserole; add skillet drippings, tomatoes, and bouillon.

Bake, covered, in 325°F oven about 2 hours, until beef is tender.

Serve with boiled rice; garnish with strips of red sweet pepper. Yield 6 to 8 servings.

greek lamb-and-pilaf casserole

2 lamb shanks, well-trimmed of fat, each cut
  in half
2 tablespoons vegetable oil
1 medium onion, chopped
2½ cups water
1 (6-ounce) can tomato paste
2 teaspoons whole allspice
½ stick cinnamon
½ teaspoon black peppercorns
1 teaspoon salt
2 tablespoons butter
1 cup uncooked long-grain white rice
1 cup plain yogurt, lightly salted

Brown lamb on all sides in hot oil in large skillet. Add onion, water, tomato paste, spices, and salt. Cover; simmer about 1½ hours.

Melt butter in another skillet. Brown rice, stirring constantly, over moderate heat; set aside.

Measure lamb cooking broth; add enough water to make 2½ cups. Return to lamb after removing and discarding whole spices. Add browned rice;

ginger beef

cover. Cook 30 minutes over low heat, until rice is tender.

Serve on large platter. Pass rice separately. Yogurt should be served in small bowl as an accompaniment and can be spooned over lamb and rice, if desired. Yield 4 servings.

ham-and-apricot casserole

1 slice (about 1½ pound) center ham, cut 1 inch thick
Prepared mustard
Pepper
1 cup dried apricots, soaked overnight
3 tablespoons seedless raisins
3 to 4 tablespoons gravy or water
6 medium potatoes, peeled, sliced
Salt
1 tablespoon butter or margarine

Preheat oven to 375°F.

Heat sauté pan. Put in ham; brown lightly on both sides. Put into deep baking dish. Spread very lightly with mustard; sprinkle with pepper. Arrange apricots and raisins on top. Add gravy; cover with potato slices. Sprinkle very sparingly with salt; dot with butter. Cover with waxed paper.

Bake ¾ hour. Remove paper; bake 15 to 20 minutes. Yield 4 servings.

hungarian lamb casserole

2 pounds stewing lamb
3 tablespoons oil
1 large onion, peeled, sliced
1 sweet red pepper, seeded, sliced
3 tablespoons flour
1 tablespoon paprika
1 chicken bouillon cube, crumbled
Salt
⅓ cup lima or navy beans, soaked overnight
3 or 4 potatoes, peeled, sliced

Preheat oven to 350°F.

Trim meat; cut into small pieces.

Heat oil in sauté pan. Add meat, onion, and pepper; sauté a few minutes. Remove to casserole.

Add flour, paprika, bouillon cube, and a little salt to pan drippings; mix well. Add 2 cups water; stir until boiling. Add drained beans; simmer 5 minutes. Pour all into casserole. Cover; cook 2 hours.

Arrange potatoes in overlapping slices on top of casserole; cook 25 to 30 minutes or until potatoes are tender. Yield 4 to 5 servings.

hungarian veal goulash

1½ tablespoons butter
1 pound onions, sliced fine
1 clove garlic, crushed
1¼ tablespoons paprika
1½ tablespoons tomato puree
1 teaspoon chopped thyme
1 teaspoon chopped marjoram
1 bay leaf
1½ pounds tender boneless leg or shoulder of veal
1 red pepper, seeded, diced
1½ cups chicken or veal stock
Salt and pepper

1 cup sour cream
1 tablespoon chopped parsley

Preheat oven to 325°F.

Heat half of butter; cook onion and garlic in covered pan until soft and transparent but not brown. Make puree by using blender or food processor or putting through fine sieve. Put into bottom of casserole. Mix in paprika, tomato puree, and herbs.

Cut veal into 2-inch squares; cook quickly in remaining butter without allowing it to color too deeply. Put on top of onion puree; add red pepper. Add enough stock to cover meat; add salt and pepper. Cook in covered casserole in oven (or simmer on gentle heat) about 1 hour, until meat is tender.

Just before serving, spoon sour cream over; sprinkle with chopped parsley. Serve with noodles, macaroni, or riced potatoes. Yield 4 servings.

italian macaroni and cheese

½ pound ground beef
1 (16-ounce) can tomatoes
⅓ cup tomato paste
1 tablespoon instant minced onion
1 teaspoon sugar
½ teaspoon garlic salt
½ teaspoon ground oregano
Dash of pepper
2 cups cooked shell macaroni (about 1⅔ cups uncooked)
1 cup creamed cottage cheese
1 cup shredded sharp cheddar cheese
2 tablespoons grated Parmesan cheese

Cook meat in heavy frypan until it loses its red color but is not brown; drain. Add tomatoes, tomato paste, onion, and seasonings. Simmer slowly 30 minutes; stir as needed.

Preheat oven to 325°F.

Combine macaroni and cottage cheese.

Pour a little sauce in bottom of 2½-quart casserole. Top with half macaroni mixture, half shredded cheese, and half remaining sauce. Repeat. Sprinkle Parmesan over top.

Bake 40 minutes or until heated through. Yield 6 servings.

jambalaya

6 tablespoons butter
6 ounces boneless chicken, diced
6 ounces boiled ham, diced
6 ounces pork sausage (smoked sausage or Polish sausage)
3 cups coarsely diced onions
1½ cups coarsely diced green peppers
2 cups coarsley diced celery
8 tomatoes, peeled
1½ cups tomato puree
4 bay leaves
1 tablespoon crushed oregano
½ teaspoon cayenne
½ teaspoon thyme
3 cloves garlic, minced
2 cups seafood stock or water
2½ cups raw converted rice, cooked

36 medium shrimp, peeled, deveined
36 medium oysters
Salt and pepper

Melt butter in 4-quart pot over medium heat; cook chicken until pink color is gone. Add ham and sausage; sauté 10 minutes. Stir in onions, green peppers, and celery; sauté until tender but crisp. Add tomatoes, tomato puree, bay leaves, oregano, cayenne, thyme, and garlic; simmer 10 minutes. Add stock; bring to boil. Add rice; stir once. Simmer 6 to 8 minutes. Add shrimp and oysters. Cover; simmer about 10 minutes, until heated through. Season to taste with salt and pepper.

Serve as is, or pack in individual round molds. Unmold; surround with Shrimp Creole (see Index). Yield 6 to 8 servings.

lamb hot pot

2½ to 3 pounds neck of lamb
2 onions, peeled, and sliced thin
1½ pounds potatoes, peeled, sliced
1 pound parsnips, peeled, sliced
Salt and pepper
3 tablespoons chopped parsley
Pinch of mixed herbs
2 tablespoons Worcestershire sauce
2 tablespoons water

Preheat oven to 300°F.

Cut meat into pieces.

Arrange one-third of onions, potatoes, and parsnips in casserole. Add seasoning and a little parsley. Add half the meat, a little more seasoning, and herbs. Repeat layers; finish with vegetables. Pour over Worcestershire sauce mixed with water. Cover; cook about 1½ hours. Remove cover; cook 30 minutes. Sprinkle with remaining parsley before serving. Yield 4 servings.

lamb-and-pear casserole

2 pounds stewing lamb
2 teaspoons ground ginger
6 medium-size cooking pears, peeled, quartered, cored
1 package frozen string beans
Salt and pepper
White wine

Trim excess fat from meat; cut into pieces. Put meat into lightly greased sauté pan; brown in its own fat. Transfer to casserole with tight fitting lid. Sprinkle ginger over meat. Add pears, beans, and a little salt and pepper. Add 2 tablespoons white wine. Juice from pears should provide sufficient liquid, but if it begins to dry, add a little more white wine. Cover tightly; cook 1¼ hours. Yield 4 servings.

make-ahead main dish

8-ounce package ruffled egg noodles
1 cup commercial sour cream
3-ounce package cream cheese, soft
6 medium scallions, finely chopped
1 clove garlic, minced

lamb hot pot

lamb-and-pear casserole

1 pound ground chuck beef
15-ounce can tomato sauce with tomato pieces
1 teaspoon salt
Pepper to taste
1 cup grated cheddar cheese

Cook noodles according to package directions for use in dish requiring further cooking. Drain; rinse with hot water. Drain again; set aside.

Gradually beat sour cream into cream cheese. Stir in scallions and garlic; set aside.

Cook beef in 10-inch hot skillet, crumbling with fork, until loses its red color. Stir in the tomato sauce, salt, and pepper; set aside.

In oblong 2-quart baking dish (11¾ × 7½ × 1¾ inches) or similar utensil, layer ½ the noodles, ½ the sour-cream mixture and ½ the beef mixture. Repeat layers in same order. Sprinkle with cheddar cheese. Cover tightly with plastic wrap; refrigerate overnight.

Bake in preheated 350°F oven until thoroughly hot, about 30 minutes. Let stand at room temperature about 10 minutes before serving. Yield 6 servings.

marengo casserole

1 (3-pound) venison roast
2 recipes Marinade for Game (see Index)
½ pound sliced salt pork
1 pound small onions
1 pound small fresh mushrooms
Butter
1 can beef consommé
1 (8-ounce) can tomato sauce
¼ cup all-purpose flour
Salt and freshly ground pepper to taste

1 tablespoon dry sherry
1 tablespoon brandy

Place venison in shallow pan; pour marinade over venison. Refrigerate 12 to 24 hours; turn occasionally. Drain off marinade. Strain; reserve. Wipe venison dry; place on rack in roasting pan.

Wash salt pork; place over venison. Pour 1½ cups water into pan. Add 1 cup reserved marinade. Roast in preheated 325°F oven 2 hours or until done. Baste with pan drippings occasionally.

Peel onions. Cook in boiling salted water until tender; drain.

Sauté mushrooms in small amount of butter until lightly browned; set aside.

Remove roasting venison from pan; place on cutting board. Let cool 20 to 30 minutes; cut into cubes. Place in large heatproof serving casserole. Add onions, mushrooms, consommé, tomato sauce, and 1 cup pan drippings.

Combine flour with ¼ cup water; mix until smooth. Stir into venison mixture. Season with salt and pepper. Add sherry and brandy. Simmer on top of stove, stirring frequently, 15 minutes or until thickened.

Serve with boiled potatoes and green beans, if desired. This can be made the day before serving and reheated. Yield 6 to 8 servings.

meat-and-cabbage casserole

1 small head cabbage (about 1 pound)
1 tablespoon vegetable oil
2 medium onions, chopped
½ pound lean pork, cubed
1 pound lean ground beef

172

1 teaspoon caraway seeds
½ teaspoon salt
½ teaspoon pepper
½ cup dry white wine
1 teaspoon vegetable oil
3 to 6 strips thickly sliced bacon

Remove outer, wilted cabbage leaves and core. Place cabbage in large pot of boiling water; simmer gently 10 minutes. Remove; drain. Gently pull off 12 leaves; set aside. Finely chop rest of cabbage.

Heat 1 tablespoon vegetable oil. Add onions, pork, and ground beef; cook until lightly browned. Drain off excess fat. Add chopped cabbage, caraway seeds, salt, and pepper. Pour in white wine; cover. Simmer 10 minutes; stir often.

Grease ovenproof dish with 1 teaspoon vegetable oil. Line dish with half the cabbage leaves; remove thick ribs, if necessary to make lie flat. Spoon in meat mixture. Cover with rest of cabbage leaves.

Cut bacon strips in half; arrange on top. Place in preheated 350°F oven; bake approximately 45 minutes. Yield 4 servings.

moussaka

2 large eggplants, peeled, cut into ¼-inch slices
Salt
5 tablespoons oil
1 onion, peeled, chopped fine
½ pound ground beef
Pepper
Pinch of thyme
1 large tomato, peeled, seeded, chopped
Cracker crumbs
1 egg
½ cup milk
¼ cup grated cheese
Chopped parsley

Preheat oven to 350°F.

Put eggplant slices into colander. Sprinkle with salt; let drain.

Heat oil in skillet. Add onion; sauté until just beginning to brown. Add meat; cook together, stirring, until meat has browned. Season with salt, pepper, and thyme. Add tomato.

Rinse and dry eggplant; sauté in 4 tablespoons heated oil until golden brown.

Cover bottom of greased casserole with thin layer of cracker crumbs. Arrange layer of eggplant on top.

Separate egg. Beat white stiff; fold into meat mixture with 2 teaspoons cracker crumbs. Adjust seasoning to taste. Arrange layer of meat mixture over eggplant. Repeat layers; finish with eggplant.

Combine egg yolk, milk, and cheese; pour into casserole. Cook 30 minutes. Sprinkle with parsley before serving. Yield 4 to 6 servings.

marengo casserole

meat-and-cabbage casserole

nasi goreng surf-and-turf casserole

nasi goreng surf-and-turf casserole

½ pound lean beef, ground
2 tablespoons bread or cereal crumbs
1¼ cups finely chopped onion
Salt and pepper
1 egg, beaten
½ cup corn oil
1 cup diced celery
½ pound canned crab meat
½ pound shelled and deveined shrimp
2 cups chicken broth
2 cups cooked rice
2 tablespoons curry powder

Preheat oven to 350°F.

Mix the meat, bread crumbs, ¼ cup onion, salt, and pepper; bind with egg. Shape into small balls, size of a walnut; leave in cold place about 40 minutes.

Heat 2 tablespoons oil in skillet; sauté rest of onion and celery. Put into large casserole.

Heat a little more oil in skillet; sauté crab meat and shrimp 2 to 3 minutes. Put into casserole with onion and celery.

Brown meat balls; add to other ingredients in casserole.

Put broth into skillet with rice, curry powder, and any remaining oil; bring to boil. Pour over contents of casserole; stir to mix ingredients together. Cover; cook about ½ hour. Yield 6 servings.

noodles and ham

3 tablespoons butter
2 tablespoons all-purpose white flour
1 cup light cream
1 cup shredded cheddar cheese
1 tablespoon prepared horseradish
1 cup cooked peas
2 cups diced cooked ham
1½ cups cooked noodles
¼ cup dry bread crumbs

Melt 2 tablespoons butter in saucepan. Blend flour into melted butter to form paste. Add cream, stirring constantly until smooth, thick sauce forms. Add cheese; stir sauce until cheese melts. Add horseradish, peas, ham, and noodles; blend well. Pour mixture into greased 1-quart casserole. Top with bread crumbs; dot with 1 tablespoon butter. Bake in 350°F oven 30 minutes or until thoroughly heated. Yield 4 servings.

osso-bucco casserole

4 meaty slices veal shin, 2 to 3 inches thick
¼ cup flour
Salt and pepper
2½ tablespoons olive oil
1½ tablespoons butter
1 medium onion, sliced fine
3 stalks celery, sliced fine
1 or 2 cloves garlic, crushed
2 tablespoons tomato puree
½ cup veal or chicken stock

½ cup dry white wine
½ tablespoon chopped basil and lemon thyme
1½ tablespoons chopped parsley
½ lemon

Preheat oven to 350°F.

Add salt and pepper to flour; coat pieces of meat with it.

Heat oil in skillet; add butter. When foaming, put in meat; lightly brown all over. Remove with slotted spoon; keep warm in casserole.

Lightly brown onion, celery, and garlic. Add tomato puree, stock, and wine to vegetables; season to taste. Pour mixture over meat. Put casserole with tight-fitting lid into oven 1½ to 2 hours. After about 1 hour add half the herbs and a few fine strips of lemon rind. Cook an hour or so. Test meat; if not completely done, cook until tender.

Transfer meat and vegetables to serving platter with slotted spoon.

Boil up sauce to reduce slightly. Add lemon juice to taste; pour over meat. Sprinkle top with remaining chopped parsley. Serve with boiled pasta or rice. Yield 4 servings.

pantry-shelf ham-and-vegetable casserole

1 (10½-ounce) can condensed cream of chicken soup
1 (5-ounce) can chopped chicken
½ cup diced cooked ham
1 (8¼-ounce) can pearl onions
1 (7½-ounce) can baby carrots
1 (8¼-ounce) can cut green asparagus
¼ cup fine dry bread crumbs
1 tablespoon butter or margarine, melted

Put enough soup in small greased casserole to cover bottom. Add layers of chicken, ham, onions, carrots, and asparagus (use half of each). Repeat, using remaining half of meat and vegetables. Pour remaining soup over mixture.

Mix crumbs with butter; sprinkle over top of mixture.

Bake at 400°F until mixture bubbles and crumbs are brown, about 45 minutes. Yield 4 servings.

paprika goulash

1½ pounds beef chuck or round
3 tablespoons oil
3 medium onions, peeled, sliced
2 tablespoons paprika
2 tablespoons flour
2 teaspoons tomato puree
2 cups beef bouillon
Bouquet Garni (see Index)
Salt and pepper
1 clove garlic, crushed
1 red or green pepper
2 or 3 tomatoes, peeled, sliced
6 tablespoons sour cream

Preheat oven to 325°F.

Cut meat into cubes.

Heat oil in skillet. Brown meat over fairly high heat; transfer to casserole.

Reduce the heat in skillet; sauté onions in remaining oil. Add paprika, flour, tomato puree, and bouillon; stir until boiling. Pour over meat in casserole. Add bouquet garni, seasonings, and garlic. Cover; cook about 1¾ hours.

Blanch pepper 2 minutes. Split; remove seeds. Cut into strips. Add with tomatoes to casserole; cook 15 minutes.

Just before serving, stir in sour cream and adjust seasoning. Serve with noodles. Yield 4 servings.

persian lamb-and-apricot pilau

½ cup butter
1 onion
1½ to 2 pounds lean lamb, cubed
4 tablespoons seedless raisins
1 cup dried apricots, halved

½ teaspoon ground cinnamon
½ teaspoon chopped thyme
Salt and pepper
2 cups long-grain rice
2 tablespoons almonds, peeled, shredded

Preheat oven to 320°F.

Melt half the butter in pan; cook onion until soft and golden brown. Add meat; brown all over slowly. Add raisins and apricots. Sprinkle with cinnamon, thyme, salt, and pepper. Pour over cold water barely to cover meat. Cover; cook gently in oven about 1½ hours. When meat is tender, if there seems to be too much liquid, boil to reduce quantity.

Boil rice in usual way 10 to 12 minutes, or follow package instructions; drain well.

Melt remaining butter; stir into rice before drying over gentle heat. Arrange rice and meat in layers in casserole. Bake 15 to 20 minutes.

Lightly brown almonds in oven. Sprinkle on top of dish; serve hot. Yield 4 to 6 servings.

pork-chop and rice casserole

tomato sauce
¼ cup vegetable oil
3 medium ripe tomatoes, sliced
2 medium onions, chopped
2 garlic cloves, minced
½ teaspoon salt
¼ teaspoon white pepper

¼ teaspoon dried oregano leaves

Heat oil in frypan; sauté tomatoes, onions, and garlic about 5 minutes, stirring constantly. Season with salt, pepper, and oregano. Cover; simmer tomatoes in their own juices about 20 minutes. Strain through sieve; return puree to frypan. Cook until liquid is reduced to two-thirds; stir frequently. Set aside.

rice
1 cup uncooked long-grain rice
Water and salt (according to package directions)

Cook rice in large amount of boiling salted water. Drain; rinse in cool water. Set aside.

chops
4 pork chops
½ teaspoon salt
¼ teaspoon white pepper
¼ teaspoon paprika
2 tablespoons vegetable oil
Margarine to grease casserole
3 tablespoons grated Emmenthal or Swiss cheese
1 tablespoon butter

Season pork with salt, pepper, and paprika.

Heat oil in frypan. Add chops; fry 5 minutes on each side.

Generously grease ovenproof casserole. Cover bottom with half the rice; pour half the tomato sauce over rice. Arrange 2 pork chops on top; sprinkle with half the grated cheese. Repeat layers; dot with butter. Place in preheated 350°F oven; bake 30 to 40 minutes. Yield 4 servings.

pork-chops and rice casserole

pork-and-vegetable casserole

pork-and-vegetable casserole

2 tablespoons vegetable oil
1 pound lean pork, cut into bite-size pieces
1 medium onion, chopped
2 pounds green cabbage, finely shredded
3 medium potatoes, peeled, cut into 1-inch cubes
1½ cups hot beef bouillon
½ teaspoon salt
⅛ teaspoon pepper
½ teaspoon caraway seeds
1 sprig parsley, chopped

Heat oil in Dutch oven. Add meat; brown on all sides about 10 minutes. Add onion; sauté lightly. Stir in cabbage and potatoes. Add bouillon; season with salt, pepper, and caraway seeds. Cover; simmer 50 minutes. Correct seasonings if necessary. Serve garnished with chopped parsley. Yield 4 servings.

sausage-and-apple casserole

8 cups cubed white bread (about 15 slices)
1 pound country sausage
1 large onion, diced
1 green pepper, diced
½ cup water
2 large apples, pared, cored, chopped
1 teaspoon salt

Use stale white bread for cubes, or dry them by putting in 250°F oven 10 minutes.

Brown sausage in large skillet. Cook until no trace of pink is in meat. Add onion and pepper; cook 2 minutes. Stir in bread cubes, water, apples, and salt. Mix together until all is evenly moist. Turn mixture into well-greased casserole. Cook in 350°F oven 30 minutes or until top crusts. Yield 4 to 6 servings.

sausage-and-rice casserole

2½ cups milk
1 teaspoon saffron shreds
24 pure-pork sausage links
4 cups thin lengthwise-sliced onions
1¼ cups long-grain rice
Salt and freshly ground pepper to taste
2 bay leaves
1¼ cups water

Heat ½ cup milk in small saucepan until warm. Sprinkle with saffron; let steep 30 minutes.

Place sausages on broiling rack in a pan. Bake 20 minutes at 350°F. Turn; bake 15 minutes.

Spread 1 cup onions in large casserole. Arrange 6 sausages over onions; sprinkle with ¼ of rice. Season with salt and pepper. Repeat layers; add 1 bay leaf. Repeat layers 2 more times, adding remaining bay leaf.

Strain saffron from milk. Combine saffron-flavored milk, remaining milk, and water. Pour over rice to cover.

Bake, covered, in preheated 325°F oven 1 hour. Stir rice mixture before serving, if desired. One tablespoon saffron, if desired. Yield about 8 servings.

seven-layer casserole

1 cup uncooked rice
1 cup cooked or canned whole-kernel corn
Salt and pepper to taste
2 cups (15-ounce can) tomato sauce
¾ cup water
½ cup finely chopped onion
½ cup chopped green pepper
1 cup cooked or canned green beans
¾ pound ground beef
4 slices bacon, cut up

Put rice and corn in baking pan or dish. Sprinkle with salt and pepper.

Mix tomato sauce and water. Pour half over corn and rice. Add layers of onion, green pepper, green beans, and beef. Sprinkle with salt and pepper. Add rest of tomato-mixture, Top with bacon. Cover tightly.

Bake at 350°F 1 hour. Uncover; cook 30 minutes. Yield 4 to 6 servings.

sausage-and-rice casserole

shepherd's pie casserole

1 cup peeled, sliced carrots
1 medium onion, peeled, sliced
3 cups diced cooked roast lamb or beef
½ cup frozen peas, slightly thawed
Salt and pepper to taste
1 cup leftover gravy (or 1 cup canned gravy)
2 cups thick mashed potatoes
1 egg
2 tablespoons milk

Place carrots in small saucepan; barely cover with water. Cook until fork-tender; drain.

Meanwhile, in separate saucepan cook onion, barely covered with water, until tender; drain.

Combine lamb, vegetables, salt, and pepper in 2-quart casserole; mix well.

Heat gravy; thin with boiling water if very thick. Pour over meat and vegetables; stir to combine. Bake, uncovered, at 350°F 20 minutes.

Place potatoes in pastry bag; pipe over top of meat mixture. (Can mound over top of casserole with spoon.)

Beat egg and milk together; brush potatoes with mixture. Return to oven; bake 20 minutes. Turn on broiler unit; cook until potatoes are lightly browned. Serve hot. Yield 4 servings.

stove-top split-pea casserole

1 pound ground beef
1 small onion, chopped
2 cups cooked or canned tomatoes
½ cup uncooked rice
½ cup water
1 tablespoon sugar
2½ cups cooked split peas
Salt and pepper to taste

Put ground beef and onion in pan. Cook until meat is browned; drain off fat. Add tomatoes, rice, water, and sugar. Cover; boil gently about 25 minutes, until rice is tender. Add split peas, salt, and pepper. Heat slowly until hot. Yield 4 to 6 servings.

veal casserole

2 pounds veal shoulder
¼ cup flour
Salt and pepper
¼ cup oil
1 large onion, peeled, chopped
2 carrots, peeled, chopped
2 stalks celery, cut diagonally
1 sprig parsley
¼ teaspoon each oregano, basil, and rosemary, all tied in piece of cheesecloth
1 cup chicken broth
¼ cup dry white wine
2 tomatoes, peeled, chopped
1 clove garlic, crushed
1 tablespoon chopped parsley
1 teaspoon grated lemon rind
1 tablespoon lemon juice

Preheat oven to 350°F.

Cut veal into 2-inch cubes; dredge with flour mixed with a little salt and pepper.

Heat oil in skillet. Brown meat, few pieces at a

time; add extra oil as required. As meat is browned, remove to casserole.

Sauté onion, carrots, and celery in remaining oil. Sprinkle over meat. Add herbs, broth, wine, tomatoes, and garlic. Cook 2 to 3 minutes; pour over meat. Cover; cook about 1½ hours.

About 20 minutes before end of cooking, uncover; adjust seasoning. Stir in parsley, lemon rind, and lemon juice. Remove bag of herbs before serving. Yield 5 to 6 servings.

veal-and-ham casserole

1½ pounds veal fillet, cut into thin slices
1½ cups bread crumbs
1 egg
½ cup milk
2 tablespoons oil
3 tablespoons butter
1 pound cooked ham, sliced thin
3 cups sliced mushrooms
2 cans (about 8 ounces each) tomato sauce
¾ cup chicken broth
2 to 3 tablespoons blanched almonds
Salt and pepper
1 teaspoon oregano
¼ teaspoon powdered mace
¼ teaspoon thyme
¼ teaspoon rosemary

Preheat oven to 300°F.

Pound veal slices thin; coat with bread crumbs. Dip in egg and milk; coat again with bread crumbs.

Heat oil and butter in sauté pan; cook veal until crisp and golden. Remove to deep casserole with a slotted spoon.

Crisp ham in same pan; add to veal.

Sauté mushrooms in remaining fat about 5 minutes; add a little extra butter if necessary. Add tomato sauce, broth, and almonds; stir well. Add seasonings and herbs. Simmer about 10 minutes; pour into casserole. Cover; cook about 1¼ hours. Adjust seasoning. Serve with noodles or wild rice. Yield 7 or 8 servings.

MEATLESS

baked macaroni and cheese

1½ teaspoons salt
4 cups (1 quart) water
1½ cups uncooked elbow macaroni
1 or 2 cups (as desired) shredded sharp natural
   cheddar cheese
1 or 2 cups (as desired) shredded process cheddar
   cheese
2 eggs, beaten
2 cups milk, whole or skim
1 teaspoon finely chopped onion

¼ teaspoon white pepper (optional)
¼ cup cornflake crumbs

Add 1 teaspoon salt to water; bring to boil. Add macaroni; cook uncovered, stirring occasionally, until almost tender, about 6 minutes; drain.

Preheat oven to 350°F.

Grease 1½-quart casserole. Cover bottom of casserole with half the macaroni.

Combine cheeses; sprinkle half of mixture over macaroni in casserole. Repeat layers.

Combine eggs with milk, onion, ½ teaspoon salt, and pepper. Pour over macaroni and cheese. Sprinkle top with cornflake crumbs. Set casserole in pan of hot water.

Bake 45 minutes to 1 hour, until browned and almost set in center. Let cool 10 minutes before serving, to allow mixture to set. Yield 6 servings.

baked macaroni in four cheeses

1 pound elbow macaroni
⅛ pound mozzarella cheese
⅛ pound sharp cheddar cheese
⅛ pound swiss cheese
4 tablespoons grated Romano or Parmesan cheese
¼ pound melted butter

Cook macaroni until barely tender; drain. Save ½ cup water. Put macaroni in buttered baking dish.

Cut cheddar and swiss cheeses into small slivers; mix together. Add to macaroni; toss lightly. Mix butter and hot water together; pour over macaroni. Sprinkle with grated cheese. Bake about 15 minutes in 400°F oven. Yield 4 to 6 servings.

baked spaghetti

½ pound spaghetti
2 tablespoons butter or margarine
1½ tablespoons chopped onion
1½ tablespoons chopped green pepper
2 cups canned or stewed tomatoes
1 teaspoon salt
¼ teaspoon pepper
⅛ teaspoon paprika
1 tablespoon sugar
1 cup grated cheese

Boil spaghetti in salted water until tender; drain.

Melt butter in pan; sauté onion and green pepper until soft. Add tomatoes, salt, pepper, paprika, and sugar; simmer 10 minutes. Add spaghetti; mix well. Add ½ cup cheese. Turn into greased baking dish. Sprinkle with remaining cheese. Bake in 400°F oven until cheese is brown, 20 to 25 minutes.

As a variation this dish can be made by adding ground sausage meat or ham. Yield 6 servings.

banana casserole

6 ripe bananas
½ cup orange sections
⅓ cup sugar
2 tablespoons orange juice
2 tablespoons lemon juice
Pinch of salt

Peel bananas; cut lengthwise. Place in buttered dish.

Remove membrane from oranges; arrange oranges on top of bananas. Sprinkle sugar over bananas. Add juices, to which salt has been added.

Bake at 300 to 350°F 30 to 45 minutes. Serve as an accompaniment to pork, ham, or game. Yield 4 to 6 servings.

broccoli casserole

1 (10-ounce) package frozen broccoli
1¼ cups milk
3 eggs, lightly beaten
½ teaspoon salt
½ teaspoon nutmeg
½ cup grated cheese

Preheat oven to 350°F.

Cook broccoli in small amount boiling water 3 minutes; drain.

Pour milk into small saucepan; bring to boil. Cool to lukewarm.

Mix eggs with salt and nutmeg. Add milk and cheese, beating constantly. Pour into greased baking dish; add broccoli.

Bake 30 to 40 minutes or until knife inserted in center comes out clean. Must be served hot. Yield 4 servings.

broccoli–nut casserole

1½ cups uncooked brown rice
3 cups water
½ teaspoon salt
1 large onion, chopped
2 cloves garlic, minced
½ teaspoon each dill and thyme
1 teaspoon oregano
½ bunch parsley, minced
½ pound mushrooms, sliced
1 green pepper, seeded, sliced
1 bunch (2 pounds) broccoli
2 to 3 tablespoons peanut or corn oil
½ cup cashews
½ pound Swiss or Gruyere cheese
2 tablespoons grated Parmesan cheese

Put rice in heavy saucepan with tight-fitting lid. Add water and salt. Bring to rapid boil; stir once. Reduce heat; simmer, covered, 45 minutes or until all water is absorbed.

Meanwhile prepare all vegetables and herbs. Trim broccoli of leaves and tough ends. Cut off florets; slice stems into ½-inch slivers.

Heat oil in large frying pan. Add onion, garlic, and herbs (except parsley). Sauté until onions begin to get soft. Add parsley; stir in well. Add mushrooms, pepper, and broccoli. Cook until broccoli is deep green; stir frequently. Remove from heat; toss in nuts.

Preheat oven to 350°F.

Spread rice in an oiled casserole. Cover with vegetable-nut mixture; sprinkle with cheeses. Bake 15 minutes, until bubbly. Yield 8 servings.

carrot casserole

3 cups sliced cooked carrots
1 (10½-ounce) can condensed cream of celery soup

broccoli cass

1 cup or 4 ounces shredded process cheddar cheese
¼ cup fine dry bread crumbs
1 tablespoon butter or margarine, melted

Preheat oven to 350°F.

Mix carrots, soup, and cheese together in baking dish.

Mix bread crumbs and butter. Sprinkle on carrot mixture. Bake about 20 minutes or until crumbs are brown. Yield 6 servings.

carrot, prune, and potato tzimmes casserole

1 onion, chopped
4 tablespoons chicken fat
1 pound brisket of beef
1 pound tenderized prunes
3 cups water
5 carrots
4 sweet potatoes
½ cup honey
1 teaspoon salt
1 tablespoon lemon juice
2 tablespoons potato flour

Sauté onion in 2 tablespoons fat.

Heat a pot; sear meat on all sides, turning until brown. Cover bottom of pot with sautéed onions. Add meat, prunes, and water. Cook 1 hour on low heat, covered.

Scrape carrots. Wash; slice into thin rounds.

Pare sweet potatoes; cut into thick rounds. Add carrots and potatoes to meat and prunes, distributing well around meat. Add honey, salt, and lemon juice; cook until tender. Shake pot gently from time to time, but do not stir. Water can be added to prevent sticking.

Make thickening by browning potato flour in 2 tablespoons melted fat, adding ¼ cup liquid from meat-and vegetable combination. Stir until smooth, cooking over moderate heat about 5 minutes. Turn thickening into the tzimmes; shake pot gently. Turn whole contents into casserole. Cover; bake in 350°F oven 2 hours. Remove cover for last ½ hour to brown top. Do not mash vegetables. Tzimmes is not attractive if "mushy." Yield 6 to 8 servings.

cauliflower casserole

1 medium heat cauliflower
Salt and pepper to taste
1 cup sour cream
1 cup shredded American cheese
Toasted sesame seeds

Rinse cauliflower; break into florets. Cook, covered, in small amount boiling salted water until tender, 10 to 15 minutes. Drain well. Place half of cauliflower in 1-quart buttered casserole; season with salt and pepper. Spread with ½ cup sour cream; sprinkle with ½ cup cheese. Top with 1 teaspoon toasted sesame seeds. Repeat layers.

Bake in 350°F oven until cheese melts and sour cream is heated through, about 5 minutes. If made ahead, allow more time to heat. Yield 6 servings.

Note: To toast sesame seeds, place in shallow pan in 350°F oven 10 minutes or until brown, shaking occasionally.

celery-and-cheese casserole

3 cups diagonally sliced fresh celery
3 tablespoons butter
¼ cup water
½ teaspoon crumbled dried tarragon leaves
2 tablespoons all-purpose flour
Salt to taste
½ cup milk
1 can cream of chicken soup
½ cup grated cheddar cheese
¼ teaspoon paprika

Combine celery, 1 tablespoon butter, water, and tarragon in large saucepan; bring to boil.

celery-and-cheese casserole

183

cheese yorkshire-pudding casserole

Reduce heat; simmer, covered, 10 minutes. Turn celery mixture into buttered 2-quart casserole.

Melt 2 tablespoons butter in same saucepan over medium heat. Stir in flour and salt; cook, stirring constantly, until lightly browned. Add milk gradually; cook, stirring constantly, until mixture is smooth and thick. Stir in soup; heat through. Add cheese; stir until melted. Pour over celery mixture, blending lightly; sprinkle with paprika.

Bake in preheated 350°F oven 15 minutes or until heated through and bubbly. Yield 6 to 8 servings.

cheese-and-olive casserole

2 cups bread, broken into pieces
3 tablespoons melted butter
1 cup grated cheese
½ cup sliced stuffed olives
3 beaten eggs
1 teaspoon mustard
¼ cup liquid from olives
2 cups hot milk

Stir bread in 2 tablespoons butter until well coated.

Line bottom of greased baking dish with ⅔ cup buttered bread. Add layer of ½ cup cheese, then ¼ cup olives. Repeat layers of bread, cheese, and olives. Top with remaining bread; brush with remaining butter.

Mix eggs, mustard, liquid from olives, and milk, blending well. Pour over mixture in dish. Bake in 350°F oven 35 to 45 minutes. Yield 6 servings.

cheese pilaf

This is a good accompaniment to roast duck or chicken.

2 tablespoons butter or margarine
1 tablespoon oil
1 clove garlic
1 cup long-grain uncooked rice
2 cups chicken bouillon
¼ cup grated Parmesan cheese

Preheat oven to 350°F.

Heat butter and oil in sauté pan. Add garlic, crushed finely with a little salt, and rice. Sauté until rice begins to color. Pour contents of sauté pan into casserole. Add bouillon; cover. Bake about 25 to 30 minutes or until liquid has been absorbed. Remove from oven. Add cheese; stir with fork until melted and well mixed with rice. This is a good accompaniment to roast duck or chicken.

For variety, some seedless raisins, seeded black or white grapes, or strips of blanched red or green pepper can be stirred into rice with the cheese. Yield 4 servings.

cheese yorkshire-pudding casserole

2 eggs
1 cup milk
3 tablespoons bacon or roast drippings
1 cup sifted all-purpose flour
½ teaspoon salt
1 cup finely grated Gruyere cheese

Beat eggs in medium-size mixing bowl until very thick and lemon-colored. Add milk gradually. Add drippings; blend thoroughly. Add flour and salt gradually; beat until smooth. Fold in half of cheese. Pour into well-greased 1-quart baking dish; sprinkle remaining cheese over top.

Bake in preheated 450°F oven 25 minutes or until golden brown. Serve immediately. Yield 4 to 6 servings.

cheesy onion casserole

6 cups onion rings, sliced thin
¼ cup butter or margarine
¼ cup flour
2 cups milk
1 teaspoon garlic salt
½ teaspoon celery salt
2 cups grated cheddar cheese

Place onion in 2-quart casserole.

Melt butter in saucepan; blend in flour. Slowly stir in milk; cook until thick. Keep flame low. Stir in seasonings and cheese. Pour over onions. Bake, uncovered, at 350°F 1 hour. Yield 6 servings.

colcannon casserole

4 large potatoes, peeled, roughly chopped
2 parsnips or small turnips, peeled, roughly chopped
1 cup cooked well-drained cabbage or kale
2 small onions, peeled, finely chopped
⅔ cup milk
2 tablespoons margarine
2 egg whites
½ cup grated cheese

Preheat oven to 350°F.

Cook potatoes and parsnips together in boiling salted water until tender; drain well. Mash; mix with cabbage.

While potatoes are cooking, cook onions in milk until soft. Mix with other vegetables; season with salt and pepper. Add margarine; pour into greased casserole.

Beat egg whites until stiff; fold in cheese. Pile on top of vegetables. Bake 20 to 25 minutes or until well browned. Yield 4 to 5 servings.

eggplant casserole

2 cups pared, cubed eggplant
2 tablespoons finely chopped onion
¼ cup water
2 eggs, slightly beaten
2 slices soft bread, torn into very small pieces
½ cup milk
1 teaspoon salt
Pepper to taste
1¼ cups shredded sharp cheddar cheese

Cook eggplant and onion in unsalted water until eggplant is tender, about 7 minutes; drain.

Combine all ingredients except ¼ cup cheese; mix well. Pour into greased 1-quart casserole.

Bake uncovered at 350°F 25 minutes. Sprinkle with remaining cheese; bake 5 minutes. Yield 6 servings.

eggplant–tomato casserole

1 large onion, chopped
2 small eggplants, peeled, diced
¼ cup butter or margarine
1 (28-ounce) can tomatoes, drained
1 teaspoon salt
⅛ teaspoon pepper
¼ cup cornflake crumbs

Preheat oven to 350°F.

Cook onion and eggplant in butter until golden brown. Add tomatoes, salt, and pepper; mix thoroughly. Pour into casserole; top with crumbs. Bake 30 minutes. Yield 6 servings.

fresh tomato–corn casserole

6 medium fresh tomatoes
½ cup chopped fresh celery
½ cup chopped fresh green sweet pepper
½ cup chopped fresh onion
Salt to taste
2 cups fresh corn, cut from cob
3 hard-boiled eggs, sliced
2 cups Basic White Sauce (see Index)

Peel and chop 5 tomatoes; place in saucepan. Add celery, pepper, and onion. Cook, stirring occasionally, 15 minutes. Stir in salt. Place half the mixture in casserole; add half the corn. Arrange egg slices over corn; add half the white sauce. Add remaining tomato mixture; add remaining corn. Cover with remaining white sauce. Bake in preheated 350°F oven about 45 minutes or until set.

Slice remaining tomato; arrange on casserole. Broil until tomatoes are hot. Garnish with parsley. Yield 6 servings.

fresh tomato-corn casserole

hot fruit casserole

1 (16-ounce) can applesauce
1 (16-ounce) can apricot halves, drained
1 (16-ounce) can pear halves, drained
1 (16-ounce) can sliced peaches, drained
1 (16-ounce) can white cherries, drained, pitted
1 (16-ounce) can pineapple chunks, drained
¼ pound brown sugar
¾ stick butter
Cinnamon
Nutmeg

Arrange fruit in layers in buttered 3-quart casserole. Sprinkle each layer with brown sugar, cinnamon, and nutmeg; dot with butter. Bake in 300°F oven about 30 minutes. Yield 10 to 12 servings.

impromptu casserole

1 (1-pound) can French-cut green beans, drained
1 (1-pound) can bean sprouts, drained
1 (5-ounce) can water chestnuts, drained, sliced
1 (4-ounce) can sliced mushrooms, drained
¼ cup Parmesan cheese
3 tablespoons butter, melted
1 (8-ounce) can tomato sauce

½ teaspoon salt
1 (3½-ounce) can French-fried onion rings

Toss vegetables with cheese in 8 × 12-inch shallow baking dish. Sprinkle with melted butter.

Combine tomato sauce and salt; pour over vegetables. Sprinkle onion rings on top. Bake at 325°F 20 minutes. Yield 6 servings.

lasagna-and-cheese casserole

½ cup seedless raisins
1 to 2 tablespoons rum
1 package (½-pound) lasagna
1 cup sour cream
1 cup cottage cheese
2 to 3 tablespoons blanched, slivered almonds

Preheat oven to 350°F.

Soak the raisins in rum.

Cook noodles in boiling salted water until just tender. Drain; rinse with cold water. Drain agian; put into deep buttered casserole. Sprinkle with a little salt and pepper.

Mix sour cream with cottage cheese and raisins. Pour over noodles; toss together lightly. Sprinkle with almonds; bake about 20 minutes. Yield 4 servings.

lasagna-and-cheese casserole

lima-bean casserole

¼ pound smoked slab bacon, diced
1 tablespoon melted butter or margarine
6 small white onions, chopped
¾ cup fresh or frozen sliced carrots
3 (10-ounce) packages frozen Fordhook lima
    beans
1½ teaspoons salt
Dash of sifted confectioners' sugar
2 cups boiling water
2 cloves garlic, crushed
Bouquet Garni (see Index)

Saute bacon in large skillet until brown; add butter. Sauté onions with bacon in butter and pan drippings about 1 minute. Add carrots; sauté 3 to 4 minutes. Add lima beans, salt, sugar, and water. Turn into 2-quart casserole; add garlic. Stir gently until mixed well. Place Bouquet Garni in mixture.

Bake at 350°F about 1 hour or until carrots and onions are tender. Remove Bouquet Garni. Decorate with canned tomato wedges, if desired; serve immediately. Yield 10 to 12 servings.

macaroni casserole with eggplant

1 eggplant (1 pound)
4 medium tomatoes
5 tablespoons oil
2 cloves garlic, chopped
½ teaspoon salt
¼ teaspoon pepper
1 stick cinnamon
¼ teaspoon allspice
½ cup red wine
3 tablespoons tomato paste
8 ounces whole or elbow macaroni
3 quarts boiling salted water
3 tablespoons olive oil
1 pound meat-loaf mixture
2 medium onions, chopped
¼ cup grated Kafaloteri cheese
2 tablespoons butter

Wash eggplant; dice into 1-inch cubes.
Peel and quarter tomatoes.
Heat 5 tablespoons oil in large skillet. Sauté eggplant, tomatoes, and garlic 5 minutes; sitr occasionally to prevent sticking. Add salt, pepper, cinnamon, allspice, wine, and tomato paste; simmer 15 minutes.

Meanwhile, cook macaroni in water until done. Drain; rinse in warm water.

Heat 3 tablespoons oil. Brown meat and onions. Combine with vegetable mixture. Remove cinnamon stick.

Grease a 13 × 9 × 2-inch casserole. Place macaroni in casserole. Add half of cheese; mix. Top

lima-bean casserole

with vegetable mixture and remaining cheese; dot with butter. Bake at 350°F 30 minutes. Yield 6 servings.

macaroni-and-cheese casserole

1 (1-pound) box elbow macaroni
1 (1-pound) can whole tomatoes
1 small onion, grated
1 clove garlic, minced
¼ green pepper, chopped
Salt and pepper
2 cups grated sharp cheddar cheese
Butter

Cook macaroni until tender. Drain; set aside.
In saucepan combine tomatoes, onion, garlic, green pepper, and seasonings. Simmer until green pepper and onion are soft. Grease large oblong baking dish with butter. Alternate layers of macaroni, cheese, and tomatoes. Season between layers. Bake at 350°F 1 hour, until brown on top. Yield 8 servings.

noodle kugel

1 package medium noodles
¼ pound cream cheese
¼ pound butter
½ pint sour cream
Seasoned salt
Pepper
¼ cup sugar
4 eggs, beaten
Cornflake crumbs

Cook noodles; drain. Run water over them. Dissolve cream cheese in noodles. Add butter, sour cream, seasonings, and sugar. Mix in eggs; sprinkle top with cornflake crumbs. Dot with pats of butter. Bake at 350°F in greased 8- or 9-inch-square pan 1½ to 2 hours. Yield 6 servings.

noodle kugel with fruit

½ **pound broad noodles**
1 **No. 1 can crushed pineapple**
1 **apple, grated**
1 **cup cottage cheese**
¾ **stick melted butter or margarine**
2 **eggs, beaten**
2 **tablespoons lemon juice**
1 **cup white raisins**
½ **cup sugar**
1½ **teaspoons cinnamon (optional)**
1 **cup sour cream**
1 **teaspoon salt**

macaroni casserole with eggplant

Boil and drain noodles. Stir with other ingredients. Place in well-greased, shallow, heavy casserole. Bake at 350°F about ¾ hour. Yield 6 to 8 servings.

noodles-romanoff casserole

1 **package (5 or 6 ounces) fine noodles**
1 **cup cottage cheese**
1 **cup sour cream**
1 **small onion, peeled, chopped**
1 **teaspoon Worcestershire sauce**
Dash of Tabasco

noodles-romanoff casserole

Paprika

½ **cup grated sharp cheese**

Preheat oven to 350°F.

Cook noodles in boiling salted water about 6 minutes; drain well.

Mix well all ingredients except grated cheese; put into greased casserole. Sprinkle with cheese. Bake about 40 minutes. Yield 4 to 5 servings.

onion–peanut casserole

2 pounds onion
3 tablespoons butter
3 tablespoons flour
1½ cups milk
½ teaspoon salt
2 teaspoons prepared mustard
1 teaspoon Worcestershire sauce
½ cup chopped salted peanuts

Boil onions in salted water until tender. Arrange in baking dish.

Melt butter; stir in flour. Add milk; stir until thick. Add salt, mustard, and Worcestershire; pour over onions. Sprinkle with peanuts. Bake in 350°F oven 10 to 15 minutes. Yield 4 servings.

pea-pod casserole

1 package frozen pea pods, boiled
1 can water chestnuts, sliced
1 can bean sprouts, or fresh bean sprouts
1 can cream of mushroom soup
1 can onion rings (optional)

Boil pea pods 2 minutes; drain. Place in casserole. Place water chestnuts on pea pods. Next place layer of bean sprouts. If canned bean sprouts are used, drain. If fresh are used, first blanch, then rinse with cold water; drain well. Cover with cream of mushroom soup.

Bake 15 minutes at 350°F. Place onion rings on top; heat about 2 or 3 minutes. Yield 4 servings.

potato-kugel casserole

8 to 10 potatoes
2 onions
2 heaping tablespoons chicken fat, melted but cool
3 eggs, beaten
Salt and ground pepper to taste

Peel potatoes. Wash in cold water; dry well. Grate potatoes and onions into mixing bowl. Combine all ingredients; blend well. Pour mixture into greased 3-quart casserole. Bake 2 hours in preheated 350°F oven. Cut in squares. Yield 6 to 8 servings.

onion–peanut casserole

spinach–artichoke casserole

1 (6-ounce) can whole mushrooms, drained
1 can mushroom pieces, drained
6 tablespoons butter
1 tablespoon flour
½ cup milk
½ teaspoon salt
Dash of pepper
1 (1-pound) can artichoke hearts, drained
2 (10-ounce) packages frozen chopped spinach,
   cooked

Sauté mushrooms in butter. Remove; separate whole crown and pieces.

Add flour to melted butter left in pan; cook until bubbly. Add milk; stir until smooth. Add salt, pepper, mushroom pieces and spinach.

Drain artichokes. Place in buttered casserole; cover with spinach mixture. Pour sour-cream sauce over casserole; top with mushroom crowns. Bake in 350°F oven about 30 minutes. Yield 8 servings.

Note: This can be frozen but do not freeze with Sour-Cream Sauce.

sour cream sauce
½ cup sour cream
2 tablespoons lemon juice
½ cup mayonnaise

Blend ingredients; heat. Pour on casserole.

spinach casserole niçoise

2 pounds spinach
1 tablespoon olive oil
1 clove garlic, minced
½ teaspoon salt
⅛ teaspoon pepper
⅛ teaspoon ground nutmeg
4 eggs
¼ cup heavy cream
Butter to grease dish
2 tablespoons dried bread crumbs
1 tablespoon butter

Thoroughly wash spinach; drain.

Heat oil in large Dutch oven or saucepan. Add garlic; cook 1 minute. Add spinach. Cover; steam 3 minutes. Season with salt, pepper, and nutmeg.

Beat eggs and cream in small bowl until well-blended. Stir in spinach.

Grease ovenproof dish with butter; spoon in spinach mixture. Sprinkle with bread crumbs; dot with butter. Place in preheated 425°F. Bake about 15 minutes or until lightly browned. Yield 6 to 8 servings.

squash casserole

2 pounds yellow summer squash
1 onion, minced
Salt and pepper to taste
1 can condensed cream of mushroom soup
1 cup fine dry bread crumbs
2 tablespoons butter

Slice squash. Add onion; cover with water. Cook until tender; drain. Season with salt and pepper. Put squash, undiluted soup, and crumbs in alternate layers in greased baking dish. Dot each layer with butter. End with crumbs on top. Bake in preheated 350°F oven 30 minutes. Yield 6 servings.

sweet-potato and banana casserole

4 medium sweet potatoes
4 tablespoons butter
1½ teaspoons salt
4 bananas, sliced
¾ cup brown sugar
¾ cup orange juice

Cook sweet potatoes in boiling water until tender but still firm; cool. Peel; slice ¼ inch thick. Place in buttered casserole in alternate layers potatoes dotted with butter and sprinkled with salt, and bananas sprinkled with brown sugar. End top layer with bananas, dotted with butter. Add orange juice. Bake in 350°F oven about 30 minutes or until the top is browned. Yield 6 servings.

spinach casserole nicoise

zucchini casserole provençale

3 medium zucchini, sliced into ovals on diagonal
1 large onion, sliced
3 large tomatoes, sliced
4 anchovy fillets, cut up
1 tablespoon capers
1 clove garlic, minced
1 teaspoon salt
Freshly ground black pepper to taste
2 tablespoons fresh basil, minced, or 2 teaspoons
    dried basil
½ cup freshly grated Parmesan or Romano cheese
Butter

Line lightly buttered ovenproof casserole with half of sliced zucchini, onion, and tomatoes. Top with half of anchovies, capers, garlic, salt, pepper, basil, and cheese. Dot with butter. Repeat layers. Dot with butter. Bake, uncovered, at 375°F 35 to 45 minutes, until zucchini is tender. Yield 6 servings.

zucchini–cheese casserole

½ cup uncooked long-grain white rice
½ cup chopped onion
¾ teaspoon salt
1 cup boiling water
½ cup water
1 pound (2 to 3 medium-size) sliced zucchini
    squash, sliced
1 (8-ounce) can tomato sauce
½ cup diced green pepper
1 cup or 4 ounces shredded sharp cheddar cheese

Add rice, onion, and ½ teaspoon salt to rapidly boiling water. Cover tightly; boil *gently* 20 minutes.

Bring ½ cup water to boiling. Add ¼ teaspoon salt and squash. Cook until squash is just tender, about 8 minutes; drain.

Preheat oven to 350°F.

Gently mix rice, squash, tomato sauce, and pepper. Pour mixture into 1½-quart casserole; sprinkle with cheese. Bake uncovered about 20 minutes. Yield 6 servings.

zucchini and cottage-cheese casserole

3 medium zucchini, sliced
¼ cup chopped onion
2 tablespoons vegetable oil
1 pound cottage cheese
1 teaspoon basil
⅓ cup Parmesan cheese

Preheat oven to 350°F.

Sauté zucchini and onion in oil.

Whip cottage cheese with basil in blender. Place alternating layers of zucchini and cheese in 1½-quart casserole. Top with Parmesan. Bake uncovered 25 to 30 minutes. Yield about 6 servings.

casserole of pigeons

2 to 4 young pigeons or squabs (depending on size)
3 tablespoons flour
Salt and pepper
¼ cup butter or margarine
1 onion, peeled, chopped
½ pound carrots, peeled, sliced
1 chicken bouillon cube, crumbled
1¼ cups water
3 or 4 tomatoes, peeled, sliced
1 bay leaf

Preheat oven to 325°F.

Split pigeons into halves; dredge with flour mixed with a little salt and pepper.

Heat butter in sauté pan. Brown pigeons on all sides; remove to casserole.

Add onion and carrots to pan; sauté in remaining fat. Put any remaining flour and bouillon cube into pan, add water; stir until boiling. Pour over contents of casserole. Add tomatoes and bay leaf. Cover; cook about 2 hours. Remove bay leaf and adjust seasoning before serving.

If pigeons are unavailable, use Cornish Hens. Yield 4 servings.

chicken and artichoke hearts

1 large onion
4 boned chicken breasts
Salt
1 stick butter
2½ teaspoons paprika
4 tablespoons flour
½ cup chicken stock
¾ cup sour cream
1 cup white wine
1 can artichoke hearts
5 slices crisp bacon (crumbled)
Slivered almonds
Salt to taste

Chop onion finely. Skin chicken; sprinkle with salt.

Heat butter in frying pan; brown chicken. Remove chicken from pan. Sauté onion and paprika in remaining butter; remove pan from heat. Stir in flour; return to heat. Gradually add stock; stir until mixture boils and thickens. Add sour cream and wine; simmer lightly.

Place chicken and drained artichoke hearts in ovenproof dish or casserole; top with sauce. Cover; bake at 350°F 1 hour. Top with bacon and almonds before serving. Yield 4 servings.

chicken and asparagus roll-ups

1 pound fresh asparagus
4 whole chicken breasts, split, skinned, pounded thin
2 tablespoons flour
1 clove garlic, minced
1 teaspoon salt
½ teaspoon dried leaf thyme
¼ teaspoon paprika
⅛ teaspoon pepper
2 cups sliced onions
3 large fresh tomatoes, sliced
½ cup chicken broth

Wash asparagus; break off each spear as far down as it snaps easily. Place 2 or 3 spears on each chicken breast. Roll; secure with food picks.

Combine flour, garlic, ½ teaspoon salt, ¼ teaspoon thyme, paprika, and pepper; mix well. Roll chicken breasts in mixture.

Place onions and tomatoes in bottom of 13 × 9 × 2-inch baking dish; reserve 8 slices of each. Place chicken breasts over sliced vegetables. Arrange reserved slices of tomato and onion over chicken.

Combine chicken broth and ½ teaspoon salt and ¼ teaspoon thyme. Pour over chicken and vegetables. Cover loosely with foil. Bake in 350°F oven 30 minutes; baste occasionally with juices in bottom of pan. Uncover; bake 15 minutes or until chicken and vegetables are tender. Yield 8 servings.

chicken breasts in sour cream

chicken barley casserole

2 cups chicken broth or bouillon
½ pound barley
3 tablespoons butter or margarine
1 small onion, chopped
½ pound mushrooms, sliced
1 cup bite-size pieces cooked chicken
½ cup plain yogurt
¾ cup shredded Monterey Jack cheese
2 tablespoons chopped parsley

Heat broth to boiling in large saucepan. Add barley; cover. Simmer about 45 minutes or until tender.

Meanwhile melt butter in frypan; sauté onion until transparent. Add mushrooms; sauté lightly just until juices appear. Remove from heat; set aside.

Combine chicken, yogurt, and ½ cup cheese.

When barley has finished cooking, remove from heat. Add mushroom and chicken mixtures. Transfer to large greased casserole dish. Sprinkle with remaining cheese and parsley. Bake in 350°F oven 50 minutes. Yield 4 to 6 servings.

chicken breasts in sour cream

1 package dried chipped beef
6 chicken breasts, boned, skinned, split
6 slices bacon, cut in half
2 cans condensed mushroom soup
1 pint sour cream

Chop beef finely; place in bottom of casserole dish.

Wrap each chicken piece with half of bacon slice. Place each piece on its own bed of chipped beef.

Mix together undiluted soup and sour cream; pour over chicken. Bake at 275°F 2½ to 3 hours.

Serve chicken on bed of hot rice or surround with Duchesse Potatoes (see Index). Yield 6 servings.

chicken casserole

½ cup butter or margarine
4 chicken breasts
Salt and pepper
1 can (about 15 ounces) artichoke hearts
1 onion, peeled, chopped
2 teaspoons paprika
3 tablespoons flour
½ cup water
1 chicken bouillon cube
½ cup sour cream
1 cup dry white wine

chicken casserole

2 or 3 slices bacon, fried, crumbled
Almond slivers, toasted

Preheat oven to 350°F.

Heat butter in sauté pan; put in chicken. Sprinkle with salt and pepper; brown on both sides. Put into casserole with drained artichokes.

Add onion and paprika to remaining fat; sauté until onion is soft. Remove from heat; stir in flour. Return to heat; cook 1 minute. Gradually add water, in which bouillon cube has been dissolved; stir until boiling. Remove from heat; add sour cream and wine. Reheat a few minutes without boiling; pour over chicken. Cover; cook about 1 hour. Before serving, sprinkle with bacon and almonds. Yield 4 servings.

chicken-cerise casserole

4 chicken joints
Salt
Paprika
½ cup butter or margarine
3 tablespoons flour
1 teaspoon sugar
¼ teaspoon each ground cloves and ground
   cinnamon
⅛ teaspoon dry mustard
1 large can (2 cups) cherries, drained
1 bouillon cube, crushed
1 small can (1 cup) crushed pineapple
Cooked rice

Preheat oven to 375°F.

Sprinkle chicken with salt and paprika.

Heat butter in skillet. Brown chicken on all sides; remove to casserole.

Combine flour, sugar, and spices with remaining fat; add cherry juice and bouillon cube. Stir until boiling and thickened; pour over chicken.

Cover; cook 30 minutes. Add cherries and pineapple; cook 30 minutes. Adjust seasoning. Serve on bed of rice sprinkled with parsley. Yield 4 servings.

chicken-cream casserole

4 cups cooked chicken
2 cups fresh bread crumbs
4 tablespoons butter
2 tablespoons flour
1 cup milk
¼ teaspoon ground mace or nutmeg
1 tablespoon chopped parsley
1 egg, beaten
Salt and pepper

Preheat oven to 375°F.

Grind chicken; mix with bread crumbs.

Make cream sauce: Melt 2 tablespoons butter; blend in flour. Add milk gradually. When smooth, bring to boil, stirring constantly. Boil 2 to 3 minutes; add mace or nutmeg and herbs. Let cool slightly.

Add sauce to chicken mixture, stir well, adding remaining butter and egg. Season well. Put in buttered fireproof dish; allow room for chicken cream to rise slightly. Cook in oven 30 to 35 minutes. Yield 4 to 6 servings.

chicken-peach casserole

1 frying chicken (about 3½ pounds) or 6 to 8
   chicken joints
2 tablespoons butter or margarine
1 tablespoon oil
1 large onion, peeled, sliced
1 green pepper, seeded, cut into strips
1 large can (about 30 ounces) sliced peaches

1 tablespoon cornstarch
1 tablespoon soy sauce
3 tablespoons white wine vinegar
2 tomatoes, peeled, thickly sliced

Preheat oven to 375°F.

Disjoint and skin chicken.

Heat butter and oil in skillet. Brown chicken pieces on all sides. Cover; reduce heat. Cook about 10 minutes. Remove chicken; arrange in large casserole.

Sauté onion and pepper in remaining fat until onion is transparent.

Drain peaches; reserve syrup.

Mix cornstarch smoothly with soy sauce and vinegar. Add 1 cup peach syrup. Pour into skillet. Stir until boiling; boil until clear. Add peaches and tomatoes. Pour skillet contents over chicken. Cover casserole; cook 30 to 40 minutes. Remove lid last 5 minutes. Adjust seasoning.

Serve with wild rice to which some cooked green peas and a few strips of red pepper have been added. Yield 6 servings.

chicken provençale

1 small stewing fowl
Salt and pepper
1 tablespoon cornstarch
¼ cup butter or margarine
3 small onions, peeled, halved
4 small carrots, peeled, quartered
1 clove garlic, crushed
4 tablespoons red wine

chicken provençale

1 cup chicken broth or water
Few black olives

Preheat oven to 325°F.

Cut fowl into neat pieces.

Mix salt and pepper with cornstarch; dredge chicken well.

Heat butter in sauté pan; brown chicken. Remove to casserole.

Add vegetables and garlic to remaining fat with any remaining cornstarch; cook a few minutes. Add wine and broth; stir until boiling. Pour over chicken. Cover tightly; cook 2½ to 3 hours. Just before serving, adjust seasoning and add olives.

If fowl is unobtainable, use 4-pound fryer. Yield 4 to 5 servings.

chicken-peach casserole

chicken–rice casserole

2½ to 3 pounds fryer-chicken parts
5 tablespoons butter or margarine
4 tablespoons olive oil
2 tablespoons sherry
1 small onion, chopped
1 green pepper, chopped
1 clove garlic, minced
1 cup raw long-grain rice
1½ cups chicken broth
1 bay leaf
½ teaspoon salt
¼ teaspoon pepper
Pinch of saffron
2 medium tomatoes, peeled, sliced
2 tablespoons Parmesan cheese

Wash chicken; pat dry.

Heat 4 tablespoons each butter and oil in large skillet over moderate heat. Brown chicken well on all sides. Pour sherry over chicken; remove chicken from pan.

Add onion, green pepper, and garlic to pan; sauté until golden. Add rice; sauté 2 minutes. Add chicken broth, bay leaf, salt, pepper, and saffron; bring to boil.

Grease 2-quart casserole. Pour in rice mixture; top with chicken. Cover casserole; bake at 350°F 45 minutes.

Sauté tomatoes in 1 tablespoon butter; place on chicken. Sprinkle with cheese; bake 15 minutes. Yield 4 servings.

chicken sorrento casserole

1 chicken (3 to 3½ pounds)
Flour
Salt and pepper
3 tablespoons oil
⅓ cup rice
1 large onion, peeled
1 orange cut in half, seeded, but not peeled
½ cup milk
1 cup water
3 tablespoons chopped pimiento
¼ teaspoon thyme
Pinch of sugar
Pinch of cayenne pepper

Preheat oven to 350°F.

Cut chicken into pieces; coat with flour to which a little salt and pepper have been added.

Heat oil in skillet. Brown chicken on all sides; remove.

Put rice into skillet; stir over low heat until brown.

Put onion and orange through food processor or grinder; use coarse blade. Mix in rice. Put mixture into casserole; arrange chicken on top. Add

chicken-sorrento casserole

milk, water, a little seasoning, and all other ingredients. Cover; cook in oven 1 to 1¼ hours. Adjust seasoning to taste before serving. Yield 5 or 6 servings.

chicken and taco-chips casserole

9 taco shells or 1 (12-ounce) bag taco chips
2 whole chicken breasts, cooked, chopped
1 (10½-ounce) can condensed chicken-and-rice soup
2 cups grated sharp cheddar cheese
1 (10-ounce) can tomatoes and green chilies

Crush taco shells or chips in bowl. Place layer of chips in bottom of greased 1-quart casserole. Sprinkle layer of chicken over chips. Pour several spoonfuls soup over chicken layer. Sprinkle with layer of cheese. Pour several spoonfuls tomato and green-chili mixture over cheese layer. Repeat layering process until all ingredients are used. Top casserole with additional grated cheese if desired. Bake 25 minutes at 350°F.

This can be prepared ahead and refrigerated before baking. It freezes well before and after baking. Yield 4 to 6 servings.

curried-chicken casserole

2 tablespoons butter or margarine
2 tablespoons oil
2 onions, peeled, sliced

1 large apple, peeled, cored, sliced
1 tablespoon curry powder
1 tablespoon flour
½ teaspoon powdered turmeric
¼ teaspoon ground ginger
Salt and pepper
2 teaspoons sugar
4 cups giblet stock or water
1 small stewing fowl
1 teaspoon curry paste
2 stalks celery, chopped
2 tablespoons seedless raisins
2 teaspoons chutney
2 teaspoons lemon juice

Preheat oven to 325°F.

Heat butter and oil in large skillet. Add onions and apple; sauté until just soft. Add curry powder and flour; cook 3 minutes, stirring. Add turmeric, ginger, seasoning, and sugar; mix well. Add stock; stir until boiling.

Cut fowl into neat pieces. Add with all other ingredients. Remove to casserole; cover tightly.

Cook 2½ to 3 hours. Stir occasionally while cooking to be sure sauce does not stick. Serve with boiled rice and chutney.

If fowl is unobtainable, use 4-pound fryer. Yield 4 or 5 servings.

flemish chicken casserole

2 large carrots, sliced
2 green onions with tops, sliced
1 heart of celery, cut into julienne strips
4 sprigs of parsley
Salt and freshly ground pepper to taste
1 (3½-pound) chicken with giblets
¼ cup butter
2 tablespoons vegetable oil
2 large onions, quartered
1 bay leaf
1 recipe Beurre Manié (see Index)
1 egg
¼ cup half-and-half cream
2 tablespoons freshly minced parsley

flemish chicken casserole

Combine carrots, green onions, celery, parsley sprigs, salt, pepper, and chicken liver and neck in soup kettle; cover with water. Bring to boil; reduce heat. Simmer until vegetables are tender. Remove liver and neck from kettle; cool.

Remove meat from neck; discard bones.

Strain liquid from kettle; reserve.

Place cooked vegetables, liver, and neck meat in blender or food-processor container; process until pureed.

Cut chicken into serving pieces.

Melt butter with oil in heavy skillet. Add chicken; fry until browned. Remove chicken from skillet; season with salt and pepper. Place in large flameproof casserole; add pureed mixture. Add reserved liquid, quartered onions, and bay leaf; cover.

Bake in preheated 350°F oven about 1 hour or until chicken is tender. Remove chicken, onions, and bay leaf from casserole with slotted spoon; discard bay leaf. Place chicken and onions in tureen.

Add Beurre Manié to casserole liquid; simmer, stirring constantly, until thickened.

Beat egg; blend in cream. Add to sauce in casserole slowly; simmer, stirring constantly, until heated through. Pour over chicken mixture; sprinkle with minced parsley. Serve in soup bowls. Yield about 6 servings.

turkey-and-broccoli casserole

2 packages frozen broccoli, cooked
⅓ cup butter
⅓ cup flour
1½ cups turkey broth or consommé
1 cup evaporated milk
1 cup dry white wine
Salt and pepper
Worcestershire sauce
3 cups coarsely diced cooked turkey or chicken
Grated Parmesan cheese

Arrange broccoli in greased shallow casserole dish.

Melt butter; stir in flour. Add broth, milk, and wine. Cook, stirring constantly, until mixture is thickened and smooth. Cook and stir 2 or 3 minutes. Season to taste.

Lay turkey over broccoli in baking dish. Cover with wine-cream sauce. Sprinkle generously with grated cheese. Bake at 400°F about 20 minutes or until bubbly. Yield 6 to 8 servings.

turkey-tetrazzini casserole

½ pound mushrooms, sliced
3 tablespoons butter or margarine
2 tablespoons flour
½ cup turkey broth
1 cup milk
3 tablespoons sherry
¼ teaspoon salt
Dash of pepper
Dash of nutmeg
2½ to 3 cups cooked turkey, cut up
1 (1-pound) package spaghetti, cooked, drained
½ cup grated Parmesan cheese
½ cup grated Swiss cheese

Preheat oven to 350°F.

Sauté mushrooms in butter 3 minutes. Add flour; mix well. Add broth, milk, and sherry; cook over low heat, stirring constantly, until sauce thickens. Add salt, pepper, and nutmeg; mix well. Combine sauce, turkey, and drained spaghetti. Turn into 2-quart casserole. Sprinkle with cheeses. Bake 30 minutes. Yield 6 servings.

SEAFOOD

cabillaud cod au gratin

1 pound potatoes
4 tablespoons butter or margarine
2 tablespoons light cream or milk
1 egg, beaten
Salt and white pepper
1½ pounds cod fillets
2 tablespoons dry white wine
2 teaspoons lemon juice
2 tablespoons flour
1 small package frozen shrimp, thawed
½ cup grated Gruyère cheese
Milk

Preheat oven to 450°F.

Cook potatoes in boiling salted water. Drain thoroughly; dry over low heat. Mash well, adding 2 tablespoons butter, cream, and egg. Season with salt and pepper.

Put fish into skillet with wine, lemon juice, and enough salted water barely to cover; poach 15 minutes. Drain carefully; retain stock. Flake fish coarsely; remove skin.

Make sauce with 2 tablespoons butter, flour, and 1 cup fish stock. Add shrimp and cheese; season to taste.

Put fish into oven dish; add enough sauce to moisten. Cover with potatoes; brush with a little milk. Bake about 30 minutes, until potato crust is brown.

Serve any remaining sauce separately, thinning it down if necessary with a little fish stock. Yield 4 or 5 servings.

casserole of halibut with almonds

½ cup butter or margarine
3 tablespoons blanched slivered almonds
2 teaspoons dry mustard
1 tablespoon tarragon vinegar
3 tablespoons sliced green olives
4 small or 2 large halibut steaks

Preheat oven to 350°F.

Heat butter in sauté pan; sauté almonds until just beginning to color. Add mustard, vinegar, 1 tablespoon water, and olives. Stir well a few minutes.

Arrange fish in shallow buttered casserole; pour sauce over. Cover; cook 25 to 30 minutes. Yield 4 servings.

casserole of shrimp-stuffed peppers

4 large red or green peppers
2 tablespoons butter or margarine
1 small onion, peeled, chopped
1 cup cooked rice
1 small can (or small package frozen) shrimp
Salt and pepper to taste
Lemon juice
1 cup broth or consommé

Preheat oven to 350°F.

Cut slice from stem end of each pepper; remove all seeds and pith.

Heat butter in sauté pan. Add onion; sauté until soft. Add rice and shrimp; season carefully. Add lemon juice.

Fill peppers with mixture. Arrange in buttered casserole; add broth. Cover; cook about 30 minutes, or until tender. Yield 4 servings.

casserole of sole véronique

2 cups milk
2½ pounds fillets of sole
2½ cups sliced mushrooms
½ cup butter or margarine
2 cups white seedless or seeded grapes
4 tablespoons flour
Salt and pepper
Lemon juice
4 tablespoons bread crumbs
2 tablespoons grated cheese

Preheat oven to 375°F.

Heat milk in skillet. When just below boiling point, put in fish; poach very gently 5 minutes.

Sauté mushrooms in half the butter 3 minutes. Put with grapes into lightly buttered casserole. Arrange drained fish on top.

Melt remaining butter. Add flour; stir 1 minute. Add fish milk; whisk until thick and smooth. Season with salt, pepper, and lemon juice; pour over fish. Sprinkle with bread crumbs and cheese mixed together; dot with butter. Cook 25 to 30 minutes or until top is golden brown. Yield 6 servings.

casserole of shrimp-stuffed peppers

deluxe shrimp casserole

¼ cup minced green pepper
¼ cup minced onion
2 tablespoons butter
2 pounds large raw shrimp, cooked
1 (6-ounce) package long-grain and wild rice,
    cooked
Garlic salt, pepper, and parsley to taste
1 can tomato soup, undiluted
1 cup light cream
½ cup sherry
¾ cup slivered almonds

Sauté green pepper and onion in butter 5 minutes. Combine in 2-quart greased casserole with shrimp (set aside 6 shrimp for garnish), cooked rice, seasonings, soup, cream, onion-pepper mixture, sherry, and ½ cup almonds. Mix well. Sprinkle top with paprika.

Bake, uncovered, 35 minutes at 350°F. Top with 6 shrimp and rest of almonds; bake 20 minutes. Yield 8 servings.

salmon casserole with corn-bread topping

1 (1-pound) can pink salmon
1 (10¾-ounce) can condensed cream of
    mushroom soup
1 (9-ounce) package frozen cut green beans,
    thawed
½ (1-pound 2-ounce) package corn-muffin mix
¼ cup finely chopped green pepper (optional)
¼ teaspoon dry mustard
1 egg
Milk

Drain salmon; save liquid. Flake salmon; distribute evenly over bottom of shallow 1½-quart casserole.

Combine soup, salmon liquid, and green beans in saucepan; heat. Pour soup mixture over salmon.

Combine corn-muffin mix, green pepper, and mustard in bowl. Add egg and ½ of milk called for on package label; mix as directed on package. Spoon 8 even mounds onto hot soup mixture. Bake in 400°F oven about 22 to 25 minutes, until topping is done and browned. Yield 4 servings.

Note: If desired, remaining ½ package corn-muffin mix can be prepared as directed on package label. Bake in muffin pans; serve with casserole.

sardine puff

2 cans (3¾ or 4 ounces each) sardines
8 slices white bread
1½ tablespoons butter or margarine
¼ cup chopped green pepper
¾ cup shredded sharp natural cheddar cheese
3 eggs
½ teaspoon salt
¼ teaspoon dry mustard
Pepper to taste
2 cups milk
Paprika

Drain sardines; cut into thirds.

Remove crusts from bread; spread with butter or margarine. Cut into ½-inch cubes. Place half the bread cubes in well-greased 12 × 8 × 2-inch baking dish. Cover with sardines, green pepper, and half the cheese. Top with remaining bread cubes and cheese.

Beat eggs, salt, mustard, and pepper. Add milk; mix well. Pour over bread; sprinkle with paprika.

Bake at 350°F 45 to 50 minutes or until firm in center. Remove from oven; let stand 5 minutes before serving. Yield 6 servings.

seafood dinner-party casserole

2 packages frozen African langostine shrimp or
    lobster tails, thawed
1 can crab meat
2 cans frozen cream of shrimp soup, thawed
1 can cream of mushroom soup
1 small can Italian antipasto (eggplant, olives,
    chopped up)
½ cup light sauterne
1 small can mushrooms
1 cup light cream

Day before serving, combine all ingredients in large flameproof casserole. Heat through, but do not boil. Remove from flame; let stand in cool place overnight. Before serving, heat again. Pour over bed of rice with Chinese noodles on the side. Yield 8 servings.

seafood supreme

4 tablespoons chopped green pepper
2 tablespoons chopped green onion
1 cup chopped celery
1 cup crab meat
1 cup cooked shrimp
1 cup cold cooked rice
1 10-ounce package frozen peas
½ teaspoon salt
½ teaspoon Worcestershire sauce
½ teaspoon pepper
1 cup mayonnaise
Crushed potato chips for topping

Mix together ingredients (except topping) in large bowl. Put into greased casserole; cover with potato chips. Bake at 325°F 30 minutes. Yield 4 to 6 servings.

shad-roe casserole with herbs

4 shad roes
2 cups dry white wine
2 cups fish stock or water
1 teaspoon tarragon vinegar
Salt and white pepper to taste
½ cup melted butter
¼ cup warm olive oil
1 teaspoon minced chervil
1 teaspoon minced chives
1 teaspoon minced parsley
1 teaspoon minced rosemary
1 tablespoon chopped shallots
¼ cup sherry

Rinse roes carefully; lay side by side in shallow earthenware casserole. Pour in wine, stock, and vinegar; season with salt and pepper. Bring stock to boil; simmer roes gently 12 minutes. Drain roes; reserve cooking stock for another use. Dry the roes on paper towel; brush with oil. Return roes to casserole.

Season butter with all the minced herbs and the shallots; pour over roes. Add sherry. Do not cover casserole. Braise roes in 350°F oven 10 minutes. Serve in casserole. Yield 4 servings.

shrimp fondue casserole

3 cans (4½ or 5 ounces each) shrimp
8 slices buttered day-old white bread
¼ cup chopped green pepper
1 cup grated cheese
3 eggs
¼ teaspoon powdered mustard
½ teaspoon salt
Dash of pepper
2 cups milk
Paprika

Drain shrimp; rinse with cold water. Cut large shrimp in half.

Remove crusts from bread; cut into ½-inch cubes. Place half the bread cubes in well-greased baking dish, 12 × 8 × 2 inches. Cover with layer of shrimp, green pepper, and half the cheese. Top with remaining bread cubes and cheese.

Combine eggs, mustard, salt, and pepper; beat with rotary beater. Add milk; mix well. Pour over bread; sprinkle with paprika.

Bake in 350°F oven 45 to 50 minutes or until firm in center. Remove from oven; let stand 5 minutes. Yield 6 servings.

shrimp and green-bean casserole

3 cans (4½ or 5 ounces each) shrimp
1 (9-ounce) package frozen French-style green beans
1 (10½-ounce) can condensed cream of celery soup
2 tablespoons chopped parsley
1 teaspoon lemon juice
1 teaspoon grated onion
½ teaspoon grated lemon rind
½ cup grated cheese
Paprika

Drain shrimp; rinse with cold water.

Cook beans according to package directions; omit salt. Drain thoroughly. Place in well-greased shallow 1½-quart casserole. Cover with shrimp.

Combine soup, parsley, lemon juice, onion, and lemon rind; pour over shrimp. Top with cheese; sprinkle with paprika. Bake in 350°F oven 20 to 25 minutes or until cheese melts and is lightly browned. Yield 6 servings.

tuna–broccoli casserole

4 eggs
1 cup buttermilk
2 cans (6½ or 7 ounces each) tuna in vegetable oil
½ teaspoon salt
1 pound (2 cups) small-curd creamed cottage cheese
2 packages (10 ounces each) frozen chopped broccoli, thawed, well drained
½ cup chopped onion
1 medium tomato, thinly sliced, or 1 cup sliced cherry tomatoes
½ cup (4 ounces) shredded mozzarella cheese

Beat eggs and buttermilk in large bowl. Add tuna, salt, cottage cheese, broccoli, and onion. Turn into large shallow casserole. Bake in 350°F oven 35 minutes. Top with sliced tomatoes and mozzarella cheese; bake 10 minutes, until set. Yield 8 to 10 servings.

tuna casserole

8 ounces elbow macaroni
1 large can evaporated milk
1 cup grated cheese
1 (7-ounce) can tuna, drained, flaked
1 teaspoon salt
½ teaspoon dry mustard
1 tablespoon minced onion
2 tomatoes, sliced
½ cup grated cheese

Cook and drain macaroni. Combine with next 6 ingredients; toss until well blended. Put into greased casserole. Top with tomato slices; sprinkle with cheese. Bake in 350°F oven 30 minutes. Yield 4 to 6 servings.

baked chicken breasts en casserole

4 chicken breasts
1 can chicken broth
½ cup dry white wine
2 tablespoons grated onion
½ cup mayonnaise
2 tablespoons lemon juice
1 teaspoon sugar
1 can cream of chicken soup
Crushed potato chips
Slivered almonds

Remove skin from chicken breasts; place in skillet. Add broth, wine, and enough water to cover. Bring to boil; simmer 15 minutes or until tender. Transfer with slotted spoon to casserole.

Boil down broth to ¼ cup.

Mix together onion, mayonnaise, lemon juice, sugar, reduced broth, and soup. Pour over chicken.

Bake in 350°F oven 20 minutes. Cover with potato chips and almonds; bake 10 minutes. Yield 4 servings.

baked chicken with marinara sauce

½ cup all-purpose flour
1 teaspoon salt
¼ teaspoon pepper
1 (2½- to 3-pound) broiler-fryer chicken, cut up
3 tablespoons butter or margarine
1 (15½-ounce) can marinara sauce or 2 cups
    homemade marinara sauce
1 teaspoon dried dillweed
2 tablespoons grated Parmesan cheese

Combine flour, salt, and pepper in brown paper bag. Add chicken a few pieces at a time; shake until coated with flour mixture. Place chicken in single layer in shallow baking dish. Dot with butter.

Bake at 450°F 25 minutes. Remove from oven; pour sauce over chicken. Sprinkle with dillweed and cheese. Reduce heat to 350°F; bake 25 minutes. Serve hot or cold. Makes a great picnic dish. Yield 4 servings.

barbecued chicken

marinade
½ cup dry white wine
2 tablespoons oil
Juice of ½ lemon
1 small onion, peeled, chopped
½ teaspoon tarragon

1 chicken (about 3 pounds)

herb butter
½ cup butter or margarine
4 tablespoons chopped parsley
2 teaspoons rosemary

Combine all marinade ingredients.

Cut chicken into 8 pieces; put into marinade. Leave several hours; turn frequently. Drain; brush with Herb Butter. Cook on rack over glowing coals; baste several times. Cook until chicken is crisp and golden.

To make Herb Butter, put ingredients into small pan; heat just enough to melt butter. Use half to baste chicken; put rest into refrigerator to firm. Cut into pats; serve on chicken. Yield 4 servings.

batter-fried chicken breasts

6 to 8 chicken breasts, boned
2 teaspoons salt
Dash of pepper

batter
1 egg, lightly beaten
½ cup milk
2 tablespoons flour
1½ cups flour for dredging chicken
Oil for deep-fat frying

Divide each chicken breast in half to make 12 to 16 pieces. Sprinkle each piece with salt and pepper.

Mix egg and milk in shallow bowl or pie dish. Add flour; mix until very smooth.

Dip each chicken piece in batter; dredge generously in flour. Put 4 or 5 chicken pieces into preheated 375°F oil; deep fry 12 to 15 minutes or until chicken is golden brown on all sides. Drain on paper towels; keep warm in very low oven until all chicken is fried. Yield 4 to 6 servings.

braised chicken with vegetables

½ cup flour
1½ teaspoons salt
¼ teaspoon pepper
3-pound ready-to-cook broiler-fryer chicken,
    cut up
3 tablespoons fat or oil
¾ cup hot water
1½ cups sliced carrots
3 cups sliced celery
¾ cup finely chopped onion
¾ cup chopped green pepper

Combine flour, 1 teaspoon salt, and pepper; coat chicken with mixture. Brown chicken in hot fat in large frypan. Drain excess fat from pan. Add water and ½ teaspoon salt. Cover tightly; simmer 45 minutes to 1 hour, until chicken is almost tender. Add vegetables; cook 20 to 30 minutes or until vegetables are tender. Yield 6 servings.

brandied cherry chicken

1 (8-ounce) can pitted Bing cherries
¼ cup port wine
1 (3-pound) broiler-fryer chicken, quartered
1 tablespoon vegetable oil
¼ cup brandy
¾ cup hot water
1 large onion, thinly sliced
½ teaspoon salt
Few grains pepper
1½ tablespoons cornstarch

Drain cherries; reserve ¼ cup syrup. Pour reserved syrup and wine over cherries; cover. Marinate in refrigerator 2 hours.

Remove excess fat from chicken.

Heat oil in large skillet over moderately high heat; add chicken; cook until lightly browned on all sides. Remove from heat. Pour brandy over chicken; ignite with match. When flame goes out, add water, onion, salt, and pepper. Cover; cook over moderately low heat 40 to 45 minutes, until chicken is fork-tender. Remove chicken to platter.

Pour juices into measuring cup; remove as much fat as possible.

Drain marinated cherries; reserve liquid. Blend cherry syrup into cornstarch; pour into skillet. Add chicken juices; cook over moderate heat, stirring constantly, until sauce is thickened. Add cherries; cook 2 to 3 minutes to heat cherries. Pour over chicken. Yield 4 or 5 servings.

breast of chicken florentine

½ cup flour
1 teaspoon salt
⅛ teaspoon white pepper
6 chicken breasts, boned, skinned
2 eggs, beaten
½ cup Parmesan cheese
¾ cup bread crumbs
¾ cup butter
1 pound mushrooms, sliced
Chopped parsley
4 packages frozen leaf spinach
2 tablespoons lemon juice
Dash of nutmeg

Mix flour, salt, and pepper; dredge chicken with seasoned flour. Dip in egg; coat with cheese and bread crumbs. Refrigerate at least 1 hour.

Heat ½ cup butter in large skillet; brown chicken on each side. Lower heat; cover. Simmer 25 minutes. Remove chicken from skillet.

Add mushrooms and parsley to drippings; stir over heat 3 minutes.

Cook spinach until tender; drain well. Season with ¼ cup butter, lemon juice, salt, pepper, and nutmeg.

Serve chicken on bed of spinach; top with mushrooms. (Chicken can be cooked in advance and heated in hot oven.) Yield 6 servings.

broiled chicken sauterne

2 (1½-pound) broiler chickens
1 onion, sliced
1 sprig parsley
1 cup cold water
1 cup sauterne
2 tablespoons lemon juice
Salt and pepper
2 tablespoons salad oil
1 tablespoon flour
1 tablespoon butter

Split broilers. Put necks in saucepan with giblets, onion, parsley, and water. Cover; simmer until giblets are tender. Add wine; strain. (This sauce is to be used for basting during broiling.) Chop giblets fine; set aside. Sprinkle chicken with lemon juice, salt, and pepper; brush with oil. Place, skin-side-down, in shallow pan; place under broiler, about 30 minutes. Turn occasionally; baste frequently with wine sauce. When chickens are tender and well browned, remove from pan.

Thicken remaining sauce with flour and butter rubbed together. Add giblets; season to taste. Pour a little sauce over each serving of chicken. Yield 4 servings.

broiled spring chicken

2 small broiler chickens
Salt and pepper to taste
½ cup melted butter
4 tablespoons lemon juice

Remove wing tips from broilers. Split from necks through breasts; leave backs together. Place on chopping board; flatten with a rolling pin. Run skewer through each chicken to keep flat. Season with salt and pepper. Place, skin-side-up, on rack in broiler pan.

Combine butter and lemon juice; brush broilers with mixture. Place broiler pan 3 or 4 inches from heat source; broil 2 minutes. Lower pan to about 10 inches from heat source; broil about 40 minutes or until broilers are tender. Turn frequently; baste with butter mixture each time. Place on platter; garnish with endive. Yield 2 servings.

203

broiled spring chicken

brown chicken fricassee

1 (3-pound) chicken, disjointed
Salt and pepper to taste
½ cup butter
½ to 1 teaspoon thyme leaves
½ to 1 teaspoon leaf marjoram
1 large onion studded with 12 cloves
½ lemon
¾ cup Burgundy
⅛ teaspoon nutmeg
⅛ teaspoon mace
1 cup half-and-half cream
¼ cup all-purpose flour
3 egg yolks, beaten
¼ cup tomato puree (optional)

Season chicken with salt and pepper; place in large saucepan. Add butter, thyme, marjoram, onion, lemon, Burgundy, nutmeg, and mace. Add enough water to cover. Bring to boil; reduce heat. Cover; simmer about 30 minutes or until chicken is very tender. Remove chicken from broth; discard lemon and onion. Cool chicken until easily handled. Remove skin and bones; dice chicken coarsely or leave in large pieces.

Mix enough cream into flour to make smooth thin paste; stir into broth.

Combine egg yolks with remaining cream; blend into broth gradually, stirring constantly. Cook over medium heat, stirring constantly, until thickened; do not allow to boil. Stir in tomato puree. Add chicken. Season with salt and pepper, heat through. Serve with baked croutons; garnish with lemon slices and parsley sprigs. Yield 8 servings.

chicken with biscuit topping

filling
2 tablespoons vegetable oil
1 small onion, peeled, chopped
½ green pepper, finely chopped
⅔ cup sliced mushrooms
2 tablespoons cornstarch
1½ cups milk
1½ to 2 cups cooked chicken, cut into cubes
Salt and pepper

biscuits
2 cups flour
1 teaspoon salt
2½ teaspoons baking powder
⅓ cup butter or margarine
About ⅔ cup milk

Heat oil in skillet. Add onion, green pepper, and mushrooms; sauté a few minutes. Add cornstarch; cook 1 minute, stirring all the time. Add milk gradually; stir until boiling. Add chicken and seasoning. Turn into deep 8- or 9-inch pie plate.

To make biscuits sift flour, salt, and baking

brown chicken fricassee

powder. Cut in butter with pastry blender until mixture looks like coarse bread crumbs. Using fork, stir in enough milk to make soft but not sticky dough. Knead lightly on floured board; roll about ½ inch thick. Cut into 1½ inch rounds with cookie cutter. Place rounds on top of chicken mixture; brush with milk. Bake 10 to 15 minutes. Yield 4 servings.

chicken with brandy cream

3 tablespoons butter
1 tablespoon oil
1 cup slivered onion
½ pound mushrooms, cleaned, sliced
¼ cup flour
Salt and pepper
4 chicken breast fillets (1 pound total) or bone and skin 1½ pounds split chicken breasts
2 tablespoons brandy

1 cup heavy cream
½ teaspoon crumbled dried tarragon
1 egg yolk

Heat 2 tablespoons butter and oil in heavy skillet over moderate heat. Add onion; sauté until tender. Add mushrooms; sauté 3 minutes, stirring occasionally. Remove from pan with slotted spoon; reserve.

Combine flour, salt, and pepper; dredge chicken breasts in mixture.

Add 1 tablespoon butter to skillet; melt over moderate heat. Add chicken; brown well on both sides.

Warm brandy. Ignite; pour over chicken. Add cream and tarragon; heat through.

Beat egg yolk well. Add some of hot sauce to egg yolk; beat. Add to chicken; mix well. Add mushrooms and onions; cook stirring frequently, until thickened. Serve immediately. (Take care not to boil mixture after adding cream.) Yield 4 servings.

chicken with biscuit topping

chicken cacciatore

1 (3-pound) chicken
3 tablespoons vegetable oil
1 clove garlic
½ teaspoon salt
¼ teaspoon pepper
1 teaspoon rosemary
6 anchovy fillets, chopped
⅓ cup wine vinegar
1⅓ cups dry red wine
3 tablespoons tomato paste
½ cup chicken bouillon

Cut chicken into serving pieces.

Heat oil in large frypan; sauté chicken and garlic 5 minutes. Turn chicken often. Remove garlic. Add salt, pepper, rosemary, anchovies, vinegar, and wine. Simmer, uncovered, until liquid is reduced by one-third.

Dissolve tomato paste in bouillon; pour over chicken. Simmer, covered, 20 minutes or until chicken is done. Yield 4 servings.

chicken and cheesy rice ring

6 tablespoons butter
2 onions, finely chopped
2 cups cooked rice
1 egg, beaten
1 cup milk
1 teaspoon turmeric
1 cup grated cheddar cheese
2 tablespoons chopped mixed herbs
Salt and pepper
½ teaspoon dry mustard
1 teaspoon paprika
4 to 6 large mushrooms
2 tablespoons flour
1 cup stock (or canned chicken broth)
3 cups diced cooked chicken (or chicken and ham)
Pinch of nutmeg
1 green or red pimiento, coarsely chopped
3 to 4 tablespoons bread or cornflake crumbs

Melt 5 tablespoons butter; cook onions 4 or 5 minutes to soften, without browning. Remove half; put into bowl. Add rice to onion in bowl. Add egg mixed with milk, turmeric, ¾ cup cheese, and 1 tablespoon herbs. Season with salt, pepper, mustard, and half the paprika.

Butter 7-inch ring mold; fill with rice mixture, packing it in well. Bake about 20 minutes. When firm and cooked, remove from oven; turn onto platter.

Meanwhile, prepare chicken sauce: Add sliced mushrooms to onion in pan; cook 2 minutes. Remove from heat. Add flour; mix well. Add stock; blend well; bring to boil. Cook few minutes. Add chicken, remaining herbs, and seasonings; flavor with nutmeg.

Boil pimiento five minutes. Drain; add to sauce.

chicken and cheesy rice ring

Keep sauce warm to allow flavors to blend. Spoon hot sauce into center of rice ring. Excess can be reheated and served separately. Sprinkle top with remaining cheese and crumbs mixed; dot with 1 tablespoon butter. Brown under broiler or in hot oven few minutes. Sprinkle with paprika; serve hot. Yield 4 to 6 servings.

chicken with chocolate

1 (3-pound) chicken, disjointed
Salt and pepper
All-purpose flour
2 tablespoons butter
2 tablespoons olive oil
1½ cups Basic Chicken Stock (see Index)
  or canned chicken broth
½ ounce bitter chocolate, melted
½ teaspoon cinnamon
½ cup chopped blanched almonds
½ cup finely chopped onions
1 cup grated carrots
½ cup raisins
12 pitted prunes
Chopped parsley
Whole almonds

Season chicken with salt and pepper; dredge with flour.

Melt butter and oil in large skillet. Add chicken; brown on both sides. Remove chicken to ovenproof dish.

Add 2 tablespoons flour to pan drippings; cook until browned, stirring constantly. Add stock gradually; cook, stirring constantly, until thick-

chicken with chocolate

ened. Blend in chocolate and cinnamon; add salt and pepper, if needed. Stir in remaining ingredients (except parsley and whole almonds); pour over chicken.

Bake, covered, in preheated 325°F oven 45 minutes. Garnish with chopped parsley and blanched whole almonds. Yield 4 servings.

chicken chow mein

1 green sweet pepper, sliced
1 red sweet pepper, sliced
1 cup boiling water
2½ tablespoons butter
1 small onion, chopped
2 stalks celery, sliced
1 tablespoon flour
1 cup chicken broth

chicken chow mein

2 tablespoons soy sauce
Freshly ground pepper to taste
1 4-ounce can sliced mushrooms, drained
8 ounces cooked chicken breast, cut into
  bite-size pieces
6 cups water
8 ounces egg noodles
Salt
Oil for frying
4 ounces sliced almonds, toasted, slightly salted

Blanch green and red peppers in boiling water 5 minutes. Remove; drain.

Heat 1½ tablespoons butter in saucepan. Add onion and celery; sauté until onion is transparent. Sprinkle with flour. Pour in broth; bring to boil, stirring constantly. Simmer 10 minutes. Season with soy sauce and pepper. Add peppers, mushrooms, and chicken. Cover; simmer 15 minutes.

Meanwhile, bring 6 cups slightly salted water to boil. Add noodles; cook 4 to 5 minutes. Drain; rinse with cold water. Set aside ⅓ of noodles. Place rest of noodles in heated bowl; add 1 tablespoon butter. Cover; keep warm.

Heat oil in skillet until very hot.

Cut reserved noodles into approximately 2-inch-long pieces. Add to hot oil; fry until golden. Drain on paper towels.

To serve, spoon chicken mixture over buttered noodles; top with fried noodles and toasted almonds. Yield 4 servings.

chicken cooked with corn

1 (2½- to 3-pound) broiler-fryer chicken
4 tablespoons butter or margarine
Salt and pepper to taste
1 (16½-ounce) can whole-kernel corn, drained,
  liquid reserved
½ cup chopped green chilies (optional)

sauce
3 tablespoons butter or margarine
2 tablespoons flour
1 cup half-and-half cream
2 eggs, separated
Salt and white pepper
¼ teaspoon nutmeg
2 tablespoons bread crumbs
2 tablespoons butter

Preheat oven to 350°F.

Wash chicken; pat dry. Cut into quarters.

Heat butter in heavy skillet. Brown chicken on all sides.

Place chicken in ovenproof casserole. Season with salt and pepper.

Add corn, chilies, and ¼ cup reserved corn liquid to juices in skillet. Stir well; pour over chicken.

Make sauce: Melt butter in saucepan. Add flour; cook until evenly and lightly browned, stirring constantly. Add cream all at once; cook over medium heat, stirring, until slightly thickened.

Beat egg yolks, salt, pepper, and nutmeg together. Add some hot sauce to egg yolks; beat well. Pour egg-yolk mixture into saucepan; mix well. Remove from heat.

Beat egg whites until stiff but not dry; fold into sauce. Pour sauce over chicken. Sprinkle with bread crumbs; dot with butter. Bake in oven 45 minutes. Yield 4 servings.

chicken cordon bleu

4 single chicken breasts
4 tablespoons chopped cooked ham
4 tablespoons grated Swiss cheese
1 small clove garlic, crushed
1 to 2 tablespoons white wine
½ teaspoon salt
⅛ teaspoon white pepper
3 to 4 tablespoons seasoned flour
1 large egg
¼ cup oil
6 to 8 tablespoons dried white bread crumbs
4 to 5 tablespoons butter

Place chicken breasts skin-side-down. With sharp knife cut a shallow slit down center of each without cutting through to skin. Cut shallow pockets on either side of these slits.

Mix ham and cheese with garlic and a little white wine to moisten. Season well. Fill pockets in chicken breasts; seal slit with small finger-shaped fillet attached to each breast. Put in refrigerator to chill 30 minutes. Coat well in seasoned flour. Brush carefully with egg beaten with 1 teaspoon oil; roll in bread crumbs.

Heat oil; add butter. When foaming, fry chicken breasts until tender, golden brown, and crisp all over. Drain on paper towel. Yield 4 servings.

chicken cordon gold

12 boneless chicken-breast halves
¾ cup flour
2 teaspoons salt
½ teaspoon white pepper
1 package Boursin herb cheese
12 thin slices ham
¼ cup melted butter
1 cup plus 2 tablespoons Galliano liqueur
⅓ cup butter
½ pound sliced mushrooms
1 bunch parsley

Dredge chicken in flour mixed with salt and pepper. Place 2 tablespoons cheese and a slice of ham on each breast. Roll up each breast; secure

chicken-corn-carrot platter

with toothpicks. Close ends with toothpicks. Brown lightly in butter. Pour in 1 cup Galliano; cover skillet. Simmer until tender, about 30 minutes.

Heat ⅓ cup butter and 2 tablespoons Galliano in second skillet. Add mushrooms; sauté until crisp. Add parsley; sauté 3 minutes. Combine mixture with chicken 5 minutes before serving. Remove toothpicks before serving. Yield 6 servings.

chicken–corn–carrot platter

6 tablespoons butter
2 (1-pound) chicken breasts, halved
4 medium carrots, thinly sliced
4 ears of corn, halved
2 tablespoons chopped chives
2 teaspoons salt
⅛ teaspoon garlic powder

Melt 2 tablespoons butter in skillet over medium heat. Add chicken; cook until browned. Place each chicken half on 12 × 18-inch piece of heavy-duty aluminum foil; arrange ¼ carrots and corn around each chicken half.

Add remaining butter, chives, salt, and garlic powder to butter in skillet; heat, stirring frequently, until butter is melted. Pour over chicken and vegetables on each piece of foil. Seal foil pockets; use double fold on top and sides. Place on baking sheet. Bake in preheated 350°F oven 1¼ hours. Arrange chicken breasts on heated platter. Surround with carrots; top with corn. Garnish with parsley. Yield 4 servings.

chicken crisps

3 tablespoons butter
2 tablespoons flour
1 cup milk
8 mushrooms, sliced
4 tablespoons stock
2 cups chopped or diced cooked chicken
½ cup cooked peas or corn
5 thick slices white bread
1 cup oil
1 tablespoon chopped parsley

Make cream sauce: Melt 3 tablespoons butter; blend in flour. Gradually add milk; when smooth,

209

bring to boil, stirring constantly. Boil 3 minutes; cool slightly.

Slice mushrooms; cook in stock 3 to 4 minutes. Chop or dice chicken; mix with mushrooms and cooked vegetables. Add mixture to cream sauce; season well. Heat thoroughly; keep warm.

Remove crusts from bread; with small cutter cut 4 crescent-shaped pieces from 1 slice.

Heat oil; add 1 tablespoon butter. When foaming, fry bread slices and crescents until golden brown on both sides; drain on paper towel.

Arrange squares on serving dish; spoon hot chicken mixture onto squares. Decorate with crescents and chopped parsley. Yield 4 servings.

chicken croquettes

4 cups cooked chicken, put through meat grinder
1 cup chopped celery
1 tablespoon grated onion
4 tablespoons butter
4 tablespoons flour
1 cup milk
1 teaspoon salt
Generous dash of freshly ground pepper
1 egg, beaten with 1 tablespoon milk
1 cup cracker meal
Oil for deep frying
2 cans cream of mushroom soup for quick sauce

Mix chicken and celery in large bowl; set aside.

Sauté onion in butter in small saucepan until onion is transparent. Blend flour. Add milk; heat, stirring constantly. When slightly thickened, add salt and pepper; simmer just 3 minutes. Add sauce to chicken and celery; chill several hours.

Shape chicken into rolls about 3 inches long. Dip into egg; roll in cracker meal. Place croquettes on waxed-paper-lined baking sheet; chill in refrigerator at least 3 hours.

Fry croquettes in deep fat, a few at a time, until brown on all sides; drain on paper towels. Can be kept warm in very low (250°F) oven until ready to serve.

For a quick sauce with croquettes, heat cream of mushroom soup over low heat; stir until piping hot. If you prefer thinner sauce, add milk by ¼ cups; stir until desired consistency is reached. Yield 4 to 6 servings.

chicken curry

1 frying chicken, cut into serving pieces
2 tablespoons vegetable oil
2 tablespoons butter or margarine
2 cups cooked barley
1 medium onion, minced
2 cups chicken broth
Salt and pepper to taste
2 teaspoons curry powder

1 teaspoon marjoram
1 cup plain yogurt
1 tomato, peeled, seeded, cut into bite-size pieces

Brown chicken in oil and butter in large skillet. Remove chicken from pan; place on bed of barley in Dutch oven or flameproof casserole.

Cook onion until transparent in same skillet in remaining oil and butter. Remove; place on top of chicken. Pour 1½ cups broth over chicken and barley. Sprinkle with salt, pepper, curry powder, and marjoram. Cover; cook over low heat 30 minutes. Remove cover. Add yogurt, tomato, and ½ cup broth, if needed. Cook, uncovered, 20 to 30 minutes, until chicken is tender. Yield 4 to 6 servings.

chicken delight

Flour seasoned with salt, pepper, and garlic salt
1 (2- to 3-pound) frying chicken, cut into serving pieces
2 tablespoons butter or margarine
2 tablespoons oil
1 small can mandarin oranges with juice
4 tablespoons lemon juice
½ cup orange juice
2 tablespoons honey
2 teaspoons soy sauce
½ teaspoon ginger

Put seasoned flour into brown paper bag. Shake chicken pieces in bag to coat with flour mixture.

Heat butter and oil in skillet; brown chicken pieces.

Drain oranges; reserve juice. Mix juice with lemon and orange juices, honey, soy sauce, and ginger. Pour sauce over chicken in skillet. Cover; simmer 30 minutes. When chicken is fork-tender, add oranges; simmer just 5 minutes more. Yield 4 to 6 servings.

chicken á la française

2 bunches celery
2 (3-pound) chickens
2 tablespoons lemon juice
2½ teaspoons salt
¼ teaspoon freshly ground pepper
¼ teaspoon garlic powder
1 cup diced onions
2 tablespoons melted butter
1¾ cups Basic Chicken Stock (see Index)
2 tablespoons all-purpose flour
¼ cup water

Preheat oven to 425°F.

Trim stem ends of celery; keep bunches intact. Cut leaves off bunches of celery; reserve for stuffing. Cut each celery bunch lengthwise into 4 pieces; set aside.

Brush chickens inside and out with lemon juice.

chicken á la françasie

Combine salt, pepper, and garlic powder; rub in cavities and on skin of chickens. Fill chicken cavities with reserved celery leaves and onions; secure openings with skewers. Place chickens in shallow dish; cover. Chill 2 to 4 hours to blend seasonings with chickens. Place chickens on rack in roasting pan; brush with butter. Bake in oven 30 minutes or until browned. Arrange celery bunch pieces around chickens. Pour stock into pan; cover pan. Reduce oven temperature to 375°F, bake 1 hour or until chickens are tender. Remove celery mixture from chicken cavities; discard.

Arrange chickens on heated serving platter; surround with the celery pieces.

Drain 2 cups pan liquid into saucepan; bring to boil. Mix flour and water until smooth; stir into pan liquid. Cook, stirring constantly, until thickened; pour into gravy boat. Serve with chickens. Yield 8 to 10 servings.

chicken with green peppers and bamboo shoots in oyster sauce

chicken with green peppers and bamboo shoots in oyster sauce

sauce
1 small onion, sliced
1 tablespoon soy sauce
2 tablespoons oyster sauce (found in Oriental food stores and some supermarkets)
¾ cup chicken broth
1 teaspoon brown sugar
1 teaspoon freshly grated gingerroot
1 tablespoon cornstarch in 2 tablespoons water

chicken-vegetable mixture
1 tablespoon vegetable oil
1 large green pepper, cut into ¾-inch cubes
¼ cup sliced bamboo shoots
¼ pound small whole mushrooms
2 whole chicken breasts, split, skinned, boned, cut into pieces
½ cucumber, peeled, cut into chunks

To make sauce, simmer together all sauce ingredients 8 to 10 minutes; stir occasionally.

Meanwhile heat oil in frypan (or wok); stir-fry green pepper 3 minutes. Remove; reserve. Stir-fry bamboo shoots and mushrooms 2 to 3 minutes; reserve with green pepper. Add chicken to frypan; stir-fry 3 to 4 minutes or until done. Return vegetables to pan with chicken. Add cucumber. Immediately add oyster sauce; heat through. Serve with rice. Yield 4 servings.

chicken kampama

3 pounds cut up chicken
2 tablespoons butter
2 tablespoons olive oil
2 medium onions, chopped
2 cloves garlic, minced
1 cup canned tomatoes
½ of 6-ounce can tomato paste
2 sticks cinnamon
¼ teaspoon ground allspice
½ teaspoon sugar
¼ cup red wine

In large skillet brown chicken on all sides in butter and olive oil; remove from pan.

Brown onions and garlic. Add tomatoes, tomato paste, seasonings, and wine; bring to boil. Add chicken. Reduce heat to simmer; cook 1 to 1½ hours or until tender. Yield 4 or 5 servings.

chicken kiev with sherry sauce

2 whole chicken breasts, split, bones, skinned
1 tablespoon chopped chives
1 tablespoon chopped parsley

212

½ clove garlic, minced
½ teaspoon salt
⅛ teaspoon pepper
½ cup grated low-fat mozzarella cheese
Toothpicks
2 tablespoons vegetable oil
1 tablespoon flour
¼ cup dry sherry
1 cup chicken bouillon or broth

Pound each chicken breast half with flat side of meat mallet to ¼ inch thick. Sprinkle seasonings evenly over chicken pieces. Cover surfaces with cheese; roll up each half breast with cheese enclosed. Secure with toothpick.

Heat oil in large frypan; sauté chicken rolls until golden brown, about 8 minutes. Place in shallow baking dish.

Preheat oven to 350°F.

Make sauce: Stir flour into drippings in frypan; stir until smooth. Remove from heat. Add sherry and bouillon. Return to heat; heat to boiling, stirring constantly. Reduce sauce by boiling until slightly thickened. Spoon over chicken; cover. Bake 30 minutes. Remove toothpicks before serving. Yield 4 servings.

chicken a la king

½ pound mushrooms, sliced
½ cup butter or margarine
½ cup flour
2 cups chicken broth
2 cups light cream
2 egg yolks, beaten
3 cups diced cooked chicken or turkey
½ cup pimiento, cut into strips
1 teaspoon salt
¼ teaspoon pepper

Sauté mushrooms in butter in medium-size heavy skillet.

Mix flour with chicken broth. Add to skillet; stir. Add cream; simmer 5 minutes. Add egg yolks, chicken, and pimiento; stir until thoroughly hot, but do not let mixture boil. Add salt and pepper. Spoon over toast or English muffins. Yield 6 to 8 servings.

chicken in lemon–dill butter

¼ pound butter or margarine
2 tablespoons lemon juice
1 teaspoon salt
1 clove garlic, minced
Dash of pepper
½ teaspoon paprika
1 can sliced mushrooms, drained
1 tablespoon dillweed
1 (2½ to 3-pound) frying chicken, cut into serving pieces

Melt butter in large skillet. Add all ingredients (except chicken) in order given; bring to boil. Add chicken; bring to boil, but do not actually boil. Cover skillet; lower heat. Simmer 30 minutes or until chicken is tender. Remove chicken to platter. Serve with noodles or rice, over which remaining liquid has been poured. Yield 4 to 6 servings.

chicken in lemon-dill butter

chicken with mandarin oranges and almonds

2 ounces seedless raisins
1 jigger Madeira
2 teaspoons paprika
1 teaspoon white pepper
1 large chicken, 3½ to 4 pounds, cut into serving
    pieces
5 tablespoons oil
1 (11-ounce) can mandarin oranges, drained
1 clove garlic, minced
½ cup hot beef bouillon
1 tablespoon cornstarch
1 tablespoon soy sauce
½ teaspoon powdered ginger
½ cup heavy cream, lightly beaten
1 tablespoon butter
2 tablespoons sliced almonds

chicken with mandarin oranges and almonds

Cover raisins with Madeira; soak.

Mix together paprika and pepper; rub chicken with mixture.

Heat oil in skillet or Dutch oven. Add chicken; fry until golden on all sides, about 10 minutes. Drain oranges; reserve juice.

Measure ½ cup juice; pour over chicken. Add garlic. Pour in bouillon; cover. Simmer 30 minutes.

Drain raisins; add. Cook 5 minutes. Remove chicken with slotted spoon; arrange on preheated platter; keep warm.

Blend cornstarch with small amount cold water; add to sauce. Stir constantly until thickened and bubbly. Season with soy sauce and ginger. Add oranges and cream; heat through, but do not boil.

Heat butter in small skillet. Add sliced almonds; cook until golden. Pour sauce over chicken; top with almonds. Yield 6 servings.

chicken marengo

2 (3-pound) frying chickens
¼ cup vegetable oil
1 onion, thinly sliced
3 tablespoons brandy
2 (1-pound) cans Italian tomatoes, drained
½ cup dry white wine
2 cloves garlic, pressed
½ teaspoon dried thyme
1 bay leaf
4 sprigs fresh parsley
1 cup Basic Chicken Stock (see Index) or canned
   chicken broth
1 teaspoon salt
½ teaspoon freshly ground pepper
1 cup small cleaned shrimp
½ pound fresh mushrooms, sliced
¼ cup butter
2 tablespoons lemon juice
2 tablespoons freshly minced parsley

Remove skin from chickens; cut each chicken into quarters.

Pour oil into large, heavy skillet; place over medium heat until hot. Add onion; sauté, stirring frequently, until golden brown. Remove onion from skillet with slotted spoon; set aside.

Add chicken to oil remaining in skillet; cook until browned on all sides.

Heat brandy; pour over chicken. Ignite brandy; flame, shaking skillet until flame dies.

Place tomatoes in blender or food-processor container; process until pureed. Add to skillet. Add wine, garlic, thyme, bay leaf, parsley sprigs, stock, tomatoes, salt, pepper, and sautéed onions. Cover skillet; simmer 1 hour or until chicken is tender. Remove chicken from sauce; keep warm.

Strain sauce, if desired. Add shrimp to sauce; simmer 5 minutes.

Sauté mushrooms in butter in saucepan until tender; stir in lemon juice. Add to sauce; heat through.

Arrange chicken on heated serving platter; pour sauce over chicken. Sprinkle with minced parsley. Yield 8 servings.

chicken with mushrooms and celery

2 tablespoons vegetable oil
1 small onion, sliced
3 stalks celery, cut into ¼-inch slices
¼ pound whole mushrooms; quarter if large
1 broiler-fryer chicken, skinned, boned, cut into
   bite-size pieces
¾ cup chicken broth or bouillon
2 teaspoons soy sauce

chicken marengo

1½ tablespoons cornstarch in 2 tablespoons water
2 tablespoons dry sherry (optional)

Heat oil in frypan (or wok); stir-fry onion and celery 3 minutes. Remove; reserve. Add mushrooms to frypan; stir-fry 2 minutes. Remove; reserve with onion. Stir-fry chicken 4 to 5 minutes or until done. Return vegetables to pan. Add rest of ingredients; heat until sauce is thickened. Stir constantly. Serve immediately with rice. Yield 4 servings.

chicken normandy

1 chicken (about 3½ pounds)
Salt and pepper
4 tablespoons oil
1 onion, peeled, sliced
2 stalks celery, sliced
2 large apples, peeled, cored, sliced
2 tablespoons flour
1½ cups chicken bouillon or water
Pinch of thyme
Pinch of marjoram
2 tablespoons grated cheese
Boiled rice

Joint chicken into small pieces; season with salt and pepper.

Heat 3 tablespoons oil in pan. Add pieces of chicken (a few at a time); brown well. Remove pieces as they are browned.

Put onion, celery, and apples into remaining oil; cook until onion is tender. Add 1 tablespoon oil. Stir in flour; mix well. Gradually add bouillon; stir until boiling. Return chicken to sauce. Add thyme, marjoram, and a little seasoning. Cover; simmer until chicken is tender. Adjust the seasoning to taste. Stir in cheese.

To serve, put some hot cooked rice onto large platter; arrange pieces of chicken on top. Pour sauce over. Serve excess sauce separately. Yield 6 servings.

chicken paprika

1 chicken, 2½ to 3 pounds
1 tablespoon vegetable oil
1 large onion, chopped
2 tablespoons paprika
1 clove garlic, minced
½ teaspoon salt
1 teaspoon caraway seeds
1 cup hot water
1 scallion or leek, cut lengthwise, sliced
1 small carrot, sliced
1 small stalk celery, sliced
2 medium potatoes, peeled, cubed
½ cup chicken broth or bouillon
3 tomatoes
1 red pepper, cubed
1 green pepper, cubed
Parsley for garnish, chopped

Skin and bone chicken; cut into bite-size pieces. Heat oil in 4-quart Dutch oven; sauté onion. Sprinkle 1 tablespoon paprika over onions; stir well. Add garlic, salt, caraway seeds, and ½ cup water. Simmer over low heat 10 minutes. Add chicken pieces. Cover; simmer 5 minutes. Add additional ½ cup water; cover. Simmer 15 minutes. Add scallion, carrot, celery, potatoes, and broth to chicken. Simmer 10 minutes.

Peel and chop 2 tomatoes. Add peppers, chopped tomatoes, and 1 tablespoon paprika to Dutch oven. Cover; simmer 15 minutes. Correct seasoning if necessary. Serve garnished with 1 sliced tomato and parsley. Yield 4 servings.

chicken parmesan with mushroom marsala sauce

2 to 3 tablespoons olive oil
6 to 8 pats butter
1 cup seasoned bread crumbs
1 cup freshly grated Parmesan cheese
1 tablespoon Herbés d'Provence (or herbs of your choice)
6 single chicken breasts (deboned)
1 cup flour seasoned with salt and pepper, on plate
2 eggs, beaten in medium-size bowl

Pour oil in center of 12-inch frying pan. Place pats of butter around oil; heat slowly to cooking temperature.

Combine bread crumbs, cheese, and herbs on plate.

Wash and pat dry chicken. Coat with seasoned flour; dip in eggs. Coat with bread-crumb mixture. Set aside on waxed paper or rack; repeat procedure for all pieces. Let stand in refrigerator 2 to 3 hours. Place all pieces in frying pan at same time; fry to golden brown. Pour sauce over chicken just before serving. Yield 6 servings.

mushroom marsala sauce
1 pound fresh mushrooms
3 to 4 tablespoons butter
⅓ cup Marsala wine (or to taste)

Clean mushrooms; sauté in butter. Add wine; stir until hot (do not bring to boil).

chicken paprika

chicken in potato nest

2 cups cooked mashed potatoes
2 tablespoons butter or margarine
2 tablespoons flour
Salt to taste
½ teaspoon pepper
1 cup chicken broth
¼ cup heavy cream
1 small can (about 3 ounces) sliced mushrooms
2 cups diced cooked chicken
2 tablespoons grated Parmesan cheese

Preheat oven to 400°F.

Line buttered 8- or 9-inch pie plate with potatoes.

Melt butter in pan; stir in flour and seasonings. Add broth gradually; stir until boiling. Add cream and mushrooms; cook a few minutes.

Put chicken into pie plate. Pour sauce over; sprinkle with cheese. Bake 25 to 30 minutes. Yield 4 servings.

chicken provençale

4 single chicken breasts, each approximately 8 to 10 ounces
3 tablespoons vegetable oil
½ teaspoon salt
⅛ teaspoon white pepper

1 medium tomato
5 black olives
1 clove garlic, minced
½ cup dry white wine
3 tablespoons water
¼ teaspoon instant chicken bouillon (or ½ cube)
¼ cup yogurt
Parsley for garnish

Bone chicken breasts.

Heat oil in large frypan; fry chicken breasts approximately 15 minutes, until golden brown and completely cooked. Season with salt and pepper. Arrange on preheated platter; keep warm.

Peel and chop tomato; slice olives. Add tomato, olives, and garlic to pan drippings. Pour in wine and water; stir in dry bouillon. Bring to boil; simmer, uncovered, 8 minutes. Cool sauce slightly; gradually add yogurt. Warm sauce over low heat if necessary. Pour over chicken breasts; garnish with parsley. Yield 4 servings.

chicken in red wine

1 (3- to 4-pound) chicken, cut into serving pieces
⅓ cup vegetable oil
¼ cup cognac
2 medium onions, quartered
1 clove garlic, minced

chicken in red wine

3 cups Burgundy wine
¼ teaspoon thyme
½ tablespoon tomato paste
1 bay leaf
½ teaspoon salt
⅛ teaspoon pepper
3 strips bacon, cut into 2-inch strips
1 4-ounce can button mushrooms, drained, or
    ¾ cup small mushrooms, quartered
1 tablespoon butter, softened
1 tablespoon flour
2 slices white bread (optional)
2 tablespoons oil
1 tablespoon butter
1 or 2 parsley sprigs

Brown chicken in hot oil in large Dutch oven; drain fat. Pour in cognac; carefully ignite. When flames subside, add onions, garlic, wine, thyme, tomato paste, bay leaf, salt, and pepper. Bring mixture to boil; simmer, covered, 1 hour. Skim off fat; correct seasonings. Discard bay leaf.

Meanwhile, place bacon in frypan; cook until done. Remove bacon; sauté mushrooms in hot fat. Drain off fat. Keep bacon and mushrooms warm until needed.

Blend 1 tablespoon butter and flour together to smooth paste (beurre manié). When chicken is done, add paste to hot liquid. Stir and simmer a minute or two.

Trim bread; cut in half diagonally. Fry in oil and butter until crisp.

Arrange chicken in casserole or serving dish. Cover with sauce. Garnish with bacon, mushrooms, parsley and croutons. Yield 4 servings.

chicken–rock-lobster kabobs

6 skinless and boneless chicken-breast halves
6 (4-ounce each) frozen South African rock-
    lobster tails
1 small navel orange, cut into 6 wedges
Salt and pepper
1 cup peach preserves
⅓ cup chopped chutney
1 tablespoon soy sauce
1 tablespoon wine vinegar

Cut each chicken breast into 4 pieces.

With sharp knife cut each rock-lobster tail crosswise through shell into 4 pieces.

Alternately spear chicken pieces, rock-lobster slices, and orange wedges on heatproof skewers. Sprinkle kabobs on all sides with salt and pepper.

Mix remaining ingredients in bowl; stir until well blended.

Place kabobs 6 inches above gray coals; grill 5 minutes. Brush with sauce; turn. Grill 5 minutes.

Brush with sauce; turn. Grill 2 minutes.

Serve kabobs garnished with chopped scallions and pineapple slices, grilled over coals on square of foil after brushing with sauce. Heat remaining sauce; spoon over kabobs or serve as a dip. Yield 6 servings.

chicken santeray

3 pounds frying chicken, cut up
Salt and pepper
4 tablespoons butter
2 tablespoons finely chopped onion
1 cup red burgundy wine
1 cup strong chicken broth
Chopped chives

Season chicken with salt and pepper. Heat 4 tablespoons butter in large skillet. When foaming stops, cook chicken, single layer at a time, until golden on both sides and ready to eat. Remove chicken from pan; cover. Keep warm over low heat while you prepare sauce.

Add chopped onions to 2 tablespoons browned butter in skillet. Cook gently 2 minutes. Add wine and broth. Bring to boil, scraping pan. Cook, uncovered, until reduced by ½ to 1 cup; remove from heat. Stir in 1 tablespoon butter in little bits. Pour sauce over chicken; sprinkle with chives. Serve immediately. Yield 4 servings.

chicken sauté in wine

¼ cup finely diced salt pork
1 (3½-pound) frying chicken
¼ cup butter
¼ cup vegetable oil
2 leeks
20 shallots or small onions
Salt and white pepper to taste
1 clove garlic, pressed
3 tablespoons freshly minced parsley
¾ cup sweet white wine
¾ cup chicken broth
½ cup whipping cream
1 (5-ounce) can black or button mushrooms,
    drained

Soak pork in enough water to cover 30 minutes; drain well.

Cut chicken into serving pieces; remove skin. Melt all but 1 tablespoon butter with oil in large, heavy skillet over medium heat. Add chicken; sauté on all sides until lightly browned. Drain off excess fat; set aside. Trim green end from leeks; discard. Cut white part into thin slices.

Combine pork, leeks, and shallots in saucepan over medium heat; cook, stirring constantly, until lightly browned. Add to chicken. Add salt, pepper, garlic, parsley, wine, and broth. Cover; simmer about 45 minutes or until chicken is tender.

219

chicken sauté in wine

chicken tetrazzini

Remove chicken, pork, and vegetables with slotted spoon; place on heated serving platter. Keep warm.

Add cream to liquid in skillet; simmer until of sauce consistency. Add half the mushrooms; heat through. Spoon sauce over chicken and vegetables; border with rice. Garnish with remaining mushrooms which have been lightly sautéed in 1 tablespoon butter.

Fresh mushrooms, cooked with pork mixture, can be used instead of canned mushrooms. Remove from pork mixture after browned; add to sauce same as for black mushrooms. Yield 6 servings.

chicken tetrazzini

1 stewing chicken, about 3 to 4 pounds
2 onions
2 carrots
Parsley, thyme, and 1 bay leaf
½ pound spaghetti
6 tablespoons butter
Dash of garlic powder
4 tablespoons flour
½ cup white wine

220

Salt and pepper
6 to 8 mushrooms, sliced
3 to 4 tablespoons whipping cream
¼ cup grated Parmesan cheese
2 tablespoons dried bread crumbs
2 tablespoons sliced almonds, browned

Preheat oven to 400°F.

Cook chicken slowly in water with onions, carrots, and herbs until tender. Let cool in stock, if possible overnight. Remove skin and bones; cook them in stock until well flavored and reduced to 2 to 3 cups.

Boil spaghetti in usual way; finish in 1 tablespoon butter flavored with a little garlic powder. Place in fireproof dish; keep warm.

Make velouté sauce: Melt 4 tablespoons butter; add flour. When blended, add 1½ cups chicken stock. Bring to boil; cook 2 minutes. Add wine; simmer few minutes.

Meanwhile, cut cold chicken into long strips. Place in mound on spaghetti; sprinkle with salt and pepper.

Cook mushrooms in 1 tablespoon butter 2 to 3 minutes; put on chicken.

Add cream to sauce; check seasoning. Spoon sauce over dish; sprinkle top with cheese and crumbs.

Bake in oven 10 to 15 minutes, until well heated and top brown and crisp. Sprinkle almonds over top. Serve at once. Yield 4 to 6 servings.

chicken with tomatoes and olives

4 breast quarters of frying chicken
½ cup flour
2 tablespoons butter
2 tablespoons olive oil
1 clove garlic, chopped
1 cup chopped onion
¼ cup chopped carrots
¼ cup chopped celery
2 cups broken-up canned tomatoes
½ cup white wine
1 teaspoon chili powder
½ teaspoon ground cumin
½ teaspoon salt
¼ teaspoon pepper
¾ cup cut-up black olives

Wash chicken; pat dry. Dredge chicken in flour; shake off excess.

Heat butter and oil together in deep skillet or Dutch oven. Brown chicken well on all sides. Remove chicken from pan. Lightly brown garlic, onion, carrots, and celery in pan drippings.

Force tomatoes through sieve or puree in blender or food processor. Add tomatoes and wine to vegetables in pan or skillet. Add seasonings; stir well. Place chicken in sauce. Simmer over low heat 30 minutes or until chicken is tender. Add olives; heat through. Yield 4 servings.

chicken with tomatoes and olives

chicken–vegetable ring

2 cups shredded cooked chicken
½ pound sliced mushrooms, sautéed
½ cup diced celery
Salt and pepper to taste
Dash each garlic and onion powder
2 eggs
¾ cup chicken broth
1¼ cups soft bread crumbs
2 cups cooked or canned mixed vegetables or
    desired combination

Combine chicken with mushrooms and celery. Add seasoning as desired.

Beat eggs into broth. Stir in bread crumbs. Add to chicken mixture. Place in ring mold. Set mold into pan of hot water.

Bake at 350°F 45 minutes or until set. Turn out onto heated serving dish. Fill center with cooked vegetables. Yield 6 servings.

chicken in wine in no time

½ cup flour
2 teaspoons salt
½ teaspoon pepper
2½- to 3½-pound chicken, cut up
¼ cup oil
1 package dry onion soup mix
1 cup dry white wine
Water

Combine flour, salt, and pepper in paper bag. Shake chicken pieces to coat. Brown chicken well on all sides in oil in skillet. Sprinkle with onion soup; pour in white wine. Add a little water. Cover; simmer until tender, about 45 minutes. Yield 4 servings.

chinese chicken with mushrooms

4 chicken-breast halves, boned, skinned, cut into
    ½-inch cubes
¼ cup dry white wine
½ teaspoon salt
2 scallions, cut into ½-inch slices
½ cup ½-inch cubes celery
1 tablespoon vegetable oil
12 snow-pea pods, strings removed
¼ pound mushrooms, sliced into "T" shapes
6 water chestnuts, sliced
½ cup chicken broth
1 tablespoon cornstarch in 2 tablespoons cold
    water
1 tablespoon soy sauce
Whole, blanched almonds (optional)

Combine chicken with wine and salt; set aside.
Stir-fry scallions and celery in oil 1 minute; push

circassian chicken

aside. Stir-fry pods 2 minutes; push aside. Stir-fry mushrooms and water chestnuts 1 to 2 minutes; push aside. Add chicken and wine; stir-fry 2 to 3 minutes, until chicken is done. Combine chicken and vegetables in wok or skillet.

Stir together broth, cornstarch mixture, and soy sauce. Add slowly to chicken and vegetables; heat until thickened and clear. Serve over rice; sprinkle with almonds. Yield 4 servings.

circassian chicken

1 chicken, 3 to 4 pounds
5 onions
3 cloves
3 stalks celery, chopped
Few sprigs parsley
1 bay leaf
8 peppercorns
Salt
2 cups shelled walnuts

222

½ cup dry bread crumbs
2 tablespoons butter
1 clove garlic, crushed
Pepper
2 teaspoons paprika
3 tablespoons oil
Pinch of cayenne pepper

Put chicken in deep pan; just cover with cold water. Add 3 onions, each stuck with a clove, celery, herbs, peppercorns, and a little salt. Bring to boil; simmer until tender, about 1 hour. Skim as necessary. Drain; keep warm. Reserve stock for sauce.

Grind walnuts finely in electric blender or food processor; mix with bread crumbs.

Melt butter; cook 2 chopped onions and garlic until golden brown and soft. Add to walnut mixture; blend carefully. When quite smooth, cook until it reaches boiling point; add more stock if sauce becomes too thick. Season with salt and a little pepper.

Mix oil and red pepper together; when oil is red, strain. Add enough oil to walnut sauce to make it a delicate pink.

Cut chicken into pieces. Put layer of sauce in bottom of fireproof serving dish; lay chicken pieces on top. Spoon remaining sauce over chicken. Reheat thoroughly.

Decorate top with remaining red oil, sprinkling over surface of dish. Serve with plain boiled rice. Yield 4 to 6 servings.

creamed chicken and ham

1½ tablespoons flour or cornstarch
1½ tablespoons butter
¾ cup chicken stock
¼ cup cream
½ cup diced cooked chicken
½ cup diced cooked ham
¼ cup chopped celery
1 tablespoon parsley
1 egg, beaten
1 or 2 tablespoons sherry (optional)

Add flour to melted butter; stir until blended. Slowly stir in stock, then cream. When sauce is smooth and to boiling point, add chicken, ham, celery, and parsley.

Remove 2 tablespoons sauce; mix with egg. Reduce heat to low; return egg mixture to heat. Stir constantly until all thickens slightly. Add 1 or 2 tablespoons sherry just before serving. Serve over corn bread squares or hot waffles. Yield 4 servings.

curried chicken

2 small chickens, about 3 pounds each
1 medium onion, chopped
⅓ cup butter or margarine
1 (light) tablespoon curry powder
3 cups boiling water
2 teaspoons salt
¼ cup flour

curried chicken

Cut each chicken into pieces.

Brown onion in butter in large skillet. Remove onion; brown chicken parts in same fat. Replace onion; add curry powder. Pour boiling water over chicken; add salt. Simmer until chicken is tender, about 30 minutes.

Mix flour with ¼ cup chicken liquid; add to chicken. Stir until thick and smooth. Serve piping hot on bed of rice. Yield 6 to 8 servings.

french chicken breasts in red-wine noodles

2 frying chicken breasts, split (about 1½ pounds)
4 ounces Canadian bacon, diced
2 cups dry red wine
2 onions, halved, sliced
1 bay leaf
¼ teaspoon poultry seasoning
Salt and pepper to taste
4 cups water
4 ounces wide noodles
2 tablespoons chopped fresh parsley

Spray large non-stick pot or Dutch oven with cooking spray for no-fat frying. Place chicken skin-side-down. Brown slowly over moderate heat until skin is crisp and well-rendered of fat. Remove chicken; discard melted fat.

Put diced Canadian bacon in pot; brown, stirring frequently to prevent sticking.

Combine the wine, onions, bay leaf, and seasonings in pot. Lay chicken breasts on top, skin-side-up. Cover; simmer gently 20 minutes. Add water to pot. Heat to boiling. Stir in noodles, few at a time. Cover; simmer 12 to 15 minutes, stirring occasionally. Uncover; simmer until all liquid is absorbed by noodles. Sprinkle with parsley. Yield 4 servings.

fried chicken with cream gravy

Salt, pepper, and garlic salt
1 cup flour
1 (2½- to 3-pound) frying chicken, cut into serving pieces
Fat for deep frying

Mix seasonings with flour; coat each chicken piece.

Heat fat in skillet; fry chicken, few pieces at a time. Cook about 25 minutes per batch of chicken, so that pieces are crisp and crusty. Drain on paper towels; set on warmed platter. Yield 4 to 6 servings.

fried chicken with cream gravy

cream gravy
2 tablespoons cornstarch
¾ cup hot chicken broth
½ cup milk at room temperature
1 teaspoon salt
¼ teaspoon pepper

Pour off most fat in skillet; leave about 2 tablespoons.

Mix cornstarch with chicken broth. Add to hot fat, stirring constantly. Gradually add milk, salt, and pepper. When slightly thickened, gravy is ready. Put in gravy boat; serve with chicken.

italian chicken in envelopes

1 (2½- to 3-pound) chicken
2 tablespoons olive oil
1 medium onion, chopped
1 clove garlic, minced
4 large fresh tomatoes, peeled, chopped (canned tomatoes can be substituted if drained and chopped)
4 large green olives, chopped
½ teaspoon crumbled dried sweet basil
½ teaspoon crumbled, dried oregano
½ teaspoon celery salt
¼ teaspoon pepper
4 bay leaves

Wash chicken. Drain; pat dry. Cut into quarters.

Cut 4 (10-inch) pieces aluminum foil; grease with olive oil. Place piece of chicken in center of each piece of foil.

Combine onion, garlic, tomatoes, olives, basil, oregano, celery salt, and pepper; mix well. Spoon some sauce over each piece of chicken. Add 1 bay leaf to each package. Fold foil into neat sealed package. Place on cookie sheet. Bake at 425°F 40 minutes. Serve from packages. Yield 4 servings.

mediterranean chicken

1 tablespoon butter or margarine
1 tablespoon finely chopped onion
½ cup chopped celery
1 (10-ounce) package frozen French-style green beans
1 tablespoon chopped pimiento
2 cups diced cooked chicken
2 cans (10½ ounces each) condensed cream of mushroom soup
½ teaspoon oregano
White pepper to taste
⅔ cup cashew or roasted peanut halves
1 tablespoon minced parsley (optional)

Melt butter in 2- or 3-quart saucepan. Add onion, celery, and beans. Cover; simmer over low

italian chicken in envelopes

heat about 15 minutes, stirring occasionally, until beans are tender. Add pimiento, chicken, soup, and seasonings. Cook 10 minutes to blend flavors; stir as needed to prevent sticking. Stir in nuts. Sprinkle with parsley before serving. Yield 6 servings.

nutty chicken

1 cup finely chopped dry roasted peanuts, without jackets
½ cup fine dry bread crumbs
1¼ teaspoons salt
½ teaspoon poultry seasoning
Pepper to taste
4 broiler drumsticks
4 broiler wings
¼ cup broth

Mix together peanuts, crumbs, and seasonings.

Dip chicken pieces in broth, then in peanut mixture; coat all over. Place in single layer on foil-lined pan. Bake at 400°F 40 minutes or until tender. Do not turn chicken during baking. Yield 4 servings.

open-roasted capon

1 (7½-to 8-pound) capon or small turkey
Butter
Salt and freshly ground black peppercorns to taste
½ cup water
1½ to 2 cups hot water or chicken broth
3 tablespoons cornstarch

Rub capon generously with butter; season with generous sprinkling of salt and pepper inside and

open-roasted capon

out. Place capon in foil-lined baking pan; place on middle shelf of 400°F oven. Roast 30 minutes. Spoon up pan juices; baste capon thoroughly. Add ½ cup water to pan. Reduce oven temperature to 375°F. Place small piece of foil over capon breast; bake about 2 hours, basting frequently with pan juices. Test fattest part of thigh by sticking with slim skewer. If juice is faintly pink, roast about 15 to 20 minutes or until done. Remove capon to serving dish.

Pour pan juices into saucepan; add enough water for desired taste.

Combine cornstarch with small amount of broth or water; mix to smooth liquid. Pour into pan; cook over medium heat, stirring constantly, until slightly thickened and rather clear, about 10 or 15 minutes. Yield 6 to 8 servings.

oregano grilled chicken

3 pounds fryer-chicken pieces
1 large freezer bag
½ cup olive oil
¼ cup lemon juice
2 cloves garlic, minced
½ teaspoon salt
1 teaspoon crumbled dried oregano

½ teaspoon freshly ground pepper
2 tablespoons butter, melted

Day before cooking, wash chicken; pat dry. Place in freezer bag.

Combine oil, lemon juice, garlic, salt, oregano, and pepper; pour over chicken. Tie bag shut; turn bag several times to coat chicken with marinade. Refrigerate 24 hours; turn bag occasionally.

Remove chicken from bag; reserve marinade. Grill 5 inches from white-hot charcoal 30 minutes; turn once. Brush frequently with marinade combined with butter. Yield 4 or 5 servings.

variation

Substitute 1 (3-pound) roasting chicken for chicken parts; marinate in same manner. Drain chicken; reserve marinade. Mount on rotisserie spit; cook 1½ hours on indoor unit or over charcoal. Baste frequently with marinade mixed with butter.

oven-fried chicken

1 young chicken, jointed
4 tablespoons flour
Salt
Black pepper
Paprika

1 egg, beaten
Fine bread crumbs
3 to 4 tablespoons oil

Preheat oven to 400°F.

Toss chicken lightly in flour to which a little salt, pepper, and paprika have been added. Brush with beaten egg; coat with bread crumbs.

Heat oil in roasting pan; put in chicken. Brush lightly with hot oil; and bake about 30 minutes. Yield 4 or 5 servings.

paella

6 rock-lobster tails
12 large raw shrimp
6 cherrystone clams
6 mussels
½ pound chorizos or other garlic-flavored sausage
⅔ cup olive oil
½ pound pork cubes
4 chicken breasts, thighs, and legs
1 onion
1 green pepper
¼ cup tomato sauce
3 cups long-grain rice
⅛ teaspoon saffron powder
1 teaspoon salt
1 teaspoon garlic powder
¼ teaspoon pepper
1½ quarts boiling water
1 cup frozen peas
1 fresh tomato, peeled, seeded, diced

With kitchen shears break centers of ribs on belly sides of lobster shells. Loosen meat from shells with fingers; leave meat attached near tail fins.

Shell and devein shrimp.

Scrub clams and mussels. Soak mussels in cold water 30 minutes to remove salty taste. Discard any that open their shells while soaking; drain. Place sausage in shallow skillet. Cover with water; bring to boil. Boil 5 minutes; drain. Remove skin; cut into ¼-inch rounds.

Heat ⅓ cup oil. Fry sausage until browned on each side. Remove from skillet; drain.

Add pork to heated oil. Fry until brown on all sides and no longer pink. Remove from skillet; drain.

Add chicken to skillet. Fry 45 minutes or until golden brown and meat is cooked. Remove from skillet; drain.

Add lobster to skillet; fry just until shells start to turn pink. Remove from skillet; drain.

Add remaining oil to skillet; heat thoroughly.

Peel and chop onion; sauté in skillet 10 minutes or until tender.

Remove seeds and membranes from green pepper; dice. Add to onions; sauté 5 minutes. Stir in tomato sauce; simmer until mixture thickens and holds its shape in spoon. Add rice, saffron, salt, garlic powder, and pepper; mix well. Add boiling water; mix well. Bring mixture to boil; reduce heat to simmer.

oregano grilled chicken

CHICKEN

Arrange lobster, shrimp, clams, mussels, sausage, pork, and chicken on top of rice mixture. Scatter peas and tomato over rice and meat; cover. Simmer 30 to 45 minutes or until rice is tender, shrimp and lobster meat turn white, and mussels and clams pop open. Remove from heat. Cover; let rest 10 minutes for flavors to mingle. Serve directly from pan. Yield 6 to 8 servings.

paella

pineapple chicken with poppy-seed noodles

4 chicken breasts
Salt and pepper to taste
2 tablespoons butter or margarine
8 ounces spinach noodles
1 chicken bouillon cube (optional)
2 tablespoons poppy seeds
3 tablespoons grated Parmesan cheese
1 tablespoon chopped parsley

Sprinkle chicken with salt and pepper; sauté in 1 tablespoon butter in large frying pan until browned. Cover; cook over low heat until tender, about 25 to 30 minutes.

While chicken is cooking, cook noodles in boiling salted water seasoned with bouillon cube just until tender, about 8 to 10 minutes. Drain; season with 1 tablespoon butter and poppy seeds. Place in large shallow ovenproof dish. When chicken has finished cooking, place on top of noodles; cover. Keep warm while preparing dressing and sauce. Divide dressing mixture equally on tops of chicken breasts. Pour sauce over chicken, dressing, and noodles. Sprinkle with cheese and parsley. Place under broiler until browned. Yield 4 servings.

dressing

1 small onion, chopped
½ pound mushrooms, sliced
1 slice whole-wheat bread, crumbed
1 tablespoon chopped parsley
¼ teaspoon thyme
⅛ teaspoon salt
1 (8-ounce) can crushed pineapple, well drained; reserve syrup

Remove all but 1 tablespoon fat from pan in which chicken was cooked. In same pan sauté onion until tender. Add mushrooms; sauté lightly. Stir in bread crumbs, parsley, thyme, salt, and pineapple. Remove from heat; set aside while making sauce.

sauce

3 tablespoons butter or margarine
3 tablespoons all-purpose flour
Reserved pineapple syrup plus water to equal 3 cups liquid
1 cup nonfat dry milk powder
1 teaspoon salt
2 egg yolks, beaten
½ cup all-purpose whipping cream, whipped

Melt butter in separate saucepan. Remove from heat; stir in flour. Add liquid and dry milk powder. Cook, stirring, over medium heat until slightly thickened. Add salt. Stir small amount hot mixture into egg yolks; add egg-yolk mixture slowly to hot mixture in saucepan, stirring. Stir and cook 2 to 3 minutes. Remove from heat. Fold in whipped cream.

roast capon with orange pecan stuffing

1 capon (5 to 6 pounds)
¼ cup butter or margarine
1 cup thinly sliced celery
¼ cup chopped onion
¾ cup water
5 cups toasted, crust-free bread cubes (½ inch)
¾ cup drained, sectioned, diced oranges
⅓ cup coarsely chopped pecans
1 teaspoon grated orange rind
1 teaspoon salt
½ teaspoon curry powder (optional)
Orange slices for garnish
Watercress for garnish

Wash, drain, and dry capon.

Prepare stuffing: Melt butter in skillet. Add celery, onion, and water; cook over moderate heat until vegetables are tender.

Combine bread cubes, orange pieces, pecans, orange rind, ½ teaspoon salt, and curry powder; mix. Add vegetables; mix carefully.

Sprinkle remaining salt over neck and body cavities of capon. Stuff neck and body cavities loosely with bread mixture. Skewer neck skin to back. Return legs and tail to tucked position. Place capon, breast-side-up, on open roasting pan. Do not add water to pan. Brush skin with melted butter or margarine. Cover capon loosely with foil, crimping it to edges of pan. (Foil should not touch capon.) Place in 325°F oven about 3 hours. Remove foil 45 minutes before end of roasting time to allow bird to brown. Brush again with melted butter. Test for doneness; continue roasting if not done. Yield 6 to 8 servings.

roast chicken

2 frying chickens, about 3 pounds each
1 teaspoon salt
1 teaspoon freshly ground pepper
2 cloves garlic, crushed
5 tablespoons melted butter
6 medium potatoes, peeled, cut into lengthwise wedges
2 medium onions, peeled, cut into wedges
⅓ cup lemon juice
½ cup water

Wash chickens; pat dry. Rub with salt, pepper, and garlic. Place in large roasting pan, breast-side-up; brush on all surfaces with 3 tablespoons butter.

Roll potatoes in 2 tablespoons butter; place with onions in pan with chicken. Roast at 425°F 25 minutes. Reduce heat to 325°F; roast 45 to 50 minutes or until leg joint moves easily. Pour lemon juice over chicken; remove chicken, potatoes, and onions to platter; keep warm.

Skim fat from pan juices. Add water; bring to boil. Pour into gravy boat. Slice chicken; serve. Yield 6 servings.

russian chicken cutlets

2 slices sandwich bread
¼ cup half-and-half cream
2 to 2½ cups uncooked ground chicken
2 teaspoons salt
¼ teaspoon freshly ground white pepper
½ cup finely chopped fresh mushrooms
6 tablespoons butter
1½ cups sifted all-purpose flour
1 egg, well beaten
2 cups fine dry bread crumbs
Vegetable oil
2 tablespoons lemon juice
2 egg yolks, beaten
⅛ teaspoon cayenne pepper

Remove crusts from bread; place bread in large bowl.

Pour cream over bread; let stand until all liquid is absorbed. Add chicken, 1 teaspoon salt, pepper, mushrooms, and 2 tablespoons softened butter; mix until well blended. Chill at least 1 hour so mixture will be easy to handle. Shape into 12 cutlets as shown in illustration. Coat each cutlet with flour; dip into egg. Coat with bread crumbs; press crumbs on firmly. Chill 1 hour to set coating.

Fill large heavy skillet ¼ inch deep with vegetable oil; place over medium heat until hot. Add cutlets; fry until browned on both sides. Drain on paper toweling; keep warm.

Combine lemon juice and egg yolks in top of double boiler; blend thoroughly. Place over hot water; add 2 tablespoons butter. Beat with whisk until smooth and thoroughly blended. Cut 2 tablespoons butter into small pieces; add to egg-yolk mixture 1 piece at a time; beat until smooth after each addition. Remove from water; stir in remaining salt and cayenne pepper. Place in sauceboat.

Place cutlets on serving platter; serve with sauce. To make this a party dish insert a toothpick into each cutlet; cover with a paper frill. Yield 6 servings.

sauced chicken in vol-au-vent shells

3 tablespoons butter
3 tablespoons all-purpose flour
1¼ cups chicken stock
2 tablespoons sherry
1 recipe Basic Brown Sauce (see Index)
Salt and pepper to taste
3 cups cubed cooked chicken or turkey

russian chicken cutlets

Melt butter in heavy saucepan; stir in flour to make smooth paste. Add stock gradually; stir constantly. Cook over low heat until thickened. Stir in sherry and brown sauce. Season with salt and pepper. Fold in chicken; heat through. Serve hot in patty shells or on toast points. Garnish with chopped parsley. Yield about 8 servings.

sauced chicken in vol-au-vent shells

roast chicken

spicy barbecued chicken

barbecue sauce
6 tablespoons oil
1 onion, chopped fine
1 clove garlic, crushed
1 medium can tomatoes (or 3 to 4 tablespoons
   tomato puree)
1 tablespoon tomato catsup
1 tablespoon chutney
1 tablespoon vinegar
½ cup stock (or water)
1 tablespoon Worcestershire sauce
1 teaspoon French mustard
1 teaspoon paprika
Juice and grated rind of ½ lemon
2 teaspoons brown sugar
1 tablespoon finely chopped parsley
1 teaspoon mixed powdered thyme, nutmeg, and
   bay leaf
4 large chicken quarters or halves

Prepare barbecue sauce: Heat oil; cook onion and garlic 5 minutes. Add sieved tomatoes or puree and all other ingredients. Cook 20 to 30 minutes; season to taste. Strain; let cool.

With sharp knife make small cuts in chicken pieces. Spoon cold barbecue sauce over; let stand at least ½ hour.

Heat charcoal grill or broiler. Place chicken pieces on hot grill; turn every 5 or 6 minutes, basting frequently with barbecue sauce. Allow 30 to 45 minutes to barbecue quarters, depending on heat of grill and thickness of chicken. Test with skewer; if juice from chicken runs clear, chicken is done.

Heat remaining sauce; serve. Yield 4 servings.

spicy roast chicken

1 cup plain yogurt
3 cloves garlic, crushed
2 teaspoons grated fresh ginger
⅓ cup lime juice

stuffed chicken-breasts athenian

1 tablespoon ground coriander
1 teaspoon cumin
½ teaspoon cayenne pepper
1 whole chicken (3 pounds)
Lime wedges
1 onion, sliced, steamed

Mix yogurt, garlic, ginger, lime juice, and spices. Rub chicken inside and out with mixture. Place in bowl; pour remaining marinade over. Cover; refrigerate 24 hours. Turn chicken at least once. Remove chicken from marinade. Roast in preheated 375°F oven 1 hour or until done. Baste with marinade during cooking. Disjoint chicken; serve with lime wedges and onion slices. Yield 4 servings.

stuffed chicken-breasts athenian

4 split chicken breasts, skinned, boned
2 tablespoons crumbled feta cheese
1 tablespoon chopped walnuts
1 tablespoon chopped parsley
¾ cup flour
½ teaspoon salt
¼ teaspoon pepper
1 egg
2 tablespoons milk
2 tablespoons olive oil
2 tablespoons butter

Cut small pocket in each chicken cutlet by making slit in each piece; do not cut all the way through cutlet.

Mix cheese, walnuts, and parsley. Put 1 tablespoon stuffing in each cutlet; seal edges by pressing together.

Mix flour, salt, and pepper. Dredge chicken in flour mixture.

Mix egg and milk. Dip cutlets in egg mixture, then again in flour mixture; refrigerate until ready to cook.

Heat oil and butter in large, heavy skillet over medium heat until foam subsides. Cook cutlets over medium-high heat until brown. Turn cutlets; reduce heat. Cook until brown and cooked through. Do not cover; chicken will lose its crispness and cheese will begin to ooze out of cutlet.

Serve chicken with Rice Pilaf (see Index); top with Kima Sauce. Yield 4 servings.

kima sauce
3 tablespoons olive oil
¼ cup chopped onion
¼ cup chopped carrots
¼ cup chopped celery
1 clove garlic, chopped
1 (8-ounce) can tomatoes, drained, chopped
2 tablespoons chopped parsley
¼ cup white wine
¼ teaspoon sugar
¼ teaspoon oregano

Heat oil in small, heavy skillet. Cook onion, carrots, celery, and garlic until limp. Add tomatoes, parsley, wine, sugar, and oregano; simmer 20 minutes or until thick.

sweet-and-sour chicken

2 tablespoons soy sauce
1 tablespoon cornstarch
2 whole chicken breasts, halved, skinned, boned,
   cut into bite-size cubes
1 tablespoon vegetable oil
1 cucumber, scored lengthwise with tines of fork,
   cut into bite-size cubes
½ cantaloupe, seeded, rinded, cut into bite-size
   pieces
1 sweet red pepper (or green pepper), cubed

sweet-and-sour sauce
2 tablespoons brown sugar
2 tablespoons vinegar
½ cup pineapple juice (unsweetened)
1 tablespoon cornstarch in 2 tablespoons cold
   water
3 ounces blanched whole almonds

Combine soy sauce and cornstarch. Coat chicken pieces thoroughly.

Heat oil in large frypan (or wok); stir-fry chicken 3 to 4 minutes. Add cucumber, cantaloupe, and pepper.

Mix together sauce ingredients; add to chicken mixture. Heat, stirring often, until sauce boils and ingredients are heated through. Add almonds. Yield 4 servings.

tangy chicken of the islands

½ cup vinegar
½ cup soy sauce
1 clove garlic, minced fine
Dash of freshly ground black pepper
1 (2- to 3-pound) frying chicken, cut into serving
   pieces

Put vinegar, soy sauce, garlic, and pepper in skillet. Add chicken; let marinate together at least 30 minutes. Heat to boil on top of stove. Cover skillet; lower heat. Simmer about 40 minutes. Liquid will be absorbed into chicken. Served hot or cold. Yield 4 to 6 servings.

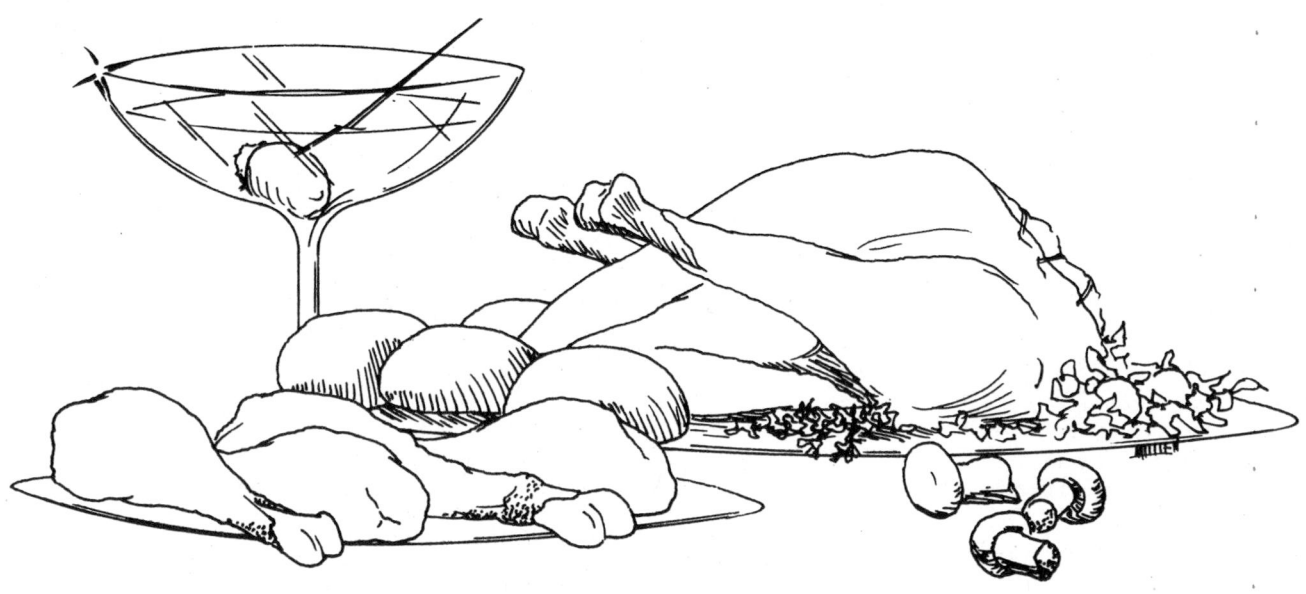

sweet-and-sour chicken

CHICKEN LIVERS

baked chicken livers

3 or 4 medium-size onions, sliced ¼ inch thick
10 to 12 chicken livers
3 strips bacon
Salt and pepper to taste
½ cup sherry

Arrange onions in flat oblong baking dish. Put 1 liver on each onion; salt lightly.

Cut each bacon strip into quarters; place 1 quarter on each liver. Sprinkle with salt and pepper. Pour sherry over.

Bake at 350°F about 45 minutes, until bacon is crisp. Baste occasionally during baking. Yield 4 servings.

chicken livers with apples and onion

¾ pound chicken livers
3 tablespoons flour
½ teaspoon salt
¼ teaspoon pepper
⅛ teaspoon cayenne pepper
3 medium apples
¼ cup vegetable oil
¼ cup sugar
1 large onion, thinly sliced

Rinse livers; drain on paper towels. Coat evenly with mixture of flour, salt, pepper, and cayenne; set aside.

Wash apples; remove cores. Cut into ½-inch slices, to form rings.

Heat 2 tablespoons oil in frypan over medium heat. Add apples; cook until lightly brown. Turn slices carefully; sprinkle with sugar. Cook, uncovered, over low heat until tender. Remove from pan; reserve.

Heat remaining oil over low heat. Add livers and onion rings. Cook over medium heat; turn often to brown all sides.

Transfer to warm serving platter. Serve with apple rings. Yield 4 servings.

chicken livers with beer

¼ pound butter or margarine
1 medium onion, chopped fine
¼ teaspoon garlic powder
1½ pounds chicken livers
1 tablespoon flour
½ cup beer
3 cups cooked rice

Melt butter in medium skillet; cook onion until transparent. Add garlic powder and livers; cook until livers are browned on all sides.

Mix flour with 1 tablespoon beer; add to livers. Stirring constantly, add rest of beer until sauce thickens and livers are done through, about 5 minutes.

Put hot cooked rice in center of platter; mound livers around rice. Yield 4 to 6 servings.

chicken livers paprikash

1 pound chicken livers
4 tablespoons butter or margarine
1 cup thinly sliced onions
1 clove garlic, peeled, mashed
1 tablespoon Hungarian sweet paprika
Salt and pepper
1 cup chicken broth
¼ cup sour cream
1 tablespoon flour

Rinse livers; drain very well. Remove fat or connective tissue.

Melt butter in large heavy skillet over moderate heat. Add onions and garlic; cook, stirring, until browned. Remove from heat. Add paprika, salt, and pepper; stir well. Add chicken broth; cover. Bring to boil; reduce heat to low. Cook 15 to 20 minutes or until livers are done to taste.

Combine sour cream and flour; stir well. Add slowly to liver mixture, stirring well. Cook over very low heat until thickened.

Serve livers with buttered noodles or dumplings; garnish with chopped parsley. Yield 4 servings.

chicken livers with sage

1 pound chicken livers, halved
1 teaspoon salt
¼ teaspoon pepper
1 tablespoon dried sage
4 tablespoons butter or margarine
2 slices raw bacon, diced fine
¼ cup dry white wine

Season livers with salt, pepper, and sage.

Heat butter and bacon together in medium skillet. Add livers; cook 5 minutes, until browned. Stir in wine; let simmer 2 minutes. Spoon livers and sauce over spaghetti. Yield 4 to 6 servings.

chicken livers on toast

1 can mushroom gravy
2 tablespoons sherry
½ cup flour
½ teaspoon dried dillweed
1 pound chicken livers
1 egg, beaten
4 or more tablespoons butter or margarine

Mix gravy and sherry in saucepan; bring to boil. Lower heat; simmer 5 minutes.

Combine flour and dillweed for batter. Put each liver into beaten egg, then into flour. Be sure to coat all sides of livers well.

Melt butter in medium skillet. Add livers; cook over moderate heat 10 minutes or until golden brown. Serve on toast squares with hot gravy. Yield 4 servings.

eggs and chicken livers

2 pounds chicken livers
**½ cup flour seasoned with ½ teaspoon salt
    and ¼ teaspoon black pepper**
3 tablespoons butter
¼ cup Madeira wine
4 large tomatoes, peeled, diced
1 cup grated cheddar cheese

12 eggs, well beaten
½ teaspoon baking powder
½ pound salted almonds

Roll livers in flour.

Melt butter in saucepan; sauté livers. Add wine and tomatoes; simmer about 4 minutes. Transfer liver and wine mixture to 1½-quart casserole. Sprinkle with cheese; broil until cheese melts. Pour eggs to which ½ teaspoon baking powder has been added into hot buttered skillet; let cook slowly until eggs become set on bottom of pan. With fork or spatula lift up eggs at edge of pan, allowing uncooked egg to run underneath. Continue cooking and lifting until eggs are set. Place eggs in center of platter; border with livers. Sprinkle almonds over livers; garnish with parsley. Yield 8 servings.

almond cookies

½ cup butter or margarine
½ cup white sugar
½ tablespoon molasses
1 cup all-purpose flour
2 cups rolled oats
½ cup flaked almonds
1 teaspoon baking soda
¼ cup boiling water

Preheat oven to 375°F.

Cream butter and sugar until creamy. Add molasses; mix well. Stir in flour, rolled oats, and almonds.

Dissolve baking soda in boiling water; add to mixture while hot. Mix to stiff dough. Roll teaspoons of dough into balls; place on greased baking pans, allowing room to spread. Press flat; decorate top of each with flaked almond. Bake 15 minutes. Remove to cooling tray; store when quite cold. Yield about 48.

almond macaroons

1 cup sugar
1 (8-ounce) can almond paste
2 egg whites

Combine sugar and almond paste in large bowl; mix with fingers until well blended. Add egg

almond macaroons

whites gradually, using just enough to moisten; mix with wooden spoon. Roll lightly into walnut-size balls; flatten slightly. Place about 2 inches apart on brown paper on baking sheet.

Bake in preheated 325°F oven about 12 minutes or until very lightly browned. Remove from oven; slide paper onto damp towel. Cool slightly; remove with spatula. Yield about 2 dozen.

almond cookies

![almond princes photograph]

almond princes

almond princes

½ recipe Basic Sweet Short Pastry (see Index)
Sifted confectioners' sugar
¾ cup ground almonds
1 egg white, slightly beaten

Roll pastry on lightly floured surface until very thin. Cut into 24 circles with 2½-inch cookie cutter; press into miniature cupcake pans. Prick bottoms and sides of shells.

Combine 1½ cups sugar and almonds in medium-size bowl. Stir in enough egg white to make mixture consistency of thick paste. Fill tart shells to just below rims with mixture. Sprinkle generously with confectioners' sugar.

Bake in preheated 350°F oven until filling is rounded and tarts are golden brown. Remove tarts from pans; place on wire rack until completely cooled. Place 2 skewers evenly over tarts; sift with confectioners' sugar to make a design. Yield 24 tarts.

almond triangles

½ cup butter
1 cup sugar

almond triangles

6 tablespoons whipping cream
3 eggs
½ teaspoon salt
2 cups flour
Chopped almonds

Combine butter and sugar in mixer bowl; cream until smooth. Beat in cream and 2 eggs. Add salt and flour; blend well. Wrap in waxed paper; chill overnight. Roll on lightly floured surface; cut into triangles.

Beat remaining egg slightly; brush over tops of triangles. Sprinkle with almonds. Place triangles on greased baking sheet. Bake in preheated 375°F oven 8 to 10 minutes or until golden brown. Yield 3 to 4 dozen cookies.

anzac cookies

1 cup flour
1 cup rolled oats
¾ cup finely shredded coconut
1 cup sugar
½ cup butter
1 tablespoon maple syrup
1½ teaspoons baking soda
2 tablespoons boiling water

Preheat oven to 350°F.

Sift flour; add rolled oats, coconut, and sugar.

Put butter and syrup into pan; stir over low heat until melted.

Mix baking soda with water. Add to melted butter; stir into dry ingredients. Put heaping teaspoons onto greased baking sheets; allow room to spread. Bake 20 minutes. Remove to cooling racks. Yield about 36.

apple–oat bars

1 cup whole-wheat pastry flour
½ teaspoon baking soda
½ teaspoon salt
1 teaspoon cinnamon
½ cup packed brown sugar
1½ cups rolled oats
½ cup butter or margarine, melted
1 egg, beaten
1½ teaspoons vanilla
⅓ cup chopped walnuts
2 cups thinly sliced peeled apples (3 medium apples)

Stir together flour, soda, salt, and cinnamon until evenly mixed. Add brown sugar and oats. Stir in butter, egg, and vanilla; mix well. Place half of dough in bottom of greased 9-inch-square baking pan. Sprinkle nuts over dough. Arrange apple slices over nuts. Sprinkle remaining dough over apples; press lightly. Bake at 350°F 25 to 30 minutes. Cool; sprinkle with confectioners' sugar, if desired. Cut into bars. Yield 18.

applesauce brownie squares

½ cup butter or margarine
2 (1-ounce) squares unsweetened chocolate
¾ cup sugar
2 eggs, beaten
¾ cup applesauce
1¼ teaspoons vanilla
1 cup whole-wheat pastry flour
½ teaspoon baking powder
¼ teaspoon baking soda
¼ teaspoon salt

chocolate–nut topping
2 tablespoons sugar
¼ cup chopped nuts
½ cup semisweet chocolate pieces

Melt together butter and chocolate in small saucepan over low heat. Add sugar, eggs, applesauce, and vanilla; beat well.

Stir together flour, baking powder, soda, and salt until evenly combined. Add to chocolate mixture; beat well. Pour batter into greased 8-inch-square baking pan.

Combine topping ingredients; sprinkle over batter. Bake in 350°F oven 30 to 35 minutes, until toothpick inserted in center comes out clean. Cool; cut into squares. Yield 16.

apricot balls

1 cup dried apricots
½ cup walnuts
½ cup coconut
2 tablespoons wheat germ
4 tablespoons orange juice
⅓ cup finely chopped walnuts

Put apricots, ½ cup walnuts, and coconut through food grinder. Add wheat germ and orange juice; mix well. Form into 1-inch balls. Roll in chopped walnuts; refrigerate. Yield 20 to 24.

bean bars

1 cup whole-wheat pastry flour
⅓ cup nonfat dry milk powder
½ cup packed brown sugar
1 teaspoon baking soda
1 teaspoon cinnamon
½ teaspoon nutmeg
½ teaspoon cloves
½ teaspoon salt
1 egg
½ cup vegetable oil
½ cup applesauce
2 cups cooked green or wax beans or 1 (16-ounce) can, well drained
¾ cup chopped walnuts

½ cup currants
2 tablespoons confectioners' sugar

Stir first 8 ingredients in mixing bowl until evenly mixed.

Place egg, oil, applesauce, and beans in blender or food processor; blend smooth. Pour over dry ingredients; mix well. Stir in nuts and currants. Pour into greased 11¼ × 7½ × 1½-inch pan. Bake at 350°F 25 to 30 minutes. Sprinkle with confectioners' sugar while warm. Cut into bars. Yield 24.

bright-eyed susans

2 cups flour
½ teaspoon baking powder
1 cup butter or margarine
½ cup sugar
2 tablespoons water
1 teaspoon vanilla extract
1 egg
1¼ cups finely chopped nuts
Jam or jelly

Preheat oven to 350°F.

Sift flour and baking powder together twice.

Cream butter and sugar until light and fluffy. Add water, vanilla, and egg yolk. Add flour; mix well. Form dough into balls about size of walnut. Roll in slightly beaten egg white, then in nuts. Place on lightly greased baking sheets. Bake 5 minutes. Remove from oven; press thumbprint in each ball. Return to oven; bake 8 to 10 minutes. Remove to cooling trays; fill centers with bright jam or jelly. Yield about 48.

bright-eyed susans

butter fingers

1 cup butter
1 cup light brown sugar
2 teaspoons grated lemon rind
1 egg
2 cups flour, sifted
⅓ cup blanched chopped almonds

Preheat oven to 375°F.

Grease shallow baking pan about 8 × 12-inches.

Cream butter, sugar, and lemon rind thoroughly. Beat in egg. Fold in flour. Spread evenly in pan. Sprinkle with nuts.

Bake in center of oven 45 to 50 minutes. Let cool a little in pan; mark into finger shapes. Remove when cold. Yield about 24 cookies.

cheese and cranberry cookies

2 cups sifted flour
2 cups grated American cheese
½ teaspoon salt
½ cup butter or margarine
¼ cup milk

Preheat oven to 400°F.

Mix flour, cheese, and salt. Cut in butter with pastry blender. Stir in milk. Roll dough in foil; chill. Roll thinly on lightly floured board; cut into desired shapes: squares, fingers, etc. Spread half the shapes with filling; cover with remaining shapes. Press edges well together. Place on ungreased baking sheets. Bake about 10 minutes. Yield about 30.

cheese and cranberry cookies

cranberry filling
¾ **cup cranberry jelly**
1½ **cups chopped pecans**
½ **teaspoon salt**
2 **tablespoons brown sugar**
¼ **teaspoon ground cinnamon**
 Break up jelly with fork. Add other ingredients; mix well.

chewy peanut–oat cookies

½ **cup butter or margarine, softened**
⅔ **cup packed brown sugar**
1 **egg, beaten**
½ **cup chunky peanut butter**
1½ **teaspoons vanilla**
½ **cup all-purpose flour**
½ **cup whole-wheat pastry flour**
½ **teaspoon baking soda**
½ **teaspoon salt**
1 **cup rolled oats**
½ **cup chopped peanuts**
 Cream together butter and sugar. Add egg; beat well. Stir in peanut butter and vanilla; beat smooth.
 Combine flours, soda, and salt; stir until well mixed. Stir flour mixture into butter-sugar mixture. Add oats and peanuts. Drop from teaspoon onto greased cookie sheets. Flatten slightly with fork. Bake in 350°F oven 12 to 14 minutes. Yield 3 dozen.

chocolate cherry bars

8 **squares dark baking chocolate**
2 **eggs**

chocolate cherry bars

chocolate fruit squares.

½ cup sugar
1 cup finely shredded coconut
½ cup candied cherries, quartered
Confectioners' sugar

Preheat oven to 375°F.

Break chocolate into pieces; melt in double boiler.

While chocolate is melting, grease well a shallow oblong pan about 11 × 7-inches. When chocolate is ready, spread over base of pan. Put into refrigerator; let set.

Beat eggs and sugar together until light and frothy. Carefully fold in coconut and cherries; spread over chocolate. Bake about 15 minutes, until top is firm to touch. Remove from oven; let cool. Refrigerate overnight.

Cut into bars; remove from pan. Sprinkle with confectioners' sugar, or sandwich 2 bars together with chocolate inside. Yield 24.

chocolate fruit squares

¼ cup drinking chocolate or instant cocoa
1 cup shredded coconut
⅓ cup sultana raisins
½ cup cornflakes or other cereal
¼ cup chopped nutmeats
1 teaspoon sherry or fruit juice
2 tablespoons crushed vanilla-wafer crumbs
4 tablespoons condensed milk
3 squares baking chocolate

Lightly butter 7-inch-square pan.

Put all ingredients (except chocolate squares) into mixing bowl; mix well together. Press into pan; smooth surface.

Melt chocolate in double boiler; spread evenly over top of mixture. Score with fork; refrigerate until firm. Cut into small bars or squares. Yield about 18.

chocolate nut cookies

½ cup butter or margarine, softened
½ cup brown sugar
¼ cup honey
1 teaspoon vanilla
1 egg, beaten
2 (1-ounce) squares unsweetened chocolate, melted
¾ cup whole-wheat pastry flour
2 tablespoons nonfat dry milk powder
½ teaspoon salt
⅛ teaspoon baking soda
¾ cup chopped peanuts (unsalted)
1 cup sunflower seeds (unsalted)

Cream together butter, sugar, and honey. Blend in vanilla, egg, and chocolate.

Stir together flour, milk powder, salt, and soda. Add to creamed mixture; mix well. Stir in peanuts and sunflower seeds. Drop by teaspoonfuls onto lightly greased baking sheet, about 2 inches apart. Bake at 375°F 8 to 10 minutes. Remove from pan; cool. Yield 3 dozen.

chocolate pretzels

½ cup butter or margarine
¼ cup sugar
1 egg, beaten
1 teaspoon vanilla
¼ cup milk
¼ cup cocoa
2 cups unsifted flour

Cream butter and sugar until light and fluffy. Beat in egg, vanilla, and milk.

Sift cocoa and flour. Mix into butter mixture until thoroughly blended. Chill dough until firm enough to handle (about 30 minutes).

Using 2 tablespoons dough, roll a rope about 12 inches long between your hands. Shape into pretzel as follows: Make loop about 1½ inches in

244

diameter by crossing ends, leaving 1-inch tails. Flip loop down over crossed ends. Press firmly into place. Place on greased baking sheets. Bake at 350°F about 10 minutes. When cool, spread with Cocoa Frosting. Yield 2 dozen.

cocoa frosting
2 tablespoons cocoa
1¼ cups confectioners' sugar
2 tablespoons butter or margarine, melted
½ teaspoon vanilla
Mix cocoa and confectioners' sugar in small bowl. Gradually stir in butter and vanilla. If too thick, thin with milk.

chocolate raisin fingers

1 cup seeded or seedless raisins
³⁄₈ cup butter or margarine
4 squares semisweet chocolate, melted
Grated rind of 1 orange
1 tablespoon corn syrup
1 cup roughly crumbled angel-food or sponge cake
Cover raisins with boiling water; leave about 3 minutes to plump. Drain; dry.
Soften butter; add with chocolate, orange rind, and syrup to cake crumbs. Add raisins; mix well. Press into oblong shape, about ½ inch thick, onto greased paper. Chill until set; cut into fingers. Garnish with slivers of orange peel (orange part only). Yield about 12 portions.

chocolate raisin fingers

chocolate sandwich cookies

2¾ cups all-purpose flour
1 teaspoon baking powder
½ teaspoon salt
⅔ cup vegetable shortening
⅔ cup sugar
2 eggs
1 teaspoon vanilla extract
Chocolate chips, melted
Confectioners' sugar
Sift flour, baking powder, and salt together.
Combine shortening and sugar in large mixer bowl; cream with electric mixer until smooth. Add eggs; beat until light and fluffy. Stir in vanilla and flour mixture until blended. Shape into ball; chill in refrigerator.
Roll small portions of chilled dough to ⅛-inch thick. Cut into rounds or desired shapes; place on baking sheet. Bake in preheated 350°F oven 12 to 15 minutes or until golden brown. Remove to rack to cool.
Spread 1 cookie with chocolate; top with another cookie. Dust with confectioners' sugar. (Placing a round cookie on a shaped cookie makes a novel variation.) Yield about 36.

chocolate tea cakes

1 (10-inch-square) Yellow-Cake layer (see Index)

chocolate tea cakes

Press circles into miniature cupcake pans; form very shallow shell. Bake in preheated 350°F oven about 20 to 22 minutes. Cool on wire rack.

Fill centers with remaining chocolate. Insert almond sliver in each dab of chocolate. Chill 5 minutes to set chocolate. Yield about 3½ dozen.

christmas cookies

2¾ cups flour
½ teaspoon baking soda
1 teaspoon ground cinnamon
½ teaspoon ground cloves
½ teaspoon grated nutmeg
¾ teaspoon powdered cardamom
½ cup finely chopped mixed candied fruits
½ cup chopped nutmeats
1 cup corn syrup
¾ cup brown sugar
1 tablespoon lemon juice
1 teaspoon grated lemon rind
1 egg, beaten
   Preheat oven to 400°F

christmas cookies

chocolate glaze
½ cup light corn syrup
⅓ cup hot water
4 tablespoons butter or margarine
1 (12-ounce) package chocolate chips

Cut cake into 2-inch strips. Cut each strip into 4 equal pieces. Cut each piece into 2 triangles.

Combine corn syrup, water, and butter in saucepan; bring to boil. Heat until butter melts; remove from heat. Stir in chocolate chips until they melt; cool to room temperature.

Place each cake triangle onto 2-prong frying fork. Spoon cooled Chocolate Glaze over cakes until well-covered. Place on cooling rack to allow excess chocolate to drip from cakes. Yield 32.

chocolate-wine cookies

1½ cups all-purpose flour
1 teaspoon baking powder
½ teaspoon cinnamon
1 egg, beaten
1 cup ground pecans
½ cup butter, softened
½ cup sugar
1 tablespoon sherry
1 (6-ounce) package chocolate chips, melted
Almond slivers

Sift flour, baking powder, and cinnamon together onto clean working surface; shape into ring. Place egg, pecans, butter, sugar, sherry, and ½ cup melted chocolate in center. Blend mixture with pastry scrapers until smooth dough is formed. Roll dough on floured surface to ⅛ inch thick. Cut into circles with 1½-inch cookie cutter.

246

christmas crullers

Sift together flour, soda, and spices. Stir in candied fruits and nuts. Add corn syrup, sugar, lemon juice, and rind to egg; mix well. Add flour-and-fruit mixture; mix well.

Cut rounds of waxed paper, about 4 inches in diameter; grease them; put onto greased baking sheets about 2 inches apart. Put tablespoon of dough on each round of paper; spread to within ¼ inch of outer edge of paper. Bake 12 to 14 minutes or until lightly browned and firm to touch. When cold, decorate as desired with plain or chocolate glaze, cherries, nuts, etc. Yield about 24.

christmas crullers

3 eggs
⅓ cup sugar
⅔ cup butter or margarine, melted
¼ teaspoon ground cardamom
Grated rind of 1 lemon
3 tablespoons cream
4 cups flour
Shortening for deep frying
Powdered sugar for topping

Beat eggs and sugar together until very light. Stir in butter, cardamom, and lemon rind. Add cream and flour. Dough will be quite buttery and easy to handle. Roll dough about ¼ inch thick. Cut with pastry cutter or knife into oblongs 4 inches long, 1 inch wide. Cut slit in middle of each oblong; pull one corner through to make knot. Or just twist oblong to make ribbon effect.

Heat fat to 360°F in skillet. Fry crullers until lightly browned; drain on paper. Store in tightly covered container. Will keep a long time.

When ready to serve, sprinkle with powdered sugar. Yield about 36 crullers.

cinnamon cookies

2½ cups flour
1½ teaspoons baking powder
½ teaspoon salt
1 teaspoon ground cinnamon
1 cup sugar
¾ cup oil
2 eggs, beaten
1 teaspoon vanilla extract

Preheat oven to 375°F.

Sift flour, baking powder, salt, and cinnamon together.

Put sugar and oil in mixing bowl; mix well. Add eggs gradually, then vanilla. Add flour mixture all at once; beat well. Shape into ½-inch balls; roll in sugar. Place on lightly greased baking sheets. Flatten with fork; sprinkle with sugar. Bake 10 to 12 minutes. Remove to cooling trays. Yield about 50.

coconut pecan cookies

1¼ cups flour
⅛ teaspoon salt
1¼ cups firmly packed brown sugar
⅓ cup melted butter
2 eggs
½ teaspoon baking powder
½ teaspoon almond extract
1¼ cups flaked or shredded coconut
1 cup chopped pecans

Preheat oven to 350°F.

Lightly grease 8-inch-square pan.

Sift 1 cup flour with salt. Add ¼ cup sugar. Add butter; mix until smooth. Press into bottom of pan. Bake 15 minutes.

While pastry is baking, prepare topping: Beat eggs well. Gradually beat in remaining sugar; beat together until fluffy.

Sift remaining flour with baking powder. Add to creamed mixture; beat well. Add almond extract, coconut, and nuts. Spread quickly over pastry; return to oven. Bake 20 minutes or until browned. Mark into squares or triangles while still warm; leave in pan to cool. Yield 16.

cornflake cookies

⅔ cup butter or margarine
½ cup granulated sugar
½ cup packed brown sugar
1 egg
1 teaspoon vanilla
1 cup corn flour
1 teaspoon baking soda
¼ teaspoon baking powder
¼ teaspoon salt
1 cup coconut flakes
2 cups cornflakes

Preheat oven to 350°F.

Grease baking sheets.

Beat butter, sugars, egg, and vanilla together until creamy.

Mix flour, soda, baking powder, and salt. Stir into sugar mixture; mix well. Stir in coconut and cornflakes. Drop dough from teaspoon onto baking sheets; space about 2 inches apart.

Bake 8 to 10 minutes, until lightly browned. Cool slightly; remove from pan onto racks to finish cooling. Yield 4 dozen.

cream-cheese refrigerator cookies

1 cup cake flour
¼ teaspoon salt
½ cup butter or margarine
1 cup cream cheese
¼ cup sugar
1 tablespoon caraway seeds

Preheat oven to 400°F.

Sift flour and salt together.

Beat butter and cheese together until creamy. Add sugar; stir in flour gradually. Shape into 2-inch rolls; wrap each in waxed paper. Chill thoroughly in refrigerator.

Cut into thin slices; put onto lightly greased baking sheets. Sprinkle lightly with caraway seeds. Bake about 6 minutes. Yield about 40.

crispy orange cookies

1¼ cups flour
¼ cup flour rice
½ cup butter or margarine
⅜ cup white sugar
Grated rind of 1 large orange
1 egg, separated
½ cup brown sugar

Preheat oven to 350°F.

Sift flour and flour rice into bowl. Rub in butter until mixture resembles fine bread crumbs. Add

coconut pecan cookies

crispy orange cookies

sugar, orange rind, and egg yolk; mix well. Knead until smooth; wrap in foil. Refrigerate ½ hour.

Roll dough to about 12 inches square. Brush with lightly beaten egg white; sprinkle with brown sugar. Fold corners to center. Form into ball; knead lightly. Cut in half; shape each half into roll about 9 inches long. Cut rolls into slices about ½ inch thick; place on greased baking sheets. Bake about 20 minutes; remove to cooling trays. Store when quite cold. Yield about 36.

danish dollars

12 tablespoons butter
1 cup confectioners' sugar
2 cups flour
½ teaspoon salt
1 cup chopped nuts (hazelnuts preferred)

Cream butter until foamy. Add sugar; mix well.

Sift together flour and salt; add to bowl. Add nuts. Dough will be stiff. In waxed paper form dough into long rolls about 2 inches round. Chill in refrigerator at least 30 minutes.

Slice roll into thin rounds; place them on greased cookie sheet. (The thinner the slice is, the thinner the finished cookie will be.) Bake at 325°F 10 to 15 minutes. Yield 40 or more cookies.

danish pastries

2 packages dry yeast
¼ cup sugar
1 cup milk
4 cups flour
2 egg yolks
½ teaspoon salt
4 tablespoons butter
Fruit marmalade or preserves for filling
2 egg yolks for garnish, beaten

Sugar for garnish
Chopped almonds for garnish

Dissolve yeast and 1 tablespoon sugar in 2 tablespoons warm milk; let this sit 10 minutes.

Sift flour. Mix yeast with flour, remainder of sugar and milk, 2 egg yolks, and salt. Work mixture with hands or dough hook until dough is smooth and elastic. Cover well-worked dough; set aside to rise at least 15 minutes.

On floured board roll dough to ½ inch thick. Dot with 4 teaspoons butter; fold dough together. Roll dough again; repeat process until all butter has been used. Let dough rest about 10 minutes.

Roll dough to ½ inch thick. Cut into 4-inch squares. Place marmalade in center of each

danish dollars

danish pastries

square; form into horn- or pocket-shaped pieces. Place pieces on greased baking sheet. Coat unbaked pastries with egg yolks; sprinkle with sugar and almonds. Bake at 400°F 20 minutes. Yield about 10.

date and almond brownies

⅔ cup flour
½ teaspoon baking powder
¼ teaspoon salt
⅓ cup butter or margarine
2 squares baking chocolate
1 cup sugar
2 eggs, beaten
½ cup chopped almonds
½ cup chopped dates
1 teaspoon vanilla extract

Preheat oven to 350°F.

Grease 8-inch-square pan.

Sift flour, baking powder, and salt together.

Melt butter and chocolate in top of double boiler.

Add sugar to eggs; beat well. Add butter and chocolate. Stir in flour. Add almonds, dates, and vanilla. Turn into pan. Bake 25 minutes. Cool in pan; cut into squares or bars. Decorate with dates or almonds if desired. Yield 16 to 20.

date-pumpkin cookies

1½ cups whole-wheat pastry flour
2 teaspoons baking powder
½ teaspoon baking soda
½ teaspoon salt
1 teaspoon cinnamon
½ teaspoon nutmeg
⅛ teaspoon ground cloves
⅔ cup butter or margarine, softened
½ cup sugar
½ cup packed brown sugar
2 eggs, beaten
1¼ cups cooked or canned pumpkin
1 teaspoon vanilla
1 cup chopped dates
1 cup rolled oats
½ cup chopped nuts

date and almond brownies

english-kitchen cookies

Stir together flour, baking powder, soda, salt, cinnamon, nutmeg, and cloves until well blended.

Cream butter and sugars. Add eggs; beat well. Stir in pumpkin and vanilla. Blend in flour mixture; stir thoroughly. Add dates, oats, and nuts; mix well. Drop by teaspoonfuls onto greased baking sheet. Bake at 375°F about 12 minutes. Remove to rack to cool. Yield 4 dozen.

doughnuts

4½ teaspoons baking powder
2 teaspoons salt
1 tablespoon granulated sugar
4 cups all-purpose white flour
⅔ cup shortening
1 cup Sourdough Starter (see Index)
1 cup milk
1 cup granulated sugar

Combine first 4 ingredients. Cut in shortening until mixture resembles dry cornmeal. Add Sourdough Starter and enough milk to form soft dough that cleans sides of bowl. Knead lightly 6 times. Pat or roll dough to ½ inch thick. Cut into biscuits, using 2½-inch biscuit cutter. Fry doughnuts in preheated 360°F grease 1½ minutes or until golden brown. Drain; sprinkle with granulated sugar. Yield 2 dozen.

english-kitchen cookies

1 pound Basic Puff Pastry (see Index)
¼ cup butter
1 cup currants
½ cup chopped candied peel
⅓ cup ground almonds

½ teaspoon ground cinnamon
1 teaspoon grated nutmeg

Preheat oven to 450°F.

Divide pastry into 2 equal-size pieces; roll each into thin square.

Melt butter. Add currants, peel, almonds, and spices; mix well. Spread on 1 pastry square to within ½ inch of edge; moisten edges with water. Cover with second pastry square; press edges well together. With back of knife mark pastry top into squares, without cutting through filling. Put on baking sheet. Bake about 25 minutes. Sprinkle with sugar; divide into squares while still warm. Yield about 12.

florentines

¾ cup sultana raisins
2 cups crushed cornflakes
¾ cup peanuts
½ cup candied or maraschino cherries

doughnuts

florentines

½ can condensed milk
3 squares baking chocoate

Preheat oven to 375°F.

Grease baking sheets; line with greased paper. Dust lightly with cornstarch.

Mix raisins, cornflakes, peanuts, and cherries in mixing bowl. Add milk; blend well. Place by 2 teaspoonfuls in small heaps on sheets. Bake 15 to 20 minutes. Leave on sheets to cool. Using spatula, remove to cooling trays.

Melt chocolate in double boiler. Remove from heat; stir until slightly thickened. Spread over flat sides of cookies; mark with fork. Let chocolate set before storing. Yield about 30 cookies.

french coconut macaroons

4 egg whites
1 teaspoon vanilla extract

french coconut macaroons

1 cup confectioners' sugar
2 cups flaked coconut
½ cup all-purpose flour

Beat egg whites with electric mixer until stiff peaks form. Add vanilla; mix well. Add sugar gradually; beat well after each addition. Beat until stiff and glossy. Fold in coconut and flour; mix well. Drop from teaspoon onto buttered and floured cookie sheet. Bake in preheated 325°F oven 25 minutes or until lightly browned. Yield 2 dozen.

fruity squares

1 (10-ounce) package pastry mix
¼ cup butter or margarine
½ cup currants
½ cup seedless raisins
½ cup chopped candied peel (orange or lemon)
¼ cup chopped blanched almonds
½ teaspoon cinnamon
1 teaspoon ground nutmeg

Preheat oven to 450°F.

Divide pastry in half; roll each half thinly into a square. Place 1 square onto baking sheet.

Melt butter in pan. Add all other ingredients; mix well. Spread evenly on pastry square to within ¾ inch of edge. Moisten edge; place second pastry square on top. Press edges well together. Using back of knife, mark pastry into squares without cutting through. Brush with water; sprinkle with sugar. Bake 25 to 30 minutes. Let cool; cut into squares when ready to serve. Yield 12.

gingerbread

3 cups all purpose flour
¼ teaspoon salt

gingerbread

2 tablespoons ground ginger
2 teaspoons mixed spice
2 teaspoons ground cinnamon
½ cup brown sugar, tightly packed
4 tablespoons milk
½ cup light molasses
2 tablespoons dark molasses
½ cup butter or margarine
3 eggs
2 teaspoons baking soda

Preheat oven to 375°F.

Grease and line baking pan about 10 × 7 × 2½-inches.

Sift flour, salt and spices together. Add sugar.

Put 3 tablespoons milk into small pan with molasses and butter or margarine, and melt over a low heat. Add beaten egg, and stir all into the flour mixture. Beat well.

Dissolve soda in the remaining 1 tablespoon warm milk, and beat into mixture.

Spread evenly in prepared pan, and bake about 50 minutes. Cool in pan; cut into squares. Yield makes 16-20 squares.

fruity squares

gingersnaps

¾ cup butter or margarine
1 cup brown sugar
¾ cup molasses
1 egg
2¼ cups flour
2 teaspoons baking soda
½ teaspoon salt
1 teaspoon ground ginger
1 teaspoon ground cinnamon
½ teaspoon ground cloves

Preheat oven to 375°F.

Put butter, sugar, molasses, and egg into mixing bowl; beat well until creamy.

Sift flour, soda, salt, and spices together. Add to creamed mixture; blend well. Form into balls; roll in granulated sugar. Place about 2 inches apart on greased baking sheets. Bake about 10 minutes. Let cool a little before removing to cooling trays. Yield about 48 cookies.

granola orange date squares

1 cup butter or margarine, softened
1½ cups packed brown sugar
¼ cup honey
2 eggs, beaten
¼ cup orange juice
1½ teaspoons grated orange rind
1 teaspoon vanilla
1 cup all-purpose flour
¾ cup whole-wheat pastry flour
½ cup nonfat dry milk powder
1 teaspoon salt
1 teaspoon baking powder
2½ cups granola
½ cup chopped dates

Cream butter and sugar. Add honey, eggs, and orange juice; beat well. Stir in orange rind and vanilla.

Stir together flours, dry milk, salt, and baking powder in separate bowl. Add to butter mixture; beat until smooth. Stir in granola and dates. Pour into greased 9 × 12-inch baking pan. Bake at 350°F 40 to 50 minutes or until done. Cool; cut into squares. Yield 24.

holiday triangles

1 cup chopped pecans
½ cup candied fruit
1¼ cups all-purpose white flour
½ cup whole-wheat flour
½ teaspoon baking soda
½ teaspoon salt
½ teaspoon ground cloves
½ teaspoon allspice
½ teaspoon nutmeg
1 teaspoon cinnamon
½ cup butter
¼ cup packed brown sugar
1 egg, beaten
⅓ cup honey
2 tablespoons buttermilk
1 recipe Bourbon Glaze
Multicolored candy sprinkles

Mix pecans and fruit.

Combine flours, soda, salt, and spices; sprinkle over fruit-and-nut mixture.

Cream butter and brown sugar until fluffy. Beat in egg. Add honey and buttermilk alternately with flour-and-nut mixture; mix well. Spread on greased jelly-roll pan. Bake in preheated 375°F oven 15 minutes or until done. Remove from oven.

Frost cake with Bourbon Glaze. Sprinkle with candy sprinkles. Cut into triangular bars; remove from pan while still warm. Yield 2 dozen.

bourbon glaze
2 tablespoons bourbon
2 tablespoons water
1 teaspoon vanilla
1 cup powdered sugar, sifted

Combine all ingredients; mix well. Yield 1 cup.

holiday triangles

lebkuchen

honey granola cookies

½ cup vegetable oil
½ cup honey
2 eggs, beaten
1 teaspoon vanilla
1¼ cups whole-wheat pastry flour
½ teaspoon salt
½ teaspoon baking soda
1 cup granola

Combine oil and honey. Stir in eggs and vanilla.

Combine flour, salt, and soda; stir into wet ingredients. Add granola; mix well. Drop by teaspoonfuls onto greased baking sheet. Bake at 325°F 10 to 12 minutes or until done. Yield 2 to 2½ dozen.

lebkuchen

1 cup chopped walnuts
½ cup mixed glacé fruit
¼ teaspoon grated orange peel
1¾ cups all-purpose white flour
½ teaspoon baking soda
½ teaspoon salt
½ teaspoon allspice
½ teaspoon nutmeg
1 teaspoon cinnamon
1 teaspoon freeze-dried coffee
½ cup butter or margarine
¼ cup packed brown sugar
1 egg, beaten
⅓ cup honey
½ cup Sourdough Starter (see Index)
Rum glaze (see Index)

Mix walnuts, fruit, and orange peel.

Combine flour, soda, spices, and coffee; sprinkle over fruit-and-nut mixture.

Cream butter and sugar until fluffy. Beat in egg. Add honey and Sourdough Starter alternately with flour-and-nut mixture; mix well. Spread on greased jelly-roll pan. Bake in preheated 375°F oven 15 minutes or until done. Remove from oven. Frost with Rum Glaze. Cool; cut into bars. Yield 2 dozen cookies.

little diplomat cakes

1 recipe Basic Close-Textured Sponge Cake
  (see Index)
1 recipe Basic Butter Cream (see Index)
1 teaspoon kirsch
1 recipe Crème Jacqueline

Prepare cake; bake in jelly-roll pan according to instructions. Cut cake into rounds with 1½-inch wet cutter. Cover; set aside.

Prepare butter cream; add kirsch. Frost rounds on tops and sides with butter cream. At this stage cakes can be stored in refrigerator in airtight container several days.

Prepare Crème Jacqueline, folding in about ⅔ of cherries and pineapple. Reserve remaining fruits for garnish.

Mound crème on top of cakes; garnish tops with reserved cherries and pineapple. Place in paper cups. Yield about 50.

crème jacqueline
1½ cups whipping cream
6 tablespoons sifted confectioners' sugar
4 teaspoons kirsch
⅔ cup chopped candied cherries
⅔ cup slivered candied green pineapple

Place cream in small mixing bowl; beat at high speed with electric mixer until fluffy. Add sugar

little diplomat cakes

gradually, beating constantly, until stiff. Add kirsch; beat until well combined. Fold in candied fruits. Yield about 4 cups.

lunch-box specials

¾ cup whole-wheat pastry flour
2 tablespoons all-purpose flour
2 tablespoons nonfat dry milk powder
½ teaspoon baking soda
½ teaspoon salt
⅔ cup butter or margarine, slightly softened
½ cup packed brown sugar
1 egg, beaten
1 teaspoon vanilla
1 cup grated cheddar cheese
1¼ cups rolled oats
¼ cup toasted wheat germ
¼ cup sunflower seeds or finely chopped walnuts
1 tablespoon flax seeds (if not available, omit, or substitute sesame seeds)
6 slices bacon, cooked crisp, crumbled

Combine flours, milk powder, soda, and salt; set aside.

Cream together butter and sugar until fluffy. Beat in egg and vanilla. Add flour mixture; stir well. Add remaining ingredients; stir until well distributed. Drop by teaspoonfuls onto greased cookie sheet. Bake in 350°F oven 12 to 14 minutes, until lightly browned around edges. Cool briefly on cookie sheet; remove to rack to cool. Yield 3 dozen.

marble brownies

¼ cup butter or margarine
1 cup sugar

2 eggs
⅔ cup cake flour
¼ teaspoon salt
½ cup chopped nuts
½ teaspoon vanilla extract
2 squares baking chocolate, melted, cooled

Preheat oven to 350°F.

Grease 8-inch baking pan.

Cream butter. Add sugar; beat until light and fluffy. Add eggs; beat until mixture is smooth. Gradually add flour and salt sifted together. Stir in nuts and vanilla. Pour half the batter into pan.

Mix chocolate with other half of batter; pour over plain batter. Swirl through with spoon. Bake 30 minutes. Cool; mark into squares or bars. Cut when cold. Yield 16.

melting moments

½ cup butter or margarine
½ cup sugar
1 egg
1½ cups all-purpose flour
Pinch of salt
Rolled oats
Candied or maraschino cherries

Preheat oven to 350°F.

marble brownies

Cream butter and sugar until soft and white. Beat in egg. Add flour and salt sifted together; mix to firm dough. Dampen hands; roll dough into balls about size of walnut. Roll in rolled oats. Put on greased baking pans; allow room to spread. Flatten a little; place cherry in center of each cookie. Bake 20 minutes. Yield 24 cookies.

chocolate melting moments

Replace 1 tablespoon flour with 1 tablespoon cocoa.

ginger melting moments

Add 1 teaspoon ground ginger; put piece of crystallized ginger on top.

melting moments

mincemeat crumble squares

1 (9-ounce) package mincemeat
½ cup water
¼ cup chopped walnuts
½ cup butter or margarine, softened
1 cup grated cheddar cheese
½ teaspoon vanilla
1¼ cups plus 2 tablespoons whole-wheat pastry
    flour
2 tablespoons wheat germ
⅛ teaspoon salt
2 tablespoons sugar
2 tablespoons sunflower seeds

Crumble mincemeat into small saucepan. Add water; cook, stirring, until slightly thickened, 3 to 4 minutes. Remove from heat. Add walnuts; cool.

Cream butter. Add cheese and vanilla; cream together until thoroughly blended. With pastry blender cut in 1¼ cups flour, wheat germ, and salt. Divide dough in half; press half in bottom of 8 × 8-inch baking pan. Bake at 400°F 6 to 8 minutes.

Add 2 tablespoons flour, sugar, and sunflower seeds to second half of dough; mix until crumbly.

Spread mincemeat evenly over baked crust. Top with remaining dough; press lightly with fingers. Bake at 375°F to 35 minutes or until golden brown. Cool; cut into squares. Yield 16.

nantes cookies

1½ cups all-purpose flour
1 teaspoon baking powder
2 eggs, well beaten
½ cup butter, softened
½ cup sugar
2 tablespoons Basic Sugar Syrup (see Index)
¼ cup finely chopped slivered almonds
1 (6-ounce) package chocolate chips, melted

Sift flour and baking powder together into mound on clean working surface; shape into ring. Pour eggs into center. Add butter and sugar. Blend well with 2 pastry scrapers until smooth dough is formed. (This process can also be done in strong electric mixer.) Roll dough to ⅛ inch thick on lightly floured surface. Cut with floured 1½-inch-round cutter. Brush cookies with sugar syrup. Sprinkle with almonds. Make firm indentation in center of each cookie with finger. Place cookies on buttered and floured cookie sheet. Bake in preheated 350°F oven 18 to 20 minutes or until lightly browned. Cool cookies on wire rack.

Drop small amount chocolate onto center of each cookie from demitasse spoon. Chill cookies no longer than 5 minutes to set chocolate. Yield 3½ dozen.

nutmeg refrigerator cookies

½ cup butter
½ cup sugar
6 tablespoons half-and-half cream
3 tablespoons orange juice
Grated rind of 1 orange
3 cups all-purpose flour
1½ teaspoons nutmeg
½ teaspoon salt

Cream butter with sugar in bowl.

Combine cream, orange juice, and rind; blend well.

Sift flour with nutmeg and salt; add to butter mixture alternately with orange-juice mixture. Add more flour, if needed, to form stiff dough. Shape into roll; wrap in waxed paper. Chill overnight.

Slice dough ⅛-inch thick; cut small hole with piping tube or thimble in one side of each cookie. Place on greased baking sheet. Bake in preheated 375°F oven 8 to 10 minutes or until lightly browned. Yield 4 to 5 dozen.

orange and cinnamon squares

2 cups flour
1 teaspoon ground cinnamon
1 teaspoon baking soda
Grated rind and juice of 1 large orange

peanut-butter nuggets

½ cup butter or margarine
⅓ cup corn syrup
3 tablespoons orange marmalade
⅓ cup light brown sugar
½ cup milk
1 egg, beaten

Preheat oven to 350°F.

Grease shallow baking pan about 10 × 7 inches; line with greased paper.

Sift flour, cinnamon, and soda together twice. Add orange rind.

Put butter, corn syrup, marmalade, sugar, and milk into pan; stir over low heat until melted. Add orange juice. Stir into flour. Add egg; beat until smooth. Pour into pan. Bake 40 to 45 minutes. Leave in pan to cool a little; turn onto cooling tray. When cold, cut into squares. Yield 18 large squares.

original tollhouse cookies

1 cup plus 2 tablespoons sifted flour
½ teaspoon baking soda
½ teaspoon salt
½ cup butter or margarine, softened
6 tablespoons granulated sugar
6 tablespoons packed brown sugar
½ teaspoon vanilla
¼ teaspoon water
1 egg
1 (6-ounce) package (1 cup) semisweet chocolate morsels
½ cup coarsely chopped nuts

Sift together flour, soda, and salt; set aside.

Combine butter, sugars, vanilla, and water; beat until creamy. Beat in egg. Add flour mixture; mix well. Stir in chocolate and nuts. Drop by well-rounded half-teaspoonfuls onto greased cookie sheets. Bake 10 to 12 minutes at 375°F. Yield 50 (2-inch) cookies.

peanut-butter nuggets

1 cup peanut butter
1 teaspoon lemon juice
¼ teaspoon salt
1½ cups (1 can) condensed milk
1 cup chopped seedless raisins

Preheat oven to 375°F.

Mix peanut butter, lemon juice, and salt together. Gradually stir in milk. Add raisins. Drop from teaspoons onto greased baking sheets. Bake 10 minutes. Yield 36.

petits fours

1 recipe Basic Close-Textured Sponge Cake (see Index)
2 recipes Basic Butter Cream (see Index)
4 (1-pound) boxes confectioners' sugar
Kirsch, cointreau, Grand Marnier or creme de ménthe
Food Coloring

Prepare cake; bake in jelly-roll pan according to instructions. Cut into rounds with wet 1-inch cutter. Keep cake rounds covered to keep from drying out.

Butter cream and icing can be divided and flavored with various liqueurs and tinted as desired, or one flavor can be used. Icing petits fours is time-consuming.

Make small amount of confectioners' sugar icing at a time, it dries quickly. Combine 2 cups sifted confectioners' sugar with 1 teaspoon desired liqueur, food coloring, and enough water to make dipping consistency. Dip cake rounds into icing, place on wire racks over jelly-roll pans to harden. Make icing and dip cakes until all have been covered.

Prepare 1 recipe butter cream at a time; pipe large rosette on top of each iced cake.

Prepare more icing; spoon carefully in circular motion over rosette of each. cake; let icing flow evenly to coat completely. If heavier coating is

petits fours

desired; spoon another coat of icing over cakes Let stand until icing has hardened. Store in airtight containers or freeze until ready to use. Yield about 100.

pistachio cookies

1 cup sweet unsalted butter
6 tablespoons confectioners' sugar
1 egg yolk
2 teaspoons cognac
2¼ cups cake flour, sifted
Pistachio nuts

Preheat oven to 350°F.

Cream butter until very soft and fluffy. Beat in sugar, then egg yolk and cognac. Work in flour gradually to form dough. Chill at least 1 hour.

Break off pieces of dough; form into balls about 1 inch in diameter. Place on lightly greased baking sheets. Press pistachio nut into each. Bake about 15 minutes, until pale golden color. When cool, sprinkle with confectioners' sugar. Yield about 36.

poppy treats

2 cups milk
1 package active dry yeast
½ cup Sourdough Starter (see Index)
2 cups all-purpose white flour
½ cup butter or margarine, melted
½ cup granulated sugar
3 egg yolks, beaten
1 teaspoon salt
3½ to 4 cups all-purpose white flour

2 (12-ounce) cans poppy-seed filling
1 cup walnuts, chopped fine
2 eggs, beaten

Scald milk; cool to lukewarm.

Dissolve yeast in warm milk. Stir in Sourdough Starter. Mix in 2 cups flour; let mixture stand long enough to develop a bubbly sponge. Add butter,

poppy treats

pretzel cookies

sugar, egg yolks, and salt; mix well. Work in 2 cups flour. Pour 1 cup flour on kneading surface. Pour sponge mixture on flour; cover with 1 cup flour. Knead until flour is worked into dough. Add flour until semi-stiff dough has formed. Knead 10 minutes or until folds form. Place in greased bowl; grease top. Cover; let rise until double in bulk. Punch down; knead 2 minutes. On floured surface roll to ¼ inch thick. Cut into 36 (3-inch) squares.

Combine poppy-seed filling and nuts. Place 1 to 2 teaspoons filling in middle of each square. Fold over corners to form triangles; pinch edges. Place on greased cookie sheet; cover. Let rise until double in bulk. Brush with eggs; place in cold oven. Set oven at 375°F. Bake 15 to 20 minutes or until golden brown. Cool on rack. Yield 3 dozen.

pretzel cookies

½ cup butter or margarine
¾ cup granulated sugar
2 eggs, beaten
2 tablespoons milk
1 cup flour
¼ teaspoon salt
½ cup brown sugar
2 tablespoons ground cinnamon

Preheat oven to 375°F.

Cream butter with ¼ cup granulated sugar. Add eggs and milk; beat until smooth. Add flour and salt sifted together; mix to smooth dough. Wrap in foil; chill 2 to 3 hours. Mix brown sugar, cinnamon, and remaining granulated sugar; sprinkle onto pastry board. Put dough on board; roll to about ¼ inch thick. Cut into strips about ½ inch wide; form into pretzel or twists. Sprinkle well with sugar mixture; arrange on greased and floured baking sheets. Bake 12 minutes or until just delicately browned. Yield about 36 cookies.

sesame-seed cookies

1 cup sweet butter
1½ cups sugar
1 teaspoon vanilla extract

sesame-seed cookies

3 eggs
5 cups self-rising flour
½ teaspoon ground cinnamon
½ cup sesame seeds
1 egg beaten with 2 tablespoons milk

Cream butter until light. Add sugar and vanilla; beat well. Add eggs one at a time; beat well after each addition.

Sift flour and cinnamon; add to creamed mixture to form soft dough. Chill several hours or overnight.

To form cookies, take scant tablespoon dough and roll into 3½-inch-long rope. Pinch ends together to form doughnut shape. Dip in sesame seeds; place several inches apart on greased baking sheet. Brush with egg beaten with milk. Bake at 375°F 15 minutes or until lightly browned. Cool on rack; store in airtight container. Yield 6 dozen.

shortbread cookies

½ pound sweet butter, room temperature
½ cup sifted confectioners' sugar
1 egg yolk
½ teaspoon vanilla extract
1 tablespoon brandy
2½ cups flour, sifted, then measured

½ teaspoon baking powder
½ cup walnuts, chopped fine (almonds can be substituted)
48 cloves
Additional confectioners' sugar

Beat butter with electric mixer until very light and fluffy. Sift sugar into butter; cream. Add egg yolk, vanilla, and brandy.

Sift flour and baking powder together. Add nuts, then flour mixture to creamed mixture; stir to form soft dough. Knead lightly; chill several hours.

Form dough into balls; use rounded teaspoon of dough for each cookie. Place on ungreased

shortbread cookies

cookie sheet 2 inches apart; place whole clove in each cookie. Bake at 350°F 15 to 20 minutes or until light brown.

Roll cookies in powdered sugar while still hot. Cool; store in airtight container. Be careful handling these cookies; they are very delicate. Yield 4 dozen.

sour-cream cookies

1½ cups flour
½ teaspoon baking powder
⅛ teaspoon baking soda
½ teaspoon salt
½ cup butter or margarine
½ cup granulated sugar
⅛ cup firmly packed brown sugar
1 egg, beaten
½ teaspoon vanilla extract
¼ cup sour cream

Preheat oven to 400°F.

Sift flour, baking powder, soda, and salt together.

Cream butter. Add sugars; beat until soft and creamy. Add egg and vanilla. Add flour mixture alternately with sour cream; set aside to chill. Divide into rolls about 2 inches in diameter; wrap each in waxed paper. Put in refrigerator; leave until thoroughly chilled.

Cut dough into slices about ⅛ inch thick; place on ungreased baking sheets. Bake about 8 to 10 minutes. Yield about 48.

three-in-one cookies
chocolate: To one-third of cookie dough add 1 square dark baking chocolate melted.
spice: To second third add ½ teaspoon cinnamon; ⅛ teaspoon each allspice, ground cloves, and nutmeg; ¼ teaspoon ginger; and ¼ cup finely chopped raisins.
coconut: To last third add ½ cup shredded coconut.

spice bars

4 eggs, slightly beaten
1 cup sugar
½ cup brown sugar
2 cups whole-wheat flour
½ teaspoon baking soda
1 teaspoon cinnamon
½ teaspoon cloves
¼ teaspoon nutmeg
¼ teaspoon cardamom
⅓ cup candied fruit
⅓ cup chopped almonds

Beat together eggs and sugars in medium bowl.

Sift together flour, soda, and spices in separate bowl. Gradually beat flour mixture into sugar mixture. Add fruit and nuts; stir to blend. Refrigerate batter 3 or more hours.

With moistened knife, spread 1 tablespoon batter into 1½ × 2½-inch bar (about ¼ inch thick) on well-greased cookie sheet. Let stand overnight at room temperature.

Bake at 350°F 15 minutes.

Cookies are best when served after storing several days in covered container. Yield 2½ dozen.

spritz cookies

½ cup butter or margarine
½ cup powdered sugar
½ teaspoon almond extract
1 egg yolk, beaten
1¼ cups cake flour
¼ teaspoon salt
1 egg white
Colored coarse sugar crystals

Preheat oven to 400°F.

Cream butter. Add powdered sugar; beat well, until soft and creamy. Add almond extract and egg yolk. Gradually stir in sifted flour and salt. Put into cookie press. Using various forms of nozzles, as available, press out shapes onto ungreased baking sheet. Brush with egg white beaten until frothy with few drops water. Sprinkle with colored crystals or with chopped nuts or decorettes. Bake about 8 minutes or until very lightly browned. Yield about 30.

struzel (horseshoe cookies)

1 cup flour
¾ teaspoon baking powder
1½ tablespoons sugar
1 tablespoon butter
1 egg, beaten
About ½ cup milk
1 tablespoon seedless raisins
Fat or oil for deep frying

Sift flour, baking powder, and sugar into bowl. Cut in butter with pastry blender or 2 knives. Add egg and enough milk to make fairly firm dough. Add raisins; shape tablespoons of mixture into horseshoe shapes. Drop into hot 360°F fat; fry until golden brown. Drain well; roll in powdered sugar. Eat hot or cold. Yield about 20.

sugar cookies

2 cups flour (approximately)
1½ teaspoons baking powder
½ teaspoon salt
½ cup butter or margarine
1 cup sugar
1 egg

spice bars

1 teaspoon vanilla extract
1 tablespoon cream or milk

Preheat oven to 375°F.

Sift 1½ cups flour with baking powder and salt.

Cream butter until soft. Beat in sugar, egg, vanilla, and cream. Stir in flour mixture. Add enough remaining flour to make dough stiff enough to roll out. Refrigerate until well chilled. Place on lightly floured board; roll about ⅛ inch thick. Cut into desired shapes with floured cutter, or use cookie press. Place on ungreased baking sheets; sprinkle with sugar. Bake 8 to 10 minutes. Remove to cooling trays. Can be served plain or decorated in a variety of ways. Yield 50 to 60.

butterscotch cookies

Substitute 1 cup brown sugar for white sugar.

chocolate crisps

Mix and sift ½ teaspoon ground cinnamon with flour. Add 2 squares melted baking chocolate to butter-sugar-egg mixture.

gingersnaps

Reduce baking powder to ½ teaspoon. Add ¼ teaspoon baking soda and 1 teaspoon ground ginger; sift with flour. Reduce sugar to ½ cup. Beat ½ cup molasses into butter-sugar mixture. Omit vanilla. Substitute 2 tablespoons water for cream.

sour-cream cookies

Reduce baking powder to ½ teaspoon. Add ¼ teaspoon baking soda and ¼ teaspoon ground cinnamon or nutmeg to flour. Substitute squeeze of lemon juice for vanilla and ⅓ cup sour cream for fresh cream.

spice sugar cookies

Mix and sift ¼ teaspoon each ground cinnamon and powdered cloves with flour. Omit vanilla.

264

sweet-potato cookies

⅓ cup butter or margarine
⅓ cup brown sugar
⅓ cup honey
1 egg, beaten
1 cup whole-wheat pastry flour
⅓ cup nonfat dry milk powder
1 teaspoon baking powder
¼ teaspoon baking soda
¾ teaspoon salt
¼ teaspoon cinnamon
¼ teaspoon nutmeg
3 tablespoons wheat germ
1 cup shredded, peeled, sweet potato
1 teaspoon grated lemon rind
¼ cup grated coconut
1¼ cups rolled oats
⅓ cup chopped nuts

Cream together butter, sugar, and honey. Beat in egg.

Stir together flour, dry milk, baking powder, soda, salt, cinnamon, nutmeg, and wheat germ. Add to egg mixture; beat well. Stir in sweet potato, lemon rind, coconut, oats, and nuts; mix well. Drop by teaspoonfuls onto greased baking sheet. Bake at 375°F 10 to 12 minutes. Cool on rack. Yield 3 dozen.

vanillekipferl

1 cup flour
Pinch of salt
¼ cup butter or margarine, cut into small pieces
¼ cup ground almonds
1 cup vanilla flavored sugar (or 1 cup white sugar and ¼ teaspoon vanilla extract)
Preheat oven to 350°F.

Sift flour and salt onto board. Add butter, almonds, and 3 tablespoons flavored sugar. Using hands, work together to smooth paste. Cover; leave in cool place at least ½ hour. Put onto board (do not add flour); roll with palm of hand into long sausage shape. Cut into 24 equal pieces. Roll each piece into a sausage; keep middle a little thicker than ends. Twist into crescent shape. Put onto baking sheets (not greased or floured). Bake until pale golden color, about 10 minutes.

Put remaining sugar onto large dish. When cookies are done, put one at a time into sugar; coat thoroughly. At this stage they are very fragile and must be handled carefully. When quite cold, store in airtight jar. Yield about 24 cookies.

sugar cookies

CREPES

basic crepe batter

1½ cups flour
⅛ teaspoon salt
3 eggs
1½ cups milk
2 tablespoons butter or oil, melted, cooled

Sift flour and salt into bowl.

Break eggs into another bowl; mix until yolks and whites are blended. Pour into reservoir in middle of the dry ingredients. (Mixing is more difficult if you break eggs right into dry ingredients.) Stir flour mixture into eggs little by little. It may be necessary to add a little milk (or whatever liquid is used in recipe) to incorporate all flour; mix liquid in thoroughly spoonful at a time before adding more. When mixture becomes easy to work (when about half of liquid has been used), remainder can be added in 2 portions. Add melted butter (and flavorings if indicated); mix. Cover; set aside at least 1 hour but not more than 6 hours at room temperature. Crepe batter can be held overnight in refrigerator. If necessary, crepe batter can be cooked immediately, but "resting" time allows flour to absorb more liquids, makes batter easier to handle, and gives crepes more flavor. Since flours vary in ability to absorb liquid, if crepe batter seems too thick when ready to cook it, a small amount of extra liquid can be added then. Consistency should be at least as thin as heavy cream.

Mixer or whisk method: Combine eggs and salt in medium mixing bowl. Gradually add flour alternately with milk, beating until smooth. Beat in melted butter.

Blender or food-processor method: Combine ingredients in container; blend about 1 minute. Scrape down sides with rubber spatula; blend 15 seconds or until smooth. Yield 24 to 26 (6-inch) crepes or 40 smaller crepes.

basic crepes

Heat 1 tablespoon oil in crepe or omelet pan or in heavy 5- to 6-inch skillet; pour out oil. (Or place pan over medium heat; brush with oil.) Lift pan from heat; pour in just enough batter to cover bottom. Swirl pan so batter completely covers bottom in very thin layer. Return to medium heat; cook until crepe is set and edges dry. Slide spatula under edge of crepe to loosen. Lift carefully; turn gently. Brown other side just a few seconds; remove from heat. Shake pan to loosen; slide crepe from pan onto oiled waxed paper. Cook crepes until all batter is used. Separate with waxed paper oiled on both sides. Seal crepes in aluminum foil; store in refrigerator or freezer until ready to use. Loosen foil and place on cookie sheet in 275°F oven to reheat.

crepes with caviar

8 to 10 (3-inch diameter) warm crepes
½ cup red caviar
½ cup black caviar
8 to 10 lemon wedges

Have above foods available; let each person make his own crepes. These are perfect for an informal yet elegant cocktail party. Yield 4 to 6 servings.

crepes with caviar

crepes with fresh mushrooms

crepes with fillings

crepes with fillings

1-pound package bacon strips, cut in half
1 pound fresh mushrooms
1 small green pepper
1 small red pepper
12 warm crepes

Fry bacon until crisp; drain on paper towels.
Wash mushrooms; fry until browned.
Clean peppers; cut into strips.
Serve with crepes; let each person fill his own.
Yield 6 servings.

crepes with fresh mushrooms

½ pound fresh mushrooms
2 tablespoons butter
½ teaspoon salt
1 bouillon cube, crumbled
2 tablespoons sherry
¼ cup dairy sour cream
1 tablespoon minced chives
8 crepes
1 recipe Tomato Sauce for Crepes (see Index)

Slice mushrooms; sauté in hot butter several minutes. Add salt, bouillon cube, and sherry; cook until simmering. Stir in sour cream and chives; heat until warm through. Spoon mixture onto centers of crepes; fold. Serve with tomato sauce spooned over tops. Yield 4 servings.

green crepes

green crepes

½ **package frozen chopped spinach**
½ **teaspoon crumbled chervil**
2 **tablespoons chopped chives**
Basic crepe batter

Thaw spinach. Add well-drained spinach, chervil, and chives to batter. Make thin crepes. Yield 4 servings.

smoked-oyster crepes

1 **(3-ounce) package cream cheese, softened**
2 **tablespoons mayonnaise**
1 **tablespoon finely chopped green onions**
1 **teaspoon finely chopped pimiento**
1 **(3½-ounce) can smoked oysters, drained, chopped**
8 **cooked crepes**

Combine cream cheese, mayonnaise, onions, pimiento, and oysters. Spread on crepes; roll up. Broil until bubbly. Serve hot for first course. Yield 4 servings.

spontaneous crepe snacks

There is no need to be confined by a recipe in formulating crepes. Almost any combination of leftovers can make a delicious snack. such as:

Slice of ham, chopped green olive, mushrooms, and sour cream;

Sardines, mixed sweet pickles, green onion tops sliced very thin lengthwise, and tartar sauce;

Cottage cheese, walnuts, raisins, chopped green onion tops, and blue-cheese flavoring.

MAIN DISH CREPES
blintzes

12 **ounces cottage cheese**
1 **egg yolk**
1 **teaspoon butter, softened**
1 **teaspoon vanilla**
18 **crepes, cooked on 1 side only**
2 **teaspoons butter**
2 **teaspoons vegetable oil**
2 **tablespoons sugar**
Confectioners' sugar

Mix cheese, egg yolk, softened butter, and vanilla. Divide filling among crepes on cooked side; roll up.

Melt remaining butter and oil in large frypan; place half of crepes in pan. Fry until golden brown; turn once. Repeat with rest of crepes; add more butter and oil if necessary. Dust crepes with sugar. Pass dairy sour cream if desired. Yield 4 servings.

cannelloni crepes

1 **medium onion, finely chopped**
2 **tablespoons vegetable oil**
¾ **pound ground beef**
2 **tablespoons tomato sauce**
½ **cup flour**
1 **beef bouillon cube dissolved in 1 cup boiling water**
⅓ **cup sliced mushrooms**
½ **teaspoon salt**
⅛ **teaspoon pepper**
2 **tablespoons butter**
1¼ **cups milk**

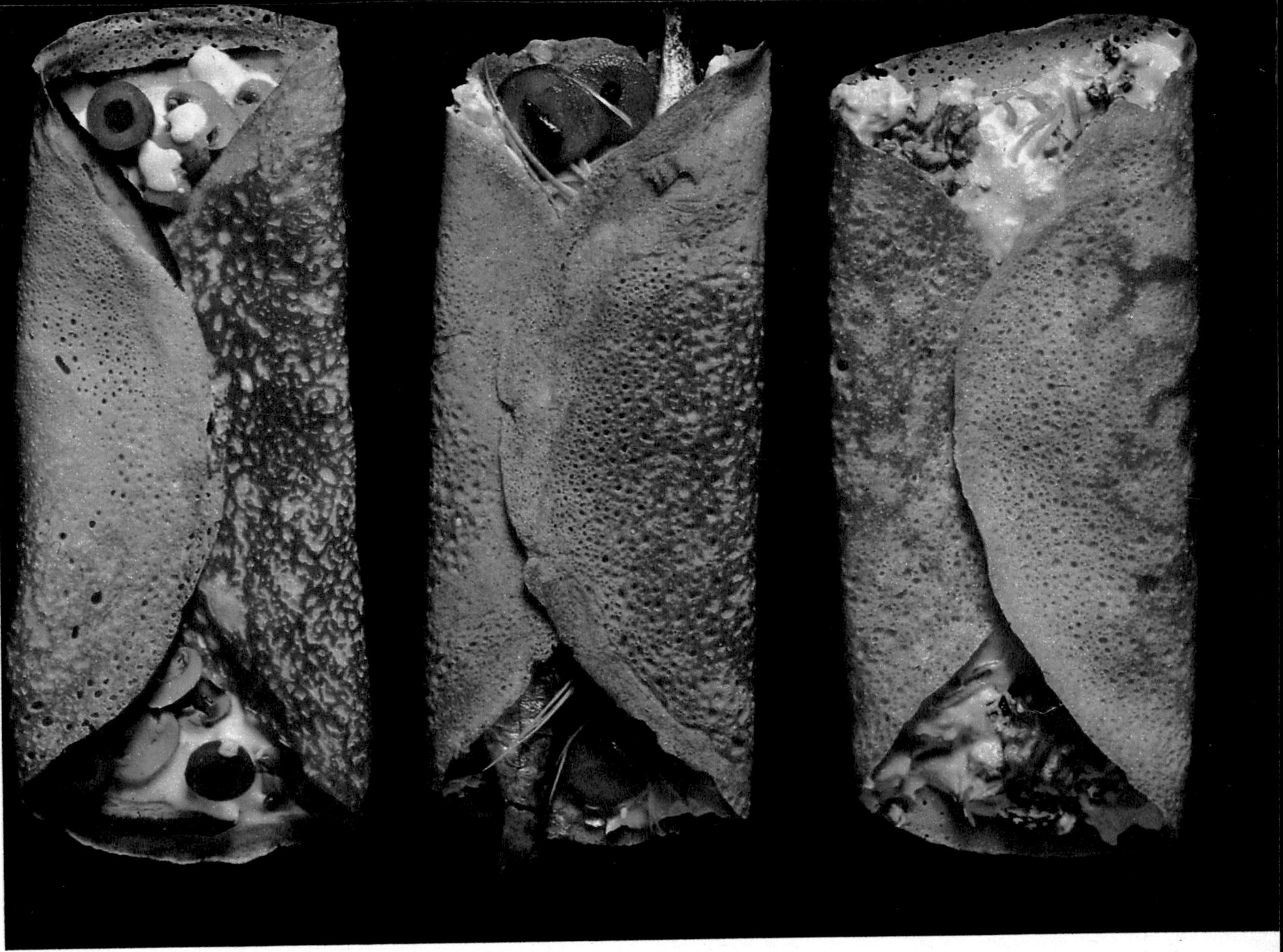

spontaneous crepe snack

⅓ cup grated cheddar or Parmesan cheese
8 warm crepes

Fry onion in hot oil 5 minutes. Add meat; cook 5 minutes. Remove from heat. Stir in tomato sauce and ¼ cup flour. Add bouillon, mushrooms, and seasonings. Cover; simmer 45 minutes.

Meanwhile, melt butter in separate small pan. Stir in ¼ cup flour; cook 2 minutes. Remove from heat. Gradually stir in milk; bring to boil while stirring. Blend in ¼ cup cheese. Remove from heat; leave cover on.

Fill crepes with ground-beef mixture; roll up. Place in baking dish; pour sauce over. Sprinkle with remaining cheese. Broil about 3 minutes, until golden. Serve at once. Yield 4 servings.

cheese, bacon, and onion crepes

1 pound thinly sliced bacon
2 tablespoons butter
10 green onions with tops, chopped
12 crepes
2 cups grated American cheese

Fry bacon until crisp. Drain; crumble. Pour off bacon fat from frypan. Add butter; heat. Stir in onions; cook 3 minutes, until soft.

blintzes

cannelloni crepes

In each crepe place small amount of onions and spoonfuls of bacon and cheese. Reserve enough cheese to sprinkle tops. Roll up each crepe; place in buttered baking dish. Sprinkle tops with cheese. Bake at 400°F 15 minutes. Yield 6 servings.

cheese layer crepes

⅓ cup vegetable oil
1 medium onion, chopped
1 pound ground beef
¼ cup flour
1 (8-ounce) can tomato sauce
1 bouillon cube dissolved in 1 cup boiling water
1 bay leaf
1 teaspoon salt
⅛ teaspoon pepper
6 crepes
1 recipe Mornay Sauce (see Index)
¾ cup grated cheddar cheese
2 tablespoons Parmesan cheese

Heat oil; fry onion gently 5 minutes or until tender. Add meat; cook 5 minutes. Drain off fat. Stir in flour; remove pan from heat. Add tomato sauce; thoroughly blend. Add bouillon, bay leaf, and seasonings. Cover; simmer gently 40 minutes.

Place 1 crepe in bottom of baking dish; spread layer of meat, then layer of sauce. Sprinkle with cheddar cheese. Continue layers; end with layer of sauce. Sprinkle Parmesan on top. Bake in 350°F oven 30 minutes or until golden brown. Yield 4 servings.

chicken-divan crepes

1 (10-ounce) package frozen chopped broccoli
1 can cream of chicken soup (undiluted)
½ teaspoon Worcestershire sauce
¾ cup grated Parmesan cheese
2 cups small strips cooked chicken
12 crepes
⅓ cup mayonnaise
1 tablespoon milk

Cook broccoli according to package directions; drain. Combine with soup, Worcestershire sauce, ½ cup cheese, and chicken. Divide mixture between crepes; roll up. Place in shallow baking dish.

Combine mayonnaise with milk; spread over crepes. Sprinkle with ¼ cup cheese; broil until cheese bubbles. Yield 6 servings.

chicken-in-white-wine crepes

3 tablespoons minced green onions
3 tablespoons butter
3 cups diced chicken
1 cup diced cooked ham
½ teaspoon salt
⅛ teaspoon pepper
½ teaspoon tarragon
½ cup dry white wine
½ cup canned mushrooms
1 hard-cooked egg, diced
1 double recipe Velouté Sauce (see Index)

12 crepes
2 tablespoons melted butter

Saute onions in 3 tablespoons hot butter 1 minute. Stir in chicken, ham, salt, pepper, and tarragon; stir over high heat 2 minutes. Pour in wine; boil until liquid has almost disappeared. Mix in mushrooms and egg. Fold in Velouté Sauce. Divide mixture among crepes; roll up. Place in greased baking dish; brush tops with melted butter. Heat at 350°F 10 minutes. Yield 6 servings.

creamed-oyster crepes

1 pint oysters
2 tablespoons butter
2 tablespoons flour
1 cup oyster liquor (add cream to make 1 cup)
½ teaspoon salt
½ teaspoon curry powder
1 teaspoon lemon juice

8 warm crepes
Chopped parsley for garnish

Drain oysters; pat dry with paper towels. Save oyster liquor.

Melt butter; blend in flour. Stir in oyster liquor slowly. Add salt and curry powder; heat to simmer. Heat oysters thoroughly but do not boil. Season with lemon juice. Divide among crepes; roll up. Garnish with parsley. Yield 4 servings.

crepes a la bellman

bouillon
2 chicken bouillon cubes
2¼ cups water
1 teaspoon salt
2 to 3 white peppercorns
1 tablespoon chopped onion
½ carrot, chopped

cheese layer crepes

crepes a la bellman

sauce

1 small veal sweetbread
2 tablespoons butter
2½ tablespoons flour
3 ounces boiled ham, chopped
1 tablespoon chopped onion
¼ cup heavy cream

8 warm crepes
2 tablespoons grated cheese

Combine all bouillon ingredients; bring to simmer.

Rinse sweetbread; boil in bouillon about 10 minutes. Skim; let cool in bouillon. Remove membranes around sweetbread. Chop sweetbread.

Melt butter. Add flour; brown lightly. Add strained bouillon; simmer 3 to 4 minutes, stirring until smooth. Add sweetbread, ham, onion, and cream. Season to taste. Distribute sauce on crepes; roll up. Place in greased baking dish; sprinkle cheese on top. Bake 5 to 10 minutes at 425°F. Yield 4 servings.

crepes with chicken-liver paté

2 tablespoons butter
½ pound chicken livers

272

2 eggs, hard-cooked
2 (3-ounce) packages soft cream cheese
1 tablespoon finely chopped parsley
1 teaspoon salt
1/8 teaspoon pepper
1 tablespoon cognac
12 crepes
1 tablespoon melted butter

Heat 2 tablespoons butter in frying pan. Add livers; cook, stirring occasionally, over medium heat 10 minutes or until tender. Drain.

Chop livers and eggs in food grinder, food processor, or blender (add a little at a time).

Work cream cheese with spoon until light and fluffy. Mix into liver mixture along with all remaining ingredients except melted butter. Put 2 spoonfuls along center of each crepe; roll. Turn seam-side-down in buttered baking dish; brush with melted butter. Bake at 375°F 15 to 20 minutes. Serve hot as first course, or slice and serve cold as hors d'oeuvres. Yield 6 servings.

crepes romaine

1 tablespoon chopped onion
2 tablespoons butter
1 tablespoon flour
1 cup light cream
4 ounces smoked salmon, diced
3 hard-cooked eggs, chopped
1 to 2 tablespoons capers
1/2 teaspoon chopped dill
1/2 teaspoon fresh lemon juice
8 warm crepes
2 tablespoons grated cheese

Fry onion in 1 tablespoon butter until soft. Stir in flour. Add cream a little at a time; let simmer 3 to 4 minutes. Add salmon, eggs, capers, dill, and lemon juice. Season to taste. Place heaping tablespoonful on each crepe; roll up. Place in buttered ovenproof dish. Sprinkle with grated cheese. Dot with butter. Bake in preheated 400°F oven 5 to 8 minutes or until cheese has melted and crepes are hot through. Yield 4 servings.

crepes with spaghetti sauce

Prepare 2 cups of a favorite spaghetti-sauce recipe. Add meat, sausage, or mushrooms. If sauce is runny, add enough tomato paste to thicken. Fill 8 to 10 crepes; roll. Place in baking dish. Spread extra sauce over tops of crepes. Sprinkle with grated Parmesan cheese. Bake at 400°F 15 minutes. Yield 4 or 5 servings.

crepes with veal

1 pound thin slices of veal, cut into 1-inch squares
2 tablespoons flour
3 tablespoons vegetable oil
1 clove garlic, minced
2 tablespoons chopped onion
1 tablespoon parsley
1/2 teaspoon basil
2 tomatoes, chopped
1/4 cup heavy cream
Salt and pepper to taste
12 crepes

Dredge veal with flour.

Heat oil; fry veal until lightly brown. Move meat to side of pan. Sauté garlic, onion, and parsley. Add basil and tomatoes; cook over medium heat until tomatoes are soft. Break up with fork. Add cream, salt, and pepper; cook over low heat until thoroughly heated. Cool. Place spoonful or two in each crepe; roll up. Place seam-side-down in greased baking dish. Bake at 350°F 30 minutes. Yield 4 servings.

egg-and-zucchini crepes

1 cup dry bread crumbs
1/2 cup butter or margarine
1/3 cup minced onion
1 large zucchini, cut into julienne strips
3 eggs, lightly beaten
1/2 teaspoon salt
1/8 teaspoon pepper
3 tablespoons minced parsley
12 crepes
1/3 cup grated Parmesan cheese
1/3 cup grated Gruyère cheese

Sauté bread crumbs in 1/4 cup butter; toss until lightly toasted. Remove from pan; reserve.

Add rest of butter to pan; sauté onion and zucchini until tender. Add eggs, salt, and pepper; with fork very lightly scramble mixture over low heat. Add egg mixture to bread crumbs. Stir in parsley. Divide mixture among crepes; roll up. Arrange seam-side-down in buttered shallow baking dish. Sprinkle with cheeses. Bake at 375°F 10 minutes or until hot and cheese is golden. Yield 4 to 6 servings.

ham-filled crepes

2 cups finely chopped cooked ham
2 hard-cooked eggs, finely chopped
1/4 cup chopped ripe olives
2 teaspoons sweet pickle relish
3/4 cup mayonnaise
8 crepes
8 slices Swiss cheese

Combine ham, eggs, olives, relish, and mayonnaise. Divide among crepes; roll up. Place in shallow baking pan with 1 slice cheese on each crepe. Broil until cheese melts. Yield 4 servings.

manicotti

3 eggs
½ teaspoon salt
2 pounds ricotta cheese
¾ cup Parmesan or Romano cheese
¼ teaspoon pepper
½ pound mozzarella, cut into 12 strips
12 to 14 crepes
3 (8 ounce) cans tomato sauce

Mix eggs, salt, ricotta, ¼ cup Parmesan, and pepper. Place about 2 tablespoons filling and a strip of mozzarella on each crepe; roll up.

Pour 1 can tomato sauce into large baking dish. Place crepes seam-side-down in sauce. Sprinkle with ½ cup Parmesan. Cover with 2 cans sauce. Bake in preheated 350°F oven 45 minutes. Yield 6 to 8 servings.

pizza crepes

6 crepes
1 tablespoon olive oil or vegetable oil
½ cup tomato sauce
½ teaspoon oregano
¼ teaspoon basil
¼ cup thin slices pepperoni
¼ cup sliced mushrooms
¾ cup grated mozzarella cheese
¼ cup grated Parmesan cheese

Brush crepes with oil; spread with tomato sauce. Sprinkle with herbs. Top with pepperoni, mushrooms, and cheeses. Broil open-face until bubbly. Yield 6 servings.

spinach-and-ham crepes

spinach-and-ham crepes

1 pound spinach
1 cup finely chopped boiled ham
3 tablespoons heavy cream
Pinch of salt
Pinch of nutmeg
1 tablespoon cornstarch mixed in 2 tablespoons
    cold water (optional)
8 crepes
2 tablespoons butter
Pieces of ham or bacon for garnish

Discard stems and heavy veins of spinach; wash to remove grains of sand. Cook about 5 minutes in plenty of boiling water; drain.

Place ham in food processor. Add spinach, cream, salt, and nutmeg; turn on motor. Return mixture to clean saucepan; stir over low heat. If puree appears too thin, add 1 tablespoon cornstarch dissolved in 2 tablespoons cold water; it will thicken immediately. Spread some ham-and-spinach puree on crepe; fold crepes into triangles. Place in buttered ovenproof dish. Dot with butter. Heat 15 minutes in preheated 400°F oven. Garnish with pieces of ham or bacon. Can be served with Mornay or Hollandaise sauce (see Index). Yield 4 servings.

tuna-with-herbs crepes

1 (6½-ounce) can tuna, drained
3 hard-cooked eggs, peeled, chopped
½ cup mayonnaise
1 teaspoon prepared mustard
¼ teaspoon salt
⅛ teaspoon pepper
1 tablespoon sweet pickle relish
1 tablespoon chopped parsley
½ teaspoon dried tarragon
½ teaspoon dried chervil
8 crepes
2 tablespoons melted butter

Break tuna into small chunks. Combine tuna, eggs, mayonnaise, mustard, salt, pepper, relish, parsley, tarragon, and chervil. Divide among crepes; roll up. Brush tops with butter. Heat at 350°F 20 minutes or until hot through. Yield 4 servings.

DESSERT CREPE BATTERS

basic dessert crepe batter

4 eggs
1 cup flour
2 tablespoons sugar
1 cup milk
¼ cup water
1 tablespoon melted butter, cooled

Mixer or whisk method: Beat eggs in medium mixing bowl. Gradually add flour and sugar alternately with milk and water, beating until smooth. Beat in melted butter.

Blender or food-processor method: Combine ingredients in container; blend about 1 minute. Scrape down sides with rubber spatula; blend 15 seconds or until smooth.

Refrigerate batter at least 1 hour before use. Yield 20 to 25 crepes.

chocolate dessert crepe batter

3 eggs
1 cup flour
2 tablespoons sugar
2 tablespoons cocoa
1¼ cups buttermilk (or add 1 tablespoon lemon
    juice to 1¼ cups regular milk)
2 tablespoons melted butter, cooled

Mixer or whisk method: Beat eggs in medium mixing bowl. Add flour, sugar, and cocoa alternately with buttermilk, beating until smooth. Beat in melted butter.

Blender or food-processor method: Combine ingredients in container; blend about 1 minute. Scrape down sides with rubber spatula; blend 15 seconds or until smooth.

Refrigerate batter at least 1 hour before use. Yield 18 to 22 crepes.

DESSERT CREPES

apricot soufflé crepes

2 cups dried apricots
1 cup water
6 eggs, separated
⅔ cup sugar
12 warm dessert crepes
2 cups Basic Egg Custard (see Index) or 1 package
    egg-custard mix
Slivered toasted almonds

Prepare apricot puree by simmering apricots in water until tender. Sieve or puree in blender or food processor; reserve.

Beat egg yolks and sugar until thick.

In separate bowl beat egg whites until stiff.

Fold ½ cup apricot puree into beaten yolks; fold into egg whites.

Spread crepes with a little remaining apricot puree; divide egg mixture among crepes. Lightly fold crepes over soufflé; place in baking dish. Cook in 450°F oven 4 minutes or until puffy. Pour warm custard over crepes. Sprinkle with almonds; serve. Yield 6 servings.

blueberry crepes

2 pints blueberries
½ cup red wine
½ cup orange juice
¼ cup red currant jelly
1 tablespoon arrowroot
2 tablespoons cold water
12 dessert crepes
2 tablespoons butter
Confectioner's sugar
Whipped cream or sour cream

Wash blueberries; put into bowl.

Combine the wine, orange juice, and jelly; bring to boiling in small saucepan.

Dissolve arrowroot in cold water; add to boiling liquid. It will thicken immediately. Remove from heat; combine sauce with blueberries.

Put 2 to 3 tablespoons blueberries in each crepe. Roll crepes; place in buttered ovenproof dish. Dot with butter. Bake in preheated 400°F oven 15 minutes. When removed from oven, dust crepes heavily with sifted confectioner's sugar. Serve with whipped or sour cream. Yield 6 servings.

chocolate-and-nut crepes

2 tablespoons cocoa
⅓ cup cornstarch
¼ cup sugar
2½ cups milk
½ cup chopped walnuts
6 warm dessert crepes

Blend cocoa, cornstarch, and sugar with small amount of milk.

apricot soufflé crepes

Bring rest of milk to boil; blend into cocoa mixture. Return to pan; bring to boil, stirring constantly until thick. Reserve ¼ cup chocolate sauce and 1 tablespoon chopped walnuts. Mix rest of sauce with nuts. Fill warm crepes with mixture; roll up. Spoon remaining sauce on top of crepes; sprinkle with reserved nuts. Serve at once. Yield 6 servings.

cream-of-almond crepes

2 tablespoons butter
2 tablespoons flour

cream-of-almond crepes

crepe gateau

1 cup milk
3 ounces almond extract
3 egg yolks
1 cup sugar
½ teaspoon salt
¼ cup Grand Marnier liqueur or rum
⅓ cup chopped candied cherries
⅓ cup chopped angelico
⅓ cup candied orange peel
12 to 15 dessert crepes

Melt butter; blend in flour. Cook 1 minute. Add cold milk; bring to simmer. Cook 2 to 3 minutes, stirring constantly; remove from heat. Add almond extract, egg yolks, sugar, and salt; beat. Adjust sweetness to taste. Add Grand Marnier and candied fruits; refrigerate until cold.

Divide mixture among crepes; roll up package-style. Place in ovenproof dish; dot with butter. Sprinkle tops with sugar. Place under broiler 3 to 4 minutes, until sugar is browned, or stack crepes with filling between each layer and top with a little filling. Yield 6 servings.

crepe gateau

24 to 30 dessert crepes
Apple sauce or various preserves and jams of
    your choice: blackberry, orange marmalade,
    gooseberry, raspberry, strawberry, grape, etc.
    or Basic Custard (see Index)
Fruit-flavored liqueur

Stack dessert crepes one at a time; place layer of applesauce, custard, or preserve between each 2 crepes. Top with liqueur; cut into quarters with sharp knife. Yield approximately 6 servings.

crepes suzettes gourmet-style

6 cubes sugar
2 oranges
1 lemon
1 stick soft sweet butter
¼ cup Grand Marnier, curacao, Benedictine,
    Cointreau or Triple Sec

12 dessert crepes
¼ cup brandy

Rub sugar cubes over rinds of oranges and lemon; combine on plate with butter. Place butter in chafing dish. Add juice of 1 orange and 1 lemon and ¼ cup liqueur. When contents of pan are hot and bubbling, add crepes one at a time. Coat each crepe with sauce; fold into triangle. Push to side of dish. When all crepes are coated, arrange over surface of dish; allow to heat through. Flame crepes with brandy; serve immediately. Yield 6 servings.

easy crepes suzettes

½ cup sweet butter, softened
¼ cup sugar

2 teaspoons grated orange peel
½ cup orange juice
¼ cup curaçao
12 warm dessert crepes
1 small orange, sliced
1 small lemon, sliced
2 tablespoons brandy

Cream butter; beat in sugar. Add orange peel, juice, and curaçao. Spread orange butter on each crepe. Fold into fourths. Decorate with orange and lemon slices. Pour brandy over; serve. (If flaming dessert is desired, heat brandy in small pan, pour over crepes, and ignite.) Yield 6 servings.

crepes suzettes gourmet-style

easy dessert crepes

Prepare dessert crepes ahead; warm in a 300°F oven 10 minutes. Be imaginative in filling and garnishing crepes.

crepes with applesauce

Fill crepes with applesauce mixed with whipped cream. Garnish with ground cinnamon.

crepes with preserves

Fill crepes with strawberry or raspberry jam; lingonberry preserves are also very delicious and attractive. Garnish with same preserve or with sugar.

crepes with marmalade and pecans

Fill with equal amounts of pecans and orange marmalade; roll. Sprinkle with sugar.

(top to bottom)
crepes with applesauce
crepes with preserves
crepes with marmalade and pecans

hot ice-cream crepes

1 pint coffee ice cream
12 cold dessert crepes
Chocolate or melba sauce

Preheat oven to 475°F. Divide ice cream among crepes; roll up. Place in ovenproof dish. Bake in hot oven about 2 to 3 minutes. Serve with cold chocolate sauce or Melba Sauce (see Index). Yield 4 servings.

mixed-fruit crepes with whipped cream

3 bananas
2 tablespoons heavy cream
1 tablespoon sugar
12 dessert crepes
1 pound fresh or canned peaches
1 pound fresh or canned pears
2 tablespoons butter

Mash bananas with cream and sugar; cover surface of each crepe.

Cut peaches and pears into small pieces; lay over bananas. Roll or fold crepes; place in buttered ovenproof dish. Dot with butter. Bake in preheated 400°F oven 15 minutes. Serve with Melba Sauce (see Index) or whipped cream. Yield 6 servings.

hot ice-cream crepes

whipped-cream-filled crepes

strawberry-cream crepes

4 cups sliced fresh strawberries
2 tablespoons sugar
1 (14-ounce) can sweetened condensed milk
¼ cup lemon juice
½ cup heavy cream, whipped
12 dessert crepes
Whipped cream for garnish
12 whole strawberries for garnish

Sprinkle sliced strawberries with sugar; set aside.

Beat milk with lemon juice until thick. Fold in strawberries and whipped cream. Divide among crepes; fold. Garnish with additional whipped cream and a strawberry centered on cream. Yield 6 servings.

whipped-cream-filled crepes

½ pint heavy cream, chilled
Sugar and vanilla to taste
6 warm dessert crepes
1 pint fresh raspberries or strawberries

Whip chilled cream until thick. Add sugar and vanilla. Divide whipped cream among crepes; fill and roll. Garnish with berries; sprinkle sugar over tops for beautiful but simple dessert. (A filling of sour cream would be a delicious variation.) Yield 6 servings.

CUSTARD

baked custard

3 cups milk
4 eggs
⅓ cup sugar
¼ teaspoon salt
1 teaspoon vanilla
Nutmeg or cinnamon (optional)

Heat milk until hot but not boiling.

Beat eggs in large bowl. Add sugar and salt. Add milk slowly, stirring all the time. Mix in vanilla. Pour into baking pan. Sprinkle with nutmeg or cinnamon. Bake at 300°F about 1 hour, until a knife stuck in center comes out clean. Yield 6 servings.

baked caramel custard

¾ cup sugar
2 large eggs or 4 yolks
⅓ cup sugar
¼ teaspoon salt
½ teaspoon vanilla
2 cups milk, scalded

Melt ¾ cup sugar in small skillet, stirring constantly until pale brown. Divide caramelized sugar among 6 custard cups; turn cups so caramel will coat sides. Let harden.

Meanwhile, mix eggs, ⅓ cup sugar, salt, and vanilla. Add milk gradually. Strain into custard cups. Place cups in pan of hot water.

Bake in 350°F oven 30 to 35 minutes or until silver knife comes out clean. Remove from hot water immediately. Serve chilled and unmolded. Yield 6 servings.

banana chocolate cream

12 Coconut Macaroons (see Index)
Juice of 2 oranges, strained
1 tablespoon rum (optional)
6 bananas
Grated rind of 1 orange
1 recipe Basic Confectioners' Custard (see Index)
¾ cup whipping cream, whipped
¼ cup coarsely grated sweet chocolate
1 can mandarin oranges

Arrange macaroons in 1 or 2 serving dishes or in individual custard cups.

Combine orange juice and rum; drizzle over macaroons. Let stand 20 minutes.

Mash bananas with fork in bowl.

Stir orange rind into Confectioners' Custard. Fold in the bananas. Fold in whipped cream; mound mixture over macaroons. Sprinkle evenly with chocolate. Can be refrigerated 3 to 4 hours before serving, if desired.

Arrange mandarin orange sections around sides of each dish as a border just before serving. Yield 4 to 6 servings.

basic confectioners' custard

1 cup milk
1 vanilla pod or 1 teaspoon vanilla extract
¼ cup all-purpose flour
½ cup extra-fine sugar
3 egg yolks

Combine milk and vanilla pod in small saucepan. Cook over medium heat to just below boiling.

Combine flour and sugar in medium mixing bowl, blending well. Add egg yolks; beat thoroughly with electric mixer.

banana chocolate cream

créme brûlée

Remove vanilla pod from milk (dry pod; store for later use). Pour milk slowly into flour mixture, stirring constantly with wooden spoon until well blended. Pour into top of double boiler. Cook over boiling water, stirring constantly, until custard is thick and smooth. Cool to lukewarm. Yield about 1 cup.

basic egg custard

2 eggs
2 egg yolks
½ cup sugar
3 cups milk
1 vanilla pod or 1 teaspoon vanilla extract

Beat eggs, egg yolks, and sugar together, using electric mixer at medium speed, about 5 minutes, until thick and doubled in bulk.

Slowly heat milk with vanilla pod in heavy saucepan until hot but not boiling. Remove pod; stir milk into egg mixture. Pour into top of large double boiler; add vanilla pod. Cook over hot water, stirring constantly, about 20 minutes, until thickened. Remove vanilla pod; rinse and pat dry for future use. Makes thin custard that can also be used as a sauce. Yield about 3 cups.

bread-and-butter custard

4 thin slices home-style bread
Soft butter

1 quart milk
6 large eggs
1 cup sugar
1 teaspoon vanilla
Nutmeg, ground or freshly grated

Lay bread, buttered-side-up, in single layer in square glass baking dish (8 × 8 × 2 inches).

Scald milk by heating until bubbles appear around edge.

Slightly beat eggs in large bowl. Add sugar and vanilla; beat just until blended. Gradually and gently beat in scalding-hot milk; strain over bread (custard mixture will look foamy). Sprinkle generously with nutmeg. Place in center of large aluminum roasting pan (17 × 11 × 2 inches). Pour enough hot water into pan to come as high as pudding mixture in dish. Bake in preheated 325°F oven until silver or stainless-steel knife inserted in center comes out clean, about 40 minutes; chill. Serve, if desired, with strawberry or raspberry preserves flavored with kirsch. Yield 8 servings.

créme brûlée

6 egg yolks
6 tablespoons sugar
3 cups half-and-half cream
1 vanilla pod or 1 teaspoon vanilla extract
½ cup light brown sugar

Beat egg yolks slightly. Add sugar; beat 5 minutes or until eggs are lemon-colored.

Place cream and vanilla pod in top of double boiler; bring to boil. Pour small amount of hot mixture over egg mixture, beating constantly. Return to remaining hot mixture; cook over hot water 3 to 4 minutes or until slightly thickened. Remove vanilla pod. Pour mixture into heat- resistant serving dish. Chill 6 to 8 hours or until set.

Sift brown sugar; sprinkle evenly over custard. Place under broiler about 4 inches from source of heat. Broil, watching carefully, 3 to 4 minutes or until brown sugar melts. Chill before serving. Yield 6 servings.

fried custard

2 tablespoons cornstarch
¼ cup all-purpose flour
½ cup sugar
2 cups milk
4 egg yolks, beaten
Dash of nutmeg
Dash of salt
1 teaspoon vanilla extract

Fine cracker crumbs
1 egg, beaten
Confectioners' sugar

Combine cornstarch, flour, and sugar in top of double boiler. Gradually add milk, stirring constantly. Cook over boiling water until thickened, then cook 5 minutes longer, stirring constantly. Gradually stir part of hot mixture into egg yolks; stir egg yolks into hot mixture. Add nutmeg and salt; cook about 1 minute. Remove from heat. Stir in vanilla. Pour into oiled 8-inch-square pan; let stand in refrigerator 4 to 5 hours or overnight.

Cut firm custard into rounds, using biscuit cutter. Dredge in cracker crumbs. Dip in egg, then dredge in crumbs again. Fry in deep hot (380°F) fat until golden brown. Sprinkle with sugar; serve hot.

Strained orange juice can be poured over each serving, if desired. Hot custard can be poured into oiled 8 × 4-inch loaf pan and, after chilling, cut into 6 strips for frying, if desired. Yield 6 servings.

fried custard

frozen christmas custard

frozen christmas custard

2 tablespoons chopped candied cherries
2 tablespoons chopped candied ginger
2 tablespoons chopped candied pineapple
2 tablespoons raisins
1 tablespoons currants
2 tablespoons chopped mixed candied peel
⅔ cup sauterne
2 recipes Basic Confectioners' Custard (see Index)
2 cups whipping cream, stiffly beaten

Combine cherries, ginger, pineapple, raisins, currants, and mixed peel in small bowl. Pour sauterne over mixture. Let stand 1 hour; drain.

Add fruit mixture to custard. Fold in whipped cream until well blended. Place in lightly oiled 8-cup soufflé dish; freeze until hard.

To unmold, let custard stand at room temperature 10 minutes. Dip bowl in hot water; turn custard out onto platter.

Pour boiling water into bowl; dip sharp knife into water. Cut custard into wedges; place on serving platter. (Dip knife into hot water before cutting each slice.)

Frozen custard can be made into balls by using ice-cream scoop that has been dipped into boiling water. Yield 10 to 12 servings.

german custard (sauce allemande)

2½ cups milk
1 tablespoon potato flour
1 vanilla pod or 1 teaspoon vanilla extract
Sugar to taste
3 eggs, separated

Make paste with small amount of milk and potato flour.

Combine remaining milk and vanilla pod in top of double boiler; bring to boiling. Stir in paste until smooth. Remove vanilla pod (rinse and dry for future use). Stir in sugar until well mixed.

Beat egg yolks thoroughly; stir in small amount of hot mixture. Return egg mixture to double boiler; cook, stirring constantly, until sauce is smooth. Remove from heat; let cool to lukewarm.

Beat egg whites until stiff peaks form. Fold ⅓ of egg whites into custard until thoroughly blended; carefully fold in remaining egg whites. Chill until ready to serve. Yield 6 to 8 servings.

german custard with raspberries

1 quart fresh raspberries
1 pint fresh currants (optional)
Sugar to taste
1 recipe German Custard

Combine raspberries, currants, and sugar in large bowl; chill until ready to serve.

Spoon raspberry mixture into serving dishes; top with generous amount of custard. Three 10-ounce packages frozen raspberries can be substituted for fresh raspberries, if desired. Yield 6 servings.

288

german custard with raspberries

hazelnut cream

1 recipe Basic Confectioners' Custard (see Index)
1 envelope unflavored gelatin
2 tablespoons rum
1 cup ground toasted hazelnuts or pecans
1 cup whipping cream

Prepare custard.

Soften gelatin in ¼ cup water; stir into custard until dissolved. Cool custard to lukewarm. Add

rum; mix well. Chill until partially set. Add hazelnuts; mix until well blended.

Beat cream until stiff peaks form; fold into hazelnut mixture until blended. Turn into lightly oiled 6-cup mold; chill until firm. Unmold onto serving dish.

Additional whipped cream can be piped in rosettes around mold and each rosette topped with whole toasted hazelnut, if desired. Yield about 8 servings.

little chocolate pots

1½ cups milk
2 cups chocolate chips
2 eggs
¼ cup sugar
Pinch of salt

Pour milk into heavy saucepan; heat to boiling.

Combine remaining ingredients in blender or food-processor container. Pour in hot milk; blend at low speed 1 minute or until smooth. Pour into 6 custard cups; chill at least 2 hours before serving. Garnish, if desired, with piped whipped cream; dust with chopped nuts. Yield 6 servings.

mexican trifle

¼ cup sugar
1 tablespoon cornstarch
¼ teaspoon salt
2 cups milk
2 eggs, slightly beaten
1 teaspoon vanilla
4 cups cubed Pound Cake (see Index)
4 tablespoons brandy
4 tablespoons apricot preserves
½ cup whipped cream
1 tablespoon confectioners' sugar
Grated semisweet chocolate
Toasted slivered almonds

Combine sugar, cornstarch, and salt in medium saucepan. Stir in milk until well-blended; cook over medium heat, stirring constantly, until mixture boils (it will be quite thin). Add a little to eggs; beat well. Add mixture to rest of sauce in pan; cook, stirring constantly, until mixture starts to bubble. Stir in vanilla; cool, covered with waxed paper.

Place cake cubes in glass bowl. Sprinkle with 3 tablespoons brandy; drizzle with preserves. Pour custard over cake cubes.

Whip cream with confectioners' sugar until stiff. Fold in 1 tablespoon brandy.

Top cake and custard with whipped cream. Garnish with grated chocolate and almonds. Cover; chill several hours before serving. Yield 4 to 6 servings.

little chocolate pots

swiss roll and custard

1 recipe Basic Rolled Sponge Cake (see Index)
1 (7½-ounce) jar blackberry jam
2 packages unflavored gelatin
½ cup cold water
1 recipe Basic Egg Custard (see Index)

Prepare sponge cake. Spread evenly with blackberry jam. Roll up; let stand until ready to use.

Sprinkle gelatin over cold water; let stand 3 minutes to soften.

Prepare custard in double boiler; stir in softened gelatin until dissolved. Place top of double boiler in bowl filled with ice. Let stand 5 minutes; stir occasionally.

Cut rolled sponge cake into 10 even slices. Place 1 slice in center of oiled 2-quart mold; arrange 3 slices evenly around side of mold. Slowly pour in custard to half the depth of the 3 slices. Place another slice in center of custard; arrange 3 slices around side between first 3 slices. Pour in more custard to half the depth of last 3 slices added. Place another slice in center of custard.

Cut remaining cake slice into thirds, so that each third has curved side; place around side of mold, straight-edge-down. Pour in remaining custard. Chill several hours or until firm.

Unmold and cut in wedges to serve. Rolled sponge cake can be made day ahead and wrapped in plastic wrap, if desired. Yield 6 to 8 servings.

swiss roll and custard

FRUIT

apple charlotte

6 medium cooking apples
½ cup brown sugar
Grated rind and juice of 1 lemon
8 thinly cut slices of bread and butter
Sugar

Grease 5-cup charlotte mold with butter.

Peel, core, and slice apples. Place layer in bottom of mold; sprinkle with brown sugar, lemon rind, and lemon juice. Cover with bread and butter. Repeat until dish is full; finish with layer of bread and butter. Cover with greased paper. Bake in 350°F oven ¾ to 1 hour. Turn out of dish, if desired, and dredge well with sugar before serving.

Alternatively, cut bread ¼ inch thick before buttering; line mold with it, buttered-side-out, so that pieces fit tightly together. Fill with remaining ingredients packed tightly; bake as above. Yield 5 to 6 servings.

apple cobbler

4 cups peeled, sliced baking apples
1⅓ cups sugar
⅛ teaspoon cinnamon
½ teaspoon almond extract (optional)
2 tablespoons butter
1½ cups sifted flour
2 teaspoons baking powder
½ teaspoon salt
¼ cup butter
1 egg, beaten
⅔ cup milk

Place apples in 1½-quart baking dish. Sprinkle with 1 cup sugar, cinnamon, and almond extract, dot with 2 tablespoons butter.

Sift flour, baking powder, ⅓ cup sugar, and salt into mixing bowl. Cut in ¼ cup butter until mixture is slightly coarser than cornmeal.

Combine egg and milk; pour into dry ingredients. Stir just enough to combine; spoon over apples in baking dish.

Bake in 425°F oven about 30 minutes, until browned. Serve with fresh cream, sour cream, or ice cream, if desired. Yield 6 to 8 servings.

apple crumble

1 (1-pound) can pie apples
1 teaspoon cinnamon
2 tablespoons sugar
¾ cup flour
½ cup packed brown sugar
3 tablespoons milk powder
6 tablespoons softened butter

Combine apples, cinnamon, and sugar; place in greased baking dish.

Combine flour, brown sugar, and milk powder; cut in butter. Sprinkle mixture over apples. Bake in 350°F oven 30 minutes. Serve with ice cream. Yield 4 to 6 servings.

apple crunch

3 medium-size apples
¼ cup packed brown sugar
¾ cup flour
¾ cup white sugar
¼ teaspoon salt
¼ teaspoon cinnamon
1 egg
⅓ cup melted margarine or butter

Pare and slice apples. Mix with brown sugar in baking pan; set aside.

Mix flour, sugar, salt, and cinnamon; set aside.

Beat egg; mix with flour mixture. Spread over fruit. Pour margarine over top. Bake at 375°F about 45 minutes, until lightly browned. Serve warm. Yield 6 servings.

apple fritters

4 to 6 cooking apples, peeled, cored
White wine to cover

Cut apples crosswise into ½-inch slices. Each slice will have a hole in center. Soak slices in wine 2 hours.

Drain apples; dip singly in fritter batter. Fry until lightly browned all over; drain on paper towel. Serve piping hot. Yield 4 to 6 servings.

fritter batter
2 egg yolks
⅔ cup milk
1 tablespoon lemon juice
1 tablespoon melted butter
1 cup flour
¼ teaspoon salt
2 tablespoons sugar
2 egg whites, beaten stiff

Deep fat for frying

Combine batter ingredients in order given by stirring with wooden spoon. Fold in egg whites last.

Heat fat in large skillet.

apple john

1½ pounds cooking apples, peeled, cored, sliced
¾ cup sugar
½ teaspoon ground cinnamon
1 teaspoon grated nutmeg
2 tablespoons butter or margarine

apple john

pastry

2 cups all-purpose flour
½ teaspoon salt
1 teaspoon baking powder
½ cup butter or margarine
⅔ cup milk

Preheat oven to 425°F.

Put apples into baking dish.

Mix sugar with spices; sprinkle on apples. Dot with butter.

Sift flour, salt, and baking powder together; cut in butter. Add milk; mix with fork until ingredients are just blended. Knead lightly on floured surface. Roll out; cut into 2-inch rounds. Arrange on top of apples; press sides down well.

Brush lightly with milk. Bake 25 minutes. Reduce heat to 350°F; cook 20 minutes. Yield 5 to 6 servings.

applesauce

2 pounds apples
⅓ cup water
¼ cup sugar

Pare apples if desired; trim away bruised or injured areas. Core; slice.

Bring water to boil; add apples. Cover; return to boil. Reduce heat; simmer until apples are tender, about 12 to 15 minutes. Stir occasionally to prevent sticking; remove from heat.

Put apples through food mill or sieve; add sugar. Mix thoroughly; chill. Yield 6 servings.

baked apples

6 large baking apples
6 tablespoons sugar
2 tablespoons butter or margarine
Cinnamon to taste
½ cup water

Wash and core apples; pare one-third of way down, or slit skin around apple about halfway down. Place in baking dish; put sugar and butter in center of each apple. Sprinkle with cinnamon; pour water around apples to prevent sticking. Bake, uncovered, at 400°F until tender, 45 minutes to 1 hour. Yield 6 servings.

baked apples with cranberry filling

4 large apples
8 tablespoons whole cranberry sauce
1 tablespoon butter or margarine
¾ cup boiling water
2 tablespoons sugar

Core apples to within ½ inch of bottoms; fill centers with cranberry sauce. Dot tops with butter. Place in 8 × 8-inch pan with boiling water. Bake in preheated 375°F oven 40 to 60 minutes or until tender but not mushy. Serve hot or cold; sprinkle with sugar just before serving. Yield 4 servings.

baked apples with cranberry filling

bananas flambé

bananas flambé

4 tablespoons butter or margarine
2 tablespoons brown sugar
1 teaspoon cinnamon
6 peeled ripe bananas, cut in half lengthwise
¼ cup rum

Melt butter in medium skillet.

Mix brown sugar and cinnamon; sprinkle some over bananas. Put bananas in butter on moderate to low heat; cook until lightly browned. Turn once; sprinkle with remaining sugar mixture. Spoon rum over bananas. Serve bananas by themselves or over vanilla ice cream. For a glamourous dessert, heat rum, pour over bananas, and ignite. Yield 4 servings.

bavarois cream with raspberries

1½ envelopes unflavored gelatin
3 tablespoons lemon juice
1¼ cups pureed raspberries
1 cup Basic Confectioners' Custard (see Index)
1 cup whipping cream, whipped

Pour ½ cup water into small saucepan. Add gelatin; let stand 5 minutes. Stir in lemon juice; place over low heat, stirring constantly until gelatin is dissolved. Cool to room temperature.

Combine raspberries, custard, and gelatin mixture; blend well. Fold in whipped cream until well blended. Pour into oiled 6-cup mold; chill until firm.

For a large party, double the recipe and put half the mixture into small individual molds or custard cups; surround the large mold with the small molds. Yield about 6 servings.

berry crisp

1 quart (4 cups) blueberries, blackberries, or strawberries
⅓ to ¾ cup sugar
¼ cup butter or margarine

bavarois cream with raspberries

¾ **cup uncooked quick rolled oats**
⅓ **cup flour**
⅓ **cup packed brown sugar**

Put berries in baking pan; sprinkle with enough sugar to sweeten.

Mix butter, rolled oats, flour, and brown sugar until crumbly; sprinkle over berries. Bake at 350°F about 30 minutes, until lightly browned. Yield 6 servings.

blueberry trifle

3 eggs
⅓ **cup sugar**
1½ tablespoons cornstarch
2 cups milk
2 teaspoons vanilla extract
24 lady fingers
⅓ **cup sherry**
4 cups fresh blueberries or dry-pack frozen blueberries, rinsed, drained
1 cup heavy cream, whipped
2 tablespoons confectioners' sugar
½ **teaspoon almond extract**
¼ **cup slivered toasted almonds**
3 tablespoons sugar

Beat eggs and sugar until well blended and foamy. Stir in cornstarch; gradually stir in milk. Cook over low heat, stirring constantly, about 10 minutes, until custard begins to thicken; do not boil. Cool; stir in vanilla.

Split ladyfingers; arrange on bottom of glass serving bowl. Sprinkle with sherry; cover with 2 cups blueberries. Spoon custard over blueberries.

Whip cream with confectioners' sugar and almond extract; spoon around outer edge of bowl. Stand almonds upright in cream; fill center with remaining blueberries. Sprinkle berries with sugar; chill before serving. Yield 6 to 8 servings.

brandied mangos

1 cup granulated sugar
1 cup water
2 (2-inch) cinnamon sticks
4 cups mangos, sliced (3 or 4 medium mangos)
1 cup brandy
1 tablespoon plus 1 teaspoon cornstarch

Combine sugar, water, and cinnamon in 12-inch frying pan; bring to boil. Turn down heat; simmer 2 to 3 minutes, until liquid is clear. Add mangos, stir gently to coat with sugar mixture. Simmer 3 minutes. Remove mangos from syrup with slotted spoon; place in quart jars, filling two-thirds full.

Add brandy to remaining syrup in pan. Dilute cornstarch with 1 tablespoon cold water; add to brandy syrup. Stir over medium heat until thick;

cool. Pour over mangos in jars. Brandied Mangos can be sealed and stored for future use.

Serve over ice cream or alone as an after-dinner fruit cordial. Yield 2 (1-quart) jars.

broiled fruit with cinnamon

3 bananas
½ **medium pineapple (or 3 slices canned pineapple)**
2 medium apples
½ **cup melted butter**
½ **cup brown sugar**
Ground cinnamon

Peel bananas.

Peel pineapple; remove core. Cut slices ¾ inch thick.

Peel and core apples; slice ¾ inch thick.

Place fruits on cookie sheet lined with foil. Brush well with butter. Sprinkle with brown sugar and cinnamon. Broil 3 to 4 inches from heat 5 minutes; turn once. Serve with sour cream or softened vanilla ice cream flavored with rum. Yield 4 to 6 servings.

brown betty

4 slices dry bread
¼ **cup melted butter or margarine**
1½ pounds rhubarb, wiped, cut into about 2-inch lengths
⅔ **cup brown sugar**
¼ **teaspoon grated nutmeg**
¼ **teaspoon ground cinnamon**
1 tablespoon lemon juice

Preheat oven to 375°F.

Cut bread into small cubes; toss in melted butter. Put about ⅓ into greased shallow baking dish. Cover with half the rhubarb and half the other ingredients. Repeat; top with remaining bread cubes. Bake about 30 minutes, until rhubarb is cooked and top is crisp and brown. Yield 4 servings.

brown betty with hard sauce

4 cups cinnamon-raisin bread cubes
4 tablespoons butter or margarine
½ **cup brown sugar**
1 jar or can applesauce (2 cups)
½ **teaspoon cinnamon**
½ **teaspoon salt**

In medium skillet sauté bread cubes in melted butter. When lightly browned, add sugar, applesauce, cinnamon, and salt; stir until hot. Serve warm with dollop of hard sauce on top. Yield 4 to 6 servings.

hard sauce
2 tablespoons soft butter or margarine
½ cup confectioners' sugar
½ teaspoon lemon or orange rind

Mix ingredients together in bowl in order given until very smooth. Sauce will melt into warm Brown Betty.

cherry cobbler

½ cup butter or margarine
¾ cup sugar
1 egg, beaten
⅓ cup milk
2 cups all-purpose flour
2 teaspoons baking powder
½ teaspoon salt
1 No. 2 can cherry pie filling

Cream butter and sugar. Add egg; mix well. Blend in milk.

Combine dry ingredients; add to butter mixture. Spread half of batter in greased 8-inch-round container; cover with ¾ can pie filling. Spread with remaining batter; top with remaining filling. Bake in 375°F oven 30 minutes or until done. Serve warm with plain or whipped heavy cream or with vanilla ice cream. Yield 8 servings.

cooked fresh fruit

6 medium-size apples or peaches
1 cup water
About ½ cup sugar
1 teaspoon vanilla

Pare and slice apples or peaches.

Put water and sugar in large pan; heat to boiling. Add fruit; cook slowly until tender. Add vanilla and more sugar, if needed. Yield 6 servings.

cool cantaloupe split

1 cantaloupe
1 quart vanilla ice cream
1 cup fresh blueberries
Fresh Lime Sauce

Cut cantaloupe in half; remove seeds. Slice into 12 equal wedges; remove rind.

To assemble splits: Arrange 2 wedges in serving dish. Place 2 scoops ice cream between melon wedges. Sprinkle with 2 heaping tablespoons Fresh Lime Sauce over all. Repeat process for each additional serving. Yield 6 servings.

fresh lime sauce
¼ cup sugar
2 tablespoons cornstarch
Dash of salt
½ cup water
1 tablespoon butter or margarine
¼ teaspoon grated fresh lime rind
2 tablespoons fresh lime juice

Combine sugar, cornstarch, and salt in small saucepan; stir in water. Cook over medium heat, stirring constantly, until thickened and clear. Remove from heat. Add butter, lime rind, and juice; mix well. Cool.

figs in brandy

¾ cup sugar
4 cardamom seeds
¾ cup cognac
½ cup raisins
½ cup blanched toasted almonds
1 (1-pound 4-ounce) can Kadota figs, drained

Combine sugar, cardamom seeds, and ½ cup Cognac in saucepan; cook, stirring constantly, until sugar is dissolved. Stir in raisins and almonds; heat through.

cherry cobbler

295

Place figs in chafing dish; pour sugar mixture over figs. Place over low flame until figs are heated through; spoon sugar mixture over figs frequently.

Heat remaining cognac in small saucepan. Ignite; pour over figs. Serve immediately. Yield about 4 servings.

fried bananas

¼ cup flour
1 teaspoon cinnamon
6 bananas, sliced lengthwise
2 or more tablespoons shortening

Mix flour and cinnamon together; thoroughly coat each piece of banana with mixture. If bananas are very long, you may prefer to quarter them.

Heat shortening in medium skillet. Brown floured bananas; slowly turn them once. Remove to heated platter; sprinkle with sugar. Yield 4 to 6 servings.

fruit bowl

1 can mandarin oranges, drained
1 apple, peeled, sliced

1 banana, sliced, sprinkled with lime or lemon juice
6 dates, cut in half
⅛ cup chopped walnuts

Place oranges in glass bowl. Combine with apple, banana, and dates. Sprinkle with walnuts. Yield 2 servings.

fruit-cocktail dessert

2 eggs
1 can fruit cocktail
1½ cups sugar
2 cups flour
½ teaspoon salt
2 teaspoons baking soda
1 teaspoon vanilla
½ cup brown sugar
1 cup dry flaked coconut

Mix together eggs and fruit cocktail. Add sugar; mix well.

Sift together flour, salt, and soda. Add egg mixture; mix. Add vanilla. Put into 9 × 13 × 2-inch pan; sprinkle with brown sugar and coconut. Bake at 350°F for 30 minutes. Yield 6 servings.

fried bananas

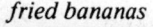

fruit bowl

fruit compote

1 can black cherries, pitted, with juice
1 can peaches, drained
½ cup brown sugar (if not sweet enough, add ¼ cup more)
1 box dried apricots
Juice of 1 orange
Juice of 1 lemon
Grated rind and fine slivers of lemon and orange

Place all ingredients in large baking dish; bake in 350°F oven 1½ to 2 hours. Cook down until caramelized. Serve cold, or, better still, reheated with sour cream or unsweetened whipped cream. Yield 4 to 6 servings.

fruit in cream

2 apples
2 oranges
2 bananas
½ cup sugar
1 cup whipping cream
¼ cup chopped almonds

Peel all fruits; cut into slices or pieces. Sprinkle sugar over fruit; let stand 10 minutes.

Whip cream until stiff; fold into fruit. Sprinkle nuts over top. Yield 6 servings.

fruit with honey sauce

2 peaches, peeled, cubed
2 cups fresh or canned pineapple chunks
2 apples, peeled, cored, cut into rings
1 cup water or pineapple juice
⅓ cup honey
1 thin lemon slice
1 stick cinnamon
1 banana, sliced lengthwise and in half
2 tablespoons sliced almonds
Whipped cream for garnish
4 cherries or grapes

Combine all ingredients (except last 4) in small casserole. Cover; cook at 350°F 40 minutes. Add banana; just heat through. Serve fruit warm. Garnish each serving with almonds, whipped cream, and a cherry or grape. Yield 4 servings.

fruit torte

pastry
2 cups flour
¼ cup sugar
1 cup unsalted butter
2 egg yolks

filling
3 to 4 cups fresh, canned, or frozen fruit
½ cup sugar if fresh fruit is used
¼ cup water, if needed
2 tablespoons cornstarch

almond coating
1 egg white
1 tablespoon sugar
½ cup sliced toasted almonds

fruit with honey sauce

hot baked grapefruit

topping
2 tablespoons sugar
1 teaspoon vanilla
1 cup heavy cream, whipped

Prepare pastry: Mix flour and sugar. Cut in butter until mixture resembles coarse crumbs. Add egg yolks; mix to form dough. Press into bottom and sides of 10-inch springform pan. Dough should come 1½ inches up sides. Bake in preheated 375°F oven 20 to 25 minutes, until pastry is firm and light brown.

Prepare filling: Drain fruit; reserve juice. Crush 1 cup fresh fruit to make juice. Add sugar to fresh fruit; let stand ½ hour. Drain juice; add water to make 1 cup.

Mix cornstarch and fruit juice; cook and stir over medium heat until thickened. Place whole fruit in baked pastry shell. Pour thickened fruit juice over top; chill thoroughly. Carefully remove torte from springform pan.

Make coating: Beat egg white until foamy. Gradually beat in sugar; beat until stiff peaks form. Spread meringue around outside of pastry shell. Press in almonds so they completely cover sides.

Prepare topping: Gently fold sugar and vanilla into whipped cream. Spread over fruit. Garnish with sliced toasted almonds, if desired. Yield 8 to 10 servings.

ginger pears

1 (29-ounce) can pear halves in syrup, drained
** (reserve syrup)**
Ginger conserve

With slotted spoon place pear halves in 9-inch pie plate cavity-sides-up. Add ½ cup syrup. Spoon ½ tablespoon conserve into cavity of each pear. Bake in preheated 400°F oven until hot, 10 or 15 minutes.

Delicious served warm with vanilla ice cream. Yield 6 or more servings.

hot baked grapefruit

3 grapefruits
6 teaspoons Madeira or dry sherry
6 tablespoons brown sugar
Butter
6 maraschino cherries

Cut each grapefruit in half; remove centers. Loosen all sections from skin with grapefruit knife; scallop or notch rims, but not very deep. Place grapefruit in shallow baking dish; sprinkle each with 1 teaspoon Madeira and 1 tablespoon brown sugar. Dot with butter. Bake in preheated 350°F oven, 1 rack above center, 25 to 30 minutes or until grapefruits are heated through and tops are golden. Place a cherry and a small fresh leaf, if available, in center of each grapefruit half. Place grapefruit on serving platter. Yield 6 servings.

melon balls with rum

2 (12-ounce) packages frozen melon balls
½ cup light rum

Thaw melon balls; drain off ½ cup syrup. Stir in rum; chill thoroughly before using. Yield 4 servings.

orange bavarian cream

1 tablespoon unflavored gelatin
¼ cup cold water
¾ cup orange juice
2 tablespoons lemon juice
½ teaspoon grated orange rind
⅓ cup sugar
¼ teaspoon salt
1 cup whipping cream
1 cup fresh orange sections, cut into pieces

Soften gelatin in water.

Combine fruit juices, orange rind, sugar, and salt; heat to simmering. Dissolve gelatin in hot mixture. Chill in refrigerator or over a bowl of ice

orange-cup dessert

cubes until mixture begins to thicken; stir frequently.

Whip cream until just stiff. Fold whipped cream and orange sections into gelatin mixture. Pour into slightly moistened 1-quart mold; chill until firm, at least 2 hours.

Unmold on dessert platter. Garnish, if desired, with piped Basic Chantilly Cream (see Index) and orange sections. Yield 6 servings.

orange-cup dessert

**Oranges with unblemished skin, as many as
     needed, 1 per person**
Fruit such as:
Bananas
Grapefruit sections
Maraschino cherries
Orange sections
Pineapple
Walnuts

Cut slice from top of orange so that remainder of insides can be scooped out.

Combine any above fruits, or others of your choice. Spoon into orange shells; refrigerate until serving time.

Can also be done with grapefruit or bananas, as pictured. If desired, a small amount of a favorite liqueur can be added to fruit. Yield as desired.

orange currant boats

2 envelopes unflavored gelatin
2 10-ounce jars red currant jelly
2 tablespoons lemon juice
¼ cup port
6 medium oranges

Soften gelatin in ½ cup water 5 minutes. Combine gelatin, jelly, and ½ cup water in small saucepan. Place over low heat; stir until jelly is melted and gelatin dissolved. Stir in lemon juice and port; set aside.

Cut hole in stem end of each orange and remove pulp with grapefruit knife; or cut each orange in half and remove pulp. (Reserve pulp for future use.) Place orange shells in foil-lined pan. Spoon enough gelatin mixture in each shell to fill to top; chill until firm.

Place remaining gelatin in half grapefruit; chill.

To serve, stir jelly in grapefruit with fork and place grapefruit in center of dessert platter. Halve or quarter oranges; place around grapefruit. Yield 6 servings.

orange wine parfaits

1 package blackberry gelatin
¾ cup boiling water
¾ cup red wine
¼ cup orange juice
**1 (11-ounce) can mandarin-orange sections,
     drained**
Sweetened whipped cream

Dissolve gelatin in boiling water; stir in wine and orange juice. Pour into 8-inch-square pan; chill until firm.

Shortly before serving, cut gelatin into small cubes. Alternate layers of cubed gelatin, orange sections, and whipped cream in parfait glasses. Keep in refrigerator until serving time. Yield 4 to 6 servings.

peach dumplings

1¾ cups unsifted flour
1 teaspoon salt
½ cup butter or margarine
1 egg yolk
3 tablespoons water
1 tablespoon lemon juice
2 tablespoons sugar
½ teaspoon cinnamon
6 peach halves, fresh or canned, drained
¾ cup sugar and ⅔ cup water*

Mix flour and salt thoroughly. Mix in butter with pastry blender or fork.

Mix egg yolk, 3 tablespoons water, and lemon juice together. Mix lightly into flour mixture with fork.

Preheat oven to 425°F.

Grease 8 × 8 × 2-inch baking pan.

Roll dough on lightly floured surface into 12 × 18-inch rectangle. Cut into 6 (6-inch) squares.

Mix 2 tablespoons sugar and cinnamon. Roll peach halves in sugar mixture. Place peach half, hollow-side-down, in center of each pastry square. Bring corners together over peach. Moisten; seal. Place in baking pan; allow space between dumplings.

Heat ¾ cup sugar and water to boiling. Pour over dumplings. Bake about 40 minutes, until browned. Yield 6 servings.

*Three-fourths cup syrup drained from canned peaches can be used in place of sugar and water. Heat to boiling before pouring over dumplings.

peaches in wine sauce

8 ripe peaches
¾ cup sugar
⅓ cup water
⅓ cup white wine

Scald and peel skins off peaches; leave fruit whole.

Combine sugar and water in medium skillet; cook 5 minutes. Add peaches; simmer 5 minutes. Add wine; simmer 5 minutes. Five minutes cooking time is usually enough to make fruit tender and syrup slightly thickened. Baste 3 times while cooking.

Transfer cooked peaches to bowl; cover with syrup. Refrigerate; serve when chilled. Yield 8 servings.

pears in chocolate sauce

1 large (29-ounce) can pear halves

chocolate sauce
8 ounces semisweet chocolate
2 tablespoons hot water
1 tablespoon butter
1 egg yolk
½ cup heavy cream
1 egg white

orange currant boats

pears in chocolate sauce

Drain pear halves; arrange in 6 individual serving dishes.

Place chocolate in top of double boiler; stir in water. Melt chocolate over boiling water; remove from heat. Stir in butter until melted. Add egg yolk and cream.

Before serving, beat egg white until stiff peaks form; fold into warm Chocolate Sauce. Spoon Chocolate Sauce over pears. Sprinkle with chopped pistachio nuts, if desired. Yield 6 servings.

pears with raspberry sauce

4 large fresh pears
3 cups water
1 cinnamon stick
2 whole cloves
2-inch piece lemon peel
3 tablespoons honey
6 tablespoons low-fat cottage cheese
1 tablespoon lemon juice
1 (10-ounce) package frozen whole raspberries
4 teaspoons sliced almonds

Peel pears; do not remove stems. Cut pears in half; carefully remove cores.

In saucepan add water, cinnamon, cloves, lemon peel, and 2 tablespoons honey; bring to boil. Add pears; simmer 10 minutes. Remove pears with slotted spoon; drain.

Puree cottage cheese in blender; spoon into bowl. Stir in lemon juice and 1 tablespoon honey; adjust sweetness to taste.

Fill pear halves with cottage-cheese mixture; arrange 2 pear halves upright on dish to form 1 whole pear. If necessary, cut small slice from bottom of each pear to make it stand up.

Puree raspberries; reserve a few whole berries for garnish. Pour over pears. Sprinkle with almonds; garnish with reserved berries. Yield 4 servings.

pêche melba

4 large firm fresh peaches, blanched
1 cup Basic Sugar Syrup (see Index)
1 teaspoon vanilla extract
1 quart ice cream
1 recipe Melba Sauce

Cut peaches in half; remove seeds.

Combine syrup and vanilla; boil 5 minutes. Poach peaches in syrup 10 minutes or until just tender; remove from syrup. Chill peaches thoroughly.

Place scoops of ice cream in 8 sherbert dishes; place peach halves over ice cream, cut-side-down. Top with Melba Sauce. Garnish with whole raspberries, if desired. Yield 8 servings.

melba sauce
1 quart fresh red raspberries, pureed
¼ cup red currant jelly
2 teaspoons cornstarch
2 tablespoons water
Sugar to taste
Brandy to taste (optional)

pears with raspberry sauce

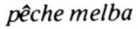

pêche melba

Combine raspberries and jelly in heavy saucepan over low heat; stir gently until jelly is melted.

Dissolve cornstarch in water; add to raspberry mixture, stirring constantly until smooth and clear. Stir in sugar and brandy. Yield about 3 cups.

pineapple fritters

2 (1-pound) cans pineapple sticks
1 recipe Basic Fruit Fritter Batter
Confectioners' sugar

Drain pineapple; place on paper toweling. Pat dry. Dip pineapple sticks, one at a time, into batter; shake off excess. Drop fritters into hot (375°F) oil in deep-fat fryer; fry until golden brown on all sides. Remove; drain on paper toweling. Place on dessert platter; dust liberally with confectioners' sugar. Yield about 8 servings.

basic fruit fritter batter

1½ cups all-purpose flour
½ teaspoon salt
⅔ cup beer
1 tablespoon melted butter
1 egg white, stiffly beaten

Sift flour and salt together into large bowl. Stir in beer until smooth; do not beat. Add only enough lukewarm water to make thick batter. Stir in butter. If not using this immediately, cover and set aside (no longer than 30 minutes) until ready to use. Fold in egg white. Yield about 2½ cups.

pineapple fritters

poached empress peaches

6 large ripe peaches
Basic Sugar Syrup (see Index)
1 teaspoon vanilla extract
2 cups hulled strawberries, pureed
½ cup sifted confectioners' sugar
3 tablespoons brandy
½ cup whipping cream, whipped

Place peaches in large saucepan; add enough boiling water to cover. Let stand about 2 minutes. Lift peaches out; dip into ice water. Slip skins from peaches; place peaches in large saucepan. Pour enough syrup over peaches to cover; add vanilla. Simmer until peaches are just tender; turn once. Drain peaches. Cool; chill.

Combine strawberries, sugar, and brandy; fold in whipped cream.

Place peaches in serving dish; spoon strawberry mixture over peaches. Garnish each peach with sliver of angelica. Yield 6 servings.

poached oranges

6 navel oranges
1½ cups sugar
¾ cup water
2 tablespoons orange liqueur

Peel rind and white membranes from oranges. Slice enough rind (orange part only) to make about 3 tablespoons slivers. Combine with sugar and water; cook over moderate heat, without stirring, about 8 minutes, until slightly thickened. Put oranges in syrup; cook over very low heat, basting constantly, about 5 minutes, until warm but still firm. Remove from heat with slotted spoon. Add liqueur to syrup. Chill oranges; baste occasionally with syrup. Serve very cold. Yield 6 servings.

purple-plum whip

1 pound purple plums, halved
¼ cup brown sugar
1 tablespoon lemon juice
2 egg whites
¼ teaspoon cream of tartar
2 drops red coloring
¼ cup sugar

Cook plums with brown sugar, lemon juice, and just enough water to prevent scorching. Cook in tightly covered pan over low heat until plums are very soft; let cool.

Beat egg whites with dash of salt and cream of tartar. Add food coloring and sugar gradually, beating until peaks form. Beat in cooked plums, small amount at a time, to keep mixture light and fluffy; use rotary beater. Chill in sherbert glasses at least 3 hours before serving. Yield 4 to 6 servings.

spiced mandarin oranges

1 small tangerine (orange can be substituted)
2 (11-ounce) cans mandarin oranges
¼ cup water
⅓ cup firmly packed brown sugar
1 (2-inch) piece stick cinnamon

Remove peel from tangerine; cut into paper-thin strips. Squeeze juice; strain.

In medium-size saucepan combine peel and juice with rest of ingredients; simmer 15 minutes.

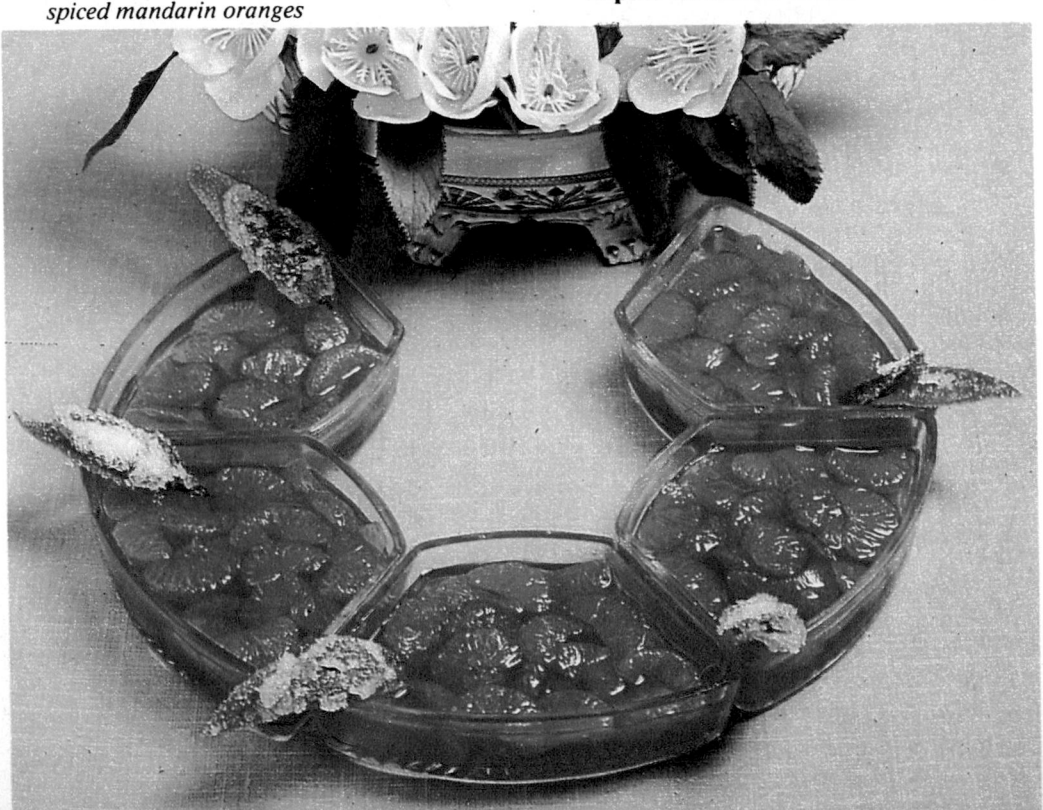

poached empress peaches

Remove from heat; remove peel and cinnamon. Chill several hours. Serve in small dessert dishes. Yield about 4 servings.

spiced mandarin oranges

strawberries romanoff

2 pints strawberries
½ pint vanilla ice cream

strawberry dringer

1 cup whipped cream or whipped topping
Juice of ½ lemon
3 tablespoons orange liqueur

Wash, hull, and chill berries.

Soften ice cream slightly; whip until fluffy. Fold in whipped cream and lemon juice.

Add liqueur to berries; fold ½ of berries into cream mixture. Spoon into parfait glasses or brandy snifters. Decorate with remaining strawberries. Yield 6 servings.

strawberry dringer

1 quart large fresh strawberries
Sifted confectioners' sugar
2½ cups whipping cream

Remove hulls from berries; cut berries into quarters. Place ¼ of berries in straight-sided glass container; sprinkle with confectioners' sugar.

Whip cream until soft peaks form. Cover berries with ¼ of whipped cream. Repeat layers of strawberries and cream; sprinkle each layer of berries with sugar. Let stand several hours. Serve over pound cake or angel food cake. Yield 8 to 10 servings.

strawberry-shortcake bowl

2 pints strawberries, sliced, sweetened to taste
¼ cup melted butter or margarine
1 (9.5-ounce) container refrigerated flaky biscuits
¼ cup sugar mixed with 1½ teaspoons ground cinnamon
½ cup chopped pecans
1 cup whipping cream, whipped, sweetened with ¼ cup sugar

Chill berries about ½ hour.

Meanwhile brush baking sheet with melted butter.

Separate each biscuit into 2 thinner biscuits by pulling apart between layers. Lightly brush both sides of each biscuit with butter. Dip both sides in sugar-cinnamon mixture; place on baking sheet. Leave about 1 inch between biscuits. Sprinkle pecans over biscuits; press into dough. Bake in preheated 400°F oven 10 to 12 minutes or until done.

Line large serving bowl with about 15 biscuits. Spoon ½ of strawberries over; spoon whipped cream over berries. Spoon remaining strawberries over cream; top with rest of biscuits. Serve immediately. Yield 6 to 8 servings.

strawberry trifle

1 white cake (see Index)
2 (10½-ounce) packages frozen strawberries
1 (3-ounce) package prepared vanilla pudding
1 cup chilled whipping cream
¼ cup sugar
¼ cup toasted, slivered almonds
Fresh strawberries

Bake cake in oblong pan as directed; cool. Cut crosswise in half. Reserve ½ for another dessert. Cut remaining cake in small pieces. Arrange ½ of pieces on bottom of clear serving bowl. Pour ½ of strawberries (with syrup) over cake; spread with ½ of pudding. Repeat with remaining cake pieces, strawberries, and pudding. Cover; chill a few hours.

Beat cream and sugar in chilled bowl until stiff; spread over trifle. Garnish with almonds and fresh strawberries. Yield 8 servings.

stuffed baked apples

6 large cooking apples
3 tablespoons finely chopped candied cherries
2 tablespoons finely chopped walnuts
1 tablespoon finely chopped almonds
¼ cup honey
½ recipe Red Currant Jelly Glaze (see Index)

Core apples. Cut thin line through peel around center of each apple, using sharp knife.

Place cherries, walnuts, almonds, and honey in small bowl; mix well.

Arrange apples in shallow baking pan; fill apple cavities with cherry mixture. Bake in preheated 375°F oven about 45 minutes, until apples are tender. Remove from oven; slip upper halves of peel from apples. Place apples in serving dish; spoon pan juices into cavities. Spoon glaze over apples. Garnish with candied cherry halves and bits of green angelica, if desired. Yield 6 servings.

stuffed baked apples

stuffed lemon apples

3 tablespoons vinegar
7 apples
¾-inch strip lemon peel
1 cup sugar
1 cup sauterne
1 (3-ounce) package lemon gelatin
½ cup golden raisins
¼ cup chopped red candied cherries

Combine 6 cups water and vinegar in large bowl.

Peel and core 6 apples; place in vinegar solution to prevent darkening.

Mix 2 cups water, lemon peel, sugar, and ¼ cup sauterne in large, shallow pan until sugar is dissolved. Bring to boil; reduce heat. Simmer 10 minutes.

Arrange apples in pan; simmer over very low heat about 15 minutes, until almost tender on bottom. Turn carefully with forks; cook 10 to 15 minutes or until tender but not mushy. Remove apples carefully to serving dish; chill thoroughly.

Prepare gelatin according to package directions, substituting remaining sauterne for ¼ cup cold water. Chill, stirring frequently, until partially set.

Peel and core remaining apple; chop finely. Place in small saucepan; add raisins and cherries. Cover with some of remaining sugar syrup in which apples were cooked; cover. Cook over low heat until raisins are plump and apple tender; chill thoroughly.

Fill apple centers with raisin mixture. Spoon about ¾ of partially-set gelatin over apples; chill until set.

Chill remaining gelatin until set; beat with fork until coarsely chopped. Spoon around edge of serving dish. Yield 7 servings.

watermelon basket dessert

A watermelon can be made into a basket by cutting through it lengthwise to within 2 inches of center. Do same at other end of melon. Remaining 2-inch band becomes handle of basket. Scoop out seeds from the portions of melon you cut off and from remaining portion that serves as the basket. Cut melon into rounds with melon-ball cutter or into small pieces with knife. Combine with other fruits such as strawberries, blueberries, seedless grapes, diced apples, pears, cantaloupe, nectarines, cherries, oranges, and cubed pineapple; fill basket. Yield 10 to 25 servings.

stuffed lemon apples

ICE CREAM

baked alaska

½ Yellow Cake (see Index)
8 egg whites
¼ teaspoon cream of tartar
½ cup granulated sugar
½ gallon cherry-nut ice cream
Spring flowers

Prepare cake recipe as directed. Pour batter into greased 9-inch-square cake pan; bake as directed. Remove from pan; cool. Cut in half horizontally. (Save half for future use.) Place on heatproof platter.

Beat egg whites until foamy. Add cream of tartar; mix in. Add sugar gradually, continuing to beat until egg whites form stiff peaks.

Remove ice cream from container; round ice-cream corners with small spatula. Place on cake. Cover ice cream and cake generously with meringue; be sure to smooth and cover entire surface.

Working quickly, fill pastry bag with meringue. Using rosette tip, decorate baked Alaska as illustrated. Place in preheated 400°F oven 3 minutes or until meringue just begins to turn brown. Decorate with spring flowers. Serve immediately. Yield 18 servings.

bavarian vanilla ice cream

2 packages unflavored gelatin
½ cup cold water
9 tablespoons sugar
1 tablespoon cornstarch
2 eggs, beaten
1½ cups milk, scalded
1 cup vanilla ice cream
1 teaspoon vanilla
1 cup heavy cream, whipped

Sprinkle gelatin over cold water to soften; heat to dissolve gelatin completely.

Mix together sugar and cornstarch. Add eggs; beat 2 minutes. Slowly add warm milk; beat con-

baked alaska

stantly. Pour into 1-quart saucepan. Cook over medium heat until custard coats spoon. Add gelatin and ice cream to hot custard; cool until slightly thickened. Add vanilla; fold in whipped cream. Pour into 1-quart mold; chill until set. Unmold carefully; serve garnished with fresh fruit. Yield 6 to 8 servings.

bing-cherry delight

1 package black-cherry gelatin
1 cup sweetened bing cherries, pitted
1 quart vanilla ice cream, softened
1¼ cups vanilla-wafer crumbs
6 tablespoons butter, melted
1 cup powdered sugar
2 tablespoons cherry juice
2 cups whipped cream
12 whole canned bing cherries, pitted

Prepare gelatin as directed. Stir in 1 cup cherries. Pour into 9-inch cake pan; chill until firm.

Mold ice cream in 9-inch cake pan; chill until firm.

Combine cookie crumbs and butter; work until all crumbs are moistened. Divide into 3 equal parts.

Just prior to serving, assemble cake in following manner: Spread ⅓ of crumb mixture on serving platter.

Unmold gelatin; place on crumb mixture. Spread second portion of crumbs on gelatin.

Unmold ice cream; place on crumb-topped gelatin. Spread remaining crumbs on top ice cream.

Combine sugar and cherry juice; stir until smooth. Pour over layer of crumbs.

Frost sides of cake with whipped cream. Score top of cake to indicate serving pieces. Decorate each piece with whipped-cream rosette and bing cherry. Yield 12 servings.

cherries jubilee

3 tablespoons red currant jelly
1 tablespoon butter
½ cup kirsch, heated
2 cups canned tart cherries, well-drained
1 pint vanilla ice cream

Melt jelly in frypan or chafing dish. Add butter; stir until melted and hot. Add cherries; heat through.

Pour kirsch over cherries; ignite with long match. Let burn until flames die. Spoon hot cherries over ice cream; serve. Yield 4 servings.

chocolate-coconut ice-cream pie

crust
1 (4-ounce) package semisweet chocolate
2 tablespoons butter
2 cups flaked coconut

Melt chocolate and butter over low heat; remove from heat. Stir in coconut; mix well. Press on bottom and sides of 9-inch pie plate; freeze.

1 quart ice cream, softened
2 cups frozen whipped-cream topping, thawed
1 cup flaked coconut

Spread ice cream into crust; spread with whipped-cream topping; sprinkle with coconut. Freeze until firm.

Remove from freezer about 10 minutes before serving; dip bottom of pan in hot water to ease cutting. Yield 8 servings.

christmas ice cream

½ gallon vanilla ice cream
1 pound coconut macaroons, crushed
½ pound red and green candied cherries, chopped
¾ cup slivered almonds
4 tablespoons cognac (optional)

Soften ice cream in large mixing bowl. Add macaroons, candied cherries, almonds, and cognac. Mix well; store in freezer. Yield ½ gallon.

creme-de-menthe ice-cream cake

2 cups chocolate-wafer crumbs
½ cup butter, softened
3 pints vanilla ice cream
5 tablespoons green creme-de-menthe
About ½ cup Fudge Sauce (see Index)

Combine crumbs with butter; press into 10-inch springform pan. Refrigerate 1 hour.

Soften ice cream in large bowl; swirl creme de menthe into it. Fill wafer shell with ice cream; freeze.

Drizzle Fudge Sauce lightly over top; return to freezer. Yield 10 servings.

fudge-sundae pie

1 cup evaporated milk
1 (6-ounce) package semisweet chocolate bits
1 cup miniature marshmallows
¼ teaspoon salt
1 quart vanilla ice cream
Vanilla wafers
Pecans (optional)

cherries jubilee

bing-cherry delight

Cook milk, chocolate, marshmallows, and salt in 1-quart saucepan over medium heat until chocolate and marshmallows melt and mixture thickens; stir constantly. Remove from heat; cool to room temperature.

Line bottom and sides of 9-inch pie pan or 2 (1-quart) ice trays with wafers. Spoon half of ice cream over wafers. Cover with half of chocolate mixture. Repeat with rest of ice cream and chocolate. Top with nuts. Refrigerate 5 hours. Yield 8 to 10 servings.

ice-cream pie I

18 chocolate sandwich cookies
Melted butter
2 quarts peppermint ice cream
2 squares bitter chocolate
1 small can evaporated milk
2 tablespoons butter
½ cup sugar
½ pint whipping cream

Roll out cookies; add enough melted butter to hold.

Butter 9 × 2½-inch-deep pie pan. Press cookie mixture onto bottom and sides of pan. Bake at 350°F 8 minutes; cool completely.

Soften and stir ice cream; put into crust; freeze.

Mix chocolate, milk, butter, and sugar in double boiler; cook until thickened. Cool completely. Pour over ice cream; freeze. Top with whipped cream, and chocolate shavings, if desired. Take out of freezer long enough to soften a bit before slicing. Yield 8 servings.

ice-cream pie II

2 large chocolate bars
⅔ cup water
2 heaping teaspoons instant coffee
1 (9-inch) baked pie shell
½ gallon vanilla ice cream, softened
1 small chocolate bar, shaved

In saucepan melt 2 large chocolate bars with water. Add instant coffee. Pour into pie shell; let cool. Fill with ice cream; top with chocolate shavings. Place in freezer; serve frozen. Yield 8 servings.

ice-cream sandwiches

1 quart ice cream
2 graham crackers (plain, cinnamon, or chocolate-coated)

Slice ice cream into 6 slices. Place each slice between 2 graham crackers. Serve immediately or return to freezer until time to serve. Yield 6.

ice-cream snowballs

1 quart ice cream
½ cup flaked coconut

Shape ice cream into 6 balls; roll in coconut. Place on tray covered with waxed paper; return to freezer. Yield 6 servings.

italian cassata

1½ quarts vanilla ice cream, softened
1 quart raspberry sherbet, softened
¾ quart pistachio ice cream, softened
½ cup diced candied fruit
2 tablespoons rum
3 large egg whites
½ cup sugar
½ cup whipping cream
1 cup whipping cream
Candied fruit

Line 12-cup mold evenly with vanilla ice cream. Freeze until firm, preferably in 0°F freezer. Cover vanilla ice cream evenly with layer of raspberry sherbet; freeze again. Cover with layer of pistachio ice cream; freeze solid.

Cover diced candied fruit with rum; set aside.

Beat egg whites until foamy. Slowly beat in sugar.

Whip ½ cup whipping cream until stiff. Fold cream and rum-soaked fruit into meringue until thoroughly combined. Spoon into center of molded ice cream. Spread to make smooth bottom layer; cover. Freeze until firm (5 hours, or will keep up to 2 weeks).

To unmold, dip outside of mold in hot water 6 seconds; invert onto cold platter.

Whip remaining cream until stiff; put into pastry bag fitted with decorative tip. Decorate with cream and candied fruit; serve sliced. Yield 12 to 16 servings.

lemon ice-cream pie

½ gallon vanilla ice cream
1 (6-ounce) can frozen lemonade
2 (8-inch) graham-cracker crusts
Graham-cracker crumbs for garnish

Soften ice cream.

Thaw lemonade. Beat together to creamy texture; pour into graham-cracker crusts. Place in freezer until serving time (several hours later or several days later).

When ready to serve, sprinkle each pie with graham-cracker crumbs. Yield 8 to 10 servings.

low-calorie ice cream

2 teaspoons gelatin
1 cup cold water

italian cassata

¾ cup nonfat dry milk
1½ cups fresh milk
3 tablespoons sugar
1 tablespoon liquid sweetener
2 teaspoons vanilla
2 tablespoons lemon juice

Soften gelatin in ½ cup water.

Mix ¼ cup dry milk with fresh milk; scald. Dissolve gelatin in milk; stir in 2 tablespoons sugar, liquid sweetener, and vanilla. Chill until slightly thickened.

Beat ½ cup dry milk with ½ cup very cold water until it begins to thicken. Add lemon juice; beat until thick. Beat in 1 tablespoon sugar until mixture is consistency of whipped cream. Fold in chilled gelatin mixture. Pour into ice trays; freeze. Yield about 1 quart.

mocha parfait

2 bananas
Juice of 1 lemon (2 tablespoons)
16 walnut halves
½ cup cold heavy whipping cream
½ teaspoon vanilla
2 tablespoons sugar
1½ pints coffee ice cream
Bitter-chocolate curls

Peel bananas. Slice; dip in lemon juice. Divide bananas among 4 parfait glasses. Top each with 4 walnut halves. Chill glasses while whipping cream.

Pour cream into small mixing bowl. Add vanilla; whip until stiff, gradually adding sugar while whipping.

At serving time, cube ice cream; divide among parfait glasses. Top with whipped cream and chocolate curls. Yield 4 servings.

orange ice cream

8 large thick-skinned oranges
1¼ cups water
½ cup sugar
2½ teaspoons grated orange rind
1 egg yolk
6 tablespoons frozen orange-juice concentrate, thawed
1½ cups whipping cream
½ recipe Basic Meringue mixture (see Index)

Cut off about ⅓ of each orange at top. Remove all pulp and juice; set orange cups aside.

Place water, ⅓ cup sugar, and orange rind in saucepan over medium heat. Let sugar dissolve; bring mixture to slow boil about 9 minutes to form thin syrup. Let syrup cool slightly.

Beat egg with fork. Add to softened orange juice. Add egg mixture to syrup; stir until well blended. Place over medium heat; cook, stirring constantly, 6 to 7 minutes. Pour into ice-cube trays; freeze to mushy consistency. Remove from freezer; scrape into mixer bowl. Beat about 4 minutes, until smooth. Half-freeze and beat 2 more times.

Whip cream until soft peaks form. Add remaining sugar to cream; beat several seconds until blended. Fold cream into orange mixture; pour into orange cups. Cover with 2 layers of aluminum foil; freeze until firm.

Prepare Basic Meringue mixture. Spoon into icing bag with large star tube affixed. Pipe meringue, in circular motion, over tops of frozen, ice-cream-filled orange cups. Place in preheated 400°F oven on middle shelf until meringue is lightly browned. Serve immediately. Yield 8 servings.

pecan ice-cream balls

1½ cups pecans
1 quart ice cream
Hot Fudge Sauce (see Index)

Spread pecans in shallow pan; bake at 300°F 15 to 20 minutes, until lightly browned. Cool; chop.

Shape ice cream into 6 balls; roll in pecans. Place on tray covered with waxed paper; return to freezer until firm.

Just before serving, top balls with Hot Fudge Sauce. Yield 6 servings.

tempura ice-cream balls

Oil for frying
4 ice-cream balls frozen very, very hard (any flavor)
Tempura batter (see Index)
Sugar and cinnamon or powdered sugar

Heat oil to medium high.

Remove balls from freezer; immediately dip into tempura batter. Fry until golden brown; serve immediately, sprinkled with cinnamon and sugar or powdered sugar. Yield 4 servings.

SHERBET

apricot sherbet

3 cups apricot nectar
1 cup chopped, canned, water-packed apricots
1 (3-ounce) package lemon gelatin dessert powder
1 tablespoon lemon juice

Mix all ingredients in saucepan; heat until gelatin is completely dissolved. Freeze until par-

orange ice cream

tially frozen. Whip with electric mixer; return to freezer to set. Yield 6 servings.

chocolate igloo

1 (9-inch-square) Chocolate Cake (see Index)
2 quarts pineapple sherbet
1 cup whipped cream
Maraschino cherry

Slice cake layer horizontally into 2 parts, using sharp serrated knife or string. Cut layers into triangular wedges.

Coat 2-quart bowl with butter; press cake traingles against sides to form a design, as illustrated.

Soften sherbet; mold in 2-quart bowl against cake lining. Cover top with cake traingles; freeze until firm.

To serve, unmold onto serving platter; garnish with whipped cream and cherry. Yield 8 to 10 servings.

lemon sherbet

1½ teaspoons unflavored gelatin
2 tablespoons cold water
2 cups skim milk
¾ cup sugar
½ cup lemon juice
½ teaspoon grated lemon rind
2 egg whites, stiffly beaten

Soak gelatin in water several minutes.

Heat milk. Add sugar and gelatin; stir until dissolved. Chill in refrigerator until just starting to become firm. Gradually stir in lemon juice and rind. Pour into freezing tray; freeze to a mush.

Turn into chilled bowl; beat with electric beater until fluffy but not melted. Fold in egg whites. Return to freezer; freeze until firm. Yield 6 servings.

raspberry or strawberry water ice

3 cups ripe strawberries or raspberries
Juice of 2 lemons
2½ cups Basic Sugar Syrup (see Index)

Rub fruit through nylon sieve. Add lemon juice. Add syrup and a little coloring if necessary. Pour into ice-cube tray. Chill; freeze. Yield 6 servings.

raspberry watermelon

½ watermelon, cut lengthwise
½ package mini chocolate chips
Approximately ½ gallon raspberry sherbet

Scoop out contents of watermelon. (Reserve for another use.) Drain the shell upside down; pat often with paper towels. Freeze shell 1 hour.

Combine chips and sherbet. Chips will resemble seeds. Spoon into watermelon shell; freeze until solid.

When ready to serve, cut into slices with sharp knife. Each serving will look like a real slice of watermelon. Yield 8 to 10 servings.

chocolate igloo

MERINGUES

basic meringues

5 large egg whites
1 cup extra-fine sugar

Beat egg whites in large mixing bowl with electric mixer at high speed 5 minutes or until stiff but not dry. Sprinkle ¼ cup sugar over egg whites; beat 3 minutes. Sprinkle remaining sugar, 1 tablespoon at a time, over egg-white mixture; fold in gently but thoroughly, using rubber spatula. Drop by heaping tablespoonfuls, 2 inches apart, onto oiled brown paper over cookie sheets. Bake in preheated 250°F oven 55 minutes. Take from oven; immediately remove from paper onto cooling racks. Yield 2½ cups.

chocolate meringues

Combine 1½ tablespoons cocoa with the sugar; beat into egg whites as directed. Bake 1 hour.

chocolate-chip meringues

Fold ½ cup chocolate chips into Basic Meringue just before dropping onto prepared cookie sheets.

basic meringues

basic italian meringue

2½ cups sugar
1¾ cups water
4 egg whites

Combine sugar and water in large saucepan over low heat. Heat, without stirring, until all sugar is dissolved. Bring to boil; cook to medium soft-ball stage or 240°F on candy thermometer.

Beat egg whites with electric beater until stiff peaks form. Pour hot syrup in thin steady stream into egg whites; beat constantly. Beat until mixture holds firm peak and is cool. Use as recipe directs.

Meringue can be covered and refrigerated overnight before using, if desired. Meringue can be piped when cold. Yield about 4 cups.

italian meringue with fruit and chantilly cream

1 recipe Basic Italian Meringue (see Index)
1 recipe Basic Confectioners' Custard (see Index)
2 fresh pears
2 fresh peaches
3 fresh apricots
3 canned pineapple slices
Red Currant Jelly Glaze (see Index)
Chopped pistachio nuts
Currant jelly
1 recipe Basic Chantilly Cream (see Index)

Cut 9-inch circle of waxed paper; spread enough meringue over circle to make ¾-inch deep layer. Let stand at room temperature until top is set. Place remaining meringue in pastry bag with medium-size star tube affixed; pipe border around edge of circle. Make peak for center by holding tube in vertical position over waxed paper; pipe remaining meringue, pulling tube up as meringue is piped. Let peak dry at room temperature.

Remove waxed paper from dried meringue shell; place on serving plate. Cover bottom of circle with custard; chill.

Peel pears; cut in half; remove cores.

Peel peaches and apricots; cut in half; remove seeds.

Arrange fruits as shown in illustration. Brush pear halves with glaze; sprinkle with pistachio nuts. Fill center of pineapple stack with currant jelly; place meringue peak on top.

Place chantilly cream in pastry bag with medium-size star tube affixed; pipe rosettes around edge of custard inside meringue border and between fruits. Yield about 18 servings.

PUDDINGS

apple pudding

5 or 6 good-size cooking apples, peeled, cored, sliced
¼ cup sugar
½ teaspoon ground cinnamon
½ teaspoon ground nutmeg
2 tablespoons butter or margarine
4 tablespoons hot water

batter
1 egg
½ cup sugar
2 tablespoons melted butter or margarine
1 cup all-purpose flour
1 teaspoon baking powder
Pinch of salt

Put apples into baking dish; sprinkle with sugar and spices. Dot with butter; add hot water.

Prepare batter. Beat egg and sugar together until thick. Stir in butter.

Sift flour, baking powder, and salt together; fold into egg mixture. Spread on apples. Bake in preheated 375°F oven 25 minutes. Reduce heat to 350°F; bake 10 to 15 minutes. Yield 5 or 6 servings.

butterscotch bread pudding

3 tablespoons butter or margarine
½ cup brown sugar

apple pudding

italian meringue with fruit and chantilly cream

butterscotch bread pudding

¼ teaspoon baking soda
2 cups milk
2 eggs
Pinch of salt
2 cups stale bread cubes (about ½-inch cubes)

Melt the butter in pan. Add sugar; heat until well blended.

Dissolve soda in milk; add gradually to sugar mixture. Stir until well blended; set aside to cool.

Beat eggs lightly. Add salt and cooled milk-and-sugar mixture.

Put bread cubes into greased baking dish; pour custard over. Bake in preheated 350°F oven about 45 minutes. Yield 6 servings.

carrageenan (irish moss) milk pudding

½ cup (½ ounce) tightly packed carrageenan
   (available in health-food stores)
Boiling water
2 cups milk
¼ cup sugar
1 teaspoon vanilla extract
Food coloring (optional)

Pick over carrageenan; discard foreign matter. Place in small bowl; add boiling water to cover. Stir; drain. Combine with milk in small saucepan; cook over moderate heat, stirring frequently, approximately 15 minutes, until thick and creamy. Add sugar and vanilla; stir until sugar is dissolved. Add food coloring. Strain to remove carrageenan; pour into individual molds, rinsed in cold water. Refrigerate several hours, until set. Unmold; serve with whipped cream or chocolate sauce. Yield 4 servings.

chocolate pudding

½ cup sugar
⅓ cup cocoa
3 tablespoons cornstarch
¼ teaspoon salt
2½ cups milk
1 teaspoon vanilla

Mix sugar, cocoa, cornstarch, and salt in pan. Add milk slowly; sitr until smooth. Cook and stir over medium heat until mixture thickens. Cook and stir 3 minutes longer. Add vanilla; stir. Chill before serving. Yield 6 servings.

coconut cream pudding

3 tablespoons cornstarch
¼ cup sugar
½ teaspoon salt
2 cups milk
2 egg yolks, beaten
2 tablespoons butter or margarine
1 teaspoon vanilla
½ cup shredded or flaked coconut
½ cup shredded or flaked coconut
Whipped topping (optional)

Mix cornstarch, sugar, and salt in heavy saucepan. Gradually blend in milk; stir over moderate heat about 7 minutes, until mixture thickens. Stir a little hot mixture into egg yolks; stir yolks into remaining hot mixture. Cook 1 minute; stir constantly. Mix in vanilla, and coconut. Serve warm or chilled in individual dessert glasses. Add whipped topping. Yield 6 servings.

coconut royal pudding

8 egg yolks
1 cup sugar

½ cup flour
2 cups milk
½ cup dry white wine
1½ cups freshly grated coconut
1 teaspoon vanilla extract
Chopped almonds

Combine egg yolks, sugar, and flour; beat until creamy.

Place milk and wine in double boiler; heat to boiling. Pour slowly into egg mixture; stir constantly to prevent curdling. Add coconut and vanilla; mix well. Cook over double boiler until mixture thickens and coats wooden spoon. Pour into bowl. Cover top with waxed paper to prevent scum from forming; cool in refrigerator. To serve, spoon into serving dishes; sprinkle with chopped almonds. Yield 6 to 8 servings.

cornflake pudding

1 quart cornflakes
1 quart milk
2 eggs, beaten
½ teaspoon salt

¼ cup molasses
¼ cup sugar
¼ teaspoon ginger
¼ teaspoon cinnamon
Vanilla
1 tablespoon butter

Stir all ingredients together, except butter; turn into greased baking dish. Dot with butter. Place dish in pan of water; put in oven. Bake ¾ to 1 hour in 350°F oven. Yield 8 servings.

creamed-cheese pudding

2 envelopes unflavored gelatin
2 eggs, separated
1¼ cups sugar
1 cup milk
¼ teaspoon salt
2 teaspoons grated lemon rind
3 cups creamed cottage cheese
Lemon juice
1 cup whipping cream, whipped
½ cup ground toasted almonds

creamed-cheese pudding

3 cups confectioners' sugar
20 ladyfingers

Sprinkle gelatin over ½ cup water; let stand 5 minutes to soften.

Beat egg yolks slightly in top of double boiler. Stir in 1 cup sugar, milk, and salt; cook over hot water, stirring constantly, until thick. Stir in gelatin; remove from heat.

Combine lemon rind, cottage cheese, and ¼ cup lemon juice; stir into gelatin mixture. Refrigerate until mixture mounds slightly when dropped from spoon.

Beat egg whites until frothy. Add ¼ cup sugar gradually, beating until stiff peaks form. Carefully fold egg whites into cottage-cheese mixture. Fold in whipped cream and almonds. Turn into 9-inch springform pan; chill until firm.

Sift confectioners' sugar into bowl; gradually add enough lemon juice to make icing of spreading consistency.

Release spring; remove side. Place pudding on serving dish. Trim one end from ladyfingers. Spread icing on ladyfingers one at a time; place around pudding as each one is iced. Garnish top with whipped cream. Tint icing, if desired. Yield about 15 servings.

eggnog rice pudding

2 cups eggnog
1½ tablespoons cornstarch
2 tablespoons milk
⅓ cup seedless raisins
½ teaspoon salt
1 teaspoon rum extract or 2 tablespoons rum
2 cups cooked rice
Whipped cream (optional)
Nutmeg

Heat eggnog over low heat.

Combine cornstarch and milk. Pour into egg nog, stirring constantly. Cook and stir over low heat until mixture thickens. Add raisins just before removing from heat. Add salt and rum extract. Fold in cooked rice. Pour into individual dishes; chill. Serve plain or with whipped cream and sprinkle of nutmeg. Yield 4 servings.

holiday fruit pudding

1 egg
¼ cup sugar
3 tablespoons cornstarch
½ teaspoon salt
2 cups milk
1 tablespoon butter or margarine
1 teaspoon vanilla
2 cups canned fruit cocktail, drained

Beat egg in saucepan. Stir in sugar, cornstarch, and salt. Stir in milk; cook and stir over medium

heat until thickened. Cook and stir 1 minute longer. Stir in butter and vanilla. Add fruit. Cool before serving. Yield 6 servings.

lemon–pear parfait

2 medium Anjou or Bosc pears
½ cup grapenuts cereal
⅓ cup coconut
¼ cup brown sugar
2 tablespoons melted butter
1 (3⅝-ounce) package instant lemon pudding

Dice pears.

Combine grapenuts, coconut, brown sugar, and butter.

Prepare pudding mix according to package directions. Alternate layers of cereal mixture, pears, and pudding in dessert dishes; chill. Yield 5 or 6 servings.

marshmallow banana pudding

1 tablespoon gelatin
¾ cup sugar
3 stiffly beaten egg whites
3 bananas, shredded

Soak gelatin in ¼ cup cold water 5 minutes. Add ¼ cup boiling water and sugar; stir until dissolved. Cool, stirring occasionally, until congealing starts. Add egg whites; beat until very light. Add bananas; stir lightly. Chill until set. Serve with whipped cream. Yield 4 servings.

mock nesselrode pudding

2½ tablespoons gelatin
1 cup cold milk
4 egg yolks
¾ cup sugar
3 cups scalded milk
¾ cup chopped raisins
10 macaroons, crumbed
1 teaspoon vanilla
½ teaspoon almond extract
2 tablespoons sherry flavoring
4 egg whites

Soak gelatin in cold milk 5 minutes.

Beat egg yolks and sugar together; pour scalded milk on them. Put in double boiler or over hot water; cook, stirring constantly until custard coats spoon. Add gelatin; stir until dissolved. Take from fire. Add raisins, macaroon crumbs, vanilla, almond extract, and sherry flavoring; mix well. Fold in stiffly beaten egg whites. Set in pan of ice water; beat until thick. Pour into 6-cup mold that has been dipped in cold water; chill thoroughly. Turn out of mold onto plate; decorate with whipped cream and maraschino cherries. Yield 6 to 8 servings.

orange pudding

2 large eggs, separated
¼ teaspoon salt
½ cup sugar
2 tablespoons flour
2 tablespoons butter
Grated rind of 1 orange
¼ cup orange juice
1 tablespoon lemon juice
1 cup milk

Beat egg whites with salt until soft peaks form. Gradually beat in ¼ cup sugar until stiff peaks form.

Without washing beater, beat egg yolks until thickened and lemon color; gradually beat in ¼ cup sugar, flour, butter, orange rind, orange juice, and lemon juice. Gradually beat in milk until smooth; fold in egg whites. Turn into 6 (6-ounce) custard cups. Place in pan of hot water

plum pudding

that comes about as high as pudding mixture. Bake in preheated 350°F oven until knife inserted in center comes out clean, about 35 minutes. Chill; turn out. Bottom will be a sauce, top cake-like. Yield 6 servings.

orange raisin-rice pudding

½ cup honey or corn syrup
4 cups cooked rice
1 cup raisins
1 tablespoon butter or margarine
½ cup orange juice
½ cup chopped nuts or peanuts (optional)

Heat honey in heavy pan until warm. Add rice, raisins, and butter; cook over medium heat 5 minutes. Stir in orange juice. Serve warm or cold. Sprinkle with chopped nuts. Yield 6 servings.

plum pudding

1 (1-pound) loaf day-old bread
½ pound suet, ground
1¾ cups all-purpose flour
½ cup firmly packed brown sugar
1 cooking apple, peeled, chopped
1½ cups golden raisins
1½ cups raisins
1¾ cups currants
2 tablespoons minced crystallized ginger
2 teaspoons ground allspice
¼ cup flaked almonds
2 eggs
¾ cup brandy
Juice of 2 oranges
Juice of 1 lemon
Grated rind of 1 orange
Grated rind of 1 lemon
¼ cup whipping cream

Process bread in blender or food processor to make fine crumbs. Place in large mixing bowl. Add suet, flour, brown sugar, apple, raisins, currants, ginger, allspice, and almonds; mix well.

Beat eggs; add brandy, juices, and rinds. Blend into crumb mixture; mix well. Mix in cream. Cover with plastic wrap; refrigerate overnight. Pack into 2 (1-quart) pudding molds or 1 (2-quart) mold. Cover with buttered waxed paper and foil. Tie securely with string; trim excess paper and foil. Cover with pudding-mold lid. Place in steamer; pour boiling water into steamer, halfway up side of mold. Cover with lid. Steam for 6 hours; add water to maintain water level, as necessary. Yield about 15 servings.

raisin-rice pudding

2 cups water
½ cup uncooked rice

½ teaspoon salt
½ cup raisins
1 tablespoon butter or margarine
1 cup nonfat dry milk (not instant) or 2 cups
   instant nonfat dry milk
½ cup sugar
1 cup warm water
1 teaspoon vanilla

Heat 2 cups water to boiling. Stir in rice, salt, raisins, and butter; lower heat. Cover; cook 30 minutes. Remove from heat.

Mix dry milk and sugar. Mix in 1 cup warm water until smooth. Add milk mixture and vanilla to rice. Stir over low heat until hot. Cool to thicken. Yield 6 servings.

rice pudding deluxe

2 cups cooked rice
½ teaspoon salt
1 (20-ounce) can crushed pineapple, drained
½ pint whipped cream, beaten stiff

Mix rice, salt, and pineapple until well blended. Add most of whipped cream (reserve some for garnish); fold in gently. Spoon into individual serving dishes; top with whipped cream. Yield 6 to 8 servings.

rum rice

¼ cup raisins
¼ cup rum
1 cup uncooked rice
1 teaspoon salt
1 cup sugar
3 cups milk
2 tablespoons chopped nuts
1 teaspoon lemon juice
1 egg, beaten
¼ pound butter or margarine
Cinnamon and sugar mixed together

The night before, or at least several hours ahead, soak raisins in rum.

Cook rice, salt, sugar, and milk in top part of double boiler or in very heavy saucepan 30 minutes. Rice will be tender and liquid absorbed. Add raisins, nuts, lemon juice, and egg.

Melt butter in medium skillet; do not let butter brown. Add rice mixture; cook until crusty on edges. Turn rice; brown other side. When ready to serve, sprinkle with cinnamon–sugar. Yield 4 to 6 servings.

sour-milk pudding

1 teaspoon baking soda
1 cup sour milk

2 cups bread crumbs
½ cup butter or margarine
1 cup sugar
2 eggs
1 cup flour
1 teaspoon cinnamon
¼ teaspoon salt
⅛ teaspoon nutmeg
1 cup chopped nuts
1 cup raisins
1 teaspoon vanilla

Combine soda and milk. Add bread crumbs; let stand 10 minutes.

Beat butter while adding sugar slowly. Beat in eggs, one at a time.

Mix and sift flour, cinnamon, salt, and nutmeg. Add to egg mixture alternately with milk mixture. Add nuts, raisins, and vanilla. Turn into greased baking dish; cover. Bake in 350°F oven 1¼ hours. Serve with any fruit sauce. Yield 8 servings.

steamed chocolate pudding

½ cup butter, softened
¾ cup sugar
¾ cup all-purpose flour
3 tablespoons cocoa
⅛ teaspoon salt
3 eggs
½ teaspoon vanilla extract
¼ cup half-and-half cream
Confectioners' sugar

Cream butter in mixer bowl with electric mixer until light and fluffy. Add sugar; beat about 5 minutes.

Sift flour, cocoa, and salt together. Beat into creamed mixture alternately with eggs beginning and ending with flour mixture. Add vanilla and cream; beat in thoroughly. Turn into very heavily buttered 1- to 1½-quart metal mold or glass baking dish. (Use 1 to 2 tablespoons butter to grease mold.) Place double thickness of buttered waxed paper over top; cover with double thickness of heavy-duty foil. Tie tightly with heavy string; trim paper and foil, leaving only about 1-inch overhang. If mold has lid, place on top. Place rack in steamer; add boiling water just to bottom of rack. Place mold on rack. Bring to boil; cover with lid. Reduce heat to low; cook at low boil 2 hours. Add boiling water occasionally to keep water level just below rack.

Remove mold from steamer; let rest about 2 minutes. Remove covers; unmold. Dust generously with confectioners' sugar. Serve plain or with whipped cream or chocolate sauce. Yield about 8 servings.

steamed chocolate pudding

½ cup pure maple syrup
½ teaspoon vanilla
3 medium apples, peeled, coarsely chopped
  (2 cups)

Melt butter in 2-quart casserole dish.

Stir together brown sugar, flour, baking powder, salt, and cinnamon.

Combine milk, syrup, and vanilla. Pour over flour mixture; blend until smooth. Pour batter over melted butter in casserole; do not stir. Place apples on batter. Bake in 375°F oven 35 to 40 minutes, until crust turns brown. Serve warm with plain cream. Yield 4 to 6 servings.

vanilla cream pudding

2 tablespoons cornstarch
¼ cup sugar
½ teaspoon salt
1 egg
2 cups milk
1 tablespoon butter or margarine
1 teaspoon vanilla

Mix cornstarch, sugar, and salt in pan; set aside.

Beat egg; add milk. Stir into cornstarch mixture. Cook and stir over medium heat until mixture thickens. Cook and stir 1 minute longer. Stir in butter and vanilla. Chill before serving. Yield 6 servings.

vermont maple–apple pudding

6 tablespoons butter or margarine
¼ cup packed brown sugar
1 cup whole-wheat pastry flour
2½ teaspoons baking powder
¼ teaspoon salt
½ teaspoon cinnamon
1 cup milk

SOUFFLÉS

belgian soufflé omelet in meringue

1 recipe Basic Italian Meringue (see Index)
Red food coloring
1 cup sliced fresh strawberries
½ cup sugar
¼ cup Grand Marnier
4 eggs, separated
Pinch of salt
1 teaspoon water
2 tablespoons butter
8 to 10 fresh whole strawberries

Prepare meringue; add about 4 drops food coloring to tint light pink. Cover with damp towel until ready to use.

Sprinkle strawberries with ¼ cup sugar and 2 tablespoons Grand Marnier; let stand no longer than 10 minutes.

Combine egg whites, salt, and water in large mixer bowl; beat with electric mixer until very stiff.

Combine ¼ cup sugar, 2 tablespoons Grand Marnier, and egg yolks; beat until thoroughly

325

mixed. Fold egg-yolk mixture slowly into egg whites.

Melt butter in omelet pan until foamy. Turn egg mixture into pan; cook slowly, pulling edge away from side of pan and leveling top to side with

belgian soufflé omelet in meringue

spatula. Pierce through omelet with tip of spatula occasionally to allow heat to rise through omelet. Cook until base is light golden brown and set but top is still foamy. Remove from heat; place, about 6 to 8 inches from source of heat, in preheated broiler. Broil about 4 minutes, until top is set and lightly browned.

Remove from oven; spoon strawberries over top. Fold in half; slide onto heatproof dish.

Place ⅓ of meringue in pastry bag with large star tube affixed. Cover omelet completely with remaining meringue. Pipe around edge and over top; pipe rosettes in decorative manner. Place under broiler about 4 minutes or until lightly tinged with brown. Remove from the oven; garnish with a few fresh strawberries. Serve immediately. Yield about 8 servings.

chocolate coconut soufflé

4 ounces cream cheese, room temperature
½ cup milk

⅔ cup semisweet chocolate chips
4 egg yolks
Few grains of salt
½ cup flaked coconut
1 teaspoon vanilla
4 egg whites
¼ cup confectioner's sugar, sifted
Whipped cream or whipped topping (optional)

Beat cream cheese and milk with rotary beater or electric mixer in saucepan. Add chocolate chips. Heat over low heat; stir until chocolate chips melt.

Beat egg yolks and salt together. Stir part of chocolate mixture into egg yolks; stir egg yolks into rest of chocolate mixture. Cook over low heat, stirring constantly, until slightly thickened. Stir in coconut and vanilla; cool.

Preheat oven to 325°F.

Beat egg whites until soft peaks form. Add sugar gradually, beating until stiff peaks form. Fold in chocolate mixture. Pour into ungreased 1-

quart casserole; set in pan of hot water. Bake 1 hour or until knife inserted into soufflé comes out clean. If desired, top with whipped cream or whipped topping; serve immediately. Yield 6 servings.

frozen patriotic soufflé

1 recipe Basic Confectioners' Custard (see Index)
1 (10-ounce) package frozen raspberries, thawed
6 egg whites
½ cup sugar
1¼ cups whipping cream, whipped
½ cup fresh or thawed blueberries

Make collar of thin poster paper to fit around entire depth and 2 inches higher than 6-inch soufflé dish. Tape together securely around outside of dish.

Prepare custard.

Pour raspberries into sieve placed over bowl; press berries through sieve with back of wooden spoon until only seeds remain. Discard seeds; set pulp aside.

Place egg whites in large mixer bowl; beat at high speed until fluffy. Add sugar gradually, beating until stiff peaks form.

Place cool custard in large bowl; gently fold in 1 cup cream, whipped, until well combined. Fold in raspberry pulp. Add ⅓ of egg whites; fold in with rubber spatula. Add remaining egg whites; fold in completely. Turn into mold; freeze about 4½ hours. Sides and top will be firm but center will be soft. Remove paper collar; serve immediately. Garnish with remaining cream, whipped and lightly sweetened; sprinkle with blueberries. Yield about 12 servings.

grand marnier soufflé

12 small macaroons
6 tablespoons Grand Marnier liqueur
½ cup milk
1 (1-inch) piece vanilla pod or 1 teaspoon vanilla
** extract**
¼ cup butter
⅓ cup all-purpose flour
½ cup sugar
1¼ cups half-and-half cream
3 egg yolks, lightly beaten
6 egg whites, stiffly beaten
½ cup whipping cream
1 tablespoon confectioners' sugar

frozen patriotic souffle

Arrange macaroons in shallow dish; sprinkle with 4 tablespoons Grand Marnier. Let soak 10 minutes or until soft. Remove with spatula; spread over bottom of buttered and lightly sugared 6- or 7-inch soufflé dish.

Scald milk with vanilla pod; remove from heat. Remove vanilla pod. Dry; store for future use. If using vanilla extract, add after scalding milk.

Melt butter in top of double boiler. Stir in flour to make smooth paste. Add milk and sugar alternately; stir constantly to keep smooth paste. Pour in half-and-half gradually; stir constantly until smooth and creamy. Remove from heat. Pour about ¼ of hot mixture slowly into egg yolks; stir constantly. Stir egg yolks into hot mixture. Add 1 tablespoon Grand Marnier; mix well. Cool mixture. Thoroughly fold in ¼ of egg whites; use wire whisk. Add remaining egg whites; fold in thoroughly but carefully. Pour over macaroons in soufflé dish. Bake in preheated 425°F oven 25 to

30 minutes or until soufflé has puffed and browned.

While soufflé is baking, whip cream with confectioners' sugar until soft peaks form. Beat in 1 tablespoon Grand Marnier.

Remove soufflé from oven; serve immediately with dollop of whipped cream. Each serving can be sprinkled with confectioners' sugar, if desired. Yield about 6 servings.

hot chocolate soufflé

Butter
Sugar
¾ cup chocolate chips
4 egg yolks
1 cup sifted confectioners' sugar
5 egg whites, room temperature
½ teaspoon cream of tartar

Grease 6-inch soufflé dish generously with but-

grand marnier soufflé

hot chocolate soufflé

½ cup lemon juice, strained
1 cup superfine sugar
1 cup egg whites
1 cup whipping cream

Soften gelatin with water in small saucepan. Add rind, juice, and sugar; stir over low heat until gelatin dissolves. Chill over bowl of ice, stirring frequently, to syrup consistency.

Beat egg whites very stiff; beat into lemon mixture.

Whip cream; fold in until thoroughly mixed.

Tie double oiled band of waxed paper around top of 1-quart soufflé dish, forming 4-inch-high collar. Pour in soufflé; chill.

Remove paper collar before serving. Decorate top with additional whipped cream, paper-thin slices of lemon, and fresh mint. Yield 6 servings.

vanilla soufflé

2 cups milk
½ cup sugar
½ vanilla pod or 1 teaspoon vanilla extract
¼ cup butter
⅓ cup all-purpose flour
6 egg whites, stiffly beaten

Combine milk, sugar, and vanilla pod in small heavy saucepan; bring to boil. Remove from heat; let stand 30 minutes. Remove vanilla pod; dry and store for future use. If using vanilla extract, add after scalding milk. Return milk to boil; remove from heat.

Melt butter in double boiler over medium heat. Stir in flour to make smooth paste, using wooden spoon. Add milk gradually, stirring constantly; cook until thickened. Pour into large mixing bowl; cool slightly. Thoroughly fold in ¼ of egg whites, using wire whisk. Add remaining egg whites; fold in thoroughly. Pour into well-buttered 6- or 7-inch soufflé dish. Smooth top; dome mixture slightly in center. Bake in preheated 425°F oven 1 shelf above center about 25 minutes, a little longer for drier soufflé. Serve immediately. Yield about 4 servings.

TAPIOCA

apple tapioca

½ cup minute tapioca
1 teaspoon salt
3 cups apples, pared, cored, sliced
1 cup brown sugar
⅓ teaspoon nutmeg
¾ teaspoon cinnamon
2 teaspoons lemon juice

Cook tapioca and salt in 4 cups hot water in double boiler 15 to 20 minutes, until tapioca is

ter; coat inside with sugar, shaking out excess.

Combine 2 tablespoons cold water and chocolate chips in top of double boiler. Place over hot water until chocolate chips are melted; beat with wire whisk until blended.

Cut 2 tablespoons butter into small pieces; add to chocolate 1 piece at a time, beating until butter is melted. Cool slightly.

Place egg yolks in large mixer bowl; beat with electric mixer until lemon-colored. Add confectioners' sugar gradually; beat until thick. Add ¼ of chocolate mixture; beat with wire whisk until blended. Add remaining chocolate mixture; beat until well mixed.

Beat egg whites and cream of tartar with electric mixer until stiff peaks form. Fold ¼ of egg whites into chocolate mixture; blend well. Gently fold in remaining egg whites until well mixed. Spoon into prepared soufflé dish; smooth top. Bake in preheated 400°F oven 35 minutes or until set. Dust with additional confectioners' sugar, if desired; serve immediately. Yield about 6 servings.

iced lemon soufflé

1 envelope gelatin
2 tablespoons water
Grated rind of 4 lemons

vanilla soufflé

clear; stir frequently.

Put apples in greased baking dish. Cover with sugar, mixed with spices and lemon juice. Pour tapioca over. Bake in 350°F oven about 45 minutes. Yield 8 servings.

blueberry tapioca

**1 pint container large blueberries (about 2 ½ cups)
  or frozen, thawed**
½ cup sugar
½ cup water
2 tablespoons tapioca

Stir together all ingredients in 2-quart saucepan; let stand 5 minutes. Stirring constantly, bring to full boil. Ladle into 5 (1-cup) individual dessert bowls. Serve warm or chilled, topped with whipped cream. Yield 5 servings.

chocolate tapioca

1 ½ cups milk
2 tablespoons minute tapioca
1 egg, separated
3 tablespoons sugar
⅛ teaspoon salt
1 teaspoon vanilla
2 squares unsweetened chocolate

Scald 1 cup milk in top of double boiler. Add tapioca; cook 20 minutes or until tapioca is trans-parent. Stir frequently.

Beat egg yolk. Add sugar and salt. Put tapioca mixture with egg yolks. Put over bottom of double boiler; cook until thickened. Remove from heat; fold in stiffly beaten egg white, vanilla, and chocolate blended with half cup scalded milk. Yield 4 servings.

coffee tapioca

1 egg yolk
1 cup evaporated milk
⅓ cup minute tapioca
⅔ cup sugar
¼ teaspoon salt
1 cup water
2 cups strong coffee
1 egg white
1 teaspoon vanilla
Caramel Sauce (see Index)

Mix egg yolk with small amount milk in sauce-pan. Add remaining milk, tapioca, sugar, salt, water, and coffee. Bring to boil over direct heat, stirring constantly. Remove from heat.

Beat egg white until just stiff enough to hold shape. Gradually fold hot tapioca mixture into egg white; cool. When slightly cool, stir in vanilla; chill. Serve in parfait glasses with Caramel Sauce. Yield 8 servings.

tapioca cream

¼ cup minute tapioca
1 cup scalded milk
⅓ cup sugar
1 egg, separated
¼ teaspoon salt
½ teaspoon vanilla

Add tapioca to milk; cook in double boiler until transparent. Add half the sugar to milk and half to slightly beaten egg yolk and salt. Pour hot mixture slowly on egg mixture. Return to double boiler; cook until thickened, stirring constantly. Add stiffly-beaten egg whites. Flavor with vanilla. Serve cold. Yield 4 servings.

tapioca custard pudding

1 pint scalded milk
2 eggs, slightly beaten
⅓ cup minute tapioca
½ cup sugar
1 teaspoon salt
1 tablespoon butter

Add tapioca to milk; cook in double boiler 30 minutes. Add eggs to sugar and salt. Gradually pour on hot mixture; turn into buttered pudding dish. Add butter; put in pan of hot water. Bake in 325°F oven 30 minutes. One cup of almost any chopped, canned, or stewed fruits or berries can be added. Yield 6 servings.

VARIETY DESSERTS

charlotte russe

12 ladyfingers
Light corn syrup
2 envelopes unflavored gelatin
1 cup sugar
¼ teaspoon salt
4 eggs, separated
2½ cups milk
2 tablespoons brandy or sherry
1 cup whipping cream, whipped

Wet base of 8-inch springform pan.

Split ladyfingers; cut off ½-inch tip of each half.

Coat side of springform pan with corn syrup. Place ladyfinger halves around side of pan, curved-end-up, to stand upright.

Mix gelatin, ½ cup sugar, and salt in 2-quart saucepan.

Beat egg yolks; stir in milk. Stir into gelatin mixture; cook over low heat, stirring constantly, about 6 minutes, until gelatin is dissolved. Remove from heat. Add brandy; mix well. Chill until mixture mounds slightly when dropped from spoon.

Beat egg whites until stiff but not dry, then beat until very stiff; add remaining sugar gradually. Fold into gelatin mixture. Fold in whipped cream; turn into pan. Chill until firm.

Release spring to unmold; remove side of pan carefully. Place on serving platter. Pipe additional whipped cream around top edge and base of Charlotte Russe; garnish as desired. Yield 12 servings.

chocolate-cream coupes

3 (1-ounce) squares unsweetened chocolate
2 egg yolks
⅛ teaspoon salt
¾ cup white corn syrup
2 cups whipping cream
1 teaspoon vanilla extract

chocolate-cream coupes

Place chocolate in top of double boiler over hot, not boiling, water. (If water is too hot, chocolate will become lumpy and hard.) Heat until chocolate is melted.

Combine egg yolks and salt in small mixer bowl; beat until light and lemon-colored. Add corn syrup; beat until well combined. Pour slowly into chocolate; beat constantly. Cook over hot water, stirring constantly, until thickened. Remove from heat; beat until cold.

Whip cream until fluffy. Add vanilla; beat until stiff. Fold ⅓ of whipped cream into chocolate, then fold in remaining whipped cream. Chill at least 4 hours. Spoon into serving dishes; mound as in illustration, if desired. Garnish with a little whipped cream or with dragonflies as illustrated. Yield 6 to 8 servings.

chocolate mousse

8 ounces semisweet chocolate pieces
2 tablespoons water
¼ cup powdered sugar
½ cup unsalted butter, softened
6 eggs, separated
1 tablespoon dark rum
½ teaspoon vanilla
2 tablespoons sugar

Melt chocolate and water in double boiler. When melted, stir in powdered sugar. Add butter bit by bit; set aside.

Beat egg yolks until thick and lemon-colored, about 5 minutes. Gently fold in chocolate; reheat slightly to melt chocolate, if necessary. Stir in rum and vanilla.

Beat egg whites until foamy. Beat in sugar; beat until stiff peaks form. Gently fold whites into chocolate mixture. Pour into individual serving dishes; chill at least 4 hours. Serve with whipped cream, if desired. Yield 8 servings.

chocolate–orange mousse

½ teaspoon grated orange rind
2 tablespoons packed light brown sugar
1 egg yolk
1 egg
3 squares (3 ounces) semisweet chocolate, melted, cooled
1½ tablespoons orange juice
½ cup heavy cream

Combine rind, sugar, egg yolk, and egg in a blender or food processor; whirl until light and foamy. Add chocolate, orange juice, and cream; whirl until well blended. Pour into individual dessert dishes; chill about 1 hour, until set. Yield 2 servings.

coffee dessert

coffee dessert

1½ envelopes unflavored gelatin
1½ cups water
1 cup milk
¾ cup sugar
¼ teaspoon salt
2 tablespoons instant coffee powder
3 eggs, separated
1 teaspoon vanilla extract

Put gelatin, water, milk, sugar, salt, and coffee together in double boiler. Stir until gelatin has melted and mixture just reaches boiling point. Add egg yolks; stir over low heat until mixture is thick enough to coat back of spoon. Remove from heat. Add vanilla; chill until mixture thickens to syrupy consistency. Stir frequently.

Beat egg whites until stiff; fold into mixture. Pour into sherbet glasses; chill until firm. Decorate as desired. Yield 6 servings.

coffee-filled éclairs

1 recipe Basic Cream Puff Pastry (see Index)
4 tablespoons Basic Coffee Syrup (see Index)
⅛ teaspoon salt
1 recipe Basic Confectioners' Custard (see Index)

2½ **cups sifted confectioners' sugar**

Prepare Cream Puff Pastry; pipe into éclairs, using 1-inch plain piping tube. Bake 10 minutes at 400°F. Reduce heat to 350°F; bake 25 minutes.

Make custard; let cool. Add half the Basic Coffee Syrup and salt; mix well.

Split éclairs on one side; fill with custard mixture.

For frosting, mix remaining coffee syrup into confectioners' sugar; add enough warm water, several drops at a time, to make spreading consistency. Spread over eclairs; chill until ready to serve. Yield 12 to 16.

junket

5 cups fresh milk
2 teaspoons sugar
2 teaspoons rennet or ½ junket tablet

Junkets are milk desserts set with rennet only, without either grain or gelatin.

Warm milk to lukewarm; stir in sugar until dissolved. Add rennet; stir. Pour at once into serving dishes; put in warm place to set. Serve with cream, if liked. Yield 6 servings.

chocolate junket

Add 2 to 3 ounces plain chocolate, grated and dissolved in a little of the measured milk.

coffee junket

Add instant coffee powder to milk to flavor; decorate finished junket with chopped nuts.

rum junket

Add rum to taste.

vanilla, almond, raspberry junket, etc.

Add a few drops of extract.

Note: When using rennet in liquid or powder form, the manufacturer's instructions should always be followed carefully.

macaroon mousse

4 egg yolks
½ cup sifted confectioners' sugar
½ cup rum
4 cups crushed Almond Macaroons (see Index)
2 cups whipping cream, whipped

Place egg yolks in large mixer bowl; beat with electric mixer until light and fluffy. Add sugar alternately with rum; beat until well blended. Add macaroons; mix well. Cover bowl with aluminum foil; let stand 15 minutes. Fold in whipped cream gradually; blend well. Spoon mixture into wet mold; chill about 3 hours, until set.

Dip mold into warm water; unmold onto serving dish. Serve immediately. Yield 10 to 12 servings.

moor in a shirt

4 slices bread, crusts removed
½ cup whipping cream
⅓ cup butter, softened
2 eggs
2 egg yolks
¾ cup sifted confectioners' sugar
¼ cup ground toasted almonds
⅓ cup chocolate chips, melted
⅛ teaspoon almond extract

macaroon mousse

moor in a shirt

Break bread into small pieces; place in bowl. Pour cream over bread; mix with wooden spoon until cream is absorbed.

Place butter in small mixer bowl; cream with electric mixer about 5 minutes or until light and creamy. Add bread mixture; beat until light and fluffy.

Combine eggs and egg yolks; beat lightly with fork. Add eggs and sugar alternately to bread mixture, small amount at a time; beat well after each addition. Add almonds, chocolate, and almond extract; beat until well blended. Turn into heavily buttered 1- to 1½-quart pudding mold. Cover with buttered waxed paper and heavy-duty foil; tie securely with string. Trim off excess paper and foil. Place on rack in steamer; pour boiling water just to bottom of rack. Cover with lid; steam 2 hours. Remove from steamer; let rest 2 minutes.

Unmold onto serving dish; dust with additional confectioners' sugar. Serve with whipped cream or a chocolate sauce, if desired. Yield 4 servings.

rich man

3 tablespoons brandy
3 tablespoons Basic Sugar Syrup (see Index)
8 to 10 Almond Macaroons (see Index)
¾ cup unsalted butter
1 cup sifted confectioners' sugar
¼ cup sherry
2 egg yolks
¼ cup ground toasted almonds
2 hard-boiled egg yolks, sieved
1 recipe Basic Chantilly Cream (see Index)

Combine brandy and sugar syrup.

Place macaroons in pie plate; pour brandy mixture over top. Let soak until soft. Lift carefully with spatula; arrange in well-buttered 1-quart mold.

Place butter in small mixer bowl; cream with electric mixer about 5 minutes, until light and fluffy. Add sugar; beat until smooth. Add sherry, egg yolks, almonds, and hard-boiled egg yolks; beat about 5 minutes. Spoon carefully over macaroons; pack down smoothly. Cover with plastic wrap; chill overnight.

Dip in hot water; unmold in serving dish. Pipe Chantilly Cream around edge and on top as desired. Yield 8 servings.

rum sponges

1½ cups water
¼ cup peanut oil
Peel of ½ lemon
1 cup unsifted flour
½ teaspoon salt
4 eggs

rich man

Peanut oil
1 cup sugar
½ cup light rum

Bring 1 cup water, ¼ cup peanut oil, and lemon peel to boil. Stir in flour and salt all at once; beat vigorously until mixture leaves sides of pan. Remove from heat. Add eggs one at a time; beat well after each addition. Beat until mixture is smooth. Drop by teaspoonfuls into deep hot (375°F) peanut oil. Fry until golden brown, about 4 minutes; turn often. Drain on paper towels.

Meanwhile heat sugar, rum and 1 cup water to full boil; cool slightly. To serve, toss balls in rum syrup. Pour remaining syrup over top. Yield 8 servings.

sicilian cheese-filled pastries (cannoli)

(cannoli)
pastry
2 cups flour
1 teaspoon salt
2 tablespoons sugar
2 tablespoons soft butter, cut into small pieces
1 egg, beaten
10 tablespoons white wine
Oil for frying
5-inch long × 1-inch in diameter cannoli forms or pieces of dowel

cream filling
⅔ cup sugar
½ cup flour
⅛ teaspoon salt
2 cups scalded milk
2 eggs, lightly beaten
½ teaspoon vanilla extract
¼ teaspoon almond extract
1 pound ricotta cheese
½ cup powdered sugar
½ cup finely chopped candied fruit
1 (1-ounce) block semisweet chocolate, grated

Prepare pastry. Combine flour and salt in mixing bowl. Make well in center; add sugar, butter, and egg. Add wine; stir with fork until liquid is absorbed. Turn onto floured board; knead until smooth. Divide dough into 4 equal parts; roll on floured surface until 1/16 inch thick. Cut into 3½-inch squares; roll squares diagonally onto forms, overlapping corners. Seal with a little water.

Heat ¾ inch oil in heavy skillet to 375°F; fry cannolis, 3 at a time, in hot oil. When light golden, remove from oil; slip off of forms as soon as cool enough to handle. Allow to cool completely.

Make filling. Combine sugar, flour, and salt in

335

sicilian cheese-filled pastries

Set aside 16 berries for garnish; strain remaining berries through fine sieve to remove seeds. Blend strained berries with cream cheese, yogurt, honey, egg yolks, vodka, and lemon juice. Stir until smooth and creamy.

Beat egg whites until soft peaks form.

Beat cream until stiff. Fold both into berry mixture. Spoon into 4 individual dessert dishes; chill until set.

Just before serving, garnish each with macaroons or almonds, walnut halves, and reserved berries. Yield 4 servings.

blackberry yogurt-cream dessert

top of double boiler. Slowly stir in scalded milk; cook over boiling water until mixture thickens. Combine 1 cup of mixture with eggs; beat well. Pour mixture back into double boiler; cook, stirring, 3 minutes. Cool; stir in flavoring. (Filling must be cold before adding ricotta.)

Beat ricotta and powdered sugar until ricotta is smooth. Fold in custard, fruit and chocolate.

Fill cannoli with small spatula, carefully packing filling. Refrigerate until serving time. Yield 30 to 35.

Note: Shells can be made ahead and frozen and filled as needed.

YOGURT

blackberry yogurt–cream dessert

1 pint (3½ cups) fresh blackberries or raspberries
4 ounces cream cheese
1 cup plain yogurt
¼ cup honey
2 egg yolks
2 tablespoons vodka
2 tablespoons lemon juice
2 egg whites
2 cups heavy cream
16 small macaroons or whole almonds
16 walnut halves

cherry yogurt dessert

1 pound fresh cherries, pits removed
½ cup honey
¼ cup kirsch
1 tablespoon lemon juice
2 cups plain yogurt
1 cup whipping cream
1 teaspoon vanilla

Combine cherries with about ⅓ cup honey, kirsch, and lemon juice. Chill 15 minutes.

Blend yogurt with remaining honey.

Beat cream until stiff; stir in vanilla. Remove 2

cherry yogurt dessert

elfin's yogurt dessert

tablespoons whipped cream; reserve for use as garnish. Fold remainder into sweetened yogurt.

Alternate layers of cherries and yogurt–cream mixture in tall parfait glasses. Garnish each with reserved whipped cream. Serve at once. Yield 4 servings.

elfin's yogurt dessert

1 cup plain skim-milk yogurt
3 tablespoons lemon juice
⅓ cup dry white wine
Grated rind of half a lemon
1 teaspoon vanilla
Liquid artificial sweetener to taste
1 envelope unflavored gelatin
⅓ cup cold water
3 egg whites

Blend together yogurt, lemon juice, wine, lemon rind, and vanilla. Add sweetener to taste.

Soak gelatin in cold water; place over low heat. Dissolve, stirring constantly. Fold into yogurt mixture; cool until thickened but not set.

Beat egg whites until stiff peaks form. Fold into yogurt mixture. Divide among 4 dessert dishes; re-

frigerate until set. Just before serving, garnish each with a few cereal flakes and a sprig of mint. Yield 4 servings.

eskimo yogurt apples

6 large red apples
Lemon juice
1 cup fresh raspberries or ½ (10-ounce) package frozen raspberries, thawed
2 tablespoons sugar
¼ cup raspberry liquor, rum, or kirsch
3 tablespoons flaked coconut
¼ cup ground almonds
½ cup plain yogurt
1 cup whipped cream or whipped topping (garnish)
Sliced almonds (garnish)

Wash apples well; polish with clean towel. Cut off top of each apple; brush with lemon juice to prevent discoloration. Set aside. Carefully cut out inside of each apple to leave ½-inch shell; brush insides with lemon juice. Dice removed portions of apples; discard core and seeds. Combine with sugar, raspberries (reserve a few whole ones for garnish), liquor, coconut, and ground almonds.

eskimo yogurt apples

Fold in yogurt; spoon into apples. Top each apple with dollop of whipped cream, a reserved raspberry, and sliced almonds. Cover with apple tops; serve at once. Yield 6 servings.

frozen melba yogurt

1 pound ripe peaches
½ pint ripe strawberries, hulled, sliced
½ cup sugar
1 quart plain yogurt

Peel, halve, and pit peaches; coarsely chop. Add berries and sugar; stir to mix. Let stand at room temperature until sugar dissolves and mixture is juicy. Stir in yogurt. Chill well in freezer but do not freeze; serve or freeze until firm and let stand at room temperature 15 to 20 minutes before serving. Yield about 1½ quarts.

homemade low-calorie yogurt

When made from 1% skim milk, yogurt contains only about 100 calories per cup. The body is a bit thin, and a 2% skim milk may be preferred for a creamier texture. The caloric value of the yogurt would then be close to 120 calories per cup.

1 quart skim milk (1 or 2%)
1 heaping tablespoon unpasteurized yogurt

Heat milk over moderately high heat almost to boiling point. Remove at once; cool to 110 to 105°F Add yogurt; stir or whisk until completely dispersed. Pour into clean jars; incubate at 110 or 105°F. 6 to 10 hours, until firm. Refrigerate at once. Chill at least 3 or 4 hours before serving or using in a recipe. Yogurt is sweetest when used within several days but will keep up to 2 weeks in refrigerator. Yield 4 cups.

raspberry yogurt ambrosia

1 pint fresh raspberries
¼ cup sugar
2 to 3 tablespoons curacao liquor
6 egg yolks
3 tablespoons confectioners' sugar
⅓ cup white wine
2 tablespoons raspberry liquor or rum
1 tablespoon lemon juice
½ cup plain yogurt

Wash and drain berries. Sprinkle with sugar; let stand 30 minutes. Divide among 4 glass sherbet or parfait dishes; sprinkle with curacao.

In top of double boiler combine yolks, sugar, wine, liquor, and lemon juice. Stir over simmering water only until thickened; do not overheat. Stir in yogurt; pour over berries. Serve at once. Yield 4 servings.

homemade low-calorie yogurt

raspberry yogurt ambrosia

strawberries yogurt san remo

1 pint fresh strawberries, hulled, cleaned, halved
3 tablespoons sugar

yogurt topping
3 egg yolks
⅓ cup sugar
1 teaspoon vanilla
Dash of nutmeg
1 tablespoon brandy
2 cups plain yogurt

2 tablespoons sliced almonds
Shaved chocolate or chocolate sprinkles

Combine strawberries and sugar. Cover; let stand 15 minutes.

Prepare topping. Beat together yolks, sugar, vanilla, nutmeg, and brandy until smooth. Fold in yogurt.

Spoon strawberries into 4 sherbet dishes. Cover with topping; garnish with almonds and chocolate. Yield 4 servings.

strawberry frozen yogurt

2 teaspoons gelatin
3 tablespoons milk
1 cup plain yogurt
2 tablespoons sugar
⅛ teaspoon salt
⅛ cup sieved frozen strawberries, partially thawed
1½ tablespoons lemon juice
½ cup whipping cream, whipped

Soak gelatin in milk in custard cup. Set cup into boiling water; stir until gelatin is completely dissolved.

Combine yogurt, sugar, and salt. Stir in gelatin mixture. Stir in berries and lemon juice. Chill until viscous; beat until foamy. Fold in whipped cream. Pour mixture into metal ice-cube tray. Cover with foil; freeze. Yield 4 servings.

strawberry yogurt sundae

1 pint strawberries, cleaned, hulled
¼ cup sugar
2 cups plain yogurt
1 teaspoon vanilla
Grated chocolate
2 tablespoons chopped pistachio nuts
Whipped cream

Reserve several strawberries for garnish. Puree remainder in blender or food processor. Combine pureed strawberries, sugar, yogurt, and vanilla. Spoon into individual dessert dishes. Garnish with chocolate, nuts, and dab of whipped cream. Yield 3 or 4 servings.

strawberry yogurt sundae

yogurt parfaits

1 medium can sliced peaches
1 cup quartered seedless grapes
2 (8-ounce) cartons yogurt
2 peeled sliced pears
1 small can pineapple chunks
½ cup cream, whipped (optional)
4 maraschino cherries

Reserve 8 peach slices for decoration.

Place layer of grapes in 4 parfait glasses. Cover with layer of yogurt; add layers of pears, peaches, and pineapple alternately with yogurt until last layer of yogurt comes within ¾ inch of top of each glass. Pipe a spiral of whipped cream over yogurt in each glass; top with a cherry. Push 2 reserved peach slices onto each glass. Fruits can be layered in sherbet glasses, if desired. Yield 4 servings.

yogurt parfaits

apricot duck

1 (4- to 5-pound) roasting duck
1 pound fresh apricots (or 1 large can, drained)
1 orange
1 onion, finely chopped
Salt and pepper
2 to 3 tablespoons oil
3 tablespoons honey
1 to 1½ cups stock made with duck giblets (or chicken bouillon cube)
3 to 4 tablespoons apricot brandy

Stuff duck with half seeded apricots and 3 strips of orange zest (the thin outer skin of orange), onion, and seasoning. Prick skin of duck with fork to allow fat to run out while cooking; season with pepper and salt.

Heat oil in roasting pan. When very hot, add duck; baste all over with oil. Roast in preheated 400°F oven; allow 20 minutes per pound. Half an hour before cooking is completed, spoon melted honey and juice of orange over duck; to give skin shiny crispness. Ten minutes before end of cook-ing, add rest of apricots to pan; heat through and brown slightly. Remove duck to warm dish; re-move stuffing to bowl. Arrange roasted apricots around duck.

Pour off fat from roasting pan. Put in stuffing; bring to boil, stirring all the time. Taste for sea-soning. Strain or blend in liquidizer, blender, or food processor. Return to heat; add apricot brandy. Serve at once with duck and apricots. Yield 4 to 6 servings.

brandied duck

1 (5- to 6-pound) duck
2 large onions, chopped
¼ cup minced parsley
1 bay leaf
½ teaspoon thyme
2 garlic cloves, crushed
3 jiggers brandy
2 cups red wine
¼ cup olive oil or butter
¾ pound mushrooms, sliced
Salt
Pepper

Clean, then cut duck into serving pieces. Place in deep dish. Add onions, parsley, bay leaf, thyme, garlic cloves, brandy, and wine to duck. Marinate at least 4 hours, preferably overnight.

Heat oil; brown pieces of duck about 15 min-utes. Add marinade, mushrooms, and seasonings. Cover tightly; simmer over low heat at least 1 hour. Yield 4 to 6 servings.

duck savoyarde

2 ducks (4 to 5 pounds each)
6 tablespoons unbleached flour
2 teaspoons salt
½ teaspoon black pepper
½ teaspoon paprika
½ teaspoon oregano
2 tablespoons oil
2 tablespoons butter or margarine
¾ pound mushrooms, sliced
4 onions, peeled, quartered
6 carrots, scraped, cut into large strips
1 clove garlic, crushed (optional)
2 to 3 cups red wine
10 ripe olives, chopped

garnish
Red currant jam or guava jelly
Parsley sprigs
Wild or savory rice

Have butcher clean ducks and disjoint them into 6 or 8 pieces each. Place pieces in paper or

apricot duck

plastic bag with flour and seasonings; shake until well coated.

Heat oil and butter in large skillet. Brown ducks on all sides; transfer to large casserole as they are browned.

In same skillet brown mushrooms, onions, carrots, and garlic; add more oil and butter if necessary. Add mixture to ducks. Add wine; cover. Bake at 350°F 1 hour. Fifteen minutes before end of cooking time, add olives. Remove ducks from casserole to heated platter. Remove as much fat as possible from sauce in pan. Pour sauce over ducks. Garnish platter with sprigs of parsley. Serve with red currant or guava jelly and wild or savory rice. Yield 8 or more servings.

duckling with oranges

¼ cup olive oil
¼ cup butter
1 large duckling
Basic Seasoned Flour (see Index)
2 tablespoons wine vinegar
2 teaspoons sugar
Strips of peel of 1 orange and 1 lemon
Juice of 1 orange
Juice of ½ lemon
1 teaspoon curacao
1 teaspoon brandy

Heat oil and butter in large frypan. Dredge duckling with seasoned flour. Place in frypan over medium-high heat; brown on all sides. Place in heavy baking dish. Pour pan drippings over duckling; cover. Bake in preheated 350°F oven about 1½ hours or until duckling is tender. Remove duckling from baking dish; place on heated platter. Keep warm. Pour off excess fat from casserole drippings.

Place vinegar and sugar in small saucepan. Cook over low heat, stirring, until sugar is dissolved. Stir in drippings, orange and lemon strips, and orange and lemon juice; cook over medium heat until liquid is reduced by half. Add curacao and brandy; pour over duckling. Yield about 4 servings.

peking duck

1 (3- to 4-pound tender roasting duck)
5 to 6 tablespoons honey
3 teaspoons wine vinegar
2 tablespoons soy sauce
2 to 3 teaspoons sherry
1 orange
1 onion
Salt and pepper

duckling with oranges

Preheat broiler or barbecue charcoal grill.

Prepare special basting sauce: In pan put honey, vinegar, soy sauce, sherry, juice of ½ orange and 3 tablespoons water. Heat together; bring to boil. Let cool.

Prick skin of duck lightly with sharp fork; pour over several pints of boiling water to soften skin; let dry. Put onion and ½ orange inside duck; season. Put bird on spit; when broiler or barbecue is very hot, cook bird, basting frequently with special sauce. Allow 20 minutes per pound; lower heat after first half hour. Test if duck is done by sticking skewer deeply into leg meat. If juice is clear, duck is done. Remove from heat. Serve with rice and bean sprouts. Yield 4 servings.

DUMPLINGS

dumplings in broth

1½ cups all-purpose white flour
2 egg yolks
¾ cup beef broth
1 teaspoon salt
¼ teaspoon white pepper
1 quart beef bouillon

Mix flour, egg yolks, broth, salt, and pepper; beat vigorously. If batter is too thin, add additional flour. Using teaspoon, drop batter into boiling bouillon. When dumplings float to top, soup is ready to serve. Yield 4 servings.

dumplings italian-style (gnocchi)

4 cups (1 quart) milk
1 cup yellow cornmeal
2 eggs, well beaten
2 teaspoons salt
¼ teaspoon pepper
1 small onion, finely chopped
1½ cups finely cut-up or shredded cheese
¼ cup melted butter or margarine

Mix milk and cornmeal in pan; cook and stir over medium heat until very thick. Stir into eggs. Stir in salt, pepper, onion, and 1 cup cheese. Pour into baking pan so mixture is about 1½ inches thick; chill. Remove from pan; cut into pieces. Place on greased baking pan or dish. Brush with butter; sprinkle with rest of cheese. Bake at 350°F about 20 minutes, until lightly browned. Yield 6 servings.

matzo balls

6 eggs
1 teaspoon salt
1 tablespoon minced parsley
½ cup melted chicken fat or top of chicken soup
⅔ cup hot water

dumplings in broth

1½ cups matzo meal

Beat eggs lightly; add salt and parsley. Add chicken fat and water. Slowly add matzo meal; mix well. Refrigerate 2 hours. Drop into rapidly boiling water or soup; reduce heat. Cook slowly, uncovered 1 hour. Yield 12 servings.

matzo balls, spicy-style

2 eggs
2 tablespoons shortening or chicken fat or mixed
4 to 6 level tablespoons matzo meal
Salt
Pepper
Paprika
Ginger
Finely chopped parsley

Cream together eggs and shortening; add matzo meal and spices. Mixture must have forming consistency. Refrigerate 2 hours. Form into small balls. Add balls to boiling soup; let simmer 20 minutes. Yield 20 small balls.

semolina dumplings roman-style

2 cups milk
1 tablespoon butter
½ teaspoon salt
Pinch of freshly grated nutmeg
Ground white pepper to taste
½ cup farina (or semolina)
2 eggs, beaten
½ cup grated Parmesan cheese
garnish
2 tablespoons melted butter
1 tablespoon grated Parmesan cheese

Butter cookie sheet; set aside.

In heavy saucepan combine milk, butter, salt, nutmeg, and pepper; bring to boil over moderate heat. Slowly add farina; stir constantly. Reduce heat to low; cook until very thick and spoon will stand unsupported in center of pan. Remove from heat. Add eggs and cheese; mix well. Spread on cookie sheet in rectangle ½ inch thick; refrigerate until firm. Cut into rounds about 1½ inches in diameter (or cut into squares or triangles, if you prefer). Arrange in greased casserole or baking dish, slightly overlapping. Drizzle with melted butter; sprinkle with cheese. Bake in preheated 350°F oven 20 minutes; serve hot. Yield 3 or 4 servings.

EGG VARIETIES

baked eggs

6 eggs
1¼ cups milk
1 teaspoon salt
2 teaspoons sugar (optional)
1½ tablespoons flour
½ cup finely diced cooked ham (optional)

Beat eggs until light.

Measure milk into 2-cup measure. Add salt, sugar, and flour; mix with eggs. Add ham; pour into buttered baking dish. Bake at 425°F 25 minutes or until center is firm. Yield 4 servings.

basket eggs

1½ pounds lean ground beef
1 small onion, chopped fine
2 tablespoons catsup
1 teaspoon salt
¼ teaspoon pepper
¼ cup milk
6 hard-cooked eggs, shelled
1 raw egg, beaten
⅔ cup cornflake crumbs
Fat for deep frying

Mix ground beef with onion, catsup, salt, pepper, and milk. When well blended, form into 6 balls. Shape each ball around a hard-cooked egg to completely cover egg, forming oval shape.

Brush each meatball with beaten egg; roll each in crumbs until completely covered.

Melt 2-inch deep fat in medium skillet. Fry meatballs, 3 at a time, until crispy brown. (They will not have to be turned if deep fat is used.) Drain; keep hot until all are done.

To serve, cut each meatball in half lengthwise; eggs will be in baskets. Yield 6 servings.

curried eggs

1 medium-size onion, peeled, chopped
2 to 3 tablespoons oil
2 tablespoons flour
1 tablespoon curry powder
Salt
2 cups stock or 1 bouillon cube and 2 cups water
1 large apple, peeled, cored, diced
1 tablespoon Worcestershire sauce
4 hard-boiled eggs
About 2 cups freshly cooked rice
Chutney
8 red pimiento strips

Sauté onion in oil until soft but not browned. Add flour, curry powder, and a little salt; stir over low heat until mixture forms smooth paste. Add stock gradually; stir until boiling. Add apple and Worcestershire sauce; cover. Simmer gently 15 to 20 minutes. Add eggs; heat through.

Put rice on large platter; arrange eggs and sauce on top. Crisscross pimiento strips over egg; serve with chutney. Yield 4 servings.

basket eggs

deviled eggs

6 hard-cooked eggs
½ teaspoon salt
½ teaspoon dry mustard
¼ teaspoon pepper
3 tablespoons salad dressing, vinegar, or light
cream

Cut peeled eggs in half lengthwise. Slip out yolk; mash in small bowl with fork. Mix in seasonings and salad dressing. Fill whites with egg mixture, heaping up highly.

For flavor variation, mix in 2 tablespoons snipped parsley or ½ cup grated cheese. Serve as an appetizer or as a salad. Yield 6 servings.

eggs benedict

6 slices (about 2 ounces each) Canadian bacon
1 tablespoon oil or fat, melted
3 English muffins, cut in half
1 tablespoon butter or margarine
6 eggs
4 or more cups boiling water
½ teaspoon salt
Hollandaise or Mock Hollandaise Sauce
(see Index)

Fry bacon in oil in frypan; keep warm.

Spread muffin halves with butter; toast under broiler.

Break eggs into saucer one at a time. Slip each egg gently into boiling salted water; water should cover eggs. Reheat to simmering; simmer, covered, until eggs are of desired doneness, about 3 minutes for medium.

Top each muffin half with slice of bacon, then with poached egg. Serve with Hollandaise Sauce over top of egg. Yield 6 servings.

eggs divan

6 hard-cooked eggs
¼ cup mayonnaise
1 tablespoon instant minced onion
¼ teaspoon salt
1 (10-ounce) package frozen broccoli spears
1 (8-ounce) jar pasteurized process cheese spread
or 1 cup Mornay Sauce (see Index)

About 1 hour before serving, halve eggs crosswise; place yolks in small bowl. Mix in mayonnaise, onion, and salt; use to fill egg halves.

Preheat oven to 400°F.

Boil broccoli as label directs; drain. In 10 × 6-inch baking dish arrange broccoli spears in 3 separate piles; place stuffed eggs in between. Spoon cheese generously over broccoli. Bake 10 minutes or until cheese is bubbly. Yield 3 servings.

curried eggs

eggs florentine-style

1 pound fresh spinach
Pinch of salt
3 tablespoons butter or margarine
cheese sauce
3 tablespoons butter
3 tablespoons flour
Salt
White pepper
1 cup hot chicken broth
½ cup light cream
¾ cup freshly grated Parmesan cheese

eggs
Boiling salted water
Few drops of white vinegar
6 eggs

Wash spinach; remove coarse stems; discard undesirable leaves. Place wet spinach in saucepan with tight-fitting lid; set aside.

Prepare Cheese Sauce. Melt butter in medium saucepan. Add flour, salt, and pepper; cook until bubbly. Add broth and cream; cook until thickened, stirring constantly. Remove from heat; stir in cheese. Keep sauce warm.

Heat 1½ inches salted water to boiling in medium skillet; add few drops of vinegar. Poach eggs in water to desired degree of doneness.

Meanwhile, sprinkle spinach lightly with salt; steam over low heat 5 minutes; drain. Place spinach in warm serving dish.

Remove eggs from skillet with slotted spoon; place on spinach. Pour sauce over eggs and spinach; serve immediately. Yield 3 or 4 servings.

eggs foo yong

2 tablespoons vegetable oil
½ cup thinly sliced scallions
¼ cup finely chopped celery
1 clove garlic, crushed
1 cup diced cooked shrimp or pork
6 eggs
½ teaspoon salt
¼ teaspoon pepper
1 tablespoon soy sauce

Heat oil in wok or frypan. Add scallions, celery, and garlic; stir-fry 2 to 3 minutes. Remove garlic; discard. Add shrimp; stir-fry until shrimp are lightly browned.

Beat eggs with salt, pepper, and soy sauce until frothy. Add to shrimp mixture; stir until blended. Cook over low heat until eggs set. Fold over; slide onto serving plate. Serve at once. Yield 4 servings.

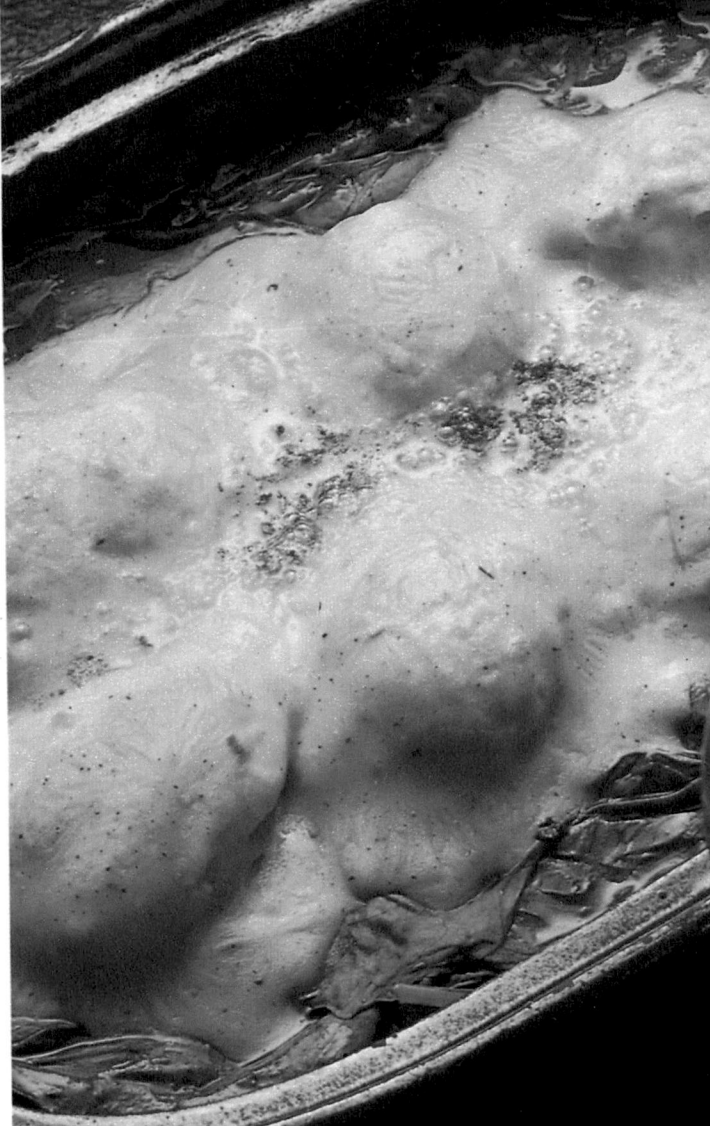

eggs florentine-style

eggs in snow

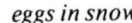

eggs in snow

2 slices bread
Butter
Nutmeg
2 eggs, separated
Salt and pepper
Grated cheese

Toast bread on 1 side; turn. Toast underside very lightly. Butter lightly toasted side; keep hot.

Add seasoning and pinch of nutmeg to egg whites; beat until stiff. Spread over buttered toast. Make slight indentation in middle; drop in egg yolk. Sprinkle with cheese; put under hot broiler a few minutes, until egg yolk has set. Yield 2 servings.

eggs scandinavian

6 eggs
3 tablespoons condensed milk
1 teaspoon salt
Dash of pepper
2 dill pickles, sliced or diced
2 tablespoons chives
2 tablespoons chopped dill
8 ounces Danish cheese, diced
3 tablespoons butter
2 tomatoes
1 extra tablespoon chives (garnish)

Mix eggs with milk, salt, and pepper in bowl. Add pickles, chives, dill, and cheese.

Heat butter in large skillet; add egg mixture. Cover; simmer on low heat 10 minutes.

While eggs are cooking, wash, peel, and quarter tomatoes.

When egg mixture has set in middle, place tomatoes on top for decoration; sprinkle with chives. Serve at once. Yield 6 to 8 servings.

farmer's breakfast

4 medium potatoes
4 strips bacon, cubed
3 eggs
3 tablespoons milk
½ teaspoon salt
1 cup small cubes cooked ham
2 medium tomatoes, peeled
1 tablespoon chopped chives

Boil unpeeled potatoes 30 minutes. Rinse under cold water. Peel; set aside to cool. Slice potatoes.

Cook bacon in large frypan until transparent. Add potatoes; cook until lightly browned.

Meanwhile blend eggs with milk and salt; stir in cubed ham.

Cut tomatoes into thin wedges; add to egg mixture. Pour over potatoes in frypan. Cook until eggs are set. Sprinkle with chives; serve at once. Yield 3 or 4 servings.

eggs scandinavian

farmer's breakfast

fried eggs

In heavy skillet heat butter or bacon drippings to ⅛-inch depth just until hot enough to sizzle a drop of water.

Break each egg into measuring cup or saucer; carefully slip eggs one at a time into skillet. Immediately reduce heat to low. Cook slowly, until egg whites are set and film forms over yolks (sunny-side up); or turn eggs over gently when whites are set and cook until of desired doneness. Yield as desired.

golden buck

golden buck

2 tablespoons butter
1½ cups grated cheese
4 tablespoons beer or ale
1 teaspoon Worcestershire sauce
1 teaspoon lemon juice
Cayenne pepper
Pinch of celery salt
4 eggs
4 slices buttered toast

Melt butter in small skillet. Add cheese, beer, Worcestershire sauce, lemon juice, and seasoning. Stir over low heat until smooth and creamy.

Beat eggs lightly; stir into mixture. Stir until eggs are lightly set; spoon onto hot toast. Yield 4 servings.

mexican scrambled eggs

8 eggs
2 tablespoons milk
1 large tomato, peeled, seeded, chopped
1 tablespoon chopped green pepper
1 tablespoon chopped parsley
3 tablespoons butter
½ cup chopped ham
2 tablespoons chopped chives

Beat eggs in mixing bowl with milk. Add tomato, green pepper, and parsley; stir well to combine.

Melt butter over low heat in large, heavy skillet; sauté ham 3 minutes. Pour in egg mixture; cook, stirring frequently with spatula, until set. Sprinkle with chives. Serve with hot buttered tortillas for brunch. Yield 4 servings.

mexican scrambled eggs

polish eggs in the shell

poached eggs

In saucepan or skillet heat water to boiling; reduce to simmer.

Break each egg into measuring cup or saucer; slip eggs one at a time into water, holding cup or saucer close to water's surface. Cook 3 to 5 minutes. Lift eggs from water with slotted spatula. Serve on buttered toast. Season with salt and pepper. Yield as desired.

polish eggs in the shell

4 hard-cooked eggs in shells
½ bunch parsley, chopped fine
3 tablespoons butter
1 teaspoon salt
1 teaspoon paprika
¼ cup shredded Muenster cheese

Cut eggs in half with large, sharp knife. Scoop eggs out of shells; save shells. Chop egg whites fine; mash yolks fine with fork. Combine chopped eggs, parsley, butter, salt, and paprika; mix well. Refill egg shells with egg mixture; sprinkle with cheese. Bake 10 minutes at 400°F or until cheese melts and browns. Yield 4 servings.

352

spanish eggs

scrambled eggs

2 eggs
2 tablespoons milk or cream
¼ teaspoon salt
Dash of pepper
½ tablespoon butter

Break eggs into bowl with milk, salt, and pepper. Mix with fork, stirring thoroughly for uniform yellow, or mixing just slightly if streaks of white and yellow are preferred.

Heat butter in skillet over medium heat until just hot enough to sizzle a drop of water. Pour egg mixture into skillet. As mixture begins to set at bottom and side, gently lift cooked portions with spatula so that thin, uncooked portion can flow to bottom. Avoid constant stirring. Cook until eggs are thickened throughout but still moist, about 3 to 5 minutes. Yield 1 serving.

variations

To egg mixture you can add grated cheese, finely chopped sautéed onions, chopped tomatoes, or chopped green peppers.

scrambled eggs with oysters

6 eggs
Dash of Tabasco
2 tablespoons butter
1 teaspoon anchovy paste

1 can oysters, drained, chopped
Freshly ground black pepper
1 tablespoon finely chopped parsley
Croutons of fried bread

Whisk eggs very lightly with Tabasco (avoid over-beating).

Put butter and anchovy paste into small skillet; when hot, pour in eggs. Stir until just beginning to set; add oysters. Season with salt and pepper. Finish scrambling eggs; avoid over-cooking. Put onto hot serving dishes; sprinkle with parsley. Serve with croutons or with toast. Yield 4 servings.

spanish eggs

2 cups Basic Beef Stock (see Index)
3 large tomatoes
¼ cup butter
1 cup finely diced lean pork

353

2 cups finely diced ham
½ cup minced onion
¼ cup all-purpose flour
Salt and freshly ground pepper to taste
5 eggs

Pour stock into small, heavy saucepan; simmer until reduced by half.

Skin tomatoes; scoop out all seeds with spoon. Chop pulp coarsely.

Melt butter in heavy saucepan; add pork, ham, and onion. Cook over low heat, stirring constantly, until lightly browned.

Combine enough stock with flour to make smooth, thin paste; stir paste into ham mixture. Add remaining stock and tomatoes; blend thoroughly. Add seasonings; simmer until thickened and heated through, stirring frequently. Pour into greased casserole; spread mixture evenly.

Break eggs carefully into casserole, spacing them decoratively; sprinkle lightly with salt. Bake, covered, in preheated 350°F oven about 20 minutes, until eggs are set. Garnish with finely chopped parsley, if desired. Yield 5 servings.

stuffed eggs mexican-style

8 hard-cooked eggs, chilled
1 tablespoon grated onion
1 tablespoon finely minced green pepper
¼ teaspoon chili powder
¼ teaspoon salt
2 to 3 dashes Tabasco
2 teaspoons lemon juice
1 tablespoon olive oil
16 small shrimp, cooked, peeled, deveined
Parsley
Lettuce

Cut eggs in half lengthwise; remove yolks. Mash yolks with onion, pepper, chili powder, salt, Tabasco, lemon juice, and oil. Stuff egg whites with egg-yolk mixture; garnish each egg with a shrimp and a tiny sprig of parsley. Place on plate surrounded by fresh green lettuce; refrigerate until serving time. Yield 4 or more servings.

OMELETS

alfalfa-sprout omelet

1 cup alfalfa sprouts
2 to 3 tablespoons butter or margarine
4 eggs, beaten
2 tablespoons water
¼ teaspoon salt
Pepper

Sauté sprouts in butter 2 minutes; remove.

Blend eggs, water, salt, and pepper in bowl.

Clean out skillet with paper towel; heat. Add more butter to pan if necessary. Pour eggs into skillet; cook slowly, running spatula around edge to allow uncooked portion to flow underneath. Sprinkle sprouts on top of cooked eggs. Fold over; turn onto platter. Yield 2 or 3 servings.

bacon and potato omelet

3 slices bacon, cut into small pieces
2 small potatoes, peeled, sliced
8 fresh spinach leaves, stems removed, sliced into ¼-inch slices
6 eggs, lightly beaten with fork
½ cup yogurt
Salt and pepper to taste

Heat bacon briefly in 10-inch skillet. Add potatoes; fry until bacon is crisp and potatoes lightly browned. Add spinach; remove mixture to small bowl.

Combine eggs, yogurt, salt, and pepper; pour into skillet. Distribute potato mixture evenly over them; cook over low heat without stirring. As eggs set on bottom, lift edges; let uncooked mixture run underneath. When omelet is set, fold with fork; serve immediately. Yield 3 servings.

basic omelet and fillings

2 eggs
2 tablespoons water
¼ teaspoon salt
Dash of pepper
1 tablespoon butter

In small bowl mix eggs, water, salt, and pepper with fork.

Heat butter in 8-inch omelet pan until just hot enough to sizzle a drop of water; pour in egg mixture. Mixture should start to set immediately. With pancake turner draw cooked portions from edge toward center, so uncooked portions flow to bottom. Tilt pan while doing this; slide pan back and forth over heat to keep mixture from sticking. Add filling, if desired. While top is still moist and creamy-looking, fold in half or roll wih pancake turner. Turn out onto plate with quick flip of the wrist. Omelets will take about 2 minutes from start to finish. Yield 1 serving.

omelet fillings
cheese: 1 to 2 tablespoons grated Swiss or Parmesan cheese
herbs: 1 tablespoon minced fresh herbs, such as parsley, chives, or tarragon
other fillings: 2 to 3 tablespoons sautéed ham or chicken livers, cooked shrimp or crab, cooked asparagus tips, raw sliced mushrooms, sour cream.

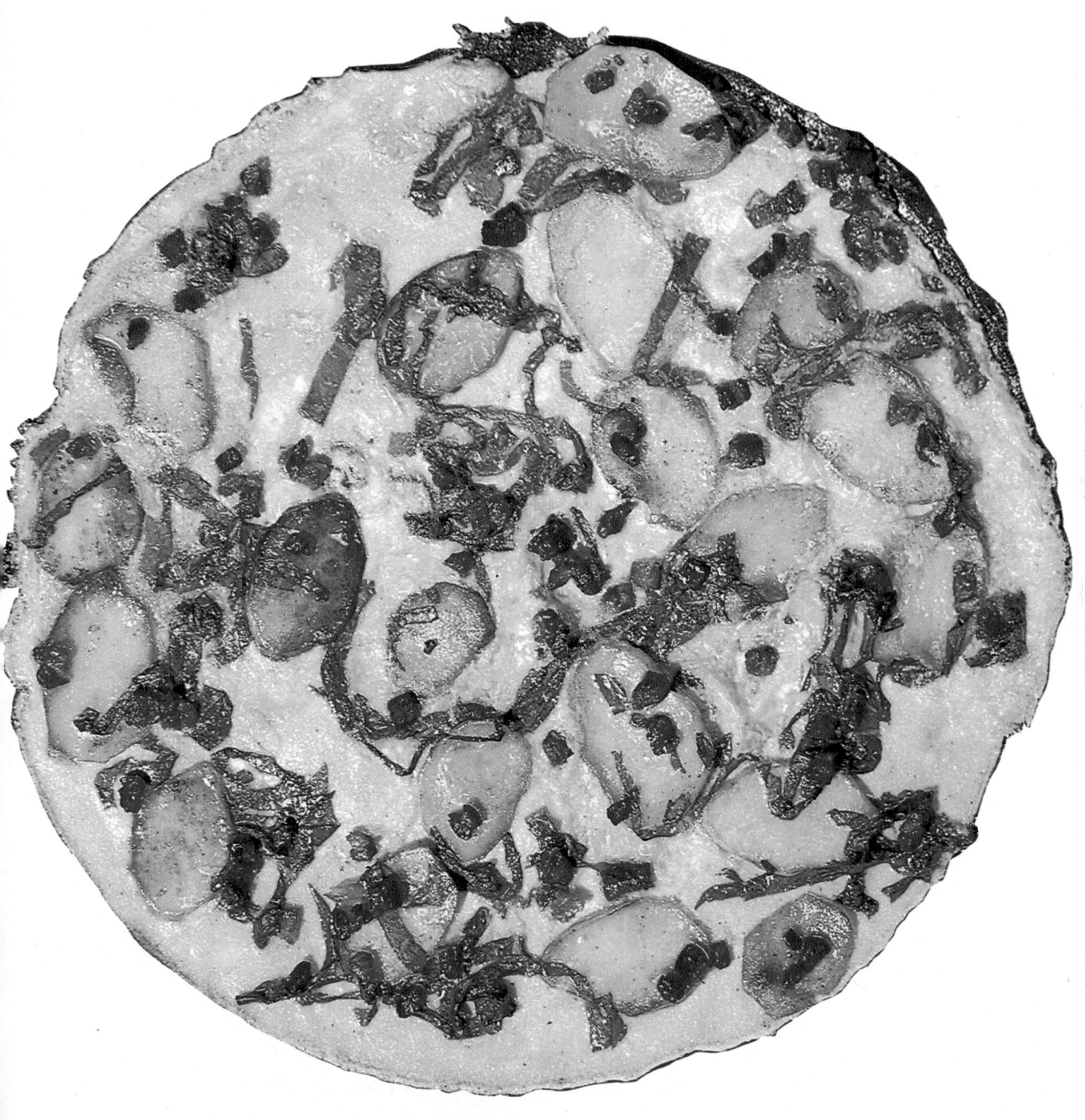

bacon and potato omelet

jam omelet

jam omelet

3 eggs, separated
1½ teaspoons sugar
1½ teaspoons half-and-half cream
2 tablespoons butter
¾ cup strawberry jam, heated
2 teaspoons confectioners' sugar

Combine egg yolks, sugar, and cream in small bowl; beat until lemon-colored.

Beat egg whites until stiff peaks form; fold in egg-yolk mixture slowly.

Melt butter in skillet. Add egg mixture; spread over skillet with spoon. Cover; cook over low heat. Remove skillet from heat occasionally, if needed, until omelet is cooked through. Broil in oven about 8 inches from source of heat until lightly browned. Spread jam on half the omelet; fold remaining omelet over jam. Lightly score top of omelet with knife; sprinkle confectioners' sugar over top. Yield about 4 servings.

mushroom omelet chinese-style

2 tablespoons butter
¼ cup sliced mushrooms
¼ cup finely chopped onions
6 eggs
Salt and pepper
Lettuce or parsley for garnish

Melt butter in wok or skillet; stir-fry mushrooms and onions over very low heat. (Butter will burn if heated over 225°F.) Remove; set aside.

Beat eggs with salt and pepper. Pour into wok; heat slowly. Lift up edges of eggs as they become

set on bottom; let uncooked egg run under. Cook until golden brown on bottom and creamy on top. Place mushrooms and onions in center; roll onto plate. Garnish with lettuce or parsley; serve at once. Yield 4 servings.

spanish omelet

sauce
2 tablespoons olive oil
1 small onion, chopped
1 clove garlic, peeled, chopped
2 green peppers, cleaned, seeded, cut into strips
1 red pepper, cleaned, seeded, cut into strips
1 (8-ounce) can tomato sauce
2 tablespoons dry sherry
½ teaspoon chili powder

omelets
2 tablespoons butter
6 eggs

Make sauce. Heat oil in saucepan or skillet. Add onion, garlic, and peppers; cook until wilted. Add tomato sauce, sherry, and chili powder; keep warm while making omelets.

In 8-inch skillet or omelet pan heat 1 tablespoon butter over medium heat until it starts to brown. Tilt pan in all directions to coat with butter.

Meanwhile, beat 3 eggs with fork until yolks and whites are well-blended. Pour into skillet; cook over medium heat until set. Fold omelet; place on warm serving dish. Repeat procedure with remaining eggs and butter. Serve topped with sauce. Yield 4 to 6 servings.

spanish omelet

spinach–veal omelet

1 (10-ounce) package frozen spinach
1 tablespoon lemon juice
6 eggs
¾ cup freshly grated Parmesan cheese
½ cup ground veal
½ teaspoon salt
⅛ teaspoon white pepper

Cook spinach according to package directions. Drain; squeeze dry. Place in blender or food processor container with lemon juice; puree.

Place eggs in medium-size bowl; whip with wire whisk until well blended. Add spinach and remaining ingredients; stir until mixed. Turn into generously buttered 6-inch soufflé dish. Place in preheated 300°F oven on center shelf. Bake 1 hour; turn out onto heated platter. Garnish with thinly sliced cucumber rings, if desired. Yield 4 servings.

spinach–veal omelet

basic custard cream filling

¾ **cup sugar**
⅓ **cup cornstarch**
¼ **teaspoon salt**
4 egg yolks, lightly beaten
2 cups scalded milk
1 teaspoon vanilla extract
2 tablespoons butter

Mix sugar, cornstarch, and salt together; stir in egg yolks. Add enough hot milk to make thin paste. Add to remaining hot milk; cook in double boiler 5 minutes, stirring constantly. Reduce heat; cook 10 minutes or until mixture has thickened, stirring frequently. Remove from stove. Add vanilla and butter; let cool. Yield 2¼ cups.

butterscotch cream filling

Use ½ cup firmly packed brown sugar instead of granulated sugar.

chocolate cream filling

Heat 2 squares baking chocolate with milk; when melted, beat with rotary beater until smooth. Increase sugar to 1 cup.

coconut cream filling

Add ½ cup shredded coconut.

cream custard filling

Fold ½ cup whipped cream into cooled filling.

pineapple cream filling

Add ½ cup crushed pineapple to cooled filling; add 1 teaspoon lemon juice instead of vanilla.

lemon cream filling

¾ **cup sugar**
2 tablespoons cornstarch
Pinch of salt
1 egg yolk, beaten
¾ **cup water**
3 tablespoons lemon juice
1 teaspoon grated lemon rind
1 tablespoon butter

Put sugar, cornstarch, and salt in top of double boiler; add egg yolk, water, and lemon juice. Cook over boiling water 5 minutes; stirring constantly. Reduce heat; cook 10 minutes or until mixture is thick, stirring frequently. Remove from stove. Add lemon rind and butter; let cool. Yield enough for 2 (9-inch) layers or 1 sponge roll.

prune filling

2 eggs, beaten
¾ **cup sugar**
½ **cup sour cream**
1 cup chopped cooked prunes
1 teaspoon grated lemon rind
1 teaspoon vanilla extract

Put eggs, sugar, sour cream, and prunes in top of double boiler; cook about 20 minutes, until quite thick, stirring constantly. Remove from stove. Add lemon rind and vanilla; let cool. Yield enough for 2 (9-inch) plain sponge layers.

BLUEFISH

baked bluefish

Place fillets into large pot cold water with about 3 tablespoons lemon juice. Cover pot; place in refrigerator overnight. This draws oil out of bluefish. Bluefish tend to taste oily, so it is important to do this before baking.

2 pounds bluefish fillets
½ cup milk
Salt and pepper
1 cup dried bread crumbs
¼ pound butter
2 tablespoons lemon juice
Seafood seasoning to taste (about ½ cup)

Heat oven to 500°F.

Dip fillets in milk; lightly salt and pepper. Dip into bread crumbs. Place ½ teaspoon butter on each fillet; sprinkle with lemon juice. Sprinkle with seafood seasoning. Place in well-buttered pan. Bake uncovered 10 to 12 minutes, until fish flakes easily. Yield 6 servings.

delmarvelous bluefish

2 pounds bluefish or other fillets, fresh or frozen
1 teaspoon salt
¼ teaspoon pepper
⅓ cup melted butter or margarine
3 tablespoons lemon juice
½ teaspoon thyme

Thaw fish if frozen. Cut into serving-size portions. Sprinkle with salt and pepper. Put into well-greased 2-quart baking dish.

Combine butter, lemon juice, and thyme; pour over fish. Bake in 350°F oven 15 to 20 minutes, until fish flakes easily. Serve with Mustard Sauce. Yield 6 servings.

mustard sauce
¼ cup butter or margarine
3 tablespoons all-purpose flour
1½ tablespoond dry mustard
½ teaspoon salt
¼ teaspoon liquid hot pepper sauce
2 cups half-and-half cream
1 egg yolk, beaten

Melt butter in saucepan. Blend in flour, mustard, salt, and pepper sauce. Gradually stir in half-and-half. Cook until thickened; stir constantly.

Add a little hot sauce to egg yolk; add to remaining sauce, stirring constantly. Heat until thickened. Serve over fish. Yield about 2 cups.

BUTTERFISH

butterfish in sour cream

2 pounds butterfish, dressed
Salt and pepper to taste
½ teaspoon salt
¾ cup flour
1 egg, beaten
½ cup milk
1 tablespoon melted butter or margarine
Fat for deep frying
1 cup sour cream
1 tablespoon chopped parsley
1 tablespoon minced green onion
1 tablespoon lemon juice

Season fish with salt and pepper.

In bowl mix ½ teaspoon salt, flour, egg, milk, and butter to form batter. Dip fish in batter to coat thoroughly.

Fry fish in large skillet in hot, deep fat until golden brown all over. Drain; set on hot platter.

In saucepan combine sour cream, parsley, onion, and lemon juice until just hot. Serve over fish. Yield 4 to 6 servings.

CATFISH

cajun catfish

6 skinned, pan-dressed catfish or other fish, fresh or frozen
½ cup tomato sauce
2 (¾-ounce) packages cheese-garlic salad-dressing mix
2 tablespoons melted fat or oil
2 tablespoons chopped parsley
2 tablespoons grated Parmesan cheese

Thaw frozen fish. Clean, wash, and dry fish.

Combine remaining ingredients except cheese. Brush fish inside and out with sauce. Place in well-greased baking dish, 13 × 9 × 2 inches. Brush with remaining sauce; sprinkle with cheese. Let stand 30 minutes. Bake in 350°F oven 25 to 35 minutes, until fish flakes easily. Turn oven control to broil. Place fish about 3 inches from source of heat; broil 1 to 2 minutes, until crisp and lightly browned. Yield 6 servings.

saucy broiled catfish

6 skinned, pan-dressed catfish or other fish, fresh or frozen
1 cup melted fat or oil
¼ cup chopped parsley
2 tablespoons catsup
2 tablespoons wine vinegar

2 cloves garlic, finely chopped
2 teaspoons basil
1 teaspoon salt
¼ teaspoon pepper

Thaw frozen fish. Clean, wash, and dry fish. Place in single layer in shallow baking dish.

Combine remaining ingredients. Pour sauce over fish; let stand 30 minutes, turning once. Remove fish; reserve sauce for basting. Place fish on well-greased broiler pan; brush with sauce. Broil about 3 inches from source of heat 5 to 7 minutes, until lightly browned; baste twice. Turn carefully; brush other side with sauce. Broil 5 to 7 minutes, basting occasionally, until fish is brown and flakes easily. Yield 6 servings.

COD

baked cod

1 dressed fresh cod (scrod), about 2 pounds
3 lemons
4 tomatoes, sliced
1 pound whole mushrooms
½ teaspoon salt
⅛ teaspoon pepper
½ teaspoon marjoram
½ teaspoon thyme
1 bay leaf
1 large onion, cut into rings
3 tablespoons vegetable oil

Wash fish; pat dry. Place in baking dish; sprinkle with juice of 1 lemon. Garnish with tomatoes and remaining lemons (sliced).

Wash mushrooms; place around fish. Season with salt and pepper; add marjoram, thyme, and bay leaf. Add onion; sprinkle with oil. Bake, covered (foil or lid), 15 minutes in preheated 325°F oven. Remove cover; and cook 10 to 15 minutes, until fish flakes. Yield 4 servings.

cod fillets in shrimp sauce

4 cod fillets, about 6 ounces each
Juice of 1 lemon
Salt
White pepper
2 tablespoons butter or margarine
1 medium onion, sliced
2 tablespoons chopped parsley
½ cup dry white wine

shrimp sauce
2 tablespoons butter or margarine
1½ tablespoons flour
1 cup hot beef broth
½ cup dry white wine
6 ounces fresh mushrooms, thinly sliced
4 ounces fresh shrimp
2 teaspoons lemon juice
Salt
2 egg yolks

garnish
Lemon slices
Parsley

Sprinkle cod with lemon juice; let stand 10 minutes. Season to taste with salt and pepper.

cod fillets in shrimp sauce

Heat butter in large skillet. Add fish; brown well, about 10 minutes on each side. Add onion; cook until golden. Stir in parsley. Pour in wine; simmer 5 minutes. Remove fillets to preheated platter; keep warm. Reserve pan drippings.

Prepare sauce. Melt butter in saucepan. Stir in flour; pour in broth and reserved pan drippings. Add wine; let simmer over low heat. Add mushrooms and shrimp; simmer 15 minutes. Season to taste with lemon juice and salt. Remove small amount of sauce; blend with egg yolks. Return to sauce; stir thoroughly. Heat through but do not boil; yolks will curdle. Pour over cod; garnish with lemon slices and parsley. Yield 4 servings.

cod and oyster scallop

1 pound cod or other fish fillets, fresh or frozen
1 pint oysters, drained, fresh or frozen
½ cup butter or margarine
2 tablespoons finely chopped onion
¼ teaspoon liquid hot pepper sauce
3 cups crushed saltine crackers
2 tablespoons chopped parsley
¼ teaspoon salt
⅛ teaspoon pepper
1 cup half-and-half cream

Thaw fish and oysters if frozen. Cut fish into 1-inch cubes.

Melt butter in saucepan. Add onion; cook until tender. Stir in pepper sauce.

Combine onion, crackers and parsley. Place ⅓ of crumb mixture in bottom of well-greased 1½-quart casserole. Place ½ fish and oysters on crumb mixture. Sprinkle with ½ the salt and pepper. Repeat layers; end with crumb mixture. Pour cream over contents in dish. Bake in 400°F oven 25 to 30 minutes, until fish flakes easily. Yield 6 servings.

coddies

¼ pound butter or margarine
3 medium potatoes, cooked, mashed
3 eggs, beaten
1 medium onion, finely chopped
1 teaspoon salt
¼ teaspoon pepper
1 tablespoon chopped parsley
3 (15-ounce) cans codfish
Fat for deep frying

Add butter to potatoes while still hot. Add eggs, onion, salt, pepper, parsley, and fish; mix well. Let stand at least 1 hour.

Shape coddies into 2-inch cakes.

Heat fat in medium-size skillet. Fry coddies until brown and crisp; drain on paper towels. Serve on saltine crackers with plenty of mustard. Yield 4 to 6 servings.

coddies

fish steaks in foil

6 cod steaks (½ pound each) or any suitable
  whitefish
Salt and pepper
6 small lemons
½ cup butter, melted
6 tablespoons dry white wine
1 clove garlic, crushed
2 tablespoons chopped parsley

Season fish with salt and pepper.

Peel lemons; remove all white pith. Cut into thin slices. Arrange half of slices down center of each foil square. Place a fish steak on top; cover with rest of lemon slices.

Mix butter with wine, garlic, and parsley; spoon over fish. Fold over foil; seal each parcel as securely as possible. Cook on hot coals or in 375°F oven; allow about 20 minutes. Serve in foil with Tartar Sauce (see Index). Yield 6 servings.

poached cod with lemon sauce

1½ pounds cod fillets
Seasoned salt and pepper
1 tablespoon lemon juice
2 shallots, peeled, chopped
¼ cup white wine
1 tablespoon butter or margarine

lemon sauce
1 tablespoon butter or margarine
¾ cup mayonnaise
Juice of ½ lemon
½ teaspoon dry mustard
½ teaspoon salt
½ tablespoon capers, drained, chopped

fish steaks in foil

Wash fish; pat dry. Sprinkle with salt, pepper, and 1 tablespoon lemon juice. Place in small, greased casserole dish. Sprinkle with shallots; pour wine over all. Dot with 1 tablespoon butter; cover. Bake at 350°F 20 to 25 minutes, until fish flakes easily.

Meanwhile, melt 1 tablespoon butter in top of double boiler. Add remaining sauce ingredients except capers. Cook, stirring constantly, over simmering water until heated through. Stir in capers.

Place fish on heated platter; top with sauce. Serve immediately, garnished with lemon slices. Yield 4 servings.

steamed cod fillets with special lemon mayonnaise

Butter
4 cod fillets, fresh or frozen
Salt to taste
1 recipe Special Lemon Mayonnaise (see Index)

Grease perforated base of steamer pan with butter; place cod (thawed, if frozen) on buttered surface. Cover pan. Pour enough boiling water into bottom pan to fill ½ full. Place perforated pan over bottom pan; steam about 15 minutes, until cod flakes easily. Remove cod; cool. Remove skin and bones; season with salt. Place fillets on serving platter; spoon mayonnaise around fillets. Garnish wtih lemon slices and cloves. Yield 4 servings.

FLOUNDER

fillet of flounder

1½ pounds fillets of flounder
Salt and pepper

¾ cup fine bread crumbs
1 egg
Butter or oil

Wipe fillets with cold, damp cloth; sprinkle with salt and pepper. Dip in crumbs, then in slightly beaten egg, diluted with water, and again in crumbs. Cook in small amount butter in frying pan 8 to 10 minutes, until brown on both sides. Garnish with lemon and parsley; serve with Tartar Sauce (see Index). Yield 4 servings.

flounder creole

2 tablespoons butter or margarine
¼ cup chopped onion
¼ cup chopped green pepper
¼ pound mushrooms, sliced
1 (1-pound) can tomatoes, drained
2 tablespoons lemon juice
¼ teaspoon dried leaf tarragon
1 bay leaf
¼ teaspoon Tabasco sauce
½ teaspoon salt
1 pound flounder fillets

Melt butter in large skillet. Add onion and pepper; cook until tender. Add mushrooms; cook 3 minutes. Add tomatoes, lemon juice, tarragon, bay leaf, Tabasco, and salt. Cover; simmer 20 minutes. Add flounder fillets; cover. Simmer 5 to 10 minutes, until fish flakes easily. Yield 3 or 4 servings.

flounder grenoble

5 tablespoons vegetable oil
1½ cups tiny cubes of white bread
6 (1-inch thick) flounder or sole fillets, folded in half
Salt and pepper

steamed cod fillets with special lemon mayonnaise

½ cup flour
4 to 6 tablespoons sweet butter
4 tablespoons lemon juice
2 large lemons, peeled, cut into ½-inch cubes
4 tablespoons tiny capers, drained
2 tablespoons butter
2 tablespoons chopped parsley

Place 3 tablespoons oil in skillet; add bread cubes. Turn cubes over and over until evenly browned. Drain in sieve; set aside.

Season fillets with salt and pepper; dip in flour so all sides are well coated. Shake off excess.

Heat sweet butter and remaining oil in heavy skillet. When very hot, add fish; be sure each fillet lies flat and does not overlap. Cook over medium to high heat about 5 minutes. With wide spatula turn fish over; cook about 5 minutes. Fish should be brown and crusty on both sides. Arrange fish on warm serving platter with nicest sides showing. Sprinkle lemon juice, croutons, lemon cubes, and capers over fish; keep warm.

Melt 2 tablespoons butter in clean saucepan until it takes on hazelnut color *beurre noisette;* pour on fish. Sprinkle with parsley; serve immediately. Yield 6 servings.

flounder a l'orange

1 teaspoon salt
Dash of pepper
2 tablespoons orange juice
1 teaspoon grated orange rind
2 tablespoons vegetable oil
1½ pounds flounder fillets, cut into serving pieces
⅛ teaspoon nutmeg

Combine salt, pepper, juice, rind, and oil.

Place fish in oiled shallow pan; pour sauce on fish. Sprinkle with nutmeg. Bake in preheated 350°F oven 20 to 30 minutes. Yield 4 to 6 servings.

flounder with oyster sauce

1 small onion, peeled, chopped
1 carrot, peeled, chopped
1½ cups dry white wine
Salt
Peppercorns
1 bay leaf
1½ pounds flounder fillets
1½ tablespoons butter or margarine
1½ tablespoons flour

363

½ cup heavy cream
Paprika to taste
1½ dozen fresh oysters
½ cup white seeded grapes

Put onion and carrot into pan with wine. Add a little salt, about 6 peppercorns, and bay leaf; simmer 15 minutes. Add fish; poach gently 7 to 10 minutes. Remove fish carefully; drain. Arrange in shallow casserole.

Strain fish liquid; if less than 1 cup, make up difference with wine.

Heat butter; stir into flour. Cook 1 minute. Add fish liquid. Whisk until smooth. Add cream and paprika; stir over low heat until sauce is thick. Add oysters; adjust seasoning. Pour over fish. Arrange grapes on top; cover. Bake in preheated 350°F oven about 20 minutes. Yield 4 servings.

flounder in wine sauce

2 pounds flounder or other fish fillets, fresh or
    frozen
2 teaspoons salt
Pepper
3 tomatoes, sliced
2 tablespoons flour
2 tablespoons butter or margarine, melted
½ cup skim milk
⅓ cup dry white wine
½ teaspoon crushed basil
Chopped parsley

Thaw frozen fillets. Skin fillets; sprinkle both sides with 1½ teaspoons salt and dash of pepper. Place in single layer in greased baking dish, 12 × 8 × 2 inches. Arrange tomatoes over fillets. Sprinkle with ½ teaspoon salt and dash of pepper.

Blend flour into butter; add milk gradually. Cook until thick and smooth; stir constantly. Remove from heat; stir in wine and basil. Pour sauce over tomatoes. Bake in 350°F oven 25 to 30 minutes, until fish flakes easily. Sprinkle with parsley. Yield 6 servings.

HADDOCK

creamed haddock and mushrooms

⅔ cup canned sliced mushrooms
2 tablespoons butter
4 tablespoons flour
½ teaspoon salt
Few grains pepper
2 cups milk
2 cups flaked, cooked haddock
1 tablespoon chopped parsley

Saute mushrooms in butter until golden brown. Add flour, salt, pepper, and milk. Cook until

thick; stir constantly. Add haddock and parsley; heat through. Yield 6 servings.

haddock chanticleer

2 pounds haddock fillets, skinned
Salt
Freshly ground black pepper
½ cup olive oil
2 tablespoons lemon juice
¼ cup chopped shallots or white part of scallion
¼ cup chopped parsley
4 tablespoons Dijon-type mustard
⅓ cup grated Gruyere cheese
½ cup fresh bread crumbs
1 teaspoon tarragon, thyme, and rosemary
    combined
1½ tablespoons butter

Wash and dry fish; season both sides with salt and pepper. Marinate in olive oil, lemon juice, shallots, and parsley 4 to 5 hours.

Place fish in buttered baking dish; coat top with mustard. Sprinkle cheese on top, then crumbs that have been combined with herbs. Dot all over with butter. Bake at 425°F 10 to 15 minutes, until fish is nearly cooked through. Run quickly under broiler to brown surface. Yield 4 to 6 servings.

haddock kedgeree

¼ cup butter
1 pound cooked smoked haddock, flaked
2 cups cooked rice
3 hard-boiled eggs
Salt and pepper
Lemon juice
5 to 6 slices hot buttered toast

Melt butter in pan. Add fish; sauté 2 to 3 minutes. Add rice, 2 eggs (chopped), salt as desired, pepper, and a good squeeze of lemon juice. Stir over heat a few minutes. Arrange on toast.

Slice remaining egg; use for garnish. Yield 5 or 6 servings.

poached haddock with mussels

2 pounds haddock, cod, or other thick fillets,
    fresh or frozen
4 pounds (about 4 dozen) mussels in shells (clams
    can be substituted)
1 cup dry white wine
1 cup water
1 small onion, sliced
½ teaspoon salt
½ cup whipping cream
¼ cup butter or margarine
Dash of white pepper

haddock kedgeree

Dash of nutmeg
2 tablespoons chopped parsley
Parslied potatoes
1 cup each zucchini, carrots, and celery, cut
 julienne style
Butter or margarine for cooking vegetables

Thaw fillets if frozen; cut into serving-size portions.

Clean mussels in cold water. Scrub shells with stiff brush; rinse thoroughly several times.

Combine wine, water, and onion in large pan; bring to simmering stage. Add mussels. Cover; steam about 5 minutes, until shells open. Remove mussels from shells; set aside.

Strain cooking liquid into large skillet; add fillets and salt. Cover; simmer 8 to 10 minutes, until fish flakes easily. Transfer fillets to warm platter; keep warm.

Reduce cooking liquid to ½ cup. Stir in whipping cream, ¼ cup butter, pepper, and nutmeg; simmer until sauce thickens slightly. Add mussels and parsley; heat. Spoon mixture over fillets. Serve with parslied potatoes and julienne strips of zucchini, carrot, and celery sauteed in butter; stir constantly just until tender. Yield 6 servings.

savory baked haddock

2 pounds haddock or other fish fillets, fresh or
 frozen
2 teaspoons lemon juice
Dash of pepper
6 slices bacon, chopped
½ cup soft bread crumbs
2 tablespoons chopped parsley

¾ cup thinly sliced onion
2 tablespoons bacon fat

Thaw frozen fillets. Skin fillets; place in single layer in greased baking dish, 12 × 8 × 2 inches. Sprinkle with lemon juice and pepper.

Fry bacon until crisp; remove from fat. Add to bread crumbs and parsley.

Cook onion in bacon fat until tender; spread over fish. Sprinkle crumb mixture over onion. Bake in 350°F oven 25 to 30 minutes, until fish flakes easily. Yield 6 servings.

HALIBUT

busy-day halibut

2 pounds (¾-inch thick) halibut or other firm
 steaks or fillets, fresh or frozen
2 tablespoons dry onion soup mix
1 cup dairy sour cream
1 cup fine dry bread crumbs
2 tablespoons grated Parmesan cheese
1 tablespoon chopped parsley
¼ teaspoon paprika
¼ cup melted butter, margarine, or oil.

Thaw fish if frozen; dry well. Cut into 6 portions.

Combine soup mix and sour cream.

In separate bowl mix bread crumbs, cheese, parsley, and paprika.

Dip fish in sour-cream mixture; roll in bread-crumb mixture. Place in single layer on well-greased shallow baking pan. Pour butter or oil over fish. Bake in 500°F oven 10 to 12 minutes, until fish flakes easily. Yield 6 servings.

Note: Seasoned Italian bread crumbs can be used in place of bread crumb-cheese mixture.

halibut with tomato sauce hungarian-style

2 tablespoons lard
1 cup chopped onion
1 clove garlic, peeled, minced
Salt and white pepper
1 (16-ounce) can tomatoes, drained, chopped
Dash of Tabasco
2 tablespoons dry sherry
2 tablespoons finely chopped parsley
4 halibut steaks, approximately 6 ounces each
4 tablespoons lemon juice
2 tablespoons butter or margarine

Make sauce. Melt lard in small skillet over moderate heat. Add onion; cook 3 minutes. Add garlic; cook until onion is lightly browned. Add salt, pepper, tomatoes, and Tabasco; cover. Simmer 15 minutes; keep warm while cooking fish. Stir in sherry and parsley just before pouring over fish.

Rub fish with 2 tablespoons lemon juice; let stand 10 minutes. Place on preheated, lightly

halibut with tomato sauce hungarian-style

greased broiler pan; brush with remaining lemon juice and butter. Broil 6 inches from heat source 5 to 6 minutes per side; baste once. Turn; cook 5 minutes. Transfer to warm platter; pour sauce over fish. Serve with boiled potatoes. Yield 4 servings.

hearty skinny halibut

2 pounds halibut or other fish steaks, fresh or frozen
2/3 cup thinly sliced onion
1½ cups chopped fresh mushrooms
1/3 cup chopped tomato
1/4 cup chopped green pepper
1/4 cup chopped parsley
3 tablespoons chopped pimiento
1/2 cup dry white wine
2 tablespoons lemon juice
1 teaspoon salt
1/4 teaspoon dillweed
1/8 teaspoon pepper
Lemon wedges

Thaw frozen steaks. Cut into serving-size portions.

Arrange onion in bottom of greased baking dish, 12 × 8 × 2 inches. Place fish on onion.

Combine remaining vegetables; spread over fish.

HERRING

pickled-herring platter

12 to 16 ounces chilled pickled herring
1 tablespoon vinegar (optional)
1 onion, thinly sliced
½ cup plain yogurt
2 cups cooked green beans
12 small new potatoes, boiled
2 tablespoons melted butter
Chopped fresh parsley leaves

Rinse herring with cold water; arrange on serving platter. Sprinkle with vinegar.

Separate onion slices into rings; arrange over herring. Top with yogurt. Place hot green beans and potatoes on platter with herring. Top vegetables with butter and parsley; serve at once. Yield 3 or 4 servings.

MACKEREL

boned mackerel with lemon sauce

5 small mackerel, cleaned
1 cup fine soft bread crumbs
2 tablespoons chopped chives
2 tablespoons freshly minced parsley
1 slice of bacon, finely chopped
Grated rind and juice of 1 lemon
Salt and freshly ground pepper to taste

Have fish dealer remove heads and tails from mackerel; bone without cutting mackerel in half. If this is not possible, cut off head and tail; slit fish down underside. Remove entrails; rinse fish. Lay mackerel open; lift out bones in one piece, using a small, sharp knife.

Combine bread crumbs, chives, parsley, bacon, lemon rind and juice, salt, and pepper in bowl; mix well. Divide into 5 equal parts; shape each part into roll that will fit in mackerel cavity. Place 1 roll inside each mackerel; place each mackerel on sheet of lightly oiled aluminum foil. Wrap loosely; seal edges. Place foil packets on baking sheet. Bake in preheated 375°F oven 20 to 25 minutes, depending on size, until mackerel is tender and flakes easily. Unwrap; arrange on serving platter. Garnish with lemon slices and parsley sprigs. Pour half the Lemon Sauce over mackerel; serve rest hot in sauceboat. Yield 5 servings.

lemon sauce
½ teaspoon freshly ground pepper
2 cloves garlic, pressed
1 tablespoon dried tarragon
1 teaspoon salt

hearty skinny halibut

Combine wine, lemon juice, and seasonings; pour over vegetables. Bake in 350°F oven 25 to 30 minutes, until fish flakes easily. Yield 6 servings.

boned mackerel with lemon sauce

2 tablespoons freshly minced parsley
2 lemons, cut into sections
1 cup vegetable oil
1 tablespoon wine vinegar

Place pepper, garlic, tarragon, salt, and parsley in blender container; blend. Add oil very slowly alternating with drops of vinegar; blend well after each addition. Place in top of double boiler.

Cut lemon sections into small pieces; add with any juice to sauce. Mix well; place over hot water until heated through. Yield About 1¼ cups.

lenten mackerel

king-mackerel steaks with sauce provençale

2 pounds king-mackerel or other fish steaks, fresh
    or frozen
2 tablespoons melted butter or margarine
1 teaspoon salt
⅛ teaspoon pepper
Paprika
Sauce Provençale

Thaw fish if frozen. Place in single layer on well-greased baking pan, 15 × 10 × 1 inches. Brush with butter; sprinkle with salt, pepper, and paprika. Broil about 4 inches from source of heat 10 to 15 minutes, until fish flakes easily. Fish need not be turned during broiling. Serve with Sauce Provençale. Yield 6 servings.

sauce provençale
4 medium tomatoes, peeled, cut into wedges,
    seeded
½ teaspoon sugar
2 tablespoons butter or margarine
¼ cup chopped green onion
1 clove garlic, minced

½ cup dry white wine
½ cup butter or margarine
2 tablespoons chopped parsley
¼ teaspoon salt
⅛ teaspoon pepper

Sprinkle tomatoes with sugar; set aside.

Melt 2 tablespoons butter in small saucepan; add onion and garlic. Cover; cook 2 to 3 minutes. Add wine; cook, stirring constantly, until liquid is slightly reduced. Add tomatoes and remaining ingredients; heat, stirring gently, just until butter melts. Yield 2 cups.

lenten mackerel

4 medium tomatoes, skinned
1 small onion, thinly sliced
4 peppercorns
2 strips lemon peel
4 thick mackerel or snapper steaks
Leaves of 4 small thyme sprigs
Leaves of 2 fennel sprigs
Salt to taste
½ cup Basic Fish Stock (see Index)
½ cup dry white wine

Slice tomatoes; arrange tomato and onion slices in well-buttered shallow baking pan. Add peppercorns and lemon peel; arrange steaks over mixture. Sprinkle with thyme and fennel; season with

370

salt. Pour stock and wine into baking pan; cover. Bake in preheated 325°F oven 20 to 25 minutes, until mackerel flakes easily.

One-half teaspoon powdered thyme and 1 teaspoon dried fennel can be substituted for thyme and fennel leaves. Bottled clam juice can be substituted for fish stock. Yield 4 servings.

pickled mackerel

3 red onions
1 cup plus 1½ tablespoons vinegar
Dash of salt
20 peppercorns
2 bay leaves
4 whole mackerels
1 bunch dill, chopped

Peel onions; slice into rings.

Boil vinegar, salt, peppercorns, and bay leaves in pot; set aside to cool.

Wash, clean, fillet, and halve mackerels; cut each piece in half again. Dry thoroughly. Put into glass pot; cover with onion rings. Spread marinade on top; let stand at least 24 hours. Serve with chopped dill. Yield 16 pieces.

stuffed spanish mackerel

3 to 4 pounds dressed Spanish mackerel or other dressed fish, fresh or frozen
1½ teaspoons salt
¼ teaspoon pepper
Vegetable Stuffing
2 tablespoons melted butter or margarine

Thaw fish if frozen. Clean, wash, and dry fish. Sprinkle inside and out with salt and pepper. Place on well-greased bake-and-serve platter, 18 × 13 inches.

Prepare stuffing; stuff fish. Brush with butter. Bake in 350°F oven 30 to 45 minutes, until fish flakes easily. Yield 6 servings.

vegetable stuffing
½ cup butter or margarine
1½ cups chopped onion
1 cup chopped celery
1 cup chopped fresh mushrooms
½ cup chopped green pepper
1 clove garlic, minced
2 tomatoes, peeled, seeded, chopped
3 cups soft bread crumbs
½ teaspoon salt

Melt butter in saucepan; add onion, celery, mushrooms, pepper, and garlic. Cover; cook until tender. Combine all ingredients; mix well. Yield 3½ cups.

pickled mackerel

PERCH

fried yellow perch lake erie–style

2 pounds (about 15) fresh or frozen yellow perch or other small fish, split, cleaned, boned
1½ teaspoons salt
¼ teaspoon pepper
½ cup all-purpose flour
2 tablespoons cornstarch
1 cup water
1 egg yolk, slightly beaten
1 egg white, beaten until stiff
Fat for deep frying

Thaw fish if frozen. Sprinkle fish with 1 teaspoon salt and pepper; set aside.

Combine flour, cornstarch, and ½ teaspoon salt.

Blend together water and egg yolk; stir into flour mixture until smooth. Fold in egg white. Dip fish into batter; deep-fat fry at 350°F 2 to 3 minutes, depending on size of fish, until fish is golden brown. Drain on absorbent paper. Yield 6 servings.

perch turbans a la newburg

2 pounds ocean perch or other fish fillets, fresh or frozen
1 teaspoon salt

¼ **teaspoon pepper**
¼ **cup melted butter or margarine**
2 cups cooked rice
Paprika
Parsley sprigs

Thaw fish if frozen. Skin fillets; cut into serving size portions. Sprinkle with salt and pepper. Roll into turbans; secure with toothpicks. Place on ends in well-greased baking dish, 8 × 8 × 2 inches. Brush with butter. Bake in 350°F oven 15 to 20 minutes, until fish flakes easily. To serve, remove toothpicks from turbans; place on bed of boiled rice. Spoon Newburg Sauce over turbans; garnish with paprika and parsley sprigs. Yield 6 servings.

perch turbans a la newburg

newburg sauce
½ cup butter or margarine
¼ cup all-purpose flour
½ teaspoon salt
⅛ teaspoon cayenne pepper
3 cups half-and-half cream
6 egg yolks, beaten
⅓ cup sherry

Melt butter in saucepan; stir in flour, salt, and cayenne. Add cream gradually; cook until thick and smooth, stirring constantly. Stir a little hot sauce into egg yolks; add to remaining sauce, stirring constantly. Remove from heat; slowly stir in sherry.

ROCKFISH

rockfish imperial

1 medium onion, cut up
2 stalks celery, cut up
1 carrot, cut up
Dash of salt and pepper
2 pounds rockfish
½ cup mayonnaise
1 teaspoon dry mustard
1 teaspoon Worcestershire sauce
1 teaspoon salt
6 drops Tabasco sauce
Paprika
Butter

Place onion, celery, carrot, salt and pepper in pot of water to cover ingredients; bring to boil. Turn to low heat. Add fish; cook gently 1 hour. Remove fish; flake. Add remaining ingredients; mix. Place portions of fish in individual baking shells or ramekins. Add 2 tablespoons mayonnaise, dash of paprika, and pat of butter on each portion. Sprinkle of bread crumbs can be added. Bake at 350°F 25 minutes or until brown. Yield 6 to 8 servings.

sweet-'n-sour whole rockfish

6 pounds dressed rockfish or other fish, fresh or frozen
¼ cup salad oil
2 teaspoons salt
¼ teaspoon pepper
Sweet-'n-Sour Sauce
3 cups cooked rice

Thaw fish if frozen. Slash fish on both sides every 2 inches about ¼ inch deep. Coat generously with oil; sprinkle inside and out with salt and pepper. Place on heavy foil on large cookie sheet or shallow roasting pan. Bake in 350°F oven

about 50 minutes, until fish flakes easily. (Allow about 10 minutes per inch of width at widest part of fish.) Remove fish to large heated platter. Pour Sweet-'n-Sour Sauce over; serve with cooked rice. Yield 6 servings.

sweet-'n-sour sauce
1 cup sugar
1 cup vinegar
2 tablespoons soy sauce
4 tomatoes, quartered
2 large onions, cut into wedges
2 green peppers, sliced
2 tablespoons cornstarch
2 tablespoons water
1 tablespoon salad oil

Combine sugar, vinegar, and soy sauce; bring to boil. Add tomatoes, onions, and peppers; bring to boil.

Combine cornstarch and water; add to vegetable mixture. Cook until thickened; stir constantly. Add oil. Yield about 3 cups.

SALMON

broiled salmon steak

4 salmon steaks (⅓ to ½ pound each)
French Dressing (see Index)
2 tablespoons melted butter or oil
Salt and pepper
Juice of 1 lemon
Chopped parsley
Béarnaise Sauce (see Index)

Brush salmon with French dressing; let stand 1 hour. Put in broiler; brush with butter. Broil 12 to 15 minutes; cook on both sides. Put on hot platter; season to taste with salt, pepper, and lemon juice; sprinkle with chopped parsley. Serve with Béarnaise Sauce. Yield 4 servings.

deviled salmon

2 tablespoons minced onion
2 tablespoons green pepper
3 tablespoons butter
1 cup canned tomato soup
1 teaspoon prepared mustard
½ teaspoon salt
1 teaspoon lemon juice
2 cups flaked canned salmon
½ cup buttered bread crumbs
6 thin slices lemon
Paprika

Lightly brown onion and pepper in butter. Add soup and seasonings; simmer a few minutes. Add salmon; pile into individual baking dishes. Top with crumbs; place lemon slices, sprinkled with paprika, on top. Bake in 400°F oven until crumbs are browned, about 15 minutes. Yield 6 servings.

italian-style salmon steaks

italian-style salmon steaks

2 pounds salmon or other fish steaks, fresh or frozen
2 cups Italian dressing
2 tablespoons lemon juice
2 teaspoons salt
¼ teaspoon pepper
Paprika

Thaw steaks, if frozen; pat dry with toweling. Cut into serving-size portions; place in single layer in shallow baking dish.

Combine remaining ingredients except paprika. Pour sauce over fish; let stand 30 minutes, turning once. Remove fish; reserve sauce for basting. Place fish in well-greased hinged wire grills or on rack in open roasting pan. Sprinkle with paprika. Cook about 4 inches from moderately hot coals or preheated broiler 8 minutes. Baste with sauce; sprinkle with paprika. Turn; cook 7 to 10 minutes, until fish flakes easily. Place on heated platter. Garnish with parsley and lemon wedges. Yield 6 servings.

normandy salmon steaks with hollandaise sauce

¼ pound fresh small mushrooms
1 tablespoon butter
½ cup white wine
6 tablespoons water
½ teaspoon salt
⅛ teaspoon white pepper
4 salmon steaks, each about 6 to 8 ounces
Juice of ½ lemon
1 recipe Hollandaise Sauce (see Index)
8 ounces fresh oysters
1 (4½-ounce) can deveined shrimp
1 ounce truffles, sliced (optional, found in specialty stores)

Clean mushrooms; cut into thin slices.

Heat butter in frypan. Add mushrooms; sauté 3 minutes. Add ¼ cup wine and water. Season with salt and pepper; simmer 10 minutes.

Meanwhile, rinse salmon under cold running water; pat dry. Sprinkle with lemon juice; let stand 5 minutes.

Strain mushrooms; reserve juice. Set aside.

Add mushroom juice to frypan. Add rest of wine; bring to boil. Add salmon; cover. Simmer over low heat 20 minutes.

While salmon is cooking, prepare Hollandaise Sauce; keep warm.

Remove steaks with slotted skimmer to preheated platter; keep warm.

Add oysters to simmering stock. Heat about 5 minutes, until edges begin to curl. Add shrimp; just heat through. Remove; drain. Spoon around salmon steaks. Pour Hollandaise Sauce over salmon. Garnish with reserved reheated mushrooms and truffle slices if desired. Yield 4 servings.

salmon croquettes

2 cups canned salmon, drained
2 cups mashed potatoes
1½ teaspoons salt
⅛ teaspoon pepper
1 egg, beaten
1 tablespoon chopped parsley
1 teaspoon lemon juice
Flour
Seasoned bread crumbs
Fat for deep frying

Mix together in large bowl salmon, potatoes, salt, pepper, egg, parsley, and lemon juice. This should be a fairly dry mixture that can be easily shaped into croquettes. (Refrigerate an hour before shaping.)

When croquettes are ready to be fried, roll in flour, then in seasoned bread crumbs.

Heat fat to 375°F in deep kettle or saucepan. Put in a few croquettes, so they will have room to brown evenly on all sides. Cook about 3 minutes each. Drain on paper towels; keep warm on heated platter until all are fried. Yield about 12 croquettes.

salmon au gratin

2 cups canned salmon
1 cup Basic White Sauce (see Index)
1 tablespoon lemon juice
¼ cup bread crumbs
1 tablespoon butter or margarine
⅛ teaspoon paprika

Flake salmon; remove all skin and bones. Combine with sauce; stir in lemon juice. Put in greased baking dish. Cover with bread crumbs; dot with butter. Bake in 400°F oven 20 minutes. Sprinkle with paprika. Yield 6 servings.

salmon loaf

1 (16-ounce) can salmon
½ cup milk
3 cups soft bread crumbs
¼ cup butter or margarine, melted
⅓ cup salmon liquid
3 egg yolks, beaten
2 tablespoons finely chopped green pepper
2 tablespoons finely chopped onion
1 tablespoon lemon juice
⅛ teaspoon pepper
3 egg whites, stiffly beaten

Drain salmon; save liquid. Flake salmon.
Heat milk. Add bread crumbs and butter; let stand 5 minutes. Add salmon liquid; beat until smooth. Add egg yolks, green pepper, onion, lemon juice, pepper, and salmon; mix well. Fold in egg whites. Pour into well-greased 1½-quart loaf pan. Bake at 350°F 40 to 50 minutes, until firm in center. Remove from oven; let stand 5 minutes. Loosen from sides of pan with spatula;

invert onto serving platter. Serve plain or with a sauce. Yield 6 servings.

salmon paysanne

2 pounds salmon or other fish steaks, fresh or frozen
½ teaspoon salt
¼ teaspoon white pepper
1 can (4 ounces) sliced mushrooms, drained
½ cup sliced green onions
¼ cup catsup
2 tablespoons butter or margarine, melted
1 teaspoon soy sauce

Thaw steaks, if frozen; pat dry with toweling. Cut into serving-size portions. Place in greased baking dish, 12 × 8 × 2 inches; sprinkle with salt and pepper.
Combine remaining ingredients; spread over fish. Bake in 350°F oven 25 to 30 minutes, until fish flakes easily. Yield 6 servings.

salmon supper ring

1 tablespoon butter
1 tablespoon cornstarch
½ cup milk
Salt and pepper
1 small can salmon, drained, flaked
1 teaspoon chopped capers
1 teaspoon lemon juice
1 package (2 cups) biscuit dough
Egg or milk to glaze

Melt butter in saucepan; add cornstarch mixed with milk. Season to taste; add salmon, capers, and lemon juice. Mix well; cool.

salmon paysanne

375

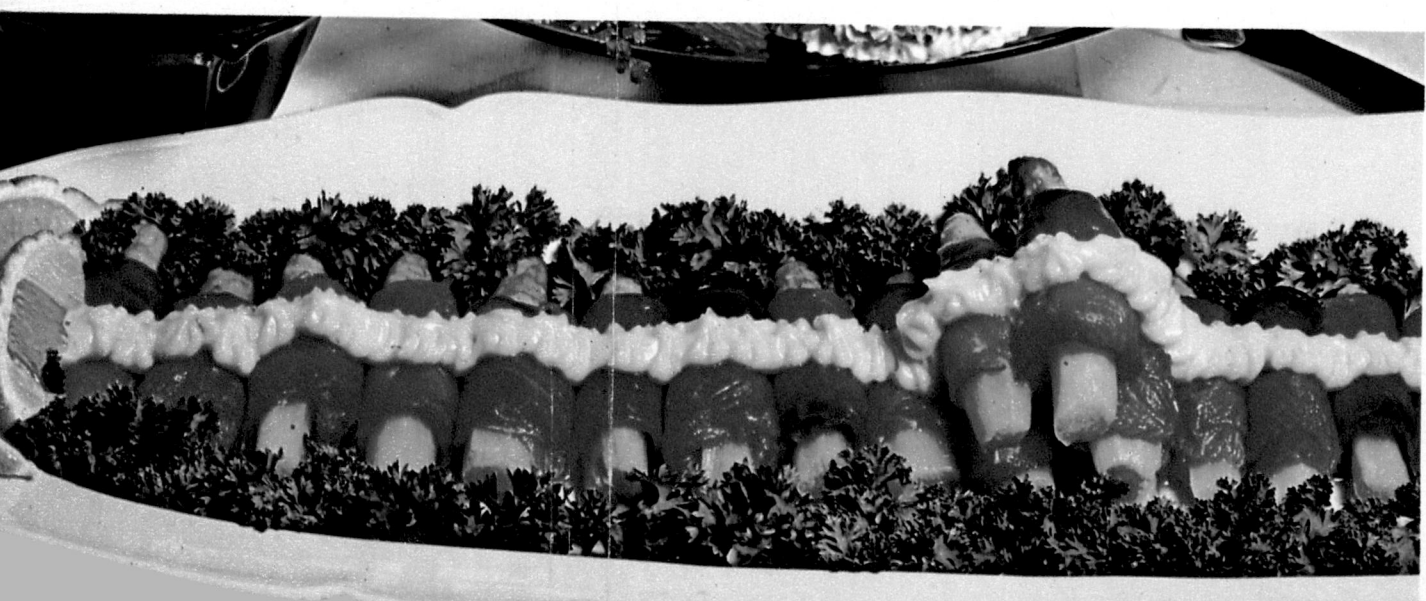

salmon supper ring

Mix biscuit dough according to directions; roll thinly into oblong shape. Spread with filling. Moisten edges of dough; roll up. Move carefully onto greased baking sheet; twist into horseshoe shape. Using kitchen scissors or sharp knife, make cuts about two-thirds of way into roll. Turn each section on its side so filling is exposed a little. Glaze with beaten egg or milk. Bake in preheated 450°F oven 15 to 20 minutes. Garnish with capers and parsley. Yield 4 servings.

smoked salmon rolls

20 slices smoked salmon
20 canned asparagus spears (preferably white),
  drained

½ cup mayonnaise
6 lemon wedges

Wrap salmon around asparagus spears; arrange on serving dish. Pipe mayonnaise over rolls. Add lemon wedges to dish; garnish with parsley. Chill well before serving. Yield 5 or 6 servings.

SARDINES

baked fresh sardines

3 pounds fresh sardines, dressed
1 teaspoon salt
½ teaspoon pepper
2 tablespoons olive oil

smoked salmon rolls

sardines with chopped eggs

2 Spanish onions, peeled, thinly sliced
2 large tomatoes, peeled, sliced
1 green pepper, seeds removed, sliced into rings
3 tablespoons chopped chives
1/3 cup dry white wine
6 large lettuce leaves (use outer leaves that are
generally throw away)

Pat fish dry; sprinkle with salt and pepper.

Grease large casserole with oil; arrange onions in layers on bottom of casserole. Layer fish over onions; cover fish with tomatoes and green pepper. Sprinkle with chives; pour wine over fish and vegetables. Cover with well-washed lettuce leaves. Marinate in refrigerator 6 hours.

Bake, covered, in 375°F oven 30 minutes or until fish flakes easily. Remove lettuce leaves; discard. Bake 10 minutes. Yield 6 servings.

sardines with chopped eggs

1 flat can sardines in mustard
2 flat cans sardines in oil
4 hard-boiled eggs
Fresh parsley

Place sardines in mustard in small bowl; mash. Place off center on large serving plate.

Drain sardines in oil; place on plate in fan shape as shown in illustration.

Separate egg yolks and whites; chop each fine. Mound egg whites on left of sardines to center of plate. Hold knife in center of plate against egg whites; mound egg yolks on right half of plate.

Remove knife. Place border of parsley around sardines. Garnish with cancelled lemon slices and strips of lemon peel. Serve with Basic Vinaigrette (see Index). Yield about 4 servings.

sea-garden sardine antipasto

3 cans (3¾ or 4 ounces each) Maine sardines
2 cans (4 ounces each) button mushrooms
Marinade
6 large lettuce leaves
24 cucumber slices
18 celery sticks
12 radish roses
12 tomato wedges
6 green pepper rings

Drain sardines and mushrooms; place in shallow baking dish. Pour marinade over; chill 30 minutes.

Prepare vegetables; chill.

Remove sardines and mushrooms from marinade; drain.

Arrange all ingredients, except marinade, attractively on lettuce leaves, dividing ingredients evenly among servings.

Lobster, tuna, crab, pickled herring, or shrimp can also be used in this recipe. Yield 6 servings.

marinade
½ cup low-calorie French dressing
¼ cup soy sauce

2 tablespoons wine vinegar
2 tablespoons water
1 clove garlic, crushed
Dash of powdered ginger
Dash of pepper

Combine all ingredients; mix thoroughly. Yield about 1 cup.

SHAD AND SHAD ROE

baked shad

1 (3- to 3½-pound) shad
Salt
Ice-cold water
Good cooking oil

Split fish down back; remove backbone, viscera, and roe (reserve roe). Pull out rib bones with pliers. Wash; cover with salt solution made in proportion of 1 tablespoon salt to 1 cup ice-cold water. Let stand ½ hour or more. Drain; dry.

Preheat oven to 500°F.

Prepare stuffing; stuff fish. Wrap with string to keep in stuffing. Place on greased baking pan; sprinkle top of fish with oil. Bake 10 minutes. Lower heat to 400°F; cook 15 to 20 minutes. Serve with sauceboat of melted butter; garnish with lemon wedges. Yield 6 to 8 servings.

stuffing
Shad roe
1 tablespoon grated onion
1 tablespoon chopped parsley
⅔ cup soft bread crumbs
2 tablespoons soft butter
½ teaspoon salt
⅛ teaspoon white pepper

Scald roe in boiling water 2 minutes; drain. Scrape eggs into bowl. Add onion, parsley, bread crumbs, butter, salt, and pepper; mix until well blended.

broiled shad

⅓ to ½ pound fish per person

Wash shad; remove head and tail. Clean; split down back. Remove backbone with as many other bones as possible. Place, skin-side-down, on greased broiler. Spread with melted fat; sprinkle with salt and pepper. Broil 20 to 25 minutes, depending on size of fish. Remove to hot platter; garnish with watercress and lemon slices. Yield as desired.

maryland shad, bones and all

1 (4-pound) shad, dressed
Salt and freshly ground pepper to taste
Lemon and pepper seasoning
3 cups water
1 cup white wine
2 ribs celery, broken into pieces
1 tablespoon instant minced onion or 1 small onion, chopped
2 bay leaves

Preheat oven to 300°F.

Wash shad; dry with paper towels. Sprinkle fish inside and out with lemon and pepper seasoning. Put on rack of baking pan. Add water and wine to level just under fish. Add remaining ingredients. Cover tightly; steam 5 hours. Baste often with liquid in pan. Yield 6 servings.

shad stuffed with shad roe nantaise

1 pair shad roe
1½ tablespoons finely chopped shallots
1 hard-cooked egg, coarsely chopped
¼ cup finely chopped parsley
1 cup fresh bread crumbs
½ cup milk
Salt and freshly ground pepper
2 shad fillets, about 1½ pounds
5 tablespoons butter
½ cup dry white wine
8 thin slices lemon for garnish (optional)
Chopped parsley for garnish

Preheat oven to 400°F.

Cut roe in half; slice through membrane. Remove and discard membrane. Put roe on flat surface; add shallots, egg, and parsley. Chop together to blend well.

Put crumbs into mixing bowl. Add milk; stir to blend. Add roe mixture and salt and pepper to taste.

Open up fillets, skin-side-down; sprinkle with salt and pepper. There are 2 flaps to each fillet. Open one; spread roe filling, smoothing it over. Bring up sides of fillet. Cover with other fillet; let flaps of fillet fall down and overlap stuffed fillet. Tie "package" neatly with string in 4 or 5 places to keep fillets and filling intact.

Butter baking dish large enough to hold stuffed fish. (Use about 2 tablespoons butter.) Sprinkle with salt and pepper. Arrange fish in dish; dot with 2 tablespoons butter. Place in oven. Bake 15 minutes. Spoon 1 tablespoon wine over fish; bake, basting often with pan juices, about 15 minutes. Pour remaining wine over all; bake and baste 15 minutes. It is imperative that you baste often as fish cooks. Remove fish. Add remaining tablespoon butter to pan liquid. Remove strings from fish. Using fingers, pull off and discard skin of fish from top. Skin comes off easily. Baste fish. Garnish, if desired, with lemon slices. Sprinkle with chopped parsley. Carve crosswise and serve. Yield 6 to 8 servings.

shad roe

Wash and dry 1 to 1¼ pounds shad roe, using care not to break skin. Let stand 5 minutes in ice water; drain. Simmer in salt water 5 minutes to make firm. Sprinkle with salt, pepper, and flour. Melt 2 tablespoons butter or margarine in frying pan. When hot, put in roe; cook slowly until brown on one side. Turn; brown other side. Cook 20 to 30 minutes. Garnish with lemon and parsley; serve very hot with crisp bacon. Yield 4 servings.

SMELTS

fried smelts

2 pounds smelts, heads off, cleaned, washed
2 eggs, beaten

2 tablespoons milk
1 teaspoon salt
¼ teaspoon pepper
½ cup flour
½ cup dried bread or cracker crumbs

Drain smelts as dry as possible on paper towels.

Mix eggs, milk, and seasonings in bowl.

Mix flour and crumbs together on large piece of waxed paper. Dip each smelt in liquid, then in crumbs.

Deep fry at 370°F 3 to 5 minutes; turn each fish once. Do not fry too many at a time. Drain on paper toweling; season.

If using skillet, sauté in butter or oil (or both), allowing 1½ to 2 minutes on each side. Drain; season. Serve with Tartar Sauce (see Index). Yield 4 to 6 servings.

svenskie smelt fry

20 medium (about 1 pound) smelts or other small fish, fresh or frozen
1 (2-ounce) can anchovy fillets
¼ teaspoon salt
⅛ teaspoon pepper
½ cup all-purpose flour
3 tablespoons butter or margarine
3 tablespoons cooking oil
4 slices rye bread, crusts removed, toasted
Svenskie Sauce
Sliced tomatoes and cucumber (optional)
Lemon twists and dill sprigs (garnish)

Thaw fish if frozen. Remove heads; clean; bone.

Drain anchovies; reserve oil for sauce. Cut in half lengthwise; place ½ anchovy inside each fish. Sprinkle with salt and pepper; roll in flour.

In large skillet heat butter and cooking oil to moderate temperature. Add fish; fry until crisp. Place 5 fish on each slice of rye toast; spoon sauce over smelt. Serve with sliced tomatoes and

fried smelts

svenskie smelt fry

cucumber; garnish with lemon twists and dill sprigs. Yield 4 servings.

svenskie sauce
Reserved anchovy oil
2 tablespoons minced onion
1½ tablespoons flour
½ teaspoon salt
1⅓ cups half-and-half cream
1 egg yolk, beaten
1 tablespoon lemon juice
1 tablespoon chopped fresh dill (or ½ teaspoon dried dillweed)

In saucepan cook onion in anchovy oil until tender. Blend in flour and salt, gradually stir in cream. Cook until thickened; stir constantly. Add a little hot sauce to egg yolk; add to remaining sauce, stirring constantly. Heat until thickened. Add lemon juice and dill. Yield 1⅓ cups.

SNAPPER

baked red snapper

1 (5-pound) cleaned, boned red snapper
1 teaspoon salt
1 pound boiled shrimp
1 egg
1 cup cream
½ tablespoon anchovy paste
Pepper
Paprika
1 cup sherry

Wash and drain fish; rub with salt.

Put shrimp through grinder or chop in food processor.

Beat egg and half the cream together.

Mix shrimp and anchovy paste; season with pepper, salt, and paprika. Stir into egg and cream. Add sherry; mix to smooth paste. Place stuffing inside fish; sew together with twine or fasten with kitchen skewers. Place in baking dish; pour over remaining ½ cup cream. Bake in 350°F oven until done, about 4 hours. Serve garnished with sliced cucumbers in French dressing. Yield 10 servings.

snappy snapper

spicy snapper

grilled red snapper steaks

2 pounds red snapper or other fish steaks, fresh or
   frozen
½ cup melted fat or oil
¼ cup lemon juice
2 teaspoons salt
½ teaspoon Worcestershire sauce
¼ teaspoon white pepper
Dash of liquid hot pepper sauce
Paprika

Thaw frozen steaks; pat dry with toweling. Cut
into serving-size portions; place in well-greased,
hinged wire grills.

Combine remaining ingredients, except paprika. Baste fish with sauce; sprinkle with paprika. Cook about 4 inches from moderately hot
charcoal coals or broiler 8 minutes. Baste with
sauce; sprinkle with paprika. Turn; cook 7 to 10
minutes, until fish flakes easily. Yield 6 servings.

snappy snapper

2 pounds skinless snapper or other fish fillets,
   fresh or frozen
½ cup frozen orange-juice concentrate, thawed
¼ cup salad oil
¼ cup soy sauce
¼ cup cider vinegar
½ teaspoon salt
Chopped parsley
Lemon slices

Thaw frozen fillets; pat dry with toweling. Cut
into 6 portions; place in single layer, skin-side-up,
on well-greased baking pan, 15 × 10 × 1 inches.

Combine remaining ingredients, except parsley.

Brush fish with sauce. Broil about 4 inches from
source of heat 5 minutes. Turn carefully; brush
with sauce. Broil 5 to 7 minutes, until lightly

browned and flakes easily. Sprinkle with parsley;
garnish with lemon slices. Yield 6 servings.

spicy snapper

2 pounds snapper or other fish fillets, fresh or
   frozen
⅔ cup tomato juice
3 tablespoons vinegar
2 tablespoons salad oil
1 (⅝-ounce) envelope old-fashioned
   French-dressing mix

Thaw frozen fillets. Skin fillets; cut into
serving-size portions. Place in single layer in
shallow baking dish.

Combine remaining ingredients; mix
thoroughly. Pour sauce over fish; let stand 30
minutes, turning once. Remove fish; reserve sauce
for basting. Place fish on well-greased broiler pan.
Broil about 4 inches from source of heat 4 to 5
minutes. Turn carefully; brush with sauce. Broil 4
to 5 minutes, until fish flakes easily Serve on
heated platter garnished with tomato slices and
lemon wedges. Yield 6 servings.

SOLE

fillet of sole au gratin

1½ pounds fillet of sole
2 tablespoons chopped onion
2 tablespoons chopped celery
Salt
Pepper
2 tablespoons lemon juice
2 tablespoons butter
2 tablespoons flour

grilled red snapper steaks

1 cup milk
½ cup grated American cheese

Place fillets in shallow baking pan; sprinkle with onion, celery, salt, and pepper. Add 2 tablespoons water and lemon juice. Bake in 450°F oven 10 minutes.

Melt butter; stir in flour. Add milk gradually; cook, stirring, until thickened. Add salt, pepper, and cheese; reserve about 2 tablespoons for top. Heat until cheese is melted; pour over fish.

Sprinkle remaining cheese over top; bake 10 to 15 minutes. Yield 4 to 6 servings.

heavenly sole

2 pounds skinless sole or other fish fillets, fresh or frozen
2 tablespoons lemon juice
½ cup grated Parmesan cheese
¼ cup butter or margarine, softened

3 tablespoons mayonnaise or salad dressing
3 tablespoons chopped green onion
¼ teaspoon salt
Dash of liquid hot pepper sauce

Thaw fillets if frozen; pat dry with toweling. Place fillets in single layer on well-greased bake-and-serve platter, 16 × 10 inches. Brush with lemon juice; let stand 10 minutes.

Combine remaining ingredients.

Broil fillets about 4 inches from source of heat 6 to 8 minutes, until fillets flake easily. Remove from heat; spread with cheese mixture. Broil 2 to 3 minutes or until lightly browned. Yield 6 servings.

sole with tomatoes french-style

1 pound tomatoes (about 1½ cups), peeled, seeded, chopped
2 tablespoons minced shallots
2 tablespoons minced parsley
½ teaspoon salt
Dash of pepper
1½ pounds sole fillets
¾ cup dry white wine
¼ cup water or clam juice
2 tablespoons butter or margarine
2 tablespoons flour
½ teaspoon sugar
3 to 4 tablespoons heavy cream

Mix tomatoes, shallots, parsley, salt, and pepper; place in bottom of greased flat baking dish. Place fillets over tomatoes. Add wine and water; bring to simmer on range. Cover with aluminum foil. Place in preheated 325°F oven 13 to 15 minutes, until fish is opaque. Remove fish to serving dish; keep warm.

Boil juices until mixture is reduced to about half.

Mix butter and flour; stir into juices. Cook until thickened. Add sugar, cream, and juices drained from fish on platter. Pour over fish; serve. Yield 4 servings.

stuffed fillet of sole

2 pounds boiled spinach or 1 package frozen spinach
1 teaspoon salt
⅛ teaspoon pepper
½ cup dry white wine
¼ cup bread crumbs
6 fillets of sole
½ cup finely chopped onion
2 tablespoons finely chopped parsley
2 tablespoons butter
1 cup sliced mushrooms
2 medium tomatoes, peeled, quartered

2 tablespoons flour
¼ cup whipped cream
1 tablespoon lemon juice

Drain spinach; chop. Add salt, pepper, ⅓ cup wine, and bread crumbs. Place mound on one end of each fillet; fold other end over it. Place in well-greased baking pan with onion, parsley, and remaining wine. Arrange mushrooms and tomatoes over top; cover with cooking parchment paper. Bake in 500°F oven 15 minutes. Remove fillets to heatproof platter.

Thicken gravy remaining in pan with flour blended with a little cold water. Simmer 2 or 3 minutes; stir constantly. Remove from heat; add whipped cream and lemon juice. Pour over fillets; brown in broiler. Serve immediately. Yield 6 servings.

TROUT

broiled lake trout

Split trout into two fillets; remove backbone. Wash thoroughly; remove all traces of blood or membrane. Place in salt solution made in proportion of 2 tablespoons salt to 1 cup water; let stand 8 to 10 minutes.

Preheat broiling oven about 10 minutes before using.

Oil heated broiler pan.

Brush fish with oil in which pepper has been stirred. Amount of oil required will be about ¼ cup with ¼ teaspoon pepper. Place trout on the broiler pan, skin-side-up, about 2 inches below heat unit. After 5 minutes skin should be turning brown; baste. Cook until skin is well browned; turn fish flesh-side-up. Baste again; cook until flesh side is well browned. Remove to hot platter; butter top of fish. Garnish to taste; crisp lettuce leaves, lemon slices, and parsley are suggested. Allow ⅓ to ½ pound fish per person.

broiled trout minceur

4 whole dressed fresh or frozen rainbow or other trout
1 cup clam juice or chicken broth
2 tablespoons minced onion
1 tablespoon cooking oil
1 teaspoon Worcestershire sauce
¼ teaspoon salt
⅛ teaspoon oregano
⅛ teaspoon thyme
⅛ teaspoon pepper
3 cups steamed julienne vegetables (any combination of carrots, green beans, celery, turnips, zucchini)
Chopped parsley

Thaw or bone trout as needed. (To bone, slit along entire length of backbone with sharp knife. Gently lift away top fillet, including bones and tail. Use knife to separate head from bottom fillet. Flip top fillet over, skin-side-down, lift away bone structure.)

Combine clam juice, onion, oil, Worcestershire sauce, and seasonings in saucepan. Boil liquid rapidly about 5 minutes, reducing to ½ cup.

Place opened fish, skin-side-down, on well-oiled broiler rack; brush with sauce. Broil 3 inches from heat about 5 minutes; brush with sauce once or twice while broiling. Carefully lift trout from broiler; center on warm platter. Surround with vegetables. Serve with lemon; sprinkle with chopped parsley. Yield 4 servings.

fried trout grenoble

4 freshwater trout, fresh or frozen (each about ½ pound)
Juice of 1 lemon
Salt
5 tablespoons flour
½ cup vegetable oil
¼ cup butter
1 slice dry bread, crumbled
2 tablespoons capers, drained
1 lemon, sliced
Parsley sprigs (garnish)

Thoroughly wash fish; pat dry with paper towels. Sprinkle with half the lemon juice; let stand 5 minutes. Salt trout inside and out; roll in flour.

Heat oil in frypan. Add trout; fry 5 minutes on each side or until golden. Remove fish carefully with slotted spoon; discard oil.

Melt butter in same frypan. Return trout to pan; fry 5 minutes on each side. Remove; arrange on preheated platter.

Add bread crumbs to butter; cook until browned, Pour over trout; sprinkle rest of lemon juice over trout. Top with capers; garnish with lemon slices and parsley sprigs. Yield 4 servings.

herb-stuffed trout with sauce

6 dressed fresh trout
2 bay leaves, halved
1 shallot, thinly sliced
4 peppercorns
2 or 3 sprigs parsley
Salt

fried trout grenoble (opposite)

herb-stuffed trout with sauce

½ cup wine vinegar
½ cup water
1½ cups soft bread crumbs
1 egg, beaten
2 tablespoons freshly minced parsley
1 tablespoon chopped chives
Pepper to taste
Melted butter
1 tablespoon capers
1 small lemon, cut into sections

Have fish dealer remove heads and tails from trout; bone without cutting in half. Place trout in shallow glass container.

Combine bay leaves, shallot, peppercorns, parsley, and 1 teaspoon salt; sprinkle over trout.

Mix vinegar and water; pour over trout. Marinate in refrigerator overnight. Drain trout; reserve marinade.

Combine crumbs, egg, 1 tablespoon parsley, chives, salt to taste, and pepper in bowl; mix well. Stuff trout cavities with dressing; brush trout with butter. Arrange in shallow baking dish; cover lightly with aluminum foil. Bake in preheated 375°F oven about 20 minutes, until trout flakes easily.

Strain reserved marinade; place in small saucepan. Stir in capers, remaining parsley, lemon sections, and marinade mixture; heat through.

Arrange trout on serving dish; pour sauce over. Serve hot. Yield 6 servings.

irish cured trout

1 (4-pound) or 2 (2-pound) trout, boned, butterflied, head removed
4½ teaspoons salt
½ teaspoon freshly ground pepper
½ teaspoon garlic powder
6 tablespoons olive oil
1 tablespoon brown sugar

On day curing process is begun, wash fish; pat dry with paper towels. Place on large nonmetallic platter.

Combine seasonings; place in small shaker bottle.

On day 1 rub fish with ⅓ of salt mixture. Cover with plastic wrap; refrigerate.

On day 2 drain any liquid from platter; rub fish with 2 tablespoons oil. Cover; refrigerate overnight.

Rub fish with salt mixture on days 3 and 5 and with oil on days 4 and 6.

On day 6 also rub fish with sugar.

On day 7 hang fish in cool, dry, breezy place 24 hours. To serve, slice paper-thin against grain. Yield 10 to 12 appetizer servings.

trout with almonds

6 brook trout
Oil

trout with almonds

¼ cup butter or margarine
½ cup slivered or whole almonds
6 slices bacon
Lemon wedges

Prepare trout; rub with oil. Cook on barbecue rack about 15 minutes; turn once.

Meanwhile, put butter into pan with almonds; sauté until butter is foaming and almonds are golden brown.

Place bacon on rack about 5 minutes before fish is done.

To serve, cover each fish with a slice of bacon. Pour foaming butter and almonds over trout; serve with lemon wedges. Tartar Sauce (see Index) is a good accompaniment. Yield 6 servings.

TUNA

tuna cakes

2 eggs
1 (7-ounce) can tuna, drained, flaked
1 small onion, finely chopped
4 slices bread, cubed
Salt and pepper to taste

Beat eggs slightly in bowl. Add tuna, onion, bread cubes, and seasonings; mix to moisten. Form into 4 to 6 patties; fry in skillet or on griddle until golden brown, turning once. Serve with mayonnaise. Yield 2 or 3 servings.

tuna au gratin

2 (7-ounce) cans tuna, drained
⅔ cup chopped onion
½ cup chopped green pepper
½ cup chopped pimiento (optional)
⅔ cup mayonnaise
½ cup fine dry bread or cracker crumbs
½ cup grated Parmesan cheese

Combine first 5 ingredients in mixing bowl; spoon into shallow baking dish (7 × 11 inches) or individual shells. Sprinkle with bread crumbs and cheese. Bake at 350°F 20 minutes or until thoroughly heated. Garnish with fresh parsley if desired. Yield 4 servings.

tuna lasagna

½ cup chopped onion
1 clove garlic, crushed
2 tablespoons butter
2 (7-ounce) cans tuna, drained, flaked
1 can condensed cream of celery soup
⅓ cup milk
½ teaspoon crushed dried oregano
⅛ teaspoon pepper
8 ounces lasagna noodles, cooked
4 slices mozzarella cheese

8 slices processed American or cheddar cheese
½ cup grated Parmesan cheese

In medium saucepan cook onion and garlic in butter until tender. Add tuna, soup, milk, oregano, and pepper.

Arrange noodles in 12 × 7 × 1½-inch baking dish. Over noodles arrange tuna sauce, slices of mozzarella and American cheese, and Parmesan. (Dish can be frozen at this point. If frozen, casserole should be baked at 400°F, covered 1½ hours.) Bake at 350°F 30 minutes or until heated through. Yield 6 to 8 servings.

tuna risotto

risotto
4 tablespoons oil
½ Bermuda onion, finely chopped
1½ cups long-grain rice
2 pints chicken stock, or bouillon cubes and water

sauce
2 tablespoons oil
2 tablespoons butter or margarine
½ Bermuda onion, finely chopped
2 tablespoons tomato puree
3 tablespoons wine vinegar
2 tablespoons lemon juice
1 (7- to 8-ounce) can tuna, flaked
Grated cheese

Make risotto. Heat oil in pan. Add onion; sauté until transparent. Add rice; stir over low heat until just golden. Remove from heat; add hot stock. Stir; return to heat. Cover; cook until rice is tender.

Make sauce. Heat oil and butter in pan. Add onion; cook until soft and golden. Add tomato puree, vinegar, lemon juice, tuna, and a little oil from fish. Mix well; heat through. Adjust seasoning to taste. Stir into risotto just before serving. Add a little grated cheese; serve extra cheese separately. Yield 4 or 5 servings.

tuna terrific

3 cups cooked rice
1 cup diced celery
½ cup diced green pepper
¼ pound mushrooms, sliced
¼ cup minced pimiento
⅓ cup slivered toasted almonds
2 (7-ounce) cans tuna in oil
¼ cup dry sherry
1 teaspoon salt
½ teaspoon rosemary
½ teaspoon marjoram
¼ teaspoon pepper

Cook rice.
Prepare vegetables and almonds.

tuna risotto

Drain tuna oil into skillet; heat. Add celery, onion, and green pepper; cook and stir 3 or 4 minutes. Add tuna, mushrooms, sherry, almonds, and seasonings. Heat thoroughly; stir occasionally. Combine with rice. Reheat; serve. Yield 6 servings.

VARIETY FISH

baked fish fillets

1 pound fish fillets (sole, flounder, or red snapper)
1 tablespoon chopped parsley
1 tablespoon lemon juice
¾ teaspoon seasoned salt
3 tablespoons olive oil
1 medium onion, thinly sliced
1 clove garlic, minced
1 large tomato, thinly sliced
2 tablespoons white wine
3 slices lemon

Arrange fish in 8- or 9-inch-square baking dish; sprinkle with parsley, lemon juice, and salt.

Heat oil in small skillet; fry onion and garlic until limp. Top fish with mixture, including oil from skillet. Arrange tomato on onion mixture;

baked fish fillets

pour wine over all. Bake at 350°F 30 to 35 minutes, until the fish flakes easily. Garnish with fresh lemon slices. Yield 2 or 3 servings.

baked fish with mushroom stuffing

mushroom stuffing
3 tablespoons butter
1 small onion, chopped
½ cup chopped fresh mushrooms
2 cups dry bread crumbs
¾ cup chicken stock
1 egg, beaten
½ teaspoon salt
¼ teaspoon pepper

4-pound whole fish of your choice, dressed
1 teaspoon salt
4 strips bacon

Prepare Mushroom Stuffing. Put butter in saucepan. Add onion; sauté until golden but not brown. Add mushrooms; cook until water from mushrooms cooks away. Remove from heat. Add bread crumbs, chicken stock, egg, ½ teaspoon salt, and pepper; mix well with hands.

Clean and rub inside of fish with 1 teaspoon salt. Stuff fish; fasten with toothpicks. Place, underside-down, in greased baking dish; layer bacon over fish. Bake in 350°F oven 1 hour or until fish flakes easily. Remove to hot platter to serve. Yield 8 servings.

batter-fried fish

1 pound fish fillets
1 egg
2 tablespoons milk
¼ teaspoon salt
½ cup fine dry bread crumbs

batter-fried fish

2 cups peanut oil
Lemon wedges
Parsley

Wash fish; pat dry.

Combine egg, milk, and salt in bowl; beat until blended. Dip fish into mixture; coat well with crumbs.

Pour oil into skillet; heat to 375°F. Fry fish until golden brown on both sides; drain on paper toweling. Place in serving container; garnish with lemon wedges and parsley. Yield 4 servings.

broiled fish fillets or steaks

2 pounds fish fillets or steaks, fresh or frozen
2 tablespoons melted fat or oil
2 tablespoons lemon juice
1 teaspoon salt
½ teaspoon paprika
Dash of pepper

Thaw frozen fish. Cut fish into 6 portions. Place in single layer, skin-side-down, on well-greased baking pan, 15 × 10 × 1 inches.

Combine remaining ingredients; mix well. Pour over fish. Broil about 4 inches from source of heat 10 to 15 minutes, until fish flake easily. Baste once during broiling with sauce in pan. Yield 6 servings.

crunchy fish–noodle bake

1 pound fish fillets, fresh or frozen
1 (11-ounce) can mandarin-orange segments
1 (10½-ounce) can condensed cream of mushroom soup
1 cup sliced celery
½ cup chopped onion
½ cup chopped salted peanuts
½ teaspoon salt
1 (3-ounce) can chow-mein noodles

Thaw fish if frozen; pat dry with paper toweling. Cut into 1-inch pieces.

Drain orange segments; save ¼ cup syrup. Save about ¼ of orange segments for garnish.

Combine soup, reserved orange syrup, remaining orange segments, fish, celery, onion, peanuts, salt, and ½ of noodles; mix. Spread mixture into shallow 1½-quart casserole. Cover with aluminum foil; crimp it to edges of casserole. Bake in 350°F oven 30 minutes. Uncover; sprinkle with remaining noodles. Cook about 10 minutes, until hot and bubbly and fish flakes easily. Garnish with orange segments. Yield 4 servings.

fast fish dinner

2 cups canned tomatoes (1-pound can) drained
2 tablespoons butter or margarine
1½ cups diced celery
2 medium onions, thinly sliced

fast fish dinner

1 pound frozen fish fillets, cut into bite-size pieces
1 teaspoon salt
¼ teaspoon black pepper
2 cups canned potatoes, drained, sliced
Parsley (garnish)

Put tomatoes and butter in medium skillet; bring to boil. Add celery and onions; simmer until onions are soft, 3 to 5 minutes. Add fish, salt, pepper, and potatoes; stir once. Cover skillet; simmer 10 minutes. Garnish with parsley; serve. Yield 4 servings.

fish cakes

1 egg
1 tablespoon lemon juice
1 onion, minced fine
2 tablespoons prepared mustard
½ teaspoon salt
¼ teaspoon pepper
1 teaspoon parsley flakes
1 pound cooked fish, boned, flaked
¼ to ½ cup cornflake crumbs
Fat for deep frying

Mix egg, lemon juice, onion, and seasonings in bowl; toss with fish. Add enough cornflake crumbs so fish cakes shape easily. Roll each cake in extra crumbs to coat outside.

Heat fat in medium skillet; fry cakes until crisp and brown on outside. Drain on paper towels; place on heated platter. Serve with sautéed chopped celery and scallions. Yield 4 to 6 servings.

fish fillets baked with sour cream

1 pound firm whitefish fillets
Salt and pepper
½ cup sour cream
1½ tablespoons Parmesan cheese
¾ teaspoon Hungarian sweet paprika
¼ teaspoon crumbled tarragon
2 tablespoons seasoned bread crumbs
2 tablespoons butter or margarine
Finely chopped parsley
Lemon wedges

Arrange fish in single layer in lightly greased shallow baking dish; season with salt and pepper.

Combine sour cream, cheese, paprika, and tarragon; mix well. Spread evenly over fillets. Sprinkle with bread crumbs; dot with butter. Bake in preheated 350°F oven 20 to 25 minutes, until fish flakes easily. Sprinkle with parsley; serve with lemon wedges. Yield 4 servings.

fish fillets in creole sauce

1 medium onion, chopped
½ cup chopped celery
1 tablespoon butter or margarine
1 (8-ounce) can tomato sauce
½ teaspoon salt
½ teaspoon curry powder
Dash of freshly ground black pepper

fish cakes

1 cup chopped green pepper
2 pounds frozen fish fillets

Sauté onion and celery in butter in large skillet. Add rest of ingredients, except fish. While mixture simmers, cut fish blocks into thirds (6 pieces). Put fish in skillet side by side; do not pile them on each other. Bring to boil; reduce to simmer. Cook about 15 minutes, until fish flakes easily. Yield 4 to 6 servings.

fish fillets india

1 pound fresh or frozen fillets
½ cup flour
2 teaspoons curry powder
¼ teaspoon salt
½ cup butter or margarine
½ cup chopped blanched almonds
Chives, chopped
Chutney

Thaw fish, if frozen; pat dry with toweling.

Mix flour, curry powder, and salt well. Thoroughly coat each piece of fish with mixture.

Heat butter in large skillet. Brown fish over moderate heat about 4 minutes per side. When fish flakes easily, it is done through. Remove fillets; put onto heated serving dish.

Add almonds to butter left in skillet; stir until browned. Pour over fish. Garnish with chopped chives; serve chutney as a relish. Yield 4 servings.

fish fillets on spinach

1½ pounds fish fillets
Juice of 1 lemon
2 pounds fresh spinach
2 tablespoons vegetable oil
1 medium onion, chopped

fish fillets in creole sauce

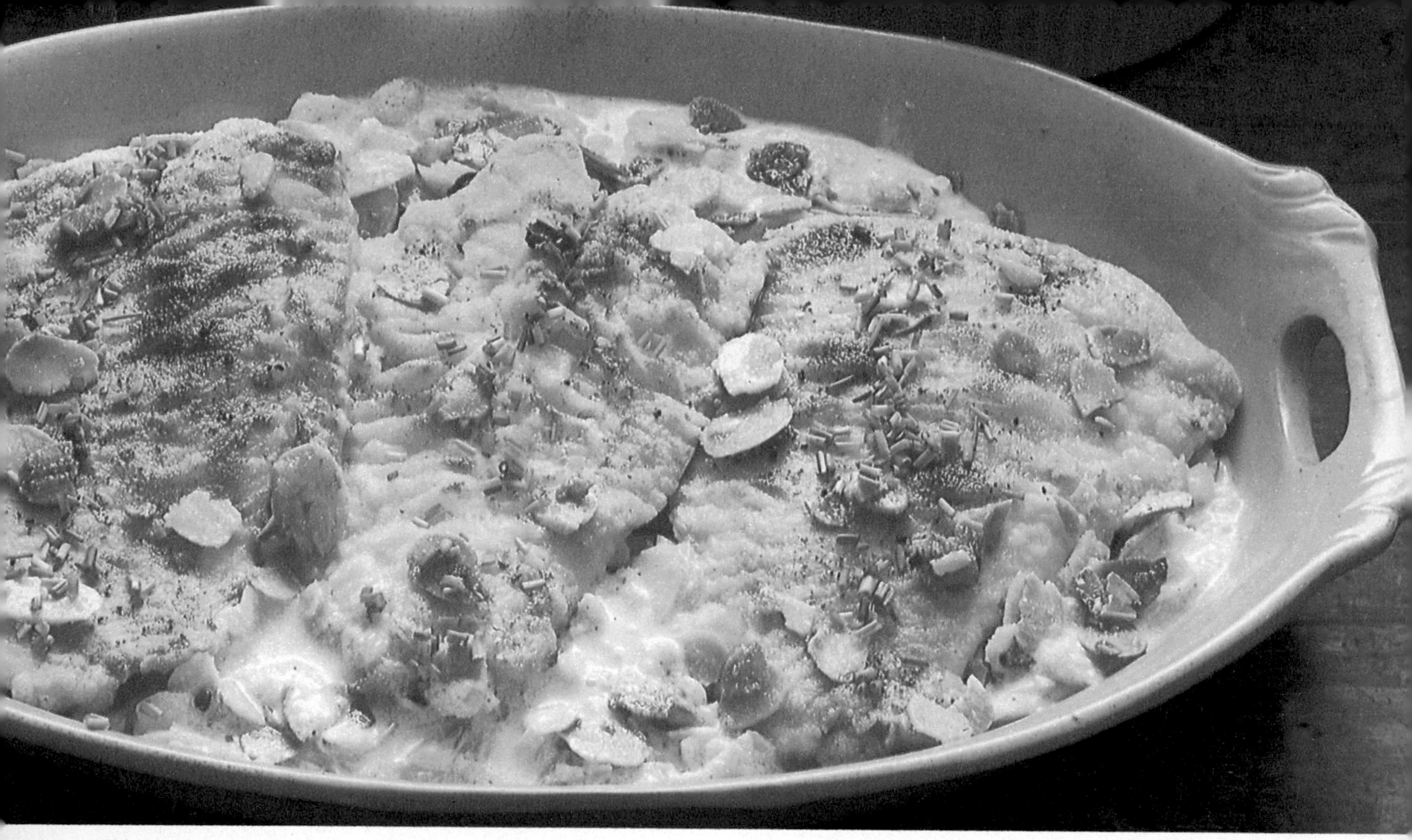

fish fillets india

1 teaspoon butter or margarine
½ teaspoon salt
⅛ teaspoon white pepper
½ teaspoon grated fresh nutmeg
2 tomatoes, peeled, sliced
¼ cup grated low-fat mozzarella cheese

Wash fish; pat dry. Sprinkle with lemon juice; let stand 10 minutes.

Wash spinach well; chop coarsely.

Heat oil in frypan. Add onion; sauté until soft. Fry fish in pan with onions a few minutes on each side, until golden brown. Remove fish and onions; reserve.

Add spinach to frypan; stir-fry 4 to 5 minutes.

Grease a casserole dish with butter; add spinach. Arrange fish fillets on spinach; sprinkle with salt, pepper, and nutmeg. Place tomatoes on fish; sprinkle with cheese. Bake in preheated 350°F oven 15 minutes. Yield 6 servings.

fish fillets on spinach

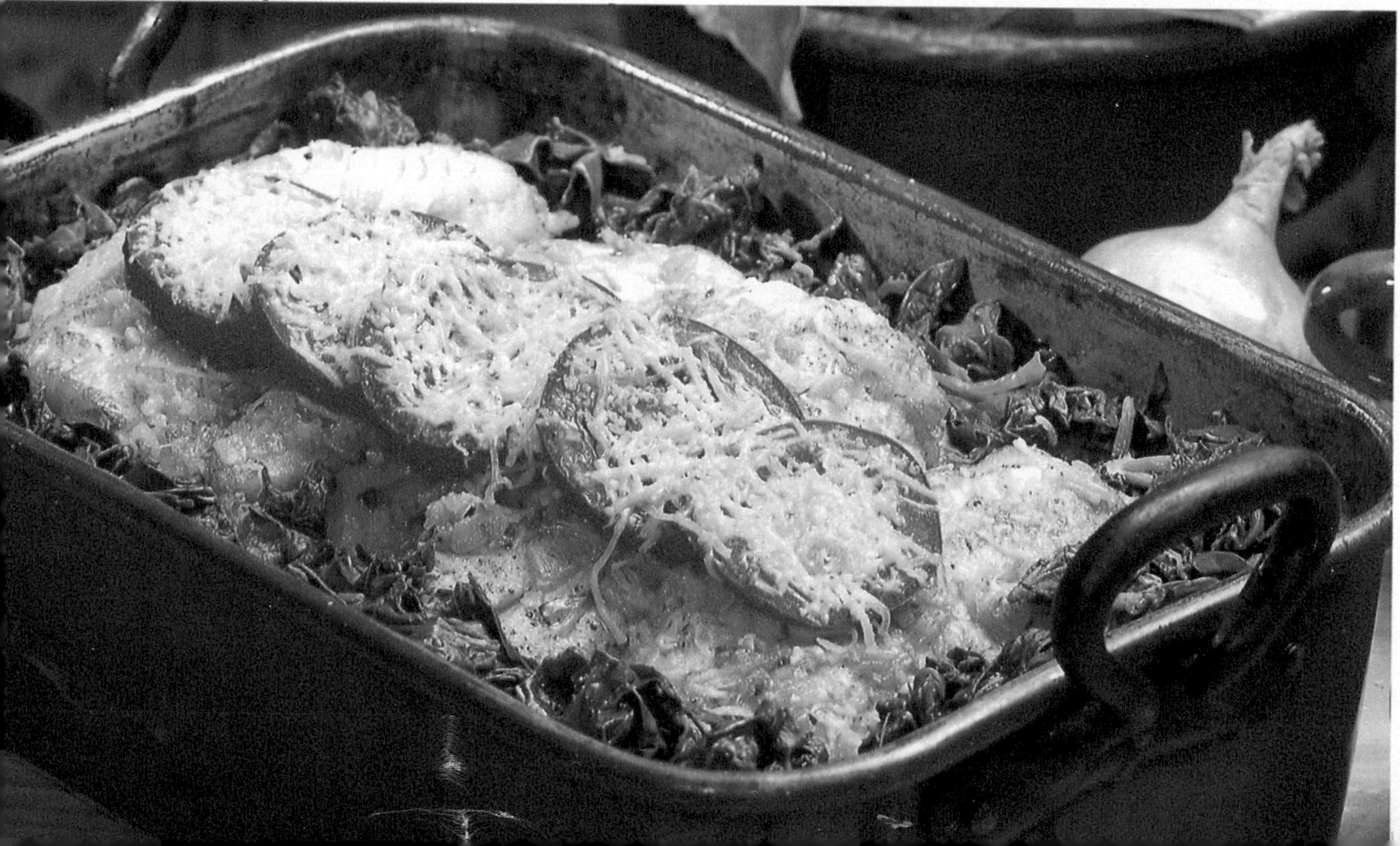

fish with herb sauce

fish with herb sauce

1 to 2 tablespoons lemon juice
1½ pounds fresh fish fillets
4 tomatoes, peeled, sliced
Salt and pepper
1 strip lean bacon, diced
1 small onion, chopped

herb sauce
½ cup plain yogurt
1 tablespoon all-purpose flour
1 tablespoon chopped parsley leaves
1 tablespoon chopped chives or thinly sliced
    scallions
1 teaspoon dried dillweed (optional)
½ teaspoon tarragon
½ teaspoon chervil

1 tablespoon dried bread crumbs
  Sprinkle lemon juice over fish; set aside.
  Line bottom of greased shallow casserole dish
with tomato slices; season with salt and pepper.
  Combine bacon and onion in small skillet; cook
until onion is golden.
  Combine yogurt, flour, and herbs; season to
taste with salt and pepper.
  Place fish fillets on tomatoes; pour Herb Sauce
over fish. Cover with bacon-onion mixture;
sprinkle with bread crumbs. Cover; bake at 350°F
about 20 minutes, until fish can be separated into
flakes. Serve at once.
  Herb Sauce can be reserved and used as topping
after fish has been baked. To use this method,
omit flour. Yield 4 servings.

fish imperial

2 cups cooked fish flakes
3 tablespoons vinegar

3 eggs, separated
2 cups milk
1 teaspoon salt
¼ teaspoon black pepper
2 tablespoons grated onion
2 tablespoons finely chopped parsley
  Preheat oven to 300°F.
  Combine fish and vinegar.
  Whip egg whites until stiff; set aside.
  Beat egg yolks. Add milk, salt, pepper, onion,
parsley, and fish; mix well. Fold in egg whites;
pour into greased baking dish. Garnish with strips
of pimiento; set in pan of warm water in oven.
Bake about 45 minutes, until silver knife comes
out clean. Yield 6 servings.

fish with lemon sauce
(low fat)

1½ pounds fish fillets
Juice of 1 lemon
2 medium onions, chopped
2 tablespoons vegetable oil
½ teaspoon salt
⅛ teaspoon white pepper
¾ cup water
2 thin slices fresh gingerroot
¼ teaspoon mace
Grated rind of 1 lemon
¼ cup lemon juice
1 tablespoon cornstarch
¼ teaspoon saffron
¼ cup plain yogurt
Chopped parsley for garnish
  Wash fish; pat dry. Sprinkle with juice of 1
lemon; let stand 10 minutes.
  Sauté onions in hot oil until golden brown. Add
fish; brown on both sides about 5 minutes. Add

fish with lemon sauce (low fat)

salt, pepper, ½ cup water, gingerroot, mace, lemon rind, and ¼ cup lemon juice. Simmer, covered, 10 minutes. Remove fish; keep warm.

Mix cornstarch with ¼ cup water; stir in fish sauce. Add saffron; simmer 2 minutes to thicken. Stir in yogurt; remove from heat. Garnish; serve immediately. Yield 4 servings.

fish and rice bake

1 pound fish fillets, fresh or frozen
1 (10¾-ounce) can condensed cheddar-cheese soup
2 cups hot cooked rice (⅔ cup uncooked)
1 egg, beaten
2 tablespoons cooking oil or margarine, melted
1 tablespoon lemon juice
½ teaspoon onion salt
Paprika

Thaw fish if frozen; cut into 1-inch pieces. Pat dry with paper toweling.

Combine soup, rice, and egg; mix well. Spread in even layer in shallow 1½-quart casserole; top with fish pieces. Drizzle with oil and lemon juice; sprinkle with onion salt. Cover with aluminum foil; crimp to edges of casserole. Bake in 350°F oven about 30 minutes. Uncover; cook 5 to 10 minutes, until hot and bubbly and fish flakes easily. Sprinkle with paprika. Yield 4 servings.

fish in sweet-and-sour sauce

1 to 1½ pounds fish fillet (cod, haddock, or turbot)
Juice of half a lemon
2 tablespoons soy sauce
Salt
3 tablespoons cornstarch

sweet-and-sour sauce
5 tablespoons vinegar
½ cup water
6 teaspoons sugar
3 tablespoons soy sauce
3 slices lemon
3 tablespoons cornstarch
Cold water
4 cups oil for frying

Wash fish thoroughly; pat dry. Sprinkle with lemon juice and soy sauce. Cut into 1½-inch-wide strips. Set aside 15 minutes; let marinate. Season to taste with salt; roll in cornstarch.

Prepare sauce. Bring vinegar, water, sugar, soy sauce, and lemon slices to boil over high heat. Reduce heat to lowest point; simmer 20 minutes.

Blend cornstarch with small amount of cold water, add to sauce. Stir until smooth and bubbly.

About 5 minutes before sauce is done, place fish in hot oil; fry about 8 minutes. Fish is done when it floats to surface. Remove fish pieces with slotted spoon; drain on paper towels. Arrange on serving platter; spoon sauce over fish. Serve immediately. Sauce can also be served separately. Yield about 3 or 4 servings.

florida fish fillets

¼ cup flour
1 teaspoon dillweed
1 teaspoon salt
4 fish fillets, skinned
4 tablespoons butter or margarine
Grapefruit and/or orange rings

Mix flour and seasonings; coat each fillet.

Heat butter in medium skillet; sauté fillets until golden brown on both sides. Remove from skillet to hot platter.

Put grapefruit slices on each fillet. Pour pan gravy over all. Serve at once. Yield 4 servings.

planked fillets or steaks

2 pounds fish fillets or steaks, fresh or frozen
2 tablespoons melted butter, margarine, or oil
2 tablespoons lemon juice
1 teaspoon salt
½ teaspoon paprika
Dash of pepper
Seasoned hot mashed potatoes
Seasoned hot cooked vegetables (asparagus,
  broccoli, carrots, cauliflower, onions,
  peas, or tomatoes)

Thaw fish if frozen; pat dry with paper toweling. Cut fish into 6 portions. Place in single layer, skin-side-down, on preheated oiled plank or well-greased bake-and-serve platter, 18 × 13 inches.

Combine remaining ingredients, except vegetables; mix well. Pour over fish. Bake in 350°F oven 20 to 25 minutes, until fish flakes easily. Remove from oven; arrange hot mashed potatoes and 2 or more hot vegetables around fish. Garnish with chopped parsley. Yield 6 servings.

poached fish with avocado sauce

1½ to 2 pounds frozen fish fillets, thawed
2 onions, thinly sliced
2 lemons, thinly sliced
2 tablespoons butter, melted
2 teaspoons salt
1 bay leaf
½ teaspoon black pepper
3 cups water
1 lemon, cut in half (squeeze 1 half; slice other
  half)

avocado sauce
2 mashed avocados
½ cup sour cream
2 tablespoons lemon juice
½ small onion, finely chopped

Pat fillets dry with toweling; cut into serving portions.

Combine onions and lemon slices with butter, salt, bay leaf, and pepper in ovenproof baking dish. Place fillets on top; add water. Cover, cook at 350°F 45 minutes. Before serving, carefully remove fish fillets with slotted spoon or spatula. Place on heated platter. Sprinkle with juice from ½ lemon; garnish with additional lemon slices.

Prepare Avocado Sauce by mixing all sauce ingredients well.

Serve hot fish with sauce, or chill fish and serve cold. Yield 6 servings.

poached fish fillets in shrimp sauce

shrimp sauce
1 pound shrimp, cooked
⅓ cup butter
⅓ cup all-purpose white flour
1½ quarts half-and-half cream
1½ teaspoons paprika
2 teaspoons salt

planked fillets or steaks

poached fish fillets in shrimp sauce

¼ teaspoon white pepper
1 cup canned mushroom caps
8 large white fish fillets
½ cup milk
½ cup water
1 teaspoon salt
¼ teaspoon white pepper
2 sprigs parsley

Peel and devein shrimp.

Melt butter in top of double boiler. Stir in flour; gradually add cream. Cook over hot water, stirring frequently, until sauce is thickened. Add paprika, 2 teaspoons salt, ¼ teaspoon pepper, mushrooms, and shrimp. Let simmer in top of double boiler while preparing fish.

Split fillets down centers. Begin at larger end of fillet; roll up. Fasten each with toothpick; place in large skillet. Add milk, water, 1 teaspoon salt, and ¼ teaspoon white pepper. Cover fish tightly; simmer gently 10 minutes. Remove fish to hot platter; remove toothpicks. Cover fish with Shrimp Sauce; garnish with parsley before serving. Yield 8 servings.

whitefish in foil

2 pounds whitefish or other fish fillets, fresh or frozen
2 green peppers, sliced
2 onions, sliced
¼ cup butter or margarine, melted
2 tablespoons lemon juice
2 teaspoons salt
1 teaspoon paprika
Dash of pepper

Thaw fillets if frozen; pat dry with paper toweling. Cut into serving-size portions. Cut 6 pieces of heavy-duty aluminum foil, 12 × 12 inches each; grease lightly. Place portion of fish, skin-side-down, on foil; top with green peppers and onions.

Combine remaining ingredients; pour sauce over fish. Bring foil up over food; close all edges with tight double folds. Make 6 packages. Place packages on grill about 5-inches from moderately hot coals. Cook 45 to 60 minutes, until fish flakes easily. Yield 6 servings.

MAIN DISH

beef fondue

1¾ cups mayonnaise
1¼ cups pickle relish
1 tablespoon minced capers
1 cup minced onions
1 cup Basic Mustard Sauce (see Index)

1 cup minced black olives
1 cup Tomato Coulis Sauce (see Index)
1 (2-pound) beef tenderloin, cut into cubes
Peanut oil
Salt and freshly ground pepper to taste

Combine ¾ cup mayonnaise, ¼ cup pickle relish, and capers; place in small serving bowl.

Place onions, Mustard Sauce, olives, remaining mayonnaise, remaining relish, and Tomato Coulis Sauce in matching serving bowls.

beef fondue

italian vegetable fondue

Place beef on platter; place on table as shown in illustration. Place onions, Mustard Sauce, olives, relish mayonnaise, mayonnaise, pickle relish, and Tomato Coulis Sauce around platter.

Fill fondue pot ¾ full with oil; place over high heat on stove until hot. Place over fondue burner. Spear beef cubes with fondue forks; cook in hot oil until of desired doneness. Season with salt and pepper; eat with desired accompaniments. Yield 6 servings.

italian vegetable fondue

1¼ cups olive oil
3 cloves garlic, sliced
½ teaspoon freshly ground pepper
2 (2-ounce) cans anchovy fillets

Pour oil into fondue pot; add garlic and pepper.

Chop anchovies; add to fondue pot with anchovy oil. Heat until bubbly. Serve as dipping sauce for fresh vegetables such as radishes, carrot sticks, small green onions, and celery strips. Yield 6 servings.

japanese fondue

bouillon
6 cups chicken bouillon
2 carrots
1 leek
1 stalk celery
2 tablespoons coarsely chopped parsley

sauce tartare
5 tablespoons mayonnaise
2 tablespoons capers
2 tablespoons finely chopped chives
2 dill pickles, finely chopped
2 teaspoons lemon juice
2 tablespoons evaporated milk
Salt
Pinch of sugar
White pepper

catsup sauce
5 tablespoons mayonnaise
2 tablespoons tomato catsup
1 teaspoon Worcestershire sauce
1 teaspoon (or less) curry powder
Pinch of sugar
Salt
2 to 2½ pounds very lean beef
2 cups boiling water

Bring bouillon to boil either in pot placed on burner or in fondue pot.

Chop carrots, leek, and celery; add with chopped parsley to broth. Cook 20 minutes.

To prepare sauce, stir together ingredients until well blended; season to taste.

Thoroughly dry meat with paper towels; cut into thin strips.

Place chicken-vegetable broth on top of burner; make sure it continues to simmer (or leave in fondue pot over low heat). Liquid will evaporate, so it is necessary to add water from time to time.

Each person places piece of meat on fondue fork, puts it in simmering broth 1 to 2 minutes, and dunks it in sauce. Pass each person separate bowl for each sauce; serve with rice. Yield 4 servings.

swiss fondue

¾ pound Swiss cheese
1 tablespoon all-purpose flour
1¼ cloves garlic
1¼ cups sauterne
Dash of pepper
Dash of nutmeg
3 tablespoons kirsch brandy
Salt to taste

Cut cheese into thin strips; place in bag. Add flour; toss well until cheese is coated.

Split garlic clove in half; rub inside of fondue pot well with cut sides of both halves. Press ¼ clove garlic; place in fondue pot. Add sauterne; place over flame. Heat until bubbles start to rise; do not cover or boil. Add cheese gradually; cook over low flame, stirring constantly, until melted. Stir in pepper, nutmeg, and kirsch. Add warmed sauterne if mixture becomes too thick. Serve with French-bread cubes, cauliflower florets, mushrooms, and rolled pepperoni slices for dipping. Yield 6 servings.

swiss fondue

tomato fondue with frankfurters

1 clove garlic
2 cups grated cheddar or American cheese
½ cup grated Gruyére cheese
½ cup condensed tomato soup
1 teaspoon Worcestershire sauce
3 tablespoons dry sherry
1 small can cocktail frankfurters
French bread

Rub inside of fondue pot with cut garlic clove. Put in cheeses, soup, and Worcestershire sauce; stir continuously over low heat until cheese has melted and mixture is creamy. Stir in sherry; cook 2 to 3 minutes. Adjust seasoning before serving.

Frankfurters are speared onto fondue forks and dipped into fondue. Serve with plenty of French bread. Yield 2 or 3 servings.

399

tomato fondue with frankfurters

DESSERT
chocolate fondue

12 ounces chocolate (any plain chocolate bar
  will do)
¾ cup cream
1 to 2 tablespoons brandy or kirsch, or
  2 teaspoons instant coffee
Dippers

Melt chocolate and cream in heavy saucepan over low heat; stir until smooth. Remove from heat; stir in flavoring. Yield 6 to 8 servings.

dippers
Apple wedges
Sliced bananas
Pieces of cake (pound or angel food)
Mandarin-orange segments
Marshmallows
Pineapple chunks

FRITTERS

assorted vegetable fritters

1 small eggplant
1 recipe Basic Fritter Batter (see Index)
1 zucchini, cut into ¼-inch slices
1 small cauliflower, separated into florets

Thinly slice eggplant; dip into batter one slice at a time. Drop several at a time into hot (370°F) oil in deep-fat fryer; brown on one side. Turn; brown other side. Remove with slotted spoon; drain on paper toweling. Place on oven-proof platter; keep warm until zucchini and cauliflower are cooked in same manner. (These can also be served for hors d'oeuvres.) Yield 6 to 8 servings.

basic fritter batter

1½ cups sifted all-purpose flour
1 teaspoon salt
2 tablespoons oil
1 egg, well beaten

Sift flour and salt together into medium bowl. Add oil, egg, and about 1 cup cold water, enough to make thick batter. If batter does not adhere to vegetables, add 1 or 2 tablespoons water to batter. Yield about 2 cups.

carrot fritters

1 bunch carrots or 2 (1-pound) cans sliced carrots
1 egg

assorted vegetable fritters

1 tablespoon sugar
3 tablespoons flour
Salt and pepper to taste
1 teaspoon baking powder
Fat for deep-frying

If using raw carrots, cook in small amount of water until very tender; mash fine. When pasty, add egg and sugar. Add flour, salt, pepper, and baking powder; stir until well blended. Drop by spoonfuls into deep fat; they will brown quickly when fat is correct temperature. Drain on paper towels; keep warm until all are done. Serve at once. Yield 6 to 8 servings.

cheese fritters

1 egg, beaten
½ cup milk
1 teaspoon Worcestershire sauce
1 small onion, finely minced
Dash of hot pepper (optional)
2 cups biscuit mix
1½ cups diced American cheese
Fat for deep-frying
Jelly or jam

Mix egg, milk, Worcestershire sauce, onion, pepper, and prepared biscuit mix in bowl; blend well. Stir in cheese.

Preheat fat in skillet; drop mixture by teaspoonfuls into hot fat. Fry until golden brown; drain on paper towels. Serve next to dish of jelly or jam fo dipping. Yield about 40 small fritters.

corn fritters

1 (1-pound) can whole-kernel corn, drained
1 egg
½ teaspoon salt
¼ cup milk
1 cup flour
2 teaspoons baking powder
2 teaspoons melted butter
½ teaspoon sugar
Fat for deep-frying

While corn is draining, mix egg, salt, milk, flour, baking powder, butter, and sugar. Stir with long-handled wooden spoon. Add corn; let sit 5 minutes. Drop by teaspoonfuls into hot fat; cook until puffy and golden brown. Drain on paper toweling; transfer to warm platter. Yield 4 to 6 servings.

mushroom fritters with rémoulade sauce

½ pound small fresh mushrooms*
1 recipe Basic Fritter Batter (see Index)
1 recipe Basic Rémoulade Sauce (see Index)

Remove stems from mushrooms; dip in batter to coat entire surface. Drop into hot (370°F) oil in deep-fat fryer; fry until lightly browned on all sides. Remove from fat; drain on paper toweling. Serve with Basic Rémoulade Sauce. Yield about 6 servings.

*Drained canned button mushrooms can be used in place of fresh mushrooms.

shrimp fritters

tomato sauce
2 tablespoons olive oil
1 medium onion, chopped
1 clove garlic, minced
1 (10-ounce) can tomatoes and green chilies
½ teaspoon salt
¼ teaspoon pepper

fritters
4 eggs, separated
½ teaspoon salt
¼ teaspoon celery salt
2 teaspoons dried parsley flakes
2 tablespoons flour
1 cup well-drained chopped cooked shrimp (fresh, frozen, or canned)
Oil for frying

Make sauce; keep warm while making fritters. Heat oil in medium saucepan. Add onion and garlic; sauté until limp. Add tomatoes and chilies, and seasonings; bring to boil. Reduce heat to simmer; cover. Cook 20 minutes.

Meanwhile, beat egg whites until stiff.

Beat egg yolks, salt, celery salt, parsley flakes, and flour. Fold into egg whites. Fold in shrimp.

In heavy skillet or deep fryer heat at least 1 inch oil to 365°F. Fry fritters a few at a time (using ¼ cup batter for each fritter) until golden; drain well. (Substitute clams for shrimp for clam fritters.) Serve immediately with Tomato Sauce. Yield 4 servings.

FROSTINGS—ICINGS

basic butter cream I

¾ cup unsalted butter, softened
3¾ cups (scant) sifted confectioners' sugar
1 egg yolk
1 teaspoon orange-flower water plus 1 teaspoon
  rose water or
1 teaspoon vanilla extract

Cream butter in medium-size mixing bowl with electric mixer at medium speed 2 minutes or until light and fluffy. Add half the confectioners' sugar and egg yolk; beat thoroughly. Add remaining sugar; orange-flower and rose water; beat until thoroughly combined. Yield enough to frost two-layer cake.

basic butter cream II

3 egg yolks
1¼ cups sifted confectioner's sugar
½ cup butter, softened

Place egg yolks in medium-size mixing bowl. Add confectioners' sugar; blend well with wooden spoon. Place bowl over hot water at medium heat; stir until mixture is very thick and creamy and free from streaks. Remove from hot water. Place bowl in pan of ice; stir until cool.

Cream butter until smooth; whip into sugar mixture a spoonful at a time with electric mixer at medium speed until well blended. Yield enough to frost two-layer cake.

basic confectioners' icing

5 cups sifted confectioners' sugar
Water
Food Coloring

Place sugar in large mixing bowl; stir in small amount of water at a time to reach easy spreading consistency. If icing becomes too thin, add more sugar to thicken. Stir in desired food coloring if desired. Yield enough for 9-inch layer cake.

basic fondant icing

2 (1-pound) boxes confectioners' sugar
½ cup white corn syrup
2 egg whites

basic fondant icing

1 teaspoon vanilla extract
Cornstarch

Sift sugar into large bowl.

Heat syrup in small pan over hot water.

Make well in sugar; add syrup, egg whites, and vanilla. Mix with wooden spoon until smooth.

Sift additional confectioners' sugar onto clean working surface. Place fondant on sugar; knead until of smooth dough-like consistency. Add sugar as needed to keep fondant from sticking.

Sift cornstarch over working surface; roll fondant to ¼-inch thick. Trim to fit cake; place over top. Decorate with desired cut-out designs. For green peppermint icing, add 4 drops peppermint oil and 6 drops green food coloring when vanilla is added. Yield enough for 2-layer cake.

butter-cream frosting

½ cup butter
4 cups confectioners' sugar, sifted
1 egg
⅛ teaspoon salt
1 teaspoon vanilla extract
2 tablespoons light cream

Cream butter until light and fluffy. Gradually add half the sugar; beat well after each addition. Blend in egg, salt, and vanilla. Add remaining sugar alternately with cream; beat until smooth after each addition. Yield 2½ cups; enough for 2 layers, 36 cupcakes, or 2 (9-inch) square cakes.

chocolate butter cream

Add 3 squares melted unsweetened baking chocolate with first addition of sugar; increase cream to 4 tablespoons.

mocha butter cream

Add 1 tablespoon instant coffee with egg.

orange or lemon butter cream.

Substitute 2 tablespoons orange or lemon juice for cream. Omit vanilla; add 1 tablespoon finely grated orange or lemon rind.

butterscotch frosting

3 tablespoons sweet (unsalted) butter
2 cups confectioners' sugar
1½ tablespoons milk
½ teaspoon vanilla extract
½ cup ground pecans

Put butter into pan; heat slowly and carefully until it just begins to brown. Stir in sugar. Remove from stove; add milk and vanilla. Stir until smooth; add nuts. Yield enough for tops of 2 (8 inch) layers, 18 cupcakes, or 8 × 8 × 2-inch cake.

cream-cheese frosting

3 ounces cream cheese, softened
2 tablespoons butter
½ teaspoon vanilla flavoring
1¾ cups confectioners' sugar

Beat cream cheese, butter, and vanilla until smooth. Gradually add sugar; beat until fluffy. Yield 1 cup.

creamy chocolate frosting

2 squares baking chocolate
½ cup milk
1½ cups sugar
2 egg yolks, beaten
1 tablespoon butter
1 teaspoon vanilla extract

Put chocolate and milk into pan; stir over low heat until chocolate has melted.

Mix sugar with egg yolks; add to chocolate mixture. Cook gently 10 minutes; stir frequently. Add butter and vanilla; leave until lukewarm. Beat until thick enough to spread. Yield enough for top and sides of 8-inch-square cake or tops of 2 (9-inch) layers.

marshmallow icing

1 cup sugar
⅓ cup water
2 egg whites, stiffly beaten
⅓ teaspoon cream of tartar
1½ teaspoons vanilla

Boil sugar and water; add slowly to egg whites. While still warm, add cream of tartar and vanilla; beat until bowl is cool. Yield enough for 1 cake.

mocha butter cream

1 cup butter, softened
6 cups sifted confectioners' sugar
3 egg yolks
¼ cup Basic Coffee Syrup (see Index)
2 squares semisweet chocolate, melted

Cream butter in large mixing bowl with electric mixer until light and fluffy. Add half the sugar; beat until smooth. Add egg yolks; blend well. Mix in remaining confectioners' sugar. Add Coffee Syrup and chocolate; beat until well combined and fluffy. Yield enough to fill, frost, and decorate 9-inch cake.

seven-minute frosting

2 egg whites
⅛ teaspoon salt
1½ cups sugar

mocha butter cream

½ cup cold water
1 tablespoon light corn syrup
1½ teaspoons vanilla extract

Put egg whites, salt, sugar, and water in top of double boiler; add corn syrup. Have water in lower pan just below boiling. Beat with electric or rotary beater 7 minutes or until frosting thickens and holds its shape when dropped from beater. Turn into bowl; add vanilla. Beat until thick enough to spread. Cool a few minutes before using, so frosting does not sink into cake. Yield enough for 2 layers, 9-inch-square cake, or 24 cupcakes.

chocolate frosting

Melt 3 squares baking chocolate; cool. Stir into frosting just before spreading on cake.

fluffy lemon frosting

Omit corn syrup; substitute 2 tablespoons lemon juice for 2 tablespoons water. Add a little grated lemon rind.

sea-foam frosting

Substitute 2 cups brown sugar for white sugar; omit corn syrup.

special chocolate icing

½ cup light corn syrup
6 tablespoons water
5 tablespoons butter
1 (12-ounce) package semisweet chocolate bits

Combine corn syrup, water, and butter in saucepan. Bring to rapid boil, stirring until butter is melted. Remove from heat; add chocolate. Stir until chocolate is completely melted. Cool to room temperature before pouring over cake, petis fours, or desired dessert to glaze; chill until set. Yield about 2½ cups.

special chocolate icing

GLAZES AND SYRUPS

anglais glaze

1 egg
1 teaspoon vegetable oil
½ teaspoon salt
¼ teaspoon white pepper

Combine all ingredients; beat well. Strain before using. Used on savory or non-sweet foods.

apricot glaze

1 cup apricot jam
1¼ cups water
¾ cup sugar

Combine all ingredients in small heavy saucepan; heat until jam is dissolved, stirring constantly. Bring to slow, rolling boil; cook until thickened. Strain through sieve.

basic coffee syrup I

5 cups brewed coffee

Place coffee in heavy saucepan; bring to vigorous boil. Reduce heat slightly; boil slowly 25 to 30 minutes, until reduced to ½ cup syrup. Cool; store in covered jar to use as needed. Yield ½ cup.

basic coffee syrup II

2 tablespoons instant coffee
½ cup boiling water

Dissolve coffee in boiling water. Cool; store in covered jar. Yield ½ cup.

basic sugar syrup

6 cups water
8½ cups sugar

Place water and sugar in large pot over low heat; heat until sugar is dissolved. Raise to slow, rolling boil; reduce temperature. Simmer 3 minutes; chill. Bottle; store.

cream glaze

1 pound powdered sugar
1 tablespoon cornstarch
1 tablespoon cream
1 teaspoon vanilla
2 tablespoons water (approximately)

Combine sugar, cornstarch, cream, and vanilla. Add water to make mixture of medium consistency.

egg wash

1 egg white
1 teaspoon salt

Combine egg white and salt; beat with fork until foamy. Used for crisp tops on savory breads.

egg-white glaze

1 egg white
Extra-fine sugar to taste

Brush egg white over surface of food to be glazed; sprinkle with sugar. Used on sweet foods to produce a crisp top.

lemon glaze

2 cups confectioners' sugar
1 tablespoon cornstarch
3 tablespoons milk
2 tablespoons lemon juice
1 teaspoon vanilla

Combine dry ingredients. Slowly add liquids; beat constantly until smooth. Yield ¾ cup.

milk glaze

2 cups confectioners' sugar, sifted
2 to 3 tablespoons canned milk
1 teaspoon vanilla

Combine ingredients; beat until smooth. Yield approximately ¾ cup.

plain glaze

1 egg
1 teaspoon vegetable oil

Combine ingredients; beat well. Strain before using. Used on most sweet items, except those you want to have a crisp finish.

red currant jelly glaze

1 (10-ounce) jar red currant jelly
¼ cup ruby port

Combine jelly and port in small saucepan. Place over low heat; stir until jelly is melted.

rum glaze

¼ cup water
1 cup confectioners' sugar
1 teaspoon rum flavoring

Combine all ingredients; mix well. Yield approximately 1 cup.

GOOSE

goose with chestnut and liver stuffing

2 pounds chestnuts
2 cups stock
6 apples
2 onions, chopped
1 goose liver
1 tablespoon butter
2 cups bread crumbs
2 tablespoons chopped parsley
1 tablespoon mixed thyme and marjoram
Grated rind of ½ lemon
Salt and pepper
1 (8 to 10 pound) goose
2 tablespoons flour
4 to 6 tablespoons oil
2 tablespoons red currant jelly
Juice of ½ lemon
1½ cups cider or stock

Prepare stuffing. Put chestnuts in boiling water 5 to 6 minutes, until both outer shell and inner skin can be removed. Keep chestnuts hot while peeling. Cover nuts with stock; simmer until tender. Drain; let cool. Reserve stock for moistening stuffing.

Peel and chop apples. Add onions; cook 3 to 4 minutes. Mix in chestnuts.

Cook liver in butter; when firm, chop; add to stuffing with 1 to 2 cups bread crumbs. Add parsley, thyme, marjoram, lemon rind, salt, and pep-per; mix together. Add enough stock to make moist but firm mixture. Stuff goose; sew up opening. Prick goose all over lightly with sharp fork; sprinkle with 1 tablespoon flour and seasoning.

Heat oil in roasting pan. Put goose into pan, on rack, if possible, to allow fat to drain; roast in pre-heated 400°F oven 20 to 25 minutes per pound. Baste every 20 minutes; turn from side to side. Reduce heat slightly after first 20 minutes. For last 30 minutes pour off most of fat. Place bird breast-up; allow to brown. Raise heat again if breast is not becoming crisp and brown. Test with skewer in thick part of leg to see if cooked. When done, remove to serving dish; keep warm while making gravy.

Skim off remaining fat from roasting pan. Sprinkle in 1 tablespoon flour; blend with roasting juices in pan. Add jelly and lemon juice; stir in well. Add cider; bring to boil. Cook 2 to 3 minutes; strain. Season to taste; serve hot with goose. Yield 6 to 8 servings.

goose with potato stuffing

1 (8- to 9-pound) young goose, thawed if frozen

potato stuffing
3 medium potatoes (approximately 1 pound), peeled
1½ teaspoons salt
¼ pound lean salt pork, diced
¼ cup finely chopped onion

goose with chestnut and liver stuffing

goose with potato stuffing

¼ **pound bulk sausage**
¼ **cup butter or margarine**
1 egg
½ **teaspoon pepper**
1 teaspoon crumbled sage leaves

Remove giblets from goose; wash well. Pat dry with paper towels. Salt lightly inside and out; set aside while making stuffing.

Place potatoes in medium saucepan; cover with cold water. Add ½ teaspoon salt; bring to boil over moderate heat. Cover; cook on low 20 to 30 minutes or until tender. Drain; place tea towel over pan. Steam gently a few minutes.

Meanwhile, cook salt pork in heavy skillet over moderate heat until lightly browned. Remove with slotted spoon; reserve.

Add onion to skillet; cook until tender. Remove with slotted spoon; add to salt pork.

Add sausage to skillet; cook until lightly browned, breaking into small chunks as sausage cooks. Remove with slotted spoon; add to salt-pork mixture.

Put potatoes through ricer or food mill or mash with potato masher.

Combine salt-pork mixture, potatoes, and remaining stuffing ingredients; mix well. Allow to cool.

Stuff goose with potato mixture; truss bird. Place in open roasting pan, breast-side-up, on rack or trivet. Prick well on legs and wing joints to release fat. Roast in preheated 325°F oven 2 to 2½ hours, until leg joint moves easily. Let stand 15 to 20 minutes before carving. Carve; remove dressing to serving dish. Serve with applesauce. Yield 6 servings.

fish sauce or gravy

2 tablespoons butter
2 tablespoons flour
1½ cups milk, scalded
½ cup Basic Fish Stock (see Index)
2 tablespoons lemon juice
1 egg yolk

Melt butter; gradually add flour and heated milk. Add fish stock and lemon juice just before removing from heat. Just before serving, beat sauce into egg yolk. Serve hot. One tablespoon catsup can be added, if desired. Bottled clam broth can be used as a substitute for fish stock in most dishes.

giblet gravy

Remove turkey from pan. Skim off excess fat; leave drippings. Sprinkle 4 to 6 tablespoons flour or 2 to 3 tablespoons cornstarch into pan; stir to incorporate brown bits. Stir in finely minced giblets from broth. Gradually add 3 to 4½ cups strained turkey broth. Add sage, salt, pepper, and Worcestershire sauce to taste. Bring to boil, stirring until thickened and well blended.

gravy

For thin gravy use 1 tablespoon each flour and fat or drippings to each cup of liquid. For medium gravy use 2 tablespoons flour and 1 or 2 tablespoons fat or drippings, as desired. If drippings are scant, add bouillon cube or a little meat extract to liquid.

method 1 (Use with fat or with drippings containing only fat and browned crusty bits.) Measure fat or drippings. Stir flour into fat; brown over low heat. Add liquid slowly; stir constantly. Cook until thickened; stir occasionally. Season to taste.

method 2 (Use with fat or drippings containing considerable amount of liquid.) Measure drippings; if necessary add water to make desired amount of liquid. Heat.

Combine flour with equal amount cold water by stirring or shaking until smooth; stir slowly into hot liquid. Cook until thickened, stir occasionally. Season to taste.

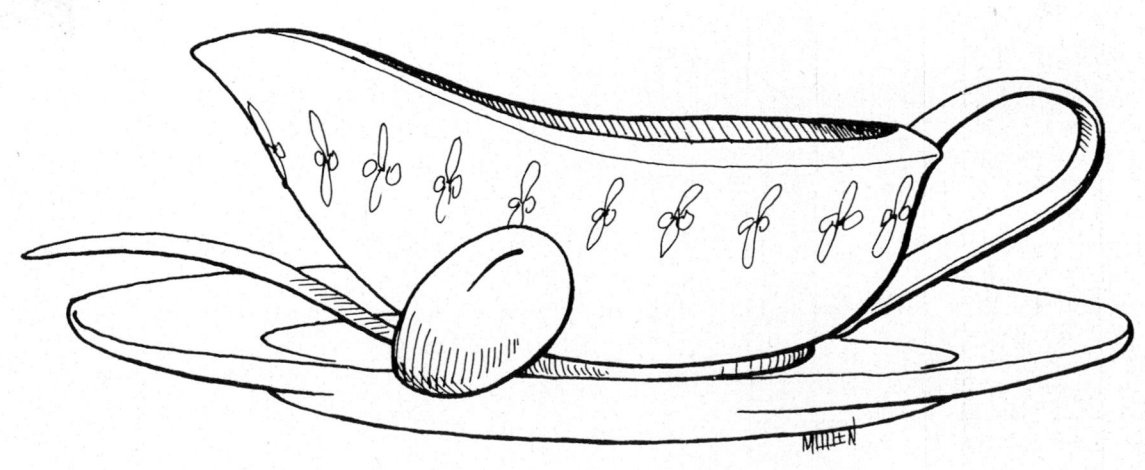

HAM

baked glazed ham

1 (2- to 3-pound) canned ham
2 tablespoons honey
Grated rind of 1 orange
1 teaspoon dry mustard
4 tablespoons brown sugar
½ cup cider or pineapple juice
1 tablespoon butter
1 small can pineapple rings
Dusting of sugar
6 to 8 canned sweet cherries

Scrape jelly off ham; reserve. Place in baking pan.

Melt honey; spread over surface of ham.

Mix orange rind, mustard, and brown sugar together; sprinkle over surface of meat. Pour cider over ham. Add jelly from ham; baste very gently over ham without disturbing sugar coating. Bake in preheated 400°F oven 30 minutes; baste after 15 minutes.

Melt butter in frying pan.

Sprinkle pineapple slices with sugar; brown in butter on both sides. Serve around ham with cherries in center of each ring.

Use liquid from baking pan to make sauce; add water and squeeze of lemon if too sweet. Yield 4 to 6 servings.

baked ham party-style

1 (6- to 8-pound) canned, cooked boned ham
1 unpeeled orange, thinly sliced
Juice of 1 orange
¼ cup anise-flavored liqueur
½ cup packed brown sugar
¼ cup dried currants
¼ teaspoon ground ginger
1 tablespoon vinegar
1 tablespoon mustard
1 teaspoon Worcestershire sauce
⅓ cup water

Heat ham in oven according to package directions.

Set orange slices to side.

Blend remaining ingredients in blender. Heat in skillet; spoon over ham. Bake ½ hour or until glazed; baste with seasoning mixture. Arrange orange slices over ham; garnish with watercress. Yield 12 or more servings.

410

baked ham slice

1 (1- to 1½-inch-thick) center ham slice
½ cup dark brown sugar
Whole cloves
1 cup milk

Place ham in greased baking pan. Spread brown sugar on top; stud with cloves. Pour milk around sides. Bake in preheated 325°F oven 1 hour or until tender.

Pears (cored and halved lengthwise) cooked with ham during last 30 minutes make an attractive garnish. Yield 4 to 6 servings.

barbecued ham slices

Ask butcher for individual ham slices weighing 5 to 6 ounces each; allow 1 slice per person.

Using kitchen scissors or sharp knife, cut through rind and fat all around. This will prevent ham from curling. Arrange slices on part of barbecue that is not too hot. Cook about 20 to 30 minutes; turn frequently. Slices of pineapple or apricot halves go well with ham. Yield 1 slice per person.

country ham with redeye gravy

6 ham slices, about ½-inch-thick
¾ cup strong black coffee

Fry ham slices 1 or 2 at a time, depending on skillet size, over medium-high heat. Fry 5 to 6 minutes per side. When done, remove to heated platter.

Pour off all but about 3 tablespoons fat in skillet. Brown remaining drippings; add coffee. Be sure to scrape up pan scrapings (these are the redeyes); bring to boil. Gravy can be spooned over ham or served separately. Serve with hot grits or biscuits to absorb gravy. Yield 6 servings.

glazed ham and rice loaf

1½ pounds cooked ham, ground
1½ cups cooked white rice
1½ cups soft bread crumbs
1½ teaspoons dry mustard
1½ cups milk

barbecued ham slices

4 eggs, beaten light and frothy

glaze
½ cup currant jelly
⅓ cup prepared mustard

Mix all ingredients except glaze in large bowl; make high rounded loaf. Place in 13 × 9 × 2-inch baking dish. Bake, uncovered, at 350°F 50 minutes.

Prepare glaze by thoroughly mixing jelly and mustard together until pasty and smooth.

After loaf has baked 50 minutes, liberally brush all over with glaze. Bake, uncovered, 20 minutes or until glaze is "glistening brown." Let cool 20 minutes before slicing. Yield 6 to 8 servings.

grilled ham with raisin and cranberry sauce

1½ to 2 pounds 1-inch-thick ham slices
Few cloves
½ cup brown sugar
2 tablespoons cornstarch
1½ cups cranberry juice
½ cup orange juice

½ cup seeded or seedless raisins

Score fat edges of ham at intervals of about 2 inches; insert 2 or 3 cloves in fat.

Mix sugar and cornstarch smoothly with cranberry juice; put into pan. Add orange juice and raisins; bring to boil. Stir constantly until mixture thickens.

Put ham on grid over hot coals away from hottest part; cook about 15 minutes. Turn; brush liberally with glaze. Cook 10 minutes. Turn; brush other side. (Can be put on broiler rack in open pan 3 inches below unit. Allow 10 to 12 minutes on each side; brush with glaze as above.) Brush again just before serving; serve any remaining glaze with ham. Yield 4 or 5 servings.

ham hocks in sauerkraut polish-style

3 large ham hocks
2 cups sauerkraut
1 large onion, sliced into thin rings
1 tablespoon granulated sugar
¼ teaspoon black pepper

Cover ham with water. Simmer 1 hour; drain. Add sauerkraut, onion, sugar, and pepper; return

ham hocks in sauerkraut

to heat. Simmer 1½ to 2 hours, until meat falls off bone. Yield 4 servings.

ham in madeira wine

1 (12-pound) smoked ham
4 bay leaves
8 peppercorns
8 whole cloves
1 bottle Madeira wine

Soak ham in cold water overnight. In large pot cover drained ham with boiling water. Add bay leaves, peppercorns, and cloves. Cook slowly 2½ hours; drain off liquid. Pour wine over ham. Simmer at least ½ hour; baste if necessary. Slice; serve.

If wine sauce is desired with ham, slightly thicken 2 cups of wine liquid. Yield 20 or more servings.

ham rolls (cold)

½ cup rice
Chicken stock or water
1 bay leaf
1 tablespoon oil
2 tablespoons butter
½ small onion, peeled, finely chopped
1 small apple, peeled, cored, chopped
1½ teaspoons curry powder
4 tablespoons light cream
Grated rind of 1 lemon
2 tablespoons lemon juice
2 tablespoons chopped cooked ham
2 tablespoons chopped red pepper
8 slices cooked ham
Lettuce
Black olives and canned pimiento (garnish)

Cook rice in 1 cup boiling stock or salted water with bay leaf in small saucepan 12 minutes; drain. While still hot, stir in oil; make sure rice is well

ham rolls

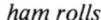

coated.

Heat butter in skillet. Add onion and apple; cook 5 minutes. Stir in curry powder; cook few minutes. Remove from heat; add cream, lemon rind and juice, chopped ham, red pepper, and rice. Set aside about 1 hour to chill.

Roll mixture in slices of ham; secure with cocktail stick or toothpick if necessary. Arrange on bed of lettuce; garnish with olives and strips of pimiento. More simply, put on platter; garnish with watercress. Serve as appetizer or luncheon dish. Yield 4 servings.

ham shortcake

1 cup cut-up ham

3 tablespoons fat (bacon drippings, ham fat, or other)
¼ cup flour
2½ cups milk
¼ teaspoon mustard
½ teaspoon salt
Celery salt to taste
4 hard-boiled eggs, cut into fourths
Hot biscuits

Brown ham slightly in fat. (Cook well if uncooked ham is used.) Stir in flour; add milk. Cook and stir until thickened. Stir in mustard, salt, and celery salt; add eggs. Heat just until hot; stir only to keep from sticking. Serve over hot split biscuits. Yield 8 servings.

cornish hens german-style

1 small cornish hen, split, or 2 chicken-breast
   halves
1 lemon
3 tablespoons cracker crumbs or unseasoned
   bread crumbs
2 tablespoons grated Parmesan cheese
¼ teaspoon ground ginger
Salt and pepper to taste

   Sprinkle poultry with juice of half the lemon.
   Combine crumbs, cheese, ginger, salt, and pepper in paper bag. Add poultry; shake until coated. Arrange poultry skin-side-up on shallow roasting pan. Place in preheated 350°F oven. Bake, without turning, until golden and tender, 45 to 50 minutes. Garnish with thin lemon slices, or serve with lemon wedges (and parsley, if desired). Recipe can be doubled or tripled. Yield 2 servings.

cornish hens with plum sauce

4 large Cornish hens
Salt and freshly ground pepper to taste
4 large oranges
1 (1-pound) can purple plums
¼ cup butter
¼ cup minced onion
1 teaspoon ginger
1 teaspoon Worcestershire sauce
1½ teaspoons prepared mustard
⅓ cup chili sauce
¼ cup soy sauce
1 (6-ounce) can frozen lemonade concentrate
¼ cup shredded coconut

   Cut hens in half lengthwise; sprinkle with salt and pepper.
   Slice unpeeled oranges; remove seeds. Place in 2 shallow, oblong baking pans. Place 4 hen halves, skin-side-up, in each baking pan on oranges. Bake in preheated 350°F oven 45 minutes.
   Drain plums; remove seeds. Place in blender or food-processor container; process until pureed,
   Melt butter in medium-size saucepan; add onion. Cook over low heat, stirring constantly, until onion is golden. Add ginger, Worcestershire sauce, mustard, chili sauce, soy sauce, lemonade, and plums; bring to boil. Stir until lemonade is thawed; reduce heat. Simmer 15 minutes; stir oc-

casionally. Spoon sauce over hens. Bake 30 to 45 minutes, until hens are tender; baste frequently with plum sauce. Remove hens with orange slices to serving platter; sprinkle with coconut. Serve remaining sauce with hens. Yield 4 to 6 servings.

roast cornish hens with savory stuffing

4 Cornish hens, approximately 1 pound each
8 thick slices home-style white bread
1½ tablespoons parsley flakes
¾ teaspoon salt
½ teaspoon poultry seasoning
¼ teaspoon freshly ground pepper
¾ cup butter
1 cup finely chopped onions
4 livers from Cornish hens
Salt and pepper
3 tablespoons melted butter

   Remove giblet packs from hens; reserve livers. Wash hens; pat dry.
   Cut crusts from bread; cut into ½-inch cubes. Place on cookie sheet. Bake at 350°F until golden; stir occasionally. Remove from oven. Combine with parsley, ¾ teaspoon salt, poultry seasoning, and ¼ teaspoon pepper; set aside.
   Melt ¾ cup butter in heavy skillet. Add onions and livers; cook until livers are lightly browned and onions tender. Remove livers; chop. Add livers, onions, and butter from pan to bread cubes; toss to mix well.
   Salt and pepper hens lightly. Pack tightly with stuffing; truss. Place in ovenproof baking dish, breast-side-up; brush with melted butter. Roast at 375°F. Turn every 15 minutes; baste with butter and pan juices. Cook a total of 45 minutes to 1 hour, until juices run clear when tip of knife is inserted in hen. Serve hot with wild rice and green vegetable. Yield 4 servings.

roast guinea hen

2 (2- to 3-pound) dressed guinea hens
1½ teaspoons salt
1 lemon, quartered
2 small onions
4 slices country-style bacon, sliced
   Rub hens inside and out with salt and lemon wedges. Insert an onion in each hen; place bacon over backs of hens. Roast in 325°F oven 40 minutes back-sides-up. Turn hens over in roasting pan; rearrange bacon over breasts of hens. Cook 35 to 40 minutes or until fork-tender. Yield 4 servings.

JELLIES

ambrosia conserve

2 medium oranges
1 large ripe pineapple
6 cooking apples
2 cups water
1 cup raisins
6 cups sugar
1 cup flaked coconut

Remove outer peel of oranges with vegetable peeler; cut peel into thin slivers with knife or scissors. Remove white membrane from oranges. Section oranges; remove seeds. Cut oranges into small pieces.

Pare pineapple; remove core. Cut into small cubes.

Peel, core, and chop apples.

Combine orange rind and pulp, pineapple, apples, and water in large kettle; bring to boil. Reduce heat; simmer, covered, 10 minutes. Add raisins and sugar; cook over moderate heat, stirring, until sugar dissolves. Add coconut; boil rapidly, stirring constantly, 20 to 30 minutes or until mixture sheets from spoon. Remove from heat; and skim off foam quickly. Immediately ladle into hot sterilized pint jars; fill to within ⅛-

Combine sugar and Burgundy in large saucepan; mix well. Stir over medium heat until dissolved; remove from heat. Add pectin; mix well. Skim off any foam. Pour immediately into 8 hot sterilized glasses; seal with ⅓-inch melted paraffin. Yield 8 glasses.

créme de menthe jelly

2½ cups sugar
1 cup water
1 cup créme de menthe
½ bottle liquid pectin

Combine sugar, water, and créme de menthe in large saucepan. Cook over medium heat; stir until dissolved. Remove from heat; stir in pectin. Yield 4 glasses.

ambrosia conserve

inch of tops. Cover tightly; invert jars several seconds. Stand jars upright to cool. Yield 4 pints.

burgundy jelly

6 cups sugar
4 cups Burgundy
1 bottle liquid pectin

416

orange jelly

1 (6-ounce) can frozen orange juice
3 tablespoons lemon juice
3¼ cups sugar
1 cup water
½ bottle liquid pectin

Combine orange and lemon juice; set aside.

Mix sugar and water in saucepan; put over high heat. Bring to full rolling boil; stir constantly. Boil hard 1 minute; remove from heat. Stir in pectin. Add fruit juices; mix well. Yield 4 glasses.

plum jam

6 cups purple plums, quartered, stones removed
1 cup water
4 cups sugar
1 tablespoon lemon juice

Combine plums and water in heavy enamel or stainless-steel pan; bring to boil. Reduce heat to low; cook until fruit is tender.

Meanwhile, measure sugar into bowl; place near pilot light to warm, or place in electric oven and set temperature on warm. Leave ele-ment on 3 minutes, turn off. Leave sugar in oven until ready for use.

When fruit is tender, add sugar and lemon juice; stir unti sugar is dissolved. Increase heat; boil 30 minutes, stirring to prevent burning, or until mixture jells when tested on cold saucer. Pour into hot sterilized jars; seal. Yield 6 cups.

quince jelly

6 pounds quinces
Sugar
Melted paraffin

Quarter quinces; remove cores with very sharp knife. Place in large kettle; add enough water to cover. Bring to boil; reduce heat. Simmer about 45 minutes, until tender.

Strain liquid through jelly bag or cloth into large bowl; do not squeeze bag. Measure liquid; place in large kettle. Add ¾ cup sugar for each cup of liquid. Bring to boil over medium heat; cook, stirring, until sugar is dissolved. Reduce heat; simmer about 20 minutes or to 220°F on candy thermometer. Remove from heat; skim thoroughly. Ladle into hot, sterilized 6-ounce jelly glasses; cover with paraffin. Yield 8 to 10 (6-ounce) glasses.

417

apricot-mint lamb

1 (6-pound) leg of lamb
2 teaspoons salt
¼ teaspoon ground black pepper
1 large onion or 1 teaspoon onion powder
¼ teaspoon garlic powder
1 bouillon cube, dissolved in 1 cup water
1 cup boiling water (approximately)
½ cup apricot preserves
½ teaspoon mint flavoring
¼ teaspoon summer savory
½ cup dry sherry
1 teaspoon arrowroot

Rub leg of lamb well with salt; brown on all sides in roasting pan over moderately high heat. Drain most of fat from pan. Blend pepper, onion, garlic and bouillon into remaining pan drippings; stir together well.

Mix boiling water, preserves, mint flavoring, and summer savory. Stir into bouillon mixture; add sherry. Roast in 350°F oven 20 to 30 minutes per pound; baste as needed. Blend arrowroot into pan liquid 30 minutes before removing from pan. Cook and stir often until sauce thickens. Yield 8 to 10 servings.

baked ribs of lamb

1 (2½-pound) strip of lamb ribs
Salt and freshly ground pepper to taste
2 tablespoons vegetable oil
1 tablespoon soy sauce
1 tablespoon tomato puree
1 clove garlic, pressed
Salt and pepper

baked ribs of lamb

Have thick, bony side of lamb strip cut through in several places when purchasing ribs.

Sprinkle ribs with salt and pepper; place on rack in roasting pan, meat-side-down. Bake in preheated 350°F oven 30 minutes. Turn; bake 30 minutes.

Combine oil, soy sauce, tomato puree, garlic, salt, and pepper in small bowl; brush over ribs. Bake 30 minutes. Cut ribs into serving pieces. Yield about 4 servings.

barbecued stuffed leg of lamb

1 onion, chopped
½ cup chopped dried apricots, soaked
3 tablespoons chopped raisins
3 tablespoons chopped dates
2 tablespoons chopped nuts
5 tablespoons cooked rice
2 tablespoons chopped parsley
1 teaspoon chopped marjoram
Little lemon rind and juice
Salt and pepper
1 leg of lamb, weighing 3 pounds after removal
   of bone
Little strong stock
1 clove garlic, slivered
Oil
Barbecue spice or barbecue sauce

Mix onion with apricots, raisins, and dates. Add nuts, rice, parsley, marjoram, lemon rind and juice, salt, pepper and enough stock to moisten. Fill stuffing into lamb cavity left by removal of bones; sew up slits. Insert garlic into small shallow slits cut into surface of lamb with point of sharp knife. Put lamb onto rod of spit; spoon oil over surface. Season well with salt, pepper, and barbecue spice or barbecue sauce. Cook about 1½ hours, until meat is tender and browned; baste with oil and seasoning when necessary. Yield 4 to 6 servings.

Make sauce with liquids from lamb and some stock and seasoning.

buckingham-glazed leg of lamb

1 (6-pound) leg of lamb
Salt and freshly ground pepper to taste
½ cup dry sherry
½ cup red currant jelly
½ cup catsup
½ teaspoon crushed marjoram leaves

Sprinkle lamb with salt and pepper; place on rack in shallow roasting pan. Roast in preheated 300 to 325°F oven 1½ to 2 hours.

barbecued stuffed leg of lamb

Combine sherry, jelly, catsup, and marjoram in small saucepan; heat, stirring constantly, until jelly is melted. Brush on lamb. Roast lamb 30 to 60 minutes or to 170° to 180°F on meat thermometer, according to desired doneness; brush with sauce occasionally. Place lamb on platter; garnish with parsley and lemon wedges. Yield about 8 servings.

Heat remaining sauce; serve with lamb.

california stuffed breast of lamb

4 to 5 tablespoons butter
1 cup chopped onion
½ cup chopped celery

1½ cups fresh white bread crumbs
½ cup raisins
1 teaspoon sugar
3 oranges
1 lemon
1 egg, beaten
Salt and pepper
3 pounds breast lamb without bones
Garlic powder
2 tablespoons seasoned flour
2 to 3 tablespoons oil
1 cup stock

Make stuffing. Melt butter; cook onion and celery slowly until soft without browning. Mix into bread crumbs; add raisins, sugar, and grated rind of 2 oranges and 1 lemon. Add juice

buckingham-glazed leg of lamb

419

of lemon and egg; season with salt and pepper. Add sections of 2 oranges; mix well. Let stand a few minutes before using.

Flatten lamb; dust over with garlic powder. Spread orange stuffing evenly over meat about ¼ inch thick. (Any left over can be cooked separately in buttered dish.) Roll meat tightly; tie in 3 or 4 places with white string. Roll in seasoned flour.

Warm oil in baking pan in oven. Add lamb; baste well. Cook in preheated 350°F oven 1½ hours; baste every 15 minutes. For last 10 minutes turn up oven to 400°F to brown outside of roll. When meat is tender and cooked through, remove; keep warm on serving dish.

Pour away excess fat; reserve juices. Add 1 teaspoon flour; mix well. Add stock and grated rind and juice of 1 orange; bring to boil. Season; serve. Yield 4 servings.

curry lamb ragout

1 pound lean lamb meat
2 tablespoons vegetable oil
½ teaspoon sage
Grated rind of half a lemon
1 medium onion, chopped
2 cups beef bouillon
1 tablespoon curry powder
½ teaspoon salt
⅛ teaspoon white pepper

1 green pepper, cut into strips
1 (8-ounce) can sliced mushrooms, drained
2 tomatoes, peeled, quartered
1 tart apple, peeled, cored, coarsely chopped
½ cup plain yogurt

Cut meat into 1-inch cubes.

Heat oil in heavy saucepan or Dutch oven. Add meat, sage, and lemon rind; brown meat on all sides. Add onion; sauté lightly. Drain off excess oil; stir in bouillon. Cover saucepan; simmer 50 minutes. Season with curry, salt, and pepper. Add green pepper; simmer, uncovered, 5 minutes. Stir in mushrooms, tomatoes, and apple; simmer 5 minutes. Cool mixture slightly; gradually add yogurt. Heat thoroughly without boiling; serve at once. Yield 4 servings.

danish blue lamb chops

8 loin or rib lamb chops, 1 inch thick
Oil
Ground black pepper
1 clove garlic, crushed (optional)
½ cup Danish blue or Roquefort cheese
2 tablespoons thick cream

Preheat broiler.

If using rib chops, trim and scrape rib bones. Brush chops with oil; sprinkle with pepper and garlic. Leave for couple of hours if possible before broiling.

california stuffed breast of lamb

Mix cheese and cream; mash well together to form paste.

Broil chops 5 to 6 minutes on each side; remove from heat. Spread cheese mixture on one side of each chop; replace under heat until cheese is light brown and bubbling. Yield 4 servings.

danish blue lamb chops

curry lamb ragout

durham lamb cutlets

½ pound or 2 cups cold cooked lamb
1 small onion
1 tablespoon butter
½ pound mashed potatoes
1 tablespoon chopped parsley

1 teaspoon tomato puree
Salt and pepper to taste
2 tablespoons flour
1 egg
3 to 4 tablespoons dried white bread crumbs
Fat for deep frying

Grind or chop meat very fine.

Chop onions finely; cook in melted butter until golden brown. Add mashed potatoes and meat to onion. Add parsley, tomato puree, salt, and pepper; cook a few seconds. Turn mixture onto plate to cool. Divide into 8 equal-size portions; form into cutlet shapes. Roll each in flour; dip into beaten egg until coated all over. Roll in bread crumbs.

Heat fat in deep skillet. When smoking slightly, put 3 or 4 cutlets into frying basket; lower into hot fat. Cook until cutlets are rich brown; drain on paper towel. Keep warm while frying remaining cutlets. Arrange in overlapping circle around hot dish; serve with vegetables and brown or tomato sauce. Yield 4 servings.

grilled piquant lamb

1 (5-pound) leg of lamb
Vegetable oil
Salt
½ teaspoon freshly ground pepper
½ cup water
½ cup red wine
2 tablespoons wine vinegar
1 tablespoon Worcestershire sauce
¼ cup lemon juice
1 teaspoon dry mustard
Dash of hot sauce
¼ teaspoon paprika
1 clove garlic, pressed
1 medium onion, grated

Rub lamb with 1 tablespoon oil, 1 tablespoon salt, and pepper. Place on grill over low coals or in 325 °F oven; cook about ¾ to 1 hour. Turn occasionally; brush with oil.

grilled piquant lamb

Combine water, wine, vinegar, Worcestershire sauce, lemon juice, mustard, hot sauce, paprika, garlic, onion, 1 tablespoon oil, and ½ teaspoon salt in saucepan; bring to boil. Brush lamb with sauce; cook about 1 hour, to desired degree of doneness. Turn occasionally; brush with sauce. If using oven, turn on broiler after final brushing to glaze slightly.   Yield about 10 servings.

hawaiian skewered sweet-and-sour lamb with rice

1 (16-ounce) can pineapple chunks
2 tablespoons soy sauce
¼ cup lemon juice

1 clove garlic, pressed
2 pounds boneless lamb, cut into 2-inch cubes
12 pitted black olives

Drain pineapple; reserve the juice. Mix reserved pineapple juice, soy sauce, lemon juice, and garlic in large, shallow dish. Add lamb cubes; marinate in refrigerator several hours or overnight. Remove lamb from marinade; drain. Reserve marinade. Arrange lamb, olives, and pineapple chunks alternately on skewers. Place skewers on rack in broiler pan; place broiler pan 9 to 10 inches from source of heat. Broil, turning and basting with reserved marinade frequently, until lamb is cooked to desired doneness.

Pour remaining marinade into small, heavy saucepan; simmer until thick. This makes a teriyaki sauce to serve with kebabs and rice. Yield about 6 servings.

lamb chops with herbs

423

lamb chops venetian-style

lamb chops with herbs on grill

4 large loin or 8 rib lamb chops
1 teaspoon thyme
1 teaspoon oregano
1 teaspoon rosemary
3 small bay leaves, crushed
6 coriander seeds, crushed
Grated rind and juice of 1 lemon
Pinch of paprika
6 tablespoons oil
Salt and pepper
Butter

Trim chops of excess fat.

Mix herbs, lemon rind, and paprika. Rub mixture well into both sides of chops. Arrange chops in large shallow dish; pour lemon juice and oil over them. Season lightly with salt and pepper; set aside in cool place about 3 hours, turning occasionally.

When ready to cook, drain chops well; put on grid over hot coals. Turn once or twice while cooking; allow about 16 to 20 minutes.

If any dried herbs are left over, a good pinch sprinkled over hot coals just before removal of chops will give delicious aroma and improve flavor.

Serve chops with pat of butter on each and plain tossed salad. Yield 4 servings.

lamb chops venetian-style

2 tablespoons butter or margarine
2 tablespoons olive oil
4 lamb shoulder chops (approximately 2 pounds)
Salt and pepper to taste
1 medium onion
1¾ pounds eggplant
3 tablespoons tomato paste
½ teaspoon crumbled dried sweet basil
½ cup boiling water
½ (10-ounce) package frozen peas
1 (8½-ounce) can artichoke bottoms (or 1 can artichoke hearts), drained, quartered

Heat butter and oil in heavy skillet.

Wipe chops with damp cloth; season with salt and pepper. Sauté in butter and oil approximately 4 minutes per side, until well-browned and almost done. Remove from pan; keep warm.

While chops cook, peel onion; quarter; separate layers.

Cut stem from eggplant; cut in half lengthwise; thinly slice.

Add onion to skillet; sauté 5 minutes, Add eggplant.

Combine tomato paste, basil, and boiling water; stir well. Add to skillet; bring to boil. Reduce heat to low; cover. Cook 15 minutes. Add peas, artichokes and lamb chops. Cook, covered, 15 minutes or until vegetables are done through. Yield 4 servings.

lamb kidneys en chemise

4 large potatoes
4 lamb kidneys
Salt and pepper
2 mushrooms
½ onion
4 slices streaky bacon
Prepared mustard
2 tablespoons butter

Wash and scrub potatoes; bake in their skins just over 1 hour in 350°F oven. Remove from oven; cut good slice from top of each. Take out enough potato to make room for a kidney.

Skin and core kidneys; season with salt and pepper. Roll in mixture of finely chopped mushrooms and onion; wrap in half a slice of bacon smeared with mustard. Place wrapped kidneys into potatoes; add ½ tablespoon butter to each potato. Replace potato tops; wrap whole in foil. Return to oven 1 hour to cook kidneys. Yield 4 servings.

peninsula lamb shanks

6 (1-pound) lamb shanks
1½ teaspoons salt
¼ teaspoon pepper
3 tablespoons oil
3 tablespoons flour
1 (14-ounce) can chicken broth
1 medium onion, sliced
1 clove garlic, finely minced
4 cups sliced celery
3 medium tomatoes, cut into wedges
1 tablespoon chopped parsley

Sprinkle lamb with salt and pepper.

Heat oil in Dutch oven. Add lamb; brown well on all sides. Remove lamb; set aside.

Stir flour into oil; brown lightly. Gradually blend in broth and 1¾ cups water; bring to boil. Return lamb to Dutch oven; add onion and garlic. Reduce heat; cover. Simmer 1¼ to 1½ hours, until lamb is tender; remove lamb to warm serving platter.

Add celery to liquid in Dutch oven; cook 10 minutes. Add tomatoes and parsley; cook 5 minutes. Spoon over lamb. Yield 6 servings.

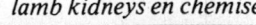

lamb kidneys en chemise

peninsula lamb shanks

roast leg of lamb

1 (6-pound) leg of lamb
3 teaspoons salt
¼ teaspoon pepper
2 tablespoons flour
1 bay leaf
1 teaspoon instant minced onion

Preheat oven to 325°F.

Wipe lamb with damp cloth; do not remove fell.

Combine salt and pepper; rub all over meat. Insert meat thermometer into fleshy part away from bone. Place on rack in shallow roasting pan. Roast, uncovered, 2½ to 3 hours, until meat thermometer reads 175°F for medium lamb, 180°F for well-done. Remove to heated platter, keep warm.

Make gravy. Pour off drippings; reserve 2 tablespoons in roasting pan. Stir in flour until smooth; gradually stir in 2 cups cold water. Add bay leaf and onion; bring to boiling, stirring constantly. Reduce heat; simmer 5 minutes. Serve hot in gravy boat, along with lamb. Yield 6 to 8 servings.

roast leg of lamb bandit-style

1 leg of lamb (4 to 5 pounds), boned, rolled, tied
2 cloves garlic, cut into slivers
Salt and pepper
2 tablespoons butter
1 (3-foot) section heavy-duty aluminum foil
2 pounds pearl onions, peeled, parboiled
2 tablespoons chopped parsley
1 teaspoon dried dillweed
½ cup white wine
¼ cup olive oil
Juice of 1 lemon

Cut slits in fat on outside of lamb; insert garlic. Rub with salt and pepper.

Heat butter in deep skillet; brown lamb well on all sides. Place lamb on aluminum foil.

Add onions to skillet; brown. Add parsley and dill; spoon mixture around lamb. Pour wine, oil, and lemon juice over lamb. Fold foil around lamb; seal tightly. Place package in large roasting pan. Bake at 375°F 2 to 3 hours, depending on desired doneness. Yield 6 to 8 servings.

roast leg of lamb with brussels sprouts and baby carrots au vin blanc

1 leg of lamb, about 5 pounds
½ teaspoon salt
1 cup currant jelly
2 (10-ounce) packages frozen brussels sprouts
½ cup dry white wine
1 (1-pound) can whole small carrots, drained
Salt and pepper to taste

Sprinkle lamb with ½ teaspoon salt; place on rack in shallow roasting pan. Roast in 325°F oven about 2½ hours, until meat thermometer registers 175 to 180°F, depending on desired doneness. After 1 hour, spread lamb with currant jelly, continue roasting, brushing frequently with jelly. During last 45 minutes of roasting, arrange frozen brussels sprouts around lamb; baste with some of wine. During last 15 minutes of roasting, arrange carrots around lamb; baste with remaining wine. Season vegetables with salt and pepper. Yield 6 servings.

roast rack of lamb with anchovies

1 rack of lamb with 8 or 9 bones
1 clove garlic, crushed
Black pepper
1 can anchovy fillets
Little milk
2 to 3 tablespoons oil
1 cup brown stock

roast rack of lamb with anchovies

Trim lamb by exposing last inch of bones and scraping them clean. Score lamb fat in trellis pattern; rub in garlic and black pepper.

Drain anchovies of oil; soak in milk 10 minutes. Rinse carefully; dry.

Heat oil in roasting pan. When smoking, put in meat; baste with hot fat. Cook in preheated 400°F oven about 30 to 40 minutes, according to size and personal preference; baste every 10 minutes. After 15 to 25 minutes place anchovies in crisscross design over fat of meat; continue cooking. When cooked, remove; keep warm while roasting liquid is heated with stock to make gravy. Yield 4 servings.

skewered lamb

¼ cup minced onion
1 clove garlic, minced
3 tablespoons olive oil
3 tablespoons lemon juice
1 teaspoon salt
¼ teaspoon pepper
½ teaspoon crumbled dried oregano
1½ pounds leg of lamb or lamb shoulder meat,
  cut into 2-inch cubes
16 small boiling onions, peeled
16 mushrooms, cleaned, stems removed
2 red peppers, cut into chunks

Combine minced onion, garlic, oil, lemon juice, salt, pepper, and oregano in glass bowl or casserole. Add lamb; stir well. Cover; marinate 3 to 4 hours (or longer in refrigerator), stirring occasionally.

Parboil 16 onions in salted water 10 minutes. Drain; cool.

Drain lamb; reserve marinade. Skewer vegetables and lamb alternately (lamb cube, onion, mushroom, and pepper chunk; repeat). Cook over charcoal or in broiler about 15 minutes; brush frequently with marinade. Serve with rice. Yield 4 servings.

variation

Substitute cherry tomatoes and green peppers for red peppers. Skewer onions and meat alternately. Skewer vegetables separately; brush them with marinade. Tomatoes can be grilled only a short time or they will fall off skewer before meat is done. Start meat first; add skewered vegetables 5 minutes before meat is finished.

snow-capped lamb or veal chops

6 (½-inch) shoulder or sirloin chops
Butter or oil
Salt and pepper
1 can condensed consommé
½ teaspoon thyme
½ cup chopped celery
½ cup green onions and tops, sliced
1 (3-ounce) can chopped mushrooms
3 tablespoons flour
1 tablespoon parsley flakes
1 cup sour cream

Slowly brown chops in small amount hot butter or oil. Sprinkle with salt and pepper; drain off fat. Add consommé, thyme, celery, and onions; cover. Simmer 30 to 45 minutes, until meat is done; stack chops to one side.

skewered lamb

Drain mushrooms; reserve liquid. Stir mushroom liquid slowly into flour; blend. Gradually stir into meat gravy; stir constantly until thick. Add mushrooms and parsley. Top chops with sour cream; cover. Heat about 3 minutes; sprinkle with chopped onion tops. Yield 6 servings.

stuffed crown roast of lamb

Crown of lamb, at least 2 ribs per person
Oil for roasting
Salt and pepper
1 to 1½ cups cooked rice
½ cup cooked peas
½ cup cooked corn
¼ cup chopped cooked red and green sweet
  peppers
1 onion, chopped
3 to 4 tablespoons butter
¼ cup almonds skinned, sliced, slightly browned
½ cup raisins
2 to 3 tablespoons sherry
Chopped mixed herbs

Have butcher prepare roast; allow 16 ribs to make a nice-size roast. Cover tips of rib bones with foil to prevent burning; crumble some foil into center of roast to preserve shape while roasting.

Heat 2 to 3 tablespoons oil in roasting pan; put in roast. Baste with hot fat; put into preheated 450°F oven. After 10 minutes reduce heat to 350°F; cook 20 to 25 minutes per pound. Season with salt and pepper; baste every 15 minutes.

Meanwhile prepare stuffing. Boil rice. When cooked and drained, mix in peas, corn, and peppers.

Cook onion gently in butter until golden brown. Add to rice, along with almonds and raisins which have been soaked in a little sherry. Add seasoning and herbs.

When crown roast is cooked, remove from oven; put on serving dish. Remove foil; fill center with rice stuffing. Decorate chop bones with paper or foil frills; serve roast with green vegetable and gravy made with roasting juices and red currant jelly. Carve down between bones; allow 2 per person. Yield 6 to 8 servings.

stuffed lamb chops

6 double-rib lamb chops
1 (3-ounce) can mushroom slices, drained
2 tablespoons mushroom liquid
1 teaspoon salt
¼ cup dry sherry wine
1 egg, beaten
½ cup bread crumbs
¼ teaspoon white pepper

Using sharp knife, make slit from bone side between rib bones into center of meat on each chop.

Drain mushrooms; reserve 2 tablespoons liquid. Mix together reserved mushroom liquid, ½ teaspoon salt, sherry, egg, mushrooms, and bread crumbs. Stuff chops with mixture. Sprinkle with ½ teaspoon salt and pepper. Broil chops 4 to 5 inches from flame 12 minutes on each side. Serve immediately. Yield 6 servings.

turkish kofte in tomato sauce

½ cup cider (or light white wine)
2 slices stale white bread
1 pound ground lamb
1 large onion, finely chopped or ground
1 tablespoon chopped parsley
1 teaspoon chopped thyme
1 teaspoon lemon rind
2 teaspoons paprika
Salt
2 eggs, beaten
2 to 3 tablespoons seasoned flour
5 to 6 tablespoons butter
Tomato Sauce
½ pint sour cream or plain yogurt

Pour cider over bread; leave for some minutes to soak.

Put meat in large bowl with onion, parsley, thyme, lemon rind, paprika, and salt.

Squeeze cider out of bread; put bread into meat mixture. Beat mixture by hand; add eggs gradually. Beating should take 7 to 10 minutes and gives meatballs their light texture. With either wet or oiled hands roll 1 tablespoon mixture at a time into rounds; cover with flour.

Melt butter in frying pan. Brown meatballs; put into ovenproof dish. Pour Tomato Sauce over. Bake in preheated 350°F oven 30 to 40 minutes. Serve with sour cream or yogurt spooned over meat; sprinkle chopped parsley on top. Yield 4 servings.

tomato sauce
3 tablespoons butter
1 medium onion, sliced
1 clove garlic, crushed
1 cup peeled, chopped tomatoes (or canned tomatoes)
1 tablespoon chopped parsley
1 teaspoon basil
Salt and pepper
1 teaspoon paprika
Cider from soaked bread

Melt butter; cook onion and garlic 5 to 6 minutes. Add remaining ingredients; heat to boiling.

turkish kofte in tomato sauce

blueberry pancakes

1 cup milk
2 tablespoons light corn syrup
1 tablespoon corn oil
1 egg, lightly beaten
1 cup pancake mix
¾ cup blueberries
⅓ cup cottage cheese

Combine milk, corn syrup, corn oil, and egg in mixing bowl. Add pancake mix; stir until dry ingredients are moistened. Batter will be lumpy. Stir in blueberries and cottage cheese carefully.

PANCAKES

Pour ¼ cup batter onto hot griddle; cook until brown, turning once. Repeat cooking until all batter is used. Yield 8 pancakes.

dollar nut pancakes

1½ cups flour
2 tablespoons sugar
1 tablespoon baking powder
½ teaspoon salt
1 egg, beaten
1½ cups milk
¼ cup chopped nuts
Fat for frying

Mix ingredients in order given; beat in nuts after rest is smooth. Drop by teaspoons onto greased hot skillet or griddle. When pancake top is covered with bubbles and edges firm, turn to brown other side. Store on hot platter until ready to serve. Yield 16 to 24 small pancakes.

griddle cakes or pancakes

2 cups flour
3 teaspoons baking powder
½ teaspoon salt
1 tablespoon sugar

blueberry pancakes

dollar nut pancakes

2 eggs
1¼ cups milk

Sift together flour, baking powder, salt, and sugar.

Beat eggs well; stir in milk. Add flour mixture; beat until smooth. Add melted shortening. Pour from tablespoon onto hot griddle or frying pan (there is no need to use grease). Cook until golden brown; turning only once. Yield about 24.

jelly pancakes

1 cup sifted flour
1 teaspoon baking powder
½ teaspoon salt
1 teaspoon sugar
2 egg yolks, slightly beaten
1 cup milk
2 tablespoons melted butter or margarine
2 egg whites, stiffly beaten

Sift flour once; measure. Add baking powder, salt, and sugar; sift again.

Combine egg yolks and milk. Add gradually to flour mixture; beat only until smooth. Add butter. Fold in egg whites. Bake on hot, greased griddle. Spread with jelly and roll, or roll around fried sausages or bacon and serve. Yield 6 (7-inch) pancakes.

puffed pancakes

2½ cups all-purpose flour, sifted
1 tablespoon sugar
¼ teaspoon salt
2 eggs, lightly beaten
1⅓ cups milk
1¼ teaspoons cream of tartar
2 tablespoons oil

Sift flour, sugar, and salt together into mixing bowl.

Beat eggs and milk together until blended. Add to flour mixture; blend well.

Sift cream of tartar over surface of batter; fold in gently.

Heat oil on heavy griddle or frying pan until drop of water sizzles when sprinkled on griddle. Drop batter by spoonfuls onto hot griddle. Cook until lightly browned. Turn; brown other side. Stack hot pancakes on serving platter; serve with crisp-fried bacon.

One-fourth cup chocolate chips can be added to batter before baking; pancakes served with 1 cup raisins heated in 1½ cups maple syrup. Yield 24 small pancakes.

rice pancakes

4 tablespoons butter, melted
3 whole eggs, beaten
2 cups cooked rice
2 teaspoons baking powder
1 teaspoon salt
1 cup flour
¼ cup milk or cream
Shortening for frying

Mix ingredients in order given, adding milk last.

PANCAKES

puffed pancakes

Heat shortening in skillet. Drop batter from tablespoon into hot fat. When golden brown on one side, turn pancake. Add extra shortening if needed. Serve with apricot preserves. Yield about 6 servings.

shrove tuesday pancakes

2 cups sifted all-purpose flour
2 teaspoons baking soda
2 teaspoons sugar
½ teaspoon salt
2 eggs, lightly beaten

3 tablespoons melted butter or margarine
2 cups buttermilk

Sift dry ingredients together into mixing bowl.

Beat eggs, butter, and buttermilk together well. Add to dry ingredients; combine thoroughly without overmixing (small lumps may remain). Bake on hot, lightly greased griddle or heavy frying pan until golden. Turn; continue cooking. Serve pancakes hot. Spread with butter; sprinkle with sugar. Yield 12.

sweet hungarian pancakes

pancake batter
2 large eggs, separated
1 cup milk
½ cup flour
1 tablespoon sugar
1 tablespoon rum (optional)
⅛ teaspoon salt
2 tablespoons melted butter

Butter or margarine for greasing

rice pancakes

¾ to 1 cup apricot jam or preserves
½ cup ground hazelnuts
2 tablespoons powdered sugar

Beat egg yolks in medium-size mixing bowl until well-mixed. Add milk, flour, sugar, rum, and salt; beat with wire whisk until smooth. Blend in melted butter. Refrigerate batter 1 hour.

Beat egg whites until stiff but not dry; fold into batter; combine well.

Lightly grease 8-inch heavy skillet or omelet pan with butter. Place over moderate heat until few drops of water sprinkled in skillet dance.

Stir batter.

Remove pan from heat; pour in 3 tablespoons batter. Quickly tilt pan in all directions to coat bottom with batter. Return to heat; cook until lightly browned. Turn; cook few seconds on other side. Transfer to warm plate. Continue in same manner; stir batter before making each pancake. Stack with waxed paper between; keep warm until all pancakes are cooked. Place 1½ tablespoons jam in center of each pancake; roll. Place side by side on ovenproof platter.

Combine hazelnuts and sugar; sprinkle over pancakes. Heat in 325°F oven 10 minutes. Serve with coffee. Yield 10 to 12 pancakes, about 6 servings.

PANCAKES

sweet hungarian pancakes

FETTUCINE

fettucine alfredo

1 pound fettucine noodles
¼ pound butter, softened
1 egg yolk
4 tablespoons heavy cream
½ cup freshly grated Parmesan cheese
Salt and freshly ground black pepper

Boil noodles in kettle of salted water.

Meanwhile beat butter until fluffy. Beat in egg yolk and cream. When well blended, beat in cheese, salt, and plenty of black pepper.

Drain noodles well; toss with sauce. Serve immediately. Yield 6 servings.

fettucine florentine

1 pound sliced bacon
1 pound fettucine noodles
3 teaspoons salt
½ cup butter
1 (10-ounce) package frozen chopped spinach, thawed, drained
1½ cups heavy cream
1 egg, slightly beaten
2 cups grated Parmesan cheese
¼ teaspoon pepper

Cook bacon in skillet until lightly browned. Drain; crumble.

Cook noodles in saucepan according to package directions; use 1 teaspoon salt in water.

Melt butter in large chafing dish over canned heat. Add spinach and bacon; cook until heated through. Add noodles; toss lightly.

Combine cream and eggs; add with cheese, remaining salt, and pepper to noodles. Toss to mix well; cover. Cook 5 minutes to heat through. Yield 6 to 8 servings.

baked lasagna

PASTA

mushroom fettucine

1 (10½-ounce) can condensed cream of mushroom soup
¾ cup milk
½ cup grated Parmesan cheese
3 cups hot cooked fettucine noodles
4 tablespoons butter or margarine

Stir soup in large saucepan until smooth; blend in milk and cheese. Heat; stir occasionally. Just before serving, toss noodles with butter; combine with soup mixture. Serve with additional cheese. Yield 4 servings.

LASAGNA

baked lasagna

pasta
3 quarts water
2 teaspoons salt
1 tablespoon vegetable oil
8 ounces lasagna noodles

sauce
1 pound ground beef
2 mild Italian sausage links (casings removed)
1 tablespoon olive oil
1 medium onion, finely diced
1 clove garlic, minced
1 (28-ounce) can peeled Italian tomatoes
1 (6-ounce) can tomato paste
½ teaspoon crumbled dried oregano
½ teaspoon crumbled dried sweet basil
1 teaspoon sugar

filling
8 ounces ricotta or pot cheese
8 ounces mozzarella cheese, thinly sliced
½ cup freshly grated Parmesan cheese

Prepare pasta. Combine water and salt in large kettle. Float oil on surface of water; bring to boil. Slowly add noodles, a few at a time; cook 15 minutes. Drain; rinse with cold water. Arrange on toweling to drain.

Meanwhile, prepare sauce. Brown beef and sausages in large skillet. Remove from pan; pour off drippings.

Add oil to skillet; sauté onion and garlic over low heat 5 minutes. Add tomatoes, broken up with fork; tomato paste; and seasonings. Stir well; add meat to sauce. Cook over low heat 40 minutes or until thick.

Lightly grease 13 × 9 × 2-inch baking dish. Ladle approximately ¾ cup sauce into pan. Top with ⅓ of noodles. Dot with ½ the ricotta and ½ the mozzarella. Add layer of sauce and ⅓ of noodles and remaining ricotta and mozzarella.

Top with more sauce; add remaining noodles. Top with remaining sauce; sprinkle with Parmesan cheese. Bake at 350°F 30 minutes or until heated through. Yield 6 servings.

easy lasagna

Garlic powder to taste
Onion powder to taste
Salt to taste
Freshly ground black pepper to taste
Pinch of oregano
1 pound ground beef
½ box (8-ounces) lasagna noodles
1 large can tomato sauce

Add seasonings to ground beef; brown meat in skillet.

Boil noodles; cut each noodle in half the short way. Place 2 or 3 tablespoons meat mixture on each noodle; roll up. Place seam-side-down in pan; pour tomato sauce over. Bake at 350°F 30 to 40 minutes. Yield 4 servings.

LINGUINE

linguine with salmon sauce

2 cloves garlic, minced
¼ cup butter
¼ cup olive oil
1 teaspoon coarsely cracked pepper
1 (7¾-ounce) can salmon
Clam juice
1 pound linguine or thin spaghetti, cooked
2 tablespoons chopped parsley

Saute garlic in butter and oil until lightly browned; add pepper.

Drain liquid from salmon into measuring cup; add clam juice to make 1 cup.

Flake salmon; add with liquid to garlic mixture. Bring to simmer; just before serving over linguine, stir in parsley. Yield 4 servings.

MACARONI

elbow macaroni goldenrod

8 ounces elbow macaroni
2 tablespoons butter or margarine
2 tablespoons flour
2½ cups milk
Salt and pepper to taste
1 pimiento, chopped
2 tablespoons minced parsley
3 hard-cooked eggs

Cook macaroni in boiling salted water 7 to 10 minutes or until tender; drain.

Melt butter, stir in flour. Add milk gradually; stir over low heat until smooth and thick. Season with salt and pepper. Add pimiento, parsley, and chopped whites of eggs. Combine sauce with macaroni; arrange on large platter. Sprinkle center with egg yolks pressed through sieve; garnish with parsley and pimiento. Yield 6 servings.

macaroni with broccoli

1 cup small-size elbow macaroni
2 cups coarsely chopped, cooked, broccoli
¼ cup olive oil
1 small clove garlic, crushed
Salt to taste

Cook macaroni in boiling salted water 7 to 10 minutes, until tender; drain. Mix with broccoli, oil, garlic, and salt; reheat. Yield 4 servings.

yankee doodle macaroni

3 tablespoons cooking fat
2 cups finely chopped onion
2 cloves garlic, crushed
½ cup sliced mushrooms
1 pound ground beef
1 can (about 1 pound 13 ounces) peeled tomatoes
1 tablespoon chopped parsley
Salt and pepper
1 (7- to 8-ounce) package macaroni
1 to 2 tablespoons margarine
Grated Parmesan or sharp cheddar cheese

Heat fat in pan. Add onion, garlic, and mushrooms; sauté until onion becomes pale yellow. Add meat; and stir until browned. Add tomatoes, parsley, and seasonings; cover. Simmer about 45 minutes.

While meat is cooking, cook macaroni in boiling salted water 7 to 10 minutes; drain well. Toss in margarine. Turn macaroni onto hot platter. Pour sauce over; sprinkle with grated cheese. Yield 6 or 7 servings.

NOODLES
deep-fried crispy noodles

1 (5-ounce) package fine egg noodles
Vegetable oil

Place noodles in large saucepan in enough water to cover; bring to boil. Cook, stirring occasionally, 5 minutes; drain well.

Fill deep-fat fryer half full with oil; heat to 350°F. Drop noodles into basket in oil; cook 2 minutes. Remove from oil; drain well on paper towels.

Heat oil to 375°F. Return noodles to deep-fat fryer; cook until golden brown and crisp. Drain well on paper towels; separate noodles, if necessary. Yield 4 to 5 cups.

yankee doodle macaroni

homemade noodles

1⅓ cups all-purpose flour
¾ teaspoon salt

2 eggs
2 teaspoons cooking oil
2 teaspoons water

Combine flour and salt in mixing bowl; make well in center.

deep-fried crispy noodles

homemade noodles

Beat eggs, oil, and water together; pour into well. Stir with fork from outside of mixture to center. Add small amount water if necessary, so that very stiff dough is formed. Turn onto lightly floured surface; knead until smooth and elastic (about 15 minutes). Let rest, covered, 30 minutes.

Divide dough into 4 equal parts. Roll 1 piece at a time as thin as possible; it should be 1/16 inch thick. Roll up; cut into 1/2-inch strips. Unroll strips; allow to dry several hours on lightly floured towel.

Bring several quarts salted water to boil in Dutch oven; add 1 tablespoon oil or butter. Add noodles; stir to keep from sticking to bottom of pot. Cook until tender; test frequently for doneness. Noodles should still be firm, not mushy; drain well. Top with melted butter; serve or use in other recipes. Yield 4 or 5 servings.

hungarian pinched noodles

½ cup flour
⅛ teaspoon salt
1 egg, well-beaten
Flour for kneading

Combine flour and salt in small bowl; make well in center. Add egg; mix to form stiff dough. Turn onto lightly floured surface; knead 5 minutes. Divide into 3 parts; roll each part, with hands, to form long cylinder about as big around as little finger. Pinch off small pieces; add directly to boiling soup, or cook in boiling salted water until tender (about 5 minutes). When done, noodle should cut easily and not be floury in center. Generally, half this recipe is sufficient for 1½ quarts soup. Pinch remaining noodles; allow to stand on lightly floured board until dry. Store airtight for future use. Yield about 8 servings, enough for 3 quarts soup.

kasha noodles

8 ounces egg noodles
⅔ cup oil
½ pound mushrooms, sliced
1 cup chopped onion
2 cups cooked kasha
1 teaspoon salt

Cook noodles until tender; drain.

Meanwhile, in large skillet heat oil and cook mushrooms and onion until tender; add kasha and salt. Add hot noodles; toss well. Yield about 6 side-dish servings.

noodle luncheon ring

1 (12-ounce) package noodles
Chicken broth
3 eggs
1 cup sour cream
1 small package cream cheese
½ cup crushed pineapple
Handful of white raisins
Pinch of salt
1 tablespoon sugar
Dash of nutmeg

Boil noodles in chicken broth until just tender; drain. Cover; let steam 1 hour.

Beat eggs, sour cream, and cream cheese. Add pineapple, raisins, salt, sugar, and nutmeg; mix well. Pour into mold that has been greased and lined with waxed paper. Bake 45 minutes at 300°F. Turn onto platter; fill with peas and carrots or mushrooms. Yield 12 servings.

noodle ring with meat sauce

2 tablespoons oil
1 onion, peeled, chopped
1 clove garlic, crushed
1 cup ground beef
1 tablespoon tomato puree
1 cooking apple, peeled, cored, chopped
Salt and pepper
¼ teaspoon sugar
¼ teaspoon dried basil
1 (8-ounce) can peeled tomatoes
12 ounces noodles
Chopped parsley

Heat oil in pan. Add onion and garlic; cook until onion begins to brown. Add meat; stir over medium heat 5 minutes. Add tomato puree, apple, salt, pepper, sugar, basil, and tomatoes; cover. Simmer about 40 minutes.

While sauce is cooking, cook noodles in boiling salted water; drain. Pack into well-greased ring mold; keep hot.

When ready to serve, turn noodle ring onto hot dish; pile sauce in middle. Sprinkle with chopped parsley. Yield 4 servings.

noodles with fresh tomato

½ pound thin noodles
Salt to taste
1 large, red, ripe tomato, about ¾ pound
2 tablespoons butter
Freshly ground pepper to taste

Bring enough water to boil to cover noodles when added; add salt.

Core and peel tomato; cut into ½-inch cubes.

Drop noodles into boiling water; cook until tender.

Heat 1 tablespoon butter in saucepan; add tomato and salt and pepper to taste. Cook about 1 minute; stir occasionally.

Drain noodles; serve with tomatoes spooned over. Yield 4 servings.

pasta with eggs and red-devil sauce

1½ tablespoons salad oil
1 (8-ounce) package mezzani
1 tablespoon olive oil
1 teaspoon finely chopped fresh sage or parsley
10 hard-boiled eggs, peeled
Red-Devil Sauce

Bring 2 quarts heavily salted water to boil; add salad oil. Add mezzani slowly; cook 14 to 16 minutes, to desired doneness. Drain; place in serving dish. Add olive oil; toss lightly. Sprinkle with sage.

Cut eggs in half lengthwise; place in shallow serving dish. Pour hot sauce over eggs; serve over mezzani. Yield 4 to 6 servings.

pasta with eggs and red-devil sauce

red-devil sauce

½ cup tarragon vinegar
1 teaspoon dry mustard
1 teaspoon paprika
½ teaspoon white pepper
1 clove garlic, sliced
¾ teaspoon salt
2 bay leaves
¼ teaspoon cayenne pepper
½ cup beef consommé
2 tablespoons butter
1 tablespoon Worcestershire sauce
1 (15-ounce) can tomato sauce

Combine vinegar, mustard, paprika, white pepper, garlic, salt, bay leaves, and cayenne pepper in saucepan. Boil until mixture is reduced by half. Strain through fine sieve. Return to saucepan; add consommé, butter, Worcestershire sauce, and tomato sauce. Simmer 8 minutes; keep warm. Yield about 2¾ cups.

soft-fried noodles with mushrooms

1 (5-ounce) package fine egg noodles
2 tablespoons safflower oil
1 cup bamboo shoots
1 cup sliced fresh mushrooms
1 cup sliced almonds
½ cup chicken broth
3 tablespoons soy sauce
1 teaspoon salt

Cook noodles in large saucepan in boiling, lightly salted water 6 to 8 minutes; drain thoroughly.

Heat oil in wok or large skillet over low heat. Add noodles; stir-fry 4 minutes. Stir in bamboo shoots, mushrooms, and almonds; mix well. Stir in broth, soy sauce, and salt; reduce heat to very low. Simmer, covered, 20 minutes or until liquid is almost absorbed. Serve with additional soy sauce, if desired. Yield 8 to 10 servings.

viennese noodles

8 ounces wide egg noodles
¼ cup butter
½ cup chopped almonds or Brazil nuts
2 teaspoons poppy seeds

Cook noodles; drain.

Melt 1 tablespoon butter. Add chopped nuts; stir over low heat until light brown. Add remaining butter, noodles, and poppy seeds; stir lightly until thoroughly heated. Serve with any creamed meat or fish dish, or with creamed mushrooms. Can also be served as an entree with tomato or any desired sauce. Yield 6 servings.

RAVIOLI

basic ravioli dough

3 cups all-purpose flour
¼ teaspoon salt
2 eggs
⅓ cup water

Stir together flour and salt in bowl; make well in center. Add eggs; beat well. Stir in enough water to form very stiff dough. Turn onto lightly floured surface. Knead until dough is smooth and elastic, about 10 minutes. Yield ????

chicken ravioli

1 recipe Basic Ravioli Dough (see Index)
2 tablespoons chopped onion

1 tablespoon olive oil or cooking oil
1 (10-ounce) package frozen chopped spinach
1 egg
½ cup ricotta cheese
¼ cup grated Parmesan cheese
1 cup finely diced cooked chicken
Spicy Tomato Sauce
Grated Parmesan cheese

On floured surface roll dough as thin as possible; cover. Let rest a few minutes. Repeat, rolling and resting until dough measures 20 × 18 inches. Let rest 20 minutes. Trim evenly; cut into 10 (18 × 2-inch) strips.

Cook onion in oil until tender.

Cook spinach until just tender. Drain; press out excess liquid. Measure ½ cup spinach (use remainder elsewhere).

Combine egg, ricotta, and ¼ cup Parmesan. Add ½ cup spinach, onion, and chicken; mix well.

Moisten 1 dough strip lightly with water; place spinach mixture by teaspoonfuls at 2-inch intervals, beginning 1 inch from end of strip. Top with second strip of dough; press gently around each mound and around edges. Cut dough with pastry wheel at 2-inch intervals to make squares centered

with filling. Repeat with remaining filling and pasta strips. Dry 1 hour; turn over once.

Meanwhile, prepare Spicy Tomato Sauce.

Cook ravioli in large amount rapidly boiling salted water 8 to 10 minutes; drain. Serve with Spicy Tomato Sauce. Pass Parmesan. Yield 6 to 8 servings.

spicy tomato sauce
1 (15-ounce) can tomato sauce
1 (8-ounce) can tomatoes, cut up
1 cup water
¼ cup finely chopped onion
2 tablespoons snipped parsley
2 teaspoons sugar
1 teaspoon salt
1 teaspoon crushed dried oregano

Combine ingredients; simmer 30 to 40 minutes, stirring frequently.

meat ravioli

basic ravioli dough (see Index)

filling
¾ pound meat-loaf mix
¼ cup dry bread crumbs

meat ravioli

2 tablespoons grated Parmesan cheese
1 egg
1 tablespoon dehydrated parsley flakes
½ teaspoon garlic salt
¼ teaspoon pepper

Prepare ravioli dough according to recipe; let rest, covered, 10 minutes.

Combine filling ingredients in bowl; mix well. Refrigerate until ready to use.

Divide dough into 8 pieces. Roll 1 piece at a time on lightly floured surface; keep remainder of dough tightly covered. Roll dough as thin as possible. If using pasta machine to roll dough, roll it to slightly less than ¹⁄₁₆th inch thick. Cut into 2-inch squares. Place 1 teaspoon filling in center of ½ the squares; top with remainder of squares. Press edges together tightly to seal; moisten edges with a little water if necessary to ensure tight seal.

Dust cookie sheet lightly with cornmeal. Place ravioli on sheet; refrigerate, covered, about 2 hours, or freeze until ready to cook.

To cook, heat 4 quarts water to boiling. Add 1 tablespoon salt; float 1 tablespoon cooking oil on surface of water. Drop ravioli into water a few at a time; stir to prevent them sticking to bottom of pan. Reduce heat so water boils gently; cook approximately 12 minutes, until tender; drain. Toss with melted butter and freshly grated Parmesan cheese or serve hot with a favorite tomato or meat sauce and grated cheese. Yield about 96 ravioli or 6 to 8 servings.

SPAGHETTI

chinese spaghetti

1 pound spaghetti noodles
3 tablespoons oil
3 cups chinese cabbage, first cut into 2-inch
   lengths, then julienne-sliced lengthwise
½ cup carrots, julienne-sliced
4 green onions, julienne-cut
4 dried chinese mushrooms, soaked 20 minutes in
   hot water, sliced (optional)
2 teaspoons salt
3 tablespoons soy sauce

Cook noodles until tender; drain well.

Heat oil in wok or large skillet over high heat. Add cabbage, carrots, onions, and mushrooms; stir-fry 1 minute. Add salt and soy sauce; stir-fry 1 minute. Add noodles; stir constantly about 2 minutes. Serve hot. If you wish, add between ½ and 1 cup shredded ham and/or shredded cooked chicken breast along with the salt and soy sauce. Yield 4 to 6 servings.

spaghetti alla carbona

1 pound spaghetti
Boiling salted water
¾ pound bacon
½ cup white wine
2 eggs, well beaten
½ cup grated Parmesan cheese
Freshly ground pepper
Chopped parsley
Extra grated Parmesan cheese

Cook spaghetti in large saucepan of salted boiling water 10 to 12 minutes, until tender but still firm.

While spaghetti is cooking, remove rind from bacon; cut bacon into ½-inch squares. Sauté in pan until cooked through but not crisp. Add wine; simmer gently 3 minutes.

Drain spaghetti well; return to saucepan. Immediately add bacon-wine mixture; blend together. Add eggs and cheese; toss together over low heat. Add a little pepper. Make sure spaghetti is well coated with egg and cheese mixture. Serve in individual dishes sprinkled with parsley and extra cheese. Yield 4 servings.

spaghetti with eggplant and tomato sauce

1 medium onion, chopped
1 clove garlic, minced
1 medium eggplant, peeled, chopped
1 (15-ounce) can tomato sauce
1 teaspoon basil
1 teaspoon oregano
1 teaspoon chopped parsley
Few hot pepper flakes or few drops hot sauce
2 tablespoons red wine (optional)
1 pound spaghetti
1 tablespoon butter or oil
½ cup Parmesan cheese

Sauté onion and garlic in oil. Add eggplant; brown lightly. Add tomato sauce, herbs, pepper, and wine; simmer 20 minutes or until tender.

Cook spaghetti in kettle of boiling salted water 7 to 9 minutes, just until tender; drain. Toss with butter. Place in heated serving dish. Pour sauce over; sprinkle with Parmesan. Yield about 4 servings.

spaghetti with meatballs

1 pound ground beef
2 onions

3 tablespoons finely chopped parsley, thyme, and marjoram
2 cloves garlic
1 cup fresh white bread crumbs
Salt and black pepper
4 tablespoons butter
1 tablespoon flour
1 can tomatoes
2 teaspoons tomato concentrate
1 cup stock
1 tablespoon mixed herbs
¾ pound package spaghetti
½ cup grated Parmesan cheese

Mix together ground beef and 1 chopped onion. Add chopped herbs, 1 crushed garlic clove, and bread crumbs. Season well with salt and black pepper. Shape mixture into small meatballs.

Melt 1 tablespoon butter; fry meatballs until brown, 5 to 7 minutes.

Make tomato sauce. Melt 2 tablespoons butter; cook 1 sliced onion and 1 crushed garlic clove 5

spaghetti with meatballs

minutes. Mix in flour. Add tomatoes, concentrate, stock and herbs. Bring to boil; simmer 10 to 15 minutes.

Bring large pot of water to boil; add salt. Curl in spaghetti; bring to boil, stirring constantly. Simmer 7 to 10 minutes, until done but still firm; drain. Wash with hot water; drain again.

Melt 1 tablespoon butter; toss spaghetti in this with black pepper. Keep warm.

Strain sauce; add meatballs. Heat through; serve with spaghetti. Serve Parmesan separately. Yield 4 servings.

spaghetti with meat sauce

meat sauce
1 pound lean ground beef
1 small onion, finely chopped
½ green pepper, finely chopped
1 (15-ounce) can tomato sauce
1 (12-ounce) can tomato paste
1 (4½-ounce) can chopped ripe olives, drained

1 (4-ounce) can mushroom pieces, drained, chopped
1½ cups water
1 teaspoon sugar
1½ teaspoons salt
1 teaspoon pepper
1 teaspoon oregano
1 teaspoon thyme
½ teaspoon basil
1 clove garlic, crushed
1 bay leaf

Combine meat and onion in Dutch oven; cook until meat is browned and onion tender. Skim off excess fat. Add remaining ingredients; cover. Simmer 1½ hours; partially cover. Simmer 1 hour or until sauce is thick; stir occasionally during cooking. Yield 1½ quarts.

2 pounds spaghetti
2 tablespoons butter or margarine
1⅓ cups Parmesan cheese
3 tablespoons chopped fresh parsley

Cook spaghetti in large kettle of boiling salted water; drain. Stir in butter and half the cheese.

Remove bay leaf from sauce; spoon sauce over spaghetti. Sprinkle with cheese and parsley. Yield 8 to 10 servings.

spaghetti milanese

2 tablespoons butter or margarine
1 slice bacon, chopped
1 small onion, peeled, finely chopped
1 carrot, peeled, chopped
3 to 4 tomatoes, peeled, quartered
1 cup stock or water
Black pepper
1 teaspoon sugar
Lemon juice
2 tablespoons cornstarch
4 tablespoons water
4 or 5 slices cooked ham
1 cup sliced mushrooms
¼ cup butter or margarine
8 to 12 ounces spaghetti
Grated Parmesan or Romano cheese

Heat 2 tablespoons butter in pan. Add bacon; cook until fat begins to melt. Add onion and carrot; cook about 5 minutes. Add tomatoes; cover. Cook gently 5 minutes. Add stock, seasoning, sugar, and squeeze of lemon juice; cover. Simmer gently about 30 minutes; rub through sieve. Return to pan. Add cornstarch blended to smooth paste with 4 tablespoons cold water; stir until boiling. Cook 2 minutes; adjust seasoning.

Cut ham into thin strips.

Sauté mushrooms in 2 tablespoons butter.

Cook spaghetti in boiling salted water 10 minutes; drain well. Add remaining butter; toss until

spaghetti is evenly coated. Add ham and mushrooms. Turn mixture onto hot dish. Pour hot tomato sauce on top; sprinkle with cheese. Yield 4 servings.

VERMICELLI
piquant vermicelli

2 tablespoons salad oil
1 (7-ounce) package vermicelli
¼ pound fresh mushrooms
¼ cup butter
1 teaspoon crushed marjoram
2 tablespoons chopped fresh parsley
Salt and freshly ground pepper to taste

Bring 2½ quarts salted water to boil; add oil. Cook vermicelli in boiling water 7 to 8 minutes, until just tender; drain thoroughly. Place in serving bowl; keep warm.

Wash mushrooms carefully in cold water; drain. Slice thinly.

Melt butter in small saucepan. Add mushrooms; cook over low heat, stirring constantly, about 3 minutes. Place over vermicelli. Add marjoram, parsley, salt, and pepper; toss until well mixed. Serve with spareribs and Basic Barbecue Sauce (see Index), if desired. Yield about 4 servings.

vermicelli with crab and ricotta sauce

To keep the cost down, this recipe calls for only 6 to 8 ounces of canned crab. If you are ready to splurge, you may want to double the amount of seafood.

6 to 8 ounces frozen (thawed) or canned king crab
16 ounces ricotta cheese
¼ cup grated Parmesan cheese
3 small scallions (green onions), chopped or thinly sliced (about ¼ cup)
6 pitted ripe olives, chopped or thinly sliced (about ¼ cup)
1 teaspoon salt
¼ teaspoon white pepper
1 (8-ounce) package vermicelli
½ cup minced fresh parsley

Drain crab; slice large pieces. In mixing bowl stir together crab, ricotta, Parmesan, scallions, olives, salt, and pepper.

Cook vermicelli until tender. As soon as it has finished cooking, stir 1 cup boiling-hot cooking water into crab and ricotta mixture.

Quickly drain remaining water from vermicelli. At once add crab and ricotta mixture; toss well. Sprinkle copiously with parsley. Serve at once on very hot plates. Yield 4 servings.

piquant vermicelli

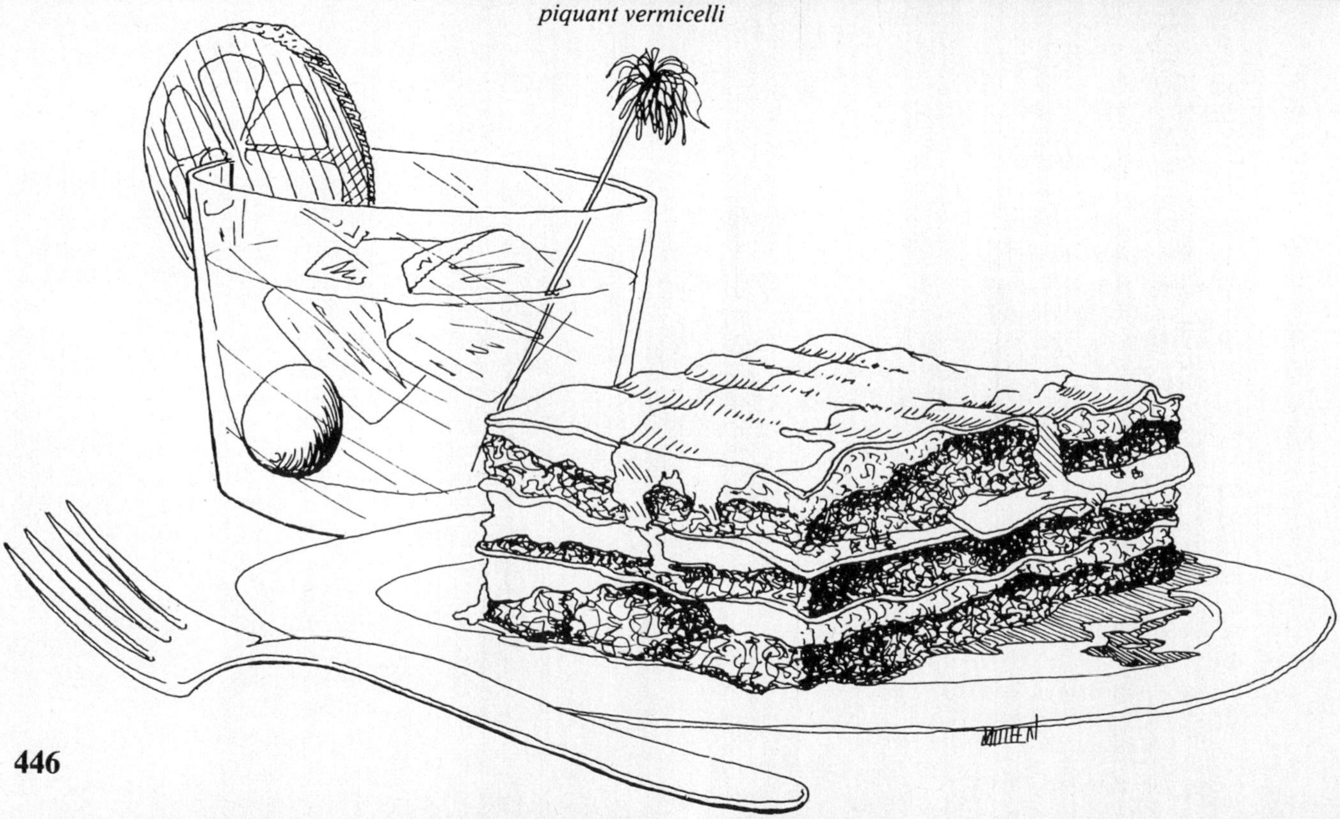

PASTRY

basic chou pastry

1 cup water
½ cup butter
1 cup sifted all-purpose flour
⅛ teaspoon salt
4 eggs

1. Combine water and butter in heavy saucepan; place over medium heat. Cook until butter is melted and water comes to boil.

2. Add all flour and salt.

3. Stir vigorously with wooden spoon until mixture is smooth and leaves sides of pan, forming a ball.

4. Turn off heat. Add 1 egg; beat until well mixed.

5. Continue adding eggs one at a time; beat well after each addition. (An electric mixer can be used to beat in eggs.)

6. Beat until smooth; cover lightly. Let stand until cool.

Spoon pastry into icing bag with 1-inch plain piping tube attached; pipe into desired shapes on lightly greased baking sheet. Do not place too close together. Bake in preheated 450°F oven on shelf above center 8 minutes. Reduce oven temperature to 350°F; bake 20 to 40 minutes, depending on size of puffs, until dry and browned. Remove from baking sheet immediately; let cool on racks. Fill as desired.

basic cold yeast dough

butter mixture
1½ cups butter
4 tablespoons all-purpose flour

yeast dough mixture
2 packages dry yeast
1 tablespoon sugar
1 cup water
1 egg, beaten
3⅓ cups sifted all-purpose flour
½ teaspoon salt

1. Let butter come to room temperature; thoroughly cut in 4 tablespoons flour with 2 forks or pastry blender.

2. Shape mixture into rectangle about ½ inch thick. Place between sheets of waxed paper; refrigerate while preparing Yeast Dough Mixture.

3. Place yeast and sugar in bowl. Add small amount of water; stir until smooth, adding remaining water. Add egg; blend well.

4. Combine flour and salt. Shape into ring on working surface; make well in center. Pour small amount of yeast mixture into well.

5. Begin working flour into liquid with 2 knives or pastry blender; add liquid as needed. Do not break flour wall.

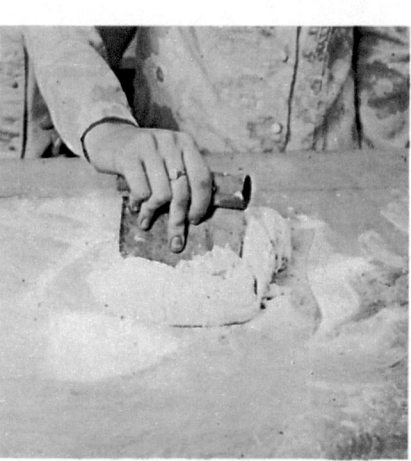

6. When all yeast mixture has been added, work in remaining flour with pastry scrapers or with hands if necessary. Work until smooth; shape dough into ball.

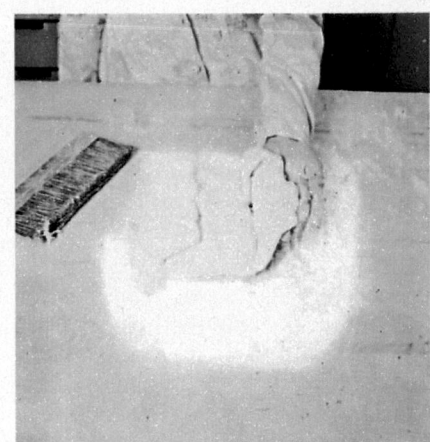

7. *Lightly flour hands; slap the dough from palm to palm across a space of about 20 inches. Do this about 100 times; reshape dough into ball when necessary. Slap dough onto counter; when it breathes perceptibly a second or two it is active and ready.*

8. *Roll dough on lightly floured board into 15 × 17-inch rectangle. Place chilled butter mixture in center.*

9. *Begin folding dough with end nearest you; fold just over center of butter mixture. Bring opposite end up over center; make ends overlap. Fold sides to center; turn folded dough over on lightly floured board so that edges are underneath.*

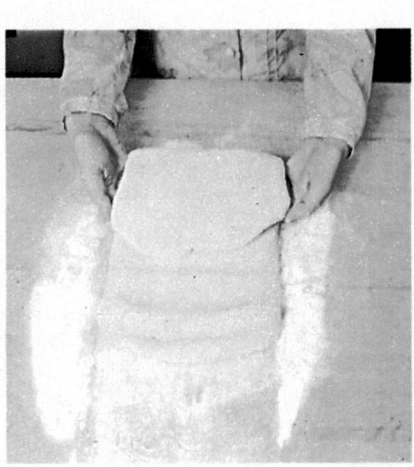
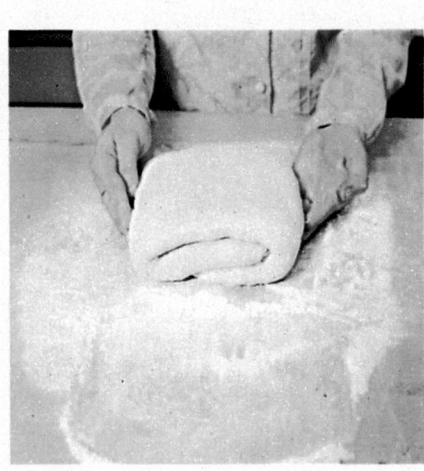

10. *Roll dough into long, narrow rectangle; use pressing, bumpy movements with rolling pin. Bubbles will appear on surface, which indicates dough is springy and active.*

11. *Fold end of dough nearest you just over center; bring opposite end over this fold. Give dough a half turn so that a folded edge is toward you.*

12. *Turn the dough over on lightly floured board so that folded edges are underneath. Roll dough 2 more times, same size; make same folds and half-turns between each roll. Place dough on lightly floured tea towel; wrap. Refrigerate a minimun of 45 minutes. Dough is ready to roll and use as recipe directs.*

basic cream-puff pastry

¾ cup milk
2 tablespoons butter
1 tablespoon sugar
⅛ teaspoon salt
¾ cup sifted all-purpose flour
3 eggs

Combine milk, butter, sugar, and salt in heavy saucepan. Cook over medium heat until butter is melted and sugar dissolved; stir constantly. Add all the flour. Stir vigorously with wooden spoon until mixture is smooth and leaves sides of pan, forming a ball. Turn off heat; add 1 egg. Beat until well mixed. Continue adding eggs one at a time; beat well after each addition. (An electric mixer can be used to beat in eggs.) Beat until smooth; cover lightly. Let stand until cool.

Spoon pastry into icing bag with 1-inch plain piping tube attached; pipe out as desired onto lightly greased baking sheet. Bake in preheated 450°F oven 8 minutes. Reduce oven temperature to 350°F; bake 20 to 40 minutes, depending on size of puffs or éclairs, until dry. Cool on wire racks; fill as desired.

basic pastry

1 cup all-purpose flour
½ teaspoon salt
⅓ cup shortening
2 tablespoons water
Yield pastry for 8- or 9-inch 1-crust pie

1½ cups all-purpose flour
¾ teaspoon salt
½ cup shortening
3 tablespoons water
Yield pastry for 8-inch 2-crust pie

2 cups all-purpose flour
1 teaspoon salt
⅔ cup shortening
¼ cup water
Yield pastry for 9-inch 2-crust pie

Sift flour and salt into bowl. Cut in shortening with pastry blender until particles are size of peas. Sprinkle with water, 1 teaspoon at a time; mix lightly with fork. Gather dough together with fingers; press into ball. Refrigerate until required.

Note: If a pie shell is baked without a filling it is referred to as being baked "blind". Line pie plate with pastry; prick bottom with fork or put piece of greased paper (greased-side-down) in bottom. Fill with rice, beans, or crusts of bread. (These can then be stored for future use.) Remove paper and beans a few minutes before end of cooking.

basic puff pastry

2 cups butter
Ice water
3¾ cups 3-times sifted all-purpose flour
½ teaspoon salt
2 tablespoons chilled lemon juice
¾ cup ice water

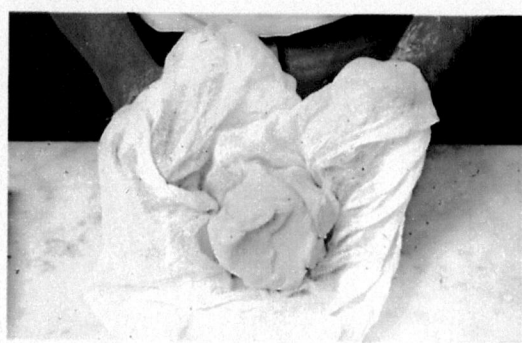

1. Place 1¼ cups butter in large mixing bowl filled with ice water. Knead with hands until butter has consistency of soft dough and is free from lumps. (You will have to remove your hands from the icy water several times during kneading process.) Place butter in double thickness of muslin or tea towel; squeeze to remove excess water.

2. Rub ice cubes over working surface to chill thoroughly. Place butter on cold surface; shape evenly into rectangle about ½ inch thick. Place on dry piece of muslin or towel. Wrap; refrigerate.

3. Thoroughly chill working surface again with ice.

Sift flour with salt onto cold surface. With fingers work flour out from center to form ring.

Cut remaining ¾ cup butter into small pieces in center of ring.

4. Chill working hand in ice water until cold; dry. Mix flour, small amount at a time, with butter inside ring by rubbing flour with butter between thumb and first 2 fingers.

5. This breaks down butter to form small granules. Chill and dry hand frequently during process.

6. Reshape ring; pour chilled lemon juice and ¼ cup ice water in center. Work flour mixture from inner ring into liquid, using 2 knives; add small amounts of water and work in flour mixture until all ingredients are moistened.

7. Shape into smooth ball; sprinkle ball with additional sifted flour. Wrap in cloth; chill 30 minutes.

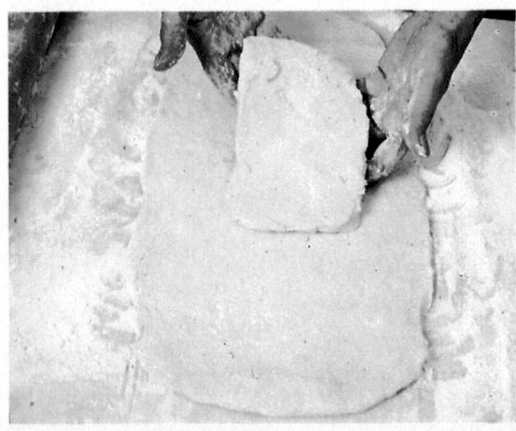

8. Again ice cleaned working surface. Place dough on chilled, floured surface; roll into long, narrow ½-inch-thick rectangle.

Remove butter from muslin; place in center of rectangle.

9. *Bring edge of rectangle nearest you up and over to center of butter. Brush off excess flour; press down gently. Fold left, then right sides to center. Brush again; press down gently. Bring top flap over; press down gently. Lift dough and re-flour surface, if necessary.*

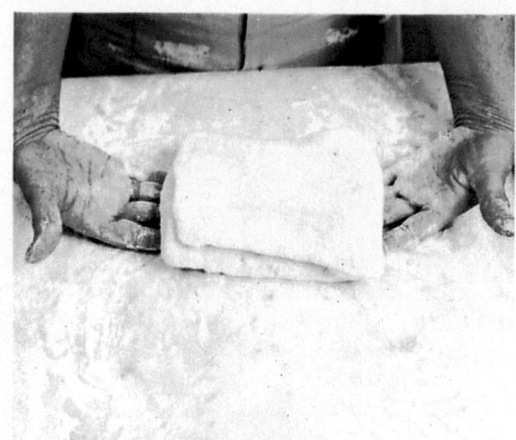

10. *Now begins the all-important part of making puff pastry—blending the butter into the dough. In all rolling and handling of dough care must be taken not to let butter break through dough, or air trapped between layers will escape. If this should happen, patch hole with small amount of flour. Air trapped between layers will expand when baked and cause pastry to puff. Roll gently, keeping rectangular shape; do not roll over ends.*

11. *Fold edge nearest you to center; fold top edge to center. Fold top over to bottom edge. Make ½ turn to right; stick finger in top edge of dough to indicate starting position for next rolling step. Wrap securely in waxed paper; refrigerate 30 minutes.*

12. *Remove dough from refrigerator; place on iced, floured surface with finger mark at top of working surface. Repeat 3 rolling, folding, and turning procedures as before; chill 30 minutes after second, third, and fourth rollings. After fifth roll, wrap; chill at least 3 hours. Roll out sixth and final roll as recipe directs; bake immediately. (After fifth roll, dough can be chilled overnight. Let stand at room temperature 30 minutes before rolling.)*

basic savory short pastry

4 cups self-rising flour
½ cup butter, softened
½ cup vegetable shortening
1 cup freshly grated Parmesan cheese
1 teaspoon salt
¼ teaspoon freshly ground pepper
1 cup cold water

Sift flour into mound on clean working surface. Shape into large ring; form high wall. Place butter, vegetable shortening, cheese, salt, and pepper in center of ring; add half the water. Work up center mixture with 2 table knives; use cutting motion. Carefully work in flour from inside of ring; add more water if needed. Mix until all flour is added and dough holds together; gather dough into ball. Place in bowl; cover with towel. Refrigerate at least an hour. Can be wrapped securely in plastic wrap or aluminum foil and stored in refrigerator for a week.

Instructions for oven temperature and length of baking time are included in recipes that call for this pastry.

basic seasoned flour

4 cups all-purpose flour
¼ cup salt
2 tablespoons freshly ground pepper
2 tablespoons dry English mustard
1 tablespoon paprika
1 teaspoon basil
1 teaspoon chervil
1 teaspoon thyme
1 teaspoon parsley flakes

Sift flour, salt, pepper, mustard, and paprika together; stir in herbs. Store in airtight container for use as needed. Yield about 4½ cups.

basic strudel pastry

1½ cups all-purpose flour
¼ teaspoon salt
1½ teaspoons butter, softened
1 teaspoon lemon juice
½ cup lukewarm water
Melted butter

Sift flour and salt together onto pastry board; shape into ring. Put butter and lemon juice in center of ring; cut into flour with 2 table knives or pastry blenders. Add water gradually, working in flour from inside of ring. Use pastry scrapers to work dough until all flour is moistened; gather into ball. Sift additional flour lightly over board; knead dough with heel of hand 15 minutes.

Dust warm baking sheet with flour. Place dough ball on baking sheet; invert warm bowl over dough. Let stand 30 minutes.

Place sheet or tablecloth on card table or kitchen table; dust generously with flour.

Dust dough lightly with flour on all sides. Roll thin on lightly floured board; lift carefully on back of hands to center of floured cloth on table. Brush dough lightly with melted butter. Place hands under dough; start working from center, palms downward, folding hands into loose fist. With slightly raised knuckles, pull gently and evenly from center to edge until tissue-paper thin. Dough will be thicker at edge. Two people working together can do this easily; but one person can stretch dough properly. Be sure to work with palms down to avoid making holes in dough. Brush with butter; let stand 15 minutes to dry. Trim off thicker edge before using as needed. Yield enough for 1 large strudel.

1. *Illustration of how to mix Basic Short Pastry. Ring has been formed with sifted flour and egg yolks, sugar, and butter placed in middle. With 2 table knives flour is worked into center mixture, adding water to form smooth, thick paste. In foreground are 2 professional pastry-cook's scrapers.*

2. *Completed pastry was placed on floured cloth. Slide pastry-cook's scraper over working surface to pick up flour and dough scraps. Shake flour and scraps into small sieve held over bowl (extra flour passing through sieve can be used again in baking). A special pastry sweeper, in the left foreground above, is useful for brushing up every bit of flour. In place of these use knife or rubber scraper and damp cloth to clean surface.*

basic sweet short pastry

4 cups self-rising flour
1 cup butter, softened
½ cup extra-fine sugar
2 egg yolks
¼ cup cold water

Sift flour into mound on clean working surface. Shape into large ring; form high wall. Place butter, sugar, and egg yolks in center of ring. Add water; work up center mixture with 2 table knives or pastry scrapers to form smooth paste. Work in flour carefully from the inside of ring; add more water if needed. Mix until pastry is thick and light; gather dough into ball. Place on lightly floured cloth; cover loosely. Refrigerate at least 1 hour before using. Can be wrapped securely and stored in refrigerator up to a week.

french pie pastry (pâte brisée)

2 cups all-purpose flour
½ teaspoon salt

453

½ cup butter
½ to ¾ cup water

Sift flour and salt; rub in butter with fingertips. Make well in center; add water a little at a time. The index finger is really best to do this, or use a fork and stir in spiral fashion, beginning at inside of well and gradually moving to outer edge. Dough should be soft enough to gather up into a ball, but not sticky. Roll in foil; refrigerate for 2 to 24 hours before using. Can be stored a week or more. Yield enough for 9-inch pie plate.

graham-cracker crust

⅓ cup butter or margarine
2 tablespoons sugar
1¼ cups graham-cracker crumbs

Stir butter and sugar together in saucepan over low heat until butter is melted. Blend in cracker crumbs. Press evenly into pie pan; chill. Yield enough for 8- or 9-inch pie.

hot-water pastry

2½ cups cake flour
½ teaspoon salt
1 egg yolk
¼ cup plus 2 tablespoons lard
½ cup water

Sift flour and salt into bowl; make well in center. Drop in egg yolk; cover with some of flour.

Put lard and water into small pan; heat slowly until lard melts. Increase heat; bring to boiling point.

Pour all liquid into flour; mix vigorously with wooden spoon until pastry is cool enough to handle. Use hand to knead until dough is smooth. Let rest in warm place 20 to 30 minutes; use warm.

never-fail short pastry

1 cup vegetable shortening
½ cup boiling water
1 teaspoon salt
3 cups sifted all-purpose flour

Cream shortening with boiling water until well mixed, by hand or with electric mixer. Add salt, and flour all at once; sitr until thoroughly mixed. Form into ball; chill in covered container at least an hour. Roll half the dough for single shell. Fit into pie pan; prick well around edges and bottom with fork. Bake at 450°F 15 minutes for single crust. Dough can be kept at least 3 weeks in refrigerator. Yield pastry for 2 (9-inch) pie crusts.

pastry made with oil

1⅔ cups all-purpose flour
½ teaspoon salt
⅓ cup vegetable oil
2 tablespoons cold water
Yield pastry for 8- or 9-inch 1-crust pie

2 cups all-purpose flour
1 teaspoon salt
½ cup vegetable oil
3 tablespoons cold water
Yield pastry for 8- or 9-inch 2-crust pie

Sift flour and salt into bowl. Add oil; mix with pastry blender or fork until mixture looks like fine bread crumbs. Sprinkle with water; mix with fork. Gather dough together with fingers; press into ball. Add a little more oil if too dry. This pastry is best rolled out between waxed paper.

Do not store in refrigerator; use at once.

rough puff pastry

3½ cups sifted all-purpose flour
1 teaspoon salt
1 cup butter
¾ cup vegetable shortening
1 cup ice water

Sift flour with salt into mound on clean working surface. Shape into large ring; form high wall. Place butter, shortening, and half the water in center. Work center mixture together with cutting motion; use 2 table knives or pastry scrapers. Work in flour carefully from inside of ring; add more water as needed. Work with knives until all flour is added and dough holds together; gather dough into ball.

Chill working surface thoroughly with ice; dust with flour. Roll pastry into long, thin rectangle. Fold top edge down to center; bring bottom edge to top fold. Fold bottom to top again, making 5 layers. Turn pastry clockwise ½ turn, so edges on left and right are at top and bottom. Repeat rolling and folding steps 2 more times. Wrap folded pastry securely in plastic wrap. Store in refrigerator at least 24 hours before using. Will keep in refrigerator up to 7 days. Bake as directed in each individual recipe.

royal short pastry

2 cups all-purpose flour
1 teaspoon salt
¼ cup vegetable shortening
1 teaspoon vinegar
1 egg
1 to 2 tablespoons water

Sift flour and salt together into bowl. Add shortening; blend with pastry blender until mixture resembles meal. Add vinegar and egg; mix. Add water a tablespoon at a time until ingredients hold together. Roll pastry on floured surface to fit 2 (9-inch) pie pans. Place in pans; crimp or flute edges. Prick sides and bottoms well with fork. Bake in preheated 400°F oven 15 to 17 minutes or until lightly browned. Yield pastry for 2 (9-inch) pie crusts.

braised pheasant with chestnut puree and orange

4 to 5 tablespoons butter
1 large pheasant
2 onions, sliced
2 small carrots, sliced
2 or 3 stalks celery, sliced
2 tablespoons flour
1½ cups stock
¼ cup cider (or white wine)
3 oranges
1 tablespoon mixed herbs
Salt and pepper
1 large can chestnut puree

Melt 2 to 3 tablespoons butter in flameproof casserole or Dutch oven. Brown bird slowly all over. Remove bird; keep warm.

Add onions, carrots, and celery; cook until they begin to brown slightly. Add flour; cook a few minutes. Add stock and cider; stir well. Bring to boil; simmer a few minutes. Add zest (outer skin) of 1 orange, herbs, and seasoning. Put pheasant back into casserole; spoon sauce over. Cover casserole; put into preheated 350°F oven about 50 minutes, until pheasant is tender. When pheasant is removed from casserole, boil up cooking juices; put into liquidizer or blender. When smooth, return to pan; if too thick, add a little extra stock. Season to taste; reheat.

Meanwhile, melt 2 tablespoons butter in pan; add chestnut puree. Heat to soften puree; add 2 to 3 tablespoons stock and seasoning. Keep warm until pheasant is tender; place down center of serving dish. Place carved slices and joints on top; spoon sauce over all.

Remove zest of second orange carefully; cut into thin shreds. Cook in boiling water a few minutes; drain. Put into cold water to restore color. Remove white pith and skin from all oranges with sharp knife; divide into segments. Arrange segments around edge of dish and strips down center. Yield 4 to 6 servings.

pheasant with grapes and white wine sauce

4 tablespoons butter
1 pheasant
2 tablespoons flour
½ cup clear stock
½ cup white wine
1½ cups white grapes, seedless if available
3 tablespoons lemon juice

Melt butter in heatproof casserole or Dutch oven; when hot sauté pheasant gently all over until golden brown. Remove bird.

Add flour, stock, and wine; blend smoothly. Bring to boil; add seasoning. Return bird to casserole; cover. Cook in preheated 350°F oven 35 to 45 minutes, until pheasant is tender; turn during cooking.

Peel grapes by dipping in boiling water a few seconds, then in cold water. Strip skins; if not seedless, remove seeds. Cover with a little lemon juice to prevent browning.

When bird is tender, remove; carve. Place meat on serving dish; keep warm.

Add grapes to sauce; cook couple of minutes. Season to taste; spoon over pheasant. Serve with mashed potatoes and peas or spinach. Yield 4 servings.

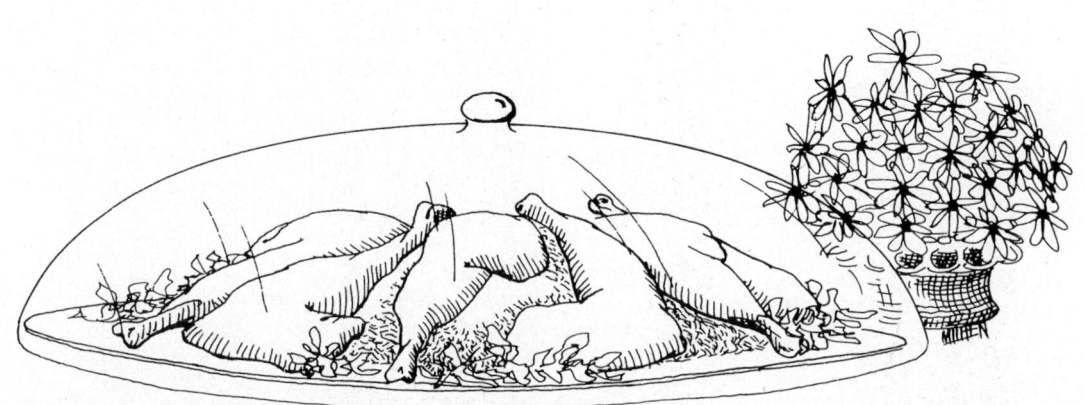

DESSERT

apple chiffon pie

crust

⅓ cup butter or margarine
2 tablespoons sugar
1¼ cups graham-cracker crumbs

Stir butter and sugar together in saucepan over low heat until butter is melted. Mix in crumbs. Press evenly into 9-inch pie pan; chill. Yield 9-inch pie, 8 servings.

filling

3 egg yolks, slightly beaten
⅓ cup apple cider
1 tablespoon lemon juice
1 teaspoon grated lemon rind
2 tablespoons sugar
1 tablespoon unflavored gelatin
¼ cup cold water
2 cups pared, shredded apples (about 2 medium)
3 egg whites
¼ teaspoon salt
¼ cup sugar
Nutmeg to taste

Mix egg yolks, cider, lemon juice, lemon rind, and 2 tablespoons sugar. Cook over low heat, stirring constantly, until mixture begins to thicken, about 2 minutes.

Sprinkle gelatin on water; let stand a few minutes. Add to hot mixture; stir until dissolved. Cool until thick but not set. Stir apples into gelatin mixture immediately after shredding.

Beat egg whites until foamy. Add salt; beat until soft peaks form. Slowly add ¼ cup sugar; beat constantly until stiff. Fold into apple mixture.

Pour filling into graham-cracker shell; sprinkle with nutmeg. Chill until firm.

apricot cheese pie

3 cups crushed sweet cracker crumbs
½ teaspoon grated nutmeg
½ cup butter
1½ cups cream cheese
½ cup sweetened condensed milk
4 dessert spoons lemon juice
½ cup whipping cream

topping

1 teaspoon gelatin
2 tablespoons water
1 cup apricot jam
2 tablespoons sugar

Butter 9-inch pie plate.

apricot cheese pie

Put crumbs in bowl with nutmeg.

Melt butter; add enough to crumbs so that when squeezed in hands mixture will form firm ball. Press firmly around sides and bottom of pie plate. Refrigerate while preparing filling.

Sieve cheese. Add condensed milk and lemon juice; beat until smooth. (Or spin the 3 ingredients in food processor.)

Whip cream; fold into cheese mixture. Pour into crumb crust; refrigerate while preparing topping.

Soften gelatin in 1 tablespoon water. Sieve jam. Add sugar and remaining water; stir over low heat until sugar has dissolved. Boil, without stirring, 2 minutes; remove from heat. Add gelatin; stir until dissolved. Let cool a little; spoon over cream-cheese filling. Refrigerate well before serving. Garnish with a little whipped cream. Yield 6 to 8 servings.

banana cream pie

½ cup sugar
¼ teaspoon salt
⅓ cup flour
1⅓ cups milk
¾ cup water
3 egg yolks, beaten
1 cup bananas, thinly sliced
9-inch baked pie shell (see Index: Basic Pastry)
Meringue

Combine sugar, salt, flour, milk, and water over low heat. When hot, add small amount to egg yolks; mix. Pour back into custard; cook 3 to 4 minutes. Add bananas. Pour into pie shell. Top with meringue. Yield 9-inch pie.

meringue
3 egg whites
⅓ cup sugar
½ teaspoon baking powder

Beat egg whites until almost stiff. Add sugar gradually, beating continuously. Add baking powder; beat until glossy.

blueberry pie

4 cups fresh blueberries or dry-pack frozen
   blueberries, rinsed, drained
¾ cup sugar
Juice of 1 lemon
1⅔ cups flour
2 teaspoons sugar
Dash of salt
1 cup vegetable shortening
4 tablespoons ice water

Sprinkle blueberries with ¾ cup sugar; squeeze lemon juice over top. Set aside.

Sift flour, 2 teaspoons sugar, and salt into mixing bowl. Cut shortening into flour. Gradually add ice water; mix with pastry blender. Chill dough. Divide dough into 2 parts. Roll out half on floured board until thin enough to cover sides and bottom of 9-inch pie plate. Prick bottom with fork. Bake bottom crust 10 minutes at 400°F. This prevents berry juice from soaking through crust. Cool bottom crust about 10 minutes while rolling out remaining dough and cutting into strips.

Fill bottom shell with blueberries; place strips of dough across top for latticework effect. Use 1 or 2 long strips around edge of plate to seal crusts. Bake no longer than 20 minutes at 400°F. If desired, top crust can be rolled in 1 piece and used to make a 2-crust pie. Yield 6 to 8 servings.

bouffant lemon-meringue pie

½ recipe Basic Sweet Short Pastry (see Index)
8 egg yolks
1½ cups sugar
⅔ cup fresh lemon juice
2 envelopes unflavored gelatin
1 teaspoon grated orange rind
2 tablespoons grated lemon rind
4 egg whites
1 teaspoon cream of tartar
1 recipe Meringue Topping

bouffant lemon-meringue pie

Roll out pastry on lightly floured surface to ⅛-inch-thick circle. Line greased 10-inch pie pan with pastry; trim along inside rim of pie pan.

Roll out pastry trimmings into long strip 1 inch wide; make folds in strip at 1-inch intervals. Place upright along edge of pastry in pie pan; overlap ½ inch. Seal strip to pastry with water. Bake blind (see Index: Basic Pastry) in preheated 400°F oven 10 minutes. Reduce oven temperature to 375°F. Bake 15 minutes. Remove from oven; remove peas and paper. Bake 4 to 5 minutes longer, until lightly browned; cool.

Beat egg yolks in mixer bowl with electric mixer until lemon-colored. Add 1 cup sugar gradually; beat until well blended. Beat in lemon juice gradually; pour into top of double boiler over hot water. Cook, beating constantly, until thickened and foamy.

Soften gelatin in ¼ cup water; stir into egg-yolk mixture until dissolved. Place top of double boiler in bowl of iced water; stir until cooled. Stir in orange and lemon rinds.

Beat egg whites and cream of tartar in large mixer bowl until soft peaks form. Fold ¼ of egg-white mixture into gelatin mixture with wire whisk or spatula to loosen gelatin mixture. Fold in remaining egg-white mixture until well blended, turn into pie crust. Spoon Meringue Topping over filling carefully, sealing to crust; twirl top with spoon. Bake in a preheated 400°F oven 5 to 8 minutes or until meringue is golden brown. Cool thoroughly. Pie can be chilled until served. Yield 6 to 8 servings.

meringue topping
5 egg whites
1 teaspoon cream of tartar
¾ cup sugar

Beat egg whites and cream of tartar in large mixer bowl until frothy. Beat in sugar 1 tablespoon at a time; beat until stiff peaks form. Use as recipe directs. Yield enough for 1 (10-inch) pie or 2 (8-inch) pies.

butterscotch pie

1 (9-inch) baked pastry shell (see Index: Basic Pastry) or Graham-Cracker Crust (see Index)
2 cups milk
1 cup firmly packed brown sugar
3 tablespoons cornstarch
2 egg yolks, beaten
3 tablespoons butter
Whipped cream

Prepare pastry shell or crumb crust.

Put ½ cup milk and sugar in top of double boiler; heat until sugar has dissolved.

Blend cornstarch smoothly with remaining milk. Add beaten egg yolks; stir into pan. Stir

chocolate marshmallow pie

until mixture thickens. Cook 5 minutes; stir constantly. Remove from heat. Stir in butter. Pour into pastry shell. Chill thoroughly; serve with whipped cream. Yield 5 or 6 servings.

chocolate marshmallow pie

1 (8-inch) baked pastry pie shell
2 squares (2 ounces) unsweetened chocolate
2 tablespoons sugar
½ cup milk
12 marshmallows
1½ cups whipping cream
½ cup chopped toasted almonds or shaved chocolate

Put chocolate, sugar, milk, and marshmallows into top of double boiler; stir over hot water until melted. Let cool; stir frequently.

Whip cream; fold into mixture. Pour into pastry shell; sprinkle with almonds or shaved chocolate. Chill thoroughly before serving. Yield 4 or 5 servings.

chocolate pie

1 (10-inch) graham-cracker or pastry pie crust (see Index)
6 eggs, separated
6 squares unsweetened chocolate, melted
¼ cup sugar
½ pint whipping cream
Prepare crust.

Beat egg whites until stiff; set aside.

Combine chocolate, egg yolks, and sugar; fold into whites. Pour into pie shell; refrigerate. Whip cream for topping. Yield 6 to 8 servings.

classic boston cream pie

cake
⅓ cup butter or margarine
1 cup sugar
2 eggs
1 teaspoon vanilla
1¼ cups unsifted all-purpose flour
1½ teaspoons baking powder
¼ teaspoon salt
¾ cup milk
Preheat oven to 350°F.

Cream butter, sugar, eggs, and vanilla in medium bowl until light and fluffy.

Combine dry ingredients; add alternately with milk to creamed mixture. Pour batter into well-greased and floured 9-inch layer pan. Bake 30 to 35 minutes or until cake tester inserted in center comes out clean. Cool 10 minutes; remove from pan. Cool completely on rack. Cut into 2 thin layers. Spread filling onto 1 layer; top with remaining layer. Pour glaze on top; let some drizzle down sides. Chill before serving. Yield 6 servings.

filling
⅓ cup sugar
2 tablespoons cornstarch
1½ cups milk
2 egg yolks, slightly beaten
1 tablespoon butter
1 teaspoon vanilla
Combine sugar, cornstarch, milk, and egg yolks in saucepan. Cook and stir over medium heat until mixture boils; boil and stir 1 minute. Remove from heat; blend in butter and vanilla. Cover; chill.

glaze
3 tablespoons water
2 tablespoons butter
3 tablespoons cocoa
1 cup confectioners' sugar
½ teaspoon vanilla
Combine water and butter in small saucepan; bring to full boil. Remove from heat; immediately stir in cocoa. Beat in sugar and vanilla (whisk if necessary) until smooth; cool slightly.

covered mincemeat flan

3 cups mincemeat
2 tablespoons brandy or rum
1 recipe Basic Sweet Short Pastry (see Index)
Combine mincemeat and brandy; set aside.

Roll out half the pastry on lightly floured board. Cut 10- to 11-inch circle.

Place 9-inch flan ring on floured baking sheet; place pastry in ring. Press pastry slightly around bottom and sides of ring, bringing pastry to top. Spoon mincemeat into pastry. Push pastry around side of ring over mincemeat; brush with cold water.

On lightly floured board roll out remaining pastry into circle; place over top of flan ring. Cut off surplus pastry by rolling pin over rim of ring. Pinch edges of pastry together to seal securely. Bake in preheated 375°F oven about 50 minutes, until top is browned. Remove ring. Dust generously with confectioners' sugar.

A 9-inch cake pan with removable bottom can be used, if desired. Yield about 8 servings.

cream-cheese pie

crust
12 cinnamon graham crackers
3 tablespoons butter, melted
1 tablespoon sugar
½ teaspoon cinnamon
Pineapple tidbits, drained
Crush crackers in plastic bag with rolling pin or spin in food processor; put in bowl. Add butter, sugar, and cinnamon; mix well. Line bottom and sides of deep 8-inch pie plate with crumb mixture. Arrange pineapple tidbits on shell.

filling
2 eggs
½ cup sugar
1 pound cream cheese
2 tablespoons sour cream
1 teaspoon vanilla
Beat eggs. Add sugar, cream cheese, sour cream, and vanilla; beat until smooth. Pour into pie pan. Bake at 350°F 25 minutes. Yield 6 to 8 servings.

covered mincemeat flan

fresh peach pie

Pastry for 2 pie crusts (see Index)
4 cups pared, sliced peaches
¾ cup sugar
1 tablespoon cornstarch
1 tablespoon lemon juice (optional)
 Preheat oven to 400°F.
 Prepare pastry.
 Mix peaches lightly with other ingredients in bowl. Put into pastry-lined pan. Top with second crust. Fold edges of pastry under; press together firmly to seal. Bake 50 to 60 minutes, until browned. Yield 6 to 8 servings.

key lime pie

1 tablespoon unflavored gelatin
1 cup sugar
¼ teaspoon salt
4 eggs, separated
½ cup lime juice
¼ cup water
1 teaspoon grated lime peel
Green food coloring
1 cup whipping cream, whipped
1 baked 9-inch pie shell (see Index: Basic Pastry)
 Mix gelatin, ½ cup sugar, and salt in saucepan.
 Beat egg yolks, lime juice, and water together; stir into gelatin mixture. Cook over medium heat, stirring constantly, until mixture comes to boil. Remove from heat; stir in grated peel. Add enough coloring for pale-green color. Chill, stirring occasionally, until thickened.
 Beat egg whites until soft peaks form. Add remaining sugar gradually; beat until stiff peaks form. Fold gelatin mixture into egg whites; fold in whipped cream. Spoon into pastry shell; chill until

firm. Spread with additional whipped cream; sprinkle additional grated lime peel around edge of pie. Yield 6 to 8 servings.

lemon-chiffon pie

2 cans evaporated milk
2 boxes lemon gelatin
1 cup hot water
1 cup sugar
Juice of 2 lemons
2 cups graham-cracker crumbs
2 packages ladyfingers
Whipped cream (optional)
 Place milk in bowl; let freeze slightly.
 Mix gelatin and water; let jell slightly.
 Beat milk and sugar in large cold bowl at high speed until thick. Add lemon juice and gelatin mixture; beat slightly.
 Butter a 9-inch springform pan. Press cracker crumbs on bottom and ladyfingers around sides. Pour lemon mixture in; chill. Unmold; garnish with whipped cream. Yield 10 to 12 servings.

lemon-cloud pie

½ recipe Royal Short Pastry (see Index)
1 envelope unflavored gelatin
¾ cup sugar
¼ teaspoon salt
1 cup water
⅓ cup lemon juice
2 egg yolks, slightly beaten
1½ teaspoons grated lemon rind
2 cups frozen whipped topping, thawed
 Prepare pastry for 1 pie crust; cool.
 Combine gelatin, sugar, and salt in saucepan. Add water, lemon juice, and egg yolks; blend well.

Place over medium heat; cook, stirring constantly, about 5 minutes, until gelatin is dissolved. Remove from heat; stir in lemon rind. Turn into mixing bowl; chill until thickened. Place mixing bowl in larger mixing bowl containing ice and water. Beat with electric mixer until double in volume. Blend in 1½ cups whipped topping. Spoon into pie crust; chill 3 to 4 hours, until firm. Place remaining whipped topping in center of pie; garnish with twisted lemon slice, if desired. Yield 6 to 8 servings.

lemon ladyfinger pie

2 packages ladyfingers
1 package unflavored gelatin
¼ cup cold water
8 eggs, separated
1 cup sugar
Juice of 3 lemons

Line sides of buttered 10-inch springform pan with ladyfingers. Line bottom of pan with pieces of ladyfingers.

Mix together gelatin and water; let soak.

In top of double boiler beat together egg yolks, sugar, and lemon juice. Cook until mixture coats spoon; stir constantly. Stir gelatin mixture into hot custard; cool slightly.

lemon-cloud pie

Beat egg whites until stiff; carefully fold into custard. Pour mixture into lined pan; refrigerate until firm. Top with sweetened whipped cream or nondairy topping before serving. Yield 10 to 12 servings.

lo-cal cheese pie

1 pound cottage cheese
1 cup pineapple tidbits (packed in own juice)
1 envelope gelatin
1 egg
5 packs sugar substitute
1 teaspoon vanilla
1 teaspoon lemon juice
Cinnamon

Put all ingredients into blender; blend until smooth. Pour into 9-inch pie plate. Sprinkle top of pie with cinnamon. Bake at 350°F 30 minutes. Cool; refrigerate. Yield 8 servings.

mincemeat tarte tatin

Mix egg yolks, sour cream, sugar, cornstarch, lemon rind, and salt in top of double boiler. Cook over boiling water until thick; stir constantly. Pour into pie shell.

Beat egg whites until stiff, adding brown sugar slowly. Fold in pecans; spread over filling. Bake at 425°F until lightly browned. Refrigerate several hours before serving. One-fourth teaspoon lemon extract can be substituted for grated lemon rind. Yield 6 to 8 servings.

mincemeat tarte tatin

½ recipe Basic Sweet Short Pastry (see Index)
1 (1-pound 2-ounce) jar mincemeat with brandy
   and rum

Roll pastry on lightly floured surface to ¼-inch-thick circle. Place bottom of cake pan with removable bottom on pastry; cut around edge with sharp knife. Place bottom back in pan.

Grease and flour cake pan. Spoon mincemeat into pan; spread evenly. Place pastry circle over mincemeat; press down firmly.

Bake in preheated 375°F oven about 45 minutes or until pastry is lightly browned. Invert pan onto serving platter; remove bottom of pan.

Dust with confectioners' sugar and sprinkle with drops of brandy or rum, if desired. Yield 8 to 10 servings.

new orleans pecan pie

1 baked 9-inch pie shell, cooled (see Index: Basic
   Pastry)
3 eggs, separated
1 cup sour cream
1 cup sugar
4 tablespoons cornstarch
¼ teaspoon grated lemon rind
Pinch of salt
1 cup packed brown sugar
1 cup chopped pecans

Prepare pie shell.

orange yogurt chiffon pie

1⅓ cups vanilla wafer crumbs
¼ cup melted butter
2 envelopes unflavored gelatin
Sugar
2 cups yogurt
1 (6-ounce) can frozen orange-juice
   concentrate, thawed
2 egg whites
Toasted coconut

Combine crumbs and butter; blend well. Press firmly and evenly over bottom and sides of pie plate; build up around rim. Chill.

Combine gelatin and ½ cup sugar in 1-quart saucepan; stir in 1 cup water. Cook over low heat, stirring constantly, until gelatin is dissolved.

Place yogurt in bowl. Gradually add orange-juice concentrate. Stir in gelatin mixture until smooth.

Beat egg whites until frothy, then beat until stiff peaks form, adding 2 tablespoons sugar gradually. Fold ¼ of meringue into orange mixture; fold in remaining meringue. Chill until mixture mounds when dropped from spoon. Turn into crust; chill until firm. Garnish with toasted coconut. Yield 6 to 8 servings.

parfait pie

1 can pitted dark cherries
1 (3-ounce) package dark cherry gelatin
½ cup cold water
1 pint soft vanilla ice cream
1 baked pie shell (see Index: Basic Pastry)

Drain fruit; reserve liquid. Add enough water to make 1 cup. Heat juice; dissolve gelatin in hot mixture. Remove from heat; add cold water. Stir in ice cream until melted. Refrigerate 45 minutes. Fold in drained fruit; put in pie shell. Refrigerate at least 1 hour. Yield 6 to 8 servings.

pecan pie

1 9- or 11-inch unbaked pie shell (see Index: Basic Pastry)
5 eggs
¾ cup sugar
1½ cups dark syrup
1½ cups pecans, chopped or halved
¾ teaspoon salt
2 teaspoons vanilla
Whipped cream (for decoration)
Prepare pie shell; set aside.

Beat eggs slightly in large bowl. Add sugar, syrup, nuts, salt, and vanilla; mix until nicely blended. Pour into pie shell. Bake at 325°F 50 minutes. When cool, garnish with whipped cream; serve at once. Yield 6 to 8 servings.

pistachio black-bottom pie

1 baked and cooled 8-inch pie shell (see Index: Basic Pastry)
1 cup light cream
1 cup milk
1 package instant pistachio pudding
1 square (1 ounce) semisweet chocolate, melted, cooled
Rum Whipped Cream
Prepare "blind" 8-inch 1-crust pie shell; cool.

Pour light cream and milk into small, deep mixing bowl. Add pudding; using egg-beater or mixer, slowly beat 2 minutes. Rapidly combine chocolate and ½ cup pudding; spoon into baked pie shell. Spoon remaining pudding over chocolate mixture; chill until firm, about 1 hour. Garnish with Rum Whipped Cream. Yield 6 servings.

rum whipped cream
½ cup heavy cream
2 tablespoons confectioners' sugar
1 tablespoon light rum
Beat cream and sugar in chilled bowl until stiff; fold in rum.

orange yogurt chiffon pie

portuguese almond pastry

portuguese almond pastry

1½ cups all-purpose flour
½ cup butter
½ cup sugar
¼ cup water
2 egg yolks, beaten
Almond Filling

Sift flour onto clean working surface; make well in center.

Cut butter into small pieces; place in well. Add sugar, water, and egg yolks. Blend with 2 pastry scrapers, gathering flour from ring, until of fine-crumb consistency. Shape pastry into smooth ball; work in additional flour, if necessary. Divide pastry into 2 parts. Roll out 1 part on lightly floured surface to ¼-inch thick; cut into circle. Use bottom of cake pan with removable bottom for pattern. Fit circle into pan; spoon Almond Filling over pastry.

Roll out remaining pastry to ¼-inch thick; cut circle slightly larger than bottom circle. Place top pastry over filling. Bake in preheated 375°F oven 45 to 50 minutes, until top crust is lightly browned. Cool 5 minutes; remove from pan. Garnish with sliced toasted almonds, then with confectioners' sugar. Yield 8 to 10 servings.

almond filling

1½ cups ground almonds
¾ cup sugar
1½ tablespoons grated lemon rind
¼ cup butter, softened
3 eggs, slightly beaten

Combine almonds and sugar in medium-size bowl; stir in lemon rind. Work in butter with fingers until well blended. Add eggs; blend thoroughly with wire whisk. Consistency of filling will be runny when mixed, but will be firm when baked.

princess ann tart

crust

½ cup flour
1 teaspoon baking powder
2 tablespoons sugar
Pinch of salt
6 tablespoons butter
2 tablespoons cold water
1 (8-ounce) jar raspberry jam

Combine flour, baking powder, sugar, and salt. Work in butter until mixture resembles cornmeal. Add water; stir into stiff dough. Roll out dough on floured surface. Place in 9-inch pie pan. Spread jam (it may need to be melted) in bottom crust.

custard

2 egg yolks
1 cup milk
1 tablespoon sugar
1 teaspoon flour
Pinch of salt
1 teaspoon vanilla

Combine all ingredients; beat well. Pour over jam in crust. Bake at 350°F 30 minutes.

meringue
2 egg whites
4 tablespoons sugar
¼ teaspoon cream of tartar

Beat egg whites and cream of tartar until soft peaks form, adding sugar gradually. Beat until stiff peaks form. Pour over cooked and cooled filling. Bake at 375°F until browned. Yield 6 to 8 servings.

pumpkin pie

1 unbaked 8-inch pastry shell (see Index:
Basic Pastry)
1 cup canned pumpkin
½ teaspoon cinnamon
¼ teaspoon ginger
¼ teaspoon nutmeg
⅛ teaspoon cloves
1 cup milk, half-and-half cream, or
evaporated milk
½ cup sugar
1 egg, slightly beaten
½ teaspoon salt

Prepare unbaked pastry shell.

Blend pumpkin and spices thoroughly. Stir in remaining ingredients; mix well. Pour into pastry shell. Bake at 400°F about 1 hour. Pie is done when table knife inserted in center comes out clean. Filling may be soft but will set on cooling. Yield 8-inch pie, 6 servings.

rhubarb pie

1 9-inch double crust pie (see Index: Basic Pastry)
4 cups unpeeled, diced, young rhubarb stalks
¼ cup all-purpose flour
1¼ to 2 cups sugar
1 teaspoon grated orange rind
1 tablespoon butter

Preheat oven to 450°F.
Prepare pastry; line pie pan with dough.

strawberry-lime pie

Combine remaining ingredients in bowl; toss well. Turn into shell. Dot with 1 to 2 tablespoons butter. Cover pie with well-pricked top or a lattice. Bake pie in 450°F oven 10 minutes. Reduce heat to 350°F; bake 35 to 40 minutes, until golden brown. Yield 6 to 8 servings.

strawberry cream pie

9-inch pastry shell (see Index: Basic Pastry)
⅓ cup flour
½ cup sugar
2 cups milk
3 small egg yolks
½ teaspoon vanilla
1 tablespoon firm butter
1½ cups strawberries

Bake and cool pastry shell.

Blend flour and sugar in heavy saucepan. Slowly stir in 1 cup milk until smooth. Add rest of milk; cook and stir over direct heat until mixture boils and thickens. Stir ½ cup of hot mixture into well-beaten egg yolks; stir together. Pour back into saucepan; cook and stir 2 minutes. Remove from heat; stir in vanilla and butter. Pour half of mixture into pie shell. Layer strawberries; pour remaining mixture on top. Cool; serve. Yield 6 to 8 servings.

strawberry–lime pie

1 baked 9-inch pie shell (see Index: Basic Pastry)
2 envelopes unflavored gelatin
1 (6-ounce) can frozen limeade concentrate
⅓ cup sugar
1 teaspoon grated lime rind
1 cup diced strawberries
1 cup whipping cream, whipped
Green food coloring

Prepare pie shell.
Soften gelatin in ½ cup cold water.

Combine limeade concentrate, sugar, and ¾ cup water in small saucepan; cook over low heat, stirring constantly, until concentrate melts and sugar dissolves. Add gelatin; stir until dissolved. Chill until syrupy. Stir in lime rind and strawberries. Fold in whipped cream until blended; tint pale green with food coloring. Chill until mixture mounds when dropped from spoon. Place in pie shell; chill 2 to 3 hours, until firm. Garnish with additional sliced strawberries. Yield about 6 to 8 servings.

sweet georgia peach pie

1 unbaked pie shell (see Index: Basic Pastry)
6 to 8 large fresh peaches, peeled, sliced
4 eggs

1 cup sugar
2 tablespoons flour
2 tablespoons melted shortening

Prepare pie shell; fill with peaches.

Beat eggs well in bowl; add sugar, flour, and shortening. Pour over peaches. It will form its own top crust in baking. Bake at 400°F 15 minutes. Lower oven to 325°F; cook 40 minutes. Let cool to room temperature. Slice; serve. Yield 6 to 8 servings.

vanilla cream pie

1 8-inch pastry shell (see Index: Basic Pastry)
3 tablespoons cornstarch
¼ cup sugar
½ teaspoon salt
2 cups milk
2 egg yolks, beaten
2 tablespoons butter or margarine
1 teaspoon vanilla
½ cup whipping cream
1 tablespoon confectioners' sugar

Prepare, bake, and cool pastry shell.

Mix cornstarch, sugar, and salt in heavy saucepan. Gradually stir in milk. Cook over moderate heat, stirring constantly, until thickened; simmer 1 minute. Stir a little hot mixture into egg yolks; stir yolks into remaining hot mixture. Cook 1 minute; stir constantly. Stir in butter and vanilla. Set in ice water to cool; stir frequently. Pour filling into pastry shell; chill thoroughly.

Before serving, whip cream until stiff; beat in confectioners' sugar. Spread over pie. Yield 4 to 6 servings.

yogurt cheese pie

crust
1¼ cups graham-cracker crumbs
¼ cup sugar
¼ cup softened butter or margarine
1 teaspoon ground cinnamon

filling
12 ounces ricotta or farmer cheese
1½ cups plain yogurt
3 tablespoons honey
1 teaspoon vanilla extract

Combine crust ingredients; press evenly into 9-inch pie pan. Bake at 375°F 5 minutes; cool.

Beat cheese well. Add yogurt a little at a time; mix well. Stir in honey and vanilla. Pour into pie shell; refrigerate at least 24 hours before serving. Yield 8 servings.

MAIN DISH
CHEESE
swiss cheese pie

Pâte Brisée (see Index)
1½ cups medium White Sauce (see Index)
3 to 4 tablespoons heavy cream
4 eggs, beaten
1½ cups grated Gruyére cheese
Nutmeg
Salt and pepper

Make pastry; chill as long as possible. Line 9-inch pie plate.

Make White Sauce; add all other ingredients. Season to taste; pour into pastry shell. Bake in preheated 400°F oven 25 minutes. Yield 5 or 6 servings.

CHICKEN
chicken and oyster pie

12 oysters
2 tablespoons butter or margarine
1 large breast chicken, cut into strips
1 cup sliced mushrooms
Oyster liquor, made to ¼ cup with water
Pinch each of salt, cayenne pepper, sugar
½ cup light cream
1 teaspoon cornstarch
Milk
1 egg yolk
7- or 8-inch baked pastry shell (see Index: Basic Pastry)
Chopped parsley (garnish)
1 or 2 pimientos (can or jar) (garnish)

Open the oysters; retain liquor.

Heat butter in sauté pan. Add chicken and mushrooms; cook quickly a few minutes.

Heat oyster liquor and water; put in oysters. Leave 7 to 8 minutes, off the heat; lift out into bowl. Add chicken, mushrooms, salt, pepper, and sugar. Stir cream (except 1 tablespoon) into oyster liquor. Add cornstarch, mixed smoothly with a little milk; stir until boiling. Boil 1 minute.

Mix 1 tablespoon cream with egg yolk. Stir a little hot sauce into it; return to pan. Add all other ingredients. Check seasoning; heat through. Pour into warm pastry shell. Sprinkle with parsley; decorate with strips of pimiento. Yield 4 servings.

chicken pie

1 (2- to 2½-pound) chicken
2 cups water
½ cup white wine

1 stalk celery, sliced
1 carrot, peeled, sliced
1 shallot, peeled, chopped
½ teaspoon salt
½ teaspoon poultry seasoning
4 slices crisp bacon, crumbled
2 hard-boiled eggs, peeled, quartered
1 medium onion, peeled, diced
2 tablespoons chopped parsley
1½ cups mushrooms, cleaned, quartered
3 tablespoons butter
3 tablespoons flour
2 cups reserved stock
Salt and pepper
3 tablespoons cream
2 frozen puff pastry shells (from 10-ounce
    package), defrosted
1 egg yolk

chicken pie

Wash chicken; pat dry. Place in large saucepan with water, wine, celery, carrot, shallot, ½ teaspoon salt, and poultry seasoning. Bring to boil; reduce heat to low. Cook 40 minutes or until cooked through. Strain; reserve stock. Cool chicken; skin, bone, and cut into 1-inch pieces. Combine chicken, bacon, eggs, onion, parsley, and mushrooms in 9½-inch pie plate; set aside.

Melt butter in medium saucepan. Add flour; cook, stirring constantly, until bubbly. Add stock, salt, and pepper; cook, stirring constantly, until thickened. Stir in 2 tablespoons cream. Pour over chicken mixture.

Lightly flour pastry cloth. Stack puff pastry shells one on top of other; flatten with heels of hands to 4-inch circle. Very carefully roll with floured rolling pin to 9½-inch circle; place on top of pie. Turn edge of crust under; do not attach to pie pan. Cut small circle from center of crust to serve as steam vent. Roll scraps for decoration. Cut into leaf shapes; place on crust.

Beat together egg yolk and 1 tablespoon cream; brush crust well.

Preheat oven to 425°F; bake pie 10 minutes. Reduce heat to 375°F; cook 20 minutes. If crust begins to brown too quickly, cover lightly with foil. Serve hot. Yield 4 to 6 servings.

chicken pie mexican-style

1 small onion, finely chopped
1 tablespoon butter or margarine
3 to 4 small tomatoes (1 pound), peeled, chopped
Salt and pepper
2 or more green chili peppers, peeled, chopped
½ cup cooked peas, fresh or frozen
1 tablespoon chopped parsley
2 cups cut-up cooked or canned chicken
Unbaked 9-inch pie crust (with thick outside edge)
    (see Index: Basic Pastry)

Cook onion in butter until tender. Add tomatoes, salt, and pepper; cook over medium heat until thick. Stir in rest of ingredients. Pour into pie crust. Bake at 400°F 20 to 30 minutes, until browned. Yield 4 servings.

chicken and pineapple pie

2 tablespoons butter or margarine
3 tablespoons flour
1 cup milk
½ cup light cream
Salt and pepper
4 slices bacon
1 can (about 8 ounces) pineapple cubes
1 cup cooked peas (or 1 package frozen)
1 cup diced cooked chicken
1 baked 8- or 9-inch pie shell (see Index:
    Basic Pastry)

Heat butter. Stir in flour; cook 1 minute. Add milk; whisk until smooth. Add cream and seasoning.

Chop bacon; fry until crisp. Add to sauce.

Drain pineapple (reserve some cubes for decoration); add to sauce. Add peas and chicken; mix well. Season to taste. Pour into pastry shell. Decorate with remaining pineapple. Put into preheated 375°F oven just long enough for pastry shell to heat through. Yield 4 to 5 servings.

MEAT
egg and bacon pie

1 recipe basic pastry (see Index) plus ½ cup
    grated cheese
2 tablespoons butter or margarine
2 or 3 onions, peeled, chopped

egg and bacon pie

6 slices bacon, chopped
3 eggs
2 cups milk
Salt and pepper
½ teaspoon dry mustard
2 teaspoons chopped parsley

Line deep 8-inch pie plate or spring pan with pastry.

Heat butter in sauté pan. Add onions and bacon; fry 3 to 4 minutes.

Beat eggs in bowl. Add warmed milk, drained onion and bacon, salt, pepper, mustard, and parsley. Pour into pastry shell. Cook in preheated 375°F oven 35 to 40 minutes. If desired, extra slices of bacon can be broiled and used as garnish. Yield 6 servings.

little meat pies

1 (10-ounce) package frozen patty shells
1 cup diced cooked roast beef
1 onion, chopped
1 clove garlic, minced
2 tablespoons butter
½ teaspoon salt
¼ teaspoon pepper
¼ teaspoon thyme
¼ teaspoon cumin
¼ teaspoon chili powder
2 dashes Tabasco
1 tomato, peeled, chopped
¼ cup raisins
¼ cup sliced stuffed green olives
2 hard-cooked eggs, diced
Milk

Remove patty shells from freezer; let stand at room temperature until soft enough to roll.

Meanwhile, prepare filling. In small skillet sauté beef, onion, and garlic in butter over low heat 5 minutes. Add salt, pepper, thyme, cumin, chili powder, Tabasco, and tomato. Reduce heat to simmer; cook 10 minutes.

Meanwhile, soak raisins in boiling water until plump; drain well.

Combine meat mixture, raisins, olives, and eggs; set aside.

Roll each patty shell on floured pastry cloth to rectangle approximately 5 × 8 inches. Moisten edges with milk. Place ⅓ cup filling on one half of

little meat pies

mexican beef pie

rectangle. Fold to form turnover. Seal by pressing edges.

Preheat oven to 450°F. Place turnovers on ungreased cookie sheet; brush with milk. Place in oven; immediately reduce heat to 400°F. Bake 20 to 25 minutes or until well browned and puffed. Yield 6 servings.

mexican beef pie

Pastry for 9-inch 2-crust pie (see Index)
2 tablespoons vegetable oil
½ cup chopped onion
½ cup chopped green pepper
1 pound ground beef
1 teaspoon salt
¼ teaspoon freshly ground black pepper
1 tablespoon chili powder
1 can (about 8 ounces) Spanish-style tomato sauce
½ cup sliced stuffed olives

Line 9-inch pie plate with half the pastry.

Heat oil in skillet; sauté onion and green pepper 5 minutes. Add beef; cook until browned, stirring frequently. Add seasonings and tomato sauce; cook over low heat 15 minutes. Let cool. Add olives. Turn mixture into pastry shell.

Roll out remaining pastry; cut into thin strips. Arrange over meat in lattice pattern. Bake in preheated 400°F oven 35 to 40 minutes, until pastry is well browned. Yield 5 or 6 servings.

pork pie

1 medium-size head cauliflower
1 tablespoon oil
2 small onions, peeled, very finely chopped
1 clove garlic, crushed
3½ cups canned tomatoes
Pinch of thyme
Salt and pepper
¼ teaspoon paprika
3 tablespoons flour
3 cups diced cooked pork
Pastry for 9-inch 1-crust pie (see Index)

Cook the cauliflower in boiling salted water until just tender; drain. Divide into small florets.

Heat oil in sauté pan. Add onions and garlic; sauté a few minutes. Add tomatoes, thyme, salt, pepper, and paprika; simmer 10 minutes. Press through sieve.

Blend flour with a little cold water. Add to sauce; stir until boiling.

Put pork and cauliflower into deep dish (about 2 quarts); pour sauce over. Cover with pastry. Bake in preheated 450°F oven about 25 minutes, until crust is well browned. Yield 6 servings.

sweetbread and mushroom pie

1 pound sweetbreads
2 tablespoons vinegar
Salt
½ recipe Basic Puff Pastry (see Index)
1 egg, well beaten
1 recipe Mornay Sauce (see Index)
¼ pound fresh mushrooms, thinly sliced
Freshly ground white pepper to taste
¼ cup freshly grated Parmesan cheese
Egg Wash (see Index)

sweetbread and mushroom pie

Soak sweetbreads in cold water 1 hour; drain.

Combine 1 quart water, vinegar, and 1 teaspoon salt in saucepan; bring to boil. Add sweetbreads; cover. Simmer 20 minutes. Remove sweetbreads with slotted spoon; place in bowl of ice water. When chilled, separate into small pieces. Remove outer membrane; cut out tubes.

Roll out pastry on lightly floured surface to ⅛ inch thick; line 2½-inch-deep oval or rectangular baking dish with pastry.

Beat egg quickly into Mornay Sauce. Add mushrooms, sweetbreads, salt to taste, and pepper; mix well. Turn into pastry; sprinkle with cheese. Bake in preheated 425°F oven, 1 shelf above center, 10 minutes. Reduce oven temperature to 350°F; bake 20 minutes or until pastry is golden brown. Brush edge of pastry with Egg Wash. Bake 10 minutes or until pastry is well browned. Garnish with toasted almonds, if desired. Yield about 6 servings.

SEAFOOD

seafood pie

Pastry for 9-inch 1-crust pie (see Index)
3 tablespoons butter or margarine
3 tablespoons very finely chopped green onions or chives
1½ cups diced cooked seafood: shrimp, lobster, scallops, etc., as available
1 tablespoon tomato paste
Cayenne pepper
3 tablespoons sherry
4 eggs
1½ cups heavy cream
¼ cup grated Gruyere cheese

Line 9-inch pie plate with pastry; prick bottom. Bake in preheated 375°F oven 15 minutes. Remove from heat; let cool.

Melt butter in skillet. Add onions; sauté about 2 minutes. Add seafood; stir over low heat 2 minutes. Add tomato paste, seasoning, and sherry; stir until boiling. Cool to lukewarm.

Beat eggs; add cream. Stir in seafood mixture; season to taste. Pour into pastry shell; sprinkle with cheese. Bake 25 to 30 minutes. Serve cut into wedges. Yield 6 to 8 servings.

tuna pie

Pastry for 8- or 9-inch 2-crust pie (see Index)
1 small can (about 8 ounces) tuna fish
½ cup finely chopped onion
1 small can (about 3 ounces) sliced mushrooms
1 can cream of mushroom soup
2 tablespoons grated Parmesan cheese
2 teaspoons lemon juice
1 teaspoon finely chopped parsley
⅛ teaspoon celery seed
⅛ teaspoon thyme
6 hard-boiled eggs, sliced

Line 8- or 9-inch pie plate with half the pastry.

Drain oil from tuna; put 1 tablespoon into sauté pan. Add onion; sauté until transparent. Add mushrooms; cook until onion and mushrooms begin to color. Add soup; stir until smooth. Remove from heat. Add cheese, lemon juice, and flavorings.

Arrange flaked fish and eggs in pastry shell. Pour sauce over; cover with remaining pastry. Crimp edges; make 1 or 2 slits in top to allow steam to escape. Bake in preheated 450°F oven 10 minutes. Reduce heat to 350°F; bake 30 to 35 minutes, until pastry is well browned. Serve hot or cold. Yield 6 servings.

seafood pie

pizza

pizza

pizza crust

1 package active dry yeast
½ cup warm water (105 to 115°F)
¾ cup all-purpose flour and ¾ cup whole-wheat
**   flour (or 1½ cups all-purpose flour)**
½ teaspoon salt
1 teaspoon sugar
1 tablespoon vegetable oil

Dissolve yeast in warm water in medium bowl.

Combine flours, salt, and sugar in separate bowl. Add flour mixture and oil to yeast; stir well. Turn out onto lightly floured board; knead until smooth and elastic, about 6 to 8 minutes.

Lightly grease bowl. Place dough in bowl; turn once to grease top surface. Cover; let rise until double in bulk, about 1½ hours. (Prepare sauce while dough is rising.)

When dough has doubled, punch down. Roll out into 12-inch circle; place on round pizza pan or on cookie sheet. Brush lightly with oil. Let rise 10 minutes. Bake 10 minutes in preheated 400°F oven. (Prepare topping while crust is baking.)

Remove crust from oven. Top with sauce, 1¼ cups cheese, and desired toppings. Bake 12 minutes or until cheese is melted and lightly browned. Remove pizza from pan; cut and serve. Yield 12-inch pizza.

pizza sauce

1 tablespoon olive oil
¼ cup finely chopped onion
1 clove garlic, minced

1 (16-ounce) can Italian-style peeled tomatoes
3 tablespoons tomato paste
1 teaspoon crumbled dried oregano
½ teaspoon sugar
½ teaspoon salt
⅛ teaspoon freshly ground black pepper

Heat oil in medium saucepan. Add onion and garlic; sauté over medium heat 5 minutes, stirring constantly. Do not brown.

Puree tomatoes and their juice in blender or food processor, or break up with fork. Add tomatoes, tomato paste, and seasonings to saucepan. Bring to boil; reduce heat to low. Cook, uncovered, stirring occasionally, 50 minutes or until thick. Set aside to cool.

pizza toppings
Cheeses:
    1 cup shredded mozzarella
    ¼ cup grated Parmesan
    1 cup thinly sliced Swiss
    1 cup thinly sliced provolone
    ¼ cup grated cheddar
    ¼ cup thinly sliced Emmentaler
Anchovy fillets
Capers
Cooked ground beef
Slivered ham
Fresh mushrooms, sliced or coarsely chopped
Pitted black or green olives, quartered, sliced, or
    chopped
Onion, chopped or sliced
Fresh parsley, chopped
Pepperoni, sliced

Green peppers, chopped
Cooked sausage
Cooked shrimp
Fresh tomato slices or wedges

pizza pineapple dessert

½ recipe Rough Puff Pastry (see Index)
1 recipe Egg Wash (see Index)
1 recipe Apricot Glaze (see Index)
7 pineapple rings
5 pitted sweet dark cherries

Roll out pastry to 15-inch circle; center in lightly floured 12-inch pizza pan. Turn edge toward center; press gently into base dough. Make diagonal cuts around edge with sharp knife; brush edge with Egg Wash. Bake in preheated 425°F oven 10 minutes. Reduce oven temperature to 350°F; bake 35 to 40 minutes. Remove from oven; cool thoroughly.

Transfer pastry shell carefully to serving plate. Spread Apricot Glaze generously over bottom of shell. Arrange 5 pineapple rings over glaze. Divide remaining pineapple rings into quarters; arrange around rings. Place cherries in centers of rings; spread additional glaze evenly over fruits. Yield 8 servings.

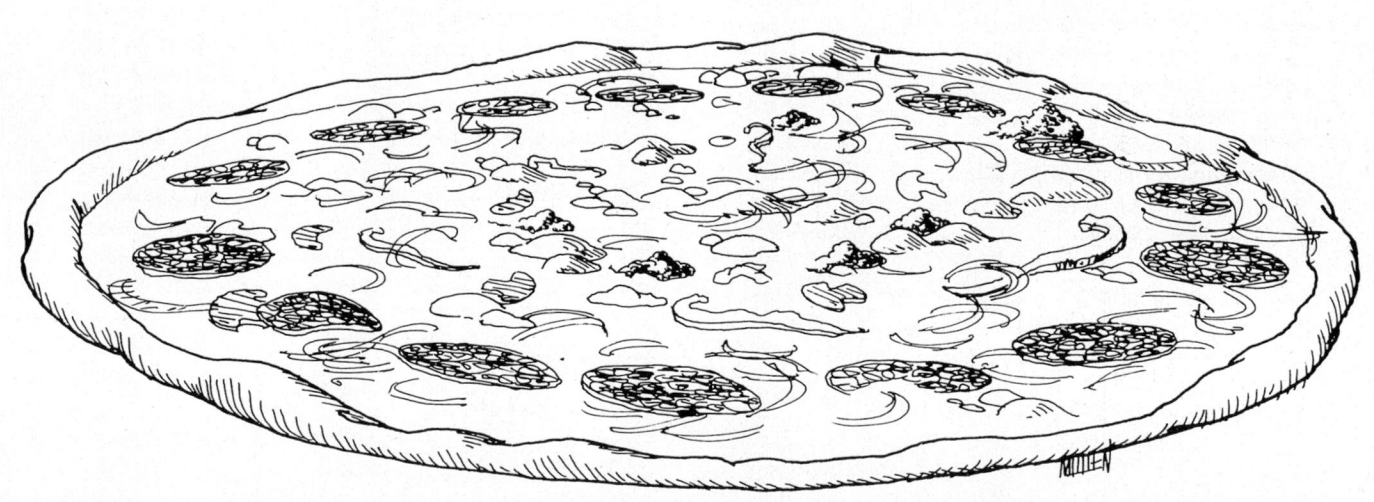

baked pork tenderloin

6 pork tenderloin steaks, 1 inch thick
½ cup flour
½ teaspoon salt
¼ teaspoon pepper
2 tablespoons butter or oil
1 cup chopped onion
1 clove garlic, minced
1 teaspoon ground ginger
1 (1-pound) can applesauce
½ cup sauterne wine
½ cup soy sauce

Flatten tenderloins slightly with cleaver; rub both sides with flour seasoned with salt and pepper. Brown in butter; transfer to oven-serving dish.

Pour off all but 2 tablespoons fat. Brown onion and garlic slightly. Stir in ginger.

Mix together applesauce, wine, and soy sauce; stir into onion mixture. Simmer 1 minute; pour over pork. Bake 1 hour in preheated 350°F oven. Yield 6 servings.

barbecued pork ribs

1½ cups catsup
¾ cup chili sauce
½ cup vinegar
6 tablespoons Worcestershire sauce
6 tablespoons firmly packed light brown sugar
3 tablespoons fresh lemon juice
1 tablespoon paprika
3¼ teaspoons salt
1 clove garlic, crushed
¼ teaspoon hot-pepper sauce
5 pounds pork back ribs
½ teaspoon pepper
Thin slices of onion and lemon (optional)

Combine catsup, 1½ cups water, chili sauce, vinegar, Worcestershire sauce, brown sugar, lemon juice, paprika, 2¼ teaspoons salt, garlic, and hot-pepper sauce in large saucepan. Heat to boiling; reduce heat. Simmer 30 to 45 minutes, until sauce is good basting consistency.

Cut meat into 3 to 4 rib portions. Sprinkle with 1 teaspoon salt and pepper. Put on rack in shallow baking pan. Bake at 450°F 30 minutes. Remove from rack; drain off excess fat. Put ribs in baking pan meaty-side-down; brush with sauce. Reduce oven temperature to 300°F; bake 30 minutes. Turn ribs meaty-side-up; brush with sauce. Top each rib with an onion slice. Bake about 1 hour, brushing frequently with some remaining sauce, until ribs are tender and nicely browned. Add lemon slices to ribs during last half hour of baking. Serve remaining sauce on side. Yield 6 servings.

chinese spareribs with glazed fresh peppers

4 pounds spareribs, cut into serving pieces
Salt
1 pineapple
⅔ cup packed brown sugar
3 tablespoons cornstarch
1 teaspoon dry mustard
1 teaspoon ginger
2 cups fresh orange juice
⅓ cup fresh lemon juice
⅓ cup soy sauce
2 tablespoons butter
½ pound small fresh mushrooms
½ cup chopped fresh onion
1 green sweet pepper, cut into squares
1 red sweet pepper, cut into squares

Place spareribs, bone-side-down, in shallow baking pan; sprinkle with salt to taste. Bake in preheated 350°F oven 1 hour. Drain off excess fat.

Pare pineapple; cut in half lengthwise. Remove core; cut into cubes.

Combine brown sugar, ½ teaspoon salt, cornstarch, mustard, and ginger in medium-size saucepan. Stir in orange and lemon juices and soy sauce; bring to boil. Cook until thickened, stirring constantly; remove from heat.

Melt butter in skillet. Add mushrooms; sauté 5 minutes, stirring frequently. Pour sauce over spareribs. Add onion, peppers, pineapple, and mushrooms. Bake 30 minutes; baste occasionally with sauce in pan. Yield 4 to 6 servings.

curried pork chops

6 loin pork chops
1 (8-ounce) can mushrooms, sliced, drained
⅓ cup finely chopped onion
2 tablespoons butter or margarine
2 tablespoons flour
1½ teaspoons salt
1 teaspoon curry powder
1½ cups milk

Trim excess fat from chops. Brown lightly on both sides in heavy frypan. Place in baking pan. Cover with mushrooms.

Cook onion in butter until tender. Stir in flour, salt, and curry powder. Gradually stir in milk. Cook, stirring constantly, until thickened. Pour over chops; cover pan. Bake in preheated 350°F oven 1 hour or until chops are tender. Yield 6 servings, 1 chop each.

chinese spareribs with glazed fresh peppers

curried pork with shrimp

½ pound pork (shoulder or butt), shredded into
    thin strips
2 tablespoons soy sauce
2 tablespoons vegetable oil
2 teaspoons curry powder
1 small onion, minced
3 celery stalks, cut into ¼-inch slices
2 scallions, cut into ⅛-inch slices
½ tablespoon cornstarch in ½ cup water or
    chicken broth
½ pound whole cooked shrimp

    Marinate pork in soy sauce 20 minutes.

    Heat oil in wok or skillet; brown curry and
onion until aroma becomes strong. Stir-fry pork
about 4 minutes or until well done; push aside.

    Combine celery and scallions; stir-fry 1 to 2
minutes. Return pork; add cornstarch mixture.
Heat until sauce is clear and thickened and shrimp
are heated through. Serve with noodles. Yield 4
servings.

fried pork japanese-style

1 medium red pepper
2 tablespoons chopped scallions
2 tablespoons ground sesame seeds
3 tablespoons soy sauce
2 tablespoons rice wine or sherry
1 pound sliced pork, ¼ inch thick
2 tablespoons oil
2 ounces transparent noodles or very thin
    spaghetti
1 medium cucumber, cut into thin strips
1 medium tomato, cut into thin strips

sauce
2 tablespoons vinegar
1 teaspoon freshly ground black pepper
1 tablespoon sugar

    Remove seeds from pepper; dice fine. Mix with
scallions, sesame seeds, soy sauce, and rice wine.
Marinate pork in mixture at least 1 hour.

    Heat oil in frying pan. Drain pork; brown well
on both sides in hot oil. Cut into smaller pieces, if
desired.

    Prepare noodles. Combine with cucumber and
tomato; place on platter with pork.

    Prepare sauce by blending vinegar, black pep-
per, and sugar. Spoon over pork. Yield 4 servings.

hawaiian pork chops

4 pork chops
1 green pepper
1 medium onion
4 stalks white celery
1 tablespoon oil
1 tablespoon butter
4 slices pineapple
1 cup chicken or veal stock
Little paprika

marinade
1 clove garlic, crushed
Grated rind of half an orange
1 cup soy sauce
¼ cup sherry or port
¼ teaspoon grated fresh ginger
½ bay leaf, crushed
Salt and pepper

    Mix marinade ingredients together; pour over
chops. Leave at least 1 hour.

    Remove seeds from pepper. Cut 4 rings; chop
the rest.

    Chop onion and celery. Mix chopped vegetables
together.

    Remove chops from marinade; dry on paper
towel.

    Heat oil; add butter. When foaming, put in
chops; brown on both sides, about 2 to 3 minutes
each side. Put into ovenproof dish with lid. Put
pineapple slice and spoonful of vegetables on each

chop.

Mix stock with remaining marinade; pour around chops. Cover; bake in preheated 350°F oven about 1 hour. If meat looks as if it is becoming dry, add a little more stock. During last 5 minutes put pepper rings on pineapple. Just before serving, dust each pineapple ring with paprika. Yield 4 servings.

mexican pork roast cooked in beer with green sauce

2 medium onions, chopped
2 carrots, peeled, sliced
1 (4- to 5-pound) loin or shoulder pork roast
2 teaspoons salt
½ teaspoon oregano
½ teaspoon ground coriander
½ to ¾ cup beer

Place onions and carrots in roasting pan.

Rub pork with salt, oregano, and coriander. Place on vegetables; add beer. Cover; roast at 350°F 2¾ hours. Add more beer if vegetables become dry. Slice and serve pork with Green Sauce. Yield 6 to 8 servings.

green sauce
2 tablespoons olive oil
1 medium onion, chopped
1 clove garlic, peeled, chopped
1 (10-ounce) can Mexican green tomatoes (tomatillos)
½ teaspoon crumbled dried oregano
½ teaspoon dried cilantro or parsley
2 tablespoons wine vinegar
Salt and pepper to taste

Heat oil in small skillet. Sauté onion and garlic until limp.

Drain tomatillos; reserve liquid. Combine tomatillos, ½ cup reserved liquid, onion, garlic, oil, oregano, and cilantro in jar of electric blender; puree.

Heat skillet over moderate heat. Pour in sauce; cook 10 minutes. Remove from heat; add wine vinegar, salt, and pepper. Chill sauce; serve with pork.

normandy pork chops

4 pork loin chops
2 tablespoons oil
2 medium onions, chopped
1 clove garlic, crushed
5 medium carrots
2 celery stalks, cut into strips
1 tablespoon flour
1 tablespoon tomato puree
1½ cups stock (or water and cube)
½ cup red wine or cider
1 teaspoon chopped thyme
1 tablespoon chopped parsley
1 bay leaf
3 medium cooking apples
1 cup quartered mushrooms
1 tablespoon brown sugar

normandy pork chops

Brown chops on both sides in hot oil, about 2 minutes each side. Place in ovenproof dish with lid; keep warm.

Fry onions, garlic, carrots, and celery until golden brown. Stir in flour. Add tomato puree and stock; bring gently to boil, stirring constantly. Add wine and herbs. Pour over chops; replace lid. Bake in preheated 350°F oven 40 minutes.

Meanwhile, cut apples into rings.

After 20 minutes add mushrooms to sauce; stir in well; lay apple rings in overlapping layer all over dish. Sprinkle with brown sugar; finish cooking with lid off dish. Yield 4 servings.

party pork chops

8 thick-sliced (¾-inch) pork chops
8 onion slices, about ¼ inch thick
8 fresh lemon slices, about ¼ inch thick, from midsections of 2 unpeeled lemons
⅔ cup brown sugar
1¼ teaspoons salt
¼ teaspoon pepper
3 tablespoons fresh lemon juice
⅔ cup chili sauce

Place pork in single layer in baking pan. Place 1 onion slice topped with 1 lemon slice on center of each chop.

Blend remaining ingredients; spoon over each chop. Cover pan tightly. Bake in 350°F oven 1½ hours or until pork is tender. Yield 8 servings.

pork chop suey

1 pound lean pork, cut into thin slices
8 tablespoons sherry
5 tablespoons soy sauce
Salt to taste
Freshly ground pepper to taste
Pinch of powdered ginger
2 ounces transparent noodles
1 stalk celery
4 tablespoons dried Chinese mushrooms, soaked in water 30 minutes
8 tablespoons oil
2 medium onions, thinly sliced
¼ cup bamboo shoots, thinly sliced
1 cup fresh bean sprouts
½ pound fresh mushrooms, sliced
1 teaspoon sugar
1 tablespoon cornstarch
Cooked rice

Mix pork with 2 tablespoons sherry, 2 tablespoons soy sauce, salt, pepper, and ginger; place in glass or ceramic bowl. Press down meat; cover. Let marinate 1 hour.

Break noodles into small pieces; boil in salted water 5 minutes. Drain; set aside.

Cut celery into thin slices; blanch 5 minutes. Drain; set aside.

Slice Chinese mushrooms into bite-size pieces.

Heat oil in skillet until very hot. Add pork; fry 2 minutes. Remove; keep warm. Add onions, bamboo shoots, bean sprouts, and fresh mushrooms; simmer 3 minutes. Fold in meat, celery, and noodles. Season with 3 tablespoons soy sauce and sugar. Stirring carefully, cook 3 minutes.

Blend cornstarch with 6 tablespoons sherry; slowly stir into sauce until sauce is thick and bubbly. Correct seasonings if necessary. Serve immediately with rice. Yield about 3 servings.

pork chops with buttered noodles

4 loin pork chops, 1 inch thick
2 cups tortellini-shaped pasta
¼ cup butter
Salt and freshly ground pepper to taste
2 teaspoons rosemary
1 teaspoon sage

Place chops on rack in broiler pan. Broil 8 inches from source of heat 20 to 30 minutes, until chops are well done; turn once.

Cook pasta in large saucepan of boiling, salted water until tender; drain thoroughly.

Melt butter in same saucepan. Add pasta, salt, pepper, rosemary, and sage; heat through, shaking pan frequently. Place on heated platter; place pork on pasta. Garnish with crisp bacon and chopped parsley, if desired. Yield 4 servings.

pork chops in onion sauce german-style

4 pork chops
½ teaspoon salt
¼ teaspoon pepper
1½ teaspoons flour
1½ tablespoons vegetable oil
4 small (or 2 medium) onions, thinly sliced
½ cup beer
½ cup hot beef broth
1 teaspoon cornstarch

Season pork with salt and pepper; coat with flour.

Heat oil in heavy frypan. Add chops; fry each side 3 minutes. Add onions; cook 5 minutes, turning chops once. Pour in beer and broth; cover. Simmer 15 minutes. Remove chops to preheated platter. Season sauce to taste.

Blend cornstarch with small amount cold water. Stir into sauce; cook until thick and bubbly. Pour over pork. Yield 4 servings.

pork chops with buttered noodles

pork chops with rice

4 loin pork chops, about 1½ pounds total
3 tablespoons olive oil
1 medium onion, chopped
1 clove garlic, minced
1 green pepper, seeded, chopped
1 cup raw long-grain rice
2 cups boiling water
2 teaspoons chicken-broth granules
2 packs cilantro and achiote seasoning mix
   (5 grams each)
2 tablespoons dry sherry
½ cup sliced black olives

Sauté pork in oil in large, heavy skillet until well-browned; remove from skillet. Add onion, garlic, and pepper; sauté over medium heat until limp. Add rice; sauté until lightly browned.

Combine boiling water, chicken-broth granules, cilantro and achiote seasoning mix, and sherry; pour over rice. Top with pork chops; cover. Reduce heat to low; cook 20 to 25 minutes or until all liquid is absorbed. Top chops with olives; serve. Yield 4 servings.

Note: Cilantro and achiote seasoning mix is sold in Latin American and Carribbean markets and is sometimes referred to as Creole seasoning. If you cannot obtain it, substitute 2 tablespoons tomato paste and ½ teaspoon ground cumin for the seasoning mix.

478

pork chops in onion sauce german-style

pork chops in white wine

4 lean pork chops, about 1 inch thick
Salt and pepper to taste
1 teaspoon bacon drippings
2 teaspoons flour
½ cup chicken broth
½ cup dry white wine
1 large onion, sliced

Season chops with salt and pepper. Sear slowly on both sides in hot bacon fat. Remove from skillet.

Stirring constantly, blend flour into fat remaining in skillet. Add broth and wine. When very smooth, return chops to skillet. Spread onion over chops. Cover skillet; simmer about 45 minutes. Yield 4 servings.

pork with cider

1½ pounds lean boneless pork, cut into 1-inch cubes
⅓ cup flour
⅓ cup vegetable oil
1½ cups apple cider or apple juice
2 carrots, sliced
1 small onion, sliced
½ teaspoon rosemary
1 bay leaf
1 teaspoon salt
½ teaspoon pepper

Thoroughly dredge pork with flour.

Heat oil in large frypan until hot. Carefully add pork; cook until browned on all sides. Remove pork; drain on paper towels. Place in casserole.

Drain oil from pan. Pour in cider; heat and stir

to remove browned pieces from pan.

Add carrots, onion, rosemary, bay leaf, salt, pepper, and hot cider to casserole; cover. Bake in 325°F oven 2 hours until meat is tender. Remove bay leaf. Yield 4 servings.

pork fillets

2 pounds pork tenderloin
1 large apple
2 tablespoons chopped almonds
1 teaspoon sugar
¼ teaspoon cinnamon
¼ teaspoon garlic powder
1 teaspoon salt
¼ teaspoon freshly ground pepper
¼ cup olive oil
½ cup dry red wine
1 cup stock

Slice tenderloin into 6 pieces.

Peel, core, and finely chop apple. Combine apple, almonds, sugar, and cinnamon; mix well.

Make horizontal slash in center of each tenderloin without cutting through. Stuff with apple

pork with cider

pork fillets

pork kebobs

filling. Press meat together; secure with metal clamps or skewers if necessary.

Combine garlic powder, salt, and pepper. Rub tenderloins with mixture.

Heat oil in deep skillet; brown tenderloins on all sides. Add wine and stock; bring to boil. Reduce heat; simmer 1 hour, turning meat at 15-minute intervals. Yield 4 servings.

pork kebobs

Juice of 1 lime
¼ cup salad oil
¼ teaspoon crushed whole coriander
¼ cup chopped onion
1 clove garlic, mashed
¼ teaspoon pepper
1¼ pounds lean pork, cut into 1½-inch cubes
1 medium zucchini, sliced
2 red peppers, stemmed, seeded, cut in chunks
½ pound mushrooms, cleaned, stems cut off

The day before cooking, combine lime juice, oil, coriander, onion, garlic, and pepper in glass or pottery bowl or casserole. Add meat; stir to coat with marinade. Cover; refrigerate 24 hours, stirring once or twice.

To cook, drain meat, reserve marinade. Skewer meat alternately with zucchini, peppers, and mushrooms. Broil or charcoal grill until done through (20 to 25 minutes), basting occasionally with marinade. Yield 4 servings.

480

pork loin with prunes

pork loin with prunes

18 small pitted prunes
1 (5-pound) boned rolled pork loin, tied
Salt and freshly ground white pepper to taste
3 tablespoons all-purpose flour
1¾ cups chicken broth
3 tablespoons sherry (optional)

Place prunes in bowl; cover with water. Soak 30 minutes; drain prunes.

With sharp knife cut slit in meat deep enough to insert prunes. After prunes are inserted, close opening with skewer, or tie with twine. Season pork with salt and pepper. Place in greased baking pan; pour 2 cups hot water into pan. Bake in preheated 350°F oven about 3 hours, or 190° on meat thermometer.

Place remaining prunes in small saucepan; cover with water. Bring to boil; reduce heat. Simmer about 20 minutes, until just tender; drain.

Place pork on heated serving platter; garnish with cooked prunes. Keep warm.

Spoon 3 tablespoons pan drippings into small saucepan. Add flour; cook, stirring constantly, until smooth and brown. Add broth gradually; cook until thickened, stirring constantly. Stir in sherry; season with salt and pepper. Pour into sauceboat; serve with pork. Yield 15 servings.

pork in orange–cider sauce

2 pounds pork tenderloin
2 tablespoons brown sugar
2 teaspoons dry mustard
2 tablespoons corn oil
1 tablespoon cornstarch
Juice of 1 orange
Cider (about ¾ cup)
Salt and pepper
1 clove garlic, crushed
6 stuffed olives, sliced
4 cloves
Pineapple

Have butcher cut tenderloin into slices; pound flat.

Mix sugar and mustard; coat both sides of meat.

Heat oil in sauté pan. Brown meat on both sides; remove to casserole.

Add cornstarch to remaining fat; stir and cook 1 minute. Add orange juice, made up to 1¼ cups with cider. Stir until boiling; boil 2 minutes. Add seasoning, garlic, olives, and cloves. Pour over meat; cover. Cook in preheated 350°F oven 30 to 35 minutes. Remove cloves; check seasoning. Serve with broiled pineapple slices. Yield 4 servings.

pork in red chili sauce

2 tablespoons lard (optional)
1 medium onion, chopped
1 clove garlic, minced
1½ to 2 tablespoons chili powder
1½ pounds lean pork, cut into 1½-inch cubes (reserve fat)
1½ cups canned tomatoes, broken up with fork
½ teaspoon salt
½ teaspoon crumbled oregano
½ teaspoon ground cumin
⅛ teaspoon ground cloves
1 small cinnamon stick

Render strips of pork fat or heat lard in Dutch oven over moderate heat. Remove strips of fat, if used. Add onion and garlic; brown lightly. Add chili powder; stir well. Push vegetables to sides of pan; brown meat on all sides. Add tomatoes, salt, oregano, cumin, cloves, and cinnamon stick; stir well. Bring to boil; reduce heat to low. Cover; cook 2 hours or until meat is very tender. Stir mixture occasionally while cooking. If sauce is quite thin, cook uncovered last 15 to 20 minutes of cooking. Serve with rice and tortillas. Yield 4 servings.

pork ribs and sauerkraut

1-pound 12-ounce can sauerkraut
1 cup chopped onion
1-pound 12-ounce can tomatoes
¾ cup firmly packed brown sugar
3 pounds country-style pork ribs

Layer ingredients in large casserole or roaster as listed, starting with sauerkraut and ending with ribs. Do not stir. Cover; bake at 325°F 3 hours. Uncover last 45 minutes of baking. Yield 6 servings.

pork roast with cranberry stuffing

Pork loin roast (8 rib chops), 6 to 7 pounds
Salt, pepper, poultry seasoning
1 cup boiling water
1 beef bouillon cube
½ cup butter
1 (8-ounce) package herb-seasoned bread stuffing
1 cup cranberries, knife-chopped
1 small red apple (unpeeled), cored, diced (¾ cup)
¼ cup finely chopped celery
¼ cup minced parsley
1 large egg

Have butcher saw off backbone (chine) of roast. Place meat, rib-ends-up, on cutting board. Holding meaty side of the roast with one hand, starting 1 inch from one end of roast and ending 1 inch from other end, cut slit between meat and rib bones almost to bottom of roast. With fingers pull meaty part slightly away from ribs to form pocket. Sprinkle inside of pocket and outside of roast with salt, pepper, and seasoning salt.

Into large skillet or medium saucepan, off heat, pour boiling water. Add bouillon cube; stir to dissolve. Add butter; over very low heat stir until melted. Remove from heat. Add bread stuffing, cranberries, apple, celery, and parsley; mix well.

Beat egg until thick and pale-colored; mix with stuffing. Spoon stuffing into pocket in roast; put any leftover stuffing into small baking dish. Roast pork on rack in shallow roasting pan in 350°F oven 35 minutes per pound. About half an hour before roast is ready, put baking dish of extra stuffing in oven to heat. After roast has been removed to hot serving platter, pour off fat in roasting pan. Spoon some drippings over top of stuffing in roast and some over small baking dish of extra stuffing. Yield 6 servings.

pork rolls with celery

2 medium onions
3 medium tomatoes, skinned
4 stalks celery
¼ cup butter
8 large thin slices pork shoulder
Salt and freshly ground pepper to taste
Grated rind of 1 large orange
1½ teaspoons crushed rosemary
¼ cup vegetable oil
2 cups Basic Beef Stock (see Index)
1 tablespoon soy sauce

Chop onions and tomatoes.

Cut celery stalks in half lengthwise, then into thin slices.

Melt butter in large skillet. Add onions, tomatoes, and celery; cook over medium heat, stirring frequently, until vegetables are just tender.

Cut each pork slice in half; sprinkle with salt, pepper, orange rind, and rosemary. Roll up; secure with wooden picks. Brown in oil in separate skillet; place over vegetable mixture. Add stock and soy sauce; cover. Simmer 30 minutes, garnish with parsley, if desired. Remove picks before serving. Yield 8 servings.

pork rolls with celery

pork spareribs in mexican barbecue sauce

mexican barbecue sauce
1 tablespoon olive oil
1 medium onion, chopped
1 clove garlic, peeled, minced
1 fresh chili pepper, stemmed, seeded, chopped
½ tablespoon salt
2 large tomatoes, peeled, cut up
2 tablespoons chili powder
2 tablespoons sugar
¼ cup vinegar
⅓ cup olive oil
¼ cup beer
4 pounds pork spareribs (country-style)

Make sauce. Heat oil in saucepan. Sauté onion until lightly browned. Add garlic, chili, salt, and tomatoes; simmer until mixture thickens. Add remaining sauce ingredients; cook 8 minutes, stirring constantly.

Marinate spareribs in sauce several hours before grilling (if possible). Grill over hot charcoal or under broiler, basting periodically with sauce, until tender, well-browned, and crusty. Pour extra sauce on ribs before serving. Yield 6 to 8 servings.

roast pork with oranges

4 pounds pork loin roast
1 teaspoon sage
Salt and pepper
1 cup water
Juice of 1 orange
½ cup sherry
1 tablespoon red currant jelly
Grated rind of 1 orange
3 to 6 oranges, peeled, sectioned

Rub pork with sage, salt, and pepper. Put on rack in shallow roasting pan. Add water. Roast at 325°F 2 hours or until thermometer registers 170°F. About 45 minutes before meat is done, pour off fat; leave pan juices. Pour orange juice and sherry over meat. Spread jelly over meat; sprinkle with orange rind. Baste a few times. When done, put meat on platter; surround with oranges. Yield 6 servings.

savory pork fillet

2 pork fillets
1-2 tablespoons oil
1 teaspoon paprika
10 to 12 mushrooms, quartered
1 small can tomato sauce (or 4 to 6 tablespoons
tomato puree, a little onion and 4 to 6
tablespoons stock)
Salt and pepper
3 to 4 tablespoons sour cream
Little chopped parsley

Cut fillets into slices; lightly brown in oil until golden brown all over, about 4 to 5 minutes, sprinkling on paprika. Remove from pan; place in flameproof dish.

Cook mushrooms 2 to 3 minutes in oil; add to pork. Pour over tomato sauce and seasonings; cook about 10 to 12 minutes over gentle heat. Spoon over sour cream; decorate with sprinkling of parsley. Yield 4 servings.

schnitzel with ham and caper sauce

4 pork loin chops, about 1 inch thick, bone
removed
2 tablespoons lemon juice
Salt and pepper
2 tablespoons vegetable oil

ham and caper sauce
1 tablespoon fat
1 tablespoon all-purpose flour

1 cup plain yogurt
4 ounces cooked ham, cut into julienne strips
1 or 2 medium-size dill pickles, cut into
small cubes
1 tablespoon capers

Brush chops with lemon juice; season with salt and pepper. Let stand 5 to 10 minutes; pat dry. Brown in hot vegetable oil in large skillet. Reduce heat; cover. Cook until done (20 to 25 minutes). Remove to warm platter.

Drain all but 1 tablespoon of fat from skillet. Add flour to remaining fat; stir to form smooth paste. Add yogurt; stir to blend and pick up browned bits. Stir in ham, pickles, and capers. Heat until thickened; stir constantly. Spoon sauce over pork. Serve at once. Yield 4 servings.

stuffed pork chops

barbecue sauce
1½ tablespoons oil
1 onion, chopped
1 clove garlic, crushed
1 teaspoon flour
1 small can tomatoes
1 cup brown stock
2 tablespoons vinegar
2 tablespoons Worcestershire sauce
1 tablespoon tomato chutney
1 tablespoon sugar
1 teaspoon lemon juice
1 tablespoon chopped parsley and thyme
¼ teaspoon celery salt

stuffing
1 onion, chopped
1 stalk celery, chopped
3 tablespoons butter
2 cups fresh bread crumbs
1 apple, chopped
4 tablespoons chopped parsley, thyme, and a
little sage
Grated rind of ½ lemon
1 small egg, beaten
Few drops lemon juice
4 good-size pork chops
2 to 3 tablespoons oil

Make Barbecue Sauce. Heat oil; cook onion and garlic, covered, 3 to 4 minutes to soften. Remove lid; brown slightly. Add flour; brown slightly. Add tomatoes and stock; bring to boil. Add all other ingredients; cook 15 minutes. Strain; set aside.

Make stuffing. Cook onion and celery in butter. Add to bread crumbs together with apple, herbs, and lemon rind. Bind mixture with egg and dash of lemon juice; if too dry, add a little milk or stock.

Make cut in center of side of each chop; be careful to make pocket without piercing top or bottom surface of meat. Push stuffing into pocket. Sew up or skewer slits in chops; pat dry. Brown both sides in a little hot oil; remove. Put into ovenproof dish. Spoon over a little Barbecue Sauce thinned with a little extra stock. Cook in preheated 350°F oven about 1 hour. Take out; remove threads or skewers. Serve with Barbecue Sauce. Yield 4 servings.

vegetables with pork chinese-style

sweet-and-sour pork

1½ pounds lean pork, cut into 1-inch cubes
3 tablespoons soy sauce
3 tablespoons dry white wine
2 carrots, cut into thin strips
1 red sweet pepper, seeds removed, cut into thin rings
4 tablespoons olive oil
1 small slice fresh gingerroot, minced
½ cup chopped onions
¼ pound fresh mushrooms, sliced
½ cup beef broth
1 recipe Chinese Sweet-and-Sour Sauce
Boiled rice

Place pork in shallow dish.

Combine soy sauce and wine; pour over pork. Turn to coat all sides. Marinate about 20 to 30 minutes; stir frequently.

Cut carrots; set aside. Cut pepper into rings; set aside.

Heat 2 tablespoons oil in wok or skillet. Add

gingerroot. Place pork in wok; stir-fry about 5 minutes. Remove pork; set aside. Add remaining oil to wok. Add carrots, pepper, onions, and mushrooms; stir-fry about 5 minutes or until carrots and pepper are tender but still on crisp side. Add pork; stir-fry 5 minutes. Add broth; mix well. Stir in Sweet-and-Sour Sauce; bring to boil. Reduce heat to low; cover wok. Cook 2 minutes. Serve with rice. Yield 4 servings.

chinese sweet-and-sour sauce
4 tablespoons catsup
¼ cup brown sugar
2 tablespoons soy sauce
3 tablespoons wine vinegar
2 tablespoons dry white wine
2 tablespoons cornstarch dissolved in ½ cup cold water

Combine catsup, sugar, soy sauce, vinegar, and wine in saucepan; bring to boil. Add cornstarch dissolved in water to sauce. Cook over low heat, stirring constantly, until sauce has thickened. Yield about 1¼ cups.

vegetables with pork chinese-style

¼ cup butter
4 cups diagonally sliced celery
1 green sweet pepper, sliced
1 red sweet pepper, sliced
½ pound fresh mushrooms, sliced
½ cup sliced onions
2 cups cubed cooked pork
1¼ cups beef bouillon
1 tablespoon cornstarch
3 tablespoons soy sauce
½ teaspoon powdered ginger
¼ teaspoon salt
Freshly ground pepper to taste
Boiled rice

Melt butter in wok or skillet. Add celery; stir-fry 5 minutes. Stir in peppers, mushrooms, and onions; stir-fry 5 minutes. Stir in pork and bouillon; bring to boil. Reduce heat; simmer 5 minutes.

Blend cornstarch with soy sauce, ginger, salt, and pepper; stir into pork mixture. Cook, stirring constantly, just until heated through and thickened. Serve over rice. Yield 6 servings.

QUAIL

quail with grapes

6 quail
Salt and pepper
6 vine leaves, if possible
6 small strips larding pork
2 cups white grapes
½ cup butter
¼ cup cognac
¼ cup consommé

Clean and truss birds; salt and pepper lightly. If you have vine leaves, wrap one around each bird; cover with thin strip of larding pork. Tie securely.

Peel grapes; remove seeds.

Heat butter in shallow pan; sear quail quickly. Put into hot oven; roast about 8 minutes. Remove from oven; untruss. Place in preheated, uncovered ovenware dish with cooking juice and grapes. Return to hot oven 5 minutes.

Just before serving, stir warmed cognac and consommé into juice in pan; baste quail with sauce. Cover; serve immediately. Yield 6 servings.

quail on toast

4 quail, split
½ cup flour
½ teaspoon salt
⅛ teaspoon pepper
4 tablespoons butter or margarine
1 cup boiling water
1 pint half-and-half cream
⅓ cup sherry
Buttered toast

Split dressed quail; roll each piece in flour seasoned with salt and pepper. Brown in butter on all sides. Pour boiling water over; cover. Let simmer until tender (15 to 20 minutes); remove cover. Add cream and sherry; simmer 10 minutes. Place birds on pieces of buttered toast. Taste sauce for seasoning; pour over quail. Yield 4 servings.

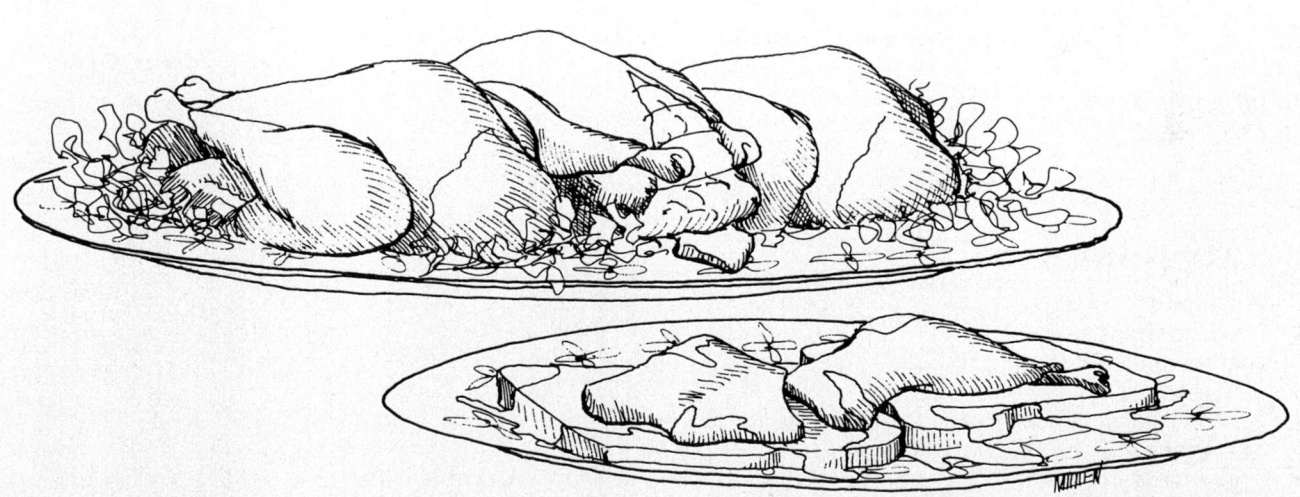

RABBIT

marinated rabbit

1 (3-pound) rabbit (fresh or frozen)
1 teaspoon salt
¼ teaspoon pepper
3 tablespoons vegetable oil

marinade
2 cups red wine
2 cups chicken broth
1 teaspoon allspice
2 bay leaves
1 teaspoon thyme

sauce
1 dozen pickled white onions (cocktail size)
1 dozen stuffed green olives, sliced
½ pound fresh mushrooms, sliced
2 tablespoons butter or margarine

Cut rabbit into serving pieces; rub with salt and pepper. Put into large bowl; add marinade. Refrigerate overnight.

Drain rabbit; do not pat dry. Strain; reserve marinade. In large frypan over high heat quickly brown all sides of rabbit pieces in hot vegetable oil. When brown, pour in reserved marinade; simmer over low heat 1 hour or until tender.

Just before rabbit is done, sauté onions, olives, and mushrooms in hot butter. Add to rabbit mixture. Serve with boiled potatoes. Yield 6 servings.

rabbit stew

1 (4- to 5-pound) rabbit
4 tablespoons bacon fat or butter
3 tablespoons flour
2 cups chicken stock
2 cups dry white wine
1 garlic clove, crushed
2½ tablespoons tomato paste
Salt
Pepper
1 teaspoon tarragon
1 bay leaf, crushed
½ teaspoon thyme
3 tablespoons sour cream

Rabbit can be found in most frozen-food departments.

Have butcher cut rabbit into serving pieces.

Heat fat; brown rabbit pieces on all sides. Sprinkle with flour; blend in well. Add stock, wine, garlic, tomato paste, and seasonings. Simmer, covered, over low heat 1½ hours. Transfer meat to warm serving platter.

Reduce sauce if necessary. Stir in sour cream; heat, but do not let sauce boil. Pour over rabbit. Yield 6 servings.

marinated rabbit

RAREBIT

chipped beef rarebit

1 cup grated cheese
1 cup shredded dried beef
3 cups canned or strained stewed tomatoes
2 teaspoons butter
¼ teaspoon pepper
2 beaten eggs
1 teaspoon Worcestershire sauce

Put cheese, beef, and tomatoes in saucepan; simmer until cheese is melted, stirring constantly. Stir in butter and pepper. Add eggs and Worcestershire sauce. Heat quickly almost to boil; serve immediately on buttered toast. Yield 4 servings.

mushroom rarebit

¼ cup butter
4 cups sliced mushrooms
Salt and pepper
2 tablespoons tomato puree
3 tablespoons stock or water
4 tablespoons grated Parmesan cheese
4 slices toast or English muffins

Heat butter in pan. Add mushrooms; sauté slowly about 10 minutes. Add seasoning and tomato puree mixed with stock. Add cheese; cook slowly until mushrooms are tender, about 5 to 7 minutes. Serve on hot buttered toast or English muffins. Yield 4 servings.

welsh rarebit

Butter
¼ cup flour
1 teaspoon dry mustard
¾ cup beer or ale
1¼ cups milk
1¼ cups grated sharp cheddar cheese
1 tablespoon wine vinegar
1 tablespoon Worcestershire sauce
Salt and white pepper to taste
6 slices bread

welsh rarebit

RAREBIT

Melt ¼ cup butter in heavy saucepan over low heat; increase heat to medium. Add flour and mustard; stir until smooth. Add beer; bring to boil, stirring constantly. Add milk alternately with cheese; bring to boil and stir until smooth after each addition. Add vinegar, Worcestershire sauce, salt, and pepper; mix well. Keep warm.

Spread butter liberally on each slice of bread; place on cookie sheet. Broil until toasted. Place each slice of bread on heatproof plate; spoon cheese sauce over each slice. Dot each serving with small amount of butter; broil until sauce is bubbly and brown. Garnish with parsley sprigs. Yield 6 servings.

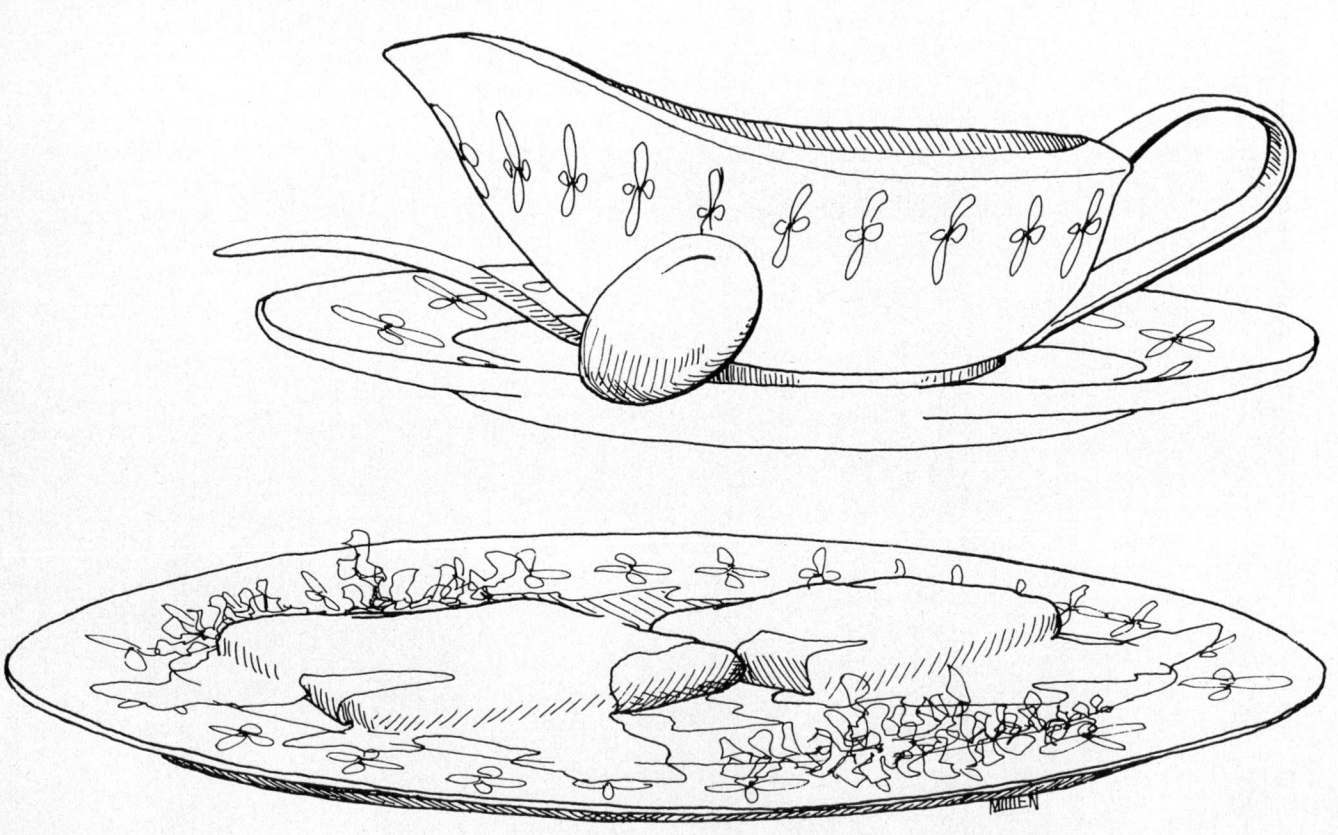

RELISHES

chow chow

15 pounds green tomatoes
5½ pounds cabbage
6 green peppers
7 hot red peppers
10 onions
1 cup salt
1 gallon vinegar
2½ cups sugar
1 box mixed pickling spices, in a bag
4 teaspoons turmeric
3 tablespoons dry mustard

Grind tomatoes, cabbage, peppers, and onions together. Put in bag with salt; let drip overnight.

Put vinegar and seasonings in large pot; add ground vegetables. Let come to boil; cook slowly 45 minutes to 1 hour. Put in jars; seal. Yield 13 to 15 pints.

Note: Be sure to put pickling spice in cheesecloth bag for easy removal after cooking. If you like hot chow chow, add horseradish to taste.

crisp watermelon rind

5 pounds watermelon rind
1 tablespoon salt
8 teaspoons alum
9 cups sugar
1 quart cider vinegar
2 lemons, thinly sliced
4 (2-inch) cinnamon sticks
2 teaspoons whole allspice
2 teaspoons whole cloves

Cut off and discard green and red portion from watermelon rind, leaving only white inner rind. Cut rind into 1-inch pieces, to measure 4 quarts. Place rind in large enamel or stainless-steel pot. Add water to cover; stir in salt. Bring to boil; reduce heat. Simmer 15 to 20 minutes, until rind can be easily pierced with fork. Remove from heat; stir in alum; cool. Cover; let stand 24 hours.

Pour off water; rinse; drain well. Add sugar, vinegar, lemon, and cinnamon.

Tie allspice and cloves in cheesecloth bag; add to rind mixture; mix well. Bring just to boil; stir constantly. Remove from heat; cool, uncovered. Cover; let stand 24 hours.

Drain off syrup into large saucepan; bring just to boil. Pour over rind; cool. Cover; let stand 24 hours.

Heat rind in syrup; do not boil. Remove and discard spice bag. Pack rind and cinnamon in hot, sterilized jars.

Heat syrup to boiling; fill jars with boiling syrup. Seal immediately. Store at least 4 weeks before serving. Yield 4 quarts.

green-tomato relish

24 green tomatoes, diced
6 green peppers, chopped
6 white onions, chopped
3 red hot peppers, chopped
4 cups cider vinegar
8 tablespoons sugar
2 teaspoons mixed spice
Salt to taste

Simmer all ingredients together about 20 to 30 minutes. Salt to taste after mixture comes to boil. Seal in pint jars while hot. Yield 6 pints.

indian relish

2 quarts green tomatoes, peeled, chopped
½ cup salt
3 cups finely chopped cabbage
3 cups vinegar
½ cup finely chopped onion
½ cup chopped green pepper
¼ cup diced pimiento
1½ cups sugar
1½ teaspoons celery seed
1½ teaspoons mustard seed
1 teaspoon whole cloves
Small piece (¼ inch) cinnamon stick

Sprinkle tomatoes with salt; leave overnight. Strain off liquid. Put tomatoes into kettle. Add cabbage and vinegar; boil gently 25 to 30 minutes. Add onion, pepper, pimiento, sugar, celery seed, and mustard seed. Add cloves and cinnamon tied loosely together in piece of cheesecloth. Mix all well; cook over gentle heat until onion is tender and relish a good consistency. Pack in hot sterilized jars; seal at once. Yield 3 to 3½ pints.

kosher dill pickles

½ bushel small, firm cucumbers
½ bunch dill, dried
Water to cover, about 3 gallons
1 pound salt
5 pods garlic, sliced
½ pound mixed pickling spices
3 pods red pepper

Wash cucumbers carefully, one at a time; any sediment left on can spoil entire batch. Place in large stoneware crock.

Break up dill; place among cucumbers.

Make brine of water, salt, garlic, and spices. Add to cucumbers; they must be entirely covered with liquid. Cover with an inverted dish weighted down with clean heavy stone. Let stand at room temperature until done to your liking. Length of time will depend on room temperature. Pickles can be eaten after third or fourth day, but well-done pickles must stand a week or longer. When pickles are to your taste, refrigerate them to halt pickling process. Yield about 10 quarts.

Note: A fresh egg in shell when placed in water will rise to surface when proper amount of salt has been added to water. This recipe gives minimum amounts of dill, garlic, and red pepper. More can be added to taste.

pickles

3 pounds cucumbers
⅓ cup salt
5 cups cold water
½ pounds onions, peeled, thinly sliced
2 cups cider vinegar
1⅔ cups sugar
1 teaspoon celery seed
2 teaspoons prepared mustard
1 teaspoon ginger
¼ teaspoon turmeric
⅛ teaspoon mace
Few dashes of red pepper

Slice cucumbers; put into enamelware or glass bowl. Sprinkle with salt; add water. Cover; let stand overnight. Next morning turn into colander; drain 10 to 15 minutes. Put into preserving kettle; add onions. Add vinegar, sugar, and spices; heat to simmering. Simmer only 3 minutes. Pack into hot sterile jars. Yield 3 pints.

tomato chutney

1 tablespoon salad oil
1 whole red chili pepper, crumbled
½ teaspoon cumin seed
¼ teaspoon nutmeg
¼ teaspoon mustard seed
4 tomatoes, peeled, sliced ⅛ inch thick
½ lemon, quartered
⅓ cup raisins
½ cup sugar

Heat oil; add chili pepper. Add cumin, nutmeg, and mustard seed. When seeds start to jump, add tomatoes and lemon. Simmer 15 minutes; stir frequently. Stir in raisins and sugar. Simmer, stirring frequently until thickened, about 30 minutes; chill. Pack in sterilized jars; seal. Yield 2 half-pints.

Note: This chutney is from Bengal. It is sweeter and milder than most. If made ahead of time and refrigerated, allow to warm to room temperature before serving.

vegetable pickle

1 medium head cabbage
4 carrots
6 onions
2 green peppers
2 red peppers
2 to 3 stalks celery
1 pint cider vinegar
3 cups sugar
1 teaspoon mustard seed
1 teaspoon celery salt

Prepare all vegetables; chop finely or put through coarsest blade of food grinder. Put into bowl; cover with cold water. Let stand about 3 hours; drain. Put vegetables into kettle. Add vinegar, sugar, mustard seed, and celery salt; bring slowly to boiling point. Remove from heat. (This way vegetables should remain crisp.) Pack into hot sterilized jars; seal at once. Yield about 5 pints.

basic boiled rice

5 cups water
2 teaspoons salt
1 cup long-grain rice

Bring water and salt to hard rolling boil in large saucepan. Add rice gradually; stir constantly. Cover; reduce heat. Cook at slow boil 18 to 20 minutes, until rice is tender; drain. Serve hot. Do not rinse before serving; this washes away vitamins and minerals.

alternate method
2 cups water
1 teaspoon salt
1 cup long-grain rice

Bring water and salt to hard rolling boil in 2-quart saucepan. Add rice gradually; stir constantly. Cover; reduce heat. Cook at slow boil 18 to 20 minutes, until rice is tender and water is absorbed.

basic fried oven-cooked rice

4 tablespoons butter
1 cup long-grain rice
1 small onion, finely chopped

2 cups hot Basic Chicken Stock (see Index)

Melt butter in frying pan. Add rice and onion; cook over medium heat about 5 minutes or until golden, stirring frequently. Turn rice mixture into 1½-quart casserole. Stir in stock; cover. Bake in preheated 425°F oven 25 minutes, until rice is tender and stock is absorbed.

busy-day rice ragout

1 small onion, chopped
1 green pepper, chopped
1 tablespoon oil
1 pound lean ground beef or veal
1 teaspoon salt
Dash of black pepper
1 tablespoon prepared mustard
2 tablespoons catsup
1 tablespoon Worcestershire sauce
3 cups cooked rice
3 cups canned tomatoes

Use medium to large skillet; stir onion and green pepper in oil until soft. Add meat, salt, and pepper; stir until meat loses pink color. Add remaining ingredients; stir until well blended. Reduce heat; cover skillet. Simmer just 15 minutes. Yield 4 to 6 servings.

busy-day rice ragout

491

chinese rice ring

1 cup converted rice, cooked
½ cup diced green onions
⅓ cup pimientos
½ cup melted butter
3 eggs, well beaten
Pinch of salt
1 can bean sprouts, drained

Cook rice as directed. Sauté onions and pimientos in butter in frypan until softened. Stir eggs, salt, and bean sprouts into rice. Put in well-greased round ring mold. Put ring mold on large baking or roasting pan filled with 1 inch water. Heat in oven about 20 minutes; unmold. Serve hot. Yield 8 to 10 servings.

curried rice

½ cup rice
2 cups hot water
½ cup canned tomatoes
¼ cup finely sliced onion
¼ cup thinly sliced red or green pepper
2 tablespoons melted butter or margarine
¾ teaspoon curry powder

Put rice into casserole; add water. Let stand about ¼ hour. Add all other ingredients; mix well. Cover; cook in preheated 350°F oven about 1½ hours, stirring occasionally. Most of liquid should be absorbed, but serve rice while still moist. Yield 4 servings.

fried rice

½ pound long-grain rice
½ pound cooked ham, cut into strips
1 (6-ounce) can shrimp, drained
3 tablespoons oil
2 tablespoons soy sauce
1 leek, sliced
4 eggs
Freshly ground black pepper

Cook rice according to package directions.
Cut ham into strips.
Drain shrimp.
Heat oil in large skillet. Add ham and shrimp; cook until lightly browned, approximately 5 minutes. Add rice and soy sauce; cook 5 minutes. Add leek; cook 5 minutes, stirring occasionally. Lightly beat eggs with pepper; pour over rice. Cook until eggs are set. Serve on preheated platter. Yield 4 servings.

mexican rice

3 tablespoons vegetable oil
½ cup chopped onion
1 clove garlic, minced
1 cup raw long-grain rice
¼ cup chopped red pepper
½ teaspoon salt
Dash of cayenne pepper
2 cups boiling water
2 teaspoons chicken-broth granules
¾ cup frozen peas and carrots, thawed
1 small tomato, peeled, seeded, chopped
  (about ⅓ cup)

Heat oil in heavy frying pan over medium heat. Add onion, garlic, rice, and red pepper; sauté until onion is limp and rice opaque. Add salt, cayenne, water, and chicken-broth granules; cover. Cook 20 minutes or until liquid is absorbed. Add peas and carrots and tomato; cook, stirring, just until vegetables are heated through.

Serve rice immediately. Yield 4 to 6 servings.

orange rice

3 stalks celery
1 onion
¼ cup butter or margarine
1 (5-ounce) package instant rice
1 cup water
¾ cup orange juice
1½ teaspoons salt
2 teaspoons grated orange rind

Chop celery and onion fine; cook in melted butter until tender but not brown. Add rice, water, orange juice, and salt; bring to boil. Cover tightly; let stand 13 to 15 minutes. Just before serving, add orange rind; fork it through gently. (Recipe doubles nicely.) Yield 4 servings.

oven-steamed rice

2 cups boiling water
1 cup uncooked rice
1 teaspoon salt

Heat oven to 350°F.
Mix all ingredients thoroughly in ungreased 1- or 1½-quart baking dish (10 × 6 or 11 × 7); cover tightly. Bake 25 to 30 minutes, until liquid is absorbed and rice tender.

Flavor can be varied by adding any of the following: chervil, curry, dillweed, onion, parsley, or saffron. Yield 4 to 6 servings.

pilaf rice

4 tablespoons butter
1 medium onion, finely chopped
1 clove garlic, crushed
1 cup rice
6 coriander seeds
1 stick cinnamon or 1½ teaspoons powdered
  cinnamon

mexican rice

6 whole cloves or ½ teaspoon ground cloves
Water or stock

Melt butter in frying pan; cook onion and garlic until soft. Add rice; cook until rice begins to take on color. Add coriander, cinnamon, and cloves. Cover with water, with about ¼ inch water above rice; simmer gently, covered, until done. If necessary, add a bit of water from time to time to keep rice from sticking. Yield 5 or 6 servings.

rice with cheese and tomatoes

1 medium-size onion
3 stalks celery
½ green pepper
3 tablespoons butter, margarine, or oil
2 cups cooked or canned tomatoes
3 cups cooked rice
2 cups finely cut-up cheese

Chop onion, celery, and pepper; cook in butter until tender. Add tomatoes, rice, and cheese; cover. Cook slowly until cheese melts and mixture is hot. Yield 6 servings.

rice marguery

½ cup butter or margarine
1 onion, chopped
1 pound fresh mushrooms, sliced
2 cups white rice
2 (8-ounce) cans undiluted consommé
2 cups water

Melt half the butter in skillet. Sauté onion and mushrooms 5 minutes. Transfer to bowl with slotted spoon.

Wash rice; drain well. Place in skillet in which mushrooms were sautéed with remaining butter. Brown; add consomme. Stir in water; add mushrooms and onions. Bring to boil; cover. Simmer about 25 minutes, until all liquid is absorbed and rice tender. Serve at once. Yield 8 servings.

rice with mushrooms

1 (10½-ounce) can beef consommé
1 cup packaged precooked rice
½ pound fresh mushrooms
1 tablespoon lemon juice
¼ cup butter
¼ cup chopped onion
¼ cup chopped fresh parsley

Combine consommé and 1¾ cups water in 1½-quart saucepan; bring to boil. Add rice; stir well. Reduce heat; cover. Simmer about 15 minutes or until rice is tender and all liquid absorbed.

Meanwhile wash mushrooms thoroughly under cold water; wipe dry. Slice thin; toss with lemon juice.

Melt butter in small saucepan. Add mushrooms and onion; sauté 5 minutes. Add mushroom mixture and parsley to hot rice; toss well. Yield 6 servings.

rice and vegetable ring

1 cup rice
½ pound mushrooms
4 tablespoons butter or margarine
4 tablespoons stock or water
Salt
Paprika
1 pound green beans or 1 head cauliflower

Cook rice in boiling salted water; drain.

Chop mushrooms; sauté 2 to 3 minutes in 2 tablespoons butter. Add stock; combine with rice. Season to taste with salt and paprika. Press rice mixture firmly into greased 7-inch ring mold; let stand about 5 minutes. Turn onto a platter; keep warm.

Cook vegetable while rice is cooking. If cauliflower is used, divide into florets. Pile vegetable into center of mold; dot with remaining margarine. Yield 6 servings.

risotto

4 tablespoons butter
1 cup long-grain rice
2 cups Basic Beef or Chicken Stock (see Index)

Melt butter in heavy skillet. Add rice; cook over medium heat, stirring constantly, until butter is absorbed. Pour in 1 cup stock; cook, stirring frequently, until stock has been absorbed. Add ½ cup stock; cook until absorbed. Add remaining stock; stir well. Cover; simmer until stock has been absorbed, stirring occasionally. Cooking time will be about 25 minutes after first addition of stock.

rice with mushrooms

skillet-fried rice

skillet-fried rice

3 cups uncooked rice
6 tablespoons oil
5 eggs, beaten
6 tablespoons soy sauce
¼ teaspoon garlic powder
2 onions, chopped
2 cups celery, sliced on diagonal

Cook rice until done; set aside to drain.

Heat oil in large skillet; pour in eggs. As they harden, cut up eggs with 2 knives. Add soy sauce and garlic powder. Add rice, onions, and celery. Stir over low heat 3 to 5 minutes, until well-blended. Yield 12 to 14 servings.

sugar-and-spice rice

1 cup cold water
1 cup whole milk
1 teaspoon salt
1 cup uncooked rice
½ cup butter
½ cup granulated sugar
2 teaspoons cinnamon

Combine water, milk, salt, and uncooked rice in 3-quart saucepan; bring to boil. Stir once; cover. Turn heat very low; cook 20 minutes or until water and milk are absorbed. Do not uncover while cooking. Spoon rice into serving dishes; top each serving with 2 tablespoons butter, 2 tablespoons sugar, and ½ teaspoon cinnamon. Serve immediately. Yield 4 servings.

sugar-and-spice rice

CHEESE

feta-cheese salad

½ pound feta cheese, thinly sliced
Freshly ground black pepper (about ½ teaspoon)
2 tablespoons vegetable oil
2 tablespoons white vinegar
3 stalks celery, thinly sliced
10 pecans or walnuts
½ teaspoon salt

Arrange cheese in shallow bowl. Sprinkle generously with pepper. Drizzle 1 tablespoon each oil and vinegar over cheese. Arrange celery on cheese. Sprinkle with nuts. Drizzle with rest of oil and vinegar; sprinkle with salt. Cover; refrigerate at least 1 hour. Mix well; correct seasoning, if necessary. Yield 4 servings.

CHEF'S SALADS

chef's salad

½ head Boston lettuce
1 large tomato, cut into eighths
½ cucumber, thinly sliced
1 small onion, grated
½ green pepper, cut into thin strips
½ cup plain yogurt
1 tablespoon lemon juice
½ teaspoon salt

⅛ teaspoon white pepper
1 clove garlic, minced
1 teaspoon chopped parsley
1 teaspoon dried dill
½ cup cooked chicken, cut into julienne strips
½ cup chopped cooked ham
¼ cup julienne strips low-fat mozzarella cheese
2 sardines, drained, cut in half lengthwise
3 stuffed green olives, sliced

Wash lettuce; tear into bite-size pieces. Arrange on salad platter with tomato, cucumber, onion, and green pepper; cover. Refrigerate while preparing rest of ingredients and dressing.

Blend yogurt with lemon juice; season with salt, pepper, garlic, parsley, and dill. Pour dressing over salad greens; arrange meats, cheese, and sardines on top. Garnish with olives. Yield 4 servings.

tossed luncheon salad

8 ounces lean cooked leftover beef, cut into
    julienne strips
4 ounces cooked ham, chicken, or turkey, cut into
    julienne strips
1 large dill pickle, chopped
1 tart apple, cored, diced
½ cup cooked or canned peas, chilled
½ cup cooked cauliflower florets, chilled

salad dressing
1 cup plain yogurt
1 tablespoon chopped fresh parsley
1 tablespoon chopped chives or thinly sliced
    scallion
½ teaspoon paprika
⅛ teaspoon nutmeg
Salt and pepper to taste
Lettuce leaves
1 or 2 hard-cooked eggs, cut into wedges or slices

Combine meats, pickle, apple, and vegetables, except lettuce.

Blend together dressing ingredients. Pour over meat and vegetables; toss lightly. Serve salad on bed of lettuce leaves. Garnish with hard-cooked eggs. Yield about 4 servings.

EGG

dutch egg salad

salad ingredients
4 hard-cooked eggs, sliced
2 anchovy fillets, diced
1 dill pickle, diced

feta-cheese salad

chef's salad

salad dressing
½ cup plain yogurt
1½ teaspoons prepared mustard
Salt and pepper to taste
Pinch of sugar
1 teaspoon lemon juice

garnish
1 hard-cooked egg, sliced
1 medium tomato, sliced
1 anchovy fillet, sliced
2 tablespoons capers
1 pimiento, cut into strips (or ⅓ green pepper)
1 small dill pickle, diced

Combine salad ingredients; place in small serving bowl.

Combine dressing ingredients; pour over salad.

Arrange egg, tomato, anchovy, capers, and pimiento on salad as garnish. Top tomato slices with pickle; serve at once. Yield 4 servings.

russian egg salad

4 English-muffin halves
Butter
4 hard-boiled eggs
16 thin unpeeled cucumber slices
1 cup cooked mixed vegetables
½ cup Basic Rémoulade Sauce (see Index)
Mayonnaise

Toast muffins in 200°F oven 30 minutes or until golden brown and dry. Cut 1-inch circle from center of each muffin. Spread each muffin with butter.

498

dutch egg salad

Cut each egg, from pointed end to just below center, to form 4 petals. Place 1 egg in center of each muffin; arrange cucumber slices between egg petals.

Combine mixed vegetables with just enough Rémoulade Sauce to moisten; spoon vegetable mixture around eggs. Pipe with green-tinted mayonnaise. Garnish with watercress, fresh parsley, and stuffed green olives, if desired; serve immediately. Yield 4 servings.

russian egg salad

499

FRUIT

apple–grape salad

2 medium tart apples, peeled, quartered, cored
½ pound blue grapes, halved, seeded
1 stalk garden mint (leaves only)
2 teaspoons sugar
2 tablespoons lemon juice
2 tablespoons brandy

Cut apples crosswise in thin slices. Arrange apples, grapes, and mint leaves in glass bowl. Sprinkle with sugar, lemon juice, and brandy; toss lightly. Cover; chill 1 hour. Yield 4 servings.

brandied fruit salad

3 tablespoons strained lemon juice
3 large apples
3 ripe pears
2 large oranges
½ pound fresh pitted Queen Anne cherries
½ pound seedless white grapes
1 small honeydew melon
¾ cup confectioners' sugar
1 cup sauterne
½ cup brandy

Combine lemon juice and 3 tablespoons cold water in large salad bowl.

Peel, core, and dice apples and pears. Place in lemon-juice mixture; turn to coat well. Let stand 20 minutes.

brandied fruit salad

Peel oranges; separate into skinless segments. Combine oranges, cherries, and grapes with apple mixture.

Peel and slice melon into narrow strips. Add to other fruits. Sift sugar over fruits.

Mix sauterne and brandy; pour over fruits. Chill overnight; serve in individual bowls. Yield 12 servings.

apple–grape salad

chinese fruit salad

chinese fruit salad

1 (4-ounce) jar ginger in syrup
1 (8-ounce) can kumquats
1 (11-ounce) can litchi nuts in syrup
1 (20-ounce) can longans
1 (16-ounce) can mangos
1 (12-ounce) can water-lily roots
1 round watermelon, chilled
1 (18-ounce) can white nuts or 1 cup slivered
  almonds
1 lemon, sliced

Drain ginger, kumquats, litchi nuts, longans, mangos, water-lily roots. Place in large bowl; mix well. Chill until cold.

Cut watermelon in half; remove meat and seeds. Cut melon meat into cubes or balls. Cut slice off base of each watermelon half; place each half in serving dish. Place melon cubes into shells. Pile ginger mixture on watermelon. Serve with white nuts and lemon. Yield about 12 servings.

creamy fruit salad

1 (3-ounce) package cream cheese
1 tablespoon syrup from canned mandarin
  oranges
1 (11-ounce) can mandarin orange sections,
  drained
1 (13½-ounce) can pineapple tidbits, drained
1 cup miniature marshmallows
⅓ cup halved, drained maraschino cherries
Lettuce

Beat cream cheese with liquid from mandarin oranges until creamy. Add oranges, pineapple, and marshmallows; combine gently but thoroughly. Lightly fold in cherries; chill. Serve in lettuce cups. Yield 6 servings.

frozen fruit salad

1 (16-ounce) can dark sweet pitted cherries
1 (16-ounce) can pineapple tidbits
1 (8-ounce) package cream cheese, softened
2 cups whipped topping
½ cup chopped nuts
Crisp salad greens

Drain fruits well.

Beat cream cheese into whipped topping. Fold in fruits and nuts. Pour into 8 × 8-inch pan. Cover; freeze.

Before serving, let salad set in the refrigerator about 1 hour. Cut; serve on crisp salad greens. Yield 12 servings.

fruit-salad combinations

Pare and section 2 grapefruit and 3 oranges. For each salad arrange grapefruit and orange sections on lettuce leaf; garnish with maraschino cherry half.

Lightly mix 1½ cups each cantaloupe, honeydew, and watermelon balls or cubes. Serve on crisp salad greens. Allow about ⅔ cup fruit per serving.

Drain 1 (13½-ounce) can pineapple tidbits; combine with 3 pared and sectioned oranges and 1 sliced banana. Place on crisp salad greens; and sprinkle with ¼ cup chopped walnuts. Allow about ½ cup fruit per serving.

Lightly mix 2 cups cantaloupe cubes, ½ cup fresh blueberries, and 1 large sliced banana. Serve on crisp salad greens. Allow about ½ cup fruit per salad.

Combine 4 peeled and sliced peaches, ½ cup halved seedless grapes, ½ cup halved and seeded Tokay grapes, and 1 large sliced banana. Serve on

fruit salad with nuts german-style

crisp salad greens. Allow about ⅔ cup fruit per serving. Yield 6 servings.

fruit salad with nuts german-style

1 small honeydew melon
2 oranges
1 cup blue grapes
Lettuce leaves
12 walnut halves

dressing
1 (8-ounce) container yogurt
1 tablespoon lemon juice
1 tablespoon orange juice
1 tablespoon tomato catsup
2 tablespoons evaporated milk
Dash of salt
Dash of white pepper

Scoop out melon with melon baller.

Cut peel from oranges; remove white membrane; slice crosswise.

Cut grapes in half; remove seeds.

Line glass bowl with lettuce leaves; arrange melon, oranges, grapes, and walnuts in layers on top lettuce.

Mix and blend well all dressing ingredients; adjust seasonings. Pour over fruit; let marinate 30 minutes. Toss salad just before serving. Yield 4 to 6 servings.

grapefruit salad

1 (8-ounce) can grapefruit sections
1 cup sour cream
1 teaspoon salt
1 teaspoon dry mustard
½ head cabbage, shredded (4 to 5 cups)

grapefruit salad

honeyed salad

Drain grapefruit; mix 2 tablespoons grapefruit juice with cream, salt, and mustard. Pour over cabbage; toss lightly. Add grapefruit sections; mix in lightly. Yield 4 or 5 servings.

health salad

1 head Boston lettuce
1 small cucumber
2 small tomatoes
1 green pepper
½ avocado
5 radishes
1 peach
1 slice pineapple (from can)
4 ounces mandarin oranges (from can)
¼ pound fresh strawberries

health salad dressing
1 small onion, minced
2 teaspoons prepared mustard
6 tablespoons lemon juice
¼ teaspoon salt
⅛ teaspoon white pepper
3 tablespoons vegetable oil
1 sprig parsley, chopped
2 teaspoons fresh dill (or ½ teaspoon dried dill)
¼ teaspoon dried tarragon
¼ teaspoon dried basil

Wash lettuce; tear leaves into bite-size pieces. Cut unpeeled cucumber into thin slices. Peel tomatoes; cut into slices. Core, seed, and slice green pepper. Peel avocado; slice. Clean radishes; slice. Peel peach; cube peach and pineapple slice. Drain oranges. Hull strawberries; cut in half. Arrange all ingredients in large bowl.

Make dressing. Blend onion thoroughly with mustard, lemon juice, salt, pepper, and oil. Add herbs; correct seasoning if necessary. Pour over salad; mix gently but thoroughly. Cover; marinate about 10 minutes. Serve in bowl or on platter. Yield 4 to 6 servings.

honeyed salad

4 dessert apples
½ cup seeded or seedless raisins
¼ cup chopped walnuts
1½ cups cooked diced carrots
Pinch of salt

honey salad dressing
1 tablespoon clear honey
3 tablespoons lemon juice

Peel, core, and dice 3 apples; combine with raisins, nuts, and carrots. Add salt. Add honey and lemon juice blended together; toss lightly. Set aside in cool place about 1 hour. Arrange in salad bowl or on platter; garnish with remaining apple—unpeeled, cut into slices, brushed with lemon juice. Yield 4 or 5 servings.

melon salad

1 Spanish melon
1 cup fresh strawberries
1 orange
2 tablespoons honey
½ cup whipped cream
Pistachio nuts

health salad

melon salad

Slice ¼ of top off melon; remove seeds. Scoop out meat from melon with melon-ball scoop; save shell. Place balls in large bowl.

Wash strawberries; remove stems. Add to melon balls.

Peel orange; slice into sections by cutting between membranes. Add to melon balls.

Drizzle honey over fruit; toss gently. Fill shell with fruit. Garnish with whipped cream and pistachio nuts; chill. Yield 4 to 6 servings.

orange and avocado salad

¼ cup fresh lemon juice
2 avocados
3 fresh oranges

orange mayonnaise
¾ cup mayonnaise
¼ cup fresh orange juice
½ teaspoon paprika
Lettuce leaves

Pour lemon juice into shallow bowl.

Peel avocados; cut crosswise into ¼-inch slices; remove seeds as sliced. Dip slices into lemon juice to keep from turning dark.

Peel oranges; cut crosswise into ½-inch slices; remove seeds.

Mix mayonnaise, orange juice, and paprika.

Line serving bowl with lettuce leaves. Place alternate layers of orange and avocado slices on lettuce; end with avocado slices. Serve with Orange Mayonnaise. Yield 6 servings.

orange and onion salad

4 large oranges
1 Bermuda onion, sliced
1 medium cucumber, sliced
1 small green pepper, peeled, seeded, chopped

salad dressing
⅓ cup vegetable oil
¼ cup wine vinegar
1 teaspoon sugar
½ teaspoon salt
¼ teaspoon chili powder

peaches filled with cheese

Peel oranges; remove as much white membrane as possible. Slice; remove seeds. Alternate layers of oranges, onion, and cucumber in serving dish. Sprinkle with green pepper. Pour dressing over; garnish with endive. Refrigerate until serving time. Yield 6 servings.

peaches filled with cheese

1 can (about 30-ounces) peach halves
3 tablespoons grated cheddar cheese
1 tablespoon grated Parmesan cheese
1 tablespoon softened butter
Salt
Cayenne pepper
Lettuce
1 (3-ounce) package cream cheese
5 to 6 tablespoons light cream
Paprika

Drain peaches.

Mix cheeses with butter; season to taste with salt and cayenne. Fill peach halves. Arrange on platter or on individual dishes on bed of lettuce.

Beat together cream cheese and cream; spoon over peaches. Sprinkle with paprika. Yield 4 or 5 servings.

orange and avocado salad

pear and grape salad

4 ripe dessert pears
1 cup cream cheese
1 to 2 tablespoons French dressing
½ pound black grapes
Crisp lettuce (optional)

pear and grape salad

Peel pears; cut in half. Scoop out core with teaspoon.

Blend cream cheese with enough French dressing to make spreadable; coat rounded side of each pear half. Place on platter, cut-side-down.

Halve and seed grapes; press into cheese close together, so each pear half resembles small bunch of grapes. Serve on lettuce leaves if desired. Yield 4 servings.

pineapple, blackberry, and strawberry salad

1 large pineapple
2 cups blackberries
1 cup strawberries
Sifted confectioners' sugar
Kirsch

Remove crown from pineapple; cut so it will sit evenly. Place on large circular serving platter at center back. Cut pineapple lengthwise into 3 sections, center section 1½-inches wide; reserve center section. Remove pineapple from each remaining section, leaving shell; dice pineapple. Sawtooth edges of pineapple shells; fill with diced pineapple. Place on platter, cut ends next to crown, at angles toward outside. Pare reserved pineapple slice; cut lengthwise to remove core, leaving 2 slices. Cut each slice in half lengthwise; place 1 pineapple slice lengthwise over diced pineapple in each shell. Cut remaining slices in half crosswise; place in center at right angles to lengthwise pineapple slices. Fill sections of pineapple slices alternately with half the blackberries and all

the strawberries. Arrange remaining blackberries on platter between pineapple shells. Sprinkle fruits generously with confectioner's sugar. Moisten with small amount of kirsch; chill until sugar has dissolved. Yield about 8 servings.

pineapple, blackberry, and strawberry salad

508

pineapple salad

2 slices canned pineapple
2 oranges
2 apples
¼ medium melon (honeydew or cantaloupe)
½ pound green seedless grapes

low-cal salad dressing
½ cup plain yogurt
1 tablespoon imitation mayonnaise (or low-calorie mayonnaise)
2 tablespoons lemon juice
¼ teaspoon salt
⅛ teaspoon white pepper
1 teaspoon honey

Cut pineapple slices into ½-inch pieces. Peel and section oranges; remove membranes; cut sections into pieces. Peel apples and melon; remove seeds; cut into bite-size pieces. Cut grapes in half. Gently mix fruit in large bowl.

Make dressing. Blend yogurt, mayonnaise, and lemon juice. Season to taste with salt, pepper, and honey. Pour dressing over fruit; mix gently. Cover bowl; refrigerate 10 minutes to blend flavors. Yield 4 to 6 servings.

pineapple salad

waldorf salad

½ cup mayonnaise
½ cup sour cream
1 tablespoon honey
1½ cups peeled, cored, diced tart apples
1 cup diced celery
½ cup coarsely chopped walnuts
1 cup halved, seeded grapes

Combine mayonnaise, sour cream, and honey. Add apples; mix well to prevent apple discoloring. Add celery, walnuts, and grapes; mix lightly. Chill well before serving. Yield 3 or 4 servings.

GREEN SALADS

caesar salad I

salad dressing
1 coddled egg
⅔ cup French dressing (see Index)
1 teaspoon salt
1 teaspoon prepared mustard
2 small heads romaine or other lettuce
2 tablespoons butter
1 clove garlic, crushed
2 slices bread, cut into ½-inch cubes
2 slices bacon, chopped
Grated Parmesan cheese
Chopped parsley

Make dressing. Coddle egg: put into boiling water 1 minute; remove shell. Mix well with all other ingredients.

Remove tough outer leaves from lettuce; wash; dry well. Break into pieces; put into salad bowl. Add dressing; toss lightly.

Heat butter in skillet. Add garlic and bread cubes; cook until crisp and golden brown.

Fry bacon until crisp; drain on absorbent paper. Scatter bacon and croutons over salad; sprinkle generously with cheese and parsley. Yield 4 or 5 servings.

caesar salad II

1 cup peanut oil
1 clove garlic, crushed
2 cups bread cubes
2 heads romaine
1 head Boston lettuce
1 bunch watercress
¾ cup freshly grated Parmesan cheese
½ teaspoon salt
¼ teaspoon dry mustard
¼ teaspoon freshly ground pepper
⅓ cup lemon juice

509

2 eggs, lightly beaten
Dash of Worcestershire sauce
1 (2-ounce) can anchovy fillets

Pour oil into jar. Add garlic; cover. Let stand at least 1 hour.

Sauté bread in ¼ cup garlic oil until golden brown; drain on absorbent paper.

Tear romaine, Boston lettuce, and watercress into large salad bowl.

Combine cheese, salt, mustard, and pepper. Sprinkle over greens gradually; toss to mix well. Gradually beat lemon juice into eggs; add Worcestershire sauce. Pour ⅓ of egg mixture and ⅓ of remaining oil mixture over salad; toss gently. Repeat 2 more times; add anchovies and croutons during last tossing. Serve immediately. Yield about 12 servings.

green salad with croutons

croutons
2 tablespoons olive oil
1 clove garlic, peeled, sliced
1 cup cubed stale Italian bread, crust removed
   (save for bread crumbs)

salad dressing
½ cup olive oil

green salad with croutons

mixed green salad

¼ cup red wine vinegar
½ teaspoon crumbled dried oregano
½ teaspoon salt
¼ teaspoon pepper

salad
1 medium head garden lettuce
1 medium head romaine lettuce or endive
¼ cup grated Parmesan cheese

Prepare croutons. Heat oil in small skillet; sauté garlic over moderate heat until lightly browned. Remove garlic with slotted spoon; discard. Add bread; sauté, stirring frequently, until golden brown. Drain on paper towels.

Combine dressing ingredients in bottle or screw-top jar; shake well. Allow to stand at room temperature.

Clean lettuce; pat dry. Tear into bite-size pieces; place in salad bowl. Refrigerate until serving time.

To serve, sprinkle salad with cheese and croutons. Shake dressing well; pour over salad. Toss well; serve immediately. Yield 4 to 6 servings.

maximilian's salad

1 large head lettuce (or 8 cups mixed salad greens)
1 medium Bermuda onion, sliced
1 clove garlic, peeled
1 teaspoon salt
1 tablespoon sugar
½ teaspoon paprika
½ cup olive oil
¼ cup lemon juice
1 (3-ounce) package Roquefort cheese, crumbled

Clean lettuce; remove brown or damaged leaves. Wash well; drain. Shake dry; tear into bite-size pieces. Combine with onion in large salad bowl.

Sprinkle garlic clove with salt; mash with blade of knife.

Combine garlic, salt, sugar, paprika, oil, and lemon juice in blender jar; whirl until blended. Pour over salad; toss. Sprinkle with cheese; serve with toasted tortillas. Yield 6 servings.

mixed green salad

1 head Bibb lettuce (or ½ head iceberg lettuce)
2 green peppers, cleaned, seeded, cut into strips
4 small tomatoes, sliced
2 small onions, sliced, separated into rings
2 hard-cooked eggs, sliced
½ cup sliced stuffed green olives
½ medium cucumber, peeled, seeded, cut into chunks

salad dressing
4 tablespoons olive oil
3 tablespoons tarragon vinegar
½ teaspoon salt
¼ teaspoon freshly ground pepper
1 clove garlic, crushed
¼ teaspoon crushed oregano
1 tablespoon chopped fresh parsley

Wash lettuce; dry. Tear into bite-size pieces; place in salad bowl. Add peppers, tomatoes, onions, eggs, olives, and cucumber; refrigerate.

Combine all dressing ingredients; mix well.

At serving time toss salad at table with prepared dressing. Yield 4 servings.

MACARONI

cheese and macaroni salad ring

1 cup elbow macaroni
¼ cup French dressing
2 cups cottage cheese
¼ cup diced pimiento
¼ cup diced green pepper
2 tablespoons very finely chopped onion
2 tablespoons chopped parsley
Lettuce
Radishes and stuffed green olives (garnish)

Cook macaroni in boiling salted water about 10 minutes; drain well. While still warm, add French dressing; mix well. Set aside to chill. Add other ingredients except lettuce; mix lightly but thoroughly. Press into quart ring mold; chill several hours.

When ready to serve, arrange lettuce on platter. Loosen mixture from side of mold with knife; turn onto lettuce. Garnish with radish flowers and olive slices. Yield 6 to 9 servings.

macaroni salad

2 cups shell or ring macaroni
2 tablespoons butter
1 cup cubed cheddar cheese
1 cup sliced gherkins
½ cup very finely chopped onion

2 cups cooked peas
½ cup mayonnaise
Seasoning
Lettuce

Cook macaroni in boiling salted water; drain well. Add butter; toss lightly. Add cheese, gherkins, onion, and peas. Stir in mayonnaise; blend carefully, making sure macaroni is well mixed with mayonnaise. Check seasoning; set aside to chill. Serve individually in lettuce leaves or on bed of shredded lettuce. Yield 6 servings.

MEAT

ham and pineapple salad

½ cup shell or other small pasta
3 tablespoons mayonnaise
1 green pepper, seeded, chopped
Salt and pepper
4 large slices cooked ham
Lettuce
4 pineapple rings
2 tomatoes

Cook pasta in boiling salted water 10 minutes; drain well. While still warm, add mayonnaise, green pepper, and seasoning; set aside to get quite cold.

Place spoonful of mixture on one half of each ham slice; fold other half over. Arrange on bed of lettuce; place pineapple ring on each ham slice. Garnish with tomato wedges. Yield 4 servings.

macaroni salad

liverwurst salad

1 cup diced liverwurst
¼ cup finely chopped onion
¼ cup diced celery
¼ cup finely chopped green pepper
½ head lettuce, torn into medium-size pieces
½ cup shredded carrots

salad dressing
⅓ cup salad oil
⅓ cup salad vinegar
⅓ cup chili sauce
1 tablespoon prepared horseradish
½ teaspoon salt

Combine liverwurst, onion, celery, pepper, lettuce, and carrots in salad bowl; chill thoroughly.

Combine dressing ingredients in jar; shake vigorously; chill.

To serve, place vegetable and meat mixture in salad bowls. Pour dressing mixture into small pitcher; pass to diners. Yield 6 servings.

marinated beef salad

salad
3 cups cubed cooked lean beef
½ cup chopped onion
2 tablespoons chopped parsley
1 sweet red pepper, seeded, chopped
1 medium tomato, chopped

salad dressing
½ cup olive oil
¼ cup wine vinegar

½ teaspoon salt
¼ teaspoon pepper
½ teaspoon crumbled oregano
½ teaspoon prepared mustard

garnish
1 head Boston lettuce
1 large tomato, cut into wedges

Combine beef, onion, parsley, pepper, and tomato; toss well.

Combine dressing ingredients; pour over salad; toss well. Refrigerate at least 3 hours.

At serving time, line serving dish with lettuce leaves; fill with salad. Garnish with tomato wedges. Serve with plenty of crusty bread. Yield 4 servings.

swiss ham salad

¾ pound cooked ham, cut into thick slices, diced
¾ pound Gruyére cheese, diced
6 tablespoons olive oil
2 tablespoons white wine vinegar
Salt
Freshly ground black pepper
Romaine lettuce or curly endive
Finely chopped parsley or fresh herbs

Combine ham and cheese in bowl.

Make dressing with oil, vinegar, salt, and pepper. Pour over ham and cheese; toss lightly. Refrigerate; leave about 1 hour to marinate.

Arrange lettuce in salad bowl. Pile ham and cheese in center; sprinkle with parsley. Yield 4 or 5 servings.

marinated beef salad

turkish cucumber salad

turkish cucumber salad

6 ounces baked ham, diced
2 large cucumbers, diced

salad dressing
1 cup plain yogurt
1 teaspoon prepared mustard
Dash of nutmeg
Pinch of sugar
Salt and freshly ground black pepper to taste
Small bunch watercress (if available, easily grown from seed), chopped
1 or 2 fresh mint leaves, minced
2 tablespoons chopped chives or scallions

garnish
Watercress
Parsley leaves

Combine ham and cucumbers.

Prepare dressing by stirring together all ingredients. Fold ham and cucumbers into dressing. Serve salad at once garnished with watercress and parsley. Dressing can alternately be used as topping. Yield 4 servings.

MOLDS

apple-lime molds

1½ envelopes unflavored gelatin
⅓ cup fresh lime juice
½ cup sugar
⅛ teaspoon salt
1 teaspoon grated lime rind
2 medium red Delicious apples
1 cup whipping cream, whipped
Green food coloring
Whole strawberries
Mint sprigs

Soften gelatin in lime juice.

Combine 1¼ cups water with sugar and salt in saucepan; bring to simmer. Stir in gelatin mixture until dissolved; add lime rind. Chill until thickened; stir frequently.

Pare and dice 1 apple; fold apple and whipped cream into gelatin mixture. Add enough food coloring for desired tint. Spoon gelatin mixture into 7 (5-ounce) oiled molds or 1 (2-quart) mold; chill until firm.

Remove core from remaining apple; cut apple into thin wedges.

Unmold salad onto serving dish; garnish with apple slices, strawberries, and mint sprigs. Yield 7 servings.

apple-lime molds

apricot ring mold

apricot ring mold

1 can (1-pound, 4-ounces) apricots
1 cup pineapple juice
1 envelope unflavored gelatin
2 tablespoons water
1 (3-ounce) package cream cheese
1 tablespoon whipped cream
½ small green pepper, blanched, finely chopped
Pinch of paprika
Pinch of salt
Watercress or lettuce

Drain apricots; finely chop enough to make ¼ cup; reserve rest.

Mix 1 cup apricot syrup with pineapple juice; heat to boiling.

Soften gelatin 5 minutes in water; dissolve in hot fruit juice. Add chopped apricots to half the gelatin; pour into small ring mold. Refrigerate until set. Chill remaining gelatin until it begins to thicken.

Blend cream cheese with cream. Add green pepper, paprika, and salt; spread on firm gelatin. Cover with remaining thickened gelatin; set aside until firm. Unmold; fill center with watercress and remaining apricots. Yield 4 servings.

avocado ring mold

1½ cups mashed avocado (about 2 avocados)
2 tablespoons lemon juice
1 package lemon-flavored gelatin
¾ cup boiling water
1 cup sour cream
¾ cup mayonnaise
1 tablespoon onion juice
Dash of cayenne pepper
2 tablespoons finely chopped green pepper
Mayonnaise
Paprika

Peel and seed avocados; sprinkle with lemon juice. Mash well; force through sieve or puree in electric blender.

Dissolve gelatin in boiling water. Add avocado, sour cream, mayonnaise, onion juice, cayenne, and green pepper.

Lightly oil ring mold; pour in mixture. Chill overnight; unmold onto large plate. Garnish with whole black olives, cherry tomatoes, and Bibb lettuce. Place small bowl in center of ring; fill with mayonnaise dusted with paprika. Yield 6 servings.

banana mold

1 package pineapple-flavored gelatin
½ pint hot water
½ pint cream
4 large bananas

Dissolve gelatin in hot water. When nearly cold, but before set, gradually stir in cream.

Peel bananas; mash with fork. Beat until light and smooth; stir lightly but thoroughly into gelatin and cream. Pour into glass dish; let set. Yield 4 to 6 servings.

Note: If mixing is done before gelatin is sufficiently cool, gelatin, banana, and cream will separate into layers.

basic emergency aspic

2 envelopes unflavored gelatin
2 cups canned beef consommé
2 tablespoons lemon juice
¼ cup sherry
¼ teaspoon salt

Soften gelatin in ½ cup cold water.

Combine consommé and 2 cups cold water in medium-size saucepan; bring to boil. Add gelatin; stir until dissolved. Remove from heat. Add lemon juice, sherry, and salt; stir until well blended. Use as desired for various congealed molds, glazes, or coatings.

basic simple aspic

5 cups Basic Beef Stock or Basic Chicken Stock
(see Index)
2 eggshells
2 envelopes unflavored gelatin
2 tablespoons wine vinegar or lemon juice
2 tablespoons sherry
⅛ teaspoon thyme
½ teaspoon parsley flakes
5 peppercorns
2 egg whites
½ teaspoon lemon juice

Measure 5 cups stock into large saucepan. To clarify stock, pull away inner skins from eggshells; wash eggshells and crush into stock. Sprinkle gelatin over stock. Stir in vinegar, sherry, thyme, parsley, peppercorns, and egg whites. Cook, stirring constantly, over moderate heat until gelatin dissolves. Beat with rotary beater, over moderate heat, about 4 minutes, until thick foam forms on top. Foam must be thick and high. Remove beater; bring mixture to boil without stirring. Reduce heat to low; simmer 10 minutes. Remove from heat; let stand 3 minutes. Place piece of wet muslin in large sieve. Pour stock mixture slowly and steadily through muslin; let drain well. Add lemon juice. Use as desired for various congealed molds, glazes, or coatings.

beet-salad mold

1 large can julienne beets, drained
2 packages lemon-flavored gelatin
1½ tablespoons grated onion
½ cup stuffed green olives, chopped
1½ tablespoons lemon juice or wine vinegar
2 tablespoons horseradish

Add enough water to juice from beets to make 2 cups liquid. Heat and dissolve gelatin in it; let cool. When just beginning to firm, add other ingredients. Beets can be chopped or left in long strips. Pour into oiled melon mold; chill until firm. Yield 6 to 8 servings.

carrot carousel

1½ cups cold orange juice
2 envelopes unflavored gelatin
½ cup boiling orange juice
¼ teaspoon salt
1 cup mayonnaise
1½ cups cubed carrots
1 (13½-ounce) can crushed pineapple

Pour ½ cup cold orange juice into blender container; sprinkle gelatin over. Let stand 5 minutes;

carrot carousel

add boiling orange juice. Process at low speed until gelatin is dissolved; use rubber spatula to push gelatin granules into mixture. Add remaining cold orange juice, salt, and mayonnaise; blend well. Add carrots; cover. Process at high speed until carrots are finely grated; stir in undrained pineapple. Pour into 6-cup mold; chill until firm. Unmold onto serving plate. Yield 8 servings.

caviar shrimp en gelée

aspic jelly
4 envelopes unflavored gelatin
9 cups cold water
3 carrots, cut up
4 stalks celery, cut up
2 onions, cut up
6 sprigs parsley
4 cloves
2 bay leaves
4 bouillon cubes
4 tablespoons sherry
Juice of 2 lemons
Salt
White pepper
3 pounds boiled shrimp
3 jars caviar
Sliced olives

Soak gelatin in 1 cup cold water.

Simmer vegetables, cloves, and bay leaves in remaining water 25 minutes. Strain; discard vegetables; retain liquid. Dissolve gelatin and bouillon cubes in hot liquid. Add sherry and lemon juice; season to taste. Put thin layer of aspic in large oiled mold. When almost firm, insert olive slices and some shrimp, cut in half down backs. Allow to congeal completely. Add caviar and rest of shrimp, cut in half or quarters if large or left whole if small. Fill ring; let chill until firm. Serve with thousand-island dressing or Russian dressing (see Index). This makes 1 very large ring mold or 2 small ring molds. Yield 12 to 15 servings.

Note: Recipe can be cut in half. Seafood can be omitted, or lobster can be substituted for some or all of shrimp.

cheese mousse

¾ cup milk
2 medium eggs, separated
5 ounces Parmesan cheese, finely grated
⅓ cup cottage cheese
Grated rind and juice of 1 medium lemon
½ cup whipping cream, stiffly beaten
1 envelope unflavored gelatin
⅓ cup water
¼ teaspoon salt
⅛ teaspoon white pepper
Generous dash of nutmeg
Dash of paprika
2 drops of hot sauce

Heat milk to lukewarm.

Blend egg yolks slightly in mixing bowl with electric mixer. Pour milk gradually into yolks, beating at low speed until blended. Stir in Parmesan and cottage cheese; blend well. Stir in lemon juice and rind. Fold in whipped cream.

Soften gelatin in water; dissolve over low heat. Pour into cream mixture gradually; stir until blended.

Beat egg whites until stiff; fold into gelatin mixture. Add seasonings. Turn into oiled 1-quart ring mold; chill until set. Unmold on platter; garnish with pretzels or crackers. Yield 4 to 6 servings.

cheese and bacon mousse

1 envelope unflavored gelatin
4 tablespoons water
2 tablespoons margarine
2 tablespoons flour
1 cup milk
½ teaspoon salt
¼ teaspoon cayenne pepper
¼ teaspoon prepared mustard
Few drops of Worcestershire sauce
¾ cup grated cheese
4 ounces bacon, broiled (or fried), chopped
½ cup cream cheese
2 eggs, separated
2 tablespoons milk

Soften gelatin in water; dissolve over hot water.

Heat butter. Stir in flour; cook 1 minute. Add 1 cup milk; whisk until smooth and thick. Add seasonings, Worcestershire sauce, grated cheese, bacon, and dissolved gelatin.

Mix cream cheese with egg yolks and 1 table-

cheese mousse

517

spoon milk; stir into sauce mixture. Beat together until smooth.

Beat egg whites until stiff; fold in lightly. Pour into loaf pan or ring mold; refrigerate until set. Turn out; serve with salad. Yield 6 to 8 servings.

cherry cottage-cheese molds

1 package cherry-flavored gelatin
1 cup boiling water
1 cup creamed cottage cheese
1 cup crushed canned pineapple
¼ cup coarsely chopped nuts
6 lettuce leaves

Dissolve gelatin in boiling water. Measure 2 teaspoons into each of 6 individual molds; chill until set. Chill remaining gelatin mixture until thick but not set. Stir in cottage cheese, pineapple, and nuts. Pour into molds; chill until firm. Unmold on lettuce. Yield 6 servings.

Note: This recipe can be made in 1-quart mold. Use ¼ cup clear gelatin mixture in bottom of mold.

chicken salad mold

1 envelope unflavored gelatin
¼ cup cold water
1 cup hot chicken stock
2 tablespoons chopped red pepper
2 tablespoons chopped green pepper

2 cups diced cooked chicken
1 tablespoon finely chopped onion
1 cup chopped celery
1 cup cooked rice
½ teaspoon salt
¼ cup French dressing
⅛ teaspoon paprika
½ cup mayonnaise
Lettuce

Combine gelatin and cold water; leave about 10 minutes to soften. Add chicken stock; stir until gelatin has melted.

Rinse mold with cold water; put in red and green peppers. Cover with 2 tablespoons melted gelatin; refrigerate until set.

Mix all ingredients except lettuce; add remaining gelatin.

When gelatin in mold is quite firm, spoon chicken mixture on top; leave until set. Unmold; serve on bed of lettuce. Fill center with mayonnaise. Yield 5 or 6 servings.

cola salad

1 large can bing cherries, pitted
1 large can crushed pineapple
1 package cherry-flavored gelatin
1 package strawberry-flavored gelatin
1 (8-ounce) package cream cheese
1 cup chopped walnuts
2 cups cola

chicken salad mold

Drain juice from cherries and pineapple; heat. Dissolve gelatins; let cool.

Mix pineapple, cheese, nuts, and cherries with gelatin mixture. Add cola last; blend. Pour into mold; chill until firm. Yield 8 servings.

crab louis mold garni

2 envelopes unflavored gelatin
1 cup water
⅔ cup chili sauce
½ cup sparkling rosé wine
½ cup sour cream
½ cup homemade or unspiced mayonnaise
½ cup tomato juice
1 tablespoon instant minced onion
1 tablespoon lemon juice
½ teaspoon salt
½ cup pitted ripe olives
1½ cups crab meat, fresh or frozen
Salad greens
Hard-boiled eggs, quartered
Tomatoes, quartered

Soften gelatin in ½ cup cold water.

Heat ½ cup water with chili sauce. Dissolve gelatin in hot mixture. Add wine, sour cream, mayonnaise, tomato juice, onion, lemon juice, and salt. Chill until partially set. Wedge olives; fold with crab meat into mixture. Turn into oiled 6-cup mold; chill until firm. Unmold on salad greens. Garnish with quartered eggs and tomatoes. Serve with dressing made of 1 cup mayonnaise and ¼ cup chili sauce. Yield 8 servings.

crab ring

3 envelopes unflavored gelatin
¼ cup cold water
1 pint tomato juice
3 (3-ounce) packages cream cheese
1 tablespoon grated onion
1 cup finely chopped celery
4 cups crab meat
1 teaspoon salt
Few grains of cayenne

Soak gelatin in cold water.

Bring tomato juice to boil; dissolve gelatin in it. Mix with riced cheese. Combine cheese mixture with remaining ingredients; pour into oiled ring mold. Chill until firm. Serve with thousand island dressing. Yield 8 servings.

cranberry salad

1 package lemon-flavored gelatin
1 cup hot water
1 orange, peeled, quartered
1½ cups fresh cranberries
1 apple, cored, sliced

1 cup sugar
¼ teaspoon salt
½ cup pecans

Dissolve gelatin in hot water; chill until partially set. Pour into blender. Gradually add orange, cranberries, apple, sugar, and salt, blending until fruits are finely chopped. Add nuts; blend just until chopped. Turn into 1-quart mold; chill firm. Turn onto lettuce-lined serving plate. Serve with mayonnaise. Yield 5 or 6 servings.

creamy golden waldorf

1 (6-ounce) package lemon-flavored gelatin
¼ teaspoon salt
⅔ cup hot water
Lemon juice
3 medium golden Delicious apples
½ cup mayonnaise
1 cup heavy cream, whipped
1 cup finely chopped celery
1 cup finely chopped walnuts
Salad greens

Dissolve gelatin and salt in hot water in bowl; stir in 2 tablespoons lemon juice. Chill until thickened.

Partially pare 2 apples; core; dice. Skin will add color to salad. Core remaining apple; cut into thin slices. Sprinkle diced and sliced apples with lemon juice to prevent discoloration. Arrange apple slices, skin-side-down, around bottom of 8-cup mold.

Blend mayonnaise into thickened gelatin; fold in whipped cream. Gently fold in diced apples, celery, and walnuts; spoon carefully over apple slices. Chill until firm. Unmold onto salad platter; garnish with salad greens. Yield 6 to 8 servings.

cucumber salad

2 cups grated cucumber
2 envelopes unflavored gelatin
2½ teaspoons salt
¼ teaspoon pepper
2 tablespoons minced onion or chives
3 cups cream-style cottage cheese
¼ teaspoon paprika

Drain cucumber thoroughly; measure juice. Add enough water to make 1 cup liquid. Soften gelatin in liquid; dissolve over boiling water. Add seasonings and onion. Stir in cucumber and cheese. Pour into individual molds or 1 large mold; chill until firm. Yield 8 servings.

egg salad mold

3 envelopes unflavored gelatin
¾ cup cold water
3 cups boiling water

519

creamy golden waldorf

egg salad mold

2 tablespoons sugar
¾ cup lemon juice
6 hard-boiled eggs
½ cup mayonnaise
¼ cup chopped parsley
½ cup chopped celery
½ cup chopped green olives
Salt and white pepper to taste

Sprinkle gelatin over cold water in bowl. Add boiling water, sugar, and lemon juice; stir until gelatin and sugar are dissolved.

Cut eggs in half; remove yolks. Mash yolks in small bowl; mix with ⅓ of gelatin mixture. Stir in mayonnaise; pour into decorative nonmetal mold. Chill until firm; sprinkle with parsley.

Chill remaining gelatin until thickened.

Chop egg whites; add to gelatin. Add celery, olives, salt, and pepper; stir until well mixed. Spoon over parsley in mold; chill until firm. Unmold onto serving plate; garnish with hard-boiled egg slices and parsley sprigs. Top can be garnished with green peas and mushrooms, if desired. Yield 6 servings.

fish mousse

fish mousse

2½ to 3 pounds fillets of fish (haddock, flounder, cod, etc.)
2 slices lemon
2 slices onion
1 teaspoon salt
¼ teaspoon pepper
2 cups mayonnaise
4 tablespoons lemon juice
2 tablespoons wine or tarragon vinegar
1 tablespoon grated onion
1 teaspoon curry powder
1 teaspoon Worcestershire sauce
⅛ teaspoon hot pepper sauce
2 tablespoons finely chopped parsley
2 envelopes unflavored gelatin

Put fish into pan with 1½ cups water, lemon and onion slices, salt and pepper; poach 5 to 10 minutes, until barely cooked. Drain; reserve stock. Remove skin from fish; flake finely.

Mix ½ cup fish stock with mayonnaise. Add lemon juice, vinegar, grated onion, curry powder, Worcestershire sauce, hot pepper sauce, and parsley. Add fish; adjust seasoning to taste. Beat until thoroughly mixed.

Soften gelatin in a little cold water; dissolve over hot water. Stir into fish mixture; pour into large mold or individual molds. Refrigerate until firm. Turn out onto bed of salad greens; decorate as desired. Yield 6 servings.

frozen fruit salad

1 (3-ounce) package cream cheese
3 tablespoons mayonnaise
Pinch of salt
1 cup whipped cream
¼ cup chopped dates (seeded)
¼ cup maraschino cherries

frozen fruit salad

¼ **cup crushed pineapple**
¼ **cup chopped kumquats (seeded)**
1 tablespoon finely chopped preserved ginger
½ **cup chopped blanched almonds**
Lettuce (optional)

Blend cheese and mayonnaise; add salt. Fold in whipped cream, fruits, and ginger; pour into refrigerator trays. Sprinkle with almonds; freeze until firm. Cut into squares; serve on lettuce. Yield 6 to 8 servings.

fruit and crab salad

1 (6-ounce) package lemon-flavored gelatin
½ **teaspoon crushed rosemary**
1 cup fresh orange sections
1 cup fresh grapefruit sections
1 pound fresh crab meat or 2 (6-ounce) packages frozen Alaskan King crab, thawed
½ **cup chopped onion**
1 tablespoon chopped fresh parsley
3 drops of hot sauce
⅓ **cup mayonnaise**
1 teaspoon prepared mustard
¾ **cup sliced celery**

Dissolve gelatin in 2 cups boiling water. Add 2 cups cold water; chill until partially set. Fold in rosemary and orange and grapefruit sections; spoon into 1½-quart ring mold. Chill until firm.

Drain crab; cut into large pieces. Place in medium-size bowl.

Mix onion with parsley, hot sauce, mayonnaise, mustard, and celery. Pour over crab; toss until mixed; chill. Unmold gelatin onto large serving plate; fill center with crab mixture. Garnish with salad greens; serve immediately. Yield 6 servings.

grapefruit salad mold

1 can (about 16-ounces) grapefruit
2 envelopes unflavored gelatin
2 tablespoons lemon juice
1 dessert apple, peeled, cored, chopped
2 or 3 stalks celery, chopped
Lettuce

Drain syrup from grapefruit; add sufficient water to make 1 cup. Soften gelatin in a little

fruit and crab salad

grapefruit salad mold

horseradish cream
3 teaspoons well-drained horseradish
½ teaspoon salt
¾ cup whipped cream

Soften gelatin in cold water about 5 minutes. Add vinegar; heat over hot water until dissolved.

Combine ham, celery, sugar, pickle relish, and mustard. Stir in melted gelatin and whipped cream; check seasoning. Pour into mold rinsed in cold water; chill until set. Unmold onto bed of lettuce; garnish with olive slices.

Fold horseradish and salt into whipped cream. Serve separately. Yield 4 or 5 servings.

plantation fish in aspic

2 pounds grouper or other fish fillets, fresh or frozen
2 cups boiling water
1 cup dry white wine
1 medium onion, quartered
1 stick celery, quartered
2 bay leaves
1½ teaspoons salt
¼ teaspoon crushed dried thyme leaves

plantation fish in aspic

syrup 5 to 10 minutes. Stir over hot water until melted. Add rest of syrup and lemon juice; leave in cold place until it begins to thicken. Stir in grapefruit, apple, and celery. Pour into prepared mold or individual molds; refrigerate until set. Serve on bed of lettuce. Yield 4 servings.

ham mousse

1 envelope unflavored gelatin
2 tablespoons cold water
¼ cup white-wine vinegar
2 cups finely cubed cooked ham
1 cup finely diced celery
1 tablespoon sugar
1 tablespoon pickle relish
1 teaspoon prepared mustard
½ cup whipped cream
Lettuce
Stuffed olives

1 lemon
½ cup cold water
2 envelopes unflavored gelatin
¼ cup tarragon vinegar
2 tablespoons lemon juice
1 teaspoon dry mustard
¼ cup chopped celery
¼ cup chopped green onion
¼ cup chopped green pepper
2 tablespoons chopped pimiento
2 tablespoons chopped parsley
Salad greens
Mayonnaise

Thaw fish if frozen. Place in well-greased 10-inch frypan. Add boiling water, wine, onion, celery, bay leaves, salt, and thyme.

Cut lemon in half; squeeze in juice; drop in halves. Cover; simmer 5 to 10 minutes or until fish flakes easily. Remove fish; set aside to cool. Strain poaching liquid.

Place cold water in 4 cup measure; stir in gelatin to soften. Add hot poaching liquid; stir to dissolve gelatin. Add vinegar, lemon juice, and enough water to make 4 cups liquid.

Make a paste of dry mustard with small amount of liquid; stir into remaining liquid. Chill to unbeaten egg-white consistency.

Remove skin and bones from fish; flake into small pieces. Mix together fish, celery, green onion, green pepper, pimiento, and parsley. Fold together fish mixture and gelatin. Turn into lightly oiled loaf pan, 9 × 5 × 3 inches, or 7-cup fish mold. Chill until firm. Unmold onto serving dish lined with salad greens. Serve with mayonnaise. Yield 6 servings.

ruby-red salad mold

2 cups cranberry juice
2 packages raspberry-flavored gelatin
1 cup pineapple tidbits
½ cup port wine
½ cup water
1 avocado, peeled, sliced
1 cup peeled, diced apple
½ cup finely chopped celery

Heat cranberry juice to boiling. Add gelatin; stir until dissolved. Add undrained pineapple tidbits, wine, and water.

Arrange avocado in bottom of 5-cup mold. Pour enough gelatin mixture over to cover slices; chill until almost set.

Chill remaining cranberry mixture until partially set. Fold in apple and celery. Pour over avocado layer; chill until firm. Yield 8 to 10 servings.

russian salad

⅔ cup diced cooked potatoes
⅔ cup diced cooked carrots
⅔ cup cooked green peas
⅔ cup diced cooked turnips
⅔ cup cooked French-style green beans
1 cup mayonnaise
2 tablespoons strained lemon juice
2 tablespoons strained orange juice
¼ cup cold water
1 envelope unflavored gelatin

Combine potatoes, carrots, peas, turnips, and beans in medium-size bowl. Add mayonnaise; toss to coat vegetables well.

Combine juices and water in small saucepan; add gelatin. Stir over hot water until dissolved. Add to vegetable mixture; stir until thoroughly mixed. Pour into oiled ring mold.; chill until firm. Unmold onto serving platter; fill center with diced, cooked vegetables, if desired. Garnish with additional green peas. Yield 6 to 8 servings.

salmon mousse

2 pounds fresh salmon, cooked, finely flaked
1 tablespoon salt
3 tablespoons sugar
2 rounded teaspoons dry mustard
½ cup scalded milk
3 tablespoons melted butter
4 egg yolks, beaten
½ cup hot vinegar
1½ envelopes unflavored gelatin

Prepare fish.

Mix dry ingredients in double boiler. Add hot milk slowly; mix thoroughly. Add butter, egg yolks, beaten with 2 tablespoons cold water, and vinegar; stir continuously. Add gelatin dissolved in 2 tablespoons cold water; cool to lukewarm. Pour over fish. Place in large mold; refrigerate until set. Yield 12 servings.

shrimp-cocktail aspic

2 envelopes unflavored gelatin
½ cup cold water
2 (8-ounce) cans tomato sauce
¼ cup lemon juice
2 teaspoons Worcestershire sauce
½ teaspoon horseradish
¼ cup catsup
Dash of Tabasco sauce
1 teaspoon sugar
½ teaspoon salt
1¼ cups boiling water
½ cup finely chopped celery
3 tablespoons finely chopped onion
2 (4½-ounce) cans shrimp, rinsed, drained

russian salad

Soften gelatin in cold water. Add tomato sauce, lemon juice, Worcestershire, horseradish, catsup, Tabasco, sugar, and salt; mix well. Chill until thick but not set. Fold in rest of ingredients. Pour into 1½-quart mold; chill until set. Yield 6 to 8 servings.

spinach blue-cheese mold

2 envelopes unflavored gelatin
½ cup cold water
1 (13¼-ounce) can beef broth, heated to boiling
½ cup chunky blue-cheese dressing
1 small onion, quartered
¼ teaspoon salt
2 tablespoons lemon juice
1 (10-ounce) package frozen chopped spinach, thawed, drained
1 cup finely chopped, seeded, pared cucumber
½ cup chopped celery

Sprinkle gelatin over cold water in blender container.

Heat beef broth to boiling in small saucepan; add to gelatin. Cover; process at low speed until gelatin dissolves. Add dressing and onion; cover.

Process until smooth. Add salt, lemon juice, and spinach; cover. Process just until smooth. Turn into bowl; chill, stirring occasionally, until mixture mounds slightly when dropped from spoon. Fold in cucumber and celery. Turn into 4-cup mold; chill until set. To serve, unmold; garnish with tomatoes and parsley or tiny spinach leaves. Yield 6 to 8 servings.

strawberry mold

3 packages strawberry-flavored gelatin
2 packages frozen strawberries
1 small carton cottage cheese
½ pint heavy cream, whipped
½ cup chopped nuts

Dissolve gelatin in 2 cups boiling water. Drain and add juice from strawberries; add enough water to equal 3 cups liquid. Refrigerate until partially set. Beat in strawberries and cottage cheese; fold in whipped cream. Can be poured into mold and served plain or slices of banana, whole strawberries, and marshmallows can be arranged on bottom of mold before pouring in gelatin mixture. Yield 12 to 16 servings.

tomato aspic

caption: *strawberry yogurt ring mold*

strawberry mousse

1 quart strawberries, washed, hulled
¾ cup sugar
½ cup white wine
½ cup cold water
½ cup boiling water
2 cups heavy cream, whipped
2 envelopes unflavored gelatin

Reserve several berries for garnish. Press remaining berries through fine sieve or use blender. Add sugar and wine; stir well; chill.

Soften gelatin in cold water. Add boiling water; stir to dissolve; cool. Combine gelatin and strawberry mixture; beat until fluffy and slightly thickened. Fold in whipped cream. Pour into oiled 2-quart mold. Chill at least 3 hours. Yield 8 servings.

strawberry yogurt ring mold

2 (3-ounce) packages strawberry gelatin
    dessert mix

2 cups boiling water
2 cups plain yogurt
Grated rind of 1 lemon
1 cup heavy cream, sweetened, whipped (garnish)
Whole fresh strawberries (garnish)

Dissolve gelatin in boiling water; cool. Stir in yogurt and lemon rind. Pour into 8-cup ring mold; chill until firm. Unmold onto large serving dish. Garnish with whipped cream and fresh strawberries; serve at once. Yield 6 to 8 servings.

tomato aspic

3½ cups tomato juice
2 envelopes unflavored gelatin
2 tablespoons celery seed
1 teaspoon salt
1 teaspoon sugar
2 tablespoons Worcestershire sauce
¼ teaspoon hot sauce
¼ cup lemon juice

Pour 1 cup tomato juice into small saucepan. Sprinkle gelatin on tomato juice; let stand 5 minutes to soften. Add celery seed; place saucepan over low heat. Stir until gelatin is dissolved; remove from heat. Strain liquid through fine sieve into small bowl. Stir in remaining tomato juice and other ingredients; pour into lightly oiled 1½-quart mold. Chill until firm. Unmold onto serving plate. Yield 6 to 8 servings.

tomato jellied pasta ring

4 cups tomato juice
2 teaspoons salt
¼ teaspoon freshly ground black pepper
¼ teaspoon finely chopped basil
1 onion, peeled, finely chopped
2 envelopes unflavored gelatin

¼ cup cold water
2 teaspoons prepared horseradish
2 tablespoons sugar
2 tablespoons lemon juice
¼ pound elbow macaroni (or noodles), cooked

Put tomato juice, seasoning, basil, and onion into skillet; heat to boiling. Simmer 10 minutes; strain.

Soak gelatin in cold water 5 minutes. Add to hot tomato juice; stir until dissolved. Add horseradish, sugar, and lemon juice; adjust seasoning. Set aside to chill until mixture begins to thicken. Stir in cooked macaroni. Pour into lightly oiled 9-inch ring mold; chill until set. Unmold onto serving platter; garnish with fresh tomato slices and black olives. Fill center with meat, poultry, or fish mayonnaise. Yield 4 to 6 servings.

tomato jellied pasta ring

tuna salad mold

1 envelope unflavored gelatin
¼ cup cold water
¾ cup hot water
2 tablespoons lemon juice
1 teaspoon prepared mustard
¼ teaspoon paprika
Salt to taste
2 (6½- or 7-ounce) cans tuna fish
1 cup chopped celery
½ cup whipped cream
Lettuce

dressing
½ cup mayonnaise
¼ cup finely diced cucumber
1 tablespoon chopped green pepper
1 teaspoon tarragon vinegar
Dash of cayenne pepper

Soften gelatin in cold water 5 to 10 minutes. Add hot water; stir until gelatin has melted. Add lemon juice, mustard, paprika and salt; set aside to chill until partially set. Add drained and flaked tuna and celery; fold in whipped cream. Spoon into individual molds; chill until set. Turn out onto bed of lettuce. Combine all dressing ingredients. Serve separately. Yield 5 or 6 servings.

turkey and grape aspic

1½ envelopes unflavored gelatin
2¾ cups clear, well-flavored turkey stock
4 tablespoons white wine
1 pound white grapes (or ½ pound and 1 can
    mandarin oranges)
Juice of ½ lemon
1 to 1½ pounds turkey meat
Few tarragon leaves
Lettuce and watercress

Make aspic. Melt gelatin in ¾ cup hot turkey stock. When melted, add wine and 2 cups stock; let cool thoroughly.

Meanwhile, dip grapes into boiling water 10 seconds, then into cold. Remove skins and seeds; put into bowl with a little lemon juice to prevent browning.

Cut turkey meat into neat small slices and cubes.

Pour layer of aspic into round mold. Arrange decorative pattern of grapes with tarragon leaves; leave in refrigerator to set. Pour over another layer of aspic. Put in layer of turkey; repeat. Layer grapes, meat, and aspic until all used; allow enough aspic to cover top completely. Put in refrigerator; leave until set. Dip in bowl of hot water to loosen jelly; turn onto lettuce-and-watercress-lined plate.

Canned mandarin oranges can be added or used in place of grapes. Yield 4 to 6 servings.

veal loaf mold

veal loaf mold

1 pound lean veal
¼ pound bacon
2 hard-boiled eggs, sliced
1 tablespoon chopped parsley
2 cups well-flavored chicken or veal stock
1 envelope unflavored gelatin

Cut veal into small strips; dice bacon. Bring to boil; drain. Rinse with cold water.

Arrange meat and eggs in layers in loaf pan or ring mold. Sprinkle each layer with parsley, salt, and pepper. Pour 1½ cups stock over meat; cover with foil. Cook in preheated 320°F oven about 1½ hours; remove to cool.

Soak gelatin in remaining stock; melt over gentle heat. Pour over meat; put in cool place to set. When cold, put in refrigerator short time or until needed. Turn out jellied veal; decorate with green salad, tomatoes, watercress, and cucumber. Yield 4 to 6 servings.

POTATO

hot potato salad

3 medium potatoes, boiled in skins
3 slices bacon
¼ cup chopped onion
1 tablespoon flour
2 teaspoons sugar
¾ teaspoon salt
¼ teaspoon celery seed
¼ teaspoon pepper
3/8 cup water
2½ tablespoons vinegar

Peel potatoes; slice thin.

Sauté bacon slowly in frypan; drain on paper towels.

Sauté onion in bacon fat until golden brown. Blend in flour, sugar, salt, celery seed, and pepper. Cook over low heat, stirring until smooth and bubbly. Remove from heat; stir in water and vinegar. Heat to boiling; stir constantly. Boil 1 minute; carefully stir in potatoes and crumbled bacon bits. Remove from heat; cover. Let stand until ready to serve. Yield 4 servings.

potato salad 1

potato and beet salad

2 fresh beets
2 medium potatoes
½ cup chopped green onion
¼ cup olive oil
3 tablespoons wine vinegar
1 teaspoon crumbled dried sweet basil
½ teaspoon dry mustard
Salt and pepper
1 head Boston lettuce, cleaned

Do not remove stalks from beets. Wrap well in aluminum foil.

Wash potatoes; prick with fork.

Preheat oven to 450°F. Bake beets 1 hour. Place potatoes in oven; bake 1 hour. Remove beets and potatoes; let cool. Remove skins from beets and potatoes; cut into ½-inch-thick slices. Combine beets, potatoes, and onion; mix gently.

Combine oil, vinegar, basil, mustard, salt, and pepper; mix well. Pour over beets and potatoes; mix gently. Refrigerate several hours, covered, to mellow flavors. Serve at room temperature in bowl garnished with lettuce. Yield 4 servings.

potato salad I

6 large potatoes, peeled, quartered
Boiling water
½ teaspoon salt
1 medium onion, minced
3 tablespoons vinegar
½ teaspoon prepared mustard
1 teaspoon sugar
2 teaspoons dill seed
Paprika

In medium saucepan cook potatoes in boiling salted water until tender. Drain; reserve ¾ cup potato water. Dice potatoes. Add salt and onion; toss gently.

In small saucepan bring ¾ cup potato water to boil; pour over potatoes and onion. Keep at room temperature 2 to 3 hours. Stir in vinegar, mustard, sugar, and dill seed. (Potato salad will be creamy.) Sprinkle with paprika. Serve at room temperature. Yield 6 servings.

potato salad II

6 cups diced cooked potatoes
3 or 4 green onions (scallions), chopped
4 hard-boiled eggs, chopped
1 teaspoon celery seed
1½ teaspoons salt
¼ teaspoon pepper
1 teaspoon curry powder
1 cup sour cream
½ cup mayonnaise
2 tablespoons vinegar

Chopped parsley

Mix potatoes, onions, eggs, and seasoning (except curry powder) together in bowl. Set aside to chill.

Mix curry powder with sour cream. Add mayonnaise and vinegar. When ready to serve, add to potato mixture. Toss together lightly; sprinkle with parsley. Serve cold. Yield 6 to 8 servings.

POULTRY

avocado and chicken salad

3 ripe avocado pears
2 tablespoons orange juice
1 cup diced cooked chicken
1 or 2 stalks celery, diced
3 oranges
¼ cup mayonnaise
Pinch of paprika
Salt to taste
1 tablespoon chopped pimiento
Salad greens

Peel avocados; remove stones; scoop out some flesh. Brush avocados with orange juice. Cut scooped-out flesh into small pieces; place in bowl with chicken and celery.

Peel and section 2 oranges; remove seeds and white pith. Cut into small pieces; add to chicken mixture.

Combine mayonnaise with paprika. Add salt; blend with chicken. Fill avocado halves; sprinkle with pimiento. Serve on bed of salad greens; garnish with sections of remaining orange. Yield 6 servings.

charcuterie salad

6 thin slices cooked chicken
6 thin slices cooked ham
6 thin slices mortadella cheese
Mayonnaise
Prepared mustard
¾ cup cooked green peas
1 tomato, skinned
Lettuce

Cut circles from chicken, ham, and mortadella with 4-inch fluted cookie cutter. Spread thin layer of mayonnaise over chicken circles; cover with ham circles. Spread thin layer of mustard over ham circles; cover with mortadella circles. Place 2 tablespoons peas in center of each mortadella circle; spoon 1 tablespoon mayonnaise over each mound of peas.

Cut top off tomato; remove seeds and pulp, leaving ½-inch shell. Cut 6 wedges from tomato

charcuterie salad

shell to resemble petals; place 1 tomato petal on each salad. Garnish each with lettuce leaf. Place salads in serving dish; place lettuce leaves around salads. Serve with paper-thin cucumber slices and whole-wheat bread. Yield 6 servings.

chicken nectarine salad

1 cup shredded cooked chicken
¼ cup grated raw zucchini
¼ cup grated raw carrot
2 tablespoons finely chopped green onion
2 teaspoons tarragon-wine vinegar
1 teaspoon salad oil
¼ teaspoon seasoned salt
2 fresh nectarines
3 to 4 tablespoons mayonnaise
Crisp lettuce

Toss chicken, vegetables, vinegar, oil, and salt together; chill.

When ready to serve, halve nectarines; remove pit; cut into thin slices. Add with mayonnaise to vegetable mixture. Spoon into lettuce cups. Yield 4 servings.

chicken salad

¼ pound mushrooms
½ cup French dressing
1 large iceberg lettuce
1½ cups diced cooked chicken
1 can artichoke hearts, drained, cut in halves
1 small red pepper, seeded, cut into strips
½ pound cooked green beans, sliced
Salt and pepper
1 cup halved, seeded grapes
¼ cup toasted flaked almonds

Wash and slice mushrooms; place in shallow bowl. Pour French dressing over; set aside 1 hour,

stirring occasionally.

Wash lettuce; discard outer leaves. Line deep salad bowl or large platter.

Combine chicken, artichokes, red pepper, and beans. Add mushrooms and dressing; season to taste. Toss lightly together; refrigerate until ready to serve. Spoon chicken mixture over lettuce. Sprinkle with grapes and almonds. Yield 5 or 6 servings.

chicken salad with bacon

1 small head iceberg lettuce
1 small red sweet pepper, cut into strips
1 cucumber, thickly sliced
1 cup small whole mushrooms
2 cups coarsely chopped chicken
2 hard-boiled eggs, quartered
4 slices crisp-fried bacon, halved
2 tablespoons wine vinegar
6 tablespoons salad oil
Salt to taste
¼ cup mashed Roquefort cheese

Tear lettuce into large pieces; place in salad

chicken salad with bacon

bowl. Add pepper, cucumber, mushrooms, and chicken; toss lightly. Top with eggs and bacon.

Combine vinegar, oil, salt, and cheese; blend thoroughly. Serve with salad. Yield 4 servings.

chicken salad with litchis

3 cups cooked diced chicken
2 or 3 stalks celery, chopped
1 green pepper, chopped
Salt and pepper
¾ cup French dressing (see Index)
Salad greens
1 can litchis
1 small can mandarin oranges

curry salad dressing
¾ cup mayonnaise
¼ cup sour cream
2 teaspoons curry powder
2 tablespoons grated onion
2 tablespoons chopped parsley

Combine chicken, celery, and green pepper. Add salt, pepper, and French dressing; toss lightly. Chill about ½ hour.

Arrange salad greens around large platter; pile chicken mixture in center.

Drain litchis and oranges. Place orange segment in each litchi; arrange around edge or down center.

Blend all dressing ingredients together; chill well. Serve dressing separately. Yield 5 to 6 servings.

chicken salad with litchis

chicken-stuffed apples

chicken-stuffed apples

½ cup heavy cream, lightly beaten
1¼ cups mayonnaise
Salt and pepper to taste
2 cups finely diced cooked white chicken meat
½ cup drained pineapple chunks
1 cup peeled, seeded grapes
2 stalks celery, chopped
4 large apples
1 teaspoon grated lemon rind
2 tablespoons slivered almonds, lightly browned

Add cream to mayonnaise; season.

Mix chicken with pineapple, grapes, and celery; mix with mayonnaise.

Polish apples; cut off top quarter of each. Scoop out flesh with grapefruit knife or spoon; remove cores. Dice remaining apple; add to mayonnaise.

Fill apples with chicken mayonnaise. Sprinkle tops with lemon rind and almonds. Yield 4 servings.

curried chicken salad

3 tablespoons instant minced onion
3 tablespoons water
2 tablespoons butter
1¼ teaspoons curry powder
⅓ cup mayonnaise
1 tablespoon lemon juice
½ teaspoon salt
Dash of cayenne pepper
3 cups diced cooked chicken
1 (1-pound, 4-ounce) can pineapple chunks,
drained
½ cup coarsely chopped nuts
⅓ cup golden raisins
1 red apple, cored, diced
Lettuce
2 tablespoons shredded coconut

Combine onion and water in small bowl; let stand 10 minutes.

Melt butter in small skillet over medium heat; stir in onion and curry powder. Sauté, stirring constantly, 3 to 5 minutes; cool. Combine curry mixture with mayonnaise, lemon juice, salt, and cayenne; blend thoroughly.

Combine chicken, pineapple, nuts, raisins, and apple in large bowl. Add curry dressing; toss gently until mixed. Line salad bowl with lettuce. Add salad; sprinkle with coconut. Yield 6 servings.

sorrento salad

curried chicken salad

sorrento salad

3 cups diced cooked chicken
1 cup chopped celery
¼ cup chopped red sweet pepper (optional)
½ teaspoon salt
½ teaspoon pepper
⅔ cup blue-cheese dressing
2 cups orange sections
2 cups grapefruit sections
½ cup diced avocado
1 avocado, cut into wedges
Orange or grapefruit juice
Salad greens

Combine chicken, celery, and red pepper in bowl; sprinkle with salt and pepper. Add blue-cheese dressing; toss to mix well. Chill thoroughly.

Dice enough orange and grapefruit sections to make ½ cup each; add to chicken mixture.

Coat diced avocado and avocado wedges with orange juice. Add diced avocado to chicken mixture.

Line large salad bowl with salad greens; spoon salad into bowl. Arrange remaining orange and grapefruit sections and avocado wedges around salad. Serve with additional blue-cheese dressing. Yield 6 servings.

turkey, celery, grape, and nut salad

2 cups chopped turkey
½ cup grapes
½ cup sliced celery
3 to 4 tablespoons almonds
Juice of ½ lemon
Grated rind of ½ orange
1 cup mayonnaise
Lettuce or endive leaves

turkey, celery, grape, and nut salad

Chop turkey into medium-size pieces. Dip grapes into boiling, then cold, water; peel. Slice celery. Dip almonds in boiling water; remove skins. Brown halved nuts in moderate oven 2 minutes.

Add lemon juice and orange rind to mayonnaise. Mix turkey and other ingredients into mayonnaise. Arrange on lettuce. Yield 4 servings.

RICE

fruited rice salads

2 tablespoons butter
½ cup diced celery
¼ cup minced onion
2 teaspoons grated orange rind
1 cup orange juice
1 cup water
½ teaspoon poultry seasoning
1 cup long-grain rice
⅓ cup golden raisins
6 orange shells

fruited rice salads

Heat butter in medium-size saucepan; sauté celery and onion until tender. Stir in orange rind, juice, water, seasoning, rice, and raisins. Bring to boil; stir well. Reduce heat; cover. Simmer until liquid is absorbed and rice tender, about 30 minutes. Remove from heat. When cool, refrigerate several hours. Serve in orange shells. Yield 6 servings.

rice salad

2 bananas, sliced
2 tablespoons lemon juice
8 ounces long-grain rice, cooked according to

rice salad

package directions, chilled
4 small tomatoes, cut into wedges
½ cup drained canned mandarin-orange sections
½ cup cold cooked or canned corn
4 ounces cold cooked shrimp
½ teaspoon dried mint leaves

salad dressing
¾ cup plain yogurt
2 tablespoons mayonnaise
1 tablespoon orange juice
1 tablespoon sugar
¼ teaspoon salt

Sprinkle bananas with lemon juice.

Place rice in serving bowl. Arrange rows of tomatoes, bananas, oranges, corn, and shrimp in starlike pattern on top. Sprinkle with mint.

Combine dressing ingredients; pour over rice. Yield 4 servings.

SEAFOOD

anchovy and tuna salad

4 tomatoes, peeled, quartered
2 small green peppers, seeded, thinly sliced
4 stalks celery, chopped
1 small cooked beet
2 hard-boiled eggs, cut into quarters
1 can anchovy fillets
1 can tuna fish, drained, flaked
Green and black olives

salad dressing
2 tablespoons white-wine vinegar
6 tablespoons olive oil

anchovy and tuna salad

Salt
Freshly ground black pepper
½ teaspoon prepared mustard
1 teaspoon each finely chopped tarragon, chives,
  chervil, and parsley

Arrange tomatoes, green peppers, celery, beet, and eggs in salad bowl or on large platter.

Combine all dressing ingredients; blend well.

Arrange anchovy fillets, tuna, and olives attractively on top. Pour the dressing over; toss at table. Yield 4 servings.

avocado shrimp boats

2 soft avocados, halved, peeled, seeded
2 cups shredded lettuce
2 cups cooked shrimp, peeled, deveined
1 cup alfalfa sprouts
16 cherry tomatoes, cut into halves
Parsley (garnish)
Lemon wedges
French dressing

Place avocado halves on lettuce bed. Spoon ½ cup shrimp into cavity of each. Serve alfalfa sprouts and tomatoes on side of plate. Garnish shrimp with parsley and lemon wedges. Serve with side bowl of French dressing made with lemon juice. Yield 4 servings.

caribbean salad

2 tablespoons vinegar
½ teaspoon salt
⅛ teaspoon white pepper
1 teaspoon honey
3 drops angostura bitters
½ small onion, grated
2 tablespoons vegetable oil
2 medium bananas
2 medium tomatoes
2 mandarin oranges (or 1 small can, drained)
1 (4½-ounce) can shrimps
Parsley (garnish)
4 stuffed olives, halved (garnish)

Make salad dressing by combining and blending vinegar, salt, pepper, honey, bitters, onion, and oil. Adjust seasonings to taste.

Peel and slice bananas; immediately add to dressing to prevent browning.

Peel tomatoes; cut into quarters.

Peel oranges; section (remove white membrane). Add tomatoes and oranges to dressing; carefully stir in drained shrimps. Arrange salad in attractive bowl; garnish with parsley and olives. Yield 4 servings.

caribbean salad

crab-chunk salad

1 cup rice
Nutmeg
Lemon juice
Olive oil
1 can crab claw meat (12- or 16-ounces), or 1 pound
   fresh white crab meat
6 black olives, pitted
1 red or green pepper, seeded, cut into strips
½ clove garlic, crushed
3 or 4 raw mushrooms, sliced
Few walnuts, chopped
Lettuce

Cook rice in boiling salted water until just tender (about 12 minutes); drain well. While still warm, add good pinch of nutmeg, squeeze of lemon juice, and enough oil to moisten. Add crab meat cut into squares, olives, pepper, garlic, and mushrooms; mix lightly. Arrange in lettuce-lined bowl or platter; sprinkle with walnuts. Yield 4 servings.

crab louis

¾ cup mayonnaise or salad dressing
¼ cup chili sauce

2 tablespoons minced parsley
2 teaspoons vinegar
½ teaspoon Worcestershire sauce
¼ teaspoon horseradish
1 pound fresh or canned crab meat

Blend all but crab meat. Toss lightly with crab meat; chill. Serve in lettuce cups or as filling for avocado halves. Yield 4 servings.

craibechan of the sea

3 tablespoons butter
1 clove garlic, peeled, chopped
1 leek, cleaned, sliced
1 medium onion, peeled, chopped
3 cups cooked seafood (Lobster, crab, and shrimp can be used, or salmon and cod make a good combination. Steam or poach fish; cool.)
Salt and pepper
Few drops of Tabasco
1 small head Bibb lettuce
1 lemon, cut into wedges
Radish roses

Melt butter in small skillet. Add garlic, leek, and onion; sauté until tender. Combine onion mixture and seafood; pass through food chopper. Season with salt, pepper, and Tabasco to taste. Refrigerate until serving time.

Line plates with Bibb lettuce; mound fish mixture in center of plate. Garnish with lemon wedges and radish roses. Yield 4 servings.

cucumber gondola salad

3 long straight cucumbers
1½ cups chopped cooked shrimp

cucumber gondola salad

fresh crab salad

¼ cup finely chopped celery
2 tablespoons minced green onion
2 teaspoons minced parsley
1 teaspoon fresh tarragon leaves or ⅛ teaspoon
   dried tarragon leaves
½ teaspoon salt
⅛ teaspoon white pepper
¼ cup mayonnaise
21 large pitted ripe olives
3 whole pimientos
6 radishes

Slice off ⅓ of cucumbers lengthwise; cut long strips of peeling from cut-off portions for garnish. Dice enough of this portion to make ¼ cup. Carefully scoop pulp from larger portions of cucumber; leave shells ¼-inch thick.

Combine shrimp, diced cucumber, celery, onion, and parsley in medium bowl. Sprinkle with tarragon, salt, and pepper. Add mayonnaise; toss lightly until just blended. Fill cucumber shells with shrimp mixture; heap along entire length of cucumber.

Cut olives into quarters, lengthwise, to form petals. Cut pimientos into equal number of matching petals. Arrange petals alternately along sides of cucumbers. Arrange strips of peeling over salad as shown in illustration. Place cucumber gondolas on bed of lettuce; garnish with radishes. Serve with a Basic Vinaigrette (see Index). Yield 6 servings.

egg and shrimp mayonnaise salad

½ cup mayonnaise
1 (½-pint) carton sour cream
1 teaspoon curry powder
6 hard-boiled eggs
Lettuce
1 cup fresh or frozen shrimp
Paprika

Combine mayonnaise, sour cream, and curry powder; chill 1 hour.

Shell hard-boiled eggs; cut in halves. Arrange, rounded-side-up, on crisp lettuce.

Fold shrimp into mayonnaise; spoon over eggs. Sprinkle with paprika. Yield 6 servings.

fresh crab salad

1 pound fresh crab meat, flaked
½ cup minced celery
1 teaspoon grated onion
1 tablespoon minced pimiento
¼ teaspoon salt
2 tablespoons lemon juice
Mayonnaise
Lettuce leaves
2 tablespoons minced parsley

Combine crab meat, celery, onion, and pimiento in bowl. Sprinkle with salt and lemon juice; toss to mix. Add just enough mayonnaise to moisten; mix well. Spoon onto bed of lettuce; sprinkle with parsley. Garnish with thin slices of cucumber and tomato. Serve with additional mayonnaise. Yield 4 servings.

german fish salad

1 tablespoon butter
1 pound whitefish fillets, fresh or frozen (cod, turbot, or haddock)
½ cup hot water
4 hard-cooked eggs
2 dill pickles
1 tablespoon capers

sauce
2 tablespoons mayonnaise
2 tablespoons sour cream
2 teaspoons lemon juice
1 teaspoon Dijon-style mustard
½ teaspoon salt
¼ teaspoon white pepper

garnish
1 hard-cooked egg
4 slices canned beets

Melt butter in frypan. Place thawed fish in frypan; pour hot water over. Bring to boil; cover. Lower heat; simmer gently 10 minutes.

Meanwhile, slice 4 hard-cooked eggs and pickles.

Drain fish; cool; cut into cubes.

Blend together sauce ingredients.

Gently mix fish, eggs, pickles, and capers in separate bowl. Arrange in individual dishes; spoon sauce over tops. Chill 30 minutes.

To garnish, cut remaining egg into 8 pieces; chop beet slices. Arrange garnish on each serving; serve immediately. Yield 4 servings.

herring salad with sour cream

sour-cream sauce
1 cup sour cream
½ cup yogurt
Juice of ½ lemon
¼ teaspoon sugar

salad
2 small onions
2 tart apples
8 marinated herring fillets
2 teaspoons fresh dill or ½ teaspoon dried dill weed

Thoroughly blend sauce ingredients.

Peel onions; cut into thin slices. Peel and quarter apples; remove cores; cut into thin wedges. Blend onions and apples with sauce.

In dish arrange herring and apple mixture in layers; cover tightly. Marinate in refrigerator 5 hours. Sprinkle with dill before serving. Yield 4 to 6 servings.

leek and lox salad

2 leeks
2 or 3 tomatoes
2 hard-cooked eggs
2 to 4 ounces smoked lox
¾ cup plain yogurt
2 tablespoons chopped parsley leaves
1 tablespoon olive oil
1 tablespoon lemon juice
¼ teaspoon dried mustard
1 teaspoon sugar
Salt and pepper to taste

Clean leeks thoroughly; cut off all but 2-inches of tops. Cut into very thin slices; separate slices into rings. Peel tomatoes; cube. Chop eggs coarsely. Cube lox. Combine all these ingredients.

Stir together yogurt, parsley, oil, lemon juice, mustard, and sugar; season with salt and pepper. Pour over salad ingredients; serve at once. Yield 4 servings.

lobster salad

2 (1- to 1¼-pound) live lobsters
2 recipes Basic Court Bouillon for Seafood (see Index)

german fish salad

herring salad with sour cream

leek and lox salad

539

lobster salad

3 cups diced cooked new potatoes
1 tablespoon diced red pimiento
1¼ cups cooked green peas
Mayonnaise
1 large lettuce heart

Cook lobsters in Court Bouillon. Split lobsters; clean. Remove meat; reserve shells, claws, and legs for garnish, if desired. Chop meat of 1 lobster; place the meat in large bowl. Add potatoes, pimiento, and 1 cup peas; toss lightly. Add enough mayonnaise to moisten; mix until ingredients are combined. Mound salad in serving dish.

Tear lettuce; place around edge of dish. Place remaining peas on salad around inside edge of lettuce. Place remaining lobster meat on top of salad. Garnish with reserved shells, claws, and legs. Pipe border of mayonnaise around outside of lettuce; chill thoroughly. The coral can be chopped and added to salad, if desired. Yield about 6 servings.

salmon and cucumber salad

2 cucumbers, washed
½ cup French Dressing (see Index)
1 can salmon
⅓ cup thick mayonnaise
1 tablespoon juice from salmon
Salt
Chopped parsley or chives (garnish)

Cut cucumbers in half lengthwise; scoop out seeds and some flesh to form shell. Discard seeds; chop cucumber taken out into small pieces. Marinate in some of French Dressing ½ hour.

Drain salmon; reserve juice. Remove skin and bones; flake salmon into small pieces. Pour remaining French Dressing over salmon; let marinate ½ hour in refrigerator.

Thin mayonnaise slightly with salmon juice.

Drain marinated salmon; mix with mayonnaise.

Salt cucumber shells lightly; sprinkle with chopped chives. Fill with salmon salad; spread marinated cucumber over top. Sprinkle with chives; top with line of thick mayonnaise. Yield 4 servings.

seafood medley

1 (6½-ounce) can tuna fish
1 (6-ounce) can crab meat, flaked
1 (4¼-ounce) can shrimp
2 tablespoons French dressing
1 cup diced celery
½ cup diced cucumber
6 to 8 radishes, chopped
1 tablespoon capers
2 tablespoons lemon juice
½ cup mayonnaise
Salt, pepper, and paprika
Lettuce

Drain tuna; break into flakes. Add crab meat and shrimp. Stir in French dressing; set aside to chill about 15 minutes. Add celery, cucumber, radishes, and capers.

Blend lemon juice with mayonnaise. Add seasoning to taste; toss all ingredients lightly together. Serve on crisp lettuce. Yield 5 or 6 servings.

shrimp macaroni salad

3 (4½- or 5-ounce) cans shrimp
2 cups cooked shell macaroni
1 cup chopped raw cauliflower
1 cup sliced celery
¼ cup chopped parsley

seafood medley

¼ cup chopped sweet pickle or drained
  pickle relish
½ cup mayonnaise or salad dressing
3 tablespoons garlic French dressing
1 tablespoon lemon juice
1 teaspoon grated onion
1 teaspoon celery seed
1 teaspoon salt
¼ teaspoon pepper
Salad greens
1 hard-cooked egg, sliced

Drain shrimp; cover with ice water. Let stand 5 minutes; drain. Cut large shrimp in half.

Combine macaroni, cauliflower, celery, parsley, pickle, and shrimp.

Combine mayonnaise, French dressing, lemon juice, onion, and seasonings; mix thoroughly. Add to shrimp mixture; toss lightly; chill. Serve on salad greens; garnish with eggs. Yield 6 servings.

simple salmon salad

1 (1-pound) can salmon or 2 (6½- or 7-ounce)
  cans tuna
1 cup chopped celery
⅓ cup mayonnaise or salad dressing
2 hard-cooked eggs, chopped
2 tablespoons chopped onion
2 tablespoons chopped sweet pickle
Salad greens

Drain fish; break into large pieces.

Combine all ingredients except salad greens. Toss lightly; chill. Serve on salad greens. Yield 4 servings.

tuna and cheese salad

8 ounces Gouda cheese, cut into ½-inch cubes
1 (6½-ounce) can tuna, well-drained, broken into
  bite-size pieces
½ cup cold cooked green beans
2 medium dill pickles, cubed
1 onion, chopped
3 hard-cooked eggs, cubed
1 red pepper (ripe green pepper)
2 small tomatoes, cubed

salad dressing
1 cup plain yogurt
4 tablespoons mayonnaise
2 teaspoons prepared mustard
1 teaspoon sugar
1 teaspoon chopped fresh dill (or ½ teaspoon
  dried dill weed)
1 tablespoon chopped fresh parsley leaves
Salt and pepper to taste
Lettuce leaves

Combine cheese, tuna, beans, pickles, onion, eggs, pepper, and tomatoes in large bowl.

Combine and whisk together dressing ingredients. Pour over salad ingredients; toss lightly.

Chill 15 to 20 minutes to blend flavors before serving.

Line serving bowl with lettuce leaves. Arrange salad on top. Yield 4 servings.

tuna waldorf salad

1 (6½- or 7-ounce) can tuna
1 cup diced apples
½ cup chopped celery
¼ cup chopped nutmeats
½ cup mayonnaise or salad dressing
Lettuce

Drain tuna; break into large pieces. Combine all ingredients except lettuce. Serve on lettuce. Yield 6 servings.

VEGETABLE

artichoke and tomato salad

2 (4-ounce) jars marinated artichoke hearts
½ cup dry white wine
Juice of 1 lemon
1 whole fennel or 1 small bunch celery, sliced
6 medium tomatoes, sliced

tuna waldorf salad

2 small onions, diced
1 clove garlic
½ teaspoon salt
¼ teaspoon white pepper
½ cup warm beef broth

Drain artichoke hearts; reserve marinade. Cut hearts in half; place in large salad bowl.

Combine reserved marinade, wine, and lemon juice; pour over artichokes.

Clean and wash fennel; slice. Add to artichokes. Add tomatoes and onions.

Mash garlic with salt and pepper; add to beef broth. Mix well; pour over vegetables. Marinate at

tuna and cheese salad

542

artichokes with cold corn salad

least 10 minutes. Serve with crusty bread. Yield 6 to 8 servings.

artichokes with cold corn salad

2 (10-ounce) packages frozen whole-kernel corn
²⁄₃ cup chopped green sweet pepper
¾ cup sliced cooked carrots

artichoke and tomato salad

2 tablespoons finely chopped onion
½ cup mayonnaise
1 teaspoon chili powder
⅛ teaspoon seasoned salt
⅛ teaspoon freshly ground pepper
6 fresh artichokes
Chili Mayonnaise

Cook corn; drain; cool. Place in large bowl. Add green pepper, carrots, onion, mayonnaise, chili powder, salt, and pepper; mix well; chill.

Remove artichoke stems; cut about ½-inch from tips of leaves with kitchen shears. Drop into boiling salted water; cook 5 minutes. Drain; shake to remove water; cool. Tap base on flat surface to spread leaves; chill. Fill with corn salad; place on serving platter. Serve with Chili Mayonnaise. Yield 6 servings.

chili mayonnaise

1 cup mayonnaise
1 teaspoon chili powder
½ teaspoon seasoned salt
Dash of freshly ground pepper
1 tablespoon lemon juice

Place all ingredients in small bowl. Mix until blended; chill.

asparagus spring salad

asparagus spring salad

¼ cup olive or vegetable oil
4 teaspoons wine vinegar
2 teaspoons finely chopped fresh basil
¾ teaspoon salt
¼ teaspoon freshly ground pepper
1½ pounds cooked fresh asparagus
1 pound cream-style cottage cheese
1 tablespoon finely chopped chives or green onion
  tops
10 pimiento strips

Combine oil, vinegar, basil, ½ teaspoon salt, and pepper in jar; shake well.

Place asparagus in dish; spoon dressing over top. Let stand at least 30 minutes to marinate.

Combine cottage cheese, chives, and remaining ¼ teaspoon of salt; mix well. Arrange the asparagus spoke-like around outside of large round platter; spoon cheese mixture into center. Arrange pimiento strips over asparagus; sprinkle cheese with additional chives. Yield 6 servings.

avocado salad vinaigrette

1 recipe Basic Vinaigrette (see Index)
8 green onions (scallions)
½ large red sweet pepper
2 avocados, peeled
Lemon juice
Watercress or chopped romaine
Bean sprouts

Prepare Basic Vinaigrette; substitute ½ cup tarragon-wine vinegar for red-wine vinegar.

Trim onions, leaving about 2-inches of green stems; cut into ½-inch lengths.

Remove seeds and white membrane from pepper; cut into thin lengthwise slices.

Cut avocados in half; remove seeds. Cut 1 avocado into lengthwise slices; dip halves and slices into lemon juice to prevent discoloration.

Arrange watercress, bean sprouts, pepper, onions and avocado on serving dish.

Shake vinaigrette to blend; fill avocado halves with sauce. Yield 2 servings.

avocado and strawberry salad

½ cup almonds
1 (8-ounce) package cream cheese, softened
¾ cup confectioners sugar
2 ripe avocados
Lemon juice
1 pint fresh strawberries, cleaned
⅓ cup fresh orange juice
1 tablespoon lemon juice

Spread almonds on cookie sheet; toast lightly in 350°F oven about 10 minutes. Place in blender; grind or chop finely.

Combine cream cheese and ½ cup sugar in small mixing bowl; beat until fluffy. Stir in almonds. Shape into cone in center of serving dish.

Peel avocados; cut in half; remove seeds. Coat generously with lemon juice to prevent darkening. Place 2 halves on opposite sides of cream-cheese cone. Arrange strawberries between avocado halves over cone.

Slice remaining avocado; place around edge of serving dish; garnish with any remaining strawberries.

Combine remaining sugar with orange and lemon juice for sauce.

Dust strawberries with additional confectioners' sugar. Spoon small amount of orange sauce over each serving. Yield 4 servings.

bean-sprout salad

2 or 3 cups bean sprouts
½ cup grated carrot
½ cup chopped spring onion
Bottled or packaged sesame dressing

Wash sprouts; place on towel to dry. Put in bowl; add carrot and onion. Toss with sesame

avocado salad vinaigrette

dressing. Serve on lettuce leaf or plain. Yield 6 servings.

garbanzo-bean salad

1 (15-ounce) can garbanzo beans, drained
$\frac{1}{8}$ teaspoon garlic powder
$\frac{1}{2}$ teaspoon chili powder
2 tablespoons oil
2 tablespoons wine vinegar

1 tablespoon dried parsley
$\frac{3}{4}$ cup chopped celery
1 (4-ounce) can pimientos, drained, chopped
3 green onions, chopped
Salt and pepper to taste
Lettuce

Rinse beans in cold water; drain. Combine with other ingredients; let stand several hours. Stir periodically to be sure all flavors are well mixed. Serve in lettuce cups. Yield 4 servings.

avocado and strawberry salad

green beans with garlic dressing

4 cups (1-pound) green beans
1 teaspoon salt
2 slices bacon
½ cup garlic French dressing
2 tablespoons minced green onion
¼ teaspoon oregano leaves

Cook beans, either whole or cut into 1-inch lengths, in ½ cup water with salt 10 minutes or until just tender-crisp.

Cut bacon into ½-inch lengths; fry crisp. Add bacon bits, without fat, to beans. Pour salad dressing over; add onion and oregano. Heat through; serve. Yield 4 servings.

kidney-bean salad

½ teaspoon salt
¾ cup sugar
½ cup vinegar
3 tablespoons cooking oil
4 cups (about 1½ cups uncooked) dry kidney
   beans, cooked, drained
½ cup diced celery
½ cup thinly sliced green pepper
¼ cup thinly sliced onion
2 hard-cooked eggs, sliced

2 tablespoons soy sauce
1 tablespoon vodka
1 tablespoon vinegar

Place bean sprouts in colander; blanch. Immediately rinse with cold water; drain well.

Combine remaining ingredients in large bowl. Place bean sprouts in mixture to marinate at room temperature 1 hour. Refrigerate at least 3 hours before serving. Yield 4 servings.

three-bean salad

1 (16-ounce) can cut green beans
1 (16-ounce) can whole yellow or wax beans
1 (16-ounce) can red kidney or chili beans
1 can apple jelly
¼ cup cider vinegar (can substitute white or malt)
4 level teaspoons cornstarch
1 teaspoon salt
½ cup sliced green onions
2 cups sliced celery

Drain all beans.

Cook jelly, vinegar, cornstarch, and salt until thickened. Stir in all vegetables. Let stand at least 2 hours. Yield 8 servings.

beet and onion salad

2 pounds fresh beets
2 teaspoons salt

beet and onion salad

Soak beans overnight; discard any that float to top. Bring to boil; simmer until tender.

Combine salt, sugar; vinegar, and oil; mix well. Add vegetables; mix gently.

Chill at least 1 hour. Pour off liquid. Gently stir in eggs before serving. Yield 6 servings.

marinated bean sprouts

1 pound fresh bean sprouts

marinade
3 tablespoons chopped scallion (green and
   white parts)
2 tablespoons sesame-seed oil

1 recipe Vinaigrette Aux Fines Herbes (see Index)
2 white onions, peeled

Cut tops from beets; leave at least 3-inches of stalk to prevent bleeding. Place in large kettle; add water to cover. Add salt; bring to boil. Cook about 60 minutes, until tender; drain; cool. Cut off tops; slip skins from roots. Cut into medium-thick slices; place in bowl. Pour vinaigrette over; toss lightly. Cover; chill several hours, tossing occasionally.

Cut onions into thin slices; separate into rings.

Remove beets from vinaigrette with slotted spoon; place in serving dish. Arrange onion rings over top. Garnish with chopped parsley. Yield 6 to 8 servings.

broadway beet salad

1 garlic clove, halved
Lettuce
1 medium-size can beets, diced
2 small onions, sliced
1 (7-ounce) can tuna
2 hard-boiled eggs, sliced
½ cup mayonnaise
¼ teaspoon salt
Pepper

Rub salad bowl with garlic. Line bowl with lettuce leaves.

Put beets, onions, tuna, and eggs in another bowl.

Combine mayonnaise, salt, and pepper. Toss gently with beet mixture; serve in salad bowl. Yield 2 to 4 servings.

cabbage salad

½ cup vinegar
¼ teaspoon salt
1 tablespoon butter
1 small onion, minced
1 small cabbage, shredded

Combine vinegar, salt, butter, and onion; simmer until onion is soft. Add to cabbage; mix well. Yield 6 servings.

cole slaw

1 head cabbage
1 cup mayonnaise
1 cup sour cream
1 teaspoon prepared mustard
1 tablespoon lemon juice
Salt and pepper to taste
1 tablespoon sugar

Slice cabbage very thin.

Mix other ingredients; stir into cabbage. Chill about 4 hours. Yield 10 servings.

hot slaw

2 tablespoons salad oil
4 cups shredded cabbage
½ teaspoon salt
½ teaspoon celery seed
¼ teaspoon pepper
2 tablespoons vinegar

Heat oil in medium-size skillet. Add cabbage and seasonings, but not vinegar; cover. Cook over medium heat about 3 minutes; stir occasionally to mix flavors. Add vinegar; stir again. Serve slaw at once, hot. Yield 4 to 6 servings.

carrot salad

2 pounds carrots (½-inch slices), cooked in salted water ½ hour
3 or 4 green peppers, sliced
2 large onions, sliced
1 can tomato soup
½ cup salad oil
1 cup sugar
¾ cup vinegar
1 teaspoon prepared mustard
1 teaspoon Worcestershire sauce

Alternate layers of carrots, peppers, and onions in bowl.

Combine remaining ingredients; heat. Beat to blend; cool while carrots are cooking. Pour over vegetables; let stand at least a day. Yield 6 to 8 servings.

cauliflower salad

1 small head cauliflower
¼ cup chopped red pepper or pimiento
2 tablespoons chopped fresh parsley (Italian flat leaf if available)
¼ cup sliced black olives
1 tablespoon chopped capers
1 tablespoon wine vinegar
3 tablespoons olive oil
½ teaspoon crumbled dried oregano

Wash cauliflower; separate into florets. Slice florets into thick slices; cook in boiling salted water until crisp but tender. Drain well. Gently mix cauliflower, pepper, parsley, olives, and capers in serving bowl.

Combine vinegar, oil, and oregano; mix well. Pour over salad; refrigerate 1 hour before serving. Garnish with anchovies if you wish. Yield 4 servings.

pickled corn salad

½ cup chopped onions
½ cup diced green peppers
4 tablespoons chopped pimiento

3 tablespoons sugar
¾ teaspoon salt
½ teaspoon celery salt
½ teaspoon dry mustard
½ cup cider vinegar
½ cup water
3 cups frozen whole-kernel corn

Combine all ingredients except corn; bring to boil. Lower heat; cover pan. Simmer 12 minutes; stir occasionally. Add frozen corn; raise heat. When boiling resumes, lower heat; simmer until corn is just tender (2 or 3 minutes); drain. Serve salad hot, or refrigerate and serve on lettuce leaves. Yield 4 to 6 servings.

dandelion salad

½ pound tender young dandelion greens
½ cup thinly sliced red or Spanish onions
2 tomatoes, cut in fourths
Cut-up or shredded cheese
Salt and pepper to taste
French dressing, or oil and vinegar

Wash dandelion greens; drain well. Cut into 2-inch pieces. Add rest of ingredients in order given; toss to mix well. Yield 4 servings.

sweet-and-sour eggplant salad

4 large eggplants, cut into ½-inch cubes
2½ cups water
¼ cup salad oil

½ teaspoon crushed coriander seed
1 teaspoon salt
½ cup lemon juice (or vinegar)
Fresh herbs and bay leaf
½ cup currants

Peel and cube eggplants.

Put water, oil, coriander, salt, lemon juice, and herbs into pan; bring to boil. Add eggplant; simmer until tender but not mushy. Remove eggplant. Boil until liquid is reduced by half. Strain. Add currants; simmer 5 minutes. Pour over cooked eggplant; chill. Yield 6 servings.

fresh garden salad

2 cucumbers
½ cup white vinegar
½ cup water
1 teaspoon salt
12 cherry tomatoes, sliced
1 green pepper, thinly sliced
1 red pepper, thinly sliced
1 small sweet onion, peeled, cut into rings
1 tablespoon chopped parsley (garnish)

Peel cucumbers; slice crosswise.

Combine vinegar, water, and salt; pour over cucumbers. Marinate at room temperature 2 hours; drain. Add remaining vegetables to cucumbers; toss lightly. Chill before serving. To serve, arrange on salad plates; garnish with parsley. Yield 4 servings.

fresh garden salad

gazpacho salad

2 large cucumbers, diced
1 large green pepper, slivered
1 large red onion, sliced
1 large Spanish onion, chopped
1 can chick peas or red kidney beans, well drained
6 to 8 ripe firm tomatoes, chopped
10 black olives, pitted
1 can flat anchovies, drained
2 cloves garlic, minced
Salt and pepper

marinade
¼ cup white or red wine vinegar
⅓ cup vegetable oil
2 tablespoons fresh chopped parsley
1 teaspoon chopped chives

Colorfully layer each vegetable in large brandy snifter, interspersing anchovies and olives. Sprinkle each layer with garlic, salt, and pepper. Layer to top of brandy snifter; cover. Refrigerate until chilled.

Combine marinade ingredients; chill. Just before serving, carefully pour mixed marinade over salad. Amounts can be adjusted according to size of glass container. Yield depends on size of container.

mushroom and sour-cream salad

2 cups canned drained mushroom slices
½ cup wine vinegar
4 heads Boston lettuce
½ cup sour cream
1 tablespoon chopped fresh parsley

Combine mushrooms and vinegar. Marinate in refrigerator 24 hours; drain.

Arrange lettuce on individual salad plates. Place ½ cup marinated mushrooms in center of lettuce bed; garnish with 2 tablespoons sour cream and fresh parsley. Yield 4 servings.

raw mushroom salad

1 pound button mushrooms
Juice of 1 lemon
8 tablespoons olive oil
Salt
Freshly ground black pepper
1 teaspoon finely chopped chives
1 teaspoon finely chopped parsley

Remove stalks from mushrooms. Wash and dry caps; cut into slices. Arrange in shallow salad bowl.

Blend lemon juice and oil. Add salt and pepper to taste; pour over mushrooms. Toss carefully; set aside to chill at least ½ hour. Before serving, sprinkle with chives and parsley. Yield 5 or 6 servings.

pallas athene salad

5 medium tomatoes
1 teaspoon oregano
Salt and pepper to taste
2 medium green sweet peppers
24 small Greek olives
1 pound small-curd cottage cheese
1 pint sour cream

Cut tomatoes into wedges; place in bowl. Sprinkle with oregano, salt, and pepper. Toss lightly.

pallas athene salad

549

pepper salad

Cut peppers in half; remove seeds and membrane. Cut into thin lengthwise slices.

Arrange tomatoes, peppers, and olives on lettuce-lined serving dish. Spoon dollops of cottage cheese and sour cream on top. Yield 4 to 6 servings.

pasta slaw

¼ cup mayonnaise
1 tablespoon sour cream
1 tablespoon vinegar
2 teaspoons sugar
1 cup pasta, cooked (any kind)
1 cup finely shredded white cabbage
3 tablespoons grated carrot
3 tablespoons diced green pepper

Make dressing with mayonnaise, sour cream, vinegar, and sugar. Add pasta and vegetables; toss lightly. Be sure all ingredients are well coated with dressing. Yield 4 or 5 servings.

pepper and pineapple slaw

1 sweet red pepper
1 green pepper
1 small firm cabbage
1 can (about 8-ounces) pineapple
1 teaspoon dry mustard
1 tablespoon lemon juice
About 1 cup mayonnaise
1 tablespoon sugar
1 teaspoon salt

Remove seeds and all pith from peppers; chop finely. Wash and dry cabbage. Cut into 4 portions; shred finely. Drain pineapple; chop.

550

Mix mustard smoothly with lemon juice; add with 1 tablespoon pineapple syrup to mayonnaise.

Mix peppers, cabbage, and pineapple in salad bowl. Sprinkle with sugar and salt; let chill until required. Add mayonnaise; toss lightly. Yield 5 or 6 servings.

pepper salad

2 medium green sweet peppers
3 large firm ripe tomatoes
Salt and freshly ground pepper to taste
½ cup olive oil
1 to 2 tablespoons red-wine vinegar
1½ teaspoons chopped chives
1½ teaspoons chopped parsley

Cut peppers in half; remove seeds and membrane. Cut into thin lengthwise slices. Slice tomatoes thinly. Arrange tomatoes and peppers in serving dish; sprinkle with salt and pepper. Pour oil evenly over all. Sprinkle vinegar, chives, and parsley over top. Yield about 4 servings.

red sweet pepper salad

6 large red sweet peppers
1 cup brown rice
1 (3-ounce) package cream cheese
2 tablespoons minced green onion
¼ cup Vinaigrette Aux Fines Herbes (see Index)
Salt and freshly ground pepper to taste
6 small thin onion rings
6 green stuffed olives
2 tablespoons minced chives
1 head lettuce
18 whole black olives

Cut tops from peppers; remove seeds and membranes. Rinse; invert on paper towels to drain.

Cook rice according to instructions for Basic Boiled Rice (see Index). Increase cooking time to 45 minutes or until tender; drain.

Dice cream cheese. Combine with rice in large bowl; toss lightly. Fold in green onion, vinaigrette, salt, and pepper. Spoon into pepper shells; place onion ring on top of each. Place green olive in center of each onion ring. Sprinkle with chives; chill until ready to serve. Arrange on beds of lettuce; garnish each serving with 3 ripe olives. Yield 6 servings.

ratatouille salad

2 eggplants
Little coarse salt
About ½ cup olive oil

red sweet pepper salad

ratatouille salad

1 onion, peeled, chopped
1 large red pepper, seeded, cut into small pieces
4 tomatoes, peeled, chopped
2 cloves garlic, crushed
12 coriander seeds
Chopped basil or parsley

Wipe and peel eggplants; cut into ½-inch squares. Put into colander; sprinkle with salt; let drain.

Heat some oil in skillet; sauté onion about 10 minutes, until it begins to soften. Add a little more oil; put in eggplant and red pepper. Cover; simmer 30 to 40 minutes. Add tomatoes, garlic, and coriander; cook until tomatoes are soft and mushy, adding a little more oil if necessary. Adjust seasoning; chill. Drain off excess oil; sprinkle with basil. Yield 4 to 6 servings.

sauerkraut salad

1 large can (No. 2½) sauerkraut
1 large green pepper, finely chopped
1 large onion, finely chopped
2 carrots, grated, or 4 tablespoons diced pimiento
½ cup water
½ cup vinegar
1 cup sugar

½ teaspoon salt

Rinse sauerkraut; drain 15 minutes. Add green pepper, onion, and carrots; mix thoroughly.

Boil water, vinegar, sugar, and salt 1 minute; let cool. Pour over kraut mixture; let set. Longer it sets, better it is. Will keep indefinitely if refrigerated. Yield 10 servings.

soybean salad

3 cups cooked, drained soybeans
¼ cup minced onion
1⅓ cups crumbled feta cheese (about 10-ounces)
⅔ cup mayonnaise (do not use salad dressing)
Dash of freshly ground pepper

Combine all ingredients; chill several hours. Serve on crisp lettuce leaves. Yield 4 main-dish servings.

spinach salad

dressing
2 tablespoons vegetable oil
Juice of 1 lemon
1 tablespoon Dijon-style mustard
1 tablespoon grated Parmesan cheese
1 teaspoon sugar

1 teaspoon Worcestershire sauce
½ teaspoon salt
Dash of pepper

salad
1 pound or 1 (10-ounce) package fresh spinach
¼ pound fresh mushrooms, sliced
1 hard-cooked egg white, sieved or chopped
¼ cup sunflower seed

Combine dressing ingredients in small jar with lid; shake well; chill.

Thoroughly wash spinach; tear into bite-size pieces. Chill in tight plastic bag to crisp. Combine spinach and mushrooms in large bowl; toss with dressing. Garnish with egg white and sunflower seed. Yield 4 servings.

spinach salad with creamy mushroom dressing

1 (10-ounce) package washed, trimmed spinach, torn into bite-size pieces
12 strips bacon, crisp fried, crumbled
4 hard-cooked eggs, peeled, sliced
1 medium onion, sliced into rings

Assemble these in layers in large salad bowl. Salt and pepper to taste. Pour dressing over; toss gently. Yield 4 servings.

creamy mushroom salad dressing
1 can cream of mushroom soup
¼ cup tarragon vinegar
1½ teaspoons sugar
¼ cup water
¼ teaspoon celery seed
¼ teaspoon marjoram
1 teaspoon dry mustard
Salt and pepper to taste
Dash of Worcestershire Sauce

Beat ingredients together; heat. Stir smooth; cool.

spinach salad with feta cheese

1 pound raw spinach
2 hard-boiled eggs, sliced
1 tomato, cut into edges
½ medium onion, thinly sliced
½ cup crumbled feta cheese

salad dressing
6 tablespoons olive oil
2 tablespoons wine vinegar
½ teaspoon oregano
½ teaspoon salt
¼ teaspoon pepper

Wash spinach well. Pick over; discard brown or damaged leaves. Remove stems; break into pieces in large salad bowl. Add eggs, tomato, onion, and cheese.

Combine dressing ingredients; shake well. Pour over salad. Toss well; serve. Yield 4 to 6 servings.

spring salad

2 kohlrabi, coarsely grated or finely diced
½ pound carrots, coarsely grated or cut into fine strips
1 unpeeled cucumber, thinly sliced
12 radishes, thinly sliced
Watercress (small bunch, if available), chopped

salad dressing
1 cup plain yogurt
1 tablespoon lemon juice
1 to 2 tablespoons honey
Lettuce leaves
1 hard-cooked egg, cut into wedges (garnish)

Combine kohlrabi, carrots, cucumber, radishes, and watercress.

Blend together dressing ingredients; pour over vegetables. Place salad on bed of lettuce; garnish with wedges of egg. Yield 4 servings.

stuffed tomatoes

8 firm ripe tomatoes
2 ripe avocado pears
Juice of 1 lemon
1 tablespoon onion juice

spring salad

tomato-accordion and shrimp salad

Salt
Black pepper
Pinch of chili powder
4 tablespoons finely chopped celery or green
  pepper
1 tablespoon finely chopped parsley

Plunge tomatoes into boiling water ½ minute, then in cold water; peel. Cut in half crossways; remove seeds and pulp. Cover loosely with foil; chill in refrigerator until required.

Peel avocados; remove seed. Mash well with wooden spoon. Add lemon juice, onion juice, salt, pepper, chili powder, and celery; set aside to chill. When ready to use, fill tomato halves with avocado mixture; sprinkle with parsley. Yield 4 servings.

tomato-accordion and shrimp salad

6 firm tomatoes
6 hard-boiled eggs, sliced
Lettuce leaves
1 cup diced boiled shrimp
½ cup sliced celery
Fresh parsley
Mayonnaise

Cut thin slice from stem end of each tomato; stand tomatoes upright on cut ends. Cut 5 deep slits in each tomato with sharp knife; fill slits with egg slices.

Line large platter with lettuce; arrange tomatoes on lettuce.

Toss shrimp with celery; mound in center of

tomato stacked salad

warsaw salad

platter. Garnish with parsley; serve with mayonnaise. Yield 6 servings.

tomato stacked salad

3 cups chopped fresh tomatoes
2 cups chopped onions
1 cup whole pitted black olives
1 cup chopped green sweet peppers
1 tablespoon sliced black olives
1 recipe Vinaigrette Aux Fines Herbes (see Index)

Place 1 cup tomatoes in tall, narrow serving container. Add ½ cup onions, then ½ cup whole olives. Place ½ cup peppers over olives; add ½ cup onions. Add 1 cup tomatoes, then ½ cup onions. Place remaining whole olives over onions; add remaining green peppers. Add remaining onions; place remaining tomatoes on top. Garnish with sliced olives. Pour vinaigrette over tomato mixture; cover. Chill overnight. Remove cover; drain tomato mixture just before serving. Yield 8 to 10 servings.

warsaw salad

2 medium-size cucumbers
6 large white radishes
2 Delicious apples
½ cup sour cream
2 tablespoons lemon juice

1 tablespoon finely chopped fresh parsley
1 teaspoon black pepper, peppermill-ground

Wash cucumbers and radishes thoroughly; slice paper-thin; combine.

Wash apples; core; slice thin. Add to vegetables; toss to mix.

Combine sour cream and lemon juice.

To serve, place vegetable and fruit mixture in serving bowl; top with dressing. Garnish salad with chopped parsley and freshly ground black pepper. Yield 4 servings.

zucchini salad

3 medium zucchini
1 medium onion, sliced, separated into rings
Juice of 2 lemons (3 tablespoons)
½ cup olive oil
¼ teaspoon oregano
¾ teaspoon salt
Chopped parsley

Wash zucchini well under cold running water. Trim off stem; slice very thin. Place in large bowl; cover with boiling water. Let stand 5 minutes: drain well. Return to bowl; add onion.

Combine the lemon juice, oil, oregano, and salt; pour over zucchini. Mix gently; marinate several hours before serving. Garnish with chopped parsley. Yield 4 servings.

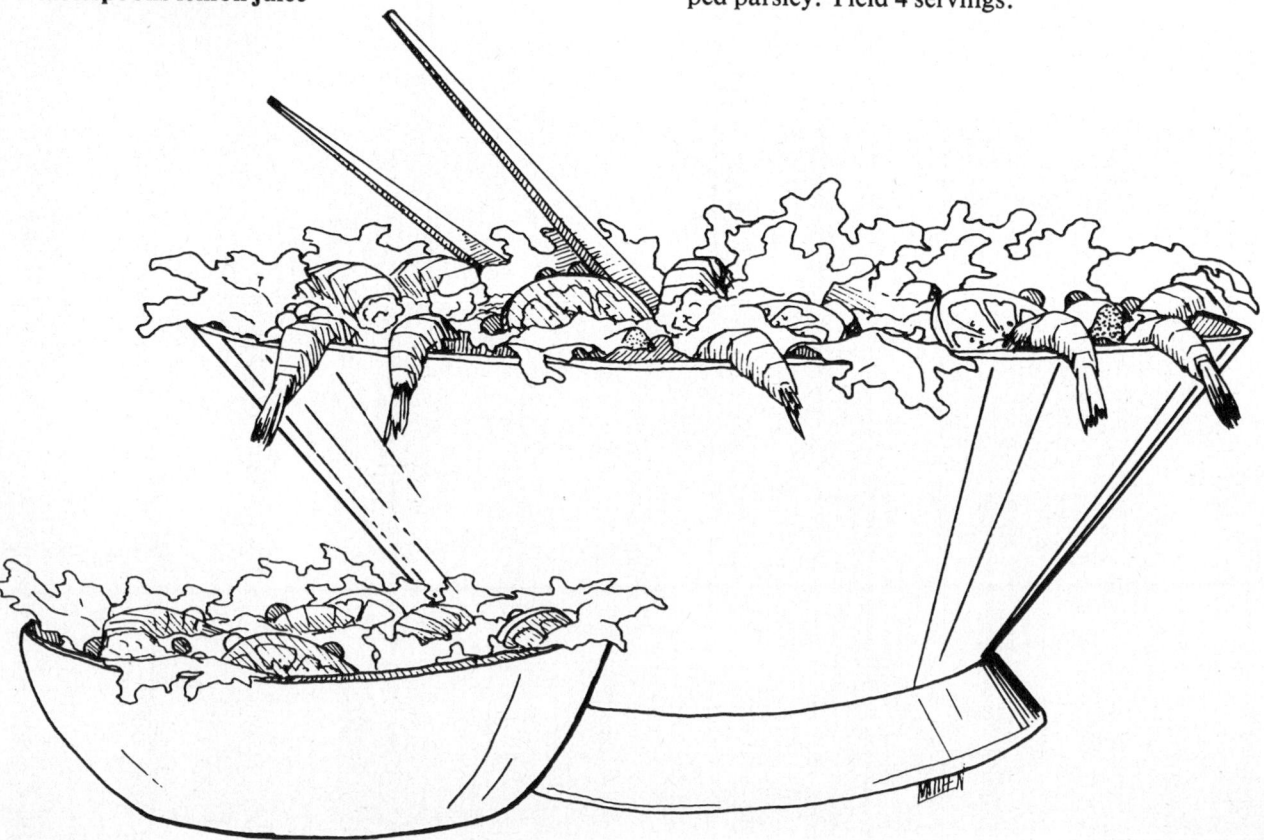

SANDWICHES

chilled pinwheels

1 loaf close-textured bread
Creamed butter, softened cheese, or any very
  smooth spread
Green-pepper strips
Pimiento strips
About 4 stuffed olives (optional)
Soft butter

Remove crusts from top and sides of bread. With sharp knife, cut bread lengthwise in slices $1/8$ to $1/4$ inch thick; discard bottom crust. Spread long slices of bread with creamed butter. Lay alternating strips of green pepper and pimiento crosswise, 1 inch apart, over entire strip of bread; or lay olives lengthwise on one end of bread. Beginning at one end, roll bread as for jelly roll. Spread a little soft butter on last lap of bread to make it stick; wrap rolls in waxed paper. Place in refrigerator to chill. When ready to serve, slice about $1/4$ inch thick. Yield 6 servings.

giant hero sandwich

1 (3-ounce) package cream cheese, softened
Mayonnaise
1 long loaf French bread
Prepared mustard
Ham slices
Salami slices
Sliced cooked pork
Bologna slices
Liver-sausage slices
Swiss-cheese slices
Fresh tomato wedges
Green and ripe olives
Small pickled onions
Gherkins
Endive
Watercress

Place cream cheese in small bowl; stir in enough mayonnaise to make smooth mixture of spreading consistency.

Cut bread in half lengthwise; spread each half with cheese mixture, then mustard. Arrange remaining ingredients on bottom half of bread; place top half over filling. Cut diagonally into 6 pieces to serve. Yield 6 servings.

greek meat pockets

$1/4$ cup oil
1 onion, finely chopped
1 garlic clove, chopped
1 small eggplant, peeled, cut into 1-inch cubes
1 large tomato, chopped
1 cup tomato juice
$1/4$ teaspoon crumbled oregano
Salt and pepper to taste
3 cups thinly sliced leftover meat (beef, lamb, or pork)
8 Mid-East pocket breads

giant hero sandwich

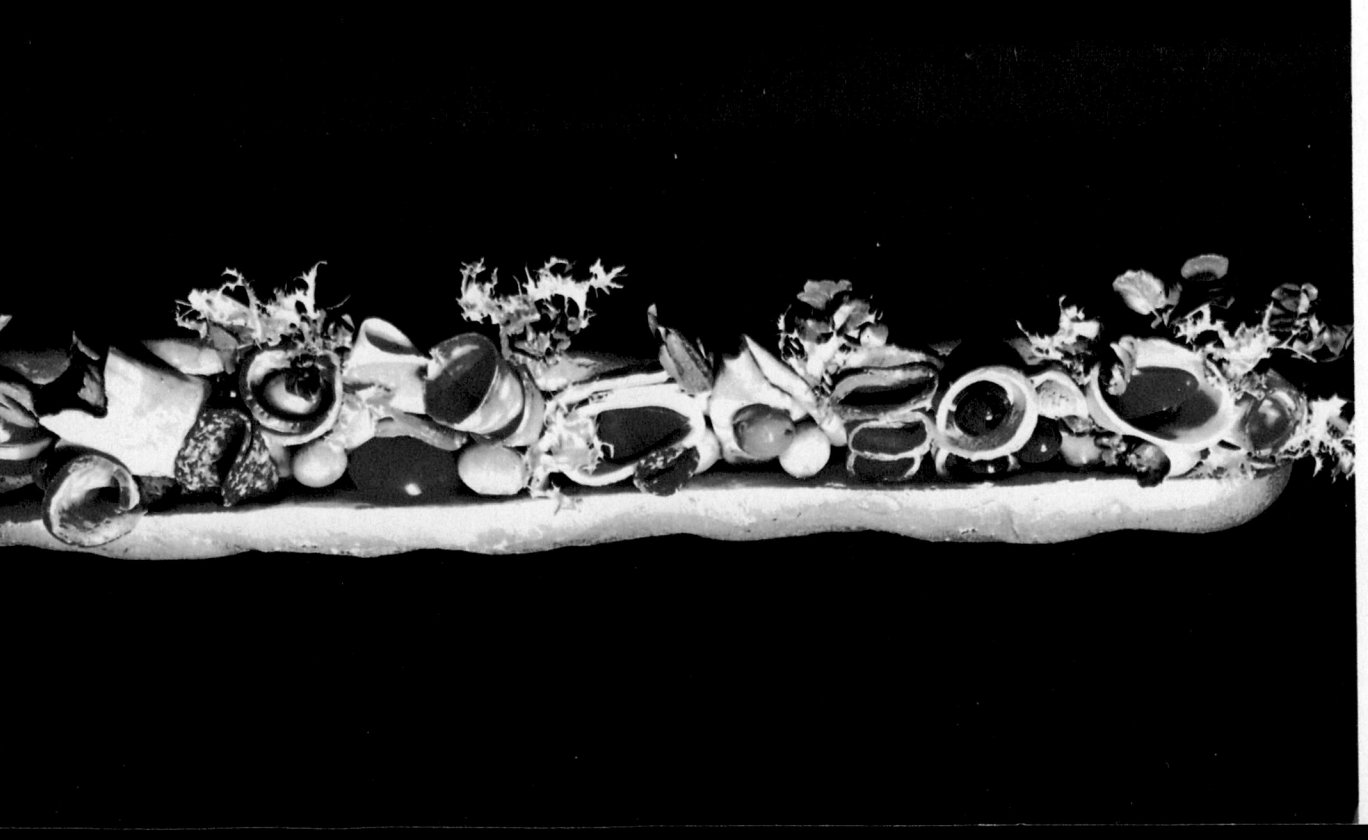

½ cup finely crumbled feta or farmer cheese

Heat oil in skillet; sauté onion and garlic 5 minutes. Add eggplant and tomato; stir over high heat until tomatoes are mushy. Stir in tomato juice and oregano. Add salt and pepper; cover. Simmer 15 to 20 minutes, until eggplant is tender and mixture thick. Add meat; stir over low heat until hot and bubbly. Heat in 400°F oven 5 minutes, if desired. Cut ¼-inch piece from top of each pocket; open. Fill with hot mixture; sprinkle with crumbled cheese. Yield 8 servings.

grilled peanut butter–cheese sandwiches

¾ cup peanut butter
12 slices bread
6 thin slices cheese
Margarine or butter for browning

Spread peanut butter on 6 slices of bread. Top each with slice of cheese. Cover with another slice of bread.

Spread a little margarine in heated fry pan. Put sandwiches in pan. Cook over low heat until cheese melts and sandwiches are browned on one side. Turn sandwiches; put a little more margarine under each. Brown other side. Yield 6 sandwiches.

ham sandwich loaf

1 loaf uncut bread
½ pound cooked ham, chopped
1 can (about 3½ ounces) pimientos, drained, chopped
Mayonnaise
1 cup sweet pickle
2 hard-boiled eggs
Butter
1 to 1½ cups cream cheese

Remove all crusts from bread; and cut lengthwise into 4 equally thick slices.

Combine ham and pimientos; add enough mayonnaise to make spreadable paste.

Chop pickle and eggs together; moisten with mayonnaise.

Spread 1 slice of bread with butter, then with half the ham mixture. Butter both sides of second slice of bread; press over first slice. Spread with egg mixture. Butter both sides of third slice of bread; press on top of egg mixture; spread with remaining ham mixture. Butter bottom of top slice; press into position. Place reshaped loaf onto serving platter; spread top and sides with thick layer of cream cheese. If this does not spread easily, soften with a little cream or milk. Refrigerate 3 to 4 hours; cut through in slices. Yield 7 or 8 servings.

monte cristo sandwich

8 slices bread
2 eggs
½ cup milk
½ teaspoon salt
Pinch of pepper
Sliced breast of chicken or turkey
4 slices cooked ham
4 slices Swiss cheese
Prepared mustard
Butter for frying

Cut crusts from bread.

Beat eggs, milk, salt, and pepper together; dip bread slices in mixture. Let soak well; drain. Arrange some thin slices of chicken on 4 bread slices. Cover with slice of ham; top with slice of cheese. Spread lightly with mustard; cover each with another slice of bread. Press down well; cut across diagonally.

Heat butter in skillet; fry sandwiches until brown and crisp; turn once. Serve hot. Yield 4 servings.

ham sandwich loaf

1 teaspoon horseradish
1 tablespoon catsup
2 tablespoons orange juice
1 tablespoon brandy
Salt and pepper to taste

topping
2 hard-cooked eggs, sliced or cut into wedges
2 medium tomatoes, sliced
8 canned pineapple chunks
2 maraschino cherries, halved

Top toast slices with lettuce. Arrange chicken on top.

Combine dressing ingredients; pour over chicken. Garnish each sandwich with egg, tomato, pineapple, and half a cherry. Serve at once. Yield 4 servings.

pizza burgers

1½ pounds ground beef
½ cup chopped onion
¾ teaspoon garlic salt
¼ teaspoon pepper

sauce
2 cups peeled Italian-style tomatoes, broken up with fork
1 (8-ounce) can tomato sauce
¼ cup chopped canned mushrooms
1 teaspoon crumbled dried oregano
6 large French rolls, split (or small individual French bread loaves)
8 ounces mozzarella cheese, sliced

Combine beef, onion, garlic salt, and pepper; form into 6 patties size and shape of rolls.

monte cristo sandwich

open-faced chicken-salad sandwiches

4 slices toast
½ head Bibb lettuce, thinly sliced
8 to 12 ounces cooked chicken-breast meat, thinly sliced

dressing
⅓ cup plain yogurt (can be part mayonnaise)

open-faced chicken-salad sandwiches

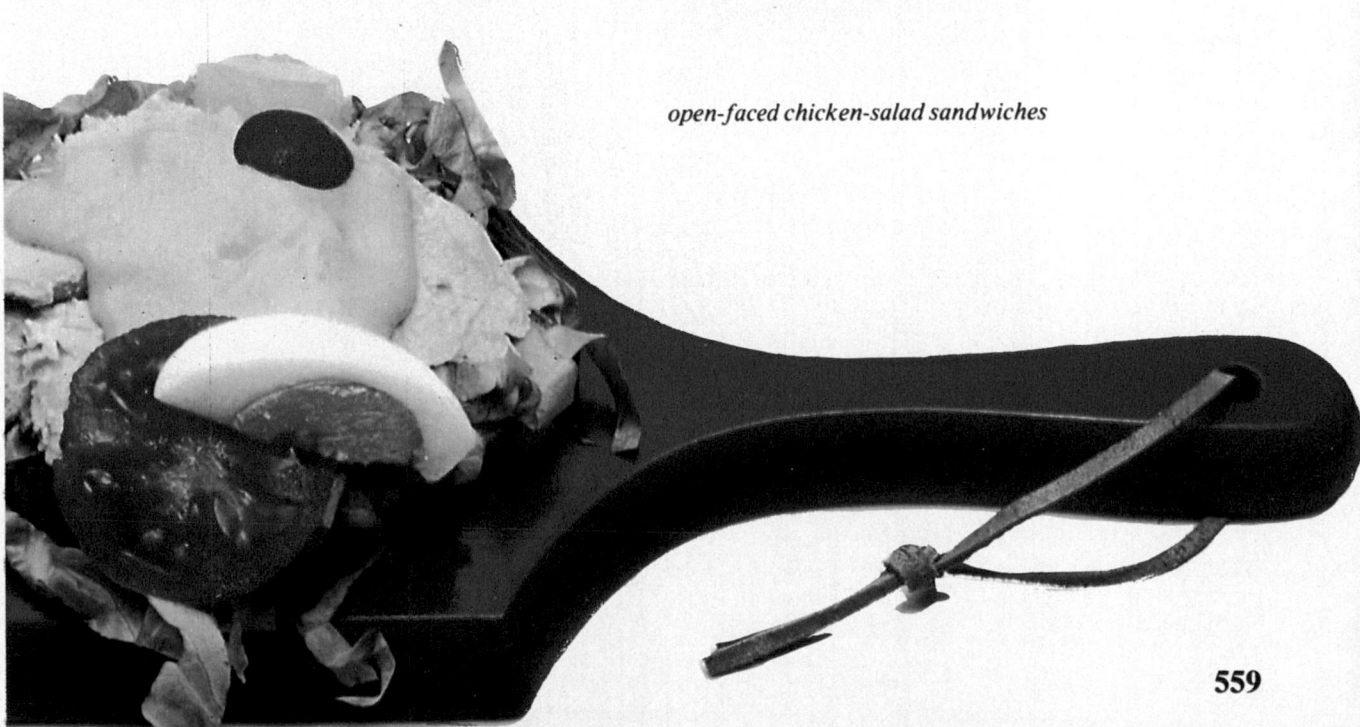

salmon and cheese rolls (hot)

Combine tomatoes, tomato sauce, mushrooms, and oregano in saucepan; heat. Broil burgers until done to taste; place on bottom half of rolls. Top with some sauce and cheese; garnish with additional tablespoon of sauce. Return to broiler until the cheese melts. Serve open-face or topped with other half of roll. Yield 6 servings.

salmon and cheese rolls (hot)

1 small can salmon
1 package frozen peas
1 small can evaporated milk
Salt and pepper
Lemon juice
4 hamburger rolls
Butter
4 slices American or processed cheese

Drain and flake fish. Add peas and evaporated milk; season with salt, pepper, and lemon juice. Stir over low heat until mixture is smooth and creamy.

Split rolls; spread with butter. Put slice of cheese on half of each one. Pile some hot fish mixture on top; cover with other half of roll. Serve at once. Yield 4 servings.

sardine, ham, and bacon sandwich

12 sardines
1 cup chopped cooked ham

2 tablespoons chopped sweet pickles
1 teaspoon prepared mustard
1 teaspoon catsup
1 teaspoon lemon juice
12 slices bread or toast
2 tablespoons shredded lettuce
1 tablespoon mayonnaise
12 slices broiled bacon

Remove skin and bones from sardines; chop with ham and pickles. Add mustard, catsup, and lemon juice; mix well. Spread on 6 slices buttered bread. Sprinkle with lettuce; dot with mayonnaise. Arrange 2 slices bacon on each sandwich; top with another slice buttered bread. Yield 6 servings.

spanish sandwiches

2 tablespoons chopped pimiento
2 tablespoons chopped onion
1 tablespoon butter
1 cup tomato juice
1 cup grated cheese
½ teaspoon salt
Dash of paprika
1 egg, well beaten
4 slices buttered toast

Sauté pimiento and onion in butter 5 minutes. Add tomato juice, cheese, salt, and paprika; cook 5 minutes or until cheese is melted. Stir small amount into egg. Return to hot mixture; cook 2 minutes. Serve on hot toast. Yield 4 servings.

sunday double-decker sandwich

sunday double-decker sandwich

8 slices white bread
½ cup butter
8 slices bacon, halved
2 teaspoons mustard (optional)
4 large tomatoes, sliced
1 cup chopped onion
8 slices American cheese (or 4 cups grated cheese)

Preheat broiler.
Remove bread crusts; toast bread on one side only. Spread untoasted side with butter; lay bacon slices on bread. Broil until bacon is cooked; spread with mustard. Place tomatoes on bacon. Brush with a little melted butter; broil a few minutes. Sprinkle onion over tomato; broil another minute. Cover with cheese. (If using grated cheese, make sure tomatoes are thickly covered). Broil until cheese bubbles. Pile one on top of another to make 4 sandwiches; broil again until top layer of cheese is well browned. Serve at once. Yield 4 servings.

tuna danish slim sandwich

2 (6½- or 7-ounce) cans water-packed tuna
1 cup coarsely grated cabbage
⅔ cup coarsely grated carrot
3 tablespoons low-calorie salad dressing
   (mayonnaise-type)
1 tablespoon catsup
1 tablespoon lemon juice
½ teaspoon salt
Dash of pepper
6 lettuce leaves
6 slices low-calorie bread, toasted
18 cucumber slices

Drain tuna; flake.
Combine cabbage, carrot, and tuna.
Combine dressing, catsup, lemon juice, salt, and pepper. Add to tuna mixture; blend thoroughly.
Place lettuce on toast. Place approximately ⅓ cup tuna salad on each lettuce leaf. Arrange 3 cucumber slices diagonally across each sandwich. Yield 6 servings.

SAUCES AND DRESSINGS

DESSERT SAUCES

basic chantilly cream

1 cup whipping cream
2 tablespoons confectioners' sugar
1 teaspoon apricot or peach brandy (optional)
1 egg white, stiffly beaten

Whip cream with electric mixer until stiff peaks form. Add confectioners' sugar, 1 tablespoon at a time, beating in gently. Add brandy, small amount at a time. Fold in egg white gently but thoroughly.

blueberry sauce

1 pint fresh blueberries
⅓ cup sugar
Pinch of salt
1 tablespoon cornstarch
2 tablespoons water
1 tablespoon lemon juice

Rinse berries; drain well.

Mix sugar, salt, cornstarch in saucepan. Add water and lemon juice; stir until dissolved. Add berries; bring to boil. Boil 1 to 2 minutes, until clear and slightly thickened; stir carefully to avoid crushing berries. Serve warm or chilled. Yield 1½ cups.

caramel sauce

1 tablespoon butter
2 tablespoons brown sugar
2 teaspoons Golden Syrup
2 tablespoons condensed milk
Pinch of salt
4 tablespoons hot water

Melt butter in saucepan. Add remaining ingredients, except water. Stir over heat until mixture is thick and turns rich caramel color. When mixture leaves sides of pan, remove pan from heat; add hot water, a little at a time. Return to heat; simmer 2 to 3 minutes; let cool. Serve with ice cream, pancakes, or cake.

flaming sauce of brandied fruits

2 canned peach halves
2 canned pear halves
2 canned pineapple slices
12 canned bing cherries
1 California orange
12 seedless grapes
2 cups syrup drained from canned fruit
6 tablespoons brandy

1 quart vanilla ice cream

Cut each peach and pear half and pineapple slice into 3 pieces. Halve cherries. Peel orange; remove all membrane; section.

Combine prepared fruit with grapes, syrup, and 2 tablespoons brandy; cover. Let stand at room temperature 2 or 3 hours. To serve, heat fruit mixture in chafing dish. Heat remaining brandy; ignite. Add, flaming, to warmed fruit and syrup. When flame dies, spoon fruit and syrup over ice cream. Yield 6 servings.

Note: Fruits can be varied to suit availability and taste.

fruit sauce

2 to 4 tablespoons sugar
2 tablespoons cornstarch
2 cups liquid from canned fruits
1 tablespoon lemon juice
1 cup crushed, drained, canned fruit (optional)

Mix sugar and cornstarch in pan. Stir in fruit liquid; cook and stir until thickened. Stir in lemon juice and crushed fruit. Serve hot or cold on pancakes, plain cake, ice cream, custard, or pudding. Yield about 2 cups without fruit, 3 cups with fruit.

hard sauce

1 cup butter, softened
1 (1-pound) box confectioners' sugar, sifted
¼ cup brandy

Cream butter with electric mixer until light. Add sugar gradually; beat until fluffy. Add brandy; blend well. Serve immediately. Store any remaining sauce in refrigerator. Bring to room temperature before serving. Yield about 3 cups.

calvados sauce

Omit brandy; substitute equal amount Calvados or strong cider.

hot-fudge sauce

1½ cups granulated sugar
½ cup brown sugar
¾ cup cocoa
¼ cup flour
½ teaspoon salt
1 (14½-ounce) can evaporated milk
2 tablespoons butter
1 cup water
2 teaspoons vanilla

Combine sugars, cocoa, flour, and salt in medium saucepan. Add milk, butter, and water. Cook over medium heat, stirring constantly, until boiling; cook 5 minutes. Cool; stir in vanilla.

lemon sauce

⅓ cup sugar
2 tablespoons cornstarch
⅓ cup lemon juice
1¼ cups water
½ teaspoon grated lemon rind
Pinch of salt
¼ cup butter

Combine sugar and cornstarch in small saucepan. Stir in lemon juice and water. Add lemon rind and salt. Place over medium heat; cook, stirring constantly, until thickened and clear. Remove from heat; stir in butter. Yield about 1½ cups.

melba sauce

2 cups fresh raspberries or strawberries
2 tablespoons water
2 tablespoons sugar
Juice of ½ lemon
1 teaspoon arrowroot or cornstarch
1 tablespoon cold water

Wash berries; place in small saucepan with 2 tablespoons water, sugar, and lemon juice. Simmer together gently 5 minutes; press through fine sieve. Return to clean saucepan; thicken with arrowroot dissolved in cold water. Chill before serving.

rhubarb–strawberry dessert sauce

3 cups 1-inch pieces fresh rhubarb
1 cup sugar
1 cup halved fresh strawberries
1 tablespoon cornstarch
2 tablespoons water

Combine rhubarb, sugar, and ⅓ cup water in saucepan; bring to boil. Reduce heat; cover. Simmer 5 minutes. Add strawberries; cook until strawberries are tender, 2 to 3 minutes.

Blend together cornstarch and 2 tablespoons water; add to rhubarb mixture. Cook, stirring constantly, until mixture thickens and boils; remove from heat. Chill in refrigerator until serving time. Yield 3 cups.

sweet cream-cheese sauce

3 tablespoons heavy cream
2 (3-ounce) packages cream cheese
1 teaspoon vanilla
1 egg white
2 tablespoons sugar
⅛ teaspoon salt

Blend cream into cheese. Add vanilla.

Beat egg white stiff. Add sugar and salt; fold into cheese mixture. This is good on fresh, frozen, or canned fruit, but is especially recommended on berries, stewed peaches, and baked apples. Yield 1½ cups.

Note: When topping is used on frozen strawberries, flavor with kirsch instead of vanilla.

vanilla sauce

2 cups milk
1 vanilla pod
3 eggs
4 tablespoons sugar
¾ cup stiffly whipped cream

Pour milk in small heavy saucepan. Add vanilla pod; heat to just under boiling point. Remove vanilla pod; wipe dry; store.

Beat eggs until lemon-colored. Pour small amount hot milk over eggs; stir constantly. Return to remaining hot milk in saucepan; cook, stirring constantly, over low heat about 20 minutes, until thick. Remove from heat; stir in sugar. Let cool; fold in whipped cream gradually.

One teaspoon vanilla extract can be substituted for vanilla pod. Add to custard after removing from heat.

GENERAL SAUCES

barbecue sauce I

1 teaspoon salt
1 teaspoon chili powder
¼ cup brown sugar
1 cup tomato sauce
¼ cup vinegar
1 onion, finely chopped
¼ cup Worcestershire sauce
1 teaspoon celery seed
2 cups water

Combine all ingredients; simmer slowly ½ hour. Use with any kind of meat; especially good with corned beef. Yield about 5 cups.

barbecue sauce II

½ cup butter
1 large onion, chopped
½ clove garlic, crushed
1 (14-ounce) bottle catsup
2 tablespoons brown sugar
1 tablespoon Worcestershire sauce
⅓ cup red wine vinegar
1 cup water
¼ teaspoon salt
¼ teaspoon pepper
½ cup cola beverage

Melt butter in saucepan. Add onion and garlic; cook over low heat about 5 minutes. Add remaining ingredients except cola; simmer about 20 minutes. Remove from heat; add cola. Excellent for meats and poultry.

barbecue sauce III

⅓ cup salad oil
½ cup finely chopped celery
1 small green pepper, finely chopped
¾ cup firmly packed brown sugar
¾ cup red-wine vinegar
2 tablespoons minced chives
2 teaspoons dry mustard
1 tablespoon Worcestershire sauce
2 teaspoons sea salt or table salt
1 teaspoon freshly ground pepper

Pour oil in small saucepan. Add celery and green pepper; simmer, covered, about 10 minutes, until vegetables are soft. Puree in blender. Add remaining ingredients; mix thoroughly. Can be stored in covered jar in refrigerator. Must be stirred before use, to blend ingredients. Use as basting sauce for barbecuing pork and chicken.

béarnaise sauce

¼ cup white vinegar
¼ cup dry white wine
1 tablespoon minced green onion
1 teaspoon dried tarragon
3 peppercorns
3 egg yolks
1 tablespoon warm water
½ cup butter
¼ teaspoon salt

Boil vinegar, wine, onion, tarragon, and peppercorns in small saucepan until liquid has reduced to 2 tablespoons. Pour liquid through fine sieve.

In top of double boiler, over just-simmering water, blend egg yolks and warm water until creamy. (Bottom of double boiler should not touch water.)

Melt butter over low heat. Add by ½ teaspoons to yolk mixture; beat well with wire whip after each addition. (Set bottom of pan in cold-water bath if eggs start to look like scrambled eggs.) After some butter has been added, up to 1 teaspoon butter can be added at one time. Leave white residue in bottom of butter pan. After butter is added, stir in vinegar mixture and salt. Yield about ¾ cup.

bouquet garni

1 parsley stalk
1 bay leaf
2 sprigs thyme
1 sprig marjoram (optional)

Combine all ingredients in small piece of muslin or double thickness of cheesecloth; tie securely with string.

brown sauce

2 tablespoons butter
¼ cup flour
4 cups Basic Beef Stock (see Index) or diluted canned bouillon
1 cup chopped tomatoes
1 cup Mirepoix (see Index)

Melt butter in small saucepan; blend in flour to make smooth paste. Cook and stir over low heat until mixture is browned. Add stock gradually, stirring constantly, until smooth. Add tomatoes; simmer 3 minutes. Add Mirepoix; simmer until sauce is reduced by half, stirring occasionally. Strain sauce through fine sieve; serve immediately.

buerre manié

A classic recipe used to thicken sauces and gravies.
2 tablespoons soft butter
¼ cup all-purpose flour

Combine butter and flour in small bowl; mix until well blended. Roll mixture into small balls. Drop into boiling liquid, one by one; stir constantly with whisk.

chili–horseradish sauce

1 cup mayonnaise
⅓ cup chili sauce
3 tablespoons prepared horseradish

Combine ingredients in small bowl; mix well. Chill before serving. Yield about 1½ cups.

chinese sweet-and-sour sauce

¾ cup sugar
2 tablespoons soy sauce
1 tablespoon dry white wine
3 tablespoons wine vinegar
3 tablespoons catsup
2 tablespoons cornstarch
½ cup water

Combine sugar, soy sauce, wine, vinegar, and catsup in saucepan; bring to boil.

Dissolve cornstarch in water; add to sauce. Cook over low heat, stirring, until sauce has thickened. Yield 1 to 1¼ cups.

chives butter

½ cup unsalted butter, softened
¼ cup finely chopped chives
Salt and freshly ground pepper to taste

Place butter and chives in bowl; beat until creamy. Add salt and pepper; mix well.

Cover top of small plate with plastic wrap. Place Chives Butter on plastic wrap; shape into ½-inch-deep circle. Refrigerate until hard; cut into circles with 1-inch canapé or cookie cutter. Remove plastic wrap from plate; push out circles from plastic-wrap side. Chives Butter can be kept in covered container in refrigerator at least 10 days.

clam sauce

2 tablespoons butter or margarine
1 tablespoon flour
1 teaspoon garlic salt
2 (8-ounce) cans minced clams with liquid
1 teaspoon parsley
1 teaspoon salt
½ teaspoon pepper

Melt butter in medium skillet on low heat; stir in flour and garlic salt with wire whisk. Add liquid from clams; continue to stir. Add seasonings; add clams last. Simmer 10 minutes. Good over cooked thin spaghetti. Yield 4 to 6 servings.

creole sauce

2 tablespoons vegetable oil
2 tablespoons chopped onion
2 tablespoons chopped green pepper
¼ cup sliced mushrooms
2 cups canned tomatoes
½ teaspoon salt
⅛ teaspoon pepper
2 to 3 drops Tabasco sauce
½ teaspoon basil

Heat oil; cook onion, green pepper, and mushrooms over low heat about 5 minutes. Add tomatoes and seasonings; cook until sauce is thick, about 40 minutes. Use with meat, fish, or poultry. Yield about 2½ cups.

curry sauce

¼ cup butter
⅓ cup finely chopped onion
¼ cup all-purpose flour
4 teaspoons curry powder
2 teaspoons sugar
1 teaspoon salt
¼ teaspoon ginger
⅛ teaspoon white pepper
2 cups milk
2 teaspoons lemon juice

Melt butter in medium saucepan over low heat. Add onion; sauté, stirring occasionally, about 5 minutes, until golden. Remove from heat.

Combine flour, curry powder, sugar, salt, ginger, and pepper; stir into onion mixture. Return to heat; add milk gradually, stirring constantly. Cook over medium heat, stirring constantly, until mixture comes to boil. Reduce heat; simmer until thick. Stir in lemon juice. Serve with poultry, rice, or potatoes. Yield about 1½ cups.

duk sauce and hot mustard

1 cup red plum jam
1 cup chutney
6 tablespoons dry mustard
¼ cup dry white wine

Combine jam and chutney in small bowl; blend thoroughly. Serve Duk Sauce hot or cold.

Place dry mustard in small bowl; stir in small amount wine until smooth. Add remaining wine gradually; blend thoroughly.

Serve sauce and mustard separately in small individual bowls. Yield 2 cups sauce; ½ cup mustard.

egg sauce

Grated rind of 1 lemon
1 tablespoon finely chopped parsley
2 hard-boiled eggs, chopped
Salt and white pepper to taste
1 recipe White Sauce (see Index)
1 tablespoon butter

Fold lemon rind, parsley, eggs, and seasoning into hot White Sauce; stir in butter. Serve with vegetables or seafood. Yield about 3 cups.

garlic butter

½ cup butter, softened
2 small cloves garlic, pressed
1 teaspoon finely chopped fresh parsley
½ teaspoon salt

Cream butter until light. Add remaining ingredients; mix until well blended. Store in refrigerator in airtight container until needed.

garlic sauce (pungent)

5 small cloves garlic, pressed
2 eggs
1 egg yolk
½ teaspoon salt
2 cups olive oil

Combine garlic, eggs, egg yolk, salt, and ¼ cup oil in blender container; cover. Blend about 5 seconds. Continue blending, adding remaining oil very slowly, as for mayonnaise. This is a thick mayonnaise-like sauce that can be served with pastas, vegetables, or bread. Yield 2½ cups.

génoise sauce

2 tablespoons butter
½ cup olive oil
1½ cups finely chopped onions
1 carrot, grated
½ cup finely diced celery
½ pound fresh mushrooms, finely chopped
1 pound ground veal
2 cups chopped skinned tomatoes
2 tablespoons all-purpose flour
¾ cup dry red wine
1 cup beef broth
Salt and freshly ground pepper to taste

Combine butter and oil in heavy frypan; heat until sizzling. Add onions; cook 3 minutes. Add carrot, celery, and mushrooms; cook, stirring frequently, about 5 minutes. Stir in veal; cook, stirring constantly, until well broken up and lightly browned. Add tomatoes; stir to mix well. Sprinkle flour over mixture; stir to mix well. Stir in wine gradually; stir in beef broth. Season with salt and pepper. Simmer about 2 hours, until thick; stir occasionally. Yield about 4 cups.

green mayonnaise tempura sauce

½ cup frozen spinach, thawed
1 tablespoon chopped fresh parsley
2 tablespoons chopped chives
1 teaspoon crumbled dried dillweed
1 cup mayonnaise

Drain spinach well; squeeze out any moisture. Place spinach, parsley, chives, and dillweed in blender container; process until pureed. Combine purée and mayonnaise in small bowl; mix well. Chill before serving. Yield about 1½ cups.

herb butter

4 ounces softened butter
1 tablespoon finely chopped parsley
1 tablespoon finely chopped chives
1 teaspoon dried chervil
1 teaspoon dried tarragon
1 tablespoon grated shallots or onion
Dash of pepper

Blend all ingredients; spoon onto sheet of waxed paper. Shape into roll about ½-inch in diameter; refrigerate until ready to use. Cut into 4 thick slices before serving. Yield 4 thick slices.

hollandaise sauce I

½ cup butter
4 egg yolks, well beaten
2 to 2½ tablespoons lemon juice
Pinch of white pepper
⅛ teaspoon salt

Melt 2 tablespoons butter in top of double boiler; pour gradually into beaten egg yolks, stirring constantly. Return to pan; place pan in or over hot water. Add remaining butter by tablespoons; stir after each tablespoon until melted. Remove from heat; stir in lemon juice, pepper, and salt.

hollandaise sauce II (mock)

3 tablespoons butter or margarine
3 tablespoons flour
1 cup milk
2 egg yolks, slightly beaten
2 tablespoons lemon juice
Salt and pepper

Heat butter; stir in flour. Cook 1 minute. Add milk; whisk until smooth. Remove from heat. Whisk in egg yolks; cook 1 minute. Stir in lemon juice; season to taste. Serve with asparagus, broccoli, or spinach. Yield about 1 cup.

horseradish sauce

½ cup plain yogurt (can be part mayonnaise)
3 tablespoons prepared horseradish
1 tablespoon orange juice
Salt and white pepper to taste
¼ teaspoon sugar

Thoroughly blend yogurt, horseradish, and orange juice. Season with salt, pepper, and sugar. Serve with beef or seafood. Yield ¾ cup.

italian meat sauce

¼ cup butter
½ cup olive oil
1½ cups finely chopped onions
1 cup grated carrots
½ cup finely chopped celery
2½ cups finely chopped mushrooms and stems
2 teaspoons finely chopped parsley
2 pounds lean ground beef
2 tablespoons all-purpose flour
2 tablespoons tomato puree
1 cup red wine
3½ cups beef broth
Salt and freshly ground pepper to taste

Combine butter and oil in large frypan; heat. Add onions; sauté 1 minute. Add carrots, celery, mushrooms, and parsley; cook, stirring frequently, 5 minutes. Crumble in ground beef; cook, stirring frequently, until lightly browned. Sprinkle flour over beef; stir until well blended. Stir in tomato puree. Add wine gradually; stir constantly. Add beef broth; season with salt and pepper. Simmer, stirring occasionally, about 1 hour, until thick. Serve with pastas. Yield about 5 cups.

italian meat sauce II

1 pound ground beef
1 large onion, finely chopped
1 green pepper, finely chopped
2 stalks celery, finely chopped
2 cups tomato sauce
2 cups cooked or canned tomatoes
1 teaspoon salt
¼ teaspoon pepper

Crumble beef in heated frypan; cook and stir until lightly browned. Add onion, green pepper, and celery; cook until tender. Add tomato sauce, tomatoes, salt, and pepper; cover. Cook slowly about 1 hour, until thickened. Serve over hot cooked spaghetti or macaroni. Yield 6 servings.

lemon cucumber sauce

1 cup mayonnaise
1 cup grated, drained cucumber
3 tablespoons lemon juice
½ teaspoon prepared mustard
½ teaspoon salt
⅛ teaspoon ground black pepper
2 tablespoons minced chives

Combine all ingredients. Serve over fish mousse, fish salads, or baked fish. Yield 1½ cups.

maître d'hôtel butter

½ cup softened butter
Strained juice of ½ lemon
Salt and pepper to season
1 heaped tablespoon chopped parsley leaves

Blend all ingredients in small mixing bowl. Shape mixture into round or square pat; refrigerate until ready to use.

marinade for beef

1 cup Burgundy
½ cup olive oil
2 parsley stalks
2 sprigs tarragon
2 sprigs thyme
1 bay leaf

Combine all ingredients in small container with lid; cover. Shake to mix well.

Can substitute ⅛ teaspoon dried tarragon leaves and thyme leaves for fresh tarragon and thyme.

marinade for fish

1 cup dry white wine
4 peppercorns
2 teaspoons slivered lemon peel
4 parsley stalks
¼ cup olive oil

Combine all ingredients in small container with lid; cover. Shake to mix well. Can be stored in covered container in refrigerator. Shake well before using.

marinade for game

¾ cup port
1¼ cups olive oil
3 sprigs tarragon
2 parsley stalks
1 large celery stalk, coarsely chopped
1 small onion, thinly sliced
6 peppercorns
⅛ teaspoon sage
1 teaspoon slivered lemon peel

Combine all ingredients in small container with lid; cover. Shake to mix well. Marinate game according to recipe directions.

marinade for lamb

Substitute Bordeaux-type wine for Burgundy in Marinade for Beef (see Index).

mirepoix (for brown sauce)

2 teaspoons butter
2 teaspoons cooking oil
1 medium carrot, coarsely grated
1 medium onion, coarsely grated
1 stalk celery, finely chopped
⅛ teaspoon dried thyme leaves
1 bay leaf, crushed
2 tablespoons sherry

Melt butter in small heavy saucepan; add oil. Add carrot, onion, and celery; sauté until soft. Add remaining ingredients; simmer until vegetables are tender. Yield 1 cup.

mornay (cheese) sauce

1 tablespoon butter
1 tablespoon flour
1 cup milk
3 tablespoons grated Swiss or Gruyére cheese
1 tablespoon grated Parmesan cheese
½ teaspoon mild prepared mustard, preferably Dijon-type
Salt and pepper to taste

Melt butter in small saucepan; remove from heat. Add flour; stir with wire whisk. Return to moderate heat. Add milk gradually; stir constantly until thickened. Add remaining ingredients.

mustard sauce

2 tablespoons Dijon mustard
1 tablespoon dry English mustard

1 cup whipping cream

Combine mustards; mix to smooth paste.

Whip cream in small bowl until soft peaks form. Stir small amount whipped cream into mustard mixture; blend well. Beat mustard mixture into whipped cream until just blended. Serve as dip for vegetables or for meat fondues.

rémoulade sauce

1 cup mayonnaise
1 tablespoon lemon juice
2 tablespoons finely chopped capers
2 teaspoons Dijon mustard
1 teaspoon minced parsley
2 teaspoons chopped chives
¾ teaspoon anchovy paste

Combine all ingredients in small mixing bowl. Stir gently with a wooden spoon until blended. Place in airtight container; refrigerate.

seafood sauce

1 cup mayonnaise or salad dressing
1 bunch watercress, chopped
1 tablespoon lemon juice
1 tablespoon minced onion
1 teaspoon Worcestershire sauce

Place all ingredients in bowl; mix well. Chill to allow flavors to blend. Yield about 2 cups.

shrimp sauce cantonese-style

¼ cup minced pork
2 tablespoons vegetable oil
1 pound cooked shrimp, cut into bite-size pieces
1 teaspoon grated ginger root
3 cloves garlic, grated
1 tablespoon Chinese black beans (dow sei), washed, mashed
1 cup chicken broth or water
1 teaspoon soy sauce
1 teaspoon salt
1 teaspoon sugar
2 tablespoons dry sherry
1 tablespoon cornstarch in 2 tablespoons cold water
1 egg, beaten
Scallion leaves, sliced

Stir-fry pork in oil until well done. Add shrimp, ginger, garlic, and beans; stir-fry briefly. Combine broth, soy sauce, salt, sugar, sherry, and cornstarch mixture; stir. Add to wok or skillet; heat until thickened. Remove from heat; pour egg in slowly, stirring with fork. Serve on rice; garnish with scallion. Serve with lobster. shrimp, fish dishes, or boiled rice.

Sauce must not be hot enough to coagulate egg as it is stirred in with fork. Purpose of egg is to color and thicken sauce slightly. Yield 4 servings.

tartar sauce

1⅔ cups mayonnaise
3 tablespoons chopped sweet pickle
3 tablespoons chopped stuffed olives
1 tablespoon chopped capers
1 tablespoon minced onion
1 tablespoon minced parsley
1 teaspoon vinegar
1 teaspoon lemon juice

Combine all ingredients; taste for seasoning. A little extra vinegar or lemon juice and a pinch of salt may be required, depending on kind of mayonnaise used. Serve with any fish or seafood. Yield about 2 cups.

tomato coulis sauce

2 cups chopped peeled tomatoes
⅛ teaspoon thyme leaves
⅛ teaspoon tarragon leaves
¼ cup chopped chives
1 garlic clove, pressed
¼ teaspoon freshly ground pepper
½ teaspoon salt
2 tablespoon olive oil

Combine all ingredients except olive oil in 1½-quart saucepan; simmer until tomatoes are tender. Turn into blender container; puree. Return to pan; add oil. Simmer 3 minutes. Serve hot or cold. Yield 2 cups.

tomato sauce I

3 medium-size ripe tomatoes, sliced
½ small onion
1 bay leaf
½ cup chicken stock or broth
1 tablespoon butter
1 tablespoon flour
1 teaspoon sugar
¼ teaspoon rosemary, basil, or oregano
½ teaspoon tomato paste (optional)

Simmer tomatoes, onion, bay leaf, and stock 20 minutes. Put into blender 10 seconds; pass through sieve to remove tiny pieces of tomato skins.

Melt butter; add flour. Add 1 cup strained tomato juices gradually; stir with wire whisk until thickened. Add sugar and herbs; simmer 5 minutes. Correct seasoning with salt and pepper. An excellent sauce for spaghetti and other foods.

Note: It may be necessary to add tomato paste in winter months when tomatoes have less flavor.

tomato sauce II

2 tablespoons olive oil
2 tablespoons butter
1 clove garlic, pressed
1 large green onion, minced
5 cups skinned, chopped ripe tomatoes
1/8 teaspoon freshly ground pepper
1 teaspoon basil
1 teaspoon chopped chives
1 teaspoon oregano
1/2 teaspoon sugar
1 teaspoon salt

Combine oil and butter in saucepan; heat until butter is melted. Add garlic and onion; cook over medium heat 5 minutes. Stir in remaining ingredients; cook, stirring, several minutes, until tomatoes are soft. Serve over pasta. Yield about 4 cups.

velouté sauce

1 tablespoon butter
1 tablespoon flour
1 cup chicken stock or broth
1 egg yolk
1 to 2 tablespoons whipping cream

Melt butter in small saucepan; remove from heat. Add flour; stir with wire whisk. Add stock gradually; stir constantly over moderate heat. Add about 3 tablespoons hot sauce to combined egg yolk and cream; stir together. Return to remaining hot sauce. Do not let sauce boil after egg yolk and cream have been added.

white sauce (béchamel sauce)

3 tablespoons butter
3 tablespoons flour
2 cups milk
3/4 teaspoon salt
1/4 teaspoon white pepper

Melt butter in top of double boiler over boiling water; stir in flour with wooden spoon until smooth. Add milk gradually; stir constantly. Cook until sauce is thick; stir in salt and pepper. Remove top of double boiler from water. Strain sauce through fine sieve; use as desired. Pour any remaining sauce into small bowl. Cover top of sauce with circle of wet waxed paper; refrigerate for future use.

For thicker sauce increase flour to 4 tablespoons. Yield 2 cups.

yogurt and green-onion sauce

1 cup yogurt
2 tablespoons finely minced green onion
2 teaspoons curry powder
Salt to taste

Combine ingredients in small bowl; blend well. Chill well before serving. Yield about 1 cup.

SALAD DRESSINGS

anchovy–cheese lo-cal salad dressing

2 cups low-fat cottage cheese
1 tablespoon lemon juice
1/4 cup skim milk
1/2 teaspoon salt
6 anchovy fillets
1 teaspoon paprika
1/4 teaspoon dry mustard

Place all ingredients in electric blender; blend until creamy. Use additional milk if thinner dressing is desired. Yield 2 1/4 cups.

blue or roquefort cheese dressing

4 ounces blue or Roquefort cheese, crumbled
1 cup sour cream
1 teaspoon lemon juice
1 teaspoon sugar
1 teaspoon instant minced onion
1/2 teaspoon salt

Mix all ingredients well. Chill, preferably overnight, to allow flavors to blend. Use within a week. Yield about 1 1/2 cups.

french dressing

2 tablespoons white-wine vinegar
Salt
Freshly ground black pepper
6 to 8 tablespoons olive and/or peanut oil

Mix vinegar with salt and pepper to taste. Add oil; beat with fork until mixture thickens.

Note: For slightly thicker dressing, add an ice cube; stir 1 to 2 minutes longer; remove ice.

caper dressing
Add 1 teaspoon chopped capers; 1/2 clove garlic, finely crushed; and a little anchovy paste.

curry dressing
Add 1/2 teaspoon curry powder and 1 teaspoon finely chopped shallots.

dressings

garlic french dressing

Add 1 peeled garlic clove, pressed or whole; let stand to blend flavors. Remove whole clove before serving.

roquefort dressing

Add 3 tablespoons crumbled Roquefort cheese; blend well. Chill before serving.

sesame dressing

Substitute sesame oil for olive oil.

tarragon dressing

Add 1 teaspoon chopped fresh tarragon leaves.

thousand island

Add ¼ cup chopped green pepper, 2 tablespoons chopped stuffed olives, 1 tablespoon chopped parsley, and 2 tablespoons chopped onion.

fruit-salad dressing

¼ cup currant jelly
1 cup mayonnaise
½ cup sour cream
¼ cup chopped toasted almonds

Melt jelly; allow to get cold. Combine with other ingredients; chill before using. Yield about 1¾ cups.

green-goddess dressing

1 cup mayonnaise
1 clove garlic, crushed
¼ cup finely chopped parsley
2 tablespoons chopped chives
1 tablespoon lemon juice

1 tablespoon tarragon vinegar
½ teaspoon salt
Black pepper
2 teaspoons anchovy paste
2 tablespoons cream

Combine all ingredients; stir until dressing is smooth. Use for all seafood salads. Yield about 2 cups.

herb salad dressing

½ cup plain yogurt
1 tablespoon lemon juice
1 teaspoon chopped parsley
1 teaspoon dillweed
Garlic salt to taste

Combine ingredients; pour over salad. Yield enough for 4 servings.

mayonnaise I

4 medium egg yolks
1 teaspoon salt
⅛ teaspoon white pepper
2 cups vegetable oil
1 tablespoon wine vinegar

Place egg yolks, salt, and pepper in medium bowl; beat with electric hand mixer at medium speed until thick, pale, and fluffy. Add 5 ounces oil in very thin stream, beating constantly, until thickened and oil is absorbed. Beat in vinegar. Add remaining oil slowly, beating constantly, until all oil is blended into mixture. Mayonnaise will be very thick. Place in refrigerator container.

Cut waxed paper to fit over top; rinse in cold water. Place over mayonnaise; cover. Refrigerate until ready to use. Yield 1¾ cups.

curry mayonnaise
Beat in 2 teaspoons curry powder.

mustard mayonnaise
Beat in 3½ teaspoons dry mustard.

paprika mayonnaise
Beat in 1 teaspoon paprika.

piquant mayonnaise
Beat in 1 teaspoon Tabasco sauce, 2 teaspoons heavy cream, and 4 teaspoons lemon juice.

tomato mayonnaise
Beat in 2 tablespoons tomato paste.

mayonnaise II

2 egg yolks
½ teaspoon salt
¼ teaspoon dry mustard
1½ teaspoons wine vinegar
1 cup olive oil

½ teaspoon lemon juice

Rinse bowl with hot water; dry well. Put in egg yolks, salt, mustard, and 1 teaspoon vinegar; beat vigorously or at low speed with an electric mixer. Add half the oil, drop by drop; and remaining vinegar. Beat in rest of oil in steady stream. Add lemon juice. Yield 1¼ cups.

Note: If mayonnaise curdles, break an egg yolk into clean basin; gradually beat curdled mixture into it.

mayonnaise III

1 cup salad oil
1 tablespoon red-wine vinegar
1 tablespoon lemon juice
1 egg
½ teaspoon salt
⅛ teaspoon paprika
¼ teaspoon dry mustard
Dash of cayenne pepper

Pour ¼ cup oil into electric blender. Add vinegar, lemon juice, egg, and seasonings; cover. Blend 5 seconds. Remove cover while blender is

herb salad dressing

running; add remaining oil in thin, steady stream. Turn off blender immediately after adding oil. Yield 1½ cups.

mayonnaise IV

1 recipe Mayonnaise (see Index)
Strained juice of 1 lemon
1 teaspoon dry mustard
1 lemon, sectioned

Place mayonnaise in large bowl.

Combine lemon juice and mustard in small bowl; stir until well blended. Fold lemon-juice mixture into mayonnaise until blended.

Chop lemon segments fine; fold into mayonnaise. Yield about 2 cups.

mayonnaise V

1 tablespoon prepared mustard, preferably Dijon
    or Dusseldorf
1 egg yolk
½ teaspoon Worcestershire sauce
1 teaspoon white vinegar
Salt and freshly ground pepper to taste
Several drops Tabasco sauce
1 cup peanut, vegetable, or corn oil
Juice of ½ lemon

Put mustard, egg yolk, Worcestershire sauce, vinegar, salt, pepper, and Tabasco in mixing bowl. Beat with wire whisk. When blended, gradually beat in oil. Add lemon juice; blend well. Add more mustard, if desired, to make mayonnaise more piquant. Yield about 1¼ cups.

russian dressing

1 cup mayonnaise
1 tablespoon chili sauce
1 to 2 teaspoons chopped chives
2 teaspoons chopped red pepper or canned
    pimiento

Combine all ingredients. Serve with egg or vegetable salads or with fish.

Note: Chili sauce varies considerably in strength. It is advisable to add about ½ teaspoon, then taste and increase quantity as necessary. Quantity given is for mild chili sauce.

vinaigrette

2 teaspoons salt
½ teaspoon freshly ground pepper
1 teaspoon prepared mustard
1 cup olive oil
¼ cup red-wine vinegar

Place salt, pepper, and mustard in medium-size bowl. Add several drops oil; blend with wooden spoon. Add several drops vinegar; blend well. Add remaining oil and vinegar gradually, stirring constantly, until all is used. Store in covered jar in refrigerator. Shake well before using. Yield 1⅓ cups.

vinaigrette aux fines herbes

1⅓ cup Vinaigrette (see Index)
½ tablespoon chopped onion
½ tablespoon parsley
½ tablespoon chopped tarragon
½ tablespoon chopped chives

Combine all ingredients in medium-size bowl; blend well with wooden spoon. Store in covered jar in refrigerator. Shake well before using. Yield 1⅓ cups.

Note: Fresh or dried herbs can be used.

zero-calorie salad dressing

½ cup wine vinegar
½ clove garlic, crushed
¼ teaspoon tarragon
1 tablespoon chopped parsley
¼ teaspoon oregano
¼ teaspoon salt

Shake well; pour over salad. Can be stored in refrigerator several weeks. Yield ½ cup.

vinaigrette

SAUSAGE

italian sausage with grapes

1 pound Italian sausage (hot and/or mild)
2 tablespoons butter or margarine
½ pound seedless or seeded white grapes

Prick sausage with fork; brown both sides in butter or margarine. Add grapes; bring to boil. Cover; cook 5 minutes. Serve with plenty of French bread and good Chianti. Yield 4 to 6 servings.

sausage and apple snack

1 pound sausage meat
2 tablespoons chopped parsley
½ teaspoon curry powder
½ teaspoon mixed herbs
Salt and pepper
2 tablespoons flour
Butter
2 dessert apples
6 thin slices bacon
Few sprigs parsley
Toast

Combine sausage, parsley, curry powder, herbs, and seasoning; shape into 6 patties. Coat lightly with flour; fry each side in butter about 5 minutes. Remove from pan; keep hot.

Core but do not peel apples; cut each into 3 slices. Fry each side about 2 minutes.

Roll up bacon; put onto skewer. Fry or broil.

Put patties on serving dish with apple ring on top. Arrange bacon rolls in center; garnish with parsley. Serve with hot toast. Yield 6 servings.

sausage pie

1 pound link sausages
3 apples, peeled, cored, sliced
2 tablespoons sugar
6 tablespoons butter or margarine
1 cup flour
1 teaspoon salt
1 egg, beaten
Milk

Preheat oven to 400°F.

Grease large pie tin.

Place sausages in skillet; prick each with fork. Cover with water; bring to boil. Simmer 5 minutes; drain off water. Brown sausages; place in pie tin. Spread apple slices over meat. Sprinkle apples with sugar.

Mix butter and flour; add salt. Stir in egg and enough milk to make stiff dough. Spread dough over apples, using fingers. Brush with butter (or some of egg). Make hole in center for steam to escape. Bake 25 to 30 minutes. Serve as is or with tomato sauce. Yield 6 to 8 servings.

sausages with braised red cabbage

1 red cabbage, about 2 pounds
2 tablespoons bacon fat or butter
1 large onion, chopped
3 tablespoons vinegar
Salt and pepper
2 cooking apples, peeled, chopped
1 tablespoon sugar
16 to 20 pork sausages

Remove and discard outer leaves from cabbage; shred rest finely.

Heat fat in casserole; cook onion few minutes without burning. Add cabbage; mix well. Add 1 cup water, vinegar, salt, and pepper; cover. Cook about 1 hour. Add apple and sugar; cook 1 hour, stirring occasionally. Remove lid; boil if necessary to evaporate extra liquid.

Broil or bake sausages until brown. Serve with cabbage and mashed potatoes. Yield 4 servings.

sausage and apple snack

CLAMS

baked clams in mornay sauce

1 pint shucked clams
Dry white wine
1 recipe Mornay Sauce (see Index)
2 tablespoons fine dry bread crumbs
1 tablespoon freshly grated Parmesan cheese
2 teaspoons chopped parsley
2 teaspoons chopped chives
Butter

Mince clams; place in saucepan. Add just enough wine to cover; simmer about 5 minutes, until wine has evaporated. Combine clams and sauce; mix well. Spoon clam mixture into scallop shells or individual baking dishes.

Blend bread crumbs, cheese, parsley, and chives; sprinkle over clam mixture. Dot with butter; place shells on baking sheet. Bake in preheated 350°F oven, 1 rack above center, 15 minutes. Yield 8 servings.

clam fettucine

¼ cup soft margarine
½ cup chopped onion
3 tablespoons flour
1 teaspoon sugar
1 teaspoon oregano
½ teaspoon salt
Dash of pepper
1 (1-pound) can whole tomatoes, undrained
1 (8-ounce) can tomato sauce
1 (8-ounce) can minced clams, undrained*
¼ cup sliced ripe olives
4 cups hot cooked seasoned noodles
¼ cup grated Parmesan cheese

Melt 2 tablespoons margarine in saucepan. Add onion; cook until tender, not brown.

Combine and mix flour, sugar, oregano, salt, and pepper; stir into onion mixture. Add tomatoes, tomato sauce, clams, and olives; cook, stirring constantly, until mixture thickens.

Combine noodles, 2 tablespoons margarine, and cheese; toss until noodles are evenly coated with cheese. Turn into deep serving dish; pour sauce over top. Yield 4 servings.

If desired, 2 (6-ounce) cans minced clams can be substituted for 8-ounce can, but 1 can clams should be drained to keep yield the same.

baked clams in mornay sauce

clam savory

Parsley flakes and paprika
Olive oil

Wash and scrub clams well to remove grit; place on baking sheet in 450°F oven until shells open. Remove meat from shell; chop. Reserve chopped clams; discard half the shells.

Heat oil and butter in small skillet. Add onion, pepper and garlic; sauté until tender. Remove from heat; cool. Add bread crumbs, bacon, oregano, cheese, and reserved clams; mix well. Fill clam shells with mixture. Sprinkle with parsley and paprika; drizzle with oil. Bake in 450°F oven until lightly browned (about 7 minutes). Serve hot. Yield 6 servings.

clam savory

3 tablespoons butter
1 small onion, peeled, finely chopped
½ green pepper, finely chopped
1 (7½-ounce) can clams, drained, chopped
1 cup grated cheese
1 tablespoon tomato puree
1 tablespoon Worcestershire sauce
1 tablespoon sherry
⅛ teaspoon cayenne pepper
Dill pickle
4 or 5 slices hot buttered toast

Heat butter in sauté pan. Add onion and green pepper; sauté 3 minutes over low heat. Add clams, cheese, tomato puree, Worcestershire sauce, sherry, and cayenne; cook a few minutes, until cheese has melted, stirring constantly.

Put thin slice of dill pickle on each slice of toast serve clam mixture on top. Yield 4 or 5 servings.

clams casino

2 dozen cherrystone clams
2 tablespoons olive oil
1 tablespoon butter
½ cup finely minced onion
¼ cup finely chopped green pepper
2 cloves garlic, peeled, chopped
1 cup dry bread crumbs
4 slices crisp bacon, crumbled
½ teaspoon crumbled dried oregano
2 tablespoons grated Parmesan cheese

pilgrims' clam pie

3 dozen shell clams or 3 (8-ounce) cans minced
    clams
1½ cups water
¼ cup margarine or butter
½ cup sliced fresh mushrooms
2 tablespoons minced onion
¼ cup all-purpose flour
¼ teaspoon dry mustard
⅛ teaspoon liquid hot pepper sauce
¼ teaspoon salt
⅛ teaspoon white pepper
1 cup reserved clam liquor
1 cup half-and-half cream
1 tablespoon lemon juice
2 tablespoons chopped parsley
2 tablespoons chopped pimiento
Pastry for 1-crust 9-inch pie
1 egg, beaten

Wash clam shells thoroughly. Place clams in large pot with water; bring to boil. Simmer 8 to 10 minutes, until clams open. Remove clams from shells; cut into fourths. Reserve 1 cup clam liquor. (OR: If using canned clams, drain and reserve 1 cup liquor.)

Melt margarine in skillet. Add mushrooms and onion; cook until tender. Stir in flour, mustard, pepper sauce, salt, and pepper. Gradually add clam liquor and cream; cook, stirring constantly, until thick. Stir in lemon juice, parsley, pimiento, and clams; pour into 9-inch-round deep-dish pie plate (about 2-inches deep).

Roll out pastry dough; place on mixture in pie plate. Secure dough to rim of pie plate by crimping; vent pastry. Brush with beaten egg. Bake in 375°F oven 25 to 30 minutes, until pastry is browned. Yield 6 servings.

pilgrims' clam pie

CRABS

astoria deviled crab

1 (6-ounce) package snow crab or other crabmeat, fresh or frozen or 1 (6½-ounce) can crab meat
1 (4-ounce) can mushroom stems and pieces, undrained
2 hard-cooked eggs, chopped
½ cup finely chopped green pepper
1 (2-ounce) jar pimiento strips, undrained
1 tablespoon catsup
1 teaspoon Worcestershire sauce
1 cup thick White Sauce (see Index)
1 (4¾-ounce) package or 2 cups crushed potato chips
¼ teaspoon salt
⅛ teaspoon pepper
3 tablespoons margarine or butter
¼ cup grated Parmesan cheese
Paprika
Lemon slices

Thaw crab meat if frozen. Drain canned crab meat. Remove shell or cartilage. Combine crab meat with remaining ingredients, except margarine, cheese, paprika, and lemon slices. Place crab mixture in well-greased baking dish, 11½ × 7 × 1¾ inches. Dot with margarine; sprinkle with cheese and paprika. Place lemon slices on top. Bake in 400°F oven 15 to 20 minutes. Yield 6 servings.

broiled crab cakes

1 pound lump crabmeat
1 teaspoon seafood seasoning, or 1 teaspoon dry mustard
1 teaspoon lemon juice
1 tablespoon finely chopped fresh parsley
2 eggs, well beaten

Pick over crab meat gently and carefully to remove shells and cartilage; do not break up lump meat. Add seasoning, lemon juice, parsley, and eggs; combine gently. Form into medium-size cakes; place in lightly buttered flat pan. Place under broiler; cook until golden brown, turning once. Serve on salted flat crackers. Yield 4 servings.

company crab

1 pound blue-crab meat, pasteurized
1 (15-ounce) can artichoke hearts, drained
1 (4-ounce) can sliced mushrooms, drained
2 tablespoons butter or margarine
2½ tablespoons flour
½ teaspoon salt
Dash of cayenne pepper
1 cup half-and-half cream
2 tablespoons sherry
2 tablespoons cereal crumbs
1 tablespoon grated Parmesan cheese
Paprika

Remove shell or cartilage from crab meat.

Cut artichoke hearts in half; place in well-greased shallow 1½-quart casserole. Cover with mushrooms and crab meat.

Melt butter; blend in flour and seasonings. Add cream gradually; cook until thick, stirring constantly. Stir in sherry. Pour sauce over crab meat.

Combine crumbs and cheese; sprinkle over sauce. Sprinkle with paprika. Bake in 450°F oven 12 to 15 minutes, until bubbly. Yield 6 servings.

crab chops

1 pound blue-crab meat, fresh, frozen, or pasteurized
½ cup butter or margarine
¾ cup all-purpose flour
½ teaspoon salt
¼ teaspoon cayenne pepper
1 cup milk
¼ cup chopped parsley
¼ cup chopped green onion
2 eggs, beaten
2 cups soft bread crumbs
¼ cup cooking oil
Lemon wedges
Tartar Sauce (see Index)

Thaw crab meat if frozen; remove shell or cartilage.

Melt ¼ cup margarine in small saucepan; blend in ¼ cup flour, salt, and cayenne. Gradually stir in milk; cook and stir until thickened. Mix in crab meat, parsley, and onion; cover. Refrigerate 2 hours. Divide into 6 equal portions; pat and shape each portion into "chop" about 5-inches long and ½-inch thick. Place each chop in flour mixture; turn to coat both sides. Dip each chop into egg, then in bread crumbs to coat evenly. Refrigerate at least 30 minutes to firm coating.

In heavy 12-inch frypan, heat ¼ cup butter and oil until hot but not smoking. Fry chops over moderate heat until delicately browned on both sides, about 10 minutes. Serve with lemon wedges and Tartar Sauce. Yield 6 servings.

crab divan

3 (6-ounce) packages Dungeness crab meat or
   other crab meat, fresh, frozen, or pasteurized,
   or 3 (6½- or 7-ounce) cans crab meat
2 (10-ounce) packages frozen broccoli spears
2 tablespoons flour
1 teaspoon salt
¼ teaspoon pepper
1 tablespoon butter or margarine, melted
½ cup skim milk
¼ cup grated American cheese
1 (1-pound) can tomatoes, well-drained
2 tablespoons crushed cornflakes

Thaw frozen crab meat; drain. Remove shell
and cartilage; cut meat into 1-inch pieces.

Cook broccoli half as long as directed on package; drain thoroughly. Place in greased baking
dish, 8 × 8 × 2 inches. Spread crab over broccoli.

Blend flour and seasonings into butter. Add
milk gradually; cook over moderate heat until
thick and smooth, stirring constantly. Add cheese;
stir until melted. Stir in tomatoes. Pour sauce over
crab meat. Sprinkle with cornflakes. Bake in
400°F oven 20 to 25 minutes, until lightly
browned. Yield 6 servings.

crab-stuffed green peppers

4 seeded green peppers
1 (6½-ounce) can crab meat, cartilage and shell
   removed, flaked
2 eggs, beaten
1 medium onion, minced
2 stalks celery, chopped
2 tablespoons butter or margarine
3 slices bacon, crisp-cooked, crumbled
1 cup whole-wheat bread crumbs (2 slices)
1 tablespoon toasted wheat germ
½ teaspoon salt
Dash of pepper

Cook peppers in boiling water until tender-
crisp, about 5 minutes.

Combine crab meat and eggs in mixing bowl; set
aside.

Fry onion and celery in butter until onion is
tender. Stir in bacon, bread crumbs, wheat germ,
salt, and pepper. Add to crab meat mixture.
Divide mixture equally to fill green peppers. Set
stuffed peppers upright in flat baking dish. Bake
at 350°F 20 to 25 minutes. Yield 4 servings.

fried crab cakes

fried crab cakes

1 pound crab meat
1 egg yolk
1½ teaspoons salt
Healthy dash of black pepper
1 teaspoon dry mustard
2 teaspoons Worcestershire sauce
1 tablespoon mayonnaise
1 tablespoon chopped parsley
½ teaspoon paprika
1 tablespoon melted butter
Bread crumbs for coating cakes
Liquid shortening for frying

Lightly toss crab meat and all ingredients (except bread crumbs) in order listed. When well-
blended, shape into cakes. Roll each cake in bread
crumbs until coated on all sides.

Heat shortening in skillet. Fry crab cakes
quickly in hot fat until golden brown. Yield 4 to 6
servings.

stuffed blue crab

hampton imperial crab

1 pound backfin crab meat
½ tablespoon chopped pimiento
½ tablespoon chopped green pepper
1 tablespoon butter

heavy cream sauce
4 tablespoons butter
5 tablespoons all-purpose flour
1 cup milk
½ teaspoon salt
1 egg yolk
¼ teaspoon dry mustard
1½ teaspoons Worcestershire sauce
Salt and pepper to taste
1 cup mayonnaise
Paprika

Preheat oven to 375°F 10 minutes before crab is
ready to go in.

Pick over crab meat; refrigerate.

Sauté pimiento and green pepper in 1 tablespoon butter.

Make Heavy Cream Sauce. Melt 5 tablespoons
butter in heavy skillet. Add flour, milk, and salt;
stir until mixture is smooth and thick.

Combine sautéed vegetables, sauce, and other
ingredients, except mayonnaise, crab meat and
paprika. Mix in ¾ cup mayonnaise. Fold in crab
meat very gently so lumps will not break up.

Spoon into shells; spread rest of mayonnaise on
top each crab filling. Bake 30 to 35 minutes, until
golden brown. Sprinkle with paprika; serve at
once. Yield 4 servings.

soft-shelled crabs

4 tablespoons butter or margarine
2 tablespoons lemon juice
6 to 8 soft-shelled crabs, cleaned
1 tablespoon cornstarch
¼ cup water

Heat butter and lemon juice in medium skillet.
Cook crabs on medium heat until browned, 5 minutes per side; remove to heated platter.

Mix cornstarch and water; add to pan juices.
Stir until slightly thickened; pour over crabs.
Serve at once. Yield 4 to 6 servings.

stuffed blue crab

1 pound crab meat
4 teaspoons lemon juice
2 teaspoons salt
½ teaspoon freshly ground pepper
3 cups coarse bread crumbs
⅓ cup dry sherry
½ cup whipping cream, whipped
1 cup fine bread crumbs
¼ to ½ cup melted butter

Use 6 buttered crab shells for baking dishes if available or 6 buttered, individual ramekins.

Combine crab meat, lemon juice, salt, pepper, coarse crumbs, sherry, and whipped cream; mix well. Spoon into ramekins; mound tops. Sprinkle fine crumbs evenly over tops; drizzle generously with melted butter. Place on baking sheet. Bake at 375°F on middle shelf, about 15 minutes, until lightly browned. Yield 6 servings.

KING CRAB

king crab–celery (low-calorie)

2 (6-ounce) packages king crab or other crab meat, fresh, frozen, or pasteurized, or 2 (6½- or 7-ounce) cans crab meat
2 celery hearts
2 chicken bouillon cubes

king crab–celery (low-calorie)

3 cups boiling water
1 cup low-calorie French dressing
6 large lettuce cups
Pepper

Thaw frozen crab meat; drain; remove shell and cartilage. Cut into 1-inch pieces.

Wash celery hearts; trim so they are about 5-inches long. Cut each into thirds lengthwise; place in 10-inch frypan.

Dissolve bouillon cubes in boiling water; pour over celery. Cover; simmer 10 to 15 minutes, until tender. Let celery cool in bouillon; drain. Place in shallow baking dish. Pour French dressing over celery; chill at least 2 hours. Remove celery from dressing; drain. Place in lettuce cups; sprinkle with pepper. Place approximately ¼ cup crab meat on celery. Yield 6 servings.

king crab krunch

1 pound king crab meat, fresh or frozen
1 (8¾-ounce) can crushed pineapple
3 tablespoons butter or margarine
½ cup thinly sliced celery
2 tablespoons cornstarch
2 cups chicken broth
½ cup toasted blanched slivered almonds
1 tablespoon lemon juice
1 (5-ounce) can chow mein noodles

Thaw frozen crab meat. Drain crab meat; remove shell and cartilage.

Drain pineapple; reserve liquid.

Melt butter in 10-inch frypan. Add celery, pineapple, and crab. Cook over low heat 5 minutes; stir frequently.

Dissolve cornstarch in pineapple juice; stir into crab mixture. Add chicken broth gradually; cook until thick, stirring constantly. Add almonds and lemon juice. Serve over noodles. Yield 6 servings.

king crab lancelot

2 (6-ounce) packages frozen king crab meat
1½ cups butter or margarine
1 pound medium noodles, cooked
2 cups freshly grated Parmesan cheese
Salt
Freshly ground black pepper

Defrost crab according to directions on box, only until pieces of meat are easily separated. Sauté chunks in hot butter until completely thawed.

Pour hot noodles into large bowl; add crab and butter. Add cheese; toss until well blended. Season to taste with salt and pepper. Yield 6 servings.

stuffed king crab legs

3 (12-ounce) packages precooked, frozen king
   crab legs
1 (4-ounce) can mushroom stems and pieces,
   drained
2 tablespoons melted butter or oil
2 tablespoons flour
½ teaspoon salt
1 cup milk
½ cup grated cheese
Paprika

Thaw crab legs; remove meat from shells. Remove cartilage; cut meat into ½-inch pieces.

Cook mushrooms in butter 5 minutes; blend in
flour and salt. Add milk gradually; cook until
thick, stirring constantly. Add cheese and crab;
heat. Fill shells with crab mixture; sprinkle with
paprika. Place stuffed crab legs on grill, shell-side-
down, about 4 inches from moderately hot coals
or place on baking sheet about 6 inches from
broiler. Heat 10 to 12 minutes. Yield 6 servings.

stuffed king crab legs

FROGS' LEGS

deep-fried or sautéed frogs' legs

deep fried
8 frogs' legs
Salt and pepper to taste
Flour
2 eggs, well beaten
2 teaspoons water
Cracker crumbs
Deep fat

sautéed
8 frogs' legs
Butter
Salt and pepper
White Sauce (see Index) (optional)

Only hind legs of frogs can be eaten. Cut off
feet; peel off skin, turning inside out. Wipe with
cold, damp cloth. Season with salt and pepper;
roll in flour. Dip in egg diluted with a little water.
Roll in cracker crumbs. (Can be dipped in fritter
batter instead, in which case omit flour and egg.)
Fry in deep, hot fat until golden brown, about 3
minutes. Serve with Tartar Sauce (see Index).

Can also be sautéed in a little butter without
egging or crumbing, in which case serve plain, seasoned with salt and pepper, or with White Sauce.

If desired, legs can be seasoned by soaking in
mixture of lemon juice, salt, and pepper 1 hour
before rolling in flour. Yield 4 servings.

frogs' legs with mushrooms

12 frogs' legs
½ cup mushrooms, canned or fresh
3 tablespoons butter
1 tablespoon flour
½ teaspoon salt
⅛ teaspoon pepper
1 cup milk
½ cup meat or chicken stock
2 egg yolks
1 tablespoon cream

Prepare frogs' legs for cooking according to
recipe for fried frogs' legs.

If fresh mushrooms are used, peel caps; cut off
stems.

Melt butter in pan. Put in legs and mushrooms;
sauté to light brown. Sprinkle with flour, salt, and
pepper. Add milk and stock; bring to boil. Cover;
reduce heat. Simmer 10 minutes.

Beat egg yolks with cream; add to pan. Stir well
but do not boil. Serve hot with buttered toast; garnish as desired. Yield 6 servings.

LOBSTER

boiled lobster

1½ gallons water
⅓ cup salt
6 live lobsters (1 pound each)
Melted butter or margarine

Pour water into large kettle. Add salt; cover. Bring to boiling point over hot coals or high heat. Plunge lobsters headfirst into boiling water; cover. After water has returned to boiling point, simmer 15 to 20 minutes, depending on size of lobsters. Test lobster by taking hold of a leg; if it detaches easily, lobster is cooked. Do not overcook. Drain; crack claws. Serve with melted butter. Yield 6 servings.

japanese steamed rock lobster

3 (8-ounce) packages frozen South African rock lobster tails
6 large mushrooms, cut into slices
6 scallions, cut into long, thin strips
1 cup thinly sliced celery
1 bunch broccoli, trimmed, cut into florets

boiled lobster

1 tablespoon soy sauce
1 envelope dehydrated chicken broth
¼ cup water

Remove thin underside membrane from lobster-tails with scissors. Push bamboo skewer lengthwise through tail to prevent curling.

Place colander over boiling water in large pot, or use steamer. Place lobster tails in colander; place vegetables on top and around tails.

Combine soy sauce, broth, and water; brush over tails and vegetables. Cover pot; steam 20 minutes or until vegetables are crisp-tender and lobster meat loses translucency and is opaque. Yield 6 servings.

japanese steamed rock lobster

lobster cantonese

2 tablespoons vegetable oil
2 tablespoons Chinese (dow sei) black beans, rinsed, mashed
2 cloves garlic, grated
1 teaspoon grated ginger root
2 to 3 ounces minced or ground pork
1½ to 2 pounds live lobster, cleaned, chopped into 1-inch pieces, or 1 pound lobster tails, split lengthwise
1 cup chicken broth or water
1 teaspoon soy sauce
½ teaspoon sugar
1 tablespoon cornstarch in 2 tablespoons cold water
Salt and pepper
1 egg, beaten
1 scallion, sliced

Heat oil in wok or skillet; brown beans, garlic, and ginger briefly. Add pork; stir-fry 1 minute. Add lobster; stir-fry 1 minute. Add broth, soy sauce, sugar, and cornstarch mixture; cover. Heat 5 minutes; remove from heat. Season with salt and pepper. Slowly pour in egg, stirring with fork. Sauce should not be so hot as to completely coagulate egg and turn it white; egg should give sauce yellowish color. Serve at once with rice; garnish with scallion. Yield 4 servings.

lobster imperial

⅔ cup ripe olives, pitted
⅓ cup butter or margarine
⅓ cup sifted all-purpose flour
1½ teaspoons salt
½ teaspoon paprika
3 cups milk
½ teaspoon Worcestershire Sauce
1 (2-ounce) can sliced mushrooms
2 cups diced cooked lobster, crab, or other
   seafood
¼ cup diced pimiento
¼ cup chopped parsley
Toast cups, patty shells, or cooked rice

Cut olives into large pieces.

Melt butter; blend in flour, salt, and paprika. Stir in milk and Worcestershire sauce; cook until mixture boils and is thickened. Drain mushrooms; add to sauce, along with lobster, pimiento, parsley, and olives. Heat thoroughly. Serve in toast cups, patty shells, or over hot cooked rice. Yield 6 servings.

lobster newburg

6 tablespoons butter
2 tablespoons flour
3 cups cut-up cooked or canned lobster
1 teaspoon nutmeg
Dash of paprika
1 teaspoon salt
3 tablespoons sherry
3 egg yolks
2 cups cream
Toast triangles

Melt butter over low heat in top of double boiler; stir in flour, lobster, nutmeg, paprika, salt, and sherry.

Beat yolks lightly in small bowl. Add cream; mix well. Slowly stir yolk mixture into lobster. Cook over hot water, stirring, until just thickened. Serve on toast or, serve in individual shells topped with buttered fresh bread crumbs and browned under broiler. Yield 6 servings.

lobster thermidor

4 live lobsters (1½-pounds each)*
1½ sticks butter or margarine
½ pound mushrooms, washed, sliced
1 tablespoon flour
1 tablespoon Worcestershire sauce
1 tablespoon chopped parsley
½ cup brandy
2 cups heavy cream
4 egg yolks
Salt and white pepper to taste
Parmesan cheese

Simmer lobsters in heavily salted water 15 to 20 minutes, until a leg detaches easily from body. Drain; cool. Crack claws; remove meat. Cut into small pieces. Remove everything from body and tail; reserve tomalley and meat. Cut meat into small pieces. Place clean shells on rack in open broiling pan; tuck tails under grid to keep from curling.

Heat 1 stick butter in skillet. Sauté mushrooms 2 minutes; stir frequently. Add flour; stir until it disappears. Add lobster meat, Worcestershire, parsley, brandy, and cream; stir until it barely reaches boiling point. Stir a little sauce into egg yolks beaten with tomalley; pour eggs into sauce. Heat well, but do not boil; season with salt and pepper. Fill shells with mixture. Sprinkle with Parmesan; dot with the remaining butter. Bake in preheated 350°F oven until bubbling. Yield 4 servings.

If live lobsters are unavailable, substitute 6 lobster tails. It will take 6 lobster tails to fill 4 shells.

south african rock lobster imperial

1 pound frozen South African rock lobster tails,
   thawed
2 tablespoons butter or margarine
½ cup chopped onion
2 tablespoons flour
1 (17-ounce) can cream-style corn
1 (12-ounce) can kernel corn, drained
¼ cup milk
1 tablespoon yellow mustard
Salt and pepper to taste
1 (10-ounce) package frozen patty shells, baked

With scissors, remove underside membrane of lobster tails. Pull out meat in one piece; dice.

Heat butter in saucepan; sauté onion. Add lobster pieces; stir until meat has lost its translucency and is opaque. Stir in flour. Stir in creamed and kernel corn, milk, and mustard; stir over low heat until mixture thickens and bubbles. Season with salt and pepper. Serve hot, spooned over patty shells. Yield 6 servings.

MUSSELS

baked mussels

Mussels
Salt
Pepper
Onion, chopped
Bacon strips
Grated cheese

Scrub mussels; open shells with knife, like

clams. Remove beard; lay in baking pan. Sprinkle with salt, pepper, and onion. Lay bacon on top. Sprinkle with cheese. Bake in 300°F oven until bacon is crisp. Yield about 8 mussels per serving.

scrambled mussels and eggs

Scrub mussels; open shells with knife. Discard beard; take mussels from shells; chop. Cook with scrambled eggs; allow 4 mussels per egg. Yield as desired.

OYSTERS

barbecued oysters

3 dozen large oysters in shells
Bread crumbs
Paprika
½ pound bacon, sliced thin

Wash oyster shells thoroughly. Open oysters; discard flatter shell. Separate oysters from curved shell, but allow each to remain loosely in shell. Cover oysters with bread crumbs; season with paprika. Cover each with bacon; place (in their shells) in one layer under broiler flame until bacon is cooked through. Serve in shells. Yield 6 servings.

broiled oysters

24 oysters
Melted butter
Dried bread crumbs
6 slices toast, cut into uniform pieces
Salt and pepper
Few drops of lemon juice

Dry oysters between towels.

Heat broiler; grease pan well.

Dip oysters in butter, then in crumbs; arrange on broiler. Broil about 3 minutes.

Moisten toast with hot oyster juice; place 4 broiled oysters on each slice. Season with salt, pepper, and lemon juice. Yield 6 servings.

fried oysters

1 pint oysters
Salt
Pepper
Flour for dredging
1 slightly beaten egg
½ cup cracker or bread crumbs

Pick over oysters, removing shell fragments; dry between towels. Sprinkle with salt, pepper, and flour. Dip in egg diluted with a little cold water. Roll in crumbs. Fry in deep, hot (375°F) fat 4 to 6 minutes. Drain on unglazed paper. Yield 4 servings.

opulent oysters

3 (8-ounce) cans oysters
1 (3½-ounce) can French-fried onions
¼ cup light cream
2 tablespoons grated Parmesan cheese
2 tablespoons butter or margarine

Drain oysters thoroughly.

Spread ¾ cup onions in well-greased round baking dish, 8 × 2 inches. Cover with the oysters. Pour cream over oysters.

Combine remaining onions and cheese; sprinkle over top. Dot with butter. Bake in 450°F oven 8 to 10 minutes, until lightly browned. Yield 6 servings.

oysters baltimore

4 slices bacon
18 oysters
3 tablespoons chili sauce
1 tablespoon Worcestershire sauce
6 tablespoons heavy cream
½ teaspoon tarragon
2 tablespoons lemon juice
1 teaspoon salt
¼ teaspoon pepper

Fry bacon until crisp; set aside to drain. Crumble into bits for garnish.

Pour off all but 1 tablespoon fat from skillet; add oysters with their liquid. Cook, uncovered, over medium heat until most pan juices are absorbed.

Mix remaining ingredients; add to oysters. Simmer no more than 5 minutes, to blend all flavors. Add extra seasonings if desired. Yield 4 to 6 servings.

oysters benedict

6 thin slices smoked ham
24 oysters

Sauté ham in frying pan until well browned. Pour drippings into another pan. Pan-fry oysters in drippings 5 minutes. Put ham on hot platter; top with oysters. Pour over Hollandaise or thick cream sauce; garnish with lemon slices. Yield 6 servings.

oysters casino

1 pint oysters
½ cup minced green pepper
½ cup minced green onion
½ cup minced bacon
1 tablespoon lemon juice
Pepper

Drain oysters; pick out shell fragments. Arrange on greased, ovenproof platter. Sprinkle with green pepper, onion, bacon, lemon juice, and

oysters rockefeller

pepper. Bake in 450°F oven about 10 minutes. Yield 6 servings.

oysters rockefeller

2 tablespoons chopped green onion
2 tablespoons chopped celery
3 tablespoons chopped fennel (optional)
3 tablespoons chopped parsley
¼ pound butter
1 cup watercress or spinach
3 tablespoons bread crumbs
3 tablespoons Pernod or anisette
¼ teaspoon salt
⅛ teaspoon white pepper
Dash of cayenne
2 dozen oysters on half shells

Sauté onion, celery, and herbs in 3 tablespoons butter 3 minutes. Add watercress; let wilt. Place this mixture, remaining butter, bread crumbs, liqueur, and seasonings into blender or food processor; blend 1 minute. Put 1 tablespoon mixture on each oyster. Place oyster shells on rock-salt beds; dampen salt slightly. Bake at 450°F about 4 minutes, until butter is melted and oysters heated. Yield 4 servings.

SCALLOPS

baked scallops

1 pound scallops
2 tablespoons chopped shallots or green onions
6 tablespoons butter
1 teaspoon lemon juice
⅓ cup fine bread crumbs
2 tablespoons chopped parsley

Wash scallops to remove sand; dry on paper towels. Place in 4 buttered shells or buttered casserole.

Sauté shallots in 2 tablespoons butter until soft; distribute evenly over scallops.

Melt remaining butter; add lemon juice. Pour over scallops; sprinkle with crumbs. Bake in preheated 375°F oven 12 to 15 minutes, until scallops are tender when pierced with knife. Serve very hot; garnish with parsley. Yield 4 servings.

broiled scallops

2½ pounds scallops
Corn oil
½ cup melted butter
Juice of 1 large lemon
3 to 4 tablespoons finely chopped green onions (scallions)

Prepare scallops; marinate about 1 hour in enough oil to coat all sides. Drain; put into preheated shallow pan. Sprinkle with salt and pepper.

Mix butter with lemon juice and onions; baste scallops continuously while cooking, about 5 to 6 minutes. Yield 6 servings.

deep-fried scallops with sweet-and-sour sauce

batter
1 cup sifted all-purpose flour
¾ cup water
1 large egg
½ teaspoon salt
2 cups oil for frying
1 pound scallops (cubed fish fillets can be substituted)

sweet-and-sour sauce
4 pineapple rings, cut into small pieces
Reserved pineapple syrup and water to make 1 cup
1 tablespoon cornstarch in 2 tablespoons cold water
2 tablespoons vinegar
¼ cup brown sugar
1 teaspoon soy sauce
1 small onion, sliced
Few strips each carrots and green pepper
2 cups hot boiled rice

Combine batter ingredients; beat just until smooth. Let stand 1 hour. Dip scallops a few at a time into batter; deep-fry in 375°F oil just until golden brown and done, about 3 to 4 minutes. Drain on paper towels.

Combine sauce ingredients in saucepan; stir constantly while bringing to boil. Heat until thickened and carrot and pepper strips are heated through.

Place scallops on bed of boiled rice; cover with sauce. Serve at once, while scallop batter coating is still crisp. Yield 4 servings.

point judith scallops

1 pound scallops, fresh or frozen
½ cup butter or margarine
1 cup sliced fresh mushrooms
2 tablespoons minced onion
2 tablespoons all-purpose flour
½ teaspoon salt
1½ cups half-and-half cream
4 egg yolks, beaten
½ teaspoon leaf thyme
¼ teaspoon basil leaves
½ cup fresh bread crumbs
⅓ cup grated Swiss Gruyère cheese
¼ teaspoon paprika
1 tablespoon melted butter or margarine

Thaw frozen scallops. Remove shell particles; wash.

Melt ¼ cup butter in skillet. Add scallops and mushrooms; cook 3 to 4 minutes, until scallops are done. Divide scallops and mushrooms among 6 individual shells or ramekins.

Melt ¼ cup butter in small saucepan. Add onion; cook until tender. Stir in flour and salt. Gradually stir in half-and-half; cook until thickened, stirring constantly. Add a little hot sauce to egg yolks; add to remaining sauce, stirring constantly. Heat just until thickened. Stir in thyme and basil. Spoon sauce over scallops.

Combine crumbs, cheese, paprika, and 1 tablespoon butter; sprinkle on sauce. Place shells on baking tray. Bake in 400°F oven 10 to 15 minutes, until hot and bubbly. Yield 6 servings.

scallop kabobs

1 pound scallops, fresh or frozen
1 (13½-ounce) can pineapple chunks, drained
1 (4-ounce) can button mushrooms, drained
1 green pepper, cut into 1-inch squares
¼ cup melted butter or oil
¼ cup lemon juice
¼ cup chopped parsley
¼ cup soy sauce
½ teaspoon salt
Dash of pepper
12 slices bacon

Thaw frozen scallops; rinse with cold water to remove any shell particles. Place pineapple, mushrooms, green pepper, and scallops in bowl.

Combine butter, lemon juice, parsley, soy sauce, salt, and pepper; pour over scallop mixture. Let stand 30 minutes; stir occasionally.

Fry bacon until cooked but not crisp; cut each slice in half.

Using long skewers, alternate scallops, pineapple, mushrooms, green pepper, and bacon until skewers are filled. Cook about 4-inches from moderately hot coals or broiler 5 minutes. Baste with sauce; turn. Cook 5 to 7 minutes, until bacon is crisp. Yield 6 servings.

scallops with bacon

1 quart scallops
½ pound thinly sliced bacon

Boil scallops, splitting large ones, in their own liquor or water until they begin to shrink. In baking pan place layer of bacon, then layer of scallops; cover with second layer of bacon. Cook in 350°F oven until bacon is crisp. Yield 6 servings.

SHRIMP

baked stuffed shrimp

1 pound extra jumbo or lobster shrimp
¼ cup milk
1 egg
½ cup bread crumbs
½ teaspoon paprika
1 pound lump crab meat
1 teaspoon Worcestershire sauce
Salt and pepper to taste
1 teaspoon Tabasco sauce
1 teaspoon mustard
1 tablespoon mayonnaise
2 slices white bread, cubed into small pieces
1 medium onion
½ green pepper, finely chopped
½ cup butter or margarine, melted

Shell uncooked shrimp; leave tail shell on. Split shrimp down back; spread apart, butterfly fashion. Dip uncooked shrimp into milk and egg mixture. Next dip in bread crumbs and paprika mixture.

Combine crab meat, Worcestershire sauce, salt, pepper, Tabasco sauce, mustard, mayonnaise, and bread cubes.

Sauté onion and green pepper in 2 tablespoons melted butter; add to crab meat mixture.

Firmly stuff breaded shrimp with crab meat mixture. Place shrimp, tail-side-up, on greased, shallow baking dish. Baste with butter. Bake in 400°F oven 30 to 40 minutes, until brown. Yield 5 servings.

beer-batter fried shrimp

2 pounds shrimp, shelled, deveined
1 (12-ounce) can beer
1 cup flour
1 tablespoon salt
1 tablespoon paprika
Dash of red pepper to taste
Fat for deep frying

Shell and devein raw shrimp.

Pour beer into large bowl. Blend dry ingredients into beer to make pancake-like batter. While using batter, stir from time to time. Thoroughly coat each shrimp with batter just before frying. Fry shrimp, a few at a time, in hot deep fat until golden brown and crusty. Drain shrimp on paper towel; transfer to hot platter. Yield 6 servings.

boiled shrimp

boiled shrimp

2 quarts water
1 tablespoon Worcestershire sauce
1/8 teaspoon hot sauce
10 peppercorns
1/2 lemon, sliced
2 teaspoons salt
2 bay leaves
1 small onion, halved
1 piece of celery with leaves

3 pounds fresh medium shrimp

Bring water to boil in kettle. Add all ingredients except shrimp; boil 10 minutes. Add shrimp; bring to slow boil. Cook, stirring occasionally, 5 minutes; remove from heat. Cover; let stand 15 minutes. Drain in colander; cool. Peel; devein. Use in recipes as instructed when boiled shrimp are needed. Boiled Shrimp can be served with hot garlic butter, a rémoulade sauce or other seafood sauces, if desired. Yield about 5 cups.

cantonese shrimp and beans

1½ pounds frozen raw, peeled, deveined shrimp
1½ teaspoons chicken-stock base
1 cup boiling water
¼ cup thinly sliced green onion
1 clove garlic, crushed
1 tablespoon salad oil
1 teaspoon salt
½ teaspoon ginger
Dash of pepper
1 (9-ounce) package frozen cut green beans, thawed
1 tablespoon cornstarch
1 tablespoon cold water

Thaw frozen shrimp.

Dissolve chicken-stock base in boiling water.

Cook onion, garlic, and shrimp in oil 3 minutes; stir frequently. If necessary, add a little broth to prevent sticking. Stir in salt, ginger, pepper, beans, and broth; cover. Simmer 5 to 7 minutes, until beans are cooked but still slightly crisp.

Combine cornstarch and water. Add to shrimp; cook until thick and clear, stirring constantly. Yield 6 servings.

curried shrimp

¼ cup butter
¼ cup flour
2 tablespoons curry powder
1 teaspoon salt
½ cup catsup
1½ cups canned milk
¼ cup sherry
1 pound shrimp, cooked, cleaned

cantonese shrimp and beans

Melt butter in frypan over low heat. Add flour; stir quickly. Add curry powder and salt; cook to thick paste. Add catsup; stir. Very slowly add milk; stir hard to prevent lumping. Add sherry; simmer slowly 5 minutes. Add shrimp; heat. Serve over rice. Yield 3 to 4 servings.

curried shrimp indienne

1½ teaspoons vinegar
1 clove garlic, minced
1½ teaspoons ground coriander
½ teaspoon salt
½ teaspoon turmeric
¼ teaspoon cumin
¼ teaspoon dry mustard
⅛ teaspoon freshly ground pepper
⅛ teaspoon ground ginger
1 small piece stick cinnamon
Dash of cayenne pepper

curried shrimp indienne

1 cardamom seed
1 bay leaf
1 pound fresh large shrimp, peeled, deveined
1½ tablespoons butter
½ cup chopped onions
½ green sweet pepper, chopped
½ cup Coconut Milk
1 tablespoon all-purpose flour
1½ teaspoons lemon juice

Combine vinegar, garlic, coriander, salt, turmeric, cumin, mustard, pepper, ginger, cinnamon, cayenne pepper, cardamom, and bay leaf in medium-size bowl. Add shrimp; mix well. Cover; refrigerate 2 hours.

Melt butter in blazer pan of chafing dish over direct flame. Add onions and green pepper; cook, stirring occasionally, until tender. Remove cinnamon stick, cardamom seed, and bay leaf; add shrimp mixture. Cook, stirring occasionally, 10 minutes or until shrimp are tender.

Combine Coconut Milk and flour; stir into shrimp mixture. Cook about 3 minutes, until sauce thickens and comes to boil. Stir in lemon juice. Serve with rice, Toasted Coconut, plumped raisins, peanuts, and chutney. Yield 4 servings.

coconut milk
½ cup milk
½ cup grated coconut

Combine milk and coconut in small saucepan; bring to boil over medium heat. Boil 2 minutes; strain. Use milk as instructed. Reserve coconut for toasting.

toasted coconut
½ cup grated coconut
1 tablespoon butter
2 tablespoons confectioners' sugar

Mix coconut with butter and sugar; spread on baking sheet. Bake in preheated 350°F oven 8 to 10 minutes, until browned.

french-fried butterfly shrimp

2 pounds large raw shrimp
1 cup sifted all-purpose flour
½ teaspoon sugar
Dash of curry powder
1 egg
1 cup water
2 teaspoons salad oil
½ teaspoon salt

Peel shrimp; leave tail on. Slit shrimp along back; remove sand vein. Flatten; make cut in back. Pull tail through; pat dry.

Combine dry ingredients; add egg, water, and oil; beat well. Dip shrimp in batter; fry in hot fat until golden brown. Remove to paper towels. Serve immediately. Yield 4 to 6 servings.

Note: For an appetizer, serve with chutney and lemon wedges. For main course serve with chili or tartar sauce.

marinated shrimp

2½ pounds jumbo shrimp
¼ bottle Italian dressing
Pancake mix
Garlic Sauce
Salt and pepper to taste

Peel shrimp; leave tails on. Place in bowl; pour dressing over. Marinate several hours in refrigerator.

Put pancake mix in paper bag; after shrimp have drained well, shake in bag for coating. Lay shrimp in large, rather flat pan; add salt and pepper. Spoon sauce over; broil each side 10 minutes. Yield 5 to 6 servings.

garlic sauce
⅛ pound (½ stick) butter
⅛ pound (½ stick) margarine
4 tablespoons minced parsley
2 tablespoons very finely diced garlic

Melt butter and margarine. Cut in parsley and garlic; mix well.

shrimp and asparagus

1 pound cooked shrimp, shelled, deveined
1 can water chestnuts, drained, sliced
1 medium onion, sliced
1 cup sliced fresh mushrooms
1 cup diagonally sliced celery
1 small can mandarin oranges, drained
1½ pounds fresh asparagus, steamed
2 tablespoons oil
¼ teaspoon salt
½ teaspoon freshly ground black pepper
2 tablespoons sugar
2 tablespoons soy sauce
Cooked rice

Prepare shrimp; set aside.
Drain and slice water chestnuts.
Arrange shrimp, chestnuts, onion, mushrooms, celery, oranges, and asparagus on large tray.

Heat oil in wok or skillet. Add onion, celery, salt, pepper, and sugar; stir-fry until vegetables are tender but still crisp. Add asparagus and shrimp; place water chestnuts and mushrooms over shrimp. Sprinkle with soy sauce; place orange sections on top. Cover; cook until mixture steams. Reduce heat; simmer about 10 minutes. Serve with rice. Yield 6 servings.

shrimp with cauliflower and chicken

1 tablespoon vegetable oil
1½ cups cauliflower, cut into florets, parboiled
  (cover with boiling water; let stand 5 minutes)
½ cup peas, fresh, or frozen and defrosted
1½ cups cubed cooked chicken
1 pound shrimp, cooked
2 scallions, cut lengthwise into thin strips

sauce
¾ cup chicken broth
1 tablespoon soy sauce
2 tablespoons chili sauce
1 tablespoon cornstarch in 2 tablespoons cold
  water
2 tablespoons dry white wine

Heat oil in frypan or wok; stir-fry cauliflower 2 minutes. Remove with slotted ladle; reserve.

Stir-fry peas 2 minutes; reserve with cauliflower.

Add chicken, shrimp, and scallions to frypan; stir-fry 2 to 3 minutes, until heated, Return vegetables to pan.

Combine sauce ingredients; add to pan. Heat until sauce boils and thickens. Serve with rice. Yield 4 servings.

shrimp creole

1 cup salad oil
1 cup flour
2 cups chopped onions
1 cup chopped celery
1 cup chopped bell peppers
2 cloves garlic, chopped
1 large can tomatoes
2 small cans tomato paste
6 cups water
3 teaspoons salt
¼ teaspoon red pepper
½ teaspoon black pepper
3 pounds raw shrimp, deveined
2 tablespoons chopped parsley
2 tablespoons chopped scallion tops

Heat oil; stir in flour. Add onions, celery, peppers, and garlic; cook until soft. Add tomatoes and tomato paste; mix well. Cook about 5 minutes. Add water, red and black peppers; simmer 1 hour. Add shrimp; cook 15 minutes. Add parsley and scallion 5 minutes before serving. Serve over rice. Yield 10 servings.

shrimp de jonghe

2 pounds fresh shrimp cooked, shelled, deveined,
  or 4 (4½- or 5-ounce) cans shrimp

shrimp de jonghe

shrimp in garlic sauce

¾ cup toasted dry bread crumbs
¼ cup chopped green onions and tops
¼ cup chopped parsley
¾ teaspoon crushed tarragon
¼ teaspoon crushed garlic
¼ teaspoon nutmeg
¼ teaspoon salt
Dash of pepper
½ cup butter or margarine, melted
¼ cup sherry

If using canned shrimp, drain; cover with ice water. Let stand 5 minutes; drain.

Combine crumbs, onions, parsley, and seasonings. Add butter and sherry; mix thoroughly. Combine crumb mixture and shrimp; toss lightly. Place in well-greased, shallow 1-quart casserole. Bake in 400°F oven 15 to 20 minutes, until lightly browned. Yield 6 servings.

shrimp with feta cheese

1 tablespoon lemon juice
1¼ pounds medium shrimp, peeled, deveined

2 tablespoons olive oil
¼ cup chopped onion
½ bunch green onions, finely chopped (use only part of green stems)
1 clove garlic, minced
1 cup tomato puree
¼ cup dry white wine
1 tablespoon butter
1 tablespoon brandy or ouzo
¼ teaspoon oregano
1 tablespoon chopped parsley
¼ pound feta cheese, cut into ½-inch squares

Pour lemon juice over shrimp; let stand while making sauce.

Heat oil in heavy skillet. Add onions (green and white) and garlic; sauté until limp. Add tomato purée and wine; let simmer 15 minutes.

Melt butter in another skillet; sauté shrimp until pink (3 to 4 minutes).

Gently warm brandy; ignite. Pour over shrimp; when flame extinguishes, add oregano and parsley. Transfer shrimp to small casserole (1½-quart).

Mix remaining juice from pan in which shrimp were cooked with tomato-puree sauce; pour over shrimp. Top with cheese; press cheese into sauce. Bake at 375°F 15 minutes or until hot and bubbly. Yield 4 servings.

shrimp in garlic sauce

1 tablespoon vegetable oil
1 small onion, chopped
1 teaspoon freshly grated gingerroot
3 cloves garlic, minced

shrimp with feta cheese

4 Chinese dried black mushrooms (soaked 30 minutes in warm water, drained, sliced)
½ cup peas, fresh, or frozen and defrosted
1 pound cooked shrimp
1 cup chicken broth
2 teaspoons soy sauce
1 tablespoon cornstarch blended with 2 tablespoons water

Heat oil in frypan or wok; stir-fry onion, ginger, and garlic. Mix in mushrooms and peas; stir-fry 2 to 3 minutes. Add shrimp; stir-fry 1 to 2 minutes.

Combine broth, soy sauce, and cornstarch. Add to shrimp mixture; heat until sauce boils and thickens. Serve at once over boiled rice. Yield 4 servings.

shrimp jambalaya

1½ pounds fresh shrimp, cooked, shelled, cleaned, or 3 (4½- or 5-ounce) cans shrimp
1 cup chopped green pepper
½ cup chopped onion
2 cloves garlic, finely chopped
¼ cup melted butter or oil
1 (1-pound) can tomatoes
1½ cups water
1 cup uncooked rice
½ teaspoon crushed whole thyme
¼ teaspoon salt
1 bay leaf
Dash of pepper
¼ cup chopped parsley

If using canned shrimp, drain; cover with ice water. Let stand 5 minutes; drain.

Cook green pepper, onion, and garlic in butter until tender. Add remaining ingredients, except parsley and shrimp; cover. Cook 25 to 30 minutes, until rice is tender; stir occasionally. Add parsley and shrimp; heat. Remove bay leaf. Yield 6 servings.

shrimp kebobs with barbecued rice

Allow about 6 shrimp per skewer
1 green pepper
1 sweet red pepper
3 or 4 small white onions
3 or 4 very small tomatoes (cherry)

marinade
½ cup oil
2 sprigs thyme
Juice of 1 lemon
Salt and pepper

Combine all marinade ingredients.
Shell and devein shrimp.

Arrange the kebob ingredients alternately on skewers, finishing with tomato; place in shallow pan. Pour marinade over; leave at least 1½ hours.

Cook over hot coals about 10 to 15 minutes, brushing frequently with marinade. Serve with Barbecued Rice. Yield 3 or 4 skewers, according to their length.

barbecued rice
1 cup rice
½ cup sliced mushrooms
1 cup water

shrimp jambalaya

½ onion, peeled, finely chopped
½ teaspoon salt
1 teaspoon Worcestershire sauce
¼ cup (½ stick) butter or margarine

Fold 36-inch length of 18-inch foil into square; seal sides to form bag. Put in rice, mushrooms, water, onion, salt, and sauce; mix carefully. Dot with butter. Fold over top edges of foil to seal bag tightly. Place on barbecue over hot coals about ½ hour. Before serving, open foil; add a little extra butter. Fluff up rice with fork.

shrimp marinara

1 tablespoon salad oil
2 cloves garlic, crushed
1 tablespoon chopped parsley
1 tablespoon sugar
1 teaspoon salt
½ teaspoon dried oregano leaves
¼ teaspoon dried basil leaves
½ teaspoon pepper
Dash of cayenne
1 (1-pound 12-ounce) can Italian tomatoes
1 can tomato paste
2 pounds shrimp
Spaghetti

Heat oil in large, heavy skillet over low heat. Add garlic; sauté until golden, about 3 minutes. Remove from heat; add parsley, sugar, salt, oregano, basil, pepper, cayenne, tomatoes, and tomato paste. Break up tomatoes; bring to boiling. Reduce heat; simmer, uncovered, 25 minutes, stirring occasionally.

Boil shrimp; shell. Devein, if preferred. Add to sauce; simmer about 10 minutes. Cook spaghetti until just tender; serve sauce over spaghetti. Yield 6 servings.

shrimp newburg

2 tablespoons butter
1½ tablespoons flour
¾ teaspoon salt
Few grains cayenne
½ cup cream
¼ cup milk
2 cups cooked shrimp
2 egg yolks, beaten
2 tablespoons sherry

Melt butter. Add flour, salt, and cayenne; mix well. Add cream and milk gradually; bring to boiling point, stirring constantly. Add shrimp. Just before serving, add egg yolks and sherry. Serve on rounds of puff pastry. Garnish with parsley and thin strips of pimiento. Yield 4 servings.

shrimp orleans

2 chopped onions
2 tablespoons butter
1 pound fresh shrimp
2 tablespoons flour
1 cup sour cream
Salt
Pepper

Sauté onions in butter to light brown.

Simmer shrimp in boiling salted water to just cover 3 minutes. Drain; reserve liquid. Shell shrimp; devein.

Dredge with flour, and add to onions. Cook slowly 5 minutes without browning. Add sour cream; simmer slowly 20 minutes. Add ¼ cup shrimp liquid; season to taste with salt and pepper. Heat thoroughly; serve on buttered toast. Yield 4 servings.

shrimp risotto

1 pound shrimp

stock
2 small onions, sliced
½ stalk celery, chopped
1 clove garlic, minced
1 cup white wine
½ teaspoon salt
¼ teaspoon pepper
3 cups water
1 small onion, chopped
1 tablespoon water
1 tablespoon dry vermouth
1½ cups uncooked rice
1 stalk celery, chopped
¼ pound fresh mushrooms, sliced
1 red or green pepper, sliced
1 package frozen peas, thawed
¼ teaspoon saffron

garnish
1 tablespoon finely chopped parsley
¼ cup grated Parmesan cheese

Peel and devein shrimp.

Put stock ingredients plus shrimp peels and 3 cups water in 1½-quart saucepan. Simmer 20 minutes; strain.

Cook onion in large saucepan in 1 tablespoon water and vermouth until translucent. Add rice and strained stock; cover. Simmer 15 minutes. Add celery, mushrooms, green pepper, peas, and saffron; cover. Simmer gently 10 minutes. Add shrimp; bring to boil. Boil 3 to 5 minutes. Transfer food to hot serving dish; garnish with parsley and cheese. Yield 4 servings.

shrimp risotto

shrimp scampi

2 pounds large shrimp
½ cup corn oil
3 tablespoons dried parsley flakes
3 tablespoons finely chopped fresh parsley
2 tablespoons lemon juice
1 teaspoon dry mustard
2 teaspoons salt
¼ teaspoon pepper
4 cloves garlic, pressed

Marinate shelled, deveined shrimp in mixture of remaining ingredients.

Preheat broiler to 500°F. Put shrimp in marinade in broiler pan 4-inches from heat 5 minutes. Turn shrimp; broil 5 minutes. Yield 4 servings.

shrimp thermidor

1½ pounds fresh shrimp, cooked, shelled, deveined, or 3 (4½- or 5-ounce) cans shrimp
1 (4-ounce) can mushroom stems and pieces, drained

596

¼ cup melted butter or oil
¼ cup flour
½ teaspoon powdered mustard
Dash of cayenne pepper
2 cups milk
2 tablespoons chopped parsley
Salt
Grated Parmesan cheese
Paprika

If using canned shrimp, drain; cover with ice water. Let stand 5 minutes; drain.

Cook mushrooms in butter 5 minutes. Blend in flour and seasonings. Add milk gradually; cook until thick, stirring constantly. Add shrimp and parsley. Add salt to taste. Place in 6 well-greased, individual scallop or clam shells or 6-ounce custard cups. Sprinkle with cheese and paprika. Bake in 400°F oven 10 to 15 minutes, until lightly browned. Yield 4 to 6 servings.

shrimp in wine sauce

2 tablespoons butter or margarine
1 pound cooked shrimp, shelled, deveined
1 tablespoon cornstarch
½ teaspoon seafood seasoning
¼ cup dry sherry
2 tablespoons water

Melt butter in medium skillet; sauté shrimp 2 minutes.

Mix cornstarch and seafood seasoning with sherry and water until very smooth. Add to shrimp; stir until sauce is thickened, about 5 minutes. Yield 4 to 6 servings.

skillet shrimp gumbo

⅓ cup oil
2 cups sliced fresh okra or 1 package frozen okra, sliced
1 pound shrimp, peeled, deveined
½ cup chopped green onions and tops
3 cloves garlic, finely minced
1½ teaspoons salt
½ teaspoon freshly ground pepper
2 cups water
1 cup canned tomatoes, drained

shrimp in wine sauce

2 whole bay leaves
6 drops Tabasco sauce
1½ cups cooked rice

Heat oil in large skillet. Cook okra 10 minutes; stir occasionally. Add shrimp, onions, garlic, salt, and pepper; simmer 5 minutes. Add water, tomatoes, and bay leaves; cover. Simmer 20 minutes; remove bay leaves. Stir in Tabasco.

Place liberal scoop of rice in each soup bowl. Fill to top with gumbo. Yield 6 servings.

sweet-'n-sour shrimp

1½ pounds cooked shrimp, or 3 (4½- or 5-ounce) cans shrimp
1¾ cups apple juice
½ cup vinegar
⅓ cup sugar
¼ cup catsup
2 tablespoons melted butter or oil
1 tablespoon soy sauce
¼ teaspoon salt
½ cup diagonally sliced carrots
½ cup cubed green pepper
¼ cup sliced green onions and tops

shrimp thermidor

sweet-'n-sour shrimp

2 tablespoons cornstarch
½ cup toasted slivered blanched almonds
2 cups hot cooked rice

If using canned shrimp, drain; cover with ice water. Let stand 5 minutes; drain.

Combine 1½ cups apple juice, vinegar, sugar, catsup, butter, soy sauce, and salt; bring to boiling point. Add carrots; simmer 15 minutes. Add green pepper and onions; cook 5 minutes.

Dissolve cornstarch in ¼ cup apple juice; add gradually to hot sauce. Cook until thickened; stir constantly. Add shrimp; heat. Add almonds to rice. Serve shrimp sauce over rice. Yield 6 servings.

squid athenian-style

SQUID

fried squid

3 pounds frozen squid
2 cups bread crumbs
1 teaspoon salt
½ teaspoon pepper
¾ teaspoon oregano
3 eggs, well beaten
Oil for frying

Thaw squid. Remove arms by cutting from head; reserve. Remove and discard head, chitinous pen, and viscera. Wash thoroughly; drain. Cut mantle into rings.

Combine bread crumbs, salt, pepper, and oregano.

Dip tentacles and mantle rings in eggs, then in bread-crumb mixture; coat well. Deep-fat fry at 350°F until golden brown. Serve immediately with lemon wedges. Yield 4 or 5 servings.

squid athenian-style

3 pounds frozen squid
1 cup chopped onions
1 clove garlic, chopped
3 tablespoons olive oil
2½ cups chopped canned tomatoes
½ cup chopped fresh parsley
½ teaspoon salt
¼ teaspoon pepper
¾ teaspoon crumbled dried oregano
¼ cup white wine

Thaw squid; remove tentacles. Chop; reserve. Remove and discard head, chitinous pen, and viscera. Wash mantle well; cut into pieces.

Sauté onions and garlic in oil until lightly browned. Add tomatoes, parsley, salt, pepper, oregano, wine, and squid. Cover; simmer 1 hour, until squid is tender. Serve with rice. Yield 4 or 5 servings.

VARIETY SEAFOOD

seafood linguine

¼ pound butter or margarine
2 cans minced clams, drained
1 clove garlic, minced fine
1 teaspoon salt
¼ teaspoon pepper
½ pound shrimp, cooked, deveined
2 teaspoons lemon juice
1 pound linguine, cooked

Melt butter in medium skillet. Add all ingredients (except linguine) in order given. Cook on low heat 15 minutes; stir occasionally. Pour over linguine. Yield 4 to 6 servings.

seafood newburg

4 tablespoons butter or margarine
4 cups fresh or frozen uncooked seafood (lobster, shrimp, crab meat, or fish fillets, all in 1-inch pieces)
3 tablespoons lemon juice
1 tablespoon flour
1 teaspoon salt
½ teaspoon paprika
⅛ teaspoon cayenne pepper
2 cups light cream
3 egg yolks
2 tablespoons sherry
6 cups hot cooked rice
Parsley for garnish

Melt butter in large skillet. Sauté seafood about 5 minutes over low heat; stir constantly. Sprinkle with lemon juice.

Mix flour, salt, paprika, and pepper; stir into seafood. Remove from heat. Gradually stir in 1½ cups cream. Return to heat until sauce comes to simmer.

seafood newburg

Combine egg yolks with remaining ½ cup cream; blend in ¼ cup hot liquid mixture. Return to skillet; stir until slightly thickened. Add sherry last, liberally if you prefer. Serve over rice; garnish with parsley. Yield 6 to 8 servings.

seafood pasquille

Tomato Coulis Sauce (see Index)
1½ to 2 pounds shrimp, peeled, uncooked
6 small lobster tails, uncooked, out of shells,
  quartered
1 stick butter
1 large onion, cut up
1 large green pepper, cut up
1 (8-ounce) can clams, undrained

Prepare sauce; use canned Italian plum tomatoes if fresh are unavailable.

Prepare shrimp and lobster.

Heat butter in large skillet; sauté onion and pepper 1 minute. Add shrimp and lobster; cook until lobster turns pink, about 3 minutes. Slowly add sauce and clams; cook 2 to 3 minutes, until well mixed. Turn off heat; let set 1 hour. Reheat when ready to serve; serve over rice or spaghetti. Yield 6 servings.

seafood scampi

12 tablespoons butter or margarine
6 cloves garlic, crushed
1 teaspoon salt
1½ pounds shrimp, cleaned, deveined
1½ pounds raw fish, your choice, cut into chunks
4 spring onions, chopped
½ cup chopped parsley

Melt butter in large skillet. Add garlic and salt, then seafood; cook 5 minutes, stirring constantly. When shrimp is pink and fish flakes tender, add onions and parsley. Cook 3 minutes. Serve over Chinese noodles. Yield 6 to 8 servings.

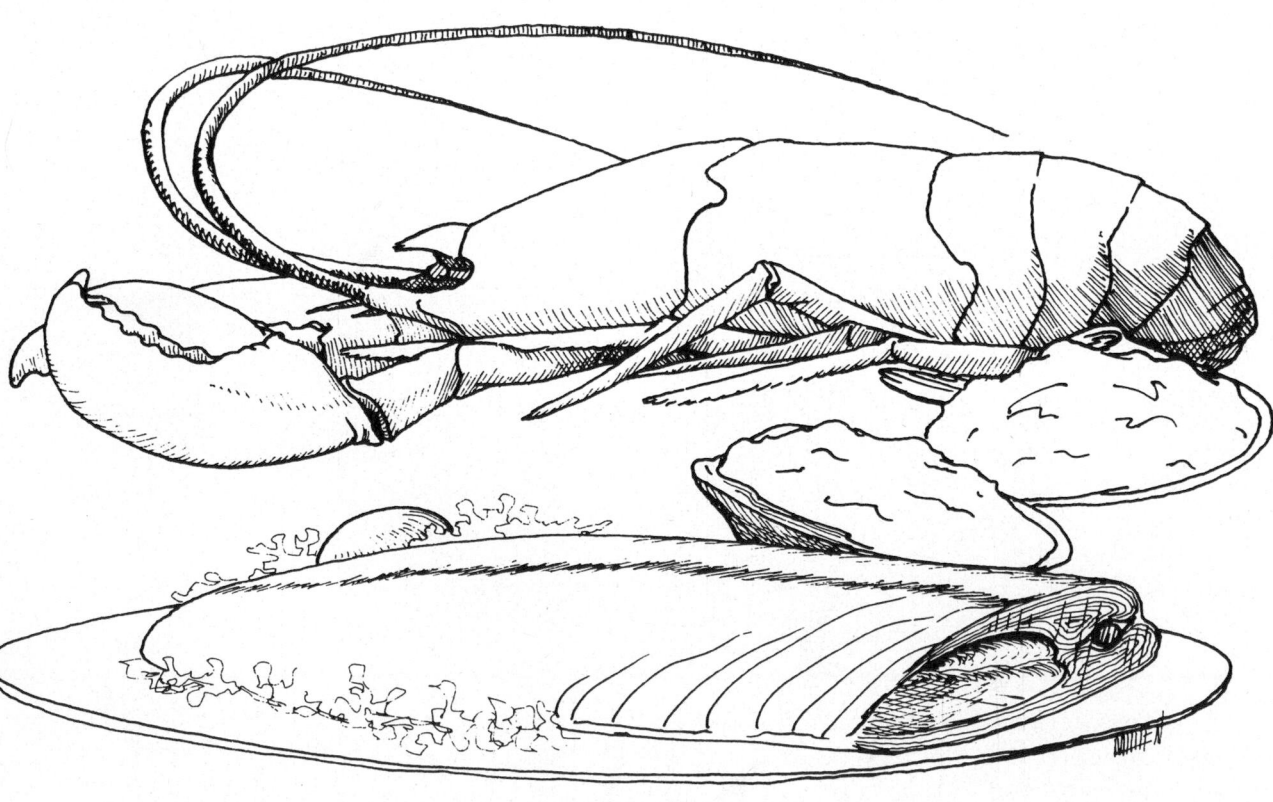

SOUFFLÉS

CHEESE

cheese and egg soufflé

3 tablespoons butter
3 tablespoons all-purpose flour
1 cup milk
½ cup freshly grated Parmesan cheese
Salt to taste
Dash of nutmeg
4 egg whites, stiffly beaten
4 eggs

Melt butter in saucepan over medium heat. Add flour; stir until smooth. Add ¼ cup milk; stir constantly until mixture clings together and forms ball. Add remaining milk gradually; cook, stirring constantly, until smooth and thickened. Add cheese and seasonings; cook, stirring, until well combined. Cool thoroughly. Thoroughly fold ¼ of egg whites into cheese mixture; gently fold in remaining egg whites. Turn half the soufflé mixture into buttered 7-inch soufflé dish; make 4 indentations in soufflé mixture, using lightly oiled tablespoon.

Break eggs, one at a time, into small dish; pour carefully into indentations. Sprinkle eggs lightly with salt; pour in remaining soufflé mixture. Smooth top toward center to form small dome. Bake in preheated 425°F oven 1 shelf above center 15 to 20 minutes, until soufflé is puffed and browned. Serve immediately. Sprinkle each serving with additional cheese, if desired. Yield 4 servings.

cheese and egg soufflé

cottage-cheese soufflé

4 eggs, separated
1 (8-ounce) container dry or pot-style cottage cheese, sieved or blended
1 cup shredded Swiss, Muenster, or Gruyére cheese (about 4-ounces)
½ cup mayonnaise
½ teaspoon dried dillweed

In small bowl with mixer at high speed beat egg whites until stiff peaks form; set aside.

In large bowl with mixer at high speed beat egg yolks until thick and lemon colored. Add remaining ingredients; beat at high speed until smooth. Fold in whites until well blended. Pour into 2-quart soufflé dish or casserole. Bake in 350°F oven 40 to 45 minutes, until knife inserted near center comes out clean. Serve immediately. Yield 4 servings.

sky-high cheese soufflé

½ cup butter or margarine
½ cup flour
1 teaspoon salt
Dash of pepper
2 cups milk
2 cups shredded sharp cheddar cheese (½-pound)
8 eggs, separated

Melt butter in heavy saucepan over medium heat; stir in flour, salt, and pepper. Add milk; cook over low heat until sauce is thick and smooth, stirring constantly. Add cheese; stir until it melts. Remove from heat.

Beat egg yolks until light; add to sauce slowly in fine stream, beating constantly.

Beat egg whites until they hold stiff but not dry peaks. Carefully fold sauce into egg whites. Pour into buttered 2½-quart soufflé dish or casserole. For attractive "top hat" effect on finished soufflé, run tip of knife around and through casserole about ½-inch deep and 1-inch from edge of dish. Bake at 475°F 10 minutes; lower heat to 400°F; bake 25 to 30 minutes, until nicely browned, puffed, and fairly firm to touch. Serve immediately. Yield 6 servings.

MEAT

ham soufflé

2 cups cold cooked ham, finely minced
6 tablespoons butter or margarine
⅓ cup bread crumbs
¼ cup flour
1½ cups milk
3 eggs, separated

½ green pepper, finely minced
Salt to taste

Sauté ham in 2 tablespoons butter until butter is absorbed. Add bread crumbs; blend well.

Melt rest of butter in another frying pan. Add flour; stir until smooth. Add milk slowly; stir constantly. Add beaten egg yolks. Add ham mixture, green pepper, and salt. Fold in stiffly beaten egg whites. Pour into well-greased 2-quart baking dish. Bake at 350°F about 45 minutes, until firm. Yield 6 servings.

SEAFOOD

oyster soufflé

1 pint standard oysters
3 tablespoons butter
3 tablespoons flour
1 cup half-and-half cream
1 teaspoon salt
¼ teaspoon white pepper
3 egg yolks, beaten
3 egg whites, beaten stiff

Drain oysters; chop.

Melt butter; blend in flour until paste forms. Add cream; cook, stirring constantly, until thick. Remove from heat; add oysters, seasonings, and egg yolks. Fold in egg whites. Pour into greased casserole. Bake in 350°F oven 30 minutes or until brown. Yield 6 servings.

salmon soufflé

1 can salmon, red or pink
2 tablespoons butter
1 tablespoon flour
1 cup milk
½ teaspoon salt
Dash of freshly ground black pepper
1 teaspoon chopped chives (optional)
3 eggs, separated
2 teaspoons lemon juice

Remove dark skin and all bones from drained salmon. Mash with fork. (You should have about 1 cup.)

Melt butter on top of stove. Add flour; blend. Gradually add milk; stir until sauce is slightly thickened. Add salmon, salt, pepper, and chives; remove from heat.

Beat egg whites stiff.

Add beaten egg yolks and lemon juice to salmon mixture. Fold in egg whites. Bake in greased mold at 350°F 45 minutes. Salmon is done when knife comes out of center clean. Delicious with a Hollandaise Sauce (see Index). Yield 4 to 6 servings.

mushroom soufflé

VEGETABLE

mushroom soufflé

2 cups finely chopped fresh mushrooms
½ cup vermouth
¾ cup milk
3 tablespoons butter
3 tablespoons all-purpose flour
¾ teaspoon salt
¼ teaspoon white pepper
5 eggs, separated

Combine mushrooms and vermouth in small saucepan. Add milk; bring to boil. Reduce heat; simmer 15 minutes.

Melt butter in saucepan; stir in flour. Cook, stirring constantly, until golden. Stir in mushroom mixture; cook, stirring constantly, about 3 minutes, until thick. Remove from heat; season with salt and pepper.

Beat egg yolks with fork until light and lemon-colored. Pour slowly into mushroom mixture; beat vigorously with wooden spoon. Bring just to boiling, but do not boil. Remove from heat; stir constantly several minutes or until cooled.

Beat egg whites until stiff but not dry; fold about ⅓ thoroughly into mushroom mixture. Add remainder; fold in lightly but thoroughly. Turn into 7-inch buttered and floured soufflé dish. Bake in preheated 350°F oven 35 minutes or until puffed, browned, and firm in center. Yield 4 to 6 servings.

onion soufflé

6 tablespoons butter or margarine
4 tablespoons flour
1 cup milk
1 teaspoon salt
½ teaspoon pepper
8 egg yolks
½ cup chopped onion
10 egg whites

Melt 4 tablespoons butter; stir in flour. When blended and smooth, add milk; stir vigorously with wire whisk. Season; when thickened and smooth, cool.

Beat yolks lightly; stir into sauce. Return to heat; cook briefly.

Cook onion in remaining butter until wilted.

603

Beat egg whites until stiff; stir half into sauce with wire whisk. Fold mixture into remaining whites; pour into buttered 2-quart soufflé dish. Bake 30 to 35 minutes in preheated 375°F oven until well puffed. Yield 6 servings.

potato soufflé

3 cups hot mashed potatoes
2 tablespoons butter or margarine
2 tablespoons chopped onion
2 teaspoons chopped parsley
1/8 teaspoon cayenne
1 teaspoon salt
3 eggs

Combine potatoes, butter, onion, parsley, cayenne, and salt.

Separate eggs. Beat yolks; add to mixture, mixing thoroughly.

Beat egg whites stiff; fold into mixture. Put in greased baking dish; set in pan of water. Bake in 350°F oven 50 to 60 minutes. Yield 6 servings.

pumpkin soufflé

1 cup canned or thick mashed cooked fresh
** pumpkin**
1/2 teaspoon ground nutmeg
1/2 teaspoon grated lemon rind
1/2 cup firmly packed brown sugar
3 egg whites
1/8 teaspoon salt

Combine pumpkin with nutmeg, lemon rind, and sugar; mix well.

Beat egg whites until stiff. Add salt; fold into pumpkin mixture. Fill greased 1-quart baking dish or individual molds two-thirds full; set in pan of hot water. Bake in preheated 350°F oven about 40 minutes for large mold, 25 to 30 minutes for individual molds. Yield 4 to 6 servings.

spinach soufflé with spicy sauce

1 (10-ounce) package frozen chopped spinach
3 tablespoons butter
5 tablespoons cornstarch
3/4 teaspoon salt
1/8 teaspoon pepper
1 cup milk
4 eggs, separated
1/4 teaspoon nutmeg
1 (14-ounce) can stewed tomatoes

spinach soufflé with spicy sauce

1 (3-ounce) can mushrooms
1/4 teaspoon dried basil leaves
Dash of Worcestershire sauce

Cook spinach according to package directions; drain well.

Melt butter in small, heavy saucepan over medium heat; stir in 3 tablespoons cornstarch, 1/2 teaspoon salt, and pepper until smooth. Stir in milk gradually; bring to boil, stirring constantly. Cook 1 minute; remove from heat.

Beat egg yolks slightly. Stir small amount of hot mixture into yolks; stir back into hot mixture. Add spinach and nutmeg; mix thoroughly.

Beat egg whites until stiff peaks form; fold 1/4 into spinach mixture. Fold in remainder; turn into 1 1/2-quart soufflé dish. Bake in preheated 375°F oven 30 to 35 minutes until knife inserted in center comes out clean.

Prepare sauce while soufflé is baking. Combine tomatoes, mushrooms, basil, Worcestershire sauce, remaining cornstarch and remaining salt in small saucepan; bring to boil over medium heat, stirring constantly. Cook 1 minute. Serve sauce with soufflé. Yield 4 servings.

BASIC STOCKS

basic beef stock

3 pounds beef brisket
2 pounds medium soup bones
5 quarts water
4 green onions and tops
1 large onion, studded with 10 cloves
1 celery stalk and leaves
1 Bouquet Garni (see Index) (optional)
2 tablespoons salt

Place beef and bones in large baking pan. Bake at 400°F about 1 hour or until well browned on both sides. Remove from pan; place in large stock pot. Drain off fat from baking pan. Add 1 cup water to pan; scrape up brown bits from bottom. Pour into stock pot. Add remaining water and remaining ingredients, except salt. Bring slowly to boil; remove scum as it accumulates on surface. Cover; simmer 1 hour. Add salt; simmer 3 hours. Remove meat and vegetables; strain through wet muslin. Chill; remove fat before using.

basic chicken stock

1 (4-pound) hen
1 pound chicken wings
2 tablespoons salt
4 peppercorns
5 quarts water
½ bay leaf
Pinch of thyme
6 green onions with tops
4 large carrots, quartered
2 stalks celery, with leaves, cut into 2-inch pieces
1 large onion, studded with 3 cloves

Place chicken, salt, peppercorns, and water in stock pot; bring to boil over medium heat, removing scum from surface. Cover pot; reduce heat. Simmer 1 hour; skim frequently. Add remaining ingredients; cover. Cook about 2½ hours; skim off fat. Season to taste with additional salt and pepper. Remove chicken and vegetables from stock. Strain stock through wet muslin; chill. Remove fat before using.

basic court bouillon for seafood

2 medium carrots, grated
1 medium onion, minced
Generous pinch of leaf thyme
½ bay leaf
¼ cup tarragon vinegar
1 quart cold water
2 peppercorns

Place all ingredients except peppercorns in 2-quart saucepan; bring to boil. Reduce heat; simmer 15 minutes. Add peppercorns; simmer 12 minutes. Cool to lukewarm; strain.

basic fish stock

2 slices lemon
2 parsley stalks
¼ medium onion
1½ pounds inexpensive whitefish
1 pound fish bones (if available)
½ cup vermouth
3 peppercorns

Place lemon, parsley, onion, fish, and bones in 4-quart saucepan. Add vermouth, peppercorns, and enough water to cover. Cover saucepan; bring to fast, rolling boil. Remove cover; remove scum. Add ½ cup cold water; bring to boil. Reduce heat; boil slowly about 15 minutes, until lemon and onion are slightly transparent and fish flakes easily. Strain thoroughly.

basic lamb stock

2½ pounds lamb shoulder bones and trimmings
1 tablespoon salt
1 teaspoon peppercorns
2 cups coarsely chopped celery and leaves
1 large clove garlic, halved
2 onions, quartered
2 carrots, coarsely chopped

Combine bones and 2 quarts water in large heavy saucepan; bring to boil. Reduce heat; simmer 15 minutes, skimming top occasionally. Add remaining ingredients; simmer 1½ hours. Strain stock through fine sieve; cool. Remove fat. Yield about 1½ quarts.

Note: Clarification is not a substitute for skimming, but an optional addition to it.

clarifying stock

2 eggshells
4 to 6 cups stock
2 egg whites

Pull away inner skins from 2 eggshells; wash; crush into hot stock. Add 2 egg whites; beat with rotary beater over moderate heat, about 4 minutes, until thick foam forms on top. Foam must be thick and high. Remove beater; bring mixture to boil without stirring. Reduce heat to low; simmer 10 minutes. Remove from heat; let stand 3 minutes. Place piece of wet muslin in large sieve; pour stock mixture slowly and steadily through muslin, draining well. This procedure makes stock sparkling clear.

605

FRUIT

apple soup

1½ pounds tart apples
2½ quarts water
½ lemon, thinly sliced
1 stick cinnamon
4 tablespoons cornstarch
¼ cup water
Sugar to taste
¼ cup wine (optional)

Wash, quarter, and core apples; do not peel. Cook until soft in 1 quart of water with lemon and cinnamon. Put apples through a coarse sieve. Put with rest of water into pot; bring to boil.

Mix cornstarch with ¼ cup water; add to pot, stirring constantly. Add sugar and wine. Serve hot. Yield 8 servings.

avgolemno soup

5 cups strong chicken stock
2 to 3 tablespoons rice
1 large or 2 small lemons
2 eggs or 3 egg yolks
4 to 6 tablespoons heavy cream
Chopped parsley

Heat stock in pan. When boiling, add rice; cook 12 minutes or until rice is cooked.

Grate rind from lemon; squeeze out juice.

Beat eggs well with lemon juice, until frothy.

Take soup pan off heat; let cool slightly before adding 4 to 5 tablespoons hot stock to egg mixture. Stir in well. Pour stock and rice into top of double boiler. Strain egg mixture into stock; stir in well. Stir over gentle heat while soup thickens; do not boil, or eggs will curdle. When soup is creamy, add lemon rind; adjust seasoning. If serving hot, pour into soup cups. Put spoonful of cream into each. Sprinkle with parsley. If serving cold, let soup cool. Add slightly whipped cream; chill before serving. Yield 4 to 6 servings.

avocado soup

2 ripe, soft avocados, pitted, peeled
1 teaspoon lemon juice
1 cup cold chicken broth
1 cup light cream
½ cup plain yogurt
½ cup dry white wine
Salt to taste

Set aside few thin avocado slices brushed with lemon juice to use as garnish. Place remaining avocado in food processor or blender; blend until smooth. Add remaining ingredients; blend until smooth. Serve very cold; garnish with reserved avocado slices. Yield about 4 cups.

avgolemno soup

avocado soup

avocado and prawn soup

avocado and prawn soup

1 small onion, finely chopped
2 stalks celery, finely chopped
1 small bay leaf
Blade or pinch of mace
3 or 4 sprigs parsley
Salt and pepper
3 to 4 cups well-flavored Basic Chicken Stock
  (see Index)
2 or 3 avocados (according to size)
½ cup peeled shrimp
1 cup heavy cream
Chopped chives or paprika
Slivers of fresh avocado

Put onion, celery, bay leaf, mace, parsley, and a little seasoning into stock. Simmer about 15 minutes to flavor stock. Strain and reserve stock.

Peel and remove seeds from avocados; chop flesh roughly. Put into electric blender or food processor; blend slowly while adding stock. When quite smooth, return to pan; heat very gently,

adding shrimp. Do not let boil; this will spoil flavor and texture of soup. Adjust seasoning.

Whip cream slightly; add spoon of cream to each soup cup. Sprinkle top with chives; add few thin slivers of another avocado as party garnish. Yield 4 to 6 servings.

blueberry soup

1 quart fresh blueberries, washed, drained
2¼ quarts cold water
½ cup sugar
Generous slice lemon rind
4 tablespoons cornstarch

Place blueberries, 2 quarts cold water, sugar, and lemon rind in 3-quart pot; cook over low heat only until fruit is soft. Stir in cornstarch mixed with remaining cold water; mixture will thicken slightly. Serve hot or cold. Yield 6 or more servings.

cherry soup

1½ pounds sweet red cherries
  (or canned equivalent)

608

4 cups water
½ cinnamon stick (or ¼ teaspoon ground cinnamon)
3 or 4 slivers orange or lemon rind and juice of ½ orange or lemon
1 cup red wine
1 tablespoon cornstarch
Sugar to taste

Pit cherries; put about three-quarters into pan. Cover with water. Add cinnamon; rind, very finely pared; and orange juice. Cover; simmer gently until cherries are tender. Put through fine food mill or into electric blender or food processor; blend until smooth. Add wine.

Add cornstarch to cold water; mix until smooth. Add a little hot soup to cornstarch mixture; pour back into soup. Stir in well; bring to boil. Cook 4 to 5 minutes; add reserved cherries last few minutes to heat through. Add sugar to taste. Serve hot with crackers, which can be crumbled into soup if desired. Yield 4 to 6 servings.

cranberry and orange soup

1 pound fresh cranberries (or canned equivalent)
2 cups light chicken stock (or water)
1½ cups white wine
2 or 3 pieces lemon rind
Pared rind of ripe orange
½ cinnamon stick
¼ to ½ cup sugar to taste
Juice of 2 oranges
Juice of ½ lemon
2 envelopes gelatin (if soup is to be jellied)
4 to 6 thin slices orange

Wash cranberries, if fresh; put into pan with stock and wine. Add lemon and orange rind and cinnamon stick; simmer about 10 minutes, until cranberries have softened. Put fruit and juice through fine nylon sieve or fine food mill after removing cinnamon stick; sweeten to taste. Add orange and lemon juice. (If using canned cranberries, it may not be necessary to add any sugar; these are usually sweetened.)

This soup can also be served jellied if 2 envelopes gelatin are softened in little stock or water and added after soup has been sieved. Reheat soup a few minutes while blending in gelatin.

Serve chilled or jellied with orange as garnish. Yield 4 to 6 servings.

pumpkin soup

2 tablespoons butter
2 tablespoons chopped onion
½ teaspoon ginger
1 tablespoon flour
2 cups prepared pumpkin
2 cups Basic Chicken Stock (see Index) (or 2 chicken bouillon cubes in 2 cups water)
2 cups milk
Salt to season

Sauté butter, onion, and ginger. Stir in flour. Add pumpkin; cook 5 minutes. Gradually add stock and milk; simmer 5 minutes. Season with salt. Yield 4 servings.

cranberry and orange soup

MEAT

beef and chinese cabbage soup

¼ pound rump steak, thinly sliced
1 teaspoon corn flour
½ teaspoon soy sauce
½ teaspoon dry sherry
2 teaspoons oil
3 cups water
2 cups shredded Chinese cabbage
1 teaspoon salt

Marinate steak in corn flour, soy sauce, sherry, and oil.

Bring water to boil; add Chinese cabbage. Return to boil; add salt. Cover; simmer 10 minutes. Serve immediately. Yield 4 servings.

beef–noodle soup

1¼ pounds beef short ribs
1 tablespoon salt
6 cups water
2 beef bouillon cubes
1 cup chopped celery with leaves
4 ounces noodles, uncooked

Combine beef, salt, and water in large pan; simmer, covered, about 2 hours, until meat is tender. Skim off excess fat; remove bones. Separate meat into small pieces. Add bouillon and celery; cover. Simmer 10 minutes. Stir in noodles; cover. Simmer 7 to 10 minutes, until noodles and celery are tender. Add a little hot water if thinner soup is desired. Yield 6 servings.

cottage broth

stock
2 lamb shanks (about 3 pounds)
7 cups water
1 onion, studded with 4 cloves
2 bay leaves
2 teaspoons salt
4 peppercorns
2 carrots, peeled, chopped
1 stalk celery, chopped

soup
3 tablespoons butter or margarine
2 leeks, cleaned, sliced
1 medium onion, chopped
2 turnips, peeled, diced
3 medium carrots, peeled, sliced
2 stalks celery, chopped
¼ cup chopped parsley
1 teaspoon crumbled dried thyme

¼ cup barley, soaked overnight in water to cover, drained

The day before serving, place lamb in shallow roasting pan; roast at 400°F until well-browned (20 to 30 minutes). Place lamb and remaining stock ingredients in Dutch oven or heavy kettle; bring to boil. Cover; reduce heat to low. Simmer 2½ to 3 hours, until meat is very tender; remove meat from broth. Strain stock; discard vegetables. Refrigerate stock overnight. Remove lamb from shanks; dice. Reserve for soup.

The following day, melt butter or margarine in large Dutch oven. Add vegetables, except parsley; cook over moderate heat, stirring occasionally, until tender.

Remove fat from soup stock; add to vegetables. Add parsley, thyme, barley, and reserved lamb; mix well. Bring to boil; cover. Reduce heat to low; cook 1 to 1¼ hours, until barley is tender. Yield 8 servings.

goulash soup

3 medium onions, sliced
1 clove garlic, finely chopped
3 tablespoons vegetable oil
2 teaspoons paprika
½ pound lean veal, ground
½ pound lean pork, ground
3 cups beef stock or bouillon
½ teaspoon salt
⅛ teaspoon pepper
2 medium potatoes, sliced
3 small tomatoes, chopped

In 4-quart Dutch oven or soup kettle, sauté onions and garlic in hot oil until lightly browned. Add paprika; cook 1 minute. Stir in ground meats; sauté until lightly browned. Gradually add stock and seasonings; cover. Simmer 10 minutes. Add potatoes and tomatoes; cover. Simmer 20 minutes or until potatoes are soft. Yield 6 servings.

gulyas

1 pound lean boneless stewing beef
2 tablespoons lard
2 medium onions, peeled, chopped
1 clove garlic, peeled, chopped
2 teaspoons Hungarian sweet paprika
Dash of cayenne pepper
3 cups beef stock or broth
2 cups water
½ teaspoon caraway seeds
½ teaspoon crumbled dried marjoram
Salt and pepper
1 (16-ounce) can tomatoes, broken up
2 medium potatoes, peeled, diced
2 medium carrots, peeled, sliced

goulash soup

2 red sweet peppers, cleaned, cut into chunks
  (green peppers can be substituted all or in part)
2 tablespoons flour
2 tablespoons water
Sour cream

Wipe beef with damp cloth; cut into 1-inch cubes.

Melt lard in Dutch oven or soup kettle. Add beef; brown well on all sides. Remove from pan with slotted spoon; reserve.

Add onions and garlic to pan; cook 4 minutes, stirring occasionally. Add paprika, cayenne, stock, 2 cups water, caraway, marjoram, salt, pepper, and reserved meat; stir well. Bring to boil over moderate heat; reduce heat to low. Cook, covered, 45 minutes. Add tomatoes, potatoes, carrots, and peppers; stir well. Return to boil; cover. Cook 30 minutes.

Combine flour and 2 tablespoons water; stir to form smooth paste. Add slowly to soup; stir well. Cook over low heat; stir until thickened. Serve in individual bowls; top with sour cream. Yield 4 or 5 servings.

hough soup

stock

3 pounds sliced beef shin
1 pound beef bones (split marrow bone or neck bone)
1 onion, studded with 4 cloves
1 bay leaf
½ teaspoon crumbled dried thyme
1 cup broken-up canned tomatoes
1 stalk celery (including some leaves), chopped
¼ cup chopped parsley
2 teaspoons salt
10 cups water

soup

1 turnip, peeled, diced
1 large onion, thinly sliced
3 large carrots, peeled, sliced
2 stalks celery, sliced
1 (16-ounce) can tomatoes, broken up
¼ cup chopped parsley
¼ medium cabbage head, shredded
½ cup long-grain rice

The day before serving, place beef shin and bones in shallow roasting pan; roast in 400°F oven until browned. Place in Dutch oven or soup kettle with remaining stock ingredients; bring to boil. Skim if necessary; cover with lid ajar. Simmer 3 to 4 hours, until meat falls from bones. Remove meat; cool. Strain stock; refrigate. Remove bones, fat, and gristle from meat; dice. Reserve meat for soup.

The following day combine stock, reserved meat, and soup ingredients in large Dutch oven or soup kettle. Bring to boil; cover. Reduce heat to low; cook 40 to 50 minutes, until vegetables and rice are tender. Yield 8 servings.

mexican soup

1 clove garlic, peeled
¾ teaspoon salt

gulyas

4 tablespoons butter
1 medium onion, chopped
1 fresh hot green pepper, chopped
½ pound baked ham, chopped
1 cup chopped unpeeled zucchini squash
4½ cups beef bouillon
¼ teaspoon crumbled thyme
2 sweet red peppers, cleaned, seeded, chopped
3 tablespoons tomato paste
1 (16½-ounce) can whole-kernel corn
Salt and pepper
2 tablespoons chopped fresh parsley

On cutting board sprinkle garlic with ¾ teaspoon salt; mash with knife blade.

Melt butter in Dutch oven or soup kettle; add garlic, onion, green pepper, ham, and zucchini. Sauté over moderate heat 10 minutes. Add beef broth and thyme; simmer 15 minutes. Add red peppers, tomato paste, and corn (with liquid from can); stir well. Cook 15 minutes more. Season to taste with salt and pepper. Garnish with parsley. Yield 4 to 6 servings.

oxtail soup

1 (2-pound) oxtail or 2 veal tails
Flour
1 medium onion, sliced
2 tablespoons vegetable oil
8 cups water
1 teaspoon salt
4 peppercorns
¼ cup chopped parsley
½ cup diced carrots

1 cup diced celery
1 bay leaf
½ cup tomatoes, drained
1 teaspoon dried thyme
1 tablespoon flour
1 tablespoon butter or margarine
¼ cup Madeira

Cut tail into 2-inch pieces; roll in flour.

In 4-quart Dutch oven or soup kettle, brown oxtail and onion in hot oil several minutes. Add water, salt, and peppercorns; simmer uncovered about 5 hours. Add parsley, carrots, celery, bay leaf, tomatoes, and thyme; simmer 30 minutes or until vegetables are tender.

Strain stock; refrigerate an hour or more.

In a blender or food processor puree edible meat and vegetables; reserve.

Remove fat from top of stock; reheat.

In large dry frypan brown 1 tablespoon flour over high heat; cool slightly. Add butter; blend. Slowly add stock and vegetables; correct seasoning. Add Madeira just before serving. Yield 8 servings.

pavian soup

4 slices white bread
3 tablespoons melted butter
5 cups Basic Chicken Stock (see Index) or 2
    (13-ounce) cans regular-strength chicken broth
4 eggs
6 tablespoons shredded Parmesan cheese

Trim crusts from bread; brush both sides with melted butter. Place on cookie sheet. Bake at 350°F 30 minutes or until golden.

Pour stock into large shallow saucepan; heat to boiling. Reduce heat to low.

Break eggs one at a time into a saucer; slide into liquid. Poach lightly. Remove with slotted spoon; keep warm. Strain stock; return to pan. Heat to boiling. Put 1 bread slice in each soup bowl; top with 1 egg. Ladle soup over egg. Sprinkle each bowl with 1½ tablespoons cheese. Yield 4 servings.

pot-au-feu

1 ham bone
1 meaty veal knuckle
1 tablespoon dried navy beans
¼ cup dried baby lima beans
¼ cup dried split peas
1 tablespoon rice
1 onion, peeled, finely chopped
½ cup finely chopped celery
1 tablespoon finely chopped parsley
½ cup tomato puree
3 pints water

pavian soup

scotch broth

Chopped chives or scallions (garnish)

Put all ingredients, except garnish, into large kettle; cover. Simmer 3 to 3½ hours. Remove bones. Cut off meat; return to pan. Skim off excess fat; adjust seasoning. Reheat. Serve sprinkled with chives. Yield 4 to 6 servings.

scotch broth

3 to 4 tablespoons pearl barley
1½ to 2 pounds neck or breast of mutton or lamb
6 to 8 cups water
1 teaspoon salt
¼ teaspoon pepper
1 bay leaf
1 leek, sliced
2 tablespoons chopped parsley
2 large onions, 1 to add whole, other diced for garnish
1 clove

3 carrots, 1 sliced for soup, 2 diced for garnish
4 stalks celery, 2 whole for soup, 2 diced for garnish
½ small turnip, diced

Soak barley several hours, preferably overnight, in cold water.

Remove as much fat as possible from mutton; put into soup pot with water and drained barley. Add salt, pepper, bay leaf, herbs, whole onion stuck with clove, sliced carrot, and 2 stalks of celery; bring slowly to boil. Simmer 1½ hours; skim off fat and scum occasionally. If time allows, let soup cool; skim off fat. If not, skim carefully while hot; remove bay leaf and as much celery and carrot as possible. Add diced vegetables; cook 20 to 30 minutes, until tender; adjust seasoning. If too much liquid has evaporated, add a little extra to make up quantity. Remove bones; leave meat in soup; reheat. Serve hot; sprinkle with chopped parsley. Yield 6 to 8 servings.

tripe soup

½ pound cooked honeycomb tripe
3 to 4 cups chicken or white stock
2 potatoes, chopped
2 onions, chopped
2 or 3 stalks celery, chopped
3 tablespoons butter, melted
1½ tablespoons flour
1 tablespoon chopped parsley
1 teaspoon marjoram
Pinch of thyme
Pinch of cayenne pepper
2 tablespoons butter
½ cup cream
Fried bread croutons

Buy ready-cooked or canned tripe; cut into small cubes. Cook gently in stock about 1 hour, with pepper and salt if necessary.

Meanwhile, cook potatoes, onions, and celery in melted butter in tightly-covered soup pot until tender, shaking to prevent sticking and burning, about 12 to 15 minutes. Blend in flour until smooth.

When tripe is cooked, strain liquid into vegetables; stir to mix in well. Bring slowly to boil; stir until smooth. Add tripe, herbs, and cayenne; simmer together a few minutes. Adjust seasoning. Add butter and cream just before serving. Serve hot with croutons. Yield 6 servings.

MISCELLANEOUS

almond cream soup

1 small potato, finely sliced
3 or 4 spring onions, finely sliced (or 2 or 3 slices

almond cream soup

ordinary onion)
3 or 4 stalks celery, finely sliced
3 cups chicken or white stock
1 small bay leaf
3 or 4 sprigs parsley
½ to ¾ cup almonds
2 tablespoons butter
1 tablespoon flour
Salt and pepper
Pinch of mace
4 to 5 tablespoons heavy cream

Put potato, onions, and celery in pan with stock, bay leaf, and parsley. Simmer gently, with lid on, until potato is tender.

Meanwhile, pour boiling water on almonds; let stand a few minutes. Drain; pop almonds out of skins. Reserve 10 to 12 whole almonds for garnish; chop or finely grind remainder. This can be done in electric blender, but a little stock should be added to liquify slightly. Add to pan; cook for 20 minutes. Remove bay leaf and parsley; pour into blender. Blend slowly until smooth. Strain through fine sieve.

Melt butter. Add flour; stir until smooth, off heat. Add strained soup slowly; stir until smooth. Bring to boil; stir constantly. Add salt, pepper, and mace; be careful not to overpower the light almond flavor.

Sliver remaining almonds; brown lightly in 300°F oven. Sprinkle with a little salt.

Add spoonful of cream to each soup cup; at last moment sprinkle with almonds. Soup can also be served chilled. Yield 4 servings.

beer soup

3 cups (2 cans) beer
6 tablespoons sugar
1 cup milk
½ inch length cinnamon stick or ⅛ teaspoon
    ground cinnamon
2 whole eggs
⅓ cup sour cream
⅛ teaspoon grated nutmeg

Put beer and sugar in saucepan; heat.

Put milk and cinnamon in another saucepan; heat. Do not boil.

Put eggs, sour cream, and nutmeg in mixing bowl; beat with whisk. Add hot beer, beating rapidly with whisk. Remove cinnamon stick; beat in milk. Pour soup into heavy saucepan; heat thoroughly, stirring constantly. Do not boil; it may curdle. If soup curdles slightly, strain it. Yield 4 to 6 servings.

buttermilk soup

2 large eggs, separated
Grated rind and juice of 1 lemon (or vanilla extract)

¼ cup sugar
4 cups buttermilk
½ cup heavy cream

garnish
Finely grated rind of half a lemon or 2 tablespoons
    chopped and lightly browned almonds

Beat egg yolks, and lemon rind and juice with sugar until light and frothy.

Beat buttermilk; stir into egg-yolk mixture.

Beat egg whites stiff; add pinch of salt.

Whip cream. Carefully fold egg whites into cream. Add to egg-yolk mixture. Do not blend too thoroughly; leave rather lumpy in texture. Ladle into soup cups; chill thoroughly. Garnish with lemon rind; serve plain crackers separately. Yield 4 to 6 servings.

cheese soup

2 medium-size carrots
2 stalks celery
1 cup boiling water
½ small onion
3 tablespoons butter or margarine
¼ cup flour
3½ cups milk
1½ cups cut-up cheese

Chop carrots and celery; cook in boiling water about 10 minutes, until tender.

Chop onion. Cook in butter until tender. Stir in flour. Add milk slowly; stir until smooth. Cook and stir until thickened. Add cheese, vegetables, and cooking liquid; stir over low heat until cheese melts. Yield 6 servings.

consommé julienne

2 small carrots
2 or 3 sticks celery, white part only
1 leek, white part only
1 cup stock
Salt and pepper
4 to 5 cups clear beef consommé
2 to 3 tablespoons sherry

Prepare vegetables by cutting into even, match-like strips. Put into pan; cover with a little stock and seasoning. Cook gently until just tender; drain. Reserve stock for use in another soup or sauce.

Heat consommé; add a little sherry. Add julienne vegetables; serve hot. Yield 4 to 6 servings.

consommé a la princesse

2 to 3 tablespoons asparagus tips
1 small cooked chicken breast
4 to 5 cups clear chicken or beef consommé
Little sherry (optional)

1 tablespoon finely chopped parsley

Cook asparagus tips, if fresh, in boiling water; if canned, rinse and heat in little liquid from can. Dice chicken meat.

Heat consommé. Add a little sherry, asparagus tips, and chicken; heat through. Serve hot, with asparagus and chicken divided between soup cups. Sprinkle with parsley. Yield 4 to 6 servings.

cream of chestnut soup

2 to 3 cups fresh peeled chestnuts (buy 2 pounds to produce this amount) or 1 large can chestnut puree (unsweetened)
3 tablespoons butter
1 large onion, sliced
2 small carrots, sliced
1 stalk celery, sliced
4 to 5 cups ham, Basic Chicken or Beef Stock (see Index) (or water and bouillon cubes)
1 tablespoon chopped parsley (or 3 or 4 sprigs parsley)
Pinch of thyme
1 bay leaf
Pinch of nutmeg
Salt and pepper
1 cup cream

apple-ring garnish
2 to 3 cooking apples
4 tablespoons butter
1 to 2 teaspoon sugar
1 tablespoon chopped parsley

If using fresh chestnuts, prepare as follows: Make small slit in top of each nut; place in well-greased pan in moderate oven 10 to 15 minutes to loosen both outer and inner skin. Remove both skins. If using canned chestnut puree, add to soup after vegetables have been cooked.

Melt butter. Add onion, carrots, and celery; mix well over gentle heat. Add chestnuts; cover. Cook 3 to 4 minutes; shake pan occasionally. Add stock, herbs, and seasoning; simmer 20 to 30 minutes, until chestnuts and vegetables are tender. Remove bay leaf. Put soup into electric blender or food processor; blend until smooth. Or put through fine food mill. Return to pan; reheat. Season to taste. Add cream just before serving, or put spoon of cream in each soup cup.

Make Apple-Ring Garnish. Peel and core apples; cut into rings.

Melt butter; fry apples until golden brown on each side. Sprinkle slices with a little sugar. Float 1 or 2 apple slices in each soup cup; sprinkle with parsley. Yield 4 to 6 servings.

cream of curry soup

3 tablespoons butter
1 large onion, chopped

1 sour cooking apple, peeled, cored
½ tablespoon curry powder or paste (more if desired)
1 tablespoon flour
2 tablespoons rice
4 to 5 cups Basic Chicken Stock (see Index) (or water and cubes)
1 teaspoon sweet chutney
2 teaspoons coconut
Salt and pepper
1 bay leaf
3 or 4 sprigs parsley
1 slice lemon
½ cup cream

garnish
1 tablespoon chopped parsley (or paprika)
Lemon wedges
½ to 1 cup plain boiled rice

Melt butter; cook onion and apple gently 5 to 6 minutes to soften without browning. Stir in curry powder; cook 1 minute. Remove from heat. Sprinkle in flour; blend well. Add rice, stock, chutney, and coconut; bring to boil, stirring constantly. Reduce heat. Add seasonings, herbs and lemon slice; cover. Simmer 15 to 20 minutes to cook rice. Remove bay leaf and lemon. Put soup into electric blender or food processor; blend until smooth. Reheat; adjust seasoning. Stir in cream just before serving. Sprinkle with chopped parsley; serve lemon wedges and boiled rice separately. Yield 4 to 6 servings.

cream of peanut-butter soup

¼ stalk celery
½ small onion
1 tablespoon butter or margarine
1 tablespoon flour
¾ cup peanut butter
1 cup milk
2 cups chicken broth or Basic Chicken Stock (see Index)
¼ teaspoon Worcestershire sauce (optional)
Salt and pepper to taste

Finely chop celery and onion.

Melt butter in large saucepan. Add celery and onion; cook and stir until tender. Mix in flour and peanut butter. Add milk slowly; stir until smooth. Add rest of ingredients; bring to boil. Lower heat; stir as needed to keep from sticking. Cook and stir 1 minute. Yield 6 servings.

hot-and-sour soup

3 cups chicken broth or Basic Chicken Stock (see Index)

niçoise soup (clear)

⅓ pound lean pork, shredded into matchstick-size
   pieces
4 Chinese dried black mushrooms, soaked 20 to 30
   minutes in warm water, sliced
2 ounces bean curd, cut into matchstick-size pieces
2 tablespoons soy sauce
2 tablespoons dry sherry
1 teaspoon salt
½ teaspoon pepper
2 tablespoons vinegar
1 tablespoon cornstarch in 2 tablespoons
   cold water

Bring broth to boil in wok or skillet. Add pork,
mushrooms, and bean curd; simmer 8 minutes,
until pork is done. Add soy sauce, sherry, salt,
pepper, vinegar, and cornstarch mixture; heat
until soup has thickened. Serve hot. Yield 4 to 6
servings.

niçoise soup (clear)

4 cups Basic Beef Stock
2 tablespoons olive oil
½ teaspoon salt
2 peppercorns
2 cloves garlic, chopped

618

1 bay leaf
2 sprigs parsley
4 poached eggs
½ teaspoon dried thyme

Combine stock, oil, salt, peppercorns, garlic, bay leaf and parsley in large saucepan; bring to boil. Reduce heat; simmer 15 minutes. Remove peppercorns, bay leaf, and parsley; ladle soup into 4 soup bowls. Place 1 egg in each soup bowl; sprinkle with thyme. Yield 4 servings.

oriental soup

1 quart chicken broth
½ cup thin strips bamboo shoots
2 ounces whole cooked shrimps
½ pound cooked lean pork, cut into thin strips
2 ounces cooked chicken, cut into thin strips
½ teaspoon salt
¼ teaspoon soy sauce

Heat broth; add remaining ingredients. Simmer 3 to 4 minutes, until ingredients are hot. Yield 4 to 6 servings.

yogurt soup

3 cups yogurt
2 cucumbers
3 green onions (approximately 4 tablespoons)
2 sprigs mint
2 sprigs basil (½ teaspoon dried)
2 sprigs savory (½ teaspoon dried)
½ cup raisins
½ teaspoon salt
¼ cup walnuts

Beat yogurt until smooth.
Chop cucumbers and green onions fine.
Mix all ingredients together; chill. Can be diluted with milk if desired. Yield 4 to 6 servings.

yogurt, shrimp, and cucumber soup

½ large cucumber, peeled, diced
Salt
1 cup natural yogurt
1½ cups chicken stock
1 cup tomato juice
1 clove garlic, crushed
Pepper
1 to 2 teaspoons lemon juice
2 teaspoons chopped dill or fennel
½ cup cooked shrimp
1 large tomato, peeled, diced
2 tablespoons diced green pepper
1 cup cream
2 teaspoons chopped dill, fennel, or paprika

oriental soup

yogurt, shrimp, and cucumber soup

Sprinkle cucumber with salt; leave covered at least 20 to 30 minutes. Drain; rinse with cold water.

Put yogurt, stock, tomato juice and garlic into electric blender; blend slowly until smooth. Add pepper, lemon juice, and dill when soup is well mixed; pour into bowl. Add cucumber, shrimp, tomato, and pepper; stir in cream. Adjust seasoning; chill thoroughly. Sprinkle with dill. Yield 4 to 6 servings.

POULTRY

chicken chowder

Carcass and giblets of 1 chicken
3 pints boiling water
1 onion, peeled, sliced
3 stalks celery with leaves, chopped
1 carrot, peeled, diced
1 teaspoon salt
1 (1-pound) can cream-style corn
2 eggs (1 hard-boiled)
1 cup flour
¼ teaspoon salt

Break up carcass; put with giblets into large kettle. Add boiling water, onion, celery, carrot, and salt; cover. Simmer about 1½ hours. Remove pieces of carcass and giblets. Cut off all meat; return to pan. Add corn; simmer 10 minutes. Add finely chopped hard-cooked egg; adjust seasoning.

Sift flour and salt together; stir in remaining egg, beaten with fork until mixture looks like cornmeal. Drop by spoonfuls into hot soup a few minutes before serving. Yield 5 or 6 servings.

chicken gumbo

3 tablespoons butter or bacon fat
1 large or 2 smaller onions, chopped
1½ cups canned tomatoes
½ green pepper, seeded, chopped
¾ to 1 cup canned okra (or ready-cooked okra)
2 tablespoons rice
4 to 5 cups strongly flavored chicken stock made with whole chicken
Salt and pepper
1 to 2 cups chopped cooked chicken
1 tablespoon chopped parsley
1 teaspoon chopped tarragon
½ cup cooked corn (optional)
Croutons

Melt butter in soup pot; cook onions gently 5 to 6 minutes with lid on until tender but not brown. Add tomatoes, pepper, okra, and rice. Pour in stock; mix thoroughly. Add salt and pepper if necessary. Cover pan; simmer until vegetables are tender, about 20 to 30 minutes. Adjust seasoning; add chicken, herbs, and corn. Reheat; serve hot. Serve as main course with croutons. Yield 4 to 6 servings.

chicken-noodle soup

3 pounds chicken, cut up
1 tablespoon salt
Water to cover
1 cup sliced carrots
1½ cups chopped celery with leaves

½ cup chopped onion
½ teaspoon poultry seasoning
1 tablespoon dehydrated parsley flakes
2 cups (about ¼-pound) uncooked noodles

Simmer chicken in salted water in covered saucepan until tender. (A frying chicken will take about 45 minutes.) Remove chicken from broth; cool enough to handle. Remove skin and bones; chop meat.

Skim most fat from broth; measure broth. Add water, if needed, to make 5 cups; bring to boil. Add chicken, vegetables, and poultry seasoning; simmer, covered, 20 minutes. Add parsley and noodles; simmer, uncovered, 10 minutes or until noodles are tender. Yield 6 servings.

chicken soup chinese-style

4 or 5 spring onions
5 cups strongly flavored clear Basic Chicken Stock (see Index)
6 small mushrooms, finely sliced
2 cups shredded white chicken meat
2 beaten eggs
Salt and pepper
2 to 3 teaspoons soy sauce

Finely slice white part of onions; reserve green parts for garnish.

Heat stock until boiling. Add mushrooms and onions; cook 2 to 3 minutes. Add chicken.

Beat eggs with a little salt and pepper until frothy.

Stir soup well. Pour eggs steadily into soup, stirring constantly, so that it remains in shreds. Let cook a minute or two to set egg. Add soy sauce to taste. Serve in soup bowls; sprinkle with finely chopped green parts of spring onions. Yield 4 to 6 servings.

chicken soup (curried)

2 tablespoons butter or margarine
2 teaspoons curry powder
1½ tablespoons flour
3 cups chicken stock
Paprika
Salt
1 egg yolk
4 tablespoons light cream or milk
¼ to ½ cup chopped cooked chicken meat or 1 to 2 tablespoons chopped chutney
2 or 3 chives, topped

Melt butter in kettle. Add curry powder and flour; blend well. Stir over low heat about 3 minutes. Gradually add stock; stir until boiling. Season carefully with paprika and salt to taste. Reduce heat. Add egg yolk and cream mixed together; stir until slightly thickened. Add chicken; sprinkle with chives. Yield 4 or 5 servings.

chicken soup irish-style

5 cups water
1½ teaspoons salt

chicken soup chinese-style

chicken soup irish-style

2 pounds chicken parts (wings, necks, backs)
2 stalks celery, sliced
1 leek, sliced
1 large carrot, cubed
2 medium potatoes, cubed
½ cup peas
2 egg yolks
¾ cup plain yogurt
½ head Bibb lettuce, coarsely chopped

Bring water, salt, and chicken parts to boil in large saucepan; cover. Simmer 1 hour. Add celery, leek, carrot, and potatoes; simmer 20 minutes. Remove chicken; cube meat; return to soup. Add peas; simmer about 8 minutes. Remove scum from surface of soup.

Lightly beat egg yolks; stir into yogurt.

Remove soup from heat; stir in yogurt mixture; adjust seasoning. Garnish with lettuce; serve at once. Yield 6 servings.

chicken soup japanese-style

½ uncooked boned chicken breast
8 fresh mushrooms
4 cups hot chicken broth or Basic Chicken Stock
 (see Index)
1 cup cooked rice
4 strips lemon peel

Thinly slice chicken meat. Wash mushrooms; thinly slice.

Put broth in fondue pot over medium-high heat. Add chicken and mushrooms; cook 4 minutes.

Place ¼ cup rice in each of 4 bowls; put 1 lemon peel strip in each bowl. Spoon in chicken-broth mixture. Yield 4 servings.

chicken soup mexican-style

6 cups Basic Chicken Stock (see Index)
1 whole chicken breast, split (about 1-pound)
¼ pound vermicelli
¼ cup vegetable oil
1 large tomato, peeled, seeded, chopped
1 ripe avocado
2 hot green chilies, chopped
Salt and pepper to taste

Early in day heat stock to boiling in large saucepan. Add chicken; reduce heat to low. Simmer 25 minutes; remove and cool chicken. Skin, remove from bones, and shred meat.

At dinner time break vermicelli into 2-inch lengths.

Heat oil in small skillet; lightly brown vermicelli. Drain on paper towels.

Meanwhile, heat stock to boiling. Add vermicelli; cook until tender. Add tomato and chicken; heat through.

Peel and seed avocado; cut into chunks. Add avocado, chilies, salt, and pepper; heat through. Yield 6 servings.

chicken velvet soup

1 whole raw chicken breast
2 egg whites
2 teaspoons salt
1 teaspoon sesame oil
6 cups chicken broth
1 can cream-style corn
2 teaspoons sugar
3 tablespoons cornstarch in ¼ cup water
1 scallion, chopped

Skin and bone chicken; mince. Combine chicken, egg whites, ½ teaspoon salt, and sesame oil; mix well.

Bring broth to boil. Add corn, salt, and sugar; cook 1 to 2 minutes. Add dissolved cornstarch; stir until thickened. Add chicken mixture to soup; add scallion. Serve immediately. Yield 6 to 8 servings.

cream of chicken soup

4 cups Basic Chicken Stock (see Index)
2 cups finely chopped celery
1 small clove garlic, pressed
¾ cup half-and-half cream
Salt and freshly ground white pepper to taste
2 cups minced cooked chicken
½ cup finely grated Parmesan cheese

Pour stock into large saucepan; bring to boil. Add celery and garlic; simmer 10 minutes or until tender. Pour into blender or food processor container; process until pureed. Return to saucepan. Add cream, salt, and pepper; bring just to boiling point. Stir in chicken and cheese; heat, stirring, until cheese is melted and soup well blended. Serve

cream of chicken soup

giblet soup

in soup bowls. Pour a dash of whipping cream into center of each serving, if desired. Yield 8 servings.

giblet soup

½ pound chicken gizzards
¼ pound chicken livers
1 pound chicken necks
Basic Seasoned Flour (see Index)
Bacon drippings
2½ quarts water
4 stalks celery with leaves
1 bay leaf
10 peppercorns
Salt
1½ tablespoons butter
½ cup chopped onions
1 cup chopped tomatoes
½ cup diced carrots
½ cup chopped celery
¼ teaspoon pepper
1 tablespoon lemon juice

Dredge gizzards, livers, and necks in flour.

Heat bacon drippings in large heavy kettle until hot. Add giblets; brown on all sides. Add water, celery stalks, bay leaf, peppercorns, and 1 tea-spoon salt; bring to boil. Cover; boil gently 1½ hours. Strain stock; set giblets aside to cool.

Heat butter in kettle. Add onions; sauté until golden.

Chop gizzards and livers. Add strained stock, gizzards, livers, tomatoes, carrots, chopped celery, pepper, and salt to taste; cover. Boil gently 30 minutes or until vegetables are tender; stir in lemon juice. Meat from necks can be added, if desired. Soup can be frozen. Yield about 6 servings.

turkey and chestnut soup leftover-style

Carcass of 1 cooked turkey
3 to 4 tablespoons or more leftover chestnut
    stuffing (or 5 to 6 tablespoons canned chestnut
    puree)
2 onions, sliced
2 or 3 carrots, sliced
2 or 3 stalks celery, sliced
Several sprigs parsley
1 bay leaf
5 to 6 cups turkey stock or water
Salt and pepper

1 tablespoon butter
¾ tablespoon all purpose flour
5 or 6 chestnuts
1 tablespoon chopped parsley

Remove remaining chestnut stuffing from cold turkey; reserve. Remove turkey meat that can be used as garnish. Break up carcass; put into large pan with onions, carrots, celery, and herbs. Cover with water; simmer until well flavored. Avoid boiling hard; this makes stock cloudy. Strain.

Put chestnut stuffing into electric blender or food processor with cup of turkey stock; blend until smooth. Turn into pan; add 4 cups stock, seasoning, and turkey meat. Cook together a few minutes. If the soup is too thin, blend butter and flour together to make paste; add to soup in small pieces. Stir until thickened. Bring to boil. Serve hot with cooked chestnuts, fried in butter and broken into pieces; sprinkle top with chopped parsley. Yield 4 to 6 servings.

turkey–vegetable soup

1 small onion, chopped
2 tablespoons butter or margarine
2 cups water
2 chicken bouillon cubes
2 cups diced cooked turkey
½ cup celery tops and pieces
1½ cups diced potatoes

1 cup diced carrots
2½ cups milk
2 tablespoons flour
1 teaspoon salt
⅛ teaspoon pepper

Cook onion in butter until tender. Add water, bouillon cubes, turkey, and vegetables; boil gently, covered, until vegetables are tender.

Stir a little milk into flour until mixture is smooth. Add remaining milk, salt, and pepper; add to soup. Simmer, stirring occasionally to prevent sticking, until soup is slightly thickened. Yield 6 servings.

SEAFOOD

baltimore crab stew

1 pound crab meat
1 teaspoon salt
1 teaspoon white pepper
1 tablespoon butter
1 pint milk
1 pint light cream
½ teaspoon Tabasco sauce
1 teaspoon Worcestershire sauce
6 tablespoons sherry
Lemon slices
Parsley snips

turkey and chestnut soup leftover-style

clam chowder new england-style

Bring crab, salt, pepper, butter, and milk to slow simmer; let simmer very slowly 10 minutes. Add cream and sauces; bring to boiling point, but do not boil. Stir as little as possible so as not to break up crab meat. Add sherry; let stand just a moment. Remove from burner. Serve in warm cups topped with lemon slices and bit of parsley. Yield 4 servings.

clam bisque

1 (7½-ounce) can minced clams
1 cup light cream
½ teaspoon Worcestershire sauce
4 dashes Tabasco sauce
Salt to taste
Chopped chives
Paprika

Put clams in blender; cover. Blend at high speed until smooth. Add cream, Worcestershire sauce, Tabasco sauce, and salt. Serve chilled; sprinkle with chives and paprika. Yield 3 servings.

clam chowder manhattan-style

4 ounces salt pork or bacon, cut into small pieces
1 cup minced onion
2 tablespoons finely chopped flat-leaf parsley
½ teaspoon freshly ground black pepper
½ bay leaf
2 cups minced celery
1 cup minced green pepper
3 (16-ounce) cans minced clams
2 (8-ounce) bottles clam juice
1 (1-pound, 12-ounce) can Italian-style tomatoes,

drained, chopped (save liquid)
4 cups finely diced potatoes
8 cups water
Salt and pepper to taste
2 tablespoons butter
Chopped parsley for garnish

In heavy soup pot cook salt pork with onion, parsley, and black pepper until pork starts to render fat. Stir and cook 5 minutes. Add bay leaf, celery, and green pepper; cook 15 minutes. Add juice from minced clams, 1 bottle clam juice, liquid from tomatoes, potatoes, and water; simmer 25 minutes. Add clams, tomatoes, and second bottle of clam juice; correct seasoning. Add butter; sprinkle top with parsley. Serve with crusty bread, garlic bread, or with oyster crackers sprinkled with melted butter and heated 2 to 3 minutes under broiler. Yield 8 servings.

clam chowder new england-style

1 quart shucked clams with liquor
3 slices salt pork, diced

2 small onions, minced
2 medium potatoes, diced
1 bay leaf
1 cup water
3 cups milk, scalded
1½ cups half-and-half cream
¼ cup butter
Salt and freshly ground pepper to taste

Drain clams; reserve liquor; chop coarsely.

Fry salt pork slowly in kettle until all fat is rendered. Add onions; sauté until golden. Add potatoes, bay leaf, and water; simmer until potatoes are tender.

Strain reserved clam liquor; stir into potato mixture with milk, cream, butter, and chopped clams. Add seasonings; simmer 15 minutes. Add more seasonings, if needed. Remove bay leaf before serving. Yield 6 to 8 servings.

clam soup japanese-style

16 small clams
4 cups boiling water
½ teaspoon salt
¾ teaspoon rice wine or sherry
1 tablespoon soy sauce
Lemon slices for garnish

Thoroughly wash clams. Put into boiling water; boil until shells crack. Add salt, wine, and soy sauce. Garnish with lemon slices. Yield 4 servings.

crab bisque

1 medium onion, diced
½ green pepper, diced
2 tablespoons butter or margarine
¼ pound mushrooms, sliced
2 tomatoes, diced
1 pound crab meat
1 teaspoon salt
Dash of cayenne
1½ cups cream
1 tablespoon minced parsley

In medium skillet sauté onion and pepper in melted butter until onion is transparent. Add mushrooms; cook 3 minutes. Stir in tomatoes; cook 3 minutes. Add remaining ingredients; heat to boil, but do not boil. Add more parsley for garnish if desired. Serve over rice. Yield 4 to 6 servings.

cream of crab broccoli soup

1 (6 to 8-ounce) package frozen Alaska King crab, thawed, or 1 (7½-ounce) can Alaska King crab
1 (10-ounce) package frozen chopped broccoli
½ cup chopped onion
3 tablespoons butter or margarine

2 tablespoons flour
2 cups milk
2 cups half-and-half cream
2 chicken bouillon cubes
½ teaspoon salt
⅛ teaspoon black pepper
⅛ teaspoon cayenne pepper
¼ teaspoon thyme

Drain and slice crab.

Cook broccoli according to package directions.

Sauté onion in butter; blend in flour. Add milk and half-and-half; stir and cook until thickened and smooth. Dissolve bouillon cubes in hot soup. Add seasonings, crab, and broccoli; heat through. Yield 4 to 6 servings.

fish soup

1 pound fish fillets
2 tablespoons lemon juice
2 tablespoons aquavit or vodka
Chives
4 onions, peeled
1 leek
2 carrots
4 to 5 medium potatoes
3 slices bacon
4 cups canned beef bouillon or Basic Beef Stock (see Index)
Pinch of saffron
½ teaspoon basil
1 bay leaf
Salt and pepper to taste
Parsley for garnish

Drain fillets; cut into 1-inch pieces. Put into deep dish. Add lemon juice and aquavit; cover.

Finely chop chives and onions. Cut leek in half, then into pieces. Peel and dice carrots and potatoes.

Dice bacon; put into pot. Cook until just transparent. Add onions and chives; cook 3 minutes. Let mixture steam. Add leek, carrots, and potatoes; steam 1 minute. Pour in stock. Add saffron, basil, and bay leaf; cover. Cook 15 minutes. Add fish mixture with its liquid; simmer slowly 5 minutes. Season with salt and pepper. Serve in bowls or in tureen; garnish with parsley. Yield 4 to 6 servings.

fish soup normandy

fish stock
½ pound fish (heads, bones, or trimmings)
4 cups hot beef bouillon or Basic Beef Stock (see Index)
Juice of ½ lemon
1 small onion, sliced
1 stalk celery, sliced
1 carrot, sliced

fish soup

Wash fish; drain. Place into large saucepan; add bouillon, lemon juice, onion, celery, and carrot. Simmer over low heat 1 hour; strain. Yield 6 servings.

fish dumplings
¾ pound white fish, cooked (cod, haddock, etc.)
¼ teaspoon salt
⅛ teaspoon white pepper
1 tablespoon butter
1 egg
3 sprigs parsley, finely chopped
2 teaspoons lemon juice
3 tablespoons packaged bread crumbs

Put fish through meat grinder (fine blade), or spin in food processor. Season with salt and pepper. Blend in butter and egg. Add parsley, lemon juice, and bread crumbs. Mix well; set aside.

soup ingredients
3 tablespoons vegetable oil
1 medium onion, sliced
5 carrots, sliced into ½ inch lengths
1 stalk celery, sliced into ½ inch lengths
2 sprigs parsley
2 cups hot beef bouillon
Fish Stock
2 tablespoons tomato paste
1 (4-ounce) can sliced mushrooms, drained
3 small tomatoes, peeled, quartered
1 teaspoon curry powder
1 green pepper, sliced
Fish Dumplings
1 (4½-ounce) can shrimp, deveined, drained
¾ cup white wine
Salt to taste
Dash of cayenne pepper
Dash of garlic powder
1 sprig parsley, chopped

Heat oil in large Dutch oven or saucepan. Add onion, carrots, celery, and parsley; sitrring constantly, cook until slightly browned. Gradually add beef broth; cover. Simmer over low heat 20 minutes. Add Fish Stock, tomato paste, mushrooms, tomatoes, curry powder, and green pepper; simmer 10 minutes.

Moisten hands; shape Fish Dumplings. Drop into soup. Add shrimp; simmer 15 minutes. Pour in wine. Season to taste with salt, cayenne pepper, and garlic powder. Stir in chopped parsley. Serve.

lobster bisque

1 large freshly boiled lobster (or 2 small, preferably female, lobsters)
5 to 6 cups fish stock
1 small onion, sliced

628

1 carrot, sliced
2 stalks celery, sliced
1 bay leaf, 3 or 4 sprigs parsley, tied together
Salt and pepper
5 tablespoons butter
2½ tablespoons flour
¼ teaspoon mace or nutmeg
1 cup cream
3 to 4 tablespoons sherry (or brandy)

Split freshly boiled lobster down back with sharp knife; remove intestine, which looks like long black thread down center of back. Remove stomach sac from head and tough gills. Crack claws; remove meat; add to back meat. If lobster is female and there is red coral or roe, reserve for garnish. Reserve greenish curd from head. Break up all lobster shells; put into pan with stock. Add onion, carrot, celery, herbs, salt, and pepper; cover. Simmer 30 to 45 minutes.

Meanwhile, cut lobster meat into chunks. Pound coral roe with 2 tablespoons butter to use as garnish and to color soup.

Melt 3 tablespoons butter in pot; stir in flour until smoothly blended. Cook a minute or two. Add strained lobster stock; blend until smooth. Bring to boil; stir constantly. Reduce heat; simmer 4 to 5 minutes. Add lobster meat. Remove herbs. Add mace; adjust seasoning. Add cream and sherry. Serve in soup cups with piece of coral butter in each cup; sprinkle with paprika. Yield: 6 servings

manhattan fish chowder

1 pound fish fillets or steaks, fresh or frozen
¼ cup chopped bacon or salt pork

fish soup normandy

½ cup chopped onion
2 cups boiling water
1 (1-pound) can tomatoes
1 cup diced potatoes
½ cup diced carrots
½ cup chopped celery
¼ cup catsup
1 tablespoon Worcestershire sauce
1 teaspoon salt
¼ teaspoon pepper
¼ teaspoon thyme
Chopped parsley

Thaw frozen fish. Remove skin and bones from fish; cut into 1-inch pieces.

Fry bacon until crisp. Add onion; cook until tender. Add water, tomatoes, potatoes, carrots, celery, catsup, and seasonings; cover. Simmer 40 to 45 minutes, until vegetables are tender. Add fish; cover. Simmer about 10 minutes, until fish flakes easily. Sprinkle with parsley. Yield 6 servings.

maryland crab soup

6 cups strong beef stock
3 cups mixed vegetables (fresh, leftover, or frozen; include chopped onions and celery, diced carrots, peas, lima beans, cut string beans, corn, okra, and tomatoes, not squash, cabbage, or potatoes)
Salt and pepper
1 pound crab meat (claw or white meat)
Seafood seasoning to taste
Claws and pieces of whole crab if available (either raw or cooked)

Heat stock in large soup pot. Add vegetables and seasoning; simmer 1 hour. Add the crab meat, and claws, and pieces 30 minutes before serving. Simmer gently, to heat through and allow flavors to blend. Serve hot in large soup bowls, with bread and butter or hard crusty rolls and butter as accompaniment. Yield 4 to 6 servings.

moules marinière

40 to 50 mussels, fresh, unopened
1 onion, or 4 or 5 shallots
1 carrot
1 stalk celery
1 clove garlic
1 cup white wine
1 cup water
2 tablespoons chopped parsley
1 bay leaf
Pinch of thyme
3 tablespoons butter
Freshly ground black pepper
2½ tablespoons flour

manhattan fish chowder

Wash mussels; scrub thoroughly to remove weed or sand. Knock or scrape off barnacles; remove beards. Examine carefully; if any are not tightly closed, discard immediately, as they are poisonous if not alive when cooked. Soak in plenty of cold water; they will expel sand from inside shells during soaking process.

Meanwhile, chop onion. Peel and chop carrot. Slice celery. Crush garlic. Add to pan with wine, water, 1 tablespoon parsley, bay leaf, thyme, and pepper. Bring to boil; simmer 6 to 8 minutes.

Drain mussels; add to pan. Cover tightly with lid; simmer 6 to 8 minutes. Shake pan frequently to make sure all mussels are covered by liquid. Remove from heat as soon as mussels open their shells. Strain off liquid; reserve. Remove mussels from pan; carefully remove half of each shell. If serving for a party, carefully remove inner part of gristly beard; otherwise, each diner can do this for himself at table. Put half shells holding fish into deep dish; keep warm.

Put cooking liquid into pan.

Blend butter and flour into paste; add to liquid. Bring slowly to boil; whisk constantly. Add remaining parsley; adjust seasoning. Pour over mussels. Serve in deep soup plates. Yield 4 servings.

mushroom–shrimp chowder (cold)

1 pound fresh mushrooms, washed, trimmed, sliced
1½ cups water
2½ teaspoons salt
¼ cup chopped fresh onion
¼ cup melted butter
¼ cup all-purpose flour
⅛ teaspoon freshly ground pepper
2½ cups milk
½ cup whipping cream
2 cups chopped cooked shrimp

Combine mushrooms, water, and 1 teaspoon salt in saucepan; bring to boil. Reduce heat; cover.

Simmer 10 minutes. Drain mushrooms; reserve liquid.

Sauté onion in butter in saucepan until tender. Add flour, remaining salt, and pepper; mix well. Stir in reserved liquid gradually; blend until smooth. Add milk gradually; cook, stirring constantly, until mixture comes to boil and thickens. Remove from heat; stir in cream, shrimp, and mushrooms. Chill thoroughly before serving. Yield about 6 servings.

oyster bisque

1 quart fresh oysters
3 cups Basic Chicken Stock (see Index)
1½ cups fine bread crumbs
⅓ cup finely chopped onion
1 cup finely diced celery
Salt and white pepper to taste
1 quart milk, scalded
2 tablespoons butter

mushroom–shrimp chowder (cold)

¼ cup sherry

Drain oysters; reserve liquid. Chop oysters.

Pour stock in soup kettle. Add oyster liquid, bread crumbs, onion, celery, salt, and pepper; boil slowly, stirring frequently, about 30 minutes. Process in blender container until onion and celery are pureed; return to soup kettle. Add oysters; heat thoroughly, but do not overcook. Stir in milk, butter, and sherry; heat through. Serve immediately. Yield 6 to 8 servings.

oyster stew

1 pint oysters
4 tablespoons butter
½ teaspoon salt
Pepper to taste
Dash of Tabasco sauce
1 pint milk
1 pint light cream
2 teaspoons butter
Paprika

Drain oysters; reserve liquor.

Melt 4 tablespoons butter in heavy saucepan; add salt, pepper, and Tabasco. Add reserved liquor to pot; stir to blend well. Add oysters; cook only until edges begin to curl, about 3 to 5 minutes. Stir in milk and cream; bring to boil, but do not boil. Spoon soup into hot bowls; dot each bowl with butter and healthy dash of paprika. Yield 4 servings.

potato–tuna chowder

2½ cups diced potatoes
2 cups Basic Chicken Stock (see Index)
2 tablespoons fresh minced onion
½ teaspoon salt
¼ teaspoon sage
¼ teaspoon paprika
Dash of white pepper
½ cup sliced fresh carrots
½ cup cut fresh green beans
½ cup sliced fresh celery
3 cups milk
1 (7-ounce) can chunk-style tuna, drained

Combine 1 cup potatoes, chicken stock, onion, and salt in large saucepan; bring to boil. Reduce heat; cover. Simmer 10 to 15 minutes, until potatoes are tender. Add sage, paprika, and pepper; mash potatoes. Add remaining potatoes, carrots, beans, celery, and milk to potatoes; bring just to boil. Reduce heat; simmer about 15 minutes, until vegetables are tender.

Break tuna into chunks; add to chowder. Simmer 5 minutes. Yield 4 to 6 servings.

scallop soup

fish stock
1½ pounds small fish, cleaned, or fish trimmings (heads, tails, and bones of mild ocean fish, or lobster and shrimp shells)
3 cups cold water

½ cup chopped onion
¼ cup chopped carrot
½ cup chopped celery
½ cup white wine
1 bay leaf
3 peppercorns
Several parsley sprigs
1 cup clam juice

Wash fish or trimmings in cold water; drain.

Combine water, vegetables, and wine in heavy saucepan.

Tie bay leaf, peppercorns, and parsley in small piece of cheesecloth. Add seasonings and fish to water and vegetables; bring to boil over moderate heat. Cook, uncovered, 20 to 30 minutes. Strain stock; add clam juice. Reserve. Yield 4 servings.

soup
¾ pound fresh scallops
2 slices bacon, diced
2 cups peeled, diced potatoes
½ teaspoon salt
¼ teaspoon white pepper
1 tablespoon chopped parsley
½ teaspoon crumbled dried thyme
2 cups peeled, diced tomatoes
Fish Stock
1½ cups hot light cream
¾ cup crushed water biscuits or pilot crackers

potato–tuna chowder

shrimp soup

Pats of butter
Chopped parsley
Ground mace

Wash scallops in cold water; if large, cut in half or quarter. Drain; reserve. Sauté bacon in large, heavy saucepan 3 to 4 minutes or until it starts to brown. Add potatoes; cook until tender. Add salt, pepper, parsley, thyme, tomatoes, and stock; stir well. Cook over moderate heat 15 minutes. Add scallops; bring to gentle boil. Cover; reduce heat to low. Cook 10 to 12 minutes, until scallops are cooked through. Stir in heated cream; do not let mixture boil after adding cream. Slowly stir in water biscuits, while cooking over low heat, to thicken soup. Ladle soup into bowls; float pat of butter on each serving. Garnish with chopped parsley and sprinkling of mace.

seafood gumbo

1 clove garlic, minced
6 onions, chopped
1 green pepper, chopped
3 tablespoons corn oil
1 (10-ounce) package frozen sliced okra, partially
   thawed
2 (16-ounce) cans whole tomatoes
3 cups water
2 teaspoons salt
¼ teaspoon black pepper
2 drops Tabasco sauce
1 bay leaf
¼ cup raw rice
1 (1-pound) package frozen deveined shrimp
1 (7-ounce) package frozen crab meat, thawed
1 dozen oysters

3 tablespoons chopped parsley
Filé powder
Rice, boiled

Sauté garlic, onions, and green pepper in hot oil in Dutch oven. Add okra, tomatoes, water, seasonings, and raw rice; bring to boil. Cover; reduce heat. Simmer 10 minutes. Add frozen shrimp; stir. Return to boil; cover. Simmer 3 minutes. Add crab meat, oysters, and parsley; simmer until heated, about 2 minutes. Remove bay leaf. Place about ⅛ teaspoon filé powder in each soup bowl. Ladle gumbo into bowls; stir gently to mix all ingredients. Add mound of hot cooked rice to each bowl. Yield 8 servings.

shrimp soup

1 medium onion, chopped
1 large carrot, chopped
1 tablespoon dry white wine
1 tablespoon water
3 cups hot beef bouillon
1 teaspoon sage
1 teaspoon tarragon
1 (10-ounce) package frozen peas
Salt and pepper to taste
12 ounces medium cooked shrimp, canned or
   frozen
½ cup white wine
¼ cup skim evaporated milk

In 4-quart saucepan or Dutch oven, cook onion and carrot in 1 tablespoon wine and water until onion is soft. Add bouillon; simmer 12 minutes. Add sage, tarragon, and peas; bring to boil. Simmer 8 minutes. Puree in blender or food mill; return to pan. Season with salt and pepper. Add shrimp; heat, without boiling, about 2 minutes. Stir in ½ cup wine and milk; correct seasonings. Serve immediately. Yield 4 servings.

VEGETABLE

asparagus soup

1 can condensed asparagus soup
Milk
1 can green asparagus tips
1 (½-pint) carton natural yogurt
Little lemon juice
Few drops of Tabasco
¼ cup heavy cream
Paprika
Cheese straws

Blend soup with liquid from can of asparagus tips; use enough milk to fill soup can. Stir in yogurt, or blend in electric blender. Add lemon juice and Tabasco. Stir in asparagus tips. Serve chilled with spoonful of whipped cream in each cup; sprinkle with paprika. Serve with cheese straws. Yield 4 servings.

baked–bean and tomato soup

1 cup baked beans in tomato sauce
1 (10½-ounce) can condensed tomato soup
1 (15-ounce) can tomato juice
1 can (2 cups) water
1 tablespoon tomato puree
½ teaspoon sugar
1 tablespoon chopped parsley

garnish
2 or 3 slices bacon, fried crisp, crumbled

Put baked beans in pan with soup, juice, water, puree, and seasonings; heat together gently, add parsley. When well mixed and hot, put into electric blender or food processor; blend until smooth. Return to pan; heat, adding remaining beans. Serve hot with bacon sprinkled on top. Yield 4 to 6 servings.

bean soup with frankfurters

1 pound dried navy beans
8 cups water
3 cups beef bouillon or Basic Beef Stock (see Index)
1 carrot, chopped
1 celery stalk, chopped
4 strips bacon, cubed
2 small onions, chopped
1 teaspoon salt
¼ teaspoon white pepper

6 frankfurters, sliced
2 tablespoons chopped parsley

Soak beans in water overnight. In 3-quart saucepan bring beans, water, and broth to boil; cook about 1 hour. Add carrot and celery; cook 30 minutes.

Cook bacon in separate frypan until transparent. Add onions; cook until golden. Set aside.

Mash soup through sieve or food mill; return to pan. Add bacon mixture, salt, and pepper. Add frankfurters; reheat about 5 minutes. Sprinkle with parsley; serve. Yield 4 to 6 servings.

beet consommé

4 to 5 cups clear jellied Basic Beef or Chicken Stock (see Index)
2 or 3 small well-colored cooked red beets, peeled, grated
1 to 2 teaspoons onion juice
Juice of approximately ½ lemon
4 to 6 tablespoons sour cream
1 lemon, cut into quarters or sixths

Prepare clear jellied stock or use canned consommé. Either chicken or brown stock can be used, or use canned jellied consommé to make equivalent quantity. Put 4 to 5 cups stock or consommé into pan with beets, onion juice (made by squeezing small pieces of cut onion in garlic press), and some seasoning if necessary, although stock should be well flavored. Bring soup slowly to moderate heat; let cook, covered, very gently 30 to 40 minutes, until well flavored and colored by beets. Do not let boil; this makes soup muddy-brown color instead of rich red. Strain through double layer of clean cloth. Add enough lemon juice to sharpen flavor; adjust seasoning. If serving hot, reheat to just below boiling point; serve with garnish of sour cream, handed separately. If serving cold, put into clean bowl; chill in refrigerator. Mix with fork before serving with lemon quarters and sour cream. Yield 4 to 6 servings.

black-bean soup

1 to 1½ cups dried black beans
1 ham bone or some ham meat minus fat
5 to 6 cups water
2 medium onions, sliced
4 or 5 stalks celery, sliced
2 to 3 carrots, sliced
1 bay leaf, 5 or 6 sprigs parsley, 1 sprig thyme, tied together
2 cloves
½ teaspoon mustard powder
Pinch of cayenne pepper
Stock or milk
2 hard-boiled eggs
4 to 6 slices lemon or ½ cup chopped ham

beet consommé

Croutons

Wash beans in several changes of cold water; cover with cold water. Soak overnight; drain. Put beans into large thick pan; add water and ham bone. Cover pan; cook 2 hours. Add onions, celery, carrots, herbs, cloves, mustard, and cayenne; re-cover pan. Cook another 1 to 1½ hours, until beans are tender. Remove bone and herbs. Put soup through fine sieve or blend in electric blender. Reheat soup; if too thick, add enough stock or milk to make good texture. Adjust seasoning. Serve hot; garnish with egg, lemon, and croutons. Yield 4 to 6 servings.

broccoli chowder

1 pound fresh broccoli
1½ cups chicken broth
1½ cups milk
½ cup chopped cooked ham
¼ teaspoon freshly ground pepper
1½ cups grated Swiss cheese (6-ounces)
2 tablespoons butter or margarine
Salt to taste

Wash broccoli; remove leaves and coarse stem ends.

Pour broth into large pot; bring to boil. Add broccoli; reduce heat. Simmer, uncovered, 3 minutes. Cover; cook 10 minutes or until broccoli is just tender. Remove broccoli with slotted spoon; chop into bite-size pieces. Add milk, ham, and pepper to stock; bring to boil, stirring occasionally. Stir in cheese, butter, and broccoli; heat until cheese is melted. Add salt to taste. Do not boil. Serve hot. Yield 4 servings.

cabbage soup

1 small green cabbage (or 2 cups shredded green cabbage)
2 slices fat bacon, chopped
1 large onion, chopped
2 small leeks, white part only, sliced
2 carrots, sliced
1 potato, sliced
1 tablespoon flour
4 cups brown stock (or water and cubes; ham stock can be used, if not too salty)
2 tablespoons chopped parsley
1 bay leaf
Salt and pepper
Pinch of nutmeg

broccoli chowder

cabbage soup

2 teaspoons chopped dill or 1 teaspoon dill seeds
3 or 4 frankfurters, fried, sliced
Fat for frying
Croutons

Wash and shred green cabbage; put into pan of boiling salted water. Cook 5 minutes; drain. Rinse under cold water.

Meanwhile, heat bacon over gentle heat until fat runs. Add onion, leeks, carrots, and potato; stir over heat a few minutes. Sprinkle in flour; blend well. Add stock, parsley, bay leaf, salt, and pepper; bring to boil. Reduce heat; simmer 10 minutes. Add cabbage. Cook 20 minutes or until vegetables are tender but not mushy. Adjust seasoning; add nutmeg and dill. Remove bay leaf. For garnish, put few slices frankfurters into each serving, or serve croutons separately. Yield 4 to 6 servings.

cauliflower cream soup

cauliflower cream soup

1 medium cauliflower
1 medium potato
1 large tomato
4 cups milk
4 minced green onions or scallions
1 tablespoon minced parsley
½ teaspoon savory
2 teaspoons salt
¼ teaspoon white pepper
1 cup whipping cream

Separate cauliflower into florets. Peel and dice potato. Skin and chop tomato.

Combine milk, cauliflower, potato, tomato, onions, parsley, and seasonings in heavy kettle. Simmer until vegetables are tender. Pour through colander; drain off liquid. Reserve liquid.

Place ⅓ of vegetables in blender container with enough liquid to blend easily; process until pureed. Repeat process with remaining vegetables; return puree and remaining liquid to kettle. Stir in cream gradually; place over low heat. Heat through; stir frequently. Serve with bowl of grated Parmesan cheese to sprinkle over top, if desired. Yield 6 servings.

celery soup chinese-style

1 heaping tablespoon dried Chinese mushrooms
½ pound pork shoulder
2 small onions, minced
1 clove garlic, minced
2 small celeriac roots with green tops (celery stalks can be substituted)
4 tablespoons oil
3 cups hot chicken broth
1 ounce transparent noodles
2 tablespoons soy sauce
⅛ teaspoon powdered ginger

Soak mushrooms in cold water 30 minutes. Cut pork into 1½-inch long, ½-inch-thick strips. Mince onions and garlic. Cut off celery tops; set aside. Brush celeriac roots under running cold water; peel. Cut into ½-inch cubes.

Heat oil in saucepan. Add pork; brown on all sides, stirring constantly, about 3 minutes. Add onions, garlic, and celeriac; cook 5 minutes.

Drain mushrooms; cut in halves, or quarters if very large. Add to saucepan. Pour in broth; cover. Simmer over low heat 25 minutes.

Meanwhile, in another saucepan bring salted water to boil; add noodles. Remove from heat immediately; let stand 5 minutes; drain. Five minutes before end of cooking time of soup, add celery leaves. Season to taste with soy sauce and ginger.

Place noodles in soup tureen or 4 individual Chinese soup bowls; pour soup over noodles. Yield 4 servings.

chervil soup

2 young carrots, finely sliced
1 small potato, finely sliced
4 to 5 cups chicken or white stock
3 sprigs parsley
3 tablespoons butter
2 tablespoons flour
Salt and pepper
¼ teaspoon mace or pinch of nutmeg
¼ cup chopped fresh chervil
½ cup cream
Croutons

Put carrots and potato in pan with stock and parsley; simmer until tender, 15 to 20 minutes.

Melt butter; stir in flour. When smooth, strain stock onto flour and butter; mix well.

Blend potato and carrots in electric blender or food processor; add to soup. Mix well; bring to boil, stirring constantly. Simmer a few minutes, adding salt, pepper, and mace. Just before serving, add chervil and cream; reheat. Do not boil; this destroys delicate flavor of chervil. Serve with croutons. Yield 4 to 6 servings.

cream of asparagus soup

1 pound asparagus, green or white
   (or equivalent amount of canned asparagus)
1 onion, finely chopped
3 or 4 sprigs parsley
3 to 4 cups chicken stock (or water and
   chicken stock cubes)
Salt and pepper
3 tablespoons butter
2 tablespoons flour
¼ teaspoon mace
2 egg yolks
½ cup heavy cream
Croutons
Little green coloring, if necessary

If using fresh asparagus, wash, scrape, and trim; remove tips for garnish. If using canned asparagus, remove tips; drain off liquid, reserving it for making soup. Chop asparagus stalks; put in pot with onion. Add parsley, stock, and liquid from can if canned asparagus is used. Add a little salt and pepper; cover. Simmer 10 to 15 minutes, until asparagus is tender. Put into electric blender or food processor; blend until smooth. Or put through food mill or fine nylon sieve.

Melt butter. Add flour; stir until smooth. Cook a minute or two; remove from heat. Strain into soup; blend smoothly. Bring to boil, stirring constantly; simmer a few minutes. Adjust seasoning to taste; add mace.

Meanwhile, in small pan cook reserved tips about 5 to 7 minutes until tender, in a little hot stock or water. Strain liquid into soup; divide tips into soup cups equally.

Mix egg yolks and cream well. Add few spoonfuls hot soup; mix well. Strain into soup; stir constantly. Reheat soup gently; do not let it boil. If soup is not good color, add a little green coloring; be very careful, as it can easily be overdone. Serve hot with croutons. Yield 4 servings.

cream of barley soup

1 cup pearl barley
1 onion, sliced
1 carrot, sliced
2 stalks celery, sliced
1 bay leaf
3 or 4 sprigs parsley (or 1 tablespoon
  chopped parsley)
4 to 5 cups Basic Chicken Stock (see Index)
Chicken carcass or ham bone, if available
½ cup cream
1 to 2 tablespoons chopped parsley (garnish)
Croutons (garnish)

Wash barley; soak overnight if possible. Otherwise, cover with boiling water; soak 2 hours. Put vegetables into pan with drained barley, herbs, stock, and chicken carcass or ham bone. Cover; cook gently until barley is tender, about 1½ to 2 hours. Discard bones and herbs. Set aside barley.

Strain soup through sieve, or blend soup and barley in electric blender or food processor. Reheat soup; adjust seasoning. Add cream just

before serving. Sprinkle with parsley; serve with croutons. Yield 4 servings.

cream of brussels sprout soup

4 tablespoons butter
1 onion, chopped
1 potato, chopped
4 cups washed, trimmed, chopped Brussels
  sprouts
1½ tablespoons flour
4 cups Basic Chicken Stock (see Index)
  (or water and chicken cubes)
2 bay leaves
3 or 4 sprigs parsley
¼ teaspoon mace
Salt and pepper
1 cup light cream or milk

garnish
1 cup cooked chestnut pieces
2 to 3 tablespoons butter

Melt butter; cook onion and potato 2 to 3 minutes. Add sprouts; cook 5 minutes, stirring constantly. Sprinkle in flour; blend well. Pour on stock; stir until well mixed and smooth. Bring to boil; stir constantly. Reduce heat. Add bay leaves, parsley, and seasoning; cover. Simmer about 20 minutes, until vegetables are tender but not overcooked, as this would give soup an unpleasant flavor. Remove bay leaves. Put soup through food

cream of carrot soup

mill, or into electric blender or food processor; blend until smooth. Adjust seasoning; reheat soup. At last moment add cup of hot cream. Sprinkle with chestnut pieces, fried in butter until golden brown. Yield 4 to 6 servings.

cream of carrot soup

4 tablespoons butter
1½ cups sliced young carrots
1 large onion, finely sliced
½ clove garlic, crushed
2 tablespoons rice
3 or 4 sprigs parsley (or 1 tablespoon dried parsley)
Thinly peeled rind from ½ orange
4 cups Basic Chicken Stock (see Index)
¼ teaspoon sugar
Salt and pepper
Juice of ½ orange
¼ cup cream
2 egg yolks
Finely grated rind of ½ orange (garnish)
2 teaspoons chopped parsley (garnish)

Melt butter. Add vegetables, garlic and rice; mix well over gentle heat 5 minutes without browning. Add parsley, peeled orange rind, stock, sugar, and seasonings; bring to boil. Lower heat; simmer 30 to 40 minutes, until vegetables are tender. Put into electric blender or food processor; blend until smooth. Or put through food mill. Return to pot; re-heat, adding orange juice. If not thick enough, add cream and egg yolks: Mix egg yolks and cream well; add few spoons hot soup. Strain back into soup; stir constantly.

cream of celery soup

Reheat soup without allowing to boil. Serve in soup cups; sprinkle with grated orange rind and parsley. Yield 4 to 6 servings.

cream of celery soup

1 slice bacon
3 to 4 tablespoons butter
2 cups chopped celery or celeriac
1 potato, sliced
1 large onion, chopped
1 tablespoon flour
2 cups water or Basic Chicken Stock (see Index)
1 bay leaf
Several sprigs parsley
Pinch of thyme
3 cups milk
Salt and pepper
4 to 6 tablespoons cream
Paprika
Croutons

Chop bacon; put in pan with butter. Cook gently a few minutes. Add celery, potato, and onion; cook together 4 to 5 minutes, stirring constantly to prevent browning. Sprinkle in flour; blend smoothly. Add stock; mix well. Bring to boil; reduce heat. Add bay leaf, parsley, and thyme; simmer 20 to 30 minutes, until vegetables are tender. Put through fine food mill or into electric blender or food processor; blend until smooth. Reheat gently.

Heat milk in another pan; when nearly boiling, add to soup pan with seasoning to taste. Serve with spoon of cream and dusting of paprika in each soup cup. Serve croutons separately. Yield 4 to 6 servings.

cream of corn soup

cream of corn soup

3 tablespoons butter
1 onion, chopped
1 medium potato, finely sliced
1½ cups fresh or canned corn
3½ cups milk
1 bay leaf
3 or 4 sprigs parsley
Salt and pepper
¼ teaspoon mace
1 chicken bouillon cube
4 to 6 spoons heavy cream
1 tablespoon chopped chives or parsley (or sprinkling of paprika)
Fried bread croutons (see Index)

Melt butter. Cook onion and potato gently, 5 minutes; shake pan occasionally to prevent sticking. Add 1 cup corn; stir well. Add milk, bay leaf, parsley, salt, pepper, and mace; bring to simmer. Add bouillon cube; cook until vegetables are tender. Put into electric blender; blend until smooth. Or put through fine food mill. Return to pan with remaining corn (if fresh, simmer in salted water until tender.) Reheat until nearly boiling; adjust seasoning. Serve in soup cups with spoonful of cream, sprinkling of chives, and croutons in each cup. Yield 4 to 6 servings.

cream of mushroom soup

8 to 12 ounces fresh mushrooms, sliced
1 small onion, thinly sliced
¼ cup butter

3½ cups milk
⅓ cup all-purpose flour mixed to smooth paste with ¼ cup cold milk
4 chicken bouillon cubes
Pinch of thyme
Salt and pepper to taste
½ cup plain yogurt

Brown mushrooms and onion in hot butter in large skillet, about 5 minutes. Add milk, flour paste, bouillon cubes, and thyme. Heat over moderate heat, stirring frequently, until soup is thickened and begins to boil. Remove from heat; season to taste with salt and pepper. Stir a little hot soup into yogurt. Stir mixture back into soup. Serve at once. Garnish with sprig of fresh dill, if desired. Yield 4 servings.

cream of pea soup with bacon

2 slices bacon
1 can condensed pea soup or 2 cans ordinary pea soup
1 can water or milk
4 tablespoons cooked peas
4 tablespoons heavy cream
1 tablespoon chopped mint
Croutons

Chop bacon slices; cook gently until crisp. Add soup and can of water; stir over gentle heat until smooth. Add peas; heat to boiling point. Pour into heated soup cups; put spoonful of heavy cream in center of each. Sprinkle with mint; serve at once with croutons. Yield 4 to 6 servings.

cream of mushroom soup

cream of pea soup with bacon

creole soup

3 tablespoons butter, oil, or bacon fat
½ cup chopped green and red peppers
1 onion, chopped
2 tablespoons flour
2 teaspoons tomato puree
4 large ripe tomatoes (or ¾ cup canned tomatoes)
4 cups stock
1 bay leaf, 4 sprigs parsley, 1 sprig thyme,
   tied together
Pinch of cayenne pepper
¼ teaspoon sugar
2 to 3 teaspoons grated fresh horseradish
   (or 1 teaspoon dried horseradish)
1 teaspoon vinegar
1 tablespoon chopped parsley (optional)

Melt butter; cook peppers and onion gently 5 to 6 minutes without browning. Stir in flour; blend well. Add tomato puree; chopped, de-seeded fresh or canned tomatoes; stock; bay leaf; herbs, and seasonings. Bring to boil; stir constantly. Reduce heat; simmer 25 to 30 minutes. Remove bay leaf and herbs; adjust seasoning. Add horseradish and vinegar. If soup color is not good enough, a little more tomato puree can be added. Serve hot; sprinkle with parsley and croutons. Yield 4 servings.

cucumber soup

2 cups milk
4 cups plain yogurt
½ cup dry white wine
1 tablespoon lemon juice
1 onion, grated
1 clove garlic, minced or crushed

2 large (about 1 pound) cucumbers, unpeeled,
   finely grated
Salt and pepper to taste
Watercress or parsley sprigs

Whisk together milk and yogurt in large bowl; gradually add wine and lemon juice. Stir in onion, garlic, cucumbers, salt, and pepper; cover. Refrigerate 1 hour before servings. Garnish with cucumber slices and watercress. Yield 6 to 8 servings.

gazpacho (jellied)

1 (1-quart 14-ounce) can tomato juice
2 envelopes unflavored gelatin
4 tomatoes, peeled, seeded, chopped
1 cucumber, peeled, seeded, chopped
½ green pepper, seeded, diced
¼ cup grated onion
4 tablespoons olive oil
4 tablespoons wine vinegar

creole soup

1 clove garlic, crushed
6 to 8 drops hot pepper sauce
Salt
Freshly ground black pepper

Heat tomato juice; add gelatin. Stir until dissolved; set aside to cool.

Combine tomatoes, cucumber, green pepper, and onion; add to the tomato juice. Stir in oil and vinegar. Add garlic, pepper sauce, and salt and black pepper to taste; mix well. Chill thoroughly, preferably overnight. Serve in small bowls set in bed of crushed ice. Yield 6 or 7 servings.

green-bean soup I

1 pound fresh green beans or 2 (1-pound) cans,
   drained
6 cups Basic Chicken Stock (see Index)
½ teaspoon thyme
¼ teaspoon savory
1 clove garlic, pressed
½ cup whipping cream
Salt and freshly ground pepper to taste

Snap ends from beans; cut beans into large pieces. Combine beans and stock in large saucepan. Add thyme, savory, and garlic; bring to boil. Reduce heat; cover. Simmer until beans are tender. Drain; reserve liquid.

Pour reserved liquid back into saucepan; boil until reduced to 4 cups.

Place beans in blender container; process until pureed. Stir into liquid in saucepan; mix well. Bring to boil. Stir in cream; bring just to boil. Remove from heat; season with salt and pepper. Cool; chill until cold. Equally delicious served hot. Yield 6 to 8 servings.

643

gazpacho (jellied)

green-bean soup II

2 to 3 tablespoons butter
1 medium onion (or 3 or 4 shallots),
  finely chopped
1 clove garlic, crushed
2 tablespoons flour
4 cups chicken or veal stock

Salt and pepper
1 pound green beans
1 teaspoon chopped or dried summer savory
Little green coloring if required
4 to 6 tablespoons whipping cream
2 slices bacon

Melt butter; cook onion and garlic 5 to 6 minutes in covered pan. Add flour; blend in smoothly.

green-bean soup I

quired. Serve hot with spoon of whipped cream on each cup; sprinkle with finely crumbled crispy fried bacon. Yield 4 to 6 servings.

green pea soup

2 tablespoons butter
1 small onion (or several young green onions), finely chopped
1 head lettuce, washed, sliced
2 cups fresh or frozen peas
4 cups Basic Chicken Stock (see Index)
Salt and pepper
Sugar to taste
1 sprig mint (or 1 teaspoon dried mint)
4 to 6 tablespoons heavy cream
2 teaspoons fresh (or dried) chopped mint
Croutons

Melt butter; soften onion and lettuce 4 to 5 minutes without browning.

Measure 2 cups peas. Add 1½ cups to soup pan; reserve remainder as garnish. Add stock, salt, pepper, sugar, and mint sprig; cover. Cook gently until tender, about 20 minutes. Remove mint. Put into electric blender; blend until smooth. Or put through food mill or fine sieve.

Meanwhile, cook remaining peas in little boiling salted, sugared water; drain. Divide among soup cups.

Reheat soup; adjust seasoning. Pour into soup cups. Add tablespoon cream to each cup; sprinkle with chopped mint. Serve with croutons. Yield 4 to 6 servings.

green split-pea soup

1 (1-pound) package green split peas
1 ham hock
12 green onions or scallions
1 cup diced carrots
1 cup diced celery

green split-pea soup

Pour on stock; mix well. When smooth, bring to boil; stir constantly. Add salt and pepper.

String beans; cut into slanting slices or break in half, depending on size. Add with dried savory to soup; cook 25 minutes or until beans are tender. Strain soup; reserve few pieces of bean for garnish (keep warm). Put remaining soup and beans through food mill or blend until smooth in electric blender or food processor. Reheat soup; adjust seasoning to taste. Add a little green coloring if re-

Jerusalem artichoke soup

1 slice lemon
½ teaspoon white pepper
Salt to taste
1 bay leaf

Place peas in colander; rinse thoroughly with cold water. Rinse ham hock with cold water.

Place peas, ham hock, and 2½ quarts water in large kettle or saucepan.

Slice onions; use about 6 green tops. Add onions, carrots, celery, lemon, seasonings, and bay leaf to pea mixture; bring to boil. Reduce heat; simmer, uncovered, 2 hours. Stir frequently to prevent sticking; add more water as needed. Avoid scorching as soup thickens. Remove ham hock, lemon slice, and bay leaf when soup is done.

Cut ham from hock; discard skin and bone. Dice ham coarsely; return to the soup. Soup can be pureed if creamier soup is desired. Yield 6 to 8 servings.

hominy soup

3 pigs feet, split, or 2 large fresh pork hocks
1 stewing chicken (about 4 pounds), cut up
1 pound lean pork (Boston butt), cut up
2 medium onions, finely chopped
2 cloves garlic, chopped
3 quarts water
1 tablespoon salt
4 red chili pods
1 (29-ounce) can white hominy, drained

garnish
1 cup sliced radishes
1 cup shredded lettuce

½ cup sliced green onions
½ cup shredded Jack cheese

In large kettle combine pigs feet, chicken, pork, onions, garlic, water, salt, and chili pods; bring to boil. Reduce heat to low; cook 2 hours. Add hominy; cook until meat starts to fall off bone (3 to 3½ hours total cooking time). Remove meat from broth; cool meat and broth in refrigerator several hours or overnight. Discard chili pods; remove meat from bones. Skim fat from surface of broth. At serving time, add meat to broth; heat. Serve hot in soup bowls with hot tortillas. Pass garnishes in separate bowls, so each diner can garnish his plate to his own taste. Yield 8 to 10 servings.

jerusalem artichoke soup

1 pound Jerusalem artichokes
2½ cups Basic Chicken Stock (see Index)
2 tablespoons butter
2 tablespoons all-purpose flour

2½ cups milk
1½ teaspoons salt
¼ teaspoon white pepper
⅓ cup freshly grated Parmesan cheese

Steam artichokes; cool. Remove skins with tip of sharp knife. Combine artichokes and ¾ cup stock in blender container; process until pureed.

Melt butter in top of double boiler over boiling water; stir in flour quickly. Cook, stirring, until smooth and bubbly. Stir in milk gradually; cook, stirring constantly, until slightly thickened.

Combine milk mixture, artichokes, remaining stock, and seasonings in heavy saucepan; cook over low heat, stirring occasionally, about 5 minutes. Stir in cheese just before serving. Serve with additional cheese to sprinkle over soup. Yield about 6 servings.

kale and potato soup

4 medium potatoes
2 tablespoons vegetable oil
8 cups water
1 teaspoon salt
½ teaspoon pepper
2 pounds fresh kale
½ pound cooked, sliced smoked garlic sausage

Peel and chop potatoes; combine with oil and water. Cook 20 to 30 minutes, until potatoes are tender. Remove potatoes; reserve liquid. Mash potatoes through sieve; return to potato liquid. Add salt and pepper; simmer 20 minutes.

Wash kale; discard all tough leaves; cut into thin shreds. Add to potatoes; cook 25 minutes. Add sausage; simmer gently 5 minutes. Yield 6 to 8 servings.

lentil soup

2 cups lentils
8 cups water
½ cup chopped onion
2 cloves garlic, minced
½ cup chopped carrots
½ cup chopped celery
¼ cup olive oil
1 teaspoon salt
½ teaspoon pepper
3 tablespoons tomato paste
2 bay leaves
½ teaspoon oregano
3 tablespoons wine vinegar
½ cup diced fried salt pork (optional)

Wash and pick over lentils; soak overnight in 2 cups water.

In Dutch oven or soup kettle sauté onion, garlic, carrots, and celery in oil. Add lentils, 6 cups water, salt, pepper, tomato paste, bay leaves, and oregano; bring to boil. Cook 2½ to 3 hours, until lentils are soft. Remove bay leaves.

At this point mixture can be pureed until smooth. Thin with water if necessary. Return mixture to soup pot; heat. Add vinegar. Garnish, if desired, with crisp salt pork cubes. Yield 8 servings.

lentil soup

lettuce soup

2 or 3 heads lettuce
3 tablespoons butter
1 small onion or 6 to 8 young green onions, finely
  chopped
2 tablespoons flour
4 cups chicken stock (or water and cubes)
Salt and pepper
½ teaspoon sugar
3 or 4 sprigs parsley (or 1 tablespoon dried
  parsley)
2 sprigs mint (or 1 teaspoon chopped mint)
1 cup creamy milk

garnish
4 to 6 tablespoons heavy cream
2 teaspoons finely chopped mint or parsley
Croutons

Chop well-washed lettuces coarsely.

Melt butter; soften lettuce and onion gently in
covered pan 5 to 6 minutes without browning.
Sprinkle in flour; blend smoothly. Add stock, seasoning, sugar, parsley, and mint. When smooth,
bring to boil; stir constantly. Reduce heat; simmer
15 minutes. Put into electric blender; blend until
smooth, or put through food mill or fine sieve.
Reheat in clean pan.

Meanwhile, heat milk in another pan; add when
on point of boiling. This lightens texture of soup.
Adjust seasoning to taste. If serving hot, pour into
soup cups. Put large spoonful of cream and a few
croutons on top of each cup. Sprinkle with mint.
If serving cold, add a little more seasoning; chill
thoroughly. Serve in soup cups with spoon of
whipped cream on top; sprinkle with mint. Yield 4
to 6 servings.

minestrone

2 tablespoons oil
2 slices bacon, chopped
3 or 4 carrots, peeled, chopped
2 onions, peeled, chopped
3 tomatoes, peeled, chopped
2 stalks celery, chopped
½ small head cabbage, shredded
5 cups Basic Beef Stock (see Index) or water
Salt and pepper
Bouquet Garni
½ cup elbow macaroni
Chopped parsley
Grated cheese

Heat oil in large kettle. Add bacon and
vegetables; sauté about 5 minutes. Add stock, seasoning, and Bouquet Garni; cover. Simmer about
30 minutes. Add macaroni; cook 20 minutes or
until macaroni is tender. Remove Bouquet Garni;
adjust seasoning. Sprinkle with parsley; serve
grated cheese separately. Yield 4 servings.

mulligatawny soup

3 to 4 tablespoons butter or oil
1 large onion, chopped
1 carrot, chopped
1 or 2 stalks celery, chopped
1 medium sour cooking apple

mulligatawny soup

onion soup

1 tablespoons curry powder or paste
1½ tablespoons flour
1 tablespoon tomato puree
4 to 5 cups stock
1 bay leaf
3 or 4 sprigs parsley
Pinch of thyme
Salt and pepper
2 tablespoons shredded coconut
1 teaspoon sugar
4 to 6 tablespoons cooked rice
2 teaspoons lemon juice
4 to 6 slices lemon
Paprika

Melt butter. Add onion, carrot, celery, and apple; stir well. Cook gently 5 to 6 minutes. Add curry; cook a few minutes. Add flour; mix well. Cook a few minutes to brown slightly. Add tomato puree and stock; blend well. Bring slowly to boil; reduce heat. Add herbs, seasoning, coconut, and sugar; simmer 30 to 45 minutes with lid on pan. Remove bay leaf. Blend soup in electric blender or put through fine food mill; return to pan. Add rice; adjust seasoning. Reheat; add lemon juice just before serving. (If preferred, rice can be served separately.) Serve hot with slice of lemon; sprinkle with paprika. Yield 4 to 6 servings.

okra chowder

2 pints okra
¼ cup bacon or other cooking fat
2 cups diced celery

1 green pepper, seeded, diced
1 small onion, peeled, chopped
2 large tomatoes, peeled, seeded, chopped
1 teaspoon brown sugar
¼ teaspoon paprika
4 cups boiling water
Bacon (garnish) (optional)

Cut stems from okra; slice.

Heat fat in kettle. Add okra, celery, pepper, and onion; sauté about 5 minutes. Add tomatoes, sugar, paprika, and water; cover. Simmer about 1 hour, until vegetables are tender. Add seasoning to taste. A little diced crisply-cooked bacon sprinkled on top is a pleasant addition. Yield 5 to 6 servings.

onion soup

4 large onions, thinly sliced
1 tablespoon butter
1 tablespoon vegetable oil
¼ teaspoon sugar
2 tablespoons flour
6 cups bouillon or Basic Beef Stock (see Index)
¼ cup dry white wine or vermouth
Salt and pepper to taste
4 slices French bread, cut ½ inch thick
2 teaspoons vegetable oil
1 clove garlic, peeled, cut
2 tablespoons cognac
1 cup grated Swiss cheese

In covered 4-quart saucepan or Dutch oven cook onions slowly with butter and 1 tablespoon oil 15 minutes; stir occasionally. Uncover; increase heat to moderate. Add sugar; sauté onions, stirring frequently, about 30 minutes or until golden brown. Sprinkle with flour; stir over heat 2 to 3 minutes. Blend in hot broth and wine; adjust seasonings. Simmer, partially covered, 1 hour.

Meanwhile, place bread slices in 350°F oven 30 minutes or until lightly toasted. Halfway through baking, baste each slice with ½ teaspoon oil; rub with garlic.

Before serving, add cognac. Divide soup into ovenproof bowls or casseroles. Sprinkle ½ cup cheese in soup. Float slices of stale or toasted French bread on soup; sprinkle with rest of cheese. Bake in preheated 325°F oven 15 to 20 minutes, until hot; set under broiler 2 to 3 minutes, until cheese is golden brown. Serve immediately. Yield 4 servings.

parsley soup

2½ cups fresh chopped parsley
3 tablespoons butter or margarine
1 onion, chopped
1 stalk celery, chopped
2 tablespoons flour
5 cups vegetable or white stock
Salt and pepper
Pinch of nutmeg
½ bay leaf
4 to 6 tablespoons heavy cream
Sprinkling of paprika
Croutons

Coarsely chop parsley, including stems, which are full of flavor.

Melt butter; cook onion and celery gently a few minutes without browning. Sprinkle in flour; mix well. Pour in stock; bring slowly to boil, blending smoothly. Add parsley, salt, pepper, nutmeg and bay leaf; simmer 25 minutes. Soup can be served as it is, blended in electric blender or food processor or put through food mill. Reheat soup; pour into soup bowls. Serve with spoonful of cream and croutons in each bowl. Yield 4 to 6 servings.

parsnip soup

3 tablespoons butter
1 onion, chopped
1½ cups peeled, finely sliced parsnips
1 tablespoon flour
3 to 4 cups vegetable or white stock
  (or water and cube)
3 or 4 sprigs parsley
1 small bay leaf
Pinch of thyme
Salt and pepper
Pinch of nutmeg
½ cup cream
1 tablespoon chopped parsley
Croutons

Melt butter; cook onion and parsnips gently 5 to 6 minutes, covered, to soften without browning.

pea-pod soup

pea soup with ham

Remove from heat. Sprinkle in flour; blend well. Pour in stock; mix well. Add herbs and seasonings; bring to boil. Simmer 20 to 30 minutes, until parsnips are tender; remove bay leaf. Put into electric blender; blend until smooth. Or put through food mill. Return to pan; adjust seasoning. Reheat, adding cream. Serve in soup cups; sprinkle with chopped parsley and with croutons. Yield 4 servings.

pea-pod soup

2 pounds pea pods
1 onion, peeled, sliced
2 or 3 sprigs mint
2 or 3 sprigs parsley
4 cups stock or 2 bouillon cubes and 4 cups water
2 tablespoons butter or margarine
1½ tablespoons flour
Salt and pepper
Sugar
4 tablespoons cooked green peas (optional)
Chopped mint

Wash pods; put into large kettle with onion, mint sprigs, parsley, and stock. Bring to a boil; cover. Simmer about 40 minutes. When outer flesh of pods is tender, rub all through sieve.

Melt butter in pan; stir in flour. Cook 2 minutes. Add puree; stir until boiling. Add salt, pepper, and sugar to taste. Add peas. Serve sprinkled with a little chopped mint or mint leaves. Yield 4 servings.

pea soup with ham

3 medium onions
3 whole cloves
1 pound yellow peas
4 cups water
1 pound ham
1 teaspoon marjoram
1 teaspoon thyme
Salt to taste
Parsley

Dice 2 onions. Peel third onion; leave it whole. Stick cloves into whole onion. Put diced onions,

651

whole onion, peas, and water into pot; cook 20 minutes. Add ham, marjoram, and thyme; cook at least 1½ hours. Remove cloved onion and ham. Cut ham into thick slices. Season soup with salt. When ready to serve, place ham slice on top of each serving of soup; garnish with parsley. Yield 4 to 6 servings.

potato and cucumber soup

1 medium cucumber
4 medium potatoes, peeled, diced
1 teaspoon salt
2 cups cold water
¼ teaspoon white pepper
1 cup heavy cream
½ cup milk
1 green onion, grated
1 teaspoon dried dillweed (or 1 tablespoon chopped fresh dill)

Peel cucumber; slice lengthwise. Scoop out seeds with spoon; discard. Dice cucumber.

In heavy 2½-quart saucepan boil potatoes in salted water until very soft. Pour potatoes and cooking liquid into sieve or food mill; set over large bowl. Force potatoes through; return to saucepan. Stir in pepper, cream, milk, onion, and cucumber; simmer gently about 5 minutes, until cucumber is tender. Add dill; season to taste. Serve hot. Yield 4 servings.

puree of turnip soup

3 tablespoons butter
2 cups sliced young turnips
1 cup sliced potatoes
1 small onion, sliced
1½ tablespoons flour
3 cups white or chicken stock
1 cup milk
1 tablespoon chopped parsley (or 1 teaspoon paprika)

Melt butter; cook turnips, potatoes, and onion gently until tender, 20 to 30 minutes. Sprinkle in a little flour; blend thoroughly. Pour in stock; mix well; bring to boil. Reduce heat; simmer 15 minutes. Put into electric blender or food processor; blend until smooth. Reheat; add more seasoning, if necessary, and milk. Sprinkle with parsley; serve croutons separately. Yield 4 to 6 servings.

sauerkraut soup russian-style

3 to 4 tablespoons butter
1 onion, sliced
2 small carrots, sliced
1 potato, peeled, sliced

2 tablespoons flour
1 teaspoon tomato puree
¾ pound sauerkraut
4 to 5 cups Basic Beef Stock (see Index)
1 tablespoon chopped parsley
1 teaspoon chopped chervil
Sour cream

Melt butter; cook onion and carrots until golden. Add potato. Stir in flour; when smooth, add tomato puree and sauerkraut. Cook a few minutes; stir constantly. Add stock and herbs; bring to boil. Simmer about 40 minutes; season to taste. Serve hot with spoonful of sour cream in each soup cup. Yield 4 to 6 servings.

soup paysanne

3 tablespoons bacon or other cooking fat
½ cup diced carrot
½ cup diced onion
½ cup diced celery
½ cup diced turnip
3 cups stock or water
1 cup canned tomatoes
½ cup diced potato
Salt and pepper
1 tablespoon chopped parsley

Heat fat in large kettle; sauté carrot, onion, celery, and turnip about 5 minutes. Add stock, tomatoes, potato, and a little seasoning; cover. Simmer 35 minutes. Add parsley. Adjust seasoning before serving. Yield 4 or 5 servings.

Note: If pressure cooker is used, put all ingredients into cooker; cook 3 minutes at 15 pounds pressure.

spinach soup

4 to 5 handfuls fresh spinach (or 1 package frozen spinach)
3 tablespoons butter
1 onion, finely chopped
1½ tablespoons flour
4 cups vegetable broth (or water and chicken cube)
3 or 4 sprigs parsley (or 1 tablespoon dried parsley)
1 bay leaf
Salt and pepper
Squeeze or 2 of lemon juice
¼ to ½ teaspoon powdered mace
½ cup cream

garnish
2 hard-boiled eggs, sliced
Paprika or croutons

Wash spinach thoroughly, if using fresh spinach; drain. Shake off excess water.

soup paysanne

Melt butter; cook onion and spinach gently until spinach has softened and become limp without browning. If using frozen spinach, let block thaw completely. Sprinkle in flour; blend smoothly. Add stock; bring to boil, stirring constantly. Add parsley, bay leaf, and seasoning; reduce heat. Simmer 10 to 12 minutes. Do not overcook; this spoils green color and fresh flavor. Put through fine food mill, or blend until smooth in electric blender or food processor. Reheat; add lemon juice. Adjust seasoning; add mace. Stir in cream just before serving. Garnish with hard-boiled egg slices in each cup; sprinkle with paprika or croutons. Yield 4 to 6 servings.

split-pea vegetable soup

1 large potato
2 medium-size carrots

2 stalks celery
½ small onion
½ cup dry split peas
2 quarts (8 cups) water
1 tablespoon butter, margarine, or drippings
1 tablespoon salt
Pepper to taste
¼ small head cabbage

Cut up potato, carrots, celery, and onion. Wash and drain split peas.

Bring water to boil. Add cut-up vegetables, split peas, butter, salt, and pepper; cover. Boil gently 30 minutes.

Cut up cabbage; add to soup. Cook 15 minutes. Yield 6 servings.

squash soup

1 large squash
6 tablespoons butter or margarine

spinach soup

1 onion, peeled, sliced
1 cup water
Bouquet Garni (see Index)
Salt and pepper
3 tablespoons flour
1 cup milk
1 egg yolk
2 tablespoons light cream or evaporated milk

Peel squash; cut into pieces; remove seeds.

Melt butter in pan; add squash and onion. Cook about 5 minutes; stir well. Add water, Bouquet Garni, and a little salt and pepper; cook until squash is quite soft. Remove Bouquet Garni. Strain through sieve; mash squash until smooth. Add to liquid; return all to pan.

Blend flour smoothly with milk. Add to squash puree; stir until boiling. Reduce heat; simmer 5 minutes.

Mix egg yolk with cream; stir into soup. Reheat but do not allow to boil; adjust seasoning. Serve with croutons of fried or toasted bread. Yield 4 servings.

tomato consommé madras

2 cans jellied condensed consommé
1 small bottle tomato juice cocktail, with Tabasco
   or Worcestershire sauce added
2 teaspoons curry powder (or paste)
Few drops of lemon juice
3 tablespoons fresh Mayonnaise (see Index)
Grated lemon rind to taste
1 to 2 teaspoons lemon juice
1 tablespoon heavy cream, whipped
2 teaspoons chopped chives

Heat consommé very slightly to dissolve. Add tomato juice and curry powder; mix thoroughly. Add lemon juice. Pour into soup cups; let chill.

Mix mayonnaise with lemon rind and juice; add whipped cream. Put spoonful on center of each cup of soup; sprinkle with chopped chives. Serve with brown bread and butter. Yield 4 to 6 servings.

tomato-juice soup

5¾ cups (46-ounce can) tomato juice
1 large carrot
1 large onion
1 stalk celery
½ cup uncooked rice
3 tablespoons flour
1 tablespoon butter or margarine
Salt and pepper to taste

Put juice in pan. Add whole vegetables and rice; bring to boil. Cover; boil gently until vegetables are tender.

Lightly brown flour in butter in pan; add to soup to thicken, if desired. Add salt and pepper. Yield 6 servings.

tomato–rice soup italian-style

2 tablespoons butter or margarine
½ cup chopped onion
½ cup chopped celery
1 (28-ounce) can peeled tomatoes
1½ cups chicken broth or Basic Chicken Stock
   (see Index)
½ teaspoon crumbled dried marjoram
½ teaspoon crumbled dried sweet basil

654

2 teaspoons sugar
Salt and pepper to taste
⅓ cup long-grain rice
Grated Parmesan cheese

Melt butter in large saucepan; sauté onion and celery until limp.

Combine tomatoes, broth, onion, and celery, and butter in blender jar; blend until smooth. Pour back into saucepan. Add marjoram, basil, sugar, salt, and pepper; bring to boil over

tomato consommé madras

moderate heat. Add rice; stir well. Cover; reduce heat to low. Simmer 15 to 20 minutes, until rice is tender. Serve garnished with cheese. Yield 4 servings.

tomato soup french-style

2 slices bacon, chopped
1 tablespoon butter
2 large onions, finely sliced

tomato soup french-style

4 to 6 ripe tomatoes (or 1 cup canned tomatoes),
    chopped
1 tablespoon tomato puree
2 or 3 strips lemon rind
4 cups Basic Chicken Stock (see Index)
Salt and pepper
1 teaspoon sugar
1 tablespoon parsley
¼ teaspoon thyme
1 teaspoon basil
1 tablespoon chopped mixed parsley and basil
Fried garlic croutons (optional)

Heat bacon in pan. When fat has run, add butter; melt. Add onions; cook gently 5 to 6 minutes, until tender and golden brown: Add tomatoes, tomato puree, lemon rind, stock, salt, pepper, sugar, and herbs; bring to boil. Simmer 20 minutes or until tomatoes are tender. Put through food mill or blend in electric blender or food processor. Adjust seasoning. Serve hot; sprinkle with parsley and basil and croutons. Yield 4 to 6 servings.

tomato soup ukranian-style

2 large beef bones
1 large carrot, finely chopped

1 large onion, finely chopped
1 cup shredded cabbage
4 cups Basic Beef Stock (see Index)
2 pounds ripe tomatoes, skinned
2 teaspoons salt
1 teaspoon sugar
½ teaspoon freshly ground pepper
¼ cup all-purpose flour
1 cup sour cream
1 cup boiled rice

Combine bones, carrot, onion, cabbage, and stock in soup kettle; bring to boil. Reduce heat; simmer 1 hour, skimming surface occasionally.

Chop tomatoes; add to soup. Stir in seasonings; simmer 45 minutes. Remove bones. Pour soup into blender or food processor container; process until pureed. Return to kettle; place over low heat.

Blend flour with sour cream; stir into soup. Bring just to boil.

Spoon rice into 4 soup bowls; ladle soup over rice; sprinkle with chopped dill or parsley, if desired. Yield 4 servings.

two-bean soup

1¼ cups dry white beans
¼ pound ham, cubed

tomato soup ukranian-style

vegetables and meat dumplings soup

1 cup cut green beans, fresh or frozen
¼ cup diced celery
1 green onion, diced
1 yellow onion, diced
1 potato, peeled, diced
1 tablespoon butter
2 tablespoons flour
¾ cup beef broth
½ teaspoon salt
¼ teaspoon pepper
1 sprig parsley (garnish)

Cover white beans with cold water; soak overnight. Drain; place in 2-quart saucepan. Add ham and enough cold water to cover beans by 1-inch; bring to boil. Simmer about 1 hour, until beans are tender. Add green beans, celery, onion, and potato. Add enough water to cover vegetables; simmer 20 minutes.

Melt butter in frypan; stir in flour. Cook, stirring, until lightly browned; remove from heat. Stir in heated beef broth; cook until smooth. Stir into soup; simmer until soup is thickened and vegetables tender. Season with salt and pepper. Garnish with chopped parsley; serve immediately. Yield 4 to 6 servings.

vegetable soup

1 cup small pieces cooked beef
6 cups beef broth
2 cups fresh or canned tomatoes
1 cup diced potatoes
¾ cup diced carrots
½ cup sliced onion
3 cups other uncooked vegetables (green peas, chopped cabbage, diced celery, cut green beans, chopped green pepper, sliced okra, diced turnips, cut corn)
1½ teaspoons salt
⅛ teaspoon pepper

Combine beef and broth in large saucepan. Add remaining ingredients; cook, covered, about 35 minutes, until vegetables are tender. Yield 6 servings.

vegetables and meat dumplings soup

meat dumplings
2 slices bread
½ pound lean ground beef
Salt
White pepper
5 cups beef bouillon

soup
¼ head savoy cabbage (green cabbage can be substituted)
1 leek
2 ounces fresh mushrooms
1 celery stalk
1 tablespoon oil
1 small onion, chopped
2 ounces (⅓ cup) frozen peas
4 ounces egg noodles
Salt
White pepper
1 tablespoon soy sauce
3 tablespoons sherry

Prepare dumplings. Soak bread in small amount cold water; squeeze as dry as possible. Mix with beef and salt and pepper to taste.

Bring bouillon to boil. Using 1 teaspoon meat mixture, form little dumplings; drop into boiling broth. Reduce heat; simmer 10 minutes.

For soup, slice cabbage, leek, mushrooms and celery.

Heat oil in large saucepan. Add onion; cook until golden. Add sliced vegetables; cook 5 minutes.

Remove dumplings from beef broth with slotted spoon; drain on paper towels. Keep warm.

Strain broth; add to vegetables. Add peas and noodles; simmer 15 minutes. Return dumplings to soup. Season with salt, pepper, soy sauce, and sherry. Serve immediately. Yield 4 to 6 servings.

vegetable soup japanese-style

1 pound lean pork
1 carrot
12 dried mushrooms
4 cups Basic Chicken Stock (see Index)
1 (4-ounce) can bamboo shoots, drained
1 tablespoon soy sauce
½ cup chopped fresh spinach leaves
1 teaspoon powdered ginger

Cut pork and carrot into julienne strips.

Place mushrooms in small bowl. Add enough stock to cover; let stand 1 hour. Remove mushrooms from stock; slice. Place in large saucepan. Add stock from bowl, remaining stock, and pork; bring to boil. Reduce heat to low; simmer 10 minutes. Add carrot, bamboo shoots, and soy sauce; cook 5 minutes. Stir in spinach and ginger; boil rapidly 2 minutes. Yield about 1½ quarts.

vegetable soup tropical-style

1 medium onion, chopped
2 tablespoons oil
1 cup diced potato
4 medium tomatoes, chopped
1 bunch spinach
1 sprig mint
5 cups water
1½ teaspoons salt
1½ cups sliced green beans

vegetable soup japanese-style

watercress soup

1 cup finely chopped cucumber
1 bunch parsley, finely chopped

Fry onion in oil until golden. Add potato, tomatoes, spinach, and mint; stir-fry 3 minutes. Add water and salt; simmer until tender. Add beans and cucumber; simmer until just tender. Add parsley just before serving. Excellent served with cheese. Yield 6 servings.

vichyssoise

¾ pound leeks, well washed, halved lengthwise, thinly sliced
1 medium onion, chopped
2 tablespoons butter
2 large potatoes, peeled, diced
3 cups chicken stock
Salt to taste
2 cups light cream
Dash of Tabasco sauce
1 cup plain yogurt
Chopped chives

Heat leeks and onion in butter in large skillet until transparent; do not brown. Add potatoes, stock, and salt; simmer until potatoes are tender, about 30 minutes. Pour into blender; puree. Stir in cream and Tabasco. Strain through sieve; chill. Just before serving, stir in yogurt; readjust seasoning. Serve very cold; garnish with chives. Yield 6 servings.

watercress soup

2 bunches fresh watercress
3 tablespoons butter
1 potato, sliced
1 small onion, finely chopped
1 tablespoon flour
3 cups Basic Chicken Stock (see Index) or water
3 or 4 sprigs parsley
1 bay leaf
Salt and pepper
2 cups milk
¼ teaspoon mace
Little green coloring (optional)
4 to 6 tablespoons cream
Watercress sprigs
Croutons

Wash and pick over watercress; discard yellow leaves. Reserve enough green top-sprigs for garnish; chop remaining cress roughly.

Melt butter; cook potato and onion together 2 to 3 minutes. Add chopped watercress; cook 3 to 4 minutes, stirring constantly to prevent browning. Sprinkle in flour; blend well. Add stock; blend together. Bring to boil. Add herbs and seasoning; reduce heat. Simmer until potato is tender, about 20 minutes. Remove bay leaf. Put soup into electric blender or food processor; blend until smooth. Or put through fine food mill or sieve. Return soup to pan; reheat gently.

At same time heat milk in separate pan. When almost at boiling point, pour into watercress mixture; this makes texture of soup lighter and more delicate. Adjust seasoning; add mace and a little green coloring if desired. Serve with spoon of cream in each cup and watercress sprigs on top. Fried bread croutons are also excellent with this soup. Yield 4 to 6 servings.

vichyssoise

zucchini soup

1 medium onion, chopped
1 tablespoon butter or margarine
4 to 6 medium zucchini, sliced
1 large potato, peeled, diced
¼ teaspoon thyme
¼ teaspoon rosemary
¼ teaspoon basil
¼ teaspoon salt
⅛ teaspoon pepper

6 cups chicken broth
1 cup skim milk

In large frypan sauté onion in hot butter. Add zucchini, potato, herbs, salt, and pepper. After mixture is hot, cook 3 minutes; stir occasionally. Add broth; simmer 15 minutes. Puree in blender or food processor. Return mixture to saucepan. Add milk; heat slightly. Serve hot or cold. Yield 8 servings.

squab and bacon brochettes

2 or 3 squabs
½ cup red wine
1 onion, chopped
1 tablespoon chopped herbs
Pepper
4 slices bacon
8 to 12 baby onions, peeled
1½ cups stock
8 to 12 baby mushrooms (use stems for sauce)

brown sauce
3 tablespoons oil
2 bacon slices, chopped
1 onion, chopped
1 clove garlic, crushed
2 carrots, chopped
2 stalks celery, chopped
Mushroom stems
2 tablespoons flour
Stock
½ cup strained marinade
Salt and pepper

Remove breasts from squabs; cut each into 2 pieces. Put into bowl; cover with wine, chopped onion, herbs, and pepper. Let marinate a few hours.

Cut bacon slices in half; make each into roll.

Cook baby onions in ½ cup stock 5 minutes; drain. Reserve stock for sauce.

Peel mushrooms. Remove stems; reserve for sauce.

Remove squab from marinade; dry. Thread ingredients alternately onto skewers.

Make brown sauce. Heat oil; cook bacon, onion, garlic, carrots, celery, and mushroom stems until golden brown. Sprinkle in flour; blend well. Add stock and marinade; bring to boil. Simmer ½ hour; strain. Add seasoning.

Heat broiler or barbecue grill; cook brochettes, brushing with butter or oil, about 8 minutes, depending on heat of broiler or grill. Squab must not be overcooked; it becomes tough and tasteless. Serve with boiled rice and Brown Sauce. Yield 4 servings.

squabs in parcels

2 large squabs
7 tablespoons butter
2 slices bacon
1 small can goose- or duck-liver pâté
1 cup chopped mushrooms
2 tablespoons chopped parsley, marjoram, and
   tarragon
Salt and pepper
Pinch of mace

1 tablespoon sherry

Cut each squab in half; brown all over in 3 tablespoons butter with bacon. Cover; roast in preheated 350°F oven 20 minutes. Remove squabs; let cool.

Mix pâté with mushrooms, 4 tablespoons butter, herbs, seasoning, and dash of sherry.

Cut 4 large squares of foil; butter. Place ⅛ of stuffing in center of each square. Place halved squabs on top; spread another ⅛ of mixture over each. Fold foil over birds; seal edges by turning over several times. Turn oven up to 400°F; bake parcels 35 minutes. Serve a parcel per person; open at table to get full effect of aroma. Yield 4 servings.

squab stuffed and baked

6 dressed squabs
1½ teaspoons salt
1 cup chopped celery
½ cup chopped onion
3 tablespoons butter
1½ cups Basic Boiled Rice (see Index)
6 tablespoons thawed frozen orange-juice
   concentrate
1½ cups chopped fresh mushrooms
½ cup raisins
1 tablespoon finely chopped parsley
¾ teaspoon marjoram
¾ cup vegetable oil

Sprinkle squab cavities well with ¾ teaspoon salt.

Sauté celery and onion in butter in large skillet until golden. Stir in rice, 3 tablespoons orange-juice concentrate, mushrooms, raisins, parsley, marjoram, and remaining salt; blend thoroughly. Heat through; spoon into squab cavities; truss.

Combine oil and remaining orange juice; blend well.

Arrange squab on rack in roasting pan; brush with oil mixture. Bake in preheated 375°F oven 45 minutes or until squabs are tender; baste frequently with remaining oil mixture. Arrange squabs on serving dish; garnish with parsley and orange slices, if desired. Yield 6 servings.

squabs with water chestnuts

2 to 4 squabs or young pigeons
3 tablespoons flour
3 tablespoons butter or margarine
1 chicken bouillon cube, crumbled
1½ cups water
1 teaspoon sugar
Salt and pepper
1 tablespoon soy sauce

squabs with water chestnuts

1 tablespoon sherry
2 green onions or 1 shallot, chopped
10 water chestnuts, sliced

Split squabs in halves; dredge with flour.

Heat butter in skillet: brown squabs on all sides. Remove to casserole.

Put remaining flour into skillet with bouillon cube and water; stir until boiling. Add sugar, seasoning, soy sauce, sherry, onions, and water chestnuts; pour over squabs. Cover; cook in preheated 350°F oven 1 to 1¼ hours. Yield 4 servings.

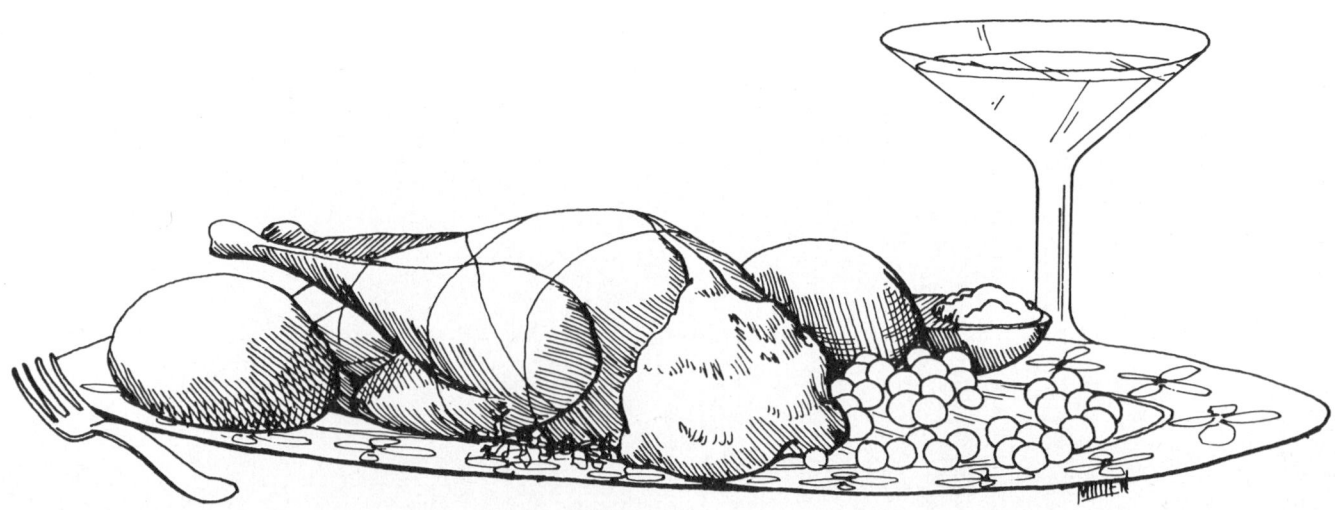

albanian lamb stew

Lean beef, chuck or round, can be substituted for lamb in this recipe to reduce costs.

1 pound lean lamb, cut into ¾-inch cubes
 (boneless shoulder or leg of lamb can
 be used)
2 tablespoons vegetable oil
1 cup water
2 eggs
1 cup plain yogurt
½ teaspoon salt

Brown lamb in hot oil in large skillet. Add water; simmer, uncovered, until water has evaporated, about 20 to 25 minutes. Place meat in greased, shallow, 1-quart casserole dish or individual ramekins.

Beat together eggs, yogurt, and salt. Pour over meat. Bake in preheated 350°F oven 20 minutes or until golden brown. Yield 4 servings.

beef goulash

1 pound lean beef (round steak)
2 tablespoons vegetable oil
1 large onion, chopped
1 pound (3 medium) potatoes, peeled, cubed
1 green pepper, cut into strips
2 tomatoes, peeled, cut into chunks
1 clove garlic, minced
½ teaspoon caraway seeds
1 (3-inch) piece lemon peel, minced
2 teaspoons paprika
½ teaspoon salt
2 cups beef bouillon

Pat meat dry with paper towels; cut into strips approximately ½-inch wide and 2-inches long.

Heat oil in 4-quart Dutch oven or heavy kettle. Add meat and onion; cook 5 minutes or until brown. Add potatoes, cook 5 minutes. Add green pepper, tomatoes, garlic, caraway seeds, and lemon peel. Season with paprika and salt. Pour in beef bouillon; cover. Simmer over low heat 30 minutes. At end of cooking time, uncover; boil liquid a few minutes, until reduced. Correct seasoning if necessary. Yield 4 servings.

beef stew mexican-style

1½ pounds lean stewing beef, cut into cubes
1 large onion, sliced
1 clove garlic, minced
4 tablespoons olive oil
3 tablespoons wine vinegar
½ cup tomato sauce
1 cup red wine
1 bay leaf
1 teaspoon oregano
½ teaspoon salt
¼ teaspoon pepper

beef goulash

albanian lamb stew

beef stew mexican-style

1 (7-ounce) can green chili salsa

Combine all ingredients in large saucepan; bring to boil, stirring occasionally. Reduce heat to simmer; cook 3 hours or until meat falls apart. Serve with Beer Rice. Yield 4 servings.

beer rice

2 tablespoons olive oil
1 cup raw long-grain rice
1 (10¾-ounce) can condensed onion soup
1 (10¾-ounce) soup can beer

Heat oil in medium saucepan over moderate heat. Add rice; brown lightly, stirring constantly. Add soup and beer; cover tightly. Simmer 20 to 25 minutes, until all liquid is absorbed.

bouillabaisse

½ cup olive oil
2 medium onions, chopped
2 leeks, chopped
2 carrots, chopped
1 or 2 cloves garlic, crushed
2 pounds mixed fish (red snapper, flounder, whiting, halibut, perch, red mullet, haddock, eel)
4 ripe tomatoes (or ½ cup canned tomatoes), peeled, chopped
1 bay leaf
1 tablespoon chopped fennel
Pinch of saffron soaked in boiling water

1 sprig thyme
4 or 5 parsley stalks, chopped
2 or 3 thinly peeled pieces orange zest
2 to 3 cups fish stock or water
Salt and pepper
¾ to 1 cup shrimp, clams, and lobster meat
1 teaspoon lemon juice
1 cup white wine
6 to 8 slices French bread

garnish

2 tablespoons butter, softened
1 clove garlic, crushed
Pepper and salt
2 tablespoons chopped parsley

Heat oil in large pan. Add onions, leeks, carrots, and garlic; cook slowly until golden brown, stirring frequently to prevent burning. Add fish, boneless, cut into chunks. Add tomatoes, bay leaf, fennel, saffron, thyme, parsley, orange zest, fish stock, salt, and pepper; cover. Cook 15 to 20 minutes. Add shellfish; leave shrimp whole; cut clam or lobster meat into chunks (canned minced clams and canned lobster meat can be used). Bring to boil; cook 6 to 8 minutes. Add lemon juice and wine; reheat a few minutes. Adjust seasoning.

While soup is cooking, cut bread into ½-inch slices; put into warm oven to bake hard.

Mix butter with garlic. Add pepper and salt; spread paste on bread slices. Put slice of bread in bottom of each soup cup or plate. Carefully spoon pieces of fish and shellfish into soup cups; divide equally. Spoon over broth; sprinkle with chopped parsley. Serve at once. Yield 6 to 8 servings.

brunswick stew

1 stewing or roasting chicken, about 3 to 4 pounds
1 teaspoon salt
3 potatoes, sliced
1 large onion, sliced
1 cup green lima beans
1 cup canned tomatoes (or 5 or 6 sliced fresh tomatoes)
1 tablespoon sugar
1 cup kernel corn

1 tablespoon catsup or Worcestershire sauce (optional)
4 tablespoons butter

Cut chicken into pieces; put in casserole with enough boiling water to cover. Add salt; simmer about 45 minutes. Add potatoes, onion, lima beans, tomatoes and sugar; cook 45 minutes. Beans and potatoes should be tender. Remove chicken bones. Add corn; cook 10 minutes. Season to taste. Add catsup. Add butter; stir well. Yield 4 to 6 servings.

chicken stew

½ cup pork drippings or other cooking fat
1 boiling fowl, jointed

brunswick stew

creamed vegetable stew

add mushrooms; remove bay leaves. Put chicken on large dish; arrange vegetables around. Thicken stock with a little extra flour; adjust seasoning. Pour some over chicken; serve rest separately. Yield 6 to 8 servings.

creamed vegetable stew

1 cup diced carrots
1 cup cubed potatoes
½ cup diced green sweet pepper
½ cup sliced green onions
1 cup diced celery
Salt
½ pound salt pork
½ cup all-purpose flour
4 cups milk

Place carrots, potatoes, pepper, onions, and celery in large saucepan. Add 2 teaspoons salt and enough water to cover vegetables; bring to boil. Reduce heat; simmer until vegetables are tender. Drain; set aside.

Wash salt pork; remove rind. Cut into cubes; place in large saucepan. Cook over medium heat until brown; stir frequently. Add flour; mix well. Stir in milk; bring just to boil, stirring constantly. Reduce heat; simmer until thickened. Season with salt to taste. Add vegetables; heat through. Yield 8 servings.

Salt and pepper
Flour
2 large onions, peeled, sliced
2 or 3 tomatoes, peeled, quartered
6 to 8 green olives (optional)
2 bay leaves
¼ teaspoon mixed herbs
Stock or water
1 cup sliced mushrooms

Heat fat in kettle.

Coat chicken pieces with flour to which salt and pepper have been added; brown on all sides. Remove chicken from pan. Add onions and tomatoes; fry about 5 minutes. Add olives, bay leaves, and herbs. Sprinkle with 2 tablespoons flour and a little salt and pepper; mix well. Replace chicken; add enough stock or water to cover. Put lid on kettle; simmer very slowly 2 to 2½ hours, until chicken is tender. When chicken is nearly done,

668

gulliver stew

2 pounds cubed lean beef
Flour
2 tablespoons fat
2½ cups boiling water
½ cup Burgundy wine
1 teaspoon Worcestershire sauce
1 clove garlic, minced
1 or 2 whole bay leaves
1 teaspoon salt
1 teaspoon sugar
¼ teaspoon pepper
½ teaspoon paprika
Dash of ground cloves or allspice
¼ teaspoon powdered saffron (optional)

1 medium onion, sliced
2 carrots, cut up
1 white potato, cut into pieces
1 medium sweet potato, cut into pieces

Shake meat with flour in plastic bag until coated on all sides. Brown meat in hot fat on all sides. In large pot add meat, water, wine, seasonings, and onion; bring to boil. Lower heat to simmer; cook, covered, about 1½ hours, until meat is tender. Add vegetables; simmer 20 to 30 minutes, until vegetables are tender. Yield 4 servings.

hungarian beef goulash

1½ pounds lean beef (chuck or round), cut into
   1-inch cubes

hungarian beef goulash

669

2 tablespoons vegetable oil
2 medium onions, chopped
½ teaspoon salt
2 tablespoons paprika
1 cup beef broth
2 green peppers, cubed
2 red peppers (ripe green peppers), cubed
½ cup plain yogurt mixed until smooth with
   1 tablespoon all-purpose flour

Brown beef on all sides in hot oil in large skillet. Add onions, salt, paprika, and broth; cover. Simmer gently about 2 hours, until meat is very tender. Add peppers last 10 minutes of cooking; remove lid so most liquid can evaporate. Add yogurt; stir only to distribute lightly. Serve at once. Yield 4 or 5 servings.

hunter's stew

3 pounds stewing-beef cubes
1 quart water
8 peppercorns
8 whole cloves
2 whole bay leaves
2 teaspoons salt
1 teaspoon marjoram
3 pounds chicken, cubed
2 medium-onions
5 large carrots
2 sprigs parsley
4 celery stalks
3 leeks
½ cup butter

½ teaspoon white pepper
3 sprigs dill
½ bunch parsley

Cover beef with water; bring to boil.

Tie peppercorns, cloves, and bay leaves in cloth bag; drop into boiling beef. Sprinkle 1 teaspoon salt and marjoram over beef; simmer 2 hours in covered kettle. Add chicken; simmer, covered.

Peel onions and carrots; cut into rings.

Chop 2 sprigs parsley, celery, and leeks.

Put butter into pan. Add vegetables, 1 teaspoon salt, and pepper; sauté over low heat until wilted.

Chop dill and remaining parsley.

Take cloth bag out of meat; discard. Remove meat from water.

Add wilted vegetables to meat stock; simmer until tender. Add meat back to stock and vegetables. Pour into serving dish; sprinkle with chopped dill and parsley. Yield 8 servings.

mediterranean fish stew

broth
1 large fish head
1 bay leaf
1 medium onion, chopped
½ teaspoon salt
¼ teaspoon white pepper
6 cups water

stew
1 large onion, chopped
1 clove garlic, minced

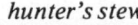

hunter's stew

mediterranean fish stew

monday's dinner

1 tablespoon white wine
1 tablespoon water
3 medium potatoes, peeled, cubed
1 pound whitefish fillets, cut into cubes
2 tablespoons lemon juice
3 medium tomatoes, peeled, chopped
¼ cup stuffed green olives
1 tablespoon capers
Salt and white pepper to taste
Chopped parsley (garnish)

Combine broth ingredients in 4-quart saucepan; simmer 1 hour. Strain; reserve broth.

Meanwhile, cook onion and garlic in wine and water until soft. Add broth and potatoes; simmer 30 minutes.

While potatoes are cooking, sprinkle fish with lemon juice; add to broth 10 minutes before end of cooking time. After 5 minutes add tomatoes, olives, and capers. Season to taste; sprinkle with parsley. Yield 4 servings.

monday's dinner

3 to 4 tablespoons margarine
1 tablespoon oil
2 medium onions, peeled, finely chopped
1 cup chopped cooked meat
1 (6-ounce) can tomato or mushroom soup
1 tablespoon finely chopped parsley
½ bay leaf
1 cup cooked vegetables (peas, carrots, potatoes, etc.)
1 cup stock or gravy
1 (7- to 8-ounce) package macaroni

Grated Parmesan or sharp cheddar cheese (optional)

Heat 2 tablespoons margarine and oil in kettle. Add onions; sauté a few minutes. Add meat; stir about 5 minutes. Add soup, parsley, and bay leaf; cover. Simmer 15 minutes. Add vegetables and stock; heat through. Adjust seasoning to taste; remove bay leaf.

Cook macaroni; drain. Toss in 1 to 2 tablespoons margarine. Turn onto large platter; pour meat and vegetable mixture on top. Sprinkle cheese on top. Yield 6 to 7 servings.

onion and beef stew

1¼ pounds stew beef, cut into 1-inch pieces
¼ cup olive oil
2 cups sliced onions or 2 cups small pearl onions, peeled
2 cloves garlic, minced
½ teaspoon salt
½ teaspoon pepper
½ teaspoon allspice
½ teaspoon sugar
1 (2-inch) piece cinnamon stick
1⅓ cups dry red wine
1 (8-ounce) can tomato sauce

Brown meat in hot oil in heavy skillet; remove from pan.

Brown onions and garlic. Add other ingredients; stir well. Add meat; bring to boil. Reduce heat to simmer; cover. Cook, stirring occasionally, 2 hours or until meat is very tender. Yield 4 servings.

672

onion and beef stew

Note: Stew can easily be done in slow cooker. Brown meat; combine with other ingredients. Cook on low heat as manufacturer directs for any stew.

pork vegetable stew

1 pound boneless pork shoulder
1 medium-size onion, sliced
3 medium-size carrots, sliced
2½ cups water
1 teaspoon salt
1 cup uncooked macaroni
2 cups cooked or canned green beans, undrained

Cut meat into small pieces; brown in large greased pan. Add onion and carrots to meat. Stir in water and salt; bring to boil. Lower heat; cover. Boil slowly about 45 minutes, until meat and carrots are tender. Stir in macaroni and beans;

seafood stew

cover. Boil gently about 10 minutes, until macaroni is tender. Stir once in awhile to keep from sticking. Add water during cooking if mixture seems dry. Yield 6 servings.

seafood stew

sauce
2 tablespoons vegetable oil
2 onions, chopped, or 3 leeks, sliced
4 cloves garlic, crushed
2 fresh tomatoes, peeled, diced
3 tablespoons tomato paste
2 cups bottled clam juice
4 cups chicken bouillon
1 tablespoon salt
⅛ teaspoon pepper
¼ teaspoon saffron
½ teaspoon thyme
1 bay leaf
6 sprigs parsley
Grated rind of 1 orange

seafoods
1 (2-pound) lobster and/or other shellfish (clams, mussels with shells, scallops, crab, shrimp)
2 pounds assorted whitefish fillets, such as sea bass, perch, cod, sole, flounder, red snapper
Chopped parsley (garnish)

Heat oil in large saucepan or Dutch oven; sauté onions several minutes, until translucent. Add remaining sauce ingredients; simmer 45 minutes.

Prepare seafoods. Cook lobster. (Place in large kettle of boiling salted water 10 minutes.) Break claws and tail from body; crack claws. Cut tail into 1-inch chunks. Remove black vein from tail

pieces; leave shell on meat. Wash fish fillets; cut into 2-inch pieces. Add lobster and firm-fleshed fish (sea bass, perch, etc.) to boiling sauce; cook 5 minutes. Add tender-fleshed fish, such as clams, scallops, sole, or cod; cook 5 minutes. Lift seafoods out as soon as cooked; keep warm in soup tureen or platter. Boil liquid 10 minutes to reduce; strain through coarse sieve into tureen. Mash through some of vegetables. Garnish with parsley. Yield 6 servings.

steak and vegetable stew

1 (1½-pound) boneless round steak
3 tablespoons butter
3 tablespoons vegetable oil
4 green onions, thinly sliced
8 round radishes, thinly sliced
½ cup diced green or red sweet pepper
1½ cups thinly sliced onions
1½ cups thinly sliced cabbage
1 Bouquet Garni (see Index)
Salt and freshly ground pepper to taste

Remove all fat from steak; cut steak into small cubes.

Melt butter with oil in large skillet over high heat. Add steak; cook, stirring constantly, until steak loses red color. Remove from skillet with slotted spoon; place in large casserole.

Reduce heat under skillet to medium. Add all vegetables to butter mixture remaining in skillet; cook, stirring constantly, until wilted. Turn into casserole. Add Bouquet Garni, salt, and pepper. Add enough boiling water to cover all ingredients; cover casserole. Bake in preheated 325°F oven, 1 rack below center, about 3 hours, until steak is

674

tender. Remove Bouquet Garni; skim grease from top of casserole. Liquid can be thickened with cornstarch, if desired. Serve with French bread. Stew can be chilled after baking, fat removed from top, then reheated. Yield 6 servings.

vegetable stew with lamb

2 tablespoons vegetable oil
1 pound lean lamb, cut into bite-size pieces
1 medium onion, chopped
1 small head cabbage, shredded
1 stalk celery, sliced
2 medium carrots, sliced
1 stalk leek, sliced
6 cups hot beef bouillon
2 medium potatoes, cubed
1 small head cauliflower, separated into florets
1 (10-ounce) package frozen green beans

2 tablespoons tomato paste
½ teaspoon salt
¼ teaspoon white pepper
Chopped parsley (garnish)

Heat oil in 4-quart Dutch oven or saucepan; brown meat about 5 minutes. Add onion; sauté until golden brown. Add cabbage, celery, carrots, leek, and bouillon; bring to boil. Simmer 1 hour. Add potatoes, cauliflower, and beans; simmer 20 to 30 minutes, until vegetables are tender.

Thin tomato paste with a little broth; add to stew. Season with salt and pepper. Garnish with parsley. Yield 6 servings.

vegetable stew with lobster

1 (10-ounce) package frozen cauliflower
1 (10-ounce) package frozen baby carrots

steak and vegetable stew

vegetable stew with lamb

1 (10-ounce) package frozen white or green
  asparagus tips
1 (10-ounce) package frozen peas
2 tablespoons butter

2 tablespoons all-purpose flour
1½ cups reserved cooking liquid from vegetables
¼ teaspoon nutmeg
Salt and pepper to taste

vegetable stew with lobster

4 or 5 ounces canned black Chinese mushrooms, drained
½ cup plain yogurt
8 to 16 ounces cooked lobster meat, cut into bite-size pieces
Chopped fresh parsley leaves

Cook cauliflower, carrots, asparagus, and peas according to package directions; drain. Reserve and combine cooking liquids.

Melt butter in large saucepan; stir in flour to make smooth paste. Gradually stir in 1½ cups reserved vegetable cooking liquids; heat and stir until mixture comes to boil and is thickened. Add nutmeg, salt, and pepper. Add cooked vegetables and mushrooms; heat through. Just before serving, stir in yogurt. Garnish with lobster and parsley. Serve at once. Yield 6 servings.

STUFFINGS

celery stuffing

2 cups toast crumbs
1 cup diced celery
1 small onion, minced
4 tablespoons melted butter or margarine
½ teaspoon salt
⅛ teaspoon pepper
¼ teaspoon sage

Toast bread; crumble into small pieces.

Fry celery and onion in butter a few minutes. Add with seasonings, to crumbs. Add a little water; mix thoroughly.

chestnut stuffing for turkey

2 pounds chestnuts
1 cup oil
2 cups consommé
6 green onions (scallions)
2 celery stalks
2 tablespoons chopped parsley
1 tablespoon chopped chives
2 cups soft bread crumbs
3 tablespoons butter
¾ pound sausage meat
½ teaspoon thyme
½ teaspoon marjoram
1 bay leaf
Salt
Pepper
¼ cup red wine
¼ cup brandy

With knife make "X" cut on flat side of each chestnut.

Heat the oil in heavy skillet; add chestnuts. Cook over high heat about 3 minutes; stir and shake pan constantly. Remove shells and inner skins as soon as possible; place nuts in pan with consommé. Cook 15 to 20 minutes, until tender; drain. Chop coarsely.

Chop onion, celery, parsley, and chives.

Make bread crumbs.

Melt butter. Add celery and onions; cook and stir 3 to 4 minutes. Add sausage, parsley, chives, and herbs. Season to taste with salt and pepper; cook and stir with fork, breaking up meat.

Moisten bread with wine and brandy. Add to skillet; mix well. Add chestnuts; mix again. Yield 5 cups.

chicken stuffing (easy method)

1¼ cups chunky-cut unpeeled tart apples
1¼ cups thinly sliced carrots
½ cup whole pitted prunes
3 tablespoons dry onion-soup mix
3 tablespoons butter or margarine

Toss apples, carrots, and prunes with 2 tablespoons soup mix. Spoon into chicken; fasten opening. Brush with butter melted with 1 tablespoon soup mix. Roast; baste occasionally. Apples and carrots stay nicely tender-crisp; in delicious contrast, prunes are moist and tender.

corn-bread dressing (for roast turkey)

½ cup butter, margarine, or turkey fat*
1 cup chopped celery
½ cup chopped onion
½ cup chopped green pepper
1 cup chopped nuts (optional)
6 cups (1½-quarts) corn-bread crumbs
6 cups (1½-quarts) soft bread crumbs
2 teaspoons salt
½ teaspoon pepper
1½ teaspoons poultry seasoning
2 eggs, well beaten
1 to 1½ cups broth from cooked giblets

Heat half the butter in frypan. Add celery, onion, green pepper, and nuts; cook over low heat 5 minutes.

Cut rest of butter into small pieces; mix lightly with corn-bread, bread crumbs and seasonings. Add eggs; sprinkle cooked broth over mixture. Toss lightly to mix. Stuff turkey lightly. Roast in preheated 325°F oven until stuffing is well heated in center (at least 165°F). Yield stuffing for 12-pound turkey.

*To make turkey fat, remove excess fat from turkey; heat slowly in frypan or double boiler. If, using turkey fat, drain and cool in measuring cup.

mushroom stuffing

¼ pound mushrooms
4 tablespoons butter or margarine
2 cups bread crumbs
1 small onion, finely minced
Salt and pepper

Chop mushrooms; cook slowly in butter about 5 minutes. Add crumbs and seasonings. Moisten with a little hot water.

onion stuffing

6 tablespoons butter or margarine
1½ to 2 cups hot water
4 cups toasted bread cubes
½ teaspoon salt
1 tablespoon sage

oyster stuffing

⅛ teaspoon pepper
¼ cup finely chopped onion
1 tablespoon chopped celery
1 tablespoon chopped parsley

Melt 4 tablespoons butter in hot water. Mix with remaining ingredients. Use remaining butter to brush on chicken. Yield stuffing for 4-pound chicken.

oyster stuffing

1 pint (2 cups) oysters in own liquid
5 cups fresh bread crumbs
1 cup butter
1 cup chopped mild onions
½ cup sliced celery
4 tablespoons (½ cup) chopped parsley
Salt and pepper
Juice of ½ lemon
Little white wine or stock

Shuck or buy ready-shucked oysters in their own salty juice.

Prepare bread crumbs made with 2-day-old loaf.

Melt butter; cook onions and celery until soft and light golden brown. Add to bread crumbs, with parsley, seasonings, lemon juice and oysters, cut in half if large. If too dry, add a little wine or stock, but stuffing must not be too soft. Fill turkey cavity; sew up carefully. Yield about 7 cups.

poultry stuffing

1 small onion
3 tablespoons butter or fat
3 cups soft bread crumbs
1 teaspoon salt
⅛ teaspoon pepper
1 teaspoon poultry seasoning

Slice onion; sauté in butter until delicate brown. Add crumbs, salt, pepper, and poultry seasoning; mix well.

rice stuffing for poultry

¼ cup chopped onion
½ cup chopped celery
2 tablespoons butter or margarine
1 cup long-grain white uncooked rice
2 chicken-flavored bouillon cubes
2 cups hot water
1 teaspoon salt
1 teaspoon poultry seasoning

Cook onion and celery in butter in large frypan until tender. Add rice; heat, stirring often, about 5 minutes. Add remaining ingredients; bring to boil. Reduce heat; cover tightly. Simmer about 15 minutes, until rice is tender and all liquid absorbed. Use to stuff 4- to 5-pound chicken or duckling. Yield 6 servings.

breaded sweetbreads

2 pairs sweetbreads
1 sprig parsley
1 stalk celery
½ teaspoon salt
1 cup fine bread crumbs
1 egg, slightly beaten
2 tablespoons butter and/or oil

Soak sweetbreads in cold water 1 hour; drain. Put in saucepan with parsley, celery, salt, and water to cover; bring to boil. Reduce heat; let simmer 30 minutes. Cool in liquor.

Take out sweetbreads. Remove fat and connective tissue. Cut into small, uniform cutlets. Dip in bread crumbs, then in egg diluted with 2 tablespoons water, and again in crumbs. Fry quickly in butter until brown; turn frequently. Serve with tomato sauce or creamed asparagus tips. Yield 4 servings.

broiled sweetbreads

2 pairs sweetbreads
1 teaspoon salt
⅛ teaspoon pepper
1 tablespoon butter or lemon butter

Soak sweetbreads in salted water 1 hour; drain. Put in saucepan; cover with water. Bring to boil; reduce heat. Simmer 30 minutes; remove sweetbreads. Discard fat and connective tissues; split lengthwise. Sprinkle with salt and pepper. Broil 10 minutes in hot (450°F) broiler; turn to brown both sides. Brush with butter; serve hot. Yield 4 servings.

sweetbreads béchamel

2 pairs sweetbreads
½ teaspoon salt

1 sprig parsley
1 stalk celery
2 tablespoons butter
4 tablespoons flour
1 cup rich milk
1 tablespoon chopped parsley
1 egg yolk, well beaten

Soak sweetbreads in salted water 1 hour; drain. Put in saucepan; cover with water. Add salt, parsley, and celery; bring to boil. Reduce heat; simmer 30 minutes. Remove sweetbreads. Strain liquor; reserve 1 cup. Remove fat and connective tissues; cut into small pieces.

Melt butter; stir in flour. Add milk and reserved stock; stir until thick. Add sweetbreads; keep hot. Add parsley and egg yolk just before serving. Serve in croustades or on toast. Oysters or veal can be substituted for half the sweetbreads. Yield 4 servings.

sweetbreads with garlic

1½ to 2 pounds sweetbreads
Juice of ½ lemon
Milk (or chicken stock)
1 cup butter
2 cloves garlic (more or less, according to taste), finely crushed
Salt and pepper
1 tablespoon chopped parsley

Soak sweetbreads 3 to 4 hours in several changes of cold salted water, until water no longer has pinkish tinge. Put in pan; cover with water, milk, and lemon juice. Bring to boil; cook 2 to 3 minutes. Drain; soak again in cold water. When cool, remove all skin and membranes; slice.

Melt butter; add garlic. Cook gently 10 to 12 minutes. Add sweetbreads; season. Turn in hot butter unitl golden brown. Sprinkle with parsley. Serve with boiled rice. Yield 4 servings.

TURKEY

barbecued turkey

½ cup chopped onion
1½ tablespoons butter
1½ cups catsup
¼ cup packed brown sugar
1 clove garlic, pressed
1 lemon, thinly sliced
¼ cup Worcestershire sauce
2 teaspoons prepared mustard
1 teaspoon salt
¼ teaspoon freshly ground pepper
1 (12-pound) fresh or frozen turkey
2 to 3 tablespoons barbecue or seasoned salt

Sauté onion in butter in small saucepan until lightly browned. Add remaining ingredients, except turkey and barbecue salt; simmer 20 minutes. Remove lemon slices. Store sauce in covered jar in refrigerator if not used immediately.

Thaw turkey, if frozen. Rinse; pat dry.

Start charcoal fire 20 to 30 minutes before cooking turkey, allowing about 5 pounds charcoal for beginning fire. During cooking period, push burning charcoal to center; add more briquettes as needed around edge.

Sprinkle cavity of turkey with barbecue salt. Insert split rod in front of tail; run diagonally through breastbone. Fasten tightly with spit forks at both ends. Test for balance; readjust spit rod, if necessary. Insert meat thermometer into thickest part of inside thigh; make sure thermometer does not touch bone or spit rod and that thermometer will clear charcoal as spit turns.

Brush off gray ash from coals; push coals back of firebox. Place drip pan made of heavy-duty foil directly under turkey in front of coals. Attach spit; start rotisserie. Cook 25 minutes per pound or to 180 to 185°F on meat thermometer; baste generously and frequently with barbecue sauce during last 30 minutes of cooking. Yield 10 to 12 servings.

curried turkey

3 turkey legs and thighs, cut at joint into serving pieces
2 tablespoons seasoned flour (add ½ teaspoon salt and ¼ teaspoon pepper)
2 onions, sliced
3 tablespoons vegetable oil
1 apple, peeled, cored, chopped
1 tablespoon curry powder
2 cups chicken broth
1 tablespoon lemon juice
2 tablespoons chutney
4 tomatoes, chopped

Coat turkey pieces with seasoned flour.

Sauté onions in hot oil in large frypan or Dutch oven until soft. Add turkey pieces; fry until golden brown. Stir in apple and curry powder; cook 2 minutes. Add broth, lemon juice, chutney, and tomatoes; mix well. Cover; simmer 1 hour or more. Cooking time will vary according to size of turkey pieces. Serve with rice. Yield 6 servings.

barbecued turkey

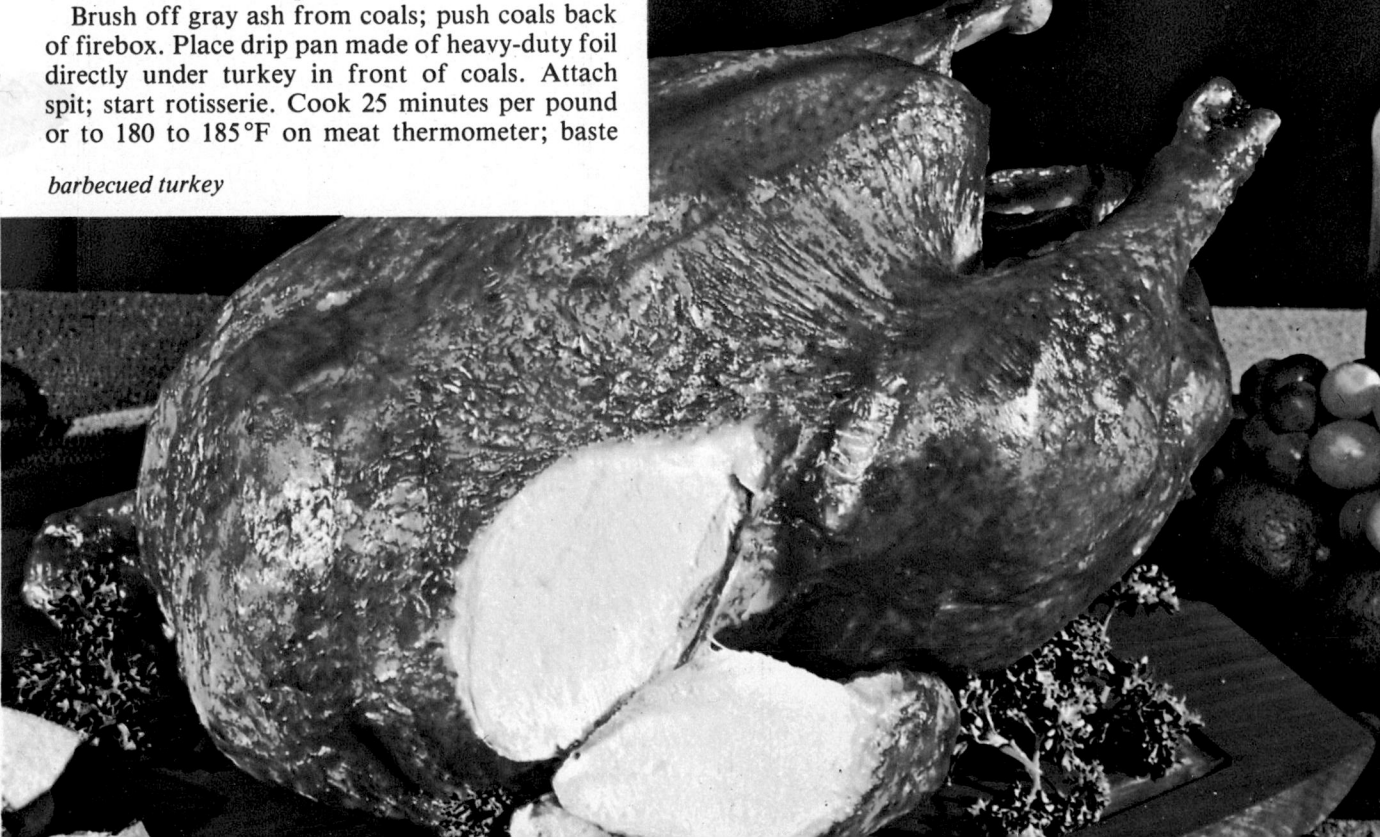

curried turkey

roast turkey with blue-cheese sauce

1 (12-pound) turkey
Salt and freshly ground pepper
Butter
20 medium onions, peeled
2 tablespoons soy sauce
½ cup chopped onions
1 cup half-and-half cream
3 tablespoons all-purpose flour
1 tablespoon red currant jelly
1 tablespoon blue cheese

Cut tips from turkey wings. Rub turkey generously inside and out with salt and pepper;

brush with melted butter. Tie legs together; place on one side on rack in roasting pan. Place wing tips, neck, heart, liver, gizzard, and whole onions around whole turkey in bottom of pan. Roast in preheated 350°F oven 30 minutes; remove turkey pieces. Roast whole turkey 30 minutes longer.

Place turkey pieces in large saucepan. Add 4 cups water and soy sauce.

Sauté chopped onions in small amount of butter until transparent; add to soy-sauce mixture. Bring to boil; boil, uncovered, over medium heat until liquid is reduced to about 2 cups broth. Strain broth; set aside.

Turn turkey to other side; brush with butter. Roast 1 hour. Turn turkey breast-side-up; roast 1 hour longer or until brown and tender. Remove turkey and onions to serving platter.

Pour pan drippings into bowl to cool. Remove fat from surface; reserve 2 tablespoons. Strain drippings. Combine 1 cup drippings, reserved broth, and cream.

Place reserved fat in medium saucepan; blend in flour until smooth. Add cream mixture gradually; cook, stirring constantly, until sauce is smooth and thickened. Add jelly and blue cheese; cook, stirring, until blended. Carve turkey; serve with sauce and additional currant jelly. Yield about 10 servings.

roast turkey with chestnut dressing

1 10- to 12-pound turkey, thawed if frozen

chestnut dressing
¼ cup butter or margarine
1 large onion, peeled, chopped
2 stalks celery, chopped
¼ pound ground veal
¼ pound ground pork
1 turkey liver, chopped
¾ teaspoon salt
Freshly ground black pepper
½ teaspoon Hungarian sweet paprika
6 cups soft bread cubes
¼ cup chopped parsley
1 pound chestnuts, roasted, skinned, chopped
1 egg, well-beaten

5 slices bacon

Wash turkey well; drain. Remove giblet pack; save liver for dressing. Lightly salt cavity of turkey; set aside while preparing dressing.

Melt butter in large skillet. Add onion and celery; sauté until tender. Using slotted spoon, transfer to large mixing bowl.

Add veal, pork, and liver to skillet; sauté until lightly browned. Season with salt, pepper, and paprika; add to onion mixture. Add remaining stuffing ingredients; mix well.

Stuff turkey with dressing; truss. Place in roasting pan, breast-side-up. Lay bacon strips in single layer over turkey. Roast in preheated 325°F oven approximately 4 hours, to internal temperature of 185°F. Let stand, tented with aluminum foil, 20 minutes before carving.

Make a favorite gravy with pan drippings. Yield 6 to 8 servings.

turkey in the bag

Rub carefully dressed bird all over with cooking oil or butter. Sprinkle very lightly with salt and flour. Rub inside of turkey with 1 teaspoon salt

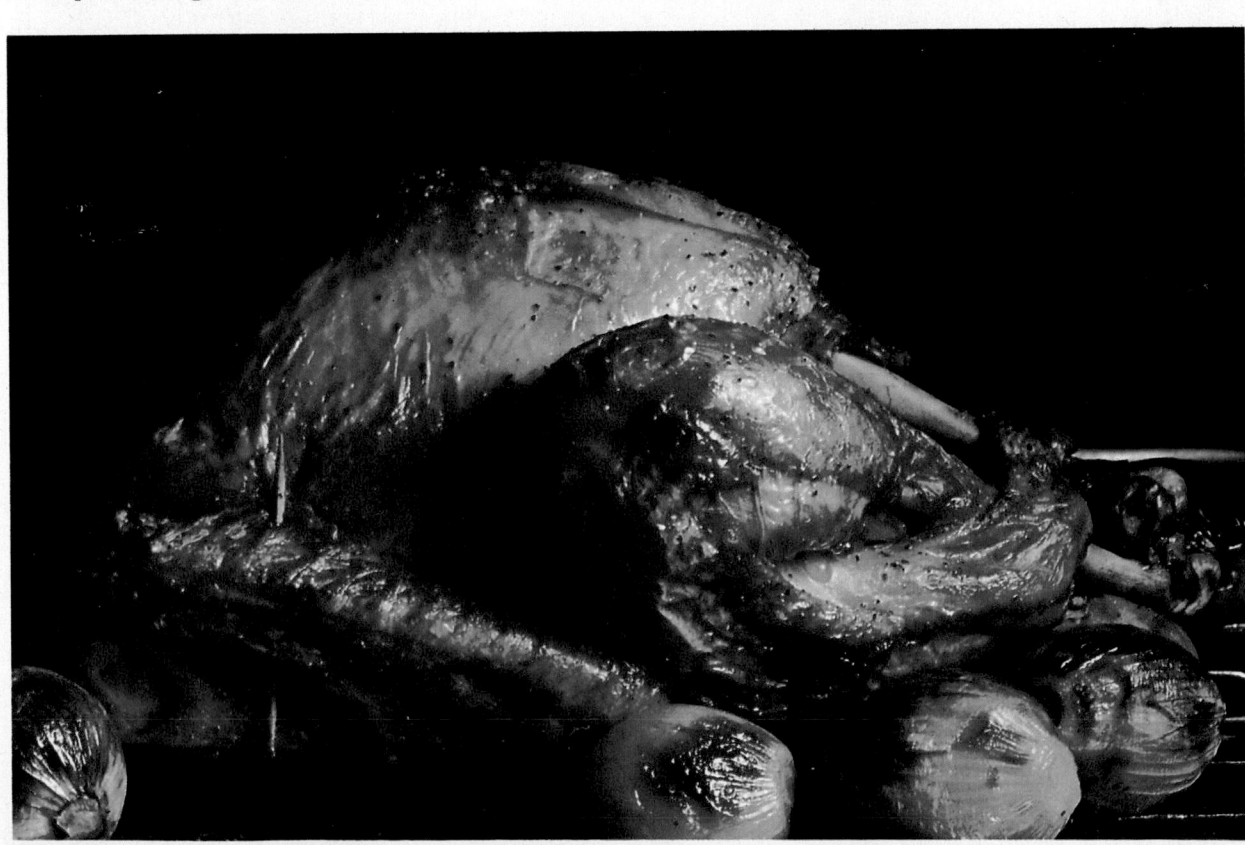

roast turkey with blue-cheese sauce

683

turkey and mushroom croquettes

for every 5 pounds dressed meat. Put into large paper bag; roll ends tightly. Place on roasting pan; set in 375°F oven. Do not open bag to baste. Here is the cooking chart:

7 to 10 pounds—30 minutes per pound
10 to 15 pounds—20 minutes per pound
20 to 23 pounds—13 minutes per pound

When turkey is done, remove from oven; let stand 5 or 10 minutes. Cut top out of bag; lift out golden-brown bird.

Make gravy from drippings.

Cook dressing separately.

turkey and mushroom croquettes

5 tablespoons butter
4 tablespoons flour
½ cup strong turkey or chicken stock
½ cup milk
Salt and pepper
Pinch of mace
Small pinch of cayenne pepper
1 tablespoon chopped parsley
2 cups chopped cooked turkey
3 to 4 tablespoons chopped mushrooms
Little lemon juice
1 egg yolk, beaten

½ cup seasoned flour
2 eggs, beated with 1 teaspoon oil
1 to 1½ cups dried white bread crumbs
Fat for deep frying

Make thick sauce. Melt 4 tablespoons butter; add 4 tablespoons flour. Add stock and milk; bring to boil. Cook until thick and smooth. Add seasonings and parsley; let cool.

Meanwhile, chop turkey into small pieces.

Chop mushrooms; cook in 1 tablespoon butter. Sprinkle with lemon juice. Add chopped turkey, then sauce; stir well. When almost cold, add egg yolk; put into refrigerator to chill and set. Divide into 12 equal portions; shape each into small roll with floured fingers. Roll in seasoned flour; coat ends carefully. Brush all over with beaten egg; cover thickly with bread crumbs.

Heat fat to 390°F or smoking hot. Fry 4 croquettes at a time until well browned; drain well. Serve at once with a piquant brown or tomato sauce. Yield 4 to 6 servings.

turkey noodle ring

½ pound noodles
5 to 7 tablespoons butter
1 onion, chopped
1 clove garlic
1 cup whipping cream
1 egg
3 to 4 tablespoons grated cheddar cheese

1 tablespoon chopped herbs
Salt and pepper
2 onions, finely sliced
1 cup mushrooms
2 tablespoons flour
½ cup stock
¾ cup milk
2 cups chopped cooked turkey
¼ cup cooked peas and corn
2 tablespoons chopped cooked pimiento
2 hard-boiled eggs, quartered
Pinch of paprika

Boil noodles in plenty of salted water until almost cooked; drain.

Heat 3 to 4 tablespoons butter in pan; cook chopped onion and garlic a few minutes to soften. Stir in noodles. Add cream beaten with egg, cheese, and herbs. Sprinkle liberally with salt and pepper; mix thoroughly. Turn into buttered ring mold; press in well. Cover with buttered paper. Put in preheated 350°F oven 45 minutes to set and to finish cooking noddles. Remove when done; turn out on hot dish. Fill with turkey filling.

Melt 2 to 3 tablespoons butter; cook sliced onions 5 to 6 minutes to soften. Add mushrooms; stir well. Sprinkle in flour; blend well. Add stock and milk; bring to boil. Simmer 4 to 5 minutes; remove from heat. Add turkey, peas and corn, pimiento, and hard boiled eggs. Season well; let stand in warm place until noodle ring is ready. Spoon into center; sprinkle with paprika. Yield 4 servings.

turkey pot roast

1 turkey hindquarter (about 2-pounds)
Salt and pepper to taste

½ cup peeled, finely chopped onion
2 small cloves garlic
½ teaspoon crumbled dried basil
¼ teaspoon dried thyme
1 cup fat-skimmed turkey broth or water
3 medium potatoes, pared, halved
6 medium carrots, scraped, cut into chunks
1 tablespoon cornstarch
¼ cup cold water
2 tablespoons chopped fresh parsley

Place turkey skin-side-up in nonstick Dutch oven. Salt and pepper to taste. Bake in preheated 450°F oven 20 to 25 minutes, until skin is crisp. Drain; discard any fat. Add onion, garlic, basil, thyme, and broth; cover. Simmer over low heat (or bake at 350°F) until turkey is nearly tender, about 1 hour. Add potatoes and carrots; cover. Cook until vegetables are tender, about 20 minutes. Remove turkey and vegetables to platter; keep warm. Skim fat from pan juices; discard.

Stir cornstarch and cold water together; add to simmering pan juices. Cook, stirring, until sauce is thickened. Spoon over turkey and vegetables; garnish with parsley. Yield about 6 servings.

turkey slices on vegetable bed

1 tablespoon butter or margarine
8 ounces fresh small mushrooms
2 (10-ounce) packages frozen peas, defrosted
4 small tomatoes, peeled, halved
2 tablespoons chopped parsley
½ teaspoon salt
2 tablespoons vegetable oil
4 thick slices cooked turkey breast

turkey noodle ring

turkey slices on vegetable bed

Seasonings to taste

Melt butter in 2-quart saucepan. Add mushrooms; sauté lightly. Add peas; cover. Heat gently 3 minutes. Add tomatoes and parsley; simmer 3 minutes. Season with salt.

Heat oil in separate pan; sauté turkey 2 to 3 minutes on each side or until golden brown. Season to taste.

Arrange vegetables on heated platter. (Use slotted spoon if too much liquid has accumulated.) Arrange turkey slices on vegetables. Yield 4 servings.

turkey sukiyaki

3 tablespoons oil
1 cup diced green pepper
1 cup diagonally sliced celery
1 cup diced green onions with tops
2 cups cooked, diced turkey
¼ cup soy sauce

Heat oil in medium skillet; add vegetables. Cook, stirring, over medium heat 5 minutes or until vegetables are tender but not mushy. Add turkey and soy sauce; stir until mixed and heated through. Serve over piping-hot rice. Yield 4 to 6 servings.

turkey tetrazzini

6 tablespoons butter or margarine
3 tablespoons olive oil
½ pound fresh mushrooms, cleaned, sliced
4 tablespoons flour
2 cups chicken broth
1 cup heavy cream

2 tablespoons dry sherry
¾ cup grated Parmesan cheese
⅛ teaspoon ground nutmeg
3 cups cubed cooked turkey
½ pound spaghetti or vermicelli, cooked, drained
¼ cup Italian-style bread crumbs

Heat 4 tablespoons butter and oil in large saucepan. Add mushrooms; sauté 5 minutes. Remove mushrooms with slotted spoon; reserve.

Add flour to pan juices; stir to form roux. Cook until bubbly. Slowly add broth; cook until thickened. Remove from heat. Add cream, sherry, Parmesan, and nutmeg; stir until cheese melts. Add turkey and mushrooms; stir well. Combine with cooked spaghetti; turn into greased 13 × 9 × 2-inch baking dish (or 3-quart baking dish).

Melt 2 tablespoons butter; toss with bread crumbs. Sprinkle over casserole. Bake in preheated 375°F oven 25 to 30 minutes. Yield 6 servings.

turkey timbale

3 tablespoons butter
2 tablespoons flour
1 cup milk
1 onion, sliced
1 teaspoon mixed herbs
Salt and pepper
2 to 3 cups finely chopped turkey meat
2 eggs
3 to 4 tablespoons thick cream

Make thick cream sauce. Melt 2 tablespoons butter; stir in flour until blended. Strain in milk,

turkey sukiyaki

previously heated with onion and herbs; bring to boil, stirring constantly. Cook a few minutes. Add seasoning; let cool.

Grind turkey finely in blender or food processor; mix with eggs beaten in cream. Add cooled cream sauce; mix well. Turn into thoroughly buttered ring mold; allow a little space at top for expansion while cooking. Cover with buttered paper; put in roasting pan of hot water. Bake in preheated 350°F oven 25 to 35 minutes, until skewer inserted in center comes out clean. (Make Mushroom Sauce while timbale cooks.) Run knife around outside and inner ring of mold; turn onto large round plate. Pour Mushroom Sauce into center; serve at once. Yield 4 servings.

mushroom sauce
3 tablespoons butter
16 to 20 mushrooms, quartered
2 tablespoons flour
1½ cups well-flavored brown stock
Salt and pepper
1 tablespoon chopped herbs
2 teaspoons Worcestershire sauce
2 to 3 tablespoons Madeira or sherry

Melt butter; cook mushrooms 2 to 3 minutes. Sprinkle in flour; cook 1 minute. Remove from heat. Add stock; blend thoroughly. Bring to boil; simmer a few minutes. Add seasoning, herbs, Worcestershire sauce, and Madeira; let flavors blend well.

bavarian veal with asparagus

2 pounds veal cubes
2 tablespoons vegetable oil
1 large onion, chopped
1 cup chopped carrots
1 tablespoon chopped parsley
¼ cup fresh lemon juice
2 cups beef broth
3 tablespoons flour
½ teaspoon salt
Freshly ground pepper to taste
2 (10-ounce) boxes frozen asparagus tips and
　　pieces or 2 pounds fresh, cleaned, cut into
　　1-inch pieces

In Dutch oven or heavy saucepan brown veal in hot oil. Add onion and carrots; cook until onion is transparent. Stir in parsley.

Mix lemon juice, broth, flour, and seasonings until well blended. Pour over meat; cover. Bake in preheated 325°F oven until 1½ hours or until meat is tender. Add more broth, if needed.

Cook asparagus until tender-crisp; stir into veal. Serve immediately. Yield 6 servings.

blanquette de veau

2 pounds veal from shoulder or breast
4 tablespoons butter
1 onion, quartered
3 or 4 medium carrots
1 tablespoon flour
2 cups chicken or veal stock
Parsley stems
1 bay leaf
Sprig of thyme (or ¼ teaspoon dried thyme)
12 baby or pickling onions
12 button mushrooms
1 large or 2 small egg yolks
1 cup cream
Squeeze of lemon

Cut veal into cubes about 1¼ inches square. Put into pan with enough cold water to cover and a little salt. Bring slowly to boil; cook 5 minutes. Skim scum from surface; drain meat. Wash well with cold water; dry.

Melt 3 tablespoons butter. Cook veal cubes slowly with quartered onion and carrots; shake frequently. Do not let them brown at all. Stir in flour. Add stock, parsley, bay leaf, and thyme; bring to boil. Place in preheated 350°F oven or simmer on stove 1 to 1½ hours until veal is tender.

Meanwhile, peel baby onions; cook in salted water 10 to 15 minutes; drain.

Melt remaining butter. Cook mushrooms a few minutes; add to onions.

Remove veal from stove; place meat in dish. Add carrots, baby onions, and mushrooms.

Strain cooking liquid; boil to reduce quantity slightly. Remove from heat; cool slightly.

Beat egg yolks with cream; add a little hot sauce. Strain mixture gradually into sauce. Add lemon juice. Do not boil under any circumstances after this point. Pour over meat and vegetables. Serve at once with mashed or riced potatoes or plain boiled rice. Yield 4 to 6 servings.

braised veal cutlets in sherry

3 veal cutlets, cut into serving pieces
Flour
Salt
Pepper
2 tablespoons butter
½ cup consommé
½ cup water
½ cup sherry
¼ teaspoon salt
2 tablespoons chopped parsley
4 thin slices boiled ham
4 thin slices Swiss or Romano cheese

Dust cutlets with flour, salt, and pepper; sauté lightly in butter. Cover with consommé, water, and wine. Sprinkle with ¼ teaspoon salt and parsley; cover. Bake in preheated 350°F oven 1 hour; uncover. Place slice of ham and cheese on each cutlet; return to oven until cheese melts. Serve at once. Yield 4 to 6 servings.

greek-style veal with vegetables

2 tablespoons flour
3 tablespoons Kafaloteri or Parmesan cheese
½ teaspoon salt
¼ teaspoon pepper
¼ teaspoon nutmeg
1 egg, beaten
½ cup milk
1 pound thinly sliced leg of veal, cut into serving-
　　size pieces
Flour
6 tablespoons butter
1 eggplant, 1½ pounds
2 tablespoons olive oil
4 tomatoes, peeled, quartered
Salt and pepper
½ teaspoon rosemary
Juice of 1 lemon
2 tablespoons chopped parsley

690

greek-style veal with vegetables

Combine flour, cheese, salt, pepper, and nutmeg. Add egg and milk; beat until well blended.

Wipe veal with damp cloth; dredge in flour.

Melt 3 tablespoons butter in skillet until it sizzles.

Dip veal in flour and egg batter; fry in butter until golden. Turn; fry other side. Remove to platter; keep warm.

Trim stem and cap from eggplant. Leaving skin on, slice ¼ inch thick; pour boiling water over. Let stand few minutes; drain.

Heat oil in medium-size skillet; add eggplant, tomatoes, salt and pepper to taste, and rosemary. Steam 10 minutes or until eggplant is tender; stir several times.

Arrange vegetables in serving dish. Arrange veal on top of vegetables.

Melt remaining butter in pan in which veal was cooked until it foams. Add lemon juice and parsley; pour over veal. Yield 4 servings.

hungarian veal chops

1½ tablespoons paprika
1 teaspoon salt
Pepper
4 veal chops
2 to 3 tablespoons butter
1 small onion or shallot, finely chopped
½ cup white wine
½ cup cream
Chopped parsley

Mix 2 teaspoons paprika with salt and pepper. Sprinkle on both sides of chops; rub in gently.

Melt 2 tablespoons butter in frying pan; cook chops about 2 minutes on each sides, until well browned. Remove; keep warm. Add onion to frypan; cook gently until tender. Add remaining paprika; cover. Cook 1 or 2 minutes. Return chops to pan; add few drops wine. Bake in preheated 350°F oven about 20 minutes; place on serving dish to keep warm.

Pour wine into pan; reduce by cooking a few minutes. Stir in cream; simmer. Stir in remaining butter; pour over chops. Sprinkle top with parsley. Serve with plain boiled noodles. Yield 4 servings.

meatballs special

1 pound veal
1 pound pork
¼ cup flour
1 tablespoon salt
½ teaspoon white pepper
4 eggs
½ cup light cream
1 cup milk
1 medium onion, chopped

meatballs special

1 tablespoon butter or shortening

Grind veal and pork together several times or have it ground by butcher. Put in large bowl. With electric beater at low speed, add flour, salt, and pepper. Add eggs one at a time, still at low speed. Add cream and milk.

In large skillet brown onion in butter just 5 minutes; add to meat. Mix enough so that meat can be easily handled; shape into oval cakes. Brown both sides; add extra shortening if needed. Cook over low heat 15 minutes. Because pork is included, meatballs must be thoroughly cooked. Yield 6 or more servings.

milanese veal rolls

1½ pounds rump roast of veal or veal cutlet
Salt and pepper
Ground sage
4 slices prosciutto
8 thin slices mozzarella cheese
3 tablespoons olive oil
1 small onion, chopped
1 clove garlic, minced
1 (16-ounce) can Italian-style peeled tomatoes
½ cup white wine
Salt and pepper
8 thin strips mozzarella cheese
Parsley sprigs

Pound meat with mallet to ⅛ inch thick; sprinkle with salt, pepper, and a little sage. Cut into 8 rectangular pieces.

Cut prosciutto slices in half. Top veal pieces with piece of ham and slice of mozzarella. Roll jelly-roll fashion; tie with string.

Heat oil in large skillet; sauté veal rolls until browned. Remove from pan. Add onion and garlic to pan; sauté until tender.

Break up tomatoes with fork; add to skillet, with wine, salt, and pepper; mix well. Add veal rolls; cover. Simmer 1½ hours or until tender. Top with mozzarella strips; cover. Melt cheese. Serve on bed of hot cooked spaghetti; top with sauce and garnish with parsley sprigs. Yield 4 servings.

saltimbocca

8 thin slices tender veal from leg
8 thin slices ham
8 small fresh sage leaves (or pinches of dried sage)
Salt and pepper
2 to 3 tablespoons butter
¾ cup Marsala or white wine
8 slices bread

Beat veal between waxed paper. Place slice of ham on each veal slice; add sage leaf. Season with salt and pepper. Roll up each slice tightly; use toothpicks to fasten rolls securely.

Heat butter; brown rolls all over about 5 to 7 minutes. Add wine and a little salt and pepper; cover. Cook gently in preheated 350°F oven (or on top of stove) about 15 minutes, when meat should be tender.

Cut bread into rounds; fry in oil and butter until golden brown and crisp.

Place each roll on fried bread crouton. Serve around dish of spinach cooked with butter. Yield 4 servings.

veal with artichokes

1 clove garlic
1 tablespoon vegetable oil
1 pound veal round, cut into bite-size pieces, pounded
½ teaspoon salt
⅛ teaspoon pepper
1 cup canned tomatoes
¼ cup sherry
¼ teaspoon oregano
1 (10-ounce) package frozen artichoke hearts

In large frypan sauté garlic in hot oil. Remove garlic; discard.

Season veal with salt and pepper; brown in oil. Add tomatoes, sherry, and oregano; mix well. Add artichoke hearts; cover. Simmer 1 hour or until meat is tender. Yield 4 servings.

veal breast with herb stuffing

herb stuffing
3 strips bacon
1 medium onion
1 (4-ounce) can mushroom pieces
¼ cup chopped fresh parsley
1 tablespoon chopped fresh dill
1 teaspoon dried tarragon leaves
1 teaspoon dried basil leaves
½ pound lean ground beef
½ cup dried bread crumbs
3 eggs, beaten
⅓ cup sour cream
½ teaspoon salt
¼ teaspoon pepper

veal
3 to 4 pounds boned veal breast or leg
½ teaspoon salt
¼ teaspoon pepper
1 tablespoon vegetable oil
2 cups hot beef broth
2 tablespoons cornstarch
½ cup sour cream

Prepare stuffing. Dice bacon and onion. Cook bacon in frypan until partially cooked. Add onion; cook 5 minutes.

Drain and chop mushrooms; add to frypan. Cook 5 minutes; remove from heat. Let cool; transfer to mixing bowl. Add herbs, beef, crumbs, eggs, and sour cream; mix thoroughly. Season with salt and pepper.

With sharp knife, cut pocket in veal; fill with stuffing. Close opening with toothpicks. (Tie with string if necessary.) Rub outside with salt and pepper.

Heat oil in Dutch oven or heavy saucepan; place meat in pan. Bake in preheated 350°F oven about 1½ hours; baste occasionally with beef broth. When done, place meat on preheated platter.

Pour rest of beef broth into Dutch oven; scrape brown particles from bottom. Bring to simmer.

Thoroughly blend cornstarch with sour cream; add to pan drippings, stirring. Cook and stir until thick and bubbly.

Slice veal breast. Serve sauce separately. Yield 6 servings.

veal cordon bleu

1½ to 1¾ pounds veal cutlets, cut into 6 thin pieces
6 thin slices boiled ham
3 slices Swiss cheese
1 egg, slightly beaten
2 tablespoons plus ½ cup milk

veal breast with herb stuffing

¾ cup fine dry bread crumbs
1 can condensed cream of mushroom soup
Paprika

Pound each veal piece to ⅛ inch thick; top each with ham slice.

Cut each cheese slice into 4 strips; place 2 on each ham slice. Roll meat around cheese; secure with wooden picks.

Mix egg and 2 tablespoons milk; dip rolls in egg, then in crumbs. Place seam-side-down in 13 × 9 × 2-inch baking dish.

Combine soup, wine, and ½ cup milk; heat to bubbling. Pour around rolls; cover with foil. Bake in preheated 350°F oven 1 hour or until meat is tender; uncover. Sprinkle with a little paprika; bake 10 minutes or until crumbs are browned. Yield 6 servings.

veal cutlets with capers

4 lean veal cutlets, about 6 ounces each
2 tablespoons lemon juice
½ teaspoon salt
⅛ teaspoon pepper
½ teaspoon paprika

1 tablespoon vegetable oil
½ small jar capers, drained
¼ cup dry white wine
1 bay leaf
3 tablespoons evaporated milk
Sliced pickled beets (garnish)
4 lettuce leaves (garnish)

Sprinkle cutlets with lemon juice; season with salt, pepper, and paprika.

Heat oil in frypan; fry cutlets 3 minutes. Turn cutlets; add capers. Fry 3 minutes; remove cutlets. Arrange on preheated platter.

Pour wine into pan; scrape loose any brown particles from bottom of pan. Add bay leaf; simmer 3 minutes. Remove bay leaf. Blend in milk; adjust seasonings. Pour over cutlets.

Cut beets into strips; arrange on lettuce leaves as garnish. Yield 4 servings.

veal kabobs

1½ pounds shoulder veal
1 clove garlic, crushed
1½ teaspoons curry powder
Pinch of paprika

veal cutlets with capers

Pinch of rosemary
Pinch of thyme
1 bay leaf, crushed
Salt and pepper
3 to 4 tablespoons oil
4 firm tomatoes
1 sweet red or green pepper, seeded, cut into strips
½ pound bacon slices, cut into squares

Cut veal into pieces about 1 inch square; put into bowl. Add garlic, curry powder, herbs, and a little salt and pepper. Pour oil over; mix well. Let stand about 1 hour.

When ready to cook, assemble meat, tomatoes and pepper on 4 skewers, putting piece of bacon before and after each piece of meat. Turn frequently while cooking. If bacon is rather lean, brush veal occasionally with a little oil. Serve on bed of rice. Yield 4 servings.

veal marengo

1 pound veal (lean breast or stew meat), cubed
2 tablespoons vegetable oil
1 medium onion, chopped
¼ pound fresh mushrooms, sliced
1 medium carrot, sliced
1 tablespoon tomato paste
½ teaspoon salt
⅛ teaspoon pepper
1 bay leaf
1 teaspoon dried thyme
½ cup hot water
½ cup white wine
¼ cup plain yogurt
1 tomato (garnish)
Parsley (garnish)

In large frypan, brown meat in hot oil several minutes. Remove meat; keep warm.

Add onion, mushrooms, and carrot to pan drippings; cook 5 minutes. Stir in tomato paste; season with salt and pepper. Add bay leaf and thyme;

pour in water and wine. Return meat to pan; cover. Simmer about 30 minutes; cool slightly. Gradually add yogurt; reheat over low heat, if necessary, but do not simmer. Remove bay leaf; adjust seasonings. Serve on preheated platter; garnish with tomato sections, and parsley. Yield 4 servings.

veal with mushrooms

2 pounds boneless, thinly sliced veal cutlet or fillet
½ cup flour
1 teaspoon salt
¼ teaspoon pepper
2 tablespoons vegetable oil
3 tablespoons butter
1 pound sliced mushrooms
6 tablespoons wine
2 tablespoons lemon juice
Lemon slices for garnish

Gently pound veal into very thin pieces.

Mix flour, salt, and pepper; lightly flour veal.

Melt oil and butter in 10-inch frying pan; sauté veal until golden brown, about 3 minutes each side. Remove; keep warm.

Add mushrooms to frypan; cook several minutes. Add wine and lemon juice; boil rapidly to reduce sauce slightly. Pour over veal; garnish with lemon slices. Yield 6 servings.

veal paprika

1½ pound veal steak, 1 inch thick
2 tablespoons bacon fat
2 or 3 onions, very finely chopped
1 tablespoon flour
2 teaspoons prepared mustard
1 can (about 2½ cups) tomatoes
Salt
1 teaspoon paprika
½ cup sour cream

Brown meat in bacon fat; put into shallow casserole with tightly fitting lid.

Brown onions in remaining fat; stir in flour. Add mustard, tomatoes, a little salt, and ½ cup water; stir until boiling. Pour over meat just to cover. Add a little extra tomato juice if necessary; cover. Cook in preheated 350°F oven about 45 minutes, until veal is tender. Stir in paprika and cream; mix well. Reheat without boiling. Adjust seasoning to taste before serving. Yield 4 servings.

veal piccata

4 pieces scallopine of veal
2 tablespoons flour
4 tablespoons corn-oil margarine
1 clove garlic, crushed
¼ cup dry vermouth
1 tablespoon lemon juice
½ lemon, sliced

Pound veal with wooden mallet until very thin (⅛-inch). Dredge lightly in flour; shake off excess.

Melt 3 tablespoons margarine in skillet. Place garlic in skillet until golden brown; discard.

Place veal in skillet; cook quickly, just until brown, about 1 to 2 minutes each side. Remove to serving dish.

Add remaining margarine, wine, and lemon juice to pan; simmer 3 minutes, scraping bottom of pan to loosen drippings. Pour over veal. Garnish with lemon slices. Yield 4 servings.

veal with rice and sour cream

1½ pounds veal, cut into small pieces
2 tablespoons oil
1 medium onion, chopped
1 clove garlic, minced
1 medium green pepper, chopped
2 tablespoons minced parsley
1 teaspoon paprika
3 cups beef broth
1 cup uncooked rice
1 cup sour cream
Salt and pepper to taste

Brown veal in oil. Add onion, garlic, and green pepper; cook a few minutes. Add parsley, paprika, and broth; simmer, covered, 15 minutes. Add rice; stir. Cover; cook 15 minutes. Slowly stir in sour cream. Season to taste; cover. Cook 15 minutes. Serve hot. Yield 4 to 6 servings.

veal marengo

wiener schnitzel

veal scallopini country-style

2 to 2½ pounds veal scallopine
½ cup flour
1 teaspoon salt
Pepper
2 teaspoons paprika
3 tablespoons butter
1 bouillon cube
1 cup hot water
1 (12-ounce) box mushrooms, sliced, sautéed
¼ cup chopped green pepper
2 cans tomato sauce
1 package noodles, cooked
Parmesan cheese, grated

Have butcher cut scallopine from leg of veal. Flatten with meat pounder; cut into serving pieces.

Mix flour with seasonings; dredge meat. Brown in butter; put in baking dish.

Dissolve bouillon cube in hot water; pour over meat. Cover with mixture of mushrooms, green pepper, and tomato sauce. Bake in preheated 350°F oven 45 minutes. Serve over hot noodles; sprinkling all with Parmesan. Yield 6 to 8 servings.

veal scallopino parmagiano

4 thin veal scallops (slices from leg of veal)
1 large egg
½ tablespoon oil
3 tablespoons flour
Salt and pepper
½ teaspoon powdered garlic
3 to 4 tablespoons grated parmesan cheese
3 tablespoons butter
Juice of ½ lemon
1 tablespoon finely chopped parsley

Beat scallops between waxed paper.
Mix egg with oil; beat.

Add seasoning and garlic to flour; mix with cheese. Brush scallops with egg mixture; press into cheese and flour until completely coated.

Melt butter; fry scallops until golden brown, about 5 to 6 minutes each side. Place on warm serving dish; keep hot.

Add lemon juice to butter in pan; reheat. Pour over scallops just before serving; decorate with parsley. Yield 4 servings.

wiener schnitzel

4 large (6 ounce) thin veal scallops
2 to 3 tablespoons flour
Salt and pepper
1 egg
Vegetable oil
5 to 6 tablespoons dried white bread crumbs
2 to 3 tablespoons butter
4 slices lemon
4 olives
4 anchovies
1 hard-boiled egg, chopped
2 teaspoons chopped capers
2 teaspoons paprika
2 tablespoons chopped parsley

Beat scallops between pieces of waxed paper until wafer-thin. Toss in seasoned flour until completely coated; shake to remove excess.

Beat egg with few drips of oil and some salt. Brush each scallop with this; toss in crumbs. (A paper bag is a good container for this.)

Melt butter in frying pan. When foaming, cook veal 3 to 4 minutes each side, until golden brown and crisp. Place on hot dish; garnish top of each scallop with 1 lemon slice. Place an olive in center; curl an anchovy fillet around olive. Surround with portion of egg white, capers, and paprika. Sprinkle all over with parsley. Decorate with sieved egg yolk, if desired. Serve at once, with remaining butter from frying pan as sauce. (Extra butter can be added.) Yield 4 servings.

VEGETABLES

ARTICHOKES

artichoke hearts in lemon butter

½ cup minced onion
½ clove garlic, crushed
2 tablespoons butter
¾ cup chicken broth
2 (15-ounce) cans artichoke hearts, drained
3 tablespoons lemon juice
1½ teaspoons salt
1 teaspoon oregano
¼ teaspoon grated lemon rind

Sauté onion and garlic in butter in medium saucepan until transparent. Add broth and artichokes. Season with lemon juice, salt, oregano, and lemon rind. Simmer 10 minutes or until artichokes are heated through.

Two packages cooked, frozen artichokes can be used in place of canned artichokes. Yield 6 to 8 servings.

baked artichoke hearts

2 (8½-ounce) cans artichoke hearts, drained
4 tablespoons olive oil
¾ cup fresh bread crumbs
Salt and pepper to taste
½ teaspoon paprika

Cut artichoke hearts in half; place in small casserole. Sprinkle with 2 tablespoons oil. Top with bread crumbs, salt, pepper, and paprika. Sprinkle with remaining oil. Bake in preheated 350°F oven 30 minutes. Serve with lemon wedges. Yield 4 servings.

boiled artichokes

6 artichokes
3 tablespoons salt
6 quarts water
Hollandaise Sauce (see Index) or melted butter

Cut off artichoke stalks; pull off hard outer leaves. Trim off points of remaining leaves with scissors. Cut off about ¼ of top, which removes many thorny pointed leaves. Place artichokes in boiling salted water; boil about 45 minutes, until base is tender but not mushy. Drain upside down. Before serving, remove choke or hairy growth in center by opening top leaves and pulling out tender center or cone in one piece. Below cone is choke; scrape off with spoon to expose tender artichoke heart. Discard choke. Replace cone upside down in center. Fill with Hollandaise Sauce, or serve butter separately.

Pull off each leaf, beginning at bottom. Dunk base of leaf in sauce; pull between teeth to scrape off tender flesh. Discard remainder of leaf. Continue this way until all leaves are eaten. Discard cone; cut base into wedges. Dip into remaining sauce. Yield 6 servings.

globe artichokes vinaigrette

Yield: 4 servings

4 fresh globe artichokes
Lemon juice
¾ teaspoon salt
1 recipe Basic Vinaigrette (see Index)

Wash artichokes; cut off stems. Remove small bottom leaves; trim tips of leaves. Cut off 1 inch from tops of artichokes. Dip cut portions of artichokes in lemon juice to prevent discoloration. Stand upright in deep saucepan just large enough to hold snugly. Twine can be tied around large bottom leaves to hold closely together, if desired. Pour in boiling water to depth of 3 inches. Add salt; cover. Boil gently 35 to 45 minutes, until base can be pierced easily with fork. More boiling water can be added, if needed. Remove artichokes with slotted spoon. Turn upside down to drain; let cool.

stuffed artichoke bottoms

12 canned artichoke bottoms
½ recipe Mornay Sauce (see Index)

Place artichoke bottoms and liquid in saucepan; heat through. Drain; pat dry. Place on baking sheet; spoon sauce onto artichokes. Broil until sauce is bubbly and browned. Garnish with tomato petals and pieces of hard-boiled eggs. Serve immediately. Yield 6 servings.

stuffed artichokes

4 medium-size globe artichokes
¾ cup dry bread crumbs
3 tablespoons grated Parmesan cheese
1 tablespoon chopped parsley
½ teaspoon garlic salt
¼ teaspoon crumbled dried oregano
¼ teaspoon pepper
2 tablespoons butter
2 tablespoons olive oil
1 cup boiling water

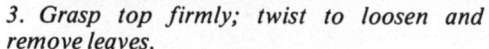

boiled artichokes

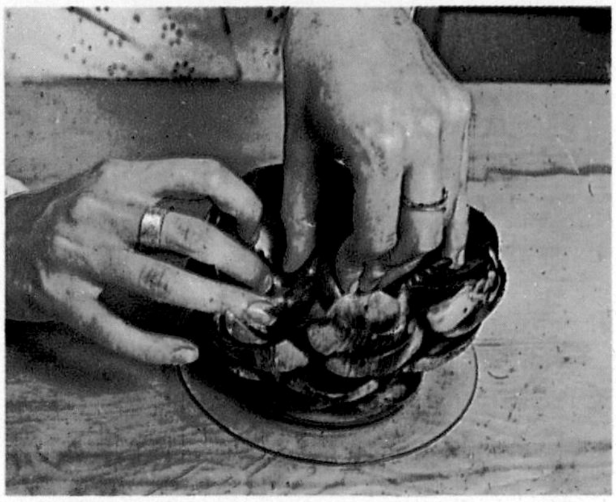

3. Grasp top firmly; twist to loosen and remove leaves.

how to prepare artichokes

1. Pull leaves apart gently.

4. Set aside cap of small, pale leaves.

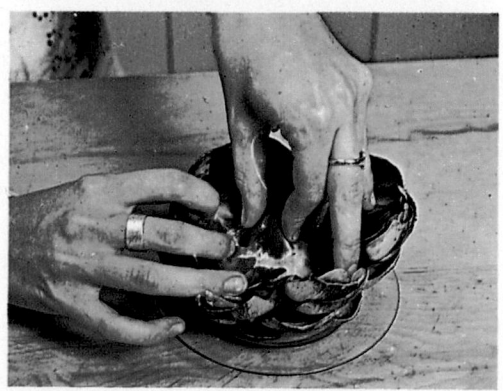

2. Spread leaves open to find peak of small, pale leaves covering choke.

5. Remove spiky choke from artichoke bottom with metal spoon.

Remove stems from artichokes. Cut about ½ inch from tips of leaves with pair of kitchen shears. Drop into boiling salted water; cook 5 minutes. Drain; shake to remove water; cool.

Combine crumbs, cheese, parsley, garlic salt, oregano, and pepper; mix well.

Tap bases of artichokes on flat surface to spread leaves. Stuff each with ¼ of bread-crumb mixture; spoon between leaves. Place in saucepan or stove-top casserole, close together so they do not tip over. Top each with ½ tablespoon butter and ½ tablespoon oil. Add boiling water; cover. Cook over low heat 35 to 45 minutes, until tender. Yield 4 servings.

ASPARAGUS

asparagus amandine

1 to 2 pounds fresh asparagus, cooked (see Index: Fresh Asparagus), or 2 boxes frozen, cooked
¼ cup butter
¼ cup slivered almonds
½ teaspoon salt
1 tablespoon lemon juice

Drain cooked asparagus.

Melt butter in small skillet. Cook almonds over low heat until golden brown, about 5 to 7 minutes; stir constantly. Remove from heat. Add salt and lemon juice; pour over hot asparagus. Yield 6 servings.

asparagus with orange cream sauce and cashews

2½ pounds fresh asparagus
1 fresh orange
1 recipe Béchamel Sauce (see Index)
Salt to taste
½ cup chopped cashew nuts

Steam asparagus (see Index: Fresh Asparagus).

Section orange; cut sections into large pieces. Add to Béchamel sauce; mix well.

Arrange asparagus in serving dish; sprinkle with salt. Pour sauce over asparagus; sprinkle with nuts. Yield 8 servings.

asparagus parmigiano

1½ pounds fresh asparagus, cooked (see Index: Fresh Asparagus) or 2 packages frozen asparagus, cooked
1 onion, chopped
1 clove garlic, minced
3 tablespoons oil
1 teaspoon salt
¼ teaspoon Tabasco sauce

asparagus with orange cream sauce and cashews

1 (1-pound) can tomatoes
¼ teaspoon thyme
1 (8-ounce) can tomato sauce
4 ounces mozzarella cheese, thinly sliced
2 tablespoons grated Parmesan cheese

Drain cooked asparagus; arrange in shallow baking dish.

Sauté onion and garlic in oil in saucepan until golden. Add salt, Tabasco sauce, and tomatoes; simmer, uncovered, 10 minutes. Add thyme and tomato sauce; simmer 20 minutes. Pour over asparagus. Place slices of mozzarella cheese over top. Sprinkle with Parmesan. Bake in preheated 350°F oven 30 minutes. Yield 6 to 8 servings.

asparagus and shrimp oriental

1 pound cooked fresh shrimp
1 can water chestnuts
1 cup sliced fresh mushrooms

1 medium onion, sliced
1 cup diagonally sliced celery
1 large can cut asparagus spears, drained, or
   1½ pounds fresh asparagus, steamed (see
   Index: Fresh Asparagus)
1 (11-ounce) can mandarin orange sections,
   drained
2 tablespoons vegetable oil
½ teaspoon salt
¼ teaspoon freshly ground pepper
2 tablespoons sugar
2 tablespoons soy sauce
Boiled Rice (see Index)

Shell; devein shrimp.

Drain and slice water chestnuts.

Arrange shrimp, chestnuts, mushrooms, onion, celery, asparagus, and oranges on large tray.

Heat oil in wok or electric skillet. Add onion, celery, salt, pepper, and sugar; cook, stirring, until vegetables are crisp-tender. Add asparagus and shrimp; place mushrooms and water chestnuts over shrimp. Sprinkle with soy sauce; place orange sections on top. Cover; cook until mixture begins to steam; reduce heat. Simmer about 12 minutes. Serve on rice. Yield about 6 servings.

fresh asparagus

Asparagus, as many as are needed; allow 4 to 6
   per person
½ cup boiling water
½ teaspoon salt
Melted butter
Lemon juice

Cut away fibrous part of asparagus stalks; tie rest together. Place in tall pot; add boiling water and salt. Cover; cook over medium heat about 8 minutes (do not overcook); drain. Pour over asparagus melted butter to which a little lemon juice has been added.

fresh asparagus with cream sauce

2 pounds fresh asparagus
¼ cup butter
¼ cup all-purpose flour
¾ cup milk
¾ cup half-and-half cream
2 hard-boiled eggs, minced
2 tablespoons fresh lemon juice

Cook asparagus (see Index: Fresh Asparagus); keep warm.

Melt butter in top of double boiler over hot water; blend in flour with wooden spoon. Add milk and cream gradually; stir constantly. Cook over low heat until smooth and thick.

Reserve 1 teaspoon egg; add remainder to sauce; mix well.

Place asparagus in serving dish; sprinkle with lemon juice.

Pour sauce in gravy boat; sprinkle with reserved egg. Yield 4 servings.

fresh asparagus with cream sauce

lemony asparagus

1 pound fresh asparagus, cooked (see Index:
   Fresh Asparagus) or 2 boxes
   frozen, cooked
2 tablespoons butter
½ cup mayonnaise
¼ teaspoon salt
⅛ teaspoon white pepper
⅛ teaspoon dry mustard
Juice of ½ large lemon
½ cup bread crumbs
⅓ cup grated Parmesan cheese

Place cooked asparagus in shallow greased casserole in single layer.

Melt butter; heat until golden brown. Blend in mayonnaise, seasonings, and lemon juice; pour over asparagus. Sprinkle with crumbs, then cheese. Bake in preheated 375°F oven 15 minutes or until browned. Can be prepared in advance and reheated. Yield 4 to 6 servings.

sweet-and-sour asparagus

2 pounds fresh asparagus
⅔ cup white vinegar
½ cup water
¼ cup salad oil
¼ teaspoon salt
½ cup sugar
3 sticks cinnamon
1 teaspoon whole cloves
1 teaspoon celery seed

Prepare and cook asparagus (see Index: Fresh Asparagus). Remove from pan; set aside.

Combine remaining ingredients in saucepan; bring to boil.

Place asparagus in shallow glass dish; pour vinegar mixture over. Cover; chill 24 hours. Drain before serving.

Equal amounts of canned, green asparagus spears can be substituted for fresh asparagus. Yield about 6 servings.

white asparagus in ham sauce

2 (14½-ounce) cans white asparagus
2 tablespoons butter or margarine
2 tablespoons flour
½ cup reserved liquid from asparagus
½ cup milk
4 ounces cooked lean ham, cut into julienne strips
⅛ teaspoon nutmeg (freshly ground if possible)
¼ teaspoon salt

Drain asparagus; reserve ½ cup liquid.

Heat butter in saucepan. Add flour; blend. Gradually pour in asparagus liquid and milk; stir constantly over low heat until sauce thickens and bubbles. Add ham and seasonings. Gently stir in asparagus; heat through, do not boil. Serve in preheated serving dish. Yield 4 servings.

BEANS

braised green beans

3 tablespoons olive oil
½ cup chopped onion
1 clove garlic, minced
1 pound fresh green beans, washed, tips removed
1 cup canned tomatoes
1 tablespoon tomato paste
½ teaspoon salt
¼ teaspoon pepper
½ teaspoon oregano
½ cup water (approximately)

Heat oil in heavy saucepan. Add onion and garlic; cook until golden. Add remaining ingredients. Juices should just cover beans in pan. If not, add a little more water. Cover; cook over low heat 45 minutes or until fork-tender. Serve with pan juices. Yield 4 servings.

brown-sugar beans

Great Northern beans
Dark brown sugar
Dry mustard
Salt
Coarsely ground black pepper

white asparagus in ham sauce

Bacon slices, quartered

Cook beans to almost-tender stage; reserve liquid. Layer beans about an inch deep in shallow baking pan or casserole; sprinkle liberally with brown sugar and several pinches mustard. Add another layer of beans; sprinkle with brown sugar, mustard, good dash of salt, and pepper. Place bacon randomly over top; add bean liquid until just visible through beans. Bake in moderate oven about an hour. Just before serving, sprinkle bacon with brown sugar; toast gently under broiler until sugar is bubbly and bacon lightly browned.

These beans make a delicious dish to serve anytime, especially for a pot-luck party. Yield as desired.

butter beans in cream

1 pound dried white butter beans
2 teaspoons salt
1 onion
1 clove garlic, pressed
2 small carrots, diced
1 cup diced ham

1 Bouquet Garni (see Index)
Freshly ground pepper to taste
½ cup half-and-half cream

Rinse beans with cold water; place in large saucepan. Cover with cold water; bring to boil. Remove from heat; let stand 5 minutes. Drain; cover again with cold water. Add salt, onion, garlic, carrots, ham, and Bouquet Garni; bring to boil. Cover; simmer 1½ hours or until beans are tender. Remove onion, if desired, and Bouquet Garni. Season with pepper. Stir in cream. Serve immediately. Yield 8 to 10 servings.

french–style green beans

2 pounds fresh green beans
1 small clove garlic, crushed
¼ cup butter
2 teaspoons salt
⅛ teaspoon freshly ground pepper
2 teaspoons finely chopped parsley

Take beans, small bunch at a time and level them at one end so that tips come together evenly. Cut off both ends so they will be uniform.

butter beans in cream

Use mechanical bean slicer, or cut each bean in half lengthwise with sharp knife. Wash beans; place in top of vegetable steamer. Pour water into base of steamer pan to just below level of top of steamer pan; bring to boil. Add beans; cover. Cook 30 minutes or until beans are crisp-tender. Remove top steamer pan from base. Pour water from base of steamer pan; turn beans into base. Add garlic, butter, salt, pepper, and parsley; mix well with slotted spoon. Serve immediately.

Beans can be cooked in colander over large saucepan with boiling water, if steamer is not available. Yield about 6 servings.

fresh green beans

2 pounds fresh pole or bush beans
2 tablespoons peanut oil
1 cup Basic Chicken Stock (see Index)
1 tablespoon cornstarch
Salt to taste

Cook beans in boiling water until crisp-tender; drain well.

Heat oil in large skillet. Add beans; cook, stirring constantly, until heated through. Stir in stock; cover. Cook over high heat 3 minutes.

Blend cornstarch and 2 tablespoons water until smooth.

Push beans to side of skillet; stir cornstarch mixture into broth. Stir beans into broth; cook, stirring constantly, until broth is slightly thickened and beans are glazed. Season with salt. Place beans in serving bowl. Yield 6 to 8 servings.

fresh green beans

fresh green beans with cherry tomatoes

1 pound fresh green beans
1¼ teaspoons salt
3 tablespoons butter
½ teaspoon sugar
Pinch of freshly ground pepper
1½ tablespoons chopped fresh parsley
8 cherry tomatoes, halved

Wash beans; remove tips. Cut into 1-inch pieces; place in saucepan with 1-inch boiling water and 1 teaspoon salt. Cook 5 minutes; cover. Cook over medium heat 10 to 15 minutes, until just crisp-tender; drain, if necessary. Add butter, sugar, pepper, remaining salt, and parsley; toss lightly until butter is melted and beans are coated. Place in serving bowl; garnish with cherry tomatoes. Yield about 6 servings.

fresh lima beans in parsley cream

3 pounds fresh lima beans
Salt and white pepper
2 tablespoons butter or margarine
½ cup cream
1 tablespoon chopped parsley

Cut off outer edge of each pod with scissors; open shell. Shuck beans into small saucepan; cover with boiling water. Add 1 teaspoon salt; cook until tender (20 to 25 minutes unless very small). Drain well; return to pan. Heat with butter and cream. Season to taste with salt and pepper. Serve in individual bowls; sprinkle with parsley. Yield 4 servings.

green beans greek-style

1½ pounds green beans
¼ cup olive oil
2 medium onions, chopped
Juice of 1 lemon
¾ teaspoon salt

fresh green beans with cherry tomatoes

green beans greek-style

¼ teaspoon pepper
⅓ cup bread crumbs
¾ teaspoon dried savory
1 bunch parsley, chopped
2 cups hot water

Wash and trim beans; cut in half.

Heat oil in large saucepan. Layer beans, onions, lemon juice, salt, pepper, crumbs, and herbs (reserve ½ cup parsley for garnish). Last layer should be beans. Add water; cook over low heat 30 to 35 minutes, until beans are tender. Garnish with parsley; cool. Serve cold as accompaniment to main dish. Yield 6 servings.

green beans with dill

2 tablespoons chopped onion
¼ cup butter or margarine
4 cups cooked beans
1 teaspoon dillseed
½ teaspoon seasoned salt

Cook onion in butter over low heat until soft and golden; do not brown. Add remaining ingredients; toss lightly. Heat; serve. Yield 6 to 8 servings.

green beans with radishes

2 tablespoons butter or margarine
1 tablespoon chopped scallions
1 teaspoon lemon juice
1 teaspoon soy sauce
¼ cup sliced radishes
2½ cups cooked fresh beans or 1 (16-ounce) can
    cut green beans, drained
2 tablespoons slivered almonds

Melt butter in frypan; sauté scallions until softened. Stir in lemon juice, soy sauce, and radishes; cook, stirring often, 5 minutes. Add beans; heat through. Gently stir in almonds. Yield 4 servings.

ham-seasoned green beans

1½ pounds green beans, broken into short pieces
    or 2 (10-ounce) packages frozen cut green beans
2 small onions, quartered
½ stalk celery, sliced
About 2 ounces cooked ham, cut into bite-size
    pieces
2 teaspoons salt
Pepper to taste
½ cup water
1 tablespoon butter or margarine

Place beans in 2-quart saucepan. Add remaining ingredients; simmer until beans are tender, 12 to 20 minutes. Yield 6 servings.

italian green beans

6 tablespoons chicken stock
2 tablespoons oil
4 peeled tomatoes, diced
1 pound string beans, trimmed, washed
Pinch of dried herbs
Salt and pepper
Chopped parsley

Combine stock, oil, and tomatoes; bring to boil. Add beans and herbs; cover. Simmer until beans are almost tender; remove lid. Simmer until excess liquid has evaporated. Add salt and pepper; sprinkle with parsley. Yield 2 to 4 servings.

lima beans creole

2 (10-ounce) packages frozen lima beans
6 slices bacon
¼ cup finely chopped onion
2 tablespoons chopped green pepper
½ teaspoon salt
Pepper to taste
2 cups cooked or canned tomatoes

Cook beans as directed on package; drain.
Fry bacon; drain on absorbent paper.
Brown onion and green pepper in 2 tablespoons bacon drippings.
Crumble bacon.
Add onion, green pepper, bacon, seasonings, and tomatoes to beans; cover. Simmer gently 15 minutes. Yield 6 servings.

lima beans and peppers

1 (10-ounce) package frozen baby lima beans
3 tablespoons olive oil
½ cup thin strips green pepper
¼ cup thin strips sweet red pepper
¼ cup finely chopped onion

Cook beans in boiling salted water, according to package directions. Drain; keep warm.

Heat oil in small skillet. Add peppers and onion; sauté 5 minutes.

Combine bean and pepper mixtures gently. Serve immediately. Yield 4 servings.

lima beans and peppers

mint lima beans

1 (10-ounce) package frozen lima beans
¼ cup chopped onion
1 clove garlic, crushed
2 tablespoons margarine
1 cup canned tomatoes
½ teaspoon dried mint leaves

Cook beans according to package directions. Drain; set aside.

In medium skillet sauté onion and garlic in margarine until tender. Stir in beans, tomatoes, and mint leaves; heat through until piping hot. Yield 4 servings.

new england baked beans

1 pound dry navy beans
1 large onion, diced
½ teaspoon salt
1 cup molasses
1 teaspoon dry English mustard
1 teaspoon Worcestershire sauce
1 cup firmly packed brown sugar
¼ pound salt pork, sliced

Rinse and pick over beans; place in large kettle. Cover with water; let soak 4 hours. Drain; place in large kettle. Cover with water; bring to boil. Cook, covered, about 45 minutes, until just tender. Drain; reserve liquid.

Combine onion, salt, molasses, mustard, Worcestershire sauce, and brown sugar.

Place about ⅓ of beans in bean pot with small amount of reserved liquid. Cover with about ⅓ of molasses mixture. Place several slices pork on top. Repeat layers; add part of reserved liquid with each layer. Bake in preheated 300°F oven 5 to 6 hours, until tender; add water as needed to keep beans covered. Yield 8 to 10 servings.

red beans and rice

1 pound dried red beans
1 ham bone (with some meat)
5 cups water
1 bay leaf
3 medium onions
1 green pepper
2 tablespoons fat
1 (10½-ounce) can condensed tomato soup,
    undiluted
Garlic salt
Chili powder
Salt

Soak beans overnight well covered with water; drain. Bring beans, ham bone, 5 cups water, bay leaf, and 1 onion to boil; simmer until beans are tender, about 2½ hours. Remove ham bone and bay leaf. Dice ham on bone; reserve. Chill beans; remove fat from top.

Chop remaining 2 onions and green pepper; cook until lightly browned in skillet with the fat; add to beans (and their liquid) with diced ham, soup, garlic salt, chili powder and salt (if needed) to taste. Reheat slowly over hot water. Serve with hot rice; use wide shallow soup plates if desired. Yield 6 servings.

roman-style green beans

1 (9-ounce) package frozen French-cut green
    beans
1 tablespoon fresh lemon juice

new england baked beans

2 tablespoons olive oil
¼ teaspoon crumbled dried oregano
⅛ teaspoon garlic powder
Salt and pepper
¼ cup sliced black olives

Cook beans in boiling salted water according to package directions; drain well.

Meanwhile, combine lemon juice, oil, seasonings, and olives in small saucepan; heat through. Pour over cooked beans; toss well. Serve immediately. Yield 4 servings.

soybeans polynesian

1 green sweet pepper, seeded, cut into ½-inch
 chunks
1 red sweet pepper, seeded, cut into ½-inch
 chunks
1 tablespoon vegetable oil
1 (8-ounce) can pineapple chunks, drained; reserve
 juice
1½ cups cooked soybeans
Juice from pineapple chunks
¼ cup catsup
2 teaspoons cider vinegar
1 tablespoon soy sauce
2 tablespoons brown sugar
¼ teaspoon salt (optional)

Sauté peppers in oil 2 to 3 minutes; remove from heat. Add pineapple and soybeans.

Combine pineapple juice, catsup, vinegar, soy sauce, brown sugar, and salt; pour over soybean mixture. Cook, stirring, over medium-high heat until mixture thickens somewhat and coats ingredients, about 5 to 8 minutes. Serve with rice.

For added flavor, prepare this dish several hours before the meal. Refrigerate while soybeans "marinate" in sauce. Reheat; serve. Yield 3 to 4 servings.

spiced green beans

2 (1-pound) cans whole green beans

lemon butter
¼ cup butter
2 tablespoons lemon juice
½ teaspoon salt
½ teaspoon dried basil
2 teaspoons dried parsley flakes

Drain beans. Bring drained liquid to boil in saucepan large enough to hold beans horizontally when re-added to liquid. When liquid comes to boil, reduce heat to simmer. Add beans; simmer 4 minutes or until heated. Do not boil. Drain beans; reserve liquid for soup stock.

Prepare Lemon Butter. Melt butter. Stir in lemon juice, spices, and parsley flakes.

Arrange beans on serving platter; coat with Lemon Butter. Serve immediately. Yield 6 servings.

string beans amandine

1 pound green beans
⅓ cup butter or margarine
½ cup slivered almonds
Salt and white pepper

Wash beans well; snip off ends. Cut into 1½-inch pieces. Boil 15 to 18 minutes in small amount of boiling salted water in covered pan. Beans should be just tender; drain well.

Heat butter in saucepan; add almonds. Cook until butter is light brown; take care butter does not burn. Toss beans with almond butter; season with salt and pepper. Yield 4 servings.

string beans vinaigrette

½ cup salad oil
5 tablespoons vinegar
½ tablespoon powdered sugar
1 tablespoon chopped sweet pickles
2 onions, chopped
2 tablespoons chopped parsley
8 small Italian green peppers
2 packages frozen, cooked French-style green
 beans

Mix all ingredients except beans. Pour over beans; chill several hours. Yield 4 to 6 servings.

winter bean sprouts

1 tablespoon butter or margarine
2 medium onions, sliced in rings
2 cups bean sprouts, 1 (1-pound) can, drained
½ teaspoon salt
1 teaspoon soy sauce (optional)
1 teaspoon lemon juice

Melt butter in medium skillet; lightly tan onions. Add rest of ingredients; stir to blend flavors. Cover skillet; simmer 1 minute. Serve at once. Yield 4 to 6 servings.

BEETS

beet baskets

6 large beets
1 cup chopped cooked spinach
1 hard-boiled egg, chopped
1 slice bacon, diced
1 tablespoon chopped onion
1 teaspoon salt
¼ teaspoon pepper
1 tablespoon butter
Parsley

Boil beets 1 to 2 hours. Scoop out centers to form baskets. Chop centers; mix with spinach and egg.

Broil bacon; add to mixture. Add onion, salt, pepper, and butter; heap mixture into beet baskets. Garnish with parsley. Serve hot. Yield 6 servings.

beets with orange sauce

¼ cup sugar
¾ teaspoon salt
2 tablespoons cornstarch
¾ cup orange juice
2 tablespoons lemon juice
1 tablespoon butter or margarine
3 cups beets, cooked or canned, sliced, drained

Mix sugar, salt, and cornstarch well. Stir in orange juice. Cook until thickened; stir constantly. Remove from heat; stir in lemon juice and butter. Pour sauce over beets; stir carefully. Heat; serve. Yield 6 servings.

grilled beets with lemon dill butter

8 medium whole fresh beets
3 teaspoons butter or margarine
1 tablespoon fresh lemon juice
1½ teaspoons chopped fresh dill

Cut off beet tops; peel beets. Place on large piece of aluminum foil; fold foil to form envelope. Add butter, lemon juice, and dill; seal edges of foil to form packet. Place on grill over hot coals; cook, turning frequently, 45 minutes or until beets are tender. Yield 4 servings.

harvard beets

3 tablespoons cornstarch
⅓ cup sugar
¾ teaspoon salt
1½ cups beet liquid (or beet liquid plus water)
2 tablespoons vinegar
1½ tablespoons butter or margarine
3 cups sliced cooked or canned beets

Mix cornstarch, sugar, and salt; blend in beet liquid, vinegar, and butter. Cook over moderate heat, stirring constantly, until thickened. Add beets; let stand 10 minutes, if desired, to blend flavors. Heat to serving temperature. Yield 6 servings.

pickled beets

3 pounds beets
1 pint vinegar
½ cup sugar
1 large stick cinnamon
1 teaspoon whole allspice
6 whole cloves
1 bay leaf
Sliced onions

pickled beets

Cook beets until tender. Allow 45 to 60 minutes for young beets, more for older variety. Skin when cool enough. Slice; set aside.

In saucepan combine vinegar, sugar, and spices (put into cheesecloth bag); bring to boil. Add beets; boil 10 minutes. Discard spice bag. Add onion; fill jars. Store in refrigerator.

BROCCOLI

braised broccoli

1 bunch broccoli
3 tablespoons oil
2 chopped scallions
2 tablespoons soy sauce
1 tablespoon gin
1 teaspoon sugar
¼ teaspoon seasoned salt
¼ cup boiling water

Remove tough ends of broccoli; cut broccoli into thick lengthwise slices.

Heat oil in skillet; sauté scallions and broccoli. Cover; cook 5 minutes over low heat. Yield 4 servings.

broccoli ring

2 envelopes gelatin
½ cup cold water
2 packages frozen broccoli, chopped
2 hard-boiled eggs, chopped
1 cup mayonnaise
1 can beef consommé
3 tablespoons lemon juice
1 tablespoon Worcestershire sauce
¼ teaspoon Tabasco sauce

Soak gelatin in cold water.

Cook broccoli according to package directions; cool. Drain; chop fine. Add hard-boiled eggs and mayonnaise.

Dissolve softened gelatin in heated consommé. Add seasonings; blend well. Let cool before stirring in broccoli mixture. Pour into oiled ring mold; chill until firm. Yield 6 to 8 servings.

broccoli spears with hollandaise sauce

broccoli spears with hollandaise sauce

1 bunch fresh broccoli
½ teaspoon salt
1 recipe Hollandaise Sauce (see Index)

Cut all but smallest curly leaves away from small heads; cut stems ½-inch long. Cook in small amount of boiling salted water about 12 minutes, until tender; drain well. Place in serving dish; cover with Hollandaise Sauce or serve sauce separately. Yield 4 servings.

creamy tuna-topped broccoli

1 bunch fresh broccoli
4 tablespoons butter or margarine
½ cup finely chopped celery
½ cup finely chopped onion
2 tablespoons flour
1½ cups milk
1 teaspoon Worcestershire sauce
½ cup shredded processed American cheese
2 (6½- or 7-ounce) cans tuna, drained, flaked

Wash broccoli; remove large leaves and tough part of stalks. Cut stalks lengthwise into quarters. Place in large saucepan with 1-inch boiling, salted water; cover. Cook 10 to 12 minutes, until crisp-tender; drain well. Reserve cooking water.

Melt butter in large saucepan over medium heat; sauté celery and onion until soft. Stir in flour; blend well.

Combine reserved cooking water and milk; gradually stir into saucepan. Cook, stirring, until mixture is slightly thickened and comes to boiling. Add Worcestershire sauce and cheese; stir until cheese is melted. Stir in tuna; heat through. Serve hot over cooked broccoli. Yield 4 servings.

paprika-buttered broccoli

1 cup water
1 teaspoon salt
2 (10-ounce) packages frozen whole broccoli

paprika butter
¼ cup butter
½ teaspoon salt
¼ teaspoon white pepper
¼ teaspoon paprika

Bring water to rapid boil in saucepan. Add salt and broccoli; boil 15 minutes or until broccoli is fork-tender but not mushy. Drain immediately.

Make Paprika Butter. Melt butter; stir in salt, pepper, and paprika.

Arrange broccoli on serving platter; pour Paprika Butter over. Serve immediately. Yield 6 servings.

sautéed broccoli

1 pound fresh young broccoli
Boiling salted water
3 tablespoons olive oil
1 clove garlic, peeled, chopped
Salt and pepper to taste

Cut off dry woody stems of broccoli; trim all discolored parts and dead leaves. Separate into small spears; peel stalks with vegetable peeler. Cook 3 to 5 minutes in 1-inch boiling salted water until crisp but tender; drain well.

Heat oil in large skillet over moderate heat. Sauté garlic until lightly browned. Add broccoli; sauté, stirring constantly, 5 minutes. Add salt and pepper. Serve topped with oil from pan. Yield 4 servings.

BRUSSELS SPROUTS

brussels sprouts in beer

1 pound fresh brussels sprouts
Beer (enough to cover sprouts)
½ teaspoon salt
2 tablespoons butter

Trim and wash sprouts; place in medium-size saucepan. Pour over enough beer to cover; bring to boil. Reduce heat; simmer 10 minutes or until tender. Add more beer, if needed, as liquid evaporates; drain. Add salt and butter. Serve hot. Yield 3 to 4 servings.

brussels sprouts in celery sauce

8 cups fresh brussels sprouts
2 teaspoons salt
1½ cups diced celery
6 tablespoons butter
6 tablespoons all-purpose flour
Milk
Dash of freshly ground pepper

Remove and discard wilted leaves from sprouts; wash. Soak 10 minutes in cold, salted water. Cook in small amount of water 9 to 10 minutes, until tender; drain.

Pour 2¼ cups water into medium-size saucepan; bring to boil. Add 1 teaspoon salt and celery; cook 15 minutes. Drain; reserve liquid.

Melt butter in top of double boiler over boiling water; stir in flour with wooden spoon until smooth.

Combine reserved liquid with enough milk to measure 4 cups; stir into flour mixture gradually. Cook until smooth and thick; stir constantly. Add celery, remaining salt, and pepper.

Place sprouts in serving dish; pour sauce over. Yield 8 servings.

brussels sprouts with cheese-noodle ring

4 cups fresh brussels sprouts
1¼ teaspoons salt

brussels sprouts with cheese-noodle ring

3 tablespoons butter
⅛ teaspoon freshly ground pepper
Cheese-Noodle Ring

Wash and trim sprouts; place in saucepan containing 1-inch boiling water. Add salt; bring to boil. Cook 5 minutes; cover. Reduce heat; simmer 10 minutes or until sprouts are crisp-tender; drain. Add butter and pepper; toss lightly until butter is melted. Spoon most of sprouts into center of Cheese-Noodle Ring; place remaining sprouts around ring. Yield 6 servings.

cheese-noodle ring
1 pound wide noodles
3 tablespoons butter
2 cups grated cheddar cheese
2 teaspoons Worcestershire sauce

Cook noodles in boiling, salted water until tender; drain. Add butter; toss until butter is melted. Pour into well-greased ring mold; place mold in pan of hot water. Bake in preheated 350°F oven 25 minutes. Unmold onto serving plate.

Melt cheese in double boiler; stir in Worcestershire sauce. Pour over noodle ring.

brussels sprouts with parmesan cheese

1½ pounds brussels sprouts
1 cup water
1 teaspoon salt
¼ teaspoon white pepper

¼ **cup butter, melted**
¼ **cup Parmesan cheese**

Clean sprouts; remove all tough and bruised outer leaves. Cover with cold water; soak 30 minutes; drain.

In saucepan large enough to accommodate brussels sprouts, bring 1 cup water to rapid boil. Add salt and sprouts; cover. Cook 10 minutes or until fork-tender; drain.

Combine pepper and butter; pour over sprouts. Garnish with Parmesan cheese. Yield 4 servings.

brussels sprouts in sour cream

2 (10-ounce) packages frozen brussels sprouts
¾ **cup sour cream**
½ **cup toasted slivered almonds**
¼ **cup chopped pimiento**
1 teaspoon sugar
½ **teaspoon freshly ground pepper**
1 teaspoon salt

Cook sprouts in ½ cup boiling, salted water 9 to 10 minutes or until crisp-tender; drain. Combine sprouts, and remaining ingredients in top of double boiler; toss lightly with fork. Place over hot water 7 minutes or until heated through. Turn into serving dish; serve hot. Yield about 6 servings.

grilled brussels sprouts

1 pint fresh brussels sprouts
Melted butter
Lemon juice
Paprika
Freshly ground pepper (optional)

Cook sprouts 10 minutes or until just tender. Dip in mixture of melted butter and lemon juice; skewer. Sprinkle with paprika and pepper. Grill or put on hibachi only 2 or 3 minutes, until browned. Yield 4 servings.

CABBAGE
baked stuffed cabbage

1 (2-pound) fresh green cabbage
4 slices bacon
1 tablespoon chopped fresh onion
3 tablespoons all-purpose flour
Salt and freshly ground pepper to taste
1 cup milk
1 cup shredded cheddar cheese
2 tablespoons chopped pimiento-stuffed olives

Hollow out center of cabbage; leave shell about ½-inch thick. Set shell aside; chop remaining cabbage coarsely.

baked stuffed cabbage

Fry bacon in skillet until crisp; remove from skillet. Drain on paper towels. Pour off all but 3 tablespoons drippings; add onion. Sauté until tender. Blend in flour; season with salt and pepper. Add milk gradually; cook, stirring constantly, until thickened. Stir in cheese until melted; remove from heat. Mix sauce with chopped cabbage; crumble bacon over top. Add olives; blend well.

Place cabbage shell on large piece of aluminum foil; spoon cheese mixture into shell. Wrap loosely; place on baking dish. Bake in preheated 350°F oven 30 minutes. Garnish with sliced olives before serving. Yield 6 servings.

cabbage with bacon and dill

1 small head cabbage
6 slices bacon
1 small onion, finely sliced
½ teaspoon salt
¼ teaspoon pepper
1 teaspoon dillweed

Wash, core, and slice cabbage; set aside to drain.

Fry bacon in large skillet until crisp; set aside.

Brown onion in bacon fat. Add salt, pepper, and dillweed. Gradually add drained cabbage; stir to blend flavors. Cover skillet; simmer on low heat. Cook until cabbage is tender, no more than 1 hour; add water if needed during cooking. When cabbage is tender, remove from pan to serving dish; garnish with bacon. Yield 4 or more servings.

cabbage curry

2 tablespoons oil
1 teaspoon salt
2 teaspoons curry powder
1 clove garlic, crushed
1 pound (4 cups) green cabbage, grated
Two 6-inch-long carrots, pared, coarsely grated
1 small onion, finely chopped (¼ to ⅓ cup)
¼ cup canned shredded coconut
¼ cup water

In 10-inch skillet over low heat stir together well oil, salt, curry powder, and garlic. Add vegetables; stir well to coat with oil mixture. Stir in coconut and water; cover. Simmer, stirring a few times, until there is no liquid and vegetables are tender-crisp, about 5 minutes. Be careful not to scorch; if necessary, add a tablespoon or two of water. Yield 4 to 6 servings.

cabbage-leaf rolls

1 medium firm head cabbage
2 cups ground cooked ham

1 cup mashed carrots
1 cup mashed potatoes
Salt and pepper to taste
Basic Beef Stock (see Index)
1 egg, lightly beaten
5 tablespoons butter
1 medium onion, finely chopped
Paprika
2 tablespoons cornstarch
2 tablespoons dry Madeira
1 (12-ounce) package green noodles
1 tablespoon crushed thyme
Peeled tomato strips

Remove core from cabbage; cover with boiling water. Let stand until leaves are easily detached; remove 16 large leaves. Cut coarse section from base of each leaf.

Combine ham, carrots, potatoes, salt, pepper, 2 tablespoons stock, and egg; blend thoroughly.

cabbage-leaf rolls

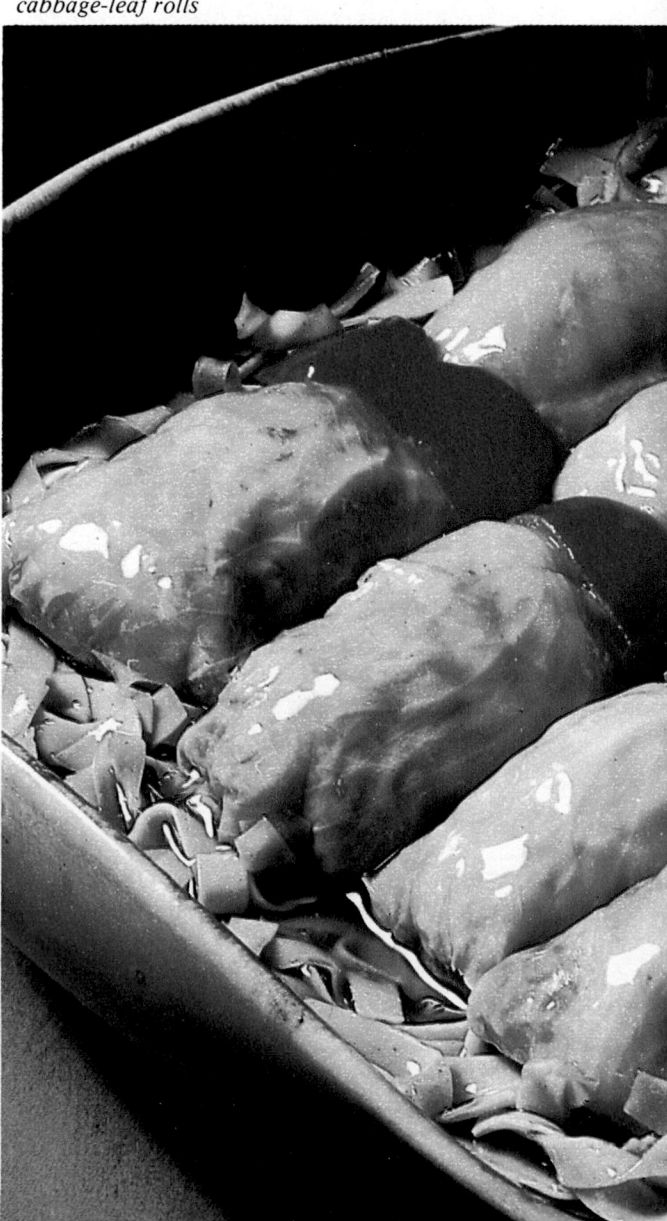

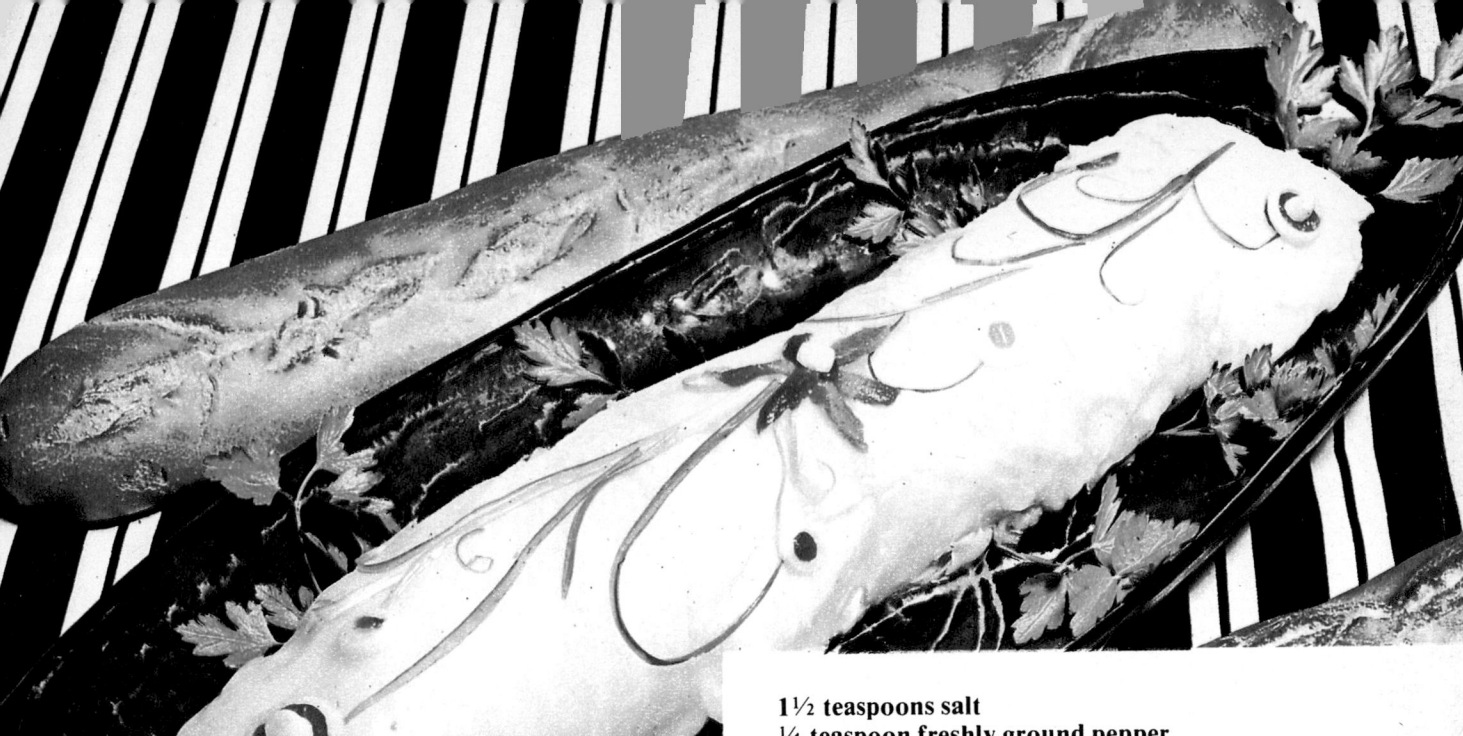

cabbage roll

Shape into 8 rolls; place in center of 8 cabbage leaves. Overlap edges; tuck in top and bottom edges. Place, fold-side-down, on remaining cabbage leaves; repeat procedure, securing rolls with string. Steam 45 minutes.

Melt 2 tablespoons butter in skillet; sauté onion until tender but not browned. Sprinkle with paprika; stir in 1¾ cups stock.

Dissolve cornstarch in ¼ cup stock; add to onion mixture. Cook, stirring constantly, until thickened. Stir in 1 tablespoon butter and Madeira.

Prepare noodles according to package instructions; drain well.

Melt remaining butter in saucepan; stir in noodles and thyme. Toss to coat well; place in shallow, heated serving dish. Top with cabbage rolls; garnish with tomatoes as shown in illustration. Spoon small amount of sauce over cabbage rolls; serve with remaining sauce.

An equal amount of ground, cooked beef can be substituted for ham, if desired. Yield 8 servings.

cabbage roll

1 medium head white cabbage
1 large Spanish onion
1 pound lean ground beef
1 teaspoon Worcestershire sauce
½ teaspoon paprika
⅛ teaspoon tarragon leaves
⅛ teaspoon rosemary
⅛ teaspoon thyme
2 garlic cloves, pressed
1 egg
½ cup tomato puree
1 cup soft bread crumbs
1½ teaspoons salt
¼ teaspoon freshly ground pepper
Melted butter

Immerse cabbage in boiling water in large kettle. Boil 5 minutes; turn several times. Plunge into ice water; peel off limp outer leaves. Repeat process; drain leaves. Chop enough remaining firm cabbage to measure 2 cups; place in large bowl.

Peel and grate onion; add to cabbage. Add ground beef, Worcestershire sauce, paprika, tarragon, rosemary, thyme, garlic, egg, tomato puree, crumbs, salt, and pepper; blend thoroughly.

Place long sheet of wide aluminum foil on working surface; cover with buttered waxed paper. Arrange cabbage leaves in 14 × 9-inch rectangle on waxed paper.

Shape beef mixture into roll about 12-inches long; place in center of cabbage leaves. Bring leaves up around beef roll; fit over each end. Brush with melted butter. Fit waxed paper around roll; wrap with foil. Fold up ends to seal; tie in center and about 3-inches from ends with string. Place in large oval roaster; add enough boiling water to almost cover cabbage. Cover roaster. Simmer 1½ hours; remove roll from roaster with tongs. Open one end of foil; pour off liquid. Remove string and foil; remove waxed paper carefully. Slide onto long, narrow serving dish; garnish with shreds of green onion, onion rings, and pimiento, as shown in illustration. Length of roll can be varied according to available cooking pans. Yield about 10 servings.

fried cabbage

3 small cabbages
Pepper
1 cup flour
2 eggs, beaten
1½ cups bread crumbs
2 cups oil

Halve cabbages; cut out cores. Cook 20 minutes in salted water; squeeze dry. Flatten out; season with pepper. Dip in flour, eggs, then bread crumbs. Fry in oil until brown. Yield 6 to 8 servings.

red cabbage

1 large head red cabbage
2 tablespoons bacon fat or oil
½ cup red wine
3 tablespoons red currant jelly
1 teaspoon salt
Dash of white pepper
Pinch of powdered cloves
1 tablespoon sugar
Wash, shred, and drain cabbage.

red cabbage

Heat bacon fat in large pot. Add cabbage; heat 5 minutes. Add remaining ingredients; mix very well. Stir a few minutes, until all flavors are absorbed; cover. Cook over low heat 25 minutes; serve hot. Yield 6 to 8 servings.

rice-stuffed cabbage rolls with melted butter

1 head cabbage
1 cup long-grain rice
1 tablespoon butter
1 tablespoon paprika
¼ cup currants
2 tablespoons finely chopped parsley
Melted butter

westphalian cabbage

Place cabbage in steamer; steam 1½ hours or until tender.

Cook rice in 3 cups boiling salted water 18 minutes or until tender; drain. Combine rice, butter, paprika, currants, and parsley; stir until butter is melted.

Remove cabbage from steamer; plunge into cold water to loosen leaves. Cut out hard core; separate leaves. Place about 1 tablespoon rice mixture in each leaf. Overlap sides; roll up. Place rolls on serving platter; pour melted butter over. Serve immediately. Yield 6 to 8 servings.

skillet cabbage

2 tablespoons vegetable oil
3 cups finely shredded cabbage
1 cup chopped celery
1 small green pepper, chopped
1 small onion, chopped
½ teaspoon salt
¼ teaspoon pepper

Heat oil in large frypan about 20 minutes before serving time; add ingredients. Cook over medium to low heat about 15 minutes; stir often. Cover pan during last 5 minutes of cooking time; stir once or twice. Serve immediately. (Vegetables will be crisp.) Yield 4 servings.

sour cabbage

1 head cabbage
2 tablespoons butter
2 tablespoons flour
1 teaspoon salt
1 teaspoon caraway seeds
2 cups water
2 tablespoons vinegar
2 tablespoons sugar
¼ cup wine (optional)

Shred cabbage into large pot; add all ingredients, except wine, as listed. Cook over very low heat at least 2 hours; add more water if needed. Just before serving, add wine; mix thoroughly. Yield 4 to 6 servings.

stuffed cabbage

1 large head cabbage
1 pound ground chuck
1 grated onion
1 teaspoon salt
¼ teaspoon pepper
2½ cups canned tomatoes
Juice of 2 lemons
1 teaspoon salt
¼ teaspoon pepper
¾ cups brown sugar

Remove large leaves from cabbage; let boiling water stand on leaves a few minutes so they become easy to roll.

Combine meat, onion, salt, and pepper; place mound of meat mixture in cup part of each leaf. Loosely fold over sides of each leaf; roll up.

In bottom of Dutch oven place a few remaining cabbage leaves. Arrange layers of stuffed cabbage, seam-sides-down.

Mix tomatoes, lemon juice, salt, and pepper in pan; bring to boil on top of range. Sprinkle with lemon; add brown sugar to taste. Bake in preheated 370°F oven, covered, 1 hour; uncover. Bake 2 hours. Yield 8 servings.

westphalian cabbage

1 head cabbage, approximately 2 pounds
3 tablespoons vegetable oil
1 teaspoon salt
1 teaspoon caraway seeds
1 cup hot beef broth
2 to 3 small tart apples
1 tablespoon cornstarch
2 tablespoons cold water
3 tablespoons red wine vinegar
¼ teaspoon sugar

Shred cabbage.

Heat oil in Dutch oven or heavy saucepan. Add cabbage; sauté 5 minutes. Season with salt and caraway seeds. Pour in broth; cover. Simmer over low heat about 15 minutes.

Meanwhile, peel, quarter, core, and cut apples into thin wedges. Add to cabbage; simmer 30 minutes.

Blend cornstarch with cold water. Add to cabbage; stir until thickened and bubbly. Season with vinegar and sugar just before serving. Yield 4 to 6 servings.

SAUERKRAUT

hungarian sauerkraut

1 (16-ounce) can sauerkraut
¾ teaspoon caraway seeds
3 slices diced bacon
1 small onion, peeled, diced
1 cup sliced smoked sausage
2 teaspoons Hungarian sweet paprika
2 sweet gherkin pickles, thinly sliced
4 tablespoons sour cream

Combine sauerkraut and caraway in small saucepan; bring to boil. Cover; reduce heat to low. Cook 15 minutes.

Meanwhile sauté bacon in heavy skillet until crisp. Remove with slotted spoon.

Add onion and sausage to skillet; cook until lightly browned. Remove from heat; stir in paprika.

Drain sauerkraut; add to skillet. Add bacon and pickles; stir well. Cook over low heat 10 minutes. Serve topped with sour cream. Yield 4 servings.

sauerkraut and apple

¼ cup butter or bacon fat
2 tablespoons flour
2½ cups sauerkraut
¼ cup vinegar
3 whole cloves
2 tablespoons brown sugar
1 large apple, finely chopped

Melt butter in pan. Add flour; stir until smooth. Add sauerkraut, vinegar, cloves, brown sugar, and ¾ cup water; cover. Simmer 20 minutes. Add apple just before serving. Yield 6 servings.

scalloped sauerkraut and tomatoes

2½ cups stewed tomatoes
Salt and pepper
2 tablespoons butter
2 cups bread crumbs
2½ cups sauerkraut

Drain tomatoes; reserve liquid. Put tomatoes in greased baking dish; sprinkle with salt and pepper. Dot with butter; cover with layer of crumbs. Add layer of sauerkraut. Alternate sauerkraut, seasoning, and butter until all ingredients are used; have layer of buttered crumbs on top. Add tomato liquid. Bake in preheated 400°F oven 20 minutes. Yield 6 servings.

sour-creamy sauerkraut

3 tablespoons butter, margarine, or oil
1 onion, chopped
1 pound sauerkraut, undrained
½ teaspoon freshly ground black pepper
Salt to taste
4 tablespoons sour cream

Melt butter in medium skillet; lightly brown onion. Add sauerkraut; stir to mix. Cover; simmer 1 hour. Uncover; drain off liquid. Add pepper and salt if needed. Just before serving, stir in sour cream. Yield 4 to 6 servings.

spareribs and sauerkraut

2 pounds spareribs
1 teaspoon salt
4 cups sauerkraut

Have spareribs divided into serving pieces. Wipe with cold, damp cloth; sprinkle with salt. Put in kettle; cover with cold water. Bring to boil; cover. Reduce heat; simmer 30 minutes. Add sauerkraut; bring to boil. Reduce heat; simmer, uncovered, 30 minutes. Serve hot. Yield 4 servings.

CARROTS

bacon carrots

1 (1-pound) bag small carrots
1 cup boiling water
½ teaspoon salt
3 tablespoons butter
White pepper to taste
4 slices bacon, crisply cooked, crumbled

Cook carrots rapidly in covered saucepan with boiling water and salt until just tender-crisp; drain. Stir in butter and pepper, then bacon. Serve at once. Yield 6 servings.

baked carrots

1 (1-pound) bag carrots, pared, coarsely shredded
¾ cup blanched almonds, coarsely chopped
Butter
4 large eggs
1½ cups milk
1¼ teaspoons salt
1 teaspoon sugar
1 tablespoon finely grated onion (pulp and juice)

Steam carrots until very tender; drain. Spread over bottom of buttered 2-quart baking dish (11¾ × 7½ × 1¾ inches).

In 10-inch skillet, stirring constantly over moderate heat, brown almonds in butter.

Beat eggs, milk, salt, and sugar to blend. Stir in almonds and onion; pour over carrots. Place in roasting pan filled with enough hot water to come about as high as food in baking dish. Bake in preheated 325°F oven until knife inserted in center comes out clean, 30 to 35 minutes. Cut in squares; serve hot. Yield 8 servings.

carrots in beer

4 large carrots
1 tablespoon butter
1 cup dark beer
¼ teaspoon salt
1 teaspoon sugar

Peel carrots; slice into long, thin slices.

Melt butter in medium-size frypan; add beer and carrots. Cook slowly until tender; stir frequently. Stir in salt and sugar; cook 2 minutes. Serve hot. Yield 4 servings.

carrot casserole

2 cups milk
1 cup cooked rice
1 tablespoon brown sugar
1 teaspoon salt
5 medium carrots, shredded
2 eggs
3 tablespoons butter
⅓ cup bread crumbs or wheat germ

Combine milk, rice, sugar, salt, carrots, and eggs; pour into well-buttered casserole.

Melt butter in pan; stir in bread crumbs; sprinkle over casserole. Bake in preheated 375°F oven 40 minutes or until top is lightly browned. Yield 6 servings.

carrots and grapes supreme

4 cups canned Belgium carrots, drained
½ pound white grapes, rinsed
¼ pound butter or margarine
½ cup cointreau

Drain carrots; rinse grapes. Place between paper towels until very dry.

Melt butter in medium-size skillet. Add cointreau, carrots, and grapes; simmer together 10 minutes. Yield 4 to 6 servings.

carrots a l'orange

3 tablespoons frozen orange juice, undiluted
2 tablespoons water
2 tablespoons orange peel
1 tablespoon flour
¼ cup butter
3 cups sliced cooked carrots

Put orange juice, water, and peel in double boiler over hot water. Cook 5 minutes; stir often. Blend in flour and butter; stir until mixture thickens. Add carrots; stir together until thoroughly heated. Yield 4 servings.

carrot mold

12 carrots
½ cup cream
½ cup cracker crumbs
3 tablespoons butter
5 eggs, separated
Salt and pepper to taste

Cook and mash carrots. Add cream, crumbs, butter, beaten egg yolks, salt, and pepper.

Beat egg whites stiff; fold into mixture. Place in buttered ring mold; set in hot water. Bake in preheated 350°F oven 30 minutes. Turn out mold; fill center with green vegetable for attractive dish. Yield 6 to 8 servings.

carrots and raisins

2 tablespoons butter or margarine
1½ pounds young carrots, scraped, cut into
    ¼-inch slices (try a diagonal slice—it's pretty)

creamed peppered carrots

⅓ cup water or dry white wine
½ teaspoon ground nutmeg
⅔ cup white raisins
3 teaspoons light brown sugar

Melt butter in medium skillet. Add carrots, water, and nutmeg; cover. Cook over low heat 15 minutes. Stir in raisins and sugar; cook 5 minutes or until raisins are plump and carrots glazed. Yield 4 to 6 servings.

carrot sticks

6 medium carrots, peeled
⅓ cup finely chopped onion
⅓ tablespoon butter
¼ teaspoon thyme
Salt and pepper to taste
1 tablespoon finely chopped parsley

Cut carrots into 2-inch sticks or julienne-style; place in top of double boiler. Add onion, butter, thyme, and 1 tablespoon water; cover. Cook over boiling water 30 minutes or until crisp-tender. Season with salt and pepper. Turn into serving dish; sprinkle with parsley. Yield about 4 servings.

creamed peppered carrots

4 cups diced carrots
¼ cup whipping cream
¼ cup melted butter
Salt to taste
1 teaspoon freshly ground pepper

Cook carrots in small amount salted water until tender; drain. Process carrots, cream, and butter in blender or food processor. (With blender, puree mixture in 4 lots.) Add salt and pepper to puree. Spoon into mound on heatproof serving dish; shape with tines of fork. Make well in center; pour additional cream into well. Serve immediately or reheat in 275°F oven if necessary. Yield 6 to 8 servings.

glazed carrots

10 to 12 small young carrots, washed, trimmed
2 tablespoons margarine
1 tablespoon brown sugar
2 tablespoons honey
2 tablespoons fresh mint

Cook carrots in small amount boiling salted water 10 minutes. When tender, drain; set aside.

Melt margarine in medium skillet. Add sugar and honey; blend. Add carrots; cook 3 or 4 minutes over low heat, stirring so each carrot is glazed. Sprinkle with mint.

Substitute parsley for fresh mint, if preferred. Yield 4 to 6 servings.

sweet-and-sour carrots

2 tablespoons vegetable oil
1 slice fresh gingerroot
1 pound carrots, cleaned, roll-cut into 1-inch
    pieces

718

glazed carrots

½ teaspoon salt
½ cup chicken broth
1 tablespoon vinegar
½ tablespoon brown sugar
2 teaspoons cornstarch in 2 tablespoons cold water
½ cup canned pineapple chunks (optional)

Heat oil in wok or skillet. Brown and discard ginger slice. Stir-fry carrots 1 minute. Add salt and broth; cover. Steam over moderate heat 5 minutes. Stir in vinegar, brown sugar, cornstarch mixture, and pineapple chunks; heat until sauce thickens. Serve at once. Yield 4 servings.

CAULIFLOWER

cauliflower with mornay sauce

1 large head cauliflower
Freshly grated bread crumbs
⅓ cup melted butter
1 recipe Mornay Sauce (see Index)

Wash; trim cauliflower; separate into florets. Place in vegetable steamer; steam until tender. Arrange around edge of baking dish; sprinkle liberally with bread crumbs. Drizzle butter over crumbs; spoon Mornay Sauce into center of baking dish. Broil until crumbs are lightly browned. Yield 4 to 6 servings.

cauliflower oregano

1 large head cauliflower or 2 (9-ounce) packages
    frozen cauliflower
¼ cup lemon juice
¼ cup olive oil
1 tablespoon chopped parsley
½ teaspoon dried oregano
½ teaspoon salt

Clean fresh cauliflower; break into florets. Cook in boiling salted water 10 minutes or until just tender. (Cook frozen cauliflower according to package directions.)

Meanwhile, combine remaining ingredients.

cauliflower with mornay sauce

Drain cauliflower; place in serving dish. Top with dressing; serve hot. Yield 4 servings.

variation

Substitute 1 large bunch broccoli or 2 (9-ounce) packages frozen broccoli for cauliflower.

cauliflower polish-style

2 hard-cooked egg yolks
1 teaspoon dried parsley flakes
2 tablespoons sour cream
¼ teaspoon white pepper
1 head cauliflower
1 teaspoon salt
¼ cup butter
3 tablespoons bread crumbs

Mash egg yolks in small bowl. Add parsley, sour cream, and white pepper; blend. Set aside.

Wash cauliflower head; remove outside leaves. Cover bottom of pan large enough to accommodate cauliflower with 1 to 2-inches of water; add salt. Bring to rapid boil. Add cauliflower; cover. Boil 25 minutes or until fork-tender; drain immediately.

Melt butter; stir in bread crumbs. Pour buttered crumbs over cauliflower; garnish with egg-yolk mixture. Yield 8 servings.

cauliflower polish-style

cauliflower with tomato sauce

1 medium-size head cauliflower, trimmed of outer green leaves
6 cups water
2 teaspoons salt

tomato sauce
3 tablespoons olive oil
2 chopped shallots, or ¼ cup chopped onion
¼ cup finely chopped ham
¼ cup canned sliced mushrooms
1½ tablespoons flour

¾ cup hot chicken broth
2 tablespoons tomato paste
¼ cup white wine
¼ cup chopped parsley
Salt and pepper to taste

Make deep X-shaped cut in base of cauliflower; place on vegetable steamer rack.

Combine water and salt in large heavy kettle; bring to boil. Lower rack into kettle; cover tightly. Cook 20 minutes; cauliflower should be crisp but tender; drain.

Meanwhile, make sauce. Heat oil in saucepan; sauté shallots in oil until lightly browned. Add ham and mushrooms; sauté 2 minutes. Remove onion, ham, and mushrooms with slotted spoon. Add flour to oil in saucepan; cook until bubbly.

Combine broth and tomato paste; add to saucepan, stirring well. Add wine, reserved ingredients, parsley, salt, and pepper. Serve hot over cauliflower. Yield 6 servings.

cauliflower with water chestnuts and mushrooms

1 small cauliflower
2 tablespoons oil
8 mushrooms, sliced
1 cup hot chicken broth
¼ cup sliced water chestnuts
2 tablespoons soy sauce
Salt to taste
1 tablespoon cornstarch mixed with cold water

Trim and wash cauliflower; break into florets. If large, slice florets.

Heat oil in pan; gently sauté cauliflower. Add mushrooms; sauté about 30 seconds. Add broth, water chestnuts, soy sauce, and salt. Bring to boil; cover. Simmer until cauliflower is tender but still crunchy.

Mix cornstarch with enough cold water to make smooth paste. Slowly add to cauliflower mixture, stir constantly until thickened. Yield 4 servings.

crisp-fried cauliflower with sour-cream sauce

1 medium head cauliflower (approximately 1½-pounds)
Boiling salted water
2 eggs
2 tablespoons milk
¾ cup dry bread crumbs
2 tablespoons grated Parmesan cheese
Oil for deep frying

Clean cauliflower; wash well. Separate into florets. Cook in large saucepan of boiling salted water until crisp-tender (12 to 15 minutes); drain well. Pat dry on paper towels.

Beat eggs and milk together in shallow bowl.

Combine bread crumbs and cheese on sheet of waxed paper; mix well.

Dip cauliflower in egg mixture; then in crumbs; coat well.

Heat several inches oil in deep-fat fryer or heavy kettle to 365°F. Cook cauliflower, few pieces at a time; in hot fat until golden. Remove with slotted spoon; drain on absorbent paper. Keep hot while cooking remaining cauliflower. Yield 4 servings.

sour-cream sauce

1 (1.25-ounce) package sour-cream-sauce mix
½ cup milk
1 tablespoon chopped parsley
½ teaspoon lemon juice
½ teaspoon Hungarian sweet paprika
¼ teaspoon Worcestershire sauce
Salt and pepper

Combine ingredients in small saucepan; mix well. Cook over very low heat, stirring constantly, until heated through. Serve over cauliflower.

dill-fried cauliflower

1 head cauliflower
½ cup bread crumbs mixed with 1 teaspoon salt,
  1 teaspoon dillweed, and ¼ teaspoon pepper
2 eggs, beaten
4 tablespoons oil or rendered chicken fat

Cook cauliflower in salted water just 10 minutes; drain. Cool; separate into florets. Dip each piece into crumbs, then in eggs; return to crumb mixture.

Heat oil in medium skillet; cook florets until golden brown. Drain on paper towels; sprinkle with more salt and pepper if desired. Yield 4 to 6 servings.

pickled cauliflower

2 quarts water
1 quart cider vinegar
½ cup noniodized salt
4 to 5 large heads cauliflower
1 tablespoon garlic powder
12 garlic cloves, peeled
24 dry red peppers
12 dill sprigs, dried

Combine water, vinegar, and salt in large saucepan; bring to boil.

Clean cauliflower; break into florets. Soak in ice-cold water.*

Sterilize 12 pint jars. Put ¼ teaspoon garlic powder, 1 garlic clove, 2 peppers, and 1 dill sprig in each jar. Fill each jar with cauliflower; cover to within ½-inch from top of jar with boiling vinegar

mixture. Adjust lids. Process in boiling-water bath 15 minutes. Remove jars; cool slowly. Immediately use or reprocess jars that do not seal. Yield 12 pints.

* Cauliflower is soaked in ice-cold water to retain its crispness when covered with hot vinegar solution.

puffed cauliflower cheese

1 medium head cauliflower
¼ cup butter or margarine
2 tablespoons flour
1 cup milk, or milk and water in which cauliflower
  has been cooked
Salt and pepper
¼ cup fine white bread crumbs
3 eggs (separated)
1 cup grated cheese

Wash cauliflower; remove stalk end. Cut into quarters; remove hard stalk. Divide into florets; cook in boiling salted water until tender; drain.

Heat butter in pan. Add flour; stir over low heat 2 minutes. Remove from heat. Add milk gradually; stir until smooth. Return to heat; stir until boiling. Add salt and pepper and most of bread crumbs. Stir in egg yolks, cheese, and cauliflower; adjust seasoning to taste.

Beat egg whites until stiff; fold into mixture. Put into greased ovenproof dish; sprinkle with remaining crumbs. Bake in preheated 400°F oven about 30 minutes, until well risen and brown. Yield 4 servings.

CELERY

braised celery

1 bunch celery
½ teaspoon salt
¼ teaspoon pepper
2 tablespoons butter or margarine
1 chicken bouillon cube dissolved in 1 cup boiling
  water
1 tablespoon finely chopped parsley

Remove green leaves from celery; cut stalks into 4-inch lengths. Arrange stalks in bottom of small pan or heatproof casserole; season with salt and pepper. Dot with butter; pour bouillon over celery. Bring liquid to boil; cover. Simmer 30 minutes or until celery is tender. Place on heated serving dish; sprinkle with parsley. Yield 4 servings.

creamed celery with pecans

4 cups ½-inch pieces diagonally cut celery
1 can cream of celery soup
1 teaspoon salt

puffed cauliflower cheese

¾ **cup pecan halves**
Buttered bread crumbs

Place celery in greased casserole; add undiluted soup. Sprinkle with salt; sprinkle with pecans. Cover with crumbs. Bake in preheated 400°F oven 20 minutes. Yield 4 to 6 servings.

sweet-and-sour celery

1 bunch fresh celery
4 slices bacon
1 small onion, sliced into rings
¼ cup white vinegar
1 tablespoon sugar
¼ teaspoon salt
¼ teaspoon white pepper

Wash and trim celery; cut stalks into 1-inch diagonal pieces.

Fry bacon in large frypan until crisp; drain on paper towels. Drain fat except 2 tablespoons. Add celery and onion to hot fat; sauté 6 to 8 minutes, stirring often. Reduce heat; cover. Cook 10 to 12 minutes or until vegetables are just tender. Stir in vinegar, sugar, salt, and pepper; heat through. Place in serving dish; crumble bacon over top. Yield 6 servings.

CORN

barbecued corn on the cob

Remove husk and silk from corn; spread generously with softened butter. Sprinkle with salt and pepper; wrap each cob in double thickness of

barbecued corn on the cob

foil, or use heavy-duty foil. Twist ends to seal. Place on barbecue grid over hot coals. Cook about 20 minutes; turn frequently. Yield as desired.

confetti corn

6 ears corn
¼ cup butter
¼ cup chopped green sweet pepper
¼ cup chopped red sweet pepper
1 tablespoon finely chopped fresh parsley

Remove husks and silks from corn. Cook in boiling water 8 to 10 minutes, until tender; drain. Cool until easily handled; cut kernels from cobs.

Melt butter in saucepan; add peppers and parsley. Cook over low heat; stirring constantly, until peppers are tender. Stir in corn; and heat through. Yield 6 servings.

corn pudding

1½ cups fresh corn
2 eggs, beaten
1 tablespoon melted shortening
1⅓ cups milk
¼ teaspoon salt
Dash of white pepper

Combine all ingredients; pour into greased casserole. Place casserole in pan of hot water in oven. Bake in preheated 350°F oven about 50 minutes. Yield 4 to 6 servings.

fresh corn on the cob

6 ears corn
Melted butter
Salt and pepper to taste

Husk corn; remove silks. Rinse each ear under cold running water; rub with hands or brush to remove remaining silks. Cut off stems as close as possible to cobs.

Fill kettle ¾ full with water; bring to boil. Add corn, one ear at a time; bring water back to boil. Reduce heat; cover. Simmer 8 to 10 minutes or until corn is tender; drain. Brush with butter; sprinkle with salt and pepper. Force a round, wooden toothpick or corn holders into ends of each ear of corn to serve.

Corn can be placed in baking pan after butter, salt, and pepper have been added, then broiled until lightly browned. Do not place toothpicks or holders in the ends of corn until after broiling. Yield 6 servings.

fresh southern corn pudding

2 cups fresh corn, cut from cob
2 teaspoons sugar
1½ teaspoons salt
⅛ teaspoon pepper
3 eggs, lightly beaten
2 tablespoons butter
2 cups milk

ranchero corn

Combine corn, sugar, salt, and pepper in bowl. Add eggs; mix well.

Place butter and milk in saucepan; heat until butter is melted. Blend with corn mixture. Turn into greased 1-quart casserole; place casserole in pan of hot water. Bake in preheated 350°F oven 1 hour or until knife inserted in center comes out clean. Garnish with fresh parsley. Yield 6 servings.

mexican corn

2 tablespoons vegetable oil
½ cup chopped green pepper
¼ cup chopped red pepper
½ fresh hot pepper, finely minced
1 (16½-ounce) can whole-kernel corn, drained
½ cup chopped well-drained canned tomatoes
½ teaspoon salt
¼ teaspoon pepper

Heat oil in medium saucepan. Sauté peppers over medium heat 5 minutes. Add corn, tomatoes, salt, and pepper; heat through. Yield 4 servings.

ranchero corn

6 slices bacon, diced
1 (4½-ounce) jar sliced mushrooms, drained

2 tablespoons finely chopped onion
2 (12-ounce) cans vacuum-packed golden whole-kernel corn with sweet peppers, drained
¾ cup grated cheddar cheese

Fry bacon in skillet over medium heat until cooked but not brown; drain off excess fat. Stir in mushrooms and onion; sauté until onion is tender. Blend in corn; heat through. Sprinkle with cheese; heat, without stirring, until cheese is melted. Yield 6 servings.

CUCUMBERS

baked cucumbers

3 good-size cucumbers
1½ tablespoons chopped onion
3 tablespoons butter
¾ cup fine dry bread crumbs
½ teaspoon salt
1½ teaspoons finely chopped parsley
1 tablespoon chopped celery
1 cup tomatoes cut into pieces

Wash cucumbers; cut in half lengthwise. Scoop out as much pulp as possible without breaking skin.

Brown onion in butter; add other ingredients mixed with cucumber pulp. Stirring constantly, cook 5 minutes or until dry. Place filling in cucumber shells. Bake in preheated 375°F oven until shells are soft and mixture is brown on top. Yield 6 servings.

cucumbers in dill

4 cucumbers
1 cup boiling water
¾ cup sour cream
¼ cup lemon juice
3 tablespoons minced dill
1½ teaspoons salt
⅛ teaspoon pepper
1 teaspoon sugar

fresh southern corn pudding

725

cucumbers in sour cream

Peel cucumbers; slice very thin. Pour boiling water over; let stand 5 minutes; drain. Plunge into ice water; drain.

Mix together remaining ingredients; pour over cucumbers, tossing until well mixed. Chill 30 minutes before serving. Yield 6 to 8 servings.

cucumbers in sour cream

4 cucumbers, garden-fresh
1 cup sour cream with chives
1 small bunch leaf lettuce, cleaned
1 tablespoon parsley

Wash cucumbers thoroughly; slice into small wedges.

Combine sour cream and cucumbers; mix to coat cucumbers.

Arrange lettuce leaves in salad bowls; pour ½ cup cucumber mixture on lettuce bed. Garnish with parsley. Yield 4 servings.

sweet-and-sour cucumbers

4 medium-size cucumbers
2 teaspoons salt
½ cup half-and-half cream
2 tablespoons cider vinegar
2 tablespoons granulated sugar

Peel cucumbers. Using potato peeler or food processor, slice paper-thin. Sprinkle salt over cucumbers; squeeze with hands to remove juice. After juice has formed, let cucumbers set in juice at room temperature 1 hour. Add cream, vinegar, and sugar; mix well; chill. Yield 4 servings.

EGGPLANT

breaded fried eggplant sticks

1 eggplant, peeled
1 egg, beaten
½ cup flour
¼ cup cornstarch
1 teaspoon salt
½ teaspoon pepper
Oil for frying

Cut eggplant into sticks about ¾-inch thick and 3 to 4-inches long.

Dip in beaten egg.

Mix flour, cornstarch, salt, and pepper; roll eggplant in mixture to coat.

Heat about 1-inch of oil in skillet; fry eggplant until golden, turning often. Remove; drain on absorbent paper. Serve with catsup. Yield 2 to 4 servings.

eggplant lasagna

2 quarts water (with 1 teaspoon salt)
1 teaspoon cooking oil
½ pound lasagna noodles
1 medium eggplant
1 (6-ounce) can tomato paste
1 cup red wine
½ cup hot water
1 garlic clove, crushed
1 teaspoon crumbled dried basil
1 teaspoon ground turmeric
Salt and pepper
2 cups chopped green pepper
10 black olives, pitted, chopped
½ cup grated Parmesan cheese

Heat salted water and oil to boiling. Cook noodles 12 to 15 minutes; drain. Arrange on platter.

Slice unpeeled eggplant crosswise into ¼-inch rounds; fry both sides in heated oil until tender. (They cook quickly and absorb considerable oil, which must be added constantly.) Drain on absorbent paper.

Combine tomato paste, wine, water, garlic, basil, turmeric, salt, and pepper to taste; simmer 5 minutes. Add green pepper and olives; cook 5 minutes.

Arrange layer of lasagna in buttered shallow baking dish. Cover with a layer of eggplant slices and several spoonfuls of sauce; sprinkle with cheese. Repeat until all ingredients are used. Bake in preheated 350°F oven 30 minutes. Yield 4 to 6 servings.

eggplant parmigiana

2 medium eggplants
Salt water
2 eggs
1 teaspoon salt
¼ teaspoon pepper
2 cans tomato sauce
½ pound mozzarella cheese, thinly sliced
¼ cup grated Parmesan cheese

Peel eggplants; slice about ¼-inch thick. Cover with lightly salted water; soak about ½ hour; dry.

Season eggs with salt and pepper; beat lightly. Dip eggplant slices in mixture; fry both sides quickly in hot salad oil. Remove slices; drain on paper towels. Arrange layers of eggplant, tomato sauce, mozzarella, and Parmesan in that order in 2-quart casserole. Bake in preheated 350°F oven, uncovered, about ½ hour. Yield 4 to 6 servings.

eggplant skillet deluxe

1 large eggplant (about 1-pound)
1 cup sliced green onions with tops
2 tablespoons butter or margarine
1 (6-ounce) can minced clams with liquid
3 cups cooked rice
¼ teaspoon pepper
½ teaspoon salt
½ teaspoon poultry seasoning

Peel eggplant; cut into ¾-inch cubes. Simmer in ½ cup water until tender; drain.

Sauté onions in butter until tender. Add eggplant and remaining ingredients; heat thoroughly, stirring occasionally. Top with grated Parmesan cheese, if desired. Yield 6 to 8 servings.

eggplant supreme

2 medium eggplant
¼ cup salad oil
1 small onion, sliced
¼ cup green pepper strips
1 clove garlic, minced
2 tomatoes, cut into wedges
1 teaspoon oregano
1 teaspoon basil
1 teaspoon salt
Pepper to taste
¼ cup parsley sprigs

Cut eggplant in half lengthwise; scoop out pulp, leaving ½-inch shells. Dice pulp; set aside. Cook shells in boiling, salted water until just tender; drain. Place in baking dish, cut-side-up.

Heat oil in saucepan; add onion, green pepper, garlic, diced eggplant, tomatoes, oregano, basil, salt, and pepper. Cook about 3 minutes, until heated through; stir frequently. Spoon into eggplant shells; sprinkle with parsley. Bake in preheated 350°F oven 25 minutes. Yield 4 servings.

eggplant with tomatoes

1 large eggplant
2 tablespoons butter
1 cup whole-kernel corn
4 tomatoes, quartered
¼ cup bread crumbs
½ teaspoon sugar
1 teaspoon salt
½ teaspoon pepper
1 tablespoon grated cheese

Pare eggplant; slice into ½-inch slices. Cook in boiling salted water 10 minutes (allow ½ teaspoon salt per quart of water); drain.

Butter casserole, arrange eggplant, corn, and tomatoes. Cover with crumbs, sugar, salt, and pepper. Bake 30 minutes in preheated 300°F oven. Sprinkle with cheese; place in oven until cheese melts. Yield 6 servings.

fried eggplant

1 eggplant
¼ cup (about) flour
Cooking oil
Salt and pepper to taste
Paprika
Grated Parmesan cheese

Peel eggplant; cut into ¼-inch slices. Spread out on board or platter; sprinkle with salt. Let sit 30 minutes to remove bitterness. Place in bowl; cover with cold water. Soak 10 minutes. Drain; pat dry.

Place flour in shallow bowl; stir in enough water to make consistency of light cream. Immerse each eggplant slice in batter; fry in 375°F oil until golden brown on each side. Season with salt and pepper. Sprinkle liberally with paprika and cheese. Yield 2 to 4 servings.

stuffed eggplant

3 medium eggplants
1 medium onion, finely chopped
1 clove garlic, crushed
¼ cup oil
½ pound mince
1 tablespoon chopped parsley
1 teaspoon salt
¼ teaspoon white pepper
¼ cup cooked rice
2 tablespoons tomato puree
1 egg

Cut eggplants in half; scoop out flesh, leaving ¼-inch around sides.

Sauté onion and garlic in oil. Add mince and chopped eggplant; sauté 3 to 5 minutes. Season with parsley, salt, and pepper; stir in rice and tomato puree. Cook 2 to 3 minutes. Remove from heat; beat in egg.

Arrange eggplant shells in casserole; fill with mixture. Pour remaining oil over; cover with lid or foil. Bake in preheated 350°F oven 1 hour. Equally good hot or cold.

Leftovers like baked beans, spaghetti, and meat sauce can be used in this recipe. Yield 3 to 6 servings.

fried eggplant

stuffed eggplant greek-style

2 small eggplants (about ¾-pound each)
3 tablespoons olive oil
2 tablespoons butter
2 medium onions, thinly sliced
1 pound tomatoes, peeled, seeded, chopped
2 cloves garlic
½ teaspoon salt
1 bay leaf
1 (2-inch) stick cinnamon
¼ teaspoon pepper
½ cup finely chopped parsley
8 black olives
8 anchovy fillets

Remove stems and caps from eggplants.

Heat oil in large skillet. Add eggplants; cook over medium-high heat 5 minutes. Remove from pan; cut in half lengthwise. Carefully scoop out pulp; leave thin shell. Chop pulp coarsely.

Heat butter in same skillet. Add onions; cook until golden. Add tomatoes and eggplant pulp; cook 10 minutes.

Crush garlic with salt; add to tomato mixture. Add bay leaf, cinnamon, pepper, and parsley; cook 10 minutes. Fill eggplant shells with mixture. Garnish each shell with 2 olives and 2 anchovy fillets. Bake in preheated 375°F oven 10 minutes. Yield 4 servings.

FENNEL

fennel italian

1 pound small fennel roots
1 tablespoon water

fennel italian

1 cup dry white wine
2 medium tomatoes, peeled, quartered
Salt, white pepper, and paprika to taste
Parsley

Clean fennel thoroughly; cut into quarters. Cook in 1 tablespoon water and 2 tablespoons wine 5 minutes; stir often. (Add more wine if necessary.) Add tomatoes, rest of wine, and seasonings; cover. Simmer 30 minutes or until fennel is tender; gently stir occasionally. Correct seasonings. Serve on heated platter; garnish with parsley. Yield 4 servings.

florence fennel

2 large fennel roots
½ recipe Mornay Sauce (see Index)
½ cup freshly grated Parmesan cheese

½ cup fine fresh bread crumbs
¼ cup melted butter

Trim fennel; wash thoroughly in cold water. Cook stalks in boiling, salted water to cover about 35 minutes, until just tender; drain well. Cut into 2-inch lengths.

Place ½ of Mornay Sauce over bottom of greased casserole. Place fennel over sauce; spoon remaining sauce over fennel.

Mix cheese and bread crumbs; sprinkle over sauce. Pour butter over top. Bake in preheated 350°F oven about 15 to 20 minutes, until lightly browned. Yield about 6 servings.

french-fried fennel

1 large fennel root
½ cup flour

stuffed eggplant greek-style

florence fennel

1 egg, beaten
½ cup milk
Salt and pepper to taste
Oil for deep frying

Slice white part of fennel into ¼-inch rings. Wash; pat dry. Save some green leaves for garnish.

Mix flour, egg, milk, and seasonings in bowl; batter will be smooth.

Heat oil in medium skillet.

While oil is heating, dip pieces of fennel into batter. Deep-fry just 2 minutes, until crusty and brown; drain. Put on heated platter; garnish with fennel leaves. Yield 4 servings.

GRITS (HOMINY)

grits with cheese

6 cups boiling water
2 teaspoons salt
1½ sticks margarine

1½ cups grits
1 pound sharp cheddar cheese, cubed or grated
4 eggs, well beaten

Bring water, salt, and margarine to boil; add grits gradually. Cook until thick, stirring constantly. Add cheese; stir until melted. Add eggs; stir rapidly. Pour into buttered casserole. Bake 1 hour in preheated 250 to 300°F oven. Yield 8 to 10 servings.

Note: Can be prepared ahead and baked when needed. Will hold in oven.

grits croquettes

2 cups cooked grits
2 cups finely chopped cooked chicken, meat, or fish
2 tablespoons chopped onion
1 teaspoon salt
Pepper to taste
1 teaspoon Worcestershire sauce
Fine dry bread crumbs

1 egg, beaten
Fat or oil for deep frying

Combine grits, chicken, onion, salt, pepper, and Worcestershire sauce; chill. Shape into 12 balls or other shape. Roll in bread crumbs; dip in egg. Roll again in bread crumbs.

Heat fat in frypan. Cook croquettes; turn once to brown each side. Yield 6 servings.

HOMINY

baked hominy and cheese

2 cups canned or strained stewed tomatoes
2 tablespoons chopped onion
2 cloves
½ teaspoon salt
1 tablespoon sugar
⅛ teaspoon cayenne
3 tablespoons butter or fat
2 tablespoons flour
2½ cups cooked hominy
½ cup mild grated cheese
½ cup bread crumbs

Simmer tomatoes, onion, cloves, salt, sugar, and cayenne 20 minutes; strain.

Melt 2 tablespoons butter; blend with flour. Add strained tomato juice; bring slowly to boil, stirring constantly.

Put layer of hominy in greased baking dish; add layer of cheese. Add layer of tomato sauce; repeat until all are used. Spread top with crumbs; dot with butter. Bake in 425°F oven 20 minutes or until crumbs are brown. Yield 6 servings.

hominy deluxe

½ pound pork sausage
3 cups canned or cooked hominy, drained
3 tablespoons chopped onion
1 cup canned tomato soup
½ teaspoon salt
½ cup seasoned bread or cracker crumbs

In medium-size skillet cook sausage until fat begins to come off. Add hominy and onion; cook until browned and blended. Add soup and salt; stir until hot. Top with crumbs. Yield 4 to 6 servings.

KOHLRABI

stuffed kohlrabi

8 medium kohlrabi
2 tablespoons butter or margarine
½ cup chopped onion
½ pound ground veal

stuffed kohlrabi

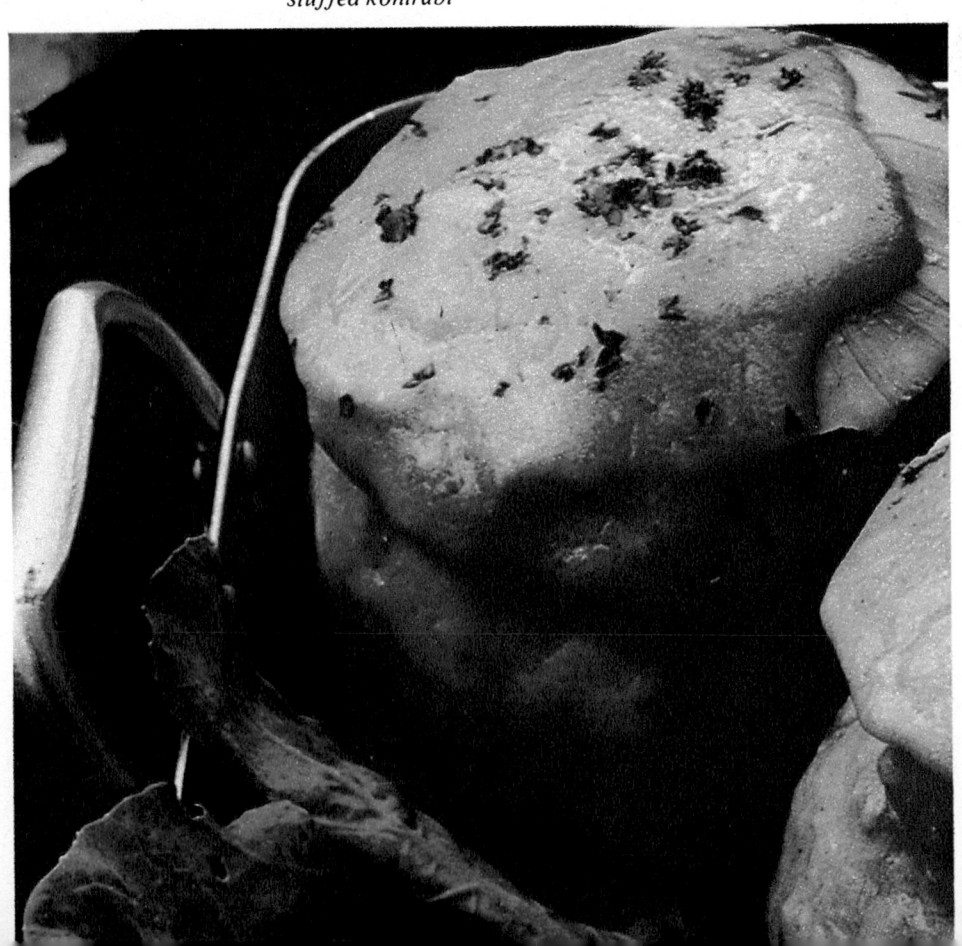

½ pound ground pork
1 egg, well beaten
2 tablespoons bread crumbs
1 tablespoon chopped parsley
½ teaspoon crumbled dried marjoram
Salt and white pepper
2 cups hot chicken broth

sauce
3 tablespoons butter
3 tablespoons flour
Salt and white pepper
1½ cups reserved broth
¼ cup heavy cream
2 tablespoons chopped fresh parsley

Wash kohlrabi. Cut off leaves and stems; reserve. Peel root; cut ½-inch slice; reserve. Scoop out pulp; leave ¼-inch shell. Chop pulp. Select tender leaves; shred. Place leaves and pulp in Dutch oven or heavy saucepan.

Melt butter in small saucepan. Add onion; sauté until tender.

Combine veal, pork, egg, crumbs, parsley, and seasonings in mixing bowl. Add onion; mix well. Pack mixture into kohlrabi shells; mound slightly. Top with slice removed in first step; place in Dutch oven. Pour broth over kohlrabi; bring to boil. Cover; reduce heat to low. Simmer 30 to 40 minutes, until shells can be pierced with fork. Transfer to baking dish.

Strain broth; reserve.

Place cooked kohlrabi leaves around stuffed kohlrabi; keep warm.

Prepare sauce. Melt butter in medium saucepan. Add flour, salt, and pepper; cook, stirring, until bubbly. Add broth; cook over low heat until thickened. Remove from heat; stir in cream. Pour over kohlrabi; sprinkle with parsley. Broil in oven until sauce is lightly browned. Serve immediately. Yield 4 servings.

MIXED VEGETABLES

fresh vegetables with pork

¼ cup butter
4 cups diagonally sliced celery
½ pound fresh mushrooms, halved
1 medium green sweet pepper, sliced
1 medium red sweet pepper, sliced
1 medium onion, sliced
2 cups cubed cooked pork
1¼ cups Beef Stock (see Index)
1 tablespoon cornstarch
3 tablespoons soy sauce

½ teaspoon salt
½ teaspoon ginger
½ teaspoon freshly ground pepper

Melt butter in wok or medium-size skillet. Add celery; sauté 5 minutes. Stir in mushrooms, peppers, and onion; sauté 5 minutes. Stir in pork and stock; bring to boil. Reduce heat; simmer 5 minutes.

Blend cornstarch with soy sauce, salt, ginger, and pepper; stir into pork mixture. Cook, stirring constantly, about 5 minutes, until heated through and thickened. Serve over rice, if desired. Yield 6 servings.

mixed chinese vegetables

5 large dried Chinese mushrooms
1 cup lukewarm water
5 ounces green cabbage
4 ounces carrots
4 ounces cucumber
5 ounces canned bamboo shoots
4 tablespoons sesame-seed oil
2 ounces frozen peas
½ cup hot chicken broth
2 tablespoons soy sauce
Salt
Pinch of sugar

mixed chinese vegetables

ratatouille I

Soak mushrooms in water 30 minutes.

Shred cabbage. Cut carrots, cucumber, and bamboo shoots into julienne strips. Cube mushrooms.

Heat oil in skillet. Add cabbage; cook 2 minutes. Add mushrooms, cucumber, carrots, bamboo shoots, and peas. Pour in broth. Season with soy sauce, salt, and sugar. Simmer over low heat 15 minutes. Serve immediately. Yield 2 servings.

oriental vegetable medley

¼ pound fresh mushrooms, sliced
Butter
1 cup diagonally sliced celery
1 cup finely slivered green onions
3 cups fresh bean sprouts
2 tablespoons soy sauce
1 beef bouillon cube

Sauté mushrooms lightly in butter. Add celery and onions; cook 3 to 4 minutes. Add bean sprouts and soy sauce. Crumble bouillon cube over all; cover. Cook 2 minutes. Be careful not to overcook; vegetables should still be crisp. Stir well. Yield 6 servings.

ratatouille I

1 medium eggplant
1 tablespoon salt
¼ cup olive or vegetable oil

2 large onions, sliced
3 cloves garlic, crushed
1 medium red pepper (optional), cored, cut into cubes
1 medium green pepper, cored, cut into cubes
4 medium zucchini, sliced ¾ inch thick
3 medium tomatoes, peeled, seeded, cut into coarse cubes
¼ teaspoon salt
Freshly ground pepper to taste
¼ teaspoon thyme
¼ teaspoon oregano
1 bay leaf
2 tablespoons chopped fresh parsley

Cut eggplant into ½-inch-thick slices, then into chunks. Sprinkle with 1 tablespoon salt; let stand 30 minutes. Dry thoroughly.

Heat oil in large frying pan; sauté onions and garlic 2 minutes. Add peppers; cook 2 minutes. Add eggplant; brown lightly on both sides (about 3 minutes). Add zucchini, tomatoes, and seasonings (except parsley). Simmer gently, uncovered, 30 to 40 minutes, until all vegetables are just tender. Baste often; do not scorch. Cover; reduce heat if necessary. Remove bay leaf. Garnish with parsley. Serve hot or cold. Yield 6 to 8 servings.

ratatouille II

Olive oil
2 onions, peeled, finely chopped

733

2 peppers, seeded, chopped
3 or 4 zucchini, thinly sliced
1 small eggplant
4 tomatoes, peeled, seeded, chopped
½ cup chopped parsley
1 clove garlic, crushed
Salt and pepper
Grated Parmesan cheese

Heat oil in heavy skillet; sauté onions until they begin to color. Add peppers; sauté a few more minutes. Add zucchini and eggplant (adding a little more oil if necessary); cook about 5 minutes. Turn vegetables into large casserole. Add tomatoes; cover. Cook in preheated 250°F oven 1¼ hours. Add parsley, garlic, and seasoning; cook 20 minutes. Sprinkle generously with cheese before serving. Yield 4 servings.

vegetable garden medley

4 potatoes, peeled
2 cups vegetable, beef, or chicken bouillon
3 medium carrots, halved lengthwise, cut into
    2-inch pieces
¼ pound snap beans, cut into ½-inch pieces
½ cup ½-inch pieces celery
2 tomatoes, halved
1 tablespoon butter or margarine

Put potatoes in saucepan with 1 cup bouillon; bring to boil. Cook, uncovered, 5 minutes; cover. Simmer 15 minutes or until tender.

In another saucepan, cook carrots and beans in remaining bouillon, uncovered, 5 minutes; cover. Cook 5 minutes. Add celery; cook 5 minutes.

Meanwhile, dot tomato halves with butter. Broil to desired doneness. Arrange on serving plate; surround with drained vegetables. Yield 4 servings.

vegetable in cream sauce

2 tablespoons butter or margarine
2 tablespoons flour
1 cup milk
Salt and pepper to taste
3 cups drained cooked or canned vegetable (such
    as carrots, peas, green beans, lima beans,
    or spinach)

Heat butter; stir in flour. Add milk slowly; stir until smooth. Cook and stir until mixture is thickened. Add salt, pepper, and vegetable; heat. Yield 4 to 6 servings.

vegetable jambalaya

2 tablespoons oil
6 to 8 ounces small mushrooms
1 cup cooked rice
1 green pepper, seeded, chopped
1 small onion, peeled, chopped
1 stalk celery, chopped
1 canned pimiento, chopped
½ cup canned or stewed tomatoes
Salt to taste
Cayenne pepper
¼ teaspoon paprika
¼ cup melted butter or margarine
Watercress or parsley (garnish)

Heat oil in pan. Add mushrooms; sauté a few

vegetable jambalaya

minutes. (If small mushrooms are used, leave whole; cut larger ones into halves or quarters.)

Combine rice, mushrooms, green pepper, onion, celery, pimiento, and tomatoes. Add salt, few grains cayenne pepper, and paprika. Add butter; mix well. Put into greased casserole; cover tightly. Cook in preheated 300°F oven about 1 hour. Garnish with small bunch of watercress or parsley. Yield 4 servings.

vegetable kabobs with seasoned butter sauce

2 medium zucchini
12 cherry tomatoes
6 pounds fresh mushrooms
½ cup melted butter
1 tablespoon parsley flakes
¾ teaspoon onion powder
½ teaspoon garlic powder
¼ teaspoon pepper

Cut off ends of zucchini; cut each zucchini into 6 slices. Arrange tomatoes, zucchini, and mush-

vegetable kabobs with seasoned butter sauce

rooms on 6 skewers.

Pour butter into small bowl. Add parsley flakes, onion powder, garlic powder, and pepper; mix well. Brush over kabobs. Place on grill over hot coals. Cook about 10 minutes, until vegetables are tender; turn and brush with butter mixture frequently. Yield 6 servings.

vegetables a la russe

1 potato, about ⅓ pound
Salt
1 small cauliflower
1 small bunch broccoli
¼ pound green beans
¼ pound carrots
¼ pound zucchini
1 cup green peas
¾ cup chopped celery
1 cup chopped scallions, green part and all
2 tablespoons chopped parsley
1 tablespoon chopped chives
1 cup Mustard Mayonnaise (see Index)

Place potato in saucepan; add cold water to cover and salt to taste. Bring to boil; simmer 25 minutes or until tender. Drain; let cool. Peel potato; cut into neat, uniform cubes, each about an inch or slightly less. Set aside.

Break off enough florets from cauliflower to make 1 cup. Use remaining cauliflower for another meal.

Break off enough florets from broccoli to make 1 cup. Use remaining broccoli for another meal.

Cut beans, carrots, and zucchini into small cubes, about ½ inch thick or slightly less. Keep vegetables in separate batches.

Cook cauliflower, broccoli, beans, carrots, and zucchini separately in boiling salted water until crisp-tender. Take care not to overcook.

Cook peas until barely tender.

As each batch is cooked, drain immediately in sieve or colander. Run under cold water to chill; drain well.

Combine potatoes, cauliflower, broccoli, beans, carrots, zucchini, and peas in mixing bowl. Add celery, scallions, parsley, and chives. Add mayonnaise; toss gently but well. Yield 8 servings.

MUSHROOMS

baked mushrooms in cheese sauce

8 large mushrooms
2 thick slices salt pork, diced
1 recipe White Sauce (see Index)
1 cup grated Romano cheese
⅓ cup finely minced green onions
1½ cups fine bread crumbs

Remove stems from mushrooms; chop coarsely.

Fry salt pork in saucepan over low heat until all fat is rendered; remove pork from pan. Add chopped mushrooms. Cook over medium heat until all fat is absorbed; set aside.

Combine White Sauce and ¾ cup cheese; stir until cheese is melted. Stir in onions and chopped mushrooms.

Arrange mushroom caps, round-side-down, in 9½-inch shallow baking dish; pour cheese sauce over. Sprinkle crumbs over sauce; sprinkle remaining cheese evenly over crumbs. Bake in preheated 350°F oven about 20 minutes, until topping is browned.

Parmesan or any hard cheese can be substituted for Romano. Yield 4 servings.

baked stuffed mushrooms

3 tablespoons butter
1 small onion, chopped
½ clove garlic, crushed
½ pound ground lamb
¾ cup fresh bread crumbs
1 tablespoon parsley
½ tablespoon chopped capers
Salt and pepper
Pinch of mace or nutmeg
1 egg, beaten
16 large flat mushrooms
8 strips bacon
2 to 3 tablespoons mixed dark bread crumbs and grated cheese

Heat 2 tablespoons butter; cook onion and garlic 4 to 5 minutes. Add ground meat; cook 7 to 8 minutes, stirring constantly. Mix in crumbs, parsley, and capers; season well with salt, pepper, and mace. Cool slightly; add enough egg to moisten mixture without making it runny.

Remove stems from mushrooms level with base. Chop stems; add to stuffing mixture. Divide stuffing into 8 parts; mold over mushroom caps. Lay other 8 mushroom caps on top; press firmly together. Wrap each mushroom sandwich in strip of bacon; place in buttered fireproof dish. Spoon 1 tablespoon melted butter over mushrooms; cover with foil. Bake in preheated 350°F oven 20 to 30 minutes; after 15 minutes remove foil. Sprinkle crumb mixture over; cook 10 to 15 minutes. If necessary, brown under broiler. Yield 4 servings.

fried mushrooms

3 dozen mushrooms, about 1-inch in diameter
2 eggs
1 tablespoon water
½ teaspoon salt
¼ teaspoon pepper
½ cup flour
1 cup Italian-style bread crumbs
Vegetable oil for frying

Wash, trim stems, and drain mushrooms.

Beat eggs, water, salt, and pepper together.

Impale each mushroom on fork; dip in flour, then in egg mixture. Coat with crumbs. Place on towel-lined baking sheet; let dry.

Heat 3-inches oil to 360°F in deep-fat fryer or deep saucepan. Fry a few at a time 4 minutes or until golden brown; drain. Serve hot. Yield 6 servings.

marinated mushroom caps

2 cups canned or small fresh mushroom caps

marinade
½ cup finely chopped onions
½ cup salad vinegar
½ teaspoon black pepper, peppermill-ground
½ teaspoon garlic powder
½ cup salad oil

Drain or wash mushrooms; pour into quart jar.

Combine marinade ingredients; add to jar. Marinate mushrooms 24 hours; shake 3 or 4 times during marinating period. Drain mushrooms; arrange on serving platter. Yield 6 servings.

mushrooms and eggs in cheese sauce

1½ cups sliced fresh mushrooms
1 tablespoon lemon juice
¼ cup butter
½ cup chopped celery
½ cup chopped green sweet pepper
¼ cup chopped onion
2 tablespoons all-purpose flour
½ teaspoon salt
Dash of freshly ground pepper
1 cup milk
1 cup shredded cheddar cheese
¼ teaspoon Worcestershire sauce
3 hard-boiled eggs
1 recipe Boiled Rice (see Index)
1 can chow mein noodles

baked mushrooms in cheese sauce

Toss mushrooms with lemon juice.

Melt butter in chafing-dish pan or blazer pan over low heat. Add mushrooms, celery, green pepper, and onion; sauté until just tender, stirring constantly. Add flour, salt, and pepper; mix well. Stir in milk gradually; cook over medium heat, stirring constantly, until thickened. Cook 2 minutes; remove from heat. Add cheese and Worcestershire sauce; stir until cheese is melted.

Reserve 1 egg yolk; chop remaining yolks and whites. Add chopped eggs to sauce; heat through. Do not boil.

Sieve reserved egg yolk; sprinkle over center of sauce mixture. Garnish with parsley, if desired. Place chafing-dish pan over low heat or over the bain-marie to keep warm. Serve over rice; sprinkle with chow mein noodles. Yield about 6 servings.

mushrooms and sour cream hungarian-style

4 tablespoons butter or margarine
1 small onion, peeled, minced
1 pound fresh mushrooms, washed, trimmed, sliced ¼-inch thick
½ teaspoon garlic salt

mushrooms and eggs in cheese sauce

mushroom and tomato bake

½ cup butter
4 cups fine soft bread crumbs
2 cups finely chopped hazelnuts or pecans
4 large tomatoes
½ pound fresh mushrooms, chopped
Salt and freshly ground pepper to taste
1 teaspoon dried crushed marjoram

mushroom and tomato bake

⅛ teaspoon pepper
½ teaspoon paprika
½ cup thick dairy sour cream

Melt butter in large heavy skillet. Add onion; cook over moderate heat 3 minutes. Add mushrooms; cook quickly over moderate heat, stirring occasionally, until tender. Stir in garlic salt, pepper, and paprika; mix well. Remove from heat; slowly stir in sour cream. Return to heat; very gently heat through. Yield 4 servings.

Melt 6 tablespoons butter in frypan. Add crumbs and nuts; cook over medium heat, stirring constantly, until crisp and golden. Set aside.

Skin tomatoes; chop coarsely.

Melt 2 tablespoons butter in frypan. Add tomatoes and mushrooms; cook, stirring, until tomatoes are soft. Place half the mixture evenly in 4 buttered individual baking dishes; season with salt, pepper and half the marjoram. Place half the crumb mixture evenly over each mushroom mixture; repeat layers. Bake in preheated 375°F oven 30 minutes or until well browned. Garnish with additional skinned tomatoes. Yield 4 servings.

stuffed mushrooms

2 (10-ounce) packages frozen chopped spinach or
   2 cups cooked fresh spinach
¼ cup freshly grated Parmesan cheese
2 tablespoons melted butter
⅛ teaspoon nutmeg
Salt and pepper to taste
12 large mushroom caps
Olive oil
12 blanched whole almonds

Cook spinach according to package directions; drain thoroughly. Puree in blender or food processor. Combine spinach, cheese, butter, nutmeg, salt, and pepper in top of double boiler; mix well. Cover; place over hot, but not boiling, water to keep warm.

Brush entire surface of mushroom caps with oil; place on baking sheet. Bake in preheated 375°F oven 10 minutes.

Mound spinach mixture inside each mushroom; garnish with almonds. Serve immediately. Yield 6 servings.

OKRA

fried okra

1 pound fresh young okra
Salt and pepper to taste
½ to 1 cup cornmeal
Fat for deep frying

Wash okra; cut into 1-inch pieces. Liberally sprinkle pieces with salt and pepper.

Put cornmeal into brown paper bag; shake okra in bag to coat each piece with meal. Fry in deep fat (375°F) until golden brown and crisp; drain on paper towel. Keep warm. Yield 4 to 6 servings.

okra louisiana

2 tablespoons bacon fat or oil
1 large onion, sliced into rings
½ green pepper, chopped
2 cups (1-pound) can tomatoes
1 teaspoon salt
Dash of freshly ground pepper
1 teaspoon lemon juice or grated lemon rind
1 pound fresh okra, cut into 2-inch pieces
¼ cup flour
2 tablespoons oil
½ cup grated cheese

Heat fat in medium skillet; tan onion and green pepper. Add tomatoes, salt, pepper, and lemon juice; simmer 15 minutes.

Dust okra with flour. Heat oil in another medium skillet. Add okra; cook until heated but not brown. Reduce heat; pour sauce over okra. Add grated cheese; cover. Simmer 15 minutes. Yield 4 to 6 servings.

okra and rice

2 cups cut okra
½ cup dry rice
1 cup water
½ teaspoon salt
2 tablespoons butter or oil
1 cup tomato sauce

Place okra, rice, water, and salt into pot; cook 30 to 40 minutes. Turn into greased baking dish; add tomato sauce. Bake 10 minutes in preheated 375°F oven. Yield 4 servings.

okra southern-style

3 slices bacon
1 cup sliced okra
1 large onion, finely chopped
1 cup chopped celery
6 tomatoes, chopped
1 green pepper, diced
1 hot red pepper, diced
Salt and pepper to taste
1 pint creamed corn

Fry bacon; when crisp, drain on paper towel.

Sauté okra in hot bacon fat to seal edges. Add onion and celery; sauté until onion is transparent, not brown. Add tomatoes, peppers, salt, and pepper; cook 3 to 5 minutes. Add corn; simmer 20 minutes. Serve hot or cold. Just before serving, crumble bacon on top. Yield 6 to 8 servings.

pickled okra

8 cups vinegar
8 cups water
1 cup salt
Several pounds fresh okra, washed, stems cut off
1 teaspoon dillseed
2 cloves garlic, chopped
2 small hot peppers, chopped

Boil vinegar, water, and salt together about 10 minutes.

Meanwhile, place okra in pint jars.

Divide dill, garlic, and peppers so that some of each are on top of each jar of okra. Pour hot liquid into jars. Let cool; seal. Put jars aside at least 3 weeks for pickling process to take place. Chill before serving. Yield about 10 pints.

stewed okra and tomatoes

1 small onion, chopped
2 tablespoons butter, margarine, or oil
1 (10-ounce) package frozen okra
1 (16-ounce) can tomatoes
½ teaspoon salt
¼ teaspoon pepper

Cook onion in butter in saucepan over moderate heat until lightly browned. Add remaining ingredients; cook until okra is tender and mixture thickens, 10 to 15 minutes. Stir occasionally to prevent sticking. Yield 6 servings.

ONIONS

beer-fried onion rings

1½ cups flour
1½ cups beer
4 very large onions
Oil for deep frying

Combine flour and beer in large bowl; blend thoroughly with wooden spoon. Cover bowl; keep at room temperature at least 3 hours.

Peel onions; slice into ¼-inch rounds. Divide into individual rings.

In large skillet heat enough oil to drop in onion rings. Dip a few onion rings at a time into prepared batter, then into hot (375°F) oil; fry until golden brown. Place on cookie sheet lined with paper towels; keep warm in preheated 200°F oven. Can be frozen and reheated in 400°F oven if desired. Yield 4 to 6 servings.

crispy fried onion rings

2 large onions
1 cup self-rising flour

Peel onions; cut into medium-thick slices. Separate into rings.

Combine flour and enough water to make consistency of heavy cream. Dip each ring in batter; drain slightly. Fry in deep hot oil (375°F) until golden brown on both sides. Yield 6 servings.

dill onion rings

4 large onions
½ cup sugar
2 teaspoons salt
½ teaspoon dillweed
½ cup vinegar
¼ cup water

Peel and slice onions; break apart. Pack loosely in jar.

Combine other ingredients in saucepan; heat until sugar dissolves. Pour over onions. Cover; chill. Yield 1 quart.

onion charlotte

4 Bermuda onions, peeled, thickly sliced
1 cup milk
2 tablespoons cornstarch
3 tablespoons butter or margarine
Salt and pepper
⅛ teaspoon grated nutmeg
⅛ teaspoon ground cinnamon
4 or 5 slices stale bread

beer-fried onion rings

740

onion charlotte

¼ cup oil or cooking fat
3 tablespoons grated cheese
2 tablespoons fine bread crumbs

Put onions into pan; just cover with cold water. Cover; boil 2 to 3 minutes. Drain; return to pan. Add milk and 4 tablespoons water; cover. Simmer until onions are tender, 10 to 15 minutes.

Mix cornstarch to smooth paste with a little extra milk; add to onions. Stir until boiling. Add 2 tablespoons butter, salt, pepper, nutmeg, and cinnamon.

Remove crusts from bread; fry in oil until brown on both sides. Arrange in bottom and around sides of baking dish; pour in onion mixture. Sprinkle with cheese and crumbs mixed together.

Melt remaining butter; dribble over the top. Bake in preheated 400°F oven until well browned. Yield 4 servings.

onions and green peppers

3 tablespoons butter or margarine
6 medium-size onions, peeled, sliced thin
3 whole green peppers, diced
2 tablespoons beef broth
Salt and pepper to taste

Melt butter in medium skillet; sauté onions about 10 minutes. Add peppers; cook 5 minutes. Add beef broth and seasonings; cover. Simmer 8 minutes. Serve at once.

A variation of this is to add 2 whole diced tomatoes just before you cover vegetables. Yield 4 servings.

onions monte carlo

2 (10½-ounce) cans beef broth
½ tablespoon dark brown sugar
½ cup golden raisins
2 pounds small peeled onions
2 tablespoons potato flour

Pour all but ½ cup broth into small, deep, ovenproof dish; stir in brown sugar until mixed. Add raisins and onions; cover. Bake in preheated 325°F oven about 2 hours, until onions are tender; remove from oven.

Mix potato flour with ½ cup broth; stir into broth in ovenproof dish. Cook over low heat, stirring constantly, until thickened. Garnish with mixed chopped chives and chopped parsley, if desired.

Two tablespoons cornstarch mixed with a small amount of cold water can be substituted for potato flour, if desired. Yield 6 to 8 servings.

onions in mushroom sauce

1½ pounds small yellow onions
1 cup water
1 teaspoon salt
1 (10½-ounce) can condensed cream of
  mushroom soup
Parsley

Peel and quarter onions; leave very small onions whole. Simmer in salted water 15 to 20 minutes, until just tender; drain. Add undiluted soup; simmer 10 to 15 minutes. Garnish with parsley. Yield 6 servings.

stuffed onions

6 large onions
2 tablespoons butter or margarine
1 pound ground beef or veal
1 teaspoon salt
¼ teaspoon pepper
1 cup beef stock

onions monte carlo

Peel onions; cut ½-inch slice from top of each. Put aside to use for topping. Hollow out centers of onions to form holes for stuffing; finely chop centers of onions.

Melt butter; brown chopped onions. Add meat, salt, and pepper; mix well. When meat is browned, stuff centers of onions with mixture. Put top slices of onions on; secure in place with toothpicks. Put in baking dish; pour stock over. Bake in preheated 375°F oven 1 hour or until onions are soft. Yield 6 servings.

PARSNIPS

parsnip puffs

5 parsnips
3 tablespoons milk
2 tablespoons melted butter or margarine
1 teaspoon salt
Few grains pepper
2 eggs
2 tablespoons water
½ cup dried bread crumbs

Cook parsnips in boiling salted water until tender. Drain; mash. Add milk, butter, salt, and pepper. Add 1 beaten egg; set aside to cool. Shape into small balls. Roll in crumbs, then in beaten egg diluted with water, and again in crumbs. Fry in deep hot fat (375°F) until brown; drain on unglazed paper. Yield 6 servings.

parsnip timbales

1 pound parsnips
2 large eggs
¼ cup milk
¼ cup fine fresh bread crumbs
⅛ teaspoon salt
1 tablespoon grated orange rind

Pare parsnips; leave whole. Steam until tender; drain. Mash in food processor or put through food mill (there should be about 1¾ cups).

Beat eggs and milk until blended; stir in crumbs, salt, and orange rind; mix well with parsnips. Turn into 4 (6-ounce) buttered custard cups; place in pan of hot water that comes halfway up cups. Bake in preheated 325°F oven until knife inserted in center comes out clean, about 30 minutes. With small spatula, loosen edges; turn out. Garnish, if desired, with orange slices and parsley sprigs. Yield 4 servings.

seasoned parsnips

1½ pounds parsnips
Small piece salt pork
¼ cup butter, melted

Wash, peel, and core parsnips; cut into strips. Add with salt pork to boiling salted water. Boil 25 minutes or until fork-tender; drain. Serve coated with melted butter. Yield 4 servings.

PEAS

black-eyed peas supreme

2 (1-pound) cans black-eyed peas, drained
1 onion, sliced into thin rings
½ cup olive oil
¼ cup wine vinegar
1 medium clove garlic, mashed
1 tablespoon Worcestershire sauce
1 teaspoon salt
Pepper to taste

Place peas and onion in ovenproof bowl.

Combine oil, vinegar, and seasonings in small pan; bring to boil. Immediately pour over peas and onions; stir gently. Refrigerate several hours or overnight. When thoroughly chilled, flavors will all blend together. Yield 8 servings.

creamed peas and corn

1 (10-ounce) package frozen peas
1 (10-ounce) package frozen corn

white sauce
2 tablespoons butter
2 tablespoons all-purpose white flour
1 cup milk
½ teaspoon salt
¼ teaspoon white pepper

Cook peas and corn as directed on packages.

While vegetables are cooking, make White Sauce. Melt butter in saucepan. Add flour; cook 2 minutes, stirring constantly. Add milk, salt, and pepper; stir. Cook until thick; remove from heat.

Drain cooked vegetables. Add White Sauce; mix well. Serve immediately. Yield 6 servings.

creamed peas and potatoes

3 medium potatoes, peeled, diced
Cold water
1 teaspoon salt
1 (10-ounce) package frozen green peas
2 cups milk
2 tablespoons butter or margarine
1 tablespoon flour
1 tablespoon water

creamed peas and corn

Salt and pepper to taste

Place potatoes in medium saucepan; add cold water barely to cover potatoes. Add 1 teaspoon salt; bring to boil over moderate heat. Cook 10 to 15 minutes or until tender; drain.

Meanwhile, cook peas according to package directions; drain. Keep warm until needed.

Add milk and butter to potatoes; heat until bubbling.

Combine flour and 1 tablespoon water; mix well. Add to potatoes; cook, stirring, until thickened. Add peas; mix well. Season with salt and pepper. Yield 4 servings.

frozen peas and beans with a fresh taste

1 package frozen green peas
1 package frozen cut green beans
4 tablespoons butter or margarine
½ cup blanched, sliced almonds (optional)

Remove peas and beans from freezer at least 1 hour before cooking.

Melt butter in medium-size skillet; sauté peas and beans 3 to 5 minutes, until hot through. Stir in sliced almonds; mix together gently. Yield 4 to 6 servings.

green peas bonne femme

green peas bonne femme

¼ pound Canadian bacon, cut into 1-inch pieces
1 tablespoon butter or margarine
3 cups fresh green peas
6 small white onions, peeled
Inner leaves of lettuce head
½ cup water
½ teaspoon salt
¼ teaspoon pepper
½ teaspoon sugar
1 tablespoon finely chopped parsley

Fry bacon in butter until lightly browned. Add peas, onions, lettuce, water, salt, pepper, and sugar; cover. Cook 10 to 15 minutes, until peas are tender; drain. Sprinkle with parsley before serving. Yield 6 servings.

hopping john

1 (8-ounce) package dried black-eyed peas
1 ham hock, halved
1 small onion, chopped
1 teaspoon salt

1 teaspoon cayenne pepper
1 cup long-grain rice

Soak peas 1 hour in cold water to cover; drain.

Place ham hock in large saucepan; cover with water. Cook 30 minutes. Add peas, onion, salt, cayenne, and enough water to cover. Cook, covered, 45 minutes; add water as needed. Stir in rice; cover. Cook 30 minutes or until rice and peas are tender. Remove ham hock; discard bone and fat. Stir ham back into Hopping John. Add 1 can tomatoes, if desired. Yield about 6 servings.

irish minted peas

1 (10-ounce) package frozen green peas
1 teaspoon dried mint
1 teaspoon sugar
Boiling salted water
1 tablespoon butter or margarine
Salt and pepper to taste

Cook peas, mint, and sugar in boiling salted water to cover 5 to 7 minutes, until peas are tender; drain. Stir in butter, salt, and pepper. Serve immediately. Yield 4 servings.

seasoned peas

2 pounds fresh peas, shelled
2 cups water
1 teaspoon salt

dilled butter
¼ cup butter
½ teaspoon white pepper
2 tablespoons chopped fresh dill

Wash peas thoroughly in cold water; drain.

Bring water to rapid boil in large saucepan. Add peas and salt; cover. Cook 15 minutes or until peas are tender; drain.

Melt butter in small saucepan; stir in pepper and dill.

Pour peas in serving dish; cover with Dilled Butter. Yield 6 servings.

hopping john

split-pea and almond whip

1 pound (2⅓ cups) green or yellow dry split peas
4⅔ cups water
4 tablespoons butter
1 teaspoon salt
⅓ cup minced onion
⅓ cup thinly sliced raw carrot
1 bay leaf, 2-inch length
¼ cup brown sugar
2 tablespoons lemon juice
½ cup light cream or undiluted evaporated milk
1 teaspoon aromatic bitters
½ cup coarsely chopped, butter-browned
    blanched almonds
2 slices broiled bacon, snipped into pieces

Wash peas in colander. Combine with water, 1 tablespoon butter, salt, onion, carrot, and bay leaf in heavy saucepan or Dutch oven with tight-fitting lid; bring quickly to boil. Reduce heat to simmer; cover. Cook 40 to 45 minutes, until peas are tender, mushy, and dry; do not stir, but keep heat low or peas will stick and scorch. If moisture is left, remove lid; dry over very low heat. Remove bay leaf. Add remaining butter, brown sugar, and lemon juice; whip with electric beater or potato masher until smooth. Add cream and bitters; whip. Fold in almonds; put into heated serving dish. Sprinkle bacon over top. Yield 10 servings.

sweet pea special

5 tablespoons butter
3 tablespoons currant jelly
1 tablespoon sugar
2 cans small peas
Salt and freshly ground pepper to taste

Melt butter, currant jelly, and sugar in medium-size skillet.

Heat peas in another saucepan; drain all but 1 cup liquid. Put peas and 1 cup liquid into jelly mixture; season with salt and pepper. Simmer very gently until ready to serve. Yield 6 to 8 servings.

PEPPERS

cold stuffed-pepper dish

2 (10-ounce) packages frozen mixed vegetables
1 recipe Vinaigrette (see Index)
2 cups ground cooked ham
10 hard-boiled eggs, ground
½ cup pickle relish
Mayonnaise
Salt and pepper to taste
6 green sweet peppers

Cook vegetables according to package directions; drain well. Mix with vinaigrette in bowl; cover. Let stand in refrigerator at least 8 hours to marinate; stir occasionally.

Combine ham, eggs, and relish in large bowl; add enough mayonnaise to moisten to desired consistency. Season with salt and pepper; chill until ready to serve.

Cut tops from peppers; remove seeds and white membranes. Arrange on serving dish; fill with ham salad.

Drain vegetables; arrange around peppers. Yield about 6 servings.

cold stuffed-pepper dish

green peppers and onions spanish-style

¼ cup olive oil
6 medium onions, peeled, thinly sliced
3 green peppers, seeded, sliced into thin rings
½ teaspoon salt
¼ teaspoon pepper

Heat oil in skillet; sauté onions 10 minutes. Add peppers; sauté 10 minutes or until tender. Sprinkle with salt and pepper. Yield 4 servings.

hungarian pepper dish

2 tablespoons lard
1 medium onion, peeled, sliced, separated into rings
1 pound green peppers, cleaned, sliced
¾ pound tomatoes, peeled, quartered
½ teaspoon sugar
2 teaspoons Hungarian sweet paprika
Dash of cayenne pepper
Salt and pepper

Melt lard in heavy skillet. Add onion; cook over moderate heat until wilted. Add green peppers; cook until crisp-tender. Add remaining ingredients; cook, covered, over low heat 10 minutes, stirring occasionally. Taste for seasoning. Serve in vegetable dishes. Yield 4 to 6 servings.

quick-stuffed green peppers

3 large green peppers
Boiling water to cover
¼ cup chopped onion
2 tablespoons butter or margarine
1 tablespoon prepared horseradish
2 (16-ounce) cans corned-beef hash
1 cup water

Cut peppers in half; remove seeds. Cook 10 minutes in boiling water; drain.

Cook onion in butter just until tender; stir in horseradish. Mix with hash. Fill pepper halves with mixture.

Place peppers in baking dish. Pour in water; bake in preheated 375°F oven 30 minutes. Yield 6 servings.

pepper pot

stuffed pepper slices

1 tablespoon chopped pimiento
1 tablespoon chopped parsley
1 tablespoon chopped watercress
1 tablespoon chopped chives
¼ teaspoon salt
⅛ teaspoon white pepper
1 teaspoon lemon juice
1 envelope (1 tablespoon) unflavored gelatin
⅓ cup cold water
Lettuce leaves

Cut off tops of peppers; remove seeds; wash.

Cream cottage cheese in blender (thin with milk if necessary); remove. Add pimiento, parsley, watercress, chives, salt, pepper, and lemon juice.

Soak gelatin in cold water; dissolve completely over simmering water. Add to cheese mixture. Fill peppers with mixture; chill in refrigerator at least 2 hours. Cut each pepper into 4 thick slices. Serve on lettuce leaves. Yield 4 to 6 servings.

stuffed peppers

4 medium bell peppers
1 pound ground beef
½ cup chopped onion
½ teaspoon garlic powder
1 teaspoon crumbled mixed Italian herbs
Salt and pepper
1 (16-ounce) can stewed tomatoes
1 (8-ounce) can tomato sauce
¼ cup water
1 cup instant (or quick-cooking) rice
2 ounces mozzarella cheese, thinly sliced

Cut tops off peppers; remove seeds and membranes. Parboil 5 minutes; drain.

Sauté beef and onion in large skillet until lightly browned; add a little oil if meat is very lean. Add garlic powder, herbs, salt, pepper, tomatoes, ½ can tomato sauce, water, and rice; stir well. Bring to boil; reduce heat to low. Cook, covered, 15 minutes.

Place peppers in 2-quart casserole; stuff with meat mixture. Spoon remaining meat mixture around peppers; top with remaining tomato sauce. Cover; cook 30 minutes in preheated 350°F oven. Uncover; top with cheese. Cook 10 minutes. Yield 4 servings.

PIMIENTO

tunisian pimiento dish

2 tablespoons butter
2 cups drained chopped canned tomatoes
1 cup sliced canned pimiento
Salt
White pepper

pepper pot

3 red sweet peppers
3 green sweet peppers
6 yellow onions
12 tomatoes
¼ cup butter
Salt and freshly ground pepper to taste

Cut tops off peppers; remove seeds and center membranes. Peel onions. Cut off stem ends of tomatoes. Slice peppers into rings; cut onions and tomatoes into wedges.

Melt butter in heavy skillet; add peppers and onions. Sauté over low heat 10 minutes; stir frequently. Add tomatoes; season with salt and pepper. Cook 10 minutes; stir frequently. Yield about 6 servings.

stuffed pepper slices

1 red pepper
1 green pepper
8 ounces low-fat or regular cottage cheese
2 tablespoons skim or whole milk

tunisian pimiento dish

baked mashed potatoes

8 medium potatoes
2 tablespoons butter
½ cup tomato puree
½ cup sour cream
Salt and pepper to taste
1 cup grated sharp cheddar cheese

Bake well-greased potatoes in 400°F oven 45 minutes or until soft. Split lengthwise; scoop out centers into mixing bowl. Set shells aside. Add butter, tomato puree, and sour cream to potatoes; mash until well mixed. Season with salt and pepper; stir in cheese. Mound mixture into shells; place on baking sheet. Broil 10-inches from source of heat until heated through. Yield 8 servings.

cheese and potatoes rissolé

2 pounds potatoes
Salt
¼ cup butter
6 egg yolks
½ teaspoon white pepper
1 pound Swiss cheese, grated
Sifted all-purpose flour
2 eggs
Soft bread crumbs

Pare potatoes; cut into eighths. Place in saucepan; cover with water. Add 1 tablespoon salt; cover. Bring to boil; reduce heat. Simmer 15 minutes or until tender; drain. Press through food mill or mash well; place in dry saucepan. Add butter; cook over low heat, stirring constantly, until butter is melted and mixture dry. Place in bowl;

⅛ teaspoon basil leaves
3 eggs
3 tablespoons milk

Melt 1 tablespoon butter in small saucepan. Add tomatoes, pimiento, ¼ teaspoon salt, ⅛ teaspoon pepper, and basil; simmer 10 minutes.

Combine eggs and milk in small bowl; season with salt and pepper to taste. Beat well with fork.

Melt remaining butter in small skillet. Add egg mixture; cook, stirring constantly, until eggs are soft and creamy.

Turn pimiento mixture onto serving dish; place eggs on top. Serve with croutons or toast points. Yield 2 to 3 servings.

POTATOES

baked potatoes

Baking potatoes
Butter

Wash and scrub even-sized, shapely baking potatoes; dry. Grease lightly with butter. Bake in 400°F oven 40 minutes to 1 hour, depending on size. When half done, pull out rack; quickly puncture skin once with fork, permitting steam to escape. Return to oven; finish baking. When done, serve at once with butter, sour cream, chopped chives or parsley, chopped bacon or ham, or grated cheese. Yield as desired.

baked mashed potatoes

cheese and potatoes rissolé

refrigerate until cool. Beat in egg yolks, pepper, and salt to taste. Add cheese; stir until well mixed. Chill well. Shape with hands into 4-inch sausage-shaped rolls; coat each roll well with flour.

Beat eggs with ¼ cup water until mixed. Dip potato rolls into eggs; coat well with crumbs. Place on cookie sheet; chill thoroughly. Fry in deep fat (375°F) until brown; do not overcook. Drain on paper towels; place on platter. Garnish with chopped parsley.

Can be kept warm in 200°F oven until served, if desired. Can be prepared and refrigerated 24 hours before frying. Yield about 8 servings.

deviled stuffed potatoes

4 Idaho potatoes
1 (4½-ounce) can deviled ham spread
¼ cup Parmesan cheese
2 tablespoons chopped parsley
2 tablespoons milk

1 tablespoon grated onion
¾ teaspoon dry mustard
¼ teaspoon salt

Scrub potatoes; dry. Pierce with fork, Bake in 425°F oven 55 to 65 minutes, until soft. Cut slice from top of each; carefully scoop out pulp without breaking skin.

In large bowl combine potatoes, ham spread, cheese, parsley, milk, onion, mustard, and salt; beat until light and fluffy. Pile mixture into shells. Bake in 350°F oven 20 to 25 minutes, until heated through and slightly browned on top. Yield 4 servings.

french potato fritters

1 pound (3 medium) baking potatoes, peeled
2 eggs
1 egg yolk
¼ cup whipping cream
2 tablespoons melted butter

french potato fritters

½ **teaspoon salt**
¼ **teaspoon white pepper**
½ **teaspoon onion salt**
1 **cup flour**
½ **cup milk**

Cut potatoes into small cubes. Cook in boiling, salted water until tender; drain. Press through ricer into mixing bowl; cool.

Combine eggs, egg yolk, and cream; beat well. Pour onto potatoes. Add butter, salt, pepper, and onion salt; mix thoroughly.

Sift flour over top; stir in with wooden spoon until blended. Add enough milk to make thick batter-like consistency. Drop from spoon onto well-greased griddle; smooth top. Cook over medium-high heat until brown; turn. Brown other side. Drizzle with additional melted butter, or

serve with freshly grated Parmesan cheese. Yield about 8 servings.

italian potato gnocchi

7 **medium potatoes, peeled**
¼ **cup butter, softened**
2 **egg yolks, lightly beaten**
1 **cup all-purpose flour**
Salt and white pepper to taste
¼ **teaspoon nutmeg**
Melted butter
1 **cup grated Gruyére cheese**

Cube potatoes; cook in boiling, salted water until tender. Press through ricer into large mixing bowl. Add ¼ cup butter; mix until butter is melted. Let cool. Stir in egg yolks, flour, and seasonings with wooden spoon; work until smooth. Shape into 1½-inch balls; flatten balls with tines of fork. Dip fork in water occasionally.

Fill kettle ⅔ full with water; bring to slow boil. Lower cakes into simmering water with slotted spoon; cook until cakes rise to top. Arrange in greased baking dish; drizzle with melted butter. Sprinkle with cheese. Bake in preheated 400°F oven 20 to 25 minutes, until golden. Oven temperature can be increased to brown tops. Yield 10 to 12 servings.

mashed potatoes

6 **medium potatoes**
3 **tablespoons butter**
1 **teaspoon salt**
⅓ **cup hot milk or cream**

Wash and pare potatoes; cook, covered, 20 to 40 minutes in boiling salted water. When tender,

italian potato gnocchi

drain well; mash with fork or potato masher. Add rest of ingredients; beat with fork or heavy whisk until creamy. Yield 6 servings.

new potatoes with herbed cottage-cheese sauce

2 to 3 pounds small new potatoes
Salt

herbed cottage-cheese sauce
½ cup plain yogurt
1 (12-ounce) carton cottage cheese, creamed in blender
1 onion, finely chopped
4 hard-cooked eggs
1 tablespoon lemon juice
Salt and pepper to taste
3 tablespoons chopped chives or thinly sliced scallions

Scrub potatoes with soft brush; do not peel. Boil in salted water 20 to 30 minutes, until tender.

Stir yogurt into cottage cheese; add onion.

Strain egg yolks through sieve; chop egg whites. Add to cottage-cheese mixture. Season with lemon juice, salt, and pepper. Stir in chives. Serve as sauce with potatoes. Yield 6 to 8 servings.

parsley buttered potatoes

1 to 1½ pounds new potatoes
1 cup water
1 teaspoon salt
⅓ cup butter, melted
1 tablespoon dried parsley flakes

Scrape skins from potatoes with paring knife.

Bring water and salt to rolling boil. Add potatoes; cover. Simmer 20 minutes or until fork-tender; drain. Turn potatoes into serving bowl; coat with melted butter. Sprinkle with parsley. Yield 4 servings.

pommes anna

2 pounds potatoes
½ cup melted butter
¼ cup grated onion
Salt and white pepper to taste

Peel potatoes; cut into paper-thin slices.

Brush bottom and sides of 6½ × 3-inch soufflé dish generously with butter. Arrange potatoes, overlapping slices, around sides of soufflé dish to form firm wall; cover bottom of dish with overlapping layer of potatoes. Brush lightly with butter; sprinkle lightly with onion, salt, and pepper. Repeat layers until all ingredients are used; cover lightly with foil. Bake in preheated 400°F oven 30 minutes; remove foil. Bake 30 minutes or until top is well browned; unmold on heated serving platter. Yield 6 to 8 servings.

new potatoes with herbed cottage-cheese sauce

751

pommes anna

potato pancakes with chives

potatoes florentine (quick method)

1 (10-ounce) package frozen chopped spinach
2⅔ cups instant mashed potato flakes
2⅔ cups hot water
¼ cup butter or margarine
2 eggs
¼ cup grated Parmesan cheese
1 teaspoon salt
Pepper to taste

Thaw spinach enough to separate leaves; drain.

Mix potato flakes and water in large bowl; let stand until potatoes soak up water. Add remaining ingredients; mix well. Fold in spinach; pour into greased baking pan or dish. Bake at 350°F 40 minutes. Yield 8 servings.

potatoes in fresh herb sauce

2 tablespoons butter or margarine
½ leek, sliced
1 medium onion, diced
2 ounces boiled ham, finely diced
1½ cups beef bouillon
2 tablespoons all-purpose flour mixed to smooth
    paste with 2 tablespoons cold water
Salt and pepper to taste

potatoes in fresh herb sauce

Sprinkle with salt, pepper, cheese, and parsley; pull edges of foil upward. Pour cream over potatoes; fold foil very tight. Bake in 450°F oven 1 hour. Yield 4 servings.

potato pancakes with chives

2 tablespoons chopped chives
4 medium baked potatoes, grated
2 teaspoons salt
Several twists freshly ground black pepper
1 tablespoon flour
2 tablespoons butter or margarine
2 tablespoons vegetable oil

Chop chives; set aside.

Peel and grate potatoes coarsely into large mixing bowl. Potatoes will accumulate potato water; do not drain. Mix in chives, salt, and pepper; work as quickly as possible, so potatoes do not turn brown. Add flour; mix well.

Melt butter in large skillet; drop potato mixture by spoonfuls into hot fat. The 3-inch pancakes will take about 3 minutes a side to become crisp and golden. Serve piping hot. Yield 4 servings.

potato patties

2 cups seasoned mashed potatoes
1 egg or 2 egg yolks, slightly beaten
1 tablespoon finely chopped onion
1 tablespoon chopped green pepper
2 tablespoons butter, margarine, or oil

Combine first 4 ingredients; mix well. Shape into 6 patties; brown well in hot fat, about 4 minutes each side. Yield 6.

roast potatoes swedish-style

6 baking potatoes small enough to fit in deep
  spoon
3 tablespoons melted butter
1 teaspoon salt
2 tablespoons bread crumbs
2 tablespoons Parmesan cheese (optional)

Peel potatoes; put in cold water to prevent discoloring. Put 1 potato in deep spoon; slice it down to edge of spoon, making slices about ⅛-inch apart. Spoon will prevent cutting through potato. Return sliced potato to cold water; slice others in same manner. Drain potatoes; pat dry. Put potatoes, cut-side-up, in large buttered baking dish; baste with some butter. Sprinkle with salt; cook 30 minutes in preheated 425°F oven. Sprinkle crumbs over each potato; baste with remaining butter. Cook 15 minutes or until golden brown and tender. Add cheese 5 minutes before potatoes are done. Yield 6 servings.

1 tablespoon lemon juice
3 tablespoons chopped fresh parsley
3 tablespoons chopped chives
2 sprigs fresh dill, chopped
2 sprigs fresh tarragon, chopped
1 sprig fresh thyme, chopped
8 to 12 new potatoes, boiled, sliced
½ cup plain yogurt
Sprigs fresh herbs (garnish)

Heat butter in skillet. Add leek, onion, and ham; cook and stir until onions and leek are transparent, about 5 to 7 minutes. Add bouillon and flour–water paste; heat and stir until mixture boils and is thickened. Season to taste with salt and pepper. Add lemon juice, herbs, and potatoes; heat through. Stir in yogurt just before serving; garnish with herbs. Yield 4 servings.

potatoes martha

4 potatoes
3 tablespoons butter
1½ teaspoons salt
Dash of pepper
½ cup grated cheddar cheese
2 tablespoons chopped parsley
½ cup heavy cream

Cut potatoes as for French fries; soak.

Cut 48-inch length of aluminum foil; fold in half. Place potatoes in center; dot with butter.

753

scalloped potatoes

1½ pounds potatoes
1 can mushroom soup
⅓ cup plus 1 tablespoon water
Butter
Paprika

Peel and thinly slice potatoes; arrange in greased 1½-quart casserole. Blend soup and water; pour over potatoes. Dot with butter; sprinkle with paprika. Bake in 325°F oven 1½ hours or until tender. Yield about 6 servings.

shrimp-stuffed potatoes

4 large baking potatoes
2 egg yolks
Half-and-half cream
4 tablespoons minced fresh parsley
2 tablespoons chopped chives
1 cup chopped cooked shrimp
½ cup grated cheddar cheese

Place potatoes in baking pan. Bake in preheated 375°F oven 1 hour or until tender. Do not turn off oven. Cut thin slice from 1 side of each potato; scoop out pulp. Leave firm shell; reserve shells. Place pulp in medium-size mixer bowl. Add egg yolks; beat with electric mixer until smooth. Beat in enough cream to make mixture light and fluffy. Fold in 2 tablespoons parsley, chives, and shrimp; spoon into reserved shells. Sprinkle with cheese; return to baking pan. Bake about 20 minutes, until cheese is melted and golden. Sprinkle each potato with ½ tablespoon parsley. Yield 4 servings.

stuffed baked potatoes

4 large baking potatoes
2 slices bacon
¼ cup milk
¼ cup melted butter
Salt and pepper to taste
2 tablespoons minced parsley

Scrub potatoes; grease with oil. Bake at 400°F 1 hour or until soft.

Fry bacon until crisp; drain on absorbent towels.

Cut potatoes in half lengthwise; scrape out insides into medium-size bowl. Mash with fork. Stir in milk, butter, salt, and pepper. Crumble in bacon. Add parsley; mix well. Pack into shells; drizzle tops with additional melted butter. Place on cookie sheet; broil 5 inches from source of heat until tops are browned. Serve immediately. Yield 8 servings.

roast potatoes swedish-style

shrimp-stuffed potatoes

SWEET POTATOES

candied sweet potatoes

¼ cup butter
6 medium sweet potatoes, cooked, pared
¾ cup grape jam
⅛ teaspoon ground allspice
1 tablespoon slivered orange rind

Melt butter in large skillet; add potatoes. Top with jam; sprinkle with allspice. Cook, uncovered, over low heat about 20 minutes; baste occasionally. Turn potatoes once. Just before serving, garnish with orange rind. Yield 6 servings.

Note: Orange marmalade to which 2 tablespoons honey have been added can be substituted for grape jam.

hawaiian sweet potatoes

1½ cups canned sweet potatoes plus 3 tablespoons juice

1 tablespoon butter or margarine
½ teaspoon salt
¼ teaspoon pepper
¼ teaspoon nutmeg
¼ teaspoon cinnamon
1 tablespoon brown sugar
¾ cup crushed cereal flakes
6 pineapple slices

Combine sweet potatoes, juice, butter, salt, pepper, nutmeg, cinnamon, and brown sugar; mix until well blended.

Crush cereal in plastic bag or between waxed paper. Drop ⅓ to ½ cup sweet-potato mixture onto paper containing crushed cereal; roll into ball. Place ball on pineapple slice in greased baking pan. Repeat potato-ball and pineapple procedure until all are prepared. Heat at 350°F 20 minutes. Yield 6 servings.

orange yams

4 pounds yams
1 tablespoon butter

sweet-and-sour yams and pineapple

1 tablespoon honey
Salt, pepper, and nutmeg to taste
Juice and grated rind of 2 oranges

Boil yams in water to cover until tender; drain. Drop into cold water; slip off skins; mash. Blend in remaining ingredients; spoon into buttered casserole. Bake at 325°F about 40 minutes, until golden. Yield about 16 servings.

spicy sweet-potato pie

1½ cups cooked, mashed sweet potatoes
½ cup sugar
1 teaspoon cinnamon
1 teaspoon allspice
½ teaspoon salt
3 eggs, well beaten
1 cup milk
2 tablespoons butter, melted
1 (9-inch) unbaked pie shell

Mash sweet potatoes into fine paste; mix in sugar, cinnamon, allspice, and salt. Add eggs.

Mix milk and butter; stir into potato mixture. Mixture will be fairly liquid. Pour into unbaked pastry shell. Bake at 350°F 40 to 45 minutes. Yield 6 to 8 servings.

sweet-potato balls

½ teaspoon salt
Dash of pepper
2 cups mashed sweet potatoes
4 marshmallows
1 cup bread or cracker crumbs
1 egg, beaten
2 tablespoons water
Shortening for deep frying

Mix salt and pepper with sweet potatoes; roll into 8 balls. Put 1 marshmallow into center of each ball; roll each ball in crumbs.

Combine egg and water; dip balls into this mixture. Roll again in crumbs. Fry in heated deep shortening about 4 minutes, until golden brown and crispy; drain. Yield 4 to 6 servings.

sweet-potato puffs

2 cups mashed sweet potatoes
2 egg yolks, beaten
1 cup cream
½ teaspoon salt
2 egg whites, well beaten

Mix potatoes, egg yolks, cream, and salt; heat in saucepan. When very hot, remove from heat. Add egg whites; beat until light. Pile loosely on buttered platter; brush with egg white. Heat in 350°F oven until brown. Yield 6 servings.

sweet potatoes in orange shells

3 oranges
1 (16-ounce) can sweet potatoes, undrained

2 tablespoons butter or margarine, melted
3 tablespoons packed brown sugar
½ teaspoon salt
¼ cup flaked coconut
6 miniature marshmallows

Squeeze oranges; save juice. Remove membranes from orange shells.

Mash sweet potatoes. Blend in 3 tablespoons orange juice, butter, brown sugar, and salt. Stir in coconut. Spoon into orange shells; place in shallow baking pan. Bake at 350°F 20 to 30 minutes, until lightly browned on top. Top with marshmallows; bake about 5 minutes to melt and brown marshmallows. Yield 6 servings.

sweet-and-sour yams and pineapple

1 (20-ounce) can sliced pineapple
1 tablespoon cornstarch
¼ teaspoon salt
3 tablespoons fresh lemon juice
2 (1-pound) cans yams, drained
Oil
4 scallions, sliced
1 small green pepper, cut into small chunks
½ cup diagonally sliced celery

Drain pineapple; reserve syrup.

Combine reserved syrup, cornstarch, and salt in saucepan; blend well. Bring to boil over medium heat; cook until thickened, stirring constantly. Stir in lemon juice.

Arrange pineapple and yams in casserole; pour sauce over. Bake, covered in 350°F oven about 30 minutes, until hot. Heat small amount of oil in skillet; sauté scallions, pepper, and celery until just tender but still crisp. Stir carefully into yam mixture. Serve immediately. Yield about 8 servings.

SPINACH
baked spinach with cheese

1 pound fresh spinach, washed, dried
¼ pound butter
1 large onion, diced
2 cloves garlic, minced
½ teaspoon salt
½ pound Emmentaler cheese, grated
1 teaspoon paprika
⅛ teaspoon nutmeg
¼ teaspoon pepper

Cut spinach into strips.

In large Dutch oven or heavy saucepot heat butter until bubbly. Add onion and garlic; sauté 2 to 3 minutes. Add spinach. Sprinkle with salt; cover. Steam 5 minutes; remove from heat.

Grease ovenproof casserole; sprinkle half the cheese over bottom. Add spinach. Sprinkle with paprika, nutmeg, and pepper. Top with remaining cheese. Bake in preheated 350°F oven about 20 minutes, until cheese bubbles. Yield 4 servings.

creamed spinach

½ cup water
¼ teaspoon salt
1 (10-ounce) package frozen chopped spinach
2 tablespoons butter or margarine
2 tablespoons flour
⅛ teaspoon garlic salt
White pepper to taste
¾ cup light cream
⅛ teaspoon ground nutmeg

Bring water and salt to boil in medium saucepan. Add spinach; return to full boil. Break up frozen spinach with fork; cover. Reduce heat to low; cook 4 minutes. Drain well; keep warm.

Melt butter in small saucepan. Add flour, garlic salt, and pepper; stir well. Cook until bubbly. Add cream; stir well. Cook over low heat until thickened. Season with nutmeg. Combine with spinach; mix thoroughly. Garnish with hard-boiled egg slices. Yield 4 servings.

fried spinach and onions

4 tablespoons bacon drippings or lard
1 large onion, sliced (1 cup)
1¼ pounds fresh spinach leaves, washed, trimmed, stems removed
Salt and pepper to taste
⅛ teaspoon finely crushed dried red chilies (optional)

Melt drippings in large, heavy kettle over medium-high heat. Add onion; fry, stirring frequently, until lightly browned. Add spinach; cook, tossing constantly, 3 to 5 minutes, until wilted and coated with drippings. Season with salt, pepper, and powdered chilies to taste. Yield 4 servings.

german-style spinach

1 or 2 tablespoons butter, margarine, or oil
½ cup chopped onion
1 tablespoon flour
½ cup water
1 (10-ounce) package frozen spinach
Salt and pepper to taste

Heat butter in large frypan. Add onion; cook until tender. Add flour; cook and stir until mixture begins to thicken. Add water; mix until smooth. Add spinach; cover. Cook about 15 minutes; stir occasionally as spinach thaws. Season with salt and pepper. Yield 3 servings.

olive spinach balls

1½ cups chopped cooked spinach
½ cup grated Cheddar cheese
1 egg, beaten
½ cup sliced ripe olives
½ teaspoon salt
1 cup buttered crumbs

Cook spinach; squeeze out all juice. Mix spinach, cheese, egg, olives, and salt; shape into balls. Roll thoroughly in crumbs; place in greased baking pan. Bake in preheated 375°F oven 30 to 45 minutes. Yield 4 servings.

parmesan spinach puree

1½ to 2 pounds fresh spinach
2 tablespoons butter
1 tablespoon lemon juice
½ teaspoon salt
¼ cup hot half-and-half cream
3 tablespoons freshly grated Parmesan cheese

Wash spinach; remove stems. Place in large pan. Add ¼ cup water; cover. Cook over medium heat 10 to 15 minutes, until spinach is tender; turn occasionally with fork. Drain well; process in blender or food processor. Add butter, lemon juice, and salt; process until pureed. Spoon into small mold; invert onto serving dish. Shape sides and level top with tines of fork. Make well in center; pour cream in well. Sprinkle cheese around sides. Serve immediately. Yield about 4 servings.

spinach with artichokes and wine

2 (10-ounce) packages frozen, chopped spinach
2 hard-cooked eggs, chopped
Dash of garlic powder
¼ cup melted butter
Salt to taste
12 drained artichoke bottoms
1 cup dry white Bordeaux wine
1 (8-ounce) package Port Salut, coarsely shredded

Cook spinach; drain. Squeeze out moisture. Stir in eggs, garlic powder, butter, and salt to taste; spoon on artichoke bottoms that have been placed on cookie sheet. Bake in preheated 400°F oven 20 minutes or until hot.

Heat wine to lukewarm. Stir in cheese a handful at a time until melted and sauce is smooth. Season with salt and garlic powder. Spoon sauce over spinach and bottoms. Yield 6 servings.

spinach chinese-style

1 pound fresh spinach, washed, cut into 2-inch pieces

parmesan spinach puree

2 tablespoons oil
Salt to taste
1 small can bamboo shoots
8 fresh mushrooms, sliced
¼ cup chicken broth

Wash spinach; cut into pieces.

Heat oil in wok or skillet. Add salt and spinach; stir-fry 2 minutes. Add bamboo shoots, mushrooms, and broth; mix. Cover; simmer about 2 minutes, until heated through. Yield 2 to 4 servings.

spinach au gratin

2 (10-ounce) packages frozen chopped spinach
3 cups cooked rice
4 eggs, beaten
1 (10¾-ounce) can condensed cream of mushroom soup
Dash of nutmeg
1 teaspoon onion powder
½ teaspoon salt
¼ teaspoon pepper
¼ cup grated Parmesan cheese

Thaw, drain, and separate spinach; toss with rice.

Combine eggs, soup, and seasonings; stir into spinach mixture. Turn into greased shallow 2½-quart casserole; sprinkle top with cheese. Bake in preheated 350°F oven 30 minutes or until firm. Yield 6 to 8 servings.

spinach fettucini

8 ounces cottage cheese, creamed
8 ounces medium noodles, dry
2 tablespoons butter or margarine, or 1 tablespoon oil and 1 tablespoon water
2 small cloves garlic, minced
1 (10-ounce) package chopped spinach, thawed
2 tablespoons grated Parmesan cheese
¼ cup chopped fresh parsley
1 tablespoon fresh basil or oregano or 1 teaspoon dried
Salt (or butter-flavored salt)
Coarsely ground pepper to taste

Remove cottage cheese from refrigerator 30 minutes ahead of time, to reach room temperature.

Cook noodles in boiling salted water according to package directions.

Combine butter and garlic in nonstick skillet over moderate heat; when moisture evaporates, garlic will begin to brown. Sauté garlic until golden. Add spinach; cook and stir over low flame until heated through.

Drain noodles; rinse under hot water.

Combine hot, drained noodles, spinach mixture, and cottage cheese. Add remaining ingredients; toss lightly to combine. Serve immediately. Yield 8 servings.

spinach in madeira

2 pounds spinach
2 tablespoons butter
¼ cup heavy cream
Salt and pepper
Dash of nutmeg
¼ pound mushrooms, thinly sliced
2 tablespoons Madeira wine
Croutons

Cook spinach in as little water as possible until barely tender. Put through finest blade of food chopper or spin in food processor. Add butter and cream; beat well. Season with salt, pepper, and nutmeg; set aside to keep hot.

Sauté mushrooms in butter until tender; add Madeira to spinach. Reheat without boiling. Garnish with croutons fried in butter. Yield 6 servings.

SQUASH

acorn cabbage bake

2 large acorn squash
½ pound sausage meat

2 tablespoons butter or margarine
1 medium onion, chopped
1 small apple, pared, chopped
2 cups shredded green cabbage
2 tablespoons slivered almonds
¾ teaspoon salt
¼ teaspoon pepper
¼ teaspoon dried leaf thyme
½ teaspoon crumbled dried leaf sage

Cut squash in half lengthwise; scoop out seeds and fibers. Place in baking pan, cut-side-down; add ½-inch water. Bake in preheated 400°F oven 20 minutes.

Meanwhile cook sausage meat in skillet until browned. Drain off excess fat; add butter to pan. Add onion, apple, cabbage and almonds; cook until vegetables are tender. Add seasonings; mix well.

Turn squash halves cut-side-up; fill centers with cabbage mixture. Return to baking pan; bake in 400°F oven 30 minutes. Yield 4 servings.

acorn squash with sliced apples

3 fresh acorn squash
Salt to taste
2 or 3 fresh tart apples
Butter
6 tablespoons brown sugar
Nutmeg to taste

Cut squash in half; remove seeds. Place, cut-side-down, in shallow greased baking dish; add ½ cup boiling water; cover. Bake in preheated 350°F oven 10 minutes. Remove from oven; remove cover. Turn squash cut-side-up; sprinkle with salt.

Peel and core apples; cut into wedges. Fill squash cavities with apples; dot generously with butter. Sprinkle each squash half with 1 tablespoon brown sugar, then with a little nutmeg. Pour ½ cup boiling water into baking dish. Bake 30 minutes or until squash and apples are tender. Yield 6 servings.

apple–onion acorn squash

3 large acorn squash
4 medium onions, thinly sliced
¼ cup butter or margarine
4 medium red apples, cored, cut into 12 wedges each
Dash of salt
2½ tablespoons packed brown sugar

Wash squash; cut into halves; remove seeds. Place, cut-side-down, in shallow baking dish containing a little water. Bake in preheated 375°F oven 20 minutes.

acorn squash with sliced apples

While squash are baking, sauté onions in butter until soft, about 5 minutes. Add apples; cook until tender, about 7 to 9 minutes. Salt to taste. Stir in brown sugar.

Remove squash from oven; turn right-side-up. Stuff squash halves with apple–onion mixture; return to oven (*without* water in pan). Bake 25 to 30 minutes, until squash are tender. Yield 6 servings.

baked squash

Small Hubbard squash
3 tablespoons butter or fat
3 tablespoons chopped onion
2 tablespoons chopped green pepper
1 teaspoon salt
⅛ teaspoon pepper
⅛ teaspoon paprika
¼ cup fine bread crumbs

Cut squash in pieces; pare. Boil in salted water 30 minutes or until tender. Drain; mash.

Melt butter. Add onion and green pepper; sauté slowly 5 minutes. Add onion, green pepper, salt, pepper, and paprika to squash; mix well. Turn into greased baking dish; sprinkle with crumbs, salt, and pepper. Bake in preheated 400°F oven 25 minutes. Yield 6 servings.

baked summer squash with almonds

6 small yellow squash
Salt and pepper to taste
¼ teaspoon sage
2 tablespoons sugar
1 cup shredded almonds
4 tablespoons butter
1 egg
½ cup toasted crumbs
Paprika

Boil squash 10 minutes in salted water; remove from water. Cut a slice from one side of each squash; remove centers with spoon. Season with salt, pepper, sage, and sugar.

Sauté almonds in butter. Add to mixture; mix well. Add egg and half the crumbs. Fill squash cups with mixture; place on baking sheet. Top with buttered crumbs; sprinkle with paprika. Bake in preheated 350°F oven 30 minutes. Yield 6 servings.

stuffed acorn squash

2 acorn squash, halved, seeded
3 tablespoons butter or margarine, melted
1 cup grated carrot
½ cup chopped pitted prunes

½ cup chopped dates
¼ teaspoon nutmeg

Place squash, cut-side-down, in baking pan with small amount of water. Bake in preheated 350°F oven 30 minutes.

Combine remaining ingredients. Turn squash cut-side-up; fill with prune mixture. Bake 25 to 30 minutes, until squash are tender. Yield 4 servings.

stuffed summer squash

3 tablespoons oil
1 onion, chopped
¾ pound chopped cooked meat
1 cup chopped mushrooms
1 tablespoon flour
1 cup gravy or tomato sauce
1 tablespoon soy or Worcestershire sauce
1 tablespoon mixed herbs
¼ cup leftover peas, beans, carrots, corn, or rice
1 summer squash, about 2 pounds
3 tablespoons dried white bread crumbs
A little melted butter
2 tablespoons chopped parsley

Heat oil; cook onion until golden brown. Add meat and mushrooms; cook 2 minutes. Sprinkle with flour; mix in. Add enough gravy to moisten; do not make too soft. Add soy sauce, mixed herbs, and vegetables.

Cut squash in half lengthwise; remove seeds. Or cut into 1½-inch-thick rings; remove seeds. Boil 5 minutes; drain. Put in buttered ovenproof dish; fill with meat mixture. Sprinkle with dried white bread crumbs. Pour a little melted butter over it. Pour remaining gravy around squash. Cook in preheated 375°F oven about 35 to 50 minutes, according to thickness of squash. Test with skewer; when tender, sprinkle with parsley. Yield 4 to 6 servings.

summer squash in cream

4 medium to small summer squash
Salt and pepper
3 tablespoons butter or margarine
1 cup all-purpose cream
1 tablespoon chopped parsley

Butter deep baking dish.

Peel squash; remove seeds. Slice squash into dish. Sprinkle with salt and pepper; dot with butter. Place in preheated 400°F oven; cover. When tender, add cream; cook, uncovered, until slightly browned. Sprinkle with parsley. Serve in cooking dish. Yield 6 servings.

summer squash and tomatoes

3 medium-size or 6 small yellow summer squash
1 small onion

2 slices bread
2 cups fresh or canned tomatoes
½ teaspoon salt
Pepper to taste

Slice squash. Chop onion. Cut up bread.

Mix all ingredients in saucepan; cover. Boil gently about 30 minutes, until squash is tender and flavors are blended. Add salt and pepper. Yield 6 servings.

ZUCCHINI

fried zucchini

3 to 4 medium zucchini, sliced into rounds
1 egg
1 tablespoon milk
3 tablespoons flour
1 teaspoon salt
1 teaspoon garlic salt
Deep fat for frying

Wash zucchini; slice into rounds about ¼ inch thick. Set aside.

Combine egg, milk, flour, salt, and garlic salt in bowl; mix well to form batter. Dip each zucchini round into batter; fry in deep fat. Batter zucchini when ready to fry, so each piece is coated; fry until crisp and golden brown. Drain on paper towels. Serve hot. Yield 4 to 6 servings.

layered zucchini

6 cups sliced zucchini, about 1¾ pounds
½ pound ground beef
1 small clove garlic, minced
1 (8-ounce) can tomato sauce
1 teaspoon salt
¼ teaspoon dried oregano leaves
¼ teaspoon dried basil leaves
1 cup small-curd cottage cheese
1 egg, beaten
1 tablespoon parsley flakes
¼ cup dry bread crumbs
1 cup shredded mozzarella cheese (4 ounces)

Cook zucchini in boiling salted water in saucepan until tender-crisp, about 5 minutes; drain.

Cook beef and garlic in skillet until beef is browned, about 5 minutes. Stir in tomato sauce, salt, oregano, and basil.

Stir together cottage cheese, egg, and parsley.

Place half of zucchini in greased 8-inch-square baking pan; sprinkle with half of crumbs. Spread with half of cottage-cheese mixture, then with half of beef mixture and half of mozzarella. Repeat layers; reserve remaining mozzarella. Bake in 350°F oven 25 minutes. Sprinkle with reserved cheese; return to oven just long enough to melt cheese, about 3 minutes. Yield 4 or 5 servings.

scalloped zucchini squash

6 cups thinly sliced zucchini squash
1 cup boiling water
¾ cup medium White Sauce (see Index)
2 eggs, beaten
1 teaspoon salt
½ teaspoon Worcestershire sauce
1 teaspoon finely chopped onion
¼ cup fine dry bread crumbs
1 tablespoon butter or margarine, melted

Cook squash in boiling water until tender, about 5 minutes; drain.

Make White Sauce. Stir a little into eggs; gradually stir eggs into remaining sauce. Stir in salt, Worcestershire sauce, onion, and squash. Put in greased 1-quart casserole.

Mix crumbs with butter; sprinkle over squash mixture. Bake in preheated 325°F oven about 35 minutes. Yield 6 servings.

stuffed zucchini

4 medium zucchini squash (about ¾-pound each)
1 pound ground beef (or ½-pound beef and ½-pound sausage)
¼ cup olive oil
1 clove garlic, chopped
1 medium onion, chopped
½ cup chopped green pepper
1 tablespoon chopped parsley
½ teaspoon crumbled dried oregano
Salt and pepper
1 cup fresh bread crumbs from French or Italian bread
1¾ cups tomato sauce
¼ cup grated Parmesan cheese

Slice zucchini in half lengthwise. Scoop out pulp; chop.

Sauté meat in oil until it loses pink color. Add garlic, onion, and green pepper; cook 5 minutes. Remove from heat. Add squash pulp, parsley, oregano, salt, pepper, crumbs, and ¼ cup tomato sauce; mix well. Stuff squash shells with mixture; place in shallow baking dish. Top with 1½ cups tomato sauce; sprinkle with cheese. Bake in preheated 350°F oven 40 minutes. Yield 4 servings.

stuffed zucchini japanese-style

Zucchini, medium size (½ zucchini per serving)

stuffing
1 pound meat (ground beef, ground veal, or leftover ground meat)
Salt
Pepper

stuffed zucchini japanese-style

Ginger
Soy sauce
Tomato sauce

Cut zucchini in half; scoop out centers. Pat dry before filling.

Mix meats as for hamburgers; season well. If desired, add a little ground ginger and small amount of soy sauce to meat mixture. Fill zucchini with mixture. Bake in shallow baking pan in pre-heated oven 350°F oven about 45 minutes, until browned. Serve with tomato sauce. Yield 4 to 6 servings.

stuffed zucchini par excellence

6 carrots, sliced
12 shallots, peeled
4 cups beef broth
4 medium zucchini
2 slices bread
¼ cup milk
1 pound (2 cups) ground lean lamb
1 teaspoon thyme

2 teaspoons salt
1 teaspoon pepper
2 eggs, beaten
¼ cup tomato paste
Melted butter

Place carrots, shallots, broth, and 1 cup water in Dutch oven or heavy casserole; bring to boil. Simmer until tender.

Prepare zucchini while vegetables are cooking. Peel each zucchini; cut in half lengthwise. Hollow out centers.

Remove crusts from bread; soak in milk. Combine bread and lamb in mixing bowl. Add seasonings, eggs, and tomato paste; mix well. Fill each zucchini half with mixture; fit halves together. Brush generously with butter; wrap each zucchini loosely in aluminum foil.

Remove carrots and shallots from broth; set aside.

Place wrapped zucchini carefully in broth; simmer covered, 1 hour. Remove zucchini.

Return carrots and shallots to broth to reheat.

Unwrap zucchini; place in serving dish. Arrange carrots and shallots around zucchini; pour broth over. Yield about 8 servings.

zucchini in bread crumbs with cheese

zucchini delight

1½ pounds smallest freshest zucchini
½ cup onion, preferably Bermuda, sliced as thin
as possible

stuffed zucchini par excellence

¾ cup olive oil
2 tablespoons minced garlic
1 large (2-pound) can imported Italian plum
tomatoes
1½ teaspoons salt
1½ teaspoons pepper
1½ teaspoons dried basil

If you have a food processor, slice all zucchini with slicing blade. Otherwise slice zucchini, skin and all, as thin as possible.

Slice onion to same thickness as zucchini; sauté onion in oil in ovenproof pot large enough to accommodate all ingredients. Onion should be soft and just turning color. Add garlic; sauté quickly.

Chop tomatoes; add with juice from can to onion mixture. Simmer 20 minutes. Add zucchini, salt, pepper, and basil. Place in preheated 350°F oven, uncovered; cook 30 minutes. After 30 minutes, if there is too much liquid, turn oven higher; let some evaporate. Yield 4 or 5 servings.

zucchini in bread crumbs with cheese

2 pounds small zucchini
¼ cup butter
¼ cup salad oil
1½ cups cooked rice
½ cup freshly grated Parmesan cheese
½ cup grated sharp cheddar cheese
Salt and pepper to taste
2 eggs, slightly beaten
Dry bread crumbs
Melted butter

Cut ends from zucchini; steam until tender. Reserve 2 zucchini for garnish; dice remaining zucchini.

Combine butter and oil in Dutch oven or heavy saucepan; heat until butter is melted. Add rice and zucchini; sauté until golden, stirring frequently. Stir in cheeses until melted. Add seasonings; let cool slightly. Stir in eggs quickly; pour into greased baking dish. Sprinkle generously with crumbs.

Slice reserved zucchini; arrange around diced-zucchini mixture. Drizzle butter over top; broil about 6 inches from heat source until lightly browned and bubbly. Yield 6 to 8 servings.

zucchini italian

2 tablespoons butter or shortening
1 onion, sliced into rings
1 pound zucchini, sliced (2 to 3 cups)
1 cup diced fresh tomatoes
1 teaspoon salt

Dash of pepper
1 teaspoon dillweed

Heat butter in medium skillet. (Use skillet with its own top.) Cook onion rings in butter until yellow. Add remaining ingredients; cover. Lower heat to simmer; cook 10 to 15 minutes, until vegetables are tender.

If you want this for company and want to make it ahead, put cooked vegetables in casserole dish; sprinkle with grated cheese. Just before serving, put into preheated moderate oven 5 minutes or until cheese has browned. Yield 4 servings.

TOMATOES

baked tomato neptune

6 large firm tomatoes
¼ cup chopped green sweet pepper
¼ cup grated carrots
2 tablespoons minced fresh onion
¼ cup melted butter
¼ cup all-purpose flour
2 teaspoons salt

baked tomato neptune

2 teaspoons sugar
¼ teaspoon freshly ground pepper
¾ cup coarsely chopped cooked shrimp
1 (8-ounce) package frozen King crab meat, flaked
1 cup coarsely chopped cooked lobster
3 tablespoons dry sherry
2 tablespoons finely chopped parsley
2 tablespoons fine bread crumbs
1 tablespoon butter

Cut ¼-inch slice from stem end of each tomato. Scoop out pulp, leaving firm ¼-inch shell; reserve pulp.

Sauté green pepper, carrots, and onion in melted butter in large saucepan 5 minutes. Stir in flour, salt, sugar, and pepper. Add reserved pulp; cook over medium heat, stirring constantly, until mixture comes to boil and thickens. Stir in shrimp, crab meat, lobster, sherry, and parsley. Spoon mixture into tomato cups; arrange in greased, shallow baking dish. Sprinkle with crumbs; dot with butter. Bake in preheated 375°F oven 15 minutes or until heated through. Garnish tops with additional parsley, if desired. Yield 6 servings.

broiled tomatoes

4 medium tomatoes

garlic butter
¼ cup butter
1 teaspoon garlic salt
¼ teaspoon white pepper
¼ teaspoon dry mustard

Wash tomatoes; place upside down on broiler pan. With sharp knife, slash skins in "X" design.

Make Garlic Butter. Melt butter; stir in garlic salt, white pepper, and dry mustard.

Brush tomatoes with Garlic Butter.

Place broiling pan in farthest slot from flame. Broil tomatoes 2 minutes; remove from broiler. Baste with Garlic Butter. Return to broiler; broil 3 minutes. Yield 4 servings.

cheese-stuffed tomatoes

4 medium tomatoes
2 ounces blue cheese
2 ounces cottage cheese
2 tablespoons evaporated milk
1 stalk celery
¼ teaspoon salt
¼ teaspoon paprika
½ teaspoon chopped chives
4 lettuce leaves

Wash tomatoes; slice off tops. Scoop out seeds.

Crumble blue cheese with fork; blend with cottage cheese and milk.

Mince celery; add to cheese. Season with salt and paprika; fill tomatoes with mixture. Sprinkle

cheese-stuffed tomatoes

chives over top; place tomato tops back on. Serve on lettuce leaves. Yield 4 servings.

dilled tomato cups with peas

4 medium tomatoes

dill butter
2 tablespoons butter, melted
½ teaspoon salt
¼ teaspoon white pepper
½ teaspoon dried dillweed
½ cup water
1 cup peas, frozen

Slice tops from tomatoes; spoon out centers, being sure not to damage structure of tomato walls.

Melt butter. Add salt, white pepper, and dillweed. Brush insides of tomatoes with Dill Butter. Bake in preheated 400°F oven 15 minutes or until tender.

While tomatoes are baking, bring ½ cup water to rapid boil. Add peas; cook 8 to 10 minutes, until tender. Fill tomato halves with hot peas. Serve immediately. Yield 4 servings.

fried green tomatoes

4 medium green tomatoes, sliced ½ inch thick
1 teaspoon salt
½ teaspoon pepper
1 teaspoon dillweed
1 cup cornmeal
Fat for frying

Wash and prepare tomatoes.

Mix seasonings with cornmeal in pie plate. Batter each tomato slice; be sure both sides are coated.

Heat fat to 375°F in medium skillet. Cook tomatoes until brown on both sides; drain on paper towels. Yield 4 to 6 servings.

green tomato pie

6 to 8 medium green tomatoes, peeled, sliced
1 lemon, thinly sliced
2 tablespoons cornstarch
2 tablespoons water
1 cup sugar
2 tablespoons butter
½ teaspoon ground cinnamon
¼ teaspoon salt
1 frozen pie shell and frozen top crust or pie-crust mix

Boil tomatoes and lemon; cover. Simmer 10 minutes, until tomatoes appear transparent.

Combine cornstarch and water; add to tomato mixture. Add sugar, butter, cinnamon, and salt; stirring constantly, bring to boil. Boil 1 minute; remove from heat.

Follow pastry instructions for baking 2-crust pie. Place filling in pie; add top crust. Seal; flute edges. Cut steam vents in top crust. Bake in preheated 425°F oven approximately 35 minutes. Serve at room temperature. Yield 8 servings.

hot herbed tomatoes

¼ cup butter
1 teaspoon brown sugar
½ teaspoon salt
Dash of pepper
4 or 5 firm ripe tomatoes, peeled
¼ cup chopped celery
2 tablespoons chopped parsley
2 tablespoons chopped chives

½ teaspoon oregano (optional)

Melt butter in large heavy skillet; add sugar, salt, and pepper. Place tomatoes core-side-down in skillet; cover. Simmer 5 minutes. Carefully turn tomatoes; spoon butter mixture over. Add remaining ingredients; simmer, uncovered, 5 minutes. Spoon sauce over tomatoes before serving. Yield 4 or 5 servings.

marinated sliced tomatoes

¼ cup salad oil
1 tablespoon lemon juice
½ teaspoon minced garlic
½ teaspoon salt
½ teaspoon oregano
4 large tomatoes, peeled, sliced

Combine all but tomatoes; mix well. Pour over tomatoes; marinate several hours. Yield 3 or 4 servings.

stewed tomatoes

6 to 8 tomatoes, peeled
2 tablespoons vinegar
2 tablespoons lemon juice
1 teaspoon sugar
1 onion, diced
1 teaspoon garlic salt
1 teaspoon basil
1 teaspoon marjoram
½ teaspoon pepper

Simmer all ingredients in saucepan until tomatoes fall apart. Yield 4 to 6 servings.

stuffed baked tomatoes

stuffed tomatoes and zucchini

stuffed baked tomatoes

4 large tomatoes
¼ cup butter or margarine
½ cup finely chopped onions
½ teaspoon salt
¼ teaspoon black pepper
¼ teaspoon oregano
2 cups bread crumbs
Parsley

Thoroughly wash tomatoes; dry on paper towel. Remove tops from tomatoes with sharp knife. Save tops for later use. Scoop centers from tomatoes; reserve ½ cup for later use.

Heat butter in medium-size skillet. Add onions; cook until tender. Add ½ cup reserved tomato centers to onions; cook until tomato pieces are mushy.

Combine spices and crumbs. Add cooked vegetables and butter. Work bread and vegetables with hands until well combined and stuffing mix has formed. If stuffing is too dry, add more melted butter. Fill tomato cavities with mixture. Place tomatoes close together in slightly greased baking pan. If tomatoes are small enough, they can be baked in greased muffin tin. Replace tomato tops. Bake in preheated 350°F oven 30 minutes or until fork-tender. Carefully arrange on serving platter. Garnish with fresh parsley. Yield 4 servings.

stuffed tomatoes and zucchini

4 medium zucchini
2½ cups fine soft bread crumbs
⅛ teaspoon oregano
4 tablespoons melted Garlic Butter (see Index)
¼ cup shredded Gruyère or Emmentaler cheese
Salt and pepper to taste
Freshly grated Parmesan cheese
4 firm ripe tomatoes
½ teaspoon minced chives

1 teaspoon finely chopped parsley
½ teaspoon chopped tarragon
Melted butter

Trim ends from zucchini; cut in half lengthwise. Scoop pulp from centers into bowl. Invert shells onto wire rack. Mash pulp with fork. Add 1 cup crumbs, oregano, 2 tablespoons Garlic Butter and Gruyére cheese. Season with salt and pepper; mix well. Spoon into zucchini shells; sprinkle tops generously with Parmesan. Place in jelly-roll pan.

Cut tomatoes in half crosswise; scoop out centers into bowl. Invert shells onto wire rack to drain thoroughly. Drain juice from pulp; reserve juice. Combine pulp, remaining crumbs and half the herbs; mix well. Add remaining Garlic Butter and enough reserved tomato juice to moisten. Season with salt and pepper. Spoon into tomato shells; sprinkle tops with remaining herbs. Place stuffed tomato halves in jelly-roll pan. Drizzle zucchini and tomato halves generously with melted butter. Bake zucchini in preheated oven 375°F oven 40 minutes; add tomatoes last 15 minutes of baking period. Bake until heated through and golden. Serve immediately. Yield 8 servings.

tomatoes rockefeller

3 large tomatoes, cut in half, seeds removed
2 tablespoons finely chopped onion
1 tablespoon finely chopped parsley
2 tablespoons butter or margarine
½ cup chopped cooked spinach, drained well
¼ teaspoon salt
⅛ teaspoon pepper
¼ teaspoon paprika
2 tablespoons bread crumbs

Place tomatoes in shallow baking dish, cut-side-up.

Mix rest of ingredients except crumbs. Divide and spread evenly over tomatoes; top with crumbs. Bake in preheated 375°F oven 15 minutes or until crumbs are toasted and tomato heated. Yield 6 servings.

tomatoes stuffed with chicken or tuna

6 medium-size fresh tomatoes
¾ teaspoon salt
1 tablespoon finely chopped onion
2 tablespoons butter or margarine
1 cup cooked or canned chopped chicken or tuna
½ cup bite-size shredded wheat, rice, or corn cereal
1 egg, slightly beaten
¼ teaspoon Worcestershire sauce
¼ cup corn, wheat, or rice flakes, crushed
1½ teaspoons butter or margarine, melted

6 sprigs parsley (optional)

Wash tomatoes; remove thin slice from stem end of each. Scoop out pulp; save. Sprinkle inside of tomatoes with ¼ teaspoon salt; invert tomatoes to drain 30 minutes.

Cook onion in 2 tablespoons butter in large frypan until lightly browned, about 5 minutes. Add 1¼ cups tomato pulp, chicken, cereal, egg, ½ teaspoon salt, and Worcestershire sauce; cook 3 minutes, stirring often. Fill each tomato with stuffing.

Mix crushed cereal flakes with melted butter; sprinkle over tomatoes. Place tomatoes on baking sheet. Bake 30 minutes in preheated 400°F oven. Garnish with parsley. Yield 6 servings.

tomatoes stuffed with spinach

4 boxes frozen chopped spinach
10 to 12 medium tomatoes
Salt
3 tablespoons butter or margarine
1 onion, grated
¾ to 1 cup sour cream
½ cup grated Parmesan cheese
Freshly ground pepper
Dash of cayenne
Bread crumbs

Cook spinach according to package directions. Drain; cool.

Wash tomatoes; do not peel. Cut off tops; scoop out insides. Sprinkle with salt; invert to drain. Scooped-out centers can be used in sauce or for stewed tomatoes.

Melt 1 tablespoon butter in skillet; sauté onion until soft but not brown. Add with sour cream and cheese to spinach. Season with salt, pepper, and cayenne. Stuff into tomato shells. Top with crumbs and dabs of butter. Place in oiled or foil-lined baking dish. Bake in preheated 350°F oven about 25 minutes. Yield 10 to 12 servings.

TURNIPS

glazed turnips

2 pounds white turnips, peeled, quartered
2 tablespoons vegetable oil
1 to 1½ cups beef bouillon
1 tablespoon butter or margarine
3 tablespoons sugar
2 tablespoons minced parsley

Blanch turnips in boiling salted water to cover 5 minutes; drain. Pat dry with paper towels. Sauté in hot oil 3 minutes to brown lightly. Pour in bouillon barely to cover. Add butter and sugar;

cover. Boil slowly 20 to 30 minutes, until turnips are just tender. Uncover; boil liquid to reduce to thick syrup. Gently top turnips; coat with glaze. Place in vegetable dish or around a roast; sprinkle with parsley. Yield 6 servings.

turnips au gratin

2 tablespoons butter or margarine
2 tablespoons flour
¼ teaspoon salt
1 cup milk
3 cups diced cooked turnips
1 cup (4 ounces) cheddar cheese, shredded

Melt butter in saucepan. Stir in flour and salt until smooth. Add milk slowly, stirring rapidly to prevent lumping. Bring to boil; stir constantly. Gently mix white sauce and turnips; pour into baking dish. Sprinkle with cheese.

Bake in preheated 375°F oven about 20 minutes, until cheese melts. Yield 6 servings.

turnip bake

1 pound rutabagas
½ pound white turnips
4 slices bacon, diced
¼ cup chopped onion

1 cup water
Salt and pepper
Chopped parsley

Peel rutabagas and turnips; cut into small cubes.

Cook bacon in heavy skillet until crisp; remove from pan. Crumble; reserve.

Add onion to bacon fat in skillet; cook until tender. Add water, salt, and pepper; bring to boil.

Combine rutabagas, turnips, and reserved bacon in 2-quart casserole. Add boiling water and onion; cover. Bake in preheated 350°F oven 45 minutes or until fork-tender. Sprinkle with chopped parsley. Yield 6 servings.

vinegar turnips

About 2 pounds turnips
1 cup sugar
⅓ cup vinegar
1 cup water
3 tablespoons salt

Peel turnips; slice very thin. Put into bowl or, preferably, crock.

Combine remaining ingredients in saucepan; bring to boil. Pour over turnips; mix gently but thoroughly. Cover; refrigerate 5 days. Yield 6 servings.

VENISON

graustark venison

1 (6-pound) leg of venison
Salt to taste
1 recipe Marinade for Game (see Index)
6 strips salt pork
3 pounds small potatoes
Butter
Salt
White pepper to taste
2 tablespoons minced fresh parsley
2 (10-ounce) packages frozen brussels sprouts
¼ cup chopped walnuts
2 tablespoons all-purpose flour
1 cup beef broth

Season venison with salt; place in shallow pan. Pour marinade over. Refrigerate 24 hours; turn occasionally. Remove venison from marinade. Strain marinade; reserve. Place venison on rack in shallow baking pan; place salt pork over venison. Bake in preheated 450°F oven 25 minutes. Reduce oven temperature to 325°F; bake about 3 hours, until venison is well done, basting occasionally with half the reserved marinade.

Peel potatoes; cut in half. Cook in boiling, salted water about 15 minutes, until tender; drain. Add 6 tablespoons butter, salt, pepper, and parsley; mix until potatoes are coated. Keep warm.

Cook brussels sprouts according to package directions until just tender; drain.

Melt ¼ cup butter in medium-size saucepan. Add the brussels sprouts; sauté 5 minutes, stirring constantly. Add walnuts; sauté, stirring, 5 minutes. Keep warm.

Place venison on one side of long, hot platter; keep warm.

Pour pan drippings into saucepan; add remaining marinade. Bring to boil.

Blend 2 tablespoons butter with flour. Add to marinade mixture; stir until blended. Add broth slowly, stirring constantly; bring to boil again. Cook 1 minute; pour into gravy boat.

Place potatoes on other side of platter; place brussels sprouts over potatoes. Serve with gravy.

One pound fresh cooked brussels sprouts can be used instead of frozen variety. Yield 8 to 10 servings.

ozark-style venison stroganoff

1½ pounds venison
1 recipe Marinade for Game (see Index)
All-purpose flour
¼ cup vegetable shortening
1 (6-ounce) can mushrooms

1 onion, finely chopped
1 clove garlic, pressed
1 can cream of tomato soup
¼ teaspoon hot sauce
1 tablespoon Worcestershire sauce
½ teaspoon salt
1½ cups sour cream

Cut venison into 1½-inch cubes; place in bowl. Pour marinade over; marinate several hours, turning occasionally. Drain off marinade. Dredge venison with flour; brown in hot shortening in skillet.

Drain mushrooms; reserve liquid. Add onion, garlic, and mushrooms to venison.

Combine soup, reserved mushroom liquid, hot sauce, Worcestershire sauce, and salt; stir into venison mixture. Simmer 1 hour; stir occasionally. Stir in sour cream just before serving; heat through, but do not boil. Serve over rice or mashed potatoes. One-quarter pound fresh mushrooms, sliced and sautéed in butter, can be substituted for canned mushrooms. Yield 6 servings.

venison loaf

2 pounds ground venison
2 pounds bulk pork sausage

graustark venison

2 medium onions, finely chopped
1½ cups cracker crumbs
1 cup evaporated milk
3 eggs, lightly beaten
2 cups Barbecue Sauce (see Index)
1 teaspoon salt
½ teaspoon freshly ground pepper

Place venison, sausage, onions, and crumbs in large bowl; mix well. Add milk, eggs, 1 cup Barbecue Sauce, salt, and pepper; blend well. Chill 15 minutes. Shape into 2 loaves; place in large, greased baking pan. Bake in preheated 350°F oven 30 minutes. Spoon remaining Barbecue Sauce over loaves; bake 45 minutes. Yield 8 to 10 servings.

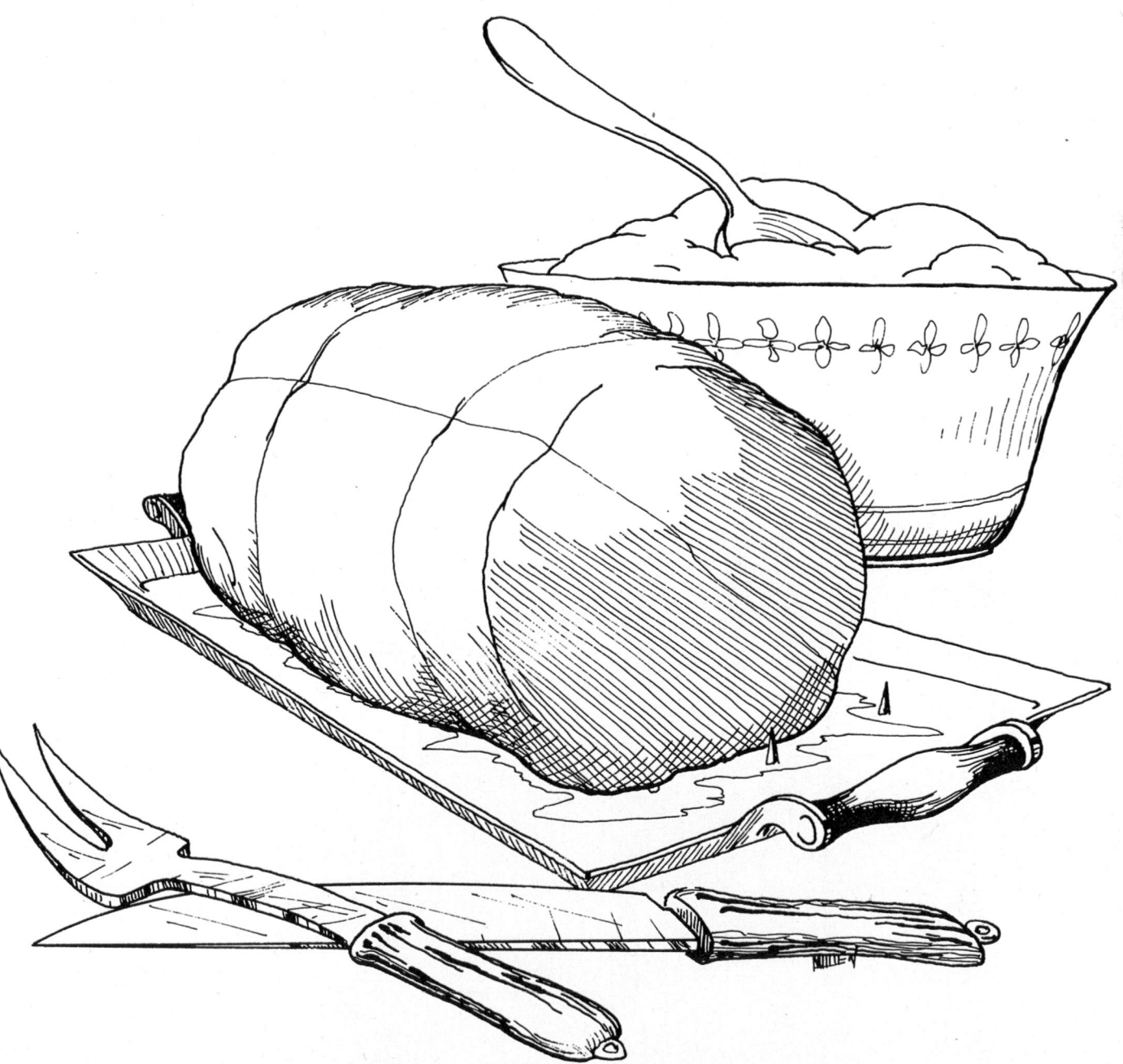

WAFFLES

basic waffles

2 cups all-purpose flour
3 teaspoons baking powder
¾ teaspoon salt
2 tablespoons sugar
3 eggs, separated
1¾ cups milk
½ cup vegetable oil

Sift flour with baking powder, salt, and sugar 3 times; place in mixing bowl.

Beat egg yolks until frothy; stir in milk and oil. Pour into flour mixture; beat with rotary beater until smooth.

Beat egg whites until stiff peaks form; fold into batter. Pour enough batter for each waffle onto hot waffle iron; bake until golden. Serve immediately with butter and syrup or honey. Yield about 8 waffles.

pecan waffles

1½ cups flour
1½ tablespoons sugar
2½ teaspoons baking powder
½ teaspoon salt
3 eggs, separated, whites beaten stiff
1½ cups milk
5 tablespoons melted butter
¼ cup chopped pecans

Measure dry ingredients into 4-cup measure; set aside.

Beat egg yolks until thick; combine with milk and butter. Add dry ingredients. When batter is well mixed, gently add pecans. Fold in egg whites. Bake in hot waffle iron. Serve with syrup or cinnamon–sugar mixture. Yield 5 or 6 servings.

raspberry sour-cream waffles

1 cup fresh raspberries
2 cups sweetened whipped cream
¾ cup strong brewed coffee
¾ cup milk
1 cup sour cream
1 egg
¼ cup vegetable oil
1½ cups pancake mix

Fold raspberries into whipped cream; chill.

Combine coffee, milk, sour cream, egg, and oil in bowl; blend well. Add pancake mix; beat with electric mixer until smooth. Pour onto hot waffle iron; bake until steaming stops. Repeat with remaining batter. Serve immediately with whipped-cream mixture.

One-half cup raspberry jam can be substituted for fresh raspberries, if desired. Yield about 4 servings.

basic waffles

Index

786